BROKEN HEGEMONIES

STUDIES IN CONTINENTAL THOUGHT
John Sallis, general editor

BROKEN HEGEMONIES

BY REINER SCHÜRMANN

Translated by Reginald Lilly

Bloomington & Indianapolis

Publication of this book is made possible in part with the assistance of a Challenge Grant from the National Endowment for the Humanities, a federal agency that supports research, education, and public programming in the humanities.

Publication of *Broken Hegemonies* was generously supported by the Department of Philosophy of the Graduate Faculty at The New School and by Jeanne C. Thayer, whose gift honors the memory of Reiner Schürmann and Irene Worth.

This book is a publication of

Indiana University Press
601 North Morton Street
Bloomington, IN 47404-3797 USA

http://iupress.indiana.edu

Telephone orders 800-842-6796
Fax orders 812-855-7931
E-mail orders iuporder@indiana.edu

Originally published in French as *Des hégémonies brisées,* Trans-Europ-Repress, Mauvezin, 1996

The paper used in this publication meets the minimum requirements of American National Standard for Information Sciences—Permanence of Paper for Printed Library Materials, ANSI Z39.48-1984.

Library of Congress Cataloging-in-Publication Data

Schürmann, Reiner, date
[Des hégémonies brisées. English]
Broken hegemonies / by Reiner Schürmann ; translated by Reginald Lilly.
p. cm. — (Studies in Continental thought)
Includes bibliographical references and index.
ISBN 0-253-34144-2 (alk. paper) — ISBN 0-253-21547-1 (pbk. : alk. paper)
1. Knowledge, Theory of. 2. Phenomenology. 3. Norm (Philosophy) 4. Philosophy—History. I. Lilly, Reginald. II. Title. III. Series.
BD162 .S48 2003
190—dc21

2002013036

1 2 3 4 5 08 07 06 05 04 03

In Memory of Louis Comtois

Dead my old fine hopes
And dry my dreaming
But still—
Iris, blue each spring.
—Shushiki

To understand the world
as based on suffering:
that is the tragic.
—Nietzsche

Only *alétheia,* by virtue
of its agonic manner of
being, makes "tragedy"
possible and
necessary.
—Heidegger

Contents

Translator's Remarks

Shortly before his death, and prior to its publication in French, Reiner Schürmann asked me to translate *Des Hégémonies brisées* into English. He provided me with the manuscript of the French as well as sections of the book that had been translated by others. While often benefiting from the work of others, I have translated the text from "scratch," often drawing on the felicitous renderings of others. Clearly Schürmann was not able to devote his final attention to the critical apparatus, for there are some errors in the citations. Where possible, I have corrected these, but this translation does not present itself as a critical edition.

Schürmann made his own translations of all non-French texts, often deviating from the extant translations that he cites; I have consulted original editions as well as their standard English translations where possible and have, in the case of German sources, translated them more or less directly. However, generally I have let Schürmann's French text guide my translations; therefore references to original editions and English translations are for the convenience of the reader only.

Schürmann wished, as do I, to thank those who contributed to the translation: David Pellauer, Peter Soares, Charles Wolfe, Alberto Hernandez-Lemus, Claudia Bedrick, and Roger Hodge. I would also like to thank Jim Mangiafico, who worked on one chapter. Early versions of some sections appeared in English before the French original was completed. All were subsequently reworked by Schürmann, and they have been translated anew. Schürmann also wished to thank the directors and editors of the following publishing houses and journals for having been kind enough to let him include these pieces here, "in the habitat for which they originally had been written": *Graduate Faculty Philosophy Journal, Research in Phenomenology,* and the State University of New York Press. In addition, I would like to thank my research assistants, Audrey Illouz and Agathe Mikaeloff, for their excellent polylingual work on the critical apparatus, Lily Davis for helping prepare the manuscript and her good sense of English and French grammar, and especially Paul Mathias, whose philosophical acumen was as helpful as was his nuanced French.

Schürmann made use of parentheses and brackets in his text. Therefore, materials placed within braces are mine. I have used translator's notes sparingly to draw attention to issues of terminology. Those notes are marked with an asterisk and placed at the bottom of the page.

VOLUME ONE

General Introduction

The pages that follow are meant to be read as a contribution to the age old "doctrine of principles." Philosophers have never stopped speculating about this principal Greek legacy. Today the business of principal principles seems to have been robbed of its heritage. What can be learned from its loss? May it actually represent a gain for us? These are good enough reasons to examine the operations that have been carried out on this legacy.*

For more or less a century, more than one nightfall has descended upon the primary facts. I believe that the nightfalls still need to be retraced. Since when—and above all in what manner—did an undertow in these facts draw them toward their ruin? All that European humanity has made of itself in the first half of the twentieth century, and all that it is in the process of doing to itself on a planetary scale in the second half that makes darkness so familiar to us, must have distant and profound origins. These are good enough reasons to suspect philosophers of shady dealings. Have they perhaps always received a return on their "principles" from dealings carried out in the dead of night?

In any event, today they are quick to confess that they know less about foundations than their predecessors believed they knew. Who, in the last analysis, makes the law? Our century has taught us much more about the troubled conditions of the law than about laws, norms, authorities, places, limpid and ultimate *topoi*. In so doing, it has squelched a profound confidence. Don't sovereign figures amount to positings? Are they not a result of ideological decrees, of an arrested questioning? Sovereign figures smack of the thetic gesture and too closely resemble investments, secure sites that are highly profitable to both inner and public life. In addition, we have learned how fragile these investments are. This is reason enough to ponder the essential fragility of the stops, theses, positings, postulates, and investments that have made the law.

The ease with which a whole age nonetheless continues to graze, in spite of exterminations still alive in our memories and planetary asphyxiations already in our throats, gives grounds for perplexity. To think is to linger on the conditions in which one is living, to linger on the site where we live. Thus to think is a privilege of that epoch which is ours, provided that the essential fragility of the sovereign referents becomes evident to it. This assigns to philosophy, or to whatever takes its place, the task of showing the tragic condition beneath all principled constructions.

The tragic is always a result of a double bind.[1] Antigone owes allegiance both to the rules of familial piety and to civil laws. The double bind of family-city remains inescapable (at least until the appearance of the modern state and its apology, the dialectic of objective Spirit), and the tragic differend remains unsolvable. Antigone ends up broken, not exactly by disparate laws but—as we shall see—*singularized*

*This last sentence, omitted from the published text, is found in the manuscript.

under one law, through a withdrawal toward the other. The tragic condition inserts one into a constituted phenomenality, and yet it wrenches one from this through an undeniable (but hubristically denied) allegiance to an other. With regard to an analytic of ultimates, an analogous conflict works upon principles. Their conditions will prove to be as irremediably incongruous, for the singular pull toward my death removes once and for all thetic reason from the coercive lights of the universal. The excess of a nocturnal knowledge in daylight, which defined the tragic hero (Oedipus, blinded, "has perhaps an eye too many. . . . To live is death, and death also is a life"[2]), has become our own excess. We owe it to the kenosis, to the emptying out of normative representations. As we know, tragedy opens after disasters have already occurred, and nothing is left to be shown but the conditions that precipitated them. In Greece such a knowledge historically preceded all doctrines of principles, and it is still necessary for us to retain it as the knowledge of a transgressive counter-strategy at work in every strategy that legislates simply. The ultimate is not simple; at the origin of everyday experience we know—though only dimly—disparate functions. There is no reconciliation between *the ultimates* of the universalizing impulse and the singularizing withdrawal. It will be a matter of examining how, from under the most solid normative constructions, the tragic pierces through. *Pathei mathos,* "to suffer is to understand."[3] How does this singularization that is *suffered* torment a *posited* sovereign?

The historical investigation therefore will only make sense if through it one fathoms tragic being.

> "There, that mountain! There, that cloud! What in them is 'real'? Merely eliminate from them the fantasm of any human *addition,* you sober ones! If only you could!"
> —F. Nietzsche[4]

To eliminate the fantasm so as to leave nothing but "there, that mountain, there, that cloud," seems impossible to us. In the following analyses I take Nietzsche literally; for us the "real" would slip away along with the fantasm. What, then, is at stake in the fantasmic "addition" and in every sobering elimination? Could it be life?

These analyses are first of all historical. They take up a debate, more than a century old, concerning epochs and the thresholds that separate them. But rather than constructing the ages and their transitions—moments of objective Spirit, constellations of the veiling and unveiling of being, epistemological apparatuses of knowledge/power—I thought it useful to read the languages that Western philosophy has spoken since its birth. At their best, philosophers have made an effort not to be carried away by the fad of the day that passes for common sense; no thought, however, has ever resisted being carried away by its own language. Far from mastering a language, concepts live on it; they are born of words. Hasn't each of our historical idioms always instituted its own fantasmic reality? I have asked myself which have been, concretely, those human additions of which Nietzsche speaks. Might they always come down to a certain organization of nouns linked in one way or another to the predominant languages? Would "reality" then exist in a Greek, a Latin, a modern vernacular? And might it be this by giving birth to the centuries that spoke those languages and relied upon common nouns as if upon courts of ultimate authority that are essentially self-evident? It will be necessary, if such questions merit consideration, to define epochs by means of the fantasmic organization instituted by a language.

The modesty of reading, however, is linked to an inevitable ambition. In order to obtain discerning answers from the tradition, one must subject it to rigorous questioning. In the following analyses I will again endeavor to discover the regimes imposed by ultimate authorities on their respective linguistic eras. Fantasms pose as an other reality. "There, that mountain! There, that cloud! What in them is 'real'? Merely eliminate from them the fantasm . . . ," and the "real" will immediately vanish. Does one not feel that that conclusion would necessarily follow? Linguistic usage maintains and activates a conflict between a given geological formation and the common figure under which we range all the peaks of the world. Is our everyday speech not naturally deceiving when we call both the Matterhorn and Everest "mountain"? Or when we call both this form passing over my apartment building and that other one disappearing in the distance "cloud"? Take away what can be spoken, and what will be left? What will be left for us? It seems the experience of speaking is the experience of not being dead.

The conflict between a given singular and its common representation is most clearly manifested in reasoning strategies. It is there, rather than in the grammar of everyday life, that I will go to pick it out. The readings to which I will devote myself will show how the "human addition" we cannot help but posit *differs* from a given fact that we cannot help but renounce. Philosophy, if it is indeed the profession of the concept, actually exacerbates the thrust toward the fantasm that every ordinary sentence posits as real. From the moment we formulate a statement we are the fake sober ones; what will it take to sober us up—a lesion, a local injury, a trauma perhaps? From the very moment we speak of things and others, these have struck us and the trauma is already present, localized as only the singular can be. From the outset, the imaginary production of thetic authorities places us in a discord where we find ourselves at the mercy of the fantasmically posited, but equally entirely at the mercy of the singular given, thus singularities. These are the incongruous ultimates that tear our being.

The investigations that will be read here are, in the end, concerned with sites. They form a topology.

A philosophical discourse pretending to be a purely historical account is not philosophy. One has the impression of hearing the voice of Sils-Maria: "You sober ones" who busy yourselves inventorying what has been said since the dawn of time, you are fantasizing a new Grand Reality—history. This is the entirely metaphysical modesty of the archivist of ideas, and the doubly metaphysical naïveté of those who claim to dismiss summarily the narratable condition and proclaim today the end of grand narratives. It only adds a chapter to an intrigue that has been declared closed. Based on the happy or unhappy outcome of the story told, one arranges it precisely according to exposition, development, and resolution. Is there anything more narratable than a drama's outcome? A "happy ending" puts the finishing stroke to the peregrinations that it entails, it brings home the point. But not the final point, for who does not know that beyond a happy ending the characters lived happily ever after and had many children? Or that the blinded hero, having been chased from the usurped throne, chose to settle the tragedy rather than conclude it, thus doing nothing but constituting it—before he too carried on through fields and deserts to shine at last in the apotheosis at Colonus? Be the narratives grand or small, the story told never comes to an end.

A philosophical discourse aspiring to a pure system, a construction *ab ovo,* is guilty of an analogous naïveté, in this case, of being oblivious to the question that has roused philosophers from dogmatic slumber ever since they began to speak their vernacular languages: What is going on with us today? Descartes and Kant understood philosophy as arriving at new and epoch-making ways of thinking nature. "Philosophy," the greatest systematician will say, "is its era, seized by thought."[5] If the turns philosophy has taken in recent times—the historicist, linguistic, and interpretive turns—have indeed implanted it on yet another new terrain, then the starry-eyed gaze pretending to look at the world anew sheds light on the *auto-da-fe* of critical reason. Out of systematic freshness, or even analytical freshness in the Anglo-American[6] sense, we forget to examine the ground under our feet. Topology, as we shall see, problematizes that ground which is the air in which we live.

Topology does this as an analysis of sites. It seeks to inscribe the "reality" that we, we moderns, fantasize in its relationship to the Greek and Latin "realities." As I intend to practice it, topology makes use of both historical and systematic tools—a distinction that is of decidedly limited import.

Before turning to the historical, to the systematic, and to their conjunction in the topological, we need to say a word about the sense in which fantasms are what is in question. This sense is inscribed between Nietzsche's minimizing injunction and the following maximizing injunction of Aristotle: "Man lives as mortal. As far as possible, he should live as immortal"[7] One would hardly know how to better formulate the traits of ordinary experience such as the analytic of ultimates seeks to extract them. First there is the immortalizing thetic attraction, then the withdrawal that singularizes us. If it wants to be wary of subjectivist entanglements, this analytic will have to go to work on historically given sites. It will have to be linked with a topology of broken hegemonies, a topology that analyzes the legislating constellations to which the ultimates have given rise.

Hoson "as far as possible"—how far exactly?

On Hegemonic Fantasms

"Say ground. No ground but say ground."
—S. Beckett[8]

The history I will attempt to retrace is the one in which the Aristotelian *hoson* was maximized: the history of *norms*. I understand this term in its strongest sense, the sense in which it names the authoritative representation that serves, during a given linguistic era, to constitute the phenomenality of phenomena and thereby to legitimize all theoretical and practical rules. In the normative sense, a fantasm cannot be exhausted in regulatory representations. It designates the sovereign principle to which the professional philosopher refers all laws of knowledge and acting, but which in turn cannot be referred to anything else,[9] the principle that serves as the ultimate reason for all generic principles, the trans-regional canon for all regional canons. This principle makes, absolutely though fantasmically, *e pluribus unum*—from many, one—not as does a major premise from which other propositions would follow, but rather as a burgeoning production center. Fantasms rule by authorizing not the deduction of a finite corpus of conclusions, but the indefinite association *of representations that require that one follow them*. Well, such representations are called laws. Hence if laws are measured against the fantasmic authority, then this fantasmic authority will be normative in the sense that one refers to it as to the law of laws.

Is it not the basics of the trade to secure a foundation, not one that is grounded but one nevertheless capable of anchoring the premises which instruct me in what I may know and what I should do? Understood in this way, a norm is not justified, and in this respect it is fantasmic. But it justifies all that may become a phenomenon during the linguistic epoch that bears its hallmark; in this respect it is hegemonic. If it may be proven that such a referent, non-referable to some superior authority, remains for as long as a language preponderates, then the history to be traced will be that of the Greek, Latin, and modern *hegemonic fantasms.*

A summary of the following pages that reads them as a contribution to the very traditional doctrine of principles would not be erroneous. It is difficult to imagine what kind of reflection could dispense with such a doctrine—whether it be developed, tacitly presupposed, or as a discourse rendered inert—at least if the reflection seeks to achieve a rigorous discourse about what we all, albeit confusedly, know. Philosophy, as it has understood itself, cannot dispense with a discourse that brings ordinary experience to a head. It must take a position on what, in the last analysis, constitutes the phenomenality of phenomena. Lest it founder under a swarm of descriptions, the search for constitutive conditions must come to a successful conclusion. There is, furthermore, if not an *a priori* necessity, at least a demonstration used by the professional to bring the investigation to a conclusion by means of a stroke of the razor, saying "only this far, not any further." The axiomatic razor's stroke—*non est procedere ad infinitum* (nothing goes on infinitely)—deals the *coup de grâce* to that burgeoning discourse.[10] It is also the master stroke of the one who recognizes that whatever pretends to be unconditioned, or that what a certain epoch-making decree wishes unconditionally, has a fantasmic status. And one ends up a winner with all these strokes. Winning what? The real, if one believes Nietzsche. A world that holds together, in any case, a livable world. A fantasm is hegemonic when an entire culture relies on it as if it provided that in the name of which one speaks and acts. Such a chief-represented (*hêgemôn*) is at work upon the unspeakable singular when it calls it a part of the whole; hegemonies transform the singular into a particular. They serve to say what is, to classify and inscribe, to distribute proper and common nouns. Since Plato, making such discriminations has amounted to obliterating the singular for the sake of the common, and to live outside this common that obliterates, ". . . if only you *could*!"

Immediately it becomes clear at what price fantasms render the world livable. Life is paid for by denying the singular; according to the vocabulary of apriorism by subsuming it under the figure of the particular. Now, what then would become of principles if the singular obliterated by the subsumptive fantasms were to be reaccredited? Would not an inextricable double bind follow?

These are the questions that an analytic of ultimates brings into play in the doctrine of principles.

Since Plato's middle dialogues, we have fixed our attention now on one particular sovereign representation, and then on some other one. These fixations have always constituted, and continue to constitute, the law. Nevertheless they have a story to tell. Therefore it is necessary, in order to understand fantasms, to ask how this came to pass—what representation assumed the role of law with the Greeks, the Latins, and then again with the moderns? How were they instituted, and how were they deposed? How did they administer their respective linguistic ages. Ours is an inquiry concerning historical sites that points to a topological question: From where does a representation promoted to the level of fantasm speak to us?

This investigation is not new. Common opinion among historians of philosophy holds that the Greeks trusted Nature (the World) in all things, the medievals God, and the moderns the Subject (Man). This opinion corresponds perfectly with the proceedings quite unanimously instituted against metaphysics, proceedings in which metaphysics is first gathered into one bloc, and then, through a somewhat curious aftereffect, is in turn accused of reification. These three Great Beings—the World, God, and Man—are distributed by common opinion along history until, with a certain critical turn in modern philosophy, they find themselves emptied of their substance and translated into simple ideas obsessing our reason (unless one were to say the Copernican turn does not exactly inaugurate the reign of Man). Opinion has a didactic utility. It serves as a reminder of the first critical requirement: to desubstantialize the contents of thought! Nevertheless, in this it continues to pursue a rhetorical strategy. Take for instance the equally plausible permutations in the epochal assignment of these Beings. It is just as reasonable, or unreasonable, to speak of a Greek theocentrism, of a medieval anthropocentrism and a modern cosmocentrism. . . . Let us call these Great Beings *supreme* referents and leave them in the care of professional persuaders.

The history of hegemonic fantasms is the history of *ultimate* referents, which are, quite literally, "nothing," *non-res.* A "supreme" standard, in political economy, would be a standard commodity (gold, oil); an "ultimate" standard would be the variable relation of goods to a factor that is itself variable. A fantasmic economy is a result of the variable relations among beings, large or small, to a referent that is itself diachronically variable; a relational referent that does not appear among beings. The doctrine of principles treats of these ultimate authorities.

An ultimate function is relevant *in principle* whenever it allows all that we are able to say, do, and know to be ranged under it. The question will be how such positings fall within the province of the ultimate functions in ordinary experience.

In order to grasp how philosophy came to involve itself with such sovereign non-beings, how it came to feed on them and feed the ages with them, it is useful to remember what has indeed been—and continues to be in certain circles—the public function of philosophy ever since the Greeks entered it on their public rolls.[11]

"We are the civil servants of humanity," Husserl said.[12] That is an altogether bureaucratized version of the philosopher-king (even though it involved, for Husserl himself, the most rigorous public probity in safeguarding the originary institution of Western rationality). Whether seated in court or in his office, what is expected of a master thinker? What does he expect of himself? What he expects are directive ideas, thus a certain kind of government. One can put it this way: He occupies the position of an expert. And he posits. What? Foundations. Be he monarchic or bureaucratic, his duties have remained technical. His *techné,* his "know-how," pertains to the deep moorings of private phenomena within, and public phenomena without. The foundation he secures must guarantee certainty in knowledge and rectitude in acting, and to life, perhaps both stability and a meaning. One sees that his job description stipulates serious responsibilities. A professional philosopher does his duty by using reasonings to excavate a knowledge concealed in each of us, a knowledge against which the darts of doubt strike and bend back as against a rock. The only condition for his expertise securing unanimity is that he tell us in plain language what we already know, but only obscurely, since we speak in common nouns. And this unanimity will have the air of a thing that goes without saying. Moreover, whoever believes that this mission has become obsolete today is helplessly deluding himself. Both the political left and right contrarily arrogate to themselves the task. The right, positing heteronomous authorities anchored in the past ("great books" in the manner of Leo Strauss,[13] institutions), strives for a rehabilitation of natural teleology. A certain left, positing future authorities that emanate from autonomy (for example, a community emancipated from communicative distortions), strives to validate arguments for the *Letzbegründung,* for precisely those ultimate foundations. The mission of these professionals is still to maximize the fantasmic work of everyday language. They promote the *koinon* to the level of a normative instance* capable of consoling the soul and consolidating the city.[14]

How is one to describe the result of this maximization, the ultimate "human addition" to phenomena? It makes an immortal halo of peace shine on them, according to a citation from Aristotle; literally a universal peace, turning phenomena toward the one. It works to focus them. It centers lines of force—strategies of speaking, life's inner dependencies—on a steady focal point. It imposes a standard meaning of being. Therefore it is impossible to describe it in the way that one describes a being; it is rather a matter of showing the mode of operation of such an epochally varying point to which all phenomena must be related if they are to have a meaning. It names, as the term for normative relations, the ultimate "reality" that makes the given singulars conceivable and in which their singularity is engulfed. It imposes on them an arch-violence. Arch-, because what is posited could not be an ultimate unless it subsumed under itself everything that may become a phenomenon; violence, because it bans from the philosophical confines all bearers of proper nouns ("Solon" and "Moses" are not definable, no more than are the objects of demonstratives such as "this" and "that"; the class in which we arrange them, however, is definable—in the present instance, "legislators"). In Platonic terms, in order for the various *hypotheses* of knowledge to have the force of regional principles, an *anhypothesis* must ground them which is not regional nor, in its turn, grounded.

The denaturation by subsumption thus inflicted on phenomena requires a very careful retracing. It is a denaturation in which an *ultimate singular* found to be the case is transmuted into an instance of a *completely other ultimate universal.* This "other," this alterity without a common noun—that is what is at stake in the doctrine of principles that is re-examined on the basis of the analytic of ultimates.

The term "subsumption" implies submission to some archic figure, a figure that conditions but is itself unconditioned, one which may not be subsumed or submitted to a still more archic thesis; it is an an-archic figure. Does this word, in its received

*The French *instance* has many of the same senses as does the English 'instance': 'example,' 'representative,' and 'instance' as well as the temporal sense of 'moment.' However, it also has the sense of 'authority.' Several of these meanings are often simultaneously at play in Schürmann's text, especially when predicated with *normative* or *dernière* ('ultimate').

sense (from the Greek Fathers for example), not sufficiently express the thetic essence of ultimate principles?

To name these principles both *referents* and *signifiers* is of course to step into the lexical conventions of linguistics. I describe a hegemonic fantasm as a referent that signifies an obligation we have—a ligature, a liaison—with regard to which there is no outside. It signals to us what we have to be. It is the most common figure of thought, it is found on the side of signifiers. By enjoining in us a way of being, norms put proper nouns in a vocative situation. But can it then still be a matter of referents? Do not referents, conventionally said to be outside language, instead face signifiers?

The question of reference entails the phenomenal origin of sovereign positions. On the one hand these indeed cannot and should not denote a particular singular, which would imply their power is subsumptive. Yet, on the other hand, the normative theses do not fall from heaven. They have their own indirect and oblique ways of referring back to the phenomena from which they were extracted.

a. The law is always a common *noun,* autonomous from the referents of which the linguists speak (or of which they have nothing to say). This is because the normative operation does not merely turn a singular into a particular but, in addition, it detaches the signifier from everything that the common noun is incapable of grasping—worldly givens. Take the "nature" by which Latin moralists were said to measure all things. For us it signifies a continuity of order which first of all unites the parts of the soul, then binds the individual to the city and all to each other, and finally links the visible world to the gods. How does such a thesis whose tissue is woven by a single and self-same principle of order deal with the givens in the world? Aristotle praised the philosophers who know how "to grow old in the familiarity of phenomena."[15] Whatever became, under the influence of hegemonic "nature," of that fidelity to those phenomenon that so preoccupied the Stoics, such as our anger and the right judgment holding it in check? What also of the city, the seasons, and the star-filled sky whose fire they so fondly evoked in order to liken it to a soul? Whatever happens to all those singulars under the positing of a continuous *ratio* running through them? Nature posited as an ultimate reason is evidently not a referent in the sense of a phenomenon in the world. According to Nietzsche's statement, positing "adds" a reality. What reality? In the present instance, the continuous *ratio.* It is an other reality, where the normative discourse takes leave of the world and plants itself on the level of the pure signifier. Is it not *in the name* of a referent that acts are judged? In acting "against nature" one is evidently not going against a being, against a thing that exists outside language. Rather, one is attacking a maximization posited in language, a reality that does not enter into the experience of the world, but nevertheless signals us what we are to do, what not to do. To maximize a linguistic unity is to "augment" its power of signification, hence to invest it with "authority" (in Latin, *auctoritas, authority* stems from *augere,* to augment). Sodomites are burned *in the name* of nature.

The genesis of such a referent is analogous to the one Kant had established for the ideas of pure reason, representations broadened to name a whole and therefore no longer corresponding to anything phenomenal.[16] In this sense, a noun that does not "render present" any sensible perception nevertheless will express a "representation."

All figures of what is common, of the *koinon,* are such representations as render the singular into a particular and the phenomenon into a signifier. It is nothing in itself, just as grammar is nothing more than words, the symbolic order no more than the acts it forbids, the structure nothing more than elements. Maximized by excessive confidence (more literally, arrogance) to the point of imposing a common noun as norm, the fantasmic thrust of language generates nothing but relations. It will not be absurd to retain this relational sense to qualify these norms, for referents as well as fantasms. A standard sense of being is always a result of a normative-nominative thesis that brings phenomena into focus, a relational sense the Greeks called a "relation to the one" (*pros hen*), that Cicero applied to nature ("*ad naturam referebas omnia*"),[17] and, in its own way, was retained by the contemporary project of an archaeology of knowledge which problematizes "that form of history that was secretly, but entirely, related to the synthetic activity of the subject."[18]

A reference is at work here in the very interior of the symbolic order that Nietzsche challenges sober realists to eliminate from the singular. In order to constitute the phenomenality of phenomena, in order to universalize them, a representational order must organize itself around a principle, a fantasmic referent measuring all representations. A hegemonic fantasm so conceived not only directs us to refer everything to it, but has, furthermore, an endless supply of significations, that is to say, normative measures. It is the position {*posé*} to which all practical and cognitive laws relate, in the final instance, all acts and all phenomena.

b. Thus, to speak of normative maximization is to indicate from the outset the indirect reference by means of which theticism still remains faithful to phenomena. In the words of Hannah Arendt: "It is easy to speak about metaphysical illusions. However, these illusions, and they are illusions indeed, have their authentic roots in some experience. In other words, even though we throw them out the window as dogmas, we would be hard pressed to know where they come from."[19] In order to maximize, one must first select, exclude. In the rarified atmosphere of these illusions one remains faithful to phenomena themselves rendered rare. In terms of a referential semiology, in what way does the *deixis* of ordinary language persist in metaphysical language?

Descartes *observes himself* thinking; then he finds in this experience the *unshakable foundation* capable of grounding universal science. Here we see the "I think" erected as mono-referent. And here, most significantly, we see the double play of maximization which obliterates the singularity of a phenomenon and raises it—thereby dephenomenalizing it—to the point where it is capable of attaching to it the whole fabric of knowledge and (in retrospect) the very way an age of the world is ordered. But how is one to posit such an all-encompassing referent unless one allows oneself first to accept a single referent upon which to support the thetic exaltation? A hegemonic referent only emerges at the end of the operation whereby one gleans such a deictic meaning of being and extends it to the totality of what may become a phenomenon—which is to say, at the end of a nomothetic operation. Subsumptive reason gets intoxicated on the fantasmic labor within ordinary language; it takes an experience and installs it on the level of language where representations age poorly; it abandons the familiarity of phenomena and transforms representations into signifiers that no longer point directly to any experience. The other reality that it posits conveys something *to me,* as a law always does.

The price to pay for such mono-reference is having to break the links to every singular capable of manifesting itself. From the moment that experience becomes possible only through its relation to the fantasmic referent—and it is for that reason that it is posited—this referent necessarily falls outside the range of any possible experience. The Greeks' synectic one, the Latins' teleological nature and modern self-consciousness comfortably continue to be referents in the sense of so-called empirical reality; but they enter the topology of hegemonies as fantasmic referents that only indirectly refer back to the experience from whence they emerged. It is the task of a retrospective topology to excavate, from under the great foundations of universal demonstrations, the phenomena that were used as their cornerstones. In distinguishing between maximization (the constitution of fantasms to subsume particulars) and singularization (the constitution of signs to exhibit singulars), topology will not destroy the foundations; it will recover those objects of exhibition and make of itself an analytic of ultimates.

Signs begin to drift when one gives *excessive* attention to reference in its being directed by some particular phenomenon. It is then that one strikes down that reference, just as I strike down my paternal relative, bearer of a proper noun, when, out of an excess of signification, I start living in the name of the father. . . .

Hence the double sense, fantasmic and deictic, of reference. Thantic singularity deprives sense itself of sense. The deictic thus introduces a poverty into the fantasmic. Sense *both* maximized *and* impoverished of sense announces the double bind. In the incongruous *both-and,* the tragic condition of being proclaims itself.

Kant was undoubtedly the first to detect the work of desire in reason. It was the duty of an emancipating critique to keep in check that work and its accompanying megalomania: "The life [of reason] is nothing but the faculty of desire in its minimal exercise." He sought to teach a minimizing sobriety to the maximizing thrust. Reason always "wants to be satisfied." But utter satisfaction is not useful. "There is so much that I have absolutely no need to know."[20] It was necessary to train reason in finitude, a task to be taken up ever anew. In these times of waning modernity, this task must be radicalized beyond the subjective presuppositions that introduce palliatives into the conflict of the faculties of reason and desire.

Under a hegemonic regime, one acts and speaks *in the name of a fantasm*—an expression we hold to be tautological. Both common nouns and fantasms direct us to de-realize the singular and maximize a thetic reality. They direct us not to accept the given, but to subsume it under a thesis.

Before turning to the epochal fantasms that have varied the sovereign reference, it is necessary to have a clear understanding about the passage beyond the genus, the *metabasis eis allo genos,* wherein reference is born. To speak of maximization is to single out abusive extrapolations as a work of language; to speak of representation is to single it out as a work of the imagination. But which path (*hodos*) does this work follow (*meta*) in its working? The elements of "method" are well known, which were at once formulated, practiced, and betrayed by Aristotle.

He formulated these elements of method as a doxographer. A narrative without a previous, methodical understanding—a narrative which he did not yet call a history of ideas—remains non-philosophical, just as a method without historical retrospection remains naïve. In reading an author, one must seek, first of all, the initial experience, namely, the experience that, before any other, roused him to think. A reading may be called good if it seeks the phenomena that the author was first in *seeing* and from which he drew his primary *facts*. But Aristotle also betrayed these precepts of reading in turning his predecessors into "philosophers of nature."[21] In the end, he practiced his precepts as a metaphysician. The region he was the first in seeing and from which he drew his primary certainties is the region of manipulable things. If in the Athenian fourth century physical change imposes itself as the key problem to be solved, it is because there was overwhelming astonishment at what human hands can accomplish. Hence the paradigmatic role of the *Physics*—"a fundamental book" (*Grundbuch*[22]), as Heidegger will say—for the whole of philosophy to come. Aristotle extrapolates the ultimate universal principles from the analysis of sensible things moved by each other, that is, from the analysis of artifacts. As for "metaphysics," the word's origin has been sought either in a classification at the Alexandria library (designating those books arranged before the *Physics*), or in the gradation of phenomenal spheres (designating a sphere beyond that of sensible things). Yet, if in Aristotle facts become clear when change is effected and observed, then the word "metaphysics" must be understood in terms of the book that treats effecting and observation. The title *Metaphysics* names a collection of "supplements to the *Physics*."

Hence, it suffices to remember the first disjunction in the *Physics*—between those things moved by themselves and those moved by others—to understand how the phenomena which were initially puzzling, and therefore extraordinary, quickly become ordinary again. Once the blueprint—which will be used for principial constructions—has been drawn by tracing them, sensible things in movement will have served their purpose. Aristotle posits the *archai kai aitiai* he extracts from them as reigning over knowledge in general. Strictly speaking, only these principles and causes are self-sufficient. Only they are autarchic. As for artifacts, once the thetic gesture has been carried out on them, they are again demoted to objects of a single science in a single one of its exercises. Therefore one may wonder whether Aristotle, more so than others, knew the art of growing old in the familiarity of phenomena.

Thus hegemonies are instituted. Representations with an epochal destiny take leave of the phenomenal world as soon as their autarchic resources have been assured—just as one leaves the paternal home. Language, which always incites maximization, is the driving force behind this departure. Aristotle also recognized this. The verbal infinitive emphasizes that which is unstable and temporal in experience; nominative constructions emphasize that which is stable and principled.[23] The singular has survived theticism, not as what by nature (*phusei*) exceeds all we can posit (*thesei*), but more clandestinely, crouched in the shadows of normative-nominative constructions. One must ask the Greek, Latin, and modern initiators: Where do you start? What region of beings do you represent first, that is to say, redraw in large after the fact? And at the price of excluding what? In order to resolutely remain in familiarity with phenomena, it will be necessary to inquire into the specific experiences and districts to which an instituting discourse proves faithful when it becomes infatuated with this or that represented thing, when it sets up the standard for phenomenalization. But one should ask above all: In what manner does the infinitive tense retain, in epoch-making arguments, both time and the singular, whereby it transgresses the universal referent postulated by nominative constructions?

These questions, which are at issue throughout the readings that follow, will in the end open to the condition that fractures every referent posited as uniformly binding: the *singularization to come*.

By reading them in the languages that the West has spoken, one finds these referents have not been few in number. The philosopher-functionary brings about, on a large scale, the conversion of the singular into a fantasm, a conversion always carried out by ordinary language on a lesser scale. It follows that one cannot rid oneself of those sovereign referents as easily as one kicks a bad habit. Hence, the task of working through the hegemonies we have inherited will be somewhat more complicated than hoped for by a deconstructive naïveté—but how then could it still be a matter of an *Abbau*—that decides to "change terrain, in an irruptive and discontinuous manner, by brutally installing itself on the outside and affirming absolute rupture and difference."[24] The task is more complicated or more modest, for from what lofty position would we be able to draw the geographic map of discontinuous planes? What field outside the terrain must one occupy in order to affirm rupture? I know of no other place than the one whereupon the waning twentieth century has planted us. A slippery terrain, no doubt, in more than one sense. But what could it mean to want to brutally leave this terrain in order to install oneself, by eruption, on another one?

The most modest and least naïve issue is, therefore, to know which have been the longest-lived normative-nominative referents in our history. We do not possess language, and language possesses us only in its idioms. That is the reason why it is necessary to read the hegemonic fantasms in their own languages. Once they take up residence, they cover a very extended space-time whose contemporary shiftings come from afar. Where is one going to go rummaging for the truth of all this if not in the Greek, Latin, and modern vernacular of their residences? The positive reality on which we have nourished ourselves since the Presocratics is recorded in the official documents drafted in those languages. Hence, the dynamics of maximization that contributed to the institutions of each epoch should be retraceable easily enough. The constructive ease with which the fantasmogenic strategy of everyday language is translated into normative-nominative referents is somewhat more stunning than even the brutal affirmation of absolute difference; but once the epitome of a fantasm has been reattached to its base—to the singular *perforce* singled out by the concept—it will be less surprising to see that, when all is said and done, the work of consolation and consolidation has satisfied its public—large or elite—for centuries.

"Perforce," because consent to hegemonic regimes is not to be taken for granted. There is here a kind of joy of violent submission to it. Perhaps this is the intoxication they wish for us, or that we wish for ourselves through them. There is, in any case, no ordinary statement that does not do violence to "there, that mountain"; it is the violence of the concept positing reality, therefore a positive violence. The theoreticians of first principles have always recognized that such violence is inscribed in hegemonic fantasms. By definition, it is said, *archai*-principles-norms-foundations are not deduced. They are only affirmed. What is it, then, that the philosopher–civil servant does? Theirs is the expertise of limiting the questions concerning conditions. This too was well understood by the brewers of words who board the rig of the last discourse quoted, slam the door on communicative reason, close their eyes, and step on the fantasmomachic gas pedal. . . . A *sacrificium intellectus* which uses the shock of fashionable words to coin the positive essences of primary principles. The less one reflects, the greater is the need to give in to thetic fantasms.[25] A philosopher–civil servant's probity is gauged by his knowing how to keep questioning, if only a little bit longer. But once the foam of fashion is blown aside, the skelature of the normative agent makes its appearance. Whether vulgarized or not, the public function of *positing* remains the same. Indeed, what limiting of questioning would not be premature? What normative doctrine is not made up of *ideas brought to a halt*?

The thetic essence of principles moved Aristotle to affirm that *archai* are negotiated but not established by force of arguments. Beckett sums it up: "Say ground. No ground but say ground." To deconstruct hegemonic fantasms, one cannot trust in interpretive throws of the dice, nor let this be produced by a fortuitous collision of signifier and insignificance, nor attack the texts from their margins. It is necessary to go straight into the thicket—to the theses upon which a text as well as an epoch rest, theses that get themselves twisted up as soon as they are declared to be legislative. Their topology deals only with places {*lieux-dits*} that are settled, formulated in an apodeictic act.

Under the *apo-deikunai*—under the thesis that there is an obvious right—the question is also how philosophy is to be understood.[26] If it is true that it essentially pleads for this or that cause (this or that representation), then arguments must be shaped according to the will of the interests in dispute. Just as a lawyer is able to argue a bit of untruth, philosophers have never stopped arguing their bit of truth—always a bit of the world, endowed with the *force majeure* (*kreittones,* Plato used to say) by arguments suiting the needs of consolation and consolidation. Under the influence of a fantasm, one associates representations according to the hysterics mobilizing the psychical or public apparatuses. If, on the contrary, philosophy is the discourse that seeks to best safeguard the originary phenomena (the phenomena of a double bind, which we will discuss), one will have at least established a point of departure from which to call an interest an interest, hysterics hysterics, and above all a thetic bond a thetic bond.

Therefore, it will be a matter of retracing a history of subjections that we have brought upon ourselves, for there is a fatality present in every speech act that makes it seemingly impossible to avoid registering the "there, that given X" as a posited meta-X. It seems impossible to let it stay the way it gives itself and to avoid projecting a common noun over it. But does the impossibility of sticking to proper nouns invariably and inescapably entail that second-order fatality in the act of philosophizing which pushes us to inscribe every datum and all speech under the influence of a signifier that is not just common, but even sovereign? Is it inevitable to say not just "mountain" but also "foundation"? And what if this positive inscription had always been an illusion? What if the positing of a *koinon,* along with the subsumption it imposes, had always tricked its public, as Kant suggested of transcendental ideas—what if they have never succeeded nor could ever succeed? What if, as if despite the referents, those who professionally *posit* referents had actually also never stopped *ignoring* here this datum, there another datum? In political philosophy these professionals say it is necessary to legitimize what is common (the state . . .) without obliterating the individual. There is great naïveté in this. What if the common and the singular both bind us—then is it not rather that we inhabit a ravaged site?

Might the singular be lodged within a truth other than the common? How, then, is one to extract it from the common? Might this require a precise rereading of the civil servants of humanity to see if, before everything and after all, they have not been the champions of the singular *even while they have pleaded for hegemony?* These are sufficient reasons warranting a review of this history.

From Difference to Differend

"Such the confusion now between the real and—how say the contrary? No matter. That old tandem. Such now the confusion between them once so twain."

—S. Beckett[27]

This examination question handed in by Beckett would surely put any philosophy professor on the spot. The contrary of the real is the unreal. And the opposite of that? An impasse. So, is not being the *same* as the real? And the contrary of being? Is it not non-being? Do we have here the old tandem of Being and Nothingness? Were we to delve into the memories of a celebrated, medieval title, in this case *De ente et essentia,* would we not find that being is the other of essence—unless it were becoming, or perhaps appearing? Or rather time—*Being and Time,* yet another title that has spoken for itself. Given that a hodgepodge of choices is not an answer, is it possible that polarity is not as natural to being as heads and tails are to a coin—that being may have no other? If this is the case, the old tandem in question could not possibly have been overtaken by confusion only just "now." It must have done so ever since being was first worked on with the help of contradiction. "*How say the* contrary?" It is still a matter of diction. Philosophers have said "here the real" and, afterwards, "there its contrary." Understood in this way, it is not merely common reality that is posited, but the old tandem in its entirety is thetic. Here the common, there the subsumed particular: Is it possible that, with this apodictic disjunction, one may have got hold of the counter position that has given rise to mortal confusions ever since it became necessary for humans to have an utmost common reality, an ultimately normative norm?

In order to grasp the manner in which such a norm legislates and reigns, it is fruitful to subject being to the question of difference, and first of all that normative difference decreed by metaphysicians and varied according to their languages (*on-ousia, ens-entitats, das Seiende-die Seiendheit*), but also to the question of the occurrent difference by means of which what is common about reality is differentiated from all else {*le reste*}, namely, what is other to the singular. One can no longer say *omnis determinatio negatio* regarding this "else" that falls outside of theticism. The singular is not anything's "determinate other." Maybe the interrogation of this new tandem—thetic reality and the "else" or "remainder"—throughout its epochal figures will teach us about the general fate that the fantasmic drives in our languages prepare for us. Being elsewise has been forgotten by the normative tradition.[28] What status does the edict of the common accord to this "elsewise" in the determinate negation by which the common is opposed to the particular?

The consoling and consolidating *chargés d'affaires* deserve the most attentive reading in view of their curious way of retaining this "elsewise" (from *diasôzein ta phainomena*[29]) which nevertheless falls outside their theses. When they impose a normative-nominative hypertrophy on singular phenomena, it is the subsumptive strategies in their thetic reasoning that leads them to forsake singular phenomena; but I will try to show, in these very reasonings, the counter-strategies by means of which the thesis fails to keep its word, difference welcomes the event, nouns yield to verbs, and the functionaries of the universal turn into the guardians of the singular. Then a tactical question must be asked of them: How does the authority {*habilitation*} to posit what is common in reality *differ* from the rehabilitation {*réhabilitation*} of the singular? It is a rehabilitation to which they also necessarily give themselves over, as their pronouncements of the law never cease to mutely echo the phenomena.

It will be necessary to demonstrate meticulously the manner in which the great instances of founding speech—namely, the one, nature, and modern consciousness—were from the outset affected by an erosion stemming from a repudiation of the singular. From the moment we put them in charge of normative constructions, philosophers have indeed answered Beckett's question in ways other than by changing the diad of common vs. particular. At the very basis of their hegemonic edifices, they have excavated the difference between *posited* reality and the singular, which, in their mode of double agent, they have simultaneously *abandoned*. In preparing ourselves to reread them, it should be clear that their double allegiance—to the subsumptive common and to the ineffable "this"—merely projects on a large scale the originally tragic condition in which our ordinary languages always place us. And none of these can be sobered up, for in the violent thrust toward the common, our lives just as violently depend on them.

Now, if life is nourished on common significations, "its" alleged other, namely, death, is signified to us by the singular. Hölderlin locates the good in unanimity, in the unifying unity and locates "the root of all evil"[30] in the singular, thereby merely resuming the doctrine of a radical evil in critical transcendentalism. Chekhov, the physician, as if administering a remedy to this, shows in what direction one is to turn before death: toward "what is called a general idea." "If this is lacking, there is nothing," are the words of a character whose end is near.[31] Further, ever since subsumptive philosophy was instituted, humans have been classed among "living beings" (*zôon logon echon, animal rationale*). They alone are fallible because only they are mortal. All other living beings—gods and animals—know no evil, the former because they do not know death (hence the artifice of the Cartesian hypothesis concerning a deceptive god), the latter because, for them, to die is to wear out.

Is this not to say that outside common representations—outside the species—there is no life? Life has to do with the general, with the common, with the species. Death, on the other hand, arrives unexpectedly in the form of a "this," and every non-subsumed "this" harbors it.

For the Greeks, tragic wisdom *singularizes* the hero to the point of enclosing his knowledge within an insurmountable silence. That sobriety to which Nietzsche challenged his friends was put on stage by Sophocles. Oedipus approaches Colonus knowing that his death awaits him there. His words have given rise to much speculation: "I shall not break the silence concerning the forbidden things. . . . Not to the people, not to my own children can I speak of them." These lines are perhaps not so enigmatic. He talks about something known only to him, of the scars he has for eyes and the approaching end of his life. Indeed, blinded, he sees: "Whatever I shall say will be clear-sighted."[32] He sees and knows that for which there is no fantasm: that singular object of monstration, his death (and, advancing toward its place, Oedipus *points it out* to Theseus). The singularizing withdrawal that death exerts on life would reduce language to zero if it were possible for us to see it in all its clarity. A radical *Aufklärung* on the subject of fantasms would deprive us of the common space where the give and take of speech proves to us that we are not dead.

The difference between reality's common and the singular's other is thus announced in a double signification that strikes us in our being. In the (common) name of the law, I know what I have to be. And, should I fail to know it, life, justly violent, will not fail to teach me. But what do I have to be in the (proper) name of my death? What does it signify to me? In what way do these two modes of signifying being combine with each other? How are they different?

So many things that we know, and this we don't know. Now, of all those things not all are of equal interest. The philosophical task, I have said, is to grasp rigorously the ultimate conditions that we already know, but confusedly. Where, then, is there such a thing as a knowledge that is as impossible to attack as it is impossible to articulate? What is there that is always known to all of us, however poorly? Our birth, our coming to being, is only indirectly known by us. Similarly for our death, it is the departure from being that awaits us. It is well known that to be a philosopher is to speak of life and death . . . as of an entry into and an exit out of the world? Is this the direction in which our knowledge tempts us? Life and death = the same and its other? Let us set aside this dubious equation. A lexical couple can entail an incompatibility of ancestry—a heterogeneity in the guise of incest. Death is always *incongruous,* for it never *throws* itself toward life as toward its twin or twinnable other. Hence, Elleatism, the Roman Stoics, and the German Reformation were all great beginnings, perhaps because in them the other of life was thought of differently.

What, then, is phenomenologically originary? In order to put it into words, I shall borrow a distinction from Hannah Arendt which has a somewhat bizarre sound in French. It is not so much the biographical facts of our birth and death that matter as it is the traits—which she calls ontological—of *natality* (*Gebürtigkeit*) and *mortality* (*Sterblichkeit*).[33] What the phenomenologists of the 1920s and 1930s taught her was that birth and death come under the jurisdiction of natality and mortality, and not the reverse.

The trait of natality carries us toward new beginnings, and it is in the character of adolescence's exasperating charm to acknowledge only this trait. No such founding institutions as bear the names of Socrates and Galileo would exist without the trait of natality. Founding the United Nations, adopting a parliamentary resolution, sitting down to start writing a book, choosing a life partner, are all examples of natality at work. Though on a lesser scale, we experience natality at every step, only it is *put into context.* Arendt, following Augustine in this ("that there might be this beginning . . . a man was created before whom no man existed"[34]), readily declared natality a sufficient reason for humans to exist on earth.

Natality translates linguistic maximization into the contextualization of everyday life. Aristotle's *hoson* well describes a supportive activity that is indispensable to life. But in denying mortality, this trait steers straight into metaphysical theticism. It then caps off the singular with ultimate contexts: genres, types, classes, and species; values, meanings, and ideas; the all-inclusive and the inasmuch-as; principles and norms . . . and there, under those caps, this trait crushes the singular.

The trait of mortality is at work on the things of everyday life. It singularizes the givens. It signifies the *decontextualization* that renders precarious all experience. The sophism of Epicurus is well-known: "Death has for us no sense. Indeed, insofar as we are, death is not there; and when death comes we are no more."[35] As do all sophisms, this one rests on a grain of truth. We do not know the fact of our demise. It is a sophism all the same, for we know quite well the characteristic pull toward our death. It leaves us essentially alone, silent, strangers. And pressured as well, for it is mortality—being towards death—that constitutes temporality. As Augustine is known to have said on the subject of time: "When nobody asks me that question I know what it is. But if anybody asks me to explain it, I no longer know."[36] And it is not fortuitous that on no other occasion does Augustine link ignorance to knowledge in this manner. Time is not just one philosophical problem among many, for it is in it that death signals us. It is as certain and obscure as death. Mortality familiarizes us with our *singularization to come.*

Here, then, is the originary singular which is not simple. It is an occurrent conjunction, not of facts but of traits. These, as will be shown, are superimposable neither upon the distentions of the soul, which are the past and future, nor upon retentions and protentions, nor finally, on the existential ecstases. This is because the future is the dimension, both of the trait that draws one toward death, and the dimension of that which carries us along from birth. By virtue of mortality, *the future solifies,* by virtue of natality, *it totalizes.* The task will be to retrace this contextualization-decontextualization back to the first conditions, "conditions" that are disparate and hence no longer *a priori,* "first" in the temporal sense and hence not in a thetic sense.

Only by doing battle does ordinary language remain familiar with phenomena. By means of a brutal syntax, it forces them under concepts. A battle ensues owing to the referential amplitude of words, for their scope always exceeds a particular given. And onto that battle—a bit like in the *Iliad,* where the gods engage in a combat strictly paralleling that taking place on the plains of Troy—the thetic profession of philosophy superimposes another, even more grandiose battle, the gigantomachia through which reason first (*primum*) grasps (*capit*), *primum captum*—therefore a principle—a known that is absolutely first because it is the most common. If today we are able to bring down onto ourselves unparalleled planetary violences, it is perhaps necessary to recognize in this the return of the singular that was pushed back outside of the normative difference. The particular is easily handled; the singular, on the other hand, never is. Here we have a violence where the "so-called general idea" is all that manages to subsume the disparate singular—a violence that consequently unmasks the fantasmic nature of ultimate referents.

Nobody (before Kant) saw more clearly than Aristotle the philosophical overdetermination that a sovereign grasp imposes on everyday figures of speech. A few of these formulae concerning the *hen* are enough here to recall the fantasmic essence of what is nominative-normatively common. We shall get a glimpse of how this Greek hegemonic fantasm, namely, the one, *differs* from the givens over which it legislates and reigns.

For Aristotle, access to the most common point of view is anagogical, it is an ascent or a taking-back-to. . . . "For every being there is a recursive ascent {*ascension-reconduite*} toward something common and like the one (*pros hen ti*)."[37] Just as decisive here as the *hen* is the *ti*, 'something like. . . ,' 'a certain. . . .' The turn of phrase is frequent in the *Metaphysics*. Aristotle notably employs it when he wants to know that toward which multiple beings converge, which is the focal point to which language refers them and which is, therefore, common to them. One may say he takes an approach similar to Kant's attempt to think the ultimate unity of experiences, though in an inverse fashion. One looks forward to what Aristotle *names* the one, but it evades us—and for a good reason, the best reason in philosophy—namely, that the principle of principles remains unnameable. It has neither a proper noun, since it is not a being, nor a common noun, for it is not a genus. Thus, the *ti* serves to muddle the concept, making it into an indirect description. Furthermore, Aristotle often describes the one as *phusis tis,* 'something like a rising' (an indetermination itself indicating that *phusis* must not be understood as nature—a supreme referent inasmuch as it is entitative—but rather as the event whereby a relation is established, an ultimate referent inasmuch as it is relational). The one "is said the most regarding all beings."[38] For them it is certainly their other but only in a way that one can neither juxtapose it to them as if it were found among them, nor as capping them off as an all-encompassing one. Were the one a being, there would be no evidence of it. Were it a genus, it would need an external differentiator to differentiate it. The one would no longer be *koinon ti,* something common to all beings. Hence it follows that the discourse that has the one as its subject matter—first philosophy—must still be "refined." No programmatic declaration more clearly emphasizes the fantasmic status of this focal referent than what the whole of the *Metaphysics* has as its mission to make known, if we are to believe the pages with which it begins.

The one seems not just unnameable. It also eludes our knowledge by not being susceptible to any specifiable concept. We can, nevertheless, think it with regard to the other upon which it works. Aristotle expressed what the one does to the other with the verb *archein*. The one commences and commands. What? The manifold ways of being, which are singled out by the various divisions in the ways being is signified. Aristotle lists four such divisions: the division according to adventitious beings (*symbebeka*), according to the true and the false, according to those signs that are the categories, and, lastly, according to power and to being-at-work (*dynamis* and *energeia*).[39] Several anagogical approaches are needed to reach the one, but alas, they are mutually irreducible! Is there not something perplexing about this for a henologic doctrine? Thus, it is according to only one of these ascents that a nameable *arche* will be found, subsuming under itself all the beings that it commences and commands. It is the division according to the categories, all of which depend on the *ousia* (a word that can be translated as 'essence' only on the strict condition that it should be understood in the sense of the Latin *esse*). There is, therefore, nothing vague about the subsumptive character of these ten ways of speaking about being. The nine which are added to the substantial mode link up in a network that literally is "subalternate." The "other" is placed "below." This is the reason why Aristotelianism quickly turned the question of being into a doctrine of substance, understood either as a being to which attributes pertain (primary substance) or a specific being to which a definition pertains (secondary substance). Of these four irreducible anagogical approaches, only the one that produces a concept was retained. But is substance not a universally known referent, and therefore identifiable as a common noun?

However, construing substance as the referential one, to the detriment of the other three approaches or ascent-leading-back's, amounts to a censoring of Aristotle's henology for sometimes being deliberately vague and interrogative; it amounts to censoring in it precisely that through which it recognizes the fantasmic status of the one. "In a certain manner (*pôs*), the one is being and being the one."[40] It is a "certain manner" which Aristotelianism will promptly set up in a certain manner through the convertibility of entitative perfections. For Aristotle, *pôs* indicates an archic-anarchic quality both of the one and of being. Since they commence and command all that is susceptible of being known—namely, beings singled out according to the categories, but also those according to the adventitious, the true and the false, power and being-at-work—they do not fall under a superior genus. Being and the one therefore can only be thought of as *archai* deprived of *arché,* and it is thus that they are different from everything that allows itself to be known according to the manifold ways we have of speaking about givens, one of which is their givenness. To have seen it, to have evidence thereof, is to keep open the split between the given and the fantasmically posited which is *recognized as fantasmic*. Therefore it is to think—not to know—the first constellation of theticism, the *henologic difference.*

Does recalling that being *qua* the one remains unknowable contain a lesson for our grasp of hegemonies? There would seem to be some necessity for a referent promoted to "sovereignty" to keep itself out of reach. Is not a condition *sine qua non* of power-wielding agents that they keep themselves inaccessible? On a scale of subordinations, the holder of a higher authority would desert its station if it were to be open to an exchange of control, particularly of that control which has been considered the most certain since antiquity: knowledge. The higher authority must remain as unknowable as the law is inaccessible. The place of knowledge is *under* the one, just as the place of the subject is *under* the law. Outside the law, as we know, there is no life. The place bestows the noun. If here there can be an obligation in the name of the one, or in the name of nature, it is because we have never examined it closely. An epochally sovereign referent gives us life only on the condition that it convey that life to us from a place that is outside our cognitive reach. This is why the law is never mastered, for to what *arche* would we subject it? To say that all hegemonic law is essentially archic-anarchic means that it predominates without any perspective dominating it. If the one were to offer itself to some perspective, or nature to inspection, or self-consciousness (the modern hegemonic fantasm) to introspection, then its rule would come undone.

The law of laws is fantasmic because it does not yield to any prehension and evades comprehension; we cannot possess it. To assign it a place would already be to make it appear before the law, and we all know that all legal appearances are made before it, not the other way around. It does not appear. Rather, it makes things appear—it makes phenomena out of beings.

The normative difference thus is opened by means of what is *called* archic. It opens up the space wherein the phenomenality of those particulars to be subsumed is constituted. "*No ground but say ground.*" The *hen* is not the *pollachôs legein,* the singling out of the manifold, rather everything is singled out with respect to it, a normative henologic difference. *Natura* is not the *naturatum,* but it is with respect to its ends that everything is arranged, a natural normative difference. Self-consciousness is not the empirical self, but it makes experience possible for it, a normative transcendental difference. Without a doubt only the theoreticians of natural law have overestimated knowledge, since they did not hesitate to declare that the sequencing of ends can be deciphered by right reason. Parmenides and Aristotle with regard to the one, as Kant and Luther with regard to consciousness, showed themselves to be more circumspect. The *pros hen* allows itself to be thought but not to be known. Similarly, the ultimate transcendental condition, apperception, indeed unifies our representations but is itself not a representation.

Were it not for our difference, we would never have a world, and perhaps today the world's normative figure has exhausted its resources. Therefore the question will be to know if one can live—and if so, in what manner—under the double bind that is recognized as originary. But the impulse toward the difference remains embedded in language. As soon as we speak according to predicative grammar—and that is the only grammar we have—we have already been situated in the middle ground of multiple configurations. We speak of it, which means we live therein. The three figures of normative difference have been our epochal homes. And if fantasms have the power to make a house arrest, it is because we have always already seen that we are lodged under the violence of the common, outside of which, to say it once more, there is no life. Accordingly, if one asks how normative regimes are to be justified, all one need do is to listen to how we speak. "That mountain over there is the Matterhorn." Just by saying "is" we are reminded of the most ancient difference constituting the law, hence of the power of persuasion belonging to speculations on anamnesis, hence of the maximizing impulse. And above all we are reminded of the power of having seen, therefore the power of the evident which moved Parmenides when he said to the Greeks: "Being is one," and Cicero when he said to the Latins: "Nature prescribes the ends," and Luther to the Germans: "Whatever you are conscious of, you possess."

So, thus domiciled, we "rational animals" have never stopped being "mortals."[41] The normative difference amply instructs us on the different ways our languages speak of and grant evidence to us, in which they legitimize, in the end, what passes for a foundation, in sum, in which they proffer to life a sequestered basis. Being-one, the natural order, and constitutive consciousness are all consolidating and consoling *archai*—their saving power lets us live, but this normative difference never says what it is that crushes life.

". . . [I]f only you could," namely, turn toward the other singular as one turns to the linguistic same—the common, the general, the universal. What if this impotence were precisely what crushes us? Such was for Nietzsche "*the mystery doctrine of tragedy,* the fundamental knowledge of the oneness of all that exists and the view of individuation as the primal cause of evil."[42] Must not difference then be thought of differently, in a way that does not construct an nth variation of that old tandem, the same and *its* other? What if a hegemonic fantasm—the Greek "one"—instead were opposed to the singular as to an other that were rebellious to subsumption? What if the one, nature, and consciousness had never satisfied the expectations invested in them, had never succeeded in turning the singular into a particular, had never posited a "reality" to save us from incongruity, had never smoothed out the disparity. One would have more than a contamination of the sovereign law. One would be dealing with a dispersive counter-strategy as powerful as the subsumptive strategy itself—one would be dealing with an ultimate other. We then would be familiars unto death, familiars till we died not only from the fantasmic strategy leading to order, but even from a strategy in conflict with it, forever disturbing the tranquility of order. For after all, our ordinary experience has taught us more about the ultimates than just to reminisce about the great authorities whose representations frame and saturate life.

Once again, a summary of these pages would not be wrong in seeing in them a testing of a suspicion, namely, that the other of life does not fit in well with it; that their discord has always been known to us, however confusedly; that death joins life without, however, forming a tandem with it, that it does not reflect life symmetrically nor oppose it with a determinate negation. A topological project requires that the verification of this suspicion be based solely on the details of normative argumentation. If the very violence of life is what institutes a hegemony, by means of what undertow does the dispersive singular work upon it? I take Nietzsche's word in its strongest sense. We *cannot* pledge allegiance to single objects of monstration. That would mean our death. Life nourishes itself on fantasms, and that obliges us to rethink the difference with regard to the function of the double allegiance that nobody has ever escaped.

Before we proceed with this new step, let us go back so as to better approach it. It is basically a matter of paying close attention. The occurrent difference between a given phenomenal economy and the singularization that is to come in it—this difference, which is no longer *uniformly* normative, will have to be liberated from under the figures of the normative difference where the color of the singular blends into the gray of the particular.

The functionaries of humanity are responsible for a rigorous reflection leading to a clear view of what we have always, though vaguely, understood. Granted, but there are also a great many ways of being rigorous, though few of any consequence, that are known to us all. For us living beings, as has been seen, no prior understanding can be more common than that by which we know ourselves to be mortal. "It was too good to last," "it had to come to an end"—so speaks that other prior understanding which is different from the one in which life grasps hold of itself in a fleeting order of subsumptions. In such turns of phrase we *know and do not know* what we are talking about. They remind us of an other, referred to as a negative. What we know without knowing is that no victory nourishes life (violence of the posited common reality) without the negative experience (violence of the singular reality that has to be forsaken). Were they to remain loyal to their mission of bringing into the open the unposited *a priori* conditions, philosophers could not help but fail in their public function. The *a priori* known to us by means of our birth and death is not edifying. Were they, on the other hand, to remain loyal to their role as servants of order, they could not help but lack by half—but would it be half?—the conditions needed to bring their rigorous discourses to broad daylight. The prior understanding of a reality, ready to deploy itself as principle, thus remains paralyzed by an entirely different reality, one for which no thought of principles could ever compensate, namely, a conflict between the linguistic impulse and the mortal knowledge that is irreducible to the old tandem. Rather, a call of death insinuates itself into the difference that ought to function as a breath of air. The normative function of each focal meaning here is shot through by a transgressive function—ultimate functions that disrupt the focal referent from the moment of its institution.

"Expropriation, to where? Neither the direction nor the drift of this question were ever pursued."[43] When Heidegger raises the question of being and time for the last time, he immediately sets aside two figures of the other. The first benefits from a non-place while the place of the second is surrounded by an epochal parenthesis, a non-place made into the other of being, namely, time; brackets are put around this second other of being, namely, beings. In the phrase "time and being," he says, the conjunction "and" indicates that which is to be thought of as the same and therefore as what is not opposed to anything, while the differential conjunction between being and beings is suspended. Heidegger seeks to understand being *as* time, which he calls an "event of appropriation" (*Ereignis*). Being's other then emerges in a new place, which permeates appropriation with the pull of an undertow (*Entzug*), and works upon it from within as an "event of expropriation" (*Enteignis*). The entire course of what follows will serve to illustrate how one must understand the crushing conjunction of strategies in being. No long journey is needed, however, to see that, so restituted, the other of being no longer enters, is unable to enter, into the artifice of thought usually associated with Heidegger's name: the ontological difference.

Expropriation, to where? Is it so difficult to pursue the question, to follow the direction in which that *ex* points? But first of all, to what does the *ap* (the *ad*) of appropriation point? By means of ever-varying and rejoined paths, Heidegger singles out and retraces the coming, the advent. Even more so than the ontological difference, it is this advent—coming to presence—that most vividly occupies his thought. In one of his numerous attempts to explain it, Heidegger follows the footsteps of language; so he says that every time and for as long as a speaking occurs, a world is produced or one is preserved. *Ad*-indicates a contextualization, the condition of possibility for every Dasein. Even before going into its internal structure, its functional modalities, much less the phenomenal site where it is born, it is evident that without "appropriation" there is no life. It is also evident that this appropriation is not among the "human additions" that language produces; it is not a fantasm. *Ereignis* is not akin to the universal or the common, the *koinon*. If it allows for life, it is not by means of general ideas that it sustains and supports us, but rather by means of more humble everyday configurations.

So, expropriation to where? Heidegger insisted all along that the only way our age will escape a violence that has become systematic and global is through a new relationship with death. "We 'rational animals' must again *become* mortal." And all along he also sought to grasp death, which is inscribed in life, not as a postscript at the end nor as an other that has been reached, nor as that wherein it results, nor as that other summarily dismissing life's demands—nothingness. Death is the revealer of a trait of being, "trait" in the sense of traction (*Zug,* a word that in Heidegger always means what the tradition called a "category of being") exerting its contextualizing attraction from within. Expropriation to where? Certainly not "toward" death, which would once again mean to place it behind a veil. Expropriation, rather, toward the singularization to come, toward that trait of being that mortality reveals, an everyday trait. What has been said here should suffice for one to have glimpsed that the *ex* points toward the mortals that we are and that we also have to become.

How does one become what one is? This can be described in relation to the "oneself," the singular other of the transcendental "I." In order to preserve the directionality of expropriation, to suggest that it furnishes the condition for all negative experience, to emphasize that it introduces the conflicting other of life into its very core, and finally, to keep the vocabulary sufficiently malleable to single out both the characteristics of experience and those of the argumentative strategies, I will speak of the singularization to come as an undertow that undermines every hegemonic fantasm.

Furthermore, one must be able to retain, by denotative precision, the full range of those phenomena that acquire descriptive breadth. What is the surplus which, at the moment when the trait of death comes to pull the question of being toward the nonsubsumable singular, suddenly serves to bracket the ontological difference (together with the normative difference that it incorporates[44])? Does this not entail something tragic? More radically than it does with regard to the "formidable" (*deinon*)[45] human essence, in Heidegger the tragic declares itself in "the attempt to think being without regard for its foundation in beings"[46]—thus, once it is suspended, without regard for the difference between being and beings. As he conceives of this difference, one would be inclined to say that being-towards-death has no place there, that in retaining it one would banish the very phenomenon that had revealed time; and inversely, that in order to safeguard (*diasôzein*) that phenomenon comparable to no other, one had to dismiss the difference. Yet in order to see that the henological, natural, and transcendental figures of the difference are essentially tragic figures, it should suffice to remember the conflict between the fantasm and the singular, a conflict that permeates every hegemony. In terms of the law, the singularization to come fractures the normative bond into a legislative-transgressive double bind.

No age before ours has known planetary violence. Consequently, no age is better positioned to unlearn fantasmic maximization, to learn and bear in mind the tragic condition. It is a privilege, which itself is a *deinon*. Therefore, the task—not exactly without interest—will be to grasp how violence is born from a trauma that thought inflicts on itself.

The heroes of Aeschylus and Sophocles owed allegiance to incompatible laws whose sub-sumptive genus is lacking. And it is from this lack that they perish—thus, from disparity, as did Dionysus. "The norm is only posited in Greek tragedy so that it may be transgressed or because it has already been transgressed; it is thus that Greek tragedy emanates from Dionysus, god of confusion, god of transgression."[47]

Our singularization to come has expelled us in advance from our every insertion into a world—we say, from every constituted phenomenality. Singularization dephenomenalizes. This is what our knowledge of ultimates teaches us. This knowledge can be deciphered best in the largest characters, which are those of the law. Topology teaches us what binds us in every normative position, not just what is represented as maximal, but also the deictic experience from which it was extracted and which will come to haunt it, destitute it. The vocabulary of difference does not express very well the ultimates which make us posit the *koinon* and let the *deiktikon* be. If it is as mortals that we know how the undertow toward the monstrable singular always works on demonstrable theses, then the strategies crossing each other in the event, instead, maintain a *differend.*

One has abdicated philosophy if one does not inquire into the conditions that make ordinary experience possible. But to respond to this inquiry with a thesis—to posit a simple *arché*—is again to enter into the megalomania of desire. The analytic of ultimates shows these conditions of possibility to be anarchic because they are at odds with themselves.

The Birth of the Law from the Denial of the Tragic

"Cruel is my lot, if I rebel; but it is just as cruel if I must sacrifice my child, the jewel of my house, and, at the altar, soil my fatherly hands with the bloody flood gushing from a slaughtered virgin. Is there a course that does not spell misery?"[48]

"Even after these painful contradictions have been eliminated, the question of being will not have been answered; but the mind, no longer tormented, ceases to ask this question it considers unjustified."

—H. Hertz[49]

On a wall in Pompeii there is a fresco representing Agamemnon sacrificing his daughter, Iphigenia. Noteworthy in the picture is the fact that the face of the koricide father is veiled.

It is Agamemnon speaking in the first quotation above, of whom Homer had said he reigned over "numerous islands and all of Argos" (*Il.* 2, 108). He was the mightiest of Greek princes. After Paris had abducted Helen, Menelaus's wife, it fell to Agamemnon, his brother, to lead the punitive expedition against Troy. None other than Zeus had ordered the operation. The fleet had gathered at Aulis in Beotia, but Artemis caused adverse winds to blow; it was she who demanded the sacrifice. Thus, Agamemnon found himself at the crossroads of two divine commands. Was this reason enough to cover his face?

Furthermore, he found himself at the crossroads of two laws, at the intersection of a conflict bleaker than those which present themselves to other tragic heroes. What law could be more important to the premier commander than to bring to a good end a war ordered by the first of the gods? And what law could be stronger for a father than the law of preserving his child's life? "Is there a course that does not spell misery?"

A rhetorical question, for woe unto the father who denies his family ties in the name of public duties, and woe unto an army commander who denies his political ties in the name of blood relations. How is one not to hide one's face in the face of such a nomic conflict.

Finally, Agamemnon finds himself placed at the intersection of two very old transgressions. The hubris experienced in the abduction of Helen strikes his *polis;* the hubris presented in the deed of the ancestor, Atrea, who had killed her own son, strikes his *oikos*. Neither of these infractions had been committed by Agamemnon himself, neither the one plunging the cities into war nor the one wrecking his home. They *befall* him. "Cruel is my lot, if I rebel; but it is just as cruel if I must sacrifice my child." Whether he deserts (*liponaus,* 212) his supreme post or whether he renounces his lineage, for him there is no way out without fault. Are these destinies of retribution crossing behind his veil, two ancient blindnesses and their sudden consequences?

But, speaking in Aulis, Agamemnon takes a curious turn and shifts his tone without pause or transition. From one to the other, the conflict of duties is lifted—one would say by the favorable winds, efficacious even before blowing. "If this sacrifice, this virginal blood, shackles the winds, one can with ardor, proud ardor, desire it without fault" (v. 214 ff.). Here, at that very moment that is still cruel in having two laws, the either-or is *severed*. Furthermore, the law that Agamemnon embraces is free of evil, it is *thémis,* righteous, just, sacred.[50]

With a single blow, one of the two laws in conflict—the law of the family—has been dismissed. And there is where we see the *tragic denial.*

And this new hubris will bear its terrible fruits upon his return to Troy. At Aulis, it inflames Agamemnon's passions. The denial is denied and anxiety gives way to audacity. "He dared become his daughter's sacrificer" (v. 225). She implored, she cried, "father!"; but "everything, she saw, was in vain." She underwent the sacrificial ordeal. Her father had her placed on the altar, "like a goat" (v. 232). To mute her imprecations—and avoid their resonance in the house—she was gagged. Then again like an animal, she is restrained with a "bridle" (v. 237), which is to say, a bit. These are Agamemnon's words. Thus he succeeds in transforming his daughter into an animal for slaughter.

Thus, above all Agamemnon constitutes himself as military commander freed from contrary allegiances. In the name of the city, which he elevates to the rank of sovereign meaning, he obliterates "there, that singular." He consolidates the union between commander and his troops. The law, uniformly obligatory, emerges in the sacrificial rapture. *Tragic denial is necessary for the univocal law to be born.*

In this light, the Pompeii fresco is not difficult to understand. What Agamemnon fails to see is seen only too clearly by the choir. Of Iphigenia, it says "The beam of her gaze will wound with pity each one of her executioners . . ." (v. 240). In the face of this human gaze that pleads for another human gaze, Agamemnon blinds himself. The painter conveys the very veil of denial.

Tragedy always maps out something like a sweep of the eyes. The hero *sees* the conflicting laws, and—at the moment of tragic denial—then blinds himself toward one of them, *fixing his gaze* on the other. Cities and armies have lived, and live, thanks to a commander's blindness. Then an *eye-opening* catastrophe ensues, the moment of tragic truth. The vision of the double bind *catches the eye* (it literally bursts the eyes of Oedipus and those of Tiresias, though in a different way) and singularizes the hero to the point that the city no longer has a place for him. In fact, there is no double bind unless the *both-and* of the two conflicting laws exhausts the field of possibilities.[51] Blindness is transformed from denial to recognition. Hubristic sightlessness is transformed into visionary blindness. Deprived of eyeballs, Oedipus sees. What? Tragic truth, the truth of the *differend.*

Like Agamemnon, the philosopher–civil servant of humanity declares the law by repressing the counter-law.

I have found the denotative rigor by which to pinpoint tragic truth—a model (or an instance) of the phenomenologically originary double bind—present in Wittgenstein's "differend." To be sure, this term functions differently than it does in what he would call the grammar of investigating being, which is where I insert it. I might add that in these investigations he in turn asked what is the ordinary use of the words one uses in these interrogations. But if usage makes the meaning, it must be permitted to introduce into a tragic critique of hegemonies a term that, even in Wittgenstein, expresses precisely the conflict between some fantasmic sense invoked in ordinary usage and the "there, that singular" which is the case. It is because of this term and this singular conflict—hence because of a lexical need—that I will here take up a few sections from the *Philosophical Investigations* dealing with the nature of philosophy, which appears in its pages as irreducible to a principial bureaucracy.

Originally Wittgenstein meant to use the remark by Heinrich Hertz, cited above, as an epigraph to the *Investigations*. Hertz wondered about the being (*Wesen*) of electromagnetic energy. Having invented the antenna—the "Hertzian relay"—he asked what those forces were that the device captured, a field of waves or a stream of corpuscles? The problem was to remain painful and insoluble. The physicist nevertheless succeeded in "eliminating" the problem by borrowing sometimes Euler's photic model, and sometimes Newton's.

But why, moreover, did Hertz consider the question of electromagnetic energy to be unjustified? Wittgenstein answers, as it were, in his stead: What disqualifies all interrogations into the inner constitution of things—all the while spurring them on—is the "tendency to assume a pure intermediary being (*Mittelwesen*) between the propositional *signs* and the facts." Language inflicts a specific injury on us. "Our forms of expression prevent us in all sorts of ways from seeing that everything happens quite ordinarily; they send us off in pursuit of chimeras."[52] Our idioms add *chimeras* to what is simply the case and is born out by experience. They traumatize the mind by exceeding experience, which alone can teach us which family of sentences belongs to which network of facts.

Thus, two types of conflicts are to be distinguished. One can be eliminated by the analysis of language signs and the features that link them to each other. This is the type of conflict in which two images of the same fact are opposed: "*Le temps s'en va.—Las!, le temps non, mais nous allons*" "Time goes on—alas, not time, but it is us that go" (Ronsard). This is a factual conflict, which can be solved by territorializing according to language games. It is eliminated by assigning signs or images to their respective usages. Following Hertz here, Wittgenstein calls this sort of conflict a contradiction (*Widerspruch*). In ordinary language, we lapse incessantly into it without much harm done to everyday praxis. Philosophy, however, demands that it be clarified. On the other hand, it is impossible to eliminate or resolve conflicts of the other sort. At most, analysis can anesthetize them. Given over to demarcations between idiomatic families, the mind takes a break from the question of being; yet, under such local anesthesia, the chimeras (the "time" of Ronsard's poem) persist. As does Nietzsche, Wittgenstein thinks we can never rid ourselves of them. Also, for him as for Nietzsche, they spring back up as soon as we speak. These illusions are no longer transcendental—no longer generated by totalizing reason as were the ideas of World, Soul, and God—but linguistic, and they remain no less ineradicable. Such is the conflict Wittgenstein called a *differend* (*Widerstreit*) between, on the one hand, a linguistic chimera and, on the other, the disparate which is the case.[53]

Witness the torments of Hertz. "A magnetic field with a given force X results from waves traveling at frequency Y"; "A magnetic field with a given force X results from corpuscles displaced at velocity Z." The contradiction between one and the other of these descriptions is painful. The former describes a field constituted by wave frequencies, the latter sees in it a moving granular mass. Yet both, however heterogeneous, prove equally workable. What is cruelly lacking is a higher set of propositions capable of subsuming them both under a demystified concept of force. "You come from *one* side and you know your way about; you come to the same place from another side and no longer know your way about" (§ 203). Faced with the *contradiction* between descriptions, Hertz found his peace by contenting himself with protocols following either one or the other image. He anesthetized the *differend* opposing, in their turn, these protocols and the chimera ("electromagnetic force") in whose pursuit language sends its speakers. The archic functioning can here be seen in operation, namely, the impulse to secure an ultimate "why." Both descriptions speak of forces in a magnetic field. Ordinary language itself thus prompts us to accept a pure intermediary being and to ask: What *are* those forces after all? If we yield to the prompting, what would we stand to gain? If we are to believe Hertz, nothing but torment. If observation were to produce an answer to the question of their being, we would know why two contradictory images can nevertheless prove equally useful. But the question surpasses experience and it must therefore be anesthetized, censured, suppressed, repressed. "We become aware of the important *facts* only when we suppress the question 'why?'" (§ 471).

The inclination toward subsumption under chimeras has, as it were, sharpened the pencils and laid out the paper for the civil servants of humanity to use. Emerging from everyday language, it has had no problem recruiting ever again a bureaucratic corps. Since we give ourselves over to it every time we speak, the impulse to maximize a meaning of being suggests itself with an obviousness that places it beyond all suspicion of trickery. And, like other repressed urges, the impulse engaged in chimeras is not satisfied with half measures, it wants totalizing measures. Philosophers at least since Diotima have endeavored to push language to its last consequences by postulating a primary grammar directing all other grammars. Thus Aristotle extrapolates from a grammar of physical change and, through a series of metabases, seeks a truly archaic science, though admittedly inaccessible.

Now, in the profession of principles, directive *grammars* have merely been the logical effect of a subsumptive *referent,* a referent to which ordinary language provides the name but which, at the end of the semantic maximization, gives rise only to a fantasm, not to a cognitive concept. Thus the notion of the differend that I am employing here takes us far from Wittgenstein. It is diverted from the analysis of language where it reveals how metaphysical assertions are born ("electromagnetic energy is undulatory") and is introduced into the topology of metaphysics itself where it reveals how hegemonies ("being is one") are born and reign. The tragic truth that names the differend serves as a vehicle to discover the originary strategies in being, strategies Heidegger describes as thrusts and withdrawals without genus between appropriation and expropriation.

Hertz's complaint therefore clearly singles out the very structure of the tragic—singular givens in contradiction, disparates; their differing from the chimerical authority that is posited so as to bestow meaning; finally, the silence in the face of the authoritative instance about which one cannot speak. . . . The epigraph fits Wittgenstein like a glove. We will also find this structure under each normative hegemony.

The disparate. Obviously, neither Hertz nor Wittgenstein speak of "contradiction" in the sense of the logical principle that carries this name. It is not a matter of a relation between two terms where one negates what the other affirms. For Wittgenstein, contradiction designates incompatibilities among linguistic usages. We indulge in a pastiche of contradiction as soon as we speak of "electric current," of "voltage pressure," et cetera. Contradictions between the hydrodynamic and monodynamic language families make up the life of language, but they also make for the unhappiness of the physicist. It is not that these two families contradict each other by being mutually exclusive and by being jointly exhaustive of a genus (physics has other parts). The principles of identity and of the excluded middle do not help one trace the ancestry of ordinary language. Language owes its life to *disparate* contradictories. These sustain our conversations, not through the disjunction between A and not-A—not by the same and its other—but through innumerable conjunctions, each of which both *follows up* on a particle of speech and opposes a *non sequitur* to it. Step by step as well as over long intervals they breed a text, a world, a texture made of bits and pieces, not in a continuous fabric. To patch things up one gradually links them together. *This* makes a text together with that other *this,* and then yet another—as zones thus woven partially overlap, touch each other, are contiguous or separated by intervals. The world expresses itself in heteromorphous prose. The gallery of images associated with water currents, from which Hertz found it so painful to go on to volts and amperes, is a good example. Such a contradictory linking-up of images helps one to make oneself understood and even to build power stations, but it does not help one make the transition to the idiom of particles that a few years later came to be called electrons. Contradictory linkups between images are those that step outside a given language game. Hence the need for an analysis demarcating idiomatic kinship relations, an operation which for Wittgenstein amounts to their justification. "Describe language games! The importance of their justification will follow" (§ 486).

To justify a language is to regulate the operations of its speakers. For Hertz, the question of being is not justified because one doesn't 'do' anything with it. There are opposing rules in the idiomatic diversity of the world, and to speak of rules is to speak of discipline and obedience. By stringing sentences together, we slide without interruption from one territorial discipline to another. Everydayness is made of successive establishments and familiar places, provisional allegiances to rules and usage and to their suspension. Nomic topography is essentially nomadic.[54] As is evident, this nomadic movement leaves a mark not only in speech but on everything we call thought and life ("What men accept as worth justifying shows how they think and live" (§ 325). One initiates first one language game then another, and already one's observance of the rules has changed. The task of philosophy is not to construct languages purified from all contradiction. As Hertz's sigh amply shows, grammatical conventions capable of disentangling the discourse on electromagnetism fall under the jurisdiction of the physicist. It is incumbent upon the philosopher not to resolve, but to make an inventory of the rules muddled in everyday language. How do we advance in a world not freed of contradictions? It is a matter of practice, of displacing the problem to the "civil" realm. What do we make of the disparity, how do we arrange it and arrange ourselves with it? "The civil status of contradiction or its status in the civil world: that is the philosophical problem" (§ 125).

A favorite opinion among the theoreticians of modernity, who either condemn it or exalt it, is that at the beginning of normative thought everything held together as in the compact ball that Parmenides evokes. At the opposite end of history, the recognition of language games is to have ended by dispersing all referents having normative force. The disparity, into which Parmenides' ball explodes, supposedly is the work of the moderns. And that work could be given a specific date of birth, perhaps that January 10, 1610, when Galileo trained his telescope on the stars. "In one night, the universe lost its center, and the next morning it had innumerable ones."[55] By retracing the legislative-transgressive strategies contained in normative arguments, I will attempt to show, to the contrary, that dispersive violence has been emphasized ever since Parmenides; it has been recognized as one recognizes one's own death, covered over again by the equally violent requirements of life.

These remarks on the disparate contradictories are sufficient to remind us of that *upon which* an epochal hegemonic regime is instituted, on an arrangement of shards of everydayness, according to new rules. Our world remakes itself with each of the great Greek, Roman, and modern beginnings. The nomadic linguistic territory—here one family, there another, and between them figures etched out by all sorts of exchanges—then suddenly appears outlined by a different silhouette. Briefly put, the rule of the Eleatic arrangement occupies itself with contrariety and contradiction in the strict sense, that of the Roman arrangement with the history of the singular, and that of transcendentalism resulting from the Reformation with the simultaneity of two perceptions of self.

However, these remarks tell us nothing about that *by means of which* a hegemonic regime is instituted, nothing about the fantasms that rearrange the world. A discourse that *speaks* "fundamentally" is an instituting discourse. The arrangement is not always what is taken to be founded. Thus it is not sufficient to grasp the disparity in its nomographies; it is necessary to seek again the differing at its place of emergence.

The differend: This is, to be sure, a polymorphous notion and therefore is opposed to what one calls, or maybe no longer calls, ideologies. Each ideology necessarily affirms itself to be *sovereign* and yet as the *rival* to all others. The reference by which to settle this differend is lacking; the superior authority remains unidentified,[56] thus providing inexhaustible grist for the great intellectual machineries. This conflict between universals, we shall see, gives rise to a diachronic figure, the historical differend between thetic referents. The disjunction distributes fantasms along a historical axis, between the early and the late, and particularly along the "too early" and the "too late." Phenomena always arrive too early for such messianic fantasms and they always come too late for the hegemonies we bemoan as one does the evils of a land.

Through their plurality hegemonies emphasize the differend, though they never produce anything but conflicts among theses. Candidates who quarrel over a prize by means of ideological satanization (as was the case in 1984, when Teheran's satanization of Washington was echoed by the latter's satanization of Teheran, Moscow, Tripoli, Managua . . .) face off against each other in the bowels of the same theticism. By contrast, a differend, in its place of emergence, expresses a conflict between a thesis of the same and a non-thetic other, the conflict of ultimates.

This differend may best be understood in terms of Wittgenstein's self-criticism. After the *Tractatus,* his thinking underwent a turn: "We turn *(drehen)* around our whole way of considering." He turned away from the logical ideal, that is, from the prejudice according to which philosophy would regulate the determining conditions of every possible language, and he turned toward the analysis of the everyday materials from which any such ideal can arise. From the requirement—"which had seduced me"—that the meaning of words be perfectly determined, the turning then leads to the examination of ordinary cases to which words apply, including those the earlier prejudice had endowed with a meaning "as pure as a crystal" (§§ 81, 108).

In the two projects, contradictories are not treated in the same way. Under the regime of the normative science, which is what logic was supposed to be, they amounted to indeterminates—to the confused, exterior, simple effects of the inner language of thought which for its part is perfectly ordered. With the renewal of oppositions of the most traditional kind—inner-outer, the law of bivalence (all statements are either true or false), et cetera—the logical order was to dissipate vagueness. In terms of contradictories, it was supposed to subsume them, resolve them from on high and redeem them. Yet, having detected in antinomian mechanics the very workings of our language, a functioning that generates chimeras, Wittgenstein nevertheless proceeds in the opposite direction, "*counter to* an impulse to misunderstand" those workings. Hence the great sobering and exorcizing project. "Philosophy is a battle against the bewitchment of our understanding by our language" (§ 109). Wittgenstein's turn toward the analysis of networks of everyday usages is no more able to put an end to the consoling-consolidating use of words than is Kant's critical turn. Even better, Wittgenstein never gave up the quest for one ultimate source of meaning, for "the redeeming word finally permitting us to grasp that which, ungraspable, has burdened our consciousness."[57] Language naturally impels us to seek the saving word. But once one detects that linguistic fantasmogenics always grow back, it becomes possible to defunctionalize the craft of philosophy. "As for *us,* we bring words back from their metaphysical to their everyday use"(§ 116).

The differend is there, where a blank space has been left by the saving word in its conflict with the diversity that is the case; and the implacable thrust in our languages to fill that blank space with chimeras—that is its place of its emergence. "A whole mythology is deposited in our language."[58] "Electromagnetic energy" would be one of those saving words, saving us from the contradictions between the models elaborated by Hertz. But that word is mythical. In order to save, it would have to express the being or essence (*Wesen*) of what it names. No doubt, the analogy with myth stirs up as many problems as it solves, which may explain why Wittgenstein did not develop it further. Nevertheless it clearly indicates what our language wishes for us, nothing less than the calm assurance of having hold of being. Such confidence can only be due to an excretion of predicative grammar, one that never leaves us. The gap between the being a word presumes and the ordinary use it serves never closes up, and thoroughly preserving this gap is a never-ending task. Witness the ceaseless struggle in the *Philosophical Investigations* against the in-itself or essence, against everything that may be grasped from within. His is a battle without end as was Kant's dispersing of transcendental illusions. The drive of idioms that speak to us as if they made us grasp things from within them—as if we were grasping them within ourselves—is a thoroughgoing drive. A sober philosophy would dissipate this double echo at the heart of everyday assertions. But perfect sobriety remains beyond the reach of analytic ascesis. Dejection occurs because the saving word seems to impose itself as a bit of natural obviousness as soon as we speak. "*Say* electromagnetic energy. . . ." Wittgenstein directs this entirely Kantianesque formula directly against the metaphysics of ineffability in the *Tractatus:* "One believes one is tracing the outline of nature over and over again, and one is merely following along the form through which we consider it" (§ 114).

Again, a reading would not be wrong that saw in the following pages primarily a document in support of the pain to which Wittgenstein and Hertz bear witness—a pain that evermore alters the pleasure of calling things by their (common) names. The document shows not only that the pain is ancient and that the differend of which it is a symptom has instituted philosophy as well as, perhaps, what is called Western civilization; in addition, it calculates into that pain an evil that is present until death. There is an evil lodged in everyday speech, manifesting itself in the dispersion of singular cases from which rises the megalomania of saying what is. Its pangs that vex everyday life are better expressed by "differend" than by "difference."

The career, more than two millennia long, of normative differences proves that no speaker escapes the mythogenic condition of wanting to say what is. Hence, it will be necessary to try to understand the difference in the differend, as well as the differend in difference. And this will happen by asking whether something like "metaphysics" has ever existed, a label that in the last century has above all served the purpose of discrediting one's contemporaries. Wittgenstein, for instance, had no qualms about ranking among them what we might call the phenomenologists of being; and Heidegger may well have repaid the favor in kind, if for no other reason than Wittgenstein's theses on the autonomy of grammar. I intend to detach the "differend" from this thesis and to use it as a tactical implement to detect how, at the idiomatic inceptions of philosophy, being was given to utter "foundation." It was given to do so when it used hegemonic fantasms to make the law, and by undoing the law through an *oblique fidelity to that very singular from which the law had been raised.* If this is the case, a certain cleistomania inherent in philosophy will prove to be thetic, which runs: The "closed field of metaphysics" merely amounts to one more thesis *in refer-*

ence to which one is situated. Read in the light of the question of being, the differend is articulated in legislative-transgressive strategies that provide mortals with their condition of being, a broken condition that philosophers—those who know how to read—have never ceased to watch over.

It is also a broken condition from which, it seems, Wittgenstein suffered until his death. In the fantasmogeny of ordinary language he experienced the very intellectual sin which for him, Ludwig Wittgenstein, amounted to a sheer loss. Yet he mocked the philosophical "festivals" stemming from this condition, where words transform what they name into chimeras more real than reality—just as the dancers clothed in a goat skin (*tragos*)—the Greek tragic dancers—transformed themselves into fantastic beings more real than reality. The transmutations by which philosophers declare first this referent, now that one, to be ultimate sharpens our *tragic condition*. Since an ailment is best diagnosed during its acute phase, it will be our task to grasp the precise figure of this tragic character under the regimes of the one, of nature, and of hegemonical consciousness.

Silence: The silence of Hertz amounted to censorship. What would be expressed were the contradictory model-images he construed of electromagnetism: waves, corpuscles. As to their differend with the "being" of electromagnetism, nothing could be said. Nothing could be *done* with being. The function of the censorship was to demarcate the field of experimentation; outside of this field there was no productive language. His was a technological silence.

Wittgenstein's silence resulted not from the incompatibility of observations and the hypotheses that are to be verified, but from the idiom and the need to describe its uses. In the *Tractatus,* this meant a silence about everything extra-syntactic (the concluding line—"Whereof one cannot speak, thereof one must be silent"—points to the ineffable character of traditional philosophical questions). In the later writings, it meant a silence about the extra-ordinary. It is necessary to dissolve the chimeras in order to grasp what usage makes obvious. This is done by analyzing the everyday use of words, including those which are inflated to normative dimensions by speculation. Usage determines sense; here, the cleaver falls on absurd turns of phrase because they go beyond the ordinary. Wherever the usage does not speak to us, there is nothing to be said and nothing to analyze. This is Wittgenstein's analytical silence.

Equally exclusive is silence in *Being and Time,* where it appears as a simple modification of that originary trait of being which is speech! In the beginning there is *Rede.* . . . Speech alone is inclusive. At most silence modifies it. Later, Heidegger seeks to recover an inclusive silence, one that would render all speech possible just as being renders possible all beings. The explicit retrieval of that originary silence would yield a "sigetics." In this *a priori* silence the private conversation (*idion*) wherein all our idioms are confined would be effaced. This then is a non-subjective but nevertheless transcendental silence.

The differend seizes upon speakers with a different kind of silence. Trapped in the double bind between disparate singulars and a subsumptive fantasm, we are rather *struck* with silence. Both technological and analytical silences amount to decisions not to take the step from phrases to habitual rules by means of phrases pretending to discover new rules, lest we sink into nonsense. The final words of the *Tractatus* give testimony to that determined disjunction between what we will and what we will not say: ". . . thereof *one must* be silent." Moreover, in the *Investigations*, the philosophical interest is even defined as the silence that excludes chimeras. "Whatever is hidden does not interest us" (§ 126). The origin of silence concerning the illusion of an in-itself is epochal in a sense inverse from that of Husserl. As opposed to Husserl, the technological and analytical practitioners suspend, not the everyday to see essences, but essences to better see the everyday. With the anti-humanist Heideggerian turn, the origin of silence comes to lie outside of all behavior and all decisions. Derived from an existential modification, silence then reaches being itself as one of its traits, namely, as the occurrence of difference in language. Like Apollo in the temple of Delphi, being speaks and keeps silent within the epochal confines—here in the sense of the history of being—of a given tongue.

Hence, if the differend strikes, it means there is a victim. "Destiny strikes," "fate has its victims"—these and many others phrases we so often encounter in reading deserve close attention. Leaving aside the question of what is understood by destiny and fate, these phrases tell the truth—at least by their predicates—about the differend on several phenomenal levels. They bespeak the violence that makes for tragic knowledge.

First, on the propositional level, the sober ones of Nietzsche declare: "There, that mountain . . ." and, in so doing, are constituted as victims, struck by the silence that separates the singular from the fantasm. The differend between the enunciative and the ostensive exhibits its violence as it severs what we say from the "this" that can only be pointed to with a finger. It is painful to speak, since we forever lack those words that might break the silence by which language zooms off from the singular event that is the case.

In tragedy, silence enters the domain of gesture. At a certain juncture, a certain hero slays *that* insolent charioteer, in a certain neighboring town marries *that* forsaken woman, and finds himself already entangled in much more than singulars, namely, in fantasmic excesses such as parricide and incest. It is said that in theater these excesses constituted suffering that was no longer—or not yet—the suffering of the hero but of Dionysus. Silence strikes when their discrepancy becomes obvious; but it has struck all along, ever since ankle irons passed over the little boy's heels, ever since he was abandoned in the desert, discovered, named Oedipus (namely, 'pierced feet')—ever since *this individual* had anything to do with the disparity that made up his life. This is the arch-silence of the Dionysian-heroic differend that commences and directs the tragedy, that moves it as its true *arché*.

Moreover, the violence that interrupts speech can furthermore be read in epochal history. The order established by hegemonic fantasms *is conquered* each time. By what? By the nameless abyss where we are devoured by negative experience (the experience of the unjustifiable, of evil, and, presupposing the experience of the ineluctable, of death[59]). Fantasmic consolations and consolidations work against that experience. The same abyss—but which is nothing other than the disparity of singulars—also plunges into vertigo the brief moments of interregnum during which a normative referent becomes indefensible—it becomes unsustainable and one cannot argue it without falling into ridicule. Such was the anguish borne by the fourteenth and fifteenth centuries. The framework of ends considered to be natural broke down, the world's rational structure crumbled, hegemonic nature was stripped bare and trivialized under the rubric of nominalism. At that time, the modern foundation, the consciousness of self, had not been expressed. At such moments, when a referential system is in that way struck moribund, the people live as if holding their breath. "Say ground," and the anguish will be dispelled. During inter-hegemonic times, one gains a clear knowledge that the function of the regime of a uniformly subsumptive fantasm is to repress. It is a knowledge about death, which can no more rise to the level of speech than "there, that mountain." This knowledge has to do with an undertow that destabilizes every law, traversing the law as its counter-law. The integrating violence of fantasms is conquered by the dissoluting violence of the singular. *We know*—and this knowledge is more accessible at times of historical rupture than it is under hegemonies. The content of a tragic knowledge of the differend is the legislative-transgressive fracture.

If the philosopher's task is to clarify a knowledge that we all possess, however confusedly, and if that knowledge has to do with the strategies of being between which our birth and our death place us, then there is no more originary certainty to be deduced than that of being as what is *capable of fantasms,* in differend with its own *ostensibility.*[60] Indeed, in the universalizing attraction of the fantasmable we have recognized the work of being-for-birth and, in the singularizing withdrawal of the ostensible, that of being-for-death.

Thus the differend reveals its originary site. What must be asked is, what is the originary condition of these disparate traits that unifies them? Hence, the question of being must remain open since tragic knowledge strikes with silence. The one certainty of mortals is that there is a differend between *this,* which is taking place before us, and what we say about it; between an Oedipus seized by just anger against an insolent charioteer and an Oedipus thereby falling first under Labdacian and later under Theban laws; between everydayness and the fantasm that frames it; between a given being and being fantasized as order. . . . The false sober-ones that Nietzsche scolds are lost in dreams if they believe that fantasms can be swept aside. Don't forget that under the legislative denial of Oedipus,[61] Thebes was made livable once again! The differend, then, constitutes the human condition—a condition in the sense of a critical transcendentalism that recognizes in fractured being—a being that breaks us—the "first known" whose evidence philosophers have always had the mission to demonstrate.

The three citations used as epigrams to this book speak of this originary breakage. The haiku of Chouchiki[62] expresses the interruption of the consoling and consolidating dream and the awakening to the singular; the definition of the tragic given by Nietzsche[63] indicates how this condition emerges in the lived world and breaks us; and finally, the Heideggerian renewal of tragedy through *aletheia*[64] affirms the agonic as ultimate.

The question of origins (but not that of principles) remains a question of conditions (but not one of the *a priori*). What condition of being is revealed in the double bind of natality-mortality? It introduces time into the unconditioned condition, even if it will be necessary to think a differend between temporal strategies. That differing will be the *discordance of times* which has announced itself under each of the hegemonic fantasms we have lived since the Greeks.

The Law of the One, of Nature, and of Consciousness

"And what if there were, lodged in the core of the law itself, a law of impurity or a principle of contamination? And what if the condition of possibility for the law were the *a priori* for a counter-law, an axiom of impossibility that bewildered sense, order and reason?"

—J. Derrida[65]

History, which is measured and talked about in terms of centuries, is a part of the topology of norms due to the fact that our directive languages each have had their epoch. This fact, however, is not proven, but merely put in relation, and in the topology of double binds, it is related to the differend manifesting itself in natality-mortality.[66]

The fact is that, when philosophy began, it spoke Greek. Furthermore, the fact is that this beginning instituted a referent, the paradigm of all normative-nominative paradigms to come, namely, the reference to the *one*. The one (*hen*) is the Greek hegemonic fantasm. It was a positive institution, and in more that one sense. It occurred at Elea during the sixth and fifth centuries before our era; Thémis, the goddess whose name stems from *tithemi* (to posit), reveals the normative one; the mortals placed under her law have in turn their own ways of positing—of placing themselves in their world and arranging the beings that occupy it. What authority could impose a more obviously normative *simple constraint* than Parmenides' one? In any case, with him the central sense of being for the Greeks was instituted.[67]

However, there is something perplexing about this. Parmenides never stops narrating. He talks about things. The extant fragments of his "Poem" depict a journey, but to give a narration instead of a proof—does that not amount to wrecking the great profession of consolidation and consolation even before that profession has been constituted into a corps? Here we have a doubly paradigmatic gesture which underscores the multiplicity wherein mortals wander, but which also establishes the point of departure for every normative position to come. Like no other, this foundational gesture sketches out a route with stopping places, with travel incidents and encounters, with tempos of displacement, an intrigue, and an outcome. Such a narrative portrays the singular and time. Does "our father Parmenides" (Plato), that first civil servant of humanity, appeal both to an *ultimate singularization* and therefore to time, even while arguing for the *ultimate maximization* and therefore the law? What can be said of that henological legislation which, in order to demonstrate that "the one that holds," must portray disparates? Does not henological legislation from the outset suffer from a transgressive strategy whose work perhaps is not fortuitous and which preserves the phenomena in their narratable singularity?

Our task will require that we demonstrate normative theticism is infested in its germ. Infested by what? By a *fidelity* to singularized, temporalized phenomena. We will have to ask if we do not recognize an essential *discordance of times* in the one which holds and which also is narrated.

However, one should not be rash to conclude that a journey, marked by a distinct time and therefore narratable, elevates Parmenides' traveler toward an extra-temporal and unspeakable point of view. The conceptions between the narrative and the argument, of the ascent (of which, moreover, there isn't one) and the summit—making the point, coiling time into a point—none of these oppositions are taken for granted by Parmenides. He just never mentions them. But what does he say? Young man, hold disparates together, an injunction the chorus never ceases to enjoin tragic heroes. Agamemnon, Oedipus, Antigone, and Creon hold disparates together. Sophocles calls this *amphinoein,* thinking from two sides.

To subject a normative argument to a topological reading is to ask "In what field have we gone to seek the signifier treated as a directive referent?" What experience, what phenomenal region, what *topos* have we turned toward in order to glean therefrom a given so as to posit it as the differential term to which all phenomena are referred? What is the domain of experience that strikes thought in the first normative argument of the West? Parmenides posits the one as giving rise—as assigning their respective places—to singulars, both present and absent. At this point, originary experience has yet to become at all selective (Aristotle will select the experience of fabrication so as to maximize its traits; the Stoics, the traits of naturally telic appetites; Descartes, those of the I think . . .). This is the experience of a radical singularizing absence permeating all that can be present, an absence in whose light humans are called *mortals.* The legislative strategy toward universals thus comes to be joined with a transgressive strategy toward singulars, one that makes us familiar with our death. This is a joining of disparates which perfectly reflects the oxymo-ronic saying "the community of mortals." The community is the fantasm; the mortals are in each instance the singulars that can never be subsumed to a fantasm. What is tragic in the initial experience is that, under the regime of the one, we are called on to "hold together" disparate, normative singulars in their disparity. Aeschylus begins where Parmenides begins. Agamemnon finds himself in the double bind between the singularizing call to prove himself commander and the equally singularizing fatherly calling. The *kouros* of Parmenides, by the same token, owes allegiance to two aggregates: an aggregate of present *thises,* and another of absent *that's.*

Therefore, the one is not maximized from things that are present. The *one* is not *uniformly* binding. Accordingly, Parmenides resigned his position in the great philosophical bureaucracy even before such a corps was constituted.

The one that holds (*hen synechés*) is not a being. Parmenides describes it in entirely functional terms, as a pure bearing, a relation, an ultimate condition of phenomena given by the fabric that alone brings them together. It is a shredded fabric, for it reminds men to keep their death, however absent, firmly present—death is ultimate. In being nothing, the one must be understood as a self-effacing signifier insofar as it names a being—it must be understood as a regulative fantasm. Under this first hegemonic referent, phenomenality is constituted by means of the entry of singulars into an adverse constellation, and in this sense, as we shall see, by means of an event in discord with itself.

What event is this? It is the event enunciated in the middle voice, which is to say, one with neither agent nor patient. Modern languages render it with the reflexive. *Phuesthai* is translated as 'to raise *itself,*' *phainesthai* as 'to show *itself.*' However, the middle voice does not thematize reflexivity any more than transitivity does. It does not express any operation of a subject on an object, or of a subject on itself. It does not give *terms* {*met de termes*} to thought. Not until the middle voice has been eclipsed can the *a quo* and the *ad quem* of either a linear (subject-object transitivity, agent-patient) or a circular (subject-subject reflexivity) movement become stakes in the matter. When one thinks in those terms, the active and passive voices have swept away the middle voice through the exclusive character of their disjunction. Beneath the self-affirmation of the grammatical subject and the institution of a normative-nominative system, it is necessary to see—or rather to hear—the very stifling of the middle voice.

But perhaps methodological and programmatic remarks are inappropriate in a synopsis, especially if these aren't the issue, for it would be better to say that all the readings we offer here lead toward being inasmuch as it is an event singularly turned against itself. It is only through being as such an event that phenomenality may be constituted without having recourse to some common, general, or universal figure, just as it is only through the intrinsically discordant event that originary phenomena may be safeguarded.

It would also be better to say that it will be impossible to give separate treatments to questions such as: What to read? How is one to read and with what program in mind? To what end? Even worse, the one of the Greeks, the nature of the Latins, and the consciousness of the moderns will be proven to be hegemonic fantasms only gradually through readings and not via some demonstration *a priori*. Inevitably, the answers I will attempt to bring to these questions will intertwine with the guiding thread of topology as a whole, a thread that binds the common places to those of the singular, just as in the person of Agamemnon it binds the public charge to the paternal obligation, or in the everyday, it bind life to death, and in normative theses, legislation to transgression.

Because beginnings are compact but ends are revealing, I will read only the opening and closing documents of each linguistic epoch. I intend to analyze the inaugural discourses that institute a law, as well as those that destitute it. When a fantasm attains hegemony, everything proceeds as if philosophy had no other strategy to follow than natality alone, maximization, tragic denial. But all this is so only *as if*, for the strategy of mortality is never obliterated—singularization is not obliterated, neither is the tragic double bind. The instituting discourses already express the double bind, and the destituting discourses will draw their final consequences from it.

I shall not stop to read instituted discourses that repeat the law for long periods. Therefore, I will say very little about the "one" as manifested in fourth century Attic thought, nor will I hesitate, furthermore, to skip over the thirteenth century scholastic apex of the Latin fantasm, nor, with the German fantasm, to take a shortcut in the trajectory from idealism to materialism and nihilism in the nineteenth century. If these philosophical summits inspire awe it is because they closely resemble the knowledge a neurotic patient imputes to his therapist. And by presuming that each hegemonic fantasm opens onto a non-fortuitous conjunction of legislation and transgression that are equally normative, the therapy effectively takes on the public function given to those who are at the summits: ideal Platonic pacification, the Thomist "grand system" (if that is the *summum* of Latin thought), the Hegelian dialectic reconciling all oppositions. But in a retrospective reading these cures prove deceptive. Neoplatonists, medieval nominalists, and phenomenologists of occurrent being are there to remind us that there is no recovery from the tragic glimpsed at the beginnings.

Hence a warning about the relative volume of the synopses: In the following pages we shall read less about the moments of fantasmic destitution than about those of institution, for at the commencement of each of the periods examined I will seek to isolate the fissure that ends up by shattering an epochal symbolic order. The ends will prove to be, if not foreseeable, at least expected.

Through centuries of usage, a language deploys the full range of resources contained in its words. As a closing document for the Greek regime, I will read a treatise by Plotinus describing the one as the event of unification which gathers the singular givens together. Here we will see a return of the middle voice in which I will discern a law of impurity, a principle of contamination, an *a priori* of a counter-law which, by virtue of our mortality, always disperses nomotheses among the singulars and time. Our limiting of the Greek one to its instituting and destituting moments should not be construed to suggest that the language of Plotinus and Parmenides were the same. But what could that mean, the same language? We do not inhabit a language the way a fossil is embedded in a monolith. Nevertheless, the semantic displacements from Parmenides to Plotinus were just shifts. By contrast, with the passage to Latin, an abrupt deployment of contiguous territories took place, a rupture. As we shall see, these contiguities will require that we diachronically stretch out the guiding thread, which is what our topology is. If we come upon thresholds of incommensurability in our history, these can only be the fractures left behind by translations. The transition into a new linguistic epoch casts an aura of irreality on fantasmic "reality." Here my interest in languages is above all aimed at rescuing the discussion of historical periodization from arbitrariness, which is why I shall pay attention to the great translators, to those who shatter historical continuity—Cicero and Luther.

To be sure, neither Cicero nor Luther may be counted among the corps of humanity's civil servants, for no giant *says* "foundation." They are listeners rather than speakers. But what do they listen to? The former listened to his Latin, the latter to his German. But a refined hearing teaches us more about normative referents than it does about ideal, synthetic, or even dialectic diction. They echoed an *incipit* at play in their languages. Speculative matters repulsed them; they posited no supreme being. Instead, they allowed a network of relations to be heard at its birth, namely, an ultimate positing–letting-be initially that was deployed in terms of language and where a new articulation of the double bind resounded. The linguistic regime speaking in them had not yet gone through the therapy of the great keepers of order. The legislative strategy of a fantasm, suddenly ascending to hegemony and having an air of obviousness in positing and imposing its reality and subsuming the particular, is best discerned in the prephilosophical discourse in which these respective linguistic regimes are instituted; but one can also see there the transgressive counter-strategy in which language lets the singular be in its temporality. There one can find the evidence of how the middle voice speaks, only to be immediately reduced to silence.

Cicero says everything refers to *natura*. The word *natura* stems from the verb *nasci*, "to be born"—the Latin form of the middle voice. Nature is not the vast dimension of beings—the World. It can be seen in the regional processes it is supposed to include—physical, political, and cosmic processes. It is necessary to understand the nature-as-referent as the operative principle in the homologizing of apparently isolated experiences. The Greek equivalent of the term *lex nature* would be monstrous. For the Latins, on the contrary, the life of the individual, of the city, of humanity, of the cosmos, is always called before an ultimate authority which, though it conjoins them, is itself nothing. In *natura,* these phenomenal regions are "born" or appear to one another. The function of this sense of being which is posited as a standard is to normalize the regional norms; it is an exigent labor that exploits the thetic violence of every fantasmic regime in successive integrations.

As with the Greek one, the law of nature—the law that nature is—has no law. It refers to nothing and is ordered by nothing. It makes an epoch by *evidently* appearing as the ultimate reason of all everyday experience. By means of this evidence, this new referent orders everything according to itself, and this presents certain difficulties when it comes to Christianizing it, which is to say, linking it up with a supreme being. The Latin equivalent of *arché anarcheos* is *lex aeterna,* the law-outside-of-the-law, which Augustine likens to the life of God. However, whether Christianized or not, Latin nature makes the law without itself following any other law. Or, to denature and naturalize Kant's view on moral law as a "fact of reason"—Latin law is the only true fact of nature.

In order to grasp a fantasm in its function as ultimate authority—hence as a norm such as I understand it—the least instructive question to ask is: When? When did people begin, in their thinking, to refer to some particular fantasmic sense of being? Should the need arise, I will not hesitate to call on the Greek Stoics (Panetius of Rhodes) from whom the Romans are said to have learned "nature"; and as we shall see, this collapsed in an author who preferred to write in middle high German. The decisive question will rather be: Where? Where does a given norm *take place*? What is its original *topos*? What experiential region was consulted for the hyperbolic deployment in it of an ultimate referent? And where some particular norm is brought to bear, what is its first place of incidence? In the relational terms that distinguish it from every supreme referent, what fields of experience were combined to produce the emergence of a fantasm in their midst? During the tragic age, Parmenides deployed the synectic one starting with the experience that contraries hold together even without a genus. These sites of both the present and the absent are incommensurable with those contemplated by the Rome-based Stoics, namely, the gradation of psyche-city-humanity-cosmos. Latin nature legislates as the principle of continuity that links these sites together.

No criterion allows for a transition from the Greek henological system of reference to that of Latin nature. The interval between the languages of our past is the no-man's-land, that singular space in which the raw other erupts in history. Hence, yet another indication that normalizing norms enjoying ultimate authority cannot be unjustified. Before what common authority may *hen* and *nature* be called to appear? What atopic judge or legislator would rule above languages? If philosophy may have been able to erect its edifice thanks to its maximization of the fantasmic thrust that always makes us use common nouns when speaking, then the civil servants of humanity have had nothing but their Greek, their Latin, et cetera, with which to posit the ultimate. Any appeal to a meta-linguistic authority would be a foolish appeal; it would be inadmissible for, as the grievances of subjects of two different countries are inadmissible, there is no *ad hoc* functionary with assigned jurisdiction over them.

From where might one derive the one and nature—nature is neither a metaphor nor a simulacrum of the one? There is no simulation nor *metapherein* that leads from the former to the latter. One may say, though it may amount to nothing but a play on words, that in the transition from one hegemonic and linguistic regime to another it is the lack of a criterion that makes the law. But this play on words does not indicate something essential, namely, that the law is instituted only by decree and by stops (*epoché*)—epochally. If this is the case, it is not only the functionaries dealing with norms who bring down the razor blade to prevent a regression *ad infinitum* in the order of reason. For one language puts an end to the language that preceded it, one fantasm cuts off its predecessor, one era or epochal ambiance replaces the one before it. From the moment we begin to speak our language, we become entrenched in a position that posits the idiom, the fantasm, and epoch that has become *terra incognita* as being elsewhere. Therefore we come to oppose it as an other that henceforth is as uninhabitable as it is irretrievable, an other whose crisscrossings only show themselves to the topologist once they have been retraced.

Nevertheless, the referential nature of the Latins, just as much as the Greek one, is fissured even at the moment of its institution. How is one to trust such a great assigner of ends if its very act of birth—and the middles voice expresses the fact that "nature" never ceases to be "born"—*falsely justifies itself* and in a number of ways?

Somewhat disillusioned, the middle Stoics devised a new gambit with which to halt (*epéchein*) opinions and debates; this gambit was the controversy about whether a sage could ever have existed. . . . Such was the Roman pragmatism consecrated by Cicero, according to whom it is necessary, in order to find the rules of conduct, to look as closely into one's own nature as into that other, universally homologizing nature. How is this *normative nature* reconciled with the "common nature" on whose teleological structure rests the whole prestige of classical natural law? In a parallel vein, a false argument confuses the first experiential region in which natural law was supposed to homologate the individual. This debate is also ancient; namely, is the city natural or not? Cicero's answer is yes, for the city of our fathers was natural! Natural politics is Rome. In what manner does this *paradigmatic singular* fit the meta-law that speaks directly to "right reason"? For Cicero, the city of the forefathers which no longer exists becomes arch-present, like a father who has been murdered by his sons. His is a labor of mourning, of guilt and canonization. A strange canon, nevertheless, of a nature that is no longer. How is one to grasp an archetype whose temporality is constituted by *the time of memories*? It is with Augustine that the counter-strategies of this argument are pursued. A particular love posits a particular law, the love of mores posits temporal law; love of joy, eternal law. Yet natural law has been praised to us as given, as non-posited! How, then, does the *thetic will* fit with the givenness upon which the whole scaffolding of these laws (natural-eternal) nevertheless rests, the lack of which would amount to a dissolution of that juridical link? In any event, nature ends up being plopped down right in front of us. The perfectly natural city that conforms to the eternal law does not exist yet. The City of God is under construction, and nature, as a result, is paralyzed by the *time of the possible*.

How can we help seeing, between these paradigmatic singulars of which one has been (Rome) and the other will be (the heavenly Jerusalem), that the natural law that is extracted from them opens up, once more, an irremediable temporal discordance?

The rational order of nature has been a cracked edifice ever since its inception. And what does it turn into at the time of its destitution? With the end of scholasticism and before a new linguistic interregnum has cut off the discourse of the Latins, the conflict between "there, that given" and fantasmic "reality" eludes the surveillance conducted by the thetic function. The heterogeneity of givenness and positing clashes without any possibility of therapy. Nature, capable as it is of homologating all experiences, proves to be only *one* nature. An infinite number of other natures could be created. Suddenly, the law of the great continuity appears doubly contingent—both to theological inspection and to the topological retrospection of which ours can serve as an example. Upon inspection, its system of mandatory ends shows itself weakened by divine freedom; upon retrospection, it proves to be genuinely suspended, struck by a syncope, by a fainting, by a halting, by a stopping, by a bracketing through the knowledge that there is no simple ultimate authority.

The spokesperson that expresses this knowledge most clearly is Meister Eckhart. On the one hand, he erects a system of continuity, no longer one of gradations like the Roman Stoics, but a system in which "the highest part of the lower touches the lowest part of what is higher";[68] in other words, one in which the end of each being is posited by the level that precedes it in rank and file. Therefore, the telic principle mandates a vertical integration. On the other hand, "only that is alive, strictly speaking, which lives without principle."[69] Eckhart's entire passion was for the condition that makes possible the quasi-feudal scaffolding in which each thing puts its feet on the head of its neighbor . . . to an indeterminate condition which supplies a different sort of normativity to subordinations. His passion was for the event in which the system of integration through submission emerges. It was for what he called the origin. The *double bind of the principle and of the origin* turns natural normativity against itself and destitutes it.

Heterogeneity is an "other birth." If the truth (for the moment we will leave aside the question of what "truth" means) of *nature* resides in the *nasci* taken literally, then it will be necessary to ask how a given singular is born. Under what conditions does it give itself and does it lend itself to my pointing to it with my index finger, "there, that mountain"? Could it be at the moment when I am also able to point to "there, that cloud," that is, when they mutually give rise to one another? In other words, is it the moment when they enter into a context, when they surround themselves with disparities and everything else that is needed to make a world (with a small "w")? Thus, an unflinching apologist of the originary indeterminate, Eckhart also makes himself into the tenacious defender of the singular—and in the same breath. Must one not retain this truth of the singular, known since Parmenides (whose poem was probably entitled *Peri Phuseos*), only now singled out by other idiomatic strategies, namely, that the deictic object is born through *phuesthai,* through 'arising'; that its birth is thus 'physical' in the sense of *phusis*-arisen; that it is *this one* that is pointed out with the finger, only insofar as it gives birth to that other *this one* and yet another one; that their pure coming together to form a constellation, emphasized by the middle voice, constitutes the temporal differend; namely, phenomenalization, ever weakened by a singularization to come?

Fantasms install themselves as universals—thetic work proclaims them to be so, a work that is always accomplished by language. None (before Nietzsche) had said this more clearly than it was said by the opposite party in the quarrel of universals—unless it were the plaintiff, claiming that justice must be done to the singular. Therefore, to recover from tragic denial does not mean to pronounce thetic universality null and void. That could never be anything but a counter-proclamation. In order for the denial to produce knowledge, it will be necessary to abandon the idea that the dialectic of opposites leads to some sovereign authority. The other that is opposable to the principial fantasm is not the singular, but the particular. For Eckhart, it follows that it is necessary to abandon principles—not negate them, but *simply* no longer to appeal to them.

Indeed, there is nature in the sense of the principle of continuity inasmuch as I *posit* a quintessential level that takes stock of what shows itself there; and there is nature in the sense of "birth" each time and inasmuch as I *let* the singular give itself. Without a quintessential positing there is no life. But—also—unless one lets the thetic paroxysms be, one will forever deny the knowledge of originary conditions. The differend of positing and letting-be, ineluctable for whoever speaks an Indo-European language, reflects the gap between a manifest order and the event of its manifestation. It reflects the tragic condition of being which the discordance of times always underscores.

Again, it would not be a mistake to read the following pages as a verification, based on textual evidence, of an incongruity between the conceptual function of idiomatic speech and the deictic function of everyday life. At least since the Scholastics of the fourteenth century we have learned that no principle of homologation will ever be congruous with the singulars that give rise to one another. And the incongruous in this case is teleology, of which Meister Eckhart availed himself as a practical *a priori* of thought. In order to allow for the occurrence of singulars, it is necessary to leave ends aside. The occurrence of that mountain and that cloud, by which a world is constituted, takes place "without a why," without normative arche-telic forceps, without a sovereign fantasm, without a standard thesis of being by which to measure beings.

Between the Greek and the Latin regimes, there is a topological shift in the general configuration of beings for the first time. The normative *hen* works on the connection between the sites of beings, the site of absent beings "firmly held" together with the site of those that are present. *Natura* is also topically posited, but its sites are different—they are linked together on the surface (or in height), psychical sites, domestic, political, cosmopolitan, cosmic sites—from "this bit of volcanic rock," Eckhart will say, up to the "loftiest angel," all these fall under the empire of presence. This is why, under the regime of the Latin fantasm, teleology could impose itself as a given. Eckhart will say quite clearly that the condition of the given is its givenness. This givenness requires us to "detach" principles from the given. What is also different is the kind of disparity which theticism forces under the fantasm. Among the regions of its Greek institution, that gap widens because of the knowledge that life and death are held together; among those of its Latin institution, it widens because of a recollection and an anticipation. But whether Greek or Latin, hegemony is fissured by singularization from the outset.

Hence, when philosophy starts speaking vernacular languages, topology, once again, moves on to a different general configuration of beings.

Here one must choose, grow poorer. What idiomatic topology ought one retrace? In my view, the genuinely foundational figure after the closing of the Latin period was Luther, the epochal translator who was the first to "reverse their manner of thinking" and institute the modern hegemonic fantasm—he was the one who, for us, said "foundation." Faith alone can bring salvation. Does this not entail displacing to a new site everything that may become a phenomenon? Is Luther not thereby claiming that phenomenality is played out on the stage of *self-consciousness*? Kant is also sometimes referred to as the philosopher of Protestantism; the epithet is apropos to Kant precisely because of what he calls his Copernican revolution through which consciousness prescribes the forms to the given according to which it can and must give itself. In order to understand the regime under which modernity has placed us, it will be helpful to read Kant together with Luther.

And finally, it is obvious that this regime of consciousness is first fractured with Nietzsche, and later with Wittgenstein and Heidegger. Here again, however, it was necessary to choose and, in so doing, to impoverish the project once again. With the aim of grasping the destitution of the hegemonic fantasm born out of the transcendental turn, I will have to rest content with the reading of a single text of Heidegger.

A word should be said about the reasons that moved me to accept the poverty involved in choosing only German language texts. They are the same reasons that an archivist or a librarian would adduce. I imagined what a bookshelf would look like that contained a coherent series of the most telling documents regarding the critical primacy of self-consciousness.[70] Both French spiritualism and English empiricism, however differently they may articulate it, operate under the fantasm at hand.

If sovereign positings center a linguistic space by imprinting it with referential relations, what would be the *topoi* that self-consciousness binds together? The answer is found in the name—self-consciousness binds me to myself.[71] But if it is defined by a self-relation, perhaps it is not necessary to reduce it to reflection from the very outset. With Luther, consciousness certainly gives rise to relations to the self, but never by way of a return to itself. *Simul iustus et peccator,* that other motto of the Reformation, puts consciousness in a double bind with regard to an authority that is outside of itself, an authority dealing more directly than ever with the law. I am both just and a sinner before God, who *appraises* me as such. The return that defines consciousness works on it by means of appraisals. I appraise God as the one who justifies and saves me, and also as the one who judges me and forsakes me. Luther pushes hard against the "rei-ism" of theology. The relational act of consciousness is wholly a matter of "regarding as. . . ," a double act—twice doubled. I see God as considering me justified, whereby I am justified; I see God as considering me forsaken, whereby I am lost. The discordant simultaneity of these two destinies of consciousness fractures the modern hegemonic referent from its inception. Phenomenalization thus operates around the "ego"; but it is crushed beforehand by a pathetic singularization around the "self."

Just as the one institutes synectics, and just as nature institutes homologation, the *simul* indicates to me a mode of being. However, it no longer addresses "mortals" nor "right reason." It addresses consciousness. With the caustic formulas of the Reformation, one is dealing for the first time with phenomena in a strict sense: with that which shows itself only in the arena of consciousness, namely, with representations. What then constitutes the phenomenality of representations in this world, deprived as it is of an obvious framework? Not without hysterics, Luther replies: "Speech, speech, speech!" Not only is critical transcendentalism born under the double bind of law. In addition, it immediately and necessarily turns all phenomena into phenomena of language. For the whole duration of its hegemony, consciousness will vary its topics according to linguistic functions.

With Kant I will limit myself to reading a concatenation of remarks that show the ontologization of the Lutheran *simul*. *Das Bewußtsein,* "being conscious"—the word bears the imprint of the question of being. Reading Kant together with Luther will clarify first of all the provenance of the legislating ego. Moreover, we will benefit, in so doing, from a distinction that becomes evident between two different forms of critical transcendentalism, one that is pre-emancipatory, the other emancipatory. But above all, we will gain a better view into the conflict that cracks the bedrock of consciousness upon which modernity was constructed. Emancipatory reason is posited from end to end as spontaneous, beginning with the forms of sensibility right up to the ideas. So now the apparatus of subjective legislation works in the service of being, which gives itself and is always singular. For the moderns, spontaneity lays down the law, and yet it is shattered upon givenness *qua* singularization.

What is being? To this question, which one could consider settled once and for all by the doctrine of modalities, Kant consistently offers two replies which gained strength for almost three decades. He replies with a positing, but also with a givenness—at the end of these decades he replies with two types of positings. Through these, as we shall see, a transcendental differend is vividly enunciated. By giving an argumentative structure (whatever there is of one) to a similar fracture in being, Kant in fact persists in breaking his contract as a civil servant of humanity. As if in spite of himself, although with unrivaled clarity, this categorical *chargé d'affaires* of categorial business never ceases to rehabilitate the singular and its temporality.

The time of the singular will prove to be the main issue in the last of the readings we will conduct in the following pages. Heidegger will bring to a conclusion the idiomatic conversation initiated by Luther and carried out over four centuries. But, after the fashion of the Greek and Latin fantasms, waning self-consciousness—bringing its hegemony to a high point and (thereby?) destituting itself—reveals strategic implications that no therapy will ever be able to expunge from discourse, implications that link the singular to time. They fracture the standard sense of being as different from beings by means of the *singularization to come*. It is on this that spontaneity, master of the world, runs aground. Fantasmic laws thereby prove to be besieged by a counter-law; the apodeictic labor of civil servants is besieged by a contradictory operation calling for the transgression of the referents that they themselves had decreed; the "reality" that we cannot help but posit is besieged by an other, unsayable reality that we cannot help but abandon; the forces of consolation and consolidation are besieged by a distressing force of dissolution; the attraction of a globe (of a globalization and of a center that affords a point of reference for everything) is besieged by a dispersive retreat toward innumerable points scattered into empty encompassing dimensions. What conflict becomes evident in all this? What double bind? Could there be a deluge of labels, the universal and particular, the same and its other. . . . The ultimate legislative-transgressive strategies within the normative referents force us to think of the other differently, to think of it according to a conflictuality that belongs to no genus, namely, the tragic conflict to which the singularization to come always gives rise.

At least one *law of the other* can, in any event, be learned from Heidegger, one that is severed from the whole problem of determinate negation—a revival of a heteronomy which, however, is not posited and which therefore is incapable of opposing autonomy. Thus, the law of the other is the link by which we are ever bound to being *qua* event. But this event has literally nothing in common. Could this perhaps be what has been furtively expressed as "that which thinks" ever since the beginning of modernity? Could Heidegger rehabilitate that voice which the obsessive fear of sovereign theses has silenced but which, nevertheless, has never ceased to haunt theticism, namely, the middle voice? The event, Heidegger will be shown to say, works on phenomena in a twofold manner. It appropriates them in a world and expropriates them by means of their mortifying singularization that is always immanent. All references posited as uniformly obligatory are fractured upon this conflictual (and therefore not simple) *singularum tantum*. Could it therefore also have been necessary to learn how to emancipate our knowledge and actions—how to emancipate life—from the great fantasized authorities? Could the original double bind—the tragic condition—have placed life, always already, outside all laws uniformly binding us?

In October 1986, an association of school-children's parents in the state of Alabama tried to bring the governor to trial on account of history, home economics, and civic education textbooks that had been approved by the state. The plaintiffs, a fundamentalist group, claimed that said manuals violated their constitutional rights to enjoy the protection of the law. In approving these programs, they maintained, the state had given its endorsement to "secularist, humanist, evolutionist, materialist, agnosticist, atheist and other religions" (a certain Southern rhetoric betrays itself here). They contended that, in so doing, the government had actually participated in the promulgation of those religions. By tacitly excluding from the history program the "contributions of Christianity to *the American way of life*" the Department of Education had deprived theistic religions of an equal protection under the law. The books in question thus favored one religion—"secular humanism"—to the detriment of other religions, namely, Christianity and Judaism. A federal court judged their grievance to be well-founded. The textbooks violated the "establishment clause" of the First Amendment to the U.S. Constitution, which reads: "Congress shall make no law respecting an establishment of religion. . . ." In failing to mention theistic religions, the state authorities "instituted the opposite belief and thereby established an opposite religion." The judge ordered the removal of forty-four titles from the programs in question and their replacement by textbooks that accorded equal value, in the number of chapters as well as in courses taught, to the "two belief systems," namely, secular humanism and Jewish and Christian theism. He nevertheless authorized the use of those history, home economics, and civic education books "as reference sources in a course of comparative religions affording equal treatment to all religions."[72]

The judgment beautifully illustrates the integrative logic of the law. In the Anglo-American system, a judicial decision not annulled by a court of appeals indeed has the force of law. The verdict shows that toward which Justice remains and must remain blind—to any figure of the other that does not fall under the schema of determinate negation. It was for good reason that Hegel, the spokesman of aprioristic isomorphism, saw in crime a systematic necessity that reveals the essence of a universal position.[73] The schema of determinate negation immunizes the law against every figure of a transgressive other which might destabilize it from within, just as the law necessarily stabilizes it from the outside—or from above it, for the only order possible is *under* the law.

Such was the reasoning of the court on the issue of the Alabama textbooks. A discourse that fails to mention certain beliefs in fact negates them, and by the same act constitutes a credo. The silence of secular humanism, particularly on the point of creation, denies "an equal force of conviction" to the doctrine that it says nothing about. It is therefore the equivalent of a faith (according to this logic, the French constitution, for instance, whose letter ignores religion, is therefore a religious document). The plaintiffs invoked the equal protection that the U.S. Constitution accords to all religions, while remaining neutral to their practice. Thus, they attacked the government's authorization to utilize "humanist" books in education, which they deemed unconstitutional. Concluding that said authorization contradicted the neutrality that the founding fathers had cherished, the judgment amounted to *effacing all possible sites lying outside the either-or* of theism and its other.

So, the law always *enforces isomorphism*. In Alabama, it deprived the interlocutors in litigation of even the possibility of speaking about anything other than credos. "For or against?" No other site is known or tolerated by the law. It gets caught up in what Wittgenstein described as territorial grammars. Having always spoken in favor of it in the face of disparate territories, the law, every law, assigns a common ground to the singular litigants. The work of the law essentially amounts to reducing plural grammars to an imperative grammar that operates by means of determinate negation. It takes stock by suppressing multiple idioms and irreducible descriptions, so it is impossible to demand any kind of extra-territoriality in relation to its *integrative violence*.

Every law, as a result of the fantasmic maximization from which it arises, is marked by its differend with singulars. Consequently, the continent of normative isomorphism is always overrun by an extra-territoriality. Therefore, if the hypothesis here presented can be verified so as to safeguard originary phenomena (natality *versus* mortality) as well as their condition (contextualization in a world *versus* an imminent and endless banishment from the world, that is, singularization to come), we will see that philosophers have annulled their mandate at the very moment they acquiesce to it—a mandate that says secure principles.

PART ONE

In the Name of the One

The Greek Hegemonic Fantasm

I

Its Institution

The One That Holds Together (Parmenides)

Parmenides, it has been said from antiquity, is the father of philosophy. He was the first to place discursive reason in the service of intuitive thought. He was also the first to designate the one problem worthy of a philosopher, the problem of being. He carried out this act of paternity by *arguing* that being is one.

His predecessors, as well as all those after him who distrust argumentation, could wage wars of unreasoned intuitions and opinions. He could have shown them the way to perpetual peace. In arguing that being is one, he taught us a sure way to proceed—the instigators of opinion speak for themselves; those converted to reason speak in the name of the universal. Whether it knows it or not, the West was trained in his school. There we have learned where to anchor discourse, all discourse, so that it may be certain. What is at stake in philosophy was prescribed by him—in arguing that being is one, necessarily, we acquire a point of reference that lasts, immutably, and that lays down the law, universally.

This necessity, this immutability, and this universality of an ultimate reference are what metaphysicians have surpassed each other in working on and reworking. With a magisterial gesture, like Alexander before the Gordian knot, "our father Parmenides"[1] bisects yes and no, being and not being, truth and error, knowledge that can be grounded and rambling assertions; he set apart the man who knows from the dumbfounded soul. Philosophy's initial argumentative tack is to oppose so as to posit better, to oppose contradictories so as to posit the one (*hen*). This ploy springs up there, moreover, with such simplicity that it thwarts all classification. How are we to understand the *hen*? As the unity making a genus, or instead as the units that compose it? As the exclusive oneness of a being, or instead as the inclusive totality of all beings, as their union that constitutes the universe? As the form of given things, hence as uniform *a priori,* or instead as this particular unified given being? If the one can be placed in one or the other of these classes (logical, ontological, transcendental), that would be the end not only of its dawn-like simplicity but also the argument based on contradictories. Each of these figures indeed introduces a certain multiplicity into the one. Parricide.

To think the one is as difficult as saying what it is. We do so constantly but in all innocence of the concept. If being is one, it will indeed be necessarily "everywhere the same"—in Greek, *isos* (*isopalés,* 8.44)[2] or *homôs* (8.49)—therefore "isomorphic" or "homogeneous." We encounter the simple one everywhere and speak of it everywhere. But if we seek to grasp what we are doing and to get it back in hand, innocence is lost and with it, the simplicity of the one. A giant would be needed in order to keep hold of it. In the "gigantomachy over being,"[3] Parmenides is the most formidable of giants.

By establishing that being makes the law because it is one, simple, isomorphic, and homogeneous, he set himself up as laying down the law for all future argumentation about principles.

We recognize this simplicity of the referent that lays down the law as a primary characteristic of the common opinion regarding Parmenides. But let us now read the words that open what remains to us of his poem. They're jolting: "The chariots that carry me. . . ." What—a thought that, in short, is to have but a single thing to say, "one,"[4] begins with the evocation of a *journey*? The calm radiance of the most austere simplicity conceivable formulated by describing a gallop, the circle of turning wheels, the screech emitted by the axle rubbing against its hub? For a text which is said to sing of the immobile splendor of the one, this is a beginning that leaves one perplexed. Whoever undertakes a voyage expects rather to be, like Ulysses, borne from here to there (*polytropos*)—involved in the polymorphic, not to the isomorphic.

One may agree to treat the assertion "being is one" as expressing not a composition but an intuition. Principles are not constructed by gathering together elements, nor by being deduced from the analysis of underlying premises—they would emerge from either of these operations particularized. Principles must be grasped in the way a person sizes up and grasps a situation in which he finds himself. Homer describes Paris trembling at the sight of Menelaus—trembling not from fear but because he suddenly understands that Menelaus is seeking revenge. Helen feels paralyzed by dread before an old woman who has come to visit; she has understood that she is receiving a goddess.[5] In the same way, we grasp what is absolutely first and is the basis upon which we can build a demonstration. We always reason in terms of propositions, that is, in terms of statements establishing a relation between at least two terms. And every predicate adds something to the subject of which it is the predicate. But we can add nothing either to being or to the one. Thus, to say "being is one" does not amount to limiting—to particularizing—one term by another, but to saying twice over the non-particular. If they could serve as the subjects of predicates in a proposition, being would no longer be being and the one would no longer be the one. Parmenides thus inaugurates discursive philosophy; he follows and he teaches a way of proceeding. Yet he immediately sets out of play the logic of predicable qualities (and along with them, the logic of convertible perfections). "Signs" are what point toward being *qua* the one. Because it is universal, what they signify can only be grasped all at once. It is the universal in the highest degree—it has to do not just with all the individuals of a species, as when one says that life and speech are universals for humans, nor with all the species of a genus, but rather with the totality of what is. Every kind of thinking other than the immediate would particularize such a signified.

This second characteristic of the common opinion about Parmenides is no less perplexing than was the first. Take his opening words: "The mares that carry me. . . ." Now, who says "I" here? When he makes the goddess speak, Parmenides assigns to her the archaic *egon eréo,* the customary, solemn expression in Homer and Hesiod[6] used to demand a respect without reservation. But when he speaks in his own name, this "I" simply says *ego,* like everyone else. The universal with the greatest extension and comprehension is thus expressed indirectly by way of the most atomized form of the singular, someone whom the goddess summarily refers to as "young man" (*koûre,* 1:24), and who says "I"? Could the daimon that carries away the young man be *Parmenides'* daimon, just as much later Socrates will be singularized in invoking *his* daimon?

There is a third characteristic of the common opinion regarding Parmenides—he is the first thinker of the atemporal. "How could being come to be? How could it have happened? For if it came to be, it is not; nor is it if it must still come to be. Thus genesis is extinguished and destruction is eliminated" (8.19–21). Here we have a new indication of the professional philosopher—he secures for our lives an anchorage that time cannot effect. It is not a question here of the commonplace according to which Heraclitus is supposed to have written as the champion of becoming and Parmenides as that of immobile being, a misunderstanding that has been dispelled by Karl Reinhardt.[7] Rather it is a matter of a condition required for any doctrine of the one, for any henology. How, after all, can the absolutely simple one be subjected to time?

And yet Parmenides hardly ever stops *giving an account.* The traveler departs from a dwelling place, covers a first segment of the route, crosses a threshold, undertakes a new segment, and finally arrives at a destination. Such a traversal so filled with movement takes time. What an odd enterprise, to turn oneself into a narrator in order to establish the most rigid system ever seen in philosophy. Parmenides describes how he initially found himself at such and such place, then at another place. What is more, he initially recounts his trajectory by tracing it from beginning to end—that is, from the land of night to that of day (2)—and then a second time, in the opposite direction, from the land of the day to that of the night (8). Whoever marks out his discourse by saying "then, and then," organizes its time span, and whoever brings this up in a second narrative has a view to temporalization, indeed they must focus upon it.

Does one pay homage to the isomorphic, the universal, the atemporal—or rather to the polymorphous, the singular, and to time? What is at issue is the law that the one imposes on the multiple. Parmenides establishes the clear and ineluctable precedence of the one. "Immobile, it rests within the conjunction of powerful bonds" (8.26). These bonds link up into a system of positions. The one rests in itself and thereby imposes an order within which mortals in turn posit names and laws. Parmenides is the first to have established a theory for the rational justification of norms. Thus one recent dependable commentator writes, "Because it is the most thoroughly articulated, the one designates the unicity and totality of the most implacable norm. *Phusis,* the law of being for all beings, is opposed to the *nomos* and to *thésis* of ephemeral, uneasy mortals."[8] In other words, Parmenides opposed the one to the multiple, as the simple, universal, atemporal law is opposed to positive laws.

There is a demonstration of a set of laws furnished with a normative referent—yet the young man who says "I" is telling us a story. Isomorphism and necessity are suited to a system wherein time is perpetuity; polymorphism and the singular are suited to the narrative in which time is a clearly delimited endurance. Parmenides introduces *his singularity* into the Fragments that have come down to us under his name, and compared to all the philosophers who come after him, he does this in a singular way. He recounts events and new departures, situating himself in a succession of places and times, constituting himself as transitory in more than just one sense; in short, he makes himself into something as worthy of attention as is the one. A spherical, unmoving system, setting out universal law—or the narrative of a voyage in the first person singular, praising the ephemeral . . . to which one are we to listen?

And what if, in order to establish his system of normative, universal legitimization, Parmenides *had* to transgress in this manner toward the other of the one that is the ephemeral and the singular? It may then be that the narrative structure of his text does not purely and simply cancel out its argumentative structure. It may be that the argument of the narrative as well as what is at stake in it reveals only a differend and not some fault in reasoning, but rather the undertow of a dispersive strategy within being *qua* one.

It is not difficult to recognize the trait of natality in the impulse to start off; as the principle of every beginning, this trait moves toward the "always more" of any content, up to the point of positing a thinkable maximum. It always moves still further, until it institutes an ultimate truth that "holds together" the penultimate truths, the almost final truths. The one that holds together is a position. The question will be whether the polymorphous, the singular, and time are the work of a mortality that works upon the name of the one, from within its lawgiving power. If so, by what necessity? Philosophy would then commence with a magnificent galloping ascension, leading straight to a sovereign thesis, an ascension, however, where in just as impressive a manner a counter-force *denies* itself, a counter-force that would immediately depose this referent and strip it of its hegemony. Such is the broken truth of a theticism that reclaims its expenses at the end of the journey.

To better see what the case may be, there is no better way than to ask about Parmenides' way, or ways. In his so-called "didactic poem," it is a question of *hodoi dizésos* (2.2), of a research trip. The major features of his legislative system (since we have to put up with a few linguistic anachronisms when it is a question of crossing over more than two and a half millennia) will appear in relation to a much disputed, however apparently elementary, question: How many are the ways along which thought may travel? What are the possible starting points for comprehending being as one?[9]

CHAPTER 1

Contradictories

Their Juxtaposition and Their Confusion

Two paths?

The question of how many paths does not seem to pose any problem. Does Parmenides not oppose "the one, which is" to "the other, which is not" (2.3 and 5)? Whatever this "one" may be which is or is not, the two propositions, "it is" and "it is not," present themselves in the form of an alternative. And the text leaves no doubt about the import of this disjunction. Its "either-or" constrains all thinking—"it is" and "it is not" indicate the only paths an inquiry may take. A contradictory relation is a relation between two propositions, one of which affirms what the other denies. This is why we have the habit of saying that Parmenides was the first to employ, with an unequaled rigor, the principle of non-contradiction. Fortified with this principle, anyone can understand that a thing is not something other than itself; that "it is" is not the same as "it is not"; that yes is not no. Moreover, he is also supposed to have practiced, and with the same steadfastness, the principle of the excluded middle by which one affirms that between two contradictory propositions—between yes and no—there is no third solution possible. One of them will necessarily be true and the other false. If these principles are not completely spelled out in his poem, the key words do figure prominently there: "It is necessary (*chreon*) therefore, either to be or (*è . . . è*) not to be at all" (8.11). Only the first term of this alternative imposes itself upon us, for "nothing is, nor will be, other than what is" (8.36f.). The first way, therefore, is "true," and the other, not (*ou gar alethês,* 8.17f.). Therefore it follows, does it not, that Parmenides teaches that there exist two ways for thinking—not one, not three—and that they mutually exclude each other as the true and the false.

"Nothing is, nor will be, other than what is." These words not only affirm (notably through the use of the future tense of the verb) the necessity that opposes contradictories, not only do they deny the possibility of a third path ("beyond" or "outside" the contradictory terms), but they also affirm one of the two words Parmenides uses in his alternatives. This word appears in the form of a present participle preceded by an article: *to eon*. This is a difficult turn of speech, of which it has been said that it indicates the beginning of philosophical thinking and to which we shall have to return. It contains a difference. We will completely miss its significance if it is treated either as an infinitive, thereby ignoring the article, or as a noun, thereby ignoring its being a verb. A "participle" is called precisely because this form of our languages participates—takes part—in both the noun and the verb. In terms of translating *to eon,* I would not hesitate to render it as 'being'—in French as *l'étant*—if this form did not make us hear only the substantialization implicit in it. On the other hand, the article in Parmenides' passage does not transform a verb into a noun, but it fractures a verb into both infinitive and nominal meanings. This duality is conveyed quite well when we say "being" {*l'être*}, even though it does not appear in the simple infinitives (*einai* or *pelein*) or in the third person (*esti*). Parmenides brings out this duality elsewhere with several unexpected turns of phrase: "beings cling to beings" (*to eon to eontos echesthai,* 4.2), "beings comes close to beings" (*eon gar eonti pelaze,* 8.25), and especially when he says, "beings-being" (*eon emmenai,* 6.1). When we name a being—Solon, Athens, eupatrids, the Council of Four Hundred, reform, money, moderation, wise man, city, law—we at the same time affirm its being. (In different terminology, we might call this simultaneous designation of a being and its being an "ontological commitment.") The duality between the nominal and infinitive meaning of being illuminates what is at stake on the first way, which remained implicit in the words cited at the beginning: "the one, that it is." "It" is in each instance a given, and "is" is its givenness. We may now complete the thought: On the first of the two ways of inquiry, what has to be thought is "what-is [dash indicates a noun] is [verb]."

In this, what has to be thought in traversing the second way of inquiry is also clarified, and apparently without any difficulty. It suffices, we might say, to supply the same grammatical subject with the negative so as to obtain this additional bit of evidence: "the other, that-which-is-not is not." Any person on the street would undoubtedly approve. And does not everyone know that the contradictories that Parmenides sets in opposition to each other are being and non-being? Thought will follow along after (*meta*) one or the other of these predicates by following the path (*hodos*) of the one or the other. It does not have just *one* method (*methodos*) to follow, but two. It has the choice between two kinds of obvious things, and this is why it requires no less than a pair of horses belonging to a goddess to prevent one from deceiving himself with the zetetic method. Parmenides could not have been clearer. He opposes two paths that one can follow—the only (*mounai,* 2.2) practical ones: the path of being and path of non-being. Hence one will be good, the other bad.

As we proceed, let us keep in mind from this text three words for speaking of being—*eon,* which speaks of the difference between being and beings; *ésti,* which tells of the givenness of being, the self-manifestation of any being whatever amidst other beings; and *pélein* (6.8). This latter verb can signify, and did so already in Homer, simply "being" in the sense of being the case. But it can also signify "to come," to show," "to raise oneself," and in general "to be in movement." For Parmenides, it expresses being as what approaches—as *coming close* (hence *pelazein,* 8.25). With metaphysical consolidations, this approaching will turn into constant presence. Hence, the more a being holds itself close to the source of all being, the more truly it will be. Beings placed far from their source will have less being. It is a matter of place and distance. For modern thinkers, a being far from consciousness will not be representable and will not be. On the contrary, *pélein* is not a matter of location but of arriving and therefore of an event. The new laws, the monetary and agricultural reforms—under Solon's constitution, all this *comes very close* to the eupatrids which, in return, come close to the newly instituted assemblies. Being *qua* approach indicates the arrival of a being nearby other beings. Endlessly, a constellation of things comes about through such a multiple arrival. Difference, givenness, and approaching are some of the initial traits of being itself the text suggests to us. Others will be added to them.

As for the paths, they would actually be two in number if non-being were thinkable. Yet Parmenides says it is "unthinkable" (*anoêton,* 8.17). It follows that the path of non-being remains impracticable, that thought *does not* have a choice between two tracks, that the contradictories between which it can wander are not so plainly being and non-being, that the additional bit of evidence we glimpsed above isn't one after all, and that Parmenides perhaps did not teach two paths of inquiry.

So let us return to our starting point, to what has been called the *proemium* (and for that reason deliberately ignored as an allegorical prelude), that is, to Fragment 2. There Parmenides states each of the paths, two times. Here is the dual statement of the first path: "that it is, and that not being is not possible" (2.3); and the dual statement of the second path: "that it is not, and that not being is necessary" (2.5). Contrary to what happens in the initial hemistiches where it is said, almost as an abbreviation, that "it" is and that "it" is not, each of the second hemistiches contains its own grammatical subject. In both cases, the subject is "not being" (*mè eînai*). Different readings have been proposed for the second parts of these statements, but those attempted translations that, owing to the absence of the article before "not being," repeat the neutral "it," hence the being, overinterpret the text to no useful end. Having posited the first modality, "it is," Parmenides, in the second statement of each path, speaks to the modalities of possibility and necessity; not to be is not possible—not to be is necessary. The consequence is that "being" and "not being" each figure in the description *of each of the paths*. To speak of the first of them, it is not enough to affirm that being is, rather it is necessary also to add that not being is not possible. To speak of the second, it is not enough to say that not being is not, rather it is necessary to add further that not being is necessary. Neither of the two ways is simple in the sense that to signify it, it would suffice to join a single predicate to a single subject. For Parmenides, thinking does not have to do with just one thing. Along what has been called the path of being, thinking also encounters non-being; there it has to learn that being is *and* that non-being is not. Similarly, along the path that has been called that of non-being, thinking also deals with being; there it has to learn that being is not *and* that non-being is. These double disjunctions allow us to grasp why non-being is unthinkable and the path that leads to it is impractical . . . why Parmenides perhaps does not propose to us two paths between which we would have to choose.

If the distinctions he makes are not in fact as simple as between yes and no, how do they really work? Let's start again. Someone who says (the dual statement of the first path) that "only being is, non-being is not possible"—what relationship does he mean to establish between being and not being? Surely, a relationship of negation. If X alone is possible, it follows that not-X remains impossible because it denies X. For another thing, when someone says (the dual statement of the second path) "what is, is not, non-being is necessary"—what relationship does that person mean to establish between being and not being? What does one claim in declaring that not-X is, if X represents "being"? One maintains that not-X equals X, something for which no advanced logical training is required in order to catch sight of the fact that here it is a question not of a negation, but of a contradiction. Between being and not being, the first statement of the second path establishes on its own a relation of contradictories. To affirm that being is not amounts to nonsense, for one makes use of the verb "being" in order to negate it. The additional bit of evidence turns out to be misleading. Concerning the route one believed to be an open option, it is said at the same time and from the same point of view that being is and is not. Of the two statements, the first claims to posit the non-being of being and the second, the being of non-being.

This is why the so-called second path must remain impractical and undiscoverable (*pana-peuthea,* 2.6). The contradictory, literally, leads to nothing. Karl Reinhardt, who at the beginning of this century established that Parmenides distinguishes three paths rather than two, somewhat oddly concluded that "the proof was omitted" that would demonstrate why, in taking the second path, one would never obtain any knowledge. This was because he understood this second path as that of non-being *per se,* and the third one as that of a mixture of being and non-being.[10] However the formulations of the second way already bring into consideration being as non-being. Thus it is clear that these two statements, the one of which affirms what it denies and the other of which denies what it affirms, come down to a double contradiction. It is this obvious fact that takes the place of any proof. Contradictories are certainly *thinkable.* Parmenides says so (2.2, cp. 8.17), and it may be a source of perplexity to observe the ease with which we are capable of clinging—in all kinds of circumstances and convinced of a rational coherence that is beyond question—to strictly contradictory positions. It is just that contradictories are not *knowable.* "You will not know what is not" (2.7). Kant will go even further. Thinking can never get beyond the contradictory claims between which it vacillates if it does not grasp them simultaneously. Knowledge comes to a halt in the face of such contradictions. They mark the end of all viability.

The conclusion seems inevitable: the so-called second path is not one. Where one cannot enter, where one cannot go, there is simply no path (at least for itinerants constituted as we are and who, along with the tradition from as far back as Homer, Parmenides calls *brotoi,* mortals). This conclusion does not imply that anyone claiming to try to pursue nothingness—who seeks to know it—does not know what he is doing. Such a person would be trying to *juxtapose* being and non-being. This kind of juxtaposition does not indicate the absence of any *krisis,* any discernment (8.15). The goddess seems, rather, to be saying to the young philosopher that to distinguish between being and non-being, and to want to know not only being but also non-being, will not get you anywhere. . . . A harsh verdict, of which it has been said that it is addressed to the Milesian "philosophers of nature" and maybe to all the thinkers before Parmenides.[11] It is also a verdict that has an air of bad faith about it since it rejects these Milesians in the name of presupposition of which they were unaware, presuppositions which the overall tone of the poem emphasizes were discovered by Parmenides alone. But whatever the target may be, it remains true that to make sense of the processes of generation and corruption observed in nature, one must deal with non-being as that from which generation arises and toward which corruption leads. Parmenides, though, does not reflect upon observation. The goddess sanctions the distinction—good, salutary, necessary—between being and non-being. The adept who acknowledges this shows thereby that he seeks to become a "man who knows" (1.3). But this distinction holds for just one of the paths.

Only one path?

As soon as the pathway of juxtaposition has been shown to be fallacious, must we not conclude that Parmenides teaches that there is just one path for thinking, just a single way of proceeding? If it were best to renounce the hypothetical coexistence of being and non-being, we might be less surprised to hear Parmenides maintain, first, that there are two "individual paths for thinking" (*noêsai,* 2.2), and second, that one of the two is "unthinkable" (*anoéton,* 8.17). This incoherence would nicely illustrate the passage from a dualistic to a monistic method—a word always to be taken literally. Properly speaking, thinking will be nothing but knowing, and knowing will be nothing but the knowledge of the one and only "it is." Thinking, properly speaking, will be to *repeat* being—which is what Parmenides does with his expression "beings-being." Will not all thinking about the one inevitably repeat in its predicates what it affirms in its subjects? Even if the word *hen* were not to be found in the Fragments (and it only occurs once in 8.6), a thinker whose sole point would consist in saying "it is" and in repeating being would still remain a thinker—the thinker—of the one. How are we to conceive the unity of the path of thinking once we exclude the juxtaposition and hence the choice between being and non-being?

Other than the disjunction between being and not being, Parmenides' text also proposes another, less harsh disjunction, one that is, for that reason, better known. To mortals who know nothing, he opposes "the man who knows." The longest Fragment that has come down to us first portrays certain signs pointing toward the one—toward the *esti*—that one must learn, then it portrays certain manners of acting which must be unlearned. Among the latter, we recognize those who are unaware of the one and who because of this know nothing. They do not know that the way called the path of nothingness is self-evidently impossible to think and to take up, that it is not really a path. The discourse of the goddess starts from this evident fact. "Thus there remains just one path to speak of: 'it is'" (8.1). This Fragment is clearly constructed. Five verses deal with these signs or testimonies, then a dozen deal with the ways of acting that are proper to mortals. It is out of the question to analyze here either these signs (I shall return to them in asking whether one of them is not part of a long line of the hegemonic fantasms that are part of our history, and whether their henology is not turned against itself as it institutes itself) or these ways of being mortal (to which I shall return in regard to two laws, the "thesis" that is Thémis and the "nomotheses" by which mortals posit a *nomos*). At the juncture of these two parts of the Fragment, the goddess says, "Here for you, I put an end to speaking and knowing, well constructed in themselves, concerning the truth. From here on, learn the opinions of mortals" (8.50f.). This is the standard translation. The words rendered as "truth" (*alétheia*) and "opinion" (*doxa*) are the guiding terms for this new disjunction between paths, a disjunction which we shall see is not superimposable on the preceding one between being and non-being. In attempting to comprehend this new disjunction, we will need to keep in mind the first verse of this Fragment according to which there is henceforth just one way for thinking.

Before examining this new disjunction and asking whether the words translated as "truth" and "opinion" name two routes or only one, let us briefly consider these translations.

Given the severity with which Parmenides places all contradictory thought at a distance from knowledge, it certainly will not be an error to array under *alétheia* the contents of every statement not invalidated by the principle of non-contradiction. The absence of contradiction is the minimal condition for a statement to be true. The most modest form of this itself modest condition would be the mere repetition "X equals X." The affirmation "being is" thus repeats in its predicate what its subject states. The reasoning here is circular, but it is not contradictory since it affirms what it affirms rather than affirming what it denies or denying what it affirms. But *alétheia* says more. In the age of Parmenides, truth had not yet been forced under the exclusive reign of the principles of non-contradiction and the excluded middle, as will inexorably happen later (and as Latin, and subsequently French, bear witness, where the words *verité* and *verrou* derive from the same Indo-European root *ver-*, that is, from *veru,* 'bar'—from that which locks). Some have sought to translate *alétheia* as "the Open that does not withdraw."[12] The ponderousness of this expression is forgivable once we perceive that *veritas* and its modern derivatives denote exactly the contrary of an opening: a closure (which is why "to open" in Latin is *ap-verio, aperio:* "I open the *pertum,* the *verum,*" the shutters.).[13] In Latin, "truth" thus came to signify the opposite of the Greek—if in fact, as most Hellenists think today following Heidegger, *alétheia* is composed of a privative *a*-and a form of the verb *lanthanomai,* 'to hide oneself.' But in order to convey the breaching (*a-*) of the closure (*ver-*, *pertum*) that is forgetting (*lêthê*), the literal translation of *alétheia* as "unconcealment" will suffice. And in what text could it be more appropriate than in this poem where it is a question of young girls of the sun "pushing aside with their hand the veils that were covering their heads" (1.10)? If it turns out that Parmenides actually teaches just one critical approach, it will entail a *progressive unveiling.* This word, "unveiling," therefore must be understood to signify both an action—the girls unveiling their faces; the goddess unveils what there is to see along the route—and a state of affairs, the faces are unveiled and because of this they are visible; as the *kouros* proceeds along the route, what there is to see shows itself. A brief examination of our other key word will confirm that Parmenides does propose just a single approach, but one in which an unveiling occurs in successive moments.

Doxa, for Parmenides, is neither opinion nor simulacrum. Nor is it a bit of conjectured advice meant to substitute for a demonstration, any more than it is a combination of things substituting for their constitution. Our speech is not the semblance of an idea, nor is our world a semblance of reality. The Parmenidean *doxa* has nothing to do with speculation about the similitude between a model and its copy, nor with the assimilation of the copy to the model, nor with their more or less deficient resemblance, nor with *seeming* in general. It is wholly a matter of *"appearing"* (*dokeîn*).

"To appear" can of course signify "to seem." So, to retain the principle of non-contradiction as "the sole guarantor of truth," inevitably some have concluded that "contradiction is the essence of all *doxa*."[14] Whether expressly or not, we understand this word by way of Plato and situate its referent halfway between being and non-being. But if non-being remains inconceivable and its way impracticable, how is one to conceive of or make use of an intermediary between being and non-being? Excluding any connotation of illusion or false pretense, "to appear" means "to show itself," and even "to show itself" brilliantly and with prestige. *Dokounta* are things accessible in their splendor. They are splendid—and not, as a long tradition will repeat, the pale reflections of entities inaccessible to us. A resplendent being promises nothing more than it gives. It manifests itself in its world, but it does not manifest any other world. This does not exclude, but rather includes as one of the ever-possible modifications of self-revelation, that it may also mislead its world by being so resplendent that its brilliance is deceiving. So there is no split here separating being and appearing. The being of *dokounta* is their brilliant appearing.

Appearing, so understood, very much reminds us what two other closely related Greek verbs signify: "to come into the light" (*phainesthai*) and "to arise" (*phuesthai*). A plot that comes to light, a growing consensus, a protest that arises, an alliance that comes to light, a book that appears are all events where a being itself takes place, not some double of it. Doxic being is manifestation. And if, as Simplicius reports, Parmenides' poem had to do with *Peri Phuseôs*,[15] and if we are willing to accept "arising" as the primary sense of *phusis*, then obviously we must not render its title as "On Nature." How then should we translate it? The being of beings is their appearing, which itself is synonymous with arising. Therefore the poem would be "On Being."[16]

After *éon*, *pélein*, and *ésti*, we then have a fourth word to keep in mind in order to speak of the being of beings—*phusis*. There isn't any being—no being differs from its being—without showing itself in the brightness of day proper to it; similarly, no being comes close to another unless it enters the daylight out of the not-day; finally, in order to give itself, a being must necessarily arise before and for other beings. Curbing the terminological tendencies of the word *phusis*, which is usually translated as 'nature' and is used to indicate an invariable essence, will, to the contrary, bring out the sense of being as difference, as approach, and as giving.

The radiance of things is nothing so long as it has not been received. In order to be convinced that appearing involves these two aspects—the radiance and its reception—it will suffice to ask about the always threatening distortion that turns it into a pretense. Here the meanderings of the "philosophers of nature" too serve as a lesson. If they could treat nothingness as though it were a being, there must be something in beings whereby we deal with them. What appears not only gives itself to be received (*noeîn,* 6.1 and 8.34), but also to be said (*legein,* 6.1), named (*onomazein,* 8.53), declared (*nomizein,* 6.8), and posited (*tithesthais,* 8.55). Every approach toward knowledge is hesitant and vacillating because it legislates in being received. The *doxai,* in the plural and an active sense, are "decrees."[17] The declarative part in them reveals the play of representation. It is necessary to represent things radiant in their presence in order to name them. Parmenides speaks of contrary positions that we assume at the risk of going astray rather than of contradictory opinions wherein we intermix being and non-being. He speaks of the denominative representations that mortals specialize in opposing in order to posit themselves all the better.

The manifest radiance of beings and a precarious decree in naming them, these are the two aspects of denominative representation, for "it is necessary to say [in declaring] and to think [in receiving] . . ." (6.1). Therefore we must guard against conceiving the relationship of these representations to unconcealment by way of the schema of an opposition between illusion and truth. *Doxai* are positions that one takes regarding anything whatsoever, by imposing on everything names wherein nothing is at work. However this work of the nothing {*rien*} is not nothingness {*néant*}. "Nothing" (a word that means *nulla res,* no thing) is not the contradictory other to being that makes every true assertion keel over into its contradictory other, namely, illusion or the false. The effect of the *doxai* does not lie in such a metabolism. The *doxai* do indeed bring about a reversal, but not of the truth. *Mortals are the ones who reverse the points of view whose complementarity remains concealed from them.* Just one misleading appearance is to be denounced—as we shall see regarding contraries and the normative structure that they introduce into the one—namely, the misleading impression that opposites exclude each other. There is no reconciliation between contradictories; they exclude one another like being and nothingness. However, between contraries unity is not only thinkable, but it is given. Otherwise there would be no contrariety at all to unveil. To the extent that the aletheiological way wends its way, the traveler learns of this unity, of which he always already has hold.

This is why the goddess does not instruct the adept in anything he does not already know. It is also why Parmenides never denounces *doxai* as futile. He makes manifest their structure of contrariety—if mortals wander here and there, it is because they come and go between extremes. In the confrontation of contrary positions, Parmenides teaches the unifying procedure; at the end of the journey through unconcealment, the "nothing" even plays an essential role in being that is nothing in comparison to unconcealed beings. Conversely, seen on the background of an unconcealed unity, the nothing has nothing to do with human decrees, names, laws, or positions, and this owing to the very fact that they are decrees stemming from the encounter with their opposites: eupatrids against Solon, war against peace, mine against yours, night against day. . . . "Everything having been *named* light and night" (9.1), never will what men establish in order to furnish a world be solid enough to merit confidence (*pistis,* 1.30). Opposing designations remain indispensable approaches so long as we do not really know of what we speak—so as long we are unaware that "everything is full both of light and obscure night, each equal to the other" (9.3f.). Yet because they are oppositional, these indispensable designations do not escape the fate of those who declare them. Like them, these designations remain mortal. The work of nothing in them is always the consequence of precarious attributions, carried out by authorities that are themselves precarious. To declare oppositions, to posit oneself as an authority, to take positions, to impose names—these are the operations constitutive of all *doxai* (positing will become constitutive of being and non-being with Protagoras).[18] Representations can serve to name things only because they first serve to oppose them.

Doxa, as the splendid radiance of things that appear and the denominative representation that opposes them,[19] helps us to understand why Parmenides teaches just one way. The goddess makes a promise (1) before she makes any revelation (8). Only once the journey has been made does she say, "you will know everything: the unshakable heart of truth, the accomplished sphere, as well as the declarations of mortals, which lack the solidity of truth" (1.28). What does she promise him? That it will be possible for him to cross the threshold separating what certainly must no longer be seen as an alternative—the approach where the step wavers and the approach where it is firm. *Doxa* is not the rival of truth. The goddess does not propose two directions to follow, the one toward the falling, the other toward the rising. Parmenides is not placed, like Hercules, at the fork in a road where he has to choose. Where, then, is he led?

To grasp this, we must first take note of a certain shift in his poem. Parmenides speaks several times of day and night. Once, as we have seen, they reciprocally exclude each other. Mortals grope around between contraries that they themselves have posited—day and night are then "forces" (9.2) that make up *doxa.* Another time, Parmenides instead links them together.[20] The goddess leads the voyager before "the gate of night and day" (1.11); that is, before the gate where the path of night ends and that of day begins.[21] What does she then reveal to him? "Here I bring to an end. . . , from here on . . ." (8.50f.). With these words, she is not only giving a commentary on her own teaching. She is revealing to him the *interlinking of the two paths.* What is more, she does so from his perspective on her, first describing the way of day, the only one worthy of his faith, then that of night, the way against which she warns him. The voyager is led to the threshold where one journey prolongs another.

Whereas the thetic way of being (more precisely, the way along which the giving of the "it is" and its reduplication, "being is," are to be thought), as well as the hypothetical way of non-being (more precisely, that along which "being is not" is to be thought) would form an alternative if they were conceivable, those of night "and also" (*te kai,* 1.11) of day *follow each other.* No doubt the way of day is the one where one learns "being is,"[22] hence it is the way of knowledge. It is not just since Plato, but since Homer, that light has been opposed to night as knowledge and life are to ignorance and death.[23] On the other hand, there are powerful reasons for doubting that the way said to be that of non-being is the same as that of night, if only because the poet *moves along* this latter way toward the gates from which he began. Also the young girls who accompany him "leave the dwelling places of night" (1.9). Therefore, the route of night is certainly practicable, whereas that of non-being has been barred as unviable. Anyone who has made pronouncements concerning his own affairs or those of others knows that the path of human impositions is suitable for travel. This path is not only open, but the ordinary run of mortals travels back and forth along it.

It is the path of the human condition. Parmenides emphasizes this in his own fashion. A *daîmon* (1.3) presents itself (as was its office, the word coming from *daiein,* "to offer")[24] to indicate this path to the voyager. Diké and Thémis accompany him. The chariot carries him, and the young girls accompany him. So introduced and with this entourage, would anyone set out along a "completely impractical" pathway? It seems more to the point to say that the goddess sets in juxtaposition the path of being and the hypothetical path of non-being; then she enumerates the path of denominative representations that mortals posit, position, and impose, and then the path of truth where the whole makes itself known through the double copulative conjunction *te kai,* that is, she places them in a series.

This serial order—which is anagogical in the literal sense (*agousai,* 1.2) but not yet in the sense of the progression concerning which Diotima will instruct Socrates—which leads from ever-hesitant decrees to secure knowledge of the "it is," means that "there remains just a single path of which to speak" (8.1). It is possible to describe the stages of this path. It starts from the house of night, the place whence come the young girls who accompany the traveler as well as, by all appearances, the traveler himself. This first segment is densely populated. Some manuscripts describe it as "leading through all the cities."[25] Here is where the mortals come in. At full speed, with the screech of the axle rubbing against the hub, the traveler traverses this segment and is brought before the gate opening on to the other segment. Diké draws back the bolt, and "here we see that, in crossing through the gate, straight along the great way, the young girls guide the chariot and its horses" (1.20f.). Thus, there is a new departure that leads "far from men and their path" (1.27). And where does this second part of the journey lead? The goddess receives the voyager "approaching," as she says, "our house" (1.25), that of day. Having arrived at his destination, he will occupy a panoptic site. He will know everything; that is, he will see lying behind him, as does the goddess, both the way of day and that of night. The second part of the journey leads to the "unshakable heart of truth" (1.29), to the unveiling that makes one know that being is.

This, then, is the only path Parmenides teaches. This way of proceeding is *consistent* in that it entails two starting points, one beginning from the house of night and the other from the gate of night and day. If this gate is described in such detail—the lintel, threshold, swinging door, bolt, bronze hinges with their screws and mounted with pins and pegs—it is because the decisive stage of the journey is the second beginning.[26] The whole is unveiled there. The concluding procedure begins when the veil is lifted that accounts for what is essential about the night. This passage is indicated by the privative *a*-in the word *alétheia*. The solemn architectural details surround the event of "privation" where *léthê*—forgetting, obscurity, veiling, withdrawal, concealment—is vanquished by the day that is truth. Unveiling, which is the one and only journey, consists of two stages, concealment and unconcealment. Which is to say that *léthê* remains operative in *alétheia* as a persistent withdrawal (and that philosophy does not yet have as its function either consolation through some uniformly normative thesis or reconciliation through some synthesis that would subsume everything under itself). The one and only path integrates concealing into unconcealing. The path along which the mares set out is "very telling" (1.2), it actually instructs the traveler both about mortal designations and about divine truth, thus we cannot separate it from research procedures[27]—the two segments of the journey *are* the two viable itineraries. Trustworthy knowledge is made manifest at the gate whose every detail assures things are going well; but also made manifest there, in return, is the function of representations from which nothing trustworthy emerges concerning being and non-being. Once again in contradistinction to Socrates who, in the *Phaedo,* undertakes a "second voyage" that *breaks* with the initial starting point, Parmenides continues to *follow* the path that will subsequently be taken as the world of the senses. He does not discover any new being that would be "over there" (*ekeî*), or other, or more true, or more originary. And the obviousness that imposes itself is not that of some being standing out among other beings. The two short sections, nocturnal and diurnal, make up just one long route. One is correct in calling this long path that of "truth," but only as regards the second segment. The one and only way that Parmenides teaches is that of concealment/unconcealment, for which the word *alétheia* suggests our wresting ourselves away from contrary representations and the conquest of a unitary point of view.

What must be born in mind in this integrative reading of the paths is that for Parmenides there is neither a monism of being nor a dualism of opinion and truth, but rather a scale of gradation and an apprenticeship in five stages: houses of the night, the doxic segment of the route, the gate of night and day, the segment of unveiling, and finally "complete knowledge" (1.28).

The second beginning brings to light what is necessary (although still only through signs which, as we shall see, do not tell the whole truth, a truth the traveler will not know until the end). But no beginning is, in itself, necessary. Being taken up by a she-demon either happens or does not happen. No one can force the gates of night and day. For a mortal, all there is to do is to accept that the unitary point of view reveals itself when it reveals itself, that this happens if and when it happens. Nothing is more *contingent* than the passage beyond assumed postures and positions taken, beyond names imposed and oppositions asserted, beyond positive laws.[28]

Or three paths?

If we now question what is essential to these positings, positions, and oppositions, we will see the validity of speaking neither of two, nor of one single path in Parmenides, but of three. We will also see how these three produce the structure by means of which the Parmenidean "it is" makes the law for every law, how it legitimizes them.

Only a mechanical application of the principle of non-contradiction can aver that Parmenides holds to a generalized thesis following the model "either . . . or . . ."; either truth or error, either day or night. Such a mechanism might have some chance of success if these disjunctions were superimposable on the contradiction between being and non-being. But we have seen that the path of denominative representations remains irreducible to the one called the path of nothingness. The path of *doxa* is that of positings, the positings by whose strength we live; but the path of nothingness amounts to an imposture. There, thought tries to make being pass for the non-being that it is not. The path of denominative representations, on the contrary, is one where the distinction between being and non-being has no place. There, being is forgotten. There, the question is not even *posed*. There, one assumes poses depending on what is advantageous at that moment, an advantage dictated by the eye, the ear, and language (7.4f.), thus a pose dictated by the pressure of beings. Mortals are essentially obsessive. Hence Parmenides is fighting on two fronts at once, against those impostors, his predecessors, who *juxtapose* being and non-being as if there were two terms between which all generation and corruption flows. And he is also writing against those mortals who *confuse* being and non-being by following the dictates of their senses (which is not to say that Parmenides is practicing some kind of "anthropology" or "psychology" as Karl Reinhardt would have it, nor that he advocates some kind of superiority of the intellect over sensibility; instead he carries out the job of a thinker by practicing discernment, by seeking out critical points, and by welcoming them). How then does the doxic confusion between being and non-being function such that we have to distinguish it both from the repetition of the same—"being is"—and from the juxtaposition of contradictories—"being is not"?

"They agreed to name two figures, as if the unity of these two could not be. In this, they were mistaken. They *opposed them like contraries* and assigned to them marks set apart from one another: here the air-like fire of the flame . . . there lightless, dense, and heavy night" (8.53–59). In these lines, night and day do not designate segments that appear in succession along the long trajectory along which the Heliades lead the traveler. They designate forces that are balanced along the doxic portion of the road. Parmenides describes how it is that humans—"they"—disregard the knowledge they have about being. They agree to divide their world into contraries. This agreement is sealed by the binomial terms jointly conferred: day/night, air/mass, etc. They err in this very postulation of opposed things, judging that there can be no unity among them. Doxic positing consists in the conviction that when it comes to knowledge, there is nothing to learn—that being is not—and when it comes to conventions, all one does is announce figures. Persuading themselves that it has no being, they make up for it. They arbitrarily assign labels to beings. "They agreed . . ." (*katétheno*). Long before any skeptics had provided the theory, humans have always already suspended judgment concerning being and have contented themselves with naming beings (*onoma* is not the "nominalist" *flatus vocis*, but rather the designation of things; the problem of nominalism does not arise in this theory of names because the question of the universal and the particular is not posed). Thus, in order to make their world habitable and useable, they have arranged these names in such a way that they can decide "for . . . against . . ."—a syntax of contraries that is much more useful for life than the harsh "either . . . or . . ." used to distinguish contradictories. These labels set apart from one another allowed them to accept that *sometimes* it is night and *sometimes* day; that sometimes this force carries the day, sometimes that one; that *here* there is mass, and *there* there is air. This oppositional granting of names has to do with seeing, hearing, and language because it always clings to what seems to be most present. The basic doxic operation consists in putting the *dokounta*, the given diversity as it appears, into an antagonistic order of forces, and an antonymic order of names. It would be difficult to find a region of these polymorphic givens where the dynamics of the contraries so granted was not marvelously successful. There is left and there is right—everything needed in order *to make a world.* "Boys to the left, girls to the right" (17).

As we shall see as regards the law, Parmenides is far from rejecting contraries established by convention (which is why we can only be surprised that Heidegger accuses him of having "explicitly leapt beyond the phenomenon of the world").[29] He is asking about their unity. We will get beyond the doxic forgetfulness of being only by understanding "the one that holds together" contrary beings (*hen synechés,* 8.6). Hence, as far as the separation of the sexes goes, it will be necessary to think about the masculine *in* the feminine, the feminine *in* the masculine.[30] Sophocles describes such a unity as *amphinoein,* "to think from two sides."

The text states clearly that it is indeed a matter of contrary *beings,* and not just of a structure of presence and absence; "absent [things] (*apeonta*)—receive them through thought as solidly present (*pareonta*)" (4.1).[31] In day, see night; in the boy, the girl; in Solon, Alcibiades; in a democratic regime, tyranny; in the right, the left. Let us keep in mind, so as to return to it below, this fifth and final aspect of being in Parmenides—after *éon, pélein, ésti,* and *phusis,* namely, the *ap-* in the *par-*, the undertow present in every present being back toward its contrary. Let us also hold fast to the rehabilitation of singular terms that thereby works against every fantasm of the common. The plural of the present participle strikes a founder's pronouncements with a disavowal that erodes the foundation as soon as it is laid down.

An order of presences subverted by the power of absences—that is the tragic condition. Creon knew something of it when, as he held his dead son in his arms, the law of family ties came to claim him and singularize him at Thebes. He learned what was already at issue in Parmenides—in the law of the city, see what there is of family ties, though it is posited as absent; in the law of family ties, see what there is of the city. Sight, vision, unbearable facts; but they *hold together* in the one.

If one understands the *doxa* one sees that there exists just one gate by which to leave the thoroughfare of positions and oppositions that there hold sway concerning beings—this is to think the absent in the present and the present in the absent. Under the hegemonic fantasm of the one, it is not a matter of being an activist for the most pressing beings—for the girls on the left and against the boys on the right. It is a matter rather of grasping the other of the same, in the same. Everything that is at stake in Parmenides, even if we still call him the philosopher of the one, lies in this unifying grasp of contrary representations. Those who fail to do so are "two-headed" (*dikranoi,* 6.5). With their eyes, ears, and above all their tongues, they follow the coming and going of representations that momentarily impose themselves as having priority. Yesterday, it was "haw" that one needed to shout to swerve to the left, and they cried "haw!" Today, it is "gee" to turn to the right, and they cry "gee!" With their two heads, one clings to "haw," the other to "gee," which is why their mind essentially vacillates (*plakton noon,* 6.6). They are good at detecting what is called for at the present conjuncture. Their prudence consists in saying everything is what it is and is not what it is (*tauton kai ou tauton,* 6.8). This confusion between being and non-being defines them as "uncritical races" (*akrita phula,* 6.7). No matter what it is, every position they can assume remains revocable, which is why the two-headed are also the swivel-headed. They always come back to their starting point, their steps closely following the back-and-forth movement within which beings are laid out for them. Making it their business to adhere to that being that is most emphatically present, they move within a circle without exit (*palintropos kéleuthos,* 6.9). Confusing being and non-being—agreeing that that means nothing more than stopping short of the "it is"—they have to remain on the alert so as not to miss any shift within the order of preponderances and precedences.

Yet these mortals "always squint at the rays of the sun" (15), whereby they betray themselves. They know better than to run after beings. Even as he travels along their route, at a gallop, Parmenides seems to say, like Kant after him, "the great multitude, whom we hold in the highest esteem. . . ."[32] It is to be held in esteem because with time mortals experience a change in disposition, and they cannot avoid using both nouns *and* verbs when speaking. The *onomazein,* the imposition of names, would function flawlessly if we were able to distribute these labels in the telegraphic, military style which has come down to us in the fragment on the sexes, that is, without any verb. "Boys to the right, girls to the left." The denominative activity would succeed if it could be just nominative. But this is not how our languages speak to us. We have seen that the participial form contains within itself the difference between the nominative and infinitive. Mortals who say "beings" (*eon*) thereby emphasize an event-like structure within sheer presence. This intimacy with the difference of beings and being has to be retained as the very essence of life (*bios, non zoé*). Aristotle reports that, according to Parmenides, we recognize the similar through the similar.[33] With the day in us, we know the day, and with the night in us, the night. This is why the dead, even if they no longer see the light, nevertheless do see the night for the night is in them. By this same affinity, when they take up *positions* as regards those givens that are beings, the living squint at the light, at the event that is *givenness*. No matter how much they try forcibly to turn their heads to adjust to the facts, every denominative representation is always inscribed in the horizon of the nominative-infinitive difference.

So as regards the disputed question of the number of paths in Parmenides, and the structure by means of which we may grasp his legislative system, it follows that the two approaches appealing to non-being—that of the pre-Eleatics and that of mortals—are thinkable only by scavenging the Eleatic path. The juxtaposing approach—as it is stated in the propositions "being is not" and "non-being is"—needs the repetitive approach—as it is stated in the single proposition "being is" (which signifies nothing more, we shall see, than "the one holds together" contraries, 8.6). In order speculatively to blaze the path called that of nothingness, which is impossible, one borrows the conceptual material and argumentative layout belonging to the path of being, the only passable path. The hypothetical alternative of being and nothingness can be constructed only at the price of treating nothingness as if it were still part of being. Thus, each time Parmenides addresses the philosophers of becoming, he does so in the form of rhetorical questions marked by a certain impatience and irony: "What genesis of it [becoming] do you seek? How and starting from what could it have grown? From non–being?" (8.6f). If yes, then non-being will still be part of being. Once deprived of their absurd contradictions, the absurd concepts and arguments by means of which these philosophers think they can undertake the path, quite closed, of non-being, must *insert* themselves among the concepts and arguments of the one path that is open, along which one learns that being is. Having shown this, Parmenides can exalt: "In this way, therefore, generation is cut off and corruption, unknowable" (8.21). Philosophy is born at high noon, not at dusk.

As for the confused approach upon the doxic thoroughfare, where do its concepts and layout come from? This is the path where thought does not conform to being but where it yields to beings. Nevertheless, we have seen there that only a thinking that has naïvely gotten in the habit of having to predicate and repeat being can make concessions to beings that are to be named and renamed. This confused approach, too, can be stated in two propositions: "being is and is not" and "non-being is not and is." We follow this approach every time our allegiance to a newly compelling being causes us to oppose our allegiance to a being previously having occupied center stage. Hence the ebb and flow of what we call ideologies today. In such about-faces, which occur amidst more or less great causes claiming to be worthy of the highest names, being and non-being are thought to be the same thing and not the same thing. The being that momentarily claims our adherence is, in effect, thereby identified with being. One is wholly for X because X is what, for the moment, most truly is. Along comes a sudden turnaround that makes everything Y, and Y will even be being itself. In the passage from yesterday's representations to those of today—or from one clan, with its totem, to another—the essential confusion in our denominative conventions makes itself manifest. If names are imposed on the basis of our sense impressions, an issue said to be archi-present in *bios*, in life, will always be only provisional. Seeing, hearing, and language maximize this archi-presence to the point of declaring it being itself. But those who so follow their eyes, ears, and tongue are following only something provisory, which by definition is not being itself. This is why, for them, "being is and is not." It is because it is referred back to some being X; and it is not because X has already yielded its place to being Y. Symmetrically, "non-being is not and is." While the great cause X is in ascendance, there is no nothingness. Strengthened by X, we know that non-being is not lying in wait for us somewhere, that it is nothing. But let Y come along and substitute itself for X, and non-being is: The being that was still supremely present yesterday has just foundered. "They allow themselves to be borne along here and there, deaf and blind are they, flabbergasted, undiscerning races, for whom being and nonbeing are equivalent and yet not equivalent" (6.7–9).

We can add that, since they result from conventions, the promotion of this or that representation to the highest rank—which are ways of identifying a being and being—is a political affair *par excellence*. The word *polis* suggests this, at least if its root is the same as that of *polos*, the 'pole' around which all names circulate, and also that of *pelein*, 'being.'[34] The first political act, in the sense of assuring the cohesion of a collectivity into a community, thus amounts to declaring what is. There is no need for a social contract to do this. One agrees to elevate one being—a natural one like the cosmic order, a divine one like Zeus, or a human one like an ideology—to the level of a standard.

The whole question will be to know whether Parmenides' one must be included among these claimants, perhaps at the head of the list, or whether it undercuts them all in advance. If the claim of the *hen* to ultimacy undercuts all doxic positing—if the *hen* links up these positions to their contraries—then this Greek hegemonic fantasm does not just bind us in any simple way. It will place us in a double bind of positions present and absent (*pareonta, apeonta*). At the end of the day it will require that we keep both the heroic code and the body of democratic laws. The *hen* will be legislative, tragically.

The confused path between being and non-being presupposes the absurd path in which being and non-being are juxtaposed, just as this path of juxtaposition clearly presupposes the path of being which alone is obvious. Therefore, our speaking of a single path in Parmenides will make just as much sense as our speaking of three paths. The path of doxa can be described only in terms of that path called nothingness, just as that of nothingness can only be described in terms of the path of being. These approaches are encompassed by a double inclusion. The denominative representations (the way of mortals), for which every critique is lacking, are subsumed under speculations about absurdly employed critiques (the pre-Eleatic way), just as these speculations on being and nothingness are subsumed under the knowledge that only being is (the Parmenidean way). However, the two subsumptions do not come about in the same way, for otherwise we would not see how the viable path of *doxa* could be encompassed by the inaccessible way, which is that of the absurd. This inclusion comes about through the *use* made of concepts as well as through their being strung together in arguments. The concepts that the goddess reveals are those of being and non-being, and their argumentative structure is that of repetition. The philosophers of nothingness expressly retain this material, due to which their approach encompasses that of mortals. But they make an absurd use of it in juxtaposing contradictions like the two terms for becoming. This same material also serves *doxic* designations, but this time surreptitiously inasmuch as the path of mortals is that of forgetting. The concepts and arguments revealed by the goddess remain veiled in the scatterbrained use made of them by the swivel-headed, who mix up contradictions. They unveil themselves, Parmenides says in the first verse of his poem, to the one who has the courage (*thymos,* 1.1) to advance beyond the ebb and flow of trends. Advance toward what? What does the double inclusion show? It shows we possess an *a priori* knowledge. Befuddled and wandering, we at least know that what is, is—that the *is* is one.

If Parmenides bars the path of nothingness and extends that of multiple designations into the path where this knowledge reveals itself, how does the one make the law?

CHAPTER 2

Contraries

The Ground for Obligation

It is not difficult to convince oneself that this double inclusion articulates the law. The goddess straightaway makes use of the one that she reveals so as to distinguish between the uses we can make of opposed concepts, namely, the absurd use of contradictions, the scatterbrained use of contraries. The one is directly put to work in order to exclude the builders of the absurd and to bring order to the scatterbrained. The goddess commands sticking with the only itinerary that she teaches. Hence her directive is not addressed just to the young traveler: "It is necessary to say and think: being-being {*étant-être*}. . . . This is what I command you to proclaim" (6.1). In this way the fundamental law that will serve as a yardstick for all others is decreed, and for those who know how to hear, made public. It may well be that in this same Fragment she counsels not just against the approach entailing non-being but also against the one entailing *doxa* (a reading that could be due to a possibly false conjecture[35]). On the other hand, it is certain that she remains implacable with regard to the upholders of non-being: "This way, I indicate to you as wholly impracticable, for it is excluded that you should know non-being, that which leads to nothing, nor will you be able to comprehend it" (2.6–8). The first effect of the fundamental law, therefore, is to constitute what is outside the law. Those who would undertake to speculate on nothingness find themselves immediately tossed out of the sphere that "powerful Necessity holds within the chains of the limit" (8.30f.). Once the law of the one is discovered, its first application is totally negative. It imposes a proscription.

In its second application, it is corrective. The goddess calls to order the mortals who agree to assign names by means of opposed figures, "as though the unity of these two could not be" (*ton mian,* 'collective,'[36] 8.54). Therefore she is more indulgent as regards contraries than as regards contradictories. To declare two figures contrary, to embrace one in order to mistreat the other—that is the recipe for advancing along the common way without paying much attention to the divine imperative: "discern with reason . . ." (*krînai logo,* 7.5). Through unexamined gestures of inclusion and exclusion, humans set up a world; this is what tragic denial always serves. They pass through their lives, strengthened by a few ready-made representations, but not too many, maintained because of the simplicity with which they dissimulate their opposites, yet—far from "the unshakable heart of truth"—always trembling, they are always on the verge of opposing representations.

Whereas contradictory declarations about being and nothingness are themselves only nothingness, contrary declarations about beings may be taken up. The *nomos* coming from convention can be integrated into the *thésis* coming from revelation. For this, it suffices that mortals take themselves back up again and adopt not an exclusive attitude, but an inclusive one in the face of contraries; it suffices that they recognize themselves as placed under the double bind of things present and absent. Ever since Parmenides, we may say, reflection on the law acknowledges the double charge to eliminate and to redress, even if redress here signifies fitting out a view with two focal points.

Accordingly, ever since Parmenides, the application of the law has justified itself by recourse to some foundation. One can have confidence in the truth that the goddess reveals (*pistis,* 1.29f.; in translating *pistis* as 'to have trust in' one already has prejudged this truth). It serves as a critical authority. Mortals are a "mob incapable of discernment" (6.7) precisely because they wander far from this standard of knowledge. However, the goddess reprimands the scatterbrained mortals not without a certain tenderness. She does not deem their laws, which are exacting by dint of being exclusive, to be at all in competition with her own divine law that is obligatory by virtue of its power of inclusion. How could there be any competition to sort through (*krinein*) between the condition and the conditioned, between critical authority and our ready-made representations? The goddess makes short work of these representations. She is hard on some, tender-hearted toward others. Even though she casts lightning bolts against the dialecticians who speculate about nothingness, she encourages mortals. Her clemency consists in prolonging, rather than cutting off, the path along which their mind wanders. She honors the doxic approach as a first stage on the path that leads to her. To make short work of the absurd is certainly divine. But if the gods save more readily than they destroy, it is even more divine to extend the route of our concealment, *léthé,* in the direction of full unconcealment, *alétheia*. There is no contest here that turns the gods against mortals. There is competition only between that zigzagging way, to which the two-headed are summoned to return, and the straight way that leads toward the absurd from which no one has ever returned for the simple reason that no one can set out upon this way. Speculation on contradictories remains confined to being and non-being, but for the struggle with contraries one arms oneself with the whole arsenal of the representable.

Parmenides designates the vast domain of contrary configurations by several terms derived from the Indo-European root *nom-*, or *nem-*. In order to "disperse and reassemble" things (4.3f.), we arrange them in terms of contrary figures with the help of names (8.38 and 19.3) and designations (8.53 and 9.1). All nominatives are at work in this, including binomials, shifting perspective (*plakton noon,* 6.6) and laws (*neomista,* 6.8). What can be posited with one name can be opposed by another. To name is to divide. How then are we to understand contraries and their conflict? Certainly not as half-portions which, brought together, would compose or recompose the one. It is only with Aristotelian logic that speaking in terms of contraries becomes tantamount to being confined within a genus (*contraria conveniunt in genere uno,* it will later be said). The age of Parmenides and the tragedians thinks otherwise, however. The parties to the conflict are not reconciled by some all-encompassing unity. Rather, contrariety deploys itself as *agon.* Therefore it would be yet another instance of overlooking the other in preclassical thought if we were to conceive of a generic identity underlying the terms that differ. These contraries without a genus do not get reabsorbed into one another in the name of the one—the union maintains their agonal disparity.

One would be wise to hear the opposed name, the name of the absent, wherever one hears the name of something present. This is why Parmenides portrays some agents charged with placing these "split" figures (*apotméxei,* 4.2) back on the right path. For everything that bears the name of the present, they recall its absent contrary. They complete the positing that is always separation (*éthento choris,* 8.55f.). They are Dike, who holds; Thémis, thesis; Moira, sharing; Ananké, necessity; and Péras, limit.

These agents work in the service of the goddess who is probably none other than Alètheia herself. They carry out her designs. And what are these divine designs? The word *theà,* 'goddess,' indicates them, at least if we note its affinity with *théa,* the 'look.' The goddess's entourage labors for a unifying view of contraries, for *sunécheia* (8.6 and 25). It teaches mortals to see whatever are opposed in terms of their reciprocal belonging together. In this we have the clearest indication of the distance that separates Parmenides from Plato's *doxa,* for with the latter, human legislation never gets beyond equivocation; it operates halfway between being and non-being.[37] In the *Republic* and in the *Laws,* to be misled in what one sees is to be misled about beings and especially about those beings that are the laws. Correlatively, to adjust one's view of what beings really are, *ontos onta,* will also be to change the laws. Hence the essential foreignness, the inner exile, of the philosopher in the city. Because it is other than *doxa,* the correct (*orthos*) view is "orthodox" in that it is directed elsewhere; it is not just another way of looking at things—otherwise Plato would agree with Parmenides—but it bears on other beings. This is where Plato breaks with Parmenides. If the "friend of the forms" happens to adopt a divine point of view on the world, he will see there the reflection of the divine laws. The Platonic threefold division—absolute non-being, doxic non-being (because mixed up with being), and being—therefore should not be confused with the Parmenidean threefold division: non-being, representations that are doxic (because they are denominations), and being. As we will eventually see, for Parmenides *doxa* does not designate a milieu where being gets mixed up with non-being. It is an approach to thinking that has to be distinguished from that of non-being, just as an unsteady step is distinguished from one that cannot be made. The goddess Alètheia and her helpers do *reunite* the contrary decrees (which is not to say that they boost them to some higher level, abolishing in these decrees what they might have of the particular and preserving in some higher mode what would be universal in them; to repeat, Parmenides does not offer a theory of the universal and the particular), but the goddess *impugns* all speculation about contradictories. The key role played by contraries in *doxa,* the law of their resolution—maintaining the absent in the present, night in day—as well as the view that the goddess, and with her the man who knows, bring to bear on these contraries . . . all these suffice to put the reader of Parmenides on guard against an anachronous preunderstanding of *doxa* based on Plato. Only a view capable of sustaining an ultimate dissension will see the origin of laws.

The divine designs, the execution of which involves holding together, thesis, sharing, necessity, and limit, are clearly stated: "Absent [things], receive them in thought as if firmly present; for [thought] will not sever being from its contiguity to being, and it will not disperse being here and there in the world, nor assemble it together" (4.1–4).

How are we to understand the one? These lines provide several indications: (a) The present and the absent remain united for "thought"; the one is therefore to be understood in terms of thought. (b) Being "clings" to being; the one is to be understood in terms of the contiguity brought about by Alétheia's normative helpers. (c) The present and the absent are not to be cut apart; the one is to be understood in terms of contraries without any genus. In articulating a threefold "holding together," a threefold *sun-*, these indications have to do with the prescriptive power of the one. The "ground" of all obligation is a "holding together." How does this bear on the way in which the one makes the law?

The "symphysis" of thinking and being

"It is the same, to think and to be" (3). "It is the same, to think and that in view of which thinking is" (8.34). These two phrases resemble each other only superficially. The first one sets up, it has been said, an equation that invalidates the pragmatic short-term point of view. Along the road of common representations, being equals being present; along the pathway that leads to the unshakable heart of truth, one apprehends that being equals thinking.[38] This is an axiom of identity by which Parmenides seems to place himself in the idealist camp. He seems to have sketched out a pan-logicist gesture, turning logical principles into a system of reality. The other phrase will assert that thought conforms to its objects, which would anchor him just as firmly in the realist camp.[39] In this way, Parmenides can please both modern schools, which are completely incompatible and which feed off each other's dogmatism. However, to their respective proselytism he opposed, in advance, a judgment of "no standing." *Who,* indeed, is it that finds nothing more natural than to ensconce thought here, right in the middle of reality, if not all mortals? To ask "where is being—on the side of the act that intends it or on the side of the intended object" is to excel in denominative declarations. Once again we have "being cut off from its contiguity to being." The "same," with which both cited phrases begin, gets understood only in terms of "holding together" (*échesthai*). In the face of the proliferation of contrary denominations, thinking keeps what is absent firmly present and in this way makes itself the guardian of the contiguity of being to being, the contiguity of its polemic unity.

"To think is the same as . . ."—a proposition that begins in this way implies several terms: thinking; then that which one affirms as the same as thinking, namely, that to which it refers (being, according to Fragment 3; the *houneken,* according to Fragment 8); beyond this is that from which thinking distinguishes itself as its other, in this particular case, the non-thinking that denominative declarations are; and finally there is that to which this other of thought refers, namely, beings arranged according to their names. These four elements form two symmetrical relations. Thinking is to being as the denominative declarations are to beings. The terms of this proportion show the crisis with which Parmenides is concerned, namely, the discrimination between antecedents (*noein* and what is at stake in it, being without a name) and consequences (*doxa* and what is at stake in it, the beings underlying their names). These are the antecedents and consequences that form the two sections of the route traversed by the young charioteer.

Through its initial analogous terms—thinking and designations—this proportion confirms the "between two beginnings" that the ample details of the gates of night and day had already indicated. Since the direction of the first segment of the route appears only with the second beginning, it would be literally nonsensical to expect the appellations by which we name beings to disclose to us the truth of the "it is." The second analogous terms of the proportion delimit the respective competencies of *noein* and *nomizein*—thinking speaks being, brings about unconcealment, joins the contraries without a genus, receives the one; denominations speak beings, bring about concealment, separate contraries, posit the multiple. These two activities together form the condition of mortals. They are never carried out in isolation. It is impossible to name beings (the first section) without also saying "it is," without enunciating being (the second section). There is no narrative of the voyage in the company of the heliades telling how the route that is far from men prolongs that of men. Yet the total itinerary that we are always pursuing in producing sentences remains, for all its familiarity, the most difficult one to retrace. In calling things by their names, we unfold a *savoir faire* as regards dispositions and oppositions, but we do not think about what we are saying. It requires nothing less than a violent abduction to bring us back to the condition closest to us. Therefore the first analogous terms of the proportion—thinking and naming—both indicate a knowledge. One is an implicit because inclusive knowledge; the other, know-how, comes off as being exclusive because it alone is explicit.

The second analogous terms—being and beings—speak of the one so long as they are not uprooted from the unity of the proportion (in other words, so long as they retain their respective places along the integral journey that leads from the dwellings of night to the unshakable heart of truth). So both of them give rise to tautologies—in the literal sense, to words about the *tauton* (8.34), about the same. Thinking is the same as being, but designations are also the same as beings. I do not speak of a tautology here in order to attribute the axioms of identity to Parmenides. The proportion reiterates "X is the same as Y." Each of its relations therefore deals with "the same." But this is not to say that these relations affirm either a coincidence A = A (strong identity) where a being is said to be identical with what it is a singular, or a correlation A = B (weak identity) where two beings are said to depend on each other through some common property. Tautology in the precise, literal sense is not the double discourse of identity; it is the simple discourse of the same. To grasp the one, we must desimplify this simplicity.

The proportion sets to work a complex interplay of exclusions (to think is not to name; being is not a name, has no name), of parallelisms (the doxic procedure is analogous to that of thinking), and of chiasms (thinking is silent about beings; designations speak of being only tacitly). These relations, however, unfold from a common origin. Thinking could not be taken up in its concerns, nor could designations, if there were not before all thinking and all designation the *aptitude* for belonging. For *noûs* and *doxa* to be able to establish their respective relations, we have to have understood "the same" as the origin of noetic and doxic acts. Nothing prevents us from reading this "same," placed at the beginning of the two phrases (3 and 8.34), as their grammatical subject. It reiterates the structure of the aptitude already announced by the (probable) title of the poem: *Peri phuseôs*. The Greek verb *phuein,* we have seen, signifies 'to arise,' just as does the Latin *oriri* (whence our words 'origin,' 'orient,' etc.). *Phusis* designates the rising movement by which something shows itself or manifests itself to another thing. As a structure of reception belonging to manifestation, *phusis* can be confined neither to the side of *noein* and *nomizein* (therefore to the side of man), nor on the side of *esti* and the *eonta* (therefore to the side of what shows itself to man). It is irreducible to some sort of basic competence "in us" just as it is irreducible to any deep structure "in things." *Phusis* is the "same" that makes thinking capable of belonging to being, and being capable of showing itself to thinking. Originarily one, being and thinking provide phenomena with the vectors upon which the functions of manifestation take place.

No one in the subsequent history of philosophy ever comes to think a phenomenal origin that was as neutral, non-entitative, purely functional, resistant to all representation and reification and therefore to all professional manipulation, as the *tauton*—the "same," from which both being (then beings) and thinking (then names) spring up. In order to explain how things can show themselves to human beings, how they can become phenomena, eventually recourse will be made to constructions based on forms—if it is not the Creator, reservoir of every form, or some subjective act quickly transformed into a "thinking thing," then on some "unknown root" underlying the subject. . . . What gets lost forever is the extreme rigor of an origin that cannot be turned into a figure, concerning which we can only state what it does. It gives the same bifocal structure to being, which holds together present and absent beings, as it does to the thinking that posits and opposes names.

In the aptitude that is preliminary to "the same," which we bring to every act of naming, the one announces itself as a simultaneous (*syn-*) arising (*phusis*) of thinking and being, as their *symphysis*.[40] This is what constitutes phenomenality. It defuses several of the possible misunderstandings that easily attach themselves to such notions as one, nature, realism/idealism, identity, simplicity.

—The one is not some thing that shows itself or that can show itself. It is neither manifest nor hidden. It is always known to us in advance as the structure of our belonging to phenomena, be they manifest or hidden. It is the manifestation at work in things present and absent. It is, thus, manifestation differing with itself.

—*Phusis,* the originary unifying arising, is not univocal—being appears to thinking as the overall bearing of phenomena, while beings appear to denominative declarations as phenomena. But *phusis* never signifies the whole ensemble of beings that makes up "nature." Instead it bespeaks the normative difference between the general henological bearing and the beings borne along.

—There is no contradiction between the two "idealist" and "realist" Fragments. "The same, thinking and being," "The same, thinking and what thinking is about." Both deal with thinking and being as symphytic. If being—the phenomenal upsurge—belongs to thinking, it does so as "what thinking is about."

—By reading the "axioms of identity"—the *tauton*—in Parmenides starting from their center, we see that what is at issue is no more a question of axioms than it is of identity. There is nothing axiomatic about these formulations since they do not serve as the starting point for any deduction, and such figures of identity as intellect (where the active intellect of grasping something is the same as what it grasps) have to do only with beings. But as vectors of manifestation, thinking and being are not beings.

—If we must speak of simplicity, this simplicity will necessarily be agonistic. Indeed, the origin of all phenomenality announces its manner of being in the *agôn* of those present and absent things it holds together. It also announces it in the *sun-*, again agonistic, where thinking and being arise for each other. Is Parmenides the father of the "doctrine of principles"? We shall see—at least if, for him, the principial function pertains to an event that turns against itself.

In order better to comprehend how the one brings into focus and thereby constitutes phenomena, it will be useful to examine *noeîn* more closely. This verb indicates both the continuity and the break between the two segments of the journey narrated by Parmenides.

Just as with *legein*—to gather together, assemble; then to say, call upon, name—*noeîn* is a procedure of mortals. In approaching the dwelling places of the goddess, the poet heard told {*se laisse dire*} the "it is." Hence the French and German expressions *se laisser dire* and *sich etwas sagen lassen* perfectly describe the sense of *noeîn*, which indicates a receiving before it does a signifying thinking.[41] This verb indicates the favor (1.22) that the goddess does in speaking and in initiating the young traveler into the truth. As for the gods, they receive nothing; they have no need of initiation, have not heard told of anyone. This is why they have only to make up those denominative tools that are names, laws, appellations, nominatives, binary oppositions, wanderings. As for mortals, they acquire what they need to know by means of the *legein* that groups things together in declarations. Their condition is as succinctly stated as possible by Parmenides: speak and to have heard it said. To speak about things or call them by their names (*legein*) does not suffice to extricate them from their doxic bobbing about. For whoever seeks to discern things divinely, "to have heard it said" (*noeîn*) is a necessity. "Thus it is necessary to speak and to have heard it said" (6.1). We thus may be tempted to schematize "to speak" in terms of the thoroughfares along which everyday opinions circulate and "to have heard it said" in terms of the narrow pathway where *Alétheia* lets everything be known.

This truly is too simple a schema, for nowhere is there a "speaking" without "receiving." Indeed, when they saturate themselves with contrary viewpoints, mortals are still receiving—namely, by seeing, hearing, and language. If they stray, it is not because their denominations shoot off into the void, unguided by some received meaning. Declarative spontaneity does not articulate all *doxa*, the whole of *doxa*.

This word, *doxa,* comes from *déchesthai,* to accept or to receive. What is more, there is even something like a corpse-like *noeîn*. The dead receive the silence, the cold, the night.[42] *Noeîn* thus is differential, with a double bearing, just as the road has two segments—ontological and ontic ones. "To think" bears on being, it is the same as being (3). It also bears on beings, as it does among the dead, since they perceive what resembles them (Parmenides treats silence, cold, and night not as privations but as beings); or among dumbfounded mortals, since they are open to the visible, the audible, the sensible; or even for the man who knows since he sees contrary things as unified (4.1). According to one indirect testimony, Parmenides is supposed to have taught that perceiving through the senses and thinking are the same thing.[43] In any case, he affirms that thinking is at work on both sides of the threshold of night and day. The double bearing of *noeîn* structures the unveiling, the unconcealment. Once this threshold has been crossed, the "it is" shows beings as present/absent and united, whence a rupture in *noeîn*. Yet the initiated does not lose sight of singular things, whence continuity. In all its procedures, thinking remains differential.

To anticipate what is ahead: If gathering in being means seeing contraries held together, then the double—doxic and aletheiological—significance of the verb will help us to respond to several crucial questions concerning the law. The conjunction of being and beings in *noeîn* will allow us to unfold the implications—which are not classical because they are preclassical—of the doctrine of the "same" for normativity. In its two uses, thinking signifies "having heard it said." Now, if the "it is" brings about the unity of what is present and absent, and if it governs what it brings about, then the recourse to the ultimate focal point that is the one will indeed sanction our prevailing laws, but only inasmuch as they are joined to their contraries, which the current regime excludes, and about which it is a question of having heard it said. . . . Consequently a focal point broken into a strategy of unveiling and another one of veiling.

From the double significance of *noeîn* it follows also that this is not a simple act. The thinking that has heard it said is not passive[44] like an empty tablet. The distinction between active and passive can only muddle the internal complexity of *noeîn*. There is receptivity (that is, preponderant, resounding, highly visible representations) in the ordinary run of mortals who, however, also speak and name, just as there is spontaneity (that is, the unifying "it is") in the initiated one, who nevertheless receives the goddess's favor. The spontaneity of the scatterbrained turns into the declarations of good sense and their receptivity into sense impressions. The initiated one is spontaneous in saying "it is," and is receptive in learning (*puthesthai,* 2.28; *matheseai,* 2.31) that the present and the absent hold together. The spontaneity of thinking is therefore not a discovery of Plato or of Kant. Along the way of *doxa,* the mind is spontaneous and receptive in the midst of beings that one knows how to name because one is accustomed to seeing and receiving them; along the way of *alétheia,* it is receptive and spontaneous in following the gift and the refusal of being, and in emphasizing these with verbs.

The spontaneous and the receptive are always conjoined in the bobbings about of *doxa,* just as they are in certain discernment. In order to comprehend in what sense thinking is the "same" as being, we have to hold on to this conjunction within the *noûs* that has heard it said and that speaks. Thinking receives nothing to which it does not also address itself. Heidegger will observe that "most often, rather than saying *legein te noeîn te,* Parmenides says simply *noeîn*."[45] There is no "noetic" act without receptivity in one way or another—be it in a scatterbrained or perfectly certain way—articulating itself in terms of spontaneity.

The conjunction of receptivity and spontaneity in *noeîn* is as originary as that between being and beings. We have seen—albeit in various ways—that along the two segments of the unveiling journey one hears it said and one speaks. The affinity between thinking and being is rooted in this structure of receptivity and spontaneity. It is a radical structure. Now, how in fact does the *sun* work as regards thinking and being?

In order better to grasp the holding together that the one is, it will be helpful to ask what happens when we "receive" something. Take a letter, for example. If we had always possessed it, we would not be able to *acknowledge receipt* of it, no more so than if it had never been delivered to us. For there to be reception, there must be an arrival or a coming that fills an absence. There must also be an acknowledgement (*katégoreîn*), the categorical statement by which we recognize that which we receive. In the case of a letter, the absence may be filled once and for all. We may expect to get other letters, but not the one that has been placed in our possession. If it is a question of food or of air, the absence or lack will never be filled for very long. And when it comes to such imponderables as love, it may be that the lack is its very food and air. For Plato, desire remains desire—Eros is the child of Plenitude and Poverty—because the object capable of fulfilling it is given as present at the same time that it absents itself. The *sun-* in *symphysis* joins the receptivity and spontaneity of thinking (which has heard it said, and speaks) to the unity of the arrival and withdrawal of being (which gives itself in present beings and withholds itself in absent ones). The originary affinity of thinking and being resides in this contrariety of the two sides of the "same." The *sun* works by a dissension of thinking and being.

Below, it will be necessary to examine further what about this dissension is normative in the ultimate authority. Parmenides, who is brought, summoned, to recognize the contrariety at the heart of every phenomena, understands how easily this can be overlooked. It may be temporarily covered over by the compulsive reign of some being, or neutralized by turns of the head so rapid as to take one's breath away. It may be feared as the threat of some imminent upsetting of the current order, or endlesssly put off as an unlikely chance occurrence. This contrariety at the heart of phenomena was not neglected by the metaphysicians. We need only recall the Platonic analyses of eros, or the Augustinian *appetitus habendi*—the hunger to possess that is always accompanied by a proportional fear of loss, *metus amittendi*. It is just that the metaphysicians did not go far enough to recognize in contrariety "the unshakable heart of truth." This is the tragic denial which defines their profession.

How then does the phenomenality of phenomena originarily constitute itself for Parmenides? Through the same undertow that runs through thinking and being, an undertow drawing back toward the receptivity in spontaneity, and toward the absence in presence. If in light of this contrariety we now reread what is called the axiom of identity, we can grasp in it more than just the vectors of manifestation. Thinking "will not cut being off from its proximity to being," *by which* "what is absent remains thoroughly present" for it. Conversely, the withdrawing of being adjoins (*échesthai*) its arrival; this is why the thinking that receives it must also spontaneously take hold of it. Being, therefore, has a structure, namely, coming into the present and departing toward the absent, which mutually hold together (*échein*). Thinking, too, has a structure, namely, to have heard it said and to speak—these too mutually hold together. We readily recognize the agonistic temperament of the Greeks, their predilection for struggle, *agôn*. Heraclitus was speaking as an authentic Greek when he affirmed that "strife (*polemos*) is the father of everything," as was Parmenides when he made the goddess invite us to "the test of a many sided struggle" (*élenchon,* 7.5). In Megara, the disciples of Parmenides placed themselves under the patronage of Eris and are said to have excelled in eristic discourse, in the art of controversy. Whatever we may make of this Fragment of the psychology of a people, and whatever we may think here about the saying of Heraclitus, for Parmenides thinking and being are "the same" through their common agonistic, polemical nature. Phenomena are born from a many-sided struggle—between "critical" thinking, because it is receptive and spontaneous at the same time, and being that is "adjoining," because it unites the present and the absent.

Does not all this strongly contradict the well-known characterization that Parmenides gives of being, namely, that it is like a sphere (*isopalés,* 8.44)? This has been nicely translated as—like a sphere "spreading out identically in every direction."[46] This is a lovely translation because of the geometrical associations of ball, diameter, radius, ray. . . . Except the word in question means "equal in the struggle," "holding the balance in some combat."[47] The association is not of some geometrical order but, once again, the agonistic. Being is like a sphere "everywhere of equal force, starting from the center." If thinking is to do what being does, Parmenides does not speak of a spreading out of thinking, but of its "holding together" (*sunécheia,* 8:6 and 25). This holding together that maintains the balance—through combat—of contraries without a genus is divine. Designations break apart what is of equal force, a break that constitutes our act of birth. The separation into contraries is mortal.

The one origin of agonistic thinking and being can be *described* as symphysis. But the goddess *prescribes* keeping the contraries unified. How does this passage from phenomena to norms come about? What joins the contraries to one another? Who is Moira, upholding this unity? Who are the additional figures, Thémis, Ananké, and the others? Doxic designations are included in the un-veiling through a subordinating conjunction that has a causal sense—*epei,* 'since'—that is as enigmatic as it is decisive for the question of law. "Since Moira upholds the attachment so that [being] remains complete and immobile, everything is only a name, which is agreed upon by mortals, persuaded that this is the truth: to be born and to die, sometimes to be, sometimes not to be, to change place and to vary in color" (8.37–41). Could it be that humans can persuade themselves that their conventions have the force of law *because* this divine consortium upholds the united contraries?

Here we see what has been taken as the framework of the normative system Parmenides puts forward. The one, the law of laws, arranges around itself all the things helping the agents of coercion, like Moira, who "upholds the attachment," Diké, Thémis, and the others. These agents are supposed to constitute the intermediaries—the "hypostases" of Alétheia, according to one commentator[48]—that impose on the world the reference to the one, a reference from which the Romans will derive the proper name for our world: the "universe," that which is turned toward the one. These intermediaries behave, in effect, like a body of female managers (just one of the names is neuter), first of all working on being, then on our conventions. Do these feminine mediators, properly speaking, unify the "nature" between the one and mortals, which the poem is said to deal with? Coercion would then pass from the one to these organizing agents, and then to mortals.

Do we have here the first construction of a theory of natural law? Maybe. But let us note under what obligation it places us. It certainly does not instruct us in the commonplace of every classical theory of natural law, to wit, the necessity of submitting our instincts to reason and our actions to some end grasped by reason. Through the intermediary of forces with, moreover, expressly programmatic names, the one certainly places us in a position of obligation. But it obliges us to honor the absent, the possible, as much as we honor its contrary, the present, the actual. It is a "law of nature" that binds us by means of an *agôn,* even an agony.

The "synthesis" of the present and the absent

When forces clash, some greater force must impose itself. This self-evident fact is at the basis of every legislative system. For Parmenides, these forces are a result of our contrary designations (9.1f.). Thus he describes how the one imprints its law on everything that bears a name, an imposition that passes through intermediaries such as Diké and the others, which ties together binomial beings. In this way, they unify being. These intermediaries are therefore still forces, albeit of a second degree. One might readily say they are forces of a natural order. Nothing seems more plausible—henology is a system of constraints. The one, the greater force, organizes around itself the forces of linking together and of obligation—nature. These forces, in turn, put the antagonisms we have posited in order. Such a hierarchy of forces, it is said, means that every philosophy of the one is equivalent to a metaphysics of order, to a natural legitimization of law, to a justification of institutions, even to their sacralization for anyone who takes this hierarchy literally.

And indeed, however clearly he distinguishes the one from beings, does not Parmenides undertake the procedure he flatters himself to have left behind, the designative procedure? Does he not *name* the one? Even if, under the problematic title *Peri Phuseôs,* he did not deal with retributive Nature (giving tit for tat), it nevertheless remains that along with a large squad of extras, the one is brought on stage as the master of contraries having no genus. A master that is certainly no thing nor anyone. It is supposed to be the simple configuration of beings in conflict, known as this configuration, but not solicited for the sake of beings in conflict. Nevertheless, does not "the one that holds everything together" (*hen sunechés*, 8.6) bear attributes? Could Parmenides' *hen* be the most spectacular of hegemonic fantasms, conversant with the eye and striking the imagination like those momentarily great causes that fill the eyes and ears of mortals along the way of *doxa*?

The setting off at a gallop reads like the purest illustration of "natality" in the history of philosophy. Who, more than Parmenides, will have shown more confidence in positing a referent, and then in maximizing this positing? Who else will have become more persuasive and with such vehemence that thought can take pride, with no fear of failure, in its thetic impulse which always aims at establishing a figure of the universal? Philosophy will have begun with the pure thrust of natality.

But toward what in fact does this thrust aim? A supreme being, ultimate focal meaning, or a broken nomic referent? It has to do with the *simplicity* of the one. We shall have to see below whether the name of the one—the name that the "one" is—does not end up in the poem designating a being and thereby turning Parmenides back against himself, by turning back against the charioteer, so to speak, on the doxic thoroughfare of positings. But first there is a question: Is it due to its simplicity that the one, the ultimate—and because of this, *simply normative*—focus "holds everything together"? The word *haploos* or any derivative of it is nowhere to be found in the poem. We might have expected to find it in Fragment 8, however. Yet can the one be simple if it holds together what is opposed? Can the universalizing work of natality, which always proceeds by theticism, remain sheltered from any contamination by the singularizing trait of mortality, which phenomenologically defeats every thesis? Would the one then turn out to be some referent broken from within, through the legislative conflict of two heterogeneous strategies?

Since it is a question of linkages and obligations, we might add that "the things present and things absent" denote things not so difficult to identify. The age of Parmenides is also the tragic age. It is so because it is the age where the ancient heroic code confronts the democratic laws of the nascent city. For future reference we may say that it won't be unreasonable to understand this in light of the following statement about things present and things absent (4.1): "Receive the absent [laws] through thought as firmly present." What if this reading is permissible, the characters we are going to see have the function of guaranteeing an allegiance to names, to laws and to incongruous sites (to *onomata*, to *nomoi* and to *nemein*[49])—to those who are descendants as much as to those of the city.

Diké, Thémis, Moira, Ananké, and Péras intervene at various moments in the poem. They all perform a strangely similar service. "Diké, not giving any slack to her reins, did not give license to being, either to be born or to die, she who, on the contrary, upholds it" (8.13f.). "Moira bound it up so that it is whole and immobile" (8.37f.). "Ananké, in her watchfulness, keeps it within the bounds of the limit everywhere encircling it" (8.30f.). "Péras being last, is the accomplice of every part" (8.42f.). We must add to this distribution Thémis who, along with Diké, sent the traveler off along the way of unveiling. In Hesiod, Diké is (with Eunomia, the good legal order, and Eiréné, peace) the daughter of Thémis, of the one who "sets in place" (*tithemi*). All these forces intervene like active powers in the service of Alétheia. All of them, also, act with regard to being, which they encircle, bind, tie together. Whether or not they are hypostases of one and the same divinity (the word "hypostates," in any case, is an anachronism), their ligatures confer on being its obligatory structure.

Does the "it is" therefore need unification? Nothing seems more absurd, for something either is or is not. Whoever says "it is" recognizes that something is *simply* the case. Kant, who also understands being as a kind of giving, will say, Either there are a hundred thalers in your pocket or there are not. Parmenides is praised precisely for having been the first to know how to divide "it is" and "it is not" as if with an ax. If with most commentators we hold that being, for Parmenides, means the fact of being, we will not see why he could emphasize these unifying forces, nor why the unity of being would be something to be *brought about.* If the one "holds together" (8.23), it will not be able to denote the being of some being that is simply the case, and we will have to ask whether the word "one" is suitable to indicate being. On the other hand, if the one is as simple as the flash of light that ends the voyager's trip, what then will the "lofty struggle" to which his ascent brings him mean?

The analysis of these unifying forces thus turns out to be crucial for grasping what is at stake in that for which this father of philosophy is said to have been the first to argue: that being is one. If *esti,* "it is" (the giving), exhausts his comprehension as well as his vocabulary for being, then we could judge that he was reasoning about the predicative value of the copula or, more rigorously, about the existential value of *einai* as a verb having to do with states of affairs. But it will be recalled that his vocabulary is more complex than this. We also have to consider again the *eon* (the difference of being and beings), *pélein* (coming toward), *phuein* (coming into presence), and the *pareinai-apeinai* (presence shot through with absence). The processes these four other words underscore explain the necessity for the mediating figures to intervene. There is no other way to comprehend the source of all obligation and its manner of being than through the binding office to which these forces with proper names devote themselves.

Through their enumeration, we are brought to renounce the cliché according to which Parmenides—yet poorly freed from the religious trappings that, up till this founder of logic, supposedly stifled the concept—supposedly fell back into personification and offered a mythological narrative. His text, as we shall have occasion to be surprised about, is certainly a narrative. But the *dramatis personae* are not these forces or these agents. His poem is not akin to those of Homer or Hesiod. He does not recount the life of gods engendering themselves or fighting among themselves. The protagonist of his narrative, singularized by its narration, is the traveler. The same may be said about its "myth." A good part of the text, indeed, constitutes a *mûthos,* but this Greek word should not be translated as "fable," as in Aesop. For Parmenides, *logos* and *mûthos,* far from being opposed to each other, both signify a way of speaking. *Logos* is a speaking that gathers together, *mûthos,* a speaking that reveals. Neither of them amounts to what Leo Strauss and his disciples call a "probable account,"[50] for neither of them is first presented by morals. The *logos,* the goddess's speech, does what being does. It gathers the contraries into the one. The "subject" for which *legein* can first be the predicate, will be the being of beings. The *mûthos* instructs the one who listens with a revelation. If its function is "verificative,"[51] it is insofar as it is a matter of a speaking that shows something. To this must be added *épos* (1.23), speaking as an act. In a text that deals with being and truth, and whose divine figures have neither a battle to win nor a life to live and whose relevant syntactical forms are a verb in the middle voice, along with the infinitive and the participles preceded by articles—in the face of such a text which is born already demythologized, to prefer occasionally an active verb or a concept to a proper noun will not mean risking disillusionment; to prefer using the verbs "to hold (or "the bearing"), "to posit" (or thesis), "to share" (or "the apportioning"), "to change" (or "the limit"), and "to clutch" (or necessity), to using proper names Diké, Thémis, Moira, Péras, and Ananké. As structures these features bear names. The function of these functions, on the other hand, is expressed with verbs.

In examining these forces we must guard against setting them up in hierarchies. Indeed, with just a bit of imagination, and by hoisting the standard, we might see them depicted as a female court: "At the center stands the goddess who governs all" (12.3). A court of rather despotic women, since what we learn from these helpers is that they bind things together. What is more, this place of sovereign women, far from mortals, is well-guarded—for the young man—who it seems is the one representative of his sex admitted to this chamber—to be able to cross the well-guarded threshold, the young women who are sent from this fortress to accompany him must first appease "Diké, who is quick to chastise. The young women flatter her with soft words and succeed in swaying her. Immediately, she lifts the bar of the gates for them" (1.14f.). The subtle levels of authority, the flattery, and the orders given evoke something like an oriental court where all the ranks would be held by women. In the traveler's place, I would not feel reassured.

Yet clearly this is not how we are required to read this text. To take only the case of Diké, she is formidable because she can grant or refuse permission. We must gather together here the various senses of a word, a word for which we do not immediately see how they belong together. *Deiknumi* means 'to show,' 'to indicate,' and *dikeîn* means 'to throw.' At first glance the bond between them is not evident. In the present case, showing and indicating are, however, not ordinary activities; Diké's place, seated next to Hesiod at the side of Zeus, suffices to prove this. It is not that the gods are subordinate to her; rather, she shows and indicates what it is divine to do. In juridical terms we say that *thémis* signifies 'family law' and *diké* 'that which applies between families.'[52] To this we must add the epic tradition where *diké* is invested with a universal authority. Showing and indicating are the acts of an authority that deal with the fate of each and every one she designates. It is easy to comprehend that this fate is "thrown" toward the receiver. Before denoting some human quality having to do with the way one acquits oneself in the affairs of the *city*—justice—*diké* originally meant the dispatch sent to each one that shows him his place and enjoins him thereto. The same root in Latin gives us *dicere,* 'to say,' hence also 'indicate.' Benveniste paraphrases the root *-dix* as follows: "[T]he fact of showing, with authoritative speech, what must be."[53] Understood in this way, this terminology may well lend itself to personification. However, in the binomial constitution of the world (*diakosmos,* 8.60), showing—in the sense of enjoining or throwing—a being to its place is the function of "holding together."

How are we to grasp the simple phenomenon underlying these juridical and epic senses of Diké? Homer describes *diké* as a force that in modern terms we would call immanent, but it is not immanent to the act of some virtuous person (this would be to comprehend it through Plato) nor to something like conscience (which would be to comprehend it by way of Saint Paul). When men turn away from the straight and narrow path, says Homer, torrential rains fall from the sky, leveling the terraces and carrying away buildings.[54] *Diké* is immanent in the very course of events. She does not give permission, we read in Parmenides; she holds back forces—indistinctly natural or human—separating one from the other. *Diké* neutralizes discrepancies. She is the force that holds and holds in all the others. *Diké* is this "holding" because she upholds each living being in the delimited place where it accomplishes the activity incumbent upon it. This is why she is allied with Péras, the limit. To move out of equilibrium, to go beyond the limits is that *hubris* for which Xerxes and Creon remain the examples that are not to be followed. That in the sixth century we are still far from a reflection on justice as virtue is attested by a fragment from Solon: "The winds stir up the sea. But when no wind agitates it, the sea is of all things the most just (*dikaiotatè*)."[55] As can be seen, "just" is not a very good translation. Rather, the sea "stays" calm. For Parmenides, *diké* conveys the traveler to the unshakable heart of truth. There he hears said, "Absent [things], receive them through thought as firmly present" (4.1f.). What is most "just," then, is the "holding together" that binds together the present and the absent.[56] It is also what is most "true," for the goddess brings about this binding together. From a point of view that is difficult to acquire, yet divine, contraries everywhere correspond to one another and thereby obey the one—this is the essence of "holding together." Certainly, from Solon to Parmenides, the equilibrium understood in this manner shifts from natural elements toward a certain arrival and undertow within being itself. "The holding together, not loosening its ties, has not given being the liberty either to be born or to die" (8.13f.). Yet the agonistic sense remains. It plays between the coming and going of those beings concerning which we say they are born when they come to presence and that they die when they move away toward absence. This has nothing to do with speculation about material things.[57] The present and the absent, night and day, masculine and feminine, are revealed to be forces in each instance "equal to one another" (9), even though mortals declare them to be contraries. Alétheia not only reveals, but she also brings about the holding together; her constraining agents cannot therefore remain external to her. This would be, indeed, to turn Parmenides into a teller of fables. Rather, Diké and her associates articulate the major features of any coherent procedure. Whoever does not snatch unconcealment from concealment does not think, and whoever does not fasten together contrary representations—one side to the other side, each for itself but against its other—to the *patos anthropon* (1.27), to the way of humankind, misses the truth for which thinking is responsible. The assigning of a being to its site is the phenomenon designated by *diké* and gathered in by whoever follows it on the pathway far from men. Such a *situation* will allow us to see no farther than the ends of our noses if we stick to individually present beings—unless, along with beings, it also "holds" being "together"; and not just with what is present, but also with what is absent.

We can understand that the holding together called *diké* would be capable of maintaining even a Zeus in his place. It unites the *léthé,* wherein all preponderances confront each other, to the *alétheia,* wherein every side has the same weight. In this way, truth holds together. Moreover, *diké* unites all pressing things (*pareonta*) to what is not given (*apeonta*). In this way, the one holds together. The holding together called *sunécheia* conveys the latter only by entailment—the things present and things absent. But this is also the way in which *sunécheia* will most expressly point toward the tragic condition. The tragic, as I have said, is an order of present things dislocated in being by an undertow toward absent beings.

Thémis, too, by her name indicates the ministry she carries out along with Alétheia. She is the one who sets in place (*tithémi,* 'to posit,' whence *thésis,* 'setting in place,' *themistes,* 'statutes,' etc.). She accompanies Diké (1.28). Therefore she links together the "then, and then" of the segments of the journey in their orderly occurrence, as well as the "here and there" of beings facing one another. From its name, we know "thesis" is essentially divine (*theos,* from *thesos,* which itself stems from a form of *tithemi*[58]). I will use a simple terminological convention to distinguish it from human "positings" (*katéthento,* 8.39; *éthento,* 8.55), from which it differs as a condition differs from what it conditions. Thémis, the principle of stable placement, stands over against our transitory dispositions and in doing so it makes them possible. It is no more external to being than is holding together. It does not go without saying that "thesis never allows being to be unfulfilled" (8.32). Yet, if there can be nothing other than being, due to the peril of treating it as a being, then *thémis,* too, speaks of being as one. Thetic unity without a contrary makes possible our positings, which themselves will be one only by winning the day over their contraries.

Thesis is divine. It unites (*sun-*) the opposites that every mortal positing makes a point of separating. Thémis has no antithesis. Only ephemeral positings set themselves off from their counter-positions and thereby nourish themselves—given some representation, are you for or against it? "The first of all the gods" (who is Eros, 13), for or against? Thémis, on the contrary, binds the for to the against. She sets the contraries in place, as one. She binds together the one as *synthesis* of the present and the absent. More than the other structuring figures, she functions as the law (*sun-*) of laws (mortals' positings and conventions).

Moira (related to *meros,* 'share,' *meiromai,* 'to receive the share that comes to you,' *moros,* 'destiny') is share and sharing out, apportioning. Thus "it is not the horses' share" to be able to talk.[59] Like Diké and Thémis, she assigns to things their places. And as regards Moira once again we can ask whether or not she sits above Zeus.[60] This is because she is the order that the gods alone attain. "Since the apportioning bound [being] so that it should be one immobile whole . . ." (8.37f.). It is not difficult to say what the dispatch, the destiny, the sharing out called *moïra* is in Parmenides. She gives contraries their share, whose jointure precisely makes up a whole. To mortals, she imparts the thoroughfare of designative representations, and to the man who knows, the path of unveiling. To present things, she imparts their manifest place, and to absent ones, their hidden place. Moira is the destiny that gives each constellation of beings its share of *apeonta* and *pareonta* that makes up a world. This allocation affects every trait of being. She apportions out the difference between being and beings, the particular giving of the givens that find themselves being there, as well as the coming and approach of beings out of absence.

The most difficult of the terms designating the interlinking of contraries into a whole is *péras*. It is translated as 'limit.' We must not take this to mean the outline that delimits a being and that marks its contiguity with another being. Parmenides says that being "is sufficient unto itself (*autar*) within the limits of strong bonds" (8.26). Limits, therefore, do not enclose a substance sufficient unto itself, nor the totality of substances in space or time that remains equal to itself.[61] The exteriority between an agent, even if it should be a divine consortium of agents, and a patient would presuppose substantial relations. But Parmenides dwells on the being that later will be called "substantial," not for its relations with other beings, but for its difference from being. Nowhere does he raise the question of the genesis and decline of beings—the question of substances and their becoming. The doctrines of becoming that he sets aside are the ones that would, absurdly, construct a genesis and a decline from the "it is." The difficult problem of substantial change will be formulated as a problem only a century after Parmenides. "Remaining the same in itself, it rests upon itself and remains without loss, for powerful necessity holds it within the bonds of the limit (*periratos*) that completely surrounds it. Its being set in place (*thémis*) forbids being ever to be incomplete" (8.30–32), and it would be incomplete if there were to be an other to being. Limit, autarky, and necessity are all ways of talking about the perfection of being such that it has neither a contradictory nor a contrary.

We might try to sum up things quickly in the following way. For the Greeks, what is perfect is that which stays within its limits. Beauty is an affair of well-proportioned shape, and the well-proportioned shape is the contour. Therefore beings only encounter each other insofar as they are endowed with dimensions. The absence of limit would lead to ugliness, indetermination, equivocation, chaos—in Hesiod's words, night and emptiness. Since Parmenides sets the limits of being in proportion to the roundness of a sphere, it is tempting to abbreviate and say simply: "Parmenides identifies true Being with the sphere of the world."[62] Plato will articulate this attitude, above all in his *Philebus*, according to which there is only finite order. Like a necklace (the original meaning of *kosmos*), the world "is" only if each one of its elements finds itself set in its place and its own way. Whence the association of limit with *télos*, and the creation of the word *enteléchia* by Aristotle: "to be" is to have in itself its own end. Whence also the idea of autarky. When they make the *apeiron* the extreme opposite of the "one," the Neoplatonists were, in this sense, only drawing the consequences of this Greek attitude that equates the perfect with the limited. Whence, finally, the Greek horror of *hubris*, of the insolence that surpasses all limits.

All this is no doubt correct. But all this—and this includes above all else the anachronistic abbreviation that reduces the praise of the limit in Parmenides to the praise of the terrestial globe and its lovely roundness—is said about beings and their complex arrangement, not about the "it is" and its simple givenness. In order to avoid the threat of overlooking the difference contained in *eon,* we need to guard against construing the limit either as the border of a whole or as that which draws dividing lines between different parts. If it is being that *péras* holds within its bonds, a vague feeling for some shapely curve is a bad place from which to begin in order to comprehend the limit. It is something quite other than the "up to here" that indicates a substance, or an individual, or the city, all as lovely as they are because they are autonomous. It is also something other than the "up to here" of being limiting itself—absurdly, as we have seen—in relation to nothingness.

The leading idea in *péras* and its derivatives is in no way that of a boundary stone, a courtyard, an enclosure, or of exclusion. It is rather that of a crossing, a passage; it is not about closure, but about opening.[63] *Péras* is that through which one exits. In "limit," therefore, we must hear *por*-and *per*-, porosity, permeability, rather than *cléis*-, from the key that closes, the wall that encloses, or the clause that forbids. It was the Romans who conceived of their *files* {*limes*} as the farthest limit of their empire, like a dike, and for whom thinking was no longer a receiving, hence, an opening of oneself, but a defining, hence a closing in. For the Greeks, who had just one word to speak of both the foreigner and the guest whom one receives, the frontier was rather the place *par excellence* of exchange and of commerce. How can we fail to recognize in *péras,* so understood, what Parmenides says about being: that it is the exchange of the present and the absent? It has no contrary; it is the very permeability that makes contraries pass over into one another.

In this way, finally, we see the necessity which Parmenides says holds being within the bonds of the limit. This necessity is nothing other than the law of the mutual belonging together of contraries without a genus. *Ananké* comes from the verb *agchô,* 'to clasp together.' Here once again, it is necessary to overcome the instincts of the physicists and guard against reading into *ananké* the intertwining or interlinking of things that make up nature. Like the holding, positing, apportioning, and limit, necessity is a law governing not things or beings, but constellations of things or beings. Ananké "clasps together" the present and the absent. We are accustomed to saying that, among the Presocratics, *ananké* and *heimarméne* (the adjectival form of *moïra* that has the same root that we translate with the abbreviated form 'destiny') constitute the two forms of constraint in the world. The former is supposed to indicate the path of the stars, the latter that of humans. Necessity, thus, would be a rule—a blind rule because it is indifferent to reason[64]—governing beings. Does not Ananké direct the course of the stars in Parmenides? You will know the heavens, says the goddess, "and how necessity directs it and has fixed the limits of the course of the stars" (*Ananke peirat' échein astrôn,* 10.6). Who suffers constraint according to these words? Not the stars, but *peiras,* the limit. Therefore we cannot rest content with declaring that necessity is determinative of things. It determines their conjunction, their mutually belonging with one another, their interchange. Each time Parmenides speaks of necessity, he says it exercises its constraint on the limit. Therefore he also describes *Ananké* as the law of a law. And one might say of Ananké that the gods, too, must submit to her.[65]

For Parmenides what is necessary is the set of traits in being that emphasize difference, givenness, the coming and approach, the permeability of the present to the absent. Being is one, yes, but this does not exclude its being structured from within; it is immobile, but this in no way entails a flat (isomorphous or homogeneous), constant presence. Immobile being as giving "it is" (*ésti,* being different from what is given, as is indicated by *eon*) turns out to be crisscrossed by a double motility, that of the event of coming to presence (*phuein, pélein*) and that of the passages between present and absent beings (*pareonta/apeonta*). For Parmenides, this ensemble of structures is necessary. We can see that, before the turn to physics in thinking about being taken by Aristotle, something like a categorical inquiry is at work in this poem. The Aristotelian categories, which are aimed at being in motion, yield but a pale reflection of the necessity discovered by Parmenides. These proto-categorical traits in no way entail a discourse that attributes, in a positive sense, something to being. Nor are they to be confused with the "signs" (8.2)—all or almost all negative—that point in the direction of being. Rather they make being into a texture of events. This texture is tightened up by the associates of the goddess. Binding the present to the absent, they show us what is obligatory.

So, the lesson of this inspection tour in the court of the goddess is as follows: If the one is such that her agents work on it, then it will not be simple. The one that Alétheia reveals will resemble something like this—it will be a "synthetic" referent, broken up into strategies of unveiling and of concealing, shoved to the side by the difference between presence and absence; finally, it will be incongruous in that it leaves out as much as it posits. If Parmenides relied upon pure natality to establish an ultimate and simple law, then philosophy indeed would commence in the tragic denial of any counter-law. However, the binding forces show that the initial impulse suffers the contretemps* of an originary *sun-tithémi*—let us say, of an originary conjunction. A contretemps that is itself polyphemous, since the trait of mortality speaks through the veiled, the absent, the letting-be. . . . Below, we shall have to ask about the phenomenal origin of this contretemps. In what way does it have something to do with time?

The law of contraries, as it results from the "synthesis" we have now seen, demands being be led back to its condition of possibility. Parmenides states this when he says that the one makes something out of the contraries without a genus: "synechia."

The "synechia" of contraries

Obligation yokes together two motifs: a divine one of the "thesis" which is essentially one, and a mortal one, of "positings" which are essentially multiple. Because it is a synthesis of the present and absent, a thesis reveals which positings are obligatory for us, namely, those which tie the absent to the present.

Each of these two motifs unfolds along its own segment of the journey. That of mortals consists in arranging a world, *cosmos,* with the facts and givens they find at

*The French *contretemps* has passed more or less wholly into the English *contretemps,* where it indicates an inopportune act, a misfire, etc. Schürmann means to indicate such a discord of an act and its time; but more profoundly, by writing the French *contre-temps* he means to indicate that there is more than one time, and these times are at odds—ultimately the time of mortality and that of natality.

hand. It follows the route of designative representations. That of the goddess consists in recalling the event by which contraries enter into a constellation—in shattering, in other words, the fixation on facts and what is given; it follows the pathway of unconcealment. How does this human arranging of the present into a world proceed, and how does the abrupt divine rehabilitation of the absent come about in this world? How does the threshold where one purpose yields to the other articulate obligation?

The mortals' motif is to arrange the present. By calling beings by their names, humans separate, disperse, and reassemble them (4.4). They arrange their world with the help of divisions and compositions, keeping this particular force as present while rejecting that particular one as absent. The two-headed come by their ideas according to what preponderates in the various mixes of contraries—"Thinking comes to men, responding in each instance to the mixture found in their members; for it is the same that thinks and that arises in their members. For each and everyone, thinking is just the more [and the less] in this mixture" (16). As Aristotle, reader of Parmenides, understood it, these combinations are no doubt of opposed materials; through the hot and cold they make temperatures known; through the permeable and impermeable, the elements; through the heavenly and terrestrial, the body; through black and white, the colors. But—contrary to Aristotle—these opposed materials always designate places of being. Parmenides is not a philosopher of nature. To conclude that there is some materialism in the genesis of thinking would be to miss the *tauton*. Instead, thinking comes to men who in each instance are responding to a constellation of topics. We recognize the rising (*phusis*) of contraries in the "the same" that situates our members and our thoughts. In all our thinking we reduce the disparate profusion of phenomena to constants by following "the most"—the force of the being most ponderously present in the given circumstance. Whether it be the mixture of contraries before our eyes or ears at a given moment, or our thought at this very moment, we live amidst and according to echoes.

After Parmenides, this *migmatic* method proper to mortals will give rise to different theories. Plato and Aristotle will rehabilitate different mixtures of being and non-being. The logicians will inventory the modes of discursive composition as opposed to the simultaneous that would be the lot of more richly endowed beings than ourselves. The condition of mortals, then, will be announced in terms of the nature of our faculties. It will be said that in every judgment we proceed by way of mixtures. Lacking an insight into the direct path, a lack that is our lot, all that is left is for us to form propositions by an indirect way, *dividendo et componendo,* by the division and composition of concepts. Theory will finally be translated advantageously into a practical use, as indicated by the well-known motto of those in power, *divide et impera*. For Parmenides, however, what is composed, divided, and mixed is not principles of becoming, nor concepts, nor factions within the city; it is the weight that in any instance we accord to particular beings. We think according to representations that take possession of our senses. This purpose of mortals—to follow the force that carries the day in any mixture—runs into that of the goddess.

The goddess's motif: "Absent [things], receive them through thought as firmly present" (4.1). The thinking in question is different and the saying harsh. The imperative it contains can't help but upset the entire enterprise of arranging things with names, laws, and posited places. It orders us to restore absent things in present things—in the idiom of the tragic age, to restore the heroic law under that of the city, or the democratic under that of the patrilineal. But the imperative orders by instructing us how to do this. The condition of mortals does not result from some facultative limitation, but from a scission that mortals practice as if by birth. They spontaneously confine themselves to the onomastic-nomic-nomadic terrain where, owing to an ever more intimate nearness, facts refer to facts. Once this land of the present has been laid out, they furnish it by means of exclusions resulting in the binary represenations Parmenides sees as the essence of all naming. The goddess thus reveals that we can separate, disperse, and mix together beings in light of some usage only by following the more radical scission between the present and absent. Every opposition between contrary designations presupposes this prior disjunction by which one "cuts being off from its proximity to being." She reveals how we make being differ from beings. When we say "it is," we conserve the non-generic union of contraries, but when we name a being, we ratify their disunion.

The same shortsighted perspective as regards opposites and farsighted view as regards their belonging together is found in Heraclitus. Those whom he elsewhere calls sleepers "are not able to put together how that which is separated from itself (*diapheromenon heautô*) is in accordance with itself (*sympheresthai*)" (Frag. 51). If only the saying Hölderlin attributes to Heraclitus could be verified: "The one differing in itself"![66] But even if Heraclitus does not name the one as the grammatical subject of separation and agreement, he too shows not just how opposites hold together, but also how sleepers/mortals overlook this holding together.

These two motifs in Parmenides also form two more motifs, two circles. Whatever path I follow—whether I am absurd and run after non-being, or so scatterbrained as to wander from here to there among the so-called preponderating forces (*dunameis epi toîsi te kai toîs,* 9.2), or if finally I accept that the uniting way shows me where contraries are of equal force—"[being] is common for me; hence, where I begin, that is where I return" (5.1f.). Wherever I may go, toward nothingness, toward the present, or toward the absent in the present, I always come back to being. This impossibility of reasoning about anything other than being gave rise to a double inclusion within concealment, an inclusion, we recall, of the representation of beings and of speculations about non-being. In this sense, any procedure concerning being will be circular. It starts from being and ends up at being. What I am seeking, I must already have hold of in order to be better able to seek it out. We can term this the precomprehension producing the hermeneutic circle. This is the actual shape of the thought of being. Parmenides calls it a sphere. This initial circle is descriptive.

However, Parmenides also draws another circle, characteristic of errant reason. It will allow us better to understand the imperative wherein the one declares itself as the origin of what is obligatory for us, the imperative of binding the absent to the present. In tracing out this circle, Parmenides becomes prescriptive.

If eye, ear, and tongue enjoy so much prestige among mortals, it is because we receive current—interesting, new, present—phenomena through these organs to the exclusion of those that remain absent because merely possible. This exclusion betrays a lack of discernment, along with the two-headedness that goes with it. The turns of our head, following the most imposing beings, always go from sheer presence to sheer presence. The equation of being and presence expressed through the prestige of the receptive (*déchesthai,* 'to receive') organs sums up, as we have seen, *doxa.* Right here is where the circularity lies. Incapable of discernment, mortals "regard being and non-being as the same thing and not the same thing; they never advance except by retracing their steps" (6.8f.).[67] This circle paralyzes thinking, for one considers any inquiry into being as amounting to busying oneself with non-being, and so the question of being therefore does not really arise. The only thing that is, is what is felt, seen, heard. Thus, "is" is initially and above all what makes for feeling, seeing, and understanding with the greatest force. But what, then, does the "it is" along the thoroughfare of designative representations signify? On this thoroughfare being is always a being promoted to the rank of supreme referent. As such it must never be equated with non-being; otherwise, how can it be said to be supreme? For anyone who gets involved in the game of promoting this or that being, being and non-being cannot, must not, come down to the same thing. Mortals lack discernment because for them "being" sometimes signifies the verb, sometimes the noun. In their first proposition—"being and non-being: the same thing"—they speak, only to reject as devoid of all interest, of the event that all verbal utterances nevertheless articulate. Yet in their second proposition—"being and non-being: not the same thing"—they speak of present beings as having more or less force. Being is not taken in the same sense in each case. This is why mortals retrace their steps each time they identify being with one of their consensual representations. They always come back to what they started from by positing it as a benchmark.

There is a double familiarity with the singular *esti* and the multiple *onta,* which manifests the normative structure of the one: contrariety. The absent multiple "is" (possible), just as the present "is" (actual). Alétheia commands no excision of the absent from the present, no devaluing of it. Hers is an imperative directed against a low regard for the possible, as though the absent lacked all force. Here once again, subsequent philosophy will bring about a strange reversal. For Parmenides, designations bring about what is actual because they mix together forces (*dunameis,* 9.2). Conversely, for Aristotle, *dunamis* will tip over entirely to the side of the possible.

In the Fragment where Parmenides traces his singular way from the dwellings of the night to that of Alétheia (1), the ample details about the gate mark the pause before the new departure. The function of the threshold and its crossing was thus heuristic, descriptive. On the other hand, in the Fragment where he traces the same way in reverse (8), the traveler, coming back from the aletheiological segment of his route toward the doxic one, henceforth knows what he has to do: *sunechein,* to hold together present and absent things. Here the function of the threshold and its crossing is prescriptive.

What always binds us as obligatory is not unknown to us. In their thinking that says "it is," mortals flawlessly observe the law of contrariety, for "what is absent remains firmly present for thought." It is just that in their designations they separate the present and absent. Thought is therefore prescriptive for designations and laws. In terms of the journey, the imperative not to separate contraries is heard at the threshold between the diurnal and the nocturnal segments. There, *noeîn* encounters the *nomizein*. Everyone knows that contrariety states our duty since thinking and naming are two activities everyone everywhere and always pursues. Thought, by which we belong to being, is prescriptive for the designations by which we come to beings. It prescribes keeping contraries united. Neither of these activities is of itself suspended or lost, nor does it invent or choose itself. One cannot maintain, therefore, that sometimes I think, sometimes I name, or that the wise person retires into his thoughts whereas the witless person loses himself in denominations. Such shifts would not agree with the unity of concealment-unconcealment. Thinking commands watching over contraries, not accidently or through some extraordinary effort, but essentially and in its most ordinary exercises. Parmenides does not describe some kind of original epistemological fall into forgetfulness and dispersion. The goddess does not teach us about "an event that happened, so to speak, in primitive times," as Karl Reinhardt claims.[68] She shows that for us forgetfulness is always joined to knowing because we are the site of the difference between being and beings.

That thought is prescriptive for what is other than thought—is this not a platitude for the entire subsequent tradition? Plato will describe *noûs* controlling the passions as a charioteer controls his horses. And for Kant, pure reason will be practical by making itself imperative for our sensibility. A commonplace, indeed, but only once reason has been conceived of as a part of the soul or as a faculty, which has to situate itself in relation to the other parts or faculties. Then it will have the mission of subduing them, which presupposes that a tragic denial will have freed reason of all internal contrariety and, in this way, made it simple. There is nothing of this in Parmenides. The other of *noûs* has nothing to do with the complex of passions, effects, senses, sensibility. It is an activity within *noûs,* deniable by it, not some rebellious impulse assailing it from the outside. In fact, how can *noûs* be uniformly normative if it is our way of comprehending being, which is not given *simply* to *noûs*. What is given is beings. Thinking prescribes retaining the contrariety of presence and absence in beings, a contrariety that is their being. As a result, *hubris* will consist in understanding being—whether expressly or tacitly—as a thing and thereby denying within *noûs* itself (all the while knowing better) the agonistic unity of legislation and transgression.

Yet it is such a reification and such a denial that mortals make their life's work. They uproot some present being from the absent and declare that for us, this is what is! However, in their *noûs,* they know the structure that is prescriptive for them whereby being unites opposites (4.1). Parmenides calls this structure *sunechia* (8, 6, 23, 25)—and Goethe will subsequently show Faust still looking for "what holds together" the universe at its core.[69] *Sun* clearly expresses the one making the law. It is a matter of relationships, yes, but not between human capacities; rather, between names, laws, and opposed sites. We can never speak of the one in itself, only of its relations—a variation of "holding together"—to beings. In all of these relations, being shows itself as prior to any being and as granting it the space where it can unfold itself. In this way, a whole series of propositions becomes formulable that, by means of the intermediary plottings of the figures of obligation, expresses the difference between beings and being, then between the differend of presence and absence. "Holding together" joins contrary beings that it preserves as contraries; a thesis puts them in place as present or absent; "apportioning" imparts being to them in these opposed places; limit opens the passageway between the present and the absent; and necessity, which in beings becomes need (*epideués*, 8.33), assures *the power* (*krateré*, 8.30) of being over against given beings, that is, over against the preponderant *forces*.

Thus, Parmenides takes aim at the conviction of the natural metaphysician in us for whom only the present truly is. Present things are the great vehicles of names, law, and places—Creon is present to his city, Antigone to her family. He would say contrary to both Creon and Antigone—"the law outside the law, receive it through thought as being as firmly present as the law."

So long as one does not make the effort to keep this normative contrariety in mind, difference will naturally seem to call for ousiology. However, to keep hold of the law of contrariety demands a great deal. Hence the denial that resorts again to metaphysics, maybe even starting with Parmenides. Still we can see how far Parmenides remains from any simply thetic ontology, how for him difference calls for a differend that is impossible to absorb into one common noun. The forgetting of being along the doxic road is an active denial. It signifies essentially saying no to all thought of an originary contrariety without genus. To acknowledge such an origin in disaccord with itself would disarm the desire for private and public consolation. "Here are our laws, here are our values, this is our yardstick for measuring meaning—they make of us a people." This is how desire speaks, the hubris that denies the legislative tragedy.

It remains true that nothing can be lacking for the "it is." What is, is—there is no greater necessity. And with the power of this same necessity Parmenides undertakes to legitimize the force of human laws. But legitimize which laws, which constraint, by which normative system, if contrariety is to be maintained in the final analysis?

CHAPTER 3

On Power and Forces

The Normative System

Parmenides, it is said, gave his native city of Elea its constitution. Like Solon, he therefore would have been a man of the law, in word and in deed (an expression that does not presuppose "the separation of theory and practice," but that, since Homer,[70] is a standard formula for speaking of the unity of a life—or, in the negative case, of a contradiction in a person's character). If Parmenides is the first to have spoken of being, he is also the first to have translated the self-givenness of every being, the "it is," into a normative system. We know nothing of the body of laws given to Elea. Yet his poem is sufficiently clear as to the direction in which we must look for his normative system. How are positive and contingent laws anchored in the ultimate and necessary referent? If this anchorage is brought about, as we have seen, through the holding together of the one, then its power reins in *essentially opposed forces*. The reference to the one, of course, attaches every human law to a single, fixed, and singular post, the "it is," but it also attaches the contrary law to this same post. It will be difficult not to conclude that henological legitimization ties down every law and undoes it at the same time.

The push contrary to the pull of the one introduces a movement of transgression into the movement of legislation. But this movement does not go toward either the multiple or the undetermined. Whatever may be said about its narrative setting, at least in its argumentative form the text does not disperse the one. It is not the multiple that becomes essentially problematic in Parmenides, but being as it is articulated in terms of giving, difference, approach, arising, and contrariety. The diction of his normative system issues from the contradiction between being and non-being, which is rendered thinkable as the contrariety of presence and absence and subsumed under the integrative dictum. The multiple becomes problematic here only secondarily, since being is the one single givenness of scattered givens. To read Parmenides as if his primary issue was "the one and the many" amounts to reading him in terms of subsequent doctrines,[71] which neutralize contrariety.

The multiple is rendered problematic for Parmenides only secondarily, but the undetermined is not taken up at all. The holding that is Diké, the thesis that is Thémis, the apportioning that is Moira, the necessity that is Ananké, and the limit that is Péras pretty much prove (against Melissus[72]) that all these universalizing figures determine being so that it holds together. In the poem, there is a transgressive strategy that, however, does not bring about either a pluralization or an indetermination of the one, but rather—as we shall see—an individualization that is in a differend with universalization. The counter-strategy results from things in an oppositional ordering.

This ordering always turns into a conflict, that is, into an event which introduces temporality into being—which will be garbled, as contrariety also will be through a similar love of order beginning with the generation of disciples. Metaphysical henologies will seek to center a body of laws upon the one guaranteeing the best of cities, yet Parmenidean normativity fits poorly with the prestige of order. His counter-strategy inevitably remains incomprehensible so long as being signifies mere presence, for in present things it requires that the absent be preserved, and in their conjunction, that time be so also.

Legality and legitimacy

The agents who bind and oblige translate the power of contrariety into contrary forces. Parmenides, of course, does not make the modern distinction between legality and legitimacy. However this distinction is useful for grasping how power comes to these forces, and for grasping the normative system based upon the one in dissension with itself.

The one measures measures. Measure, having power due to its givenness, legitimizes these measures which have force through conventions. What is susceptible of being (or not being) legal will always be an act (or a situation made up of acts). The conformity of these acts to the law that is in force makes up their *legality*. But everywhere and always the law can be and has been called into question. In order to resist this, it must, in turn, be able to shore itself up with arguments. The law, directly, and the acts, indirectly, have need of an authority capable of assuring their *legitimacy*.

To achieve this, we seek a fixed point that cannot be called into question, and we argue for a link, if not of necessity at least of propriety, between this fixed point and the law in force. The authority referred to will not be legitimizing unless it qualitatively differs from any human legislator.

Since Parmenides, the candidates for this sovereign post from which laws and acts receive their measure have continued to substitute themselves for one another. Here are some examples. "[T]he supersensible World, Ideas, God, the moral Law, the authority of Reason, Progress, the Happiness of the greatest number, Culture, Civilization."[73] It is not a simple-minded anti-metaphysical truism to say that the Parmenidean "it is" is irreducible to these subsequent figures whereby one in each case severs the legitimate from the illegitimate by referring to a being. Parmenides was not just the first to raise the question of legitimization, he remains the only one to have answered it without declaring some being as preponderant, outweighing all the others because it serves as their guarantor. The most closely held fact, so closely held that it seems to have no weight at all—the "fact" that what is, is—confers on laws and contingent customs the same relative necessity that the path of truth guarantees to designative appellations. Being, which according to the "thesis" is one, legitimizes the laws which are always ready to turn into their contraries, into multiple laws through *nomotheses*.

Parmenides' triumph as the one who declares everything holds together, however, bears as much on the *nomoi,* laws—therefore, as well, on institutions—as it does on the *onomata,* names—that is, on language. To legitimize the former and justify the latter through recourse to a simple *ésti* is the task he thinks he has accomplished. To reduce this triumph to the discovery of great logical principles, as a number of interpreters have done and continue to do, is once again to split henology in two—no longer, as in the nineteenth century, between realism and idealism, but this time between the life world and language. If we speak of the life world, the one is seen as the norm for all communicative agreement; if of language, it is seen as the principle (of non-contradiction) of all logical principles. The reason Parmenides remains foreign to us is that he knew how to anchor phenomena—how to legitimize institutions and justify language—without promoting some being to the condition of an origin itself without an origin. Such a conception of what makes law necessary and universal cannot be found anywhere else in the history of philosophy.

Laws and customs come and go, but the focal point for centering them must present itself as an unchanging and continuous point of reference. It must also allow us to discriminate between a good and a bad law, which means that, uncontested, it must itself finally impose the order that all essentially challengeable legislators endeavor to translate for their subjects, who are essentially submitted to a time span where much changes and halts.

a. Does Parmenides' being, which is one, dwell with beings, which are many? How should a point of reference be constituted so that it remains constantly present for the terms that refer to it? Experience nowhere encounters a constant presence. What I desire is certainly present to me, but only so long as I desire it. What I am aware of is given to me only so long as I am aware of it. As for my presence to myself, it no doubt is felt to be point-like, in each instance accompanying the things I desire and of which I am aware. There is a kind of poverty to our experience where nothing endures. More enduring are those figures of presence that are not directly experienced but constructed, those of form and substance, of the creator and his creation, of the subject and its objects, of the mind to its world. . . . How did the metaphysical reflex come up with such Great Presences? It has always been a matter of beings beside other beings, and quite often inhering in them. If these Great Presences remain consistent with the beneficiaries of their presence, forming a whole with them, it is because they imposed a cohesive authority on them. These Great Presences have been those dominant forces in our history to which we have clung and which we have seen as a list running from the supersensible world to civilization. But the "it is" of a being does not force adhesion, nor cohesion, nor inherence. How can what is nothing be close or present? How can it dwell near to things and their representations? Parmenides is as clear as one can be regarding presence. He speaks of it in the plural of the present participle (*pareonta*). Presence classifies some beings, but it does not determine being. If there is one lesson in his poem that we cannot call into question, it is that he calls "being" the jointure of two classes of beings, those that are absent and those that are present. This does not mean that being is to be understood as the presence of the absent ones to the present ones. In no way is being presence. Absence and presence intersect in being like two strategies.

And yet, the *ésti* must produce itself everywhere and every time there is a being. Otherwise we would have to yield to the opinion of those who say, absurdly, that only nothingness is. It follows that the temporality of the giving is irreducible to that of the present givens. Being holds together the many beings, but it does not remain alongside them. What it does do is preserve the two intersecting strategies. In their conflictual conjunction, the way being occurs is as an event.

In this we immediately see the consequence for the legitimization of the laws. Are you pleading the case of the city? Hold firmly present the heroic code that nevertheless you must exclude from it. Are you pleading the case for this former code? Firmly hold the laws of the city as things present in this code. We call this intersection the *tragic chiasm*.

b. As for the discrimination between good and bad laws, it clearly constitutes the decisive charge of which any argument aiming at legitimacy must acquit itself; it is literally decisive, since it is a question of deciding between which collective pronouncements should be adopted or which should be rejected. For such decisions, *sunécheia* once again provides the key. The one "holds together" the contraries without a genus. The law, then, will be all the better if it translates into common language what *péras,* the limit within which strategies intersect, accentuates within the one, namely, the opening of opposed stipulations to reciprocal permeability. The good law will retain within itself its contrary, will affirm it. This would doubtless mean that the work of the legislator will endlessly be resubmitted to deliberation. If we are to believe Fustel de Coulanges, this was in fact the way it was with Greek laws. In the ancient city, free men "spent their lives in governing themselves."[74] On the other hand, the bad law, stipulation, constitution, or institution is the one that claims to be perennial. The prestige of a dominating force is born from a double subtraction brought about by the metaphysical instinct—it does the illusions of an unalterable duration the favor of stealing away the time of givenness, the event; and it favors the promotion of privileged beings to the rank of sovereign by obliterating the contrary of some given—be it a law, a pronouncement, an axiom, a principle, or an ideal, a cause or an end, or any other representation momentarily taken as supreme. To retain its contrary would be to undermine the promotion.

c. The centerpiece of the whole argument aimed at the legitimization of laws governing acts consists in establishing the order imposed by the ultimate referent. How does the one impose its law? We can see this by setting aside two misunderstandings, both of which tend to get spontaneously associated with the idea of a normative system maintaining itself by reference to a focal point (whether it be simple or not) common to the terms that make up such a system (whereby it differs from a reticular system of terms maintaining itself only through the correlation among them, and where, consequently, such a focal point is missing). One of these misunderstandings concerns the law, the other that which legitimizes the law.

The first misunderstanding will become clearer through a linguistic reference. In the epoch when Parmenides was writing, the word *nomos* still had a fairly broad sense, broader, for example, than it had for the Sophists. It signified the received social order, taken as valid. The expression *nomos estin,* as does the middle voice of the verb, *nomizetai,* means that something "makes a law" because it is "worthwhile."[75] At the end of the sixth century, Cleisthenes speaks of Athens' laws as *nomoi,* whereas Dracon and Solon still said *thesmoi.* In Parmenides, the verb *nomizein* means 'has value' (a translation that brings in value and in this sense is perhaps less happy than the German *gelten*) or 'currency' (another unhappy translation, for it does not allow us to distinguish positive laws, posited as the strongest case, from any other representation soliciting the "two-headed creatures" we are). The best solution is to render this verb in Parmenides by "makes a law," in the sense that one says "necessity makes the law." Every *nomos* is the result of an agreement, but not every agreement "making a law" requires the legislative mechanisms of the political regimes as these are eventually discussed. So, what we must keep in mind is that Parmenides accords to laws and customs the same status that he accords to designative appellations. They are precarious, the result of conventions, always on the point of tumbling into their contraries but not, for all that, false, nor unrecoverable for the procedure of unconcealing. As contradictory as they may seem, divergent laws and customs only amount to *contraries.* The issues mortals declare to be opposed are always beings, and hence reconcilable within being, whose essence is to reunite what is opposed. When understood in this way, contraries mutually imply one another, polemically. We cannot name them without saying "it is." Thus the man who has been warned, who does not forget the absent in the present, will see them in their conflictual unity. We have to wait for Xenophanes, a vulgarizer, a rhapsode drawing on a vocabulary that seems to have escaped him (and in whom since Reinhardt we no longer see the master but an epigone of Parmenides), to find *nomoi* relegated to the rank of erroneous beliefs, only good for nourishing the disdainful and bitter verve of an itinerant poet who spews out invectives against *custom.* After all, did not custom demand that athletes receive more honor than did sages, at the head of whom Xenophanes did not hesitate to place himself?[76] Here we have *nomos* reduced to the contradiction of the true and the false.

For Parmenides, on the contrary, *nomos* is integrated into the progressive unveiling of the true. To legitimize the laws agreed upon by mortals will be to push beyond the gates of night and day, to grasp the possible other of the same, and to grasp it within the same. Yet the integration of the overly short, doxic segment into the long route of unveiling no more legitimizes any laws or customs than it justifies any particular denominative representations. It does not legitimize one institution rather than another any more than it justifies one appellation over another. The sanction it accords to institutions, therefore, fits just as well with other possibilities as it does with those that happen to exist. What is more, if the "man who knows" receives the absent in the present, recourse to the one legitimizes, along with the laws and institutions currently in force, their contraries as well. This is an inevitable consequence of the comprehension of being for Parmenides. Since he refuses to reduce being to presence, it would be a useless effort to seek where, in the light of unconcealment, the present wins out over the absent, democratic laws over heroic laws, or the heroic laws over the democratic.

The result is the radical contingency of all laws, whether we hold them to be customary, natural, divine, or merely current (distinctions that Parmenides clearly does not yet draw). Always, the law that some consensus sets aside is as imperiously commanding as the new law that is adopted in its place. The man who respects the laws in force violates their contraries, which the goddess, however, commands him to hold as having equal force. Conversely, the one who observes these contraries that the consensus rejects violates the laws in force. Parmenides detects something like a transcendental illusion in *doxa*—the fiction that being would be equivalent to being present, a fiction that it is impossible to dissipate, from which it also follows that, whatever rule we heed, we remain at the same time under and outside the law.

His emphasis on contraries shows, moreover, what extension must be given to the concept of "law." His henology as a whole, because it shows the constraining attraction of the one, is a thinking about the law. What Parmenides says about *nomos,* therefore, has a literally universal bearing, one that turns all "words and actions" toward the one—in a later terminology, theory as well as practice. The rigorous parallel between *nomos* and *onoma* also suggests that these two words cover the whole domain of the nameable, everything we can represent to ourselves. To comprehend the economy of representations that the one imposes, we must first grasp that Parmenides' henology is what it has always been said to be: a system of order that implants normative reflection elsewhere than in regions of specifically practical knowledge such as ethics or politics. However, we must also realize that it implants this non-regional knowledge in the non-generic unity of contraries. This entails two consequences that apply to the order that is at issue here. In Parmenides we do not find contraries coming together in some final harmony. Other than contrariety there is no economy of present and absent that reveals the transgressive undertow at work in their normative jointure. It follows that Parmenides' henology as a whole thinks not only what arrives on the scene but also its contravention. Therefore, to understand the intersecting of strategies imposed by the one, we must also see that it introduces the other of the given, into the given. Parmenides' henology does more than remind us of the absent in the present. It summons the other that is contrary to the present—the body of laws contrary to those to which one adheres—as having equal force. In this way, it joins to the legislating attraction an inverse pull that violates every position and disposition, every positive law.

To place *nomos* just on the side of what is currently posited would amount to a misunderstanding of *alétheia* and of the integration of concealment within unconcealment, which is what makes up its essence. Unconcealed starting from the heart of well-rounded truth, laws, but also what can negate them (laws, customs, institutions, actions, opposed situations), are shown to be upheld by the "holding together" that is the one. This is a god's eye view of our world, and only courage (*thumos,* 1.1) can help us to prepare for the great path of mortals. But it reveals itself only to those who let themselves be carried along. From this point of view, there can be no legitimization of a body of laws or customs without incorporation of the contrary other to these laws and customs. To mortals thus prepared and thus borne away by it, such an incorporation of the other has to signify returning to the tragic denial that every preponderance posits—sustaining the double bind.

The second likely misunderstanding concerning the one—a misunderstanding that can be found even in the better commentators on Parmenides—has to do with this legitimizing authority itself. To impose its measure, must not the one govern like an agent? And does not Parmenides, therefore, name this agent in what has been passed down to us as the title of his poem? This argument is tempting. In a poem entitled "On Nature," he speaks of conventions, and he declares them to be held together by the one. Can this "one" be anything other than nature? Do we not have here an agent capable of measuring, of limitation, and finally of retribution? Do we not have evidence here that Parmenides opposes to all positive law the law of nature as a norm? That it is impossible to remove all naturalistic connotations from the title *Peri Phuseôs* is demonstrated by the passage about the members of the body (16.3). Is not *phuein* 'to grow'? Nothing could be more normal. To speak of coming to presence is to speak of what happens between the germination of the seed to the dehiscence of the fruit. . . . Yes, this seems normal in every sense of the word. We should look for the normative in nature. There we shall find a norm that applies to everything. To know what its members are for, it will suffice to ask why some particular organ developed, grew—why it came to presence? There is no need, therefore, for extravagances with a subversive air. It is enough to cling tightly to the teleological goal of natural acts. Parmenides is the father of natural law.

This slippage of the one toward nature can appeal to a long tradition. For Democritus, qualitative sensory perceptions are called *nomô*. And does this not mean illusory, subjective, unreal—hence, doxic? And do we not have here a truth that some modern thinkers will rediscover when they call hot and cold, sweet and sour, and so on "secondary qualities"? For Democritus, only quantitative "primary" perceptions are *phusei*. Therefore he opposes laws, senses, and opinions *in toto* to nature. Even if this proto-materialist only dealt with the one, is this not sufficient to associate him with that proto-idealist, who would be Parmenides, in terms of the same rejection of *doxa* in favor of nature?

Aristophanes pokes fun at those who proclaim the laws to be against nature. He may well have had Parmenides in mind, if only indirectly, taking him as the ancestor of this conflict between *phusis* and *nomos*. It is the Sophists of the sixth and fifth century, apparently, that he had directly in mind. He depicts them, for example, as consoling the spouse caught in adultery *in flagrant delecto*. Sophistic, "unjust reasoning" will comfort the accused: "You slipped, you loved. . . . You were caught in the act, and here you are lost, for you are incapable of speaking. But if you are with me, give free reign to your nature (*phusei*) and don't worry about what is shameful according to the law (*nomize*)."[77] It was Antiphon who most clearly drew a line between the "necessities of nature" and the laws of the city, which were taken to be essentially arbitrary. From here, the opposition passed into the vocabulary of some of the Sophists and to Aristophanes and other tragic playwrights. Thus, in a plainly Eleatic tone, Antiphon lays out four terms. He subordinates the *nomoi* to *phusis* just as he subordinates *doxa* to *alétheia*. Just like designative representations or opinions, human laws exist as posited (*thései*). Whence the parallel between laws and opinions. He then recalls the great problem that had begun to be considered during the age of Parmenides: How can one be proud of what was shaped by human hands? The Sophists answered: One cannot be. The only laws that bind us are those of nature, which, in this proportion based on two relations, corresponds to the true. Understood in this way, the law of nature recalls Parmenides' "unshakable heart of truth." Antiphon, it could be said, only draws the consequences of the Eleatic distinctions between *doxa* and *alétheia,* just as he distinguishes between names/ laws/customs and the unconcealment leading to the truth (in this he diverges from Sophists such as Protagoras and Gorgias who, in the debate over nature and law, would choose the law over nature). He announces that one can well do without human laws. "On the contrary, whoever violates those laws planted in us by nature, even if no one sees us, does a great evil. Exposed to view and known by all, the evil would be worse. Indeed, the harm that comes to us comes not from the representations we might make but from the truth. Whence the general maxim that most legal prescriptions are the enemies of nature."[78] Hippias and Callicles will go so far as to reject purely and simply all positive laws in order to cling only to natural law, undeformed by human intervention.[79] The content of the Sophists' injunction to "follow nature" surely differs from the *synechia* of contraries recommended to Parmenides the charioteer. Still, like the Sophists, does he not refer to the necessity that nature, that ineluctable equalizer, imposes on mortals? No, given that agreements between unsteady minds are always revocable, Parmenides' *ananké* cannot refer to nature as the law of all laws, as the norm of every convention.

Nature—or the tragic chiasm, the intersecting of opposed strategies? How are we to decide between such rival readings of the one if not by referring to being with which the poem deals, as we have seen, *inasmuch as it is one*? Being is to be understood there as givenness (*esti*), difference (*eon*), upsurge (*phuein*), approach (*pélein*), and contrariety (*pareonta-apeonta*). These categories all imply the other of the given, they make it enter into the given; and they all emphasize the event of this entry. Depending on the way in which a being is said to be, they indicate an interference {*ingérance*} in the management {*gérance*} of current affairs. Having been absent, a being is given as present; however, it gives itself as differing from this givenness, as arising from and approaching out of absence, retaining, in the end, the absent. This interference of the absent is what the naturalist misreading seeks to erase.

The intersecting strategies, which make up the one, could be erased only by a sleight of hand. For the conjunction of contraries—for the law of the one—it would be necessary to substitute the teleology of natural functions, the law of nature such as the Greeks understood this.[80] Being would then be passed off as an organization of beings. Such a substitution finds no support in the text of Parmenides and can be pulled off only by an anachronistic reading of its title. *Phusis* and truth—Parmenides does set them in parallel. But he does so only in order to emphasize the internal structure of unconcealment. The upsurge, *phuein,* signifies that one being always rises up against another, and *alétheia* signifies that contraries, which are disjointed under the doxic regime of concealment, are joined to one another under the polemical regime of unconcealment.

As a result, the contrary, contrary-making interference of the absent in the present destabilizes every *nomos*. This latter is transgressed in and through the recourse to the one whose power, however, gives force to rival laws and founds them. What then will legitimize the body of laws that a city may give itself? Parmenides' answer is clear: To legitimize the legislative activity itself is one thing, to legitimize these particular—democratic, for example—laws against those—oligarchic—is another thing. This latter legitimization falls only to the political actors.[81]

Hence it follows that, as legislator for his native city, Parmenides had been able only to think differently than he did when he argued the tragic chiasm. The legitimization of *nomoi* as such—which, whether present as given or absent as possible, have the same force—actually belongs to the one that he does not yet call the philosopher (why he could not do so is perhaps clarified by the epithets Heraclitus applied to Pythagoras, the inventor of the word "philosopher," so as to apply it to himself: "impostor and arche-charlatan . . ."[82]; the word was born with a bad reputation). It is not sufficient to say that reference to the one legitimizes democracy just as much as it does the heroic code. We need to add what is essential. The normative reference *calls for* the contrary of what turns out to be the case. By making mortals realize that their designations divide things, the reference to the one restores what *doxa* rejects. When democracy (Athens, the assembly, isonomy) plays with the force of the present, ancestral retribution (the Furies, the areopage, the *deinon*) will have the force of the absent, *the same force*. The henological power holds together both forces. The strategy toward the transgression of positive law thus is an integral part of every legitimizing strategy that has recourse to the one.

How can we live while retaining night even in the daylight we call civilization, a daylight given to the West by Greek legislative genius? Dos not Parmenides' goddess reveal too much to the mortal, just as that "dark light" did to the demigod who "received the gods more than he controlled them"?[83]

But what is there in the one, in its well-rounded sphere, that itself necessarily fractures the whole domain of the positive that it nevertheless legitimizes?

The logos, *condition of laws*

Parmenides' normative system is best reconstructed by attending to the continuity that the Fragments establish between "nomic" phenomena, in both senses of the word "nomic," *onomata,* which applies to the whole domain of language (and which posterity will call "theory"), and *nomoi,* which applies to the domain of action, ways of doing things, institutions (what will later be called "practice"). The nomic is our world of lovely beings in its totality.

Now, for those phenomena which are especially dependent on language, *logos* designates the specific condition of their functioning. Before showing this, however, it is important to ask in what sense we can speak of conditions and conditioning with regard to Parmenides.

a. How does the procedure of unconcealment proceed that legitimizes laws and customs, all the while calling for their overturning? It *retro*-ceeds. The argument goes from the laws currently in force to the norm that is the one. In order to assure its normative power, this argument passes through intermediaries that bind together all contrary forces and thereby obligate us. Starting from those beings that make up laws on the basis of varying nomotheses, the argument moves toward being as what makes up *the* law through an unvarying thesis. So, no longer treating non-being as if it were being, and not yet admitting a mixture of being and non-being, Parmenides has to structure being in terms of regions of beings—present and absent beings. Hence the pivotal role of *sunécheia*. The double retrocession toward the focal point, which "holds together," is the spinal cord of his normative system. It is double in that the analysis moves away from preponderant beings toward the binding forces, namely, Diké and her companions that allot places, and then moves toward the one. We need to try to trace out the two movements of this analysis as clearly as possible.

Whatever may be said dogmatically or critically, philosophy has been and remains the search for the know-how by which to carry out just one procedure: the argumentative competence to get from the conditioned to its unconditioned condition. This is what philosophy has been since Parmenides. We can even say that none of the metaphysics that will follow, which look for what must be prior to all experience, are equal in rigor to Parmenides because they have all looked among the contents that we possess even prior to any experience, contents that *a priori* furnish the mind or the different regions of the life world. Parmenides' henology, on the contrary, is a preliminary mode of thinking ("where one must first go"), prior to all questions concerning experience; but in Parmenides, it does not apprehend any content where it goes. All that it apprehends is the integration of the paths that make up the long path of unconcealment. The procedure that retroceeds by crossing the threshold of night and day is neither *a priori* nor phenomenological.

If the analysis that leads back from what is given were *a priori,* it would reveal to us a knowledge that we would possess even before any encounter with givens. This knowledge would speak to us from *elsewhere* than our world; for example, if it spoke from the world of ideas, the *a priori* that it revealed would be dogmatic. Were it to speak from *within* our world, for example, from the world of acts of consciousness, then it would be critical. Parmenides' procedure certainly does lead toward a thinking and even toward speaking prior to experience—one cannot name beings without thinking the absent in the present (4.1), nor without speaking of "beings-being" (6.1). It would not even be wrong to say that Parmenides anticipates the Aristotelian distinction between two kinds of priority. Denominative representations then would be first "for us," whereas synechia—the mutual belonging together of these representations—would be first "in itself." Still we can see the vast distance that separates Eleatic philosophy (and, it must be added, Ionian philosophy) from Attic philosophy. The one and its structure, the contrariety of places, are first in themselves. But this priority has nothing to do with any forms—the (Platonic) ideal or (Kantian) categorial—decked out with the *a priori*. The Parmenidean reference to the one, it should be especially noted, remains irreducible to the *pros hen,* be it participatory (Plato) or attributive (Aristotle). It is distinguished from them not only due to the nature of its henological focal point, but also in that both participation and attribution only come into play in the present to the exclusion of the absent. *A priori* schemas allow us to say that a thing is this rather than that. But the one is not the idea of some genus, it is the not bearer of accidents, nor is it a universal concept nor the cause of any effect, nor the premise of any argument, and not at all the starting point for a deductive demonstration. Above all, everyone thinks it, but no one *knows* it through his own efforts. Knowing it is not the result of any observation or reflection on the one. It "comes" to us or it does not come. For all these reasons, it would without doubt be wise not to attempt to deal with the one as something *a priori.*

And yet the very coherence of a normative system requires a relation between the anterior and the posterior. No positive law will be legitimate without being backed up by some ultimate authority from which it derives its constraining force. Does the step backward that Parmenides so powerfully carries out lead then to phenomenal *regions* (which should not to be confused with the *sites* of present or absent beings)? There would be something elegant about postulating and elaborating a phenomenology of at least the two domains that Parmenides treats in parallel, that of denominations and that of laws. Yet if the step back from phenomena does not justify one phenomenon against another—not one language against another, or one institution against another—is it really toward the domains of language and institutions that the synechic regard turns? With the distinction between *onoma* and *nomos,* Parmenides does indeed trace out something like regions of beings. They are the result of a diversity in our declarative activities: names here, laws there. Beings give themselves to us in the way that we receive them. In this sense, *déchesthai* ('to receive') is to be differentiated in terms of our different acts. Here lies what is essential for any regional phenomenology: givenness, its diversity, the origin of this diversity in our manner of receiving the given, without overlooking the ultimate target imparted by the goddess which embraces her perspective.

Beyond its elegance, such a construction seems plausible. But this appearance is misleading. To be convinced of this, we need only ask: Of what absence can a regional phenomenology speak? The study of language in terms of its concepts, judgments, and forms of argumentation—the region of knowledge we call logic—just like the study of institutions based on regimes and governments—politics—is not something that forces itself upon Parmenides because these inquiries limit themselves to the present. They seek to answer questions about matters of fact: How do we talk? How do we govern ourselves? Acts such as speaking and governing constitute zones of what is present for us. It is true that such inquiries easily include what is possible, and in this way a certain absence. When we ask: "How should we speak, what should we do?" we are asking about what ought to be but is not. In passing from what is given to what is ordained, our gaze does turn toward a certain absence. So a language that effectively followed self-evident formal principles or a city that would fully realize a pre-existing rational ideal are certainly two figures of the absent. But these absences are not the contrary of the present, and here is where a phenomenological reading of Parmenides would go wrong regarding absent things.

b. The Parmenidean one cannot be turned into an *a priori* for epistemic disciplines or into the origin of phenomenal regions. Yet it provides the condition for every science and every phenomena. We are intimately acquainted with this condition, which is the one. Parmenides' poem opens with an energy that we bear within ourselves and that nevertheless requires a revelation. We must have within ourselves that by which we can advance as far as what holds everything together, and it must come to us. "The mares that bear me to where my courage is heading. . . ." (1.1). Some translate "courage" as "desire." It determines the end of the journey, but if the mares do not come from elsewhere, the trip will not take place. Therefore the revelation made to Parmenides teaches him only what everyone knows, namely, the most elementary condition of activities along the thoroughfare—so elementary that we must make ourselves leave the thoroughfare in order to learn to talk about what goes without saying. The "wise mares" (1.4) drawing the young man are wise because they know the way from night to day, just as a horse knows the ford across a river from having crossed it many times.

The movement of thinking that goes from the conditioned to its condition is carried out by Parmenides a number of times in his text, and in terms of a number of different phenomena. We can see this in terms of the parallel between laws and denominations. As regards the latter, his procedure is quite explicit. Parmenides retrocedes from scattered speaking to the condition of all speaking: the one, which gathers all statements into an order. By "tongue" (*glôssa,* 7.5), he does not mean the organ in our mouths nor, in association with hearing and seeing, some faculty (in general, our sensory capacity), any more than *noûs* means intellect over against such sensory faculties. A reading of early philosophical texts in which one does not try to free oneself as much as possible of commonplaces would be condemned in advance to produce nothing new, only more commonplaces. Parmenides does not oppose tongue—language—to intellect, as will happen in "rational psychology"—but to *logos*. "As habit, do not train yourself to give free reign to the eye or you will see nothing, to an ear and to a tongue ringing with echoes; rather, in gathering (*logo*) it together, discern the test of the lofty struggle" (7.4–6). This lofty struggle, it is clear, is the contrariety that characterizes the conflicting forces along the road of designative representations. The goddess invites the young man to gather together those forces that mortals assert are contrary to one another. *Legein* is the task she assigns him. Opposed to this is the dispersion that is the work of "tongues" (The eye that sees nothing is not an agent of dispersion; only the ear and the tongue are—speech heard and proffered). The opposition between "tongue" and *legein* is clearly odd since the latter verb, if its root signifies 'to gather together,' can also mean, at least since Homer, 'to speak.' Where then does the retrocessive step lead?

Glossa disperses as much as it unites, not only when we talk nonsense, but—as with every doxic effect—essentially so. Denominative representations clash in our statements. *Legein* is what gathers them together.

On a first reading, *logos,* too, has to do with discourse. Thanks to it, the daughters of the sun flatter Diké (1.15). The goddess offers a *logos,* a teaching (8.50), and this word thus signifies the same thing as does *mûthos*—'discourse,' precisely speaking. For mortals, this is a speech most necessary to acquire. For what will that speaking be that unifies things instead of pushing already mixed-up things to the highest degree of confusion? What speech will be the condition of all our words? Parmenides answers, in the clearest fashion: "It is necessary to speak by gathering it together, and in conserving and receiving it, beings-being" (6.1). The speaking that disperses things is a speaking that follows the rise and fall of the flow of significant forces, just as according to Cleisthenes, sometimes one praises the healthy instinct of a people, and sometimes those received values for which the natural elite among us serves as guardian for the greater good of all. . . . The speaking that gathers together (*legein*), however, is neither populist nor democratic, nor oligarchic. It authorizes the one tragic chiasm, not sometimes the laws of the city and sometimes patrilineal laws. It is simpler, since it is but one singular word, *éon,* "beings-being."

At first sight, therefore, the picture is all too familiar. A young man has been raised up, it has been put into his head that what he hears around him is only empty prattle, and now he returns, claiming that there has been a divine kidnapping, and repeating the unintelligible phrase "beings-being." One incantation is as good as another.

However, we shall have less a sense of déjà vu if we reread more attentively what Parmenides opposes to a loose tongue: ". . . discern instead, through the *logos,* the test of lofty struggle." *Logos* here is not a tool. Parmenides is not proposing to us some instrumental theory of language. We should hear the imperative: Discern *by having recourse* to *logos,* just as one has recourse to an ultimate authority. The phrase the initiated recounts indicates that it is this authority. It speaks of the being of beings. It sets discourse on the long sojourn of their difference instead of on the short pathways that link beings. And what do we learn along this long differential sojourn? There we learn the sure reference. The *pistos logos* (8.50), therefore, is not simply the instruction that is offered. It is that about which the adept finds himself being instructed—being-one as ultimate authority. This is why one can say that the *logos* here is "the very name of being.[84] And if this long sojourn consists of two segments—concealment and unconcealment—it is clear that in following them we do not disengage ourselves from those battles for preponderance that characterize the first segment. Such would be to disengage ourselves from our mortal condition. Rather, we also receive (*noeîn*) the other, contrary to those doxic affirmations that seek our votes. *Logos* speaks of the contrariety within being thus gathering beings together. It emphasizes the order of those equal forces that are the absent and the present. This order is normative for "tongues." It obliges us to speak about current affairs without cutting them off from their possible contraries, without disjoining them from their opposites for which the one is the conjunction. *Logos* is this conjunction in terms of synechia. It is what establishes the relation—the *ratio*—between the two segments of the aletheiological thoroughfare.

The normative intermediaries—holding together, thesis, apportioning, limit, necessity—explicitly extend the "logical" order, so understood, to practice. They articulate the bonds between linguistic and ordinary phenomena. Through their function of binding and obligation (through *-leig* in all its forms), these agents diversify *logos* (the *-leg* in all its forms). The same step that retrocedes from the *legein,* which is speaking, to the *legein,* which is being, also reveals the condition of everything that binds us, every law and every custom.

As with *nomoi,* laws, so with *onomata,* names. Born of ever-revocable agreements, laws, too, carry on a "test of lofty struggle." To sustain this struggle is to discern, as in the case of contraries, among apparently contradictory laws; it is to gather them once again into a knowledge where opposites reciprocally imply one another. Therefore it is, finally, to preserve these beings, which are conflicting laws, in their contrariety wherein they change places. The dangerous legislator believes he can *rule* the lofty struggle among contrary laws, either in a friendly fashion or by a sovereign decision. Here is the wisdom intended for those powers that legislate: Receive the other excluded by the laws set forth along with the laws set forth. Here is the wisdom intended for those from whom one can extract obedience: Remember the other excluded by the laws pronounced to you along with those laws pronounced to you.

To understand the status of laws for Parmenides, it suffices to hold firmly to their parallel with denominative representations. That common opinion opposes this appellation or denomination with some other, or this law with some other law, is all the same in the short run. Such shortcuts run the risk of always being the same. If Parmenides does not treat things as they appear (*dokounta*) to us as semblances of things, or with the representations or statements by which we deal with them, as misleading illusions—if the segment of unconcealment where positions clash is indeed the main road where we call things by their names—it is also the route where one advances guided by well-founded laws. *Nomos* is no more an evil than are *onoma*. The only evil lies in separation and in the denial that there has been a separation. "They [the mortals] were agreed to give names to two figures, as though the unity of these two could not be. In this they were mistaken. They have opposed them as contraries and assigned them marks set apart from one another" (*chôris ap' allélôn,* 8.53–56). According to the lexicons, this passage contains the first appearance of the term translated as "separation" and destined for celebrity in the debates between Aristotle and the Academy. To set apart what one names and to deny that the figures so opposed are really one, here is the forgetfulness whence is born every position claiming authority. They all have in common that they separate the inseparable by positing each thing "everywhere as the same for itself, but not the same for the other" (8.57f.). Determinate negation is the very model of every doxic figure (in this way playing on individual contrary terms but not—contra Hegel—on contradictory ones). Like names, laws disunite what the *logos* gathers only to make it, polemically, one. This is why laws hold only along the nocturnal portion of the path. The reciprocal belonging together of opposites is what constitutes diurnal knowledge, which "trusts in unconcealment." Thus the legitimization of names and laws comes about through their integration into this unitary knowledge; unitary because it is, literally, "logical."

Is the law of the one "the most implacable norm," as one commentator puts it? Yes, but implacable in terms of its double bind, obliging us to preserve in each thing posited its opposite. A modern mind, which has initiated the dialectic that suppresses and preserves contraries in sublating them, cannot help but fail to see how much the one calls for the transgression of current laws. Parmenides' one, however, neither reconciles nor sublates positions and their negations. It accentuates their struggle. If we must comprehend the one and its binding forces in terms of *logos,* and *logos* as conjoining contraries without a genus, then this will mean cutting short that kind of validation that seeks to base all laws on one monovalent referent. Normative power does not just give value to a consensual agreement alone. How could the one exercise its legitimizing efficacy with regard to the sole present body of laws if being is to be understood as the order of the present and the absent mutually sustaining each other? With an appeal to the absent opposite, in every present law and institution, Parmenides expresses the truth of tragedy from Aeschylus to Sophocles: In democratic law, receive the heroic code as firmly present, and with the heroic code, democratic law. The vocabulary of being (*pareonta-apeonta*) thereby emphasizes the version whose one side expresses in ontological terms Michel Foucault's observation: "Only a fiction can make us believe that laws are made to be respected. . . . Illegality constitutes an absolutely positive element in social functioning, whose role is foreseen in the general strategy of society."[85]

For Parmenides, it is the sphere of "equal forces," *homoîos*—an order whose elements have the same strength, extent, or size (as in the Latin *par*)—that most exactly describes the conflictual function of *logos*. But does the normative system then delegitimize the present in order to legitimize the absent? Does the goddess call for an uninterrupted succession of putches? Or does the disposition (*logos*) into opposites indicate something else, something quite other? Something that the verb (*legein*) expresses better than does the noun {*logos*}?

Does not the one—a power that disposes forces and that preserves their struggle—suggest too much causal efficacy for it to have the role of a pure condition? If the one amounts to a cause, and if Parmenides endows it with attributes, does this not turn his henology against itself? Would it not be fitting then to set Parmenides at the head of the promoters of entitative, supremely efficacious, uniquely divine referents? Yet it is one thing if Alétheia turns the normative one into a double bind, and therefore against itself, and another if our reading discovers an ambivalence in the one and thus turns Parmenides' henology against itself. We shall have to distinguish further these two turnings (chapter 4).

The first one fractures the *simply* normative power of the one. Would Parmenides then have discovered the fragility of referents even before the metaphysicians inaugurated their reign? Like all the proto-categories, *legein* is a verb. As concerns being, it speaks of a non-simple process that the obligating figures (Thémis, the thesis; Moïra, the apportioning, etc.) do not convey. Would it then be the event accentuated by the verb; would it be time that could immediately depose the posited hegemony? What bearing does this have on the story of the journey and the individualization that it brings about (chapter 5)?

The status of Parmenides' henology as well as that of the narrative itself will, moreover, be clarified by having recourse to one and the same criterion: the singular path taught by Parmenides and the manner in which its stages are linked together.

CHAPTER 4

Henology Turned against Itself?

"'It is': along this path, signs abound."
—Parmenides (8.2)

The "it is" joins contraries in a struggle; hence the precariousness of the world for Parmenides. To an ear divinely instructed, the undertow toward the absent makes itself heard with as much sonority as the tumult of the present. There is a double dictate whose pulls are opposed without a common genus and that ceaselessly vary their configurations. Taken up, heard, obeyed in isolation, neither of these two dictates—neither the unconcealed dictate of the unconcealed obsessive present that constrains us nor the concealed dictate of what is absent by exclusion, constraining us—tells us what is necessary. The apodicticity in the chiastic dictate of a double bind, this is the law of the one according to Parmenides.

The conjunction of contraries without a genus is highlighted by every verb and every verbal form for speaking about being (*esti, éon, pelein, pareinai-apeinai,* as well as by *legein*). This conflictual union is produced wherever something manifests itself, wherever there is a phenomenon. It is phenomenality producing itself, and in this sense, an event. Yet do not the signs that mark out the path of inquiry deny, resoundingly, that being is to be understood as the event of a double bind? Without retracing here all the details of their abundance,[86] it is easy to see that by way of these signs being bears witness to itself (*sèmata:* testimonies, attestations) with a new duplicity. This double path of speaking has nothing to do with contradictories, or with contraries, or with their union apart from any genus. It has nothing to do with the *one* polemically turned against itself. However, it has everything to do with subsequent history. The question is whether these signs turn *henology* against itself. Their equivocation is perhaps perceptible only to us, who have lately come on the scene. Yet it is indeed striking, and this in more than one way. It is flagrant, but also has long-term repercussions. In any case, it has affected all thinking about being since Parmenides.

"Since this is, it was not engendered and is indestructible. It is one frame, unshakable, needing no end. This neither was nor will be, for it now is. Everything in it is the same size, and insofar as it is one it holds everything together" (8.3–6). "This," namely, the givenness "it is," bears witness to what it is. By itself it itself bears witness to its attributes—but is it a question of attributes? Such is the instruction given by Alétheia. Here the "it is" unconceals itself. Signs abound along the path of unconcealment. One may immediately wish to object: Does not the accumulation of predicates militate against this unconcealment that they are supposed to articulate? This objection would hardly matter if it challenged the predicates of the one and only plurality. What gives rise to a problem is these predicates as predicates.

The list of such signs seems to cast us adrift. We thought we understood what Parmenides meant by being, the *singulare tantum* that is the entry of contraries into a constellation of presence and absence. This is an event that demands concerted thinking, for what is best-known to us because it takes place around us at every moment—the phenomenalization that brings near what is present and sets afar what is absent—is also, for this very reason, what is most difficult to grasp in all this. Do not these signs fit better with a being? Indeed, what can we call unengendered, indestructible, of one piece, a whole block, etc., if not some "thing?" How can we state such predicates without emphasizing qualities, directly or indirectly attributable to a thing in this sense? Does not a quality require the support of that which it will be the property? Is not to hold forth in predicative propositions while at the same time denying that there is any referent subject to speak vacuously? Is it not to hang on to the present alone, and thus to turn thinking into a kind of representation? Worse, or even more simply, since no argument can make the "it is" play the role of a bearer of attributes, is it not simply to give oneself over to nonsense?

Or into an aporia. If the signs that mark out the way of the "it is" amount to so many attributes, then this way is closed. "Aporia" means impasse, closed passage. For Socrates, this seems even to have been the very goal of dialectical questioning in order to engage and hold on to his listeners. In the Platonic aporia, on the contrary, one already glimpses something of how to get out of the aporia; the situation where the ignorant person grasps his ignorance, understands where he must go, and begins to question himself. For Aristotle, it is simply the inquiry into what one says based on opposite yet equal reasoning, an inquiry that prepares its own solution. Having been a state in which one was to persevere, aporetic reasoning becomes a conflict of opinions that has to be transcended.[87] For Parmenides, however, aporia means something else again. It announces itself in the following either/or, from which there is apparently no escape. *Either* by "being" we are to understand the event of the "it is" that makes manifest the conflictual union and of which, since it is not a thing, we can predicate no quality; and yet, by all evidence, signs denote qualities—therefore they remain unintelligible. How is one to attach them to the event of concealing and revealing? *Or* these signs denote real predicates that add certain qualities to their subject. But that to which one can add real predicates belongs to the order of substance and in this case it is the "it is" that becomes unintelligible, for, beneath this verb in the middle voice, without a subject, we then must understand there to be a being. But such an aporia in Parmenides, arising as it does from the *predicative function* of signs, could provide neither a goal nor a starting point for a process of reasoning—Parmenides would thus seem quite simply to be the victim tripped up by his own henological project. Thinking about "the one that holds together" would not hold up. . . .

In fact, by drawing on these considerations concerning the status of predication it was possible to turn henology against itself beginning with the generation that followed Parmenides. His disciple Melissus[88] took over the list of signs in order to catalogue the properties of a supreme being. The subterfuge that reduces being to a being is therefore an ancient one. One cuts up what is written in such a way as to extract some key words—in this case, the impersonal *esti* (8.1) in the first phrase of the Fragment, that is taken to be a reasoned account, after the prelude that is taken to be simply allegorical—and to put them along with others in a group of consecrated appositions. Melissus, for example, consecrates "the world" as the supreme referent topping off beings. Once this shift in favor of something representable is made, he can treat the one as the sum of spatio-temporal magnitudes. One consequence is that the "powerful limit" is turned into the unlimited, the *apeiron*. For this disciple, this means that the exact, overall extent of the physical world escapes us. Another consequence is that the "now" in the lines we just discussed turns into a perpetual duration. In this way, thought about being is turned into a doctrine about beings. If such a doctrine defines "metaphysics," and if we seek to date the beginning of such a thing, the answer is obvious. It happens with Melissus's claim to succeed Parmenides. (Let me add that the partisans of Heraclitus were not inactive. They carried out a similar operation, making him hold just the opposite thesis of what was attributed to Parmenides. The history of philosophy began, then, like the movies: in black and white. In order to sharpen the contrast, and out of filial piety, they then tampered with the sound track. Henceforth one will speak as the proponent of change, while the other will defend the unchangeable.)

If this aporia leaves no way out, we need to seek (a) to situate it within the topography indicated by the Fragments. Then we need to inquire into the status of its (b) negations and (c) affirmations.

a. Topography—In the text, "signs" are put in the position of predicates. Therefore they denote the attributes of something. But what? Melissus said the world; others, God, etc. What is certain is that it cannot be part of the occurrent *hénôsis* because it is conflictual, for it is nothing at all and thus cannot provide any basis. Conclusion: If signs point toward the one, and if they are to have a meaning, we have to understand the one as a being. Signs thus effectively turn henology against itself.

This is the problem. After two and a half millennia of interrogating it, I am hesitant to say: Here is the solution. . . .

Still, here is at least a proposed solution. "'It is': *along this path* signs abound." It suffices to recall the most uncontestable fact about this poem, namely, that in it Parmenides recounts a journey. Along exactly what path, then, do signs abound? Along what section of the one path, along what portion? We recall that above in integrating the doxic segment into the aletheiological one, it was possible to set side by side the rival Platonizing solutions, the dogma of a monism of being and a dualism of opinion and knowledge. In place of such anachronisms we stick to the stages of the itinerary, which constitute so many paths of being. These stages were the dwellings of night, perhaps Hades; the broad path of denominations, our everyday world; the gateway of night and day, the moment where one is struck by another way of seeing; the narrow path of unconcealment; and finally a panoptic site from which the adept receive instruction "in all things" (1.28). Signs mark out the fourth moment of the journey, the narrow road that *leads* to the site where the plain, completely round truth is apprehended. They signify the "it is," *such as it presents itself along the approach route.*

But to advance along an approach route is one thing; to arrive at the end is another. Their enumeration, therefore, is not the last word in the teaching given by the goddess. Along the approaching segment the "it is" reveals itself. The whole question is: How? In its conflictual truth it cannot be a matter of unconcealment/concealment, for this defines the knowledge obtained at the very end. Nor can it be unconcealment in terms of *doxa,* and certainly not yet in terms of *alétheia.* . . . What then? The road signs tell us precisely. At least on a first reading, all of them point toward a present being. Along the approach route, they signify the "it is"—therefore, the one—as if it were a present being. Yet over the whole journey taught by the goddess, it will in fact be a question of unlearning the prestige of presence. If the signs rough out a doctrine of a founding being, then this proto-metaphysical tremor passes over the *kouros* at a precise moment of the voyage, the moment that *precedes* the goddess's favor, a favor that will be the last word and through which—alone—he will know the all.

Hence the provisional status of the signs. If they resembled real highway signs, it would be correct to write (passing over the mixed metaphors) that they can be compared to the rungs of a "ladder that one must throw away once one has climbed it."[89] After all, what relevance would a signpost still have if it bore a plaque saying "Elea" followed by an arrow, which one then transported into the town to set up right in the middle of the marketplace? Such would be a gag causing a certain effect. Seen from within the city, with its streets and squares, Elea is no longer the cream-colored spot against an olive-green background it seemed to be when seen from afar, along the route where the traveler kept an eye out for signposts.

We must therefore take literally the word "signs" and their being placed "along this way." In reading Parmenides, no one has ever thought of equating being with any of the other moments of the journey, with Hades, or with doxic denominations, or even with the gate with two doors. Yet these equations, where being amounts to being non-being, representations, and then to the initial moment of unconcealment, may be just cruder and thus less speculatively appealing than the equations that identify being with what along the narrow route is indicated *from afar* as like a being. Once the end is reached, the semiotic function will prove to have been reifying and thus will have exhausted its relevance, just as the equivalences established between being and the house of the dead, or with the thoroughfare of denominations, or with the gateway that opens on the day, will have lost their relevance. The charioteer will have learned nothing if he does not abandon these equivalences as he proceeds along his way. The last equivalence to abandon is the one that would have it that the signs point toward the one as toward a describable being.

Well, then, what provisional figure of the one do the signs describe? It is not easy to say; it could be the cosmos, understood as the place where tragic denial takes place: the exclusion of the absent. We would then see, along the doxic section of the route, that which fills the cosmos and makes us turn our head. Along the section of unconcealment we would see the cosmos as the *place* where this filling-in occurs. The word *kosmos* has a variety of senses in the poem (4.3; 8.52 and 60), but they all have to do with some kind of disjunction or some form of denial. The cosmos is not the physical world (contra Melissus). The world order comes from unilateral appellations that are imposed on what we accept as being manifest. Nor is the cosmos any longer the sum of beings. It is rather their site which itself is manifest. It is the result of a separation of day and night. Its unfolding (*diakosmos*, 8.60)—which is not a cosmogony—consists in the division of the indivisible. What matters is that for Parmenides the question of the world is posed exclusively as that of the present, appearing in all its splendor and set in opposition to its contrary. The problematic of beings in their totality, on the contrary, is touched upon nowhere in his poem.

In order to test this reading of the signification of the signs as the *penultimate stage* of the itinerary, and therefore as provisional, let us see what follows if the signs instead were actually to describe the very end of the journey. It is true that a list of these signs outlines the head figure for all onto-theologies yet to come, necessarily descriptive and speculatively entitative. In this sense, it is easy to convert the negations among the signs into strong affirmations. Even without including, as this would have implicitly, the all-powerful, or explicitly mentioning the eternal (*aéi*, Melissus), the catalogue of attributes more than manages to describe a being, and it wouldn't matter which: permanent ("unengendered and indestructible"), constant ("unshakable"), perfect ("needing no limitation"), ceaselessly present ("neither was nor will be"). If we were to take the penultimate point of view for the final one that makes the summit, what would become of the legislative system here? It is indeed necessary to realize that by gaining a normative basis, the operations both beyond and before the gate where one begins for a second time end up by resembling one another. But then we do not get beyond the conferring of proper nouns. In front of the gate, because "on each individual thing men have imposed a name that draws attention to it" (19.3); beyond the gate, because "either it is total or it is not at all" (8.11). Through representations, we name particular beings; through provisional unconcealings, particularizable beings, therefore totalities.

However these totalizations will bring about a double loss. On the one hand, what is lost is the necessary anchorage of the system. The evidence that what is, is—the necessity of the "it is"—will be quashed in favor of the encompassing one. Parmenides will be made into the promoter of a preponderating force open to subrogation. He will have spoken as a mortal. On the other hand, what is lost is the unity of legislation and transgression. Contrariety will have lost its structuring role. *Hénosis* as originary dissension will be split in two to allow one univocal force to be instituted. A spirit desirous of norms will feel itself assuaged in that the attraction of the absent will thereby have disappeared from the heart of any referent—and therefore any anti-law from the heart of every law. But whether we judge as comforting or disturbing this shift toward subsumption under a name, which is transferred from being to beings honored by the troupe of Diké, Thémis, Moira, Péras, and Ananké, with the eclipse of contrariety what follows is the development of substitute references. The same spirit that is the friend of norms will find it difficult to rejoice in either this eclipse or this elevation, which nevertheless is its consequence.

To sense the equivocation—the double voice—that risks shattering Parmenides' henological way of speaking into an aporia, we need only to compare the list of signs (unengendered, indestructible, of one piece, unshakable, etc.) with what I have called the proto-categories (*esti, eon,* etc.). The aporia could then be described as that between thinking and knowing. The unity that the proto-categories point toward, the polemical unity of being, is the same unity as that of concealing/unconcealing—that is, *of thinking*. In this way, the so-called identity of thinking and being in Parmenides limits itself to the conditions for thinking and being, conditions that are, here and there, originarily separate traits. The one so understood leaves us free to follow or not to follow the impulse to think (1.1). Thinking thereby differs from *knowing,* which never allows for choice, for one no longer discusses what one has recognized to be true. The signs, then, would describe a being and in this way make it known. What follows from this as regards thinking? Would the signs limit thinking to agreed-upon referents? If so, they would have to underscore the event that comes with conflict. But their predicative function shows that this is not the case. Do they instead aim at purifying what is normative of all internal dissension? Such is undeniably the tendency when they signify. Due to their predicative nature, these signs run the risk of stripping all normative aspects from Alétheia—Concealment/Unconcealment—so as to immediately reattach them to some (present) being or to the site of uniformly unconcealed presence, the world. If this were Parmenides' final word, the *sèmata* would do more than just signify one source of the laws. They would link these laws to some ontic, subsumptive totality.

The signs posit a form of knowledge as if it were ultimate, *fata morgana* arriving on the scene. But this anticipated knowledge is also a displaced, a dislocated knowledge. Until the goddess takes the right hand of the traveler into her own hand (1.22f.), there are only false places and false knowledge. To "know everything," he must wait until she tells him everything.

b. Negations—Here is how the positive signs indicate the "it is"—from afar, from the path of the approach. Negative signs allow us to take another step in the direction of ultimate knowledge.

As savvy readers, we know what it means to deny a quality. We master the various movements of negation without any trouble. One can negate one quality in order to affirm other ones. Take for example the clever trick of Melissus. The sum of things is unengendered, but it is eternal. Here negation works in the service of a distribution of predicates. One says that for being S, predicates *a* and *b* do not apply, but *non-a' and non-b'* do (prime, so as to mark the free association in Melissus). One can also negate a quality as being deficient so as to rediscover it whole at some higher level. This procedure produced the formula for what ancient thinkers had not yet named as "negative theology." In it, negation or apophasis works toward a higher restoration of some predicates, toward cataphasis. One says that for some being S, predicates *a* and *b* do not apply, but A and B (the same predicates, but hyperbolized, "super," supreme) do. A quality may be negated twice over and thereby be restored at some higher level—this is the modern operation, successfully carried out under the well-known name of "negative dialectics." Here negation works in the service of a kind of sublation, a "hyper-elevation." One says that for a being *s,* the predicate *a* negates the predicate *b,* but once both have been maximized into *A-B, s* unites with it.

The next step in the direction of the "it is" does not preclude that a proposition made up of negative signs might end up by ensnaring the one in a vice with an odd sort of jaws: predicative/non-predicative. It would therefore form a sort of amphibology. But before we conclude there is some kind of categorical error at work here, it would be a good idea to reread it. We can avoid these difficulties only if we rid ourselves as much as possible of the confining walls of a prefabricated reading. What then would a negation of predicates be that did not amount to weighing beings in terms of their attributes and to declaring one of them as dominant, the one that would unify (from some point of view) as many of these attributes as possible? What would a negation be that did not engage in a mechanical process, whether of the distribution, or the restoration, or the sublation of predicates?

Yet none of these three learned figures of negation, no more than any of the others developed by philosophers, can be injected into Parmenides. Indeed, all of them combine a certain negation with a certain affirmation. The impossibility of such a mixture of yes and no has already marked off the Parmenidean *doxa* from its Platonic form. Our examination of the "ways" has shown that no gray zone can be conceived where being and non-being would commingle. Similarly, no gray zone can be carved out where affirmation would combine with negation. Such zones are precisely the half-day between day and night (1.11) where, before Parmenides, the "philosophers of nature" labored and where, after him, the parricide will be committed.

We must therefore seek to think negation in terms of a prescientific simplicity. Then the negative attributes would apply to being through the negation of all attributes. Unengendered, indestructible, unshakable, with no need of completion, without "was" or "will be," indivisible (8.22), immobile (8.26 and 38), without beginning or ending (8.27), lacking nothing (8.33), neither stronger here nor weaker there (8.44f.), not being a bit more here, a bit less there (8.23)—these predicative negations would then bear on the "it is" *through the reiteration of the one and only negation,* not through the negated predicates. If we are to avoid misconstruing the status of negation before the Platonic turn, we will have to guard against reading this battery of predicates as sketching the outlines of the portrait of being thereby turned into an all-encompassing being. Another anachronism would be to see one and the same negation striking again and again and thereby indicating that being is not being. If a portrait does emerge, it will be only through a kind of counterpoint *differentiating* being from the marks suited to a being.

Read in this way, the negative signs, all of them, denote just one and the same signified: that being differs from beings, that it cannot be described. In this they reinforce the proto-categories rather than being in discord with them. The *traits of being*—givenness, difference, etc.—cannot be assembled into a portrait because they remain irreducible to attributes. Rather, they join together, as we have seen, into disparate pushes and pulls. Beings do lend themselves to attribution and therefore to description. They are engendered, destructible, disfigured, shakable, needy, in time, divisible, mobile, etc. Only such *traits of beings* can come together to make up a portrait. Negative signs speak of being through the "not" in such traits; and their negated contents (engenderment, destruction, . . .) set forth the possible portrait of a being with a subsumptive name. Read in this way, the negative signs repress attribution and provide access to unconcealment/concealment.

c. Affirmations–Still, the signs are supposed to say something about the one. In Greek, "to say something about" is *legein ti kata tinos*. For Aristotle, this turn of phrase indicates the way in which a universal is related to a particular—it indicates description by subsumption. Parmenides, on the contrary, before actually saying anything about the one, gives us the double warning we have just considered. On the one hand, it will be a question of "signs," not of predicative attributes; on the other hand, signification will work starting from "this way," therefore, from afar. This excludes the logic of subsumption twice over. To affirm a predicate as belonging to a subject always comes down to the doxic operation, to naming beings, by subsuming them under a representation indicated by a common noun. How, then, do the signs nevertheless speak of the one?

We need to see what is at stake here. If the one that is being can be described, this will be due to an internal necessity. Traced back to some representable authority, in the name of which one acts, it will find itself weighed down with debts toward those who have promoted it. Perhaps what is at stake is the public position of the philosopher. If his knowledge consists in a kind of expertise—that is, if his business is to know how to elevate some referent to the dignity of being the supreme yardstick—then (whether crowned king or not) he will come first in the management of collective affairs. And once the competence of the philosopher has been recognized, we shall have a new reason, even if it is of a wholly different order than that of dissension, for speaking of the unity between legislation and transgression in Parmenides: The one will have fallen into the haphazardness that characterizes every cultural consensus. The law of all laws will be immediately struck by an imminent obsolescence. For a retrospective reading of the epochs, norms become precarious at the very moment when an era sees them as stable. The philosopher's purpose is to hear and to fulfill the general aspiration of his time for a firm handhold. He carries out his mission by anointing some fantasm eminently rich in attributes. Is this what happens in Parmenides? If yes, he will have been the first of the "civil servants of humanity." If it turns out that, despite everything, affirmative signs name the attributes of the one, the swerve toward hegemonic fantasms will have begun with Parmenides.

Beneath several of these signs, we can easily recognize being as dissension. In the "it is," contraries (present/absent, light/night) "hold together." This is why there everything is "of the same measure," why it "holds everything together," why it is "closest to itself" (cf. *pélein*), and consists of "equal forces starting from the middle." For these signs, the saying-something-about entails neither attribution nor description. These latter would presuppose that we separate the present from the absent. Only by splitting apart the one to the profit of singularly present things do we bring about the "stronger here, weaker there." As in cell division, where pairs of chromosomes divide themselves and separate from each other (meiosis), such a scission would engender unequal forces because they are freed from their contraries. Following such a division (*diairésis*, 8.22), nothing would any longer hold together.

The signs we are reading protect the "it is" from such a division from which are born unequal and therefore dominant forces.

Among other of these signs we recognize those who accompany Alétheia. Péras is named, Moira binds being so that it is "total" (8.37), Ananké makes it remain the "same, reposing in the same," "solidly founded" (8.30). And where these three are found, Diké and Thémis cannot be far off. If we read them as witnesses to the "it is," the normative traits also signify that by being we are to understand the conjunction of contraries in their reciprocal holding together.

So we have two *classes* of affirmative signs. The first ones depend on what I have called proto-categories, the second ones on those agents of subsumption that link every denominative representation and every law to their contraries. We may say that categories and normative traits specify the genus-affirmative "sign"—the categories bear witness to being in generally articulating its relation to beings; the normative traits do so by stating this relationship as an obligation.

Among the affirmative signs, the "now" by itself forms a third class. We must read it as such, namely, as a new testimony, also peculiar to it, that being gives about itself. We will see below apropos of narrativity how time precisely determines the henological understanding of being. The sign *nûn̦* (8.6) in any case confirms that we entirely misunderstand Parmenides if we place him among the philosophers of the atemporal. Quite to the contrary, always and in every "now," a being gives itself, differs from being, arises, draws near, retains the absent; and always and in every "now" the holding together, thesis, apportioning, limit, and necessity unify the unconcealed nameable under the unnameable law—unnameable because it is itself disparate—of unconcealment/concealment. Here once again only a reader shaped by some subsequent school could amalgamate eternity (a word, we have seen, that is not found in Parmenides) with the now and speak of an "eternal now."[90] The adverb "now" instead expresses how this union occurs, namely, *in every* now.

There remains the one. Some manuscripts make it the grammatical subject of the predicate "holding together" (*hen sunechés*). Others have the word followed by a comma, thereby enumerating it as one element among others on the side of the "holding together" (*hen, synechés,* 8.6).[91] For the former reading, which we have followed up until now, holding together is part of the list of signs, but not the one. *Hen* is treated instead as a synonym of *esti,* and the signs will be said of *the one, that is, of the "it is."*[92] For Parmenides, the problematic of the whole and its parts arises only when (thanks to a comma) we make the one into a predicate: "being is one." What is more, the problematic of the one and the many rebounds against the grammatical subject, "being." Here is where the properly metaphysical arguments about the divisibility and indivisibility of being start. But none of this applies if we treat the one instead as a synonym of *esti* and make it into the subject for the predicate "holding together." Then the one benefits from all the negations we have seen to benefit the "it is." Like the latter, it will be a grammatical subject without being the ground for attributes.

Whether directly or indirectly, from near or far, it turns out that all the signs bear witness to being without transforming it into a being. This is why it is so difficult to follow a reading according to which Parmenides "thinks the very being of beings as a being."[93] To do so would be to condemn the father of the reism fabricated by the son. It is a difficult question to know whether to charge a founder with all the "isms" that, following him, come to invoke what he said (ought we hold the great names of nineteenth-century Germany responsible for the consequences that occurred in the twentieth century?). Still, there remains one last difficulty by which Parmenides' henology may be turned against itself into an onto-theology. It has to do with the status—and the station—of the divine in his poem.

"In the middle stands the daimon who governs all things" (12.3). Here is one popular reading: Parmenides draws near to a figure who governs (*kybernâi,* 12.3), who starts and commands (*archei,* 12.4); yet the end toward which the signs mark out the road is not submitted to a beginning nor to a command (*anarchon,* 8.27). The end, therefore, is this figure. Moreover, there the traveler learns "all things" (*panta,* 1.28), but it is the figure placed in the center that governs everything. Thus Parmenides approaches the "anarchic *arché*," set in the middle—of the sphere, no doubt of the sphere—about mastering the totalities through its gaze. Is not the theocentric construction obvious here? The gaze to which the traveler assimilates himself follows the lines of force of an absolute power that directs, almost like gravity, the activities on the surface of the sphere. One could also affirm without hesitation that such a figure sees the absences united to the presences. Who indeed, if not a goddess or a god, could grasp everything originarily without separating them? Furthermore, this figure itself will be both present and absent. Present, in his governing of the whole, absent through its station far from the whole. A subsequent tradition doesn't hesitate to postulate and equip with signs an ecstatic kind of knowing over to which the totality of things will give itself—an extraordinary knowing and pleasure, exploiting an equally extraordinary experience. Parmenides will then have inaugurated a sequence of supreme representations leading to Philo, then to the Greek fathers such as Eusebius or John of Damascus. The *kouros* will participate in the joy of an absolute witness. Having learned the signs, he will bear witness to a proper noun worthy of universal influence, universal authority.

Our verse would be less enigmatic and its theocentrism more plausible if Parmenides actually said what almost every translator, inexplicably, has him say—if the *goddess* Aléthia (as in 1.22) rather than the accompanying daimon (as in 1.3) were placed at the center. But this is not the only difficulty. The happiness of discovering the first speculative theology in these Fragments comes at a high cost. It costs, point by point, a misinterpretation of every concept:

(1) The feminine figure who begins and commands "in the middle" is the same one who gets the journey under way. Now, whoever it is that shows the way, which is the job of the daimon, from where does she derive her authority? It is this figure that governs the trajectory one can undertake. The *archein* is therefore to be understood as *daiein,* as the "demonic" opening up of the way (obviously this hardly clarifies the obscure Fragment 12). I have suggested, following the example of Socrates' daimon, that the daimon here indicates the singularity of Parmenides, or of the voyager. It singularizes him in opening the route to him. There you have his *archein,* his beginning and governing.[94] The daimon functions as an expediter rather than as a feminine Pantocrator; Pantocratess.

(2) No combination is possible between the *archein* (12.4) and the *anarchon* (8.27). The former is said of a being, the latter of being. To amalgamate them in order make them into the predicates of a supreme government would amount to annulling the difference between beings and being (6.1) in which, since antiquity, the paternity of Parmenides' philosophy has been recognized.

(3) What are *all the things* that the charioteer sees, having arrived at his destination? They are the segments of his route and their interconnectedness. And what are all the things placed in the center that the daimon governs? Probably the cosmic "rings," out of which no commentator seems to have been able make much sense.[95] In no case, however, should the panoptic site that the traveler reaches be confused with the origin, concerning which an ecstatic visionary will affirm "[t]he one who would grasp things in their initial upsurge must grasp them all equally."[96] It is from the henological standpoint that we see the procedures that led to it; it is from the mystical site that one sees every creature filling time and space.[97]

(4) For Parmenides, the origin that itself is without origin is not a *cause*. It is being, and certainly to be sought among the everyday. Subsequent descriptions of a Beginning/Commandment/Principle without a beginning, commandment, or principle always have to do with some efficacious being. Now, the daimon is efficacious in pointing out the road, but that does not make it originary. Being is originary, but none of its proto-categories authorize attributing any power to it.

Have we dispelled every ambiguity from the positive signs that risks turning them into attributes when we recognize different classes of *sèmata* and tie them to being *qua* event—that is, to the one, understood as their union? Can we somehow gain the wherewithal to cut through the hesitations of Heidegger, who reads Parmenides sometimes as a premetaphysician, sometimes as the first metaphysician?[98] And does Melissus (who manipulates the text just enough to produce some solid attributes of the one) thus turn out to be a traitor and misleading as regards this recognition of classes among the signs? This would be to make things simpler than they really are. If we follow the order of his itinerary, henology does not turn against itself, beginning with its institution by Parmenides. The *aporia* is removed by following the *poros*.

"A single speech henceforth remains the way—'it is': along this way signs abound" (8.1f.). Signs are placed along the way (*odos*) or the passage (*poros-peras*). They mark it out and they clear the way. It is certainly a misreading to translate this as "proofs."[99] This would obligate us to read not just this or that line of the Fragment, but all the Fragments in terms of the "genre" by which they begin: as a narrative of a journey. Such a rereading would have nothing to do with its consequences for literary effects, for literature. It is just that, neither with Parmenides nor with those who follow him, has philosophy been able to proceed on the basis of proofs in the strong sense of this term, on the basis of deductions from a self-evident first premise that puts an end to conflict. Philosophy proceeds not on the basis of proofs that force one to accept them, but by arguments calling for consideration.

Among these arguments, some proceed formally—for example, by syllogisms that conclude "*then* all C is A." Parmenides too says *then* along his itinerary. First, the traveler leaves the dwellings of the night to set out upon a segment of the road, then he crosses a threshold, setting out upon a second segment, and *then* he arrives. Both "*thens*"—logical and narrative—imply time. Victor Goldschmidt speaks of a "logical time."[100] But each "*then*" does not imply the same time. Logical time is not narrative time. The former particularizes whereas the other singularizes. The former "*then*" lays out propositions to lead reason to assent. It determines the particular using universal premises. The latter lays out the events of a plot. It portrays the singular, the individual and its ephemeral shadings.

CHAPTER 5

The Disparate

Narrative of a Journey

The power of the one gives force to laws. It legitimizes the absent forces, excluded by a nomothesis, just as much as it does the present ones, retained by this thesis. A double strategy is thus at work in the justification of norms. Henology expresses the dissension of forces—a dissension that is, and that must be—by placing us amidst the chiastic legislative/transgressive push and pull. Now, what is it that runs through the one, destabilizing it in this way? Since the one must be understood as union, phenomenalization, manifestation, could time be doing this?

It is difficult to set this suspicion aside once it no longer suffices to observe the world and to reflect on our observations in order to effect the anchoring of *onomata* and *nomoi,* of everything that has a name: The unity of being shows itself only to someone for whom it appears as a sort of abduction. Then it shows itself as the ultimate referent, polemically turned against itself. We have seen how this reception is at work, not just along the ways of *doxa* (as *déchestha*) and unconcealment (as *noeîn*), but also in the the very last revelation made to Parmenides (as *punthano-mai* and *manthano*). But what is it that "appears" to the charioteer? A sequence of passages. And where episodes succeed one another, there is time.

To take the measure of the importance of this temporalization, we must seek to establish (a) the role of narrative in the poem; (b) the time proper to this narrative; and (c) its consequences for any *Normenbegründung,* the search for an ultimate ground for all norms.

Narrating gathered singular things

Our first question amounts to taking stock of the respective "literary genre" in the principal Fragments (1 and 8). The problem is an old one. The classical solution was formulated by Hegel: One of these Fragments of Parmenides constitutes "an allegorical entry into his poem on Nature" (a formulation with which I cannot at all agree), the other contains "his main thought" according to which "thought is identical to *its* being."[101] This solution is not very convincing. To be thought is not the same as the being *of* thought. We have seen the sequence of courses and stopping points that the charioteer (1) makes: dwellings of the night (the doxic segment of the road), threshold of night and day (the segment of unconcealment)—the heart of truth, that is, the unity of unconcealment and concealment. This is a journey "toward the light" (1.10). Now, when the goddess comes on the scene to expose the "main thought," how does she go about doing this (8)? She begins by stating the *esti* that is the heart of truth, since it covers both the *pareinai* and the *apeinai.* Then she describes the signs along the path that leads there, that is, that mark out the way along the diurnal portion of the journey. Next she says: "For you I put an end here to speech and to knowledge, solid in themselves, concerning the truth. From here on, learn the denominative representations of mortals" (8.50f.). Through her discourse, she crosses the threshold of the same gate, but in the opposite direction, passing from day to night. Also, since she teaches the adept these denominative representations, her speech sets her on the road of *doxa* where mortals "declare these figures to be contrary, as if the unity of these two could not be" (8.53f.).

As for the end of her discursive descent, at the dwellings of the night, it is difficult to establish just what she is talking about. We must recall that these dwellings cannot be either a place posited by humans as is the night-figure (8.59), nor are they the region of the absurd where one treats nothingness as a being. It is most probably the domain of total *léthé.* For several reasons, I would readily conjecture that the realm of complete concealment is that of the dead. First of all, Léthé, Forgetting, was the name of a plain, of a well or of a source of water in Hades; next, in legends, the dead appear as veiled (Heracles leads Alcestes out of hell covered with a veil). What is more, the humans who frequent this road come from these dwellings and are called "mortals" by Parmenides. Finally, we may ask whether mortals are the only ones capable of declaring night and day (8.55ff.), or at least of having some prior knowledge that naturally sets them midway between the two (1.11). Knowledge of night as an attachment to a place is, in any case, connatural to them. The perfectly sedentary are the dead. They alone have no use for roads.

If this is correct, we can note that the departure recounted at the beginning of the first Fragment will beautifully illustrate the *thrust of pure natality.* One flees far from mortifying attacks. This strategy of being, which always makes a beginning and that essentially maximizes, will therefore appear there as the courage (*thumos,* 1.1) of putting death behind oneself and advancing toward a pure, absolute position. Natality is the thetic fervor in us that, if it could rule alone (or if it could subsume under itself the counter-strategy of death), it would produce an ideal frenzy. It would affirm the figures of an unrestrained, all-encompassing holding together. The charioteer, we may recall, advances toward a point of view from which he will see all (1.28). If he had described just this ascent, Parmenides would have left us the most beautiful document of metaphysical megalomania. But the goddess does not have in mind any such apology of the universal. She comes to constrict the limits of the end. She reminds the horseman of his mortal condition. What does the young man actually see upon arriving at the end? She shows him the singulars of his one and only world (6.6). Singularization thus underscores the trait of mortality. It is the counter-trait that holds "thumotic" frenzy in check. Like all the gods and goddesses of the sixth century, this woman is divine by virtue of her restraint.

But whatever the case may be regarding the impulse to leave death behind oneself and the lesson concerning natality and mortality that follow upon them, the reader is left to conjecture, as much with regard to the starting point from which the wise mares draw the charioteer up as with regard to the end point where the words of the goddess come down. What is not left to conjecture, however, is that in every detail *the ascent in the wagon and the descent in discourse balance each other.*

Some have emphasized the parallel motifs in the *Odyssey* and in Parmenides.[102] Like Ulysses, the *kouros* may try to return home (*nostos*). But no one has noted the perfect topographical symmetry, in Parmenides, between the traveler's narration and the instruction given by the goddess. This symmetry obliges us to read the two principal Fragments as both recounting one and the same journey: once from the beginning to the end, once from the end to the beginning. This entails several consequences.

The goddess qualifies her words sometimes as *épos* (1.23), sometimes as *mûthos* (8.1), and sometimes as *logos* (8.50). If, under these denominations, she is always telling a story, the discursive activities emphasized by these words will all have the same narrative essence. Parmenides recounts, and so does the goddess. To him, she "tells everything"—*everything that he just went through.* The speech that inaugurates philosophy says "first. . . , and then. . . , and therefore. . . ." And it matters little if we call it epic, or mythic, or logic. Hegel, therefore, was wrong about elevation in Parmenides. "With Parmenides," he writes, "the philosophical activity properly speaking began: the elevation (*Erhebung*) into the kingdom of the ideal. . . . To this is joined dialectic."[103] The goddess is just as much a narrator as is Parmenides. Thus philosophy begins with an elevation where we find, not antitheses leading to an ideal, but incidents leading to a place.

As for the course Parmenides recounts, it resembles not so much that of Ulysses as that of Oedipus. It leads to no reconciliation, whether speculative or domestic. Rather, as with Oedipus's wanderings, it leads to a site where the conflict among laws—in which the tragic is summed up—is seen and accepted. Parmenides' journey ends with tragic knowledge.

The double narrative furthermore confirms that the decisive moment of the journey is the reversal of fortune, the *episode,* occurring at the gate of night and day. It has been said that every narrated story has to do with a reversal of fortune, whether for the better or the worse.[104] But unlike the tragic hero, the charioteer has the luck of a *peripeteia* or rather of a *metabolé* for the better. This is described in terms of hinges and pivots, and it constitutes the hinge or pivot point of the poem. At the same time, no direct allusion is made to a movement of elevation. The schema of rising results only indirectly from the traveler's destination, since his route leads to a panoptic place. Only a regard from on high "teaches him everything" (1.28)[105]—the pathway by which he drew near to knowledge, the critical threshold, the route of the dumbfounded, and finally the houses of the dead (in that order).

Another consequence is that the synechic point of view bears on the *variety* of the ephemeral givens. The gaze from on high unites beings, not principles of beings. It in no way obliterates the singular or the individual. Only an itinerary that is neither abstractive nor dialectical can lead to a holding together of contraries without subsuming them and thereby universalizing them. The ascension practiced by this father of philosophy only brings on stage the singular, a young man who says "I," a goddess who also says "I," the stages of a journey, things present and absent. . . . And none of these singulars is maximized into an absolute representation. The whole range of these remains without a highest commandment. We cannot be sufficiently surprised that the philosophy of being begins with a narrative that shakes the primacy of knowledge with regard to universal principles. Parmenides opens philosophy like a narrator opens his story, but also like acid cuts into iron.

The one is devoted only to an experience that comes to you, and that also may not come to you. This rules out that the procedure may lead toward the one as toward some first cause. Rather, being *qua* the one "is in accord"—even if in differing ways—with the course of the journey. The event of phenomenalization happens everywhere and always, but its internal conflictuality is retained only rarely and with difficulty. Indeed, along the way of denominations, this event happens by way of theticism, and we thereby honor the partial by its partial maximalization. Along the way of unconcealment, it happens by way of signification; it is there that we know the similar through the similar. Finally, at the panoptic site, the event is recognized in its originary dissension, and then we know the same by way of the same. Each time, what resembles itself assembles itself. Wherever we may go, we know only what we experience. But the traveler has no experience other than this journey in order to know the one. What can we say regarding this, namely, knowing the same through the same? A journey gives one an experience of time. It seems difficult not to conclude that the "methodic" affinity with the one introduces into it *time, as well as being.*

Nomadic and eonic procedures

"The advancing mares that carry me along as far as my courage will go" (1.1). What is the time at work in such a narrative in the first person? It matters little whether this person be human or divine, or that his voice belongs to one character in the narrative or to the narrator. Nor do the later theories of *diagésis,* of narration, in Plato or Aristotle really matter. To begin as Parmenides does is to commit oneself to a diagetic form of discourse and this is to commit oneself to time in more than just one way. Can we, must we, read in the *temporal configurations of what is said* an indication that will teach us something about the temporal condition of being as one?

The charioteer initially finds himself torn away from a scattered kind of time. Dumbfounded mortals go from here to there; their wanderings cover an entire field. Nomadic wandering is related to the names and *nomoi* they declare. The Indo-European root *nem-* once designated the occupation of land by a clan, its distribution among the clan's members, and its exploitation.[106] Hence takings, distributions, unpredictable exploitations of spaces and times which are realized through impulses and relapses, reorientations, exchanges, ruptures, good times and bad times, shifts, everything that gives rise to an open space without boundaries or borders (Parmenides places road signs, it will be recalled, along the segment of the road beyond the gates of night and day.). The topographical schema of *doxa* is bidimensional like nomadic territory whose shifting frameworks escape any attempt at mapping them. No semiology can capture and tie down the nomadic impulse. A place is chosen, then one moves on again. To be mortal is to choose a point of view, then move on to another one. Vagabond minds advance by upsurges of unequal speed, with hasty moments and delays. We cannot ask them where they are, since they are already elsewhere. Their displacements and their connections lay out—at least provisorily—*nomadic time*.

The narrated "I" reconfigures this dispersion into a *chronology*. The charioteer as well as the goddess link together incidents that happen in succession. Both of them say, "At first . . . and then . . . and then." The incidents are the same ones. Also the two speakers coordinate these incidents into the same series, except that they are traversed in opposite directions. The sequence of events sketches a line—the path of Parmenides. The episodes unfold as well, and inseparably, in time and space. The two speakers spell out the places to be crossed. The consecutiveness of what they relate gives a breadth to the details. And almost as if emphasizing that what they are presenting is not fiction but rather a history that actually took place, they recount these events as occurring in the past. Parmenides makes this history into an autobiography for which the goddess is a biographer. Chronological time determines the syntactical tenses: aorist, perfect, imperfect, present. The future intervenes only in the passages where the goddess comments on the teaching she is giving ("you will know everything," 1.28). In so doing, she does not break off the chronology, but rather indicates her authority over it.

Nomadic and chronological time are reconfigured once more by the end point that closes the narrative. This last figure organizes time into a beginning, intervening moments, and an end: "At first . . . and then . . . and finally. . . ." To indicate this figure, Greek had the word *aiôn*. Therefore we may call such a configuration drawn toward a resolution as if by a magnet, *eonic time*. The *aiôn*, or *eon*, must be understood in its original sense, not as the antonym of *chronos*, in which case it would designate the unlimited or the eternal. Rather, what the word *eon* speaks of better than any other term is the holistic character of a time structured from within. In opposing eonic time to nomadism (a time with innumerable beginnings) and to chronology (an open time, with neither a beginning nor an end), I am following this initial sense of the word *aiôn*, which signified the whole of a complete life, with its ages going from infancy to old age[107]—not hope for life in the demographic sense, but the completed cycle of its phases. Eonic time cannot be defined in terms of chronometric units. Rather, it determines these units. Thus, for example, the periodicity of the seasons shapes the eon that is the year. Zeno, the disciple of Parmenides, will establish with a *reductio ad absurdum* this quasi-Gestalt-like unity of time in natural movements like that of the flight of an arrow.[108] An analogous holism integrates the stages traversed by Parmenides.

Eonic time reunites within itself heterogeneous factors, most of which contributed to establishing the agenda of subsequent philosophy: Hades (if it is what we are to understand through the reference to the "dwellings of the night"); the denominative representations that the metaphysicians will turn into "opinions"; the "ready" spontaneity aided by divine favor in the first departure; the drive later transmuted into a gradual ascent; the solemn passage across the threshold; the second journey; the signs soon to be consecrated as "ideas"; the arrival at the fatherland with regard to which, for the entire subsequent tradition, our own world is like a place of exile. The eonic time of the journey integrates these stages into one organized figure. The moments of the journey stop being just episodes arranged in chronological order and become a story or history. The lapse of time is oriented as a function of the destination where the plot, brought to a head by the charioteer and his female consorts, finds its denouement. The peripeteia lead somewhere.[109] The final point to which they are brought by the conclusion breaks off the linearity of the chronology. Without closure there is no eonic time, and without eonic time, no narrative. The *aiôn* is the henological figure of time, the *simple* one temporalized. It will reappear as *arithmos* in Aristotle's definition of physical time: not as "number," but as numerically articulated "configuration."[110] A chronology remains essentially open-ended, in the sense that tomorrow one must add the episode of a new day; eonic time is closed. If it were not closed, there would have been neither journey, nor narrative, nor divine instruction. Without the destination that is the place of Alétheia, the *kouros* would not have been able to change from having been a receiver to being a sender, an initiator. Eonic time alone allows the play of iterative inversions. In the succession of verses, Parmenides gives an account, and the goddess recounts; but as the poem claims to relate a history, the journey must have taken place first, then the goddess retells it to the hero, and then the charioteer turns himself into a poet and inverts things another time, into his text in hexameters, into the tale told.

As a provisional summary, let us bear in mind three forms of the "then" statements: the many "thens," laid out like a surface with no geometrical measuring points; there are the pluriform "thens," spread out into a surface without geometrical reference point; there are isomorphic "thens" this time lined up in indefinite fashion to form a chronology; and the unique "then" at the end, indicating the safe arrival at our destination, which closes the narrative so as to make the eonic figure. As in any narrative, what is stated also brings into play a mimetic "then."[111] Parmenides passes from the world of everyday life—the things recounted about his journey—to the explicative discourse of the goddess, then to the narrative verses of the poet. However, we shall comprehend the relevance of all this for henology only still later on, through the relation of the time of his utterances to that of their uttering. Still, in this preliminary summary, certain features contributing to the temporal condition of being as one already announce themselves, but only announce themselves. Most notably, for Parmenides, the one is not simple. And time shows itself to be eonic, therefore already on the approach-way, not just at the aletheiological site.

The nomadic dispersion and chronological "et cetera" thematize the one, but they do not give us knowledge of the time of the one. The question of atomic units and of their alignment or agglutination does not arise for Parmenides. The one, therefore, cannot be related in any way to indivisible temporal elements, either as staking out some territory or as succeeding one another. As for a mimetic reconfiguration, which we enlist to save the referent of a narrative, it will not help us either in this regard. In reading the narrative of a journey in this poem, the question is not: How is the world of everyday life presented there? Nor: Did Parmenides' journey really happen? Nor:

What is the road that Parmenides took to leave Elea, as indicated by archeological excavations?[112] The question is: How is the temporal condition of being as one conveyed in his poem?

This question about the time of being, however, must be raised if it is true that we speak only about what happens to us, and that a story happened to Parmenides' *kouros*—perhaps to the *kouros* Parmenides. As *told,* this story is one owing to the *eon* (and not because a text with a beginning and an ending is assumed "ontologically" to imitate the one; to speculate on the "form" would be once again to commit parricide against Parmenides). But what is the condition of temporal unity that here brings about a story? Parmenides' emphasis on the first person singular obliges us to take into account the telling of the story, more so perhaps than with any other document in the philosophical tradition. The temporal condition of being as the one reveals itself a bit more through the way in which the eonic time of what is told is articulated in relation to *the time of the telling.*

The eonic time of what is said already temporalizes the one. If the *aiôn* organizes itself into a closed configuration because it has an ending, and if this ending is the panoptic site, then only the recounted journey, in its totality, is reliable. The eon is the most reassuring of times. Not only does it not contravene all order, it even founds it. Through the closure it indicates, we may be confident that in the end discovery *wins out* over concealment. Yet this victory—which would be indicated by the privative *a-* in *alethéia*—wins out following the temporal parceling out of what is asserted. Plato's formula "all is one," *hen to pân,*[113] is undoubtedly a schoolroom summary, stemming from a problematic that no longer is that of Parmenides. Yet, as we have also seen, the goddess proposes to teach the traveler "all things" (*panta,* 1.28). What is this, exactly? It is the thoroughfare crowded in all directions by the ordinary run of mortals that stretches into a footpath far away from humankind. "All things" signifies the integral path by which the traveler has come, furnished with bits and pieces, that he organizes into a coherent narrative: house, "every city," the squeaking axle, the young women who unveil themselves, the gate, the sections of the road, the signs, and let us not forget normative agents singularized by their names—all these are bits and pieces irreducible to any one genre. These *panta* are "one," yes, but only in and for the journey as recounted. They are one, but a singular totality. Were this totality to be thought of as universal, there would be no need for Parmenides to turn to a narrative. The one that the goddess teaches to the charioteer cannot be dissociated from the narrated journey, or from eonic time, or from the singular totalization that this time brings about.

The temporal closure that always defines the eon certainly instructs us about the one. The question is whether the eonic configuration suffices to express, without anything else, what the time of the one is. We shall see where this *singularization* leads (it leads to the one, and in so doing splits any ordering power). We reach this point if we look at how the time of telling disconnects itself from the time of what is told.

The statements of the charioteer and the goddess incorporate the same intervals of the journey: Their times of telling, on the other hand, remain wholly heteromorphous. The two speakers do not extend over the same time spans. They do not even extend over the same segments of time. The traveler takes a short time to recount his journey along the long road of mortal denominations, and then takes a disproportionately long time to tell how he hastened to cross the threshold. The goddess hardly dwells on this crossing, no doubt because for her to cross discursively the gate of night and day takes no courage. She even sums up in just a few words the road that the mortals built. On the other hand, she lingers over the diurnal portion, marked out by the road signs. This is the segment where unconcealment begins, and according to tradition her name is Unconcealment-Concealment. In her time of telling, she distributes the time of the recounted trajectory in terms of the uprooting from *léthé* she brings about. Each of these speakers, therefore, governs the rhythm of his or her speaking in terms of what he or she does (their times agree only in what they do not speak about, the ellipsis at the beginning of the journey). Such is their *poiésis* and such also the distortion that they inflict on the time span of telling. The crossing that is granted the traveler and the unconcealing brought about by the goddess make a *poietic time* of their respective times of telling. At each turn it is a time of a doing, an acting. Hence the "I" who speaks and acts thereby singularizes him or herself.

Due to its configuring effect, this poietic time of telling resembles eonic time. It is a different temporal figure, however, in that it does not subsume the given into a closed order. The telling is articulated onto the time of what is told through a complex, changing constellation of singulars.

Such a constellation *makes itself* {*se fait*}. The protagonists' doing {*faire*} is but one of many ways in which a being—any singular—enters into relation with others. In Parmenides' itinerary, it is not yet a matter of moving through appearances toward their essence, but rather of traversing stages and incidents toward a singular point of view on singulars that is won by the singular traveler who says "I." This is neither an ascension of the soul toward its true Homeland nor an *itinerarium mentis* toward its Creator, but rather a constellating event. The subsequent schemata of a Great Return will claim to teach the mind a necessary procedure that leads to universal authorities. Parmenides only speaks of himself. His unifying view is born from a variety of singular factors. The goddess's grace (*prophrôn,* 1.22) responds to the vehemence of his *thumos* (1.1). His zetetic spontaneity (2.2.) encounters an anagogical benevolence (1.2). Parmenides' text is woven from such fulgurations that we might think to associate rather with the name "Heraclitus." They produce themselves, and owing to this their temporality is originarily poietic (which is also a better reason than its use of hexameter to speak of this text as a "poem"). Such instantaneously occurring relations are called events.

It seems to me that if one asks about the time of the one, this is where we must look: toward *singular, ephemeral constellations phenomenalizing singulars into an event.*

Where does this first philosopher of being, advancing thus along an explicitly singularized route, speak in the name of the universal? Could it be in his relation to the reader? Even though he relates an imagined or actual undertaking, by putting himself into the scene as "Parmenides the traveler *kouros*" (the narrated agent), he actually remains other than Parmenides the producer of the scene as "poet" (the narrating agent). This distinction helps us not to confuse the conversation between fictive "I's" on the one hand, and that between narrator and reader on the other. But in this sense, this distinction comes up against the specific problems raised by "the path of Parmenides." Does the universal, then, form itself in the reader's imagination or in his reflective judgment? There is another solution that is addressed to the fictive genre in general and that also runs up against these problems. The distinction between character and narrator, with its concomitant appeal to imaginative reconfiguration in the reader, extends even further the list of instances where the singular is encountered in this narrative. Whether we examine the recounted peripeteia, the proffered narrative, the narrator, or even the hearer/reader who receives the narration, in every case we have something singular. The time of telling—be it that of the narrated agent or the narrating agent—the time of what is told, and the time of reading or of application (what Paul Ricoeur calls *mimesis*$_3$) all converge on the singular. Which is why Parmenides' narrative makes one think, not of later anagogical schemas, but of Nietzsche's Zarathustra: "'This is *my* way—where is yours?' This is how I replied to those who asked me 'the way.' For *the* way doesn't exist."[114]

The temporal condition of being as one is confirmed in the occurrent articulation of the telling onto what is told. It only remains to locate its source.

In reading these Fragments as the narrative of a journey and in seeking to trace how they articulate different times, I do not mean to follow that school of literary criticism for which texts are to be illuminated purely by other texts. I am not interested in dismissing the referent. But neither do I think that the triangle constituted by the author, the reader, and the world—a triangle based on subjectivity—can really teach us what happens in Parmenides' texts. I would say that in reading Parmenides as relating a journey, the referent remains, at every moment and for every point of view, something singular—like the "I" that I say here. Thus Parmenides speaks of the event in which disparate individuals reunite so as, by chance, to compose a world. This implies, first, that it is difficult to turn Parmenides back against himself by making *esti* the ancestor of every referent posited with a view to eliminating contingency. Another implication: It will be more difficult than ever to legitimize the current laws, for the event in which singulars join together provides only a neutral reference point as regards good and evil. This implies, finally, that Parmenides understands *being turned against itself* into a differend.

We can see the work of natality in the initiatory impulse that opens the poem. The young man's impulse goes "as far" (*hoson*[115]) as his courage will carry him (1.1). How far, exactly? To the point where he hears the injunction to hold together contraries with no genus. If he had *denied* this injunction—hence if he had maximized pure presence—Parmenides would have had to follow natality to its final height. He could have done this only as have others since: by positing one simple principle. But the goddess comes to cut off the desire for such final simplicity. She instructs the mortal about his condition. *Doxa* is no more abolished than is mortality abolished when one passes from night to day. To remain courageous to the end therefore is to learn an incongruous, yet ultimate holding-together. The search for "first things"—philosophy—therefore begins with the assent to what holds us without hope of a simple beyond—the tragic double bind.

The henological differend: the phenomenalizing and singularizing one

The "signs," I admit, could be rigorously read as indicating a being, to which it then would be difficult to deny the highest rank. But we have seen that even when they are read this way, they remain topographically remote from the one. Therefore, they alone cannot convey the manner of being of such a being. Signification, in any case, is only the penultimate moment of the pathway on the course of which knowledge is imparted. It would certainly be a misreading to take the road signs about what is coming simply for the ultimate revelation of the truth.

It follows that if we want to comprehend the mode of being proper to the one, we will be wasting our time by investigating these signs. What then are we to investigate? Precisely what Parmenides says of the one: that it "holds together." Let us return briefly, therefore, to synechia, having learned about the narrative status proper to this text.

Here it is no longer possible to deny the ultimate incongruity. According to the *argument* (4), the one holds contraries together; its mode of being is contrariety apart from any genus. According to the *narration* (1 and 8), the one holds what is diverse together; its mode of being consists in making disparate singulars enter into constellations. And there is nothing stable about such constellations. They vary from stage to stage. The narrative makes it impossible to ignore what the one, understood as a sort of union, has already stated: If its stake is contextualization, then henology erases the name, breaks apart the encompassing, shatters the principle. The one is cloven not just in terms of contrariety, but in terms of innumerable lines of fissuring.

Diagetic temporality lines up events in the plural. But as we also have seen in his highly elaborated vocabulary for being, Parmenides speaks of one wholly other event, incomparable to the episodes or peripeteia of his narrative. This is the neuter, anonymous occurrence in which always and everywhere arise economies of disparate givens—phenomenalization through contextualization. There is a difference between this occurrence and the givens. The *one event* gives rise as much to the ontic-ontological events that are to be thought as it does to the fictive events that are to be narrated. It is the one saying that differs from any concatenation of statements; the one now, which differs from the diegetic configurations; the one being, which differs from the constellations of beings. This event—a *neutral tantum,* says Heidegger,[116] and also a *singulare tantum*—is emphasized by all the proto-categories. The narrative puts on stage the interlinkage of individuals that the argument makes known.

Read in this way, the two textual regimes—argumentative and narrative—do not at all work against each other. We have seen that the argument for the oneness of being is based entirely on singularities. The category of "contrariety" requires keeping hold not of absence and presence, but of what is absent and what is present without a genus. The "is" always bespeaks a singular. The difference between "beings and being" no longer transforms the singular into a subsumable particular. The same may be said about the categories of "rising" and "approach." They emphasize the entry of contraries—then of disparates—into constellations. Being as ephemeral configuration of these disparate things is always one. Thus, at the moment when he announces the one,

Parmenides also underscores its temporal aspect: "the one is a whole, [at each turn] now, holding [everything] together" (8.5f.). Being as one holds together singulars in each case and owing to the fact that they occur as an aggregate. Alétheia unveils this occurrence; she is what she does. With all the veils cast aside, the argumentative and narrative regimes converge on the crossing of the gates of night and day—on the event that is itself unconcealment—and then they converge on the knowledge that at the heart of unconcealment brings about the concealment at the heart of natality, namely, mortality.

The narrative regime of the text not only makes sense of the strategy of dissolution in the argument, but it aggravates it. The argument requires the simultaneous affirmation of contraries; the narrative, for its part, calls for the affirmation of disparates. From contraries to disparates, the law agonizes. The narrative renders this *agôn* inescapable. The hermeneutical dilemma shifts in further aggravating matters: The dispersive gap does gape between the argument that being is one and the sequence of narrated peripeteia; it gapes between the argument based on signs and the same argument as taught by the narrative (as one teaches a procedure). This figure of difference between beings and being, where the names of beings enter into strife with the verb just as the strategy of legislation enters into strife with that of dispersion, of transgression, and therefore already with that of destitution—this figure will be a differend.

This differend is *henological* in that the one both centers and disperses singulars. The narrative confirms that the one gathers phenomena into innumerable constellations that ceaselessly make and unmake themselves. To acknowledge this motility does not amount to abandoning the house of Alétheia for nomadic wandering. It does, however, set Alétheia on the only plateau where there is something to unveil: on that stretch where splendid gatherings of things come about, then dissolve. The one remains held like the "and" in "present *and* absent things"—held like a conjunction.

The one rules by strategies of conjunctions, but as a non-universalizing conjunction of singulars it maintains the disparate and therefore also disperses them. What we call reality is itself conflictual. Along the way of *doxa* we extricate ourselves from this by generally-agreed-upon tactical moves. The way of unconcealment reveals these conflicting strategies, with no law of resolution. "And what if the stake of thinking were the differend, rather than consensus?"[117]

As the first hegemonic fantasm, based on "signs," the one seems to transcend the many. Perhaps there is even a mediation by way of opposites. The one would then posit outside itself, first all the contraries (the dyad, 8.53) and then the innumerable (where the *doxai* are formed). Its double transcendence would mean that to raise ourselves to the heart of truth we would have to pass through an initial dyad, through the absent united to the present. With or without such mediation, the transcending one would oppose to itself another world, our world. The latter is "similar" (*eoikôs,* 8.60) to the first world. This is why we will cling to being only by way of signs. The divine bestowal then would amount to an epiphany: In passing through the gate of night and day, we would see the night of the image-world pull back and the day of the model world arise. The divine concession would also amount to an ontophany: For this "father of everything fixed," being would reveal itself as "the rigid one"[118] indicated by the sphere. Such a sketch of a one beyond everything does not prejudge in any way the *type* of relations that attach the world of the many to that of the one, relations that Kant, for example, examined in the third and fourth antinomies of pure reason. For Parmenides, *if signs amounted to attributes,* being would transcend beings.

None of this holds, however, if the signs point toward the still distant endpoint of the journey and if we must understand the one as a conjunctive event. Then the *kouros*'s procedure would take him far from becoming, yes, but only to those *traits* of the singular, the individual that are neither born nor perish. Parmenides describes several instances of these traits. The attraction of the present, joined to the withdrawal toward the absent, is one of them. Sexual attraction is another: The daimon who blazes the way (1.3 and 12.3) also shows the way to "coupling, sending the female to the male and the male to the female" (12.5f.). Yet another instance is the braiding of the rings that gives texture to the cosmos (12.1f.). Several centuries later, such conjunctions will be treated as so many instances of a union *with* the one. This is a completely different way of thinking from Parmenides, who instituted the union that *is* the one. What then happens to becoming? If "being one" means "phenomenalization happening," there is no brake that will be able to immobilize becoming. And we know its condition: appearing *per se* in each instance of union. The arrangements of disparate beings do not stop happening; their occurrence as such is what alone neither changes nor becomes. The proto-categories designate this appearing, and the "sphere" describes it—an adequate description since the sphere is the most perfect figure conceivable. Movement within it does not harm its perfection, any more than the categorical instances harm the integrity of the categories.

If being is one as a conjunctive event in every gathering of beings, then the most relevant of its descriptions will be the *nun,* the now. Not the immobile instant, the *nunc stans,* toward which one flees time, but the association of associated givens. The occurrent one will be found in language as the time of telling, of enunciation, from which derive the enunciated figures of time: nomadic, chronological, and eonic. This time indicates not the *homo viator,* the human being on his or her way toward a better, because stable, condition, but the being that unveils the path of Parmenides. Time is not opposed to the originary *tauton,* it constitutes it as originary.

Is this what the father of ontology understood by "being"? To answer we must hold fast to the ensemble of dualities emphasized by the proto-categories. We must also hold fast to the time that they all shape, whether directly or indirectly: the *nun* of conjunction. Finally, we must hold fast to *alétheia* as the truth of this splendid, because disparate, multiplicity. To the simple question "what is being," we may answer by surrounding it with questions about beings and time:

What are beings? Always the given singular.

What is being? The ephemeral aggregation of singulars *qua* aggregation.

What is time? The event of their entering into this aggregation.

To the question about beings, Parmenides replies with words in the plural: "the present and the absent things," or "all things." To the question about the being of these beings, he replies with the expression "beings-being" (*eon emmenai* or simply *eon*). To the question of the time of being, he replies with verbs for "being" (*einai, phuein, pélein*). The ephemeral gathering of singulars into a constellation therefore constitutes the being of beings.

In what way is being one? As cumulative and "re-cumulative," as constantly recurring. The one that being is, is thinkable only as the crystallization of beings (which has nothing to do with atomism), a crystallization thought not in terms of beings, but as an occurrence, hence in terms of time. The one is what occurs through an aggregation. Beings and being are articulated in the *henological difference.*

How does this difference make law? Our analysis of contraries has shown that they essentially conjoin and disjoin with one another. Therefore we cannot think of being as arrival without also thinking of it as leaving. There is no centripetal aggregation without a centrifugal disaggregation. To use Heidegger's words once again: no appropriation without expropriation.[119] In the idiom of an analytic of ultimates—no universalization without singularization. In terms of the law—no legislation without transgression immanent within it. In one fell swoop, and necessarily, the henological difference makes the law by binding us both to the dissolution of the phenomena of the world and to their consolidation that is under way. As soon as he understands the one as a process, Parmenides *has to* establish both attraction and withdrawal as equally normative. This double bind is embedded in our condition as mortals. We can call it the *henological differend.*

Parmenides argues for and recounts a knowledge that before him Homer had put in a poem and that the tragic authors will put on stage a short time after him (Aeschylus is his contemporary). In this differend, something else is at work than a predilection for paradoxes (as with Zeno). The most splendid of heroes, Achilles, plays with his force, feeds his anger, savors his vengeance, all the while aware of his own death. Antigone and Oedipus are not victims "crushed by the terrible wheel of fate"; they live the dissolution at the core of every consolidation, and they affirm it (*Oedipus at Colonus*). For Parmenides, what has the man who knows, learned? He has known that by its very normative function, the one reunites and disperses. Because the one reunites, we always find ourselves inscribed in configurations and in some order. In its legislative strategy, the one is the condition for the nouns in our languages and the laws in our institutions. But because it is not a being—because it is only a tendency in beings—the one does not substitute a homeland for the diaspora. This is why every configuration and every order calls for its overthrow. As Hölderlin understood, in talking of "dark light," life *calls for* its contrary, death; it enters into a constellation with it, is one in synthesis with it (which does not mean that being calls for its contradictory, which is nothingness). In this transgressive strategy, the one is the condition for the verbs in our language and for the reversals in our history.

The two sections of the path will be quickly transformed by tradition into two worlds, just as it will transform the gateway of the peripeteia into the separation of the sensible and the intelligible, or "names" into opinions and the "signs" into ideas, "being conducted" into "ascension," and the end point into one supreme, simple being. . . . In this way, originary time will be repressed and *the singularizing counter-law denied.* The ultimate dissension will have been covered over with a principle of order.

But Parmenides breaks in advance, like a contract that has not yet come into force, the most serious office with which philosophers later will find themselves charged: the double office of consoling the mind and consolidating the city. The differend unmasks the official charge to edify as hubris. Whoever seeks to take on this charge will spin around the (vicious) circle of denominative representations. Givens are consolidated only by other givens, therefore by the express reduplication of beings-beings. Will the mind that would console itself by thinking the difference of beings and being be engaged in this very same reduplication? History is not lacking in examples where "being," in a less explicit way to be sure, has served as the cornerstone for political or spiritual edification. But a cornerstone is always a represented being. . . . Difference has been co-opted in the service of hegemonic fantasms and their regimes.

The critical procedure practiced by Parmenides has forever lost sight of the archaic Greek smile. A century later, Democritus will know a new pleasure. He will be called the laughing philosopher. He found more happiness, it is said, in discovering a causal connection than he would find in occupying the imperial throne of Persia.[120] But then nothing defends normative edifices better against the tragic than do representations of a cause.[121] In them, Democritus will find his peace and Greece a well-being that turned into a school. There is no joy more exalted and exalting—exalting the reference points into ultimate authorities—than that which makes one say: "I understood why. . . ." As for the differend, it exalts nothing. It neither consolidates nor consoles. It speaks of order, incongruously disturbed by an additional authority. The necessity of the differend, argued for and narrated by Parmenides, binds us not to the edifying clarity of a cause, but—like Oedipus blinded and *sophos*—to the excess of light that is also night.

II

Its Destitution

The One Turned against Itself (Plotinus)

Introduction

When we now read some of Plotinus's texts our study will involve addressing precise questions to these texts which stem from the reading of Parmenides: Above all, how does the initiatory impulse of natality suffer the *counter-blow {contre-temps}* of mortality (chapter 7), and more generally, how does *time {temps}* effect the stable referent which is the one (chapter 6).

Thus for the moment Plotinus will thus speak on behalf of the closure of the Greek epoch,[1] that is, for the destitution of the *hen-fantasm*. This may seem surprising, for indeed who instituted the metaphysics of the One, if not Plotinus? And yet . . .

First of all, there is here an instituting which for all that does not depart from the sphere of the Greek language. In the third century of our era, the Greek language surely was no longer that of Parmenides. Nevertheless, the latter's vocabulary can be found almost intact in Plotinus, broadened by numerous tributaries of which some, particularly the Alexandrian ones, remain mysterious to us. Subsequently the architecture bequeathed by Plotinus was quickly furnished and inhabited by squatters: the Christian theologians. This appropriation by a foreign dogma will institute its own "efficient history"; but before the guardian of the Acropolis could make Proclus say "Had you not come, verily I would have closed"[2]—before Proclus, then, was officially designated as the last Greek philosopher—Plotinus *began anew*. Neoplatonism means, with him at least, new Platonism. In Plotinus we have a creative recommencement that more truly marks an ending than does the learned recapitulation of a Proclus.

So it will not be so much a matter of submitting some texts to the law of the One, but rather of subjecting the law to some texts. This court appearance will pair up two gestures.

On the one hand, the One that holds together—the principle of order—will be exposed to some Plotinian statements (on *union*, first; on voluntary impetuses, *thelémata*, next) in order to see how it "defends itself." We may say straight out that the defense, that is, the legitimization, which Plotinus provides of this fantasm will exhaust henology as a metaphysics of order. Posited as trans-noetic, the One indeed fulfills its organizational function outside all rational control. This follows from the very architectonic of the universe in which the movement of ascent passes from the hypostatic Soul (of which the visible world is the border) to the hypostatic Intelligence, and from there, by a backwards step which is incomparable to the first, it passes to the One. The "second departure" of the *kouros* in Parmenides, beyond the gates of night and day, is translated here into a second transcendence: into a surpassing of the Intelligence. Hence, by exposing the legislating One to these texts we will have to grasp how, in the new arrangement, the One makes and undoes the law; we will have to learn to think it other than as being in the service of order.

On the other hand, in summoning the law to appear in front of texts I will expressly have recourse to Heidegger, especially in the beginning. The debt is greater here than in any other of the readings in which I will try to arouse the poignancy of the "legislating tragic." Summoning the law before the letter of the *Enneads* would indeed not have been thinkable without anticipating—if only as a simple reading tool, displaced over seventeen centuries to foreign surroundings—the *occurrent singularization* in which one will recognize, at the end of the journey with Heidegger, the contretemps of mortality which has always broken hegemonies.

As was seen in Parmenides, nothing so purely attests to natality as the impetus which brings one to think the One. To follow this impetus to the end, we must ask the Plotinian One: How do you make the law? *Uniformly,* it will be said. We shall see.

Only one question haunts Plotinus: "How did the One not remain in itself?" (*En.* V, 1, [10] 6, 6)[3]. The question concerns pure and compact simplicity, not the multiple other stemming from it.[4] The enigma of enigmas can be seen precisely in that the One was not able to be content with its self-possession (he uses the mythical preterite tense which indicates, as is often the case in Plotinus, a priority of order). Let us step back so as to situate it better.

When metaphysicians speak of a supreme being, they call it "the Good," "the Beautiful," "Truth," or "the One." Each of these epithets results from a specific theoretical experience which gives rise to the cognitive point of view from which one considers this being. It appears as the Good insofar as the desire for possession maximizes it in order to find rest in it.[5] It appears as the Beautiful insofar as, maximized again, it orders all things into a cosmos, an arrangement whose proportions can be mastered by mathematical reason.[6] It appears as the True by maximizing the transparency felt when the mind returns to itself. . . .[7] What gives the point of departure to these maximizations? Each time, it is a determinate interest—appropriation by desire, domination by reason, and reflection by the mind. But in virtue of what interest, what intellectual temperament, have metaphysicians called the supreme being "the One"? To be sure, it is due to a need for order. But metaphysicians have not gone to such lengths to accumulate negations for any of the other maximized representations. No doubt the most profound answer will be that they called this being "the One" so that it might dwell—rest and remain—in itself; that it might be what it is.

Negative theology has no more ardent desire than that. To the question: Why did the One not remain in itself? it will answer: Not by necessity, but because it is love. Going against this profundity, I wish to suggest that the Neoplatonic *hen,* at least according to some decisive texts by Plotinus, is not primarily to be understood as a predicate of the supreme being, nor moreover of any *being* (accordingly, from now on I will use capital letters only for the hypostases of the Soul and Intelligence, but not for the one—which in fact is not a hypostasis). There is a double enigma in the words referred to here. If the one, as Plotinus never ceases to say, is beyond beings; if it is neither some thing nor some being (*oude ti, oude on, En.* VI, 9 [9], 3, 38), then what is being spoken of when it is described as entitatively present to itself—as "remaining in itself"? A turn much more enigmatic than the causes and conditions one inquires about when asking "Why?"

So as to retain the density of the enigma, let us immediately discard three false solutions, three metaphorical ways of speaking which are nevertheless widespread even in the texts of Plotinus himself.

The one does not "descend" so that the world may be. Such a descent would signify an action to which a first principle abandons itself in degrading itself, in emptying itself of itself. Now, the one does not act, and nothing is more repugnant to henology than such *kénose.*[8] The one "remains what it is, even while it becomes other than itself." (*En.* V, 5 [32], 5, 1).

Neither does the world appear by "emanation" (a bad translation of *proodos*, 'procession'). According to this metaphor, the principle would remain in itself, rich and overabundant like a headwater, and yet it would pour out by an intrinsic necessity. There is no headwater without water flowing from it. To speak of emanation is thus to connect the principle to the world. Now if Plotinus is the first to sketch a thought of freedom, it is precisely to preserve the one from all these connections and ties binding it to what is other than itself.

Analogous remarks hold for the richest metaphor, that of "light." This is an excellent metaphor in that it suggests a communication, without any diminishing of the one. Minds lit up and illuminated bodies unfurl in colors (in *lumen*, according to the medievals) the pure clarity (medieval *lux*) which light is in itself.[9] But as suggestive as the metaphysics of light may be, the one does not shed its incandescence on a scale going from pure whiteness to black. The Plotinian universe degrades itself by hypostases, not by a continuous diffusion. The metaphor is good for emphasizing the otherness of the second transcendence, so long as it conceives of our world as a non-isotropic realm. Intelligence shatters continuous propagation. Thinking arises when light produces its own reflection (*phôs ek phôtos*). If this refraction is missing, one may well be commenting on Marsilio Ficino,[10] but not on Plotinus.

These three images are as popular as they are deceiving. All three *trace discontinuous transcendence back to a continuous transcendence.* They neglect the *epekeina* which in Plotinus keeps the ultimate referent far from the numerous ideal, penultimate references.

If metaphysics is the doctrine of the nature of things and of their grounding—and, furthermore, if the problems of nature and ground find their answers at the level of the subsistent Intelligence, which is penultimate—then a discourse about the one, a henology, will have nothing to maximize. The one will not be the supreme *noumenon*; its way of being will have to be sought among phenomena, but not in light of them.

It will be first, not by maximization, but by purity. It will not provide a ground, either for things, or for our knowledge of them. Rather we find the one in things and knowledge being purely configured. As their impulse to be contextualized, *as pure natality,* the one is first.

CHAPTER 6

The Temporalizing Event

"... what is purely and simply singular, what, by its singularity, is unique and, as unique, is the sole and unifying one that precedes all number."[11]

—Heidegger

The one is not a being, not a something. This is clearly indicated in the first lines of Plotinus's treatise *On the One:* "It is due to the one that all beings are beings." (*En.* VI, 9 [9], 1, 1). Why can one not say of the one that it is something, a being? "The one is in all respects first, but Intelligence, ideas *and beings* are not first." (ibid. 2, 30; my emphasis). The derivative status of beings follows from their chief quality, intelligibility. All that is or exists can be understood. But the one, which is what is most intimate for us, nonetheless escapes our comprehension. Hence it is not a being. Conversely, beings are secondary since they are of the same order as Intelligence (*noûs*) and the ideas.

By thus upholding the incognizability and the non-being of the one (ibid. 3, 39), henology turns Plato against himself. Agreeing with Plato, Plotinus holds that to be is to be intelligible. But contrary to Plato, he discovers that when we speak of intelligible things we always speak of multiple things, be it only of the duality of knowing and known. Now, nothing which implies otherness—or, even more so, multiplicity—can be first. Intelligence and being will be derivative because they are intrinsically multiple. This is why, in the Plotinian universe, no being can claim supreme standing. Thus, if it is "due to the one" that all beings are beings, the one is not itself to be found among them.

The one is without content, it owes nothing to the mechanics of maximization: therefore it is not a thesis. Rather, it centers all things, a centering in which one can recognize pure natality. To be a centering is less than to be a being. Intelligence, the second hypostasis, gives beings their being (more precisely, borrowing from Heidegger, their "beingness"). But the one gives a simple direction. The expression "supreme Being" thus amounts to nonsense, and the expression "supreme being"—which is perfectly adequate for the maximizing metaphysics of the Good, the Beautiful, and the Truth—is here a contradiction in terms.

Only a hasty reading will see in the declarations concerning incognizability and non-being a negative discourse about a divine First, a negative theology in the train of Philo. Nevertheless, such is the received opinion about the Neoplatonists: Since the one transcends Intelligence and beings, it is "above" them, more intelligent, "more of a being" than them. Its simplicity makes it unknowable to us, but supreme vis-à-vis what is other than itself. The distinction between the one and intelligible beings results in a few conceptual equations for which one would find ample support in the Neoplatonist corpus, be it Christian or non-Christian: To be one is to be *inconceivably* actual, spiritual, intelligent, permanent, powerful, causative, eternal, a being. . . . Henology would be a metaphysics of radical transcendence, but the one would remain something after all. It would only be beyond the reach of intellection: being beyond being, mind beyond mind, cause beyond causes. Despite its negations, such an exaltation remains squarely onto-theological, a discourse about being "as such" which derives its legitimization from a being—from a being that is inaccessible, but foundational nonetheless: supreme and divine.

Yet by distinguishing between the one and being, Plotinus disrupts the collusion between the function of an ultimate focal point and the official charge of grounding. He thereby retrieves a trait of being that had been lost under the predominance of etiology—of the discourse on causes—ever since Plato. The English participle "being" and the Greek participle *on* harbor an ambiguity. A participle is the grammatical form that "participates" in both the noun and the verb. *On,* or the archaic *eon,* is an essentially equivocal concept. About this equivocity, Heidegger writes: "'*On*' says 'being' in the sense of '*to be*' a being; at the same time it names a *being* which is. In the duality of the participial significance of *on* the distinction between 'to be' and 'a being' lies concealed."[12] In Plotinus, the '*on*' of the second hypostasis is meant as a noun: beingness, hence its derivative character. It "is" *par excellence.* In the subsisting Intelligence, beingness coincides with beings; in this it is supreme, foundational, intelligible. But due to these very perfections, it will not be first. If we consider the ambiguous pedigree of Neoplatonism given the Heideggerian repetition of the question of being, one may well think of Christianized Plotinianism when Heidegger deplores that the identification, since Plato, between the nominal *on* and the supreme being has obscured the verbal connotation of the participle *on,* and thus being.

In any case, in Plotinus the one and beingness are separate strata. Therefore they require distinct strategies of thinking. Their *chorismos* makes it impossible to reduce the first condition of all things to the nominal form of being—to *ousia,* as Plotinus also says.[13] For him the *on* assuredly is God, *theos* (for ex. *En.* IV, 7 [2], 8 (3), 12). But Plotinus's onto-theology is his penultimate word. The search for a ground is not his last word. This search does not constitute henology, the discourse on the one. Onto-theology differs from henology as the second hypostasis, *noûs,* does from the first, *hen.* Plotinus has seen that any discourse which seeks to anchor phenomena in an unconditioned foundation falls into a vicious circle. To seek the reason of beings in another being is to spin around among what is representable. In other words, he has seen the strategic difference between an entitative *cause,* which is representable and knowable, and a non-entitative *condition,* which is unrepresentable and only indirectly thinkable.

One must direct the question of conditioning to the condition which the one is: If not in the manner of a grounding being, how does the one condition what is?

"It is due to the one that all beings are beings." Contrary to the classical metaphysics of form, Plotinus thus holds that it is not due to their substantial form that all beings are beings. The reference to the one displaces the difference by means of which Plato and Aristotle had isolated divine or sensible substance in the beings. The one is a condition by virtue of its difference with the foundation. The central nerve of all henology is, indeed, the difference between the *one* and beings. Thus, since the one is a non-being (*mè on*), it would be better to speak of negative henology.[14] It can be negative only because *logos* constitutes the thresholds between the hypostases and thus occupies an inferior position in relation to the one. In negative henology, the difference does not separate beingness and beings, but the one from beingness and conjoined beings.

How should the henological difference, a normative condition, be understood?

The henological difference

The discourse of negative henology feeds on this difference between condition and foundation, a difference unthinkable for negative theology. It translates into aprioric terms the split in the present participle between the infinitive and the nominative, between "being" and "beings". The one differs from Intelligence as a process or an event differs from a thing; or, speaking grammatically, as the verb differs from the noun. Plotinus himself never equates *to hen* with *to einai* so as to oppose them to *to on*. Nevertheless, in the work of a later Neoplatonist, we read: "The one that is beyond substance (*ousia*) and beyond beings (*ontos*) is neither being, nor substance, nor act, but rather it acts and is itself pure acting, so that it is itself being (*to einai*), that which is prior to beings (*ontos*)." The editor of this striking text first attributed it to Porphyry, and then to the "Anonymous of Torino."[15] In these lines the one is not only called "pure acting" and thereby desubstantialized, but it is made synonymous with "being." Here the difference between the first and the second hypostasis appears as clearly as that which separates being from beings, or the pure, indeterminate "it is" in the middle voice from the determinate sum of all beings—the difference between the verbal and the nominal.

The desubstantialized concept of the one (which is not, strictly speaking, a concept) designates no transcendent reality—no thing—and in that sense, nothing. The "verbal" understanding of the one expressed in it is also irreducible to the subsequent notions of *ipsum esse subsistens* or *actus essendi*. Although these notions rehabilitate the infinitive in ontological discourse, the verb there serves to emphasize the principle of intelligibility—the *second* Plotinian hypostasis.

Essential truths never suffer from being repeated. . . . Thus we must distinguish between two versions of the ontological difference. Because of the profound influence that Aristotle's *Physics*—"the hidden foundational book of Western philosophy"[16]—has had over the entire tradition, the ontological difference has remained confined to the realm where it applied to observation: the realm of production. Metaphysicians have not "forgotten" the ontological difference, but, at least within the Aristotelian tradition, they have understood it as a physical difference. They have had recourse to it to answer the question of technology: How is one to produce a universal *eidos* in individual material? This origin here determined the received terms: difference between *ousia* and *on, entitas* and *ens,* or, in Heidegger's idiom, between *die Seiendheit,* beingness, and *das Seiende,* beings. Here we have the *metaphysical* difference. Its function was to give an account of physical change. In Plotinus, it constitutes the realm of *noûs*. Indeed he writes, "The first substance," that is, Intelligence, "has all things and is all things." (*En*. I, 8 [15], 2, 16 and 22). The physico-metaphysical difference rules over this onto-theological territory since the actual substantiality of things, *ousia* (*energeia*), is treated there as a being, as the hypostatic Intelligence, as the subsistent act, as a God.

Plotinus takes a step backwards from this *metaphysical* difference between substantiality and things, a step which leads to the one or—following the Anonymous of Torino cited earlier—to being. What appears with this step can be called the *phenomenological* difference. The phenomenological difference secures no supreme ground, nothing which transcends a deficient reality toward a complete reality. It is only the transcendental condition of appearing. The Plotinian henological difference between the occurrent *one* and substantial beings exhibits, as we shall see, the decisive characteristic of the phenomenological difference between occurrent *being* and substantial being, namely, temporality. Anonymous ties together two heteronomous trajectories, of which the first leads from beings (from the *on* or the *onta*) to "beingness," *ousia*, and the second from beingness to being, *einai*. Now, to speak in verbs means to expose what one speaks of to time. Contrary to this, to call the one "more that beings" (*hyper-on*)—as this will come to be used in the Neoplatonic school after Plotinus—is to completely miss the heteronomy between the two passages and thus to lose sight of originary time. As a result, one can no longer see how the one overcomes, as it does in Plotinus, the physical difference—how it transgresses, since that is the *mot d'ordre*, the metaphysics of closure.[17]

We can draw a hypothesis for reading from the "one" brought near to the infinitive "being"—a bringing together which, to say it again, is not to be found literally in Plotinus.

Plotinus does not mention Parmenides' poem. But his commentary on Plato's *Parmenides* must be included among those revealing places where he takes up the distinction between the one and beingness. There, Plotinus establishes a system of equations, where each of Plato's hypotheses equals one of the three hypostases. The first hypothesis[18] is that "the one is one." Plotinus correlates it to absolute unity, the primordial one (*En*. V, 1 [10], 8, 23–26). Saying "the one is one" amounts to saying that we cannot speak of it because, not being any thing, it does not bear a name.[19] On the other hand, the proposition "the one is" that Plotinus correlates to the hypostatic Intelligence emphasizes a unity made of multiple beings. "For whatever has existence, whatever is, is numberable. . . . As multiplicity [in the second hypothesis] has some unity, it is not absolutely multiplicity, since it is one; and a multiple thing is less than the one, since it possesses multiplicity."[20] The Parmenidean issue—the one and the multiple—finds itself shifted toward a measurement according to greater and lesser, and is thus redrawn as stratified (and thereby rendered unrecognizable, one fears, for a Parmenides). Subsistent Intelligence is less than the one. Its unity is made up of the intelligibles to which it gives coherence; this coherence defines it in turn as a first substance. It *contains* beings without *subsuming* them. Subsumption would be a sovereign function. In this commentary on Plato, the argument for breaking up the identification between the one and beingness thus rests not on the distinction between the universal and the particular subsumed under it, but on that between unity and the multiplicity that it contains in it. *Ousia*—beingness—will be a derived unity because it gathers together multiplicity. By implication, substantial being cannot in any way be predicated of the one. The henic function later will be ultimate without being subsumptive. For it to be otherwise, the one would have to rule over beings. Yet, as will be seen concerning the *arché,* nothing could be more foreign to it, since it is itself foreign to beingness.

Faced with the distance opening up between intelligible foundation and ultimate condition, one may be tempted to give up. If the ultimate referent puts attributive logic out of play—what more can one say? To say something, for us, means to modify a grammatical subject by a predicate. Once predication is declared to be inoperative, what remains to be done but fall silent, or break into incantations?

What remains is to understand the one otherwise than by entitative attribution. Now, and this is the sense of what will follow, the other manner of thinking by which Plotinus goes beyond ousiology can best be read when he puts the one to work: as a *singular event of union.* To do justice to the affinity of the *hen* with the verb "to be," one must understand the one as union (*hênosis,* for ex. *En.* VI, 1 [42], 26, 27), and union not just as *epekeina,* going beyond beingness, but also as *hapax:* occurring in an event.

It is the verbal sense of *on*—and, more indirectly yet more decisively still for the question of the law, of *hen*—which relegates all the substantial notions of the one to the rank of derivatives: beingness first, life next.

The full ontological difference, embracing both what served as (metaphysical) foundation and its (phenomenological) condition of possibility, thus includes three terms.[21] In the vocabulary of Plotinus they are "beings, substance, one." In the vocabulary of his fourth century disciple, they are "beings, beingness, to-be." In these descriptions, the third term is to be understood as a verb: *uniting, being,* then, following Heidegger, *coming-to-presence, phenomenalizing, self-manifesting.*

I add these words from the Heideggerian lexicon especially to dispel a misunderstanding. "Union" actually covers a vaster—and on the whole more modest—field of occurrence in Plotinus than does ecstasis. One says that, if he has an "ethics", it includes three activities: purification at the level of the Soul, being illumined at the level of the Intelligence, and unity in the one. But in the phenomenological sense, unity takes place wherever beings enter into a constellation. "Uniting," "being," "coming to presence," "phenomenalizing," "self-manifesting," to which one may add "making a context," "making a world"—these verbs thus describe one another. We must recall this semantic network so as not to be mistaken about the connection made here between the one (as union) and being.

The reading hypothesis according to which the Plotinian one is understood in its *otherness* will have to be verified textually as well as systematically by placing it together with being in the verbal and thus temporal sense—this hypothesis.

The one as event

The one is to be understood neither as a being (it is *mè on*) nor as beingness (it is *epekeina tès ousias*), but as being (*to einai*). These distinctions allow us to discard an alternative that, in one form or another, preoccupied the Neoplatonists as well as their disciples. It encloses the one within the opposition of inside-outside; but does it orient the beings on the outside—like a vanishing point that would give the phenomenal constellations their "sense of direction"—or does it orient the being on the inside, like the "grain" in wood? Stated in this way, the gigantomachia between transcendence and immanence is not only desubstantialized, but it has already lost its pertinence. If the one—as must now be examined—has to do with time in some sense, then the shadows of both these giants will find themselves dispelled. What will remain is the phenomenal constellat*ing*. Such was, anyway, the lesson drawn from the verbal sense of being. It invites one to understand the one as a singular event: a non-datable event, an innumerable singular. If it unifies, better, so as to exclude the connotation of "doing." If it unites—, that is not its act in the way that thinking and speaking are the acts of a human substance. In the absence of an agent, the singular event "happens" without any bearer of responsibility. Nevertheless, thanks to this constellating all things are: "Separated from the one, beings do not exist. The army, the chorus, the flock will not exist if they are not one army, one chorus, and one flock. The house and the ship themselves are not if they do not possess unity; for the house is *one* house and the ship is *one* ship. If they were to lose that unity, there would no longer be either house or ship" (*En.* VI, 9 [9], 1, 3–9).

Union as considered here is not the act of the one, and even less what I might feel toward it. The one neither effects nor causes anything. It is, rather, entirely and essentially union. *Hen* is *henôsis*. Plotinus never calls the one a hypostasis. And as for union (even if this word cannot always be avoided), union is not "uni-fication" There is no "doing" in the one. The example of the army in movement, drawn from Aristotle,[22] suggests how it is, and is not, a singularizing event.

An army in disarray scatters: *bad singularization*. "The multiple breaks up" (*En.* V, 3 [49], 12, 14). This always imminent breaking makes for the suffering—both spiritual and ontological—from which Neoplatonism received its impulse. It is an ontological suffering because divisions fragment beings starting from the sensibles up to the intelligibles and even up to the Intelligence, which thinks and is thought. If it is suitable to describe the one as singular, it will evidently not be in order to suggest dissipation, disarray, and separation into atomic singularities. The singular which unifies, Heidegger says in the above epigraph, "precedes all number."

Similarly, if the one is described as an event, it will not mean a rehabilitation of contingency. Such an army which, on such a day, took heart again after the first losses and which, at such a time, came back to order: *the bad sense of event*. We are far from the peripeteia of the young Parmenides on his carriage. Plotinus does not at all exclude "such a being," "such a day," "such a place" from his discourse. Even the spiritual simplification he teaches can only be recounted. The soul which purifies itself crosses phases and strata. Moreover, as will be seen, he gives the account of it in the first person. Thus, we will come back to *singularization* apropos of the contretemps of mortality. But that is not what is at issue when we try to understand the one in terms of natality, which is to say, as union. The time of natality is apparent in what the one always contextualizes. It is *singular* contextualization: pure natality, an event that is formulated in the middle voice—not the transitive, nor the episodic, nor the causative, nor the active, nor the responsive (in unifying itself and becoming simple, everything answers to the one; but it answers to nothing).

"Singularity" does not signify dispersion, nor does "event" signify an incident. Which will the good singularity be, here?

And first of all, in what sense will union be an event? In that it ceaselessly brings back—without even the possibility of ceasing—the bricks to make a house, the soldiers to make an army, the cities to make an empire. The one is the *self-configuring* by virtue of which—but without virtue or force—there are figures. As the occurrence in all that comes to be, "it did not come, and it is there! It is nowhere, and there is nothing where it is not!" (*En.* V, 5 [32], 8, 23ff.). The one is the factor with which all things are coordinated and in the absence of which they would disintegrate. It is their pure entrance into constellation. But far from holding the epitome of power, as the *trait*—as traction and attraction—in coming-to-presence, it is what in presence is most slight and most precarious.

The good singularization answers to the "each time" in the following quasi-tautology (which is a figure that is as apophatic as are the negations): "Union happens each time that there is an entering into presence."

But apophaticism itself has traditionally served the interests of maximization. Allied to onto-theology, it eclipses the discovery one wishes to term phenomenological and from which negative henology is born. This discovery is stated by Plotinus in the text quoted above: It is thanks to union, thanks to their entering into mutual relations, that beings are beings. Negative theology, on the contrary, teaches us that the one is the supreme being; we do not know what it is, but only that it is. Now, if it is permissible to read in the one *qua henôsis* a resurgence of the verbal connotation of the present participle, then we are able to think—if only "from below," and thus without knowing—what it is. We are able to think its "nature." And literally it is precisely that—*nasci, phuein,* the very movement of coming to presence in all that is. It is the *phainesthai,* the appearing as such, of all phenomena; it is their origin in the sense of pure *oriri,* rising. These verbs, *phuein, phainesthai,* and in Latin translation *nasci, oriri,* indicate how the one is an event: like the upsurge by which any phenomenon, whichever it may be, enters into a constellation with others, into an economy of presence. These terms also indicate how apophatic negations are to be understood in Plotinus. The one, he says, has neither "form" (*eidos*) nor "substance" (*ousia*), nor "this" (*tode ti*), and "even this name, the one, contains no more than the negation of the multiple." To speak of it, he adds, it might be more appropriate to use "the symbol Apollo," composed of the privative *a*-and *pollôn,* "of many." It would be better to call it "without-multiple." These negations have but one goal—to keep us from conceiving the one as position, as *thesis* (*En.* V, 5 [32], 6, 6f. and 6, 26–31). One can see which other thinking will succeed in deterring theticism: only a thinking faithful to pure natality. At the risk of confusing the otherness of the one with a hyper-maximization, negations should also dissuade us from conceiving it simply as a mode of being more intense than anything we experience phenomenally, whether of a sensible or an intelligible phenomenality.

The second movement of transcendence, the *epekeina,* which leads from the intelligible to the one, actually remains heteronomous in relation to the movement leading from the sensible to the intelligible. It is not enough just to repeat this. To understand it one still has to learn to think otherwise. It is true, as the commentators say, that Plotinus's originality resides in this heteronomy, this other law which thinking follows when it raises itself up—but how can one still speak "there" of place, *ekeî*—from *noûs* to *hen*. Here we have the first consequence of this nomic otherness, namely, that since beings are located at the second hypostasis, the first will neither be a crypto-being (Plotinus calls it a god only by concession, the Intelligence being more properly a god[23]), nor a pseudo-being (the one alone would be true, if our world was posited as false; but it would be false, if our world was posited as true), nor a hyper-being (it would encompass the world in its stratifications).

There are many reasons why the trans-noetic procedure is difficult. Leaving aside the spiritual motifs, there remains mainly the difficulty of dissociating it from all causal representations. The one assigns things their sites within a given constellation of presence. It "does" that, not as a demiurge (and even less as a creator), but in the manner of a process without agent. This is why the one may be described as the entrance of phenomena into commerce, as their contextualization, as the happening of their mutual relations. But it is still difficult to think otherwise than with causal representations, if only because Plotinus and all the Neoplatonists after him only recognize a "descending" causality. The sensible remains deprived of any ascendant effect on the intelligible, and there it will not be able to have any noetic effect on the one. But what do we mean when we say that the one is the only true cause, that it is the "cause of the cause," which Intelligence is? If we again keep ourselves here from lumping together the otherness of the transcendences into an anagogical continuity, then the one offers to Intelligence—to the second hypostasis—an orientation so that it may be able to unite beings by rendering them intelligible. It is Intelligence which "makes" unity. As for the one, it is no more active than a geometric law is active when three lines *enter* into a certain relation to make up a triangle. That entrance is what is to be retained. It happens wherever there are phenomena—as such the one is an event; and it always occurs in *this* phenomenon—the event is, as such, singular. In preclassical Greek, as was seen,[24] such a configuration was termed *aiôn*.

This discordance within union—incongruously universal and yet eonically singular—renders the best-known terms of henology problematic. Take mediation for example. In meditation Intelligence, as the active fullness of reality, is *immediately* unified. It brings about its unity by containing within itself the ideas which are ideas "of" subsistent Intelligence. And it unifies all things *mediately* by having recourse to its model: the one. According to this scheme, the one spreads out in causes, directing them toward the bottom. It also gathers them, directing them toward the top. It orders substance below by manifesting it, and above by harboring it. The one thus prescribes a dual path to substance, a bidirectionality (as one speaks of a two-way street). Regarding this function, we may indeed call the one the "cause of the cause," the "eminent cause," "the veritable cause" (*En*. VI, 8 [39], 18, 37).

This manner of speaking is nevertheless just as eminently problematic. It silently passes over the heteronomy—and therefore the homonymy—of the "cause." The causality from the one to the Intelligence is other than that from the Intelligence to the Soul. Consequently, describing *noûs* by its mediating function is again a ruse to equalize the transcendences. Otherness is preserved, on the other hand, by distinguishing between *singular union*, in the middle voice, and *transitive particularization*. *Henôsis* "is made"; but *noésis* makes something: it "makes the true." Union occurs here, and here, and here again; as such, it is singular. Intellection produces ideas; as such, it is particular. The singular thus falls outside of the congruous universal. The latter arches over the lone particular, and there are no effects other than particular effects: A cause (that is, an idea, of which each is first in its series) is the subsumptive agent *par excellence*. Thus to speak of singularity is in no way to argue for the principle of individuation. Nothing would be more absurd than to present the one as the precursor of hecceity. The *haec* can only become problematic in a theory of substances . . . which, to be sure, is not absent in Plotinus. But for him, individuation is done by the Soul and the last individuation, by matter, as well as temporal and spatial extension, which are traces of the Soul.

It can be said of this set of premises—the one as event of union, not as a hyper-being; the one as emphasized in the participle by the verb in the middle voice, not by the noun; the one as the singular "direction" of phenomena, not their particularizing cause; and the one as the (Alexandrian) *motus* of pure natality—that they unharness Plotinian henology from metaphysics, the scaffolding of ultimate reasons. The one therefore would not appear in the long list of these reasons; it would not fit in the catalogue of the referents which uniformly make the law. Why? Because beginning with the subsumptive forces which the ideas are, and beginning with their substance which the Intelligence is, another backwards step is required to think the one: a backwards step which is not inscribed in continuity with the regression toward the causes. One will only miss the way in which the one is first, and thus its "primacy," so long as one seeks to seize hold of it by some causal procedure. Plotinus, it is true, is far from rejecting etiologies.[25] But when it comes to etiologies, all of the schemes of effectuation, attribution and predication are to be used within quotation marks.

So, if the premises we have seen in fact agree with the hypothesis according to which the one can be understood in its otherness only by drawing it closer to being, then—remembering that verbs always emphasize time—we cannot help but ask "In what way does the one have to do with time?"

Originary time

The issue, then, is to confirm the understanding of the one as singular event by raising the most arduous question—heretical within the Neoplatonic tradition—of the temporality of the one. Before seeing how far we can and must push the question of temporalization, it will, however, prove useful to briefly recall the three decisive moments in the Western philosophies of time. A well-known setting, but one helpful for succinctly situating henological time.

The first of these moments results from the key experience that strikes the Greek mind in the classical age—namely, the experience of change effected by our own hands. Substantial motion effected in workshops had arisen to the level of discourse in Aristotle's *Physics*. The notion of time that really will take hold thus remains tied to motion:[26] *kinésis* as first produced by means of tools, and thus handcrafts; then—by derivation—it happens on its own, a natural *kinésis*. There is here no time without motion. There is no "before" or "after" without instants following themselves in an observable becoming. The Soul certainly plays a role in this observation, and even experiences movement in its own life; nevertheless, this concept of time is formed in terms of the change in the sole domain in which sensible substances are set into motion by someone else, and secondarily, by themselves. Thus, outside of these substances, time can be an issue only by analogy.

The second moment is the interiorization of time. Augustine is not unaware of the concept of time that arises from the observation of physical change. Following Aristotle in this, he states that we arrive at it by numbering the formal "mutations" in matter.[27] But the primary experience of time shifts. Its proper place is no longer manual production, but the life of the mind. "It seemed to me that time is nothing else than extension; but of what sort of thing, I do not know. It would be surprising if it were not extension of the mind itself." In much the same fashion as the physicalist concept of time, this spiritualist notion is applied only to the world here below. Eternity is beyond time because it does not undergo change or extension. Mutability is the essence of time,[28] which is therefore not simple: "Time is threefold, the presence of what is past, the presence of what is present, and the presence of what is to come."[29]

The third moment in this history of conceptions of time is the discovery of ecstatic temporality. In a way, this notion can still be viewed as an offspring of the Augustinian *distentio animi*.[30] However, the ecstatic understanding of time breaks with the spiritualist tradition in more than one way: The ecstases by which human existence goes out of itself into what we call the past, present, and future replace the representation of a linear temporal flux; the pre-eminence of the future replaces the traditional pre-eminence of the present; and the three co-originary, "equiprimordial" dimensions of time henceforth prevent the construction of the past and future as prolongations of the present. In the metaphysical tradition up to and including Husserl, these elements—the *linear* sequence of "nows," the genesis of the stream from the *present,* as well as the formation of the past and future by acts comparable to *retentions* and *protentions*—form a system. When eternity (a fixed "now," or perpetuity), from which time is distinguished like the unstable from the stable, is added to these, one has the metaphysical system of time.

To these points of interest in the journey of the Intelligence in search of time, two more must be added in order to properly grasp *henôsis* as a singular event. Both are breaks in the itinerary of Heidegger's thought. He describes the first of these breaks as the transition from time as the "sense of direction of being" to time as the "history of the truth of being." This break constitutes the "turning" (*die Kehre*) in his thinking. Briefly, it results from the discovery that being-in-the-world is diversified according to *Menschentum,*[31] the epochal type of man, for example, the Greek, Roman, Medieval, modern, and contemporary types. Thus ecstatic temporality turns into epochal temporality. The continuity with the Existential Analytic is nonetheless striking. An epoch is the sudden establishment of a constellation of presence and absence that unites the three dimensions of time in the *non-linear* upsurge of a phenomenal arrangement that henceforth will mark the age. And since it is the advent of such a new arrangement of things, the *epoché* remains *future-oriented.* Lastly, as the phenomenal origin of past, present, and future, the epoch unifies these dimensions *co-originarily.* In the movement of Heidegger's thought from ecstatic temporalization to epochal temporality, the basic features in his understanding of time become historicized and yet also preserved, as will be seen.

The other break is described by Heidegger as the transition from "the truth of being" to "the topology of being."[32] At this last stage, his reflection on time touches on what might be called the "primordial" condition—the universal and necessary condition of all previous notions—were it not for the impossibility, directly resulting from it, of a "first order." Time here is the "direction" of being inasmuch as being assigns phenomena their site in a given economy. Such assigning is not the deed of any agency. It is nothing other than the entrance of beings into an arrangement which makes up an epoch. This entrance, for which Heidegger still has recourse to verbs such as *phuein,* 'emerging,' and *phainesthai,* 'appearing,' is the phenomenon which the term *Ereignis* is supposed to capture. As we have seen, this may be translated as 'event,' so long as we understand by this both appropriation and expropriation. The "proper" (*eigen*) points to the way singulars belong to one another in a world, a mutual belonging which is always made fragile from within by the *ex-* of expropriation (by the *Ent-* of *Entzug,* etc.). The proper thus designates the movement by which things render themselves mutually and provisionally proximate—which does not mean unfailingly close by, or fully present. Here, just as in ecstatic and epochal temporalities, it is *Sinn* as directionality, and not as "significance," that is at stake here. But if time thus gives a "sense of direction" it is no longer to human existing, or to historial *epéchein.* For of what is *Ereignis* the sense of direction? It can only be in relation to presence and absence. Time as the event of appropriation-expropriation gives a sense of direction to coming to presence, a sense of direction which turns the latter against itself by coupling universalization—the law of salvation (*Heil*)—and singularization—the counter-law of havoc (*Unheil*).

It should be clear in what way Heidegger, up until his last writings, remains indebted to the transcendental tradition. Time as event makes possible ecstatic as well as epochal temporality.[33] However, Heideggerian transcendentalism abandons the ancestry of self-consciousness—thereby destituting modern hegemony. The event is originary time, operative always and already in lived time (through existence or in history), and it makes possible all the concepts of time the tradition has transmitted to us, be they physical or spiritual.

Time as bad eternity

How does Plotinus fit into this history of concepts of time? At first sight his place is obvious. It is indeed from Plotinus (via Porphyry) that Augustine learned to seek out time in the life of the soul rather than in physical motion. Augustine repeats Plotinus regarding the soul's *distentio* toward past, present and future. After having rejected all the ancient definitions of time, particularly the Aristotelian one, Plotinus offers his own: "It is the extendedness (*diastasis*) of life that takes time, and the ceaseless forward movement of life takes ever new time, quite as life past took past time. Would it then not be appropriate to define time as the life of the Soul in movement as it passes from one state of life to another?"[34]

Even if this definition concerns extension and motion, Plotinus in fact dismisses the conceptions of time derived from spatial representations, inasmuch as he refused to identify it either with motion (Aristotle), or with a thing moved (Pythagoras), or with some aspect of movement (Stoics). To understand time in terms of itself, he turns inward—a move that presages not only Augustine, but Kant as well. Time, then, is the life of the Soul. This definition also excludes the Platonic demiurge from having produced it: "It is the Soul . . . that generates time" (*En.* III, 7 [45], 13, 47). As the Soul's life, time "precedes" the sensible world. Without it, such a world would not exist. For the classical Greek tradition, there was no time without the world. On the contrary, says Plotinus, the soul temporalizes *itself* and in so doing temporalizes the world.[35] This is a new way of thinking that he states with some apology to his predecessors: "Possibly [these thinkers] did not yet think in this reversed fashion, and possibly we simply no longer understand them" (ibid. 13, 13). The apparently obvious place of Plotinus in the history of the concepts of time is the moment of its interiorization.

But what exactly is his "reversed fashion" of thinking? Time "manifests itself in it [the Spirit], it is in it, and it is unified with it, as the eternal is to the intelligible being" (ibid. 11, 64). His new way of thinking can thus be stated by this proportion:

Eternity : Intelligence :: Time : Soul

The reversal in the manner of thinking consists in understanding time in terms of eternity. What separates Plotinus not only from the authors of Greek antiquity but also from those of Hellenic antiquity is his understanding of time as tied to eternity. Properly speaking, the definition—time, the life of the Soul—depends on and follows from this new priority. Indeed, the Soul can know itself only once Intelligence is known. The "definition" is thus not originary. It depends on the more fundamental premise stated in the above proportion. The new way of thinking requires an examination of the *model* of time in the second hypostasis, Intelligence. This model is eternity.[36] So Plotinus tells us that it too is derived. If we are to follow his new manner of thinking, we therefore will not be able to skirt the question, "What is the model of eternity in the one?" Plotinus cannot avoid the question of originary time.

His "method" always consists in following a *hodos,* a path, of descending explanation. In a world where a phenomenon is understood only by resorting to a higher level which more fully possesses its qualities, any action of the sensible upon the intelligible remains necessarily inconceivable. It is for this general methodological reason that interiority cannot be Plotinus's last word about time. He does not at all conceive of time in relation to sense experience, be it internal or external. It is true that his inquiry—the *modus inveniendi* as opposed to the *modus explicandi*—proceeds from the exterior by way of the interior to the superior, but this itinerary does not properly constitute an ascent. Plotinus retains only the heuristic function of *anagogé,* at least as far as the problem of time is concerned.[37] Thus he describes how the perception of an external movement, for example growth in an animal's life, *reveals* the inward movement of psychic life, that is, time. In turn, the life of the Soul reveals the life of the Intelligence, eternity. The one discovered at the end of this regressive movement obviously is affected neither by time nor by eternity. It is the immediate source of eternity and the mediated source of time. If we recall now the equivalency between *to hen* and *henôsis,* between the one and union (leaving being at the second hypostasis, forgetting for the moment Anonymous of Torino, who equates it to the one), then the issue of originary time can be formulated in another, more developed proportion:

one : Intelligence : Soul :: uniting : being : becoming :: *X* : eternity : time.

The first triad names the hypostases. The second gives the verbs that correspond to them in Plotinus. In the third, where the terms are "temporal," how might the unknown *X* be described?

We may learn something about this, at least indirectly, by examining how eternity refracts the one—but does not mediate it—as life of the Soul. Indeed, eternity separates the realm of this unknown and that of time. Now, refraction only occurs on a threshold which participates in the two realms that it connects. The refringent hypostasis must include two *logoi;* it must be two-sided, one turned toward the realm concealing the *X* and from which it proceeds, the other toward the realm where the hypostasis disperses it as the life of souls. Thus Proclus will later say that from the point of view of the one, the ideas are "henads," but from the point of view of the multiple, they are "monads." Furthermore, given the general framework of participation by deficient similitude, the lower degrees of being—the images—manifest the higher degrees—the models—whatever the hierarchical level might be. Eternity is the image of the one and the model of time. Plotinus must therefore describe these two sides of eternity, which look upwards and downwards, in "temporal" terms. "*Perpetuity* is the state of being pertaining to the substrate, a state of being that stems from it and inheres in it; *eternity,* on the other hand, is the substrate itself, together with that state of being which is manifested in it." As the image of the one, eternity is a *hypokeimenon,* even a god. But as the model of time, it is a state, a simple way of being (*katastasis*) near to that substrate, and it is a world. "Eternity . . . is God himself, showing and manifesting himself as he is, namely, as being (*to einai*), immutable, self-identical, and thus endowed with a constant life."[38] If perpetuity is "the state which brings [eternity] to manifest itself," then eternity *appears* as perpetuity, as constant duration. Christian followers of Plotinus will conclude from this distinction between the essence of eternity and its appearance that perpetuity is only an inadequate analogy of the *nunc stans* in which "all is possessed simultaneously." In appearing, eternity both manifests and conceals itself.

A certain surplus is thus passed over silently when eternity is treated *inductively* as a model of time. Any inductive proposition about the second hypostasis remains incommensurate with it: the measure of eternity is the one. Only a *deductive* way of thinking about eternity would match its measure and would capture this surplus. When time is defined as the image of eternity, this deductive approach therefore is commensurable with it. A phenomenon, be it sensible or intelligible, is fully understandable only in the light of the degree above it—which is the reason why there can be no knowledge of the one. Plotinus's reversed way of thinking is deduction.[39] Anagogic reasoning keeps its simply heuristic function, and it follows that the treatise on eternity is a negative treatise on the one as *condition of any temporal figure.* "Eternity is around the one."[40] The ascending procedure which passes from moving time to its stable yet complex cause, and then to the stable and simple condition—this ascent is stated by Plotinus as an order of discovery, as opposed to the descending order of grounding: "It is now appropriate to state how *time* should really be understood. To this end we must go back to the state of being which we affirmed was *eternity;* immutable life, given all at once, infinite, absolutely fixed, at rest in and directed towards the *one*" (ibid. 10, 16–11, 4). In thus rising up again by "allusion"—by an approaching and approximative (*ad-*) game (*ludus*)—from time to eternity and to the one, what is the originary condition of all the derived temporal concepts that are reached? Which unknown surplus does the approach and allusion touch upon?

Being as time

We saw that each of the traditional metaphysical attributes of the absolute—the good, the true, the beautiful—originates in a specific, maximized experience. In Plotinus it is a general axiom that we can only philosophize about what we also "touch": "How could we understand [eternal things] if we had no contact with them? And what contact could there be if they were utterly alien to us?" (*En.* III, 7 [45], 7, 3ff.). We are indeed in communion with each hypostasis: Through the experience of need, we are in contact with that of the Soul and thus time;[41] through intellectual intuition and (already) discourse, with that of the Intelligence and thus eternity;[42] through "going forth from the self (*ekstasis*), the simplifying (*haplôsis*) and renouncing (*epidosis*) of the self; reaching towards contact (*haphé*) and rest (*stasis*)" (*En.* VI, 9 [9], 11, 23ff.) we are in communion with the one and originary "time" (in quotes to suggest the model of the model of time, the life of the Soul).

Since maximization is excluded, "touch" itself has a heuristic function. It is true that the description of contact with the one may appear to be a moral one. Thus there is a Plotinian imperative: become simple. Nonetheless, such an injunction is possible only because we always touch the one by means of a more elementary conveyance than need and intuition, which, according to the order of descending dependence, rather refract the touch which brings us to union. It is not difficult to understand which impetus is at stake. *Natality* appeared to us as this primary spontaneity without which there would be neither phenomenalization nor world.

The one as singular event of union is natality—not maximized, but retained in its purity (natality, being the "principle" of maximization by representation, itself knows neither maximum nor minimum; neither does the one, not being representable, know greater or lesser). Just as at the outset of the journey in Parmenides, the one is natality excised from mortality, and this more efficiently than under any hegemony *with content.*[43] This is why there is no more austere thinking than that of the one—it is neither consoling nor consolidating.

To think the one, which everywhere is the issue of our elementary experience, we must unlearn the fascination for everything that can be represented. The natural metaphysician in us lives off representations, exalting this or that one of them and positing it as supreme according to circumstances. He lives off theticism. On the contrary, one need not posit anything to think the one. Thus, Plotinus says, we impoverish ourselves and we become wise. The imperative thus enjoins us to live according to our way of being and, *following the example of the one,* to "let all things be unto themselves" (*En.* V, 5 [32], 12, 49). Simplification and union in Plotinus thus constitute the essential traits both of man and the one. This is why the latter is best described by processes: not just "uniting" (*henoein*) *but* also "letting-be" (*eaein*).[44]

This affinity between natality in us and the event which the one is is also emphasized by other words. Consider *dunamis.* The one makes all things possible (*dunasthai*). As such, it lets all things emerge from itself without suffering any diminution.[45] Rendering all possible, letting appear (an entirely un-Aristotelian notion of *dunamis*) is an "event" which occurs neither in eternity nor in time. This event—letting appear—is rather the condition of eternity as much as it is of time. It is thus the *one* condition, conditioning the totality of the intelligible and the sensible, which yet is *singular,* and occurs whenever there is appearance. One and singular is the event by which each being—ideal beings first, then material ones—receives the site assigned to it. One and singular is the event as assignment. It "eternally" occurs in Intelligence; but also "here and now," in the Soul. Thus understood as a power, the one differs from all beings. By which difference? It does not add itself to them, any more than it sums them up, but it does differentiate their union.

Now, to unite is to phenomenalize—this is the very definition of natality.[46] If the one is too close to us to think it easily, it is that . . . I raise a pen, and already I do what the one does: a world sets itself in place, where a little paper, a lot of endurance, and some small black signs enter into a constellation. Union is the being of phenomena, their appearing in a context according to laws. We must not go on to conclude (as modern readers might) that there is being only where humans are acting or knowing. Plotinus wards off such subjectivism in advance. He distinguishes between "the one in itself," "the one of Intelligence," and "the one of the Soul." Here, one plus one plus one does not make three. One and the same union is brought about everywhere, "before any number." Therefore, if it is nothing but an event of contextualization, the *hen* is the law of phenomenal laws. It is so due to a process that is at every turn singular.

The anonymous author quoted above said of the one that "it itself is acting." This is a perfect description, again, of natality. Said of the one, it must accordingly be understood as appearing as such—the actor behind the acting remaining irrelevant for henology, under pain of falling back into ousiology. The one is manifestation. In Plotinus, the difference between the manifest and its manifestation is in play exactly when he seeks to exclude all substantialist connotations from the one. In ousiology, *dunamis* signified virtualities as yet unfulfilled in the cosmos. In henology, on the other hand, nothing is left "in *potentia*": "Nothing else can be born; and there is nothing which is to come into existence, because it [the one] generated all things. It is not all these things itself . . ." (*En.* V, 5 [32], 12, 46–49). *Dunamis* is this "acting" without an agent by which all becomes the uni-verse: turned toward the one, unified, contextualized, existing world. Henology is the discourse on this *vertere* in the uni-*verse,* on the "direction"—the directionality—of things making a world; on the event of the world making itself.

As such, it can be described as *originary time.*

Union is also emphasized as *arché*. This term always refers to the one when used without a restrictive attribute. It is often followed by a genitive: The one is "origin of emanation, origin of life, origin of the Intelligence as well as of all things." It is an origin which is not foreign to us: "[W]e indicate it by virtue of what in ourselves is like it" (*En.* III, 8 [30], 9, 39f., and 24). What is it in us that is like the *arché* without qualifier? What is it that, in us, is always beginning? Again, it is natality. It brings us to unite first the body, the Soul with its levels, and the Intelligence, integrating them into a human being; then, most of all, a life returned from dissolution. If the one is very familiar to us, it is through natality—the "principle" of unity in us of the incessant establishing of a world. The word *arché* implies, besides, a motility that neither its Latin equivalents—*princeps, principium, primum,* but also *imperium, regimen,* etc.—nor its modern ones preserve. In the text quoted earlier from Aristotle, this motility was likened to a battle that is forming. When an army is in route, the disarray does not stop because one or two soldiers take heart again. But as soon as the combat order is re-established, the activities of each turns into the action of all. So it is that the one is the *formation* of order, absolutely. The same for natality. So long as the *arché* designates to us the attribute of some being that dominates, the Neoplatonic discourse about the one indeed reverts to negative theology. But if the origin is essentially *oriri*—or the *arché,* essentially *archein*—then henology does not speak of the divine world-government, but of something with even greater bearing: of the event which is coming to presence. This event is impossible to objectivize into a hypostasis or a deity, for although it is "temporal" in the sense that it renders all the figures of eternity and time possible, it occurs neither in time nor eternity, properly speaking (without quotes). Neither can this event be conceived as the emptiest genus, embracing all types of unification, since through the natality in us we "touch" it. Above all this event is not inserted directly into an ascent which would go from the visible and the Soul, pass through the intelligible and the Intelligence, and end in the solely "touchable," which would be the one. Such an ascending continuity would answer to the maximization from which hegemonies are born. It would however lack the heteronomy of *epekeina:* the discontinuity of the one-Intelligence *logos* in relation to the Soul-Intelligence *logos*. Natality purifies itself in this discontinuity. It loses all content, representations, images, ideas, causes, and theses that are to be advanced.

The very matter, *die Sache selbst,* of henology is the entrance of a multitude of factors into a constellation, the advent of such a constellation—in other words, originary time.

Let us add that the heteronomy of the two transcendences—first toward the *noûs,* then toward the *hen*—puts metaphysics in its place. The backward step from the visible, the first transcendence, is metaphysical. The *epekeina,* the backward step from the intelligible, is no longer metaphysical in this sense. It leads neither to the first nature of substances, nor to their ultimate foundation. To pass beyond the hypostatic Intelligence thus is to work through the scaffolding of reasons and causes, the scaffolding of etiologies which makes up metaphysics. Beyond the scaffolding, reason loses its wits. Then for once, one may thus speak peacefully of *delimited* metaphysics: From the hypostatic Intelligence to the one we no longer go in the same direction as from the Soul to the Intelligence—we do not continue toward reasons. Plotinus traces the limit where reason no longer grasps any direction, where direction changes direction and becomes temporal directionality.

Is it not a very minimalist reading of the *Enneads* to want thus to think the one as the simple event of phenomenalization? Is it not utter functionalism to so desubstantialize the one to the point that a verb describes it better than a noun? Don't the best-known and maybe most disconcerting texts testify to a highly personal and datable experience of the one? Porphyry recounts that his master "reached the supreme goal four times, not just in potency, but by the ineffable act."[47] If it is a simple event of phenomenal placing into presence, how can the one inspire a confession such as this one?: "Often I awaken to myself by escaping from my body; a stranger to any other thing, in the intimacy of myself, I behold a beauty as marvelous as possible. I am convinced then, more than ever, that I have a higher destiny; my activity is the highest degree of life; I am united with the divine, and, having attained this activity, I station myself in it above the other intelligible beings. But, after this rest in the divine, I must descend again from the Intelligence to reflective thinking. . . ." (*En.* IV, 8 [6], 1, 1–10).

The reduction, if that is the word, from the one to union does not in any way bespeak a functionalism. Here Plotinus speaks of those rare moments when it was given to him to "let all things be" quite as the one lets them all be. This experience is the end toward which the imperative to become simple points. The question of causes and effects is not pertinent there. The experience is located at the antipodes of the etiological experience as it was analyzed in Aristotle's *Physics:* the experience of making, manufacturing, and already of the mastering (*kratein*) of nature. Plotinus stands at the margin of this predominant tradition in the West inasmuch as, to all sovereignties erected by maximization, he opposes union, which one experiences by letting-be. This "time"—the "letting" which is the very way of being of the one—concludes the reduction for which *henôsis* cannot mean union *with* the one (since the one is not entitative), but union *which is* the one.

Recalling now Anonymous of Torino, and translating, as he does, "uniting" as "being," we may still be able to recognize in the occurrent one the "time" of being. *Einai*—but it is no longer Plotinus who is speaking—would then signify the motility in all manifestations: its occurrence .

It is said that, due to the trans-noetic *epekeina,* henological discourse remains necessarily negative. Its object joins together auto-revelation and auto-dissimulation, whence the profusion of negations in all the Neoplatonists. The one withdraws, which means that it withdraws outside of *the Intelligence.* This is true, of course. But if it "temporalizes" phenomena through their singular entering into presence—if it is the singular event—then it especially withdraws *outside the universal.* And so it singularizes itself.

After the question of the time of the one, here is another one that at first sight is just as inadmissible in henology: whence comes the singularity by which union was described? Might it have to do with that "movedness" in the one which has always bothered the commentators, even to the point that Porphyry relegated that treatise to the end of the *Enneads*? Might it be there that the "good" singularity of phenomenalization—uniting—is allied with the "bad" singularization—willing? Might there be a labor of mortality in the one itself? A disparate contretemps in the originary "time" which natality is?

CHAPTER 7

The Singularizing Contretemps

> "Nondescript is the figure of pure singularity.
> Nondescript singularity has no identity,
> is not determined in relation to a concept . . . ;
> the nondescript is a singularity plus an empty space."[48]
> —Giorgio Agamben

"How did the one not remain in itself?" (*En.* V, 1 [10], 6, 6). Even though this question seems, by all rights, a source of insoluble perplexity, Plotinus nonetheless answers. The treatise which gives the answer—and which in turn has all it needs to perplex the reader—is entitled: "On the Freedom and the Will of the One" (*En.* VI, 8 [39]). How did the one, immobile beyond eternity, not remain in itself? Here is the disconcerting answer: "It alone is in truth free" (ibid. 21, 31). To the law of the one, and within it, is added another law: that of a free willing.

The reader encounters formidable difficulties here. At the levels of being inferior to the one, freedom signifies the productive act of an essence which communicates itself. Consider the essence of the Intellect. It produces its reflection—its "idol" (*eidôlon*)—and its essence lies within its act (*energeia, En.* V, 2 [11], 1,12). The act is a principle of formation and, in this sense, free. The Soul thus owes its form to the freedom that is communicative of the level of being which it imitates: to the freedom of the Intellect. Psychic form results from a noetic act that endows it with essence. In the architectonic of the world, freedom thus manages the abundance of formal communications.

If Plotinus advanced from the Soul to the Intellect and to the one, as if from the small to the great and to the greatest—if his universe held, without rupture, by a *formal anagogic continuity*—many problems would vanish. To speak of the freedom of the one would then amount to speaking of the act by which a hypothetical greatest essence would discharge itself outwards. At stake in the treatise on the freedom and will of the one would be the essence of the world, the idol of the one. Plotinus would give his solution to a problem for which others had recourse to the demiurge or the creator. But Plotinus denies that there is an essence (and with it, any ontological issue) in the one. As a result, freedom will not serve to answer the question (which in any case is not Plotinian): How did the world appear? Freedom does not thematize communication. The freedom of the one does not produce anything which "goes outside," neither form nor reflection, neither copy nor idol. Neither does it produce anything which "remains within," like a turning back on oneself. The willing of the one is not modeled on reflexivity. If it were, to unite would mean to think, and this would be a confusion between hypostases which would render the reading invalid. The free willing of the one is inscribed entirely in rupture with the noetic and psychic freedoms. For marking this rupture—the second transcendence of freedom—one will profit from keeping in mind the key formula: "An act is free, in the pure sense, which is not subjected to essence" (*En.* VI, 8 [39], 20, 18).

The free willing of the one—it is not the attribute of a subject, and yet it is an act. But it is a non-communicative and non-reflexive act. It is an inessential and yet—because of that—pure freedom. How should this be understood? In the one, there is some sort of temporalizing occurring in the one that disconcerts hegemony.[49]

One had believed to have found a solution by declaring the *Enneads* a collection of diverse teachings brought back from Alexandria, intended to show to the Emperor Gallian how to successfully manage an *aggiornamento* of paganism, or even a patchwork where optimism struggles against pessimism. . . . The commentator who delivers these noteworthy insights[50] adds, moreover, that in the end with Plotinus, optimism won out over pessimism. Now, if what one calls optimism depends phenomenologically on the trait of natality in us, and what one calls pessimism depends on the trait of mortality, then their struggle remains rather unresolved in the dying man who says: "I strive to make what is divine in me rise towards what is divine in the whole."[51] Unresolved, because—the cited statement says it in all precision—death is not the happy outcome. It appears there as work. It marks the tragic effort (*peirâsthai*) to affirm the divine whole while in the factual grip of the singularization imminent in that hour.

Taking the example of the dying man, it is necessary to endure the difficulty of reading and, with it, the suffering of the double bind. They have a revelatory power. Might the *peiran* (the word from which "peril," "experience," "pirate" . . . come) which befalls the dying man, and differently the reader, reveal something of the condition which is the one? To be an event and thus a conditioning time, the one would have to singularize—singularize itself and singularize the conditioned—in the same contextualization by which it gives meaning to that which it unifies? Freedom means then that contextualization and manifestation would always and only dissolve. It would bespeak the precariousness of the one as union: whatever there is of the nondescript, of the non-manifest, in every manifest context.

In any case, through the *energeia* of freedom and the will we descry something that compensates for the one, from within.[52] The energetic supplement works counter to the univocal normativity that a referent must exercise to be ultimate. Porphyry, in his editorial caution, ranked the treatise on the freedom and will of the one as the penultimate of the fifty-four *Enneads* (a bit like one places the most problematic piece right before the end when making the program for a musical *soirée*). He made it into the penultimate word of the master. In this he was followed by the commentators who smooth over the bumps of the text by applying to it the balm of "metaphorical sense"—consequently they would have us understand that the sense stripped bare has nothing rough about it. Hence the treatise which Porphyry made into Plotinus's last word denies again that there may be a willing in the one (*En.* VI, 9 [9], 6, 40). Thus naked, univocal normativity re-establishes itself.

Union supposes free willing; it needs that which nevertheless savages the *simple bond.* And what can it mean for the origin thus to inseminate itself with some wild, mad, perhaps medicinal herb? What *other bond* does free willing introduce into the one? The interest of normativity can only reply to these questions by denial: with the ready retort and a No. All readings that see the final word of Plotinus in "the purely one" (*to katharôs hen, En.* V, 5 [32], 4, 6), in the axiom "the origin of all beings is simpler than them" (*En.* V, 3 [49], 16, 7)—as if the pure and the simple *terminated* the effort to apprehend the conditions of the manifest world—effectively denying the double bind. But thought cannot stop there. To the "purely one" Plotinus adds, as we will read, the "purely free" (*katharôs eleuthera*): an addition which creates a problem. To be sure, the thinking which removes from the one all material, psychic, and noetic qualities—a negatory thinking which erases even the predicates from the *logos* (for example, even the predicate "purely one" which offers nothing to conceive)—goes far. No being, even if it is a reflection of the one itself and thus an idea, ever penetrates into the one. In this rigorous sense, "heno-logy" remains forever an impossible project. And yet here we have Plotinus announcing, peremptorily one might say, an entire treatise "On the Freedom and the Will of the One." Does this then go even *further* into an a-logical discourse than does affirming the free and willing one? Does this not take it too seriously as a law-making noun? Does this not cling to it as to the Father? This further step can only move one further away from formal anagogic continuity and attributive logic. From this arise some questions; those dealing with the law will interest us most. By following Plotinus in the further step toward an act of pure freedom, will the one retain its uniformly compulsory force? Will it be able to bind simply? In a word: Will hegemony survive unbroken with a free will traversing it?

When we understand the one as union—*hen* as *henosis,* sense of direction as manifestation, being as event—the questions that have already been raised become more poignant. Here it is no longer a matter of describing essence by its attributes, but of thinking the other beyond (*epekeina*) that, in Plotinus, makes the essence transcend hypostasis. To uphold the tragic here would mean to understand that the one is an event because its non-submissive act (non-subjected, non-subservient, non-enslaved: *ou douleusasa*) is not subsumed under anything. Within the one, something—but it is not any thing—refuses to be subjected to the principial function, to subsumption, to the reference which uniformly makes the law. It is difficult not to conclude that for Plotinus the ultimate condition is an event with incongruous tractions: a phenomenalizing-singularizing event. Henology here would be the discoures *of* ultimates.

If this is the way it is, one will have other motives than metaphysical ones for describing the Plotinian one as anarchic. The traditional motifs of ontological anarchism are summed up in the observation, contained analytically, moreover, in principial theticism, that the absolutely first cannot in turn be preceded by any origin. If it were thus preceded, it would not be first.[53] In this sense, all metaphysical referents are anarchic: the non-originated originary (*arché anarchos*). On the other hand, following the other motifs that may appear here, the one will be anarchic because in itself it does not possess what is needed for it to be an absolute *arché*—simple normativity. It is not that it exceeds all power, nor that it would lack power. But the *dunamis* of the one combines with the unsubmitted *energeia,* which is therefore not the "actuality" of that "power,"[54] so as to counter-invest the stasis. Power and acting do not go together very well with thetic monism. A dissension belabors the one from within. It lacks a simple essence. The *arché* is not all its own. It is anarchic by virtue of an act of otherness which troubles it. Phenomenological anarchism always results from an originary *différend* between conditions. The consequence is that Plotinus does not fall—at least, not without catching himself—into the thetic monism of which historians of ideas make him the champion.

Could it be that the one is deposed by the obviousness of its own truth? Could it be that with Plotinus, lover of the one if there ever was one, it had to speak of ultimates?

One should not lunge toward hasty conclusions. The distance between essence and quality is used by Plotinus, in certain contexts, to explain evil, or in any case, a certain concealment. Does not freedom as that which "is not subjected to essence" strangely recall that very distance?

Introducing a non-submissive act into the origin does not for all that amount to exalting—in the face of the diurnal principle that the one or the good would be—the nocturnal complex of evil-sin-corruption-ugliness-death. The one is neither *duarchon* nor *poluarchon*. The co-originary free will does not set itself up over the absolute good, defying it. Neither defiance nor *assumption* either. As we will see, we know quite a bit about unsubjected liberty as the pull of mortality. But to retrace this trait all the way back to the ultimate conditions of all manifestation is not necessarily to glorify death or to attribute it to the absolute. Such an attribute would require that the one offer itself to phenomena as their subject, hireling, substance, and substrate; it would have to offer this very entitative repose that ruins transcendence beyond essence. The other in the one therefore does not signify otherness (*heterotês*) in the sense of the first product of the one; nor is the last product of the one—evil—implied or folded into the good, coiled up in it in one way or another, endorsed or exalted.

It is a more ancient logic which brings Plotinus to contaminate the one by a free willing, a tragic logic, in the sense of incongruous and irreconcilable laws. More than ever, he thinks otherwise than do the subsumptive philosophers. The focal point that is the one will remain extrinsically *pure* (there is no second focal point, no henads), but not intrinsically *simple* (it bears a seed of audacity and therefore freedom). Hence subsumption is dislocated. Hence again the question—would this hegemonic fantasm be deposed by the obviousness of the ultimates in which its truth resides? Hence, in any case, the dislocation of the resignation of the functionaries of humanity faced by this referent in which liberty begins to split open order.

On an insubordinate act that makes the law

A discourse on the origin beyond the beyond is called apophatic: a "negatory" discourse on transcendence which makes the intelligible world secondary. In Plotinus, the excess of hyper-transcendence first sets into motion—obviously—the "spiritual" work on oneself (quotation marks are implied in the following—the *pneuma* marking the spot, so to speak, in the strict grid of *nous*[55]). But Plotinian apophatism begins elsewhere. The less obvious motive here is phenomenological rather than spiritual and is relevant to an analytic of ultimates. Plotinus remains attentive to the dispersion that is necessarily imminent in a given empirical or ideal contextual manifestation. Whence this very same excessive origin, shattered in its simplicity by a yet-to-come. The *coming dissension* renders any entry into presence and any union precarious. With the free will, Plotinus discovers an originary endangerment. The one binds us, both by union and by this perilous other. Such is the new configuration of the double bind, whose legislative character we must try to understand.

When he affirms the simplicity of union, his discourse, says Plotinus, is necessarily situated "short of" that about which he is speaking.[56] "Short of" will make all the more sense when it comes to the differend, which is the one shot through with freedom. The reason for saying "short of"—like Romeo to Juliet on her balcony, with the poor visibility this involves—is, firstly, speculative. Excess can never, and yet can solely, be described in the terms of that which it exceeds. But strictly speaking, anarchy—and consequently, Plotinian learned, ignorance—does not result from speculation any more than from introspection. Tragically disparate laws must necessarily exceed the concept. Such laws remain inconceivable due to their very disparity. In Plotinus the reason for which the *logos* remains short of the one stems from the originary differend. The gaze rises no longer toward a simple sparkle, as of a young girl, but toward a conflictual labor which catches sight of itself, all ratiocinations fallen away, on its deathbed.

Primary freedom is willing but unruly; *it does not will in the name of the one*. It wills audaciously, Plotinus will say (*En*. VI, 9 [9], 5,29). Even though, in the name of the one, the law "gathers to put into order" (*sun-tassein*), it still calls for another "syntax." There is a conflict of "tactics," which exceeds the conceptual grasp. By understanding this excess through insubordination, we will have simultaneously grasped the impossibility of denying singularization in the one so that the universal can shine forth exclusively, the impossibility of denying mortality and "pessimism" to the benefit of pure natality and "optimism," the impossibility, at last, of slipping out from under the two mutually inadmissible laws, laws that can also be described as those of manifestation and concealment.

The *and* that places them end to end is precisely where we see the ultimate referent supplemented from within by pure freedom.[57] The *and* signifies traits of functioning and dysfunctioning, in differend. We see that, in relation to the Greek tradition, the law of the one not only displaces itself, but it dislocates itself. The text that explains how the one did not remain within itself (*En*. VI, 8 [39]) clashes with this tradition, just like it clashes with the *Enneads*. Nevertheless it is a decisive text. In it, Plotinus gives the genuine reason for apophatism and anarchism, namely, that *the one is not simple*. More harshly than any other in the philosophical lineage of Parmenides he emphasizes the incomparable traits which turn the one against itself.

The traits are incomparable because, despite lexical symmetries, they are unopposable. Henology seeks to pass beyond the intelligent-intelligible dyad and, thereby, all oppositional logic.[58] It seeks, in other words, to pass beyond reconciliation, with the result that the Intellect—the second hypostasis—functions as the ultimate subsuming principle. But phenomenalization and singularization are never coupled in a dyad. They are not coordinated. They are not positioned as contraries, or as contradictories. They can never be reconciled or subsumed, because they do not hyperbolize the self-reduplication that defines the Intellect.

The fantasmic *attraction* of the one comes from our immediately trusting in the strategy of desire that natality is: we ponder a position that is not darkened by any negation. For example: Up above reigns a sovereignty to which no servitude corresponds; a joy without correlative pain; a production without destruction. . . . These are so many theses deprived of their determinate negations, to which must be added freedom and the will, deprived of their antitheses, which are necessity and automatism.[59] If the freedom of the one were opposed to some necessary thing—and its will to some involuntary thing—its legislating attraction would be done in. It is an attraction which is not "etiological," but "dynamic"—the freedom of the one calls into question the regime of causes,[60] its will being pure power.

The *retreat* of the free will, on the other hand, thrusts a telling bit of evidence into the midst of union, namely, that there is another strategy of desire that dares the death of the perfect stasis. Audacity in the one will not mean "opposition to the one." The ultimate position dislocates itself without the dislocating act negating it head-on. Neither does the act modify an essence by some attribute or accident. Rather, it institutes the incommensurable and thereby it strips the regime of the purest referent of commensuration that metaphysics has ever fantasized.

In this beginning of the Greek end, which bears the name Plotinus, speculative dialectics are thus muted. Fresh attention to phenomena reveals more elementary truths. It reveals that, in union, something clouds over the simple normative reference, something that has to do with time and the singular, that therefore the *singularization to come* threatens each manifest constellation of givens from within. Plotinus pays attention to these originary phenomena with a method, to be sure, that is highly overdetermined by a concern to answer the philosophers. But the new attention does not restore in them the mortality that everyone knows as aptly as they know natality—though they know them poorly since both reach too close to us.

Plotinus (a) advances from the oppositional theticism broken up by the *epekeina*, toward the *conflictual event* which, in the one, turns singularization against phenomenalization. Then he (b) inquires into the originary audacity, the instigator of this conflict—he sees in it the work of the *free will*. Before further retracing the figures of the singularizing audacity through the hypostatic architecture, let us go over these two stages.

a. There is no transcendence beyond the Intellect without oppositional logic, and with it the logic of extension, vanishing in the face of an a-logic of accomplishment. By opposing the universal and the singular as more or less extended magnitudes, one might gain *in abstracto* a hyperbolic continuity going from beings to the one (perhaps, because the one unifies all things without itself being a genus). But one would miss what occurs in the one, because Plotinus reasons otherwise than with common names. So as not to posit genera and hand over his henology to the historians of ideas like a carcass, one must speak of processes emphasized by verbs. Therefore, both *uniting* and *singularizing* occur in the one. We have recognized the tragic function in such a law-making dissension. Now, whoever expresses processes and speaks in verbs expresses times and conjugates tenses. Union is an event due to the time of natality. And whoever expresses singularization expresses a *contre-temps*—time without time, another time, the time of death, time of mortality. If the non-subjected act in the one gives shape to singularization, Plotinus will have complicated from within the event that is union. The Greek fantasm will have destituted itself, not as a result of extraordinary speculative adventures, but due to his faithfulness to the most ordinary phenomenological "first known": the double bind of natality and mortality. The referent posited as universal will have turned out to be not just an event, but a conflictual event.

Under the law of union, everything appears as birth, spontaneity, novelty, beginning, life. Duration is the life of the Soul; eternity is the life of the Intelligence; coming to presence, lastly, is the life of the one. How, now, does the disparate other of natality appear, under the law of the singularizing contre-temps—if it is true that non-essential *energeia* installs that law at the heart of the origin? The counter-law is discovered by an argument which is still ascending. Therefore it is through time (the life of the Soul) that eternity (the life of Intelligence) is discovered, just as through the latter the event, the "life" of the one, is discovered. Here is a triply productive life, since each time and insofar as there is a manifestation, the Soul, Intelligence, and the one come to pass by themselves. Each hypostasis comes to be by an act (*energèma*). Which one? The Soul, by distending itself toward the past and the future, the Intellect, by reflecting on itself. And the one? Here is how Plotinus concludes the ascending argument: "Intelligence is the product of an act; similarly [the one] is the product of an act. Now this act cannot be that of an other. [The one] is thus the product of its own act." (*En.* VI, 8 [39], 16, 16 ff.). *An act other than that of union,* but not the act of an other. How is this otherness to be understood? How should the purely one and the actually other be thought without thinking a discordance therein? Would purity thus be only exterior?

b. Mortality, the instigator of all discord, still must be recalled. Of which act is the one the product? "It is such as it wills" (ibid. 16, 22). The one "is" in virtue of its free willing. An anagogic terminus which is unexpected, to say the least. Plato would not have understood—the one so simple that it obliges one to close one's eyes, to flee the tumult (*taraché*), to turn one's ears away again from the tumult within, to become immobile, to cease speaking and even reasoning: this one is precisely what is described by action verbs. It wills. Even more, while Plotinus is usually careful to remove what is serious from the attributes that he confers upon the one—which is "so to speak" (*oion*) the gaze, life, being, support . . . —here, there is nothing of the kind. In the face of the freedom of the one he lets down his guard. To say that the one produces itself then seems more than a manner of speaking. Is it not to inquire into the one in the constative, like we seriously inquire into this and that thing? To be sure, it is not like taking note of one thing and *its* other, but rather like taking note that a thing is *already* other: *media vita*. What is serious will no longer be univocal theticism, no longer the norm in its nudity.

If the freedom of the one responds to the problem of the yet-to-come in phenomenal constellations, then the mystery is redoubled. To the mystery of a safekeeping, which the Christian Neoplatonists will reify to better exalt its name and still master it by discourse, is incongruously adjoined the mystery of a non-safekeeping which, formerly in Colonus, reduced Oedipus to silence. The event of putting in constellation, which preserves phenomena, is mysterious and exalted (but not entitatively) above time and eternity. There is an unfathomable *mystery, that there is coming-to-presence,* that there is manifestation. But just as mysterious is the becoming-other in it—mysterious by a law unto itself: In such a manifest order, the nondescript (not just any and every thing, nor the contingent) is possible which undoes the safekeeping. As such, *the nondescript remains as unfathomable* as union. The nondescript to come in what you live is what singularizes in advance the phenomena gathered into a world temporally given as livable. That there is this world remains as unthinkable—as "trans-noetic"—as the seed of otherness which already, from within, ruins its safekeeping.

We gladly speak of the mystery of time, meaning by that how quickly things are no longer what they were. Here the mystery of time is more complex. By its complexity, it provides the conditions for the forward course (unless it rushes backwards) of which one likes to sigh—the "radiant event which is union endangers itself by its imminent insubordination, and thus its dispersion and its concealment." If in the truth of the one there were not this peril, if it glowed in a tranquil splendor, it would not be an event.

Plotinus emphasizes the peril and power of the future by ontologizing—by over-ontologizing, rather—the free will.

Which ontologization? It describes the second hypostasis, namely, the idealities as possessing being better than our realities. Take for instance a geometric point and its determinate other, the line. The Intellect, site of determinate negations, *wills* to pass from the point to the line. It punctually determines the distension of the Soul. Herein consists its audacity. An extraverted noetic will, "action-curious," "resolved to acquire more," an "agitated power, willing to spread out amidst the other that which it has contemplated," "not satisfied that the whole be totally present to it." This is a will which is antithetical, and thus classified as derivative. It is also a will which is adrift—not satisfied "with remaining in itself, it dissipates the one" (*En.* III, 7 [45], 11, 15–26). Here we have the secondary will that as such allows us to answer the question, itself secondary: How does the multiple descend from the dyadic being (intelligible-intelligent; matter-idea)? It does so by a noetic will of exteriorization and alienation, exercising itself on intelligible matter. The passage from beings that are genuine because they are intelligible, to beings which are mimetic because they are sensible, exhausts the ontological program.[61]

Originary will, on the other hand, does not relate the one to its other. No intelligible matter is found there, and that is why that will is trans-ontological. It relates the one to itself. But by which relation (*pros*)? This is a crucial question, as soon as reflexivity is excluded and otherness is included. It is a legislative question as well. What makes the relation, and, accordingly, the law?

The other in the one can only be thought of from "this side" of the one. How, then, does that trait disastrous to order appear? For us, the dystaxic counter-strategy is called mortality; in the Intellect, it is called exteriorization; in the one, lastly, it is called freedom and will. What must be pondered here is an ascent. It does not dispel the discontinuities between hypostases. All that continues through the levels of being is the differential *traits* of natality and mortality. Therefore, how could one not conclude that, with the relation (*pros hauton*) which turns the origin against itself (but not in contradiction with itself, nor into a reflection directed at itself), the other of the one penetrates all the way into the one? The text would then emphasize in the one this other—singularization—that, formulated from "this side. . . ," would draw us, draw us toward death. The *undeniable,* the trait of mortality, would pull us from under the free will.

Traditionally we speak of freedom and the will in ethics and morals. The ancient solutions to the problems which are posed there—the Platonic solution by the assimilation to the Good; the Stoic solution by the absorption of affects into reason—are preserved by Plotinus while transmuting them so as to tear them away from ethics and morals. Here we have assimilation: "Plato says very aptly that one must go search for the good up there, and that to become wise and happy, the gaze must turn towards That up there, to which one must assimilate oneself and according to which one must live" (*En.* I, 4 [46], 16, 10ff.). The key word is no longer "the Good," but "That up there" (*ekeîno,* three times). To go in search of the good, one must conform to the unnameable up there—which we have seen is not the Idea of all ideas.

As for absorption of affects into reason—the ancient Stoics did not allow for any attenuating circumstances: It charged reason to shed light on the appetites—inferior judgments—until they were entirely transformed into rational judgments. Thus desire and aggressivity would be absorbed into the *logos*. At the end of a hard struggle, they would become as transparent as a clear thought. In the ascetic combat man takes "the whole"[62] which is truly linked together only by *logos,* as his measure. So as not to become discouraged in the face of such rigors, a dose of hardness toward oneself might be required. Hence, later on, the middle Stoics will come to doubt that the sage thus conceived could ever have existed, or that he might ever exist.

In Plotinus, our dealing with affects is placed under the sign not of the struggle between parts of the soul, nor of the effort to make rational judgment, but under the sign of gentleness. For him, the principle of a universal continuity[63] leads to an injunction that inverts that of the ancient Stoics: Do not annihilate the singular in the logical universal, but "leave" it with gentleness; rehabilitate it in its singularity. Like others, Plotinus prescribes that the free will "follow the nature of the whole" (e.g., *En.* I, 4 [46], 7, 41). But to grasp what he means by that maxim and thus by the free will which submits itself to it, one will first have to know how to understand the one by which "the whole" holds together. If it is true that it—the one, itself—suffers from an originary dissension, the maxim will fall elsewhere than into the fields of ethics and morals, fields which are plowed and replowed by cutting principles, notably that of a telic continuity which compresses the "whole." The one turned against itself, on the other hand, could not serve as a principle for such a compression. To make a point about natural finalities, simply to posit as a final point and final end is not, at least in the treatise in question (VI, 8 [39]), the way in which the one wills, constitutes, and belabors phenomena. Its way will be to bring them into configuration and thus to the world, *and* to leave them to the disfigured, to the insubordinate, to the precarious, to distance, to the nondescript, to concealment: to the singularizing dispersion. The Stoics, we can see, did not provide Plotinus with much more than an idiom—which furthermore allowed him to turn against Zeno and Chrysippus.

Freedom indeed, Plotinus repeats it often enough, always wills the singular, whereby one has hold of the "energy" (I transcribe the Greek) in the one, which obliges us to speak of union and of event, rather than of the one and its stasis (see the preceding chapter). Now if this is so, the simple henological bind is not only temporalized by the event, but *replicated by the undeniable.* All that stems from the one, all that can become a phenomenon, *also* stems from the inessential freedom. This "also" places it under a double bind without relief. To understand it, we must try to retrace the ascending procedure which leads from freedom in the Soul to freedom in the Intellect, and then to the singularizing energy in the one. The ascent—which, if to rise up means to maximize an essence, is not an ascent—bridges the disparities between phenomenal *givens.* But it does not lead to a simple origin without remainder, nor to an archic positional initiative. For the act of the one aggravates the disparity of the phenomenalizing-dephenomenalizing *traits.*

At each stage of this ascent, we will therefore see a strategy of singularization affirmed. We will also see the discontinuities hollowed out in the hypostatic architecture, for detachment singularizes otherwise than does solitude; and solitude otherwise than originary audacity. We will finally see if we can or cannot say that the one destitutes itself as a hegemonic fantasm through the obviousness of it own truth.

From detachment to solitude

For the Soul, being free means having the liberty to choose. It is different for the Intellect, which is free to reflect. Now, in Plotinus there is no generic concept of freedom embracing psychic and noetic acts, and even less the henic act. From choice, to reflection, then to the act originarily unsubmitted to essence, we do not rise to the comparative, then the superlative, of freedom.[64] The inquiry into conditions does not lead to any privileged meaning. But neither does it collapse into a pure and simple empirical observation of plural freedoms (not into a metaphysical *libertarianism*). Knowing that the one is always a union of multiple *givens* is not what will strike a blow at the henological administration; the blow comes rather from a counter-appearance, from a pull other than toward appearance and the obvious, which endangers the way in which the givens *give themselves.* The one becomes phenomenologically true through the knowledge of a condition which dephenomenalizes what appears. Anarchy wins here because throughout the whole architectonic, insubordination persists. From (psychic) detachment, to (noetic) solitude, to the audacity of inessential free willing (in the one), the *arché* withdraws to the extent that these polymorphic liberties press forward.

From detachment to solitude, I return from external to internal things; it is the only moment where I choose. In Plotinus it is also the only domain where one can speak of ethics. Once the return within has been accomplished, ethics has nothing left to say. The poles of the Soul and the Intellect stake it out and delimit it—poles of the *soul* and the *intellect,* rather, for this ethics sets up levels in the individual, not hypostases. Thus the only anagogic stage where one can say "I" and "we" is from detachment to solitude.

Some consequences for ethical discourse follow from this. Firstly, because this discourse is of very limited pertinence, only the soul has choice. The intellect, properly speaking, does not have any choice. Next, choosing is not just the act of the individual soul, it is above all the act by which the soul individualizes itself into "I" and "we." Finally, contrary to the subsequent notions of *arbitrium* or even *Willkür,* here choice is not directed toward this or that particular object of desire. It is not directed toward anything in the world, but on the world itself, as well as our relation to it.

We have a (psychic) choice between two ways of being. The individual soul can belong to the world of "expiring times," of "falling due" and thus of *caducités;* and it can gather itself up from its fall and falling due. What it cannot do is desire, either this particular being or any other one. The either-or does not place objects in front of a faculty of choice. Rather, freedom becomes its own issue. Thus putting myself at the mercy of incidents and vicissitudes—of what "falls within" and what "falls all around"—I abdicate all freedom. On the other hand, by retreating from their mercy, I acquire a (noetic) freedom where nothing befalls me. . . . I can either attach myself to the world until I blend into it in one mechanism, or I can detach myself from it until this mechanics no longer has a hold over me. When its grip relaxes, the other freedom is won—a reflexive, *principial* liberty.

When the soul chooses in this way, the ideal ordering supplants the representational automatism—it is a supplanting in which principial liberty is granted. "In someone who is filled with seminal liquid other images form themselves; and it is thus for all the vital liquids of the body. Now those who act according to those representations, we will not count among those who act from out of the autonomous principle (*eis archèn autexousion*)" (*En.* VI, 8 [39], 3, 15ff.). If we let ourselves be determined by delegates (they are not just imprints) of foreign forces that are in us, it will be the hydraulic regime of secretions that are binding us by imaginary scenarios. On the other hand, if we determine ourselves from out of ourselves (*eph' hêmin, ep' autois*[65]), it will be the archic regime of reflections that unbinds us by obvious idealities. More or less agitated saps arouse representations; by paying attention to them we become lost in the heteronomous. More or less centered reflection soothes the representations; paying attention to the forms reveals "that which depends on us," whereby we gain autonomy.

Here is how the soul-intellect gap delimits ethics. The loquacious discourse of the latter falls beyond *noûs.* The otherness of noetic freedom halts it—this is essential freedom which, alone, merges with necessity. The intelligence that hearkens to ideas is supremely free; it knows no other measure than the return to itself whereby it accomplishes what alone is necessary. It initiates and directs the choices of the soul, which amounts to saying that by determining it, principial freedom ends the ethos.

In the Intellect, the practical framework of choosing disappears; beyond the Intellect, it is the framework of freedom-necessity which becomes irrelevant. In Plotinus, one cannot act "in the name of the one" (not ethically or morally, in any case;

tragically, it will be another question, but one in which the noun is effaced). The noetic function, since it determines ethics in the last instance and ends it, is thus also a disruptive function. The whole semantic field of the noun, with the semantics of authority that it holds, is applied to *noûs* alone.

So the nominative power is eclipsed, as we always say in henology, because the one is ineffable. Because it does not appear among beings, it cannot be named. But more profoundly and phenomenologically, the authoritative noun is lost, because the one is not simple. It never unifies without there being a remainder or future. "Freedom," "will," "audacity," "nondescript" are so many words to suggest what remains—the ultimate that remains, the one once it is grasped as union. "Singularization to come," "always imminent dephenomenalization and demanifestation," "transgression," "mortality" are words that indicate a contretemps in the union that would also belong to this group.

The semantic ruptures which vary "freedom"—and which break its univocal concept—problematize the singular in diverse ways. One advances toward solitude like one moves from allo-determination to auto-determination and like one moves from *I* and *we* to *types* of "me" and "us."

Allo-determination singularizes us most evidently. The other draws us outside, but it does not attract us *from* outside. If Plotinus explained heteronomy by a theory of stimulants and of their impressions, then he would open the way to a causality inconceivable in henology—a material causality, efficacious from outside and below. Common people (*phauloi*) do not exactly yield to stimuli coming from elsewhere. The liquids in their vessels and communicating capillaries cause singular images to appear in them, by which their willing (*thelein*) lets itself be solicited in turn. Images nevertheless have being only through the freedom that wills them. They are nothing unless we follow after them and cultivate their connections and linkings so as to magnify the agreeableness or disagreeableness felt by the circulation of humors. These foreign delegates exercise influence only so long as we grant them an abode. To cultivate them is to establish oneself in a world which is essentially null and void.

Through *freedom of choice* either I singularize myself by assenting to the world, or I universalize myself out of the world. Ethical knowledge exhausts itself in this alternative (the freedom of the one does not therefore signify anything anthropomorphic—the one neither chooses nor reflects). Abandon your thought, your memory, your discourse, and your acting to imaginary associations and your autonomy will be gone. The indistinct influx of images, an influx which accompanies inflammations, drowns this *principial freedom* which the ancient Greeks already used to distinguish and discriminate (between citizens and slaves first of all): *eleutheria*. Choice intervenes in the associative current which threatens to inundate the evidence; choice revolves around the either-or of a certain dependence with regard to that current, and around a certain independence; and it results either in subjugation to waves of images, investment, and fixation, or in principial freedom. It is a matter of *arché,* again: I chose—and chose again, according to habit and training—either hetero-archy, or autarchy.

In allo-determination, the force of the singular can be seen without difficulty. This is so because by freely abdicating principial freedom, we yield to the constraint of fantasms (*phantasia anankazousa,* ibid. 2, 17). These come to us, diversely pathogenic. Some of them are easy to relinquish, others less so. In all of them, we look at ourselves "in Dionysus' mirror, so to speak."[66] If choice intervenes in the associative flow, it is that the matter of the letting-be—in which Plotinian ethics can be summarized—is given by plural affects (*ta pathêmata*). And whoever says "plurality" says "aggregate of singulars." The worldly "I" is constituted by accumulations. That is why it keeps changing.

Faced with dispersion, which the soul sticking to the world wills, auto-determination appears first as a conquest of the universal: as auto-universalization. The intellect rules in ethics because it is the bearer of types. Whence follows the task of leaving images and holding to types. Necessarily bound by ideas, the soul must still become what it is. This axiom, as old as Platonism, states the condition, as much as the goal, of theoretical conversion. The soul must choose to think of itself in terms of its archetype which frees it, rather than in terms of the images which affect it and consign it to the world. Then it becomes detached, as it already is naturally. Hence the question: "If by principle the soul is not subjected to affects, why then seek to deprive it of affects by means of philosophy?" The answer: "If we admit that the soul is a principle which uses the body, we separate it."[67] By nature, the soul is separate from the world, that is, from the body and society. It is present to them only by mixture, by compromise and compromising. Hence the exhortation to separate it from them further still; an exhortation to solitude, under which Plotinus places all that one calls practice. The ethical good thus consists in advancing from a bad singularization to another, good one.

Strangers to that through which we fantasize, we must still become strangers to our fantasms. We must detach ourselves from the hallucinatory singulars (pulling ourselves "to and fro") and from their swarm whose droning drives us wild. Whoever would go to the end of that *mad singularization*—to the end of dispersion through allegiance to images—would lose their identity. Whereas by detaching myself from images, I constitute myself in my *ethical singularity.* On this hinges the life of the soul, which is *theôria*—the consideration of the world in its intelligible architectonic. By hearkening to fantasms, we make death belabor us. The soul dies to what it is "in principle." A loss and a death which, in truth, are always and already borne. Hence the stronger call, which aggravates choice, to mature with an eye toward another birth.[68] To advance the cause of natality is to advance according to the trait of natality down to and including causes. . . . This is the soul which, as this trait has it, remembers that the hypostatic Intellect—the site of all causes—will conquer the universal and thereby defeat death. It will defeat *its* death, the death of the soul, the extinction of the idol in it. Solitude will be salutary for it.

That is how, in ethical choices, formal *attraction*—literally in-forming and so conforming—struggles against the deforming *retraction.* By anagogic displacements, Plotinus will carry the struggle all the way into the origin beyond the ethical principle, up into the one. In ethics, noetic freedom is what begins and commands. Yet, this freedom is not ultimate, and that which is ultimate neither begins nor commands. Rebellious against essence, it disrupts any formation from within. Its audacity gives rise to the nondescript, the ineffable and yet best-known figure of the singular.

This can be seen in certain thetic incoherences in the "will of the self," which bear witness to how the one cannot be simple. They notably affect auto-eroticism (*hautoû erôs*), in which the entire treatise on the freedom and will of the one appears to be summed up: "It is at once [the object] which arouses love and loving desire, for it is self-love" (*En*. VI, 8 [39], 15, 1). To say it straight off: The return to oneself that these lines imply breaks the simplicity of the one, but not by the ethics of *erôs,* or by the dialectics of *noûs*. What breaks it is that freedom withdraws from the one. This drawing away situates noetic reflexivity, just as it again situates psychic dispersion. This breach in the one thus begins any singularization tearing phenomenalization asunder. Originary audacity fractures archic simplicity. At the start of freedom, there is an act which wills the counter-law of the rebellious nondescript.

At first, the various formulations with *'auto'*- may be able to suggest to certain readers a rough sketch of the "self" in Plotinus. By focusing on the intellectual part in the soul the individual would become himself, conquering the singular self—a stable form behind the I, acquired by assimilation to the idea. Doesn't Plotinus say, for example, that "to be immaterial, isolated from the body. . . ," is "to be in oneself" (*kath' hauto, En*. V, 1 [10], 10, 20)? Analogous formulas abound. Don't they paint a picture that describes autarchy as it results from detachment? Might one not have here a premodern candidate for the self—interior man, emancipated from the servitude of images, in conformity with his own *eidos*? Plotinus would enlist such a self each time he opposes the detached soul to the soul combined with the body.

Such a retrodictive reading from a concretion—in this case, the self—of the modern hegemonic fantasm always remains a highly risky operation. It is easy to dissipate. To be brief and to note only the grammatical misinterpretation, here this reading tends to confuse the pronoun and the noun. In the affirmations of immateriality, the "being in itself" is *predicated* by the soul not mixed with the body (principial freedom is thus "subjected to the noetic essence"; that is why it will not be pure). Plotinus does not speak *of the self.* And of the individual, he prefers to speak in the plural, thus underscoring its essential ideal multiplicity.

More difficult to dissipate is the schema of reflexivity behind self-love. Plotinus draws and redraws this schema and then he erases it just as diligently. During the course of this sketching, reflexivity changes its profile and is transmuted into transgressivity. In order to notice this, we need only observe how the self-willing structure is sketched out in the hypostases so as to undergo such distortion in the one that the drawing comes undone. Let us take it up again, then. What remains, in effect, is the problem of noetic singularization. The solitude of spirit thematizes in a barren way the incongruity of the one loving itself—and thus willing itself—but not reflecting itself.

From which premises does detachment result, and where does it lead? If the soul were to separate itself from the body entitatively, that would be death; but if it were to separate itself from the body by learning solitude, that would be the life of its life.

The premises are easy to see: The soul is from elsewhere; by being combined (*syntithêmi*) with the body, it only finds a lesser good; by dying, it accedes to its native good. "[L]ife in the body is by itself an evil, but by virtue, the soul enters into the good, no longer living a life of combination then, but already preparing to separate itself" (*En.* I, 7 [54], 3, 19ff.). The soul can be more or less alive, detaching itself more or less from the calls which disperse it. It is a question of mixture, for by giving way to affects, it follows forces which do not come from itself. Mixture thus opposes itself strictly to separation, and requires it. The secret of life lies in the distancing of oneself—and the secret of principial freedom resides in the insubordination toward the world which binds us through the accommodations we have already made. Non-entitative separation is detachment (which is the translation of *chôrismos,* and is more appropriate in Plotinus than "separation," since in him the word answers first the question: How are we to live?). If one wishes to speak of Plotinian ethics, it must be brought back to detachment. To love oneself well, one must withdraw from desires and mixed inertias. Images to which we are always already attached arise from concessions to this jumble; detachment itself, and with it principial self-love, is always yet to come.

If ethics, the doctrine of living well, is summed up in detachment, it also risks becoming muddled there, but not because of some hostility to the body which would betray itself in detachment. Such a hostility would hardly be in accord with the praise of gentleness. Rather, detachment runs the risk of muddling living well insofar as Plotinus ties it to the will, and, it seems, to a will folding back on itself, coming close to itself with love—and thus that he ties it to a reflexive will. Eros abolishes distances better than does vision. Self-love does not require that one maintain distance as does looking at oneself.[69] Only, erotic proximity harbors ruin along with joy. Plato, for good reasons, abolished desire in the possession of the good. Eros is terrified and terrifying: If it comes to possess that which it loves, it will have to disappear. The suitor collapses in the grasp. Desire then slips into memory; as for willing, it shifts to the pluperfect. The summit of happiness belongs to the gods alone who know neither the distance of willing, nor the withdrawal into oneself of self-willing, and thus neither the collapse of the having-willed, nor the terror of the having-willed to come. The soul on the path of deification "will have willed." Deified, it will have erased all traces of desire, love, and will from itself. Inversely, for the love of the good to subsist, desire must remain desire, and will must remain will; the distance must remain gaping and the cessation of willing—the having-willed—to come must remain terrifying. There is a consequence of this erotic dialectic—if Plotinus means that the origin *wills itself,* he could hardly posit it as *possessing itself* as well. To will oneself is to desire oneself and thus *not* to possess oneself. In the one "which loves itself," then, something other than a resumption of the dialectic of Platonic eros will occur. The one taking pleasure in itself (Eros, son of Abundance) will not be able to will itself as well (Eros, son of Lack). Auto-willing would be the undoing of auto-possession. Hence the terror (*ekplexis*[70]). We have been able to say that, in the Plotinian one, "the will attains its highest goal: itself." The one would be understood as the "auto-desiring principle."[71] Such a reflexivity of the will and of desire always only amount to an extrapolation of the structure of *noûs*. As such, we are not really speaking of the one. If there is here a willing in the one, reflexivity proves inescapable, but nevertheless it is impossible, if the one is to be a simple position. Incongruity undoes structuration through a return to self. It is an utter mistake, a powder thrown into eyes fixed on Principles, to maintain that in the one, to will oneself means to posit oneself simply. Reflexivity will never salvage archic theticism. On the contrary, it ruins its simplicity. Unavoidable and yet impossible, the relation to oneself indicates well and truly that the free will opens a breach in the one through which a non-dialectical otherness filters, together with terror. As for the powder, we shall return to it by examining that which rightly menaces the one: atomism.

The argument which seeks to explain simple auto-position by the reflexive will nevertheless has, at first blush, something plausible about it. The same rearrangement of Platonism which gives to separation a reflexive sense—when "to separate" means "to detach *oneself*"—inaugurates once more the problematic of the self-will. Furthermore, according to the hierarchical scheme which passes for being the substantial core of Neoplatonism, that which lies at the bottom of the scale must be found at the top; the structure of the return to oneself would thus be imprinted on each hypostasis. Reflexivity in the one would be paradigmatic for the other levels of being. Just as the soul detaches *itself* and the intellect reflects *itself*, according to their nature, so does the one will *itself* (willing-willed, it is even termed "cause of self," *En.* VI, 8 [39], 14, 41). If the structure of a reflexive willing were to hold, it would extend a fundamental voluntarism throughout the architecture of the world. Such a reading would go only too well with the repeated insistence on the auto-engendering of the one (*En.* VI, 8 [39], 7, 53, etc.). Thus one would not be wrong to suspect that the discovery of detachment entails the discovery of the intransitive will (and, in a sense, of the will *tout court*), and not the reverse. This double discovery marks the turning toward interiority in late antiquity. One would be completely mistaken, on the other hand, to suspect that the soul should, or even could, increase the distance; that precisely in their simultaneous entrance on stage, detachment and the will would get configured as voluntarism, and that the interiority of the will would trace out the reflexivity of the Intellect by spreading it throughout the levels of being. The return to self, an act proper to the noetic hypostasis, puts an end to ethical discourse and consequently shuts off the problematic of willing essences. The one wills itself, it loves itself, but *therein* lies nothing essential anymore. It would be absurd to maintain that "the beyond" of essence becomes thinkable by projecting into it principial freedom, and thus the structure of the (Aristotelian) Intellect knowing itself. A corollary to this absurdity: If the act of the one meant the actualization of a power—and if, consequently, the phenomenal world "objectified" the will of the one as originary reflexive power—then Plotinus would be offering something like a formative metaphysics, and the title "Of the Freedom and Will of the One" would propel him straight into nineteenth-century Germany. In Plotinus, the origin wills itself; but, devoid of an essence, it *is* not willed, and there is no design organizing it. In the absence of essence and of structure, the one does not dialecticize anything at all—neither eros, nor intellection. In nevertheless positing an originary willing, Plotinus thus disturbs, at once and in the same thetic gesture, the metaphysical serenity of the one.

This is so because, as he posits it, the will of the one is not inferred, then maximized beginning with a theory of human powers. In order to see how much this free will disorients us, all one need do is ask where detachment leads. The answer: to solitude through interior autarchy, which is the life of our life of the mind. Now, in a system of descending causality, this fecund solitude can only result from ideal imitation. The soul detaches itself from the images-fixation-world-body-affects-attachments-tumult-dispersion-multiplicity-suffering complex by turning back toward its idea, and thus toward subsistent reflexivity. It is a return and a turning which transmute freedom of choice into principial freedom, and detachment into solitude. The latter will be transmuted in turn by *epekeina* beyond the Intellect. Already in the self-sufficient solitude of the mind, the will has nothing more to do with an attribute of a subject, with a faculty of a substance, nor with the perfection of an essence. In the one, it has nothing more to do—or only by misuse—with the return to self. It is a poor reading of Plotinus to detect in him some hyperbolization of anthropological will and freedom, then of noetic reflection. In the one, will and freedom will signify a distance-taking in the same. The lesson of solitude teaches that the Intellect only *re*flects because it *in*flects an originary otherness which is impossible to subsume under the scheme of reflexivity. In terms of an analytic of ultimates, there is spiritual solitude only because a coming disintegration first of all belabors from within every aggregate making a world.

Although it is non-reflexive—or rather, *because* it is non-reflexive—the breach in the aggregating one remains open. Freedom will have to be grasped there otherwise than according to the ethics of *erôs* and the dialectics of *noûs*—it will have to be grasped as an audacity that disintegrates because it temporalizes.

How then does the singular appear going from detachment to solitude?

The Soul's step backwards toward the Intellect, from which it differs and which it imitates, suffices to show how little *thelêma* is voluntaristic. The solitude in which the Intellect is singularized breaks hypostatically with the detachment in which the Soul is singularized. This is why detachment is thinkable only in a *differential theory of the singular.* This theory gives the—non-modern—context both to freedom of choice, that is, to attachment converted into detachment, and to principial freedom, that is, to a psychic appetite that has passed over into noetic willing. But there are differences and singularities only because in the one, there is first of all a differend.

Thus, at the level of the Soul, bad singularization consists in being dispersed according to the affects endured, and good singularization in being detached; at the level of the Intellect, bad singularization consists in being curious about innumerable ideas, and good singularization in received solitude, ". . . for one must not act" (*deî de mêden prattein, En.* I, 9 [16], 10). This is still an ethical axiom, but, as one can see, it is hardly "voluntaristic."

Plotinus describes the psychic singular which one must abandon, preferably as an *eidôlon:* 'idol,' deformed idea, impoverished image, reflection, copy. The detachment which leads from bad singularization to good solitude begins with the gaze. For deformations to disappear and for the soul to return to good form, it must stop watching out for compromising situations. The soul learns to detach itself by practicing at looking elsewhere: "It lets its copy go, not by cutting it off from itself, but insofar as [the copy] ceases to be; now, it ceases to be when [the soul] directs its gaze entirely up there" (*En.* I, 1 [53], 12, 29ff.). The difference between *eidôlon* and *eidos* marks out the ethical field. Outside of this field occurs the utterly other singularization where free willing renders phenomenality precarious by the imminence of the nondescript.

What sort of singularization does curiosity effect? At the level of the Intellect, *the infinite is redoubled.* Plotinus has devoted a treatise to the question: "Are there ideas of singular things?" (*En.* V, 7 [18]). Its answer argues for their profusion. Plotinus allows for ideas, not only for each thing, but also for the singular properties of each singular soul. He reassures his audience twice: "[O]ne must not be frightened by that infinity" (ibid. 1, 26 and 3, 21). Thus there is something frightening about it . . . it is a non-Pascalian fright, for we lift our gaze not toward the immensity of space, but toward the models. What do we see there? "Once again, infinity" (*to apeiron anapalin,* ibid. 3,23). The amassing of noetic singulars replicates that of psychic singulars and intellectualizes curiosity. Individual forms form two swarms. And it is indeed numeric infinity which is multiplied by two. It is a counter-strategy of noetic *profusion,* which does not easily go with the *centering* function proper to the Intellect, and from which the good noetic singularization results. The discrepancy between these traits introduces a struggle right into solitude. Reflexive presence to self, to which detachment leads, thus does not equal peace. It equals the *agôn,* the model for detachment. The return *to* myself not only universalizes me, it singularizes and also even disperses me; in this, the return conceals in itself a return *against* the self.

Singularization makes all the difference, and all difference. Psychic hallucination is geometric suffering: images pour in, obeying no order. Noetic fright is arithmetic suffering: ideas are strung together, not obeying number. Henological terror, lastly, is logical suffering: the one posits itself and juxtaposes to itself an act, but here this other of the one is not the other of the same.

"Fleeing alone towards the Alone." On these words the *Enneads,* as arranged by Porphyry, come to an end (*En.* VI, 9 [9], 11, 50). Now, there is solitude and solitude, and yet again solitude . . .

a. "When souls turn away from the whole and, as if tired of the community, turn towards their singular and proper being, then each retires into its reserve" (*En.* IV, 6 [6], 4, 10ff.). Souls tired by dispersion are *isolated* . This is a bad solitude, a consequence of corporeal mixture.

b. Inversely, the soul finds a good singularity when it returns to the whole by regaining courage, when it takes hold of itself so as to reintegrate the ideal community. Let the soul be detached from images, return into itself by reflection, appropriate noetic being, and it will find fulfillment, sheltering, rest: the solitude which is plenitude.

In the Intellect emancipated of all action, we may grasp "what depends on us" (*En.* VI, 8 [39], 2, 34). We are principially free in the genesis of our thought. A life rendered thoroughly transparent will thus find its principle in itself. It will have reached the supreme goal toward which all the Ancients strove, whether they gave priority to political life or contemplation—the goal which autarchy is. Being *solitary* is an essential description of the Intellect. It separates singulars and gathers them under their genera, their ideas, their laws—this is precisely what constitutes principial freedom.

Hence there is a solitude beneficial to freedom which is like the test for authentic experience. Whoever reflects is detached and becomes solitary with happiness. For the Stoics, such was the first test of the wise man (an ordeal which no one ever passed, but that is another problem . . .). Ontological separation, like ethical detachment, approaches this solitude. And reflection does not stop at its edge. That solitude is beneficial which brings about a return to self and which, thereby, makes one independent. The Intellect finds in itself everything that is—essentially reflexive, it escapes need.

Now, solitude can only be *ethically* good for the soul because it is *essentially* good for the intellect. The good of the soul consists in becoming stabilized on the originary idea of itself in itself. It accedes to its freedom when it consents to let the origin it bears in itself reign in it alone. "Origin" should always be understood in the strictly hypostatic sense: As delegates of the world, coming from outside, the images that the soul harbors distract it; but these very images, as reflections originating above it and linked together according to the laws discovered by reflection, center the origin. As we have seen, the Intellect contains the individual models;[72] for that, the ethics of the return does not first require a universalization,[73] but an ethically good singularization; the happiness of the solitary.

c. The one, itself, is not solitary, but *alone*. So, the final word of the *Enneads,* already quoted, can also be translated as "flight from the solitary towards the alone."[74] All in all, the one is in a way outside genera.[75] But there too, from psychic isolation to the noetically solitary, then to henic aloneness, solitude is not maximized. The one is alone in that the world to which it grants phenomenality at every turn occurs here and now.

From the Intellect to the one, solitude thus undergoes a discontinuity of sense and direction. This new incidence of *epekeina* must be examined because it deals with the opposing argument, to which Plotinus devotes the major part of the treatise on the freedom and the will of the one.

We will understand this argument and its premises poorly unless we remembers that, from the Soul to the Intellect, henology moves back toward the essential *conditions* of phenomena—but also that the step back from the Intellect to the one is *heterogeneous* with regard to this search for conditions. It leads to an event, to the manifestation—the coming to presence—of a manifest world. This event is not simple. It situates all things under the phenomenalizing attraction of the one as well as under the singularizing retraction of the free will in it.

From stabilizing solitude to temporalizing audacity

Here is the opposing argument which gives Plotinus so much difficulty: "[the one] is only by chance the way it is; it does not possess sovereignty over what it is; what it is, it is not from out of itself; consequently, neither freedom nor self-disposition come back to it" (*En.* VI, 8 [39], 7, 11–15). The one is only one by chance—this sums up the objection. Given the vehemence with which Plotinus refutes it, it hardly can have been formulated by him in a sort of thought-experiment.[76] Having doubly cut off the *hen* from the mobile world, he would hardly have devoted fifteen chapters out of twenty-one to toying with the hypothesis of its contingency. Let us immediately add that the hypothesis of originary chance is doubtless inspired by atomism—if not by a specific school (it could only be that of Epicurus, then), at least by that tradition in general.[77]

Now, why would atomism, the theory of an originary powder ceaselessly configuring and reconfiguring the world, stir Plotinus so deeply? Might there be something in henology to which atomism *comes very close* but whose proximity, neglecting a certain decisive discontinuity, would *distort* everything? Could it be that the abyss that separates the nondescript from the contingent is the smallest of abysses—of which Nietzsche will say that it is also the most difficult to cross and, at first, to recognize as an abyss?

It so happens that Plotinus names what happens on both sides of the abyss. The abyss is actually not large: The same word designates what takes place on both sides. Therefore the smallest abyss will separate two senses of the same noun, but two dissymmetrical, incongruous senses irreducible to some determinate negation: there is a sense that is, so to speak, "maladjusted," and then another one. The fault line cuts straight into the denotation of the word *tolma*. It may be translated as 'courage,' 'audacity,' 'temerity'. . . . How should the atomist argument be characterized? "*Tolmèros*" (*En*. VI, 8 [39], 7, 11). It is a reckless argument. And how does Plotinus counter the argument? In the *Ennead* that follows the one on the freedom and will of the one, he takes up the polemic against the holders of "chance and luck" in the constitution of the world.[78] His reaction is just as lively: "To those people we do not speak" (*En*. VI, 9 [9], 5, 1ff.). Then he addresses his own "people." Why speak to them? So that they learn to consider the Soul, then to understand that it comes from an other nature, the Intellect. They have to know that the Intellect is not simple. This knowledge will make them grasp "the marvel which is before the Intellect—the one." His people therefore know, or are ready to learn, that the world is stable and hierarchical, and that it culminates in a pinnacle able to overjoy whoever receives the grace of considering it. Now, how is one to grasp that marvel beginning with the Intellect? He gives a rather unexpected answer—by understanding that the Intellect "had the audacity to withdraw from the one" (ibid. 29ff.). *Tolma,* again. But it no longer is a matter of the temerity proper to such and such group of maladjusted persons or to some particular reasoning about the composition of the world. It is about an audacity which is not a human audacity; which is predicated by nobody; which is not even conceived according to anthropological, ethical, or metaphysical schemes. We recall that the hypostatic Intellect puts an end to all of these schemata. The word *tolma,* 'audacity,' says a commentator, describes here "the particularization of the Intellect beginning with the one."[79] It describes an originary process in the one, from which the first production emerges: otherness. It is *the* originary process, for, step by step, with otherness winning, audacity spreads. The ascending way, along which Plotinus just led his audience with a view to their spiritual regeneration, is also descended by him to show them the penury in which their adversaries are vegetating. The descent follows the guiding thread of audacity. Thus the Intellect comes from the one, by audacity; souls in turn distance themselves from the Intellect, by audacity again (*En.* V, 1 [10], 1, 4). The first otherness is in relation to the Intellect, followed by a second alterity, on the margins of the universe. There, where everything crumbles, the Intellect has the audacity to make itself an "other intellect." Taking the most extreme distance from the light that it bears in itself, it "sees what does not belong to it"—the obscure, the shapeless, the material (*En.* I, 8 [51], 9, 15–19). Audacity designates the "spirit" which, from the one all the way to matter, fractures each hypostasis so as to make possible that which will succeed it.

Let us note that if the Intellect can thus make itself other to the extent of even seeing the night, it must be because it already bears the night within it. The henology which, to give an account of otherness, cannot do without the audacity in the one, can neither, in the Intellect, do without an obscure depth, "shapeless and undetermined." This is intelligible matter. It is "entirely black [. . .], it being understood that, from the intelligible to the sensible world, obscurity differs totally." This is a differential conception of matter; as sensible, matter is the "mysterious principle"[80] of all extension in space and time; as intelligible, it is a mysterious principle again (co-constitutive, here, of forms as plurals). *And in the one*? Plotinus himself suggests the question. Black intelligible matter as well as formal light, he says, "*have both come to be, insofar as they have an origin*" (*En.* II, 4 [12], 5, 1–14 and 25). Would it be pursuing the differential conception of matter too far to ask what is, in the one, the origin of the formless and the indeterminate? Is this not where the most urgent question lies once we understand that otherness is not foreign to the one? Otherwise, isn't the answer all too obvious? Indeed, how could we not trace the formless back to the inessential act which, in the one, withdraws from pure light and prefigures there—or, since no figure is there yet, prepares there—all darkenings? Then, with audacity, the night would penetrate even into the sun of the sun. Moreover, it would arise there, it would stem from there.

Understood in this way—and it is now the key to glimpsing the manner in which the free will indicates originary time—audacity is just one word among others for suggesting the motion of withdrawing in the one, a movement that is inevitable precisely because the one must be posited as simple. It is precisely through its auto-position that the one loses simplicity and institutes the double bind. The free will, like audacity, expresses this counter-law in the one: "The origin of evil [for souls] was their audacity, their entrance into becoming, the first otherness, therefore the will to belong to them" *En.* V, 1 [10], 1, 4ff.). Audacity, the will to belong to oneself, entrance into becoming, obscurity, shadow of the first night, otherness: Plotinus enumerates a series of conditions which express how the ultimate focal distance becomes disarrayed. Indeed we have to see that the disarray results from the very theticism according to which the referent "is posited" or "willed" as simple. Its relation to itself blemishes its simplicity.

We have to rely on the very terms of a series when seeking to understand the one by way of the other. As for the title of the treatise, *On the Freedom and Will of the One,* it inserts only two members into the series of contrary factors which serve to separate the one from itself. The title must be understood in terms of other constituent elements. It says, in the one, there are two allies of audacity.

Plotinus divides up the semantic field of this word in such a way that maladjusted *tolma* answers to henic *tolma*. Reckless argument answers to the audacity in the one, from which all disjunction, all otherness, all incongruity, all disarrayment of the world arises—in short, from which its tragic condition stems.

We can see how, regarding the archic question, atomism might indeed come dangerously close to henology.

Ancient atomism responded to the dilemma of the immutable and motion. It claimed to resolve this dilemma by explaining the mutability of phenomena in terms of absolutely primitive elements entering into variable constellations. These particles remain invariable in themselves. The rudimentary indivisible constituents assure the immutability in change: Identical to themselves, they ceaselessly shift around to form, deform, and reform groups of every magnitude—the visible world. Most of the consequences ensuing from atomism obviously have nothing which might threaten henology or even touch a nerve. Gods composed of atoms; the plurality of universes and their periodic disintegrations; the absence of qualitative multiplicity and thus of hierarchies; the impossibility of a divine agent guiding events. . . . There is in all this no affinity with henology. The world of Plotinus is stable throughout, and only the individual soul can move around in it. Above all, in a universe which holds together by the simple presence of the one, there will be no place for an originary dust. In it, the origin can be only one. And it is a tautology to say that henology is opposed to atomism like a doctrine of the one is opposed to a doctrine of the multiple.

And yet, we have seen that for the one to be posited as the law of laws, an inessential surplus of actuality is necessary *by which* it would thus be posited—therefore, *which* would posit it thus. This results from what Plotinus describes as desire, as love, as willing to take pleasure in oneself. There is a surplus of an act, which contaminates and destitutes the "marvel," even while it is refining and instituting it. The surplus can only keep desire unsatiated, love burning, will unexhausted, and *erôs* terrified. For the one to be one, the free willing "of" the one (subjective genitive) must keep its distance "from" (objective genitive) the one which it wills and posits. If that distance were obliterated in a uniformly successful theticism, therefore in some First taking pleasure in itself fully, that would be the undoing of love. The double genitive function spoils thetic simplicity. Through the erotic will, terror turns the one against itself—not a human terror, but rather a structural, henological terror. It follows from the *hautoû erôs,* from positive auto-eroticism. The will, however, is posited to make the one radiate in its pure originary sufficiency—the one is free because it wills to be such as it is and because it is such as it wills to be (*En.* VI, 8 [39], 18, 49; 13, 55). This will, on the contrary, can only obscure the brilliance of the one and transgress its focalization.

Atomism would threaten henology if freedom, self-love, will to belong to oneself, audacity, entry into becoming, otherness . . . designated *forces* in the one.[81] Then this ultimate referent indeed would owe its institution to a configuration of indivisible elements. Hence the treatise opens with the question of forces: "Is it possible, even for the gods, to inquire into whether something depends on them? Or, rather, must such a question be restricted to humans and their doubtful forces?" Plural forces which, so they can be spoken of with regard to the one, Plotinus hastens to reduce to the singular: "Or should force only be granted to the one?" (*En*. VI, 8 [39], 1, 1 and 5). This is a rhetorical question, which, for the first six chapters, staves off the hypothesis concerning conflicts in the one.

The hypothesis is imposed anew at the moment Plotinus lays into the reckless objection. "How would we trace the one, from which all beings draw their forces, back to that which is in your free disposition or in mine" (ibid. 7, 8)? This is again a rhetorical question, and again it is supposed to stave off the hypothesis that would make the one fall under the jurisdiction of plural forces. He never treats this hypothesis on its own.

This does not prevent there being an ambiguity beginning with the title: the freedom *and* the will . . . how should this "and" be taken? Moreover, what should be done with the series of factors that put the focal distance in disarray: audacity *and* otherness *and* obscurity *and* entry into becoming *and* self-love *and* will to belong to oneself *and* freedom. . . ? Coordinating conjunctions do not accumulate through mere literary redundancy. Nor are they brought into line by invisible equal signs. For the one to be posited as one, plural strategies are required in the one itself.

We see that atomism might strike a sensitive nerve in Plotinus. We can also speak of audacity in the one as if it were a force.[82] To be sure, the hypothesis would only be authentically atomistic if the forces had engendered the one. Now, nothing entitles one to speak of forces in the sense of primitive entities. Then does the repeated *and* amount to an amassing? All along, I have treated the *and* which appears in the title as signifying "that-is-to-say"—"The freedom, that is to say, the will, of the one." Understood as such, the title would straightaway and synthetically denote the "free will." It seems to me that the same reading must be applied to the enumerated series. Only then does the question rebound: If they do not substitute a dust cloud of atomic forces for the one, but *vary one single originary dislocation,* toward what do these counter-strategies in the one point?

In order to offer an answer, we need to read it again: "The Intellect had in some way the audacity to withdraw from the one" (*En*. VI, 9 [9], 5, 29). An alienating audacity *in the one* that produces the other of the one (*prôtê heterotês*). The Intellect first had the audacity of an essential otherness, that which defines beings—the otherness between intelligent and intelligible. Then it dared to be multiple, abounding in forms. Audacity is the *logos* which makes one pass[83] from the one to beings; it is thus the co-*logos* of beings. This is an audacity which gets worse as it goes along, since it spreads throughout the whole architecture. It digs out the intervals—the "apostases"—between hypostases. Audacity is the very principle of all that distances, alienates, pluralizes, and, in this direction—a descending direction, the outcome of which is matter—of all that singularizes. In the descending direction, separation—again—has nothing good about it. To be is audacious from the point of view of the one, and the singularization that ensues, is a work of death.

Does the will to be other then signify a sort of revolt against the one? Might willing arrive on the philosophical scene in the form of a No? Beings would be rebelling against the one, willing to be the non-one.

Such an oppositional dialectic, as we have seen, is not the thought of Plotinus. If it were, the will would introduce antithesis into the one itself. Now, it introduces singularization, the work of death, and therefore *time* into it. Audacity must be thought otherwise than as negation. It emphasizes the principle of overabundance throughout the entire hypostatic architecture. Auto-eroticism exists not as something sterile, but as hyper-fecundity itself. What follows is the necessity to think of death, as well as singularization which is its effect, as something other than as simple extinction. Souls do not die; only their idol dies. Plotinus obliges us to think the trait of mortality as a trait of glory. He sees the originary flash spreading throughout what we know only as the strategy of death—a flash which he describes as the audacity and free will of the one. Literally a "flash," for union is always made suddenly (*exaiphnes*). It is an instant out of time, which is not simple—the strategy of centering on the one (natality) is allied with the *contre-temps* which singularization (mortality) is. It is an originary instant as well, from which all memory and all hope come to us.

This is a difficult and perhaps unprecedented thought: The origin gives a "theoretical" coherence (that is, "considerable," "presenting itself to be considered") to the universe, but only at the price of an initial incoherence. It is a thought of mortality which does not at any level abolish the counter-strategy that is in dissension with natality, nor does it reify immortality. Indeed, the Intellect implicates and replicates the trait of mortality, as solitude; but originarily this trait is folded into the one as the free will. Death as we know it, itself, deploys this trait ontically.

The step backwards from the Intellect toward the one always destabilizes the ascending movement from the Soul. Herein lies the spirit of Plotinian thought. Hence, to withdraw from principial freedom toward the free one is to break with ethics. It is to pass outside the demarcated and demarcatable spheres. Generic descriptions, which are most germane to the physics and metaphysics received from Aristotle, must be expunged, as not germane, in order to think the freedom of the one. Even "negation" will not be the clever word for this other step backwards. Differing from the procedures at which the pseudo-Dionysus will excel, Plotinus moves back toward a referent which is neither supreme due to being maximized, nor above all simple and giving rise to adoration. The anagogic procedure which follows the clue of freedom instead arrives at a strange originary supplement. It arrives at the one compared to which there is nothing more universal—*and again* at the act of willing to be, an act compared to which there is nothing more singular, singularizing, or perturbing to simplicity. Ethics, religion, psychology, metaphysics, suffer no harm from it, which is fortunate. . . . We have indeed seen that from the Intellect—in which the discourse of those disciplines ends—to the one, the mimetic continuity comes undone. The rise toward the one is not etiological. It does not make one pass from the positive to a comparatively causal mediation, and then to the superlative causal instance. To conceive it as cause of the world is to have already misunderstood the freedom of the one. Something entirely other occurs when, from principial and noetic freedom, Plotinus rises back to the freedom and will of the one. An *originary dysfunction* occurs, which subjects the one to the attack of the nondescript and of time.

"*Quodlibet ens* is not exactly 'being, little matter which', but 'being, which matters in every way'; in other words, it already presumes a reference to the will (*libet*): indefinite being maintains an original relation with desire."[84] The desirable *begins* with the nondescript, a beginning which, in Plotinus, is described as free willing. Free willing designates the one, like a pencil stroke directs attention toward a point marked on a white background, indicating "This is important." Which "this"? The "this" that is the event of union—of phenomena entering into constellation—each time and everywhere it occurs. This occurrence is turned by willing into the ultimate desirable singular. The one is nondescript in the strong sense: *in willing.* Free willing (which has nothing to do, to say it again, with the arbitrary, the faculty of the good, or some psychic or noetic power) thus overloads the one with an indetermination. The nondescript clouds it over, not by a first evil, but by the *singularizing contre-temps* which the satiated-insatiable will introduces into it. Thus penetrated by night, the one becomes nondescript.

Desire and will of what? Love of what? Which freedom? With transitivity lacking in the one, and reflexivity aborting itself there, there remains the singularizing dysfunction which is inflicted on it. Through free willing, the one threatens all phenomenal constellations with disintegration. What is at stake in the treatise translates advantageously into Latin: *quodlibet,* the nondescript which maintains the will all the while depriving it of an object, including itself. By taking possession of the one, by fixing phenomenalization into a stable presence, free willing would collapse. Now, affirming itself over and above the one—since it is its act,even an ultimate authority—it is the very figure of a willing on the verge of satisfying itself by possession and thus extinguishing itself as willing. This extinction would mean the congealing of the world. *Having to keep desiring in order for the one to remain normative,* the nondescript keeps the distance which introduces less than a counter-norm, but more than a predicate into the origin: an ultimate other, a troubling operator. It introduces into it the originary strategy of mortality. Free willing, love, audacity, signal not only the formless and the indeterminate in the one, then, but also and especially the dephenomenalizing counter-strategy at the heart of all constituted phenomenality.

There is the "ascent" that sets forth from the soul isolated in dispersion, and that passes through the solitary spirit; it leads to that audacity that originarily *temporalizes in the opposite direction of what happens* in manifestation. With this movement, henological theticism has finished playing, finished legislating. In Plotinus, non-dogmatic spiritual experience makes the referential one burst open, and that because of what it reveals about theticism itself. The philosophical act of "positing a first" always introduces the conflict between positing and posited. In the words of Plotinus—willing and the willed. The henological regime is not even thinkable as an unconditional position. Here we see the condition that institutes this conflict, that nourishes and sustains it, but which, right at its institution, also has ruined it. The ruin becomes obvious in Plotinus, who does not content himself with "positing" a universal, but who again "lets" the singular phenomena be given. It appears therefore that any union, in the sense of settings-into-constellation, is originarily adjoined to a contre-temp—to singularization by audacity and free willing.

But all of that, is that the truth of the one?

The one, destituted by its agonic truth

Many times it has happened: lifted out of the body into myself; becoming external to all other things and self-encentered; beholding a marvelous beauty; then, more than ever, assured of community with the loftiest order; enacting the noblest life, acquiring identity with the divine . . . Yet, there comes a moment of descent from intellection to reasoning, and after that sojourn in the divine, I ask myself how it happens that I can now be descending, and how did the Soul ever enter into my body, the Soul which, even within the body, is the high thing it has shown itself to be. (*En*. IV, 8 [6], 1, 1ff.)*

It is well-known that the soul cannot last "up there." After a moment of happiness in immediate contemplation, it must come back down. Why? Nothing could be clearer. Combined with and dependent on the body, wouldn't the soul experience a moment of violence when given to be one with the divine? Its rank is fixed two rungs below the one. Its normal condition is the time which is measured in successions and simultaneities. Plotinus even coins a neologism to describe this condition of the soul: The activity—better still, the life—of the soul is *chronoûn,* "temporalizing" itself and thereby temporalizing the world (*En*. III, 7 [45], 11, 30). It must strip itself of this one fact by turning toward its immediate model in the Intellect: "Take everything off!" (*En*. V, 3 [45], 17, 38). From the second to the first hypostasis, what remains for it to remove? The idea or the very form of soul. It must become without idea, without form (*aneideon, amorphon, En*. VI, 7 [45], 17, 36). What could be more convincing as an answer to the question, "How is it possible to descend thus?" asked by Plotinus. Of course, it is because the soul has need of its form. To hold firm in simple presence at the simple source of all presence is asking for too much nudity. The soul cannot do it.

Before acquiescing to these conclusions which pass for common sense in the history of ideas, it is useful to look closely. Have we not just read that *the one itself has enough to endanger* everything which is other than it? And is it not alienated by its own audacity? The treatise on freedom and the will would then oblige us to seek the conditions of the "redescent" and of distance, not first of all in the falterings of the soul, but in a certain agonal truth of the one.

What is important is that the one is not passive when the soul rises toward it. We cannot help thinking of the young man in Parmenides, carried off and brought toward the goddess Alétheia: "Then, leaving there all reasoned knowledge, led up to the beautiful, residing in it and thinking it so long as he resides there, he is swept away (*exenechtheis*) by the rising wave of the Intellect. Raised up to the top by the swelling flood, all of a sudden he sees" (*En*. VI, 7 [38], 36, 17ff.). Abduction, sudden vision—it is difficult not to remember the departure and the arrival of the Parmenidean charioteer. Especially if one must admit, as one commentator says, "an activity of the one itself, which seizes and bears beyond" the Intellect.[85]

Here we come to an unavoidable question: Under what conditions can such an activity of the one take place? Are we supposed to think that the one that is willed to

*Plotinus, *The Enneads,* trans. Stephen MacKenna (London: Penguin, 1991).

be pure by theticism goes off, so to speak, kidnapping souls? This pushes the limits of the act by which the one constitutes its other. Rapture singularizes the one: it is an indispensable strategy for what one calls ecstasy (by itself, the soul is too weak to bring off the ascent). It is also a strategy which introduces a shadow once again into the pure glow of the one. Here is a new indication, that it is impossible to posit, that this referent is itself always *appropriated* without emphasizing at the same time that it *is expropriated* toward the nondescript. It remains to be seen if, and how, Plotinus recognizes in this originary double bind the truth of the one.

Now, in the treatise Plotinus names this shadow. He uses the word *alétheia*[86] just once. The context is remarkable. He asks: These things which owe their being to the procession from the one—the intelligibles first, the sensibles next—by what do they continue to revert to the one? The answer: "Each being which exists in *alétheia* and which has come to be through that nature [the one], even if they are in the sensible world, is what it is by virtue of its provenance from that [nature]. Now, by 'is what it is,' I means this: Namely, that together with their essence, beings possess the cause of their existence" (*En.* VI, 8 [39], 14, 17–21). In other words, it matters little if one speaks about intelligible or sensible things (and it matters little what the etiological schema is), all plural beings possess their proper singular being *and also* the universal cause of being, a cause that is the one, origin of processions.

These lines describe two sites: that of the source of being which is beyond what is, and that of the singular beings which is what it is. Now, this "is what it is," Plotinus has just said is double: singular-universal. Therefore, if every being gets its "is what it is" from the one, and if this "is what it is" links the disparates which the singular and the universal are, then the one itself is disparate in that way. The one itself occupies two sites. Not inside/outside of itself, but twice in itself: a universal cause singularizing itself {*se singularisant*}.

After the preceding chapters in this *Ennead,* we are no longer surprised to see the one thus taking some distance in relation to itself. What is new here is that the discordance which passes throughout it is expressly described as the truth of the one, its *alétheia.* Should one conclude that from the series of schisms at the heart of the law—audacity, otherness, obscurity, entry into becoming, self-love, will to belong to oneself, freedom . . . —that from this series something is missing as long as one does not add to it the *lêthê* which forms the heart of the *alétheia*?

The text hardly allows one to dwell on that word. It remains that the dissension of concealment and unconcelament binds the two senses of union—as event of manifestation and as rapture. In manifestation, withdrawal means that an order of appearance gathers beings, but also is always already preparing to expel them and abandon them to their singularity; in rapture withdrawal demonstrates the soul as it frees itself from its form, passes beyond relation and difference, instantaneously beating a retreat. This idea "at once" (*exaiphnes,* suddenly), in which union is made, veils and splits asunder full presence just as it unveils it and lets it flash. Hence we have the conflictual, agonal truth of the one—as singularizing contre-temps, it devastates all forms and configurations to which it gives birth as the phenomenalizing event.

Now, in all simplicity, how are we to trust an ultimate referent whose truth is such as this? As soon as it implies a temporal conflict and a dissension in manifestation, the henological normative reference can only shatter. "The other way of seeing" (*En.* VI, 9 [9], 11, 22ff.) destitutes the Greek hegemonic fantasm: The one shows therein an inessential act, essential to its truth, and thereby it loses the authority of the common noun.

The *hen* here does not make the law any more uniformly than it does in the beginning in Parmenides. One lets phenomena be given clearly only by remaining attentive to the *heuristics of dysfunction.* When a tool breaks, when the body becomes decrepit . . . then there is something to be understood. Plotinus dared this clarity by rehabilitating the originary double bind under the apparently monofocal sense of being. What Parmenides' *kouros* glimpsed long ago, what has subsequently been denied under the simple bonds of the subsisting Good and the subsuming Genera, in Plotinus ends up by imposing its undeniable truth: the tragic that legislates.

PART TWO
In the Name of Nature
The Latin Hegemonic Fantasm

The Romans are not considered to have been particularly sensitive to the tragic. But if sensibilities are one thing, the argumentative strategies therein are another.

The Latin hegemonic fantasm does not follow—any more than will the modern—from the discovery of some previously unknown phenomenon. Of course, the idea of an order that administers both human action and what there is of the extra-human, an order that makes nature the dispenser of justice, dates back to preclassical Greece. Long before the linguistic turn from Greek to Latin, the tragedians had put this nature, this ordering force, upon stage. They had represented nature as an agent of sanctions. There are heroes that bring upon themselves sufferings that nature inflicts indirectly. Others would appeal to her for self-justification. However, it suffices to recall the either-or between *phusis* and *nomos,* notably in ancient sophistry, to understand that a pure and simple apposition between these two terms would, for the Greeks, amount to nonsense.[1] "Natural law" is the Latin hegemonic fantasm.

In Greek, *'phusis'* (as do its modern translations, by the way) generally signifies two things: on the one hand, a certain region of phenomena, and on the other, a principle of production. It refers to that region of beings that are not made by the hands of men, as well as to the principle by which these natural beings, plants and animals, come to be. The semantic ambiguity actually arises in modern languages; witness the slightly mean-spirited comment circulating through London about a member of the royal family: "Princess Anne likes nature a great deal; this is somewhat surprising when one considers what nature has done to her." The word is based upon an amphiboly. Anne likes nature, which is to say the phenomenal region in which she finds trees, prairies, and horses, but not buildings, asphalt streets, and cars. As for what nature has done to her . . . like all bipeds, the princess in question came to be through the same principle of production which brings forth the trees, the prairies, and the horses, an agent whose results might be more or less pleasing to the eye. According to Aristotle's vocabulary, *phusis* itself is amphibolical. It designates a kind and a cause that does not rely upon man: the kind of beings other than artifacts and the sort of causes different from any sort of craft or art.[2]

What does not appear in the Greek polysemy of the word is the sense of a great concatenation of things encompassing *all domains* and encompassing them according to *the continuity of ends.* Well, such is the "natural law" of the Latins.[3]

It is true that in the pre-classical Greeks *phusis* denotes 'rising,' 'becoming,' 'arrival,' 'growth,'[4] and thereby all that shows itself. This giving or donation includes what a thing will have become, its essence (which is a relation of inclusion that inverts the Platonic doctrine of ideas[5]): *Phuein* includes the mature state where what grows ends by displaying its latent qualities. It is nevertheless a fact that, understood as the arrival into presence of what is virtually or simply present, *phusis* cannot serve as a norm in the sense of a maximized phenomenon, and for the simple reason that it is not a phenomenon, but rather, the showing itself, the *phainesthai,* in all that shows itself.

The Latin protagonists of natural law did not translate the Greek. They take up a position elsewhere by playing upon the ambiguity: natural encompasses *both* the city *and* the natural domain. Take the definition given by Cicero: "Nothing so conforms to statutes and to the order of nature—by which I mean the law and nothing else—as does this power of command (*imperium*) without which no family, no city, no nation, nor even the human species, nature or the world would be able to subsist" (*Laws,* III.1[6]). Nature thus ceases to represent any region other than that of man and his works. It looms over and sanctions all regions through the sovereign authority of ends. The great chain of individual-family-city-nation-humanity-nature-world forged by the principle of a teleocracy continues—such is the new guiding fantasm.

It is above all the third link in the Ciceronian sequence that marks the innovation. Prior to the Romans, one would not have *been able* to dream of declaring the nation—and this goes equally for the human species—the end of the city (and not only because there never had been a Greek State). In this grand linking together, the Latins found their common place *par excellence,* the place where all played their part, where all lived, and in which they obeyed and were made to obey without question.

A description that one considers germane thereby possesses a prescriptive value. Accordingly, the law was not added on to the great chain of regions where each serves as an end to what comes before and finds its end in what comes after. To know this chain is to know that continuity is imposed upon us and enframes us through its "objectivity"—or, in Latin: through its *castitas.*[7] This is a practical knowledge that give rise to a "great and immutable joy."[8]

Systematically speaking, nature can *link together* the phenomenal regions only because from the beginning it *controls* the principles therein. It serves as the ultimate principle for regional principles. Teleological law looms over specific laws and subsumes them. Hence the joy when each part of the soul deliberately engages in that for which it is made—intelligence in the truth; the will or love in the good . . . this is happiness. It will be immutable, for the great telic chain "naturally" leads to first truths, to the gods. Happiness deifies us. This is a continuity that extends the principle of internal consolation into a principle of public consolidation. Here is the power of consolation and consolidation which belongs to the principle of continuity as the principle of principles. For the Latins, this all-encompassing character is what governed meaning; they found in it their tutelary meaning: the meaning of meaning.

Even better, if it encompasses the gods, then natural law could not be placed alongside other first truths. Rather, it assigns to them—to "eternal reasons"—their epistemic site. An example of this is the principle of non-contradiction, the specific realm of which is called "logic"; for the proportions which are obvious because they are seen as invariables, that of mathematics (which is to say, for the ancients in general, axiomatic geometry); for the generic structure of reality, that of theology; for the ontological deficiency of evil, that of morality. Logic, mathematics, theology, and morality stood as proof of nature's sovereignty. Their common locus is their common noun: *lex natura.*

The telic linking together of regions of experience, governed by these eternal reasons—that is the nature-law. A Roman Stoic was supposed to die for it.[9]

To grasp this Latin innovation, it will be useful to begin by very clearly demarcating *natura* posited as legislative in this way, from the law that *phusis* imposes, which is the ordering force according to Aeschylus and Sophocles.

Nevertheless beforehand, and to announce the double bind, let it be said immediately that something wrecks the almost unanimous homage which, since Cicero, the Latins paid to nature as what makes the law. Several argumentative counter-strategies traverse nature by virtue of the very maximization that institutes it. The effective tethering that we assign to this referent is counter-invested from within, as we will see, by forces that so obviously work to untether it. The unanimity in question leaves one somewhat perplexed—especially when one takes the pleasure of invoking it in the twentieth century. The idea that nature could be an organizational directress can count, so it seems, on our spontaneous sympathies. These are more than historical reasons to show the fissures in this common edifice from which escape those truths it was designed to imprison, the truths of the singular and of the disparate, of time and of differing, of all the traces of death and dissension in being of which nature is the sign, truths obliterated by the agents of normativity. Incidentally, in Rome these agents will be functionaries in more than one sense.

Latin nature rules uniformly, and at first glance, exclusively. On a second look, this fantasm simultaneously turns its regime in on itself and deploys it. Its turning back on itself is just as systematic as is its deployment. It is said that Cicero was the creator of Latin philosophical language. From Cicero to the medieval nominalists, each advance in the articulation of the natural law is accompanied not just by resistance but by a counter-measure, a transgressive step that implacably distorts the legislative procedure.

In a word, nature is established as normative by extrapolating it from a specific singular. We will see which. Fidelity to this precise singular shatters the *simple telic bind* which the universal is reputed to impose. It is an indirect fidelity that, in their theticism and in their theses, makes the Latin philosophers fulfill, as if despite themselves, the oldest mission which is to preserve the phenomena.

Common sense in the history of ideas requires that premodern reason conceive an order of ends to be attained as *given* whereas modern reason, if it occurs to it to conceive of such an order, instead postulates this order as *posited*. One receives and contemplates that which is given; but that which is posited, one makes. As a network of laws, as Kant will say, nature is possible only on account of a legislative subject. For the moderns, the contemplation of a pre-established order is "sterile and, like a virgin consecrated to God, brings forth nothing."[10] That which is given comes from another; what come from us will necessarily be posited. According to doxographic good sense, givenness and positing would be as distinct as heteronomy and autonomy, or again as subjection and sovereignty. Premodern nature would impose an order which transcends us and in which we are inscribed, while modern nature would be transcendental, an order spontaneously written and imposed by us. Consequently, behind this writing that occurs spontaneously it would be necessary to see the writing subject, whereas ancient nature would instead be "inscribed in our hearts." The primary source of all laws and the ultimate authority for their legitimacy would be sought by the ancients in the nature which has us in its *grip* and by the moderns in the human that *grasps*. Grasps what? Precisely those measures by which to prescribe its ends.

As far as nature as the ultimate Latin referent is concerned, the disjunction between givenness and positing is distressingly oversimplified; the manner in which it is simplistic and the manner in which it is fatally distressing are exactly what will have to be elucidated. Here the manner shall count as much as the fact, because the counter-strategies within Latin "nature" follow directly from a *positing* required by its own hegemony. Since the days of Aristotle, it goes without saying that givenness and positing are the two processes, conjointly exhaustive and mutually exclusive, needed to conceive an order.[11] However, if it turns out that nature, attaining hegemony with the passage from Greek to Latin, cannot lay claim to a givenness uncontaminated by positing, then it will be useful to examine its inability to bind us and bind us together, to oblige us and knot the bindings, as desired by both common sense in the history of ideas and our contemporary nostalgia for order.

The fantasm speaks of a victory in the great crossing-over that connects the individual to the city and to the world. This is desire speaking, perhaps more overtly even than in the Greek or modern hegemonies. Nature asserts herself as the ordering force that we always triumphantly desire and that always triumphs. For the Romans, nature is the *force majeure* that has the edge over all disorderliness. As they desired it, so they stated it. It is a voluntarism that by itself causes one to suspect a thetic play {*jeu*} under the reign of *natura*. The gambit {*jeu*} of the thesis remains, moreover, indifferent with regard to the stakes {*enjeux*}—whether the philosophers were Christians or not, their love for natural law follows from the same positive gesture: the double gesture of the physiothete posing as the physiologue. They claim to retrace the given telic organization even though they organize and draw up (and thereby erase) what they want to be the outlines of nature. These strategies establishing the principle of continuity will appear, once disentangled, to be so many crippling counter-strategies. Theticism will announce itself *as allegedly given* at the heart of the new focal meaning of being, whereby pure givenness is rendered null and void. Several texts from Cicero and Augustine will allow us to observe the apprenticeship of this false movement.

Nature is a thesis: Like all other normative referents, it is a phenomenon selected from experience and then promoted to be the law of laws. It will not be difficult to free this play of positing from under givenness, to outplay, that is, the postulated givenness. Indeed, whether the stake is ancestral Rome (Cicero) or the heavenly city (Augustine), it is always a particular represented being that determines what one declares to be "natural," "by nature," "in conformity with," or "contrary to" it. There is a narrowing of the *diasozein ta phainomena,* which will gain widespread acceptance. Up until the end of the Latin era, nature will remain a singular fantasmically exalted into a paradigm. The metaphysician in us finds it difficult to shake off such an exaltation, even if the Scholastics of the waning moments of the Middle Ages dismantled it with a subtlety and rigor never equaled.

The Romans are perhaps not known for their sense of the tragic. However, their philosophers (there were two: Cicero and Augustine) made themselves the most faithful guardians of the normative double bind. They posited an archetypal singular *without ever repudiating the singularity therein.* And it is this that we must train ourselves to hear in their instituting discourses. They oblige us to think with a new freshness about the arguments in whose terms fantasmic nature looms over the sum of all that is the case. On account of their lack of speculative sophistication, on account of the turn we would like to call "naïve" in which they reinvested language with a maximizing thrust as well as imagination with a representative thrust—in other words, on account of their oblique fidelity to the differend between given and fantasm—these two great Latin innovators adhered most closely to the tragic condition of being.

Here again we have the exaltation which burgeons in tragic *denial*. It owes its rich philosophical career to the power of denial. With a gesture that the West has never forgotten, Antigone placed herself under the authority of that which she called not the natural law, but the law of the gods. The authority and denial from which it stemmed proved to be enduring enough to eclipse, in a certain manner, the effective history of all other normative fantasms. Antigone must decide between conflicting laws. On account of her univocal allegiance—at least until the fleeting moment in which she has a clear vision of the double bind—to the law inscribed in the heart, Antigone's gesture has gained a widespread acceptance more tenacious than that of statesmen such as Agamemnon and Creon.

Nature, principle of telic continuity, is thus not to be confused with *phusis,* the ordering force upholding justice. This principle displaces and amplifies this force. In order to see how, we will briefly recall the birth of normative nature, through thetic denial, in the history that recounts how Antigone perished *for* it, and Xerxes, the most notorious transgressor, died *from* it.

Excursus: Xerxes punished by nature

"In youth's rash temper he conceived the plan
To stay the sacred Hellespont with fetters
As though it were his slave. He strove
To alter the stream where ran the God, Bosporus,
And enchaining it with hammered links he
Prevailed, making this coursing God
A highway for his great army.
Nay, was it not madness that held sway over my son?"[12]

Aeschylus describes the defeat suffered by the Persian army at Salamis as having been incurred by the recklessness (*thrasei*) of it leader, Xerxes. To him who goes too far, nature metes out punishment. The Greeks called such an excess *hubris,* a word that stems from *huper,* meaning 'beyond.' Xerxes, by means of his inventions for traversing the Hellespont, transgressed the bounds fixed by nature. He took on more than his match. First he had two boat bridges placed across the strait. Then, after a tempest had destroyed those, he had the sea whipped as punishment and the pontoons rebuilt. Last of all, he undertook an engineering work of enormous enterprise, having a channel dug so that his fleet might round a dangerous promontory. His mother sees more clearly: to take nature thusly in hand, is that not madness? Hubris is arrogance. It arrogates to oneself rights to which one has no lawful claim. Accordingly at Salamis, the usurper will in the end get what he had asked for. But the lesson will only be clear once the price has been paid, a price that only the invincible ordering force of nature can levy.

What is to be learned from this lesson? It suggests several traits of normative nature, traits that are rearranged during two millennia of speculation about this order but which are never truly abandoned by that posterity that will ponder the nature in the law.

The nature offended by Xerxes appears as man's other; were it not so, Xerxes would not have been able to whip, chain, and humiliate nature. Furthermore, nature is the other that transcends human action and its limit; were it not so, Xerxes would not have been able to be accused of disrespect. Nature is, moreover, a well-ordered other, resembling a society in which there are superiors and inferiors; were it not so, Xerxes' war stratagems could not have appeared as an effort to reduce the strait to slavery. This natural order is, in addition, rational; if it were not, it would not be madness that Aeschylus perceives in the work of Xerxes' Persian expedition. Finally, as a limit, nature shows itself to be immutable. The second bridge does not constitute any less of a transgression than the first. Otherness, transcendence, order, rationality, immutability: Here are some of the characteristics of that law which is imposed by *phusis* as a region of givenness and a principle of production. It is an active *phuein,* the avenger itself, that teaches Xerxes at Salamis, at his own expense.

Creon also is taught by this law. Like Aeschylus, Sophocles portrays a force (*sthenos*) that confronts an incommensurable other. Just as were the Persian strategies, the interdiction against burying Polynices is in conflict with more ancient, already given, and more surely established regulations. Antigone describes these as the "unwritten and immovable laws of the gods."[13] In the works of Aeschylus, tricks and a barbaric (that is to say, lawless) force are opposed to that other force that is nature, a region and agent that strikes the transgressor. In the works of Sophocles, conflict more clearly opposes two laws, or rather two kinds of laws. Creon's edict is a law *also,* but it dies with its legislator. Other is that law which lives always in man and even occupies a precise place within, not reason (*nous*), but spirit (*phren,* v. 683), whose seat is the diaphragm—the "sense" which Creon recognizes, all too late, to have lost when he carries in his arms his dead son and pities his own "senseless spirit" (*phrenôn dysphronôn,* v. 1261). As for Xerxes, Aeschylus calls him simply, "sick in spirit" (*nosos phrenôn,* v. 751).

That the natural law implanted within would be more certain, and in that sense stronger than all edicts issuing from power, does not mean that it would also be easier to fathom. Antigone remains uncertain in respect to this law: "Who knows whether all that I have done is also held sacred in that other abode?" "And which law do I follow in pronouncing these words?" (v. 521, 908). We "sense" the ultimate measure, but we do not know it. At least that law decipherable in the flow of the Bosporus does not inflict such uncertainties on the hero. It is the advantage of the visible which makes the madness of a Xerxes that much more flagrant. But whether it speaks within or without, nature returns the favor, only more massively, through a reflux of that which had been transgressed. Nature returns the violence which we inflict upon it, multiplied. To Creon it returns Hemon soaked in blood. So, only *oimoi*[14] remains, "alas," for which there can be no Platonic idea nor Aristotelian category. Aristotle's *Physics* will hearken to this *phusis,* much better than does his theory of catharsis in the *Poet-*

ics: we only tear things away from their natural place provisionally. Anti-nature is the loser, if not from the start, at least in the final account—at Salamis.

This is where nature enters into contradiction with the laws, through an excess of that figure to whom Greece owes her institutions and ascendancy: the human legislator. Xerxes legislates through brute force; Creon by arbitrary edict. The superior force equally *counters* both of them with unequaled blows. The conflicting forces—nature and the laws which exceed it—thus oppose each other in an asymmetrical manner. There is a conflict between disparate forces, but not a sublation of this disparity under some sort of sovereign focal point. Contradictories remain deprived of a genus, without recourse to authority. This is one of the reasons I find it difficult to maintain simply that the standard (normative) Greek referent would be *phusis.* Another reason is the literal sense of *phusis,* which I have said does not evoke any such thing as an ideal order or a principle of continuity. The tragics portrayed *phusis* as a power of retribution, but they did not extend it so far as to make it encompass the laws and their spheres. It governs certain beings, like the times for example, and it acts like a cause—those whose effects man can only endure. It is a force—and a formidable one—but it does not oversee all representable forces as does a metarepresentation. The tragics did not postulate any genus above the individual. Aeschylus and Sophocles leave the archaic site, where subsequent philosophers will locate consoling and consolidating referents, empty. They address to these sites questions without response, and thus remain forever ahead of us. In the silence which they portray—which settles over waning modernity as a result of a different knowledge[15]—there speaks loudly the *differing.*

It speaks there through what I have called, with regard to Parmenides, the tragic chiasm. Commentators have often remarked (again, notably in Hegel's footsteps, so as to postulate a reconciliation that cannot be found there) that the confrontation between Creon and Antigone leads to a crossing of their respective positions. At the beginning of the piece, Creon condemns the young girl for having violated the laws of the city. She did not know how to separate herself from the family and "arrive in the city." In the end, on the other hand, Creon swears that he will nevertheless respect "the established laws" (v. 1113). Here we have the protagonist of civil order making himself the advocate of family religion, of the heroic code, of burial rituals, of ancestral piety. It's as if he changed sides. The unbounded defender of the city pleads for the household. The overly political man recognizes that he himself was under the obligation to bury Polynices, a member of his family. Conversely, Antigone, who was equally excessive in championing the *oikos,* suddenly aligns herself on the side of the *polis.* "Oh, city of my fathers in the land of Thebes. . . ." (v. 937). I suspect that the very name "Antigone" (*anti, genos*) indicates this chiasm—she is the one that is "born against"—against the city; but at the end of the journey, she—of everyone!—turns out to be, furthermore, "against birth," against the order founded on birth. The chorus calls this double knowledge *amphinoein,* 'to think from two sides' (v. 376).

Just like Parmenides, Sophocles requires the chiasm of unilateral positions—in the isonomy of free citizens, see the ancient heroic code; in this code, see the new democracy. The preclassical Greeks left the site of the ultimate authority blank. Therefore, if archaic "nature" makes the law, it is primarily as the *force majeure* dispensing justice and secondarily through the argumentative chiasm between *oikos* and *polis.*

That Aeschylus and Sophocles treat nature as a force does not mean that it is to be counted among beings in the same way as is the current of the Bosporus or the nocturnal rite to which Antigone devotes herself. They portray it perfectly as a network of contextualization—but a partial network. Moreover, there is another way of contextualizing beings—namely, the city which is an artifact of man. This fact will be decisive for grasping how a force is transmuted into a fantasm when, with the Latins, the natural measure will be identified with this or that singular being, gleaned from and lifted above all other singular beings and then universalized. I will attempt to retrace this transmutation, not as the result of a certain mentality, nor of the reification effected by Christianity, nor even of the forgetfulness of being (theticism being an oblique manner of safeguarding being in its double bind), but as an effect of translation. As soon as the expressions *lex natura, lex naturalis,* etc., are coined, nature will fulfill the needs of consolation and consolidation. It will impose a simple focal meaning wherein tragic knowledge will be obliterated. Focalized, knowledge will be, on the contrary, quite comforting—"Those who know will never be unhappy."[16]

The rearrangement of *phusis* into *natura,* with all of its thetic character, can be best discerned in the emergence of a singular archetype: the hyperbolic conversion, strictly anti-Greek, of a real city into something given by nature. The concept of a paradigmatic individual certainly was not foreign to the Greeks. The Aristotelian *phronimos* is just such an individual, and in political matters above all, opinion cannot dispense with having recourse to such models ("a sage like Solon," "courageous like Achilles"). But the singular finds itself accentuated altogether differently, when Cicero declares Rome—as Augustine declares Jerusalem the heavenly city exiled on earth—the natural city, such that one might say: nature made the city. For a Greek, it would have been a flat-out absurdity to posit some empirical city thus as natural. On one hand, whether they considered man as "naturally" political or not, the Greeks were in agreement that the *polis* comes to be only through the gesture of the legislator; on the other hand, an archetype that can be pointed to with a finger—there it is, we can visit it on the seven hills of Latium; it is there, where some people gather in Its Name—for the Greeks could only amount to a monster, to an atopia, or a categorial mistake. For Plato, the typic city could not be visited because its being was only in speech. And if for Aristotle the virtuous man united the ideal and the singular in a model visible to all, such a conjunction remains impossible for the city. It would be to make truth out of plasma.[17]

That which is born on its own is natural. But a city is not given to having been born on its own. It is founded, and made in its singularity (to honor this singularity, Aristotle will compile 158 constitutions.) The estime attached to such a founding gesture can only guard a Greek from the stupidity that consists in idealizing his own *polis.* A Roman, on the other hand, draws his pride from the archetype fully present in the singular. Let us add that this full presence does not exclude historical time but rather, as we will see, invokes it. Accordingly, the differend that fissures the new ultimate referent still holds, though differently than it does in Greek henology, to the time of the singular. It holds to the singularization that leads back to earth and destitutes idealized Rome as much as it does the heavenly Jerusalem.

What happens beginning with the moment when the first Latin philosophers declare a perfect coincidence between the ideal and the deictique in a city which can be, if not visited (already in Cicero's day the Republic is well on its way to being destroyed), at least described? Nature makes a spectacle of her law in some particular "this." It is true that it already exposed itself in a like manner in accordance with Aristotelian astral theology. Order, unity, permanence, possession of the end and all the other predicates with which the metaphysicians of natural law endowed *natura* had appeared to be realized in the *visible* revolutions of the celestial bodies. He who wished to know *phusis,* the region of givenness and principle of production, had only to lift his eyes. For Aristotle (as it will be for Kant, but in a different way), the starry sky was the sole phenomenon in which the divine showed itself for observation. However, in coinciding with the universal, this very singular excluded time. Now, the ancestral Republic in which Cicero reads the natural law *was still intact* just a generation before; the heavenly city, in which Augustine reads the eternal law, *will be shortly,* after several more generations of exile. That which was there but is no longer, like that which is not yet there but will be shortly, is called the contingent. Rome and Jerusalem might not have been; and in being no longer, or not yet, they may be otherwise than they actually are not at the present time. For Cicero and Augustine, that contingency of "previously" and "not yet" will be systematically necessary with regard to the natural law. If the Rome of old and the Jerusalem to come were there as is the night sky—in motion, made of singular bodies, and nevertheless eternal—then the exhortations to which these two Fathers of Latinism devoted themselves would lose their nominative-normative referent and, thus, their sense. For lack of being given, all that is left for nature is to be posited. The patently given gives way to posited representations. Likewise, verbs in the middle voice (*nasci*) emphasizing particular singulars being manifested as being the case give way to the name (*natura*) that is particularizable according to cases. Overdetermining the singular given—positing—immediately makes normative nature a victim of the double bind. It confers an obligatory force both to the singular and to the universal.

Inserting the paradigmatic into the represented contingent—this is the specifically Latin theticism. Compared to Greek astral theology, which was perhaps Aristotle's[18] point of departure, it is not the visibility of the law in singulars which is out of place, but rather their contingency. For in the end, how are we to speak of a figure nominatively and normatively posited, which was or which will be, if not with verbs in the past and future tenses? Consequently, excellent rhetoricians that they are, Cicero and Augustine at every step recall the "being born" that lies underneath nature. Rome was born, Jerusalem well on its way to being born. . . . The middle voice here breaks the name in the vocative "Rome!," "Jerusalem!," just as the return of a suppressed denial breaks the voice of the leader who declares the law.

The Latin era opens with the nomination of a monster to the post of sovereign—the nomination of a thesis that makes the law naturally. Beginning with its very institution, hegemonic nature is contrary to nature. What is monstrous is not only that a willed thesis is passed off as if it were natural, but also that an archetype that is traversed by contingency.

We again find this contingency stated, preserved, and exalted in the last century of Scholasticism. Scholasticism thus will put the finishing touches on the double play of a positing passing itself off as givenness. In the so-called nominalists and in Meister Eckhart, the fantasm of nature collapses by virtue of an originary indetermination, one seen as breaking the great principle of telic continuity from within. This is what makes it therefore difficult to maintain that this *force majeure* is simply, absolutely given. From beneath "de facto" created nature, the Scotists bring into the light of day one part of affirmation as the sole proof. In the eternal law, they discern an act. This law, they say, has been posited, contingently, through a freedom—what for the ancients would amount to a pure violence against justice-dispensing nature. Occam does not exactly destroy nature; rather, he expresses its destitution through the conflictual strategies that have belabored the hegemony therein since its institution. As for Eckhart, he absolutely does not envision the questioning of telic continuity; but in constructing it in the way he does, he again sees it incongruously dissolving from within. Nature becomes soluble—in more than one sense, as we will see. Simultaneously indeterminate origin and determinate principle—such a broken reference would appear to the fathers of Latin thought—Cicero and Augustine—as madness. In them the referent will equally manifest the singularizing truth (in a differend with normative nature), singularization, and the differend that can easily be shown at work *ab urbe condita*.

The name *natura* first of all signifies the uterine orifice, the place where birth occurs. The natural is what follows from being-through-birth—from natality. Now, this concept, such as I have borrowed it from Hannah Arendt (signifying the impulse toward referential institutions and toward principial maximization) states well enough the linguistic inclination through which theticism shifts from the *natural* singular to universally telic *nature*. It shifts from nature-birth to the nature-orientation-orientor and then to the orientation of nature toward ends. But natality is phenomenologically ultimate only when joined to its dissymmetrical other, which is being-towards-death or mortality. Seneca declares in all candor that by grasping the order of ends one "leaps over one's own mortality."[19] For us it will be a question of understanding how, in the name of the systematic dependence of the contingent singular, nature must lower itself to the level of normative simplicity; how here again natality—the strategy of universalization—takes on, without a hitch, morality, the matchless strategy of singularization; consequently, how in Rome the ultimates as well as the ultimate references to which they gave rise, are rearranged; how the simple bond that posits the intended telic concatenation immediately runs aground on the legislative-transgressive double bind that is undergone.

I

Its Institution

The Principle of Telic Continuity (Cicero and Augustine)

When philosophy began to speak Latin, nature came to exert a regulative force in it. For a millennium and a half, nature will determine the conditions according to which what is must show itself. It became normative with Cicero, who prides himself on having brought philosophy, "that source from which all flows," home to Rome.[20] More precisely, there is a new beginning when Cicero gives a Latin rendition of the middle Stoics. Thus, in the freshness of a new linguistic aether impregnating representations, nature finds herself instituted as an ultimate reference henceforth constitutive of phenomenality—a hegemonic fantasm.

Beginning with its Roman institution, an ensemble of counter-strategies inhibit, contaminate, and damage the legislative activity that one takes to be natural. With originary natality, contrary traits arise and are emphasized by the Latin language. They are reflected, at a normative level, in the arguments reappropriating these ultimates. A play of organizing attractions and dispersive withdrawals shreds the texture that envelops the individual, the city, humanity, the cosmos, and the gods. In what follows, I will seek to bring into relief the most flagrant of the double binds inserting us into the order and then wrenching us out of it. The subsequent wrenchings away result from the knowledge of death, whose systematic denial is the responsibility of the "functionaries of humanity," as well as from the labor to remain faithful to what one finds to be the case—a labor that this knowledge forces upon the everyday.

To know me as moral is first of all to know me as singular and, therefore, to know us as plural (*'ad plures ire'* we thus say for 'to die'); consequently it is necessary to begin by raising the question of the singular, which is what is natural for us. (A) Singulars are not subsumed—their plurality makes up a mass. If some morally binding significance is attached to this singularity, it can only raise the specter of a certain normative dispersion (a specter to be counted among the offspring of that monster that is the desire that is raised up from and maximized over the givens that are found to be the case). Hence a different counter-strategy has to be liberated, resulting from *natures that tell their story.* (B) Temporality is, again, rooted in the knowledge of our death. Wherever this rebounds onto politics, it draws the principial authority out into a history. Whether they are Christians or not, the founders of Latin philosophy historicize nature. They subvert nature, and not fortuitously, by retracing an errancy: Visible Rome just as much as invisible Jerusalem has gone astray in datable deeds and gestures. Consequently, it will be necessary to analyze nature, erring in her paradigms, and nevertheless sanctioning action under a singular which was—republican Rome—and then under a singular which will be—the heavenly Jerusalem. These are counter-strategies which here indicate an *erratic differend.* (C) Consequently one last trait will express the truth of theticism—normative nature is essentially posited, not given. Its legislative power follows from a voluntary action and not from an innocent perusal of phenomena. It will be necessary to examine the obliqueness by which the thetic will nevertheless safeguard the phenomena and thereby, as if despite it, transgress the fantasm beneath which it nevertheless forces them. In other words, it will be necessary in the normative argumentations to take note of the *will turned against itself.*

Hegemonic nature will collapse when it appears as the singular effect of a singular will; when it appears as a posited figure making the world, second in relation to a pre-positional condition and in a differend with it; when it enters into the history of a wandering because—and this word that the Scotists will set loose is used only to summarize the rest—it was *produced* by freedom; whence it will finally follow that the will is indeterminate and will make nature indeterminate—ergo the dissolution that will mark the end of the Latin epoch.

Before unknotting this bundle to detail its elements, a brief reminder is in order to demarcate hegemony. Doxographs who distill "the" philosophy outside of its languages are by this very act led to treat "of" the concept of nature. This is a synchronistic takeover by force, from which the concept in question emerges diversely overdetermined—a good forty times if we are to believe the lexicons. Already polysemic for the Greeks, with the Roman turn this concept is endowed with new connotations and complexes that previously were inconceivable. The distillate that supposedly is perennial nature itself obviously results from a highly partisan operation. Now, even if the linguistic turn made it seem otherwise, it is with *phusis* that *natura* breaks. It is, moreover, a different nature by which the intellect just as infallibly escapes diachrony. But there is a rupture, and this by virtue of the fledgling canonicity of the principle of continuity on the one hand, and on the other by virtue of multiple factors corrupting its youthfulness. Hence the importance of a toxicological analysis, so to speak, of this Latin reference beginning with its rapid development as a criteria for what is and what is not healthy, most notably in the social body.

This toxicology would be destitute of substances as much in the works of the Greeks as in the works of the moderns. It is not that nature—non-perennial, epochally different—rules there uncontested; before and after the Latins it doesn't rule at all. We have seen that as a "symphysis," nature upholds the rule of the one; and as we will see, as a web of *a priori* laws it will uphold the rule of self-consciousness. But that is already to say that both here and there—in synectic henology and in critical transcendentalism—nature signifies in each case something entirely different than a telic concatenation. "The concept of nature"—this does not exist. There is *phusis,* then *natura,* and lastly *nature/Natur* . . . even if it is necessary to make accommodations by translating it, in most of instances, as "nature."

It follows that there is a Greek encompassing, then a Latin encompassing, and then again a modern encompassing. Without here going into the third sense, we can say that the kinetic notion of *phusis* encompasses phenomena that are such because they show themselves through their own coming to presence. This notion denotes the sum total of self-moving beings, and it also encompasses them in that it connotes the principle of their movement, a principle that imitates human "know-how." The denotation and connotation certainly make Greek "nature" a law. Nevertheless, it is a regional law opposed to that of "technical" productions. It is not the law of laws, but—and this is not an equivalent—the *force majeure,* the avenger, the dispenser of justice, retributive, stronger than any rival law that emerges from political know-how. Kinetic *phusis* therefore has nothing by which it may lay claim to hegemony. It covers only one of the two movements that the *Physics* analyzes: growth, not fabrication.

The denotative-connotative arrangement of nature is completely different.

CHAPTER 8

Concerning Singular Given Natures

"There exists a true law, it is that of right reason, which conforms to nature, is prevalent in all humans, and is subject neither to change nor to perishing. This law calls us to fulfill that which is fitting, and by its interdictions it turns us from offense. . . . To this law no amendment is permitted, it is not lawful to abrogate this law either totally or partially. Neither the senate nor the people can dispense us from obeying it, and there is no need at all to search for a Sextus Aelius to explain or interpret it. This law is not one thing in Athens, another in Rome, one thing today, and another tomorrow. It is always one and the same law, eternal and immutable, which rules all peoples and in all times . . . Whosoever does not obey this law flies from himself, having mistook human nature."

—*Republic,* III, 22, 23

Do not these lines read as a paraphrase of Antigone justifying herself before Creon? She had invoked the "unwritten and unshakable laws of the gods." It is all there—immutability, eternity, and the intelligibility of the true law; also a quasi-religious fear, seeing that it would be contrary to the *fas* to abolish or reinstate the application of the law; and again the limit of the law traced through its interdictions; and there is its obviousness as well: the law in question is none other than the *recta ratio* itself. Among the similarities one finds there is the impossibility of a conflict with human decrees, for neither the Senate nor the people, no more than Creon, can strike a blow against this law. These lines of Cicero seem to show admirably well the unity of ancient—Greek and Latin—philosophy as well as the univocity of nature making the law.

And yet. To turn away from the unwritten law here is to misunderstand human nature—law and nature as being equally universal. Cicero adds a feature to the description of Antigone that Sophocles omitted: the congruence between the true law and *our nature,* by which it is now necessary to understand the rational constitution of man. How does this rational constitution legislate?

The Latin *ratio* means something other than the Greek *phren*. To stick to the words for a moment, the latter dealt with "sense" or with the "heart"; the former, however, dealt above all with an "account" that one demands and one gives. Right reason is that which gives a fair account. In myself, right reason takes account of the other forces or instincts; and with respect to what it tells me to do, it takes account of the totality of the *civitas communis hominum et deorum.*[21] The principle of continuity between well-ordered man and the human genus is the reckoning of right reason. The tendency toward ends is right, and it is right that I should watch over the finality in the economy of my own forces as well as of those in the city and the species. Such is the nature inscribed in us: a principle of exact reckoning, of dosage, of telic adjustment; a principle of maximized amplitude which is beyond all phenomenal regions. Hence, a *norma* ('leveling').

Now, this is the new conceptual strategy that reorients the totality of argumentation—this principle obliges us to take account of the singular "I" as was never done in Greece. Roman pragmatism reckons with the natural individual to the same extent as it counts on universal nature. We portray our own proper manner of being. A Greek would never have been able to entitle a book *Pathways toward Myself* (*Eis heauton,* Marcus Aurelius). How does right reason conjoin the singular and the universal? It conjoins them "as is proper"—proper to what?—to my nature, which, no sooner had the Roman Stoics denied it than, driven away, it always returned at a gallop. Is this simply a bit of good sense? In any case, it can only annul this law of laws according to which nothing could be more natural than the reason in me, homologated by successive cross-checkings with all that is reasonable and rational outside of me. The ultimate normative leveling twists itself to conform to me. Let us consider this matter more closely.

On the nature that returns

The singular and the deadly torsion it introduces into the system of nature can be quite clearly discerned in certain key translations established by Cicero. The most pertinent is made by the very title of his perhaps best-known work, *De Officiis*. Cicero borrows his theme from the Stoics.[22] *'Officium'* is the Latin translation of the Greek *'kathékon',* which is usually rendered in English as 'that which is fitting.' The Greek term designates the type of action in which we listen to and follow that which is in accordance with our "nature" in the sense of "character." What occurs with the passage into Latin?

In order to really see here the effect of translation it is first necessary to have grasped a shift in Greek Stoic ethics. In this shift the austerity of the ancients Stoics gets effaced. Zeno of Citium, we say, introduced into morals the law of reason which declares: "you must."[23] Implacable, this law summons each one to transform their impulses into judgments. Austerity depended on the exclusive reign of what, in the third century before our era, the founders sometimes call "common nature" (*koinè phusis*), at other times *logos,* and at yet others *nomos*—three terms whose significations become greatly obscured in their works. What will be morally good, then, is that, and only that, which serves the practical goal guiding one's work upon the self: the immaculate sovereignty of reason (*kathortoma*). What will be morally bad is that which impedes such work. The sage is the one who will have succeeded in transforming the entire range of his impulses (*hormai*)—instincts, affects, passions, desires. He will have rendered them "logical" without remainder.

A similar austerity is effaced two centuries later with the middle Stoics. It is then that what is held to be natural begins to be displaced. Individual nature is *also* declared to be *normative,* notably with Paneatius of Rhodes. It is necessary to examine this shifting by which an ethic of individual[24] sites broaches the principle of an encompassing telic continuity at the very precarious moment at which this system is being put into place. Unless we have experienced the slope upon which the Greek Stoics were engaged until the Roman age, we will not understand what happens when, half a century later, Cicero translates *kathékon* as *officium*. At the edge of that slope, the universalist morality of the "you must" is eclipsed in favor of an ethic based upon the economy of impulses and abilities.

Kata hêkein, 'to have occurred' and in this sense 'to be suited to,' expresses, in the works of the Greek language Roman Stoics, a morally indifferent act, but of which one is able to give an account because it has been performed in conformity with the physical processes of life. Such an act is *eulogon,* 'well-founded.' The ideal of the sage who had reabsorbed all of his instincts into his intellect inspires nothing but irony: "we shall speak of the sage some other time. . . ."[25] What is suited to a plant is the production of chlorophyll; to all living things, the search for health rather than illness, for life rather than death; what is suited to humans is the desire for honors, pleasures, and riches rather than dishonor, pain, and poverty; for a public personage, to never lose the mastery of himself as when becoming winded during a speech. . . . The fitting proceeds from those dispositions which belong to us by nature and from the positions that life affords us. Through birth and training, *kathékon* is domestic, proper, and familiar (*oike on*) to us. It is an ethics of the empirical character where an act is justified by fitting into the picture with the other acts following from nature. If the middle Stoics only distinguished between sages and the senseless, if both are likely to live "properly," it is because here the success of a life is measured by the accord between deliberate deeds (of *bios*) and vital deeds (of *zoé*). Through the harmonious development of these tendencies, everyone can make his life "just" in the ancient sense of equilibrium. The indicators of order, which are the city and the cosmos, first of all serve to stabilize the individual life and to make of it a work.

How are we to understand "nature" within this instinctual economism? At first, certainly, it names the group of specific talents to be acquired within an individual life. But there the accent is already displaced. These talents of the species no longer reside in the triad *logos-phusis-nomos*. They reside in the goods pursued by all the representatives of the species, such as public respect or private pleasures. Yet much more characteristic of "nature" are the individual dispositions not issuing from the species. That which is originally ours (*to prôton oikeîon* is what Cicero translates, by way of an allusion to the nature that we become at our birth, as *quod natum est*)[26] encompasses specific as well as singular qualities. This is how the injunction to live according to nature now tells me *also* to live according to *my* nature. The native—the innate—is composed of an essential nature and of the natural, about which Roman pragmatism understood that it can no more be chased away than can the desire that pushes for maximized references.

Even before these translations by Cicero, a drifting that will carry the Latin hegemonic fantasm afar is taking shape in this shift toward individual natures. We will divine the import of this in recalling that for Plato nature and the individual form precisely the beginning and the end of diaeresis: a method which restricts the application of a concept to *particular* cases. According to this method, every analysis worthy of the name starts out from the genus, which it divides by successive dichotomies, until it arrives at the *atomon eîdos,* which might be translated as "indivisible nature." This notion enters into Platonic reasoning only as a culminating point, but never as a co-principle. Now, that is precisely what it becomes in Rome. There the natural *singular* is affirmed as an additional principle.

This principle is expressly stated as such when Cicero translates *kathékon* as *officium.* Two etymologies have been proposed for this word.[27] The prefix *of-* comes from either the proposition *ob-* or the noun *opus.* In the first case, *officere* means 'to do something to someone'—to render him a service or to inflict an injustice upon him. In the second case, the word would first have been *opificium* and would have originally signified the 'fabrication of a work.'

All one need do is recall the Stoic injunction—"make your life a work"—to suspect that the second sense is the one we must bear in mind. This conjecture is corroborated in the works of Cicero by two associated notions. On one hand, he also defines *officium* as 'to give an account'—that of which one can give a plausible account is proper.[28] The articles that have to be taken into account are above all the functions that one exercises in life. Thus it is plausible that a senator makes speeches and a lady makes weavings. (But she does not do the cooking. That is a labor not proper to her and thus one of which, if the idea came to her to try it, she would not be able to give a plausible account to her husband.) To fulfill one's office is to accomplish one's proper work.

On the other hand, Cicero associates "office" with *persona.* The section of *De Officiis* dealing with individual nature begins with this distinction: "We should understand that nature has endowed us as if with two *personae:* one is universal, stemming from the fact that we are all equally endowed with reason. . . . The other *persona* is assigned to individuals in their singularity."[29] The common and the proper are *personae* (de *prosôpon*), a word behind which Cicero evidently hears its primitive sense of 'theatrical mask.' To fulfill one's office means to play one's role well. For a Roman fully in pursuit of a dazzling and prominent public image, it is less a matter of being than of beautifully executing one's part. "When each speech or action is in accord with each *persona,*" then there is *decorum* (97). In the theater, a celebrated actor can mime a beggar and the king might be played by a stand-in. Both must get into the skin of their part . . . to which Cicero correlates individual nature. Thus he comes to speak of natures in the plural—an inconceivable idea for the ancient Stoics. "Among natures and customs, there exist innumerable differences" (109). What has happened to the absolute teleocracy imposed by reason? The spectacle of dissimilar natures has relegated it to the role of an onlooker. For the morality which identifies the good and the rational, Cicero substitutes an ethic of characters, of talents that are native and on that account natural; an ethic of naturalness. It doubly provokes the agent. This morality draws ever closer to cosmopolitanism and, beyond, to a conformity to the cosmos; but while exhorting me to remain faithful to *that which is the case in me* it in turn extracts me from this encompassing order. In the *natura* that makes the law (but is no longer either one or simple) is combined an attraction that produces universals and a certain singularizing withdrawal.

As individual nature rules and measures, such is a life. "We measure our efforts by the standard of our nature, because it is of no use to struggle against one's nature" (110). This is a remarkable formulation both in what it links together and what it refuses to link. It links the ancient metaphysics of measure to the role which each has been assigned to play upon the world's stage; and it detaches the singular from the domain of the modifiable where more rationalist ethics have taken care—or have had the candor—to place it. Here it would no longer make any sense to require that one follow the sole rule of subsumptive *logos*. Once one hears that "it is of no use to struggle against one's nature," once one observes that nature always returns, all that remains is to take it into account. It is necessary to recognize in this a standard of actions that is just as normative as the universal reason that defines us. The idea of *persona,* of role, suggests well the shift toward the natural singular as a co-regulator of life. In the theater of the world, each is born with a role destined for them; similarly, each should carry out their deeds and gestures "just as they are born" (*quo modo quisque natus est*) (119). The etymology of "nascence" and "nature" is one of the favored twists through which Cicero likes to prop up the hybrid concept of a *normative nature*.

The practical question is of knowing what our obligations are to the natural. For the moment, let us bear in mind the single parallelism between the natural and nature, both of which are normative without, however, belonging to the same matrix. Which *persona* should one follow in each action? This is what is "amongst all decisions, the most difficult" (117). Cicero certainly does not doubt that our first obligation is to the common *persona* in us that separates us from the animals. However, each, "as he is born," should also satisfy the idiosyncrasy of his psychic makeup and social standing. Cicero makes a catalogue of characteristic traits,[30] not as a descriptive anthropologist, but rather to show from whence secondary obligations come to us. Only one thing can exempt us from an incompatibility between two prescriptive orientations—the *personae* must be adjusted with a view to the singular formal principle of non-contradiction. As long as our individual nature does not contravene the normativity of rational nature, actions that follow this manner of being are proper. "Each should hold resolutely to the talents that are proper to him. . . . There is no propriety when one acts 'against the grain,' which is to say, in opposition to one's nature" (110). The obligation which we have to follow our natural talents is not a matter of morality in the sense of a deductive discourse, but of *decorum*. Not of decor: the Latin word "decorum" translates as the Greek word *prepon,* 'correctness.' It is even less a matter of duty. The singular is normative in order to make of our life a "correct"—and in that sense "just"—work, where everything sticks together because all is in its place. Here also will be the place to ask whether making the natural secondary with regard to nature clears up their normative incongruity as elegantly as Cicero would like, which is to say, as elegantly as he *posits* it.

The theoretical question is actually altogether different, and more revelatory in another way: What is the originary experience from whence the double bind of nature and the natural is imposed upon this first Latin, who is Cicero? We fashion for ourselves a face, the singular *persona,* through constantly making choices. Amongst these choices, those that add a trait that can be integrated into our already acquired profiles will be encouraged, and those which disfigure it will be avoided. Choices are made through assenting or refusing assent to solicitations. Now, for the man of politics, who is again Cicero, all of this happens at first and before all in the highly visible arena of power. There is here something like a metaphysical determinism: Whether Cato adopts an obstructionist tactic to defeat a law or not, both decisions will proceed from what is natural as this is bequeathed by his destiny (*heimarménê, fatum*). However, there is still an ethical indeterminism: From Cato's own point of view, his tactical choices are free. For the Greek who passes his days solely in Rome, such as Paneatius, the natural signifies the psycho-portrait of each person. For the Roman such as Cicero, the natural follows from the site that each person occupies in the *Urbs*. The normative singular of which one can give a plausible account is the *public site*.

Thus it is that nature, understood as the principle of ordering ends according to their continuity, is first denatured. Moreover, Cicero shows himself to be perfectly aware of the topological adjustments he effects. From the point of view of destiny—understood in terms of the cosmic *topos*—he does not hesitate to describe a harmony extending from a life perfectly balanced in all its parts to the extremity of the globe and to the gods, a harmony in which nature does not leap about randomly in linking together the ends pursued by each person. "If, in setting out from the beings first sketched out, we wish to progress to the last and fully realized beings, we shall necessarily arrive at the divine beings."[31] If we wish . . . but that is precisely not what Cicero wants. He speaks from another point of view: that of the statesman. By means of the topological schema through which he writes his *apographa*, he distances himself from the Stoics' teachings on purpose. The *topos* for his teaching is the Roman magistracy. There is a distance between the Greek *kathékon* and the Latin *officium* about which he seems very pleased. He justified his translation to a friend: "I have no doubt that what the Greeks call *kathékon* is our *officium*. That same word of which you doubt, does it not square clearly with the republic itself? Do we not say 'consular office,' "senatorial office'? The word fits perfectly. Now, then, give a better translation of it (*aut da melius*)."[32]

His interlocutor does just as good a job of putting his finger on this denaturing. Atticus proves to be a better expert of the Stoics. He objects that *kathékon* means, for all that, something other than the visible public place with its conventions; namely, it means the subsumption of tumultuous drives under the universal that resides in us: under the rational nature that is essentially at peace. Cicero, the translator, does not seek the equivalent word, but the equivalent usage, a usage that is as much institutional as linguistic. One could hardly better emphasize the displacements of sense owing to language. The mutual imbrication of the Latin language and its Roman institutions in a single *usage* ends by transmuting the morality of rationality into an ethics of naturality.

The two *personae* born in us, from whence speaks a common nature that is singular, appear curiously confounded in the lines cited above in the epigraph. "There exists one true law, which is right reason that conforms to the nature distributed among all humans, subject neither to change nor to perishing. It calls us to fulfill that which is fitting (*quae vocet at officium iubendo*). . . ." This is an admirable description of the double bind of nature and the natural! The Stoics ranged the "fitting" on the side of life in accord with the instincts. On the side of life in accord with reason, they ranged "that which is well done" (*kathorthoma, recte factum* or *recta effectio*): the acts deducible by reason that are commonly done everywhere, in other words the virtues. Now, obviously one would expect that the true law would give us a prescription for the virtuous life. Was this in a sense not already the lesson of Antigone? But in the works of Cicero, this law calls us to fulfill well our public function, to play well our singular role. Whether it is the urbanity, the pragmatism, the cosmopolitanism of Rome, or some other so-called cultural factor which makes what is properly one's own enter into the normative work of common nature, the individual will continue to be strengthened in regard to and against the law distributed in the human genus. The proper *persona,* to which I ought to adjust myself, has a place only within me. It is located outside of the great telic linkage. This call to follow one's own proper voice more than the common voice—*this singularizing extraterritoriality*—does this not resonate with Sophocles?

Her denial of the city singularized Antigone, just as Creon's denial of the family singularized him—until late in life, too late, there came to them the clear vision of the originary dissension. Does philosophy have any means by which to forestall this "too late" of tragedy?

The millennium and a half which will follow Cicero will instead occupy itself with positing the sort of nature that *subsumes* the natural. Theticism is supposed to become voiceless against the "too late" and against every trenchant delay, just as it is supposed to bring to a definitive conclusion all conditions and all insistent questioning. Recourse will be made to grand measures to deny the transgressive counter-strategy by which the singular corrodes the edifice of natural law from within. This corrosion, a temporal and temporalizing breach, is the work of death that nevertheless destroys the genus, annuls the denial, gives new impetus to the question of conditions beyond a premature conclusion, renders incontrovertible the normative double bind as ultimate authority, and extracts in advance the phenomena from the hegemonic fantasm. As is always the case with the metaphysician within us no matter what the language may be in which it bathes, the Latin philosophers *will realize* the universal. Thus, faithful despite themselves to the ancient lesson to follow the phenomena, they will refine the realism of the universals without ever truly reaching the point of transmuting the singular into the particular. Certain among them will declare the singular destitute of all being, and this will be a theticism of the most hubristic sort.[33] But at the end of this journey, in the fourteenth century, the singular will end up by getting the better of nature. This amounts to a reterritorialization of the tragic structure if ever there was one—nevertheless it is a return of this knowledge, and in force. Its force will be such that it will then break our history in two—into ancient and modern history.

At the very moment when a vocabulary is constituted for systematically invoking nature as an ultimate referent, *natura* is scaled down and ends up by arranging ethics around the portrait conforming to the public site a man occupies. The fissure in the rational edifice of the *lex natura* becomes more severe in the political writings of Cicero where he speaks more of his own authority. There, in treating a created constitution—the Roman—as a natural being, he endows the singular with the strongest normativity.

However, before considering this, let us see how, when this referent is instituted all in one piece, the singular is placed neither at the beginning nor at the end. How does it speak under the name henceforth making the law? Would expressing the *I* singularly be a discourse capable of forestalling the tragic "too late"? Would the singular expressing itself thus essentially deal with the early and the late? How does it refer to what was and to what will be? How does it refer to time over and above the natural?

On self-narrating natures

Prior to the modern era, no thinker had said "I" in a more resounding tone than St. Augustine. Neither had anyone denounced so violently the culture of "I." To fabricate an individual *persona* is as such both the sign and reality of sin. This is because individual nature is always fickle, uncertain. Hence, a consoling remedy is given: "If you find that your nature is unsettled, go then beyond yourself."[34] From *my* nature, whence? Toward *His* nature, responds Augustine. This is a new singularization owing to what is called "interiority."[35] It is also a new scaling down of the referent, for this time it is not in universal-singular nature, but in singular-Singular nature. Augustine goes about the speech that is his confession as if he were fathering something. What transpires there is the *erratic production of a singular other.* Nature is "this me" at the beginning of the confessional wanderings confessed, and it is still "this me" at the end, but then mediated by "That one who is there" or by "You." This whole production works by way of deictic givens, arranging and rearranging them until the "I" is an other. To grasp how Christian Latinity broaches hegemony—institutes it and undermines it—it is necessary to follow the itinerary of this production recounted by Augustine.

He relates his past and his story fills him with horror before the inconstant. It is a salutary horror in that it makes him turn toward that place where all is only order and constancy—toward the law whose immutability he never wearied of touting. Now, this law that he calls eternal and that will have to be examined—under what figure does it stabilize him? This is a question of normative authority.

The narratable singular figures into the confession first of all by way of the changing nature of the protagonist; but the intrigue with which I find myself bound up when placed before the horror of my nature is tied together by the pacifying *force majeure* of a nature that is also singular. Hence the recitative mode. It has a systematic necessity that is more tenacious than a memory trying to keep the wanderings of the "I" going. Above all, what must be narrated is how You make the law, measuring me through singular interventions. The law will prove to be integrative through this truly strange principial organization whose strangeness must be scrutinized—the strangeness of narratable subsumptions. The normative bind will be knotted in a story between *natures that narrate only themselves.*

The stages which the "I" traverses in its confession can easily be spelled out: There are vicissitudes far from the law; then a reflective looking back upon and into the self, whereby a reflection of the law is discovered; and finally a return to the law neither reflected nor reflected upon, but fully radiant. The conquest of a stable interiority proceeds from exterior to interior things, then to superior things. However, through these anagogic stops one more story gets expressed, a story that is not anagogic.

On first glance, Augustine retraces the dialectical production of a *single bond,* going from the singular (the wandering "I") to the universal (the law—later we will take up how it is eternal and how it is natural) so as to return to the universalized particular (to the "I" subsumed under the law). In this dialectic, nature is encountered in three sites, though it is not the same in each. Only in the second site is nature common and commonly imposed, that is to say, normative. The vicissitudes at one pole can only be shown—these are conspicuous objects. At the other pole, the concluding point is what has to be created—it will come into being through subjection. Only the mediating term can be demonstrated; it is the object of reflection. Let us briefly follow the course of this apparent dialectical production of a subjected "I." How is the nature which makes the law to be understood here?

The first site is that of desire. Augustine talks about drives and about attempts at holding on and holding off, about the offensive things, in his estimation, suffered, or menacing him, and about desirous impulses mixed with fear. Individual nature is changeable because desire pursues first one relief and then another. The search for possession defines love in all its forms.[36] The search for variable possessions defines "appetite." Furthermore, individual nature, being dispersed among multiple appetites, swerves and spins with the least excitement. Augustine recounts his pursuits and finds fault therein, less on account of their diversity than on account of the impossibility of possessing them. Horror declares itself each time in his fear of losing that which he has touched. There is no desire to possess (*appetitus habendi*) without the fear of loss (*metus amittendi*). A jumble of ardors and relapses make up the history of the *persona* fashioned by character and social role. There is a moment of exteriority whose chronicling is most clearly of concern for the "genre" of autobiography.

The access into the second site is complex. The story that continues is now that of a certain free rein given to stimulants. Giving free rein requires that the "I" be turned in another direction, elsewhere. This is a moment of reflection through which the singular simultaneously affirms and annuls itself.

The singular affirms itself here as a protagonist who has given leave to the chase and all grasping: *intus ibam,* "I have re-entered into myself." Which "I"? The heart restless through all its impulses. The story fulfills the conversion that it relates, which is why Augustine must keep talking endlessly. Endlessly he gives leave to the aberrations of his individual nature by endlessly recounting his giving leave to them. The narrative no longer retraces a visible gesture. Statements in the first person constitute, in a strong sense, the moment of interiority. They constitute it in and through the narrative. For the narrator, to make a U-turn and enter into himself is to recount his dissoluteness as well as his return to rule. The restless heart singularizes me otherwise than do my impulses; it singularizes me through a pathological heightening of memory. Augustine confesses an obvious fact within him and the interminable recollections of neglecting this obvious fact. The heart returning to itself would remain null and void if it could not say and resay "I," to the point—such is the goal of this completely other pursuit—of displaying a life obviously centered. The "I" is then always decentered under the desired dissimulation of the obvious. How is it then constituted? It lives and resonates in the single enunciative act. Thus, if we want to speak of an Augustinian "self," it would be necessary to place it within confessional activity. *There is nothing common* in this effective memory of the self, there is no removal of individualizing conditions, no *via remotionis* leads the heart—a technical term in Augustine for what, anachronistically, we may be tempted to call the self—to untroubled possession.

Full presence will be brought into harmony in and through the narration itself. Consequently the self that is brought about there will be all the more precarious.

But, in returning to itself, the singular also annuls itself: "I re-entered into myself and I saw with some eye of my soul . . ."[37] Bound by the *anima mea* (or, according to the perspective, by the *animus meus,* the *mens mea*), the "I" is transmuted. *There is nothing more common* now than this eye of the soul which Augustine seems not to know how to name. The "some" dissolves the proper noun. The common eye sees, and it is devoted to seeing spectacles. The spirit and its eye form the object of a memory neither chronicling nor effective, but rather speculative in the sense of reflection. It is an inspection that is no longer exactly introspection. It no longer discovers a changeable nature, and it no longer constitutes a precarious self. Turned inward, the "I" becomes reflective and grasps the functions which are invariable. Bringing these into focus—a focusing that we call, again anachronistically, the Augustinian cogito—secures a fixed platform for the dialectic. It is always and again a question of me, but it is insofar as I see these functions with a clearer and nevertheless anonymous eye: with a focal, non-contingent eye that remains open whether or not I give it any attention. In topographical terms, this focusing is operative otherwise than in the enunciative act. It is operative in the act conjoining the functions which are (the content of this triad, however, is not important here) being, knowledge, and willing (XII, 11, 12). It then signifies in us another nature than the conspicuous one. "I have re-entered into myself": the fact is datable. "I have seen": this fact no longer is so, its issue being "the immutable light" that focuses the gaze and reveals the interior topography. I have seen that which, according to the law, is obvious for all and always. This interior gaze normalizes me, as it normalizes each person everywhere. The Augustinian institution of natural laws holds completely to the non-episodic radiance of the subsisting truth. This means that in making a return to the self, the singular "I" is annulled in a sort of proto-transcendental "I" that can be described in terms of a certain mental structure and its functions. If it is urgent to return from the dispersion outside, it is that the "I" inside pulls and attracts the *a priori* centering that it effects—by its common nature. Reflected light is natural since it always clarifies the plexus of *a priori* functions in us. But I can turn myself to these functions through conversion just as I can turn myself away from them through aversion. When converted in this sense, the "I" will be different.

In its first site, the singular finds itself denounced. It is struck down on account of the attention given to the *persona*. In its second site, it is legitimized by the activity which in this case defines it: confession. However, it is precisely through this that it is also universalized. *Natura* here no longer signifies an unstable nature, born November 13, 354, but the innate law, "written in the hearts of men and which inquietude itself does not efface" (II, 4, 9). This law—notably but not exclusively of trinitarian directives—is discovered in reflection. It commonly constrains me without ambiguities or ambivalences and in plain language. Now, a bundle of *a priori* functions cannot serve as the ultimate unity. The "I" is still a manifold unity. Therefore, there is, lastly, a third site reached by the history recounted—"I have re-entered into myself, and I have seen with some eye of my soul above this eye of my soul, above my intelligence, the immutable light." The above puts me in my place. It brings reason into line, making it into the *recta ratio,* and it straightens me out. The "I" finds its footing in subjecting itself to this rectificatory, normative, normalizing constraint. A similar setting up of the singular is effected by subjection. It generates the particular, which is the effect of a uniformly constraining nature in plain language. The *normed particular* is produced starting with a *dispersed singular* when introspection gives way to speculation, and speculation to mirroring. The "I" is known as the reflection of the true light. It reflects *upon itself* and gains certitude because it reflects *it.* Such is, briefly, the journey of the singular, universal, and particular.

It is here that we must look more closely to see that the mere semblance of a similar dialectic proves, if not a false semblance, at least only the half of the itinerary confessed.

What we must look at more closely is the third site, the axis, around which the dialectic in question arises, bends, branches off, and breaks indeed under the weight of history itself. It bends in that the singular heart subsists in the particular. It branches off because it leads thought toward the Singular functioning as universal. It is broken under the incongruity of the singular that is mine and the Singular that is its, which are irreducible both to the particular and to the universal. To say "I" and "You" in such a resounding manner is to make the incongruity in the ultimate authority ring out—the tragic condition.

The entire work of the *Confessions,* or almost, is expressed in direct discourse. Augustine says "You," who are more real, more of a *res,* than are desire's external lures; "you," who are more stable than the passing interior respites in the ever-fragile return to self, or return to the self; "you," who are still more luminous, which is to say, truer, than the obvious facts in which the spirit is certain of its proper manner of being. . . . When the supremely singular gives itself to be possessed, it takes away the fear of loss. One would have expected that the guarantee of perfect stability would condense the dissolute singular from above, that it would inhale it like a pump sucks up and compresses a liquid. Does such a work not sketch out the return to the self, such as we have retraced it, as a natural confluence that is normative because it gathers up in advance my dissolute life into its most ordinary compactness? Doesn't the theory of radiance or influx—a theory of the truth flowing from above, and in this, the supremely influential—point in this paradigmatic direction? We aspire to the immutable, and it breathes us in—isn't this the recipe for all philosophical consolation?

No doubt. But in Augustine something else happens, something altogether different. With the aprioric platform scarcely won, the "You" begins to deflect the universalizing optics, or hydraulics. In its third position, the Singular allows itself to be touched by singular hearts: "And whilst we speak and breathe it [wisdom] in, here is what we touch, though barely, from the rapid and total upsurge of the heart" (IX, 10,

24). A return, then, to the narrative mode. A trembling heart which touches its pacifier, if only in an *ictus* (or so it is, above all, in this case), has something to recount. But subjection and narration are not in accord with each other.

Here we see how the differend opens up. This pacifier, so singular that the appeasements it provides can only be recounted, is the very model of natural law, a model Augustine calls eternal law. The wisdom of God denotes the intra-divine life which the triadic organization in us imitates. In Augustine, the great founder, the entrance of the "I" and the "You" into nomothetic discourse denatures nature, not just because the uneasy heart persists there in its disquietudes, but because Augustine affirms a *natural law about which the work of subjection is recounted as only the singular recounts it.* With the entry of philosophy into the Latin patristic, the ultimate referent must answer both for Greek pragmatism and biblical interventionism—the "both-and" which is resolved in favor of biblical interventionism. Augustine has only to make a distinction between natural light and the light of revelation. Similarly, he has only to make a distinction between rational law and revealed law—there is no law more rational than active wisdom. Whatever may be the consequences for this *supreme* referent which is God, the *ultimate* referent, which is nature, is found shot through with singularizing strategies that will prove to be explosive among the Augustinians at the close of the Middle Ages.

Augustine does not run out of *givens.* "I," "you," these pears which I stole, this city, Milan, this little girl who sings "Take and read" such and such a book, the thirty-first year of my life, then "my heart," that other day when near to a window in Ostia, my mother. . . . The whole gamut of givens runs from a sack of pears to "the wisdom which You are." All are singulars, retained as such—which is proof of a perspicacious fidelity to phenomena. Perspicacious because singularization is expressed *sub specie mortis.* This fidelity is won and it must constantly be rewon in the face of death. Witness the beginning of the scene at Ostia: "Well, the day was imminent when she [mother] would take leave of this life. . . . We spoke together, forgetting the past, concentrated on the future" (IX, 10, 23). Made to ascend, normative discourse is placed under a maximizing thrust—or as we say, under that of natality. But in only portraying various "thises," and stretching them out in the direction of the future, this discourse also situates itself resolutely under that of mortality. The double bind of the universal and singular—we have seen it elsewhere and we see it here—divides imminence in two. It places Augustine *before* the eternal law and *before* death. Hence the "I," unheard of until then, is temporalized in the very search for the authority making the law.

From here it is not difficult to see that in this institution of a hegemony, the fantasm is only posited in order to be deposed. The singular given does not suffice to console the soul (no more than it will to consolidate the city in the last writings). This is so because the range of givens always has time as its key. The non-temporal is not given to him, but posited. Time, which inspires either contempt (*contemnenda temporalia*) or praise (the wisdom in the history of the heavenly city is gathered together on earth)—time, therefore, anguishes and individualizes. Hence the enormous work of overdetermination—"the wisdom that You are" turns into the *lex aeterna;* and fidelity to phenomena turns into the nomothesis. However, inasmuch as it is engaged here, theticism is dismantled in advance by the act of confession. There is a double act, confirming the wandering which forms my nature and praising the wisdom which is His nature. Thus the Augustinian dialectic in no way concludes with a subjection. The disparate sites of singulars—me here, You there—thwart the normative subjection by means of the same gesture that inquires into it.

Placing the singular and Singular into a series calls for the narrative. In subordinating the subject to the law, confession raises itself up to the intelligible, but in linking together the "I" and the "You" it instead repeats the obvious. Beginning with its institution as a normative referent, *natura* places singulars in a topical disparity while placing particulars into nomic subjection. This double bind appears ten years before in the *Confessions,* when Augustine addressed sharply and familiarly the stable law which was supposed to relieve anguish—namely, in the dialogue *On Free Will* begun a year after his conversion to philosophy. This is the document *par excellence* that establishes natural law. Yet the principle of telic continuity is on this account legislative, and, on account of its being cracked there by a singularizing fissure, it is transgressive.

The vocabulary of this dialogue remains largely Stoic.[38] The natural law is the object of a choice (*liberum arbitrum* translates the Greek *eklogé*) and thus, for Augustine, of the will. Beginning with his readings of Cicero, Augustine posits the will shot through by a division: "The happy life is accorded to the will which is good and the miserable life to the will which is wicked" (15, 31). A boldly generalizing axiom of an impeccable dualism: "It is evident that there exists one kind of man who is a friend of eternal things, and another kind who is a friend of temporal things. So there are here two laws, one eternal and the other temporal. . . . Those that the love of eternal things make happy act under the eternal law, while the unhappy remain subject to the temporal law" (ibid.). Augustine works and reworks the division between these two wills. He enlists its opposing strategies in a dialectic that, once again, runs aground on the singular.

In the terms of the interiority being born here, those human beings whose will is good turn themselves inward in order to contemplate an order there which does not change, and those whose will is wicked turn away from inwardness, are outwardly restless, endeavoring to obtain those goods that are strewn about and know only the inconstant, which is without order. There is no gray zone where either-or would be blurred. Among human beings there are those who obey the eternal law and those who obey the temporal law. This is a disjunction admitting no concession to which Augustine—to his ultimate regret—abandons himself, since whosoever lives under the eternal law *does not live* under the temporal law and whosoever lives under the temporal law *does not live* under the eternal law. "Those whose good will attaches itself to the eternal law have no need of the temporal law" (ibid.). If you are counted among the wise, you will be exempt from civil laws. Here, in this beginning of its long philosophic career, the task assigned to free will is no more complex than to distinguish between the day and the night, between day and night without any intermediate twilight and as peopled by two distinct human families. In the subsequent writings of

Augustine, the incidence of these two types of laws will instead intertwine the two families. As for his change of heart, the more Christian he becomes, the more will he see each of what he will then call "cities" as subject to two types of laws, even though these cities also remain always clearly opposable through the respective loves which found them. The blunt formula of the young Augustine will establish authority: The wise choose the eternal law, the foolish the temporal law.

Let us note that this dualism fractures not the referent posited as supra-individual, as in the works of a Manichean, but the individual will. Augustine no longer places man under two principles, the one eternal, the other temporal. Rather, he opposes the election and abandonment of one and the same principle: The eternal law presents itself to the choice of each individual. Even though one can always turn away from it, it rules uniformly, solely normative, sunlike. The dialectic that is supposed to produce the standard sense of nature, we will see, nevertheless does not, for all that, come to an end in simple subjection. Just as everyone orients themselves toward this referent, everyone gets what they have chosen, whether it be the regime of the eternal law from which one gains liberty, or whether it be that of the temporal law, the sanction of which is coercion. This is a much more urgent choice than was ever made by the Stoic *eklogé,* whose stakes sharpen the point, also normative, of disparate singulars. A specific, individual possession is to be won or lost: the being who said, "I am the light, I am the life." And it is here that the fissures become multiple.

From a doxographic point of view, the treatise on free will and the eternal law are split apart for the first time by the conflict between two preponderating forces—Stoic right reason and revealed wisdom. According to each of them, it is a matter of disciplining love, turning away from the pleasures which one is always at risk of losing as soon as they have been satisfied. But according to Stoic reasoning, the imperative follows from the fact that "spirit (*mens*) also is able not to rule" (10, 20); and when it rules, individuals "are at peace with themselves because they have made the passions subject to the rule of the spirit" (9, 19).[39] According to Christian argument, which is still undeveloped in this dialogue, the *imperium* is altogether other. A singular which gives life reigns over the singular existence—over the "heart," the proper term, as we have seen, for designating the individual before God. This tone will become dominant in Augustine's more dogmatic writings without the Stoic tonality ever being obliterated in his works. Only, each heart will be situated more and more expressly under the practical authority of "wisdom," which is the proper term by which to array the interventions of God. Within the edifice of the law, these interventions introduce a fissure no longer doxographic, but systematic. If these interventions are arrayed, it is because a certain geometric ideal is dispersed into points irreducible to any sort of continuous natural telocracy—into erratic singularizations.

Wisdom indeed exerts itself intermittently, tracing the dotted line which is the history of salvation while being concerned with individuals, whereby the telic continuum is perforated. For the Stoics, for whom Cicero makes himself the spokesman, the morally fine individual was constituted through reason's influence over the other faculties. Augustine derives from this influence what we might call an integrative definition of natural law: "When reason governs the irrational energies of the spirit, then there dominates in man that which, in conformity with the law we have recognized as eternal, should dominate" (8, 18). This is an integrative definition in that the law prescribes the homologating of faculties in terms of their end, namely, their domination by reason. Its retributive definition is quite different: "God sets punishments upon the wicked, just as he recompenses the good" (1, 1). Here the Stoic *heimarméné* ('destiny,' 'apportionment') is turned into a principle of *ad hoc* interventions. Practical wisdom transmutes the eternal law into the singular law according to which the singular agent acts. Once again the divine will as well as the moment of its acting belong to the semantic field of wisdom. We can see the consequence, which is, with just a shade of difference, parallel to the *Confessions:* The retributive conception breaks with the integrative just as the will breaks with the linking together of ends and the moment of acting breaks with duration; and just as the singular rebelling against subjection breaks with—and indeed breaks—the subsumptive universal. With just a shade of difference, on account of the persistence of eidetic paradigmatism. Nevertheless, it is a rather curious persistence for the status of the eidos from which the integratable would arise reverts to a singular (to God who assigns the recompenses) and the status of the copy to the aftereffects of a universal (to authorizing reason). Now, for Augustine, what sense would there be in lingering over these aftereffects if not ultimately to exalt the agent capable, in its will, of saturating the moment with its full presence? But once this retributive-volitional-instantaneous exaltation is posited, what sense could there ever be to have *universal nature subordinated to the singular*? Thus we have here the requirement of a praxis which cuts short the ascension toward the subsumptive summit. No sooner is it won than the platform of an anagogic dialectic is abandoned in favor of an agent. The law inscribed in hearts, which then is called, strictly speaking, the "natural law," remains universal, but nonetheless derives from the "eternal law," the sole founder. Now the latter, as divine practical wisdom, arises intermittently since a will is always intermittent. The absolutely free will is erratic—and here again the Scotists proved to be excellent Augustinians.

So here we see that to which the translation leads when *eklogé* comes to connote *voluntas*. The distracted will is normed by a willing that brings it into focus—each are singulars, and incongruously mediated by the principle of universal telic continuity. Similarly, what norms the wanderings of desire are erratic rectificatory interventions mediated just as incongruously by the law. As a result, we no longer know very well how to respond to the question of what makes the law. Indeed, what are we to say faced by this monster of a universal that encompasses without remainder all phenomenal regions and nevertheless is secondary in relation to a singular agent? This difficult position in which we find ourselves is a very fine example of the disparity that cracks normative nature from within at the moment of its epochal institution. In the *Confessions,* this disparity keeps a singular *force majeure* at a distance away from a singular that wanders from one enticement to another. In *On Free Will,* this disparity separates this same *force majeure* from a universal compared to which nothing more integrative can be conceived, and which strangely is placed *under* it. What is clear is that the *ontic agent* of individual retribution looms over natural law, and the *universal principle* links together the genera. Indeed, this is a lovely example of originary disparity—we could also say, of a universalizing and singularizing double bind.

The double bind is wholly in force in this apposition of dissimilars—practical exemplarism. The apposition effaces neither the singular—intervening freedom—nor the universal—the greatest model of extention, marking the genera. The archaic figure that lays down the natural law punishes and rewards. Now, with nature thus made secondary in respect to a singular will, we would like to know how a *uniformly* subsumptive work can be sustained. According to the Stoic principle of continuity, nature homologates the universe through systematic dependencies; in the name of its integrative law and due to right reason, everything holds together. But here universal consistency results from a dependency as if through suspension: The integrative law according to which right reason guides the human genus is caught under the retributive law according to which all abides by, and due to, the act of a singular. Each law aspires to normativity. Whence the conflict in the ultimate authority.

This conflict is in the ultimate authority, for Augustine does not hesitate to identify normative nature and divine will.[40] The singular that incongruously is attached to nature is the core issue of a narrative to the extent that it deals with a life. Referential nature then signifies, above all, the law of this particular life that Augustine describes in terms of plans, or in terms of the relation in God between intelligence and the will, or even of trinitarian processes—which are so many groups in a *relational* referent, and thus an ultimate, non-*entitative* or supreme referent. Singular exemplarism projects into God the model of natural law, an ontic projection operating on the relations that an action brings about. What happens once Augustine identifies normative nature and divine will? The rational texture homologating beings is ripped at the very place that he seeks to attach it—at an act singularized by the will and in turn singularizing the one to whom it is addressed. It is a curious exemplarism that is stated in the second person: "You have all disposed within yourself."[41] What is the observation in terms of which Augustine exalts nature, the measure of given ends? He maximizes it beginning with the free choices to which the happy and the miserable have given themselves. Just like the confession of errant wanderings which passes from things exterior to things interior and onto superior things, the demonstration of the law begins from an ontic given (the will through which human beings classify themselves) and then it discovers a condition (sanctioning nature), only to shatter this nature on account of a positing and an apposition that once again is ontic (the retributive will). Under this version of theticism, the narrative showing the "thises" thus irremissably decontextualizes the world which the demonstration was supposed to contextualize. It is necessary to keep perplexity alive before these asymmetrical moments and before the ultimates to which they give rise. Manifestation erupting in demonstration—this is the most phenomenologically authentic thing, in the sense of a grasp of ultimates, that Augustine has to offer.

The erratic production of the normative singular introduces a double strategy into the fantasm of nature: A pull toward the continuous order but also a pull back toward intermittent interventions. The double bind can only frustrate the perturbed heart. The rough sketch of an ascension toward nature, the principle of all principles, places the heart in the right place to await *the consolations of the genus*. Certainly the heart obeys an ultimate law, but it is the will of an agent denaturing these very consolations. As an ontological chain linking beings together, nature is life-giving; but as the ontic motivation of an action, nature is in great danger—and it threatens quite concretely—of taking back that which it gave. Augustine indeed repeats this along with the Platonists: the singular is the principle of death.[42] This counter-principle exacerbates inquietude. The disparity of ultimates makes the work of consolation, promised by the nature that homologates nature, miscarry.

It is in this respect that Augustine is a better philosopher than he might appear to be. We will see further on how the referent which is nature is supposed to consolidate the city. As for the consolation of the heart, because it remains suspended from a singular will, it turns instead to panic. Augustine is a better philosopher than one might suspect judging from the amalgam of Greek philosophic remnants with Christian doctrine. As integrative, nature is life-giving; as retributive, it threatens with punishments, loss, death. In this *magister mundi,* we have remarkable proof of the fidelity to phenomena among those outside the regime of functionaries. The phenomena which speak so loudly through this great initiator are those which everybody knows best, but which everyone is poor at recognizing: the incessant advent of death in the thrust that makes life. With an immediate simplicity possible only before the construction of grand conceptual edifices, Augustine follows the ineluctable conjunction of natality and mortality. As in Cicero, though according to another arrangement, the singular intervenes in the law of nature as the undertow of a counter-law that throws it into turmoil by temporalizing sense and order.

This temporalization is best discerned in the history where such cities wander.

CHAPTER 9
On the Erratic Differend

The transgressive strategies that topple a hegemony result from singularizations and from a temporalization which renders them capable of being narrated; such is the work of indetermination—and therefore of death—which inevitably ruins the determinant work of life erecting normative constructions.

In order to grasp how the time of the singular breaks the *natura,* let us first recall the expectation inherent in the ultimate referents. The fantasmic maximization departs from a singular, relational given—my nature, my voluntary choices, thus the confessed "I"—and inflates its intrinsic relations to subsumptive dimensions without remainder. The point of departure of this operation is only shown or described; it escapes the rational grasp. As theticism has always maintained, the singular is ineffable. As for the end point, it also escapes reason. If it could be deduced without error, a simply constraining authority would remain ineffable due to its very simplicity, its unicity, its supremacy {*archie*}, its primacy. An ultimate principle serves as a referent for all reasoning, but only an intuition brings it to a halt. One might as well say that it is posited, a positing whose well-foundedness is negotiated (in the sense of the Aristotelian dialectic) in the see-saw of preponderances in representation. The topology of fantasms informs us directly of the thetic standards which gave order and life to an epoch by providing it with the law; and indirectly, it also informs us of the singular from which their maximization started out. There is no genus for the traits of natality and mortality, which are ultimates. Hence there is a fracture in thetic edifices, whatever their intuitive underpinnings might be. To the positive and sovereign triumph is joined a different triumph: The temporalizing undertow of the singular that erodes all sovereignty from within. Philosophy has never ceased to bear in mind this work of death, even if it does so by a fidelity that is rather oblique to the ultimates as the originary phenomena.

Now, time has never more clearly destabilized theticism than in the discourse of the early Latin world which *posits a particular city as natural*. For Cicero, it is Rome; for Augustine, heavenly Jerusalem. In their politics and ethics alike, it is not exactly a particular being that persists in the maximizing work and that resists subsumption. Rather, it is "offices" in Cicero and divine "wisdom" in Augustine that are the relational terms raised up to the superlative. They are "terms" because they stop the proliferation of references; they are relational because they sometimes connect certain roles and other times certain rewards; they are "raised" to the superlative, finally, because compared to them nothing higher can be conceived on the normative scale. The same is true with respect to the political. In the singular republic that was Rome, the system of telic relations is natural, a system of continuity or equivalence that we call its constitution. The promised Jerusalem is natural as well, and is just as singular in its telic homology that we call charity. In its institutional beginnings the political discourse that speaks in the name of nature maximizes the laws of a city, one that was and another that will be.

For Aristotle, the guiding phenomenal region that incited archic investigation was that of the change brought about by man and studied by physics. The region from which the early Latins extracted their hegemonic fantasm is altogether different. It is the political. It entails a different temporalization of being that is no longer that of the observable kinetic processes, but is that of narratable mnemonic processes. Discourse must keep alive the memory of the ancestral city as well as that of the Jerusalem to come. Both will serve as antidotes for the pains of the present inasmuch as *memoria* draws up its faithful chronicle. Cicero puts it simply—"through discourse we retain the republic of which for some time we have not been able to retain the public thing."[43] Caesar having abolished the *maiorum instituta,* the temporalizing act is to have piety for the city that was. In the theticism of republican Rome, time is constituted by the memory of the past. In Augustine, it is constituted by the memory of the city that will be.

It is now necessary to inquire here into that temporality from which singularization arises.

On a normative singular that was

In the most patriotic epic left to us by antiquity, the *Aeneid,* Vulcan makes for Aeneas a shield "of an indescribable texture." (VIII, 620ff.). One sees in it the she-wolf who has just given birth, the twins sucking at her teats, the rape of the Sabine women, the bloody punishments inflicted on the enemies, "the descendants of Aeneas rushing to arms for liberty," the Gauls and the goose that announces them, Numa, Cato . . . much more than just a list, it is a chronology. Virgil shows how Rome progressively created perfect laws capable of civilizing the world. At the moment when only the carcass of these institutions remains, he acts as a historian whose aim is a revival that would inspire *pietas* toward the ancestors. Moreover, the incarnation of this revival is in the very center of the shield. It is Caesar Augustus.

Let us contemplate the Homeric model of this description, and the obvious exaltation of the city that was. In the *Odyssey,* Hephaestus forges for Achilles a shield that is also of an indescribable texture (XVIII, 478ff.). It represents not a particular city and its history, but the world: the stars, the *okéanos,* the cities with their feasts, civil projects, markets, assemblies, quarrels, and wars. In the middle there is not a person, but the earth, the sky, and the sea (*pontos*). The representation arises from what is observed: the plane surface of the earth, the vault that looms over it. But Homer further constructs that which the eye perceives: this sphere and its geometrical divisions. Virgil also starts off from an observation: Rome is no longer what it was. He constructs, in recounting it, the origin of the perfect city. The narrative exalts the city that was to the level of a model. Virgil posits Rome. The Greek constructive genius, put in the service of paradigmatic idealities, was geometric. That of the Romans is political. They put it in the service of their own city that is promoted as an archetype to be imitated by all people.

A generation before Virgil, Cicero had devoted himself to a similar promotional work (only similar, because it turns the republicanism of the ancients against the Empire). How does the fantasmic maximization function that he uses to benefit republican Rome?

Cicero proceeds by a series of linguistic mediations which admittedly are a little eclectic. The gods speak through the voice of the world; they address the earth and sea so as to put it in an order. Similarly in the republic, the law speaks through the magistrates; it addresses the life of men in order to submit them to rule. Moreover, "the guide which is nature" determines the ends that each person follows, thereby prescribing their actions. Finally, and in order to make the model explicit, "speech interprets the mind"—a mediation that operates through words.[44] The speakers—gods, laws, nature, mind—form the conceptual ensemble that Cicero calls, in short, the "natural law."

The middle terms—world, magistrature, individual practical goals, words—name the regions to be integrated, that is, to be made continuous. These are the universe, the city, the individual and language (this last one serving, in addition, as a structuring model for the rest). But where is one to take hold of this patched fabric so as to form a whole that could hold together? Cicero responds by *recounting the genesis,* a procedure that obviously cannot be used to explain the first, third, and fourth regions, namely, the arrangement of the continents and the seas, ethical teleology, and the syntax of language. The sole domain where "nature" is to be taken literally as signifying "that which is born," is the second region listed, the *res publica*. Only there, when we ask "What is nature?" do we inquire into the origin in the sense of *naturality.* By relating its birth, the account is supposed to provide the proof that the republic was natural. Cicero therefore has Scipio recount the steps through which Rome came to achieve the one natural government, an amalgam of the three best constitutional forms.[45] When it is a question of genesis, an answer can be given only in the narrative mode. Now, it is in order to retain the singular that one recounts stories. The region of the political—that of the laws and of the magistrature—therefore introduces into an uninterrupted nature a discontinuity that calls for reflection. No other phenomenal domain has a history, none is self-determined by its being born. Consequently, perhaps the most well-known passage in all of Cicero comes to sanction this discontinuity. In this passage, Scipio dreams that in return for his life of service to the republic, he finds himself transported to the skies of philosophical contemplation. By recounting the birth of Rome under Romulus and Remus, then its growth, he "found an application for the Socratic doctrine come from abroad."[46] He acted as a philosopher, better than the best of the Greeks. Of the city that he idealizes, he made himself an effective servant both as consul and as friend of the forms. Here is the singular city, enthroned in the sky of ideas.

Rome owes its normativity to the seduction of its language. Beware of the slippage, more than etymological, that posits its "nature" beginning at "birth."

Today the apologists for the "classical theory of the natural law" attach great importance to the narrative status of the *Republic* and the *Laws*. Cicero serves their fundamentalists thesis that a city will be good only through the trickery of an elite—through the regime (by which these theoreticians mean the unity of private and public, a society and the state). The dialogue on the republic takes place in winter, they observe, while that on the laws takes place in the summer. The participants in the first seek the sun, "looking at political affairs in the light of eternity"; those of the second seek the shade. The moral that these apologists infer from this is that the search for the best regime is more important than that for the best laws.[47] Do not worry too much about the methods that lead there, we must integrate the private, civil society and the state. But, upon closer inspection, the argument of the dialogues instead runs in the opposite direction. The inversion is worth being noted because it shows which norm Cicero actually holds to be natural and how it invalidates the principle of telic continuity.

The dialogue of the *Laws* consists of three books. The first deals with the constitution, the second, religion (which is a fabrication of the masters *ad utilitatim vitae*), and the third, the magistrature. The decisive turning point occurs with the transition from the first book to the second. The characters are discussing the constitution in the shade of an oak. To take up the question of religion, they leave the shade and settle in the sun near a river. The first part of the dialogue has not succeeded in resolving the nature of the laws, and from this arises the need to "seek another beginning" (*Laws* II, 1, 1). They then consider *lex* as an intelligible cause of positive law, *ius*—following the example of the "second voyage" in the *Phaedo,* in which Socrates lifts his gaze toward "something beautiful that exists entirely by itself" (*Phaedo,* 96d-105c). When ascending or inductive reasoning that sets out from the constitutions fails, it becomes necessary to find a fixed point for descending or deductive reasoning. And whoever wishes to search the intelligible causes for a fixed point will benefit from placing himself under the open sky. . . . Cicero insists, citing a well-known verse: *"A Iove Musarum primordia,"* "Let us depart therefore from the Jupiter of the Muses." But Jupiter is an invention for the maintenance of public order! He and the Muses will be bad candidates for the rank of unchanging landmarks. Hence any "supreme" referent is ruled out. Conclusion: "Let us therefore set out from this highest law which was born [nata, and hence "natural"] before all time" (*Laws* I, 6, 19). The sought-after condition is "the positive law stems from nature" (*Laws* I, 13, 35). With *natura,* Cicero has the systematic beginning which alone will guarantee order. Moored in this way, *lex* can serve as an axiom for all reasoning on *ius* and on the commonwealth. Praise of the regime instead of praise of the laws? The situation is more complex. Cicero posits the continuous regime and declares it "founded in the nature of things" (*Laws* II, 4, 11). But he posits it as law, as the ultimate referent. But the question is: Which law? Where does he come across it? How is it foundational?

The Latin hegemonic fantasm does not leave behind, in the moment of its institution, the world of given things any more than does the Greek fantasm. Like the second departure in Parmenides, and contrary to what happens in the *Phaedo,* that of Cicero amounts to seeing the visible in another way, not to seeing the other of the visible. But the law that shows what positive law is all about *was* visible for Cicero only a generation earlier. Here we see that historical time is what weakens this nomothesis in the positive gesture that institutes it. The argument temporalizes nature exactly where its modern apologists establish their fundamentalism: in the narrative. The Rome that was was natural, and in this it forever serves as referent, as rule, and as norm. It serves as a referent by virtue of the inclusive force (*vis*) of its law become reality in the republic (*Laws* II, 4, 8); it serves as a prudential rule, because this law alone permits one to distinguish between the just and the unjust (*Laws* I, 6, 19); it serves as a norm, finally, for good or bad *ius* (*Laws* I, 16, 44). The Ciceronian thesis consists in declaring the totality of received institutions to be the referent, rule, and norm. The natural law that reason discovers in itself is what constituted the constitution of the largest of the republics. It is normative as long as one keeps it in memory, as long as one recounts its birth-nature.

Thus maximized from a singular institution, nature not only consoles, it also and above all consolidates. "My entire discourse tends to consolidate the States, to strengthen the forces, to cure the peoples" (*Laws* I, 13, 37). Ancient is the question of whether man becomes social under the constraint of needs or if he is so naturally. Cicero's thetic insight has to do with what had never been seen: Life in a city is natural, yes, but it is so—or rather, it was so—in a single city. The law serving as universal axioms had its place and its time, namely, the place marked by the Seven Hills, and the time separating the Twelve Tables from the Empire. The aporetic character of such an axiomatism does not escape him. Fearing that they will wreak critical havoc in the edifice that he believes nevertheless to have constructed with skill, he asks the representatives of the New Academy not to look too closely (*Laws* I, 13, 39). The aporia nevertheless leaves its mark on the entire tradition of natural law (a tradition in which, in the twentieth century, the fundamentalism in question would like to be monolithic): a *Latin* tradition stemming from Cicero, running through Lactance, Augustine, and Thomas Aquinas, up to its breakdown in the face of the evidence of the disparities and of the differend which it has not ceased to patch over as one cheats death. Then—at the end of the middle ages—nature, the universal principle of telic continuity, collapsing precisely in the individual (*haec*) nature.

By retracing these disparities and this differend, we will see that Cicero's great leap forward is a false movement, a *false movement more true* that the posited principial continuity. Its truth allies it with the other instituting gestures of the hegemonies and keeps Cicero faithful to the absolutely first phenomenon, namely, to the double, universalizing-singularizing bind that is ultimate in ordinary experience. In the nomothesis first set out in the Roman republic, the disparity is easily seen by following the play of "forces" in it. The law is essential because it always prevails. Hence the regret of the *instituta maiorum:* Under the republic, the force of the law was natural and the dictatorship does violence to it. The law actually is "the force of nature" (*naturae vis, Laws* I, 6, 19). Law, nature, force—Cicero sometimes almost equates these three terms (*vis naturaque legis, Laws* II, 4, 8). Nevertheless we can doubt that the three terms are really equal. Does not the weakening of the republic suggest that what gives the impetus to the "law of nature" is neither the experience of the law nor that of nature? Toward what normative authority does the syntagm "force of nature" point, an authority whose normativity declined with the ascent of Julius Caesar?

If it is susceptible to weakening, then the force of nature will no longer be able to be understood according to the schema of Aeschylus, as the attribute of the Bosporus whose course one does not divert with impunity. Nature-as-law will now signify this completely different *force majeure* against which one would have risen in vain as long as the institutions *were intact.* Cicero, the translator, has a word for a constellation such as law-nature-force. The Stoics had taught that reason reigned and that for this reason it must reign. Among the human faculties, the rational soul is the *hêgemonikon.* As we have seen, Cicero renders this word with *imperium.* But here again, to translate is to change the framework of a word and to redistribute its significations. The Greek notion described the continuous fabric enveloping spiritual well-being. The continuity is quite different when Roman supremacy binds together the destinies of an entire age—when the world lives under the empire (lowercase "e") of a city. From this nodal point, Cicero (like Augustine) follows the guiding thread to arrive at the nature which gives force to the law, a thread that leads to an *imperium* not only singular, but even contingent—and that nevertheless imposes its law as nature.

Let us reread the statements on natural law where Cicero expressly defines it by way of the principle of continuity (*Laws* I, 10, 30; III 1, 2f). The spheres of life are linked to each other through the *imperium.*[48] The *imperium* forces individuals under the order of the household; particular interests beneath those of the city; and as for people, the *imperium* forces them into the horizon—new and totally anti-Greek—of cosmopolitanism; it forces earth and sea into their respective places; and celestial bodies, finally, are forced under the cosmic order. But where did a Roman have his original experience of the law? For Cicero—the politician, lawyer, orator, and republican destroyer—the question does not even arise. He had his first systematic experience of force in his own city. The state of nature (in the premodern sense of order, obviously, not in the Hobbesian sense which signifies the opposite of order) is the *libera res publica populi Romani* that its *de facto* supremacy—legislating for everyone, everywhere and forever—promotes. Through its proven force, this condition tolerates no exception. Right reason and right discourse align themselves with the empire, which is the natural law . . . of the Roman republic now without force. One could say that there is in this an *imposing* double overdetermination; namely, that which was becomes constantly present, and the conspicuous becomes essence. Rome equals nature as today America equals freedom (no quotation marks) when it greets its immigrants with "*Welcome to freedom*" (no capitalization).

Even before the Empire, the Latin epoch thus begins with a new and decisive experience: the imperial experience. Here is its *arché,* here is its principle and its name. Roman thought extends this experience over everything it touches. The phenomenality of phenomena is constituted therein in the name of the *imperium.* Consequently the imperative essence of theticism (as we will see in detail in relation to Luther and Kant, then, in a critical light, in relation to Heidegger) maintains itself throughout the twenty centuries that have followed Cicero. In this sense, the great break in our history is produced perhaps when Greek gives way to Latin, and less, whatever the moderns may think, when Latin gives way to our vernacular languages.

Thus the triumph over Plato on which Cicero prides himself. The *politeîa* need only remain "the shadow and the image of a republic." Rome, on the other hand, allows one to "see in reality how what reason and discourse describe is constituted" (*Rep.* II, 30, 52 and 39, 66), for the effective *imperium* lacks a shadow and an image. The test of the laws comes from the *de facto* government. The Platonic republic had been posited and was incapable of passing this test, by which it is patently obvious that it was contrary to the natural condition. How would laws which are impossible to enact be in accordance with nature? How would right reason speak or recognize itself in this nature? To what force could a constitution and institutions, which had not passed through the Roman singularization, lay claim? But—a neuralgic point that makes theticism tremble—the constitution and institutions having passed through it, how will nature still make the law?

This is the normative singularization whose tragic character Rome, in the middle of which Cicero sees himself living, spreads out before the eyes of everyone. Rome has strayed far from its origins. It placed itself outside of right reason, which amounts to a loss of its reason, which is to say, of its constitutional *imperium* that has corrupted its institutions forever. The republican model is striking for its incongruity of natural-birth and nature-as-law. Just as in Aeschylus, this conflict is still resolved only through denial—not in diverting the Bosphorus, but through the hubristic denial of nature, stigmatized by Cicero, that will institutionalize the first Triumvirate. As always, this is dysfunctional, and the fact that Rome could have strayed in this way reveals something about its being. It reveals in which way singularization here makes the fantasm indeterminate and breaks the hegemony. It reveals the *erratic tragedy.*

So we see here the false movement and the shape of the differend that follows. Facing the dictatorial denial of a Caesar, Cicero invokes the natural law as a *force majeure.* He recalls the institutions of the ancients in order to oppose them to the unbridled ambitions of his day. But unlike Xerxes, who would pay at Salamis the debt contracted at the Bosphorus, no retributive reflux of nature comes to engulf the arrogant Caesar. Consequently, Cicero maximizes into a fantasm that nature *qua force* that was struck with incapacity. The republic has failed. The equation *lex* = *natura* = *vis* also failed the test of effective government. Hence the immense work of idealization. We must understand this movement in order to see the breach open in the edifice of natural law, a breach that will take more than a millennium to ruin natural law.

Cicero has nature passed from one sovereignty to another. The first, under the *proper noun,* was highly effective. With it Rome had become for the people what the Aegean Sea had been for the Persians: the force dispensing justice. This force being exhausted, the narrative discourse invests nature with a second, and now achronic, sovereignty. This is a revisionism that makes Rome into a paradigmatic singular and makes "nature" into a *common noun.* Its imperative law is removed from the conflict of disparate forces where it should have prevailed and is installed as the most common referent. The site of ultimate recourse, which the Greek tragedians had had the wisdom to leave blank, is here occupied and named. Above I said the "one" in Parmenides—and below I will say self-consciousness in the first thinkers of modern, critical transcendentalism—are not posited as accessible to the understanding. They can only be thought. The Latins, on the other hand, extrapolate imperative nature from a clearly delimited region of observation. Whence the confidence in its intelligibility. Perhaps the confidence would not have resisted the critique that Cicero foresaw only too well if Christianity had not come to clarify reason with an unexpected light, for it is truly a stroke of luck for the metaphysics of natural law to have come to the point where Thomas Aquinas, for example, is able to express its universal reach through a schema of participation in the divine *imperium* (an empire that at the same time is both nourished and ruined by the disparity between an agent that, according to the interventionist wisdom, is singular and an essence that, according to subsumptive universality, is subsistent).

The false diachronic-achronic movement in Cicero—the transmutation of a historical force into a fantasm—causes, among the hegemonic referents, *natura* to remain the only one that could be declared known by everyone. This is not to bring it back to a "supreme" referent or to a being. Its "ultimate" or relational character results, on the contrary, from its very definition according to which nature wants "everyone to be firmly established in their rank" (*Rep.* I, 45, 69). If its common name is at once distorted by the persistence of the proper noun and therefore of the ontic, it is because it has been instituted beginning with a group of laws that had been the case and that can be dated.[49] The law of nature is natively proper to Rome, just as the natural is to an individual.

A differend opposes a meaningful illusion (and one toward which language pushes) to the disparity that is the case. This disparity in ordinary experience remains phenomenologically contradictory and without an encompassing genus. The Latin language is irresistible in the maximization to which it lures its speakers. We have seen it pass from the middle voice (*naître,* {'to be born'}) to the noun (*natura,* {'nature'}). The differend opens up between the singular givens, between the nature of someone in particular, the birth of some city—and the fantasm of a continuity that ties its ends together. This is an *erratic differend* since, according to Cicero, there would have been no need for the teleocratic maximization if the singular serving as the point of departure (Rome) had not strayed.

The truth of this false movement is that Cicero *lets* the singular show itself. But his fidelity to what shows itself is oblique in that he posits it as a universal. The concept of nature then loses in comprehension what it gains in extension. The safeguard of the phenomena is observed in all its philosophical beauty in that Cicero refuses to make the singular into a particular. Rome is subsumed under nothing. Thereby, he can boast that his *Republic* remains closer to the phenomena than does Plato's. But his fidelity is indirect in that it takes the great detour through the fantasmic maximization of the singular—a universal subsumptor, one nevertheless retained as singular. The nomothesis is thwarted. A transgressive effacement sabotages the subsumptive effect.

This is an effect and an effacement in which one sees a fidelity that is just as oblique to time. The singular alone dies. Once defunct, the Roman republic becomes familiar with idealization (in which its posthumous destiny recalls to some extent Freud's Moses). Here factual death constitutes time in the mode of a memorial; it is not a possible death, in the mode of anticipation. Where, then, does the panegyrist stand to accuse Rome of having strayed? He "fabricated an idea" of the republic that is no longer and posited it, according to his own standards, where he saw nature. Conversely, where in nature is the city measured by an idealized yardstick? There would be no hegemonic nature if the Rome where Cicero lives had not strayed far from its birth. The same instituting act thereby establishes the archetype and effaces it through the erratic. Nothing else is needed to make manifest the legislative-transgressive unity of the founding gesture. The institution does not attach to the norm a corruptible body that would affect it as *its other.* Rome no more embodies nature than it particularizes it. Its law was nature, and to the normative universal the institution attaches *the disparate other* that is the singular. Even as the hegemony under which the Latins live puts itself in place, the city that was draws the new reference outside of its vocation into full presence. The revocable title delegitimizes in advance and from within—and necessarily—the fine title of nature.

To anticipate a lexicon that will only be formed little by little by other readings below:

We see where theticism wants to go with the *natural difference.* Every final authority, uniformly posited as a *force majeure,* differs from the dispersed mass whose dispersion it neutralizes. Its normativity normalizes the givens. As the Latin metaphysicians think of it, the organizing nature *is not* the disparate natures, nor is it natural-birth. It legislates over both. The Romans direct themselves toward a nature that is common, intact, and untouchable, a nature that is a subsumptive difference that reduces the singular as it was born (the individual, Rome) to an instance of the common.

But if Cicero likes to attach the noun *natura* to the verb *nasci,* we still recognize therein a profound fidelity to the *purely descriptive difference* that each language of philosophy opens in its own way. It accentuates the nominative-infinitive duality. It keeps and preserves the narratable singular in the middle voice without transmuting it into the particular other of someone who is represented in the name of a guardian. This extra-tutelary surveillance is essential to its inaugural gesture, as it is to each institution of hegemony where one takes up listening to a language and, in the persisting absence of the ideological edifices, trusts in it in order to think differently.

Heard and understood in this way, the difference gives time a more complex figure than one would suspect from the nostalgic tone of the republican orator. As naturality, nature points to the birth of a singular from long ago, after the she-wolf had suckled the twins. But as—let us say—nativity, it points to another birth: every phenomenon, always, "is born." It shows itself, becomes manifest, comes to presence. And notice, Cicero seems to say, how our city makes itself present to the modern spectator: a pity. No more than Augustine after him, Cicero need not fear the experts' quibbling about his linguistic competence. His is a competence of the ear as much as of the glottis. Because of his occupation, he still hears the verb under the noun and the appresentation under the represented. He preserves and articulates this complex figure of time that is the duality between the bearer of a proper noun having persisted through four centuries and the event of appropriation by which a phenomenon is born to presence, is contextualized, and enters into the world. This is the *temporal difference* between the "formerly" of the lamented republic and the "now" of the deplored Caesarism, where chronological succession differs from arrival to presence as duration differs from the pure now.

This pure now is not surrounded by other instants forming a line, and nevertheless is a now that is fissured. Indeed, from the moment the republic is no longer and nature puts its regime into effect, in what time does one live? Answer: In that time where the republic is no longer and where nature reigns. . . . In other words, there is no "now" without a singularizing withdrawal dispersing us toward that which was, nor without the universalizing attraction toward that which always is (posited as being). There is a double tug where an infrangible *discordance of times* is declared. It suffices to recall the two senses of *archein,* 'to begin' and 'to command.' Rome had begun with the nature-birth—which is why after the collapse nature-as-law rules. A similar *non sequitur* will turn out to be essential to the constitution of all temporality, the trait of natality always being added to mortality by a *non sequitur.* There is a gap between the principial reference, posited in order to command and to measure commonly, and the originary reference to the singular beginning. The discordance between the dispersive and the normative remains without common measure. Such is the temporal figure of the legislating tragedy.

If I now examine how the Latin Christian nomothesis is put in place, it is less to compensate for the possible philosophical shortcomings of a Cicero than to understand a phenomenal time being formed in terms of a "not-yet." The city of God is not yet given; but its anticipation constitutes all that is found to be given. Being the subject of a narrative and a description, not of a reasoning or a deduction, it will be singular as was the Rome of the ancestors. The counter-strategy that this singular future inflicts on natural law will confirm—even though by a completely different conflict and a completely different errancy—the dissension that time introduces into the new hegemony. And again in Augustine, the dissension makes the law into a final authority.

A singular empire, the empire of a singular, is put into effect in the name of nature when Augustine confesses the coming of the heavenly city. The hegemony is established, no longer in the name of a given that was, but of a given that will be. Therefore nature then signifies a time other than the singular and, consequently, a rearrangement in the erratic differend.

On a normative singular that will be

"Two loves made two cities: the love of self even to the point of contempt for God, the terrestrial city; the love of God to the point of contempt for self, the heavenly city."[50] The cities thus described by the respective act which founds them, *against what shall we measure them* to distinguish them? The question is important in order to know what serves as a normative focal meaning when Latin philosophy places itself in the service of Christianity.

The aging Augustine suffered something like a relapse. The black-and-white world, whose facility for responding to the "problem of evil" had seduced him during nine years of his youth, reappears. Two loves, two contempts, two cities . . . there is no need to hesitate, it seems, to recognize two figures of the common, two principles. To love oneself to the point of contemning God, is this not the principle of Darkness in us? To love God to the point of contemning oneself, is this not the principle of Light in us? Conclusion: The two cities, equally irreducible, are measured against each other.

However, everything becomes more complicated with this conclusion. If one of the two terms put in opposition is good and the other evil, the heavenly city obviously enjoys a position of priority. But then this is the effect of the antagonism between two irreducible principles. The terrestrial city is posited *in relation to* the heavenly. Its subordination dissipates the principial dualisms, and at least saves Augustine from that relapse. Still it is an affair of "nature"; love, though divided, does not therefore divide what he understands as nature. Nature remains unitary, always good.[51] The normative focal meaning therefore is "the nature in which God originally created man" and it is back to nature that his designs will end up leading him (XIX, 15). The conflict of the two cities cannot revert to a gigantomachia between natures. Rome, or "Babylon," is not nature. This puts an irrevocable end to the idealized naturality of the terrestrial city—to all terrestrial cities. To Rome, decomposed in this fifth century beyond the worst apprehensions of a Cicero, we could indeed add others. Which would be the city uncorrupted by love of self? Would it be the one for which God originally created man? Also, will the teaching be imposed only once the celestial city is established because in it nature is intact, and hence finally gives us an undamaged norm: a representation in the name of which we will judge the decadent Rome, militate against the consequences of Sin and re-establish the telic continuity between the individual, humanity, and the universe?

As such, Augustine would thus give a new turn to the oppositional figure most amenable to metaphysical recycling: two ideal types, posited in such a way that one poorly imitates the other. He would have *put into place* the two cities, and doubly so by placing them in opposition and yet placing them out of danger of the contingencies where time carries singulars away. He would have obtained a normative place, one and complete—an authority owing nothing more either to the topography of the Latium or to the complex network of sites of power (royal, aristocratic, popular), sites precisely contingent which could be lost and whose loss the reign of Caesar had sealed. Is it not patently obvious from this that the promised Jerusalem serves to measure life because it reigns removed from the consequences of sin? In it we would have an integrating canon "without Sin," much like nature before the weaknesses of Eve remains canonical for fallen nature. The doxographs emphasize the Neoplatonism in Augustine which overdetermined Roman pragmatism as a realism of universals. We no longer risk here the hesitations of a Cicero: It seems there is no longer the paradox of a singular posited as an archetype. As a symbol for a love that conforms to nature, does not the Jerusalem to come clearly take its place on the side of subsumptive agents? Does it not totalize without the fissures that singularization opens in the normative edifice? Consequently, the description of it given by Augustine would satisfy the demands of a prescriptive discourse; and the opposition of the two cities would be that of the sought-after normative difference.

One of the two cities serves as a referent for the other. This bit of information will not only astound no one, but it remains above all plainly formalist. The platitude in this consists in declaring that theticism amounts to positing the same and *its* other, and then, upon this great discovery, in closing the case. If on the other hand we do not content ourselves with such formalism, it is really necessary to consider the case of the naturally normative city. It will be necessary to ask not only *how* we speak, that is, by which differences and oppositions, but also *about what* we speak.

Is Jerusalem really an unfissured measure? Augustine describes this Jerusalem as a *parallel city* which is built in hearts. More than a topography, his description sketches a diachrony. The normative city is built slowly. Memory holds present the blueprints beginning with Abraham and up to the great founder that was Paul. Memory even anticipates its full presence to come. For the present, this city being built parallel to visible cities remains a construction site. It is not yet a given. Ontically present and absent, it holds its citizens in perpetual alert. They must keep themselves ready for the day when they will inhabit it. The future, more than the present, falls to them; hence waiting, destiny, and risk—above all, risk. Unlike the Rome that was, the Jerusalem that will be still only has to be in the mode of a possibility. Cicero speaks to remind; Augustine to urge to vigilant preparation. Time affects this city in the form of growth, and it orients it essentially toward an abrupt arrival to come. It is difficult to see how such a contingency as "When?" could apply for ideality. It is even less clear how the pre-eminence of the future could be in accord with some totalizing principle, even if it were the immanence of the "everything in everyone" by which the Jerusalem to come is defined. We especially do not see what the phenomenal origin of this parallel city could possibly be. It was "made" by a certain type of love. One might as well say that love—that is, the will—posits it: a positing contingent (there exists another love) upon a contingent referent (which does not yet exist). Here again we have the return of the maximized singular and of time resingularizing it from the inside which, together, point in the direction of a double normative bind.

From Rome to Jerusalem, Augustine changes the subject, but not the predicates. In both, the model city gives order. How?

Rome "was never a true republic" (II, 21, 83). Such is the judgment that Augustine makes in opposition to Cicero concerning the best laws and their chances of realization. On what basis does he arrive at this verdict? His reasons involve the city that he posits as naturally perfect, a positing which, in its turn, depends on the anticipatory mode under which he conceives normative nature.

The representation of the measure given by that nature undergoes a transmutation from the dialogues of the young Augustine to the late dogmatic treatises. We have seen the Stoic ancestry of the natural law: imprinted in our minds, it constrains the will to render life *ordinatissima*. But, as we have also seen, the natural law only reflects the eternal. The divine intellect contains in itself the law of all laws. Order emanates from "wisdom" as a practical, divine attribute. It measures all things against the economy that it synthesizes in itself and that it spreads over what is other than it.

Now, with the rigidifications in Augustine's thought, the ultimate measure—and the timelessness that was this measure—turns more and more into what later will be called the eschatological. The new terms offered as choices to the will not only summon time and the singular, but their call is made more pressing than ever in the erratic production of the "I" and the "You." The choice is no longer between the eternal law and the temporal, nor between the pacified heart and the fragmented, but between the heavenly city *inchoately* present and the terrestrial city *externally* present. What is lacking is plenary presence; however, it is a provisional lack inasmuch as the city-as-measure is constituted from fragments in the cities measured by it. The application of the law thus precedes its full presence. The normed city is before our eyes; the norming city remains a rough sketch. These are literally new "terms." Augustine opposes the true term, the Jerusalem that will be, to the false term that applies to the restlessness of heart in the Rome that was. Each of the two cities, normed and norming, has its imaginary geography: one, the dispersion without perspective or outlet; the other, the diaspora where every advance is only errancy but where there is a coming perspective. Each also has its time: one, the appresentation to the mind of the things that are, but which come only from the outside; the other, the representation in the mind of those things from within, but which only will be.

And as in Cicero, the norm serving as measure is the strongest singular. Jerusalem will conquer. Its force is unmistakable. Is Rome not crumbling already? It is therefore not natural. The only one that is natural is this other city whose growth—visibly, for those who can see what is inchoately—has been overflowing the banks of the Mediterranean since the time of Paul. Hence there was a decisive transmutation in the definition of time once Augustine became a man of the Church. The normative difference which separates the city of God and that of men is temporal, the difference of a temporality no longer constituted in mind and memory, but publicly.[52] Augustine follows Cicero in defining the *res publica* as *res populi* and the people as a collectivity united by law and justice. But what is this justice founded by the ancestors? It is the emptiness due to its *imperium*. In the Ciceronian republic, one does not give to the one God that which is his due. This is why all normativity is lacking in this republic. It is rotten at the top. "There is no true justice except in this commonwealth of which Christ is the founder" (II, 21, 83). To him, before all others, it is proper to "give that which is owed him." Now, this other commonwealth, still fragmentary but subject to the divine empire, is 413 years old at the moment when Augustine begins to write *The City of God*. What does the definition of the future as "presence of future things" mean at that time? The anticipation of those things in the mind, soul, memory? How could it be thus, when it is a matter of a city having been born on earth some years ago, at present extending everywhere to the detriment of its Roman rival, and promised victory in a number of years (only the exact number of which remains uncertain)? *Praesenta* and *futura:* as in Parmenides the plural of the neuter indicates the distribution of singular givens in sites that are themselves just as singular.

To the dispersive forces of the singular is joined that of diachrony. In order that the justice natural to man be established, human history must first arrive at its resolution. Then all will live as God originally created them, as they were *born* before sin. In order that they live under the empire which is nevertheless *natural* to them, time is necessary. What is more, only then will this norm, which always and everywhere already orders the life of everyone, fully come into being. We can see the historicization of nature. "Presence of future things"—the definition now signifies the parallel city, provisionally present in the form of an exiled one, but promised full and complete future sovereignty. Augustine makes a public act of anticipatory memory. He addresses himself to this normative authority in the process of gestation, as if he were one of its *chargés d'affaires*. The authority always signifies "nature" in the sense of "being born," but of a naturality where the *nasci* prior to the fall is anticipated in the mode of a public that is not-yet.

One need not be a fourteenth-century expert to detect the disparity between the integrative regime of nature and its factual singularization to come. The universal which we cannot not posit and the singular which we cannot not abandon turn normative nature against itself, a turn that breaks the concordance of times; for how would the regime whose presence one posits be paired up with the singular that one lets come? *Without* future singularizations, there is no binding regime; but *with* it, there is no uniformly binding regime.

Temporality thus remains essential to this ultimate referent. It carries along a fantasmic upsurge. Rarely short of sarcasm when concerned with the false Roman splendor, Augustine notes that Cicero considered his contemporaries to be like bad art collectors. They had received the republic like a magnificent painting, half-effaced by the ages, and they neglected to restore the colors (*Rep.* V, 1, 2). Augustine comments: The panegyrist of the ancestral city did not see things clearly. Could it indeed be that already in the time of the ancestors the Roman republic had been "not living by its customs, but painted in color, according to the word Cicero inadvertently let slip?" (II, 21, 82). This gibe aims to undermine the historical base of the alleged Roman normativity, to expose the theticism there, to turn it into a fantasm. But what can be said about the city to come? Does not it, too, produce a painting? Cicero could very well say the same thing about it. The city that conforms to nature is for later. Love, a particular love, makes it. It posits it in advance and, in the same thetic gesture, places it out of full presence, out of reach. Furthermore, this city is recounted as only the singular is recounted. One might as well say that it is depicted. Temporality, voluntary positing, gap of absent and present, narrativity, painting: What more is needed to prove the fantasmic maximization imposed here again on the singular?

Augustine, as well, fantasizes the natural city through a division beginning with the visible Rome. Through a displacement in time he augments and promotes a factual being to an archetype. The preamble to his severe judgment of Rome ensues from the fantasizing of a singular focal point toward which honest wills converge. It is true that this city is no longer a place that could be visited. It is located neither on the Seven Hills nor at the foot of Mount Hymettus nor, as historic Jerusalem, on a watershed such as between the Mediterranean and the Dead Sea. But neither is it supposed to exist only in discourse, for then the historic drama that Augustine intends to narrate would be over, namely, the discordance, the plot that this city weaves through the ages, and the denouement.[53] How would the narrative which recalls and anticipates this course produce an achronic referent if not by a grave, fantastic, fantasmogenic metabase? Normative nature is constituted by an anticipation in parallel to the cities arising from fallen nature. It follows that the diachronic is posited as achronic, loved as such, willed as such, "made" as such. This is the metabasis. The *ante* of things last in time passes for the *coram* of things ultimate in rank. This is not to say that, idealized from out of diachrony, the achrony produces a supreme, entitative referent. The fantasized norm is still nature extrapolated from city life—an ensemble of relations, an ultimate referent. The condition that makes this norm stands out from all the cities is its fantasmic status. As such it responds to them and offers rejoinders.

We see it in the apocalyptic work by which Augustine puts the Ciceronian-Stoic program of peace into effect. The *imperium* no longer signifies reason's control over private urges and public interests, but that of a future political plan over all present political plans. The preponderant force (*pondus meum*) is temporalized by an economy of individual and social characters. There was a Stoic delight in maintaining the balance of the instincts. Henceforth the wait defers pleasure. The futurity that comes through the postponement of delight is seen most clearly when Augustine appeals to Paul against Cicero. It should suffice to raise briefly this appeal with regard to the "primordial goods of nature"[54] and the "sage."

The terrestrial city is born by the infinite cares given to the *persona* that are as much private as public. Is it not the love of self that founded it? Now, its days are numbered. The goods that are natural to us therefore cannot coincide with the instincts and their wonderful economy. Where does one go, within the eschatologization of nature, to look for natural goods if not in the *eschata,* the ultimate things? Thus these goods are found denaturalized as givens in the soul and renaturalized as gifts to come. We *will attain* these goods which are nevertheless natural (XIX, 4, 5). Here is the new normative site. It will only be given with beatitude, at the end of time (*beatitudo finalis*). Releasing the presently actual world, nature recaptures another world that will be. Cicero boasted to have brought philosophy back to earth against the Greek's seeing in our world only a pale reflection of an elsewhere. Augustine raises this antithesis even higher, so to speak, in positing a new "elsewhere." However, it is not a better universal. The city-referent to come has a history, and it is an aggregate made of singulars wherein it repeats the Ciceronian city-referent. But the goods that are natural to us wait for us outside the compass of our sight and outside the era of our life. If we are holding a deposit for them, it is only through the anticipatory aggregation of hearts invisibly making a republic.

This elevation toward a future singular results in a curious return of the sage in the "commonwealth." "That the life of the sage be a social life, we approve. Whence indeed would the city of God have been born, would it advance in its development and would it attain the ends that it deserves, if the life of the saints were not a social life?" (XIX, 5). This is an entirely Roman portrait of the sage. Much like Cicero's Scipio (and against the ideal of a Chrysippus), the sage devotes himself to the republic. Rome really does remain the phenomenon from which the nomothesis departs. But this nomothesis immediately moves away from the heuristic phenomenal given. Earthly society will no more make life wise than the influence of reason will make it honest. It suffices to look at it: "What restlessness, enemy of peace, does not threaten the sage in his body?" (XIX, 4, 2). Consequently, the sage is recruited for the construction of the heavenly city: a moment of eschatologization which not only collectivizes the singulars, but also orients time. The future singular owes its coming to a process of concrete socialization which here defines the time of history. With these new sages—the saints—we have the first builders of better tomorrows in the history of philosophy. They make the city advance and finally reach the city that measures all cities. Their intervention best indicates how Augustine projects in advance the "natural difference" between the two cities.

This difference owes its normativity precisely to the not-yet. So long as man strays far from the ends that are his due, the force of the law—nature-as-referent—has need of supplements. In a land of exile, it remains to be completed by the temporal laws that administer the armistices. Any provisional peace, however, refers back (*refert*) to "the well ordered obedience under eternal law" (XIX, 14). The end will be this law in full force, without supplement. This is not to deny that the empire of nature is already deployed as a *force majeure:* "the heavenly city uses, in its exile, terrestrial peace" (XIX, 17). The normative difference, rather, comes down to a dual effect of imperative nature. It reigns partially now, and it will reign fully at the end of time. The *referre* indicates a measurement. The provisional aggregate—which is the case, but a scattered case and one parallel to Rome—is measured against the definitive aggregate that is not yet the case but which, when it is, will absorb under its empire what is parallel to Rome and scattered. The normative reference is established between two diversely treated singulars: between the present Rome, degraded into an *ectypon,* and the Jerusalem to come, maximized into an *archetypon.*

The not-yet gives force to nature through the readjustments imposed on Cicero. Nature falls twice; it is a norm displaced and with a dual effect. First, each individual consciousness experiences the not-yet. The *res publica* of believing consciousness, socialized by charity, is precisely where we find the present effect of the positive Latin archetype in the way that the upsurge of a promise arranges it henceforth; the edification of the fully natural city begins with the aggregation of hearts. But their collective memory makes present the commonwealth to come. This is the plenary effect to come, which the collective will posits in advance of the society without charity (diachronic *ante*) and in front of it (achronic *coram*). The Augustinian nomothesis therefore consists of anticipating the final stasis of history, a stasis (only) as concrete as its fluctuations but nevertheless normative because it alone is shielded from these fluctuations that are measured in terms of antecedence.

Natural law therefore signifies the slow birth of a commonwealth, as it anticipates the restoration of the nature in which God originally created man. The metabase is profound for the relational principle of final authority, which thus amounts to *the nature that will be.*

In Augustine, nature is fissured by an erratic differend similar to the one that Ciceronian theticism denies. Only, the thesis of a parallel city is maintained by a labor, no longer of mourning, but of *a postponement whose temporality we deny.* Is it not the charge of the everlasting philosophical bureaucracy to find arguments to deny time? Is this not the impulse which prompts one to posit normative structures? Augustine also conceives nature according to the principle of continuity. It encompasses the created and the non-created in a single *telic* empire. But the continuous fabric is torn under the attraction of the singular to come.[55] There is a wandering of hearts because, between the contradictory cities, love can make mistakes and is constantly mistaken. And there is a differend because the maximal linguistic fiction—the common noun *natura,* obliteraing the middle voice of the verb *nasci*—produces the illusion of an encompassing one. This is an illusion which we are permitted to call "transcendental" since language sweeps speakers off to the transcendental, apparently with no possibility of coming back to earth. We have seen its origin. It is the irresistible totalization that begins with an aggregate of givens; with the "these" that Augustine calls "hearts." The double bind always results from a singular given, completely held together as singular and universalized to the normative level. Therefore it remains to be seen how the splitting of the parallel city is articulated in a differend.

This splitting results directly from the erratic production of normative nature. In the dialogue on free will, the institution of nature passed from the unstable singular that "I" am to the normative singular that "You" are, then to the singular where "I" is an other: stabilized, rectified, normed. No generic authority was hanging over these disparate arrangements of deictic givens. In the same way, here, no common authority hangs over the describable givens, which are the crippled hearts aggregating themselves today by impulses and interests, and the indescribable normative, which will be the republic of these very hearts that are then restored. To subsume them now and then, there is but one *name:* "nature." But we have seen that it names these hearts in their state to come. By leaving it up to the name of nature so understood, the subsumptive place indeed remains blank—and it is here that the differend turns out to be irreducible to a determinate contradiction and the proper name impossible to pass off as a common denominator. In the absence of a uniformly binding principle, the mediation is historicized. Now, who or what performs the mediation between the observed terrestrial city and the anticipated definitive republic? It is the inchoate republic of hearts aggregating themselves under the sign of faith-hope-love, that is to say, it is still deictic.

The argument pivots on the parallel city as on an ostensible, erratic middle term. The aggregation through internal affinities ("Jerusalem dispersed") replies to the aggregation through external interests ("Rome"). The love of God to the point of contempt of self moves away from the corrupted city. There is a spatial gap, where one city replies to the other as if in response or as a rejoinder, but this gap is where it also answers *it* as if by repetition or reproduction in another site. Space is hollowed out in history since the aggregate of restless hearts in their dispersion precedes, moreover, the site of tranquility ("heavenly Jerusalem"). There is a temporal gap, this time between the question that I have become for myself and the anticipated pacifying response.

How then does this spatio-temporal differend produce the thesis of normative nature? Answer: By the removal and the maximization of the singular that is set aside. "The end where the city will find its sovereign good can be described either as peace in eternal life or as eternal life in peace" (XIX, 12, 1). The peace that sanctions the phenomenal regions is in the future: Both descriptions that Augustine offers here thus deploy, in a principial and achronic continuity, a singular that is thinkable only as the final point in a diachronic sequence. The normative authority results from a genesis. What is more fantastic than such a fabric, unfurled from a "this" and enveloping, at the end of genetic time, the totality of phenomena?

The symmetry between this false diachronic-achronic movement and that of Cicero is striking. To measure existing societies, Augustine places nature ahead of them, as Cicero had placed it behind them. With the subsequent political Augustinianism,[56] the future city is endowed with the sharpest normativity. But with the maximization of the parallel republic being born in hearts, the earthly *imperium* has already lost its autonomy and is absorbed in the heavenly. Nature, thus nascent, shapes fallen nature as a *force majeure*. God is more present to the soul (*maxime intus*), says Augustine, than the soul is to itself. So it is as well with the natural city. It is more present, internally, to the city of Rome than that city is identical to itself in accordance with the principle of identity. This is an empire spatialized and historicized, obviously, as it is seen in the precarious armistices of the balanced interests which, while waiting for the denouement, pass for peace. These armistices manifest no less the force of the fully natural city to come. If (against Mani and with the Neoplatonists) evil has no proper being, then even a diabolical city tends to imitate the order of the perfect city (Kant will have an analogous formula)—so strong is its empire. An imitation through deficient similitude, as the copy imitates the idea? Yes, by oppositions such as fragile–stabile, *uti–frui,* precarious peace–perpetual peace; no, for the two cities are separated by the *time of history*.[57] This "yes and no"—this is the false movement and here we have the double bind.

The republicanism that Cicero had set off to collect in a recent past so as to exalt it as a natural order is what Augustine restores in time. Rome had the wrong *imperium*. It was never a republic. We must look for the perfectly ordered city elsewhere and in another time. Under the program of restoration as under that of anticipation, the elements of theticism remain no less the same: the removal of a singular, a historical distance, an institution at the level of "nature," a totalizing reference, a positive archetype, an erratic figure of the normative difference, and finally a double bind of the ultimate posited referent and of the singular from which the positing departs.

What we must now watch at work are the ultimates that link us to maximization as well as to singularization, along with the double bind to which they give rise—watch them at work in the will.

CHAPTER 10

On the Natural Double Bind

The Will Turned against Itself

The historians of ideas teach that the will became a philosophical issue at the end of antiquity.[58] If we recall the difficulties the Neoplatonists had in saying, if not why, at least how the one was not content in its solitude but exteriorized itself in order to constitute what is other than it, then we may be tempted to chalk this innovation up to Alexandrian henology. Some have even taken this for a philosophical effect of Christianity, such that Augustine supposedly was driven to discover the will, especially by way of the simultaneous and incompatible impulses in the individual *mens*—in the confessional spirit in line with Paul: "the good that I want I do not do, and the evil that I do not want I do" (Romans 7:19). The will then is thought to be born in the drama either of henological exteriorization or theological interiority.

But it is one thing to establish on a diachronic line the place and date of the emergence of some gambit of thinking, and it is another to understand the newly urgent questions in response to which it emerges. Such is the case with the will. A new epistemic arrangement was necessary so it could appear. Neither Cicero nor Augustine decided to make it a theme; and that the Greeks have no word with which to expresses it is hardly a sign of interest on their part. In waning antiquity the will is constituted as a response—it remains to be seen to which preliminary, but nevertheless fundamental, questions in the new legislative structure it responds.

So it had to become an issue, perhaps even the decisive issue at the moment that eidetic principles determining the genera yield, like great authorities for reasoning, to telic relations that determine beings. From where does the systematic appeal to the will in the continuous fabric of ends that is *natura* come?

To be able to answer this we may recall the very ancient prestige of ends.[59] These ends have been and remain normative, both before and after the rupture between the Greek and Latin linguistic eras. But they do not remain so in the same capacity. Teleological prestige changes its phenomenal surroundings. The new positive referents—the Rome which was, the Jerusalem that will be—formally substitute for Aristotelian eidetic principles in that they accomplish their archic function, but within a telic framework. On the other hand, in Aristotle the genera of knowledge converge on the ends; they accomplish their telic function within an archic framework. In order to know how the Latin fantasm of a network saturated by finalities summons the will, it will be helpful to briefly recall the manner in which, in Aristotle, teleology names the principle of all principles. In other words, what *telos* in Aristotle serves as the first *arché*?

"By principle, I understand in each genus those truths whose existence it is impossible to demonstrate."[60] The knowledge of these principles would complete knowledge, for "he who knows the universal in a certain manner knows all the particular cases that fall under this universal"[61]—in a certain manner, which is to say, only potentially. Principles are not demonstrated. This follows from a double modesty of archic thinking: Not only does it grasp only more or less universal essences, whereby it passes to the side of *ultimate singulars,* but it also grasps these essences in the plural, whereby it passes to the side of the *ultimate universal.* For Aristotle, the poverty of philosophy above all consists in this second shortcoming. He makes up for it with a mimetic principle, which is really a stopgap in the epistemic doctrine rather than its crowning moment, namely, teleology, which orients all knowledges toward a wisdom nevertheless beyond reach.

Formulated as axioms, principles or "first things" (*ta prôta)* in each case govern only one science. Knowledge comes to us fragmented according to the various sorts of phenomena. To have hold of the principles of a science is to know, potentially—even if by way of deductions that themselves must be completed by abstractions—all the cases that fall under the purview of a particular regional experiential referent. Nevertheless it is impossible to subsume the phenomenal regions under some chief referent. Hence in Aristotle the modest standing of the first science in Aristotle. It is condemned to remain "under study." The genera cannot be summed up by a maximal universal; being is not a genus. A science of principles, if it were within our reach, would have to begin with a single "first thing." From this all-inclusive referent one then has to be able to deduce not only the generic, subordinate axioms, but even further down the line, the species, then the singulars all the way down to those that are only possible. "Such a science would be a science in a high degree, or even at the highest degree." But, Aristotle adds, "it is clear that the principles proper to each thing are not susceptible of [deductive] demonstration."[62]

Consequently, scientific discourses can be subjected only to an uncertain to-and-fro among conceptions that are never definitive. Metaphysics is here confined, in the words of one commentator, to the level of a "substitute and stopgap measure."[63] Since a deductive ontology remains unattainable, it is necessary to put together a substitute. If worst comes to worst, it means having to undertake the dialectic. In terms of criteria of truth applicable to first things, one will not be able to establish anything more certain than probable doctrines—which is what most people think is relevant in a given genus. "In the various sciences [. . .], principles are discussed only by way of probable doctrine (*endoxa*), a task that belongs to the dialectic."[64] The most solid thing that the discourse about being *qua* being offers us, but yet does not colidate into a science, is the body of dispersed axioms governing politics, ethics, etc. Aristotle recognized preponderating forces only in the plural[65] (which is why the twentieth century would lose nothing in following the thirteenth-century usage by calling him—at least for the dispersion that he recognized in principles, not for the thetic centering that he has effected in substance—"the philosopher"). Regional principles are not universalized under any *principle of subsumption*. They are, however, gathered together thanks to a *principle of imitation*—that is, teleology.

The science of the absolute *arché* remains an ideal of epistemic unification. Only as such will it serve as *telos* for all research. Consequently it certainly goes beyond the genera, but as imitable, though irrealizable. It goes beyond them in provoking the desire to know—an early Greek sign of the Latin will, one of whose functions obviously will still be to motivate the erotic ascent to the causes. We would not even set out to seek a first knowledge if our diverse knowledges did not always aim at an ideal unity; but since this unity is denied to intuition, the inquiry remains interminable. The Aristotelian dialectic is a stopgap measure measured by this ideal of Greek "luminaries" (which anticipates the modern Enlightenment in that, anew with Kant, the ideal dispatches the understanding in an infinite inquiry). We possess something like a preunderstanding of what would be knowledge whole and complete, a preunderstanding that mobilizes the anagogic *erôs* in epistemic pursuits *of all genera*. Lacking this preunderstanding, there is no inquiry. By virtue of the goal of a discourse that is not wholly—and not dialectically—one, the genera resemble each other. The heteromorphic sciences have a tendency toward this impossible plenitude. To attain the gnostic pleroma would be to perfect our narrowly circumscribed knowledges under the guidance of an integrative epistemic authority. Therein they would possess (*echein*) their end (*telos*). In the "entelechy" of an immediate knowledge, we have precisely the mimetic principle unifying the sciences. Apprehension does not grasp this principle, but it has already brought itself to bear in every inquiry that it moves even though it refuses to yield itself to it. To motivate desire from a distance as only an end motivates, such is the principle of resemblance that unifies the sciences. What does knowledge desire—or, to coin a translation drawing on what is most problematic here—what does knowledge want? To imitate unity. Under the Greek hegemony so understood, the end is the beginning in that the epistemic one moves the passions of knowledge. The genera carry out their telic function under an archic form. In place of the impossible integration, there is imitation.

Quite different from this is the conjunction between teleology and volition at the beginning of Latin philosophy. There the will enters the philosophical scene as *actually integrative*—or at least it is posited as such. The separating of hegemonic fantasms that thus inserts the will into the center of *natura* seems most brutal, if one listens to the arguments of those who deny that there has been a rupture.

Were one to compare the modesty and even the failures in the Aristotelian inquiry into the principle of all principles with what came to pass in Rome, one would have reason to be perplexed by the ingenuineness of a Leo Strauss, for whom "classical philosophy"—Greek and Latin—portrays the philosopher as an advisor of men in power. In Greece as in Rome, or so we hear, this expert advises politicians about natural law. He teaches them to raise their eyes toward (*pros*) the "first things," and then to reason on the basis (*apo*) of them.[66] Very well. But we have seen what the "first thing" is in the reasoning of a Cicero and an Augustine (and what other philosophers did the Romans have?): in each instance it is a singular being. To direct one's gaze toward the Rome that was, or toward the Jerusalem that will be, then to judge the present in terms of these representations, is altogether a different program than the one that proposes to think toward and on the basis of axioms that have to be negotiated, axioms acclaimed, moreover, only for their mimetic affinity. The champions of Greco-Latin classicism are able to maintain the fiction of the premodern normative monolith only at the cost either of an absurdity, or of a paralogism, or even (and in Strauss it is the completely interested motive of the operation) of a more or less noble lie in order to constitute an anti-modernist corps in the twentieth century.

The absurdity would be to claim that the greatness of Rome or that of the promised Jerusalem is related to the totality of possible regimes in the same way an axiom is related to its subordinate propositions, or again as a principle is related to the experiences that it unifies. The paralogism here would be to speak of "first things" in its premises, but not to do so in the same manner: The major premise of the argument would repeat the Aristotelian *archai* whereas the minor premise would name beings—cities. In the lie, finally, reason would be subjected to the interests of executive power.[67] The absurdity, the paralogism, and the lie—all three indicate that, from the Greek to the Latin, the telic-archaic function passes through different standard meanings of being. So let's call a rupture a rupture. Beginning with Latin philosophy, the world is phenomenalized in reference to ends, only the final function no longer is a matter of principles, but of represented singulars, then fantasms. The latter fulfill their archic function within a telic framework.

That *one* form—the teleological form of thought—endures does not mean that Rome or Jerusalem finally answers the question of the genus of all genera, nor that their proper nouns are direct measures outside the political and ethical domains, nor above all that they constitute the object of a science susceptible in some manner or other of synthesizing knowledge. These empirical cities determine what must be understood by nature. Here teleology is not born from a give-and-take among opinions administering the totality of regional sciences—it is imposed by a single regulative being which is itself represented, which is to say, repainted in normative discourse. To declare the Roman regime, or that of the heavenly city, to be the natural integrators of ends is to overwork the frail relations of the dispersive epistemic mimesis to the point that they project a positive fantasmic force.

It is to *want* a given singular to be normative. The issue of the will was not able to arise prior to the Latins because none of the telic arrangements prior to them had been conceived in terms of a singular saying "we" (as does Cicero) or "I" (as does Augustine). So the thetic will comes forward as an inescapable agent only with these discourses in the first person. But the agent of what? It must *will against* the singularization that has happened (the Rome which is no more) or the singularization to come (the Jerusalem which is not yet). In order to institute the principle of continuity, the will can only deny the given—all the while loving it, holding onto it, willing it from the start—from out of which the principle is extrapolated.

Demonstrating which constitution is the naturally better, Cicero refers every political phenomenon to ancestral Rome; demonstrating which law is naturally infrangible, Augustine refers everything to the heavenly Jerusalem. In both, phenomenalization is made up of ontic relations that are observed in a being that is represented, then ordained normative. Demonstrations are based upon a monstration that, in the name of posited nature, it must obliterate. Hence the allegiance to the singular willed by an abiding love (*diasôzein*) immediately introduces entropy into the subsumptions willed by a nomothetic love. Whence the double appeal: the natural double bind is the effect of the will turned against itself.

For Aristotle, principles at most received a semblance of legitimization through the dialectic of opinions. How will the ultimate Latin reference be legitimized? If it is a matter of relations observed in singulars, Cicero and Augustine can only name some particular city and declare it integrative. They can only overdetermine the proper nouns by means of the most common nouns. Legitimization passes through a rhetorical investiture. This is where the fractured force of theticism is revealed. The truth of the will, which renders it systematically necessary under the new hegemony, resides in the dual demand of extremes. This is the contradictory work that, by *instituting* the principle of continuous phenomenalization, persists in denying the withdrawal of singularization.

Willing one's own as well as the common

The will was bound to become a philosophical issue as soon as the ultimate authority boiled down to monstrable singulars that were described, then maximized, by rhetoric. It will not be surprising that Husserl's philosophical civil service is, then, a job for the recognized professionals of eloquence of this or that particular city: for a Cicero, advocate for the republic which was, and for an Augustine, bishop of the city that will be. In retrospect, we certainly can say that the will secretly arranges every thetic system. It is only with the Roman orators that its normative effect comes out of hiding—an unsteady emergence but revelatory as such, for the incipient will attaches all things to the common noun only because it remains attached to the bearer of the proper noun. And with the Romans it suddenly appears, finally thematizable and thematized. There again it is immediately turned against itself in that the nomothesis keeps hold of a particular singular with its *ad hoc* relations (to want the singular is to love it with loyalty, to let it be, to preserve it, to remain faithful to it), and that, as normative, these relations are again applied to the totality of givens, turning their network *ad unum* (to want the norm is to love it with fealty, to posit it, to universalize it, to authorize it to subsume, to give it influence). This is an institutive procedure but is also a mistake; it is an institution, then, that subverts itself.

More explicitly than any other ultimate referent, Rome and Jerusalem owe their paradigmatic status to a *fiat:* There is no simpler way of putting it—the imperative-imperious-imperial way—and it was a completely Roman pragmatic way of escaping the indeterminations of a reason that inquires into the principles of all principles. The will is explicitly required when it is a question of fleshing out a portrait of the ultimate archic locus—that Aristotle had the wisdom to leave empty and of which he opened only certain surroundings to dialectical negotiations.

There you have it, fidelity to phenomena under a thetic cloak. Latin "nature," such as rhetoric invests it, is not a common noun. It is a predicate. For Cicero, as we have seen, *lex natura* indicates that the law of republican Rome was *born naturally.* The normative-nominative operation plays upon the proper noun "Rome," followed by the attribute "natural." Under the thetic cloak, the verb—like Penelope—never ceases to unravel the fabric of ends.

No doubt Roman thought has little patience for questions remaining questions. It has no use for essentially problematic and literally interminable questions about being in the middle voice. It prefers to conclude research, and it expects answers rather than more questions. Here, the deictic gesture shows what one *wants*. Regarding the relations ruling such a city we can see, as Augustine says with disarming openness, the natural law is "made" by love: since this love dictates the norm, we might say "posited and recognized as posited."

Teleology has lost nothing of its very ancient prestige. But if your sympathies do not carry you toward the absurd, toward the paralogism or the lie, it is all the more worthwhile to know *what* Cicero and Augustine are speaking about when they exalt ends. Here is what: In each case they will their own city as the normative sense of being. This is a transmutation of ends by the will if there ever was one.

This transformation extends the principle of inner consolation into a principle of public consolidation. Hence the fantasm of continuity is extrapolated from it beginning with the balance of forces in one's conduct toward the self—by ethics. The singular stubbornly persists through the paradigmatism conferred on such a city—through politics.

To grasp how the institution of hegemonic nature turns the will against itself as soon as it begins to develop, we need only indicate the work upon the self that, in Cicero, nature finalized in this way imposes on Stoic man. The demonstration is easy, and also disarming. He counsels his son, Marcus: choose *your* nature . . . only to immediately go on to say: follow *nature*. Will what is your own and also what is common. One pities the son placed under the double bind of such paternal injunctions. Nonetheless they reveal a genial philosopher (in the sense of the word that caused a frenzy during the age of Kant and Goethe: the genius unable either to learn or to explain how his knowledge came to him) who refuses to give in to dogmas, just as he will refuse to give in to compromises with Caesarism. We have seen the discord in the equation between Rome and nature, a discourse that underscores, in the imperfect tense, the ostantive proper noun beneath the normative common noun. The injunctions of the father come to translate this very discord into terms of the will. Paternal advice aims to *contextualize* Marcus in the teleological framework of soul-city-cosmos-gods, but also to *singularize* him in choosing the situation that best suits him in the city. At the moment that the Latin legislative fantasm is instituted, the will is there, which is what the incongruous work of contextualization-singularization is all about.

a. The selective will. The beautiful contexture of the parts of the soul is what is most likely to be disrupted on those occasions that Zeno called a "fresh madness": the instantaneous outburst of an affect, without a moment's hesitation, provoked by an overturned oil lamp, an insult, but also by a flattery. . . . Such is the occasion for the logical spark in us to reassert its hegemony. The *hêgemônikon* in the soul is the part that "guides" the others toward moderation.

It can always be this to the extent that it is their natural end. And yet, integrated as I am by nature, I still must become so. Hence, the old ascetic ideal required that one absorb the affects purely and simply into the *logos*. "My" nature being always a mixture of forces, nothing is more traditional than to call, in this mixture, for the victory of reason. *Recta ratio* protects the instincts from dispersion. Ethics is perfected in morality by uprightness, namely, by reason leading every force in us back to its harmonious insertion into the psychic apparatus. Thus there will be in me an ardor against nature, the insult by which I react to the overturned oil lamp. In allowing invective to burst out, I will have allowed anger to become autonomous. The quantum of force released by a mechanism fragments the apparatus. Were one impulse thus to be affirmed in this way, the ideal of the wise person would be more than besmirched; some of this will be done from wisdom, for some of it will be due to the conformity to nature, the principle of an endless contextualization.

Now, with the Roman Stoics this perfecting of ethics through subjection to right reason is not something that goes without saying. In a satisfactory moral theory, as theirs is, that involves stopping short of a uniformly normative discourse, the task of securing the equilibrium of forces then becomes the responsibility of the will. It selects among the instincts in order to make a life into a work. The more beautifully its choices fit together, the better the work holds together. The ethical end of the will is the portrait: "my" nature.

This displacement (which was at work at Rhodes in the last two centuries before our era[68]) weakened the subsumption not only in its prestige, but in its very labor. What is it that spoils the portrait in advance? How does "fresh madness"—we have awakened from the dream of outfitting ourselves against it—reveal itself as a condition of impossibility that in the end is the work-portrait (an individual *energeia* is inconceivable for the Greeks)? Following the example of the ancients, the directive faculty was still supposed to gain the upper hand over every other force. To impede dispersion is what remains the task, and yet reason nevertheless reveals itself incapable of transmuting the instincts and incorporating them. Once its task is recognized to be impossible, and the psychic tumult implacable, the path of selective choice (of the *ekologé*) climbs at the same rate that the side of assimilative reason declines.

The selective agent will no longer claim to metamorphose the instincts into their other. The will, more modestly, will fit their proclivities together. This is how directive reason gives way to the coordinating will. The latter will balance the micro-politics of impulses, and afterwards, in the Roman macro-politics, will make a great show of a well-made portrait. So, it suffices to have recognized a mad impulse as *possible,* like a wisp of hair in a portrait, in order for such a micro-singularization to have enough force to disturb in advance the contextualization of instincts. The art, from which the work will eventually emerge, will consist henceforth in an appropriate selection of present forces. This Ciceronian résumé of the "moral mean" testifies to this: "to choose the things conforming to nature as long as they are not opposed to virtue."[69] We understand this to say, "choose the things conforming to *your* nature as long as they are not opposed to *nature.*"

Conceived according to free choices, the *hêgemônikon* functions as a perpetual Congress of Vienna where the powers conduct their affairs with a view to a stable balance. The middle Stoics certainly will hold that only the influence of reason is right (*orthos*); but the emphasis henceforth will lie on influence, thus on the will, before coming to rest on reason. The one who acts "according to what is right" will manifest, in good and bad fortune, an imperturbable homeostasis of faculties—a homeostasis that must extend to the forces in the city, in the human race, in the universe. Thus when, in the lines cited in the epigraph to chapter 8, Cicero speaks of right reason, which is the one true law because it is in accord with nature, he has in mind the doctrine of *katorthoma,* thus toned down in view of the portrait. The law "summons us to carry out what is fitting": above all, to choose and to cultivate in us—to will—the impulses susceptible of a portrayal. In contradistinction to what today we would call voluntarism, the Stoics do not turn themselves inside out pursuing this or that determinate good. Of course they preferred to have a good reputation. But if it did not result from their own efforts, it is then the hour of truth: How have I constituted my *persona* with the material given to me—tendencies, aptitudes, etc.? In fashioning this given, *I make my nature the singular object of a singular will.* The will will be selective only in rejecting the overdeterminations of the passions whose vivacity would muddle the functional continuity. It will avoid *pathos,* which means, "what refuses to obey selective reason" and thereby "transgresses the duty."[70] The call to "apathy" too is changed when reason is instrumentalized to homologate the psychic forces. Through its choice, reason become voluntary retains, among the affects, those to which we can acquiesce without losing peace of mind. This is what nature as measure now demands. It is the principle of a judicious development through appropriate and gradual interventions in the self with a view to the balance of forces.

Now, the Greek vocabulary hardly allows for the articulation of the balanced organization of psychic forces. In *proairêsis,* in deliberation, choice arises from logos. But for the Roman Stoics "whatever may be the personality that we choose (*velimus*) to retain, it will be decided by our will (*voluntas*) (*Off.* 115). Is this a consequence of Roman cosmopolitanism? In any case, the "selection" is displaced. Its issue now is . . . the career, a phenomenon unknown in the Greek city. "Above all," to follow Cicero in his address to his son, "we must decide who and what sort of man we want to be (*velimus*) and what vocation we wish to pursue in life. Here we find the most difficult of all our deliberations" (*Off.* 117). How, in the Greek polis, would the beautiful young man thus have been able to sense that he was at the crossroads of possible lives? The choice of life would boil down to just one. Learn the art of politics (*politikê arêtê*). Such would have been the only paternal response to the torments—hence in this it is beyond the scope of this epoch—of the professional orientation. We see how the attention to the singular militates against the thetic will, and from its interior, even though it is supposed to impose a universal congruence of ends.

b. The integrative will: Consequently we see in what respect Cicero was driven to name the will from the moment the singular gave rise to a normative differend more explicitly than it ever had in antiquity. In the nineteenth century it will be good form to laugh at the philosophical ambitions of Cicero—and does he not confess his relative lack of substantial cultivation? But in his candor he preserves the phenomena more faithfully than do the systematizers. He said he was philosophizing even when he didn't look like it, for example, in pleading at the forum for the *concordia ordinum,* a continuity integrating the orders of life. Therefore he can be understood as an *actor veritatis,* making a political work out of the truth. What truth? The truth that nature links together and orders all regions of experience. Now, this linking together—the maximization of psychic conditions in one's conduct toward oneself, expanded into the maximization of Roman conditions, out in one's conduct toward the people—passes through rhetoric—more precisely, through the forum.

To see that it is *the thetic will that calls for rhetoric,* it is necessary to take note of a certain Roman defeatism in relation to the principle of continuity that nature is supposed to be, which is the counterpart to the triumphalism that posits the equivalence of "Rome" and "nature." This is because, already in the psychic apparatus, the continuity proves impossible to sustain either as given or as what has to be imposed as ordained. Things are no different in the sphere of politics. In the concordance of orders, attention to the singulars immediately sows a certain discord. At the time of Cicero, the Stoics had become a skeptical school. Philosophy in general seemed to them impoverished, not only in its incapacity to answer the most burning questions concerning truth, but also in that it had never produced with much certainty the wise man described so long ago, under the Portico of Polygnotus. The endless work of psychic contextualization, the labor of right reason, had never been but a fantasm—that is the defeat with which, in Rome, the Stoics deal. Their gallery of portraits upon which entelic nature sparkles was, and would remain, empty. Normative rectitude ceased to constitute a problem. The class of morally indifferent phenomena—the "fitting" was a class discovered by them—is what preoccupied them. A bright mind can resign itself to the fact that impulsive discharges last, being invincible; the selective will can compensate for wisdom, in other words, through a psychic pragmatism. But it is not good to expose minds less sure of those impulses to this philosophical poverty. A collective awareness of the uncertainties about thought processes could only spell injury to the good functioning of institutions. Thus, all in all the will is responsible for the (ethical) selection which is to cultivate the singular nature and (political) integration so as to deploy the standard sense of being beginning with the forum of the singular city.

As a result, the normative is conceived not without some second thoughts. The *epoché* of the Stoics, their suspension of judgment, subverts their thesis that nature is normative because it is continuous. Hence, to the masses they plead for the texture of soul-city-world-gods. Nature changes from a *given* into a *willed* homologating principle. Here we see the other employment of the will, where it posits the universal even while, in polishing the portrait and commemorating Rome, it cultivates the singular. For this maximization Cicero needs the rostrum; Augustine will need the pulpit.

From the height of the speaker's rostrum the concern for general tranquillity had to restore, for large consumption and with a view to public safety, to the Stoic luminaries the referent that they dismantled. In their exoterism, they showed civic sense is most demanding. Animated by a heightened sense of responsibility for the common good, they readily write, moreover, popular texts for wide circulation. The key concepts of this rehabilitation aimed at the majority are precisely reason "guided" in its influence over the self and the "concord" in the concatenation of orders outside the self.[71] In their rhetorical exoterism, these terms highlight the thetic will.

With the Roman Stoics, whose spokesman Cicero makes himself, a voluntary posture thus does not refute the natural law; hence this quasi-transcendental influence of a *nature that my will posits as common,* and which in turn obliges me as a principle of the universal telic continuity. However, it is an influence destabilized from within by another nature—the natural—*that my will cultivates as my own* and that, as a singular given, obliges me.

A uniformly normative morality would resolve such a conjunction of the naturally given and the voluntarily posited by means of subsumption. It would say: Seek the greatest good so as to subject to it both the given and the willed. Now, *natura*—the only candidate for this integrative post—proves to be doubly knotted. The ethical knot: I want my nature, but also the universally finalizing reason. The political knot: I want my city, but also universally contextualizing humanity. In these knots—in this "but also"—consists the metabasis for which Cicero did not see the problem. Nevertheless, in retrospect it is difficult not to detect in this the gravest of problems: of not recognizing therein the most ancient differend. The law of the common *would* not even be if, in order to be extrapolated from it, it were not based on one's own law. The will turns against itself in that the singular wants *its* law, with and against (and at the origin of) *the* law.

Willing one's own as well as what is exogenous

Comparable knots, as well as those also incurred by the will, complicate nature in Augustine.

If I try to describe what excited me ten, twenty years ago, and then what matters in my life today—in the event that this could be of interest to someone—and if thereupon I were to tarry over questions a bit antiquated since Augustine, of the sort "Did I stay the same?" "Have I changed?" then I would no doubt notice that the representational I's are hardly a matter of there being new sides, but rather that there have been redistributions and redispositions. The great neurotic ships keep circulating, but they circulate according to slightly different codes. In the arsenal of psychic forces, those that weigh the most today bear down on us differently and elsewhere.

And so it is with hegemonic economies. From *De Officiis* to *The Confessions,* the weight of the singular rips through the telic continuity which is *natura,* but it weighs down upon it differently and elsewhere.

We have seen the "political" differend through which a represented city ontologizes the eternal law, all the while folding up its encompassing fabric like an umbrella on an ontic given. In terms of the will, *amor* makes the city normative while *dilectio*—a technical term in Augustine indicating the real love for a bearer of a proper noun—singularizes it.

Hegemonic nature is deployed and folds up just as inevitably in the "ethical" sphere—in that of the me and the you. The normative argument here is remarkable for the play between the universal within and the singular outside, a play that prefigures in certain respects the double bind in modern critical transcendentalism. Augustine postulates a systematic continuity within the mind that transgresses just as systematically by singularization occurring from the outside. The distribution of forces in a differend will actually be analogous in Kant, since for him the normative universal will result from positings within the subject, and since the singular will transgress the subject through givens from outside.

My will turns against itself in aiming at nature as my *own* good, but in aiming at it in the form of a singular *different* from it—in the form of the "You."

Thus it is a matter of full possession. The will is naturally capable of appropriating God (*capex Dei*); it is made to be totalized by and through itself. The supreme good that one must grasp and possess, Augustine repeats frequently enough, resides in oneself. God, as the the inner master, offers understanding; as the light spread out in the mind, he offers vision; as the truth that lays out the eternal reasons (the ideas), he serves the intellect as the sufficient condition for knowledge; as the inner word, he says and effects the unity of soul-knowledge-love. . . . Here we have the mental functions toward which it would be enough for the will to turn itself in order to be fulfilled, as is its nature, through its own good. It would then possess the truth that brings all ends into focus—the ideal order present in us and linking us together as the principle of continuity among domains of experience.

Now, original corruption has diverted the will from this possession in which it would find in itself the absolutely universal. Our factual *velle* dissipates short of our rightful *posse*. However natural, the totalization remains beyond reach. As a result, the will will need to go through a series of contingent facts in order to grasp its good, and to grasp it in the form of an exogenous gift. In the place of possession there is (a) a precarious contextualization of singulars which are (b) heteronomous.[72] The natural link, uniformly obligatory, doubly inscribes me—under the universally radiant truth outside me but concealed by sin, and the side of the singular that comes to me from outside but is shot through with contingency.

The singular and the heteronomous fragment presence into partial glimpses, into the scattered and successive "this here's"—on the first view, precisely what Augustine abhors. One need only to have opened the *Confessions* in order to know how much the disparate, which is our fate, distresses and irritates him. His impatience toward the individual goes quite far. Did it not make him frankly obliterate, in the core of his "ethics"—in his theory of friendship—what was irreplaceable in the friend. Take Alypius, a friend. If Augustine felt well in his company, it cannot be, it must not be, because of the qualities that make him unique; nor because his nature makes for an agreeable portrait. Rather it is in order "to cure Alypius of this plague," namely, his passion for the gladiatorial combats—a cure which would end with the consecration of Alypius as a bishop (*Conf.* VI, 7, 11ff). As we have seen with regard to the parallel city, without a *contemptus mundi,* there is no friendship. In the eyes of God, we are all equal in the strongest sense of the term, which is to say, mutually indifferent.[73] And the "world" is to be scorned, precisely as a place where the "this here's" and those different ones there solicit us. Whether Platonically I love the idea in you, or, as Augustinian, I love uncorrupted nature, there will be no love except as covered over by the gauze of these generalities—the idea, nature.

Augustine strikes down the singular in the culture of the self with still more intolerance. As we have seen, he shares nothing of Cicero's passion for the cared-for *persona*. On the contrary, it falls among the direct consequences of original corruption. To make of myself a personality, to refine my diverse tendencies to the point of harmonizing them into a personality that one would hasten to greet at the forum would be to leave embedded in me impulses forever disordered, be they camouflaged under a brilliant exterior—in that case even more so. The great manufacturer of second nature is habit. Hence the deduction of the verdict against the attentions and refinements brought to bear on my nature is expeditious: "The law of sin is the violence of habit"; so, if habit debilitates, it is because the will is not centered on its end, is not in order; second nature, "fabricated, so to speak,"[74] thus results from an uncentered will that makes us into children of this world, given to chasing after the *thises* and the *those* according to the whims of vanity, of cupidity, and all the rest. Hence the verdict: The individual personality is against nature. It is a mask affixed, ever since the fall, to the "immutable law of nature,"[75] the *ordinatissima*.

Here we have situated the singular that is the worldly city, if it is not that of the devil. And yet . . .

a. On phenomenalized and dephenomenalized singulars. The vituperations against the singular are, of course, all that is left of the Augustinian. In analyzing the proposed remedy, notably in the *Confessions,* we have nevertheless seen that under the intact and ordered hegemony of nature a gap nonetheless opens up between two *thises*. It is now necessary to see in this gap a twist that the will brings to bear on itself. The gap separates the singular me—into the heart blessed with primordial possessions (which means, possessing the "first order"), but with a dowry squandered by wrongdoing, which has broken its zest of self-possession—and into this henceforth exogenous singular: you, master who teaches, light that clarifies, word which speaks the knowledge that the soul has of itself. These are the rubrics of an intact nature that have come to describe a bearer of a proper name other than myself. The natural order collapses in the distance willed between two deictic beings. They polarize the will and are thinkable only one through the other, but without being contained with a common genus. Doubly binding desire, they rearrange the Ciceronian conflict between the natural (natal property) and nature (the harmonizing of orders). We see here how Augustine states this new arrangement, reduced to two pivot points: "To know God and the soul, that is what I desire. And nothing more? No, absolutely nothing."[76]

Pivot points standing naked, *telê* without texture—this arrangement inscribes us otherwise and elsewhere than the telic concatenation *wills* it according to the "classical" theory of natural law. One really has to grasp this reduction of nature to the simple field of tensions between I and You that is also willed. *Thises* never manifest themselves except in a context (a phenomenologist would prefer to say "in a world," were it not for the risk of confusing it with the Johannine and Augustinian *mundus*.) To manifest beings by ceaselessly linking them together according to their ends—that is the very role of hegemonic *natura*. Therefore, the decisive question from here on out is: The rejoinder ("and nothing more? —No, absolute nothing") having disentangled the I and the You from the telic tissue that is nevertheless posited as all-encompassing, how are beings phenomenalized in the pure asymmetrical counter-posing of these two singulars?

When he works on the one and only space between these singulars, phenomenalizing them according to the one and only gap that separates them, Augustine abdicates the principial civil service, and this through his fidelity to the givens that are found to be the case. They are still cases and cadences of the will, but here the will falls otherwise than in its integrative relapses.

One has to call it a minimal legislative arrangement. The gap between me and You opens up due to the will singularizing me. Now, as an affair of the "heart" (of what today—but not in Augustine's Latin—one would call the "person"), singularization can only be alarming to the quest for tranquillity and order. If making a second nature that is noticed in society is freely to turn away from the first nature that no one notices, that we do not make for ourselves and which despite the disorders suffered is never lost, and if desire—the will—cleanses this first nature by reducing the primordial continuity to the pure distance between me and You, then one cannot help reading the invectives of Augustine against all dispersion, dissolution, distance, and dissimilitude as so many symptoms of a panic in the face of the possible loss of all contexture. He speaks as if ceaselessly threatened from one moment to the other by the loss of the phenomenality making up the world. The minimal relation of me and You poses the problem by its nudity. It portends the definitive decontextualization. With *natura* reduced to a bifrontal insertion, the heart indeed has something to worry about. To take possession of our end and thus to close the phenomenalizing gap is out of the question. All one can do is confess it. All that is left, consequently, is an act of the will that not only allows two beings to subsist in nature, but that in turn receives them contextualized without recourse to an encompassing homology. Knowing the imminent loss of the world, thus knowing mortality, I want to be singular before You. Later, the Scotists—and Luther—will show a comparable self-confidence in their fidelity to singulars factually phenomenalized by received interventions (they will say by heteronomous freedom) without resorting to a normative primordial nature. In this they show themselves to be excellent Augustinians.

The gap opened up between singulars—between me and You—reduces possession to desire, namely, to non-possession. But this gap itself opens up through desire. One must bear in mind this twist of decontextualization-recontextualization, for it is through this that the will turns against itself. Whoever speaks of desire speaks of the possessive, the unappeased will. How is one to appease it under the regime of factual alterity? Here we have the whole program of "knowing God and soul," that is, of traversing the distance between me (the *this* normed by You) and You (the normative *This*). This is a rephenomenalization at a different level, but not the mending of the telic fabric. Rather, as we have seen in Augustine, the ascending pathway *serializes* sites. It leads things on the outside to those on the inside, then to those that are above. In other words, the conversion not only drives along disparate singulars, but even those sites that are ruptured.

The remedy for the singularization that diverts (*avertere*) me toward the outside consists in returning (*convertere*) to the gap alienating me from myself from within.

To save oneself from singulars by singulars is the formal paradox of a phenomenalization that keeps fractured domains (*foris, intus, supra*) apart. On first blush it is true that the route toward God unfolds without a hitch within an interior setting: The agent that makes the transition from outside to inside is the will, and the goal, since it is a question of straightening things out, is the right will. Thus to be converted means first of all to work on the will, by the will. But what it seeks in the interior sphere so as to be perfected—teacher, light, truth, the word—it can only desire at a distance that forever deprives it of possession and peace. Thus what remains for it is a serialization of sites that are not continuous, but discontinuous; not to be effected, but received; not one's own, but exogenous, never phenomenalized once and for all, but always threatened with being dephenomenalized.

Accordingly, interiority does not contain what it promises. The totalizing return to myself fails. Interventions are needed that place the inside within a series between the outside and the above, interventions that can only come from elsewhere. "You have pierced through my deafness . . . you have taken away my blindness . . ." (*Conf.* X, 27, 38). The serialization that reorients the will, emerging first from a singular other and an exogenous site, is produced or not produced. The return, the straightening out, the paradox maintained, the alienating fracture that is willed, the belonging recovered without wiping away the topical intervals—all this, which abrogates the invariability and thus the ordinariness of metaphysics, can only be recounted, parceled out by thanksgivings and the heaving of sighs.

Thanksgivings, since the gap between me and You relocalizes the world—a rudiment of world—even as the heart was worried it might not be dismantled; nevertheless there is a heaving of sighs, for the dislocation and delocalization always remains to come.

We see the epochal semantic shift from *erôs*—rising from, elevating, rising over the particulars—to *voluntas* taking in recontextualized singulars as disparates. There is no sort of escape toward the universal, the general, the generic, the common, that consummates the conversion and the confession. The joy of integrated ends does not appear at any moment in the phenomenalization effected by the will that Augustine calls *dilectio.* How then does the will work on singulars? It works on them through *systematic breaches of the principle of continuity.* In order to will the *telos,* however natural it is, a girl was needed who plays ball and sings "take and read"; then it was necessary to read and understand, thus to give credit to this exterior authority, a book; also necessary were the words of an Alypius and a Monica; and finally it was necessary to say "You converted me to You" (*Conf.* VIII, 12, 29f.). In other words, it was necessary that a number of *thises* suddenly be arrayed so that You are found therein, though all the while occupying an exogenous site. The rectified will embraces the heteroclite that is given. From me to You there is no ascension of the particular to the universal, but the unstable phenomenalization of incomparable singulars.

A love affair. Whether or not it is one explicitly, Augustine hardly ever stops recounting his changes of heart. His will, at first misdirected outside in the love impulse, returns to the inside where it is transmuted into right love. What force is at work behind this about-face? "To love is nothing but to tend toward a thing for itself."[77] The force is a certain *res*—"You"—that draws and attracts. The will turned outside settles in a region of things that are described, like the *persona,* in terms of fabrication. "Do not take up residence in what is fabricated, but live in the fabricator."[78] The divinely fabricated is the world full of traces of its artisan; the humanly fabricated is the world of twisted love that disfigures the traces of nature. How is one to cure the twisted ones that we are and who create natures in order to fashion personalities? By leaving it up to You who spreads out your rectifying light above. And how is one to discover this light? This happens in the story that posits the You and that lets it be. Confession posits the recontextualizing other, the spiritual exercise (*exercitatio animi*) lets it be. The antidote to the twisted will is a history whose intrigue is summed up in the gap that opens up between the singular that I am—myself—and this other singular—the singular of another cite—that You are, yourself. Confession comes down to saying that, once the continuity of orders has been broken by sin, do like I do, love the *res* that came to me and that I have loved in return.

Here we see the singular and the disparate no longer abhorred, but rather as purveyors of salvation. The will lets itself produce and love the interruptions that mortify its natural, native megalomania.

But this is not to say that the will never recovers from the maximizations which natality induces. For its part, nature-as-law recovers, but spaced out from within and slowed down till the end of time. The spacing and the slowing down defer the law. They singularize it at the expense of a metabasis, and they universalize it at the expense of an aftereffect. Here is the metabasis: Love would neither receive nor choose anything at all if the gladiatorial combats, the charms of Alypius, the careful brilliance of Augustine, the rhetor, had not revealed that the love was for singulars that free us from hyperbolic effects, just as it—love—is love for common nature, communally binding us. *Amor* is a neutral power (comparable in this to the Kantian *Willkür*) which is determined in accordance with the object. The other bond imposed by a different singular, namely, the prescription that binds otherwise and comes from "You," would remain null and void, if *thises* were not loved with horror at the circus and other *thises* loved with friendship at Thagaste and Cassiciacum. The metabasis is a passage from one's own *this* to the exogenous *This.* And this is the effect of the aftereffect: Continuous nature works on us beginning with the true light that exceeds our reason just as it also works on us beginning with the final restoration that exceeds our time. The battle of the will against itself therefore is first of all neither psychological nor spiritual. It is the functioning of normativity itself beginning with a hegemonic fantasm that is applied to the ideal order spaced out within ("eternal reasons" grasped in the natural light) and slowed down beforehand (the joy of ends grasped in the revealed light), an order that is *demonstrable* and nevertheless leads back to a being that is *monstrable* in spatio-temporal interventions. Such is the differend to which the ultimates here give rise.

Moreover, we can only be perplexed by the ease with which, in the argument about the legislative authority, the usual interpretations of Augustine unfailingly follow this shift from the demonstrable to what is only monstrable. Does this ease indicate the impulse of the natural metaphysician in us, fantasizing despite everything, or does it instead indicate that, familiars of the originary differend, we are so profoundly in accord with the tragic condition that there is nothing left to say when the spacing and the slowing down prove to fracture a nomothesis?

Whatever the case may be, *natura* remains intact but at a distance; it furnishes the condition to the mental functions that summon light, glowing, mastery, the word. . . ; now, errancy makes possession something remote from these personal functions, functions that are clearly closest to me; errancy is what sets these functions far away. Hence, the only singular interventions, spacing out and temporalizing nature, will transmute this distance into salvation. Thus the universal principle of telic continuity here comes to be affixed to a pronoun and to exacerbate the normative incongruity: You, master; You, the word; You, the light; You, the truth.

Cicero had envisioned a more or less strictly symmetrical reduction when he apprised his son of "the most difficult" question: which career to choose? He placed the will of Marcus in the double bind of one's own nature and common nature. Augustine sharpened both the point of departure in the singular and the double bind that follows from it. The point of departure is this restless heart, dispersed among singulars which solicit him; the double bind is the love of the *proper order* that this very heart finds inscribed in itself, then the desire of the *exogenous singular*—You—whose episodic interventions transgress in advance the continuous order, all the while weaving it together. With this love and this desire being equally legislative, the will ceases to grasp our ends in complete beauty and simplicity.

Hereby we are in the grip of the differend, the minimal sense of being involved in that exercise known as confession. In confession, the will enters into conflict with itself through a decontextualization-recontextualization that plays on the disparate singulars that are always threatened by isolation. Hence the prayers: do not leave me. . . . Being is, there, only in the gap thus opened. The singular I wants—desires, loves chooses, adores—the other than itself, such that this consoling other manifests itself as a deictic male (*princeps*) rather than as an apodictic neuter (*principium*). The natural law is not abolished, but it passes over to being an attribute to a personal pronoun. It inscribes being between two singulars that are affirmed as such in disparate places and times. With neither enclosure nor genus, it is the law only by virtue of the single *interval* between me and You. This is a new indication that universally homologating nature is pushed to the end, beginning with its own institution, and that there the erratic differend immediately exhausts the uniformly normative power.

It is only an indication, for the work of the thetic will is more complex than this interstitial play. The complexity has to do with the spacing and with the slowing down.

b. On a normative parallax. You go down a river in canoe. On one of the banks there is a house and next to it, a little downstream, is a poplar tree. At first the house seems to be in front of the poplar, thus bigger. When you have passed both and turn back to look at it upstream, the poplar seems to be in front of the house, now being bigger than it. This optical phenomenon is called a parallax: the apparent movement of one object relative to another as a result of a change in the point of observation with a correlative inversion of sizes.

The whole problem in hegemonies of *obvious facts* and of their backside can be described in these terms. With every hegemony it is a matter of a relation *seen* as determining the large and the small, as a result of a position taken. In Augustine, the disparate that is posited and deposited in levels is preserved in the singularity of these levels, and turns up again with each advance toward the ultimate referent—and even in the advance into the ultimate referent, which is the decisive advance.

The dual labor of the will—to posit the great referent, to let the singulars go—appears most clearly when Augustine places virginal nature *beside* societies and individuals so as to measure them by it. This is a juxtaposition that opens up a "not yet," since the two cities become comparable through a false diachronic-achronic movement. This movement punctuates and punctualizes the telic continuity from within. But the leading edge of what is "to come" remains parallactic in that an imperative fixes its angle of measurement. By grasping how this punctuality is turned against duration, we will better understand how the will turns against itself when it posits the large and the small.

As Hannah Arendt[79] analyzed so well, the heavenly city in gestation on earth *does not meet up with* existing societies that are gathered together under a body of consensual laws so as to temper and make up for a plurality of interests. For Augustine, such societies become, on the contrary, manifest for what they are, solely through their relation to the heavenly city. As much as their temporal succession, the spatial juxtaposition of the two communities has produced a long history of worldly affairs that have been arranged by the thetic will such that they cannot have very much weight. The preponderating forces come from elsewhere. Arendt has shown how—despite, notably, the elegy of friendship and in virtue of its very conception—such a doubling in the Augustinian notion of love, and thus of the will, is translated into a remarkable indifference toward others. "We no longer experience it in concrete, intra-worldly encounters: for example, as friend or enemy."[80] All that counts is the relation of each toward the postulated, posited, willed measuring point. All that counts is the parallactic angle. To love one's neighbor "in God" means to wipe out the very possibility of an interpersonal choice, to hamper the understanding and thus the rationality in a society marked immediately by sin; in sum, it means to strike down human relations as such as being worthless.

Arendt, however, does not address herself to the institutive gesture through which Augustine endows nature-as-law with normative attributes; it is a focusing that fixes, in large scale, the parallel city, the only city that conforms to this law. In the first as in the last study published in her life,[81] Arendt sought instead to grasp the belittling of "our city" through having recourse to the legislative-transgressive play of *motifs,* a play stated by Paul ("the good that I want I do not do, and the evil that I do not want I do," Romans 7:19 already cited). Now, in Augustine the conflict of the will is a matter of the normative before being a matter of the motif. The *velle-nelle* is concerned with the postulate of a present that is posited because of its durable universality, but fractured by the event, which is loved because of its singularity. In order to understand (as the moderns say) the philosophical genius of Augustine better than he himself understood it, one must remain as attentive as possible to this double bind that the thetic will brings to bear. Thus we briefly pester nature with transformative tactics, first according to space and then according to time; first by observing the will putting the universal and the singular in place, then by following it into the blows and aftereffect that open up the differend of presence-event.

By placing it before the truth (*coram veritate*), before the virginal nature from which it was able to fall, fallen nature shows its dissolutive power. The parallactic *coram* indicates how the two cities meet up without ever being confused. Placing the one before the other is precisely what also indicates their common ontic status. To place one *this* in relation to another, and to play the role of the philosopher in such a manner that one of the two seems larger and the other smaller—this is precisely the same optic effect that instituted first one focal meaning of being, then another one according to epochs. Who could not share the incredible sigh of relief, after centuries of the sort of treatment one has received there, that we hear in Wittgenstein when he assures us: but no, "things are going on quite normally . . ."

The corrupted state of the worldly city indirectly emphasizes the positivity of the city true to natural law (whereby, by systematizing Augustine a little bit, one can understand the invisible effect of the eternal law on common life). The two societies make use of the goods of subsistence, but even though they act visibly in concert, invisibly they pursue two disparate ends: "This world is there to make use of, not in order to enjoy it."[82] The inhabitants of the worldly city are responsible for the management of goods, wherein the visible republic finds its end. The inhabitants of the heavenly city are the ones who make use of these same goods with a view to a larger republic, even if it remains invisible. While the ones are occupied with "providing for the needs of mortal life," the others "do not hesitate to obey the laws of the worldly city that assure its good administration" (*City* XIX, 17). The key word is *administrare*. It pertains as much to material services as to the laws that regulate them. Civil legislation does not come into contact with the natural law that is in force within oneself (at least this is the way it is in the state where the members of the two societies rub shoulders without being confused; on the other hand, these societies do not rub shoulders in the household where the *paterfamilias* determines the religion of each). In the public domain, the law of charity becomes, at most, effective through interiority. If the young Augustine could discriminate between two groups of men—sages obeying the eternal law, witless ones the temporal law—and if the *City of God* restores the worldly laws of the two communities without exemption, it is because in the meantime one of the communities has been rendered invisible. The heavenly city in the process of growing cannot be distinguished by any trait that can be verified by the naked eye of the civil society where pagans and Christians live under the same government and the same laws, making use of the same institutions and establishments, making exchanges on the same markets and pursuing there the same possibilities of profit. The parallel city is fashioned by a different fate (*sors*), which makes for different companions (*consortes*). Their association hearkens to a body of laws (to honor only one God, etc.) that is larger because more interior (*melius quod interius, Conf.* X, 6, 9). Everything happens as if the inner eye saw the most important laws inscribed in the mind, belittling those of society. The two regimes are equally posited and positive, but, as a result of an optical angle, one of them completely dominates the arrangement of inside and outside. Such is the imperative that governs the parallax.

Now we have the passage to the interior (in which the Augustinian project is summed up). There the positivity of the large and the small is confirmed by Augustine's positing, opposing, superimposing the disparates that are the universal and the singular. This is most obvious with regard to justice. For each of the two cities he gives a precise definition to the one in it who is just. As for the one who is concerned with worldly affairs, he *couldn't help* but follow Plato and Aristotle: "The function of justice consists in rendering to each that which is due him, whence it arises that in man himself a certain equitable order of nature (*iustus ordo naturae*) is established that subjects the soul to God, the flesh to the soul and, consequently, the soul and the flesh to God."[83] He couldn't help but follow them . . . were it not for sin, which everywhere and always ruins the equitable order. Where, then, and in whom might such an order actually have existed? One never finds out. As a result, for those who know they are in exile on earth, justice "consists in the remission of sins" (*City* XIX, 27). Here we have a new angle, the eternal passes in front of what nevertheless is supposed to be natural: "[W]e are able to live in justice only by virtue of the eternal law which preserves the natural order."[84] Equity is made according to another parallax, but it is just as concrete and just as applicable to the diversity of cases as is the standing positive law that is executed by public forces. The thetic gesture posits the eternal as universal; and it also posits *the gesture* of the city being constituted here-below as singular. And so we have the parallactic disparity interiorized. Justice will be fully done when the eternal law is naturally obeyed—in the final city. In willing the universal constraint as well as the singular, the love that builds cities turns against itself, and this in its legislative function.

The double bind above all smites this great Augustinian discovery—freedom. External society is born of necessity; the internal from free choice. The passage to the interior discovers a land of emancipation unknown until then. Now, if others can become a question for me as I have become a question for myself, this will always be only as a function of this other, parallel justice. Only there will my fellow creatures have weight. But freedom intervenes only to open the access to a dominating, willed necessity. The inhabitants of the new land quickly reveal themselves to be of the same temper—more than fellow creatures, they are equals. Augustine wants them to be free, but this in such a manner that, as bearers of a proper name, they immediately lose their newfound openness. Free, yes, but to choose only God. At the very moment their identity is taken into consideration humans thus recognize themselves as peers under a regime that looms over them and that suppresses anew their freedom. At the most concrete level of charity, individual differences become blurred. The heart—a technical term in Augustine, as we have seen, for designating the singular—of the other is of interest to me only insofar as it is also *capax veritatis,* whereby we are all from the same mold. Barely discovered, freedom is covered back over by the common. However, under cover, it never stops working on the nomothesis, so much so that the nascent hegemony absorbs the equally nascent freedom, just as an organism absorbs a poison. The period of incubation will last until Duns Scotus.

Consequently we see here how convulsed the will is that posits, necessarily and at the same time, eternal law and freedom. As an organizational faculty (through the obedience which the believers take over from the wise men), the will institutes the principle of homology; but as an elective faculty that gathers together bearers of proper names, the will immediately destitutes this principle. Augustine tries hard to efface the singularizing work of freedom. To love the differences among the singulars—and outside of these differences, free choice has no object—would be to retain only the outer appearance of humans. Differential choice subsists there no less when it is a matter of abducting others toward the truth (*rapere ad veritatem, Conf.* X, 43,70), thus toward the spiritually subsumptive authority. Thus an essential function in the normative argument—that of a recruiting agent—amounts to selective freedom.

Accordingly it is not difficult to see that once *libre arbitre* is engrafted in telic nature, singularization can't help but continue asserting itself in the constitution of nature as an inexorable moment, to such an extent that in the fourteenth century it will be precisely this (divine) free choice of singulars that will ruin from the within the edifice of natural law.

The Augustinian ascent passes from exterior sites to interior and superior ones. Now, the normative will *posits and permits* the disparate at all these anagogic levels. In the exterior city, this will is why all that counts are the opportunities for promoting the parallactic cause of the true, interior city—a promotion that requires that one advance into the framework on which obvious facts are superimposed, at first from the small to the large (from the exterior to the interior), then from the singular heart to the universal city-nature (from the interior to the superior). These superimpositions lead from a crumbled framework outside to the adjusted angle inside, then to the sole mensurative perspective above. In this optical trajectory *the singulars* (in the plural) are integrated into *the large* singular, which is the co-opted city where hearts once again become, after a fashion, stones—but a mason's stones. Normative obviousness is thus born from a dual view. We see what we want to see. Double vision is a result of the will that posits the city-as-nature as encompassing but which, since this positing incorporates hearts, also can't help but let it go, incongruously singularized by ineffaceable freedom.

Before passing on to the matter of time, we will take one last look at the thetic will. *Voluntas* turns against itself (the formalism is only apparent), not only in loving the universal as well as the singular, and not only in maximizing the singular as universal, but also in willing the universal *qua* singular.

This is a completely different matter, a divine matter. The Scholastics tried their best to distinguish more clearly than Augustine between eternal law and natural law, then between these two taken together and positive laws. The latter will be of two types: the human laws that result from customs and conventions, and the divine laws that concern the qualities attaching to certain times, places, persons, acts, objects . . . laws that are inaccessible to an intellect that is left to its own devices and are accessible only through revelation. All positive law presupposes a legislator endowed with a will and who intervenes in the course of events. Now, in the Augustinian nomothesis it is also one of the distinctive traits that even the eternal law is ordained by the will. As an ordered order, it is a matter of the wisdom of God; but as an ordering order it is a matter of his will. Thus God commanded (*praecipit*) the first content of the eternal law, namely, in such a way that the body, the soul, and intellect are supposed to be harmonized: "It is some praiseworthy influence that the soul seems to exercise over the body and reason over the vices, if the soul and reason themselves are not subjected to God as God commanded of them, they no longer have a just influence over the body and the vices" (*City* XIX, 25). The eternal law is the very idea of preformed order, and nature the overall concept of the totality covering all that can be harmonized according to this order. If God harmonizes the ends through voluntary acts, through precepts, then nature will be the divinely willed *par excellence.* It results from the right rule (*recte imperare*) of God.

Every efficient cause is voluntary (*City* V, 9,3); so (the shifts that orient an argument intervene in the minor premise) the efficiency available to the intellect is always only the effect of a revealed efficiency; thus the revealed cause is exceedingly voluntary. It is so in its particularities, as in the reward for good conducts, as well as in its generalities, such as the composition of the human makeup. In such a reduction of eternal law, thus of nature in the normative sense, to a positive law we see the universal willed as a precept, willed singularly.

This turn appears again through the selective love in those who take up residence in the one or the other city. In the case of love, the will enters into the very definition of what is "the thing of a people" (*City* XIX, 24). The two cities are born from a voluntary act posited by their respective members. The love of concord under divine injunctions founds the heavenly city; the love of concord through the homeostasis of libidinal impulses founds the worldly city. Thus, both for the laws and for the acts that conform to them, the will adjusts the parallactic angle. Its extracting from the field of empirical forces a force that it declares preponderant is what makes for the autonomy of those left over, the minor forces.

Here again the will posits and cuts off. It posits a normative singular, and it cuts it off from the *singulars* in the worldly city which it then serves to *particularize.* Straight off, the conflict between the cities shapes up as a battle of subsumptions. The two cities are linked together only apparently: today Rome, tomorrow the heavenly Jerusalem. If "two loves have made two cities," it is the case that one of the two loves functions as a landmark in terms of which the other will be able—but also will not be able—to align itself. It is a landmark which shows the will split in two against itself. Augustine, the sinner, does not choose the city that he loves, and the one he chooses—in stealing the pears in the neighbor's garden: his paradigm of the heart divided against itself—he does not love.

The order that a Cicero could praise as natural because it best realizes general justice is here downgraded. Another is juxtaposed to it, to which the prestige of being natural reverts. Nature changes places, but it hardly changes its description. It remains a concrete arrangement, magnified to exceed in obviousness every arrangement accessible to observation. The parallel city, administered only by true justice, remains a nomothetic singular.

If we now ask here, once again, what is the phenomenal region in which the preponderance of one city over the other originarily manifests itself, it can only be the sphere of the conflict in which the will never ceases opposing itself to itself under the positive divine law: to believe even while not believing, to hope beyond hope, to love out of charity but without loving out of desire. This is again a sign, but only a sign, that thought is passing under the vantage point of the will. To think here is *to proclaim nature* as one proclaims someone to be leader: you, bearer of a particular proper noun, you will be the law of laws. . . . This inflection precedes and determines dogma, and not the reverse.

At its Greek apogee, philosophy was astonished by what the hands could accomplish. Since Aristotle, fabrication had remained the key phenomenon, the observation of which furnished the schemes for all branches of knowledge. Beginning with Latin philosophy, the great beginners were astonished by another making—by the cosmopolitan republic, unique in history and so obviously crowned with success. The phenomenon that compels Cicero's admiration is his *urbs*. Perhaps this is philosophical astonishment, even though it is more reminiscent of the astonishment of the lover who says "how beautiful you are"—or rather "how beautiful you were just a little while ago" . . . whereby Rome became a fantasm. Similarly for Augustine. The one destined to receive his admiration is the parallel city, which is the core issue of a declarative act because it is not yet. "To grow old in the familiarity of phenomena" (Aristotle), such is no longer the program. The metabases set off from the *imperium* that henceforth is originary.

Referential exaltation still preserves, in the work of the maximizer itself, the singular upon which it exerts itself. Hence the double bind of the *posited* normative and of the singular that is *left alone*. We have never forgotten—for it cannot be forgotten in the everyday—the lesson according to which to philosophize is to cultivate, to follow, to greet the beings that are given. Only, to bear in mind some preponderant particular being as "the very concern" of thinking is to apply the lesson with a censorious heaviness already found in Parmenides: with the very heaviness of the *force majeure* that weighs down on our acts once the overdetermination of the singular is accomplished.

With regard to the Latin speculations on nature, nothing could be more false than to denounce it for having forgotten to be faithful to phenomena. According to Freud, like the sons of Moses toward the father they assassinate, the Latin metaphysicians of natural law remain so faithful to this singular that falls to them (republican Rome) that they exalt it as alone worthy of safeguarding. Hence the natural normative difference between the heavenly and the worldly, between the inside and outside. They are not guilty of directly forsaking the singular. But they do show themselves there to be faithful infidels by turning the will against itself, whereby they emphasize, in their own way, the legislative tragedy.

Now, with the singular inserted into the normative telic continuity, the focal meaning of being, which is nature, is temporalized.

On natural contre-temps: the law suffering singularizations

Once Latin philosophy was Christianized, where did it go to look for its ultimate referent? For the moment let's admit that Augustine confesses as the spokesperson of the coming millennium (an assumption which, at least with regard to the legislative tragedy, and at least for the final moment of this millennium, will be soon verified).

If this is so, the answer has just been given: Augustine turns toward the life of the mind so as to grasp there the linkages of pristine nature; so the big "But" of the sinner spaces out and slows down this arrangement, it places it beyond reach. As a result only interventions from outside will make up for nature, henceforth displaced and singularized—displaced, for far from finding them within itself, the mind receives these landmarks from elsewhere; singularized, for nature, the telic network linking by right all phenomenal regions, shrinks down to the simple distance between me and You. Augustine went looking for the normative referent in this gap of places and of agents. Nature is instituted as the principle of universal consistency imprinted in my intellect, but it is just as quickly and also necessarily destituted by the call to another stranger, contingent in its governing interventions. These interventions singularize the enveloping texture to the point that nothing remains of this text except the long personal pronouns. In confessing a focal meaning of being received intermittently, Augustine invokes a broken referent—one that is legislative due to the universal ordering, and transgressive due to singularization.

For the will this signifies that in positing the topological heteronomy of me-and-You, it is again turned against itself and not as it was with the Roman Stoics. There is, then, a rearrangement of the Ciceronian double bind in which the will clearly determines the whole ensemble of *my* nature and *nature* as ultimates. This is the philosophical faithfulness of Cicero, seeing that the will conforms, without denying it, to the differend instituted by it, just as always and everywhere—denied or not—life conforms to requirements of a common fantasm and of *thises*. These are all tragically dislocative requirements. No asceticism will ever check the thetic impulse in thought, just as no speculative flight will ever tear us away from deictics.

There is also Augustine's philosophical fidelity in whom, throughout his work but more obvious than ever in the *Confessions,* the cleavage of what is one's own and what is foreign rips the will apart. The gap that the conversion at the same time postulates, reveals, and turns to the good separates two co-originary but incongruous terms of the will: the universal concordance of orders which is mine by right because it is communicated to the mind by emanation, and the bestowing of a singular concord—the peace of my heart—that occurs like a fact of grace and thus remains foreign to me. Lodged in discontinuous sites, this law and this counter-law make the willful search for joy erratic. The law is posited as fully present in me and summing up nature; but the counter-law radically alienates nature since it returns this arrangement to me as the object of tender love coming from elsewhere, reduced to "You," singularized.

And thus temporalized. The gap of the positive-loving will does not work on time differently than it works on space. Just as topological heteronomy turns the singular against the telic continuity, so the temporal differend turns the event against that form of chronological continuity that would be constant presence. We have seen the normative singularization through the preterite tense in Cicero and by the future tense in Augustine. But it is recounted even in the origin of the law, where we find a twisted temporalization whose originary twist is obvious in Augustine, and is even more noticeable in those arguments of Augustine that have underlayments of Cicero in them.

With the law originarily turned back against itself, a discontinuity infects the presence (the presence of things past, presence of things present, present of things future, *Conf.* XI 20,26) from which time is deployed.

If being is essentially presence, and if in other respects this essence is constituted by singular occurrences, then we have a hard time seeing how the focal point will be simple. Presence and occurrence obviously are not to be understood either historically or psychologically. They bear on nature that makes the law. Prior to the history of anagogic ages,[85] and prior to the time of psychological distensions, the double bearing of presence-event *naturalizes* disparates without a common condition, namely, the everlasting principle of continuity as the unforeseeable interventions that intermittently revalidate this principle beyond the fall. How does the continuous and eternal order in reason arrive in nature, singularized in this way? How is one to describe the manner of being of a law which, while remaining universally normative, can nevertheless only fall to us as contingent?

It is not difficult to see that such a manner of being temporalizes the cleavage where philosophy produces idealism—a word that now more than ever must be wielded with caution, like something fragile one borrows and precisely what the double bearing comes to break. Intact, idealization would open the space where the first order (nature-as-fantasm) would be fully, durably, continually present. To idealize would be to maximize some given phenomenal order, to institute it as primordial. The argument that posits an ideal norm starts off from a changeable given and ends up at an unchangeable representation thereby capable of bringing a regime to bear. From Plato to Husserl, idealization has thus worked on things in movement. In them the ideal order is *posited* as *given* for discovery. The present requires only an intuitive linking together in order to be grasped, sheltered from the time that passes. Plenitude and Poverty hold to the two terms of erotic invention—invention in the sense that the Platonic ascent leads from specific insights to generic insights. Were it to possess its object of desire, *erôs* would cease to be; but if it did not already possess the beginnings of what it desires, it would have no precomprehension of it and wouldn't even have thought to move. Without an obscurely glimpsed possession, just as without any clearly desired possession, *erôs* would lose the space of its path of invention. It is an agent of pursuit. Son of Plenitude, it holds what it loves, even though, son of Poverty, it aspires to it, remaining at a distance.[86] From the Greeks up to the first phenomenologists, the gap productive of ideality gives rise to a normativity we could call "inventive."

There are other figures of normativity, but in terms of a temporalization hardly any other than that of full presence. Thus with Kant the idealizing mechanism will be ascribed to practical reason without undermining (at least in that which concerns the "fact of reason") presence. As transcendental, reason gives itself the ideal of the good will; as empirical, it approaches it without ever coming into full conformity with it. There is preunderstanding, not of a good, but of a "fact" always present. The gap, itself also shielded from time, gives rise to a deontological normativity.

Now, we have just seen that conversion again works on a normative gap. Only, where does this path lead here? To a hyper-present Idea, an *eidos* beyond all the *eidê*? To something like a principle of coercive presence constantly speaking to me from within? What in the normative authority would resemble these archaic, temporally intact figures when Augustine speaks of the end as not having recovered from something that *happens* to him? The old gap between what is given and ideality, where ideality subsumes the givens, is here transmuted into a purely descriptive gap. A normative positing that is intact in its full presence is called a universal. Now, the *this* that I am and the *This* that You are, being phenomenalized thanks to and beginning with heteronomous places, thwart the ancient and the modern sovereignty of universals. By what speculative turn, indeed, could one of its singulars particularize another one? Good luck to whoever would attempt such a subsumption. The journey that is conversion surely leads to a normative authority, but where neither archetypic intervention nor deontological spontaneity binds us and where the shelter against time falls into decay. The terminus of the journey is emphasized in the middle voice: *oriri* of the origin, *nasci* of nature, "to happen" of the double bind. The arrangement of eternal reasons is posited, present in us as our natural condition by right; but the putting into force of the law fails as a result of the original contravention that in fact deposes it. It is henceforth law turned back to us, in an event that is or is not produced.

It is impossible to dissociate the law, consequently, from these interventions that deny the durably encompassing continuity. Between the *terminus a quo* and the *terminus ad quem* of the confessed ascension, there comes to be a sudden occurrence which places a singular—"You"—outside the orbit of all other singulars. What is at play in such exorbitance is a *res* that, in distinction from both inventive and deontological morals, acts, gives an account of itself, and is found in the lists of things that happen. The will that posits the legislative gap advances neither toward a universally discovered law in the wake of such an experience (a particular body loved for its beauty, the *Symposium*) nor toward a universal and obligatory condition as a result of some particular sentiment (Kantian respect). It advances in pursuing a more originary temporal contortion.

The erratic condition of being in Augustine results from willing (of which loving, positing, and letting go are forms) *submitted* to time (of which presence and the event are figures). The order of reasons posited in the mind, punctualized by singulars that occur, turns the will against itself. But if there is a temporalizing submission, the contortion will not originally be exactly a matter of the will. It will segment it into position and spiritual love because at first it segments time into presence and occurrence. To understand how this is so, it is necessary to detach *voluntas* both from *erôs* and *agapê* and from the *Wille*.

The erotic strategy (in Augustine's youthful dialogues) says—I love in you the universals that are beauty, truth, etc; the agapic strategy answers (notably in the *City of God*)—I love in you these wholly other universals that make of us builders of the city to come. Both strategies instrumentalize the universal, which is what removes, for all that, a good dose of interest that we have been able to find in the distinction between *erôs* and *agapê*.[87] As for the subsequent *Wille*, it subjectivizes the function which, here, is the responsibility of the other, which is You: that of the absolute good.

We have briefly glimpsed how *voluntas* makes a gesture in the direction of time by the necessity in which Augustine is found to pass from the argumentative register to the narrative register. His will suffers an about-face that he dates on a diachronic line. During the month of August in 386, he heard someone singing to herself: "take and read. . . ," an event that set the stage—put things in time and place—with deictic beings. Now, the heteronomic intervention made, so to speak, time move along. Take, read, hear, believe. By such imperatives the will gets ahead of itself. It posits the legislative gap as faith, it submits itself to it as love, and it institutes the future and thus is temporalized as hope. To be on the point of producing itself is the very status of singularization. Hence the unending prayers of "come," "intervene," as if ever-immanent singularization signified death for us.

The idealization failing in this signification succumbs to time. In the gap between "me" and "You," the "me" designates the heart natively social, far from You, but singularized from the world by You who are to come; "You" designates normative nature, natively mine but alienated and singularized by Your sudden occurrence. The same sudden occurrence that is immanent isolates me in the world and again makes me invoke the name of nature, in the second person singular. Immanence breaks social steadfastness as it breaks ideal strength. To this steadfastness and strength the differend opposes—but outside of them—a co-originary intermittence. It strikes down lasting sociality and stable eternity all together. Both are undermined by, and for, sudden occurrences. In Augustine these *natural contretemps* are best read in certain key episodes (take for instance the scene in the garden in Milan, *Conf.* VIII, 8, 19–12, 30) where the heteronomous intervention both confirms and enfeebles nature-as-law. It confirms it as present, intact within, beyond the fall. But it also enfeebles it by submitting me to the name of nature solely under the mode of the singularization to come.[88]

Once the differend of present and future is recognized, it will hardly be all that will bind us to "the immutable law of nature." The latter will be impossible to establish on the basis of its own obviousness, as providing the standard sense of being, constantly present in homologating regions and obligatory for it before every other prescription.

The Augustinian thetic "nature" instead has need of circumstances and immanences in order to rise to the normative rank: circumstances allowing singulars to be phenomenalized according to a scale of willings spread out by Augustine with an unequaled subtleness, and immanences temporalizing both the heart and the city. The differend that is announced in these natural contretemps sets up singulars that one cannot not let go against the fantasm that one cannot not posit. Here we have normative authorities that are incomparable and yet indissociable.

Hence this amphiboly of recognition: Reason is recognized as clarified by an ultimate postulation, and it makes itself recognized by what happens to it. Incongruously recognized, nature will never satisfy the conditions of universality and of simply constraining necessity. It will be doubly constraining, since it is nothing without the passage of audible speech that binds us to it just as to the fastasmized postulate. When Augustine gives his recounting so as to indicate "the law written in our hearts," nature owes its hegemonic status to this passage and this postulate. The return to the self (*redire ad memetipsum, Conf.* VII, 10, 16) indeed discovers a first order, thus a primordial presence, but this return is no less marked out there, from one end to the other, by beings loved for their sudden occurrence: ball girls; the book that invests authority; the pears that I confess having stolen in my youthful folly; my restless heart; the tranquillity sensed inside; "you, my God."

The final exclamation, "You are my God," gathers up all the force of a declarative proposition. The performative "are" *declares* the law. But we see the dissymmetrical terms that it unites. In the exclamation the same Augustinian nomothesis is expressed that emphasized the most singularizing singular—"You"—and the most encompassing universal—"God." The double allegiance imposes on me a fidelity to the case that happens, as it again subjects me, as a case, to the fantasm that holds. This is presence touched by singularization, whereby the temporal differend binds us.

It is nothing new to say that in Augustine the will enters on the scene broken. Again it is necessary to have grasped in the natural contre-temps the condition of any such breakage. Modeled on other extremely rare instituting figures to which thought *comes*—Parmenides before him and Luther after him—Augustine pursued with equal vehemence both the flash of the suddenly occurring singular and arrested presence. The sudden occurrence bursts in advance such arrests: a flash and bursting through which hegemonic nature finds itself, from its first emergence, placed back at the level of the event.

In his vehemence, the Yes to nature is thus split in two. Yes to regulation—to the continuing order of eternal reasons in us—and Yes again to the irruption and the contre-temps. Thetic love regulates and regularizes; tender love singularizes. Their normative disparity is precisely where we see the Augustinian figure of the legislative tragedy. Kant, while apparently banishing the heteronomous and the singular, will change few of the terms of this conflict. Regulation will then become the responsibility of the spontaneity that organizes through ideas and categories; the irruption becomes the responsibility of the giving of the *thises* that suddenly occur in time. Hence in Kant we will see again an incongruity in being.

Augustine is not only aware that the will is multiple, but he even makes this multiplicity the very issue of his confession. But it will be useful to keep in mind the manner in which the will posits and deposits nature: appropriating the order of reasons constantly present, all the while letting itself be expropriated by singular interventions. Such is the originary temporal condition that turns the will against itself.

It will also be useful to bear in mind that the hierarchizing disjunctions in Augustine—heaven-earth, large-small, true-false, high-low, happy-miserable, inside-outside, enjoying-using, centered-dispersed, saved-lost . . . —are only his penultimate word on the question of conditions. His final word adds to the exalted terms (heaven, truth, high, happy . . .) disparate and nevertheless co-originary terms: tender love, monstration, irruption, intervention, singularization . . . So many names in which the middle voice speaks. They emphasize not some symmetrical other of nature (not some offshoot of *techné* pairing up with nature, an offshoot of *phusis*), but the odd other *in* nature-as-law. They introduce a subtraction into the very origin which therefore is not pure. Moreover, the subtraction does not in the least work on the nomothesis at its margin, not in the least in substituting a withdrawal for it. Rather it fissures the great telic continuity and warps the homologating, normative gesture. This is how

Augustine remains faithful to these ultimates which are natality carrying us toward the law and mortality leading us back, not to the determinate other *under* the law (to the worldly, the small, the false, the low, the unhappy . . .), but to the contre-temps *within* it, irrecuperable for every univocal law. The pure origin whence the law would come to us does not exist in the institution of the Latin referent.

II

Its Destitution

The Double Bind of Principle and Origin (Meister Eckhart)

Introduction

At the end of the Middle Ages the *natura* which for a millennium had been called upon to legitimize all laws of knowing and acting disintegrates. From under its simple bond that was posited as an ultimate authority, a double bind reveals itself which from then on is undeniable. In order to see how this happens, it is necessary to interrogate the spokesmen for the fourteenth and fifteenth centuries who, with a clear awareness of what they were doing, knew how to give clear expression to the destitution they were suffering. They knew how to *cast aside the denial* on which hegemonies feed. There are three candidates who, above all, could help us understand what incongruous potential Latin theticism set free.

First, there is Meister Eckhart. He takes over the neo-Aristotelian thesis of universal con-naturality, the thesis that there is a network of affinities among beings linking them solely by virtue of their actual being. Compared to certain predecessors, he even strengthens its prescriptive rigor. At the same time, however, he pushes that thesis to extremes where the arrangement of affinities topples into something else, something incompatible with any uniformly normative configuration. Legislative connaturality gets disfigured and slips away. This is obvious in his best known exhortations—"pierce through everything representable," "give birth to the Word of God," "in your ground become one with God's ground." . . . These are so many processes that breach the connaturality in the ultimate authority, but which result from the very argument by which Eckhart, too, maximizes this referent.

In William of Occam, nature, obviously hegemonic, would be the concept of that universal under which come all other universals. Now for Occam, a concept signifies a singular offered to apprehension. Nature collapses into the given *of which* it is the nature. This shuts off the path of normative recourse. It is true that he, too, on the one hand constructs nature and on the other demolishes it resoundingly. In its construction he pursues practical ends; it was a matter of justifying the imperial claims of King Ludwig of Bavaria who had granted him asylum against the papal authorities in Avignon. "Emperor, defend me by thy sword, and I will defend thee with my pen," he is said to have told him. Therefore, from Munich Occam writes those treatises of political philosophy in which, as if nothing were amiss, public order is once again guaranteed by the force of natural law. The name of nature remains intact, obligatory, legislative. On the other hand, of course, his common noun ranged nature among the figments of the mind (*quoddam fictum*), established by convention (*tantum ex institutione*), which we believe has universal significance, but through which we speak always and only of what is given to sensible intuition in immediate apprehension. The category of relation, on which rest all systems of continuous nature, has only subjective being–and this is why Occam merits being called *inceptor venerabilis*. What then do we speak about when we speak of nature? Always and only of the *this* given in experience, which remains the only knowable object. Under Occam's razor, nature no longer extends beyond the monstrable, deictic object, be it through univocity or analogy. Only the singular is. With that the principle of continuity is destituted.

And finally we have Nicholas of Cusa. He is called the last of the Scholastics—he still posits the primacy of an encompassing concatenation where each thing extends its essence into every other thing (*quodlibet in quolibet*) but, as it were, already has left the School by disengaging the I from that entailment. With this, another swerve toward finite spontaneity is made. He starts off on the road that will eventually lead to the transcendental subjectivism of the eighteenth century in that individuality appears as a task (albeit in an altogether different manner than for the Stoics). The I begins to assert its primacy—that is, its spontaneity—through a certain creative power and a certain freedom. To nature's anchorage in God another anchorage is thus opposed, neither a rival nor, strictly speaking, even a comparable one, but a heterogeneous anchorage. Thereby we belong and do not belong to the grand organization of ends which is nature. We belong to it since finite spirit, after the fashion of absolute spirit, contains all forms rolled up in it and can unfold them. In this we imitate God, who deploys nature by "explications" and "complications" of forms: number deploying the one; the complex, the simple; extension, the point; movement, rest; time, the now; diversity, identity; etc. Nature links regions together by gradual involutions. Accordingly, in the spirit that carries the forms, be it divine or human, opposites coincide. Hence the need for a "better I" above the individual I to ward off dispersion and chance, the arbitrary and the meaningless. This ideal power (the individual *posse*, not the absolute *possest*) that singularizes me is normative, a singularity that does not allow itself to be swept away by the great explicative-implicative tides. I assert myself as other than nature, an otherness that is guaranteed ideally. Here as well, then, denial is weakened, and the singular emerges from ostracism.

Still, when all is said and done the choice among these three witnesses is not difficult. Let us not forget that it is a matter of showing how hegemonic nature, *by virtue of the very thetic gesture that posits it,* inflicts the double bind whose evidence, repressed until then, brings the Latin era to a close. To put this briefly, in Nicholas of Cusa the singular acquires a certain normative pertinence solely in the ethical sphere (in an opposition to nature without a genus and without being elevated, an opposition that should have disarmed in advance his later admiring dialecticians.); conversely and to put it just as briefly, in Occam it is the universal that retains its normative pertinence solely in the political sphere (a debt of personal recognition paid in a Latin intellectual's currency, at the same time that he pays the Latins back in the coin of—already—a good English empiricist). If it is a matter of seeing how an ontology relies on nature through and through, and *in doing so* splinters nature through and through, it is Meister Eckhart one has to read.

The more distinguished a hegemonic thesis, the more its logic manifests the tragic. Those who put forth the harshest strategies of order are also the ones who highlight the most evident counter-strategies. Hence the interest a topology of normative double binds has in Parmenides, Plotinus, Cicero, Augustine. Hence also the interest in Eckhart. He too shows in all clarity—a clarity *sui generis,* it is true, which demands patient reading—how at the end of the Latin era the argument that supports referential nature tilts by its own logic into an argument which, at the same time and with the same vehemence, destitutes that referent.

It goes without saying that the reading of Meister Eckhart[1] is meant as a paradigm for understanding the breakdowns through which the Latin era reaches completion. Eckhart is a good spokesman for this catastrophe since he draws extreme consequences from the traditions that confront each other at this beginning of the very learned fourteenth century. He takes hold of the "surest" themes in the premodern theory of natural law and turns them against that theory. Whatever his intentions,[2] such treatment had the effect of dissolving the hegemonic bases of the Latin epoch.

Nature lays down the law by ranking the ends that preside over our cognitive and moral activities. But Eckhart does not just order that telic edifice differently. He also ruins it. In an explicit critique of theticism, he observes that a normative argument posits the standard of organization. The demonstration of nature-as-law thus serves to turn the principle of continuity back against itself. This turning back and turning against is essentially phenomenological, inasmuch as in order to see a thing for what it is, it is necessary to cease overpowering it with positions, impositions, propositions, theses. Only one kind of knowing counts, and it is practical—it is not knowing how to posit, but knowing how to let be. But this is what wrests phenomena from their concatenations according to ends. In order to let singulars be, the universal that frames them with ends has to be let go. To remain faithful to phenomena, one has to live "without why."

Eckhart calls into question the denial with which the theoreticians of natural ends have struck down phenomena—as well as thoughts—irreducible to order. In his critique of theticism, as we will see, he rehabilitates an ultimate temporality and an ultimate singularity. He strikes back at the very spot where the natural ordering lays down the law, that is, at the representation of ends. In this representation Eckhart preserves something of Neoplatonism, namely, that each being finds its immediate natural end in the superior rank that it desires, contemplates, and poorly imitates.[3]

So Eckhart takes a twofold step back in relation to the natural teleology thus erected. First he points to its systemic condition—God as the "foundation" (*begin,* DW II,502; S II,148) that posits it. Then he shows its extra-systemic condition: "nothingness," "desert," "ground" (*grunt*), "godhead," "origin" (*ursprunc, ursprinc*), that lets nature be. In what follows, I am interested only in this twofold quest for conditions; only in the God-foundation and in the ground of God. This does not amount to digging up the *a priori* for some still more *a priori* anteriority. This would be an absurd task. But the *a priori* here is not simple.

Once he has set up the system of natural subordinations, and with a rigor that barely leaves a space to breathe, Eckhart proceeds to call into question the tragic denial upon which all such systems feed, and he does so with a rigor that provokes sighs in him. Accordingly, in the two steps back from nature toward the foundation and toward its ground, the word "condition" is not to be taken in the same sense—the arrangement anchored by the God-foundation and finalized by the principle of continuity comes unanchored and definalized in the originary ground. The foundation and the ground are disparate conditions, as disparate as earth and sky ("God and godhead are as disparate as heaven and earth," Pf 180[4]). My only aim will be to trace the dislocating work of the two conditions that ensue, namely, the principial condition over which the foundation presides and the ground as the originary condition.

By "godhead" Eckhart understands God's being.[5] He interprets this being in accordance with Aristotelian *energeia* (*actus* or *actualitas;* in Middle High German *gewürke*). One can in general say that in his legislative strategy he follows certain schemata borrowed from Christian Neoplatonism, while in his counter-strategies he follows—taking liberties—rather those of neo-Aristotelianism.[6] The liberties notably concern the Aristotelian difference between being and beings.[7] The whole interest in reading Eckhart stems from his urging audiences to "pierce through" the being which is God and to penetrate into being which is the godhead. This is no longer a differential thought, but one that is doubly normative. God is supremely normative; the godhead is normative as well, although otherwise. Such disparate normativity reveals the intermittence by which the Latin era lived. It is without doxographic antecedent.

For Eckhart the continuous network of ends depends on one primary being that *disposes it* (principial condition). But in its turn, this first in the order of nature is "uttered" or "stated"—it is the "fruit of nothingness," it "becomes," "pours itself out," "issues from," "is born from" another source and in a provenance that is other whereby the principial regime *deposits itself* (originary condition). Hence the incongruity of principle and origin. In differing they put man, here again, in the tragic double bind.

It is thus necessary to start by analyzing the *principial* relations by which Eckhart constructs the system of legislative nature (chapter 12). Taken by themselves, these relations tighten fabulously the iron collar of order. Eckhart seems to hear in them only denial, and he adds to it by subjections. After having spelled out one such legislative and ordering strategy, I will indicate briefly how it slides immediately into an originary and thus transgressive strategy. In making his theses on order slide that way, Eckhart calls denial into question.

It will then be necessary to try to grasp how that source of another obligation, which is singular and singularizing, binds us—but is a freeing—and which Eckhart calls the *origin* (chapter 13). Only then will Meister Eckhart have made himself heard. What determines us in the final instance is the origin in dissension with the principle. The ultimates of ordinary experience give rise to a new configuration. This new configuration will appear in tracing a metabolic effect; nature destitutes itself as a simple referent when the fantasmic maximization topples over into temporal singularization.

CHAPTER 11

Nature, Principle of Subordinations

Certain texts in the history of philosophy gather together and articulate the great strategies of life and thought that made up an epoch. There are others which, in addition, reshape received configurations and thereby disrupt the epoch. These are texts of transition. Among the latter one may count Plotinus's *Enneades,* Heidegger's writings, and certainly the German sermons of Meister Eckhart. Indeed, it is the case with what is called speculative mysticism that, while medieval knowledge acquires a breadth difficult to master and while the game of conceptual overdeterminations turns into filigree, an epoch comes to its end. At the same time, and in more ways than one, these sermons are literally exorbitant texts. Still situated in the doctrinal orbit of Scholasticism, they nevertheless contradict its enunciative regularities and do so by more than one strategy. One must remember in Eckhart not only the arguments that repeat and reshape the common noun that lays down the law ("nature"), but also the arguments that shake this noun's position by a gesture piercing through to the very end of conditions, a gesture itself denied under the hegemony of the noun. It will be a matter of tracing how, to the noun that lays down the law, Eckhart adjoins this other figure: a singularizing figure with neither name nor genus which speaks through verbs and undoes the law. To the question: What is it that in Eckhart's thinking lays down the law? The answer thus will be: The telic principle, incongruously turned against itself by the origin.

For this question to remain germane, one must avoid giving it a sense that is either too broad or too narrow.

Too broad (that is, confusing a text from the metaphysical tradition with metaphysics itself) would be the question: Whence this reflex of always thinking in reference to some sovereign position? This question would not only be too broad. With it one would miss in Eckhart both the nominative mark and the infinitive counter-marking, both the force of orbit and that of disorbiting; in other words, both the legislating diction and its transgressive contradiction. For a reader at the end of the twentieth century, to read Eckhart is to witness the fading away of principles by which an age has lived. The strategies that constitute the law and the counter-strategies that destitute it are asserted in him without any authority in whose name the singular, as well as time, would be brought back into order. The conflict that Eckhart reveals in theticism derails the principial economy. The speculative trajectories that Latin philosophy had followed since late antiquity no longer work toward imparting, *nemein,* a dwelling, *oikos*. They no longer work to arrange life according to one "economy." In Eckhart, law and counter-law do not form a system. They are not reconciled in some superior point of view that would preserve both of them, even if cancelled in their particularity and hence inflated. With Eckhart we are—just as formerly the *kouros* in Parmenides was—placed at once under the law and, by this very fact, outside the law. In Eckhart's own life there were moments when he found himself rather under the configuring law and outside the singularizing counter-law. At other times, he placed himself clearly under the singularizing law and outside the configuring law (one may think of the *Entweltlichung,* decontextualization, inflicted on him by the various trials, notably those before the Inquisition). But whatever the import of these empirical incidences, the conflict of the law and its other in Eckhart is not some simple dispute. Here again it is a differend. As such it remains *a priori,* if this term is appropriate; it is not primarily empirical, biographical. Latitudinal considerations about the reflex most widely shared among metaphysicians, the reflex of always seeking what is first in the order of foundations, are bound to miss this conflict.

Too narrow, on the other hand—because fallaciously non-violent—would be a question interrogating the index of words: What did Meister Eckhart have to say about the law, its essence, its regime and eventually its effects? Remembering the two senses of the Greek word for "origin"—to "commence" and to "command"—one might survey the passages in which Eckhart speaks of the various legislating agents, from the Creator down to the princes, passing Moses and Jesus along the way. One might thus learn how—with which being—natural, divine, and positive law begin. One might then look for what he has to say about obligation, and one might learn (perhaps[8]) in what manner the law commands. But what one thinks of the law is one thing and the law according to which one thinks is another. In the present chapter I will try to verify the "rush" (rushes that do not meet, advances that do not fit or befit, moves that do not converge, are "incongruous") with which Eckhart refers, without derogating, to nature as to a sovereign representation. I wish to verify how "nature" functions in his texts as a hegemonic thesis, how in giving the measure to this thought nature lays down its law.

As a transitional thinker, Eckhart is at home as much in the era that draws to a close as in the one that he senses opening up and to which he responds by saying "I" in another fashion.[9] Now, even when he speaks and writes in his mother tongue, German, Eckhart remains to a large extent a Latin, and entirely a medieval. To philosophize thus is to apportion places and perform insertions. What is medieval is his search for a continuous ordering that assigns us our place and inserts us. Eckhart can in no way dispense with the referent that is nature. This referent guarantees there is truth in knowing, rightness in acting, and immutability in being. But of this search he expresses, moreover, the tragic condition—which does not make him a proto-modern, but a medieval who *cancels the erratic denial.* Remaining faithful to the impulse of natality, he "posits" the encompassing; but remaining faithful as well to the withdrawal of mortality, he "lets" singulars be. Between these disparate ultimates the question must once again be inscribed: In Eckhart's thinking, what lays down the law?

Are we setting out onto a vicious circle by tracing the law's nominative-infinitive figures of the law, only to discover that the noun always configures it and the verb disfigures it? Is this not selling the shop before having set it up? Answer: Eckhart always speaks from a certain experience—whereby he resembles at least Plotinus, even if their experience itself cannot have been the same (since in Eckhart it remains still more enigmatic than in Plotinus, I will not dwell on this point; there are specialists for this). Tragic knowledge arises here again from an "I have been seized," whereby Eckhart belongs to the lineage of those whose eyes have been opened by a reversal in history; those to whom knowledge *came* because something *occurred* to them. The abduction suffered by—or in—Parmenides, the simplification experienced by Plotinus, the political defeat endured by Cicero, the "take and read" heard by Augustine, the words that made Luther feel reborn, the fault from which Heidegger awakened: These are just so many experiences, ungraspable in themselves, by which these Great Beginners (René Char's phrase[10]) and their twins, the witnesses of closures, found themselves in the state of tragic knowing. In German, *finding oneself knowing* what previously was denied is *innewerden* (above all not 'to interiorize'; rather in a sense it is the opposite: to enter into). It is already a great deal if, as readers, we succeed in desimplifying this knowledge. Readings do not suffice for one to enter into a knowing. A certain *pathein*[11] is needed. But readings may indicate its conditions.

Noun and verb, then, spell out a difference. Nature as the configuration of beings differs from nature as the process of dissolving any given configuration and order. In Eckhart this difference turns into the *"natural" differend,* a differend that is impossible to resolve. For him, nature as process remains the other which resists being integrated into nature as ordering. A break without appeal separates the position of the noun laying down the law, from what he describes by verbs such as, above all, "being born" in the ground of the soul, as well as "giving birth" to the Word, "letting" what is one's own, "detaching oneself" from self and images, "liberating oneself" from the world, and most of all "piercing through" beyond every system of beings. These counter-strategies undo the subsumptive edifice with the very gesture that erects it. They lead *natura* back to the event of a certain birth in man, designated by verbs such as *nasci* (which may serve as one indication among many others that he often thinks in Latin even as he speaks in German).

From the moment of its institution until its destitution, *natura* certainly did not remain the same. To better grasp the first term—the nominative—of the nominative-infinitive differend, it is thus necessary to begin by asking: How is nature recast here as laying down the law? Only then will I return to the counter-strategies and to the double bind that results from it, so as to show how there would no longer be a legislative, nominative, thetic strategy without the transgressive work of the counter-strategies.

The rotation of elements

Eckhart conceives of the continuous order linking ends together in many ways. I will follow here the conception that reveals best the manner in which nature lays down the law, namely, nature as the subject of the "great work" in alchemy. Continuity will be the principle of this work.

There are several advantages to this approach.

First, it shows, at the very heart of the Latin era, how far away one is from the fantasm of nature as derived from the political realm, that is, how far one is from Rome. Nature has been recast. It still displays a continuous fabric, organized by ends that are *posited as given*. But the great concatenation now deploys nature from a point of departure quite different than the public and the republican. Its deployment sets out from an experience best exemplified in metallurgic and psychic transmutations.[12] Therefore what we have is a new arrangement under the same epochal hegemony. This hegemony still consists of the telic continuity that binds man to phenomenal regions. But now nature imposes itself through a different teleology, as well as by a different continuity—a teleology and continuity whose very positional logic will lead it to topple over into the incongruous "without why" and singularization.[13]

Indeed, to point this out right away, just as the alchemist returns a metal to a formless liquid state in which all metals are indistinct so as then to confer on it the noblest of singular forms, that of gold,[14] so the non-attachment that Meister Ekhart teaches leads the soul back to a formless state (in which it becomes "without property," "as it was when it was not," DW I,25; S I, 52 {W I,71}), a state in which all beings are equal ("in God, no creature is nobler than another," DW I,55; S I,60 {W I,199}), so as then to confer on the soul the noblest of forms, that of the Word ("from the very ground where the Father begets his eternal Word, thence [the soul] becomes fruitful and begets with him," DW I,31; S, I,53 {W I,73}). The hierarchy of beings is posited for the sake of a liquefaction in which the high and the low melt and fuse. The resulting moment of identity ("the soul's ground and God's ground are one essential being," Pf 467) is metabolical for the law, since from this dissolution singulars issue ("'Brother Eckhart, when did you leave the house?'," Pf 181; {W II,81}) freed from the teleological framework, temporalized. So this is that toward which we will be headed. The alchemist's motto for this work of indetermination, then of singularization, is *solve et coagula*. For now, however, what counts in Eckhart is the thetic scaffolding, to be liquefied below . . .

The "great alchemical work" furthermore demonstrates how far *natura,* which is that work's principle, remains removed from any notion of nature familiar to us today.[15] To look at nature as it commands the alchemic rotation of elements is to examine it as though through the lens of an inverted telescope. It recedes. There is another advantage here. The strangeness indicates the extent to which the normative referent under which we late moderns are situated remains incommensurable with the one that preceded it until the fourteenth and fifteenth centuries. By leafing through alchemic recipe books it becomes obvious that one is wasting one's time in still wanting to invoke "the natural law" as being one and evident, from Parmenides down to

Pufendorf (or to the Fundamental Law of the German Federal Republic as intended by its authors in 1949).

In addition and above all, the nature to which the alchemist submits himself requires of him certain practices in order to be understood.[16] A practical *a priori*, it will be recalled, was required to think the *hen* (in Parmenides, to turn away with "courage" from mortal dwellings; in Plotinus, to "let" the manifold "be"). In still a different way, such an *a priori* will appear in Heidegger, at the moment of diremption. Now, there are hardly any systems of ultimate reference which connect the individual to the encompassing teleology by a work on oneself that is as practically demanding as the one required in alchemy. The masters want to spiritualize their bodies. If they liquefy metals and make them pass one into the other, in truth they work on themselves in order that their own body become light, fluid, extendible, and that their spirit in turn take on bodily qualities such as resistance to fire and immobility. Universalization followed by singularization, they say, realizes our originary nature. Such is the goal of the great work. Eckhart does not express himself otherwise when he indicates the goal of non-attachment.

Lastly, the institution of a hegemonic referent appeared to us as a fantasmic maximization, through selective fidelity to a single phenomenon or a single phenomenal region. Natality—the thetic instinct of "always more"—attaches itself absolutely to one representation, relativizing all others, and conferring upon it a hyperbolic prestige. Natality cannot but deny the plurality of singulars, which the trait of mortality is there to keep alive. Now, which is the principial representation that Meister Eckhart simultaneously posits as most certain, closest, most encompassing, strongest—the one through which he then urges his audiences to "break"? To answer simply "natural order" would be too vague. Accordingly, it is no exaggeration to claim that the natural order as presupposed by alchemy well describes the region of experience from which Eckhart sets off in his normative thesis. I am saying, and only saying, that alchemical "nature" is *useful to describe* what goes without saying[17] at Eckhart's point of departure.

This thesis of nature he then denatures out of faithfulness to singulars and to time. Here, alchemical "denaturation" will therefore prove useful as well to describe the what-does-not-go-without-saying by which Eckhart will call into question the denial that sustains all hegemony.

> "It is thus clear what the philosophers mean when they describe the production of our stone as the alteration of natures and the rotation of elements. You now see that by 'incorporation' the wet becomes dry, the volatile stable, the spiritual embodied, the fluid solid, water fiery, and the air like earth. Thus all four elements renounce their own natures and, by rotation, transform themselves into another. . . . Just as in the beginning there was one, so also in this work everything comes from one and returns to one. This is what is meant by the retransformation of the elements."[18]

Retransforming the elements, such is the project of the "chemical philosophers." For some among them, this is to be achieved with the help of what they call the philosopher's stone: not a stone at all, but rather a technical and spiritual knowledge.[19]

For all of them, rotation leads somewhere—not to the gold they produced and which was yellow copper (brass), but to what gold signified for them: the better metal, the better state of the soul. They seek to induce the elements to renounce their own natures. In other words, they bring them into a process for which the elements are not made. Water becomes fiery, fire liquid, earth loses its weight, air becomes solid. The elements undergo retransformations that are not physical, but rather contrary to *phusis*. Likewise for the metals (the traditional criticism lodged against the practitioners of the great work was that nature "forbids this gold"). This anti-physicalism makes it all a question, literally, of a *great* work. For all of them, know-how implies a return to a unity which, by right, precedes the diversity of elements—to an *unum* in the sense, not of trans-noetic union, but of material indistinction. The elements come from the one and return to the one, not by a hypostatic *exitus-redditus,* but by liquefaction or sublimation. To allow for these operations upon nature, the thesis on continuity had to be rearranged. The hegemonic principle now needs to be posited in such a way that it allows nature to overcome nature. Accordingly it is necessary to understand the hermetic maxim (which can seem a catch-all phrase)—"whatever is below is like what is above, and whatever is above is like that which is below"—as an operational framework.[20]

These general characteristics should suffice to demarcate the chemical philosophers' work, in spite of obvious affinities, from any proto-scientific, neo-Aristotelian as well as Neoplatonic project.

According to one received etymology, "alchemy" would derive from the "black earth" of Egypt, or more precisely, from the alluvial silt of the Nile. The word itself would thus point to the undifferentiated: to the "one" in the text quoted, which is also called *nigredo.*[21] The rotation supposes that earth, water, air, and fire can pass into one another by *going through* this indistinction, the work's first stage. Likewise for the seven metals: lead, zinc, iron, mercury, copper, silver, and gold. They are not treated as simple bodies. In a work such as leading the metals, notably the most ignoble which is lead, back to uniformity so as then to be formed into the most noble which is gold, the elements can obviously no longer be conceived as unalterable substances. Hence the two moments that interest us: *first* reducing the elements to indistinction, *then* producing from this the best of them all. I linger on alchemy only for this sequence expressed in the maxim *solve et coagula.*

It is an operational sequence, which leads from reduction to what is called clarification. Gold is clear, solar, leonine. The masters see this sequence inscribed in man's way of being as well as in the rest of nature. Gold, Eckhart states without hesitation, *is* the natural end of all metals; similarly, the glitter of gold—marked by the aureole—*is* the state at which all activities of the soul aim. Just as is lead, the soul is a substance to be reduced and purified. These terms are here to be taken in an almost materialistic sense. Minerals are considered spiritually and the soul is considered materially, which is to say that the distinction between matter and spirit is erased. Indeed, in alchemy God is never the issue. As we have seen, both Albert the Great and Thomas Aquinas associate alchemy with physics—the one as its twin science, the other as the art of its application. Theology never mentions it. Alchemy acts upon the principle of continuity in the mineral and the psychic domains. In both, it teaches the *solve et coagula.* It rearranges that principle in such a way that, in minerals just as in the soul, nature displays the normative order between elementary indeterminacy and the greatest of singular elements.

About the first moment, indeterminacy, one is bound to miss it altogether, just as one is bound to miss the alchemic work itself if it is seen as *only* metallurgic liquefaction or *only* psychic purification. To work on minerals is to work on oneself. And to return to one's own ground, one has to return minerals to their ground. There is no gold-making without calcination of metals and volatilization of cinders. Likewise, there is no coagulation of the soul without the "dis-agulation" of psychic states and the sublimation of its properties. Moreover, in line with their (non-Aristotelian) conception of prime matter, alchemists do not hesitate to declare that the indeterminate they produce by successive roastings in the cucurbit and by adding mercury *is* the soul in its indeterminate state. It is the soul led back from its thought activities, its sense impressions, its biological functions and movements, to a state of total receptivity. Eckhart no doubt does not have prime matter in mind when he, too, outlines a similar reversion and declares that in the work (*werk*) of non-attachment "the soul must become as virgin as it was when it was not." Still, the masters of the great work speak a very similar language. Metals, like the soul, carry in themselves the power of returning to pure receptivity, to virginity. "In this work, everything comes from one and returns to one." Everything—materials as well as souls—is to be *led back* to the indistinct prior to order, as everything issues from prime matter prior to order. Metals as well as the soul are allowed to reform themselves, ennobled, beginning from the indistinct.

In its second moment, singularization, the work produces a *this.* Duped princes take gold-making literally, and they expect to fill their coffers. The masters who know, on the other hand, understand it figuratively and persevere in inner purification. But whether fraudulent or spiritual, the work always comes to an end *out of the ordinary.* Reduced to its "pure nature," the soul receives the better of singular forms—the Word—outside of all ordinary nature.

Such is the principle of continuity, industriously recast. The alchemist uses his industry to produce the best of singulars, and in this his work becomes therapeutic. To reduce metals or the soul to the indeterminate and then to educe a singular is to bring them back to their most common ground and then to ennoble them (in Eckhart, *edelkeit,* 'nobility,' designates not only the degree of being, but altered being: we are to transmute ourselves into the nobleman, cf. DW V,109ff.; T,139ff. {W III,105ff.}). Rotation heals the elements in conferring upon them the nobility inscribed in—preinscribed, prescribed by—the species, healing lead by converting it into drops of gold; healing tuff by converting it into a precious stone (see below); healing oats by converting them into bushels of wheat; and finally, healing the soul by converting it materially into a singular, that is, by begetting in it the Word. Eckhart accordingly speaks of the "bitterness" of all minerals other than gold and of all grain other than wheat. Hence, metals and grasses need to be "sweetened." When he speaks of sweetness, nothing mawkish is intended, but rather alchemic processes. Similarly, the soul must heal itself from its specific bitterness. This therapy Eckhart calls *abegescheidenheit.* When the Word is born in non-attachment, it expels psychic bitterness, just as gold expels the bitterness—the privation—defining lead. Singularization through indetermination is demanded by nature inasmuch as all species seek to return to their indistinct "pure nature" (*weselôs, formelôs,* without particular being or form), so as then to receive singular excellence. The great work presupposes a natural teleology that constructs the elements. But the work breaks its point of integration since it terminates in drippings, in a *this*.

This is what happens to the methods the reductive-decanting metallurgist uses. He cooks, roasts, calcinates. . . , but above all he distills. In the still, reduction happens in the cucurbit and clarification at the lip of the serpentine called the canthus (hence to "decant"). In the retort, elements are reduced at the vessel's bottom while they are clarified at the tip of a long and narrow curved beak. All these devices drip singulars from their spouts.

The rotation of forces

Reduction to formlessness, production of a singular form: such are the two stages of the alchemic work.

Such also are the two stages of non-attachment as taught by Meister Eckhart.

We will see how it ricochets on the fantasm of nature. Beforehand it should be noted, however, that in these two steps know-how escapes from the conditions of definitional knowledge.

Indeed, on the Aristotelian epistemic scale, the unknowable blocks knowing at two extremes. Arguments cannot but founder both upon a hypothetical genus of all genera—upon the undetermined space that envelops the genera—as well as upon singulars. The former escapes science since it does not involve distinctions and the latter escapes since singulars do not involve compositions.[22] Aristotelian science advances between the ineffable of greatest extensivity and the ineffable of deepest intensivity; between the pure, trans-conceptual extendedness in which all concepts are inscribed and the infra-conceptual singular that all concepts circumscribe. At both ends, obscurity remains systematically impossible to cast off. The natural order begins signifying with the universal, and it signifies the particular. Beyond as well as on this side of their separation, meaning will be either too diluted or too condensed. Reasoning is possible only between the two fringes of night, between the indistinct that is beyond genera and the too distinct on this side of the particular. In that in-between, our arguments divide and compose ideas. Their back and forth guides life from generic to specific clarities. The evidence of the universal thus spreads open a zone of free exchange between one sense that is too extended to be grasped and another that is too contracted.

In this intermediary, the impulse of natality posits master ideas such as nature, understood as the order of syllogistic objects that is knowable via thetic abstraction. As for the trait of mortality, it takes us back to the unknown outside nature, far from the particular and the subsumptions producing it, far from order and its daylight, toward an extensivity and an intensivity for which we lack words because determinacy is lacking.

Argue away the dark of night that surrounds the master positions: such is the denial from which all metaphysics of order have derived their persuasive force. The denial provides a reason, albeit atrophied, for betting blindly on order and exclusively on the natality that posits order. The trait of mortality, however, makes us know (makes us familiar with, not cognize) the indeterminate—both trans-epistemic and infra-epistemic.

Accordingly, this dual labor of the indeterminate is what destitutes the hegemony of Latin "nature." The fracture between the *naturally particular* and the *singular outside of nature* is the same fracture that separates both the indistinct and the too distinct from the determinate. That fourteenth-century monk speaking from his pulpit is particular inasmuch as all sorts of specific and generic subsumptions posit him to be knowable as a substance; he is singular in that he is given in a manifestation that is narratable as an event. And what he preaches is to come back from particularization; to return to the trans-epistemic indeterminate, so as then to singularize us in the infra-epistemic indeterminate, in a *this*.

Meister Eckhart not only recovers from tragic denial but he also recognizes the nameless singular *in* the equally nameless space of all signification.

It is as if he said: You *will know the singular,* pure intensivity, if here and now the Word is born in you; likewise you *will know the pure space prior to significations,* pure extensivity, in piercing through the representable God toward his being which is the godhead. In the order of genesis, Eckhart follows the two stages of *solve et coagula*. But in the order of being, my singularization is "God's pure being" itself. To understand Meister Eckhart is to understand that these are not two ineffables.

For the alchemist, the singular drip-by-drip of the philosopher's stone is ineffable *as is* the formless distillate in which forms are liquefied. For Eckhart, such an *analogical "as"* does not suffice. He asserts that the soul's ground is the very ground of God. Therefore it is necessary to try to think the indeterminate in which here and now I become departicularized, identical (it will be necessary to see what sort of identity) to the indeterminate in which God suffers depersonalization.

In the great work of non-attachment, I as singular lose all particular predicates, and this by the same process by which God loses all his divine names. If the opaqueness at the two extremes of the epistemic scale amounts to one and the same indeterminacy, it can no longer be maintained that the "birth of the Word in the soul" and the "breakthrough beyond God" constitute in Eckhart two incompatible teachings. They follow the genetic sequence of *solve et coagula*. But in passing from the genetic question to that of being, Eckhart passes from the philosopher's stone to the philosophical. Accordingly, if there is any necessity to think indeterminacy as one, then the nature-as-law that allots ends will in turn have a non-place outside ends as its condition of possibility. And if non-attachment means living in accordance with this "non" and this "outside," then the continuity principle will no longer be able to exercise the simple bind to which it owes its hegemony.

All this is indeed what Meister Eckhart teaches, including this consequence aimed directly at "nature": "Strictly speaking, only that is alive which is without a principle" (*hoc enim proprie vivit quod est sine principio,* LW III,16).

Thus we see, by way of an overview, how according to Eckhart the indeterminate intrudes into the very core of Latin natural law and dislocates its determinations.

This hard core is the fantasm of a soul with its powers in order. Eckhart describes it as "right nature" (DW II,244; S II,53 {W I,221}) in the sense of the "right ordering" of forces (DW II,191; S II,35 {W I,275}). One feels as if one were reading a middle Stoic, or Cicero, warning his readers against the illusion of ever reaching complete impassivity of the senses and of reaching a state in which one is no longer susceptible to suffering: "Now our good people imagine they can reach a point where sensible things no longer mean anything to the senses. But they never get there" (DW III,491; S III,179 {W I,88}). Our good people are the nuns given to discipline and to whom he is preaching. The quite Roman pleasure of fighting pleasure,[23] too, is echoed in Eckhart: "This much however must be attained: that the will, well ordered and God-conformed, neglect all natural pleasures. . . . Lo, then the strife would change into pleasure" (DW III,491s.; S III,179 {W I,88}). From the subordination that ranks the soul's faculties, he even infers *apatheia*—impassiveness, if not of man in his entirety, at least in spirit: "Suffering of the senses and of the lower powers are no concern [to the spirit]" (DW V,271; T 75 {W III,43}). Lastly, what he calls "right intention" (*rehte meinunge,* perhaps a loose translation for *recta ratio*), repeats the ancient three-phase schema according to which the created issues from God, remains governed by him, and returns to him. "The beginning of that intention is God, and the execution of that intention is God, and . . . it terminates in divine nature" (DW I,164; S I,109 {W II,141}). In the idiom of the Roman doctrine of natural law, the dominion of reason over the senses is grounded in God's dominion as the beginning and end of any well-ordered soul.

Eckhart, however, makes these thought models his own, but not without deflecting them. Impassiveness turns into non-attachment, his one topic and one passion. Natural order itself demands *abegescheidenheit.* In his impetuous rigor, he does not content himself with stating what would not be unprecedented: Detach yourself from your salient features. He goes further and says what is unprecedented outside, precisely, of alchemy: Detach yourself from both the specific as well as the generic salient properties. What does it mean to "let" particular properties "go"? And what does it mean to "let" specific and generic properties "go"?

In a sense, the doctrine of non-attachment rests on an axiom as ancient as Platonism: The more universal a concept, the better its referent. From this it follows that *lex natura* itself prescribes that we become as detached from all images and from all particular forms as we are in our specific nature. "I hold humanity in itself more dear than the man I carry about in me" (DW II,18; S I,215 {W I,95}). The imperative of turning away from the particular and turning toward the universal strikes at our practical concerns. What must be unlearned are not forms and images themselves, but the modes of behavior attached to forms and images. Eckhart urges us to let go of the *Eigenschaft,* to consider no attribute our own. This means to possess qualities such as learning and know-how without making them belong to us the way attributes belong to a substance. There is, then, something like a natural imperative that bids us to become our nature as it has been posited by its species under its genus. A detached man will be "void of all alien images, as virgin as when he was not [yet]" (DW I,25; S I,152 {W I,71}).

The same axiom, applied not without temerity, again makes Eckhart push beyond all species and genera. His temerity here is altogether alchemic: "As I have often said, the soul cannot become pure unless it be reduced to its initial emptiness, as God created it—just as gold cannot be made from copper by two or three roastings unless the copper be reduced to its primary nature." Such is his urging to become detached even from specific and generic qualities. Accordingly, Eckhart goes on to the alchemical rotation of elements. To draw gold from the alembic, metals "must be wholly reduced to [the state of] water and be completely rid of the nature in which they are found" (DW II,599; S II,179f {W I,202}). The species is to be reduced to its proximate genus and the genus, to the nameless expanse in which any conceptual extensivity is inscribed. This metal here—copper—must lose its specific nature and return to generic nature, "metal." The piece of copper will then have become again what it was when it was not yet. But this nature, in its turn, is to be dissolved into pure liquidity: "water," "prime matter." Liquefaction will then have purified and detached it of all qualities, be they particular or specific and generic.

What is he talking about? The lesson of non-attachment would be roundly missed if one sees in it some psychological recipe of Stoic inspiration. We are far from the Stoa and Rome. After the fashion of the alchemists to whom he refers, Eckhart is speaking of a different system of nature. This system is organized by concepts interwoven according to the extension of the meaning—as universals are in realism. But contrary to that realism, the singular referent is never omitted: lead and charcoal are worked upon, and so is the self. Accordingly, what is essential can be understood only when one applies oneself to reductions. Moreover, the essential is the *indeterminate condition of all naturally determined conditions;* this indeterminate condition becomes thinkable only in the course of a doing. Non-attachment thus relativizes normative nature by also taking for *normative* the indeterminacy of "pure emptiness." The God-foundation determines all things in accordance with their ends; but God's ground renders them indeterminate. This is the reason why he is also non-ground, groundless, abyss (*ungrunt, gruntlos, abegrunt,* e.g., DW II,309 and 493; S II,79 and 146 {W II,238 and 271}).

What does it mean to reduce the soul to its initial emptiness? Further on, Eckhart will exhort his listeners to return to the absolute freedom which is the pure actuality of being. Initial emptiness, groundless ground, absolute freedom, actuality of being, if Eckhart seeks to think some normative indeterminacy under these names—but names they are not—does one not have good reasons to avoid mysticism like a pestilence upon clear and distinct ideas? What does taking "initial emptiness" as one's standard mean if not that it is necessary to dissolve in some vacuum? Or if such are your tastes, does it mean that as necessarily conditioned, you can arrive at some sort of experiences that will astonish your friends? Or even that Eckhart, preaching the origin as an act of being, had what is called an intuition of being?

Red herrings all. The normativity of the initial emptiness, of absolute freedom, of the actuality of being, only make sense when *linked* to the principle *against nature:*

counteracting the impetus of natality and quashing the fantasm that it maximizes. It is a coupling reminiscent of the ones practiced by those terrible Maniote pirates who would lash their prisoners face to face with a corpse and abandon them on an island, thus tied together, to their fate. Theirs is a brutal lesson in the singularization to come; too literal a double bind; still, it deals with tragic knowledge. To think would be to anticipate this kind of lesson.

The double bind of the indeterminate origin and of the determining principle will provide the singular issue of the readings below (chapters 12 and 13).

As co-normative, pure emptiness (*blôze lûterkeit,* DW III,341; {W II,39}) points, we have seen, both beyond genera and on this side of particulars. Now, the reduction to formlessness terminates in the adduction of singulars. The final goal of non-attachment by successive roastings is precisely not the indistinct liquid; it is a distinct singular, namely, the best: the philosopher's stone, gold, myself. Concerning final distillates, Eckhart recalls what I have called the "it goes without saying" of the High Middle Ages: "The nature of all grains aims at wheat, that of all metals aims at gold, and all generation aims at man" (DW II,228; S II,48f {W I,215}). Thus there is a descent from the placeless to the genera, then to species and to *particulars* as allocated to their respective sites. But what above all goes without saying under the regime of medieval "nature" is that, in any process of purification by universalization, the end will be a *singular.* The descent goes through forms that it organizes according to the criterion of privation ("weakness," "bitterness," "imperfection"): "All grain is nothing but weakness and bitterness compared to the perfection and form of wheat. . . , all metal, but weakness and bitterness of gold. This is why the alchemists can boast of transforming any metals into genuine gold by purifying them of their bitterness. Such is also the relation of man, the most perfect among living beings, to the other living beings, such that each animal is an imperfection and a bitterness of man" (LW I,285). Now, what is man's goal in purification through non-attachment? None other than what it is in alchemical purifications, namely, being the best singular—here, the Son of God. "Where the Son is re-imaged, the soul too is to be re-imaged. All creatures are subjugated to the soul that is thus introduced and enclosed and locked up in God" (DW I,399; S I,200 {W II,71}). To determine is to particularize; but through the indeterminate that singularizes him, man is united with the indeterminate in God. As the system of determinations stands subordinated to the best of singulars, indetermination through non-attachment takes one outside that system, outside nature.

So posited and transgressed, one could say natural teleology is recast from the Romans on. The primary end of alchemical distillations is to reduce to indistinction all that can be molten; their final end is a distinct, deictic "this." Likewise for non-attachment. Its primary aim is to pierce through the scaffolding of nature; its final and practical aim is to unite man with the Son, outside-nature, that is the being of God (the godhead).

The primary task of any apprentice distiller, as well as of any soul seeking to put order into its drives, is to reduce metals into a formless liquid; the soul into the ground where all its forces are indistinct and "equally noble" (DW I,173; S I,112 {W II,146}). This comes to pass with the breakthrough into the godhead. In piercing through beyond specific and generic forms, the soul is denatured. Its concrete aim remains, however, singularization. This comes to pass with the birth of the Word in the denatured soul. Thus the trans-conceptual unknowable and the infra-conceptual unknowable are linked together—the pure extendedness that lodges all subsumptive genera, and the singular that dislodges the subsumable particular. By "being," Eckhart understands the identity of these two non-determinates. This identity through depredication is difficult to think. It will be thinkable only by the depredation it brings upon graduated nature.

We see how the classic imperative of ordering the soul's powers gets displaced. The organization becomes rotation. "With all its might the soul must break into the divine order" (DW II,121; S II,9 {W II,33}). The alchemist reduces metals by liquefaction so as to produce one piece of the most excellent metal; likewise the soul's forces must return to indistinction in God's ground so it may become excellent in being singularized. Such identification, such "theosis," would have been anathema for the Platonic tradition.

And how is this divine order itself to be understood? Alchemically, here again. In God as well, rotation makes the determined pass into the indeterminate, and from indistinction it brings back the distinct. This is a trinitary alchemy, which Eckhart describes in geometric terms as the loss of one's proper place on the periphery of a circle and as the piercing through toward the non-place of the godhead, the center.

Just like psychic ordering, trinitary ordering is organized into forces: power (Father), wisdom (Son) and love (Spirit). These forces emerge from the godhead and are engendered in accordance with the *filioque* at their proper loci on the periphery. "What is the divine order? From divine power there bursts forth wisdom, and from them both there bursts forth love, [their] conflagration. For wisdom, [which is] the truth, and the power and the love, which is their conflagration, all stand on the periphery of being, which being is supereminent, pure, without nature. It is [God's] nature to be without a nature" (DW II,119s.; S II,9 {W II,32}). By "supereminent being" (*überswebende wesen*), Eckhart translates the Neoplatonic *huper-on,* the divine being that remains unthinkable as it is incomparable to all beings. He also describes it as "non-natured nature," opposed to the "natured nature" of the Trinity (Pf 537). The intra-divine ordering thus consists in that the godhead, *natura non naturata,* emits the threefold *natura naturata*. Pure being puts the natures of Persons in place, just as the center of a circle puts in place the proper loci on its periphery. Natures and places thus become knowable, but not pure being and the center. Here again, there is a configuration (of the three natured natures, power-wisdom-love) only because of a prior indistinction. In effect, pure being has neither nature nor any perfections of its own, and it is the principle of nothing. The echo of the "pure act" in Aquinas is obvious. No less obvious, however, is the distance with regard to Aquinas, who would hardly have thought of wresting (in the strict sense of a non-static *epekeina*) the *actus purus* away from the *summum ens*. Trinitary alchemy does demand just such a wresting away. Divine ordering is brought about by the rotation between the indeterminate of the largest extensivity—pure *esse* without a nature—and the indeterminate of the deepest intensivity, the threefold singular *ens*. "Such is the divine order. Now when

God finds the soul to be on par with this order, there the Father begets his Son" (DW II,120; S II,9 {W II,32}). The rotation of forces terminates in singularization, in us.

Nothing less than God's being is distilled in my singularization. "God must needs seek us, as though his godhead depends on it—as indeed it does!" (DW II,34s.; S I,221 {W I,101}). His godhead depends on it, which is to say that the ineffable extensivity of being is identical to the equally ineffable intensivity of the singular.

Thus we are to identify the rotation of forces in our soul with their rotation in God. Not to be missed is the moment of indistinction, without which there can be no singularization. "Now we speak of the soul's order. A pagan master says that the soul's supereminent natural light is so pure and so clear and so elevated that it touches the angelic nature. At this point it is so faithful [to angelic nature] and so faithless and hostile to the lower powers that it will not flow into these or illumine the soul [in them] unless these lower powers be subordinate to the higher powers and the higher powers to the highest truth" (DW II,121s.; S II,10 W II,33).

The soul's order mirrors God's. To pure being, to the pure nature in God, corresponds in the soul the exalted natural light. However, as happens when Eckhart advances an argument of authority by relying on some source—"A master says"—he ends up being poorly served. The pagan master, in this case Maimonides, understood superior, intuitive reason to be the inner light. The model according to which higher reason unites us with the truth that is God is ancient. Emanation effects the continuous, vertical integration. Now, Eckhart calls the light so communicated by emanation the spark in the soul—something "in" the soul, he will say in his defense, not "of" the soul.[24] To what then does the soul's exalted natural light remain faithful? What is highest in us is "equal to [God] and to his nature, and he has so given it to the soul as its own that it is part of the soul" (DW III,428; S III,147 {W II,114}): In its spark, the soul is faithful to divine, "non-natured" nature. Eckhart is being served poorly by a model of participation in graded perfections, while he seeks to suggest an identity with the godhead beyond all gradation. In his ground, man is united to pure being which is indistinct with regard to proper being and proper natures.

Hence a theory of the two natures that is more alchemical than Nicean. Above all it concerns man. The *epekeina* separates the spark of pure actuality in us from the powers that constitute our "other" nature, other than being. "Where the intellect breaks forth from the soul, it enters as into another nature." It enters into stratified nature, as is determined by the law. The break is analogous to the one in which "God breaks forth into his Son" (DW III,253; S III,85 {W II,329}). Just as the godhead, the spark as center—the trace of indeterminacy in us—breaks forth again upon the periphery where it is surrounded by the faculties of the soul: intuitive power, discursive reason, and love. So it is that the soul stands ordered under the double bind of indeterminate nature *in us* and *our* determinate nature.

What follows from this double bind for natural law? Continuous vertical integration produces but one of the two disparate binds that hold us. The principle of continuity reigns in all its efficacy when the senses submit to the three higher powers, that is, "when the sensible power obeys inferior reason, watches it and aims at it; when [this inferior reason] attaches itself to superior reason and holds on to it; and [superior reason], to God" (LW I,612). The right order results from subordinations. Yet these are then erased by non-principial "pure nature." It follows that, under the indeterminate, I am bound and held otherwise: bound and held *by* the identity between God's ground and the ground of the soul; bound and held *to* break—I, singularly—beyond nature-as-law, beyond its principle.

The urgency one feels in reading Meister Eckhart comes from this double link, a linkage that is disparate and yet ultimate. If there is anarchy, this word would indicate the impossibility of an ultimate, *simply* normative referent.

It remains that in his strategy of natural normativity, Eckhart thinks in an entirely archic fashion. Otherwise, he argues, how is one to ward off evil? Only perfect continuity would prevent evil: "Where order reigns, there can be no evil. Now, here is natural ordering, that the highest [part] of what is below touches the lowest of what is above. But the highest that the soul has is reason in us" (ibid.). From this it follows that the soul is ordered and sheltered from evil when reason fixes itself on the intelligible above it. Obviously the ancient telic strategy remains perfectly intact. It requires that each rank submit to the one that precedes it. Such was the kernel of classical natural law. In Eckhart, however, we will see that this strategy does not remain simple. A different, incongruous strategy, a trait that pulls toward the indeterminate and thus toward death, cuts across this strategy and makes it precarious. To understand how the double bind of principle and origin destitutes nature, it will be necessary to retrace some of the slippages that the determinate-indeterminate normativity—a normativity differing with itself—inflicts upon order (chapter 12).

Here the indeterminate is not the ancient *apeiron* nor the modern *das Unbestimmte*. In the taxonomy of proper allocations, it neither stands opposed to the determinate nor mediates it. It works on the determinate through dislocations. It takes a practical task, an elsewhere, and a condition and joins them to the order.

Here it is a practical task since, according to this double bind, I must indetermine myself. In a static world as is the stratified universe, only the individual soul is capable of movement. Hence, since Plato, the warning not to let oneself be misled about one's happiness by heading in the wrong direction; hence also the injunction to assimilate oneself to God (*theosis*). Now, in Eckhart to singularize oneself by indetermination does not mean to "ascend." It is a matter of piercing through (*durchbrechen*) outside of nature, not to climb from one state to the next up to the Supreme Good, to the heart of nature. Eckhart also speaks of "sallying forth" (*ûzrucken*), a term from chivalry. The soul must sally forth outside the peripheral ranks toward the center where there stands neither any idea nor any other being. "For one point to get nearer [the center], it would have to sally forth outside its place" (DW III,294; S III,103 {W II,280}). There is no coincidence of opposites here, but rather an advance toward originary indeterminacy. Now, as the origin of the circle and of sites, the center itself has no site. It is non-natured nature: "The essential point, which is God, stands there in the center, equally far from and near to all creatures, and the only way for me to get closer to it is for my natural reason to sally forth with a light above it" (DW III,298; W II,281)—a light, as we have seen, that signifies the work of reduction to the non-natured.

Moreover, the indeterminate opposes an elsewhere to order. We have seen that "where there is order, it is impossible that there be evil."[25] The opposition of order and elsewhere thus does not amount to a negation. The indeterminacy of the ground is to be thought of otherwise than in terms of either good or evil. Eckhart twists received figures of opposition so as to think a disparate condition. The indeterminate, the place without a place, the center, extensivity, the godhead, non-attachment, the singular ... *do not mirror in black* the determinate, the place, the periphery, intensivity, God, the proper, the particular. What the terms of the first series designate touch us from elsewhere. To the discursive regularity that sustains order, Eckhart does not oppose a contrary one that would incite to disorder. All the while laying out nature-as-law, he displaces his discourse outside of its problematic and speaks otherwise. Singularization by non-attachment *has nothing to do* with particulars and the proper. It requires that one return to the elsewhere, to the blank prior to every figure.

Whereby, lastly, the indeterminate points to the condition of nature-as-law. "Condition" does not mean here what it means in every metaphysics of order, namely, the archetypal model and its paradigmatic splendor. Eckhart moves up the ladder of models, then pushes it away. Order and its principle can only take shape by appearing out of a non-figure. So, Eckhart does not think this for the sake of figuration, as is evident from his usage of the metaphysics of light. Subordinations bind man, as much from inside as from out; as much in fact as by law. "Whatever is ordered must be subordinated to that which is above it. No creature pleases God unless the natural light of the soul, from which they get their being, illumines them from above" (DW I,313; S I,166 {W I,257}). That creatures receive their being from the soul does not mean here that in the soul they become intelligible through the splendor of their paradigm. The natural light is identically the soul's being and God's being. Eckhart thinks of being in its pure emerging, of natural places in their pure allocating, of light in its pure shining, and of order in its pure manifesting. In the same manner, the condition of *natura* that is other than the principle of continuity is nature's pure *nasci*. These are so many "pure" processes inasmuch as they are not conceived for the sake and in the service of beings, places, intelligibles, order, nature. They can darken. Only then does being serve beings. We can "dim being" (*wesen bevinstern,* DW II,120; S II,9 {W II,32}). This is stated in the possessive genitive; manifestation then means manifestation *of* the natural order. The condition that is other than archetypal or paradigmatic is the event of coming-to-light as such.

In these points—plus a fourth one, which together constitute his "program"—Eckhart outlines as many counter-strategies which, prompting a discordancy without recourse, turn nature-as-law against itself (chapter 13).

In *denying the indeterminate,* one keeps moving from beings to beings and from level to level within continuous nature. Thus its condition remains unthought. Whoever wills the law must blind himself to its origin. Of just such a denial, now, a beautiful example can be found in a certain nervousness in the author who has produced the most rigorous deduction of Latin natural law: Thomas Aquinas. In that nervousness I see a symptom showing how theticism calls for the indeterminate as its condition and at the same time obliterates it.

Thomas Aquinas: nerves on edge

"Every soul must submit to the authorities holding power over it, since there is no power except coming from God."

—Romans 13:1

"To say that the divine will does not proceed according to the order of wisdom is blasphemous."[26]

—Thomas Aquinas

With these two citations we hold both the thesis ("there is no power except coming from God") in the defense of which Aquinas's nerves are put on edge, and the terms of the defense itself—as well as those of his nervousness. The defense posits in God a priority of wisdom over will, a priority which supports the thesis. To will is to be able to act, on the condition that a determination is given. The will is the telic power *par excellence.* But it does not itself select its ends, which is why it needs to be guided by reason. It is therefore a telic, yet undetermined, power. In itself the will remains unfocused. That is why an ordering power must precede it so as to articulate and orient it. The conclusion of the two premises can then be formulated like this: "Therefore power proceeds from God's wisdom." Conversely, if power—any and all power—does not come from this determining order, then all is lost . . .

Why this rawness of the thetic nerve on the precise and rather "scholastic" point of God's wisdom getting the upper hand over the will? To get all worked up and cry blasphemy is one of the ways of denying a knowledge that we have. It seems as if Aquinas had seen, and profoundly so, that power might also not come straight from the intra-divine order. Otherwise why would this author, little inclined to outbursts, fret as he seems to do?

In briefly outlining here his Grand Deduction of the law (a remarkable treatise), precisely one question will be at stake. It regards the first position in graded nature. This question and this position both concern the neo-Aristotelian meaning of being: actuality. How does that originary meaning delimit and bear upon the principle of continuous gradation, upon nature-as-law? In other words, how can the pure act provide a starting point for the deduction that is to legitimize the existing authorities? How does *esse* come to found power?

If there is a gap between being and power, then the first in rank will harbor a certain indetermination which the early fourteenth-century Scholastics will develop by assigning normative primacy either to the absolute divine will or to the godhead in the sense of God's ground and abyss. For them both these later figures make the principle indeterminate. When Scotists posit it as absolute, the will is disengaged from the order emanating from reason; and the godhead, as conceived by Eckhart, sets off into a desert in which determinations are lost. A metaphysics of order will always be maddened by the unthought obviousness of a principial foundation denaturized by the origin.

Ever since Augustine, we saw, nature has laid down the law through the created order that is prefigured in the uncreated. Thus again in Aquinas: "The plan of divine wisdom which moves all things to their due end has the character of law" (II-I, q. 93, art. 1). That teleological order is divine, that it cannot be but rational, and that it pertains therefore to intellect or wisdom, all this is held quasi-unanimously throughout the Latin Christian millennium[27]—until, precisely, Aquinas glimpsed a fissure in the apparatus stringing powers together and hastens to patch it up in hurling the verdict: blasphemy.

Posited as first and prefiguring the created, order is called eternal law; as participant, it is called natural law. Following this received disjunction, Aquinas develops a deduction of the law that is inseparably a deduction of power. It traces a precipitation—Eckhart's term—of law and of power, from the initially posited down to its last effects on acting. So deployed, *natura* serves above all to discriminate among positive laws. A positive law "that deviates from natural law is no longer a law but a corruption of law" (II-I, q. 95, art. 2). But nature binds legislators only because it first assures them that their power is founded. The principial decree authorizes their decrees. It guarantees the exercise of power through a series of mediations that issue in a four-leveled cascade.

1. *Eternal law.* The deduction begins by positing an arch-order. This is variously described as the convertibility of God's being with perfections (goodness: I, q. 6, art. 1; truth: I, q. 16, art. 5); as his creative science ("God's science is the cause of things," I, q. 14, art. 8); or again as God's wisdom inasmuch as it contains the world's "plan," that is to say, the ideas (I, q. 15, art. 2,2). Of these descriptions, to state matters quite dryly, the first emphasizes the unity in the arch-order; the second, its sovereignty (and using power); and the third, its intrinsic plurality. Divine wisdom is a "plan," in that it assigns to all things their ideal ends. It is a law in that any end attracts what it moves, just as the proper use of a bodily organ moves it as it attracts it to its particular function. Eternal law is best described as the network of ends that incites—that excites—all movements and all actions.

In a first mediation, the intra-divine order communicates itself by *imprint.* As a middle term does always, this one conveys the workings of the system. Law and power are transmitted according to two schemata: that of participation by deficient similarity and that of teleology ("It is evident that all things partake somewhat in the eternal law in so far as, by its imprint, they incline towards their proper acts and ends," II-I, q. 91, art. 2). God's imprint upon the world is its teleological order. As a result of these schemata, the lower levels of being are marked by both dictates (*dictamen*) of, and submission to, law; both regulative spontaneity and regulated receptivity.

2. *Natural law.* By virtue of this law, the beings that act, as well as those that only move, partake in the arch-order. There is no action unless there is purpose, no movement unless there is a goal. By the rule of ends, the *lex naturalis* deploys the imprint in a graded arrangement. Nature is harmonized vertically according to the greater or lesser mastery (*dominium*) one holds over oneself and others. It ranks agents that submit to power even as they exercise it. Depending on one's place in this array of subordinations, each is a "subject" both subjecting and subjected. Participation in the

first power is thus organized in terms of a mixture of domination and obedience that is infinitely varied according to ends. Together, teleology and graded participation serve to affirm that in nature all works for the best. The system of subordinations is just. "God saw that this was very good." Very good indeed, for natural law orients us essentially toward the good in general. More specifically, it turns us toward ends above us in the hierarchy, then those equal to us, and finally to those below. Thus nature demands that in turn we do justice to each rank. Hence three domains of justice are incumbent upon us, each of which is regulated by its own principles (II-I, q. 94, art. 2).

By a second mediation, starting now with this system of natural principles, the body of positive laws is *deduced* in a narrower sense. This does not mean that nature contains analytically whatever can be required of us, nor that, by some demonstration, it suffices to extract from it what is right. To deduce in the narrowest sense means here to empower plural laws through the communication of forms. It means in-forming positive laws.

3. *Positive law.* This body of laws organizes social customs by revelation (divine law) and legislation (human law). Only at this level is the law a writ: one holy, the other judicial. If, then, actual customs conform to the natural good—as a living organism conforms to its ends—and if the "public person" promulgates them as laws, then they assume the power of obligation. "The law is nothing else than an ordinance of reason in view of the common good, conceived and promulgated by him who has care of the community" (II-I, q. 90, art. 4).

A last mediation, finally, assures that positive laws are *applied.* These laws inform situations. Here subjects no longer exercise any dictate. In its last incidence the law is characterized only in terms of its reception.

4. *Acting.* It will conform to the law habitually through virtues and contingently through coercion.

Without entering into the details of this huge scaffolding, it is not difficult to see where the shoe pinches. The crucial strut obviously is the point of departure. What is it that Aquinas has seen there, yet denies, hence recognizes and banishes, but which returns to unnerve him and make him cry blasphemy? This cannot be just one or another part in the vast setup, nor even, properly speaking, the relation tying together the folds in the initial bundle. Rather, a relation *within* the compact thesis lends itself to blasphemy. That is what he says, and that is why his panic admits of no remedy—there is no appellate authority. What is maddening is a withdrawal that loosens from within the power that commences and commands—a withdrawal without which the footings of the law could not be posited and through whose effect they can only be weakened.

What commences and commands order is here pure act. At the top of the scale as well as at each rank Aquinas posits actuality as the tutelary sense of being. Now if tutelary power somehow belongs to being, such a property raises certain questions. Pure *esse* guarantees the arch-order in its unity, in its efficacy, and in its intrinsic plurality, which is to say in everything that connects the teleology of law with the participation in power. How, then, is one to think the step from actuality to tutelage?

Is *esse* opposed not rather incongruously to tutelary administration, whether this be to exercise or submit to it? If it should turn out that the evidence both recognized and banished by Aquinas has to do with this incongruity, then one may suspect that he *saw correctly* in seeing the system's keystone fissured. The overdeterminations that establish the why of order will be able to work only on the actuality of being through the perverted powers that be. These overdeterminations will be able to counteract its purity, discredit it, even while having to lend it credence. What indeed could one predicate of purity without, by the very fact of doing so, already having lost it?

Aquinas does not hesitate to append a whole list of predicates to what is posited first. Take for instance the "true," the formal object of the intellect. God's *esse* is "in conformity with his intellect" (I, q. 16, art. 5). This does not seem like much. Who would deny that God's being is true? But with such predication, pure being is *determined* through its convertibility with perfections. The same applies to causality. Pure being is furthermore said to function as "measure and cause" (ibid.), whereby it is overdetermined in one stroke by Neoplatonic exemplarism as well as by Aristotelian kinetics. As for ideal plurality, it determines God's being through the one axiom that makes theticism appear at its rawest: the axiom that God's essence is his *esse*.[28] Now, "in accordance with his essence, God resembles all things" (*est similitudo omnium rerum,* I, q. 16, art. 1,3). Here, then, pure being is ordered by ideas. Does the why of order, this *quia* laying down the law, apply the discourse on being to the *quia*?

Aquinas charges and surcharges essence with determinations guaranteeing order. On the other hand, the act of being—*energeia,* God's essence—has to remain pure. Thus the axiom in question conjoins the *principle of order* incongruously with the *energetic origin.*

In any case, the perversion is obvious. Aquinas twists the infinitive and originary sense of being around into the nominative and principial sense. This again may not look like much, but the ever-ongoing and cursive operation of predication can only miscarry if *esse* is to be understood as pure actuality. It is necessary to try to follow that cursive course that carries determinations far away from pure act.

To glimpse where the flight leads—it leads to being "without why," relinquishing order with its why—and without leaving the scholastic idiom, let us retain in passing the *sed contra* with which Meister Eckhart counters the very thesis of an intra-divine order. He, too, understands God as being (and being as God). But he no longer hesitates to recognize that the act of pure being is hostile to archetypal order: "God scorns working through images" (Pf 8; {W I,8}).

And what if Aquinas's nerves were put on edge precisely by the evidence he saw best and for which he remains a great philosopher: the evidence that "being" signifies the pure actuality of a being which is always singular?[29] Being is given singularly in simple apprehension. The deduction forces this singularity under the being that is common to natural beings. It forces the purity of the Yes in actual givenness under the altogether different purity of being a maximum at the top of a graded scale. Due to its purity, however, actuality can only remain unamenable to determinations, be they cognitive or volitional, causative or ideal, determinations that are crucial since they must establish the "why" of the world. Is this the result of an Aristotelian-Platonic syncretism? No doubt. Yet beneath the syncretistic allure and fact, it is a question of something else that is still more difficult to think. Could it be that Aquinas did see pure actuality as introducing an *originary indeterminacy* into the very principle that deploys the law? His panic in the face of a hypothetical primacy of the will in God would then betray an inevitable slippage in the very source of order—the will being among the faculties the one that does not determine itself. What man of the law would want to see the law falling under the jurisdiction of a condition that is indeterminate with regard to ends? The law's simplicity would be done for, and it would cease to impose uniform obligations. Concerning this threat, one is tempted to salute Aquinas, saying—"good eye."

The grand deduction of the law starts from a principle without which there would be no deduction. Which principle is it? "The things that come from God, inasmuch as they are beings, are assimilated to him as to the first and universal principle of all being" (*primo et unversali principio totius esse,* I, q. 4, art. 3). The deduction translates into terms of law the hierarchy that analogy posits in being. From top to bottom, this hierarchy results from additions to the act. As co-constituent, the act does not mix with anything in the continuous chain of degrees. Aquinas speaks of additions and compositions precisely to preserve the purity of the originary element. But things turn out differently when *esse* comes to command the order by natural subordinations; that is, when it comes to exercise power.

What then happens is this. Aquinas must not, and yet he must, posit actuality as such as a natural principle. He must not because of the unicity of the pure act wherever it occurs. But yet he must posit it so as to guarantee that the natural chain of powers is anchored in the arch-order that is compact, fully saturated, absolutely primal, universal, and intelligible by rights. In his idiom: God's subsisting being (*esse subsistens*) must not coincide with the being common (*esse commune*) to the created. But actuality is necessarily one. Whatever is, is. God, for example. . . . How will this necessity organize the uncreated or the created? Only a *coup d'état*—a seizure of order—can enthrone the evidence of the simple act and make it wield power. Aquinas would have gotten all worked up for having to commit, in the name of nature, such a coup. Conversely, the evidence that *being is against nature* is equally enervating.

To state it in an idiom from the history of ideas: In its archic position, neo-Aristotelian *energeia* does not pair off with either power or essence. But as the Neoplatonic hierarchy comes to modulate it, being inevitably gets conceived as an essence. In the deduced hierarchy, *esse* reigns as the essence of power, whereby it lays down the law. Still, by what affinity with the proper will the act come to exercise power? The necessity that actuality be one produces manifestation, whatever the manifest being may be. But the necessity of a first principle produces order—essentialist, nominative necessity is altogether at odds with the necessity of being in the infinitive.

Anchoring power in the act of being again obliges Aquinas to distinguish between two disparate types of universality. Being ("verbal") remains distinct from the beings ("nominal") of which it is the act. Being is what is most universal, but not in the manner of an abstract essence. Thus it is a different universality that remains irreducible to the problematic of universals. It is a different perfection as well, one that remains irreducible to determinations. It is a different purity, finally, disparate in relation to all ideal purity.

Is there not a problem then when the pure act, *origin* of all being, serves as a *principle* for nature? Being changes purity. To anchor the law, Aquinas posits being as pure the way essentialism posits a universal—which is precisely how power is posited. In the deduction of the law, he distinguishes between power *in abstracto,* pure as is any essence, and power *in concreto,* determined by who has possession of it and by the use he makes of it. In what way is power pure, taken abstractly or in itself? It is pure the way any other universal quality is, for example, just as "living," taken abstractly or in itself, is specifically determinable by "warm-blooded," and particularly by "red-haired." Thus, abstractly, "there is no power except coming from God"; it becomes specified by natural law and particularized by positive law and application. Exercising power is thus just as *universal because it is natural,* as is willing the good and knowing the true.

Entirely other is the act of being, which is *universal because in each instance singular* in beings. The question, Does X exist or does it not? can only be answered with yes or no, nothing more and nothing less; there is no hierarchy. Something either actually is, or it is not.

Thus the otherness between origin and principle opens up. It results directly from *energeia* torn from kineticism and reappropriated by Aquinas as the act of being. This act is "complete" in each being of which it is the act. What kind of positional initiative will ever turn being into the law of laws? The question can only remain open and set one's nerves on edge.

Power and the act of being are conjoined with the most blatant incongruity when Aquinas distinguishes between particular and singular. As we just saw, power gets particularized by subsumptions. The singular, on the other hand, cannot be subsumed under anything. It can be characterized only by the "dominion of its act" (*dominium sui actus,* I, q. 29, art. 1). I read in this phrase a subjective genitive. For Aquinas the act itself is dominion, mastery, power, sovereignty. Of course the "person"—which here means the singular—governs his act, but only because the act itself is first of all governance. But is this not to treat the act as that with which it above all must not be compromised, namely, whatness? The forceful takeover closes the gap opened by the infinitive sense of *esse,* between being as singular act—hence as singularization—and as common perfection. One has to see clearly that without such a forceful takeover the deduction would lose its moorings and that, quite simply, normative nature could not be. The little crisis of nerves concerns the principial order in God as *ipsum esse.* If he does not contain, folded up in himself, the laws that the world unfolds in graded diversity, then what is left to make them hold to and, most of all, what is left to hold on to? Without an order in God, there is no order on earth. There is only desolation. The stakes in the principle of continuity are formidable, as much for consoling the soul as for consolidating the city.

The divine intellect posits in itself the exemplary order; now that alone can be exemplary which is absolutely first; whoever denies that in God firstness pertains to the intellect would therefore ruin the world order. But as we have just seen, the indetermination by the singularization of being brings about this ruination in the order precisely at its point of departure. Indeed, this is something about which to get worked up.

Aquinas cries blasphemy because he *both* sees, and does not want to see, that (1) what is at issue in the so-called deduction is in fact a nomothesis; that nature is posited, not given, (2) theticism always requires an indeterminate space *in which* to posit a normative referent together with its consequences, and (3) the pure act of being, which here provides the space in which the law is inscribed, is belabored by a differend. Originarily and principially incongruous, the law governing nature is a broken law.

If one wishes to posit the law above all suspicion, one is forced to deny such conditions. This tragic denial is explicitly undone by Meister Eckhart.

CHAPTER 12

Feet on One's Neighbor's Head

Eckhart in no way contends that "God's will is above his intellect." Rather, this is the way the Scotists speak when they deprive the natural order of its source in the divine intellect and thereby render it essentially contingent. Eckhart, in a way, does worse. He argues that this order depends on God and does so with such a passion for immanence that this order has to pre-exist in God's very ground—where it necessarily is undone, liquefied. His argument amounts to displacing the issue of law all the way from the formal and principial scaffolding up to its originary presence in being.

To understand this displacement it is necessary to see first how Eckhart accounts for formal order and the continuity in its transmission. He does so by distinguishing between reposing and positing. We will then see what follows from the displacement toward the problematic of being, the neuralgic point that Thomas Aquinas lives through well enough, but that he had to deny.

The distinction of reposing and positing reflects the distinction, classical since Augustine, between eternal law and natural law. Eternal "right order" pre-exists in God's ineffable bosom; outside it is posited as natural law. "In that place which is nameless, all creatures bud and blossom in right order, and all creatures are themselves posited from out of the ground of this place where right order [pre-exists] . . . This place is God, who gives to all things position and order" (DW II,191 and 201; S II35 and 38 {W I,275 and 278}). There will be continuity inasmuch as divine 'insitting' (*einsitzen*)—the seating—translates into 'setting-forth' (*setzen*), into positing and ordering (*setzunge und ordenunge*). To put it less oddly but also less precisely, it is a matter of distinguishing between God's reposing in himself and his positing of order outside himself.

To seat {asseoir} (*setzen*) something is to assign it its place and in this sense posit it there. The "composed" (German collocative *Ge-*, translating the Latin *com-*), the whole of what has been so set forth (past participle *das Gesetzte,* 'the posited') is ordered by the law (*das Gesetz*) of assigned places. Eckhart reduces the normative gap between natural law and eternal law by tracing the former back to the latter, tracing what has been "set" or "posited," i.e. created, back to an immediate incidence of divine "insitting," divine "repose." We will see that, since it designates the originary being of God, order dissolves in this repose.

Here is a text reminiscent of Aquinas's grand deduction but completely different from it—vertical continuity is expressed in terms of presence, hence in terms of being rather than power and law.

> Whatever stands on something else, its lowest part touches the highest part of that which is below. God touches all things yet remains untouched. God is above all things an instanding in himself, and his standing in himself sustains all creatures. All creatures have an upper and a lower part, but God has not. God is above all things, and nowhere is he touched by any. All creatures always seek outside of themselves: each seeks in the other what it lacks. This God does not do. God seeks nothing outside of himself. What all creatures have God has entire within himself, all in one. He is the ground and the encirclement of all creatures. It is true that of these, one comes before the other, or at least one is born of the other. Still, no creature passes on its own being. Each retains something of its own. God, on the other hand, is a simple instanding, an insitting, in himself. As for every creature, according to the nobility of its nature, the more it is seated in itself, the more it gives itself out. A simple stone, such as tuff, points to nothing more than that it is a stone. But a precious stone, which has greater force because of its instanding, indwelling and inseating, thereby raises its head and looks out above itself. (DW I,224f.; S I,130 {W I,193f.})

Here we can say that nature is reconfigured. The Romans, haunted by the fantasm of the city, would not be able to recognize themselves in this feudal edifice where rank is everything. Hegemonic nature will be overthrown when the carefully articulated strata of this edifice are liquefied in originary identity. The normative gap will thereby close up, and (as the judges of the Inquisition sensed, rather than understood) nature will have lost the space in which to unfold its regime.

Now, such reduction to the identical is common stock in alchemy. Using the lines quoted as a guide, it is possible to draw out the framework of forces in which the "chemist philosopher" plies his trade. In order to describe their system, these philosophers like to refer to the symbol of the "Seal of Solomon," the star of David composed of two superimposed equilateral triangles.[30] They make it serves multiple purposes, which may allow one to adapt it with a degree of liberality and irony. May its six angles evoke here some abstract alembic, to be used further below to distill the singular elixir . . . (chapter 13). After each of the six points, I will briefly indicate how the principial strategy gives way to the originary.

The immediate communication of the law

Transmitting the law is what is most problematic in an arrangement of elements that stand in continuity. Counter to mediations by impressions, participations, or deductions, Eckhart asserts immediate transmission: God "touches" all things and thereby maintains each at its rank. Were it not for his "insitting"—which depends on nothing since no being touches him in return—there could be no "seating" upon which created beings directly depend. God's insitting posits the seat that maintains in existence all that is other than he. To understand how the principle of continuity recasts nature here, the feature that needs to be addressed is the immediate communication of being. This communication connects the being that is uncreated with each created thing. God lends being to all that he sets outside of himself. Yet *all being remains his,* for as a divine possession, being excludes mediations. Following Eckhart's example, no living thing can communicate to its offspring the being it holds to be its own (*eigen*), since neither parents, nor any ideal intermediary, can be interposed in the direct transmission of being from the creator. Moreover, needing to be perpetually maintained by another's bearing means that one's being is borrowed, but that it can never be appropriated (*eigenen*). Thus living creatures, which are posited above inanimate ones which they touch with their lowest part, the body, and which are posited beneath spirits which the best among them touch with their highest part, the intuitive apex of their thought, still belong individually and immediately to him who so posits and disposes all things in this manner. The theory of borrowed, not appropriated, being militates against all constructs of mediation. Eckhart indeed erects a hierarchy of beings, but there the problem of being is dissociated from the question of form; as for the problem of the law, it is extricated from the question of formal participation and reabsorbed into that of being. The hierarchy established by a progressively deficient likeness of forms to divine ideas goes without saying. Being, however, is not transmitted this way. "What is mine I have from nobody. For if I take it from another, it is not mine but belongs to him from whom I got it" (DW II,108; S I,247 {W I,151}). Diverted only as a loan, so to speak, being remains one and the same. The law of positing thus ends not in an alterity but in an allotropy.

What is at stake in this theory of immediate bestowal is above all identity. This appears from the way the law allocates property (*eigenschaft*[31]). Posited beings do not acquire being. The created remains the other of being. Property is the prerogative of a being in repose; there alone is there uncontested possession and identity without allowances.

According to this ontology of loans (*borge*), something borrowed belongs essentially to the one who owns it and accidentally to the borrower. The same holds for natural law. It relates to eternal law as the borrowed good to the lender. The bearing—namely, the law—is communicated to the one maintained, *in fluxu et fiere* (LW II,652), by influx and becoming. The loan always is nothing but an extension of the proper, of property, of full repose. Hence two modes, uncreated and created, of one identical presencing. By his insitting, God is present to himself, a presence that his "setting-forth" only extends by allotropy. "No creature has any being, for their being depends on God's presence. If God turned away from all creatures even for an instant, they would be annihilated " (DW I,70; S I,65 {W I,284}). "Insitting" and "positing outside the self" designate two aspects of one and the same presence, whose conjunction exhausts the modes of being and whose disjunction designates the spheres of the law. A loan is but a consequence of one and the same asset. Being is one, and it is God (LW I,156). Likewise for the law: There is one instance of ownership; the incidence of lending imparts it.

The principle of continuity here rests on an identity thesis that is much stronger than in any of Eckhart's predecessors on this point, including the Stoics. To transmit the law means to manifest it as one and the same in its primary stance—its primary insistence—as well as in its secondary instances. Self-identity through one's bearing becomes, in self-manifestation, identified with an other that is maintained. To say that this maintenance must be renewed at each moment is to say that, like being, the law of nature is not *of* nature. In the created, the law of allo-position is the same law of uncreated self-possession, but "touching" what is other than God. The law of *Setzen* is the same as *Einsitzen,* effectively manifesting itself.[32]

The law of nature—of having a posited, borrowed being, flowing in from elsewhere—is thus summed up in the eternally identical law befalling the borrower. If presence, and along with it the law, signifies a process of borrowing, then we will no longer be able to speak of deriving or deducing the law in Eckhart. There is only the one bearing, and it translates into the maintenance of the created. To be sure, such unicity does not mean its univocity. But just as being is given on loan by what commentators term the analogy of attribution,[33] so in Eckhart the law acquires multiple incidences by an analogy of position. "Whatever stands on something else, its lowest part touches the highest part of that which is below." One has to be wary not to read into this distinction of high and low some theory of emanation. Otherwise the immediacy of transition would be done in. Analogy of position means rather that each being is directly allotted its natural site. There it puts it feet on the head of the one that occupies the level beneath it; but it communicates to it neither being nor presence nor possession nor derived law. On this footing, each is a single inductive object for fantasizing nature. Through primary presence, each fits directly into the natural configuration.

One would be hard pressed to imagine a more rigid system of natural allocation. Its strength resides in the identity of the non-identical: in the identity of being *in the ground.* Still, as a mere corollary to that identity and as a topography of its incidents, the law of nature courts catastrophe. If it rests on borrowed being alone, presence cannot but disrupt its hegemony. Nature, as what lays down the law, will turn out to be no more than a surface effect—and the denial that sustains it will be overcome, lost in advance. As Eckhart's gaze moves back from the order of incidences toward the instance of the *grunt,* the ground of the soul that is nothing other than the ground of God, the allotment of natural sites, *will lose its simple legislative function.* In this move from principle to origin, identity has to be thought of otherwise than according to the fixity of "A = A," and normative nature, made secondary to the identical ground and liquefied in it, even ceases to be an issue. It will no longer make sense to speak of law and of property. Eckhart, we will see, does not hesitate to say as much.

A poietic law

The unicity of the law and the graduated multiplicity of its immediate incidences entail a second trait that dissolves the normative order which is nature: insitting and setting-forth are a making (*poiesis*). Aquinas's grand deduction was meant to justify power and its exercise. Such justification becomes impossible as soon as Eckhart emphasizes the *werk*—the operation or the work—rather than the transmitted *potestas.* The non-identical—the uncreated and the created—is identical due to order being set into work—poietically. God holds himself in himself, and as an activity, this bearing maintains that which is other than it in its place. It is therefore necessary to resist the temptation of reducing *Einsitzen* in Eckhart to a pure and simple echo of the Neoplatonic *aut'hypostaton* of Pseudo-Dionysus. Primary self-possession is here neither static nor hypostatic. God determines himself through an acting that also determines his other.

Here we have a beautiful demonstration for understanding how the fantasm of continuous nature follows directly from theticism. The positive act proceeds in one direction—"God touches all things yet remains untouched." To be touchable, reachable, is to fall under the sway of an other. For the created, the act that posits is a "hoop," holding and keeping it. Thus it is a thetic act. By thinking identity as activity, as an effective positing, Eckhart seeks to account for natural order and its preservation without having recourse to such representations as omnipotence. He has recourse rather to the logic of theticism. A single act posits the same and its other, whereby this unicity of act inscribes the (created) other in continuity with the (uncreated) same. What keeps things in place is God's intermittent activity through which he makes himself present to every one of them.

The series possession–bearing–insitting–autonomy thus emphasizes an effecting whose effects are the series loan–maintaining–setting forth–heteronomy. The center "touches" the excentric. It is a touching that is already a tangling and continuation of the same into its other. Rather than severing the autonomous being from heteronomous beings, this act dethematizes their ontological otherness. The poietic law thematizes how *energeia* erases the *chorismos*.

This is what Eckhart describes when he distinguishes not between given regions (created and uncreated), but between two acts: creating and procreating. He seeks to grasp a "making" that is at work everywhere and thus guarantees trans-regional presence. The being that insits does not withhold itself, does not hold back what is his own. Only living creatures hold on to what is theirs. "No creature passes on its own being." If parents are incapable of communicating their being to their offspring, this is not only because they possess it on loan, but also because a borrowed existence is never "a bearing, an insitting"; it is never effective regarding its own being. Whoever lives by borrowing borrows only for himself. He can only pass along a being that is equally borrowed through divine creation rather than appropriated through human procreation. The most marked hereditary traits are created, they do not result from procreation. Presence alone is poietic. One has to note the incompatibility between "being posited" and imparting one's (human) being, and that there is an equivalence between "reposing in oneself" and imparting (divine) being. The dyad of insitting and setting-forth refers to one single operation.

Here again one step will suffice to devastate nature. If presence as *werk*—as actuality of being—is one and the same in the uncreated and the created, then between God and man there obtains an originary unity in operation (*ein in disem gewürke,* DW I,114; S I,86 {W II,137}). To think such a unity, not only does the regionalization of uncreated-created become useless and obsolete, but so does the whole representation of a graduated universe. That classical edifice with its degrees collapses into the presence–actuality–activity–operation–work of being.

Moreover, we can see see how the neo-Aristotelians, for whom the actuality of being is one and unique—prepared this devastation of the order. Both Aquinas and

Eckhart translate Aristotelian *energeia*. But when Eckhart understands it as *gewürke* rather than as *actus*, an identity between man and God (not substantial but operative) becomes thinkable that no longer appeals to some difference in composition. Here is this operative identity: "Acting and becoming are one. . . . God and I are one in this operation: he works and I become" (DW I,114; S I, 86 {W II,136f.}). The vast natural continuity sinks into this identity. When the order appears on the ground of an operational identity, the denial of the double bind becomes unsustainable and nature is destituted.

Rather than the legitimization of power, Eckhart retains the *poiesis* and *energeia* in the imparting of being. Hence there is no longer any *reason* to put one's feet on the neighbor's head; there is no longer the principial contiguity of places, but the originary temporality of an event.

The temporality of natural law

"What all creatures have, God has entire within himself," whereas among things created "one is there before the other." By opposing the "all together" and the "one after the other," Eckhart again invokes the natural order, this time with a view to a more clearly Neoplatonic problem.

The *Einsitzen* that is one, turning itself into multiple *Setzen,* is deployed not only in a hierarchy but also in a chronology. The thesis spreads out continuity both in the manner of an encompassing fabric and as a series of occurrences. If nature consists in this topic-chronology, which needs to be posited anew without surcease, then it is configured all together through subordinations and successions.

"What all creatures have . . .". Indirectly, this phrase suggests the ideal preformation of created properties, both universal and individual. If, as an ancient Greek dream has it, we were able to adjust our gaze to the divine "all in one"—if we were capable of extricating a certain exercise of thought from the law of "one after another"—then spatial juxtaposition would collapse into a full-blown "here." Likewise the sequence of "nows" would coalesce into simultaneous givenness. Eckhart not only entertains the possibility of such a panoptic view. He states that, by virtue of God's compact acting in us, such synopsis is part and parcel of the loan. "What lies beyond the seas is no more distant to this power than what is now present" (DW II,34; S I,221W {I,100}). In a single breath, time and space are syncopated in the compact power of immanence. In terms of the analogy of position, man is the stage where the eternal law of *tota simul* refracts into the natural law of the spatial and temporal *hoc et hoc.* Created seatings disclose what uncreated "insitting" encloses.

The thesis thus distributes spaces and times. The circle placed around each thing demarcates one as the carrier of meaning here, another there; one time is denoted now, another later. What are the possessions rolled up into the single fold of the "all in one" that nature unfolds? It is the sum of the complements that "each creature seeks in the other" because it misses them in itself. Man lacks the plants' chlorophyll, while plants need man's cultivating talents. Of these deficiencies, some can be fulfilled simultaneously, others only intermittently over more or less long lapses of time. All reappear always anew. To so depend on exterior complements points to our temporality (*zîtlicheit,* e.g. DW II,309; S II,79 {W II,238}). "Holding oneself in" is the eternal law inasmuch as in the first compactness all reciprocally complementary qualities are one. "God seeks nothing outside of himself." He does not fall under the law of "one after the other" because he does not fall under the law of needs and need fulfillments. What is at issue, although unstated, is privation—in the compact cause of all forms there can be no *sterêsis*. By contrast natural law organizes—positively and thetically—time spans according to compositions always changing forms, privations, and matter.

Here again, then, we see how principial strategies slip off toward the originaries, and thus simple normativity off toward the double bind. This slippage results from the oldest of philosophical questions, the question of conditions. In Eckhart, to inquire into the condition of temporal succession amounts to disfiguring the configuration that is nature. Here is how.

In the Neoplatonic tradition, the condition for occurrences to succeed one another lies in their paradigmatic and stable simultaneity, that is, in their cause. For Eckhart—as much a neo-Aristotelian, we have seen, as a Neoplatonist, hence neither one nor the other—reduces paradigmatism to theticism and principial stability to originary *energeia*. The quest for conditions thus does not make him go beyond space and time to some atopic and achronic cause, but rather to an event, namely, to the one we have encountered as an identical loan and as an operation. Here "loaning" and "borrowing" describe one and the same process, the condition of all spatial and temporal manifestation. The spreading out of nature ceases to be an issue in thinking this event. The originary event—the condition of successions and simultaneities—does not circle, sustain, nor maintain anything. In it, the principle of continuity becomes untenable.

The instance of self-possession

Eckhart's main argument concerning order, both in its source and in its refraction, is that nature "holds" by God's immediate thetic activity. This theticism, which is a doing, is identically the condition of divine insitting as well as of each posited thing (*gesetzt,* hence also of positive law, *Gesetz*). Refraction does not, cannot, mean diffraction, dispersion, patchwork. Rather, nature is organized like a feudal society ruled by the principle of *noblesse oblige*. "The more it indwells in itself, the more each creature gives itself outwardly." Its degree of in-standing measures its degree of *ec-stasis,* its standing-out. Beings must possess themselves a little, a lot, or entirely, in order to offer themselves up a little through speech (humans), a lot through "wakefulness" (angels), or completely through creation (God). The instance of self-possession is the organizing criterion for normative nature.

Insitting in itself thus denotes a bearing that essentially imparts itself. Eternal law is what the perfect instance yields perfectly outside itself. Natural law stratifies the ecstatic loans. Self-possession remains the differentiating factor among these instances, these highs and lows that make up the world. The principle of continuity demands that self-possession—the criterion for spatial inclusion and exclusion for the Greeks[34]—here turn into a criterion for successively encompassing, hierarchized, inclusions. The more a being possesses itself, the more generous it is in giving itself over to the outside, to the dispossession of itself. Now, that through which it offers itself to the outside, but only to the outside, is its name.

In beings posited outside the creator, autonomy mixes with heteronomy. These mixtures, in turn, go outside themselves in an exiting from the self that is neither originary nor principial because it does not lend any being nor maintain any "seating," but in an exiting of the self that makes for knowledge. What does it make known? The name ("'Brother Eckhart, when did you leave the house?'" quoted above). The possibility as well as the necessity of names appears with the emergence of "God" as the supreme referent, beginning with the godhead in which all references are effaced. The name is thus the general correlate of theticism. It is necessary to explain how this is so.

For Eckhart all nouns are proper names. They denote an *Eigenschaft,* a property, be it generic, specific, or individual. If the created "offers itself outside," it does so by displaying properties. It offers what it has—what distinguishes it and makes it nameable. The name will show its proper, appropriative function when retracing the dialectic between possession and position; between reflexive self-possession and denominative generosity.

The attribution of names suffices to establish the general fact of natural subjection. In the name of nature, I am named human; in the name of the father, I am named son. . . . However, such attribution of names does not suffice to organize these subjections into a system. For that, Eckhart resorts to the most reliable provider of order, namely, dialectics—a certain dialectic. Here, this dialectic moves between possessing itself through intrinsic reflection and offering itself through extrinsic denomination. Such a dialectic assigns places and determines the ranks. The formal hierarchy does not impart being. If it did, being would literally degrade itself by composition. It could no longer guarantee identity throughout nature, nor would being be God. Rather, the hierarchy distributes being-nearby-oneself and its modes. Titles of nobility are established by balancing (as one balances the books) a soul's capacity for possessing itself *ad intra* with its concomitant modes of dispossessing itself *ad extra*. These titles are ethical, for all beings are situated in relation to another and act in keeping with that site where they have been placed. As we know, the Greek *ethos* designated the "site." In their derivative manner of being outside themselves, the created agent reveals itself not through "a bearing, a simple instanding" where being is imparted prior to any juxtaposition and succession, but through a sustained bearing where the agent manifests itself in extension and duration. Such self-manifestation cannot be simple because of the complex constitution of created beings of which each "has a lower part and an upper part." Divine positing is received in them (for Eckhart just as for Thomas Aquinas[35]) according to the capacity of the mind to return to itself. The principle of continuity thus determines the series of beings more and less capable of entering into themselves and of offering themselves outwardly to other beings. This dialectic forges a "golden chain" in which "the foot of the highest is set on the head of the lowest" (DW I,211f.; S I,126 {W I,187}). The capacity for outward self-manifestation is never lost with any of the links in the series—except that, possessing neither life nor intelligence, "a simple stone points to nothing more than that it is a stone."[36]

At the top as at the bottom of the scale, for a being to return unto itself *is* to manifest itself outwardly. In the limit-case at the top, self-return is perfect. In the limit-case at the bottom, exiting out of the self is perfect. Natural law produces a *catena aurea* in which beings follow upon each other according to their capacity to show outwardly what they harbor inwardly, an aptitude that indicates their more or less perfect self-possession.

Hence the remarkable status of names. Does not "mysticism" present itself as the delirium of effacing the name? To liberate in oneself the ineffable, to become united with the ineffable, to flee exteriority, to act in the name of nothing, all this indeed describes the discursive strategies dearest to Eckhart, on the condition, however, of seeing first how the violence of the name is at work. To name is to demarcate sites by stratifying subjections. In a scale where the name signals the varying intensity of self-possession, it will go without saying—it will be *natural*—that each occupant of a rank puts its feet on a neighbor's head. The dialectic between reflexive self-possession and denominative dispossession thus intervenes to gauge the degree of subjections thus fixed by names.

As is usual in classifications such as this, we are ourselves everywhere in the picture, or almost everywhere. We are almost at the peak, since if we were not endowed with intuitive thought within, there could be no public life outside; we are almost at the bottom as well, since our corpse is never very far off. Beings—like a stone—for which the name emphasizes nothing more than the genus, are also the ones least capable of governing themselves. Each thing has possession of itself according to its rank. But the less it can impart itself, the less it resembles the first being which both possesses and imparts itself completely and for which the name, in order to do this, ceaselessly conveys full self-possession; as the only proper name that does not mix with anything specific or generic, it is the one that needs most urgently to be erased.

Thus the single act, possessing-positing, marks not only a system of subordinations where antitheses (such as inside-outside, possession-dispossession, having-giving, reflection-revelation) measure all allocations. Inasmuch as self-positing posits everything else, which is the first thesis, that act again makes of the name an effect of theticism and confines it to the thetic.

Now this dialectic, and with it the classification of names, does not survive the moment of indistinction. The fantasm gets destituted as Eckhart steps back from the thetic order toward the conditions of theticism. This move retrocedes from borrowing to lending, from actuality to action, from *natura* to *nasci,* from the nominative subsumption (i.e., from subsumable nouns and names) to the infinitive (i.e., to verbal process). It is essentially a step that leaves positions and oppositions behind and leads outside the determinate. Where indeed—an old question—must one be in order to describe a closed system? Eckhart responds without circumlocution: outside of the system. This is another "outside," to be sure, than is at play in the antithesis of "inside-outside." Eckhart lays claim to a singular place, other than the natural, from which to deploy nature. It is always from that place, the extra-natural condition of the natural system, that Eckhart speaks. By piercing through to the conditions of possibility, one no longer occupies any site that can be "called by its name," one no longer stands within any "nomenclature." This elsewhere Eckhart describes as *lûterheit* (vacancy, void, vacuity, purity, limpidity), *wuestunge* (desert, wilderness, waste), *einoede* (solitude), *vinsternisse* (darkness), *nihts* (nothingness). . . , a place without a name.[37]

The *epekeina*—and this in God himself—is substituted for the *chorismos,* which is the separation between creator and creature that effaces continuity. There, the beyond opens up the abyss between "God," the name of names, the ontic foundation of teleology, and the "godhead" (*gôtheit*) which is without name and beyond principle. As we will see, only non-attachment allows one to cross this abyss, and Eckhart does not hesitate to add: then *got entwirt.* Just as all other beings, the highest, too, makes itself indistinct as a result of the counter-strategies already encountered: operation, loan, event. For if God wants to look inside a detached soul "it will cost him all his names" (DW I,43; S I,56 {W I,77}).

Eckhart could not have better stated that the conditions of any given order are to be thought otherwise than as nameable entities and comparable representations; they must be thought otherwise and elsewhere than within the dialectical framework that nevertheless he himself so solidly cast.

Nature as laying down the law suffers its fatal reversal as soon as one inquires into the antitheses that it authorizes and on which it rests its authority. These antitheses stratify things "naturally." But, Eckhart asks, what is the condition of this natural framework? It cannot in turn figure among the properties that participate in "the more and the less." The question of conditions can therefore be phrased thus: What is the condition of borrowable being according to the dialectic of self-possession? What is essential being (*wesenlich wesen*)? The answer is once again topographical, but in such a way as to point to an originary topos in differend with all natural antitheses: "I pray God that he rid me of God, for, as far as we take God as the foundation (*begin*) of creatures, my essential being is beyond God" (DW II,502; S II,148 {W II,274}). Rid of the foundational God, I will be rid of the principle of continuous insertion, rid of nature-as-law.

From a pure place to proper places

If auto-possession and allo-position amount to two aspects of the same act, what kind of causality regarding nature is Eckhart ascribing to the foundation-commencement-commandment-*begin*? It seems difficult to speak of creator, creature, and creation as he does, all the while denying, on the one hand, that things created have a being of their own and, on the other, that God posits them in an act distinct from the act by which he possesses himself. Indeed, either this single act is a creative one and then God creates himself, which would be more astonishing than any of the condemned propositions, or this act consists in the divine life—trinitary or otherwise—and then the intra-divine processes would extend to the whole of extra-divine relationships. In this case, those later critics who accused him of simply extending divine being to nature will have been right.

The question is one of middle terms. It is a matter of seeing that in nature-as-law it is order, not being, that is transmitted as mediated from level to level—or from place to place, for the argument here is entirely spatial (we will come back to the unicity of being below in reference to the limit). Continuous allocation (a) situates beings *already constituted*. From this follows (b) the necessity of a *space before all allocations*—something like a blank page, without borders and extended indefinitely—preceding a grid that covers it, a non-saturated white space before proper places and that secondarizes the grid that allocates places. This grid and hence the initial order will be normative for every sketched plan {*dessin-dessein*} of nature. Thus, (c) to *think the inscription* of order, the tracing itself of the grid, will be to think this (which makes the doctrine of the principle monstrous), to think the condition from which the principial instance is born. This is monstrous, for by thinking such a condition Eckhart would have to sap the principial foundation. *Natura* as order will be reduced to the *nasci* that Meister Eckhart prefers to express in the imperative: give birth!

a. There is no doubt that, in the argumentative strategies for supporting natural law, exemplarism prevails over efficient causality in Eckhart. An investigation centered on law does not, however, have to deal with the problem of effective action *ex nihilo*. Rather, such an investigation has to account for the principle of order in the world. The conceptual pair of "insitting" and "seating" at least furnishes a tool for making an argument justifying it. For Eckhart to assert a *thetic* act that is one and the same—to argue one and the same nomothesis for God and the created—is to avoid the contradictions that would follow were he to claim one and the same *causal* act by which God acted on himself as well as on his created other without, for all that, flatly suggesting that the distinction between creator and creature is only a verbal concession and that the world is God. In Eckhart there is indeed an identity between God and world, as we have seen, but the identity of an operative presence. The terms "creator" and "creature" do not so much emphasize an efficient cause and its effect as they name the duality of this presence. Normativity thus pertains to the allotropy "self-presence—presence to the other." Eckhart does not efface the demarcation between creator and creature, but in his legislative strategy Eckhart states that full and constant presence determines the causal schema, not the other way around. Following the interest in presence, the foundational God as well as nature-as-law will be beings; their continuity will be established through "precipitation" and they both will occupy their proper place.

Whether one reasons from (neo-Aristotelian) efficient causality or from (Neoplatonic) exemplary causality, one always reasons about representable, distinct beings. Both as a mover and as a model, the cause is a being that is present to other beings. Whether metaphysicians speak of production out of nothing or of procession out of the One (which, when henology becomes Christian, is endowed with noetic perfections such as subsistence), they always form representable beings. Now Eckhart posits, and does not posit, a synonymy between *ipsum esse*—a verbal phrase which, we saw, he renders as "operating"—and the nominal phrase *summum ens*.

He posits precisely this synonymy in his legislative strategy. Among beings, some are big and others small, but first of all there is this ontological kinship, this connaturality, where all of them are beings. The capacity to *posit*—in the sense of formally placing and ordering—can be transmitted just as the capacity to exhibit outside what a thing carries inside can be transmitted: "What is most clearly above orders and posits what is below" (DW II,178; S II,30 {W I,248}). It is unlikely that Eckhart recalled the two corresponding Greek terms but (as indicated by the editor of this text), behind the noun *taxis,* 'order,' one cannot help hearing the verb *tassô,* 'to posit.' What is obvious, however, is the chain of mediations that Eckhart took care to exclude precisely with regard to being. *Any* being that stands higher than another "orders and posits" this other by descending causality.[38] Such a communication of attributes presupposes that the source as well as the beneficiaries of the ordering thesis are a representable, distinct being. Between giver and receiver there has to obtain the affinity that both are "something," that is, "some things." Likewise the benefit bestowed, namely, the good which is order, too will be a "something." In the arrangement of formal participation, the relations between founding and founded mediate among beings. To invest the below with the ordering capacity that properly belongs to the above still amounts to reasoning about things. When he argues for order, Eckhart necessarily treats the foundational God as a thing as well. The order that is nature, he says, is composed of "divine things" and of "temporal things" (DW V,266; W III,41). The principle of continuity envelops God and the world.

The way he takes up the ancient question of natural places shows very well, moreover, that his stake in the opposition between possession-bearing-insitting-autonomy and position-maintaining-seating-heteronomy is in no way the system of causes and their effective power. At stake is a system of presence and its allocative effect.

b. But Eckhart again undoes the synonymy between "being itself" and "the supreme being." He opens up the same gap as between origin and principle, between godhead and God, or between pure place and proper place.

Here is how he steps back toward space, the *pure place of proper places both for the foundational God and for nature-as-law:* "God has no proper name. He is a place and the position of all things, and he is the natural place of all creatures. In its highest and purest, the sky has no place; in its precipitation, however, where it becomes efficacious, it is the place and position of all corporeal things, which are beneath it" (DW II,200; S II,38 {W I,278}). In itself, the sky *has* no place. It *is* pure place. Spatiality belongs to it only as the canopy of light overarching the conglomeration of things beneath it, allowing it to orient them by the cardinal points that are to be found nowhere in the sky itself. In like manner, God's *is*—hence the godhead is—pure place, "the place and the 'where' of all things" (LW III,168), itself without name or description.[39] If God determines the proper places of created things, this will be in another capacity, namely, inasmuch as he answers to names such as "creator," "eternal law," "foundation." . . . Not to have a place implies pure magnitude, extendedness without end or limits, namely, the extra-systemic condition of the topical system which is nature. In the lines quoted, God without a name differs from God that is position, as the sky without a place differs from the precipitation into higher and lower places. Accordingly, places (in the plural) only appear with the position of the created and its order. Then God "becomes" the foundation and natural place of everything. Nature becomes the scale, grid, square and hence the norm, the world map with its cardinal points that are natural ends.[40]

Efficiency appears with the inscription of order in pure extendedness—formal efficiency in cosmology; creative efficiency in theology. The inscription remains incongruous since no continuum encompasses, on the one hand, the foundational God along with the topical grid that he traces, and, on the other, the pure space of manifestation in which nature is inscribed. When Eckhart says the foundation of order "becomes," one must appreciate the monstrous bifurcation he intends to inflict on all normative theory. He thinks an ultimate principle which in its turn has an originary condition. In his words, positing himself at the heart of the pure godhead, the foundational God becomes. The inscription of order is normative or archic in that it commences and commands the *Niederfall,* precipitation, into natural strata.

This is neither a fall nor a decline, to be sure. The thetic act to which the created owes its order is not an act by which beings are precipitated from the height of some intact spiritual condition to the bottom of a corrupt material condition. By translating *Niederfall* as 'precipitation' we preserve and stress the spatial sense of the term. Solid bodies materialize in a descending movement, as in atmospheric precipitation. This metaphor, almost a technical term in Eckhart, designates the establishment of degrees of being that are literally inferior to superior ones in terms of "in-fluence" (*in fluxu et fieri*). The pyramid of beings establishes itself by stases of the formal effluence allocating rankings.

Both the foundational God and nature-as-law take shape for each other through participation so understood. They are configured into one regime: "In the order of nature, higher beings dominate naturally and govern the lower ones, while the lower ones obey naturally and submit to the higher ones" (*Commentaries on Genesis,* I n. 121[41]). To posit a being is, in all rigor, to put it in its place. Since in such thetic allocation the decisive factor is governance, it is clear that causality can only function in a descending direction. The "order of nature" encompasses the eternal law of perfect divine self-possession as well as the natural law of graduated self-possession all the way down to the last piece of tuff.

The hierarchized stases thus have their commencement and commandment in the authority that posits them—in the foundational God, at one and the same time the source and summit of natural law. The argumentative move from the caused back to its cause keeps moving among beings. The gaze moves back from steads or stations to their highest instance. Beyond this, it is impossible to conceive of any being or any class of beings capable of mastering and regulating.

Beyond the foundational God one must, however, think an altogether different condition: the originary "instance" (quotation marks, for there is no longer a being there that "holds itself in itself") prior to both eternal and natural law.

c. That condition must be thought since every inscription thematizes the black grid laying out positive order as much as the blank space—desert, nothingness, solitude, godhead . . . —*on the ground* of which order can at all be posited. God's ground therefore concerns neither what he is as a being, nor his rank in respect to all other beings, nor even his action concerning them, the action of ordering everything that is manifested in "precipitation."

Eckhart describes God's ground as *ursprunc,* 'origin,' as that from which emergence occurs. Now, speech is emergence *par excellence.* Hence his new description of originary *energeia:* not only as operation, but also as locution. "Being is the Word" (*esse enim verbum est,* LW III,190). Eckhart thus gives an ontologizing reading of Saint John, which takes the *pros ton theon* literally ("and the Word was turned towards God," John 1:1), but he cannot express it—the turn, or the turning toward the foundational God arises from the ground of God. He thinks the originary emergence, which configures nature and its ontic foundation, as utterance. The system of nature refers back to its origin in the same manner nouns refer back to the *verbum:* word, speech, enunciation.

The imperative to give birth to the Word amounts to saying to act out of your ground. Just as the alchemist first reduces metals to formlessness in order to then confer on them the best of forms (gold), so does the reduction of nature to namelessness precede the enunciation of the best of names (the Word). We have seen how Eckhart's two great themes are organized—following the example of *solve et coagula,* the breakthrough beyond God toward the godhead is accomplished when the Word is born in the soul. The Word, however, is a noun like any other. It is the singular noun *par excellence.* For the Eckhart who declares that being is the *verbum,* Word-Verb, the indeterminacy of pure openness in which nature stands inscribed is none other than the indeterminacy of the singularizing enunciation. This allows one to think more precisely this difficult identity by *depredication* that I have said is thinkable only by its effect of *depredation* upon graded nature. We will understand the originary instance prior to natural law if one succeeds in understanding being as a verb in the middle voice. Instance has to be thought as without any positive stasis. But since it is the condition of every position, we have recourse to it each time we trust in nature and its ends—hence, all the time. An action that pertains to the principle will pertain, and by the same token, to the origin. It is our incongruous condition to always act "in the *name* of the *verb.*"

Thus, to destitute referential nature does not mean, once again, to abolish it. God's intransitive insitting and his transitive setting do set square a world governed by the law of status. Nature remains an inescapable normative fantasm because the transitive-intransitive posits a closed system. They articulate the whole and its parts in an infrangible, feudal structure of proper places. There is normative legislation insofar as the thetic condition is the final one at the heart of the closed system. But in order for there to be closure, there also has to be an extra-systemic condition, a condition outside the law, legislating differently. This other condition makes the natural configuration indistinct just as the act of enunciating renders indistinct an utterance by singularizing it—by drawing attention to the performative, by turning being into an event.

Limitation, delimitation, illimitation

The last element to be considered in this outline of the legislative system is limit. Which is, in Eckhart, the limit that really counts, the one that cuts, sets apart, separates, that varies the *chorismos*? As opposed to the Platonic *chorismos,* it no longer integrates the laws. On the contrary, it will make them slip away. Stepping beyond the limits that integrate nature is the very gesture of the freedom that Eckhart called non-attachment. Accordingly, non-attachment reveals the limit that counts precisely by transgressing it.

According to the thesis of vertical integration, the limit that circumscribes knowledge is not the separation between the world and "its" God. Rather, we have seen how these two co-thetic figures envelope each other. The limit that makes nature tremble will be the gap between the God proper to the created and the godhead impossible to appropriate. This is where understanding comes up against the incongruous. Still, what escapes every arrangement—the differend between beings naturally integrated and the event of being—nevertheless is not unfamiliar to us. Indeed, we ourselves are traversed by this separation. For the soul "to find itself and God is one and the same deed, and is timeless. It is . . . not included, not united, but rather is identical" with the godhead (Pf 85f.; W I,164). This identical deed is the work of non-attachment. The limit that it reveals in crossing it is therefore the one that incongruously splits in two the final instance into principle and origin.

There is no law without theticism; and to posit is to limit. The law essentially limits. Whoever transgresses, passes bounds. Whoever contravenes it passes boundaries—in the idiom of natural law, a transgressor is one who steps out of the place where he has been "seated." To their misfortune, five Labdacides and four Atrides so left the natural place where each had been seated.

If eternal law differs from natural law as "insitting" differs from "seating," they also differ as delimitation and limitation. Eckhart, as we have seen, carves the most severe natural boundaries. The normative order is stratified in strict contiguities. "Whatever stands on something else, its lowest part touches the highest part of that which is below." The posited, positive stases follow each other in such a way that the lower fringe of one traces the other's upper fringe. This amounts to a reciprocal *limitation,* as a stairs' landing ends a flight of steps for which it is the ceiling and begins the flight whose floor it is. The edifice constructed in this way is called natural law. Only one level in the continuous stratification suffers no reciprocal limitation of being. This is the supreme referent which determines and orders its other, the world. "God touches all things yet remains untouched." Putting things in place through "touching," or *delimitation,* is called eternal law.

Now it suffices to follow the instantiations so delimited to see the whole body of law that is imposed by limit slip away. Delimiting is a *transitive* act. The foundational God, who posits the seats with a view to ends, delimits his other. Continually creating it, he preserves the world in its limits. A being untouched in its insitting by what it posits inevitably exceeds all thetic delimitations. As both principle and end (*principium et finis idem,* LW III,190), he sustains the natural law. Delimitation thus puts the created in a position of receptivity. It circumscribes it by the dialectic between self-position and allo-position.

Delimitation is moreover *reflexive.* This results as much from perfect self-possession as it does from imperfect positions. The creator possesses himself in limiting himself in relation to the ideal possibles that are posited in him (perfect positions) yet are not translated into things actually created. He limits himself as well in relation to actual things (imperfect positions) since he is creator only over against the created. In Eckhart's words, divine insitting is entirely for the sake of "seating" the created. Outside the stratified edifice that reflects him, God is neither *begin* {beginning} nor end.

This entails a consequence that shatters the edifice. Divine delimitation, i.e. eternal law, is really quite *passive*. "I am a cause of God's being God. If I were not, then God would not be God" (DW II,504; S II,149 {W II,275}). This now is the limit on which our knowledge stumbles but which for Eckhart is what his thought is all about—the limit between foundation and ground. Eckhart boldly puts the foundational God and the created I in a parallel receptivity. If opposite the first being there were no other beings that he founds, there would also no longer be a first being. "Before there were creatures, God was not God" (DW II,492; S II,146 {W II,271}). This "before" here signals the condition. It points to the ground of God which is energetically identical with the uncreated ground of the soul. The duality of God and man appears only as I step out of this one, originary ground. Hence the passivity of the foundation; the created I delimits God as creator.

Transitive, reflexive, and passive, the law by reciprocal delimitation of order (not of being) is lastly *telic by subservience*—mercenary. "Those who seek anything in their work or act for any 'why' are serfs and mercenaries" (DW II,253; S II,57 {W II,97}). In the telic edifice of nature, the immediate end naturally desired by all things is the level of being that precedes them in rank. As their ultimate "why," the highest rank, the foundational God, serves as their magnet. Serving such a God, however, I make of myself a serf and a mercenary, a slave fettered in the teleocratic shackles called the order of nature. Eckhart has seen that in the relation between master and slave, roles get reversed as soon as they are fixed. As I ask of God salvation, as I desire God, I have already reduced him to a provider and hence to a slave.[42] The "natural desire for God" which, for Aquinas, pointed to our connaturality with him here only indicates a *perversion* in the system of ends, a system where the supreme end serves as the guarantee for natural coherence and where, consequently, the first being is degraded to the last of the serfs. Such instrumentalist perversion, it is true, has infected the principle of telic continuity from its very institution on.[43]

With these multiform delimitations, the slippage of the law toward the origin has already occurred.

From where indeed can a closed system—such as this one, marked by transitive, reflexive, passive, mercenary trajectories—at all be described? Hardly from within that system. Continuous teleology necessarily refers back to a condition itself not conceivable in terms of ends. This condition remains a-topical, the incongruous other of nature, an other prior to the law and "its nature is to be without a nature" (DW II,120; S II, 9 {W II,32}). In order to think the *principle* and its self-limitation by position, Eckhart compares God to the commander-in-chief of an army, stationed at the head and followed by commanders subordinated according to their rank (DW II,122;

S II,10 {W II,33}); subordinated, that is, by the principle of gradation. However, to think the *origin* without relation to the posited, he can only speak from a non-place that does not figure in the hierarchy of degrees, places, contiguities, limits, and hence of nature as well as of law.

For the Roman philosophers, memory was this non-place from which nature could be described as a closed system.[44] In Eckhart, things are more complicated as he takes account of normative nature so it can be enclosed, disfigured, erased. For that he has to show how *non-attachment,* the originary activity (not opposable to any passivity), is one and the same as the *godhead,* the originary actuality (not opposable to any potentiality).

In order to describe nature, it is first of all necessary for Eckhart to step outside of that construct that he, as a theoretician of natural law, put together to posit nature as he does. And he has to do so not to occupy some Archimedean point, but rather to let nature become a phenomenon. This activity of letting-be (*lâzen*), which alone permits one to see, is what Eckhart calls "non-attachment." This is the philosophical attitude *par excellence,* to withdraw one's hand from the phenomenon so as to see its conditions. It is opposed to arguing claims. Accordingly, the natural teleocracy is just an issue about which people advance claims. One has to be strongly attached to the will to make a case for the common good, which is its natural end; strongly attached to drives to make a case for procreation, which is the drive's natural end; attached to life, to make a case for the supreme being, which is its natural end. . . . But whoever makes a case for finality does a poor job of describing phenomena. Advocacy is not the work of thought. Philosophy begins where advocacy leaves off,[45] and where it seeks to see its conditions, which are without "why" (*sunder warumbe,* DW I,90; S I,78 {W I,117}).

Now, divine actuality is without a why, too. The foundational God has a why, namely, the system of limits by which he determines hegemonic nature. The "without why" renders the system indeterminate. It introduces discontinuity and illimitation into it. Hence it halts the normative functioning of the play of limitations and destitutes the hegemony.

Just as previously with the Milesians, *peras* here becomes secondary compared with *apeiron.* The abyss that separates them runs between the godhead, which has neither opposites nor subordinates, and God as the foundation and end of nature. Eckhart's contemporaries proved more disturbed by this gap between the boundless and all figures of the limit than would have been his distant Greek initiators. Being is without limits since it is without nature and without place. It is the other to all beings because it is dislodged from every and all natural places. To the descriptions of the origin as identity, operation, event, "being" as verb, and enunciative birth it is thus necessary to add *apeiron*—illimitation in the active sense of "letting ends be." *Peras* presides over the rhythm of limitations. If the law is essentially concerned with limits—limits posited by a legislator and observed by subjects—then not only all limits are engulfed between *peras* and *apeiron,* but so too is all law.

The identity of God's ground and the soul's ground as Eckhart seeks to think it can then be described furthermore as the identity of one and the same "letting." Both a detached man and the godhead "let the world be." For man, this does not entail a conflict with whatever he may come to possess. I could be the most cultivated of men, says Eckhart, but as long as I do not cling to this mental wealth "with its before and its after"—with the bedazzlement into which I anticipate stunning an audience before opening my mouth in public and fondly recalled long thereafter—and so, if I cultivate my refinement "without the shackles of any images" it may stir in me, I would nevertheless be detached. Likewise for the godhead. It is the fullness of possible being, but by its illimitation it remains unattached to any being or any world.

This already amounts to thinking differently and elsewhere. In order to question position, opposition, and all positivity, one has to detach oneself from the thetic gesture and hence from arguing claims "in the name of some noun."

Eckhart says non-attachment and letting-be (*gelâzenheit*) together make up a single thing. He, the architect of one of the most rigid systems of natural legislation there is, thus essentially seeks to disturb the attitude that clings to "whys," that posits referential beings and pleads causes. Not that his left hand does not know what his right is doing. We have seen that normative nature *cannot but* be erased as soon as the conditions of theticism are opened to inquiry. Eckhart maximizes the work of natural limitation, and he makes it abort. One could not stress more clearly the legislative tragedy in these conditions.

This, then, is how far one can and must push the description of the legislative system, which is nature, namely, to the point where its very coherence proves to depend on an origin transgressing the system. In order to lay down the law, the telically definite presupposes an indefinite outside the law. In terms of what would be a mechanical metaphysics, for one force to be able to subjugate a rival force and hold it in its rank, subordination requires more than a *force majeure* establishing ranks. Such a relation in a mechanical system can only be conceived from a viewpoint outside the system. In terms of the logic of opposites, the arrangements of contraries such as insitting-seating, delimiting-limiting, untouched-touching, etc., are not even thinkable as dividing a whole unless a place be given—but which is not the place of any element in the arrangement—prior to all items placed in opposition. Where then does Eckhart place himself as he posits the subordinations that make up nature? Perhaps because he comes at a moment when one thetic era is closing upon itself, he seems to know better than others in his tradition that all reasoning about principles presupposes a point of departure outside principles. For Aristotle, this point of departure was opinion and its reasoning, dialectics. In Eckhart, the point of departure is the double bind of a determining principle and an indetermining origin. If it is true that a system can be thought and posited only out of some extra-systemic knowing, then this double bind is the legislative labor of a nature that demarcates differences and that we know at the same time to be broken in advance by the lack of differentiation.

This knowing acquaints us with *the natural differend*. In order to see how it plays itself out, let us return to a text already partially cited, this time, however, not for the singularization that it emphasizes ("Brother Eckhart . . ."), but for the *chorismos* that it traces between the originary godhead and the principial God:

> God becomes. Where all creatures declare him, God comes to be. When I stood in the ground, in the bottom, in the river and fount of the godhead, no one asked me where I was going or what I was doing: there was no one to ask me. But when I departed by flowing forth outside, all creatures cried out: 'God.' If anyone asked me: 'Brother Eckhart, when did you leave the house?' this would prove that before I was still inside. (Pf 181; {W II,81})

These lines do not mention nature. Still they point no less rigorously to the differend between origin and principle, or between *nasci* and *natura*. If *nature* designates the totality composed of "God" and "all creatures," then the metaphors such as "ground," "bottom," "river," "fount," "house," and "godhead" point to *being-born*. These metaphors suggest a rising movement, an emergence outside nature. "I *departed*" in flowing forth outside, "'when did you *leave* the house?'" Here again, nature is originary (*oriri*, to rise) inasmuch as it is born (*nasci*, to be born). Among these metaphors, the two that have drawn the most attention—"ground" and "godhead"—are perhaps also the most misleading since they express less directly this upsurge or this egress. It is not enough, then, to remember that Eckhart teaches a certain identity between God's ground and the soul's ground as well as a certain separation between the foundational God and the ground of the godhead. It is furthermore necessary not to misconstrue the originary ground that is "prior" to foundation. To better grasp the double bind imposed by the natural differend, it will be useful to clarify what is meant here by priority, by identity, and by difference. The lines cited supply some indications.

The metaphors clearly suggest two disparate figures to which primacy belongs in the order of things—one too many, according to the precautionary axiom not to step back indefinitely in the search for conditions, but to secure some last instance that is simple. Creatures cry out to their concordant other: "God"; but God comes to be from out of the discordant other, the godhead. It is evident that each of these figures signifies God, and it is equally evident that a substantial becoming of the one from the other is excluded. If becoming is here to be understood as a process, as a rising, a movement of manifestation, then from *natura* regulating the relations between creator and creature, on the one hand, to the *birth* of the pair creator/creature, on the other, there is a break in the manner of being. Principle and origin are set apart as are a thought entity and an event. A conceptual strategy indicating which relations of subordination are to obtain is necessarily a nominative strategy; it names beings so as to dispose of them according to an order. A conceptual strategy that tells the manner in which an order manifests itself stresses, rather, the givenness of the order; it follows the contrary of the name and is infinitive. It speaks in the middle voice that always thematizes being. Eckhart's statement concerning God as origin can thus be underscored by the following two parenthetical terms: "It is his nature [*nasci*] to be without a nature [*natura*]." The disparity so introduced in God, which for seven centuries has disconcerted readers of Eckhart, signifies the differend between a nominal understanding and a verbal understanding of being. From the God that is topical because it occupies a rank—the summit—in the system of nature, to the atopic, anonymous God without nature, there is a differend, since no common law covers being *qua* entity and being *qua* event. Eckhart also speaks of life to designate this event. "Life is a kind of outpouring in which something first ferments and flows into itself, discharging all that it is into all that it is, before pouring forth and spreading outside" (LW II,26). Thus "life," too, bespeaks a disparity, namely, between the originary (non-determinate, non-limited) boiling of possibles and the boiling or principial precipitation into an actual order (determined by delimitations and limitations). Moving freely among other possibles, I have nothing with which to compare myself.[46] Once interposed between higher and lower strata, freedom gets stifled by comparisons, standards, and norms. This is a non-symmetrical disparity, emphasized in Eckhart by a "before" that postpones nature, constitutes it after the fact.

Needless to add, this differing does not oppose "insitting" and "seating in the other"; not the thetic same and its equally thetic other. Creator and created are mutually exclusive, but they are jointly exhaustive of the incidences—"eternal" and "natural" in the narrow sense—of nature laying down the law. A differend, to restate it, does not separate the same and *its* other within a genus, but separates these contraries as a whole and *an* other; so one has the congruent pair creator/created and the incongruous event of their originary rising or appearing, i.e., of their manifestation. An irredeemable differend under the law of contraries since it cleaves the generic block of an im-pertinent alterity, outside of genera.

The series of metaphors also allows one to grasp the *genesis of the differing*. Eckhart is explicit. It arises from an act of utterance which "declares" (*erklaeren*), that is, which "renders very clear." The foundational God comes to be at that place where all creatures render his name very clear, where he is there *for* them, *their* other. Eckhart would have provoked less tumult if he had stated the opposite, which nevertheless says exactly the same thing: Creatures come to be at that place where the foundational God declares and names them, where they are there *for* him, *his* other. The two "declarations" are strictly equivalent. They articulate the same genesis of the genus creation, with the contraries—creator and creature—that exhaust that genus. The declaration of names here is not to be confused with the enunciation of the Word, which is originary in regard to God and me (and the world). As opposed to enunciation, Eckhart conceives declaration as playing itself out between these two antitheses. Creatures declare God—they "cried out"—but they do not utter the godhead. The distinction between the two types of utterance allows one to grasp better what otherness is at issue between the cluster of metaphors pertaining to "godhead" (*ursprunc,* origin, ground, house, bed, river, source) and those pertaining to "God" (*begin,* principle, foundation, creator/creature, trinity, natural law). Between these two clusters there is not even the continuity that would tie a speaker to the "communication," as we say, in which he expresses himself. For Eckhart there is communication only among pledged ranks. On the other hand, it would be difficult to imagine a continuum that is more tenuous—neither substantial nor even formal in any case—than the one between a speaker and his expression; and yet it is just such a continuum that Eckhart takes good care not to construe between the "boiling" life that is the godhead and its boiling over into creator/creature.[47] This latter pair presents itself "outwardly" by *reciprocal declarations*. Between the creator declaring the creature, and the creature declaring the creator, there is continuity through a give and take, the great concatenation which is nature-as-law. But if the genesis by which these contraries separate themselves from the "inward" accumulation is not even comparable to expression (and even less to some emanation), then otherness between originary *birth* and principial *nature* indeed separates into disparate and nevertheless ultimate functions.

The six traits of the legislative system that I have pointed out suggest in which sense nature is a normative fantasm in Eckhart. The law's communication, its poietic character, its sequential incidents, the formal hierarchy resulting from the greater or lesser capacity a being has of externalizing itself, the primacy of topographic over causal schemes, and lastly a certain reciprocity between limitation and delimitation—all these traits make nature an order. We also saw that such an order can only be spoken of from a viewpoint that does not figure in its arrangement. In this sense nature is indeed a fantasm: a totality of representations, but a generated totality. Eckhart repeats unremittingly, to the point of incurring the most official reproofs, that to satisfy the very requirements of systematicity, the genesis of the legislative system which is the natural order of beings demands an origin exterior to that order. But as this origin cannot be found among beings, for then it would also be found within the arrangement, it cannot be named either. It subverts the system even as it gives rise to it. By positing the principle, Eckhart argues "for" nature. But since it is a closed system, this organization demands moreover a condition that breaks with its constituents, a condition at odds with and that gives rise to it. Following Eckhart in his description of that origin as the pure event of giving, an event other than beings and in a disparate otherness, one would be arguing both "for" and "against" nature. The dissension cannot be settled either by appeal (there is no last resort above the "for and the against") or by amicable agreement (God is amiable, lovable, but one cannot love the godhead) or by rejection (destituting nature does not mean jettisoning it). Eckhart places us both under the law and outside it.

One may call this condition "tragic," or whatever one pleases. In any case, the disparity between normative nature and the equally normative (though in a different manner) piercing through nature remains striking. The principial bond maximizes the fantasm, and it particularizes us. As to the originary bind, it singularizes us. I call "tragic" the ultimate conflict between the thetic, integrative impulse and the expulsive effects of mortality that are time and the singular, the singularizing event. Eckhart recognizes we are bound by a gap between beings and being that is more disjoining that the "ontological difference." He recognizes a double bind impossible to ratify, hence a differend.

The transgressive strategy announced itself in the slippages toward this differend that have been pointed out. Where do these slippages lead us? The task now is to grasp in which way their strategy singularizes us even as the legislative impulse universalizes natural ends and, by subsumption under them, particularizes us. The very program that Eckhart claims to follow in everything he says is summarized in being as a singularizing event.

The thought of being does not meet up with the metaphysics of order. How, then, does Eckhart understand being?

CHAPTER 13

Nature Denatured by the Origin

> "When I preach it is my wont to speak about non-attachment, and of how man should become free of himself and all things. Secondly, that one should be re-imaged back into the simple good that is God. Thirdly, that one should remember the great nobility that God has put into the soul, so that man may thereby come marvelously to God. Fourthly, I speak of the purity of the divine nature, for the brilliance of God's nature is unspeakable. God is a word, a word unspoken outside." (DW II,528f.; S II,151 {W I,177})
>
> —Meister Eckhart

In these four points, Eckhart outlines as many strategies for thinking otherwise than in the name of nature. The group is obviously less than systematic. But on each point, the principle of continuous integration loses its power of univocal legislation, a loss due to the intrusion of an occurrent sense of being. In the exhortation to non-attachment, this descriptive event signifies "becoming free." The points that follow this first one develop its implications. The content of non-attachment is to be "re-imaged"; its terminus, "coming to God"; and its logic, the neutrality of a "word unspoken outside"—that is, as we will see, of a word uttered within. There is a neutrality to this fourth point since it is the only one where Eckhart does not state that something "should" happen. Understood on its own terms, apart from any protreptic interest, non-attachment thus leads to an event already thematized by the other points, but more obliquely, an event that *happens* (the birth of the Word within), that is described in the middle voice, and which—as the goal of that peculiar great work—renders us indeterminate even as it singularizes us.

These counter-strategies exclude us from nature. To summarize these just as briefly, they dissolve the correlative theses by which the fantasm had maintained its hegemony, the theses of a certain possession of self, of an image measurable against its model, of an intra-psychic order organized according to nobility, that is, to rank; and lastly, of an intra-divine order serving as the eternal law for nature.

Thus not only the magnetic pull exerted by a city that was or will be slips away, but so does the teleology of an order through gradations of subjection. Eckhart seeks to think an ultimate authority traversed in its very position by a nominative-infinitive dissension (in the word *ursprunc* one could then hear "originary fissure" just as well as "originary upsurge"). On each of the four points, the slippages of theticism due to a verb in the middle voice injure the sovereignty of the noun. Thus there are dissensions between the proper end and 'detaching oneself' (*abescheiden*), that is, 'becoming free'; between the *a priori* order and 're-imaging' (*înbilden*); between a certain mimesis and 'piercing through' (*durchbrechen*); and between nature and 'uttering' (*sprechen*).

These pairs, which don't really pair up, help render more explicit the double bind under which the principle and the origin place us. The origin is indeed best spoken of through verbs in the middle voice, each of which thematizes the verb "to be."

"Detaching oneself": against the appropriation of ends

"Detach yourself": One would be hard pressed to find in the history of philosophy an imperative that enjoins more clearly to *return from tragic denial*. The imperative strikes the principial regime in its originary condition.

The denial, it will be recalled, accounts for and will always account for the force of the natural metaphysician in us. Denying that there is dissension in the ultimate authority is a hard blow by the metaphysician. He strikes a name endowed with authority as one strikes a plaque; and he strikes out of existence any allegiance not hailing that plaque. He sustains his fantasm through strokes of incorporation and exclusion. He—who exactly? The man of the law who severs what is proper from what is inappropriate because it is inappropriable under the name. In the face of these regulative strokes and these regimental cuts, to detach oneself would mean to receive the improper that does not bring with it the hegemonic blow. The man of non-attachment is not a friend of the man of law; but both of them are me. Similarly, expropriation is the enemy of appropriation. But both of them constitute me and put me at odds with myself.

As the counter-strategy that exerts a different pressure on the gradation, non-attachment takes something away from us. Eckhart does not describe this taking away for its own sake, but always as *a departure from the principial strategy*. Still, this retraction must not be misconstrued. Originarily, to detach oneself does not mean to withdraw into one's inner retreat. Eckhart has little patience for interiority, nor does he invite one to a retreat. On the contrary, it is Martha, the active, who has the better part, not Mary, the contemplative (DW III,481–492; S III,171–79 {W I,79–89}). Nor does he withdraw from normative maximizations as, when infatuations for some sovereign name have collapsed, one proceeds to criticize it. We have seen Eckhart ardently maximizing the integrative continuity and hence the name of nature—but not its hegemony, which would be univocal. Rather, he traces, carves out, and pursues a withdrawal leading outside the *simple* attraction for this continuity that seems most evidently to bear the imprint of common sense. In non-attachment, the natural metaphysician remains what it is: a metaphysician of nature. But he retracts absolute theticism. He posits the proper, and yet he lets it be.

When Eckhart speaks of *abescheiden,* one has to know how to read in order to avoid becoming enmeshed in the web that is to be undone. The first imperative in the text quoted states that man should become free of himself. This is to say, he is to free himself from what he has—from what he is—*properly*. One is to free oneself from the name: "The name 'I' is suppressed since [God] and the soul are so entirely one that God cannot have any property," no more than can the soul (DW III,338; S III,118 {W II,38}).

Thus understood, non-attachment *differentiates the determinations* that nature integrates by subsumptions and that the intellect reflects in concepts and judgments. Stated otherwise, it works in the service of specular reflection. In the following we will see the manner in which an *originary indetermination* is at work in these integrations.

With the specific character, as with the emancipation that strips it away, it is a matter of the "me." Here and there—which me?

For Eckhart, the speculative mystic, the me is *that from which* one must become detached. The nature that returns when we drive it away, the character that we fashion in society . . . all that is bad singularity. As for Augustine, that sort of singularization disperses us externally. Reason is what recenters us. It seizes what it is looking for internally. When non-attachment serves as the differentiating factor, there is thus quite a retreat to the inner tribunal. It initiates the *intus ire:* "The more [man] detaches himself from all things and returns into himself, and the more he apprehends all things clearly with his reason without recourse to the external, the more he is human" (DW I,250 S I,141). Here the verb to detach is constructed in the reflexive and denotes the return of reason to itself; it connotes interiority, describes the intuition of forms and thus ideal ends, in brief, it shows the way to the human nature in each of us. The imperative—of the most classical sort—thus tells us to live in accordance with this nature, not in accordance with our particularities.

The man that does all this is speculative. He knows that the intelligible mirrors the degrees of being and that they are more valuable than the sensibles. Following this gradation, non-attachment universalizes me just as the concept and judgment universalizes the impression. Witness: "Relinquish that part of you that represents man and what you are and apprehend yourself purely in accordance with human nature." Non-attachment would thus be the condition not only for the grasping of essences by pure reflection but also for becoming human in accordance with the pure species. Why the appeal to nature? Because it is "more intimate to man and more closely related than he is to himself" (DW I, 420). Human is the species *that* you are. It is not being human *who* you are: not "you."

In what we call speculative mysticism, non-attachment is thus taken up by the system of subsumptions; and it is done so by Meister Eckhart himself. What is human, therefore, is he who is not fixated on his assets, he who has assumed and subsumed them. The specific character here is thus the particular. Eckhart also calls it the "dowry"; the universal species is "clarity." The dowry particularizes and encumbers our clear nature. In accordance with this differentiation, Eckhart speaks, in the first point of his programmatic declaration, of a practical *a priori* for attaining a speculative *a priori:* that man should liberate himself from himself *qua* specific substance, and that he should understand himself as a universal substance. In Aristotelian terms, non-attachment would mark the passage (this is excessively Aristotelian as it translates into practice an epistemic distinction) from primary to secondary substance, the passage from the me rendered opaque by all forms of composition, to the clear quiddity by definition.

But what exactly can it really mean to rid oneself of primary substance? It is strange advice: "You should detach yourself and leave behind all those things in you that cause a difference. Man [the individual] is in effect an accident of [human] nature. Therefore leave everything that is accidental in you and thus understand yourself in terms of human nature, free and indivisible" (DW II,381; S II,201). Whosoever follows this advice is really detached. He "wants nothing, knows nothing, possesses nothing" (DW II,488; S II,145). Here again, the epistemic Aristotelianism is displaced by the practical. To want, to know, and to have all figure among the inferior analogues, more precarious than are the superior ones that are the bounty, the truth, etc. The former belong to nature only by accident; the latter—the transcendental qualities—belong essentially. Following this idiom, to detach oneself means to pass from inferior analogic perfections to superior ones.

When it comes to interpretations of non-attachment, we are tempted to stop at this theory of the concept and of judgment that is extended—Eckhart says in his defense[48]—to morality. Eckhart teaches disdain for the singular—which is too impoverished ever to be reflected in a concept. He would speak as a metaphysician of the spirit bearing eternal reasons, as a rationalist placed midway between Augustine and Leibniz. His preference for the archetype rather than the ectype would be "ethics" because it would show that with which we should identify ourselves, to the bearer in us, not of the proper noun but of the common noun.

Nevertheless, what we have done here is to read these texts in reverse order. The *reflected* usage of the verb "to detach oneself" appeals to abstraction, to absolutization, to the mobile and thus to ends, to effort and thus to the will: to an agent. The *middle voice* indicates a way of thinking otherwise. It indicates that something "is going on," nothing more. It is descriptive, and of a process in which the agent is not master. Conjugated in the middle voice, the verb "to detach oneself" plunges the appropriating agent into anonymity. It emphasizes an expropriation that happens all the time.

It is a process that is incommensurable with the imperative of advancing from inferior degrees to superior ones. The originating strategy now in question does not lead to wanting, knowing, or having reasons in place of their replicas; it leads to wanting, knowing, having *nothing.* The thread of non-attachment fits in with a grand nomic construction only because, in this enveloping fabric itself, it speaks of an other, heteronomous condition. Followed for itself, it does not lead to a plenitude of determinations remote from the singular—to nature, the arsenal of essences that the intellect, reservoir of ideas, reflects—but always straight to an indeterminate given. *Straight,* since the originating point is distinguished from the principle in that it removes us from the intermediary points; *to an indeterminate* for, as a neutral process, non-attachment can no longer aim at speculative objects of definition or composition; it aims at the *given*—singularly.

Thus, in medieval Aristotelianism, what is it that gives of itself directly and always in an event affected by no agent, and thus outside of all subsumptive operations? Of what do we speak when we telescope the grades and say: Outside of X, this particular being has no more qualities than another?—"outside this pure nature, the angel has no more knowledge than this [piece of] wood here" (DW I,212; S I,126)? What is this "X" for the lack of which nothing would be left of it? It is, as we have seen, the actuality of being. Eckhart, we saw as well, rightly designates it by the liberated and pure nature (*die bloze, lautere nature,* ibid.)—pure, that is to say, without taking account of its composition. Just as for Thomas Aquinas the act of being is not modified according to the hierarchy of beings, but is only limited, so it is also in the originary strategy of non-attachment. Eckhart renders *esse* as *wesene* and speaks—Thomas would find nothing to fault in this—of the "simplicity and nudity of being." Where Thomas Aquinas would find a great deal to fault is when Eckhart adds: "Thus turn away from all things and apprehend yourself purely in being" (DW II,266; S II,59). Whosoever apprehends themselves thus can do without sovereign positions and subordinations.

But then again, what can be said about it?

"It is promised, I will live detached": Thus we do not speak in terms of having to apprehend oneself purely in being. There is no mention of *metanoia,* nor do we ask ourselves to what specific property we should devote ourselves: to the particular that lowers me or to the common that elevates me. In the eyes of non-attachment, all determinations—common or specific—are removed from the specific. Accordingly, to detach oneself will mean to allow oneself to expropriate determinations; to recognize a condition that renders us *indeterminate.*

In reducing nature to naked actuality, Eckhart erases the fixation on the principle of continuity. It is an erasure that he repeats in the equation-refrain "nature and being" (*wesen und nature*[49]). Can an orator that speaks in terms such as these be talking about extraordinary things? He will instead be speaking of our most ordinary condition, not of experiences that are literally ravishing, but of a knowledge evident to each and everyone. What is more ordinary than being and nature? To detach oneself is thus to turn to things and ourselves to the extent that they are actual; it is to turn from them and ourselves to the extent that these are bearers of a speculatively graspable being-such. Non-attachment is not a little piece of speculative mysticism.

Who detaches himself? If it is a question of an ultimate condition, the response would be: All that is detaches itself in its own manner of being. And if this manner of being is naturally subsumptive under ends, then nature always detaches itself from the subsumptions that nevertheless fashion it. Thus fashioned, it is not pure. These fashions limit it through ends. *Pure nature* and nature as a *telic arrangement* differ, says Eckhart, as being differs from nothingness. Whence the two philosophemes that result from the analogy of attribution (from creation as "loan"): "Being is God" (LWI,156), just as the consequence that follows from this: "All creatures are a pure nothingness" (DW I,69; S I,65). It is not the ordering of forms that is something. Thus the appropriation of the basis of ends cannot be the last word on nature. Non-attachment adds to it the condition of expropriation, whereby it denatures nature.

We can certainly say that this counter-strategy is also "moral." The knowledge of our expropriation outside all constituted existence is indeed a practical knowledge. But if morality implies a choice, then here it is not just one more either-or. It is not just that either you like your particular features, or you appropriate the species and love all that is human. But rather: *both* the normative appropriation *and* the subtractive expropriation. Non-attachment thereby alienates proper ends.

He that attaches himself to no form and keeps himself free from natural ends is *in this* necessarily of one single and the same pure nature with God. Eckhart describes this necessity as a constraint that only the free man knows "when a free spirit maintains itself, as it must, in non-attachment, it forces God [to come] toward its being. If it could maintain itself without form and without any accident, it would revert to the [being] of God."[50]

"If it could. . . ," but it cannot.[51] This is a way of saying that the condition without form or accident is always nothing but a co-condition. It leaves the nomothesis intact while detaching itself from it. The principial law posits the uncreated here and the created there; the originary law leaves the positions there in "one being and one nature." Non-attachment unites man without form in his actuality to the God without form in his actuality. Eckhart does not thus propose two beings to compare their respective being, finding the one that pertains to God greater than the one that pertains to man, and then to undertake an abstraction in which that which is "naturally" unequal ends up appearing equal nonetheless. He has no such intention of denying the inequality of essences. He would never deny the subordinations that compose nature-as-law. He denies that with the inequality of essential properties we would have said something regarding being. He *denies that in denying* the undertow outside constituted phenomenality we know the legislative condition in its final instance.

What, then, does it mean that non-attachment wants us? We must recall again what we know, even if poorly: That the proper ends do not uniformly lay down the law, but that an other law always evicts us from the world where ends rule. Non-attachment keeps open the differend between the principle that integrates phenomena and the origin that dephenomenalizes them, singularizes them.

"Re-imaging oneself": against the a priori *imagination of order*

As the second point of his program, Meister Eckhart states that we should "re-image ourselves in the simple good that is God." According to all evidence, "re-imaging" runs against the grain of a program of imaging. What program, how against the grain, why "oneself" and "in"? A number of interests intersect here in any case: the visible world, the image of the intelligible; man, the image of God; the concept, the specular image of the thing; the multiple, the composite image of the simple; fiction, the twisted image of the true; evil, the exhausted image of the good. . . . Eckhart accordingly gives a number of meanings to the pair of "imaging, re-imaging." Here again the slippage of the transitive voice to the middle voice will be critical for the question of nature and its law. It will mark the sliding of difference into a differend.

In order to understand this, it is first necessary to follow Eckhart pushing the prestige of the image to its peak, then keep pushing a point so as to topple it; in other words, maximizing nature and then denaturing it.

Obviously his primary interest has to do with paradigmatism. Now Eckhart posits this paradigmatism and erases it in the same gesture: "God carries all images in himself—not as the soul or some other creature, but as God: in him there is nothing new nor any image" (DW II,600; S II,180). God carries in himself all images and no image. The full is the empty. This is an aporia that must be followed up to the point—precisely at that point—where the mechanics of opposites is broken.

This aporia serves to distinguish paradigmatism from another manner of carrying images in oneself: "as the soul or some other creature." Eckhart makes a division between archetypes and concepts. In the archetypal world and in the simple fact that is God, there is never anything new. On the other hand, in the soul there is something new, namely, the images (*bilde*) that it acquires. It amasses them, being fabricated from opinions and in entertaining ideas, in abstracting concepts, in cultivating views and fictions, in exalting convictions. A man cultivates himself (*bilden*) if he can see in his imagination ever-new things and if he stimulates these representations. God as well possesses images but he is not cultivated. They are his without his receiving or activating them. He does not acquire them. At the pinnacle one does not work. We do not make anything, no image in the sense of *bilden*. He harbors in him images not as representations or as copies (*abbilde*), but as models (*urbilde*). In this he is the simple good. The multiple goods demand of man that he activate himself and hoard them; the good, in which the images we can accumulate are prefigured, is simple, without any activity. The copies are hierarchized violently and roughly; the models smooth out the bumps. "In God, the images of all things are equal, but they are the images of unequal things. The highest angel and the soul and the mosquito have an equal image in God" (DW I,148; S I,102). Moreover, they are God himself: "Man is fully the equal [to God] and entirely the same as [God]" (DW III,343; S III,120).

Here we have the prestige of the paradigm or the archtype pushed to the peak. Eckhart takes on the job of promoting the fantasmic, the most classic job in philosophy, and raises the images in grades, from inequality to equality to identity. The plenitude creates emptiness by unity, that is to say, by identity. "[T]here, further than a thousand miles but also as close as the place where I am at present; there is where there is abundance and plenitude. . . , there, there is single unity" (DW II,86s.; S I,240).[52]

It is no different when it come to the concept and its prestige. We see it in the aporia according to which the full is the empty. God carries images in himself; at the same time there are no images in him. What does this mean unless that the ideas are not abstract? The pure good gathers ideas together. Thus we, in order to make the forms of things of a varied morphology enter into our soul, should resort to diverse acts, notably abstraction. "Image" thus translates simultaneously—but separably—the idea pre-existing experience as well as the abstract concept of experience. According to this last scheme, identity unites the knower with the known, in one single *energeia*.[53]

Thus the aporia of carrying with oneself all images and no image is applied to man as well. Our representations have a mode that follows from the work put in to acquire them. It is the labor of imaging which, pertaining to the beings outside of us, engages in abstraction; pertaining to the inside concepts, in deduction; and pertaining to the beings below us, in intuition. The labor of representation does not end in something simple and it does not provide reassurance. It causes flight; the soul "cannot find rest in any mode, and it always hastens to pass beyond all modes" (DW II,64; S III,22). The man who no longer takes flight, the detached man, is "liberated from all the images of which he never knew" (DW I,12; S I,46). The work of receptive-active cognition ceases. I find myself a participant in divine fullness and emptiness. The Meister Eckhart that situates himself midway between Augustine and Leibniz, as we saw, brings the concept to its height in emptying it of representations and in filling it with eternal reasons or ideas.

On the two roads of promotion—of filling up or evacuation—we deny the indeterminate, and we exalt the same simplicity. In both instances the pinnacle is the "simple good." Accordingly, the consummation of the eidetic hierarchy in simple incandescence in no way incinerates paradigmatism as such. To the contrary, the concentration of modes at their acme is an integral part of it. The summit of a pyramid is its integrating part.

Eckhart also shows that the fullness of images is the void along a more Aristotelian scheme. "A carpenter who builds a house pre-images it in himself" (DW II,397; S II,107). The image is neither ideal nor abstract, but guides and accompanies—and in this sense integrates again—production. As a directive image, it exists at first in the imagination of the builder, then in his plan; it directs each phase of the construction and finally is offered to the view of all, realized in wood and stone. It directs the technical enterprise. It anticipates its end—the function that it loses at its height, that is to say, once the building is in fact crowned. Similar to anagogic *erôs,* technical teleology loses its plenitude in reaching it, in entelechy.

Finally, the last scheme according to which Eckhart has the image contribute to serving hegemony is a trinitarian scheme. Man will rule over all things, in the image of the Father: "Where the Son is re-imaged, the soul also must be re-imaged. All creatures are submitted to the soul thus introduced and included and enclosed in God" (DW I,399). But as thus introduced and sovereign, it is one with God and consequently no longer an image.

In these diverse positions the *eidos* auto-erases itself in being folded back into the archic fold where it deployed itself. This is where the dialectic of the full and the empty does quite a nice job of sustaining sovereign nature. So, Eckhart pushes these figures of identity again, so much so that the eidetic foundation topples over into the "ground without ground"; and that the denial promoting hegemony finds itself revoked.

As the intellectual known for heading up his generation,[54] Eckhart departs from the rank and file where with great panache he did not avoid a good fray with adversarial theses. He confounds them by leaving representation . . .

We see this in the *impossibility of thinking the ground in terms of images* or the images in terms of ground. In place of entirely feudal subordinations there is indetermination.[55] We always ask for products of the imagination; Eckhart asks of desire. Thus "desire" is here called "imagined fulfillment." But desire imagines itself replete with gifts only if it has posited beforehand the giver and the receiver: the lord and the serf. We can desire the peak only after having posited subordinations. Concerning this aprioric position, Eckhart says that it should not be like this. In arguing against mediation by images he takes the principle of continuity as his target. The imagination desires the peak in positing continuity from the bottom to the top; that is, in making itself an aprioric imagination of order. The argument challenges nature as a fantasm.

In place of this fantasm and his principle, in the place of order, of images, of feudal allegiances, of nature—what? The "pure" nature of images. In it there is no longer giver or receiver. "The ground of God is my ground and my ground, the ground of God" (DW I,90; S I,78). We can see this is an altogether different identity than the simplicity in which hierarchies culminate. God is no longer the lord of anybody nor the foundation of anything. He is an identity prior to attributes and appropriations, "before [being] takes a name, before it erupts" outside of the ground without ground (DW III,179; S III,65)—before the fantasmic imagination had credence. This new strategy of discrediting the name attacks the possessive genitive. If the ground of God is my ground, it is no longer only that of God; and if my ground is the ground of God, it is no longer mine. To the extent that the ground is one and the same, it can be neither a divine nor human *eidos*. It would be necessary that it be both at once; but then the eidetic function that is to determine something in terms of its proper end is plunged into the absurd. The determinative sinks away with the possessive. Pure nature is not the nature "of" something or "of" someone. Indeterminate, it disables the genitive function. Accordingly, to say that in the ground God and man are *entbildet,* unimaged, deprived of images, eidetically expropriated, is to pre-empt transitive theticism. It is to weaken the aprioric imagination "of" order.

From here there is an answer—a negative one, but we cannot convey it more clearly—to the question: What to do? The single ground that is not a common ground proves to be unfit to serve as the directing *eidos,* as the aim, as the "why." Accordingly, in regard to the question of what one should do, Eckhart can only answer by alluding to the aim in sight: "Without why you should accomplish your work from your most interior ground" (DW I,90; S I,78). Without why means the basis will not indicate where to go, nor what to do. The word disabuses us of the *eidos*. It is an illusion of reaching that which assigns an end to action. The word disabuses us both about the acting and about the making that perceives the *eidos* as end. *Praxis* carries it in itself, *poiesis* posits it outside of itself. The diverse functions of the image traditionally converge precisely on this assignment of ends.

The imperative of "without why" dispossesses the aprioric imagination. In the principle of continuity that it varies, it deadens the nerve: finality.

During these most active years, Eckhart was a prior in Strasbourg. Not long before, stained glass windows executed in the style of the new realism had been installed in the wings of the cathedral for the instruction of the people. What should happen when a spectator said: "There is Charles the Bald and Louis the German at the Strasbourg Oath"? Eckhart's answer: "The image is not of itself, and it is not for itself" (DW I,269). The spectator that stops himself at the new techniques and colors misses it as an image. The image *of* somebody does not have its own being. It is not from itself—not from, nor departing from itself—but from and starting from what it represents: Charles, Louis. It is not for itself either, but for the spectator. There is a double non-existence of the image[56] that for Eckhart results from the very status of being created. What is created receives its being without any mediation, as does the image. "It receives its being immediately, over the will, it naturally leaves and pushes outside of nature, as a branch pushes out from a tree" (DW I,265s.; S I,149). In a faithful portrait, a face is offered just as immediately as a branch outside a tree. The being of an image is neither glass nor color; its existence is manifestation. If we stop at the image for itself, we will not understand what is going on when we say: "Here is Charles." The existence of the image is understood only as event—or, in Eckhart's words—as "suffering" (DW III,438). The portrait of Charles suffers Charles. As an image, it is entirely suffering, it submits what it is to him. It is nothing more than a process of showing, a process of *imaging.*

The anti-teleologic, extra-teleologic strategy substitutes a verb for the noun "image." The program stated in its second point "that we should re-image ourselves in the simple good that is God." This is a succinct formula where the verb "to re-image oneself" is in the reflexive. Now, to designate the occurrent identity in the ground, he can hardly place himself in the reflexive—no more than the simple good can serve as an eidetic image to some being or to all beings. To re-image oneself is a process where what occurs is the same thing that happens in non-attachment and distillation. The forms reduce themselves to formlessness; the images to imagelessness. It is a process that in no way functions to reintegrate my model into God. It consists of losing both the model and God and of rediscovering the image without image as well as God without God; the detached man "is in turn re-imaged in the first image without image" DW II,456; S II,129). The first image is first just as the godhead is first in relation to divine characteristics, without an image, just as the godhead is not the idea of God. It is a primacy that no longer designates the pinnacle out of which flows the forms that are to be appropriate. Eckhart topples the primacy by removing the attributes.

In the process of re-imaging, the image is not exactly erased. It loses its canonic eminence. In Eckhart's idiom, it is "left to be." In the Aristotelian idiom, which is also that of Eckhart, it is degraded to an accident. The principle that organizes nature—the continuity of ends—integrates the *eidos* in its multiple positions. The eidetic posits and arranges the modes of existence. Fabrication, species, hypostatic genera, transcendental perfections, divine persons: everywhere the proper end determines the mode. For Eckhart, this means everywhere the image determines the why. It maximizes teleology, institutes it as a principle. Thus "only the accidents establish a why" (DW II,266; S II,58 for *zuoval* and *mitewesen,* cf. DW III,341; S III,119). The great principle of telic continuity is here reduced to an accident.

Is this a hopelessly tortuous confusion? Not at all. Eckhart completed his School lessons. Where then is he situated, and from where does he speak, he who declares the principle is an accident? In his place on the scale, properly, in the modes of existence? Yes and no. Yes, since there is no site where one does not make use of you and where you wouldn't make use of another, even if just in "imaging" him. The natural order desires that the highest part of the inferior touches the lowest part of the superior. And no, for—we saw it as well—the integration by subjection can be described only from elsewhere. We imagine, we "image," the ground; but we "re-image" ourselves in the ground from which we speak of the foundation, from which it is articulated (middle voice).

From the second programmatic point it is certainly necessary to retain the vertical gallery of images. But it is also necessary to retain *the elsewhere* that is the process of re-imaging. Not that it adds to nature some non-integrated site. We will understand this programmatic point when we understand how the "re-imaging," in its transitive usage (re-imaging the soul, DW I,39; S I,200) harmonizes the uniformly legislative apparatus attribute-image-end-why-nature, and how, in the middle voice (tortuous, but as in the cucurbit), it once again dissolves this apparatus.

Thus, there is a sliding from the transitive and from the reflexive to the middle voice. This indicates a condition, as in "this is," "this is going on," "this happens," "this is shown." In an analogous fashion, the imperfect announces the condition of being—man should become "free from all images, as virginal as he was when he was not" (DW I,25; S I,52)—the condition that the aorist would more appropriately express.

"To re-image oneself in the simple good"—the phrase certainly cuts short the theory of the return to the *eidos* of all *eidé* in a Christianized Neoplatonism. Such a return would tighten up the continuous gradation by focusing all things on their last end. For them this means re-integrating their models. Accordingly the model of all models would be abysmal by virtue of its plenitude. The eidetic God is the sufficient reason—determined and determining—of all created things. It is their ultimate "why." But as such it will not be primary. He is creator only for the created, just as the lord is only lord over the serf. Only the indeterminate will be originary—God in "the abyss of all his godhead" (DW II,68; S I,234). The origin is indeterminate because it is unimaginable. "No image opens up the godhead to us" (DW III,323; S III,113). And it is unimaginable because it is not "for" anything. It does not pair up with any being, and nothing faces it. Without why it no longer has a place among beings. All one can say of it is that it dispossesses us of beings and of all that these have in their train—the image, the why, the sufficient end, and continuing nature. Eckhart jettisons this train when he speaks of re-imaging, of the godhead, of the abysmal ground, and of pure nature.

"The soul [must] be re-imaged in the first vacancy" (DW I,56; S I,60). What is passive in it is not one. If in the godhead God is not anybody's God nor the foundation of anything, then he will no longer be a psychagogue either. Negation is not apophatic either. Negation does not speak of qualities of existence—not of images—even if these are negated in the last instance. It speaks elsewhere and otherwise. The elsewhere is the process of indetermination and of disappropriation; the otherwise is the middle voice.

To re-image oneself means, therefore, losing these means. The neutral process eclipses mediations and leads to "nature without ground" *gruntlose nature* (DW III, 113; S I,42). "Leads to" is poorly formulated. Rather, this dispossession of ends is a process without *telos*. It unveils the originary condition where the common teleology withdraws. As withdrawn, it is an uncommon trait.

There is a difference between the verb "to image" and the noun "image." Eckhart conceives of it—rather, he practices it—as he practices the difference of being born and nature when the being-born is said to be *of* nature.

It proceeds otherwise than from the form of "to re-image oneself." Between the reflexive and the middle voice, there is a differend. The trait outside of the proper and the common, outside of the continuously imagined world, does not underscore the constituted phenomenality naturally attractive by means of its ends. The trait of subtraction pulls toward the ground, but not a common ground. This trait no longer emphasizes telic attraction, neither to affirm it, nor to deny it, nor to overexalt it. The cataphatic, the apophatic and the hyperbolic express precisely the being-born *of* nature.

On the other hand, the occurrent character and thus the differend here again appears in an argument that is more Aristotelian than Neoplatonic. Eckhart then explains "re-imaging" in terms of being. Re-imaging signifies detaching oneself from images—no longer to find their plenitude, but to *suffer,* he says, "naked being," the "pure nature" that, as we saw, are not the being and nature *of* anything. The identity of the ground of God and of the ground of the soul therefore is no longer to be understood in an eidetic manner. "When all images are detached from the soul and it observes only the single one, then the naked being of the soul finds, in suffering it, the naked and formless being of the divine unity" (DW III,437s; S III,151). The identity of non-identity is "suffering." Man is pulled elsewhere, expropriated, he suffers something like an injury, and is alienated from what is proper to him. This is "re-imaging oneself."

Thus the top, the bottom, and the intermediate that deploys the natural difference collapse. They collapse not into something isomorphic,[57] but into the differend of the traits of appropriator and expropriator.

In accordance with this second point of the program, what "should" we do? Nothing less than what the image does: annihilate one's own being, render indeterminate the stratified eidetic order; we should recognize as primary this dissension by which the *imagination* places us in nature and gives us the *knowledge* that anticipates expropriation and thus, literally, death: death plain and simple—the knowledge that wrenches us out of nature.

"Piercing through": for absolute freedom

"We should remember the grand nobility that God has deposited in the soul by means of which man can marvelously reach God." As we have seen, by nobility we must generally understand that which integrates the principle of continuity: *rank.* This has a top and a bottom because, as in the game of the hot hand, the top of the inferior touches the bottom of the one who is superior. According to this scheme, nobility augments either with universality or with the capacity a being has to exteriorize itself, or again with the proximity of the image in the eidetic model: so many "marvels" that permit man to climb in grades and to reach God. Some specific faculties of the soul turn it upward, such others turn it downward. When nature lays down the law through vertical integration, nobility is what theticism decisively posits. It decides your level.

So, pursued to its excess, this integrating logic—just as is the case with the image—completes in two ways the structure that it serves to erect. It puts the finishing touch on it by compressing the levels into an identity at the summit; and it also completes it as a nudge in the right direction can suffice to stabilize a wobbly structure not yet standing on its own.

Perfection: Ours is the first rank. "The soul that tastes divine nobility . . . wants what there is of the most elevated, so much so that it is incapable of tolerating anything above it. I even say without beating around the bush that it cannot tolerate God above it. If it was drawn above all things until it came to its highest freedom—so far, that it touched God in his pure divine nature—then the soul would never find repose at least until God did not convey himself in it and it in God" (DW III,401; S III,140). Eckhart, it seems, speaks of a certain excessiveness in the will. It is impossible to stop the will midway. Once it is set in motion, it wants everything and the best. It wants the peak of the scale. There alone, nothing would limit it from above; it would touch the bottom fringe of nothing with that which in it is the superior. It matters little whether such an "up to the end-ism" is an act of the will or of the intellect;[58] its fine point would confer on the soul its real nobility. Its rank would place it naturally at the top. God in it, it in God. Is this not what Eckhart states in the third point of his program, that the soul should recall the grand nobility in itself so that man can reach God?

Completion, decay, destitution are the work no longer of the intellect or will, but of freedom. Indeed, what has freedom done in this push to extremes that is all too reminiscent of the megalomania of desire? At the beginning of the cited lines, the most elevated part of the soul is the will. In the end, the soul hoists itself—is hoisted—up until it reaches "its highest freedom." Without warning, Eckhart breaks off his argument. The highest part of the soul, and thus *its nobility, is its freedom*. And one cannot go on too quickly to say that being free defines the will. It will be quite instructive to read attentively, for Eckhart traces an interference of argumentative regularities in which the double bind, under which "nature" places us, is announced anew and in another way: the bind between the apogee of the determining integration and then again of indetermination. The "highest freedom" of the soul touches God in his "pure nature"—not as one would have expected, in his supreme nature, not in his nature that is supreme, in his nature of being supreme. Having tasted his freedom and pure nature, the soul cannot bear anything above it, not even God. Freedom and pure nature—did Eckhart get the century wrong? The whole nineteenth century will struggle with this opposition. Does his arguing for a freedom that strips away any taste for determinations stem from his having seen in this opposition a false question?

Reducing Eckhart to problems of psychologisms is a pitfall one must avoid. In order really to keep guard against this it is enough to bear in mind the affinity between human freedom and *pure* divine nature. If there is an affinity, freedom will also be "pure." But pure in what way? Eckhart beats anthropomorphism at its own game. He does not say the soul reaches God because, among the psychic faculties, there is the will capable of choosing what is the best; because it is free to choose God. It is not through a partiality for ends that he combines freedom, will, and nature. Nor does he project such a conjunction in God. Pure freedom will not be able to be construed teleologically or transitively.

Eckhart appears alerted to the Scotist metaphysics where freedom belongs to a forked transitive power in which, by necessity, it belongs to the absolute power of God whose will could aim at and create other natures, and by contingency, it belongs to his relative power, in what it aims at and wants as our own.[59] This does not prevent Eckhart from linking together in a very different way pure nature, freedom, and the ground of God, or from adding to this the divine will, innumerable possible worlds, and number (certainly quite differently than the moderns would carry on about nature and freedom as two heterogeneous types of efficiency). Hoisted up into the godhead, freedom does not crown a system of acts that is transposed beginning with human experience and absolutized in such a power. It is here that we find all the difficulties and all that is of interest in Eckhart's argumentative slippages. He remains resolutely implanted in the metaphysic of degrees (in which the metaphysic of faculties is only a case), and at the same time, he does proceed no less resolutely elsewhere, and he does so with disastrous consequences for hegemony.

Is the nobility in the soul a matter of the culmination of the highest rank, or of equalized positions? If it designates a rank, then reaching God would mean to imitate the preceding level and, at the limit, to identify oneself with the supreme level; if on the other hand it designates pure freedom, then it will pierce through to elsewhere, breaking the scale. To which case would the defection of hegemonic nature be genuinely the work of freedom—of a freedom? So would it be imitation or piercing through?

This is a categorial question. The principle of hierarchization is constituted by the triumph of the last of the Aristotelian categories, namely relation, over the first, namely substance.

According to this principle the bottom is in relation with the top which it "touches," "tastes," by an imitation that is deficient and mediated by its place in rank. This means that substantial being is not endowed with relations, but rather that it results from them. Thus, piercing into the godhead is to escape altogether from imitation, from deficiency, from mediation, from identity, from measurement , and from subsumption—from the whole polymorphous work of relation. Here there is an excess, but it has nothing to do with the ends of desire or some other power. Rather, it is an excess that destitutes measure and power.

"The grand nobility that God has deposited in the soul"—we remember that it is necessary not to confuse what is "in" the soul with what is properly "of" the soul.[60] *Inside,* as we have seen, is the actuality of being which we have also seen is *of* God; it is borrowed. The only thing that is hierarchized is what is of the soul, namely, the acts that turn it toward the top or the bottom. What there is of God repels all relation, since being is God. The actuality of being renders relations inconceivable, deprives them of a space in which to distribute the ranks. These unthinkable relations make the ranks atopical. Thus one can talk about the absolute and the relative only on condition of splitting these concepts. "Nobility" is not forked in some way. Rather, it creates amphiboly. Through a relative employment it situates man on a continuous scale. Nobility is something pertaining to man, namely his essential quality. But taken absolutely, it indicates in him something completely different—*actuality, which is to say, freedom.*

In man, not of him. The absolute in the sense of the detached, of the absolved, and of the indeterminate, describes the pure nature that is incomparable to stratified nature and incompatible with it. Indeed, understood in this way, relations are obsolete due to absolution. "God indicates . . . the altitude of his nature in which all that is a creature is absolved. There, [man] knows nothing save for God and himself" (DW III,241; S III,83). The altitude is incomparable, so much so that in its turn it does not enter into relations with the relationally more or less. Comparisons and oppositions are asphyxiated by virtue of the same loss of space that smothers the stratifications—just as, according to the distortion of the Aristotelian view mentioned above, space polarized by kinetic ends (heaven-earth) in Eckhart disappears in the heavens as a pure space of inscription deprived of reference points. Absolute altitude neither relates to nor opposes anything. Between the nature that liberates and the nature that subsumes, there is no common measure. Thus to speak of God *and* of me in nature where relations are absolved amounts to a simple compromise. Whoever lets himself be dispossessed of rank reaches his real nobility. He knows that actuality is his liberty; it is a space that is too open to be furnished. He traverses the imitable and the juxtaposable. He absolves, *absolvere,* natural mimesis. He crushes nature, sees it being crushed. He pierces through.

What can it really mean to take absolute freedom and the act of being as a norm without there being some sort of thing correlatively normed? Is this still some dissolution in the Great Indeterminate? No, this does not signify anything beyond the double bind between origin and principle. Whoever knows that no noun can be the last word has recognized his norm in the absolute freedom *that is* the act of being. The last word about our condition amounts to a subtraction that happens to us and that is announced in the middle voice. Descending from the proud line of von Hochheim knights, Eckhart would never even have dreamed of doubting that things are determined as the particular things we know them to be: overlords and vassals, precious stones and earth included. But he no longer doubts that we know a great deal about our condition of being. The passage from awareness to knowledge is what he calls piercing through.

To pierce through is to go from the God-foundation to the ground of God. On this route the ensemble of relations and identities that they conclude are blurred. In this context Eckhart still speaks of "me" but in such a way that in piercing through beyond the foundation I am "neither God nor creature" (DW II,504; S I,149). To remind me of freedom, I am dispossessed of identity, of attributes, of the God and of the creatures that have a place—that have their places—only as terms of the founding relation. Mutually determining themselves, the uncreated and the created remain bound by this relation; they are not free. When it comes to "piercing-through" it is first of all necessary to speak in the imperative mode. It is a matter of retaining the freedom that alone is freedom "for" nothing, without why: the actuality of being. You should "pierce through outside of all things and above all things and reach into divine freedom" (DW III,401; S I,140). It is divine liberation in that it surpasses all measure, both the "why" and the "for-oneself." The freedom that it brings to light belongs to no one. Like being, it is God—understood as the godhead. It becomes absolute with the removal of attributes. The imperative of "piercing through beyond God" can thus be translated as "let yourself be removed." In doing so, the imperative has already given way to the middle voice.

Inversely, unless the attachments that bind us to proper ends are undone, there will be neither freedom nor happiness. Indeed, freedom is "the greatest happiness that nature is capable of effecting, [namely] that at the peak [of the soul] it [pure nature] produces itself in accordance with itself" (DW III,401; S III,140). This is a remarkable formulation. It renders happiness indeterminate *in its ground*. Being free means allowing pure nature "to produce itself." Here the middle voice quiets the others: the imperative, transitive, reflexive voices. We will not know freedom producing itself—likewise the actuality of being—unless by always "piercing through." In the middle voice, this verb thus indicates the knowledge that the origin always renders the principle indeterminate. It indicates the knowledge of their incongruous normativity.

We should add that, as a neutral production of the originary condition, piercing through disengages mimesis. The world deployed in images that imitates the first fold and reproduces it in ordered foldings, a world in which the law of nature reigns, this is an ignoble world. Through the ordered ranks of feudal nobility it silences—it denies—another nobility in which we come to recognize the originary event of being. To unfold and be refolded, *exire* and *redire,* is always to reproduce the end. Thus, when we describe it as nobility, actuality, or freedom, the originary event does not have an end at which to aim. A little laboriously, Eckhart points out the neutrality of this event in relation to telic degrees. The soul "seizes the pure absolution (*die lûter absolûcio*) of the free being, that is without a 'there'; [it seizes it] where nothing is received or given; where there is naked isness {*estance*} deprived of all being and of all appearance. There [the soul] lays hold of God purely according to the ground —there—as it is beyond all being. If there were still being there, the soul would take [this] being in the [absolute] being, where there is nothing but a single ground" (DW III,133; S III,50). Eckhart sets freedom back on its feet with a tourniquet that connects it not only to purity, to the atopical ground, to *epekeina,* to the reiterated *ekeî,* to nobility, and to the actuality of being, but also to a process which is neither reception nor a giving, he says here, but, as he says elsewhere, which is letting-be—in the middle voice. So this is what makes God and man neither man nor God.

The contortions that Eckhart inflicts here on the dialectic of negation play on the infinitive 'to be' (*wesene*) and in the third person singular (*ist,* from here the noun *isticheit,* isness {'*estance*'}). "Is" and the "isness" always refer to a subject. Thus absolute being is pure isness, *estance*. Absolute, absolved of determinations, it belongs to God alone (the created only borrows it). But it does not belong to God as does a predicate to a subject. The apophatic schema that deprives being of all being and of all isness rather arranges it so that it does not excite the excess of piercing through. Consider the last about-face, altogether traditional in that he exalts and thus reinstitutes the measure, but by liquefying it and thus by destituting it—being is altogether *über allez wesen,* beyond and distinct from all being, and *wesen in wesene,* being indistinct in being. This is the normative restitution and normative destitution that make up what Meister Eckhart is all about.

Piercing through, in the sense of returning to our originary condition, is something we do all the time.[61] In all acts we return to a knowledge as elementary as that of happiness: "Our happiness resides in this, that man pierces through and traverses all that is created as well as all temporality and all being: that he passes into the ground that is without ground" (DW II,309; S II,78f.).

Thus, rendered indeterminate—alchemy is never far away—the ground becomes clear in singularization. Happiness here proves to be henceforth more complicated. A mortal undertow constitutes it and undermines it at the same time.

"Articulating oneself": for singularization

In the last point of his program, Eckhart speaks of "the limpidity of divine nature, what brilliance there is in divine nature cannot be expressed. God is a speech, and a speech expressed externally." In the limpidity or brilliance in question we have recognized the actuality of being as such. Here Eckhart seems to want to situate it. It is seated, he states, in pure nature, not externally. Actuality *takes place* even where the speech that is the Word is expressed. As a new instance of the spatial *chorismos,* Eckhart thus separates the pure space in the godhead from natural space. As a new instance also of the identity through *energeia,* he describes the pure actuality of the godhead (but this is not a description properly speaking) as immanent expression. The "place" of actuality is that of an expression.

How is this to be understood? When it comes to oppositions such as inside-outside, at issue is something other than symmetrical disjunctions, and even something other than trinitarian speculations. Rather, originary actuality is itself gathered up in this event of language we call "enunciation"—just like, in the alchemist's alembic, prime matter, which is the indeterminate in its greatest extension, is gathered up in the singular, which is the indeterminate in its greatest intensivity.

The last aporia only indirectly thematizes the particular features—nominatives or adjectives—with which the detached man has to pay. It thematizes the singularization—in the middle or adverbial voice—that in thus paying he makes his own. The double bind of the nominative and infinitive expresses the secret of happiness (tragic, in the sense of incongruous ultimates), just as it first expresses the mystery of being (agonal, in the sense of being and beings in a differend). Neither happiness nor being is designated simply, plainly, by name.

We should add that this secret and this mystery overdetermine the *abescheiden,* a word that, perhaps already in Eckhart's time, also signified "to die."[62] The *ars moriendi,* the training to auto-universalize oneself spiritually by following the telic sequence that, from the Romans[63] up until Eckhart's principial arguments, constitutes the natural law—this *ars,* this know-how, here is wrenched from the fantasm of the great continuity of ends. The *morietur,* the withdrawal of mortality, detaches in advance the bonds that insert me in a continuous world. For the Eckhart that transgresses the principle of a graduated nature in the direction of an origin, knowing the event of being means knowing that any gesture positing an ordered completion turns against itself just as *to articulate oneself* turns against the *articulation*. To articulate something is essentially to interrupt an ordering. Similarly, when one understands it in terms of the Word, the origin interrupts nature-as-law. It dephenomenalizes phenomena in advance; it singularizes them in their sudden emergence that Eckhart names "pure being," "pure nature." When he approaches, as we have just seen, the actuality of being and the activity of articulation, there is an abeyance of nature. Both ordered nature and its abeyance therefore will make the law without there being any common recourse.

Following the example of the preceding aporias, this last aporia again is elucidated by non-attachment. The *abescheiden* is a labor, and precisely a labor to disengage pure being from beings: "Where you find yourself [plunged] into multiple affairs rather than in pure, limpid, simple being, there is where you should begin your labor" (DW II,107; S I,246). The imperative has something about it that leaves one perplexed, especially since it does not spare the foundational God. He also will have to work, to disengage himself, desubstantialize himself, to sacrifice his nominative particularity. "If God should never penetrate with his gaze [the bottom of the soul], it will cost him all his divine names" (DW I,43; S I,56). What one must bear in mind about this perplexity is that to speak of God by name, we silence the originary actuality. Hence the interest in verbs such as "detaching," "working," "being born," "piercing through," "casting a gaze," and "seeing" . . . to which is added another that expresses the process *par excellence* where being is event: "listening." In the actuality of listening, the speech proffered and the speech heard have one and the same *energeia*. With phrases in the middle voice, notably with "being born," it is always a matter of this energetic identity. To beget and to be begotten—the event of birth is one and the same. Also the non-metaphysics of the Word is wholly dependent upon a non-metaphysics of articulation. It allows Eckhart, who rarely fears generous affirmations, to rake over with one great gesture the terms that the natural metaphysician in us can't help but posit separately from one another, and to place beneath the sign of the same—but of a *same* that *happens*—both the ground of God (the abyss) and pure being as well as pure nature, both articulation and begetting. Here is this gesture: "The unfathomability of divine being and of divine nature, [God] creates {*faire naître*} it entirely in his only Son. Here is what the Son understands of the Father. He has revealed him to us finally so that we would be the same Son" (DW II,84; S I,239). "Nature": a single "birth" {*naître*}. One more time, *natura* comes down to *nasci*, as a noun always comes down to the verb as soon as one detaches oneself from the articulation so as to hear what is *being articulated*. And so again, order refers to a process of *putting* in order while we ponder the emergence of its signifying structure. All Eckhart's vehemence has to do with the being-born–self-articulation–placing–being that, as an originary event, engages nature-as-law but that, because of its incongruity with order, also destabilizes it.

The cited lines end in our becoming singular, ". . . so that we would be the same Son." The dislocating condition effected for us by the *same that happens* is a condition that can only remain incomprehensible to the extent that we separate it from the non-attachment accomplished singularly, effectively. For Eckhart, this is the reason for speaking of an "only" Son. What one must learn from Eckhart in this bold gesture: Unfathomable, indeterminate being is singularized—but yet is not determined—in non-attachment. Inversely, when detached we return to the indeterminate that we are: *wesen und natûre* of God that at the zenith of the Latin era are posited as the act of being.

Such is the thesis that we saw serves to anchor the deduction of the law. Therefore, at the heart of this theticism, Eckhart liberates a denied knowledge, a knowledge that the infinitive *esse* does not agree with the noun *ens,* any more than does the origin (*urspringen*) agree with the principle (*begin*). Hence the knowledge that liberates non-attachment introduces into nature-as-law the mortifying dissension between the indeterminate singular and the common determination in accordance with the telic principle of continuity.

The spatial *chorismos* also marks this same dissension. When Eckhart speaks of the radiance in pure being and pure nature, he coils back up, so to speak, the spectral rays that deployed nature. He looks above the prismatic diffraction where the continuous scale of colors is harmonized. He returns to the event in which the light is *emitted* {*s'émet*} that *puts* {*met en place*} the visibles in place. The pure luminous space thus differs from the natural space organized by graduated refractions. We saw how Eckhart (after others[64]) identifies pure space and light. We can go further by saying that in the natural arrangement of proper places there are no holes, and yet we had understood that the being of God is pure space, desert, emptinesss; so this being is not inserted in the space of layered, spectral space—no more than the event of *being spatializes* figures among the naturally disposed places. Here is how the two incommensurable spaces each in their own way underscore the interval between principle and origin.

What is going on when Eckhart describes the origin as "speech not articulated externally"? The opposition of inside and outside does not divide some genus into symmetrically posited elements. It serves to delimit the infinitive from the nominative. To "articulate" oneself, just like the other cited verbs, signals the event of being that denaturalizes nature that is externally articulated according to the syntax of proper ends. It is a denaturalization in the origin, *by* the origin. What is going on? Articulating oneself, that is what is going on. Work without a worker, non-attachment without an ascetic, pierced without bravery, birth without father or mother. As for a best friend, there is no one. At the origin, there is *nothing at all.* Accordingly, to think the ultimate normative authority, one must suspend the question: *To what* does primacy amount? When, under the articulated order (under the law deduced from the pure act treated in *ens*), Eckhart has in mind the event of articulation (the actuality of *esse*), when he thinks God deprived of his perfections and man deprived of his specificities, the *solve et coagula* transmutes the nature laying down the law. If it had interested him, he would have deduced this just as implacably as Thomas Aquinas. But he is more interested in reducing it again—as in the alembic—so that from it the singular, the only Son, the detached me, will arise. To think the origin we must therefore pay the price by renouncing our attachment to assets deduced from the species, from the nameable, from properties, from entitatives—thus paying not to set out upon some anagogic and universalizing route, so as not to exhaust ourselves in normative comparisons by running through all the reference points from the top to the bottom of the scale. He who thus ceases chasing nouns and properties knows himself as mortal because he is singular. He knows himself as expropriated from nature, while altogether occupying his allotted, appropriated place. Thus he knows himself doubly bound. To lose *in fact* the noun and the proper is entitative death; as for non-attachment, it liberates the non-factual *knowledge* that the trait of mortality always draws us toward our singularization to come. It frees the ultimates that make the final instance not simple.

Eckhart compares nature to the taxic spectrum, to taxonomic space, and even to a syntax. Each time, he invites his listeners to abandon these constituted orders. Thus, when the *same* signifies the articulation and the hearing of the articulation ("that which the Son hears of the Father, so that we should be the same Son"), it is necessary to understand it as that upon which the natural metaphysician in us stumbles. Originary being—as far from the foundational God as the sky is from the earth—is singularized just as an articulation singularizes language and syntax. The contents of our dictionaries and our grammars are not engulfed by articulation; they survive it. Thus the God-being is not engulfed in the godhead-event. But the godhead-event does not take place within the graduated order that is nature—an order of which the God-being is the pinnacle—any more than does articulation take place in our dictionaries and grammars. The verbs "to be articulated," "to be born," *wesen,* state a unique process between distinct beings. God "effects me as his being: one, but not similar" (*sîn wesen ein unglîch,* DW I,111; S I,86).

Surely in all this the model of thought, or in any case, one of the models of thought, is Johannine. Now, according to trinitarian theories, what does the Son "hear?" Eckhart first of all establishes a sort of proportion in which being born refers to begetting, just as hearing refers to speaking. There is nothing more traditional than identifying the manner of being of primary analogies, and afterwards those of secondary analogies: "The speaking of the Father is his begetting, and the hearing of the Son is his being born" (DW II,53; S I,228). For the Father, to speak is to beget; for the Son, to hear is to be born. On the other hand, what is hardly traditional is the identification between the consequent terms: "In the eternal speech, the one who hears is the very one that is heard" (DW I,193; S I,121). The Son hears that the Father is God and that he, the Son, is the Son of God. He hears the divine being in which all alterity is exhausted, including the alterity of God and me, and in which universalization is settled. The aporia that separates the singular *wesen* from distinct beings (*sin,* DW III,387; S III,134) is not resolved. It leads thought elsewhere. It leads it to the place where "being" is nothing other than "articulating oneself." On this point, the Johannine *legein* is not foreign to the Aristotelian *energeia*. Hence the ease with which Eckhart passes from the articulation to the begetting, and then to being. The occurrent sense that ties these affinities together—and this alone counts here—is not on a par with the articulated, conceived, and ontic sense.[65] Eckhart shows that he who advances toward the only question in philosophy—What is being?—loses here his bonds to syntax, ascendance, law, sense, and world. He shows what it is in the knowledge motivating this question that singularizes you, that pulls you toward death.

We must still circumscribe more closely this singularization that we gain (if to know is to gain). What then does man hear and make his own when he detaches himself from images and leaves behind assets and attributes? "His being and his nature and his whole godhead, reveals them to us completely in his only Son and instructs us so that we should be this same Son; a man that would have departed from himself in such a way that he is the only Son is the one that would possess what the only Son possesses" (DW I,193; S I,121). In the non-attachment that renders one singular, we make the very same process that defines articulation and hearing our own process. The detached man—and it is something quite different than an exercise in dialectic—appropriates the expropriation outside of the specific character constituted by the *Eigenschaft,* that is, by attachment, possession, specificity, ownership.

Here is the counter-strategy of thought from which fealties and stratifications—the whole graduated universe—has disappeared. This entire vassalage is here obsolete. What one calls the analogy of attribution does not allow for treating created being as the being *of* the creature, as turning it back into a specific character. The created being remains an assumed being, impossible to appropriate. Accordingly, in his argumentative counter-strategies Eckhart annuls natural subordinations by *expropriating* us toward the one in accordance with being. "You are one with [God] in accordance with being and nature, and these [being and nature] you have in yourself as the Father has everything in himself; you got it from God, not in vassalage, as God is your proper good" (DW II,383; S II,103). In other words, it will be my proper good if I allow myself to be expropriated from my being to the extent it is mine.

The expropriation in no way wrenches me from this or that particular object that has nominative or adjectival significance. It does not even wrench me from God, the final cause as "my proper good" (a key concept in telic and principial speculative strategies that seems to have been lost here in the originary counter-strategy). The natural ordering of causes as well as the natural pursuit of ends are kept intact by the expropriation that at the same time suspends their function. Eckhart suggests this placing of nature in abeyance in all his phrasing in the middle voice, phrases he says sum up his program of instruction.

It is through a process of dispossession that we enter into a possession. Here again, how do we think it? Only as an event that the "articulation" conveys least poorly. "Articulating oneself": The middle voice puts into place neither a speaker nor a listener. It is not acroamatic, not destined to be heard. It startles order, causes it to break open, for according to the transgressive counter-strategies in Eckhart, there is no more order as soon as "being" is described as "articulating itself." There is no more order, no more subordination, telic appropriation, or nature. If appropriation essentially has to do with what authorizes the law, then the event of "articulating itself" signifies an expropriation outside the law. This is something in Eckhart that can only cause fear. Fear in the man of the law, in the natural metaphysician in us.

To mark the event in being, he says *wesen und wesunge* (DW II,383; S II,102), as if to say being, that is to say, event. This will be understood only by working at it. "Loosen," "leave," *"laß los.":* One says these words to someone who is dying. Eckhart speaks as if to the dying: "Work in all things, this means: . . . detach yourself from all that is yours, belong to God, and then God will be properly yours" (DW II,107s.; S I,246). What will be yours is not the nameable God—nor moreover the unnameable—but the one that already is yours as long as you listen, understand, be: the event of being, the disparate condition of all beings. Of the trinitarian theories, Eckhart maintains that the Word is articulated and gives birth. The filiation that *comes to be* thus furnishes him with the vocabulary with which to speak of the ground of God, the disparate condition of both the trinitarian and the natural ordering.

To articulate oneself, to be born, the event that emphasizes the middle voice demands to be cleared out in me, even as it inserts me in stratified nature. It has to be freed by a work of singularization that does not confine itself to any of the strata in the great natural sedimentation of the layers of beings. This work burns the deposits. Eckhart calls it the piercing through.

To understand by working is an alchemist's recipe. We grasp the great work of transmutation only by working to transmutate ourselves. "The man that should understand this should be very detached" (*DW* II,109; *S* I,247). What the alchemist always said is that in all metallurgic decantings it all has to do only with you.

The Latin "nature" is destituted as, a millennium earlier, the Greek "one" had been destituted, by the eruption in broad philosophic daylight of the most ordinary knowledge. The philosophic day is the day of the universal that spreads out the *hen* or the *natura*. Ordinary knowledge adjoins to it incongruously a more nocturnal undertow, due to the singularizing familiarity that each has with his death. As a phenomenologist of ultimates, Michel Foucault formulated this knowledge, saying "An obstinate relation to death prescribes to the universal its singular face."[66]

VOLUME TWO

Preface: Analytic of Ultimates and Topology of Broken Hegemonies

With desire we take hold of a law
That can serve as the weapon for our passion.[1]
—Goethe

Is the law, as these lines suggest, a weapon to brandish in the defense of our passions? A passion turned into a weapon, perhaps? A singular passion—the passion for some singular—which desire would promote, exalt, institute as a universal rule?

If this is the way it is, if the law first of all protects this or that particuar private passion, then public law will prove of rather modest extraction. As in all dazzling ascents, the humble conditions of the beginnings will continue to make themselves felt even in the effects of fame and renown. The singular point of departure from which the law arises, a singularization, will fracture from within the universal endowed with the force of obligation. Renown {*Renom*}—the word well describes the career of the law. A proper noun named anew, renamed {*re-nommé*} for the purpose of subsumption, carried to the level of the most common name, maximized: that is what the law will be.[2] Speaking "in the name of" will always amount to speaking of the proper name or noun, and then of renown.

The whole problem of normativity, of principles, of appellate recourse, of the ultimate authority, is lodged in this "and then." It will be useful to reflect on the persistence of the singular, the object of passion, at the heart of the common referents that enjoy the renown of law. To reflect thus means to put into question the rallying names in which we trust as if their legislative prestige went without saying: names such as "progress," "people," "race," "freedom." . . . By submitting ourselves—you and I—to such common representations, we become capable of understanding each other—which is, by the way, why anomy is bound to remain a dream.

The prestige of the common makes for *actual knowing,* and it prompts *thinking.* The persistence of the singular under the law, however, with the various senses of "passion" that follow from it, is something that we *fathom* {*savior*}.

We *actually know* things in calling them by their name. Knowledge grows and gains strength in the light of the common. Without specific and generic names expressing laws, the world would remain impenetrable to us. Cognitive laws state the necessary relations linking phenomena. On the other hand, we *think* when we ask ourselves and others: In the name of what do I do what I do, say what I say, judge as I judge? Here, where meaning is at stake rather than kinds, we use a different name and a "common" that is different. Consequently we use a law that is different, one which states not relations that are, but those we are convinced ought to be. Thought relations always remain more tenuous than cognitive relations; an understanding that rests on a common thought remains more precarious than one imposed by a known truth. In the absence of names that give it meaning, the world would become unlivable for us.

Cognition and thinking are not everything. The laws that regulate the true and those that regulate meaning do not exhaust all the law that we call normative. Our understanding cannot but comply with the true that constrains it—it is a hard law. Reason, on the other hand, debates convictions—it is a more supple law in which freedom enters. This is to say that both in their turn depend on conditions. Consequently philosophy has as its mission to seek the unconditioned that renders possible the conditioned. Outside of this, it lapses into some "theory of," into the theory of knowledge or theory of correct meaning, as well as some other such theories. None of these is philosophy. As for the unconditioned, we have a *knowledge* of it. Neither hard nor soft, this knowledge can be neither demonstrated nor even discussed. What, then, do we know of the law, prior to demonstrations establishing the true and discussions negotiating meaning?

Not all *a priori* knowledge is ultimate (which is why, in Kantian terms, our theoretical as well as practical makeup is arranged according to an order that deductions trace; the only ultimate function being apperception). Could the ultimate that we know bear both on the common which desire promotes, exalts, declares, and institutes as law, and on the singular which pertains to a passion? Could this bear upon a double bond of the law—one that is subsumptive and deictic? If we maximize, and cannot but maximize, proper nouns into common nouns, could this be because an unconditioned condition that is known to everyone (more about this later) leads us to posit principles just as it keeps us at the same time inevitably faithful to deictic objects? Put differently, when we elevate a singular passion—a passion for some particular singular—and brandish it as a law, could it be that we know of ultimate*s*? Do we obey a universalizing-singularizing double bind, one that is ineluctably originary?

If such is unconditioned knowledge, then we will learn more about the law by analyzing these ultimates of ordinary experience.

What would an analytic of ultimates be? I say "would be" because if the topology of broken hegemonies, which is my topic, calls upon such an analytic as upon a propaedeutic, it does not elsewhere or otherwise develop it. The connections linking the two projects nevertheless are not difficult to see. Therefore we will make do with a sketch. What is at issue is the question that is decisive in all philosophical undertakings: Where to begin? The analytic of ultimates begins neither thetically nor—we will say—by randomly chosen cases.

In a thetic beginning of discourse one states: "I posit that X, from which follows Y and Z." In positing the supreme good, substance, or the principle of sufficient reason, one occupies a point of departure that will allow one to understand (such is at least the expectation invested in theticism) the good life, physical change, or the impetus that moves essences toward existence. A thesis is always a thesis with a view to subsuming and explicating consequences that have proved problematic at the outset, which is the reason why a thesis is never absolutely first; but this is another question. In any case, nothing serves better "as the weapon for our passion" than theticism in its innumerable forms. It provides interlocutors with common concepts and agents with general ideas. Theticism constitutes the force of the natural metaphysician within us. Thus to the extent that, to live, it is necessary to speak and act, to understand and think, we will never extricate ourselves from poses and positions assumed, from theses put forth, and stops that are posited. . . . We will never extricate ourselves from legislative maximizings.

It would be a matter of randomly chosen cases if a philosophical discourse were to begin by saying: "Positions have abounded and overabounded, and they continue to abound; their profusion alone demonstrates that none of them is compelling, necessary, or even legitimate; let us then start more modestly with the *casus*, the contingent site that happens to be our own and let us ask: What is happening to us today?" From such a beginning with random cases, one will be able to note deconstructive questions in the margins of transmitted systems. One will be able to annotate our institutions archaeologically and genealogically, thus subverting them.

The analytic of ultimates begins quite differently. Its point of departure is the knowledge from which no one escapes and which escapes no one, even if the natural metaphysician in each of us closes his eyes to it (and even if the thetic metaphysician closes them due to professionalism): the knowledge that we arrive by our birth and go to our death. Those are the originary phenomena to which it would not be useless for philosophy, if it is weary of thetic controversies, to remain faithful. Their analysis indeed posits nothing; its point of departure is therefore "legitimate," legitimized by ordinary experience. Yet it is a point of departure that does not ground anything either. Indeed, this analysis says *one word too many* to be able to ground understanding, ideals, systems, and institutions. The origin, as known by the mortals that we are, is not simple. What conceptual edifice could be erected upon the basis of originary phenomena in dissension, as are being-towards-birth and being-towards-death? Such edifices can only crack at their base. Therefore the topology of hegemonies reveals in detail the fissures that follow from their normative constructs. It shows these not out of malicious pleasure, nor in order to repeat the history of an error or that of a straying, but rather to know better the condition of being. I will not conceal the fact that if there is an urgent task for thinking, it is, for me, to better know the tragic condition. To learn to love it.

The point from which the analytic of ultimates sets out differs moreover from all points of departure that are cases. It does not ask: What is happening to us today? Rather, it asks: What is happening to us as mortals? In that, it deepens the analytic of *Being and Time*. It deepens it inasmuch as one cannot but wonder how the strategies of being-towards-birth and being-towards-death are at all to be "rooted originally" in Dasein if, as Heidegger suggests, they are ultimate. Were one to bear in mind rather their disparity, then all rootedness, all grounding, all origin as one, would be fractured—just as Heidegger develops this, as we will see, beginning in the mid-1930s.

The topology of hegemonies is articulated on the basis of the analytic of ultimates a little bit like epochal history in Heidegger is articulated on the basis of the existential analytic. A little bit . . . for on the one hand, in Heidegger this very articulation remains highly problematic. On the other hand, according to some of his texts, two or three more centuries would suffice to wean us from thetic investments. Thus the impulse that carries us toward subsumptive fantasms would not be phenomenologically co-ultimate with the impulse that always singularizes us. Focal meanings would, as it were, be incurred historically, and the day could come when we will no longer speak of them—just as, for two centuries now, one has not heard of phlogiston or of aether.

The analysis of ultimates "precedes" the topology of broken hegemonies in that it reveals strategies in unconditioned knowledge which turn the conditions of thought against themselves.

The impulse that prompts the understanding to look for subsumptive concepts and thought for ideas imparting meaning—this impulse I described in the first volume as that of being-towards-birth or "natality" (*Gebürtigkeit,* not my coinage[3]). It is the strategy that always leads us to posit the common. If it is of interest here, it is not as the moving force in understanding, but for the effect it has on thought, for the figures of a law of laws, by which the West has lived and continues to live, thus for the names of meaning in which it has found rest—in short, for its hegemonic fantasms.

So it is neither wild ramblings nor venturing outside of the knowledge that is shared most widely to say that everyone knows at least one thing, namely, that the clarity of a posited common is never the whole of experience, never all of experience. Something else is mixed in with it that ruins the repose promised by subsumptive nouns. Familiar in advance of any destabilizations in a universe of meaning that is stabilized fantasmically, we are not really surprised when a world comes undone which, for a while, had gone without saying. Rather, what is surprising is that things hold together. This is what we somehow know, if neither by the understanding nor by reason. It is a knowing that comes to us from elsewhere than cognition and thinking. The strategy of withdrawal, which wrenches us in advance from any constituted world, reveals being-towards-death or "mortality" (*Sterblichkeit,* also not my coinage). We know, albeit poorly, that in all experience the tug of death is at work in whatever can become a phenomenon. A withdrawal undermines the order of things. Mother of all contingencies, it escapes understanding and allows itself to be thought only with difficulty. Still, it is this strategy of dephenomenalization, incongruously at work in all phenomenal arrangements, that must be thought and that I seek to think.

Such, then, are the ultimates of experience. They are disparate pulls on the knowable as well as on the thinkable, hence on any phenomenal constellation. They show to where the regression toward conditions leads: to tragic knowledge.

The impulse that comes to us from our birth, which leads us to posit figures of the common, has something irresistible about it. Natality—the mother of all desires—can but want the maximum. It cannot but posit a maximal protection, seize a truth that saturates the understanding and a meaning that gratifies thinking, deploy an encompassment of the vastest extension and a significance of the densest intensivity. In brief, natality makes us posit hegemonic fantasms.

The project of the present study is to grasp natality and mortality as they are joined in these fantasms; it is to rehabilitate the originary double allegiance, to lend a voice to the tragic condition silenced by the theticism of meaning, to try to comprehend the broken hegemonies. The fantasms of the common indeed are fractured upon this condition of phenomena that singularizes them as only death singularizes.

From Parmenides until certain motifs still in Heidegger, thinking means to grasp one *simple* originary reference. Now, our remaining faithful to the ultimates that we know because we are born and die will do away with any simplicity in the ultimate authority; it will do away with all simple ultimate authorities. Rather, a disparity will originarily hold us and bind us. The conceivable, the sayable, all that allows for communication and which gives life, does not pair up with singularization—notwithstanding whatever there is in our languages that, fashioned by the mechanics of determinate negation, *opposes* to life the inconceivable and the unsayable that singularizes and kills.

This disparity turns time against itself. An analytic of ultimates concerns the future in two ways. Natality pushes me to project the morrow. . . . But I know mortality, too, in the mode of the future, that is, as my singularization to come.

The disparity of ultimates also turns language against itself. From this point of view—or rather, from the standpoint of listening—words possess a double import. They subsume *particulars* as cases of a universal, and they point out deictic *singulars.*[4] The vital force of natality makes words signify the common. Hence, it opens up the space in which subsumptions occur outside of which no one would hear anyone. It is a space that no one who speaks will ever succeed in abandoning (if metaphysics amounts to the labor of subsumption, then one would have to say that there exists no non-metaphysical language). Yet the undertow of mortality also makes words point to singulars and singularizes us (if words always have this ostensive, monstrative bearing, if they signify not only a universal but still signify *to me* what to do or whom to be, then metaphysics never constituted a closed system). Hence the appellative and performative character of speaking, which strips language of overdeterminations.

In normative arguments it is a matter of hearing—of "repeating"—the fidelity to tragic knowledge, and this through the very din of theticism. Therefore it will be necessary to wrest the originary double allegiance from texts and theses bequeathed by tradition. The analytic of ultimates serves as a set of tools for such wrestings from univocal law. Faced with authorities posited as uniformly normative, this analytic serves to set free the singular and singularizing prescription that has been obliterated. We must not shun detailed analyses for such liberation. They are the price to pay, if not in order to unlearn, at least to observe at work the most widely shared reflex, which is much more than a professional idiosyncrasy of philosophers: the reflex of denying that beneath all law and obligation, it is the tragic that legislates. Thus we may hope, certainly not to cure ourselves, as one does a twitch, of the ancient reflex that posits and that denies, but to reveal, in the fantasms this reflex exalts, the work of the ultimates that breaks their hegemony.

Observing how tragic denial functions requires a topology. If subsumptive positings are indeed maximized from out of rather humble experiences,[5] they will be more easily understood when led back to their places of extraction. What phenomenon is being preserved, albeit hyperbolically, under this or that posited normative referent?

Here is the first sense in which I speak of *topos,* a useful sense for any reading of a text as long, of course, as one does not place too much emphasis on it. When the good attains the rank of being truly a being and thereby fulfills the function of the one, the *topos* of extraction is the more modest question: How is one to live well? Likewise, when substance becomes the terminus for all *pros hen* relations, its hyperbolized function no doubt arises from the marvel before man's technical know-how. How striking the transformations are that our hands (of fifth- and fourth-century Athenians) are capable of effecting upon materials! Topology seeks to go back to the given, under the posited. It inquires into the places of birth from which the impulse of natality emanates.

But topology is concerned with other places as well. Hannah Arendt described natality as the "principle of beginnings" that empowers us to embark upon the new. Consequently, for two centuries now—ever since Kant saw in the French Revolution the proof of an undeniable moral progress—there has been no lack of theories that locate historical beginnings, for carving out eras to think the epochs. Besides revolutions, the spiritual development of the people, advances in the means of production, discoveries that render normal science incommensurable with a preceding science, and inventions rearranging a configuration of knowledge and power, have been invoked as indices of a new beginning. It had seemed to me that the most obvious and the least thetic beginnings are marked when one natural language yields to another in our history. Everything begins differently as we change language. The *topoi* of which the topology takes inventory are then the Greek, the Latin, and the modern vernacular sites from out of which philosophy has spoken.

These two senses of *topos*—a phenomenon from which a thesis is set up, and natural language which for a time lends its parameters to theticism—converge on the hegemonies themselves. It is evident only retrospectively, of course, once the chips are down and fantasms have collapsed; only then can we venture the hypothesis that the Greeks relied on the one as on *their most common place,* and the Latins on nature.

What happens today, however, and has been happening for a century and a half (roughly since the deaths of Hegel and Goethe), is more than a destitution of one or the other such fantasm. Our lot is the diremption of any representation functioning as uniformly and simply normative, a diremption about which it would be wise to be wary of concluding that the end of metaphysics has come. . . . For such an end even to be thinkable it would indeed be necessary to suspend the impulse of natality, to disengage thought from that impulse. One might just as well ask desire to rid itself of its megalomania.

Diremption requires a new discipline in thought, not only to comply with norms, but also not to betray the deictic phenomena in their places of manifestation. We have yet to learn how to live in worlds where this singularizing undertow would no longer be denied. Phenomena are betrayed as they are subsumed under the one among them that gets saved and cultivated excessively. And we save phenomena (*diasôzein ta phainomena*) by letting them manifest themselves, by allowing the diremption of theses that console the soul and consolidate the city, by letting diremption legislate.

In the chapters that follow I will seek to understand such diremption in examining the manner in which the last of the thetic fantasms got instituted, then destituted. This last hegemonic fantasm, to state it straight out, is self-consciousness. As all that counts here are the opening and closing moments of a fantasmic regime, I will not hesitate to leap with both feet over the speculative career enjoyed by self-consciousness in the nineteenth century.

Just as the earlier ones, modern hegemony too will prove broken from its institution. Where, then, is one to look in order to learn how it put itself in place? There is, it seems to me, no more of a choice here than there was regarding the discourse instituting the *hen* (Parmenides) as well as the one instituting *natura* (Cicero and Augustine). It was Martin Luther who, after the breakdown suffered in the fourteenth and fifteenth centuries, started anew "watching the people's mouth speak" and listening to the living idiom; it was he who named the *locus noster* that the moderns will inhabit; and it was he who, with vehemence, pointed to the work of mortality in the institution of the new referent. Martin Luther, a "genius" rather than a professional of theticism, was this instinctual philosopher who begins epochally.

Endurance is required to follow in Luther the brute force of thinking. But what lessons in return! With his ardor, the vernacular shifts the parameters that went without saying on to a new territory (and this even when he writes in Latin); consciousness abruptly establishes itself as that territory that all henceforth inhabit; and since the Greek tragedians, no one has enunciated with comparable passion the double bind that holds us. He suffers singularization, and wills to suffer it. At stake in that passion is salvation. In Luther the modern pathos first bursts forth—autonomy and heteronomy, disparates that pull on self-consciousness, which from now on constitutes all phenomenality.

Kant will give to this pathos (not to be confused with the "pathological" but which renders it possible) figures of freedom and of being. In reading the *Critiques* these figures do not immediately leap to the eye. They emerge there however by a systemic necessity. The spontaneity in self-consciousness is broken along different lines of fracture that run in the opposite direction from Luther. While running in the opposite direction, the Kantian fault line will remain essentially related to it. This is why I will read "Kant with Luther."

Seeking to think the diremption of theticism—the conflict in being, the dissension which is being—Heidegger will finally rehabilitate the tragic condition. He will have us think the diremption that is our lot—the legislative diremption.

Passion thereby rids itself of the disguises under which it maintains theticism. Goethe's lines on *Leidenschaft* can also be read as addressing a *Leiden,* a suffering that seeks to arm itself. Now, the wound suffered by the law comes from its other which does not fall within its regime, which shares no common genus with it, and which nevertheless inhabits it like an irritant. The other to all genera is the singular. To say yes to the legislative diremption will be to rehabilitate the singular under common nouns, to affirm the *pathein* that singularizes us "to death," to understand all figures of the *arché* as figures *punitively* {*passiblement*} turned against themselves, and in this, as anarchic figures.

PART THREE

In the Name of Consciousness

The Modern Hegemonic Fantasm

Introduction

A century before Descartes, Luther recognized, circumscribed, and resolutely occupied the site upon which every thought process and every conceptual strategy of the next four centuries were to work. Self-consciousness is the philosophical terrain where the moderns believe themselves to be at home. Here they find a certitude capable of assuaging their pangs of doubt, an achievement sufficiently neutral to lend itself to being concretized in a moral conscience, a strategic instrument with a view to critical and revolutionary emancipations, also as a guarantee of an enclosed garden, interior and ultimate, and finally, as a source of new sciences. Three centuries after Luther, the topography of this terrain conceals hardly any more secrets. By then, it will already have been converted into a home for the "I-think" into which it invites phenomena so as to render them true. From the sinner lost through his deeds, but saved through his faith (Luther), to the world spirit disjointing all things as it creates them, but reconciling all things as it thinks them (Hegel), the subject who is conscious of himself will have grown up somewhat. . . . But the site where these dramas—individual salvation, universal reconciliation—unfold remains self-consciousness. The young Luther installs himself in this *locus noster*. He does not, however, install himself there alone: "Our place, where we ought to live with God, is consciousness."[1]

However, in order to grasp that which has been held to be a normative referent in a linguistic age of philosophy, it is not enough to situate it in its place. The *hen* certainly designates the site where the Greek nonomachies were played out; but in terms of forces in conflict, the one had normative power only insofar as it held these forces together (*synéchein*, Parmenides). The same goes for *natura*. It is assuredly the site where the Latin conflicts between laws was instituted, for example, the conflict of my nature against what is reasonable; but here again, this referent is normative only insofar as it imposes an order, the continuity between the *logos* of the soul, the city, and the world. It does not work any differently for modern self-consciousness, which traces the horizon inside of which all the dramas of the law are played out for us; and self-consciousness itself lays down the law insofar as—insofar as what? This is precisely the question. It will make the law neither as the one "holding together" contrary phenomena, nor as nature, "homologating" the phenomenal regions. Rather, consciousness makes the law; it makes the law in the manner of a condition "determining" all phenomena, a condition which is perhaps not altogether opposable to a cause effectuating phenomena.

As early as the sixteenth century it was said, "Luther is the father of the German language as Cicero was of the Latin language."[2] The linguistic era of modern philosophy opens up when Luther "sees the mouth of the people speak" (*dem Volke aufs Maul schauen*). Luther is thought to have unified the dialects and, above all, to have fashioned High German through his translation of the Bible. That translation, says Nietzsche, "has remained up until today the best German book." Luther's speech forms one body with his language. "In Germany, the preacher alone knows how much a syllable weighs and also how much a word. . . . The master work of German prose is, then, quite naturally the master work of its greatest preacher."[3] Or, in the words of the Grand Ferryman of the Rhine, Heinrich Heine: "Luther not only gave us the freedom of our movements, but also the means by which to move. He gave a body to the spirit; and to thought he gave speech. He created the German language."[4] He was an incarnation who brought to an end the instrumentalist practice of language and who, in the words of another commentator, despite his Latin "is entirely imbued with German."[5]

Above all, however, the modern vernacular age begins with an overturning of references that prefigures the revolution in the manner of thinking that occurs in the works of Kant and the Idealists; after Luther, "to be" means "to be for consciousness." The origin of all phenomenality is displaced toward self-consciousness. Without a doubt, a similar shift informs the works of Meister Eckhart. But it would be false to maintain in Eckhart that self-consciousness was a normative measure for representations and actions. Here, then, is what is first broached in Luther—and, as we will see, "broached" {*entamer*} in more than one sense. For two centuries now, the order considered to be natural has not been upheld. Manifold in itself, nature has crumbled under the weight which gave it millennial gravity: the weight of teleology. From the moment when the nominalists recognized the "absolutely" free creator—the Christian figure of the *telos* as ultimate authority—nature has been recognized as only relatively obligatory. Teleological nature was only *one* nature among innumerable possible natures. Accordingly, it is enough to understand nature in this way in order for its bankruptcy to be recognized by all and its hegemony to collapse from its system of ends. Thus, amidst the vertigos of the fifteenth and sixteenth centuries, when the absence of an ultimate referent became intolerable, Luther secured a new foundation. Only, like Parmenides and the Roman Stoics before him, he secured it without attenuating the anguish. Rather, he aggravated it. He broached the *locus noster* as one undertakes an occupation, but he also broached it as the sea corrodes the base of an island. No one will have more dramatically emphasized in consciousness—henceforth hegemonic—the *transcendental differend* that inaugurates the conflict of contrary attractions than does this first of the moderns.

Luther translates into an ontological reference what his contemporary, Copernicus (probably unknown to Luther), established as an astronomic certitude: the regularity in which we trust will in no case be that which we observe, but always and only that which we construe. Luther radicalizes the "Copernican" revolution by seeking the standard for all truth no longer in an originary order of essences, but in an originary act of consciousness. This act will be constitutive without, however, being spontaneous, and it will be nomothetic without being autonomous. It is an act in which death and life are conjoined with a violence not experienced since the birth of Greek philosophy and since that of Christianity. The modern referent is born fractured—and here again it is in this that our most intimate knowledge rises to speech. It cannot be said more simply nor more bluntly than Luther does: *simul,* we are simultaneously alive and dead.

He articulates this transcendental differing with a pathos which betrays the work of a hegemony at its birth. Yet he makes only a rough sketch of how this new referent and its inner cleavage are in their being. The guiding modern fantasm will be fully instituted only with Kant. Hence—whatever Kant says of this in his own declarations of intention—the strategies of life and of death are conjugated expressly as two strategies of being. Following the thread of an entirely coherent concatenation of arguments (even though it has escaped the attention of most commentators) from the precritical writings up to the *Critique of Judgment,* we will see that a conflict between two senses of being splits self-consciousness; that the referent from which the moderns expect supreme legislation produces, simultaneously and necessarily, its own transgression; and that the most ancient knowledge takes shape in this differing. Only the *singular* is, but it is unsustainable except when subsumed under some universal, hence as a *particular.*

In reading Kant with Luther, we are not in the least concerned with retracing the influence (impossible to establish) of one doctrinal corpus upon another. Nor are we concerned with recounting the hold that Lutheranism had over Kant's formation (easy to establish). Even in Luther it is necessary to look into the law otherwise than by picking away at the *pollachôs legetai* of this law. The dissension between legislation and transgression works on and breaks the ultimate fantasm that makes the law of all laws. One should not expect, then, an analysis of the complex body of laws as it is according to Luther, a body that requires works beyond human reach—that, consequently, we are not able to keep from transgressing and hence which thrusts us into sin. Finally, one should not expect a spectroscopy of practical reason freely procuring the moral law and submitting to it. I wish neither to disentangle an influence so as to sort out the history of ideas, nor to strip down a system to its bones in order to extract a framework of concepts. The conceptual structure in the works of a Luther or a Kant teach us nothing more about the specific constraints on modernity than can the history of ideas. I wish to show not what has been said *about the laws* (including that through which pure reason determines the will) in the sixteenth and then in the eighteenth centuries, but how the modern age, after the fashion of the preceding ages, springs into life with a new *law for all laws:* self consciousness, the condition both of the laws called theoretical or scientific as well as for practical and positive laws.

One last precaution: In reading Kant with Luther, we do not lay claim to a community of doctrine. On the other hand, it is indeed my understanding that the ascendant under which both of them work remains the same—the disposition which Luther institutes ardently, but also hesitantly, and which Kant *upholds* with the hand of authority. Perhaps Kant is, actually, "the philosopher of Protestantism."[6] In any case, self-consciousness remains the *locus noster* up to and including Husserl. Yet it is still necessary to know how to read Luther as the founding thinker of modernity. In the interior of the common arena delimited by the disposition of modernity, the key factors are completely different for Luther than for Kant. For example, crucial for all that can happen in the new *locus* is the opposition between autonomy and heteronomy; these terms are switched from Luther to Kant. In the works of the former, authentic self-consciousness receives its *nomos* from elsewhere. Saved through an extrinsic initiative, consciousness is essentially heteronomous and must remain so. In the works of the latter, a reason placing itself under the regime of heteronomy would thereby surrender its capacity to govern itself as a law unto itself, as well as its capacity to submit itself to the cause by which it is aware of being for itself. Modern self-consciousness, as we will see, is always consciousness of a cause over which we have no hold. Kant calls it a "fact of reason." By submitting ourselves to it we know in advance that reason is efficacious toward itself. Each "pathological determination" that we do not give to ourselves in advance would inhibit transcendental freedom understood as absolute spontaneity. Thus, heteronomy, the origin of salvation in Luther, becomes the root of all evil in Kant; inversely, autonomy, the tendency which is radically evil for Luther, in Kant turns into the supreme good of the person. This chiasm changes everything in the site of hegemonic self-consciousness, but it causes neither the site nor the disposition to change. Hence, "Kant with Luther."

The modern age begins when self-consciousness is established as the source and measure of all laws. This is not to say, contrary to what one reads from time to time, that the moderns "discovered" it. It is one thing to have a discourse, as old as Homer, which treats self-consciousness as one phenomenon among others; it is quite another thing to have a discourse that promotes this self-consciousness into an ultimate referent, into the source of the phenomenality for all that can become a phenomenon, into the dominant fantasm of an age. To dissipate the foolishness according to which this phenomenon would itself be counted among the "acquisitions of modernity," I will briefly indicate its veritable place of birth. Like all phenomena belonging to the world in which we live, self-consciousness has certainly known a moment when it was rendered especially problematic—in this sense, invented, discovered, acquired. But this occurred before Luther and Descartes, namely, in the passage from the first to the second poet-authors of the *Odyssey.*

Excursus: the consciousness of Ulysses

Muse, tell me of the man of innumerable feats
Of him, the destroyer of sacred Troy,
who was thrown about hither and thither.
He knows the towns of so many men
And has learned from them their customs.
How when at sea he did experience torments in his heart
Striving to save his life and to bring his comrades home!
But in spite of the fullness of his desire, he could not save them.
The ruin they endured was nothing other than their proper forfeit
Senseless as they were, they devoured the cattle of the Sun
And so were deprived by him of the day of their return.
To us, Goddess born of Zeus, recount that according to thy
good pleasure. (1, 1–10)[7]

In these verses which open the *Odyssey* there is something which ought to take one by surprise. All begins and is brought to a close with an invocation of the Muse. Not, undoubtedly, of that Muse found in the new catalogue, but quite simply of the *moûsa,* whose function it is to remember.[8] "Remind us," is the prayer that frames the prologue. Then, in broad strokes, the text situates the events the memory of which the poet asks be preserved. Some are placed before the moment in which he speaks, others afterwards. Her memory of things to come is turned toward the man tossed hither and thither; her memory of things past toward the destruction of the city in Ionia. The second and third verses thus fix the pivot linking the *Odyssey* to the *Iliad.*

A brief survey of a very condensed series of events follows: the wanderings to come. They lead the hero through apprenticeships in the towns and torments at sea. This summary, in its turn, draws to a close so as to establish the stake of these events: for Ulysses to save his own life and to bring his companions home. The *nostos,* the return home, is what will be treated in the poem. The poet's statement a bit further on (1, 87) concludes the proem and gives to the original narrative its title.

The summary draws to a close once again through the citation of a decisive episode. Obviously one expects the major episode which will pave the way for the entire story: "the day of return." The prologue can be ended only by going straight for this target and naming it. Does not its quasi-geometric rigor demand that the opening of the poem be tied together by where it will be concluded? Only an anticipation of the recoveries at Ithaca would be in accord with the extreme precision of its concentric circles inscribing, first, the key episode within the pursuit of return, then this return itself within the general fresco of Ulysses' adventures, and finally this very fresco within the program of the two epics.

Well, the prologue places a completely different episode at the center of these thematic circles. The geometric target is absent.

The return is certainly named, but following an episode portraying the oxen of Helios, their slaughter by the companions, and the resultant loss of those men to the sea. This interlude—four verses of the ten—is discordant. Not only does it deviate from the rigorous nutshell summary of the prologue, but in addition it introduces, into the grand plan of Homeric epics, something like a moral lesson. If the companions perished in the storm, they did so because they were looking for trouble. As demented as they were, by killing and eating the cattle of the son from on high, they, through "their own infamies" (*autôn gar spheterèsin atasthalièsin olonto*) laid a hand on the wealth of a god. Accordingly, Helios delays not in rendering them the same treatment by putting an end to their days. Their drowning is tantamount to a penal sanction. This is that upon which the prologue is centered. It is, then, a question of homecoming only indirectly; of direct importance is that the impious will be justifiably deprived—and for Ulysses this will be so most of all.

The reader remains cheated of the point for which the text prepares him, while nothing in the preceding lines permits him to expect what he ends up reading. Beginning with the sixth verse, a completely different interest is substituted for the synthetic survey of the narrative framework. This interest does not stem from anywhere in the *Iliad.* On the other hand, it dominates entire sections of the *Odyssey*—almost a third of the poem. Since the 1920s, there has been agreement that we read here the hand of a second poet, the Deutero-Homer.[9]

What is at stake, once again, is the "negative experience." Why do terrible things such as storms befall us? The response of the first poet is that they are the apportionment (*moîra*) of mortals, imparted by the gods (*theôn moîra*) and distributed on earth according to their council. This response is embodied in Moira who attributes to mortals their lots in return for the blindnesses that befall them and the angers which seize them (the *Iliad,* fully an account of allotments of suffering ceaselessly redistributed, opens with the anger of Achilles). Not even the immortals are sheltered from the provocations of anger. Accordingly, even without naming Moira, the first poet of the *Odyssey* portrays her along with any number of characters as early as the proem, following the prologue. Here he places the council of the gods. Why expose Ulysses to so many vicissitudes? Because in his blindness he has put out the eye of the Cyclops Polyphemos who was, by the way, the son of Poseidon. Ulysses brought upon himself the wrath of a god. It is on this account that the master who girds the earth and the sea relentlessly pursues him, seeking if not to utterly destroy him (a course the council refused to authorize), at least to deprive him of might, renown, ships, companions, clothes, and identity (in this Poseidon shall twice succeed: with the storm, carrying him to the home of Nausicaa, *Odyssey,* 5, 339ff., and in debasing him to the point of a beggar upon his return to the home of Penelope, *Odyssey,* 13, 341ff). None other than Zeus establishes this etiology. Before the united council, he states the reason Ulysses continues to wander far from Ithaca: the blindness—the negative portion—on account of which he allowed himself to be led along, as well as the wrath of Poseidon which followed upon it. Poseidon who girths the earth, driven by an implacable anger against him to avenge the Cyclops whose single eye he has put out (168ff).

From the beginning of the performance, the *Odyssey,* such as we have it, thus retraces two plots. They follow the same scheme: Ulysses strikes Polyphemos—the anger of Poseidon—the storm which takes from Ulysses his companions and his boats (9); the companions strike down the sacred oxen—the anger of Helios—the storm and the loss of the companions (12). The two series proceed from an infraction which gives rise to the anger of a god, which ends in a disaster. However, the two series are not *connected* to the initial infraction in the same manner. The first plot (of Homer) establishes an etiology entirely in accordance with Moira, while the second (altered by the Deutero-Homer) brings another etiology into play. It is through the construction of a justly earned pain that he overdetermines the second plot. As a result, the initial infraction does not have the same sense in the two authors. I leave to the side the plot involving Polyphemos and Poseidon, which is not thusly overdetermined (here Ulysses, in the face of grave danger, blinds the Cyclops in legitimate defense). To see how, for the first time in the Occident, self-consciousness becomes problematic, all that is important here is the revision in the plot involving the cattle of Helios.[10]

The original account of this plot connected events in the same manner as the metopes of a Doric frieze are connected. Undeviatingly, the author of the *Iliad* and of the major part of the *Odyssey* unfolds episodes by forming the scene around two or three characters.

The metope before the infraction on the isle of Thrace: The exhausted companions entreat Ulysses to touch land, for the duration of the night only. This metope places one worn-out man, the supplicant, before another: "You are hard, Ulysses! Your strength is without measure. / Your limbs never suffer weakness. Your skeleton is of iron. / Permit your companions who fall from exhaustion and drowsiness to set foot upon the land" (12, 281f). Ulysses concedes. However, a gale arises which lasts for an entire month. The living are spent, the fish and the birds are difficult to catch, stomachs are gnawed by hunger. Thus, Ulysses withdraws to implore the assistance of the gods.

The metope of the infraction: While Ulysses sleeps off to the side, the companions set upon the cattle of Helios. They skin the cattle, "detaching the thighs from the two sides, covering them over again with fat, / . . . and they grill the mass of viscera." (12, 360f).

The metope after the infraction: Helios, seized with anger, places himself before Zeus, seeking satisfaction.

The final metope: the storm. "Borne by the waves around the black ship, they resembled crows, / And by the god they were deprived of their return" (12, 418f).

According to this metopic reasoning, misfortune *happens* to the transgressors, just as exhaustion, the tempest, hunger, and even the decision—the fated share—to nourish themselves with forbidden flesh happen. Certainly they are struck down by a just return of things, but *diké* intervenes in this sequence only to re-establish an equilibrium,[11] and not at all to penalize a crime perpetrated with full knowledge of the facts. According to Moira, the etiology describes the slaughter of the cattle as a necessity born of distress and this distress as the due lot the companions share. The straying and the loss are "destined" to them. Who is the memorialist who, in the face of these cog-like turnings of circumstances, is deeply moved? No one is there who might sympathize. Like the Doric friezes, the Homeric metopes portray some sort of spectator that is quite other than a divine one.

On the other hand, the second wording of events traces an etiology which introduces into the narrative—and renders it henceforth problematic—self-consciousness.

The second poet, fully eclipsing the character at the end of the prologue, unfolds the events before the attentive gaze of Ulysses. In the scene on the isle of Thrinacia (Sicily?), Ulysses seems aware to the point of prescience (*eidôs aipyn olethron*). Even before setting foot upon land, even before the gale has arisen, he extorts from his companions an inviolable oath of abstinence. "Swear to me, every one of you, a powerful oath: / That if we come upon a herd of cattle or sheep, / That none of you, through a disastrous transgression, / Shall kill either oxen or sheep" (12, 298f). An oath hardly plausible in the circumstances, given that they still enjoy favorable winds and abundant provisions. Now, once having given an oath, what is it that the companions will do when they decide to set upon the cattle? They will take no notice of their own words. They will violate a pledge solemnly taken. They shall no longer act as if compelled by the mechanical turnings of distress. Rather, they will commit "a horrible crime" (*atasthalièsi kakêsi,* 12,300). No longer have they lost their way; they are guilty. Through all kinds of literary operations, the Deutero-Homer returns to this: Their ruin has the value of a penal sanction.

To grasp self-consciousness at its birth, it will be enough to try briefly and schematically to restore several of the traces that follow from this new insistence. What does the gaze that Ulysses casts over events, at the moment when he imposes the oath of abstinence upon his companions, imply for the epic scene? How is one to describe this gaze?

First of all, we shall look beyond the scene. Ulysses speaks suddenly as though from an observation post. While they are still sailing in absolute tranquillity, he already sees the troubles which await them on the isle. The parallel with the proem is glaring. There, the worldly comings and goings parade themselves before the arch-spectator: Zeus. In the second poet one can read a compositional maladroitness in the quasi-Olympian prescience of Ulysses.[12] The fact remains that in making his friends swear not to overstep the limit, Ulysses detaches himself from them so as to reach a panoptic site. What is it that, from out of this site, pushes him to demand the oath? The concern that a good captain has for the well-being of his crew? The caution against the "horrible crime" leads us to doubt this. His concern also makes him Olympian. From his place beyond the scene, he speaks as the guardian of the measure.

Afterwards, his is a gaze productive of a fault. In forcing them to take an oath, Ulysses *renders* his companions perjurers. By explicitly warning them (*proeipeîn*), he binds them in advance. Their act of despair is transformed into an act of moral failure. Zeus is made the chronicler of this other manner which humans have of going wrong—other than through the ancient cog-turnings of destiny. "With what ills do mortals not charge the gods./ It is from us, to listen to them, that their evils derive. Yet they themselves / through their own disastrous crimes (*sphêsin atasthaliesin,* third occurrence), strike themselves again with more suffering than their share (*hyper moron*) has reserved for them." (1, 32f). Zeus remains the serene spectator of the faults through which mortals inflict death upon themselves. A parallel serenity is not within human reach. Ulysses himself will suffer in his body the offense committed by his companions. "It is most needful that another / In the name of the gods is stirred and shares in suffering" (Hölderlin[13]). In the Deutero-Homer, this other is stirred because (like Zeus) he sees unhappiness in advance, and he feels compassion because (differing from Zeus) he knows suffering, his own lot. In trying to ward off *hubris,* Ulysses places his companions in a situation of bringing it upon themselves. He exposes them to the stinging wound of a fault. Through this he justifies in advance their catastrophic end.

Finally, the reflexive gaze. The linking together of events according to the difficulties brought about deliberately unfolds the scene before the eye of Ulysses. The observer now becomes a part of the scene. Ulysses figures here both as protagonist and spectator. He is observed giving in to pressure: "It is easy for you to force my hand, I who am alone" (12, 297). Then he contemplates the consequences and becomes indignant. With this reflexive gaze, we have the elementary trait of self-consciousness. The hero of the second poet is a character capable of returning to himself. He knows himself as a leader of men and as a guardian of their lot (*moros*). He is no longer the victim, cast first to one side, then to the other, always struggling as a thoroughbred actor. He sees and foresees the verdict which the weak are capable of bringing down upon themselves. He grasps the full sense of their possible transgression, he dreads it, beseeches them—and through this thrusts them into it. His reflexive gaze centers the metopic succession on a focal meaning. It is he who transmutes the infraction into a crime. The centering of the narrative and the transmutation of its argument are brought about starting from the same point: Ulysses knowing himself to be Ulysses. The lesson in responsibility that the Deutero-Homer administers is only possible given this gaze beyond the scene that is productive of the fault and reflecting it along with its consequences—the gaze which is the consciousness of Ulysses. Consciousness works upon situations otherwise than do the cunning of spirit, intuition, or tragic knowledge.

Even the name of Odysseus is a ruse, and when the occasion presents itself, doubly so. The word originates from the verb "to fly into a passion." At the birth of the boy, his father declared: "He will be called Odysseus, the one who flies into a passion" (*odyssamenos . . . Odysseus,* 19, 407f). Now, differing from an Achilles, Ulysses (*Oluxes,* the alternative form of the name) possesses the singular nature of knowing how to master his impulses. He never leaves, so to speak, the reflexive observation post. In following his anger, he would have nimbly settled the lot of Polyphemos. "Then, in my heart seized by anger, arose the thought / of my approach, of drawing my pointed sword the length of my thigh, / of plunging it into his stomach, there where the diaphragm envelops the liver, / after having felt the place with my hand. But another impulse restrained me" (9,299ff). The hero is then completely contrary to what his name leads one to believe. Essentially, he is cunning (*polutropos, poluméchanos, polumètis*). It also occurs to him to push a ruse to the point of subterfuge. "You wish to know my famous name, Cyclops? So, I will tell it to you. / . . . Nobody, such is my name" (9,364ff). The name "Outis"—from all the evidence, a variation of *Odusseus*—will earn the blinded Cyclops the derision of his brothers—and will give Ulysses his life. In this maneuver one has wanted to see the mark of an "inside" opposing itself to an "outside," an opposition inconceivable for someone such as Achilles. In taking on an appearance which denies his being, Ulysses confers upon himself a subjectivity differing within itself. The lie would then indicate the genesis of a dialectical subjectivity.[14] That is perhaps going too far. Be that as it may, self-consciousness works on events by means of a difference which is other than the spirit of cunning. It works on them through a difference between that elsewhere from which one considers the world—"Where are we when we think?"[15]—and the world considered.

Self-consciousness is furthermore distinguished from "noetic" intuition. The original epic most certainly abounds with scenes where a hero suddenly sees an ensemble of circumstances in which he finds himself caught. The plot which is knotted together around Ulysses, Polyphemos, and Poseidon is related by Homer in the form of an indirect narrative. Ulysses recounts it to the Phaeacians. The hero thus already embraces his past through a synthetic gaze, as one might regard the sequence of a frieze. Ulysses recounts that when escaping, with great difficulty, from the dwelling of the Cyclops, he heard the blinded Polyphemos invoke his father: "Fulfill my wish, Poseidon . . . / If I am truly yours, and if you glorify yourself in being my father, / that never shall Ulysses return home. / . . . However, if it is his fate to see his own again

/ . . . then grant that this might be only after a long time, after many proofs and the loss of his companions, / carried on a foreign vessel" (9,528f). Ulysses understands that henceforth he is involved with Poseidon himself. To grasp suddenly all of the details and implications of a situation is precisely the Homeric sense of *noein.*[16] Self-consciousness, however, is not episodic as is this *noein*—a synthetic intuition, abrupt, arising from a surmise.

Finally, self-consciousness is something other than tragic knowing (*anagnôrisis,* recognition), the great clarity of which blinds the heroes of Sophocles. The whole of *Oedipus Rex* traces the slow rising of this knowledge throughout compressed confrontations. When Jocasta understands what series of reversals has led her to marry this man, and who he is, she sees more than a frieze narrating a sequence of ever more coherent scenes of misfortune: the oracle announcing to Laius that he will die at the hand of his son, the newborn whose feet are pierced and who is left exposed in the desert, the parricide rashly committed in anger. . . . Jocasta sees *herself* otherwise to the extent that this knowledge arises in her. Self-consciousness, here again, transmutes an infraction—the murder at the fork of the road—into an offense, into deeds of death and love amongst those of the same blood. However, her gaze does not *produce* the offense; it is pure dejection. Ulysses speaks a lot. To Jocasta—as to Oedipus a short time afterwards—there remains only silence. Before withdrawing forever (the sequence in *Antigone,* 1235), she implores Oedipus: "Do not seek" (1064). The shepherd who formerly brought the child into the desert did not seek to question him. This is because she has already "seen." From this moment on, she possesses the knowledge which makes the hero tragic. Reflexivity accuses the heroine herself. The consciousness of Ulysses, rendered problematic as it is by the Deutero-Homer, works on the event by producing the perjurious companions. The consciousness of Ulysses says "you will do, you have done that." Jocasta's consciousness makes her a self-accuser in saying "I have done that."

The gaze which is self-consciousness can produce an accusatory effect only because it is at first reflective, referring deeds and actions, according to their measure, to the companions (the Deutero-Homer) or onto the self (Sophocles). The responsibility which overwhelms, so emphatically underlined by the second author of the *Odyssey,* is always only a derivative phenomenon in relation to reflexivity. To grasp a moral evil in which one is implicated supposes a grasp of one's self. It would not be difficult to show that philosophers, the ancients as much as the moderns, have been consistent in recognizing this phenomenal priority of self-consciousness over moral consciousness.

This does not mean that they have unanimously exalted self-consciousness into a standard by which to understand all other phenomena. The Deutero-Homer recognized the phenomenon that only much later will be called self-consciousness; he did not in the least, however, construe it to be an ultimate referent. For that to occur, he would have had to take a step back with respect to phenomena, a step not permitted by ancient thought on account of the very proximity of phenomena. It would have had to have been a step going from full consciousness—Ulysses knowing himself to be a leader of men; Jocasta knowing herself to be mother and wife—to a pure, formal consciousness. The problematic of a *referent ultimate by itself* will give birth to philosophy in the interval which separates Homer from the Tragics; the promotion of *formal self-consciousness* to the rank of ultimate will be possible only two millennia later.

I

Its Institution

On the Consciousness That Determines (Kant with Luther)

With Luther and Kant, self-consciousness comes to exercise a *regime*. For an entire epoch, which is hardly past, it will govern the manner by which every object of experience must be constituted. This comes to pass in the time of Copernicus. Self-consciousness thus finds itself promoted to an ultimate referent, constitutive of phenomenality as an ultimate authority—a hegemonic fantasm.

Its institution passes through two gestures, successive but strictly commensurable, of "Copernican" inversion. Their common measure resides in the I, serving henceforth as a principle. The two gestures of inversion do not culminate, however, in an I endowed with the same functions. These inversions discover the I as at first subject to an extrinsic determination, then as exercising its own determination. To establish its epochal regime, self-consciousness becomes passive before it becomes spontaneous. The first gesture is an inversion in the subjective apparatus forming the experience of speech or the word (Luther); the second gesture is a parallel inversion in the subjective apparatus of sensible experience (Kant).

The fantasm through which the moderns will live is instituted with much struggle and many pains. As an I, formally one and identical to itself, it governs our epoch. Its struggles and its pain result, however, from a differend which traverses it from the moment of its accession to a subsumptive position. The new receptive apparatus for the experience of speech is such that there the subject discovers itself living and dead ("justified and a sinner"), simultaneously. Throughout several of Luther's brief texts, I will seek to discover how this identity and this differend are articulated in the regime of passive consciousness. Above all, I will choose these texts from his two systematic works, the *Commentary on the Letter to the Romans* and *De Servo Arbitrio*.[17] I will then ask whether under the regime of spontaneous consciousness the identity of the I continues to be traversed by a differend. To see here with clarity, I will read the series of rare passages where Kant makes a statement concerning his comprehension of being. There is good reason to interrogate these closely, seeing that here "to be" signifies sometimes the active positioning of a given (through a category of modality—in German, the act of *Position*), while at other times the givenness of the given (*Setzung*). The question will be to know whether there is a systematic necessity to this duality, a necessity having something to do, perhaps, with the very promise which the moderns invest in self-consciousness.

The single and formal I rules over experience in legislating for it. If, however, subjective legislation must give rise to a differend in its own dominion—thereby making it impossible to govern through recourse to the I—then the law of laws to which the moderns submit themselves will not fulfill the normative expectations invested in it any better than did its Greek and Latin antecedents.

Before looking at some of these passages in Kant, we will first see how self-consciousness in Luther accedes to its hegemonic rank (first chapter), and then what it is in the *simul* that immediately breaks its hegemony (second chapter).

A

The Regime of Passive Consciousness

'An Obedient Spirit that Lets Itself be Broken . . .'

CHAPTER 1

The Identity of the "I"

Transcendental logic and consciousness in a differend with itself impose upon Luther a single necessity. What is the obvious fact that gives rise here both to a new logic and to a new sense of the tragic?

*Topography of speech**

The logic of the formal I and the aporia of the differend that is its consequence are not only announced by Luther in a single breath; he puts them forth with autobiographical accents betraying an urgency which is at first neither theological nor psychological. The new logic is allied with a new sense of the tragic as early as his *Commentary on the Letter to the Romans.* In this text, the young Luther still follows medieval practice. For each verse commented upon, he offers a short analysis of words (*glose*, from *glossa,* 'tongue'), then a doctrinal explication (*scholies*, from *scholion,* 'annotation'). In such a setting, one does not expect confidences. Accordingly, the autobiographical "I" only rarely pierces through here. On the page which is the most remarkable in this regard, he expresses himself with crude formulas (in this period, these were not yet Luther's stamp, as they would progressively become with the progression of the controversies). These are the lines where Luther repudiates the logic of things and solemnly affirms the tragedy of the *simul.* "Either it is me who has never understood anything, or the scholastic theologians have . . . dreamed." Both of these seem to have been the case: "Foolish as I was, I remained incapable of seeing. . . ." "I struggled with myself without knowing that pardon is real, even though, for all that, it does not cleanse us of sin." The context is that of pardon. Does it wipe away sin or not? The Scholastics believed that it did. Thus to them he says "O you senseless ones! O Theologian pigs! Here I say to you: Get a move on! Now, I pray you, stir your hands! Be men! Place there all of your strength that evil desires may no longer be in you!" (*sch.* 4,7 cor.). If these desires are allowed effectively to be uprooted, then pardon will render man as innocent as Adam before the Fall. If, on

**Speech* here translates *parole*. Occasionally it will be rendered as *word,* especially when it is understood in its theological context as well as when it is necessary to de-emphasize the abstractness of the noun "discourse" in favor of the concrete event of hearing.

the contrary, they persist, even seeking occasion to be inflamed like matches (*fomes,* from *fovere,* 'to heat'), then foolish will be the one who claims our will is capable of stripping them away. What will follow from this, then, is that we still remain corrupted by a "radical evil" (ibid.) that cannot be extirpated. These accents signal that it is essential to read attentively.

What do the dreamers maintain? That all species of sin—original sin transmitted since Adam, as well as actual sins committed according to occasion—can be wiped away. How, then, do they understand these sins? "As if here it were a matter of certain things that could be whisked away in a split second." It is a question of presence and absence, where the entire problem of injustice—which is to say of evil—will be about knowing whether justice "is found to be given or to fail to appear." But, asks Luther, what is it that can be found either as given or as failing to appear? What is it that is sometimes present and sometimes absent? In what region of experiences does one encounter these phenomena susceptible of being the case here and now, but not there or later on? Luther says that it is in the region of those phenomena that are called *res,* things. Do we not qualify as "realist" those doctrines which call true that which concerns things and their ways of being? In Luther's time the science of "saying the truth," of *vere loqui,* is logic (coupled with the science of *recte loqui,* grammar, and that of *ornate loqui,* rhetoric). But what logic? That which examines the signifying modes (*modi significandi*) manifesting the modes of understanding (*modi intelligendi*) which, in their turn, manifest the modes of being (*modi essendi*). What are these last modes? They are divided first into being present and, as Luther puts it, being "lifted off and swept away"—being absent. Such a logic is a logic of things, the most robust preconception that helps one makes one's way through life.

To that, Luther opposes "the consciousness of being unjust," whose great vitality serves to underline the fact that pardon does not efface injustice. There is in consciousness a constitutive element which does not fall under the "either-or" of present and absent. Through a great effort of retrospection upon his years of apprenticeship, years of introspection into the knowledge of belief, of infractions even in academic style, not to forget polemics, he reorients the axis of received questions. "One could know neither that which is sin, nor that which is pardon." This is because one would be questioning them according to a poorly oriented axis. Thus, the contents which begin to become a problem with Luther are not new. Rather, the ancient contents are found to be rendered problematic in a different way. A "new result in the research into evil," then? In seeking to understand the minute questions of daily life or the less minute questions such as those concerning good and evil, what we happily call research results are determined beforehand by the manner in which we raise the problem, that is, by how it is problematized. It is there that naïvete lies in wait for us. The axis which orients our questions is, in its turn, the most difficult to render problematic. Nevertheless, it is here that one is deceived about the very type of responses one will obtain. Copernicus and Luther discover at the same moment that those who rely upon sound good sense in their problematizations risk obtaining soundness to the detriment of sense. This is because good sense is the natural ally of things which are seen. In regard to Copernicus, Fontenelle will describe the project of the moderns as a struggle against confidence in the eyes: "One does not easily persuade men to put their reason in the place of their eyes."[18] Treating the minute and the less minute "as if it were a matter of certain things that can be whisked away in a split second" still remains the way of posing the question—or of not posing it—of what, for reason, is going to have the prestige of good sense. Luther qualifies this *prestige of things present* as "pure madness." One will have difficulty accusing him of not knowing what he is doing. He knows, and he says, that he is reorienting an entire mode of thinking; he does so by directing the axis of inquiry elsewhere, thus rendering the old problems problematic in a different way; and he is no less explicit about the old orientation, hereafter senseless, than he is about the new, henceforth the only sensible one: to think no longer according to "things," but according to "consciousness."

Why such anger against the theologians? Because they understand nothing about sin. They treat it as a task which you set for yourself (or with which you are born) and which is lifted from you. They count it amongst the *entia,* beings, claiming "that sin can be removed as long as man lives . . . as if sinful deeds were removed, in the metaphysical sense, just as one removes a layer of paint from a wall" (*sch.* 7,1 cor.). It is the 'havingness' {*ayance*'} (*habitus*) which, according to the Aristotelians, "sticks to the soul like paint to a wall" (*sch.* 7,18). In this polemic against the logic of things, self-consciousness is instituted as the focal point of another logic: transcendental logic.

Until we are more fully informed, the opposition between things and consciousness obviously is not sufficient for maintaining that we are dealing here with a transcendental logic, or that this logic dispenses with entitative logic, or that such a turn can implicate what is beyond Luther and the specific problems to which he addresses himself, or, above all, what the necessity is in claiming this new logic and, the case arising, a new sense of the tragic. However, the opposition between things and consciousness that Luther highlights all along suffices to render his procedure of consequence. His transcendentalism (if it proves to be that) remains inchoate because it is inimical to autonomous reason. Notwithstanding, he is not in the least tentative in respect to his presuppositions and implications. He immediately takes cover under the naïvete that characterizes reasoning through systematic doubt—a reasoning which in complete meditative candor wanders from the act of "I think" toward the *thing* thought: "Thus, while I wished to think that all was false, it was necessarily obligatory that I, who thought it, was something."[19] To this Luther gives the pre-emptive retort: Leave the domain of consciousness and not even *scientia* will remain for you, but only *entia*[20] —a reversal of perspective, however, that should have disturbed its unquestionability.

"Foolish as I was, I remained incapable of seeing. . . ." The birth of the modern hegemonic fantasm occurs in a crises arising from terrors and ignorance, following from a new way of seeing. The terrors of Luther had been unleashed by Paul: "The justice of God is revealed" (Romans 1:17). Indeed a terrifying little phrase for an age in which the last judgment was dramatically heightened as never before[21]—a drama fixed a few years later (thanks to the funds extorted, above all in Germany, through the sale of indulgences) on a wall of the Sistine Chapel. Terror: where is my place in this fresco—amongst those who ascend or who descend? If God is "entitavely" just, if his justice, wisdom, etc. are "perfections," if at the end of time, he will apply these and settle the final question, if he is the just judge who will have in any case, the last word, then I am lost, "in my reality a sinner," "sick unto death." The Luther overwhelmed by this nightmare preferred that there be no God at all and consequently no damnation. Despair and anguish will accompany him throughout his writings. Whether or not he had *causes* for such persistent anguish,[22] his systematic *reasons* stay in the background of his consciousness of the subject: a sinner, but nevertheless justified; simultaneously rendered just without any excess of sin and being rendered a sinner without there ever being an ultimate justification. In understanding justice otherwise than as a quality of a being, I cease being foolish. But I remain—I become—the healed-diseased, the living-dead, thus anguished in my very roots. Once a new logic is established and the epochal threshold passed over, the reist stupor is driven out. As for the terror, it gets much worse.

What, then, is the new critical vision separating one epoch from another? The key definition is "By the 'justice of God' one should understand not that through which He Himself is just, but that which comes from Him and by which we are rendered just" (*sch.* 1,17). Read in this way, Paul speaks of God not as he would be in his being, but as he appears in terms of what he does within our consciousness. Even more—and here is the constant in the Lutheranism that marks the epoch—Revelation never speaks of God, but it always and only speaks of modifications in the way we understand ourselves. It speaks only of the phenomenal God that appears, rendering us just.

The question is no longer "Who is just and in what manner?" (ibid.), which is a speculative, Greek question because it presumes that justice is the result of our actions, and it is also a mortal question because it condemns these actions to remain deficient. The justice which one can fulfill is always justice *before* a moral law, be this given from outside by some legislator or inscribed within hearts. Now, on account of this very exteriority, no human effort will ever make us unfailingly obedient to the moral law. In trying on one's own to become a just agent, one can only fail and be lost (hence the ineliminable anguish). Consequently, the judgment is foreseeable. If God is like a just judge, and if we remain always and necessarily lacking in regard to the demands of the moral law, then the judgment can only be disastrous. Through his reading of Paul, Luther learns to pose the question otherwise. The question is no longer one of our rendering ourselves just, but of seeing us, of recognizing us as justified by a new understanding that we have of ourselves—rendered just, already placed *within* divine justice. This is the breakthrough. It consists in an inversion. From protagonists of a justice which destroys, we become beneficiaries of a justice which restores. "Then I felt entirely reborn, entering through the great open gates of paradise."[23]

By regarding myself according to my own works, I can only be lost through the whole of my nature (phylogenetic); by regarding myself according to the works of God, however, I am saved through the whole of my nature (ontogenetic). The conflict of this double perspective doubly encompassing me, makes up the transcendental tragedy in Luther to which we will have to return. The eye here is "full," directed to works and their consequences; in this respect it resembles the eye of Ulysses. I see the whole of my nature twice: as corrupted and as saved. Only, the inversion within this way of thinking does not stop here. In reorienting the axis of inquiry, Luther renders problematic the very gaze that the subject directs upon itself. This time it is an empty, formal, pure gaze that henceforth makes for transcendental logic. The eye which is self-consciousness sees with an efficacy heretofore unknown, an efficacy that is *a priori* because it is constitutive of self-comprehension.

Ever since the Vienna Circle at the beginning of the twentieth century, there have been those who like to speak of a "linguistic turn" that philosophy supposedly took, declaring that all valid propositions depend on elementary propositions of which they are the functions, and that philosophy is no longer a body of doctrines, but the activity through which we attempt to clarify what we say, etc. . . . Others, less inclined to renounce systems, trace this turn back to the Idealists, in whose work language is constituted as the medium of intersubjectivity. Or rather, if every judgment is an affair of language and if synthetic *a priori* judgments constitute the key issue in Enlightenment criticism, then was not this turn taken, properly speaking, with the *Critique of Pure Reason*? Now, transcendentalism is concerned essentially with language. Thus, this linguistic turn would have been taken as early as the sixteenth century, when self-consciousness achieved hegemony, an ascension effectuated through *speech*. In being addressed to a listener, language becomes central, first of all through its exterior function. It is the medium of appeals—of an announcement—going from one endowed with vocal cords to a listener endowed with an intact eardrum (Luther). Only later can it become the milieu of the secret judgments of reason (Kant), then of intersubjective recognition (Hegel), and finally, of grammatical usages (Wittgenstein). The breakthrough beyond the logic of things occurs through living speech, speech reaching us from outside.

It is not difficult to grasp the implications of this breakthrough for the new epochal referent. The law which condemns and the law which saves, what do these signify? Both command obedience. Accordingly, only those phenomena that have the character of speech can demand to be obeyed. The law which presents us with a moral requirement and the faith which situates us inside such a requirement (as he who makes use of all of his civil rights is *within* his rights) are the two modifications of hearing that exhaust the range of speech capable of soliciting us. The new epochal referent is essentially concerned with speech, with the authority by which it calls on the subject and with the milieu—self-understanding—in which it speaks to the subject.

Luther distinguishes "the utterances of the law from those of promise." The first make sin known; the others snatch us from despair and from the death which follows. The former as well as the latter strike self-understanding. The question is to recognize myself, or to not recognize myself, as incapable of perfecting myself (just as the ancients searched to make themselves into works of art). "The voice of the law is heard by those who know not their sin. . . . While the word of grace only comes to those who, conscious of their sin, are overcome by despair." If self-understanding is movable, it is because it is entirely a matter of hearing. The word which it is capable of hearing is essentially one and is refracted into the law and into grace. In a state of latency, consciousness despises this single word. "Those who have not yet experienced the workings of the law, who neither recognize their sin nor feel death, scorn the mercy promised by that word" (*SA* 683f). The period of latency thus resembles a prelinguistic stage. The law presents consciousness with the word, and grace places it within the word.

The stage prior to the word is also that prior to all authority. Hence it seems fitting to distinguish three *sites* that we are able to occupy in respect to the word: the site of infants and monomaniacs (*monii*) ignorant of the law, without sin (the moment of latency on this side of good and evil); the site of the adolescent awakening to reason, discovering within himself the law and, with it, sin (the moment of anguish and despair, where the law reveals to us our incapacity to ever realize the good without miscarrying); and finally, the site of the adult "cured" of the battles of adolescence through an extrinsic intervention, thanks to which our faults are no longer reckoned upon us (the moment of salvation through faith) (*sch.* 7,8). When the law makes itself known, it seems to place a crippling obstacle over against justice; when we receive the revelation that justice has been fulfilled in the law through the same act which renders us just, we are placed within the authority of the accomplished law.[24] Thus, the *topoi* are, prior to, in the face of, and in the word, what constitute authority. In this *topography of the word,* the liberating breakthrough is produced in passing from the second to the third sites. It is there that "the freedom of the Christian" is born.

The description of these steps follows that given by Augustine. It is as though they are moments of a process of maturation. Now, Luther proposes yet a further description, better suited to his dramatic temperament. It also thereby becomes clear not only what the first effect of the law is (an antagonisms that consumes me), but even what the agent is that at first has neither morals nor faith and then morals, and finally is a believer. "To make a comparison with fire in limestone: there it sleeps, hidden; one does not even know that fire can be found there; but if water is poured there, the fire will have something of what it needs to show itself. Not that water puts fire in limestone; all it has done is in its way make us recognize what is there; without the fire seeking it, the water has come to illuminate it. It works the same way for the will of man and the law. He finds himself already in sin, but he is unaware of it until he knows the law and receives it. Then, without it being the fault of the law, he burns white hot. As oil extinguishes the living coals of limestone, so grace extinguishes the furnace" (*gl.* 7,8). The latency of fire in active limestone, combustion through hydration, and finally, the appeasing effect of hydrocarbons, an example, clearly medieval, of processes which postulate metaphorically a subject that has such experiences. This subject, on the other hand, is not a medieval subject, for one learns nothing about it except processes. Let us call this non-entitative subject the "I" and understand by this whatever in us hears the word and is affected by it. Often in his texts (notably in *De Servo Arbitro*), the function of the I understood in this way amounts quite simply to the will inasmuch as it resembles hearing. Our will is *pathetic* in that it submits to callings, it suffers; that it passes from latency to confrontation, then to obedience, where it accepts the non-imputation of failures. And what is the first effect of the *pathos* effectuated through the word? Man "is already in sin, but he is unaware of it until he knows the law." When the word affects us (*pathein*) with its authority, it makes us understand ourselves differently. I, hear, self-understanding, as these are arranged prior to, in the face of, and in the word—that is the sustaining framework on which an epoch will be built.

The new site that we inhabit is delimited by this constellation of one stable pole of identity (the I), one constitutive act (hearing) and one medium capable *a priori* of being modified (self-understanding). In Luther, only that which manifests itself on the stage marked out by these cardinal points—on the stage of self-consciousness—can become a phenomenon.

Self-consciousness is structured from within through the effects of the word. Accordingly, in the expression "topography of the word," the preposition "of" signifies the subjective genitive, not the objective. In describing the regions of indifference, then of morality, and finally of salvation, Luther does not seek to define the terms of his statements. He seeks to give a topology of the enunciation which carves out these regions, and not of the statements which pertain to these regions. His new logic is supposed to retain the efficacious assignments of subjects to these sites, while the old logic, when it comes to treating the word and its effects, confines itself to defining essences. He does not ask: *What are* the irresponsibility prior to, the moral responsibility in the face of, and the healing response within, the word? He asks: *How* does the word situate us in relation to itself? It situates us then, as we shall see, by giving rise to the facts of consciousness.

The scene of the *topoi* where one and the same word is given to be heard, saying at first, "you must," and then, "you can"—this scene may be called transcendental. In adopting this term, I do not mean to include Luther within some doctrine concerning man, God, or the world. Rather, the term designates the project of discovering in experience the *a priori* part borne by the subject. Obviously I am orienting myself here with the help of Kant.[25] Luther circumscribes the scene where the Kantian critique will operate. This does not mean to say that he anticipates the architectonic details.

His breakthrough is simple, as was the Copernican revolution. It is also charged with formidable difficulties. To elucidate several of these, let us bear in mind the topography of the word. Further on, in regard to the "radical" evil and to "perverse" teleology—and again in regard to Kant—I will return to the relation, which has nothing fortuitous about it, between the will and self-consciousness. Here I will content myself with bringing up several of the difficulties which bear directly on the transcendental status of a thought for which phenomena are modifications in our manner of self-understanding, modifications effected by speech. As it is practiced by Luther, the transcendental method is not applied to the type of experiences that become problematic beginning with Descartes and Hume. He has no interest in these, which are not verifiable and of which the spiritualists (*Schwärmer,* exalted spirits, more numerous and influential in his epoch than in Kant's) take advantage. The pivotal experience, which renders his transcendentalism essentially veritable, is not lodged in sensibility, but in language. As for the difficulties, they have to do with the relation between phenomena and consciousness, with the systematic role of speech, with the new status of causality, and finally, with the unity of the I.

Luther's inquiry into the modifications our self-comprehension undergoes ends in a web of subjective conditions preceding every actual experience of latency, of law, or even of faith. But these modifications that affect the I in coming from outside, and the justification in which they culminate, will be passive, received, "imputed." Differing from a critique of autonomous reason, his *critique of the I capable of listening* discovers a web of functions organizing modes, not of spontaneity, but of obedience.

Being-for-consciousness

In a critique of the I capable of listening, how is the phenomenality of phenomena constituted? Phenomena themselves, which become problematic for Luther, have been so ever since Christian revelation. In resonant tones they allude to the question: Where am I going? . . . With the discovery of passive justification, however, these phenomena are now deployed in a field of tension marked by two certitudes: that of going to ruin, in which phenomena are abandoned to the understanding of ourselves that we are able to conceive ("works"), and that of being saved following the understanding of ourselves which we can only receive ("faith"). The question of knowing whether Paul, Augustine, and others also understood revelation in this manner is here beside the point. The only issue is the new hegemony that has no antecedent: my accepting or not accepting recognition by the gaze that saves. All phenomenality is constituted between these poles.

In the field thus marked out, the old phenomena are rearranged by their reference to the understanding that the I can have of itself, and in this sense, by reflection. Now, to refer something to my reflection is to represent it to myself. At the prelinguistic stage, on this side of good and evil, I see the world otherwise than I do once wrenched forth from the sleep of innocence, and differently still again, according to whether the law terrorizes me unto death or faith gives me life. This new phenomenality is constituted by representations stemming from my being placed prior to, in the face of, and in, the word. The dreamed-of immediacy with "things" is here rent apart; the modifications in the self-understanding determine representations and for the first time in history we are concerned with phenomena in the critical sense. Thus there are *phenomenal worlds,* worlds of infantile self-satisfaction, of the pressure toward the moral good, and finally of the tranquillity in received justification. Because they owe their being to representation, the phenomena that fill out the constituted worlds through speech or the word are no longer things, removable through grace. Precritical, they remain of a manipulable order. One washes away sins as one does color from a wall, sells indulgences like merchandise, administers salvation as one supervises a dependent. When it is a question of removing, buying, or supervising, beings can only be placed either within reach or beyond it; thus their essence (*Wesen*) consists in that they "are given or are absent," which is to say, it consists in their presence. In Luther, on the other hand, the critical understanding of phenomena—through reflection and thus through representation—desubstantializes things.

This understanding also desubstantializes the I. If the I boils down to the activity of consciousness accompanying the modifications in self-understanding, then, with this, every notion of the entitative I ceases. Luther does not let himself polemicize against the Aristotelian definition of man in which "speech" specifically modifies the genus "living." This definition understands nothing about living speech. Living speech strikes the eardrum and tells us who we are. It strikes also as a sight can strike us. We are "just through the sight of grace." (*sch.* 4,7 cor.). The essence of phenomena consist in their mode of appearance to the I; likewise, our own essence consists in our appearing beneath the gaze of God. Following our self-understanding, we appear there as either accepted or rejected. Because it translates a hearing, a seeing, and an understanding, such an "either-or" is opposed *in toto* to all entitative conceptions which translate into a doing and a taking. I see and understand phenomena according to the way in which I see and understand myself: lost in the face of the law or rendered just within faith. And where will that be placed which can be regarded only in its being represented? Nowhere else than in consciousness. If Luther discovers the possibility of regarding the self as it is regarded by God, he has already reassigned all that is to a new place. "Our place is consciousness." There, in this place, the site of phenomena is no longer determined by being within reach; nor their essence by constant presence. Their site is determined through the modifications in self-understanding, and their essence through their relation to the I.

Finally, the Lutheran critique desubstantializes God himself. "What signifies: To have a God, or, What is God? Answer: One calls a God that from which one ought expect every good and near to which one should seek refuge in every distress. Thus, to have a God is nothing other than believing in him and placing full-hearted trust in him. I have often said that only trust and faith produce both God and idol. If faith and trust are just, your God is also just. Inversely, where trust is false and afoul, there the just God can no longer be found. These two questions actually are only one: faith and God. As I say, that to which you give your heart and to which you entrust yourself, there is that which is, properly speaking, your God."[26] Luther could not have better summed up his phenomenal notion of God. He never expresses himself about the thing itself that would be the *supreme* referent (who remains "hidden").[27] He inquires solely into the *ultimate* reference, namely, self-consciousness. There are two relations in which God is made a phenomenon—through the law, he avows death; and through faith, he saves.

The methodical inversion is here again obvious. When the I comes to occupy the referential center in every phenomenal constitution, things in themselves can only remain beyond reach. Moreover, to show themselves to us, phenomena must submit themselves to the formal conditions proceeding from the I. Kant will formulate it, saying, "The conditions of the *possibility of experience* in general are also the conditions of the *possibility of the objects of experience*."[28] Although he understands something different both by experience and by object, Luther subscribes in advance to this principle of identity between subjective and objective conditions: "The justification [coming] from God and the adherence to God (coming from us), these are both one" (*Iustificatio dei et credulitas in deum idem est, sch.* 3,4). Could one hope for a more precise formulation, before the Kantian accomplishment, of the supreme Principle of all synthetic judgments? The justifying God and the subject adhering to him are constituted according to the same *rules*—the "prior to–in the face of–in" the word. For Kant, the subjective conditions rendering sensible experience possible are the very ones which render possible objects as phenomena. For Luther, the subjective conditions rendering the experience of justification possible are the very ones which render possible the object which is God insofar as he is a phenomenon. To this identity of conditions, Luther does not hesitate to give a further twist: "Faith is creative of divinity"—adding, to mark precisely the phenomenality (and what Feuerbach will neglect in his reading), "not in his person, certainly, but in us."[29]

Luther inaugurates the transcendental turn by taking up a single question in reference to God: How does he become a phenomenon? In a strict sense, a being becomes a phenomenon only by entering into our consciousness and submitting to the rules of reflection. In Luther, these rules are a matter of the capacity to hear the word. His transcendentalism is a *critique* in that he separates the functions which necessarily and universally form parts of listening, either (both) to obey the word which renders guilty or (and) that which renders innocent. According to both of these modifications, the being of beings is the very being of the consciousness in which it shows itself.

The history of philosophy before the modern age has not been lacking in formulas positing some sort of identity of the non-identical. "Thinking and the thought are both one," repeats Aristotle.[30] They are so in the experience of movement and thanks to the mediating role of the intelligible form. The identity of transcendental conditions is different. For Luther, they render possible not kinetic experience, but metabolic experience, the experience of a sudden reversal. Now, in this *métabolè*, which is not a *métanoein* for it is no longer a question of "being" converted {*"se" convertir*}, nothing mediates between a subject here and a God there. The word is God himself becoming phenomenon, addressing himself to the listening I. From here on out, formulas of identity signify the absence of mediations. The whole question will be to know what the originary act of the receptive I must be, if the conditions of the possibility of listening are also the conditions of the possibility of the word that is heard. Starting from this act, one will proceed to grasp better how the two modalities of the word—the law and the gospel—modify the understanding that I have of myself. Indeed, it is impossible to uphold the transcendental turn in the absence of an initial act within the subject, diversifying itself *a priori* according to the modes of possible experience.

The identity of being under the new hegemony can be seen in terms of the understanding of truth that results from it. For what Luther calls "metaphysics" (*sch.* 7,17)—speculation about things—the truth consists in the conformity between a statement and a state of fact; now, in the constitution of phenomena through reflection, truth still signifies a conformity, but it is the conformation of my vision of myself to the gaze which God turns upon me. In the "metaphysical" constitution of phenomena, error is the contrary of conformity; in their constitution through representation, however, the contrary will be altogether different. It is useful to pause briefly here to grasp better that in which self-consciousness determines phenomenal being.

In Luther, truth becomes problematic in the same manner as justice does. He interrogates the limits of a single self-understanding in each. Accordingly, both are explained in terms of the reversal that makes him feel "entirely reborn and entered through the great, open gates of paradise." It is first of all necessary to understand the justice of God as that through which he renders me just and acceptable in his eyes. Now, by this it is also necessary to understand that God "is justified" (Romans 3:4). A Pauline turn which might surprise. It is the same for truth: "That God is truthful" (ibid.). Is not this prayer absurd? He states in the optative what should only be in the indicative. But this wish is addressed to ourselves. Having been rendered just and true, it is still necessary for us—but this is not still one more act—to recognize our having been so rendered. The active justification of God, that through which he renders us just, is a divine *operation;* on the other hand, the "passive justification of God" (*sch.* 3,4 cor.), that through which we recognize what he has done for us, is a human *confession*. The same goes for truth also. In forbidding speculation upon the thing-in-itself which would be God, Luther likewise has to remain silent about truth as a divine attribute. To say that God is true—or that he has spoken the truth in his promises, that he is truthful—signifies, then, that he has treated *us* effectively according to his promises. But this amounts to nothing so long as man does not confess it as such. Hence the imperative: "God must be truthful." The commandment is not addressed to God, but to the beneficiary of justice and of operative truth. "God himself becomes just and true in his word . . . through one's acceptance of them and holding of them to be just and true" (*sch.* 3,5 cor.). Luther insists that "God is mutable at the highest point . . . As each is in himself, thus is God for him in His coming to him: just for the just, pure for the pure, wicked for the wicked" (ibid.). Here it is neither a question of divine intrinsic qualities, nor of qualities he bestows upon us, but only of those we render to him in recognizing him, to him, according to what makes us us. *"Mutatio extrinseca"* (ibid.) is the phenomenal manner in which the constitutive absoluteness of self-consciousness is betrayed. The anger of God is shown only to a consciousness "in the face of" the world. His fidelity appears to a self-consciousness "in" the word. As is self-consciousness, so is that which can become phenomenal in it. Indeed, the phenomenal God is mutable at the highest point, namely, in being able to veer from the principle of life to the principle of death. Here are the two empirical modifications of consciousness whose *a priori* conditions we must search for further.

It follows that the contrary of truth as conformity cannot be error. It is damnation. Not to render passive justification to God, not to render him truthful, amounts to being condemned by oneself. Again, it is a matter of the gaze: "The disbelief with which [the recalcitrant] judge and condemn His words, He regards as [their own] injustice and damnation." (ibid.) Above all, a matter of valuation. God esteems as justified those who esteem him just and truthful. "The whole weight of this conversion resides in our valuation (*in aestimatione nostra*)" (ibid.). Self-consciousness—accepting justification or refusing it—determines phenomenal being by assessing it as conforming or not conforming to the word. Moreover, the phenomena include both exterior givens, such as the written and transmitted word, and interior givens, such as desire, which is always the aim of this word. With the accents of a great beginning and with constantly varied phrases, he affirms that these phenomena receive their being from the consciousness that I have of myself.

But can one, for all this, speak of "*being*-for-consciousness"? One knows with what vehemence Luther derisively twists all theories of being. They always result from "our human wisdom . . . from the presumptuous claiming of truthful being" (ibid.), that is, from our being impostures. More precisely, derision strikes all statements in the indicative which pretend to speak of God "in himself." (ibid.) But what can the prayer

"That God be truthful" signify for that which in this epoch is not yet called ontology? Several of Luther's remarks about the verb *ginésthô,* which the Vulgate renders as 'is'—to my knowledge the only ones which he consecrated to this question—indicate the direction in which it is necessary to seek the answer. "*Is*. The Greek word signifies above all 'that this may be'." (ibid.) Does metaphysical hubris (*frivolum et delyriosum commentum*) disappear, then, through an optative discourse about being?

A proposition "S is P," where a subject is linked to a predicate through the assertive copula, does not thematize the receiver. It does not matter to whom such a proposition is addressed. It works differently than a proposition such as "That S may be P," where a subject is linked to a predicate through the copula of desire. Such a proposition expresses a longing. It can concern a state of fact. Witness Luther's wish that the end of time would come! The wish can also concern the receiver of the proposition, however. Then this proposition turns into an imperative. It asks not only that some state of fact be produced or be the case, but rather that the content which it affirms, that which this proposition proposes, be recognized as true. It is addressed directly to the recipient, soliciting his adhesion. And who is the recipient? De facto, everyone. Taken in this sense, the optative seeks to make proselytes. This is the role that Luther has it play. Luther says that the manner in which Paul uses the verb "to be" "does not so much express the truthfulness of God as the confession of this truthfulness." (ibid.) This is a confession demanded of one and all. "It is just that all confess and recognize Him . . . That we hold him to be truthful, that he may be reputed to be faithful. . . . That this may be proclaimed to all: you are just and truthful. . . ." (ibid.) The copula of desire, substituted for the copula of assertion, brings about the revolution in the mode of thinking just as the invectives against the "reist" conception of sin bring it about. In both cases, the one who is guilty is Aristotle. Against him, Luther maintains that the being of phenomena depends upon givens—on "facts," as we shall see—within self-consciousness.[31]

An ontology in the optative is an ontology of estimation. Phenomena are nothing in this ontology so long as I do not esteem them as high or low. So it is for "works." It is not a question of dismissing them purely and simply, but "of not esteeming them, evaluating them (*talia aestimemus aut tam digna reputemus*) such that they suffice" for rendering us just. (ibid.) The award for the discourse upon being thus will no longer go to those who recite *ens, unum, bonum, verum,* but to those who esteem God's faithfulness to be supreme and who proclaim their assessment. The heir to the discourse about being as being is the preacher. He holds the active justification and truthfulness of God in esteem and by confessing these publicly, he returns them to him through passive justification and truthfulness. The theoretical science that in Aristotle is "refined" is found by Luther literally to be reformed. With this new form, the discourse about being no longer belongs to a science, nor to any theory. Rather, this is the discourse of a knowing (concerning the justice and the truth communicated) and of a praxis (concerning obedience to the word of another, having satisfied the law). A similar reform, reformation, revision, is at play in the "as." Then, as what does being manifest itself? It certainly remains that which is given to experience. But to what experience? I have said that the decisive problem posed by Aristotle is that of physical movement. The apophantic "as" is to be understood only in terms of that. *On hè on* first of all means being as *being in motion.* But that will no longer be the guiding meaning once my relation to the word determines what can become a phenomenon for me, as well as, through the metabolism we have seen, the manner in which it can become a phenomenon. The "as" now works differently. If being creates a problem for valuations, it is problematic as *being for consciousness.*

Once the constitution of phenomena in consciousness is recognized, major problems remain to be solved before one can speak without hesitation of critical transcendentalism in Luther. On the one hand, there exist the doctrines which trace being back to thought and things back to the processes of thought. Such doctrines are called idealist. Does not Luther commit a reduction of this sort? Phenomena are what they are *through speech.* In seeking the being of phenomena in their appearance to consciousness, does he not trace the real back to the ideal? On the other hand, in every self-understanding, the word remains the word of law, directly when it reveals me to be guilty of some lack, indirectly when it reveals me as saved because another has already made good on this in my stead. Now, the consciousness capable of placing itself prior to, in the face of, or within the law—prior to, in the face of, or within the good that is obligatory for it—is called moral consciousness. In order to have transcendentalism, it is necessary not only for self-consciousness to be left clearly dissociated from moral consciousness, but also that the diverse situations regarding the law be reduced to a morally neutral act, to an originarily synthetic unity analogous to the simple act which Kant calls pure apperception. Self-consciousness accompanies all thought about contents, but does not itself have a content. It is not a thought, but consciousness of . . . of what, in Luther? Of the efficacious word, thus of a *causality.* But how is the extrinsic causality, which is first of all law, here articulated in respect to the subjective condition without this law immediately taking on a moral character? If, without doing harm to the text, one manages to show the neutrality of listening in relation to the moral consciousness, one will have established at the same time the concomitant character of this originary act and, in this way, its affinity with transcendental apperception. Finally, it will be necessary to ask what, in the context of passive justification, do "to give" and "to receive" mean? God gives and I receive; but, are to give and to receive thinkable without any *auto-givenness,* however formal, on the part of the I? In response to this difficulty, a duality in being will take shape, but here it will only take shape there (since it is no longer employed in the differend of the *simul*). To take up again the topology of possible sites vis-à-vis the word, if justice is not given to me from outside, the law will never be satisfied. However, if I am secured within the accomplished law, without there having been any appropriation on my part, then the law will not be satisfactory for me; hence, an aporia. Either justice is something which is offered to me and which I appropriate for myself, but then morality's remedy to being lost seems to result from my own efficacy; if salvation comes from works then Luther's crucial—in all the senses of the word—discovery is null and void. Or justice is granted to me from outside without any initiative on my part (faith is the work of God in me), but then one can no longer see the point of the vehement exhortation "to justify God." This aporia bears upon givenness. It seems that givenness can be neither heteronomous nor autonomous. That it harmonizes the two—a little bit of heteronomy with that portion of autonomy which is needful—remains excluded by the premise of passive justification.

These difficulties—consciousness *through* the word, *of* the sole divine causality, *according* to received, not produced, givenness—result, like so many corollaries, from Luther's understanding of being, namely, that being means being-for-consciousness. The continuity with Kant rests upon this understanding of being. Accordingly, it will be necessary to await the *Critique of Pure Reason* to see the question of being raised for itself. Then it will be raised precisely in the terms of a transcendental dissension inherited from the Lutheran *simul,* even though with neither noise nor forebodings.

*Consciousness through the word {parole}**

The new hegemony will impose itself as an obvious fact only if it responds to a need dimly felt. If he had not emphasized in clear words and coherent propositions a prior knowing which everyone already possesses, though less clearly and coherently, Luther would have provided only a new springboard into the speculation in which we are here immersed. He would have changed the theses, but without escaping from thetic games, nor, consequently, from the metaphysical arbitrariness which he condemns. This is the difference between philosophy and all other literary genres. The latter allow one to indulge in being astonished. Philosophy, on the other hand, should not astonish. It should clarify a knowledge possessed by all. Kant, for his part, will escape without hardly any suspicions of having an arbitrary point of departure. The need that moves him to implant himself on the terrain of self-consciousness stems from a fact whose universality we can deny only with difficulty and which, on that account, he never puts into question: the fact of sensible experience. In Luther, what is that fact that is indubitable because it is commonplace, prereflexive because it is of the practical order, positive in the sense of a given, known flawlessly by those to whom it is addressed and precisely for that reason serves as the *beginning* of his transcendental critique?

No one will be delivered from great anguish in the face of the law if not through promise. This breaks the cycle in which the law and sin are mutually reinforced to the point of the despair of a certain loss. Promise opens "the great opening of the gates of paradise." Past deeds and actions, avouched for by the Scripture, will remain null and void as long as an experience does not reveal their immanence for me. So, what experience? "But what? The word, the word, the word."[32] It is necessary to examine the extrinsic efficacy of the word. Even in Luther it has to do with the point of departure. In Kant one can certainly say that the philosophy of consciousness continues to bathe in the matrixed medium of language inasmuch as the categorial deduction has made it so through judgments. However, this is a mentalist conception of language and is phenomenologically derived from the living speech from which Luther sets out.

**Parole* is the French word used preponderantly in this section and always has the sense of "spoken word"; used in the theological context it conveys more of this verbal sense than does the English "the word of God," which, moreover, conveys more strongly the sense of a single word than does *parole,* which implies a discourse.

Only the word proffered in an act is efficacious; hence to bring the Lutheran project down to the sole principle of *sola scriptura* would be to disfigure it. Certainly, Luther equally dismisses both metaphysical arbitrariness and the delirium of private experiences in availing himself of a contract which links him to the written word: "I have made a contract with my God: He begrudges me neither visions, nor dreams, nor even an angel, because I content myself with the gift which I have in the Holy Scripture."[33] Nonetheless, written words never give us anything more than a dead discourse. Only the spoken word is living.[34] This word alone frees and delivers. Luther understands the plenary word to be the public statement of revealed promises. In the actual act wherein a voice makes itself heard, the "hidden" speech, the Word {*Verbe*}, is rendered audible to our ears. The proffered word which shows and instructs is the "complete, perfect" effect. The word justifies, "grasps rather than being grasped." The proffered word differs from another effect of the same Word, namely, that "announcing only a part, not the whole; only fulfilling man partially, in his flesh." This other word—"imperfect, stretched . . . pushing always further towards the flesh" (*sch.* 9,28)—is the law in all its forms. It, too, is essentially oral. It says: "you must." Thus, the word is one, and it is living; however, we receive it either as derived, condemning (the law), or as full, as liberating (promise).

Now, usually Luther is content to say simply "the word," so as to oppose it to "the law." That is, there is freedom and freedom. The law doesn't make anyone free, not even that law which removes us from the falsity of happy, infantile irresponsibility. The transition, amidst many struggles, through which one passes from primitive immunity to the rule of law marks the period of mourning for the *freedom of indifference,* lost forever to those who have been awakened to responsibility (*sch.* 8,15). *Liberation,* for its part, demands yet another passage, beyond the always negative account of merits and derelictions. The liberating word will be, quite simply, the word. Thus the freedom of which we are made aware cannot be conceived. It can only be received. If the word which conveys this did not suddenly occur in history, or reach our ears, then we would remain without appeal before the law. Nothing is more contingent, nor more factual, than receiving the promise (whereby in Luther every semblance of idealism is set aside[35]). Consciousness lacks every resource needed for producing consciousness of the promise. The liberating word comes necessarily from the outside.

However, the problem of universality in Luther's point of departure is not thereby put to the side. Rather, it is rendered all the sharper. If a contingent word, dated because it is *data,* given in a moment of history, is required to instruct us of our possible freedom, then in the name of what does it speak? No longer, one fears, in the name of an experience known by all, as is sensible experience. It speaks for a certain group—the believers—of a certain society, namely, the one moved by the history of biblical efficacy. There is a major difficulty, it seems, in his trying to escape this cultural provincialism through a different way of reading. The "book of nature" instructs us in a natural knowledge of God, revealing his "vestiges" in nature and his "imprints" in consciousness.[36] Isn't this bit of Augustinian metaphysics absurd according to Luther's own premises? Indeed, how could we justify such a substitution of books when it is only a word coming from the outside, a word as contingent as a gaze that glances, that can liberate us? On the other hand, is this change of books not to abandon the linguistic medium as the originary phenomenal region of the transcendentalism for which one seeks a point of departure in the obviousness of statements that one may or may not have understood? The impasse is perfect: Either Luther begins with the liberating word, effectively heard, and then his transcendentalism takes account only of selective experiences, but then this will have the programmatic effect of inverting his entire way of thinking, or he begins with self-consciousness, natively imprinted with the word, but then we thereby revert to a Christian Platonism of the most classic kind.

This impasse, however, is not one. For Luther, the word is not, no more than is consciousness and its contents, a being. Neither nature nor Scripture harbor words or any sort of obscure discourse that it would be a question of deciphering. Indeed, they do not harbor characters at all; they don't speak at all. Words are no longer of the world. No similitude, be it manifest or hidden away, erects a bridge of adequation between the visible and that which one says of it. Words enter into correspondence, not with the figures of the cosmos, but with the figures of the I. As for their place, I either give it to them or I do not. With vehemence, Luther disengages himself from the sway of the *co-presence* of words and things and takes refuge under the sway of *reflection*. The word no longer signals any fatal state, nor does it give an account of any observation. It signals to me what I can be, but in itself it is the sign of nothing. Hence the polemic against Erasmus: It is useless to take up a word as one does a pebble and go on to read the tropes and analogies inscribed in it. In itself, it is empty (one day, Luther will lose patience even with the Bible and will write: "Ach, Bible Bable Bouble!"). Such as I hear it, so is the word. Its being is embodied in its appearance. If it were otherwise, how could the same word be both terrifying and sweet?

Now, a reflexive structure does not work unless there is a spontaneous energy in it. There is no capacity to listen unless I can reflect for myself—make my own—on the revealed word, or any other word. Here is the Copernican turn in the mode of thinking: to look, not toward the perceived or understood contents, but toward the receptive structure rendering possible the reflection of that which is given to perception or understanding. Every decisive philosophic question one can and should pose to Luther concerns, in one way or another, the possibility and the status of this spontaneity in the subject reflecting on the extrinsic word (to pose philosophic questions to Luther does not mean to place Luther within philosophy[37]).

The structure of listening bears within it two moments, two types of givenness. One is receptive, the other active (*sch.* 10,17). Through the first, Luther centers the subject upon an event given from the outside. Through the other, he centers being upon the reflecting subject.

The *primacy of exteriority* renders us entirely dependent upon contingent events; accordingly, in the critiques of the I capable of listening, only what is given auditorily liberates us. Even Kant who, to preserve an exteriority systematically first and analogous to that of the auditory, will subordinate the understanding (against all idealism) to a given; in the critique of the spontaneous I, only the sensibly given gives us access to the world. Apropos of the modifications in self-understanding and their conditions, Luther thus quite clearly anticipates the distinction between the subjective *a priori* structure and the empirical *a posteriori* contents. Observe, he says, a person who depends, body and soul, upon rumors and reports poured from the mouth into the ear—such a person shows that the word is all we possess for finding our way back to the world. And, he concludes, the same thing goes for the believer. "We too, we have nothing other than the single word whose contents we are, however, unable to produce" (ibid.). Receptivity with regard to the word is something which we "have," that is ours. Like gossip, we necessarily and universally lie in wait for that which is said. However, we remain necessarily and universally "incapable of producing" what is said and can be given wide report. The capacity to listen is an *a priori* subjective condition for understanding our world, whereas the word making itself understood in its actuality will always be adventitious. The primacy of exteriority places us at the mercy of linguistic events upon which we never have a hold. The capacity to listen remains void as long as "the pronouncing of the word produced in the present, which is to say, the event of the word passing before our ears," is missing (ibid.). It is a mark of our extreme finitude that hearing is our natural condition for having a world and for situating us in it; but the world that gives it to us and situates us can either suddenly arrive or not. Moreover, it can arrive unexpectedly as opaque (to the man of the law), or as transparent (to the man who is promised).

Only the second moment allows *interiority* to intervene, an interiority through which, no doubt by reason of the new prestige of self-consciousness, we typically characterize as "reformed" thought. The word that modifies my self-understanding is such that "no one can grasp it unless they receive it through listening and faith" (ibid.). The word works on the new grasp—resumption, representation, reflection, reflexion—in a manner analogous to the work performed by the Kantian categories. In both, the given "is" only to the extent the I can make it mine. In Kant, being is a category and making mine means to subsume; in Luther, being is the effective word and making mine means to obey. The tone rises, the anti-scholastic polemics resume, the autobiographical "I" is put forth anew. Here again, these are so many indices that one must read attentively. What is at stake is the bond between the moment of exterior giving and that of interior estimation—in other words, the modification in the self-understanding that expresses the formula of Paul such as it is related by the Vulgate: *fides ex auditu*, "faith comes from what one hears" (Romans 10:17). The role of *appropriative spontaneity* in hearing is what poses a problem here.

"The doctors of more recent times . . . speak without the witness of Scripture" (*sch.* 7,18). Between Aristotle and Paul—between reason only and speech—they have held in esteem reason only, holding the word for naught. They sought to understand God "in his being," not "in his speech" (*sch.* 3,7). Is this an underestimation only of God? One may readily imagine some sort of division of labor between faith and reason. Speech would generate obedience to God; reason would generate the knowledge of nature. Such an administrative distribution already amounts to more of an amputation of reason than one finds among the nominalists. By transmuting it, linguistic assessment would be confined to the sphere circumscribed by Augustine:

"'To know God and the soul, this is what I desire.' 'Nothing more?' 'No, absolutely nothing'."[38] Luther's transcendentalism remained embryonic because it excluded the domain upon which it will later exercise its "competence" equally exclusively: the domain of nature. Now, Luther's eloquence swoops down on precisely the fiction of such a distribution of competencies. The Scholastics, quite literally, have not *listened to* nature. "Creation in its entirety groaned" (Romans 8:22). To these groanings, philosophers turn a deaf ear. Their logic of things remains a logic of the manipulable and the visible, forgetful of the audible. They "do not believe in that which we can retain only through hearing, but do not point out with the hand or [see] with the eyes" (*gl.* 10, 16). At their best, philosophers know only how to look—"to look so profoundly at the present state of things that all they can do is to speculate upon the essence and properties of things. . . . I believe that I owe to God the obedience of crying out against philosophy and of recommending Scripture. . . . But it is the case that we greatly esteem the science scrutinizing the essence of things, while the things themselves detest their essence and groan. . . . Sages and Theologians, they erect, with smiles, powerful and stunning conceptual edifices upon that which is full of groaning" (*sch.* 8,19). In every phenomenal region, including that of the study of nature, there is the problem of spontaneity appropriating a word.

What are these groanings of nature? Something like the laments of children being made to eat by adults? Are these groanings emanating from things? Nothing of the sort. They issue from an assessment coming "from the outside" of things (*sch.* 8,20). "Those who appropriate [creatures] differ" according to their manner of assessment (ibid.). The creatures turn out to be as mutable as that which has been said of God. Their objective groanings are our subjective groanings. Those who know only how to see and to touch take their provisional character for their being; those who knows how to listen retain their provisional character as provisional. "Through an erroneous evaluation . . . man esteems them as higher than that which does not go back to them" (ibid.)—higher, by endowing them with an "entelechy," as if they already carried their end, their *telos,* within themselves. However, none have yet seen that for which they are destined—their end to come. There are those, however, who have heard it pronounced.

The revolution in the mode of thinking "at which reason balks" (*SA* 695) consists here in understanding being as the transformative efficacy of a word. If I am able to undergo modifications in my self-understanding, then the consciousness that I have of myself is essentially a matter of a call. The philosophers, even when they speak of God, "do not believe" because they are only concerned with the word so understood—with the word *understood.* They trust "only those words signifying something visible or created . . . satisfying the hunger of only one part of man—his flesh" (*sch.* 9,28). There is a double "carnal opacity" to every word directed toward the visible. Not only does it exclude the audible, but it still passes for the whole of speech, filling the whole man. There is even an opacity to the law. Whosoever seeks to satisfy the law through his own resources is closed off toward the liberating word which (and this is never put in doubt) nevertheless comes to the ears of all; also, for all the law, he will never hear that he is thus enclosed. This double enclosure of the self results from an assessment exclusively in favor of the present, excluding the word. The new assessment will consist in "opening up the space to revealed words" (*sch.* 3,4) and, since these are words of promise, to the opening up of the space to time.

To grasp the Lutheran character of this new manner of thinking, it is necessary to bear in mind the appellative essence of being-for-consciousness, without confounding free obedience either with some exercise of autonomous spontaneity or with some type of subjective efficient causality. It is in this respect that appropriative spontaneity poses a problem. The estimation by the "spirit" which declares the end of time truer than any telic end, is assuredly a subjective act taking hold again of the exterior word. Even more, this estimation translates into acts which, in no matter what other critical context, one would not hesitate to call spontaneous. It is a matter of "*making oneself* conform" to the word (*sch.* 6,17), of grasping the election offered (*gl.* 9,6), of "*renouncing* all things, of dying to oneself and to all" (*sch.* 10,10). Luther does not hesitate to add that he who does this "*has satisfied* God and is just" (ibid.). To conform oneself, to grasp, to renounce, to satisfy: How are we to see there only the work of an other? Luther even states what resemble genuine hypothetical imperatives: "If we . . . offer ourselves to hell, . . . then we have, in truth, satisfied justice and He . . . will render us free" (*sch.* 9,3). In other words, if you seek to be free, offer yourself to hell. Such an imperative is a practical rule indicating the means to be used (the *resignatio ad infernum* marking the maximum of detachment just as predestination marks the maximum of heteronomy) to attain a fixed goal (freedom in regard to the condemnatory law). And yet, we have seen that if liberation occurs, it comes from outside. It follows from the vicarious satisfaction of the law, a satisfaction given by another. The word that communicates this to us thus shows and must show that all spontaneity in man is illusory. Justification results from "an effort which is not to be attributed to free will" (*SA* 680). Thus another, dogmatic motif is added to the phenomenological motifs preserving the exteriority of the word. "The words coming from the mouth of no matter which pious man" reach our ears from the outside because, in the first place, "the word resonating from the high heavens" (*sch.* 10,6)—revelation—comes to us from the exterior; in its turn, this exteriority results from that of the Word, which satisfies the law without any initiative on the part of humans.[39] Such are the strong reasons for not corrupting pure receptivity.

What is problematic here is neither resignation to hell (an edifying theme taken up again by Tauler), nor even the apparent conditional through which it suddenly seems that "works," such as renunciation, can produce justice and guarantee us salvation (a conditional excused by commentators as a lapse in a thought still searching for itself[40]). Rather, the systematic problem holds to the fact that a listening (passive) unaccompanied by a grasp (active) hears nothing at all and consequently isn't a listening at all. Even gossips require vigilance to grasp who has done what with whom . . . and this attention is paid, given. A deaf ear, even this, is something which we, in turning, lend. We *receive* a word on the subjective condition of *grasping* it also—of getting hold of it again, representing it, reproducing it. It is systematically impossible to do without a faculty by which I give myself to that which gives itself to be heard and through which *I give it to myself* through a mode determined by self-understanding. Luther calls this subjective determination an estimation. How are we to conceive of this if not, at least, as quasi-spontaneous?

Hence, it is in what might appear to be an incoherence in his text that Luther shows, to better advantage, the activity of the "re-." What does Luther call these "works"? In the first place, they are the practices demanded by the moral law, and then, observances. But none of the active verbs in the active voice I just cited designate such productions of contents. To the contrary, all speak of a re-production, a response. They emphasize acts that one can describe only as formal, quasi-spontaneous acts ("quasi" because they do not yet emanate from the subject freely giving itself its law). Far from "remaining a medieval at heart"[41] because he attributes all spontaneity to God, Luther opens wide the gulf between *subjective, formal, quasi-spontaneity* and *divine, efficient spontaneity*. The first connotes neither causality nor autonomy. It emphasizes nothing more than the faculty for again getting hold of that which is given to be understood (a faculty rendered autonomous only by Kant, precisely under the name of the understanding). It institutes the I, referring all phenomena to it as a formal act. It opens the modern era, the era of reflection through estimation. But it also divides the estimating subject into receptive-passive and receptive-spontaneous subjects. It divides receptivity into a suffering and a doing, a duality which we will see breaks the new hegemony.

It is first of all important to distinguish the formal spontaneity in the reception of the liberating word from all other spontaneity, whether it be causal or, more generally, autonomous. Afterwards it will be necessary to examine what, in Luther, the act is through which the I is placed at the center of that which it represents to itself and guarantees through an *act*—thus, while fracturing—the unity of *passive* consciousness. Once we have understood and then named this spontaneity that nevertheless the exclusive efficiency of God is supposed to have in hand, we will have the needed terms by which to raise the question of pathetic consciousness in discord with itself (chapter 2).

The consciousness of a causality

Self-consciousness rises to hegemony in a position of complete dependence. There is nothing paradoxical in this. With Luther it becomes the hegemonic *condition*, the ultimate referent in the constitution of all phenomenality; but it remains dependent on a supreme referent in which it recognizes the *cause* of its destiny.

At the birth of modernity in Luther, self-consciousness does not yet possess either autonomy or efficiency. It is born doubly nomic, for it is already the formal law for representation; but also, more than ever, it is the consciousness of the efficiency of God alone (*Alleinwirksamkeit*), materially theonomous. In terms of being, consciousness values that which, for it, is; but that which it can value as high or low—efficient speech—is given to it from outside. The being of the given depends formally on its reception. Being as estimation of the given (later it will be as categorization) institutes self-consciousness as the horizon in which all that can become a phenomena must inscribe itself. Luther pushes theonomy further than medieval piety. The spontaneity of the anagogic itinerary of which, a century earlier, the spirit could take advantage to elevate and appear before God is seen as nothing more than hubris.[42] Self-consciousness lacks the wherewithal to elevate itself above the state of receptivity in which subsists the one who alone can set it free. Nevertheless, in order to produce deliverance in it, God must appear before it and make the justificatory speech effective. He must become phenomenal for it. As a new ultimate referent, self-consciousness is *consciousness of a causality.*

The two philosophers—Aristotle and Kant—who alone, perhaps, knew what they were doing in deploying a hegemonic fantasm, both set it to work in the service of causality. With Aristotle, philosophy is the science of principles. The discourse that proceeds on the basis of deductions will be scientific; in order for it to be first science, philosophy thus must place us in a position of reasoning deductively on the basis of an absolute first principle. Now, this first principle remains unknowable. From where would a deduction depart so as to establish it as the first principle? This could only be done by beginning with a referent anterior to the one that we seek to recognize as the first. Here we have an infinite regression that shows that a first principle cannot be found in the conclusion of a deduction. The guiding science thus must remain "sought after"; dialectic and the ultimate referent will be recognized as fantasmic. In our reasoning we must be content with principles that are relatively first: relative to physical movement and to the origins from which it sets out. The origins are first only in their respective genres (*ta prota kai aitia,*[43] in the plural), but they do not allow themselves to be reduced to a single origin. The philosopher will negotiate principles as we negotiate a turn. He advances in a straight line only when he reasons on the causes of the movement. As for Kant, he is awakened from a dogmatic slumber—"in order to make an attempt . . . in a reverse direction"[44]—in discovering that no inherent necessity to things obliges us to link two events with the relation of cause to effect; this link and its necessity comes rather from us. Thus, among the principles, causality is the only one governing both human action and natural processes (see below). This reverse manner of thinking will be all-encompassing in that it encloses the phenomenal regions within the supremacy—"attempted," thus explicitly established, constructed as hegemony—of consciousness as the origin of principles. These regions, separating the types of causality, are two in number: nature and freedom. The inversion in the manner of thinking was provoked not only by the problem of causality (as formulated by Hume), but it raises it up to a guiding problem for all rigorous procedures. But the *causes* nevertheless have *conditions.* Accordingly, the condition to which one would appeal—the I, freely acting in its syntheses—by rights remains unknowable. This is where Kant recognized the hypothetical, fantasmic status of the ultimate authority.

Luther also orients his thought entirely in relation to a certain causal conception. By the ontology of estimation, he puts an end—provisional, we will see in reference to evil—to the ancient prestige of kinetic causality. The justificatory word that the believing consciousness holds in high esteem nevertheless acts as an efficient cause. Such was the crucial discovery in regard to the justice of God. Thus, in Luther as well as before and after him, causality remains the guiding problem. Only, it became impossible to conceive it as a natural cause once being no longer signifies a substance, but an act: effective estimation. Conceiving causality as subjective and autonomous, on the other hand, is not yet possible, for estimation must conform to a word coming from outside. Accordingly, Luther construes this estimation as subjective and heteronomous. The sites in which consciousness is implanted by the word are so many *effects* of this word that is imposed as law in those who discover good and evil, and that offers a promise to those who discover freedom. In Luther, only the word is the originally efficient cause that through the law binds, or through the promise sets free.

The anguish of predestination is too bitter for one ever to be able to insist on the entirely *ontic* character of heteronomous efficiency. "The anguished disquietude of the heart is most heavy with the idea that God could think better of it and do something else" (*gl.* 4,18). The word is efficient but it "pushes away and rejects one, as it accepts and crowns the other" (*sch.* 1,28). In these unforeseeable interventions, we recognize the Scotist heritage[45] in which the divine will is not guided by any "eternal law." It chooses who it chooses. The contingency in elective efficiency is coupled with the ignorance about the addressee. "Not more than we know God and his guidance, do we know our justice, as it depends entirely on him and his guidance" (*sch.* 4,7). Divine efficiency is intermittent, both in its cause and in its effect. It does not presuppose any essential quality in God, and it does not establish any in man. It does not articulate any sort of constant presence. Philosophers who make a profession of observing only the present state of things understand nothing of this. The liberating action suddenly happens like the occurrence of a word passing close to the ears; the ultimate condition of its effect remains fantasmic because it, too, is "attempted."

So, what is the—for lack of a better word—"ontological" condition of these ontic interventions? In seeking an answer, we will see outlined anew the reversal in thought from which critical, modern subjectivism is born.

To inquire into a "cause" is to inquire into an agent that effects a change. When one asks "Who did what?" one will always be able to call this agent as well as its action a cause. As for the one inquiring into "causality," he no longer seeks to know who or what produces what effect. He seeks to know if, or if not, there is a cause, and in what manner it functions. Thus he inquires into the being-a-cause of some particular cause. Now, in Luther's "exclusive efficiency," what is the being-a-cause of this cause that is the word? We will attempt to retrace the consequential points.

In his doctrine of singular divine efficiency, Luther follows, all the while transmuting it, a schema that goes back to the heights of John the Evangelist and to the Neoplatonists of the first centuries. Consider what Augustine said about this. In the (neo-)Platonists "I read, no doubt not in these terms, but the meaning was absolutely the same . . . that in the beginning was the Word, and the Word was in God . . ." and so it goes for almost all the Prologue of the fourth gospel. "As for this one: 'He came in his own domain. . . ,' I have not read it in these books."[46] Thus in both places, in the philosophers as in John, he read that the Word resided close to God, that it was made exterior to him, and that it came back close to him. What he did not read in the Neoplatonics—that the Word was exteriorized even to the point of becoming flesh and dying—constitutes an excess in the becoming-other that does not break, but rather reinforces, the triple incidence of the Word that are the *moné* (residence), the *proodos* (procession) and the *epistrophé* (conversion). Thomas Aquinas makes this schema the plan of his *Summa.*

Luther no longer escapes this ternary schema, but he inflicts on it the violence of a transmutation, a violence that strikes a blow to the phenomenal God, thus to the second and third moments.

The transmutation is none other than the very discovery that Luther states made him feel reborn. That there had been a transmutation insofar as there was a discovery—interpretive violence insofar as there was a reading—can, moreover, only reinforce the impression of experimentation, of a reversal in the manner of thinking. Everything happens as if, faced with the text on the justice of God that terrifies him, Luther also says "let's try, then, to read in the opposite direction. . . ." By following this tack, we already have hold of the new version of the *proodos* and of the *epistrophé.* What actually "proceeds" from God according to this new understanding? "Our own justification, the one that God accomplishes in acting upon us." The old "emanation" of beings resembling less and less their source to the extent they take distance from it and increase their limitations, is changed into *imputation.* God gives no longer perfections, but a reputation. Thanks to his efficient word, I am reputed to be right next to him. And what is it that "returns" to God? "The passive justification of God, the one by which he is justified by us." The old conversion of beings, by which they recover their lost resemblance in losing their limitation, is changed into conversion by *estimation.* God brings back to himself no longer the totality of beings placed high or low, but a totality of acts by which we actualize the high or low: "When we interrogate ourselves about God, it is God loving himself and so much so that we want and love him" (*sch.* 3,11). Our estimations are also themselves the work of God. The same goes for the types of justification, so that like the active, the passive too is the work of God. "He justifies by being justified, and he is justified by justifying" (*sch.* 3,4 cor.). In accordance with the received speculative schema, the descent constitutive of the universe as well as the climb leading it back to its origin are surely the effects of God reposing in himself; but if it is a question of biblical origins in John and Paul (*Ph* 2, 6–9), or of their metaphysical resumptions from the Alexandrines up to Duns Scotus, the medium of this work remains precisely the universe with its degrees of being. The logic of the divine work remains the logic of things, and this is precisely no longer in accordance with the new sense of justice that desires that "I" be the addressee of God's active justification, and that his work come to fruition when "I" render to him his passive justification. If Luther can hold up for derision the abysmal gaze of metaphysicians who scrutinize the ground of things, it is because he himself has cast an eye into another abyss, namely that of the consciousness that he has of himself. The descent and climb back up are confined there; they are at work *pro me.*

The game of procession-conversion has changed milieu. Essences have given way to the word. Divine efficiency is no longer addressed to existing beings, but to a hearing in its singularity. The negative proof for this is that, in the old *itinerarium mentis,* the spirit came to man as a trace of the Spirit that converted the intellect by retracing Its arrival in reverse. Now, only a being can come from another and return to it. The intellect had been understood in the same way one does a thing—after the manner of

God and all creation. With Luther, nothing emanates from God who effects beings; nothing goes back to God that proceeds from beings. The active-passive justification, in its conjunction, abruptly addresses us such that "the path of man is not his path. . . . The course is not the concern of he who runs, but is the concern of God who gives it and maintains it" (*sch.* 9,16). The *itinerarium mentis* reflecting the course of things is thus transmuted into the divine guide steering my journey: "In going outside of himself, God directs us to enter into ourselves, and by the knowledge he has of himself, he brings about in us the knowledge that we have of ourselves" (*sch.* 3,4 cor.). The procession-conversion is "for me." Here lies the inverse manner of thinking. Its "place" is self-consciousness, and so we have the site of the new manner of thinking; self-consciousness is "effected" by the word, and so we have here the new causality; and finally, the reflecting consciousness, entering into itself, recognizes "the workings of God that maintain it." The consciousness that I have of myself is the consciousness of a causality.

Taken in isolation, none of these points are entirely unprecedented in the tradition before Luther, and some of them have come to the surface since Deutero-Homer. But the focus is new.

Here is the great principle upon which this new focus is based: "So as they believe it, so they [humans] shall have it" (*SA* 778, cf. 769). This principle transmutes the masterpiece of all Aristotelian naturalism, the efficient cause. The being of the justifying cause, the causality of this ontic cause, is to be sought out in self-consciousness. This determines both the fact (*hoti, an sit*) that God is the cause, and the manner in which he is (*ti, quid sit*). We see it as the key concept in the theory of singular divine efficiency, the theory of strength or power (*virtus*). In Thomas Aquinas, we recall, power is a perfection of God distributed according to a diminishing intensity across the levels of being in creation, which is a naturalistic conception of power. In Duns Scotus, we recall as well to the contrary, power constitutes the essence of the absolute will of God, which is a voluntarist conception of power. Now, according to the Lutheran theory of singular divine efficiency, the power of God resides nowhere other than in the *confession* of this power—neither in the divine being, as in the teaching of the Aristotelians, nor in its manifestation, as in the nominalists. "By the 'power of God,' one must understand not that through which it is powerful in itself according to its substance, but that through which it makes powerful and strong" (*sch.* 1,16). Not that he is strong, but that he makes strong. It involves a change of place, a translation that makes for an epoch is an epochal translation. So where do we now find the strength or the power, the force, all those elements that constitute the causality of a cause? "All these are named after God, not because they are in him, but because they come from him and are in us" (*sch.* 1,19). Once more, Luther refuses to talk of God, for talking is always and ever again only the understanding that we have of ourselves. Does divine power exist? Yes, "in us." In what manner does it exist? "Named after him," by a reputation that is a giving back. We are strong because he holds us as such, and he is strong because we name him—we confess him—as such. In this imputative and reputative exchange, power as an entitative quality slips away. How could it be otherwise when the being of this exchange is self-consciousness?

"Efficiency of God alone" means that he alone has the power to save. But this power itself, and not only its effect, only exists when consciousness undergoes the modification—faith—that saves. The being of the "efficiency of God alone" thus resides in self-consciousness, not in the agent that saves. Moreover, the same thing goes for this other power, which is the law. Through the modification that liberates consciousness, "we die to the power and the domination by the law, but not to the law in itself and as such" (*gl.* 7,5). This is because the law in itself and as such, no more than God in himself and as such, does not become at any time the central concern in this theory. Its unique concern is *self-consciousness as the consciousness of a causality.*

But even by thus displacing efficiency, Luther no more escapes the kinetic schema than he escapes the triadic schema of residing-procession-conversion. He finds the most striking formulas, marking the "Copernican" displacement in which the ascendancy of consciousness is substituted for that of nature, in reference to *movement* and its cause. Thus Aristotle's *Physics* enjoys a curious return in a context where one would least expect it, namely, in the context of evil. Luther's convictions here again are clear. The fact of evil goes back to the idea of original sin; accordingly our nature has been evil since Adam. Now, in his continuous creation of the world, "God maintains everything in everything, so much so that without him, nothing can be produced or effected", thus if he acts perpetually in all beings, "he does not cease to form and to enhance corrupted nature as well." It follows that "he combats evil with evil" (*SA* 708f.). Such an instrumentalist conception of evil—"the defect is found in the instruments" that we are (ibid.)— is inevitable given the extremism and the efficiency of God alone and also the extremism of the passivity on the part of the subject. If, following original sin, human free will "is nothing" (*SA* 651), and if "since the loss of freedom . . . we desire sin and evil, we will speak sin and evil, we will do sin and evil" (*SA* 670), then there is a necessity, not "of constraint" but of "immutability," of committing evil. What does this mean? This means that the efficient cause *moves* the created, whether it is good or bad, without moving—altering—nature. This is a return of kineticism, only here it is interiorized, transcendentalized.

It is stated from the mouth of the Prime Mover: "By a universal movement, I want to move myself from inside this evil will in order that it continue to desire by its own spirit and its own path, both that I will not cease to move it, and that I cannot do otherwise." This moving from within is no longer that of living beings (Aristotle) such that they carry in themselves the principle of their growth, but it is that of the will, such that it carries in itself the principle of impetus and orientation. The kinetic schema does not remain here in any less identical a form: "In itself, the will could not move itself . . . but the all-powerful mover moves it in a movement from which nothing can be subtracted." The Aristotelianism can be seen even in the archic, double function of the *prôton kinoûn akinèton*. This not only initiates the progress of the movement (by the elective word that selects), but it also commands it (by the imperative word that binds). The unflinchingly anti-Aristotelian Prime Mover is what Luther is after: "By the force of my omnipotence, I myself set evil in motion." The effect of this mover is "universal" without being cosmic, which would signify a twist in the transcendentalist project. Universality encompasses individual wills. This can be seen in the objection raised by the ingenue as well as the response that it evoked. Objection: "Why doesn't God halt the efficiency of his omnipotence that moves the will of the impious, to the extent that said will continues to be evil and becomes ever more so?" Answer: "What you are desiring here, for the good of the impious, is that God cease to be God, since it is to wish for an interruption of his force and efficiency" (*SA* 711f.). To stop moving the impious from doing evil, God would have to cease to be the universal mover. He would also have to cease moving his elected from doing good. And who would want such a thing? . . . Nothing establishes the kinetic essence of the *Alleinwirksamkeit* so well as this univocity of the word as efficient cause. According to a Lutheran parable, the *one* word comes to be for me, or God, or Satan.[47] Thus, univocity confirms transcendentalism (this term is used for the time being in a provisional sense until the question of the I and its unifying act is resolved). The word is phenomenalized for me, be it as divine or as satanic. As I believe, so I will be.

Luther leaves untouched the systematic influence of the moving cause but he reinscribes it in reflection. The cause is efficient in me, no longer because it would be *present* in its effect, but because I *represent* it to myself as efficient, and such as I represent it to myself. *Kinesis* is henceforth in play elsewhere than in living beings and artifacts. Accordingly, it comes to be other. One and the same moving causality is apparent in one single type of phenomena—movement: here in the case of the impious on their road to ruin, there the justified entering through the great open gates of paradise. At the risk of missing the nexus between language and self-consciousness in this nascent transcendentalism, it is necessary to bear in mind, in this theory of efficient speech, both the persistence of the kineticism and its revision according to reputation and imputation. It is worth noting that the causality whose being is constituted by reflection and representation is still kinetic causality.

Ludwig Feuerbach thought he saw his own anthropologizing critique of religion anticipated in the Lutheran displacement toward reflection and representation. Luther would have recognized that the subject produces the idea of God from out of unsatisfied desires.[48] He would have demonstrated the generative mechanism of sublime fictions. Yet one must say that nothing is more foreign to him. If Luther upheld a similar subjective production, he would not, when all is said and done, just substitute one ontic cause for another. This would be no longer to have God producing freedom, but man producing God. But Luther says something quite different. He is concerned with the cause-being—thus with the causality—of this cause which is the word (the phenomenal God). The being of the word resides in consciousness where all words must be assessed in order to become efficient. This in no way diminishes the otherness between the human subject and the cause of his liberation. The systematic place that Luther reserves for the positive word suffices to show that he intends to safeguard this otherness more resolutely than anyone before him. It is a *non sequitur* to trace assessment back to production and, as a result, to fiction. When Kant states explicitly what Luther only indicates—namely, that existence is a category of the understanding—the determining activity in the subject certainly does not signify a fabrication. It does not follow from the categories of modality that the understanding "produces" being.

But in Luther a formal, subjective quasi-spontaneity does follow from this. Recognizing this does not amount to postulating some causal efficiency in consciousness. The *labor* {*travail*} of a transcendental act is not a *work* {*œuvre*}. But for all that, can one deny any activity in the subject that would "open" a space for the word, that would "conform" to it, "seize," "renounce," "satisfy" what it demands, in short, which would appropriate it? Luther's abrupt response (a reprise of the Rhenish mystics, but in whom it did not exclude human activity[49]), namely, that God effects all of this in us, raises more problems than it solves. It is difficult to see in this anything but a gesture cutting questions short, so much that we will not know how self-consciousness is supposed to be constituted so as to undergo the extrinsic determinations situating the I prior to, in the face of, and in the word. The alternative is even more abrupt. Either the I is passive and capable of being saved—or the I actively and substantially posits itself, training itself to "havings" and walled up in itself even unto damnation. Luther repeats a similar either-or for many pages. But polemic is one thing. Another is to understand the manner of being of a consciousness essentially at the mercy of the word.

The consciousness that harbors a precursive practical knowledge in its activities, brought to bear on its obligations and prohibitions, is called moral consciousness (*Gewissen*). It is the voice of an inner judge, keeper of the knowledge concerning good and evil. Be this materially (in the ancients) or formally (in the moderns), the moral consciousness contains in itself the idea of an order of the good as a "fact." Therefore, where there is precursive knowledge, all extrinsic modifications will be accidental. Self-consciousness (*Bewußtsein*), on the other hand, remains neutral toward its contents. Its function amounts to accompanying all subjective modifications. In Luther, as well, moral consciousness is "partial" in relation to self-consciousness, as the word that judges is partial in relation to the word that justifies. In the law, even when speaking to us from inside, he hears the muffled voice of the promise that speaks to us clearly only in the mouth of an other. Since the essence of language is embodied in its efficiency, the law inscribed in the heart will have the status of a simple limit case, imperfect, of the word essentially coming from outside. Whether or not the word binds us or frees us, consciousness produces nothing, above all not an order of good and evil.

How then should a consciousness be constituted that is placed in a passive situation by a word that states first: "You must" and then "You can"? It is precluded from deducing some "I can," contained analytically in the "you must." The inevitable and universal defeat in the face of the law shows well enough that on my own, regarding by intact being, I can do nothing at all. A deduction of power from out of duty, in which Kant will see the factual proof of our autonomy ("you should, thus you can"), appears to Luther as the very gall of all impious reasoning. Does causal heteronomy entail the foreclosure of all originarily subjective acts? This is what it will be impossible to sustain in view of the literally critical function of reflection: the function of *estimation,* separating the law and faith.

At stake is the capacity of resuming, of representing, of reproducing, the word. There is no transcendentalism without such an act of pure apperception by which I make the modifications occurring in the field of the consciousness my own. But how do we understand such an active appropriation in a consciousness that is essentially passive? The issue here, then, is of the kernel of critical transcendentalism in its birth in Luther.

The unity of receptive consciousness

The major problem of all critical transcendentalism has to do with the unity of self-consciousness. In this respect it matters little whether the rules governing my representations end up assuring my submission (Luther) or, to the contrary, my emancipation (Kant). These subjective rules must be such that they actually make the contents they serve to organize my own. "Making my own." This is the originary act without which the critical turn is null and void. In Luther the contents of consciousness are the modifications that I submit prior to–in the face of–in the word. How do these sites become mine?

Luther speaks of a "mathematical point to grasping justice."[50] He could not have better described the unifying act, the ultimate subjective condition for appropriation (he could have better described, on the other had, the *object* of the grasping—not only justice, but every word, whether it condemns or justifies). To better understand this intermittent act of appropriation, we return to the topography of the word. The mutations that it effects remain, in Luther, the experience of the departure that is impossible to prove, but whose conditions demand to be elucidated. The passage across these *topoi* is the alpha and omega. The subjectivist turn begins with these sites and is embodied in them. Critique can at the most disengage their functioning.

Now, this functioning is not at all generative. Luther seeks a geometric point capable of centering consciousness, not an algebraic point added to others to constitute the line of a genesis. The positionings of the I do not succeed one another in a diachrony. Thus the mobile subject is not stretched along the length of a series of psychic acts as if across so many episodes. If there is any line traced by the I prior to–in the face of–in the word, as one commentator well observes, it can be only a trait that "strikes out the totality of our psychic resources only so as to leave the I entirely empty, purely receptive."[51] The command "you must" wrenches consciousness from its infantile slumber in which it does not yet know either good or evil. When it enters into the age of reason, it posits itself as autonomous. It experiences the moral law that speaks to it within (if not from within). Thus the *moral agent* is native to us. The "natality" in us posits it. This first modification of consciousness thus produces a semblance of auto-givenness. That it is only a semblance is what the second modification teaches. That justification comes to us from elsewhere signifies that the *justified patient* is not native to us. It is given from the outside when the word reveals the essential incapacity of the agent to affirm itself—when it reveals itself as the usurper of autonomy, necessarily failing in its usurpation. In its second, non-usurpatory modification, consciousness experiences the reality of allo-givenness. In this it undergoes its singularization, the index of our "mortality."

For Luther, justification is offered to all as the possibility of an upright self-consciousness, rectifying the consciousness turned back toward itself. Whatever the dogmatic difficulties inherent in a similar universalism may be, the giving of the rectifying and liberating word remains a trait of consciousness as such. This is why Luther can cast a synchronic eye on the sites prior to–in the face of–in the word. Accordingly, the full givenness of the word is not just one trait among others. Self-givenness proves to be fictive only in the light of allo-givenness, and this sufficiently demonstrates the *originary status of this heteronomous givenness*. In justification, the truth of morality appears; in the word that sets free, the truth of words that binds; in the patient, the truth of the agent; and in heteronomy, finally, the truth of autonomy. Thus it is necessary to examine once again the issue of passive justification and to ask, this time from the point of view of the unity that poses a problem, that if self-consciousness is essentially the consciousness of an extrinsic givenness, then isn't it necessary that a quasi-spontaneous act accompany it that is capable of unifying consciousness?

A candidate for this unifying role has already presented itself: the act of hearing. But hearing consists of many things. If this candidate proves capable—if it is possible to smooth out its rough edges by resolving some of the difficult problems regarding the unity, the simplicity, and the synthetic nature of the "I hear"—then we will be able to speak without hesitation of critical transcendentalism in the birth of the referential consciousness. We will have hold of the originary function in the subject, the *sine qua non* of the revolution that turns away from the logic of things so as to turn toward an aprioric logic. It will be necessary to see next if, and in what manner, this primary function is diversified, according to Luther, into acts that are equally formal, but emphasizing more specifically the two positionings of the awakened I: "in the face of" and "in" the word.

Kant will conceive of a single givenness of diverse givens—singular, because it is uniform, and uniform because it is always formed by time. In Luther, the given is not diverse as is the sensible multiple; rather, it is heterogeneous. The moral agent is posited as autogenous in the face of the law, and the justified patient is received as allogenous by faith in the efficiency of the word. The two givennesses do not originate in the same world. Yet they are equally immediate. Hence, there is an absence of all schematizable form in their reception. Hence also, if there is a categorization or proto-categorization in Luther, its place is not the understanding, but self-consciousness as a whole. The two givennesses, as we have seen, determine all consciousness, torn as it is between a fictive but inextirpable autonomy and a real but undemonstrable heteronomy. The pathos that follows from this strips away the *simplicity* from this referent (see further, chapter 2). But where in this lies its *unity*?

A hypothetical imperative—in any case, a sequence of acts—is expressed, it seems, in appropriation: "make yours" the justice offered, and you will be justified. It is necessary to understand by "condition" a conditional: whosoever desires salutary heteronomy should fight against fictive autonomy. Is this how consciousness is unified? Does the unity of the I result from a making, from a "making mine"? Will the I be one—will I be one—by *making myself* heteronomous?

When he explains, one more time, that divine justice signifies that through which God makes us just, not that through which he is just in himself, Luther places reception under two conditional clauses. One concerns fictive autonomy, the other salutary heteronomy. The conditional clause regarding the position of the autonomous agent says that the passive justification appears in broad daylight only "if our injustice has become our own, that is to say, known and recognized (*agnita et confessa*)." It seems nothing could be clearer. We should recognize our injustice—self-affirmation in the face of the law—and, as a result, we will be accorded justice, acceptability regardless of the position of the self. He will be saved who confesses that he is rotten to the core with egotism. And do we not see in Luther the new pathos of confession, in Protestants the new pathology of culpability, the pathogenesis of the Reformation that wins over all modernity like the microbe does an organism, leading straight to the Freudian couch, etc.? Or again Luther's instructions for preaching: Push people to despair of themselves, only then extend to them the saving arm . . . "for our injustice hurls us headlong at the feet of God." Now, does not the weight of the moral agent come from the fact that, on his own, he remains quite incapable of recognizing himself and of recognizing himself as unjust? That he thinks of everything—consolidating his autonomy—except of hurling himself headlong at the feet of God? Accordingly, a few lines later, Luther affirms the contrary of what we believe from reading it as a conditional clause regarding fictive autonomy. "That our injustice can bring to light the justice of God . . . only the men of the pulpit think this" (*sch.* 3,5). To say "How I am low!" so that God would raise me up is also to say "How far will I not climb!" As a result, the hypothetical imperative collapses and with it the empirical status of the condition for receiving justification.

The conditional clause concerning salutary heteronomy and its givenness says, "Having received [justice], we glorify God as the one who gives." First we receive salvation, then, knowing what he is capable of giving, we praise him. We see what he does, and then we make known what he has done. This time, the hypothetical series of moments reverses that of the first clause. Before, it seemed it was necessary to recognize in order to receive; here we seem to receive, then we recognize. The reception of salvation would be the empirical condition of its recognition and of our recognition. But here again the aporia lies in wait. For, for Luther, praising, glorifying, recognizing, is all one—namely, *confiteri*. As in Augustine, in confession we simultaneously admit being a sinner and we praise the savior. "Confession (*confessio*) glorifies Him and praises Him because it confirms how salutary is His justice" (ibid.). It is the act in which is expressed the subsumption of the agent positing himself as autonomous under the patient that is being received as heteronomous. To say "How low I was, I who have been raised up," is the same thing as saying "How far *did* I not climb!" As a result, the temporal sequence of moments collapses and with it, as before, every empirical condition of salvation by justification.

The question is decisive in order to discover the gesture on which Luther centers receptive consciousness. The impression of an empirical sequence here arises from the double sense of the same verb. We will *confess* (namely, our injustice) in order to receive (justice), after which we will *confess* again (namely, the giving). But if the same word is found at the beginning and end of the chain, it is because we are performing one and the same act—confessing. There are no hypothetical conditions linked together. The progression indeed passes from the conditioned to its condition, but in an altogether different sense. In this sequence that really is not one, where does the *conditioned* appear? It is designated as a whole by the double sense of the verb "to confess." What are the two objects of this transitive verb? Confessing injustice and confessing justice. The same double meaning is also at play in appropriation. We make our injustice ours—we receive justice as our own. The two objects are injustice and justice. Now, we saw that the first is the essence of posing as autonomous agent, and the second is the essence of salvation by heteronomous granting. Consequently one confesses or appropriates both the postures and the salvation. It is impossible to know the former without recognizing the latter that overcomes them. And what is the simple *condition* of this double conditioned? The text states it as well: "We glorify God as the one that *gives*." The detail was foreseeable, one will say. In a theory of the efficiency of the one God, who "gives" if not God? The vicious circle is obvious. If God alone is efficient, he alone gives. One concludes that God is the exclusive cause of that for which God is the exclusive cause. A vicious circle, without a doubt. But in what manner does this efficient cause come here to us? As a being lowering itself and raising another being? Luther's anger is always directed at the same fiction, with the reist illusions that it entails, that of a confrontation between two beings, one human and the other divine. In what manner then? It suffices to read: ". . . God as the one who gives." The condition both of fictive autonomy and salutary heteronomy is singular, and it comes to us—it is the givenness of self-consciousness even before it is diversified into lost or salutary self-understanding. We become its addressees that we are by confessing it.

The "I confess" is properly the act that says what is. It says that self-consciousness is one through the extrinsic efficiency of the word. It says that it is one through its constitutive receptivity.

The act of "I confess" can pride itself on a noble theological tradition. Yet as a candidate it is still too weak to function as a mathematical point centering the I. Through its double referent of the object—the injustice of works, the justice of the faith—the act emphasizes the unity of self-consciousness; it also emphasizes receptivity and therefore heteronomy; finally, it is clearly of a linguistic nature. On the other hand, it does not express the moving force itself in Luther's transcendentalism, namely, the metabolism—the *metaballein,* the overturning—in self-understanding with its either-or. The act of "I confess" covers a phenomenal territory that is too narrow for localizing the new hegemonic center. The act "I hear" covers a territory that is too large since it passes over the specificity of the event that the word is for Luther, namely, its efficiency.

The work that the candidate for being the originary function in consciousness must accomplish is described best as *heteronomous apperception.* "Apperception" is meant to designate the self-consciousness accompanying the modifications effected by speech, and heteronomous is meant to express that in the subject there is no spontaneous production to be accompanied, but only an alien work. When, thanks to living speech, consciousness is illuminated—the terrifying light of the law, and/or the rectifying light of faith—heteronomous apperception is empirical. We recognize the diverse modifications as our own, saying "I am lost," "I am saved." But how do we make the giving our own unless by an act of *a priori* reception that is constitutive of consciousness and is diversified according to the effects of the word? Whether or not the light of the law lights up, heteronomous apperception remains the intermittent act, empty of any content, in this sense pure, for grasping the efficient word. Only such an act will satisfy the criteria of formalism and unity defining all critical transcendentalism.

It is one thing to describe the formally unifying mission of the originary act in consciousness for centering the I. It is another to name it and to disentangle the systematic difficulties in it. These problems all have to do with the *a priori* status of the originary act. Below it will be necessary to examine the traits by which apperception is diversified downstream, following the relations of the I to the word. There is here a transcendental formalism, since the word could never guide consciousness in its infernal and celestial vagaries unless the originary act prepared its *a priori* avenues. Heteronomous apperception therefore must be diversified in advance in order to bring out these two effects. Here we are examining this act upstream, namely, in its theonomy, its relation to the *nomos* that makes it heteronomous. There is also a transcendental unity here, since consciousness would remain incapable of recognizing topological modifications as its own if, throughout its positionings effected from the outside, it did not know itself as one. This necessarily alien effectuation and this knowledge equally necessarily mine make up heteronomous apperception.

But is it not a contradiction in terms to speak of a self-consciousness determined by an alien *nomos*? Doesn't extrinsic givenness cleave consciousness? This is not even to mention the problem that wells up in Luther, namely, if heteronomy follows from a received givenness, how will self-consciousness exercise any sort of hegemony? The major difficulties that are raised here by apperception—concerning nothing less than the fate of critical transcendentalism, as one will see in Kant's autonomous apperception—are due to the *simplicity* of the formal I in its originary act. Its unity can only be synthetic. But what is this synthesis?

Before returning to Luther for a response, we should note that the transcendental subject is born, certainly not as a solipsist (since it is constituted by its relation to the word), but indeed barren of any world. It is born decontextualized. The world remains the great void of transcendental logic, an absence to which Kant will provide the beginning of a remedy in the form of the sense receptivity with which his critical enterprise will begin.

Again we should note the fate that will make transcendentalism—and hence the modern hegemonic fantasm—into an originary synthesis of the two *nomoi,* namely, the law of autonomy and the law of heteronomy, whatever the manner may be in which, for the moment, these are to be understood. If he conceives of the I as a "mathematical point for seizing justice," Luther opens up in consciousness a break between what comes from God and what comes from myself. It would be difficult not to see the I cracked between an alien act and another that is mine that makes the alien gift mine. Accordingly, such a cracking will not disappear automatically when the outburst of Enlightenment thought dispels the beyond in the constitution of reason and when the other of the I, whose place will have been evacuated by God, henceforth is the sensible given that one must undergo. Whether the primacy in experience is accorded to God or to the perceived, the other—some instance of the other suffered, endured—continues to dictate its law to the I. The end of theonomy therefore does not necessarily signify the sweeping away of all alien interference in the purity of the I. In the terms of law, if heteronomous apperception in Luther proves to direct consciousness against itself, the legislating strategy will come to us from outside, but a transgressive counter-strategy will be opposed to it from the inside. When, after a switch between autonomy and heteronomy from Luther to Kant, the legislating strategy issues from subjective spontaneity, from the inside, then the perceived given with which the Kantian critique begins will oppose to this spontaneity a transgressive counter-strategy coming this time from the outside, but with effects that are no less fracturing than the Lutheran autonomy. Obviously it will be necessary to understand that sense receptivity is no longer the same thing when the critique proceeds from the absolute primacy of divine heteronomy to the primacy of the perceived given, which is relative to empirical consciousness. Nevertheless, under the reign of heteronomy in Luther, as under that of autonomy in Kant, there will be a break between the *auto-* and the *hetero-*, a break that is systematically inescapable. If, in a nutshell, it is here that we have the birth of modernity, hegemonic self-consciousness will immediately constitute phenomena through a broken spontaneity. The issue overwhelms Luther—to know if it is only possible that, in the singular giving, divine heteronomy reigns without the I introducing into it anything of its own; and to know if, in spontaneity proper, the received singular introduces into it a suffering and thus something improper. In short, to know if self-consciousness, be it receptive or spontaneous, is not necessarily broken when it comes to exercise hegemonic legislation.

Now, it is easy to see that, in accordance with the very revolution that leads Luther to transfer the drama of salvation into the arena of consciousness, absolute theonomy remains a wish—fulfilled empirically by predestination and election, but transcendentally counteracted without appeal by the necessity of a receptive act "to seize (*arripere*) justice." There is no givenness without reception. Recognizing this does not amount to erasing, but, to the contrary, emphasizing the distinction between the *a priori* structure of receptivity and the empirical fact of passivity.

In Luther, the topical argument establishing active receptivity in empirical passivity is concerned with the gift of light to the mind (not to reason, of which the *lumen naturale,* always finite, illuminates only according to the sensible which is given to it). Regarding *illumination* and his "view," Luther forces divine exclusivity even beyond that of the theonomy, however it is propped up, governing the word and its efficiency. The light illuminating our spirit comes from God, as also does the vision with which we receive it. We see with the eye of God—whereas Luther never says that we hear the word with the ear of God (which would be a *novum* in the tradition). This is a forced theonomy that shows how consciousness is joined with an *a priori* illumination, and the passivity in this illumination is joined with an active reception.

We are already illuminated (prior to the law) in our infantile situation. "The words of God are something open that is accessible to all and illuminate even children" (*SA* 654). "Words" are the law and the promise. The capacity to be illuminated by it is the condition of self-consciousness in everyone. Thus the eye of God in me is desubstantialized and demythologized. Luther traces seeing back to the understanding that I have of myself. The eye of God signifies heteronomous apperception. The illumination becomes empirically efficient in effecting modifications in the manner that I understand myself, namely, efficient in condemning, in situating me in the face of the word "you should"; efficient in saving, by situating me in the word "you can." Here we have *a priori* illumination diversely modifying the consciousness.

In this illumination, the joining of passivity with receptivity is completely different. In learning that the law has been accomplished by proxy, we find ourselves the uncooperative beneficiaries of justification; *passivity* characterizes the effective bestowal that is contingent on justice, its experience in this sense. But this bestowal can only be produced if consciousness first has the wherewithal to grasp the offered justice; *receptivity* characterizes the power of receiving the word, a necessary and constitutive power. Divine exclusivity is most marked regarding sight rather than hearing, for the mind sees the justifying light with "the eye of God" himself.[52] Hence the illuminationism of the *mens* is demetaphysicized by the transcendentalism of consciousness.

So it is by means of an extrinsic light and an extrinsic visual organ that we receive what is given—as salutary efficiency, as the word understood, light seen, or even as vision—and that, it seems, cannot escape heteronomy pure and simple. Does not the theory of illumination assume an unmitigated passivity on the part of the subject? In Augustine, of whom Luther states that he "is mine, entirely mine" (*SA* 640), this theory would support the evidence of *contents innate* to the spirit, eternal reason. God illuminates them naturally, and this is the reason that through training we can learn to see them. The contingent *exercitatio* is only possible for us by virtue of the passivity constitutive of reason. Lacking a turning back on the self that may or may not happen, the ideal evidence remains latent. The Augustinian theory serves to account for the origin of ideas in us. These are imprinted on our essential nature. The imprint that subsistent truth engraves in our mind is passive according to the Augustinian theory. Now, Luther amputates this model from its essentialist framework. Illumination is brought to bear on God as we alone can experience him, namely, inasmuch as God modifies consciousness—man "would never see his ugliness were it not illuminated."[53] When *a priori* illumination is actualized in an event—when "God illuminates himself" (*sch.* 11,8)—what do we see? Neither God, nor some seeds of eternity. We always and ever again see ourselves, but in a new light. Not as beautifully spontaneous, full of initiative, autonomous, but ugly in our spontaneity, our initiatives, and our very autonomy. Thus what we see is our disgrace, self-consciousness placing itself over against the law, and that is what we henceforth contemplate through the divine eye. The theory finds itself thus amputated from the ideal objects and from their entitative source that in the Augustinian tradition it served to prove. As a result, passivity is no longer the final word of experience.

The final word is receptivity. There is nothing ontic nor contingent about receptivity. Luther states this even where he pushes theonomy to the extreme. "The eye of God" is found "inside us." This amounts to saying that it belongs to consciousness as a function. It is *the* apperceptive function, the one that becomes diversely operative as we find ourselves magnificent in the light of the law or forsaken in that of faith. Accordingly, Luther opposes this eye to "our eye,"[54] to reason left to its own means, illumined only by its natural light. The rational organ in us that is ours receives the impressions by which we find it once again in the visible world; the spiritual organ in us that is of God always receives this other imprint by which we know ourselves in actually hearing. Latent, the light-word keeps us infantile; bursting, it displays beneath our eyes the ugliness of the one magnified, with the possibility of finally finding oneself "reborn entirely and entering through the great open doors of paradise." Thus self-consciousness can remain troubled, and as a result the mind is positioned in relation to its duty; it can be illuminated, and, as a result, it finds itself as forsaken-saved. In one light as in the other, receptivity remains the *aprioric function of self-consciousness*—the strict pendant illuminating *a priori* "even children." In receptivity, the passivity that always places consciousness on the lookout for a word arising from outside is joined with the appropriative quasi-spontaneity.

If he thus emphasizes heteronomy as co-constitutive of self-consciousness, then the schema of illumination obviously only varies the schema of hearing. The word is the "most illuminating light" (*SA* 654). In the two schemas, it is a matter of the same receptivity in consciousness. Whosoever wakes from the sleep prior to the law, opens his eye to good and evil. Whosoever finds himself wrenched from the sleep of good consciousness in the face of the law opens the other eye, despairs of what he took to be the light—but thus would no less despair of having already recognized himself as capable of seeing a light and hearing a word that saves. The Augustinian metaphysical commonplaces about the height of the mind, emptied of their essentialist connotations and restituted in a topography of functions, serve here to set up all *empirical activity* on the side of the cause outside the I. But yet they reveal that, to receive its effect, it is necessary that there be in consciousness a *transcendental receptivity* that resumes, represents, and reproduces the object given and thereby makes it its own. In the absence of such an approporiative "re-," the understanding that I have of myself would not be modified at all. We see and hear only that which we make our own by sight and hearing. We only receive that whose reception we acknowledge. Heteronomous apperception is a function accompanying consciousness in the face of the law as in faith. This act will not be simple, otherwise how is heteronomy to be understood? But in order to unify consciousness, it must be one. It must be able to express itself as singularly as the "I think." However, as a matter of words, it resembles the "I hear" instead. Furthermore, and due to the very fact that its *a priori* receptivity joins consciousness to an efficient, alien work being carried out in it, this act analogous to the *cogito* will synthesize an allogenic givenness and an autogenic reception, as is stated by the "I confess."

Therefore, by which act will I make the extremely affected linguistic work my own? The moral stage here is the more enlightening. Show me just one, states Luther, who in all their acts has without fail satisfied the law. Such a hero of duty is found nowhere. Hence the Protestant and modern intoxication with culpability. Self-affirmation insinuates itself even into the most devoutly submissive spirit, as in the case of ice that causes the rock to crack. Now, there can be no obedience or disobedience in empirical matters unless there is a formal act through which we have submitted ourselves beforehand to the word as such. The previous candidates to this unifying position—the "I hear" and the "I confess"—did not express this submission. They did not express what the law and revelation have in common, namely, what they require to be observed. More clearly than the verb "to hear" (*hören, horchen*), its intensive—the verb "to obey" (*gehorchen*)—indicates as much the prescriptive nature of the word as it does the efficiency of God alone. It expresses the heteronomy in the act producing self-consciousness, precisely the heteronomy that the future emancipating "I think" will have to dispel. In Luther, the condition of all subjective modification—the place where his critical transcendentalism takes shape—is *the act "I obey."*

In order to bring the transcendental turn to a conclusion, what still must be examined is the synthesis by which I absolve myself by this act. All critical transcendentalism understands itself in the *a priori* synthetic work that self-consciousness accomplishes. Accordingly, in Luther, there is a synthesis at the origin of all possible modifications of the subject. Whether it is on the road to ruin or whether it lets itself be found and swept off toward its salvation, the formal I is delivered unto its other, that is, unto an allo-givenness in the midst of language. It is necessary to bear in mind this essential handing over of the self as the absolutely first *a priori* synthetic act. Whether the extrinsic efficiency of the word remains concealed in the "you must" or whether it reveals itself in the "you can," the I entrusts itself to the word. The handing over of the self to the word *makes* obedience synthetically receptive. The synthesis is formal to the extent that the "I obey" provides the condition as much to the arrogance of the empirical deed, which damns the man of duty, as it does to the humility of the deed, which is again empirical, that saves the man of faith. Nothing better underscores the innovative problematic of Luther than this *synthesis of the "I obey" and the word,* the synthesis that is heteronomous apperception. With the "I obey" thus understood, we have his founding gesture for the new hegemony.

Nor does anything better mark his distance in relation to the emancipating project of Kant.[55] The "I obey" implants the I in a place in which authority not only reigns untouched, but even receives a transcendental legitimization. All praxis remains heteronomous and must remain so. Luther's oratorical vehemence aims to exclude the "I obey" from ever being able to signify some "I do." From there to Kant, although the key elements of transcendentalism scarcely vary, their respective functions will change entirely. In Luther, the *a priori* synthesis is pre-emancipatory because it results from the intervention of an other; in Kant, it will be *our originary deed.* In it resides the very nerve of subjective autonomy and, consequently, all potential of emancipation, intellectual as well as practical, individual as well as collective.

The synthetic unity of consciousness is the problem *par excellence* that haunts all critical transcendentalism, and for architectonic reasons. Kant will seek to dissipate this obsessive fear—the fantasmic presence of a fissure—through the deduction of categories beginning from the "I think." Indeed, in the critique of the autonomous I the unity of consciousness will have to prevail over the two roots of *Gemüt,* and the transcendental deduction will have to show how the forms of understanding (the categories) are applied to those of sensibility (in time and in space) as well as, through their intermediary, to the perceived manifold. This is the attempt at an autonomistic solution in which it will be necessary to interrogate the counter-strategy introduced by the *being of the other,* namely, by our affectivity in relation to the sensible given.

Obsessive fear is no less obvious in Luther, even if, to the contrary, he clings to the being of the other and wants it so. At what stage of the pre-emancipatory transcendental edifice does the fissure declare itself? Above heteronomous apperception, in the order of the conditions of possibility, there is only the light of God illuminating the eye of God in us. Now, "that which illuminates the eye is neither obscure nor equivocal" (*SA* 654); there is no fissure there. The unity of consciousness remains except at its source. On the other hand, seen from the positionings to which consciousness is awakened—, the positionings prior to and in the word—it is decidedly lost. Where then does the dyad appear in heteronomous consciousness? It can only be in the act that constitutes it as heteronomous, in the act of the "I obey." Moreover, these words express this act when it submits the quasi-spontaneous, apperceptive I to the word-as-light received, which alone is purely spontaneous. The synthetic unity of consciousness is split by the reception that the I combines with the giving. Luther avoids the specter of a double self-consciousness by the practical imperative: "God demands an obedient spirit . . . that allows itself to be broken" (*sch.* 7,8). This is the attempt at a tutelary solution into which the passive I, allowing itself to be broken, introduces a counter-strategy that we must now examine.

Self-consciousness will be one only to the extent that it is *passive* even if, as *receptive,* it is not simple, synthesizing the efficient word and the act of conformity effected. Where do the traits that cross in the I point—the arrival of the illuminating word and the I which gives itself over to it? They point downstream from the synthetic "I obey," where heteronomous apperception is diversified into the conflict of the *simul* "in the face of–in the word." For the consciousness *in the face of the law,* receptive quasi-spontaneity necessarily turns into thetic spontaneity. But "*in faith,* we can act against our moral consciousness" (*sch.* 14,23); moreover, all thetic acts are broken by faith in the efficiency of God alone. The traits crossing in the I are translated into two sites—the "moral" and "faith"—which are equally constitutive of consciousness. How can we not conclude that the conflict opened up by heteronomy inevitably develops into an aprioric differend in the subject itself? If this is so, it will be necessary to seek out the categories emphasizing such a differend. In his great discovery, Luther saw himself "simultaneously" as moral agent confused in the face of the word and as justified patient, finding rest in it. This is because the quasi-spontaneous act of reception naturally—natively, by the natality in us—pushes consciousness to fashion itself simply as spontaneous. What in me *posits* itself in the face of good or evil is not the same as what *allows* efficient speech to act. The latter does not let itself be singularized, and in this the work of mortality in us is always apparent.

Thus the justification effected by the word breaks consciousness in its constitutive and even unifying act, the "I obey." We have just seen how the modern hegemony is instituted. What remains to be seen in detail is how, through fidelity to the tragic ultimates, it is broken.

CHAPTER 2

A Pathetic Differend

If Luther institutes the new fantasmic authority in declaring "only by faith," he institutes it as immediately broken, declaring its subject "simultaneously justified and sinner." After having seen the modern hegemony, it is now necessary to see what is the modern tragedy.

Candor *prior to* the word is forever lost with the discovery of good and evil; we will even see, from the transcendental point of view, that it never really existed. Can we free ourselves from terror *in the face of* the law? Or be released from it? Luther indeed says that, as justified, we die to the law. Will the efficient word then install us *in* the consummated law as one raises a ward and installs the liberated one in his own right? Doesn't Luther speak incessantly about liberation? And what would a semi-freedom be, a freedom under semi-tutelary surveillance, if there is no freedom at all? But it suffices to recall the inextricable anguish with regard to election, the polemic against the fiction of a constant presence, and above all the necessarily extrinsic character of the new freedom for understanding that nothing is ever left behind this freedom, neither the law nor its universalizing drive that posits it, nor its effects. It requires a saintly will to *fulfill* it—which visibly our will is not. In relation to the law, we remain minors.

We will never get over the law as we get over a pubescent trauma. It has its own logic, and as is suggested by the bond of *logos-lex,* it is even the sphere of logic properly speaking. What then are its durable effects? Its "No" gives a content to the transcendental "I obey." "You will not do it." A statement that in the first place has a heuristic function. It "forces us to recognize our impotence" in producing our own justice (*sch.* 8,3, cor.), so much so that it "declares all men are unjust" (*sch.* 3,19), "accuses them of being sinners and renders them guilty" (*sch.* 4,14). But, as is well-known to whoever passes from the self-aggrandizement prior to good and evil to the self-positing in the face of the law, this is exciting. It incites one to carry on regardless. Its "No" is acerbic, it wounds narcissistic innocence. Thereby it does more than reveal our culpability to us. It goads the self-affirmation that it nevertheless condemns and carries it to paroxysm. It exacerbates it. "Rather than strengthening the will against sin, the reign of the law incites it to sin" (*sch.* 2,12). The No that reverberates with the knowledge of good and evil proscribes what we desire and prescribes what we do not desire. The No whips up the "desire for transgression" (*sch.* 8,15) in two senses of the word: it thrashes it and kindles it. How could it be otherwise as long as the law summons us to affirm ourselves as autonomous? But the summons perverts the "I obey."

It is not difficult to see where the logic of the law leads—straight to death. The law "worsened the sin as well as the deserved remuneration: death" (*gl.* 5,20). Worsened death? Yes, by annihilating all rational structures for circumventing it. Reassuring constructions did not remain the privilege of the Greeks. They even infiltrated the ancient Fathers who, according to Luther, nevertheless valued speech highly. Any serenity conceivable by reason is simply artificial. The law does not only reveal our impotence in the face of its prescriptions and proscriptions. It *produces* self-affirmation: the lesson of impotence, exacerbated guilt. In reducing to nothing the chances for immortality, the law thrust us headlong into death, without recourse. It produces death. It "reveals to man his death."[56] Negative experience no longer allows for the framing of other consoling experiences. Luther sees little more than a system of "snares" (where life and death occupy neighboring ranks serenely made up of material goods [*sch.* 8,7]) in a comforting enterprise like the anagogic schema that has, nevertheless, proved itself. The law as understood by Luther renders us, for the first time in the West, really mortals.

The undertow created by naked death is a differend with the life granted from the outside. The modern tragedy that is born here opposes death to life without an arbitrating authority and in the form of two givings emphasized by the I: the one autonomous, the other heteronomous. Now, a subject that is held by life and death, as much by the one as by the other, is a subject who suffers. *Simul* is the name of extreme suffering, of the pathos whose agents ineluctably work on consciousness. The *simul* describes the condition of modern man, a condition which is no longer exactly tragic, nor erratic, but *pathetic*.

In order to grasp the conflict well, a terminological convention suggests itself. It will be useful to speak of the "I" only in terms of the transcendental unity of subjective functions, a unity which we have seen already in Luther is neutral in relation to all the contents of the consciousness (a small difficulty, however, since in the French expression 'consciousness of the "I"' {*conscience du je*}, for *Ichbewusstsein,* tends to substantialize the I, it is necessary to describe the unifying act that is the "I obey" as "self-consciousness" {*conscience de soi*}).

The object of the heteronomous giving is the "self." It is born from the justification that confers a new being.[57] Luther describes the efficiency of God as the communication, by the word, of the divine self becoming our own. God "emptied himself out" (*heauton ekenosen, PH.* 2,7). In the somewhat airy terms of the speculative tradition inspired by this kenose, the justifying word is the milieu in which God conducts, in us, his conversation with himself. Luther retains from this tradition the linguistic character of the self that is bestowed. He devotes all his passion to bringing about a consciousness from this statement addressed to us—to bringing about self-consciousness. We are to understand by this the effect of the word that saves. Thus the self is neither pregiven like an imperishable kernel in the soul, nor acquired by some interaction with others.

I *suffer* the self, the principle of life.

We call the ego, moreover, the agent behind every position that makes itself out to be autonomous. Luther describes it as *Eigensinn* (*sensus proprius, sch.* 2,22). This is not born in the face of the law; rather, it affirms itself against it. In the pathos of consciousness, it intervenes as the agent of autonomous positions as much as it does as their object, as what posits and what is posited. Yet its autonomy is nothing but a fiction, and a doubly mortal fiction. It suffers death, but puts it to death as well. It is struck down for not fulfilling the law, which demands "none have ever done it, thus none have its life" (*sch.* 10,15). The ego is no longer either pregiven as a congenital task in the soul, nor acquired by compromising with the evil of the world.

The ego is what I *make* of myself and, because of its impotence, the principle of death.[58]

"The self," "the ego"—the article designates not a thing, but rather pronominal traits. Also, neither the self, nor even the ego are to be understood here first in a moral sense. One must not think of impulses emanating from the subject, as in the love of the self and *amour-propre* in Rousseau. Rather, these are two ramifications of the I—like the two blades of a pair of scissors, pivoting on the joint of the I. To the Luther who cuts away metaphysics and who prunes Christianity, these scissors are provisionally useful for cutting the dead wood of the old logic of things, cutting into Porphyry's tree . . . (provisionally, for—as we will see—although these two blades form a pair, these two branches do not work symmetrically). To the Luther who carves out the preliminary modern profile, the pair serves to open an epoch. The pathos of all transcendental dualism is indeed born in the gap between the self and the ego. Where do we get these two modes of being near to ourselves? Only the promise reveals them, the one that "bears on the facts that we do not see" (*SA* 633). The self and the ego are *facts of consciousness.*[59]

Moral consciousness is nothing but the voice of the ego in us. While according it credence, the subject still awaits the salvation of its works. The voice of the ego rises from the ashes of Narcissus where the freedom of indifference is lodged, and it lures us—lures the ego, essentially—toward the ashes of the self where the "freedom of the Christian man" will go up in smoke. Accordingly, with regard to the ego and its principles, liberation through extrinsic intervention appears immoral. "The word of God . . . comes beneath the outward appearance of evil" (*sch.* 12,2). Inversely, with regard to the self, all moral motivation remains captive to the law, disgusting: "To speak of myself, such a disgust seizes me each time I hear this word 'justice,' that if I were completely burgled I would feel less pain" (ibid.). The old definition of justice, *sua cuique tribuere,* makes up the vocabulary of the ego as it shapes its catalogue of virtues. All weight, be it of acts or souls, can only disgust. Equity, through virtue, smacks the inventor of morals. Giving to each their due is the Siren's call seeking the collapse of the self.

The ego and the self are no longer the first markers of experience. Luther does not exhort one to pass from awakening to Awakening: awakening to the law, then the Great Awakening to the self; death to immediate and undifferentiated pleasure, followed by some Great Death to egotism. Saying that salvation does not come from works amounts to saying that there is "no technique"—of awakening, of concentration, of mastery, of resolute detachment, of abnegation—he will never liberate the self from ego. There is no refuge, neither on the side of the ego nor on the side of the self. Rather, these are the transcendental facts of consciousness, opposed one to each other to the point of annihilation. Reflexive facts—those that we want, and then those for which we hope.

We should also add how the ultimates of experience—natality and mortality—are at work here. Natality, we will recall, is that drive that always pushes the natural metaphysician in us toward universalizations. Natality is encouraging to principles and is the principle in us that posits principles. Now, in Luther, the whole complex of principles-universals-laws, the whole thetic complex, is the province of the ego seeking to consolidate itself. Thus natality here produces the contrary of what it promises. It produces death. Inversely, mortality is that trait that always draws us toward our singularization to come, whose datable occurrence is called death. Now, in Luther, the promise undoes theticism, and it does this by singularizing me. The self, which is an effect of mortality, thus becomes the source of life. One may see in this inversion of ultimates the first gesture in the history of ideas for disabusing the natural metaphysician in us. We will see its outcome below in Heidegger (with which this book will end) where the singularization to come, recognized and borne in mind for itself, will mark the *diremption* of every hegemonic fantasm and thus the chance, if that is the word, of recovering from tragic denial.

As Deutero-Homer had discovered, moral consciousness is but a modification of self-consciousness. Accordingly, the conflict between the inhibitive protestations of the ego and the liberating intervention of the self is played out elsewhere than on the moral terrain. It is played out on the "spiritual" terrain.

All that is of interest here in this term, highly overdetermined in Luther, is its conflictual sense. "Spirit" first of all is another word for the transcendental site that Luther meant to occupy[60] (whence will be born the ethic one calls interior disposition, *Gesinnung*). In this sense, the word designates consciousness as a whole, but divided against itself. The key formula is "The spirit makes (*facit*) the good, but it does not fulfill (*perfecit*) it" (*sch.* 7,18). Spirit does so according to the intention of the self which is co-extensive with it; but God alone fulfills it—not the ego, which is also co-extensive with the spirit. The good is the law satisfied. The spirit knows the alien origin of the good so understood, but the ego arrogates it to itself. This is a doubly blind usurpation; it cannot help but preclude the liberating knowledge, a preclusion by which the ego constitutes itself as the other of the self; and, enclosed in the cycle of *perficere*, of performance, the ego cannot see the preclusion that nevertheless defines it. The ego nowhere reads the intention of the self since it is not exteriorized by performance. The ego and the self confront each other on the only terrain that they share, on the *Gesinnung*. "Spirit" thus does not here designate a being—neither the fine point of the soul, nor God or one of his persons, nor something infused, flowing from God to the soul. It designates "the whole man," but "intentioned," *gesinnt*, according to the ego or the self (*diverse sentiant*, ibid.). From here, there is a shift in the transcendental notion of the spirit.

In the cited formula, spirit is consciousness as a whole modified by the justifying word. Now, the *transcendental* conception of the spirit is revealed only beginning with its destinal conception; it is the destiny of the whole man to become spiritual. Who, indeed, can speak of the spirit as the arena in which the conflict between the ego and the self plays itself out, if not the one who already believes that the self can triumph? As justified, we *are* in the spirit, as is indicated by this hermeneutic principle for the reading of Paul: "The apostle speaks of spirit, which is why he can be understood only by those who are in the spirit" (*sch.* 3,5). In this destinal sense, the spirit is opposed to the "flesh" as the self is opposed to the ego, as heteronomy is to autonomy, and as the promise is to the law.

Are these disjunctions opposing, in so many figures, the same and *its* other?

In the stampede for shocking words, a good number of our contemporaries not long ago rallied around "deconstruction"—a half century after this word had been coined (*Abbau*), and just a little while ago they flocked together under others standards. The deconstructionists made a livelihood of bringing to light binary symmetrical opposites in a text: Evil is the other of the same that is good, the object is the other of the same that is the subject, etc., and they worked on these disjunctions, in which "the other" supposedly designates the domination of one posited term by its opposite, as gaps, as marginal alterities, as differences {*différances*}. Do the self and the ego call for such treatment, or do they by themselves oblige us to think the other in a different way? By what alterity is the ego the other of the self?

We will better see it by examining their respective *times*. The shift of meaning toward a destinal notion of the spirit indicates that we can lack the self. We can miss our destiny. The ego, for its part, even if it is a fiction, never leaves us. Indeed, good and evil are symmetrically opposed on the terrain of the ego; but is such a symmetry a characteristic both of the "spiritual" good that is the self, and this other that is, for Luther, the ego, namely, radical evil?

The time of the ego and the time of the self

Evil is born when I affirm and desire *in the face* of the law that which I automatically do *prior to* it. I breathe—for whom? I inhale oxygen for myself. Each throatful and each mouthful that I take sustain me, myself. The discharges of the body and of energies relieve me, myself. The newspaper that I read, the diplomas I work toward, the money I earn—are for me. And what is there of me in the coin that I drop into the hat that is held before me, or the present that I bring to a lover? In the moment it is what beckons me, appeals to me. At other times, due to mechanisms that are more subterranean, I can reward myself in doing what has no appeal at all. This is the automatism of the ego in the state of infantile latency. No effort will ever dismantle it.

In contrast, placed *in the face of* the law, I affirm it and desire it. Again, nothing shall dismantle this affirmation and this will . . . and philosophers heap praise upon these, those who exalt autonomy.

Accordingly, as contained *in* the law, autonomy had better prove itself a fiction, and in order to thwart it, the law has to be annulled so as to pass beyond good and evil. It goes without saying that, for Luther, such a passage remains inconceivable. The self places us neither outside the law, nor above it, but *in* it, fulfilled. The "freedom of the Christian man" does not nullify good and evil. Free in that way, we know that the good is not something that is effected. It is something that is received. To do good will henceforth nauseate, as will every pursuit of virtues and "havingness" {*ayance*} (*habitus*). Luther has seen that, beneath the techniques for driving it away, the fictive ego strongly risks raising itself to its own multiple (whence his rejection of the monastic institution). The law remains, and with it the illusion of being able to satisfy it. Consciousness, making itself out to be autonomous, carries on a conflict unto death with the consciousness that accepts itself as heteronomous. The ego anticipates, not what Kant will mean by the autonomous "I"—namely, the *a priori* function of giving myself cognitive and practical laws—but the substantial "I" that the metaphysical instinct in us endows with attributes both great and small, and whose persistent illusion plunges reason into insoluble paralogisms. Luther discovers the phenomenon of the transcendental illusion, but he detects it precisely in the place that, for subsequent philosophy, it cannot nor should not contaminate: in spontaneous self-positing. At its birth in Luther, the autonomous ego is a transcendental fiction because it pretends to fulfill the law by its own means. It has the status of a desire for being, pledging us to evil and death.

Does evil have any bearing on the spirit? If it does, is it grafted on the spirit by a figure of time?

A desire does not encumber itself with mediations nor does it delay itself with detours. And so it is with this transcendental fiction, namely, that the will to mimic the extrinsic givenness of the self and to work against it from a spontaneous position sends (*ligat*) us immediately and directly to perdition. Extrinsic efficiency delivers us (*solvit, SA* 630) from it only at an altogether different register. We remain dispatched unto death, in a posture "prior to" the word; we are delivered from it in a situation "in" the word. Dispatching and deliverance—the ego and the self as non-entitative facts of consciousness—thus do not maintain any sort of good equilibrium in the subject. The law and faith each determine all of man. They simultaneously have hold of consciousness. The *simul* (*simul iustus et peccator, sch.* 4,7) fractures self-consciousness from the moment it mushrooms into a hegemonic fantasm. We will see that the ontological dualism that results from this is the very condition of this hegemony. The scissors of double determination in consciousness will not close itself again so long as the I reigns. A transgressive counter-strategy opposes itself, from within the new fantasm, to its legislating strategy. It breaks it beforehand by opening up a gap in it. Luther *pathetically* describes the counter-strategy discovered in the mechanism of the transcendental fiction as the mortal tendency to fabricate an ego. The ontologic dualism of modern transcendentalism takes shape from the outset as a differend.

It is a differend between the self and the ego, not between good and evil. If Luther feels nothing but "disgust" for moral considerations pretending to discriminate between good and evil, it is because they arise from the "wisdom of the flesh." But we will understand nothing of the ego, nor all the more so the differend in which it engages with regard to the self, unless we dig down to the very root of evil. This root thrusts down elsewhere than into moral soil. It thrusts down into the "spirit." It does so in such a way that only the word of promise makes it comprehensible. Moral consciousness is fixed in the ego, is nourished by it, and speaks in its name; but this enrootedness and this delegation shows itself only to self-consciousness. The roots of evil thus grow in the soil prepared by the extrinsic intervention offering salvation. After Adam and Eve, "the wisdom of the flesh discriminates between good and evil. . . . Inversely, the wisdom of those that are spiritual know neither good nor evil, but they always and exclusively look to the word" (*sch.* 10,6). Good and evil show themselves in the light of the law. The self does not suffer them—not because it supposedly has raised itself higher, beyond good and evil, but because it does not know their root. Evil is rampant in the flesh, from which it is nourished and which speaks throughout all discourses professing to be discriminating; but it is rooted in the "spirit"—both understood as *Gesinnungen,* as the dispositions of all men. A self-consciousness that is delivered, from the outside, from the cruelty of the law, will know how to speak of evil by contrasting it, not with the good, but with the spirit. It speaks of "radical evil" (*sch.* 4,7).

All the missions that the ego arrogates to itself, notably the one of fashioning oneself according to any one of the popular conceptions of good and evil—the mission of "saving itself through works"—are lodged in the ramifications of this evil. These are ethical projects in which the ego relies upon its own resources. I leave the matter in my hands alone, regard myself as reliable, entrust myself to my own powers, put my confidence, my loyalty, my faith, in sovereign action, defying the exteriority of my word—these forms of *fides* turned back on the subject describe the root of all evil that Luther calls the "curvature" (*incurvitas, sch.* 6,6). This is because, in its moral athleticism, the ego is not training for the good; it is training always only for itself. Thus, the good of the ego is not the good. Even more resolutely than Duns Scotus, Luther refuses to attribute evil to some deformity due to matter, to a negation or evanescence of the moral good, or even some privation. Evil is born elsewhere than in the self—the only genuine good—and it has a different history. The good of the ego is the evil of the self.

The coiling up of trust around the ego allows for the description of radical evil, but it does not allow us to know it as that which gnaws at us (if we were to know not in this way, we would know where we stand in relation to the only efficient, extrinsic cause; we would be able to adjust ourselves in relation to it, but as a result there would then be a second liberating cause, the adjustment finally accomplished—the very fiction against which Luther never ceases to fight). "This, contrary to God, is rooted in an abyss that is so deep that no man will ever know it" (ibid.). Again, an opposition fractures the ultimate referent; and in the abyss of a nascent dualist transcendentalism there grows an unknown root, already . . .

And already also, evil is a tendency (*Hang, pronitas,* 1,24, cor.). The desire to make the "I obey" work for the ego, which nevertheless is destined to conform to the self—this desire does not resurge every once in a while. It does not wait for any occasion to spring up. As the word *pro-num* (*nuere,* to incline) says, it is inclined beforehand and even before any occasion. To say that man is a sinner is to say that man in his entirety, "all his senses and all his faculties," at all times and everywhere, leans toward that which earns him his death, that he is struck with a "mortal illness" (*sch*. 5,14). This inclination is incomparable to any other. It is the very condition of all desire. It is why Luther speaks, in a nutshell, of "evil desire" (*die bose Lust,* gl. 7,23). In a nutshell, it is not a faculty that is evil, but its use. Evil is a problem not of structure, but of function. Here, all the means of the ego desiring itself as autonomous are good, and the best means for this are also the best developed for positing oneself as such. The best *instrument* above all is the "spirit" as a disposition for obedience. Using this as a function in the service of the ego represents the curvature, the perverse refolding back that pledges us incurably to death. The instrumental connotation of the spirit is grafted onto its destinal notion. Just like the intellect and the will, the spirit can put itself just as much at the service of feigned autonomy as of salutary heteronomy. It remains "weak," always ready to submit itself to the ego. For Luther, radical evil resides in this tendency to give full reign to the ego, an inextirpable tendency.

Those who fabricate their own justice "seek that which is theirs, even in God" (*SA* 694). The folding up is never unfolded, neither by the force of ascetic discipline, nor by moral deeds. "By nature, on our own, we are evil. . . , for man can only desire that which is his own; he can only love himself above everything" (*sch*. 3,10). Contrary to the permutation, perpetrated *in fact* between use and joy (*uti–frui*), where Augustine saw the essence of sin (and in spite of the number of references that Luther makes to it [*sch*. 5,4.]), the curvature designates a trait of our *being,* not of some particular taste or some particular act. This trait that previously withdrew all attraction for heteronomy places us in a double bind. The ego withdraws us from the self that attracts. Were we to know this withdrawal vitiating our very being, the despair would be fatal. Even worse—or rather, even more clearly—all that our reason knows of it is the heavy stench of such intentions that otherwise are moral. Life will be livable whereas the root plunking deep into the abyss of contrariety will remain unknown to us.

The instrumentalization of the spirit points toward the time of the self and the time of the ego. The self and the ego are both natural to us, but diversely temporalized. Was the attraction for a word that saves anonymous because it was not satisfied by an effective hearing, and was it of a different nature than the vitiating withdrawal of consciousness—radical evil?

To speak of the "nature" of consciousness first of all means to speak of the *I*. For Luther, the pure expectation of the word harbors a natural awareness of God. His argument for flushing this out is buttressed by the necessary and universal submission of consciousness to the *auditum*.[61] "Nature," in this sense, designates the very opening that makes apperception heteronomous. Submission to a transforming word defines consciousness; now, the words to which we submit ourselves can only be partially efficient (*sch*. 9,28). Therefore, it is in the nature of consciousness to wait for an entirely efficient word, transforming with no remainder. The argument for this natural expectation of God does not rest on any generalizable experience, be it of the good or of the true. It is not of a moral but a transcendental order. The opening for the obedience to the word that causes rebirth and the reception of the theonomous self—this opening is natural to us in the sense of an *a priori* receptivity. A similar receptivity, as we saw, defines consciousness as spirit. The natural attraction for the fulfilled "I obey"—for the self—thus no more depends on the fulfilling speech actually occurring than does the opening, which is hearing. Being able to listen, and to be carried beforehand toward a word that can eventually seize us completely, is all one and it is a condition preceding all experience. Lacking such an anticipated seizure, consciousness will not even allow itself to be wrenched free from its freedom of indifference prior to the law. In its posture in the face of the law, it knows naturally that a liberating word can come to require it and to annul shortcomings. The nature of the *I* has nothing of the temporal about it. It commits us to two imputable destinies, to two disparate times.

On the one hand, it commits us to the time imputable to the *ego*. Radical evil that can be ascribed to us is "natural" in the sense of the lineage from which we come. In the genetic terms inspired by Augustine, the ego is natural to us due to our phylogenesis. In biblical terms that are more remarkable here: "Original sin is confused with the actual sin committed by Adam. . . . To all, Adam transmits his nature, and with it, his sin" (*gl.* 5,15). *His* nature, *his* sin. For Luther it is a matter of setting aside the specter of a common, irreparably ruined nature. Original sin remains properly one's own, as does the act that it corrupts and as does the name of the one who perpetrated it, Adam. Accordingly, as is "his" sin, so is "his" nature: his own. The first man transmitted to us his lack of individual submission and with it his equally individual nature. This is the nature that radical evil vitiates, not human nature as essence. "The curvature is *now* something belonging to our nature" (*sch.* 8,3, cor.). "Nature" here is neither postulated as a quiddity, nor construed as a unity of entitative characters, but is incurred. It can only be related, be narrated, the day after the transgression of someone in particular, seduced by some other particular, beneath a particular tree. . . . Man enters in this story of evil, not as a particular allowing himself to be subsumed under a species, but as an individual instance of condemnation and death, and that can be grasped by the word. He enters into a concatenation of individuals that has lasted since the fall. The period of the ego is this stippled time.

On the other hand, the "I obey" commits us to the time imputable to the *self.* This is born from the election. Its nature results from an ontogenesis. The destiny of the spirit is to find itself invested with the promise that fulfill the *a priori* expectation (at least, if that is what predestination reserves for me). The self that is ascribed to us depends on an event; namely, the statement in fact heard that effects justification. By nature it is no less temporal than is the ego. But its time is not at all linear. It is an intermittent immanence. It turns the now toward what is promised to come.

The necessity imputed to the ego is unconditionally general (non-universal). The ego is in fact natural to all the subjects corrupted since Adam. We are born *with* him—as in the twenty-first century our children will be born with an atmosphere rendered unbreathable by us. This is a completely different conception of radical evil, either from the one that would bring in its train the old logic of things, or the one that would corrupt the universal formalism—necessary by right—characterizing the "I obey." The necessity imputable to the self, for its part, is conditionally general (no longer universal); the self in fact is natural to all subjects on the condition that justification seizes them. We are born *for* it as for a promise. In both cases, facticity is on an anthropological order and must not be confused with the spiritual facticity according to which, independent of imputation, the self and the ego are "facts that we do not see."

Thus the time of the ego and the time of the self are out of sync. This is because, according to the synchronic order of conditions, the ego has no life of its own. In Luther, time, the only time, is that of the instantaneous efficiency of the word promising life. The time in which we fashion our profile by training our 'havingnesses' {*ayances*} (*habitus*), thus the moral time, follows from the same transcendental fiction of the ego. The story of Adam, prolonging itself in us as a stretch of time, lives on the promise that causes an eruption, that suddenly occurs in us as an event. Their *simul* places them nowhere in parallel, or in polar coordinates. It signifies, not symbiosis, but parasiticism. Is it to such a temporality in dissension with itself that the divided man *par excellence* at the beginning of modern times—Hamlet—alludes when he observed, "*The time is out of joint . . .*"?[62]

The ego is a fact of consciousness because it is fabricated (*factum*); the self because it is effected (*effectum*). In the same manner, moral justice mimics justification. The time that lasts mimics eventful time. Thus, once again the time that lasts mimics the event to come.

These disparate times constitute the basis of our being. One must not take 'being' (*Wesen*) to mean substance, for then the curvature would make salvation impossible (it would literally make us something else), or pointless (it would taint us accidentally). The *incurvitas* affects the being of consciousness. But with which pathology? How will evil radically pervert consciousness without also compromising apperceptive neutrality? Given the heteronomy of the I, it is out of the question that this pathology could amount to a conflict between subjective powers: "*Nothing is in our power.*" (SA 691). How then can the proper that defines the ego affect, and durably, self-consciousness? The word "proper" give us an indication: as a desire for self-possession. We *understand* the particular bearer of the common noun, but we *desire* a particular bearer of the proper noun—and first of all, myself. A desire, even setting itself up to serve the good in consciousness, does not for all that reify it (as is done by all the psychologies of "powers"), nor does it muddle its pure transcendental concomitance (the consciousness "accompanying" the desires). Such a living desire is called a tendency. To say that Martin Luther had the tendency to crush friends and enemies is to describe precisely such a particular individual affected in his self-consciousness by a penchant precisely for some specific behavior. Luther understands the being of consciousness as a battle of affects. The *simul* signifies that the I is both self-affective and lets itself be affected.

Pathogenesis consists in our counting on the continuation of time and in our imputing it to ourselves as an asset. The object of desire that consciousness wants in its own affect is the ego that lasts. Radical evil makes me give a high estimation to the permanence of the ego—the constant presence of this singular for which, since Adam, the singular individual has a singular penchant.

From where comes its strength? From the law, once again. The penchant for positing oneself, affirming oneself, possessing oneself as autonomous and durable is not one penchant among others. Nobody, nowhere and at any time has ever circumvented this incline nor failed to get their footing on it. This impossibility stems from the very itinerary of the ego in relation to the law. In contrast to a conception that would see in the prohibition an obstacle in the face of that which the "me" is born into, breaks the motivating happiness, and adapts the living being to reality, the stage prior to the law is not characterized here by the anonymity of a "that" still deprived of identity or of "heart." "In our heart, we remain always inclined to evil, and because of this, rebels against the law" (*sch.* 3,9). The ego is a rebel against the fulfilling-fulfilled occurring through primary processes. In discovering the law, it discovers death, and primary automatism veers toward willed autonomy. The ego posits itself from then on as immortal. Prior to the law, time does not exist. There is, then, neither autonomy nor heteronomy; nor polymorphous perversions either, but monomania, a closed, exclusive, mechanical structure of the ego. The No breaks the happy orbit of consciousness. It drives it to consolidating itself against exorbitant intrusions. As a tendency, evil is thus quite the opposite of a type of regression. The project of stable autonomy comes to the surface with the first heteronomy, that of the law. In the face of the exorbitant posited (*gesetzt,* hence, *das Gesetz,* the law) in front of it, imposed upon it, the ego has no choice. It can only seek to posit itself in turn, and forever. Prior to the word that says No, it is and takes pleasure in being; in the face of the word, it posits itself, unhappy until death and desiring itself as permanent beyond death. In the promise that says Yes, finally, the ego enjoys a strange satisfaction, but without the law, for all that, disappearing, for the ego does not, once again, have a choice. It was and would be better off without this law as well as without this promise. Because the law remains, the self intermittently bestowed is the intruder that needs to be expelled. Whence a storm of hostile affects. Whence again the event *changed* into a duration. Whence above all the temporality that turns the incongruous promise against duration. At the beginning of the philosophy of consciousness, the time that lasts was a transcendental illusion, non-congruent with the time of historical facts. The alterity signifies here, not the determinate negation of the same by its other, but an alteration.

Concretely, in this pathetic *Wesen,* the other of the ego is not absolutely the driving apparatus, the source of unforeseeable and troubling irruptions in the stable succession of daily life. The other of the ego is the self. The intruder is this new man, born elsewhere. A friend to the event, he pulverizes the transcendental illusion of linear time. This foreigner must be loved or destroyed—he cannot be tolerated or else the force of the "either-or" will be blunted. To love requires a saintly will that annuls the law in fulfilling it. With the law remaining, there is nothing left to do but destroy this other.

As was known by the second author of the *Odyssey,* and as rediscovered by the age of *Hamlet, Macbeth, Lear,* and *Richard III*—the age of Luther—when we are our own worst enemy, self-consciousness becomes cunning. In Luther, the ruse of the pathetic consciousness perverts the reception of the self. Of the two protagonists in the fight to the death, the ego is much more familiar than the self. The latter, arising from the outside, also makes itself known only from the outside. As with all events, it remains ineffable. The ego itself is effable as are all things that last; it suffices to have lived in order to have encountered it. The law subsumes me through an *ever-present particularization.* It applies itself to the ego as to a case. But it is necessary to have heard in order to anticipate the self. The promise elects me through an *ever-immanent singularization.* It is addressed to the self as to an addressee. Even better, it addresses my self to me, to me the addressee.

The differend in consciousness that makes it simultaneously sinful and justified thus arises only from the previously stated justification. Without it, there is no self, and without the self, no incongruous time. Accordingly, radical evil manifests itself from the point that the ego is driven to desire itself as lasting in the face of the word that binds, namely, in the face of the law; but it manifests itself as perverse only when the ego is driven into a corner a second time, by the word that unbinds. It enlists this in its own cultivation. It enlists the *kairos* to function as a point on the line of the *chronos*. It spreads itself out. . . . Not happy to fashion itself as it prefers to see itself, the ego fashions a God that sees me as I prefer to be seen. I affirm myself as just by tracing the offered heteronomous justification back to my autonomous ends. Luther describes this corruption for each of the constitutive acts of the subject. "Malice is the perverse motivation of the *spirit* by which man inclines to doing evil" (*sch.* 1,29); it consists in "the perversity of the *heart*" (ibid.), "the perversity of our *will*" (*sch.* 3,21). It reorients their interaction, the *Gesinnung;* it is the "perversity of the *interior disposition*" (*sch.* 1,29). Thus reoriented, "*nature* inclines to evil" (*sch.* 2,22), that is, our inherited nature, not the one on the basis of which we can speculate in placing man halfway between extreme degrees of being. Placed under the sign of the *simul,* it is seated in the middle of nothing at all. The scene of a desire pointed toward death, directed against the life bestowed, is what corruption is. The scene of the desire for a cunning death, since it recuperates life to its proper ends, is what self-consciousness is; it is itself its own mortal enemy.

We will have understood the Lutheran pathos when we understand that permanence equals death; but that, equally fictive though it be, the posited duration nevertheless has more force than received life. Its force makes us the agent that posits it—the ego—forever better-known than the self.

It even seems more real than the self: "Sinners in reality are just by the divine reputation that give them grace" (*sch.* 4,7). We might call this a slip on Luther's part. Does Luther ever stop repeating that only the granting of life is real, the event? It is not a slip but a transcendentalization of reality. The real is reputation. We should thus understand (just as elsewhere): Sinners, esteeming themselves as stable in the face of the law, are in reality still just because they esteem themselves as destabilized by faith. It remains that the abridged formula—"sinners in reality"—suggests by implication the time of the self, its essential fragility. The being of the self depends on the possible hearing (no necessity forces the word toward us) of a possibility (no necessity forces the imputation). Thus there is nothing more precarious than the self.[63] However, it possesses a power *sui generis*. It reveals the ego. Its power is critical. It aims not to destroy, but to make one see. No more so than, in Kant, the critique of the thinking thing dissipates the idea of a substantial I, the critique of permanence in Luther does not make the ego disappear. It only unmasks the fictive character of autonomy. The word-promise is this critical light by which the same, in referential consciousness, is opposed to an incongruous other.

We can easily see why there can be no resolution in this pathetic differend between the ego and the self. Their *general* natures remain different. However, it is important to see better how they are linked to the *universal* originary condition, the act "I obey." A similar linking of givens to the first subjective function is the very mainspring on which the Copernican turn functions. In order to point out that which in fact is given to me, apperception must be diversified into acts of consciousness making these givens mine. In Luther, what are these acts? What are the *(proto)-categories* that maintain the differend dividing the hegemonic modern fantasm at its root?

Positing and letting-be

The formal I concretizes itself in two disparate facts of consciousness. As the ego it feigns to be educated; and it is effected as a self, educated by the word "that all teach" (*sch.* 1,1 cor.), which is to say, that those whose word is right teach. Luther considers the subject exclusively at the end of this double genesis where the autonomous fiction and the heteronomous effect become imputable. Sinners and the justified "simultaneously"; the word sufficiently states the synchronic usage that Luther makes of an originally genetic model (infantilism prior to the word—adolescence in the face of the word as law—maturity in the word as promise). To the extent that they are imputable, the ego and the self are givens that are *invariable because they are general.* In contradistinction to the application to the sensible given by which Kant will seek to verify how the I is found immersed in the world, for Luther the concrete is not the empirical. The concrete is the two modes of self-understanding in the face of the word and in the word. But for their simultaneous givenness to be possible, does it not require acts in the subject that are *invariable because they are universal,* acts which emphasize these facts of consciousness?

In accordance with the very anti-reist demarcation of Luther, there cannot be other assorted universals than the categorial. The facts of consciousness will be givens, constituted only by those processes where there is still some spontaneity. In the subject, acts are distinguished from facts just as the universal is distinguished from the general and as the *determinans* is from the *determinatum.* Luther will have taken the critical turn if the originary act "I obey" is diversified *a priori* into acts of which one determines the ego and the other determines the self. Any application to the sensible remains outside this perspective by reason of the heteronomy in apperception. We saw the decontextualization that results from this absence of any extra-subjective application. Accordingly, when it comes to the manner of thinking from which modern hegemony is born, its type of reversal will be played out elsewhere than in an application. This reversal will either substitute a logic of *a priori* acts for the logic of things or it will be null and void. If nature proper is generally corrupted, what universal act in consciousness will emphasize the ego? Similarly, once the promise of a heterogeneous justification has been heard, by what act will consciousness receive it? These transcendental questions concern the universal and necessary processes that compose the *Wesen* (in the verbal sense) of consciousness.

It goes without saying that in speaking here of categories, we do not re-enthrone the metaphysical ego that seeks to submit the visible and the invisible to the "wisdom of the flesh."[64] The ancient categorial discourse, starting from substances, was nothing but hubris in the eyes of Luther since ousiology consolidates in its present state the creation that "groans" nevertheless toward another state (*sch.* 8,19). On the other hand, a categorial discourse starting from the "I obey" neither substantializes nor consolidates anything. The prestige of presence is broken here by the event of a word that must be obeyed, a word that is always at the moment of arrival.

Now, Luther not only establishes the aprioric functions to single out (*kategorein*) the ego and the self, but he also provides the schemas for deducing these functions, beginning with the neutral act that is heteronomous apperception. Without at least the rough outline of such a transcendental deduction, self-consciousness would serve perhaps as the *scene* for the representation in which the differend between the ego and the self plays itself out; it would have a hard time effecting a *regimen*. The Copernican revolution is won or lost in the deduction of pure subjective acts beginning with the originarily synthetic "I obey." So that consciousness can be modified by the No of the law and the Yes of faith, it must determine beforehand and through quasi-spontaneous acts these facts that are not seen. We will examine here the acts themselves through which we determine *a priori* the two facts of heterogeneous consciousness. Which are these *a priori* acts? How are they deduced from the originarily synthetic "I obey"?

What one must bear in mind is that it is one thing to reduce the acts determining the ego and self to their common source—or, what comes to the same thing, to deduce them beginning with this source—and it is another, impossible thing to sort out the conflict between these subjective facts. The conflict would disappear only if consciousness produced the law and the promise instead of meeting up with them. If that were the case, we would be in full-blown idealism, in which everything would be reconciled. The differend would be transformed into the dialectic. The tragic would be found serenely trapped in one of the "moments" of the absolute coming to itself—for a critical mind, this is more a miraculous solution than a marvelous one. In any case, no mediation reconciles the terms of the pathetic differend in Luther. In light of the incongruity of the facts of consciousness, the ego resists being subsumed under the absolute by some mediating agent. A heteronomous word, whether it condemns or saves, always speaks to us immediately. It strikes without warning. Prior to the law, nothing heralds this. When it is there, all one can do is stand fast in the face of it. The same goes for the liberating word; no subsumption implants us in the fulfilled law. What is specific to the imperative word is that it does not wait to be made true, neither by psychic antinomy nor by some empirical verification, nor by a speculative overelevation. A simple capacity to listen makes its arrival possible, but the capacity to listen amounts to a formal anticipation—it is neither a power of the soul, nor the faculty of spatio-temporal intuitions, nor mediation. The living word carries in itself the criterion for its truth.[65]

The "one-plus-one equals one"—the *simul*—suits tragic intuition. One plus one is a double holism; the tendency to affirm oneself in the face of the law until death has hold of the whole man, as does the liberating promise (if he accepts himself as justified). It is literally a "paradoxical" double hold since the entire man of promise is "contrary to the opinion" of the man of the law, and the man of the law is contrary to the man of promise. No more so than in Parmenides, under the new fantasm the conflictual hold is not resolved. However, in contradistinction to Parmenides, it does not oppose contrary beings, but discordant subjective acts. Only on condition of such a transcendental discord will self-consciousness be able to modify itself entirely in accordance with one *and* the other word.

"Without my preparing or contributing to it, the word of God comes to me."[66] There would be preparation if, as taught by the tradition before Luther, some preamble were required in order for faith to take root, and there would be a contribution if it fortified itself, as also is demanded by the tradition, by means of some meritorious conduct. A formal condition like the "I obey" remains evidently irreducible to such antecedents and consequences. It is also evident that the apperceptive condition does not cease to be formal if it is diversified in accordance with the different words that must be obeyed. What act is necessary for consciousness to be able to hear the law that binds? And what other act is necessary for it to receive the promise that unbinds it?

The *a priori* act by which consciousness anticipates the moral imperative results from the quasi-spontaneity in apperception. It is the "quasi" inflated to exclusivity. The I, as we saw, would neither grasp nor present anything unless it *re*grasps and *re*presents. The "quasi" is legitimized by the reduplicating activity of the I that defines reflection, an activity in which the I makes the contents of consciousness its own. Reflecting, it originally finds in itself the means to posit itself.

We have also seen that in the face of the law the I must affirm itself. The moral consciousness has only the appropriative *re* to constitute itself and consolidate itself. The law requires nothing more from me but that I posit myself. The law asks, "What type of subject do you want to make of yourself?" And it asks this while commanding, "You will do it! You will not do it!" In this sense, the imperative answers to the ego that asks, "How do I posit myself?" "You will posit yourself in such a way so as not to commit evil and to do good. You will, simply, posit yourself." Lacking self-positing, how is one to call an act, or the one committing it, moral or immoral? Moral judgment is always brought to bear on what is posited, what is assessed in terms of a position that one takes and occupies. In order for it to be able to judge good and evil, the subject in the face of the law must originarily be such that it could posit itself, that the *tithemi* belong to it as a function—at least this goes for beings constituted by our phylogenesis and our factual ontogenesis—as a transcendental function. The I of the hyperbolic position, affirming itself in "hurling itself beyond" apperceptive quasi-spontaneity, is essentially thetic.

The ego posits itself on par with the law, and it posits acts by which to measure itself against the law. Accordingly, always and at each stage it is only a pure *thesis;* prior to the law, it is neither autonomous nor heteronomous, but latent due to the pleasure that it finds in itself; in the face of the law, it is autonomous due to its desire for life; and in the law, it negates the heteronomous self through a desire for death. The quasi-spontaneity in the I swells up into a thetic tendency, a murderer of the self, only in a consciousness already reoriented by extrinsic efficiency. It is indeed necessary to note that this tendency—radical evil—does not leave the ego in any of these situations. "You are entirely curved back on yourself. . . . This perverse essence is seen in that what we seek in all things is what is our own" (*sch.* 15,2). Redemption does not mean peace. Heteronomy displaces violence, it does not temper it with anything.

In what way is this thesis—the positing that is curved back upon itself—to be understood as an anticipatory act *a priori*? Luther translates the phylogenesis since Adam in a strictly parallel religious typology. Religion prior to the law would be pagan; that in the face of the law would be Judaism. Only Christianity, because it teaches the substitutive fulfillment of the law, would situate man in this law. The self-positing, henceforth, is the act by which I set myself up as the symmetrical *de-*

termined other of God. But as Kant will observe, in the alterity between the same and *its* other, the conditions that make experience possible will also be the conditions making the object of experience possible. The ego has "its" God. Whether religious consciousness seeks to exalt itself, to humiliate itself, or even to annihilate itself before God, it always posits itself facing him. It pretends to fashion for itself a relationship, even there where it posits itself as a pebble crushed on the path. It never escapes from the tendency to endow this other with attributes or to strip them away, to treat it as dissimilar, similar, or even identical to itself, to place it among the beings outside them. . . . It never ceases positing itself as autonomous even there where it lays claim to an immaculate heteronomy. "Nature posits before itself no object other than itself" (*sch.* 8,3 cor.). The thetic act is the inextricable tendency that the ego has to constitute itself, beneath the aegis of the exterior that is as subtle or not as we desire, as an active moment in the fight between life and death. If, through all the topographical sites, the subject was not so ready for the thesis, if he did not naturally anticipate positing himself, radical evil would remain incomprehensible. Then to where does the undertow of death pull, flowing as if it were life? Regarding Kant's emancipatory transcendentalism, it will be important to remember that radical evil draws self-consciousness to posit itself as autonomous.

What now is the transcendental act by which consciousness anticipates and determines the self? To get a good look at it we ask, inversely, "What human subject would be deprived of the imputable self?" We saw what a subject deprived of the imputable ego would be: any subject before the sin committed by Adam. Are there subjects deprived of an imputable self? It is enough to recall the genesis, not of the collective nature inclined toward evil, but of the individual sites "prior to–in the face of–in the word" to remember that the self is bestowed at a precise point of the progression. It is born allogenously when the promise of justification appears. By what act does consciousness determine the self?

Luther responds, but not without having previously reorganized the series of stages—the "prior to–in the face of–in the word"—into so many simultaneous instances. This discrete correction aims at Augustine, the only one among the doctors to benefit from his respect and, therefore, his consideration. The story of the relations to the word (infancy-adolescence-maturity) comes from Augustine. Luther corrects its diachronic cadence: "We can understand this in even a deeper sense." The deeper sense is the synchronic sense, as shown by the list of recalcitrants that follows, all exposed to the word but obstinate toward it: "Jews, heretics, sectarians and bizarre monomaniacs that have no sin." Denying that they are lost—which, however, is what the word reveals to those who want to hear, at the same time that it offers them justification—they pretend themselves to be without sin. On the other hand, "A heart which is not propped up by its own meaning . . . lets itself be led" (*sch.* 7,8). Luther turns away from all genetic explications in naming the two *a priori* traits diversifying the I: the proper meaning that *posits* itself as an ego, and that brings about the positing in innocence, militates against the self that agrees to receive its direction and that *"lets"* (*sinere,* sch. 3,7 cor.; *cedere,* sch. 10,10; *locum dare,* sch. 3,4) the direction be given.

No concept heralds the transcendental design more clearly than the verb "to let-be," with all its connotations. It belongs to the mystical Rhenish vocabulary, whose teaching amounts, we can say, to calling for *Gelassenheit,* for "letting-be." Luther again takes up this call at the decisive threshold of his procedure, where he must describe how extrinsic intervention liberates consciousness from the condemnatory influence that the law exercises over it. The promise frees the subject that lets it take effect. "To let" thus designates, first of all, the practical subjective condition for there to be passive justification. Also, this verb literally gives the measure of any such liberation. "Deprived of all knowledge, of all sentiment and all understanding, we should let ourselves be given over to what is required of us" (*sch.* 10,2). The measure is not to be found in some force imposing itself in the world. Luther appropriates here, for transcendental ends, the *contemptus mundi.* Knowledge, sentiment, and understanding orient us toward the world; the "letting" neutralizes these extraverted functions and orients us toward the only measure, that of consciousness. What is it a matter of "letting-be"? Certainly not the contents that these functions grasp. To empty knowledge, sentiment, and understanding of their objects would only amount to stupefying them. Just as Meister Eckhart repeated throughout his sermons, it is a matter of letting the attachment to these contents sink away. Letting go as detachment signifies that nothing in the world can serve as a landmark for the spirit. Where Eckhart had spoken of property, *Eigenschaft,* Luther says *sensus proprius.* The call to let everything go points exclusively in the direction of the new standard of measurement, namely, self-consciousness, rather than toward such and such a "thing" that it would be a matter of giving up. Here there is a new connotation. The imperative of the *lassen* is addressed to the ego. By definition the ego is attached. To what? To itself. Its thetic essence huddles up. If it is true that the offered heteronomy lays a claim not to some part or superior power in us, but to the entire consciousness, then the imperative to let everything go amounts to the imperative to let go of *oneself.* Now, consciousness, as affirming itself, totally and in everything, is the ego. But on the other hand, a consciousness that let itself be given a self would thereby disarm the ego. "Letting be given" is a possible strategy in consciousness, whose "positing" can only end in failure. The strategy of *letting* arises from the word, whereas the counter-strategy of *positing* arises from us. Accordingly (the last connotation in the phenomenal order, but the first in the order of the unique theonomous efficiency), this letting is embodied in the attitude that "opens space" to the word.[67]

Attitude? An attitude is something we adopt at certain times, or that certain people adopt, or that we do not adopt. It is a type of behavior. Accordingly, letting-be certainly also counts as a possible behavior. It is the contingent condition that enables the word to be obeyed. We can, or cannot, open a space for it. If it were otherwise, there would be no need for exhortation. As an attitude, letting-be is an *empirical* condition for understanding the word and obeying it.

But as sinners and as justified "simultaneously" we have always already understood this in accord with the synchronic relations to the word. As we saw, even infantile games without good or evil are already pursued in the light of the word that saves. For subjects with our phylogenesis and our factual ontogenesis, the justifying word is a constitutive factor of consciousness. It holds us wherever our contingent pursuits lead us. Only on this condition can Luther see all mankind straddled either by God or by the devil. This is why there also has to be in consciousness an act *a priori* that singles out the word even before divine efficiency makes us accept it or diabolic efficiency makes us reject it. Divine efficiency is the concern *of* the self; diabolical efficiency is the concern *for* self. It this sense, letting-be is the *a priori* condition for understanding the word and conforming to it—the transcendental condition of the self. We single out every word, both in positing (us/it) and in letting (us/it) be.

In order to account for the word and its diverse efficiency, Luther can no longer have recourse to the naturalist schema of a Logos subsisting nearby God, then being manifested in the world, history, and reason, and finally conducting all things back to that point where it has subsisted eternally. Such pantocratic constructions have lost their hegemony. The fantasm of a supreme Plan, annexing every possible experience under the sway of an order that supposedly Nature or Logos is to have imposed, also collapses along with the logic of things. How, as a result, is one to render intelligible experiences such as condemnation by law and liberation by the promise? This is a question of categories and their provenance. After having overwhelmed the metaphysics of substance with injuries, to what categories should we turn? The Gothic fresco of *gubernatio mundi* held, by the grid of categories, to ousiological provenance. Now, the turn toward self-consciousness can no more do without categories than it can renounce hegemony. In Luther, no phenomenon can escape the struggle between positing and letting-be, which means that the pathetic consciousness finds itself elevated to be the law of laws, the fantasmic law for every imperative word, whether it says "you must"—namely, dying—as is stated by the moral commandment, or "you can"—namely, living—as is stated by the justifying promise. The turn signifies that henceforth everything knowable will be determined on the basis of forms issuing from the I. Everything knowable—thus, there will be a new hegemony of determinative forms, and they will come from new categories as well.

Descartes will resign in the face of the problem of categories so posited.[68] The pure act of the *cogito* would be originary only if it analytically contained pure secondary acts. In the place of developing its concepts, Descartes will seek help close to the authority from which he has already drawn the *cogito*—that of Augustine—and will fall back upon *innate contents*. Ideas are "objective realities," "things."[69] Here we have the originally modern way of drawing a veil over critical reason. The decisive problem of the constitution of the object consists in turning from a transcendental logic back to a logic of things. The sleight of hand is hardly trifling, since reason emerges from it as master of a world, prescribing to extended things not only their rules, but their contents. It is not hard to see what sort of power it abrogates to itself by this trick. Behind the curtain it transforms itself from the regulator of all knowledge—making things conform to the act "I think"—into the master of nature, making it conform to clearly and distinctly perceived contents. Certainly this constitutes a step made toward subjective emancipation. But reason prescribing objective realities to the world knows what is essential even before experience. Here lies its violence. Such contents possessed in advance have been made into the weapons of every dogmatism. The Cartesian version of material autonomy leads directly to projects like Condorcet's "mathematizable society." One should compare this with the project of emancipation through the more modestly regulative exercise of reason: "The maxim of always thinking by oneself is the project of the *Aufklarung*. . . . It is easy to emancipate individual subjects through education; for that it is enough to begin early by getting young minds used to this reflection. But emancipating a whole age is long and arduous."[70] Long and arduous: Regulating reason does not know in advance the content to prescribe to its world of experience. In this regard formal autonomy tempers the violence both of formal heteronomy (Luther) and material autonomy (Descartes).

Transcendental formalism actually is, if not established, at least sketched out in Luther. As the critical turn requires, positing and letting-be are functions only *anticipating* possible, imputable contents. Due to the manner in which the ego and the self are given, formalism remains pre-emancipatory. These facts belong to us neither *a priori* in the sense of defining consciousness through a universal endowment (as the categories defined it), nor *a posteriori* in the sense of coming to us by a contingent givenness (as their imputation comes to us). They are given, one to our historical nature by the law that binds, the other to singular individuals by the promise that unbinds. Luther is already in league with Kant against Descartes, in that heteronomous apperception tolerates no transcendentally pre-existent contents in consciousness. The act "I obey" formally anticipates the event of a doubly contingent givenness: phyletic and ontic. It is true that Luther always addresses himself to subjects who are already exposed to revelation and plunged in the torments of the *simul*. Through this factuality of the ego and the self, he establishes himself elsewhere than does Descartes or even Kant. The *facts* of consciousness remain unassimilable either to innate elements or to the pure regulation of reason. Because of their double bond to the contingent, they can serve neither the mastery of nature nor emancipative progress. Mastery and progress are ruses of the ego. The *traits* of consciousness—positing and letting-be—will nevertheless comply with transcendental exigencies. They diversify the originary act of the "I obey" into derivative acts. Here there is no longer any ambiguity that muddles categorial formalism.

To see this, all one need do is ask how, from the *locus noster* that is consciousness, Luther comes to positing and letting-be; one sees how, in a systematic reconstruction, these secondary acts can be deduced. "Our place" is where we say "I obey." This primary act synthesizes apperception and heteronomy. The deduction then consists in examining to where both of these traits lead. We have seen the essence of apperception in (quasi-) spontaneity; taken to its extreme, it leads to the ego. We have also seen the essence of heteronomy in passivity; taken to its extreme, it leads to the self. The deduction develops the logic of apperceptive spontaneity to the point of pure positing and that of heteronomous passivity to the point of pure letting-be. The *a priori* acts are deduced by analyzing what is contained in the originary synthesis of the "I obey."

Thus, to open a space for the word means to formally constitute phenomena, to anticipate them as the subject anticipates the *transcendental object*. Capable of suffering the other that I do not produce, I open the space where something can show itself, which is a critical definition of the transcendental object that, here, obviously is of the linguistic order.

The discomfort of the modern *locus* is concerned with its synthetic nature. In Luther, the originary synthesis is hybrid. It excludes every simple givenness as beyond compare. If the ego and the self were presented to us in the manner of the sensible manifold, their givenness would be one, and consciousness would be whole. There would be no breakdown affecting the subject in its dealing with its object. Givenness would remain formally one. Being would be given to experience and would be singled out as such by a corresponding *a priori* act. Now, the ego and the self determine the whole of each consciousness, so their status remains irreducible to that of empirical givens. This follows from the originarily hybrid synthesis. It follows that givenness is not one, that the real is not to be sought on the side of the perceived manifold, that the categorial acts aggravate the breakdown of the formal I, and that the pathetic differend cleaves the modern foundation, namely, normative consciousness. Being as a whole is singled out, both by positing it and by letting it be; accordingly, being is in itself disparate as are these incongruous traits.

Perverse teleology

What follows as a result are torments the likes of which had never been known before modernity. What is "nature," presently? The facts of consciousness are born in two irreducible histories. The genealogy of the self does not proceed in parallel with that of the ego; their genesis does not fall in the same genus. The self and the ego therefore differ, not as the same differs from *its* other, but as disparate facts differ. This is precisely the torment ("that which compels the departure from peace," *ex-fridare*).

And so after Luther there is an influx of palliatives. Nature must be healed, returned to peace. There was never a shortage of such therapeutic verve in the philosophies of the twentieth century. In the face of torments, one has sought comfort in "classical philosophy" (Leo Strauss). This epithet then covers, more or less explicitly, all thought from the Milesians to the Eliatics up to the High Scholastics. The comfort that is found here takes shape quite explicitly. It concerned the systematic prestige of teleology. This prestige arose from the certitude that ends—that for which all things are good—are given, not posited. The "rediscovery of teleological thought"[71] then consists in a rehabilitation of necessary ends, physical ends given in the causal structure of natural processes and ethical ends given in the structure of human faculties. It was a matter of grave interest—that of the pacifying, functionary philosopher-king. The credit accorded to ends consoles and consolidates. Little matter that a credit must always be an advance on which we borrow—that the champions of natural ends postulate first of all the telic order that they then feign to discover.[72] The "rediscovery" points elsewhere; it is addressed to the moderns who receive the torments that they merit. No matter the ease with which the "classical" epithet causes one to overlook the rupture between the Greek and Latin linguistic eras as well as the change in attitude or hegemonic horizon that results from it; whatever may be, again, the unexamined clichés concerning the status of the given and the posited from Parmenides to Occam; and whatever may be, finally, the nostalgia that recovers these versions of the quarrel of the ancients and the moderns,[73] a quarrel that happened to be dogged by the very reason of its simplicity, the fact is that teleology lost its obviousness beginning with the sixteenth century when one began to think in one's mother tongue and philosophy changed its attitude. The darling of the "classicals," teleology, is also a problem child. Until Nietzsche, no one had stated it more clearly than Luther: natural teleology is "perverse."[74]

Perverse, literally and doubly so. On the one hand, it turns heteronomy back into a system in the service of the ego. In this manner it better shows how radical evil vitiates the ego. The curving back of the faculties comes from the fact that they can seek only that which is their own, the ends given with the ego—thus, posited ends. Teleology as natural offers only a pseudo-heteronomy.

On the other hand, it infects moral consciousness with a ruse. This consciousness, nevertheless thetic through and through, labors under the illusion of freely choosing between good and evil. By vocation, the ego (speaking to Luther through the voice of Erasmus) acts as if positing signified choosing. But all it ever posits is itself. Heteronomy is distorted a second time when we imagine the free will in the face of its ends, free to realize its nature or to violate it. The comfort fabricated by consciousness coiled up on itself pertains to the ruse of the free choice. Perversion here does not mean the corruption of a noble, spiritual faculty put in the service of base instincts. The perverse is not what goes against nature. Quite to the contrary. It is perverse to call spontaneous and free those energies that *naturally* conform to a system of telic necessities. If by free choice we understand a capacity to direct oneself, be it toward good or toward evil, then we have succeeded in the loveliest camouflage operation. How do the ends to which the agent cannot not aspire become subject to choice? They are assuredly natural, but *natural to whom*? Luther answers: Those ends of which the tradition speaks unanimously were never natural except to the ego. In them it found its pleasure. It rolls itself up around them and finds relief in relation to them. It is the same as saying that they subject themselves without possible evasion. Free choice is a serf's choice, duped by his captivity due to the pleasure he derives from it (a pleasure that is perpetually frustrated, but that is another problem[75]).

But didn't Luther write a famous treatise on the freedom of the Christian man? It being a matter of promise, must there not be a free choice that chooses to believe? Where can it be housed? There is nothing more plausible than going to find it on the side where Luther claims to have found liberty pure and simple: in the "good" heteronomy of the self. The ends of the self would be natural to it in the sense of nature prior to the Fall or after the great promised restoration; the mind (speaking in Augustine's voice) would desire them naturally, and wisdom would consist in contenting itself with the "eternal law." But heteronomy is only good without conditions or concessions. The self is a fact of received consciousness, not posited or willed. The agent works on it from the outside, not from within. If there is any sort of power to choose, it can only belong to this extrinsic agent that saves us by freeing us from the law, or that condemns us by chaining us to it. In no case can liberty signify a power in us. Accordingly, Luther's conclusion is abrupt: "The force of the free choice is nil, . . . it is wholly a divine name and can belong to no other person" (*SA* 636).

The self can thus no more choose its ends than the ego can. The will remains servile, both in its folding back on itself and in the alien intervention that causes its unfolding. Hence the term (which lends itself to misunderstanding, but once again that is another problem[76]) that it straddles like a beast of burden. The *object* of a teleology originating elsewhere and plunging into the ego, the will governed by the passive regimen, will never be the *subject* of a process coming from itself, where it would fix itself upon some end, would pursue it, then grasp it. Certainly it is itself a *telos,* but only by divine efficiency.

In the two modifications of consciousness, the will remains obsessed, literally; it always follows the force that "prevails" over it. On its own, it goes nowhere. There is no intrinsic verve directing it. If it leaned toward a certain good, it would be *noluntas,* non-willed, rather than *voluntas* (*SA* 635). We will have come upon the nerve of Lutheran anti-teleology when we have understood that the will cannot be said to be either powerless because constrained by ends (that which would negate it), or powerful because it selects them (which would absolutize it), nor neutral because powerful/powerless with regard to them (which would deprive it of sense, as in the syncretism of Erasmus), but that it nevertheless acts by necessity (*SA* 714). The will is servile because it is necessarily obsessed—*either* by the ego, *or* by the self. In consciousness exposed to the word, it is in fact obsessed *both* by the ego *and* by the self. Ethical theories of free choice never describe anything but the will obsessed by the ego. They erect, as a natural orientation, a drive coming from the ego that presides as master.

The uses that have been made of the Augustinian "free choice" demonstrate it perfectly. On the eighth of April, 1341, Petrarch, whom we call the first humanist, had his day of glory. Adorned for the occasion in a royal mantle, he was crowned Poet Laureate of the Senate and the Roman people—the first title signed "SPQR" for more than a millennium. Furthermore, the king of Naples later named him *magnum poetum et historicum* with the right of crowning other poet laureates, consecrated him as Master, accredited him as honorary professor, conferred on him Roman citizenship and formally approved all his writings, past, present, and future! After such honors, hardly had Petrarch returned to his retreat at the foot of Mount Ventoux than he sank into a profound melancholy. He recalled Augustine's *Confessions* and, as a therapeutic exercise, drafted the three dialogues entitled *The Secret Conflicts of my Concerns.* The interlocutor is none other than Augustine. He reprimands Petrarch for the weakness of his will. The first dialogue opens with this reprimand: "Man of little strength, what are you doing (*Quid agis, homuncio*)?" A lack of effort, that is what this melancholy represents. Augustine thus invites the sick man to a *meditationem assiduam,* a mobilization of all his resources, since "whosoever seeks is also capable of attaining what he wants." He shows Petrarch "the root of salvation," an unshakeable will. "Augustine: No man desiring to be delivered from his miseries will fail to obtain what he desires, provided that he puts all his sincerity and all his heart into it. . . . The ascent leading to the goal of our desires is simple. . . . Instead of saying: 'I cannot,' you must say: 'I do not want'." A will closed up in an assiduous meditation is "the path to arrive at the unique, singular, supreme Light."[77] Luther would have scarcely recognized in this champion of the will the Augustine that he claimed as "entirely his."

Luther's polemic against teleology perfects the hegemony of consciousness by extending it to the nature that we term extra-mental. The subjective constitution of this extra-mental nature remains a peripheral issue for his transcendentalism. But without such a constitution, Luther would find it more difficult to defend himself against the prejudice that passes for the received wisdom with regard to him, namely, that he is "modern" in his altogether new need for certitude.[78] Concerning nature, he puts the blame directly on the presumed comfort that the natural order would offer to the torments of conscience. In order to destroy the teleological lure, he dismantles Aristotelianism—synonymous, in this polemic, with ends held to be natural.[79] The teleological lure consists in imagining ends adapted to our own powers. Thus the good would coincide with happiness and with our natural disposition exercised without reserve. It is a teleological ethic because it is a eudaemonic one, in which the word *energeia* indicates the whole perversion; the *erga* are our works. Now, to trust in them so as to realize their ends amounts to taking oneself as an end, in which the word *entelecheia* expresses the primary perversion with perfect precision. Imagining oneself as "having one's end in one's self"—this is radical evil. Philosophers have found nothing more pertinent to describe the will than to define it as the faculty that carries its principle in itself (*hekousion*). Such is the perspicacity of Aristotle, as if in spite of him. Does he not thereby show that we are totally corrupted?

As for extra-subjective nature, it enters into consciousness through the dual influence of the self and the ego; therefore, it enters it doubly. The revolution in the manner of thinking can best be seen in these simultaneous modes of constituting in us the being of the nature outside of us. The efficiency of God "*pulls* everyone's will powerfully so that they desire and do either good or evil" (*SA* 747). God does not first constitute nature and then man through it, but first of all the will and nature through it. The pullings of the ego and the self constitute nature, which thus is no longer originary (neither of the two traits leads *ad fontes;* with Luther, nature ceases to be the medium of a return to sources, it ceases to be a source).

When and since the ego attracts all to itself, it posits nature in conformity with its ends. Therefore, the subjective constitution signifies a telic constitution, legitimate in regard to our resources. Under the influence of the ego, the will does as it pleases with regard to "what is beneath it: man knows that he has the right to make use of his money and possessions, to do or not do with it what seems good to him" (*SA* 638). My fortune, as the end outside the subject, has its being in that I make use of it as I wish—a position and use legitimized by the fact of consciousness due to the fall. Animal nature inside us is assimilated to these "inferior" goods outside of us; "the baser affects . . . the flesh, blood, the marrow . . . that animals also have" (*SA* 780s). The ego amalgamates all nature as the other of self-consciousness to its thetic measure. "In that which concerns the being of nature, . . . we know that the free will brings about certain things, such as eating, drinking, procreating, governing" (*SA* 752). The transcendental turn is marked here not by the amalgamation of the instincts, of physical and governed goods, an amalgamation where we rediscover, to the contrary, a constant in the premodern dualisms. It is rather that the other of consciousness is constituted in its manner of being by the reference to a fact of consciousness. Nature as objective spreads out and displays only the ego. It lends to it a network of branches and circulation. The reference to the ego does not destroy the reign of natural ends, but it alters its understanding. To see it, one need only recall to what this reign offers support and comfort: to the ego itself, that posits it. Here lies the teleocratic comfort that is as traitorous as it is solipsistic. How, indeed, does some end *posited* by the ego absolve itself of its coiling up on itself?

When and since the self attracts everything to itself, it lets nature be in accordance with completely different ends. "It is the mad who consider [the created] only in its preparatory mode and in no way in view of what it will be in the end" (*sch.* 8,19). The self's constitution of nature is also telic, but only according to ends that are yet to occur. Things do not already possess their end. They aspire to it. We saw in regard to the polemic against philosophers and their equating of being with presence that they sigh while waiting to reach far (*apo*) from the present, close to God (*theos*); the natural end that lets the self be is the promised apotheosis. Here the subjective constitution signifies hope. Under the influence of the self, the will does not submit to any thing; it submits itself to a promise, to the time of a certain history. To whom does this other teleology offer comfort? To the self that allows the ends yet to come to rule. It is a precarious comfort, moreover, since the self can be taken from me, the promise can be withdrawn, and the election refused. Teleocratic constitution by the self no more has what it takes to reinstitute normative nature than does the ego. Rather, following the Copernican inversion, what measures nature is the self and the ego—letting-be and positing. Those who are nostalgic for order through ends have good reason to be, for with the transcendental turn nature no longer offers either shelter from time and history or a measure against egoism. It has changed from being the one that norms to being the one normed, and doubly so.

The work of time reveals an incongruous normativity. If it marks all of nature, how must being be understood? Since consciousness engages in a pathetic differend with itself, it is no longer enough to speak *uniformly* of being-for-consciousness. Being will be shot through with strategies of positing and letting-be—it will be in dissension with itself.

Normative consciousness broken

The hegemonic sense that is instituted with Luther can no more simply acquit itself of the responsibilities that have been assigned to it than can the Greek "one" and the Latin "nature": to console individual life and consolidate public life. Consciousness does not provide a simple measure. Accordingly, by way of a conclusion concerning the differend between the ego and the self, it is necessary to ask what are its consequences for the modern fantasmic regime. After the upheaval of the sixteenth century, self-consciousness assigns to being the only scene where it can come to pass. How does this assignation function in Luther? With what sort of normativity does the receptive I mark being in that scene? Beyond Luther, how does the apperceptive act impose its unstated and unstatable law on every law that can be expressed?

In order to better grasp what sort of cleavage the self and ego use to split apart this law of laws, we will focus on three questions: (a) How, in Luther, does consciousness as an ultimate referent legislate the word, the supreme agent? (b) Is there some systematic *necessity* that the modern *arche* turn against itself in strategies that break its archic power and that, in so doing, render the new hegemony anarchic? (c) If yes, how do these strategies work on consciousness so that, beneath its regimen, being institutes a pathetic differend with itself?

a. Whether it is always on our lips or whether we never mention it, an ultimate referent essentially goes without saying. Acquired in advance, it always seems certain. It secures our theoretical and practical acquisitions which in this sense are subsequent to it. As what is active first in an epoch, this referent imparts value to the experiences of which we speak. These experiences become the issues at stake and constitute a resource only in reference to this fantasm. This referent forces them to come back {*revenir*} to us—they are like the income {*revenu*} that it produces. We know this ultimate source of enrichment and are even constantly making use of it, but we have no knowledge of it. Nothing that we represent to ourselves is more obvious than it; if there were just one represented thing, it would dislodge the ultimate referent from its hegemony. But none is better hidden either. Unquestionable and at the same time ungraspable, normative authorities are the most difficult to debunk. They serve as a measure for all phenomena, but by what yardstick is one to measure them?

Luther transfers *in toto* the issues of received Christianity from an order of things to an order of consciousness. For him, Christianity is organized in a fractured, bifocal system around the word as commandment and the word as promise. These "two words of God" measure all that is representable. They fracture the coherence of the hegemonic system since they work diversely on the subject, creating in it incommensurable facts of consciousness, inscribing it in two geneses and charging it with two heterogeneous times. The question is whether, in a manner that is sure even if hidden, these word-measures are in their turn measured by self-consciousness. Should we say that heteronomous apperception serves as an ultimate *norm* for these two supreme norms?

Whatever the answer that will have to be given to this question, in any case it will not signify that the I *gives itself* the two word-measures. I do not "take" the measures of the commandment and the promise under which I find myself, to the contrary, always already placed. Luther argues for the regimen of the receptive consciousness. The exteriority of the word remains for him the very gauge of its efficiency. The normativity of the I will instead be disjunctive. It would separate that which is a sensible phenomenon (because it can be received by apperception)—returning from it, enriched with meaning—from that which has no meaning because it does not enter into the originary heteronomous synthesis.

How is one to describe more precisely this *a priori* synthesis? It determines beforehand the order of the event-bound contents in consciousness. It decides not what these contents are, but in what manner they should be organized. It imparts a topographic rule. It prescribes where beings will be situated in order to be represented; only that which resides in the passage from the word that binds to the word that releases will arrive in consciousness. In terms of categories, the *a priori* synthesis claims that only what can be singled out, both through "positing" it and by "letting it be," becomes a phenomenon (the sale of indulgences has no place in this trajectory, and therefore is, so to speak, nothing). The regimen of passive consciousness commands the conformity of all phenomena to the subjective modifications in relation to the word. In this topographic sense, apperception is the norming norm; the law and the promise are the normed norms.

How are they normed? How does the "I obey" function? If it demands conformity, it does so by imposing a practical rule for the constitution of phenomenality. This rule is not difficult to grasp. The "I obey" reattaches (*religare*) the I to the word-measures, and it submits to it religiously (*religio*). All apperception does is accompany the phenomena dealing with the sites "in the face of" or "in" the word, whereby this apperception remains heteronomous. But is it not clear under what normativity the two modifying words of consciousness—the law and the promise—are placed. The I is defined by the synthetic function of obedience. Now, every act of obedience that I demonstrate analytically implies an injunction that I give myself. As an *a priori* imperative, it cannot come to the I from outside. The I enjoins itself with obeying the words that can interpellate it. Thereby it traces the horizon of their being. To be, show yourself in consciousness. This injunction also signals the norm for the being of all possible linguistic phenomena. To be, show whether you condemn me or save me, whether you modify the I into an ego or into a self. *I enjoin myself* a priori *to receive as phenomena only those efficient words, either my condemnation by the law or my salvation by the promise.* This rule is a transcendentally imperative act. It does not contradict, but on the contrary completes the "I obey."

Because it is heteronomous, originary apperception in Luther designates an inseparably obedient-imperative act, an act in which I order myself to obey.

This is not to say that it turns the law and the evangelical themselves into imperatives, for then we would be dealing with a religion within the limits of pure reason.[80] It is a matter of something completely different, and has a historical significance that is much larger than the moralistic rationalization of monotheism. Neither ethics nor religion come into play, but—and if the expression has turned to cliché, the fate that a mass culture inflicts on its most pertinent concepts does not take away from this pertinence—the destiny of modernity. It is not enough to describe modernity as the era of representation. From its birth in Luther, self-consciousness imposed a regimen because it is essentially an *imperative*. This follows from the new function of categories which no longer describe what is, but prescribe it. Consciousness is prescribed to hear only the words ordering it—"you must," "you can." This means that its quasi-spontaneity is legislative, for only that which is related to this autonomous duty and this heteronomous power will be.

Self-consciousness, in is very receptivity, attains in Luther the rank of ultimate referent because in its *a priori* legislation it dictates what, for it, will be and what will not be.

b. Once the ego has been posited, the self that requires its death is also there; once the self has been given, the ego that desires its death is also there. This sums up the systematic necessity for self-consciousness, promoted to the phenomenalizing *arché*, remaining riddled with conflictual strategies. The self is that which hopes for being, the ego is that which desires being. The necessity can best be seen by examining the functions that the ego assumes in this hope and in this desire.

It is stricken by, but also the carrier of, death. The strategy of hope dooms the ego to death, for the subject must be lost to it in order to be won. On the other hand, in the desiring counter-strategy the ego imparts death, for it leads the subject to its condemnation.

The moral task generates the force of the ego. Placed on the bench of the accused by the self, it has something with which to defend itself: the law pure and simple. A single phrase has awakened it from the freedom of indifference: "You should." Afterward, it observes itself living. It is also condemned by a single phrase: "I can." It congratulates itself. The anarchy-breeding transgression thereby enters into normative consciousness. Luther describes the linkage of these two phrases—thus the necessity of the false transgressive movement—in many ways: as an overdetermination of ordinary language, then as a strategy of affects, and finally as a conflict of causality. Promise-law, ego-self . . . each time the incongruous one-plus-one contaminates the *arche* itself and breaks it into an archic referent.

Take a direct imperative, for example, "Raise your hand." It becomes complicated, for Luther, on the side of the addressee. "If we take these words as they resonate, and if we leave behind all that consists of tropes or deductions, they signify that we are called upon to raise our hand, nothing else. . . . [On the other, hand, whoever] interprets it thus: 'Extend your hand,' which is to say, 'By your own power, you can raise your hand'—is one who adds force to deductions and tropes" (*SA* 701). The link that goes from the command "Do! " to the affirmation "I can" overdetermines language. It abandons "the simplicity of words" (ibid.). When an imperative is stated in the second person, the addressee implies nothing but "the usage of the language already turned completely upside down" when it makes use of the first person indicative (*SA* 704). So the law states always and alone: "You must!" There is nothing in these simple words that authorizes the addressee to conclude "thus I can." The ego is the transcendental noun—and Kant is its advocate—of this binding that does violence to words in their simple sense. It overdetermines language by deducing power from duty.

This is an unavoidable inference for subjects burdened with our history and phylogenetic time. The ego that ceases to infer for itself a power would be as good as dead, and then we would be good even beyond death. The self would be won, the differend resolved. Just like the nominalists before him and upon whom he claims to draw[81]—and, in another manner, just as Nietzsche after him, but who scoffs at him for this "earnestness in objects of knowledge"[82]—Luther identifies and situates the linguistic operation from which universals are born, with their pretended consequences (*sequelae*) passing for constraints with respect to reason. He discerns this "Babylonian captivity" of the mind[83] in the overdetermination of language, and he situates it in its distance with regard to "simple words." We think again of the words of Nietzsche: ". . . if only you could!"[84] Could what? Cease to conclude that you *can*, because you *must*. If only you were able not to infer an efficiency for yourself. Here is the nerve of "reformed" thought.

It specifically attacks principial theticism, namely, the effect of that ultimate of experience, which is natality. And in the archic strategies it rehabilitates the effect of mortality that the natural metaphysician denies but that is that alone from which life comes, for Luther. There is a permutation of coefficients: The Lutheran *arché* singularizes me "for life," whereas the subsumptions bearing metaphysical salvation universalize me "to death." All the anarchic vehemence in Luther springs up from this permutation and from the *simul*.

In the archizing strategy, the self lets itself be grasped by the event of the word that is addressed to it and singularizes it. The archizing strategy frustrates the promised *arché,* for the ego infers for itself an enduring essence and deduces for itself a power, beginning with words set up as universal premises.

While instituting a new hegemony, Luther thus put his finger on the mechanism that generates fantasms. He even demonstrates its ineluctable mortal constraints. The inferential mechanism imparts death to those who depend on it (thus to all, since all are entirely ego), but its essentialist products are subject to it also. The justifying word annuls the overdeterminations and with them all subsumptions under theses. It imparts life to the singulars that we are, but it causes the particulars that we feign being to die. According to thetic self-understanding, I have in my possession an efficient power since I belong to the species of living beings endowed with free choice. . . . The strategy of overdetermination produces the particular, and with it the subsumption machine, the machine that kills.

It is indeed necessary to grasp this permutation of the coefficients of life and death. Life comes to me through the strategy that puts me in a position of receptivity, that singularizes me, that refers me to what is to come; for its part, death comes to me through the strategy that universalizes, particularizes, subsumes. How are we not to recognize in this "who loses gains" an extreme formulation of tragic knowledge?

Language does not follow any strategy here other than that of *affects*. The lure of the free will corresponds with the overdetermination of the imperative "You must" by the indicative "I can." The ego posits itself as free to say "I desire the good," "I do not want evil." It posits its freedom to choose, and it posits itself as capable of turning itself spontaneously to its other, which it chooses. For such an archizing strategy, the word alone is efficient, there is no place in us for such a spontaneity; for the anarchic counter-strategy, the will dreams itself as efficient, as cooperating with salvation, as anagogic. The illusion of possessing a power that one does not have is called megalomania. What is its object here? That the will has choice, that it has the role of choosing where to go and to go where it chooses.

In its megalomania, the will takes itself to be a force, "as if, from the moment we command it to do something, it would therefore necessarily be capable of accomplishing it" (*SA* 677). But "all imperative words . . . never signify anything other than what men ought to—not what they can—accomplish" (ibid.). "The will being present, by what consequence, I ask you, must the power be the there as well?" (*SA* 691). "The impotence of the free will" to wrench itself from the ego, along with the gap that follows between "what should be done and what it is possible to do" show that no task can be accomplished if not "by an alien force" (ibid.). All substitution is but an affect

(*SA* 733), a passion of consciousness affected by the duty and affecting the power. Whether it follows from linguistic or anthropological schemas, the inference that deduces power from duty lacks probity. It is opposed to passive justification with the same necessity that, in Kant, the dialectic of illusion is opposed to the truth.

The reason for this is that the inference from positing to efficacy—an inference on which the ego is nourished—itself lacks probity. It is not enough to understand self-consciousness as the consciousness of a causality. It is still necessary to see that for Luther this consciousness of causality is true as affecting the singular, and false as a perfection of the particular. The subject is inscribed in *disparate causalities* that the linguistic and anthropological schemas do nothing but refract into the midst of words and faculties.

In the archizing strategy, the self remains singular as does the addressee of a causative word. Not only is it never really given, it is never a given. It is given in the mode of the future, as the singularization always yet to come. In the anarchizing counter-strategy, the ego's specialty is to fake the particular; by positing itself freely in the face of its destiny, it includes itself within the species of living beings for whom the free will would be the distinctive mode of being a cause.

To translate this conflict into causal terms, Luther unquestioningly follows what the Aristotelian tradition, so mishandled in other respects, quite dogmatically takes too far: the kinetic understanding of being. "The words as they resonate" and the "duty," he states, indicate "the manner of being about which we mean to speak." They indicate the strategy of the self, lieutenant of the prime mover in consciousness. In what does this manner consist? In that "God powerfully makes, moves and draws all things." The being of all things consists in being moved and drawn toward the future, natural being drawn by sighs, the being of consciousness by the promise.[85] Faced with this new being-in-movement, free will "is nothing, which means that it can do nothing" (*SA* 751s.). Reasoning that goes beyond simple words, as well as the bursts of will that goes beyond the straddlings it undergoes, are nothing. The only one that will aspire to their efficiency is, by profession, the one that claims to be a cause—the ego.

The double necessity of being—that of the occurrent singular and that of the enduring particular—thus allows us to specify in what sense being-for-consciousness remains tied to causality in Luther. It will only be that which receives its phenomenality through its relation to the received singular and to the posited particular, for the causality that is divine efficiency constitutes the self, and the counter, subsumptive manner of this causality constitutes the ego. The two facts of consciousness thus amount to *effects*. One is moved immediately by God and the other mediately by way of the detour of the radical tendency for hubris. To be, for Luther, thus always and again means being in movement. But in passing from substance to consciousness, kineticism is altered. Strictly speaking, only the self is, because the pure causal power, the *Alleinwirksamkeit,* is revealed in it. The ego, that on its own cannot move itself where it nevertheless is supposed to go, is reduced by this to nothing. Being-for-consciousness remains causal being, but represented, phenomenalized. For Luther, to say that God makes, moves, and draws all created things does not amount to abandoning the transcendental terrain, but to reinscribing the ancient causal schema in it. The being of the justified being takes shape in the self that waits (". . . choosing nothing, but only waiting for the efficient God," *SA* 633). If Luther denounces thetic being as idolatrous, it is because the thetic ego as kinetic movement mimics the efficiency that brings salvation. The created being's being moved is traced out in the positing of the "I can." But thetic mimicry functions only because God moves the megalomania of desire, just as he first moves hope.

From this perspective, the necessity of the differend results from the fact that God's exclusive causality, modifying our consciousness, can only be refracted in our own—feigned—causality. Accordingly, in a pamphlet against the free will, there is a systematic appropriateness to tracing the efficiency that moves the world back to that that saves souls. How is one to denounce the fiction of a free will (how is one get its back against the wall: "either-or") all the while recognizing the inescapable character ("and-and") of this fiction? Luther can only do it by assimilating the force that pretends to be subjective to that which the natural metaphysician in us posits as moving the world—by assimilating egology to ousiology. We say that plants grow and animals run, and already we have surreptitiously conferred on them the moving force that can be attributed to God alone. As we have seen, to include them in the class of things that can move themselves is to understand plants and animals in the same way one does the ego. Rather, they constitute the domain of signs, futurized as is the self. One finds this fraud among the physicists as much as among those who say "I can." Both the former and the latter use a fraudulent language. It is also an inevitable linguistic fraud.

If such is the reason to make an appeal to physical movement, it is that the will proceeding directly to evil is, for Luther, the first kinetic phenomenon—not the world proceeding in its cycles of life (in which there is nothing to do). The order of foundations is thus the inverse. The efficiency of the creator moves the rest of the world *just as it first moves the megalomania of the ego.* If we did not lean toward the transcendental fiction of a spontaneous power, and consequently toward evil, we would never have any knowledge of kinetic mechanisms. Thus natural processes become problematic only beginning with the big problem of the ego unfailingly positing itself as an autonomous agent. It follows that the category for understanding nature is the very one that makes us know the ego—"positing." In both instances, the being poses as the agent. Accordingly, does not all critical transcendental philosophy teach that we understand natural movement and its causes only because our consciousness finds in it the rules by which to single them out?

Self-consciousness reigns, anarchically, because it unites, without any possible reconciliation, the disparates that are the law and the promise, the ego and the self, positing and letting-be, presence and imminence, particularization and singularization.

c. A hegemonic fantasm decides what can be for an era. If the modern fantasm institutes particular dissensions, one will have a hard time avoiding the decisive question, namely, how does the legislative fracture announced in these dissensions affect being-for-consciousness?

What is being? With perfect clarity, Luther nevertheless answers this question, which he would abhor for its paganism. The being of the ego is a fiction, for, by taking a stance in the face of the law, I usurp it. The being of the self is an effect, for, placed in the fulfilled law, I let myself be granted it. The light of this granting alone is true (namely, the truth that is the Word). Its clarity reveals that I posit and I let-be, simultaneously. What is being? The categorial *simul* of these two acts. Can we conceive of a sharper conflict than that between being as fiction, thus as false, and being as election, which alone is true?

Yes. And not only can we, but if there really is a differend, we must do so. Luther conceives of the alterity in consciousness otherwise than on the model of determinate negation. With the same insistence that he uses to affirm the *simul* of these subjective acts, he repeats again: *either-or.* He thinks a figure of the other that is hostile to all subsumption. I posit *and* I let-be, simultaneously—I am, *either* ego, *or* self. How are we to understand this?

The elegant solution would be to retain the facts, but only in their imputation. They would come to me only *a posteriori*, by virtue of a free, alien desire. This will, Luther repeats frequently, *either* condemns me, *or* saves me—hence the ever-sharp anguish. The ego and the self would be embodied in two realities, one of which God imputes to me. According to the contingency of divine accountability (to impute is to bring to account), self-positing will be attributed to us or not attributed to us. The solution is elegant in that damnation will indeed be able to break being ontically, to the extent that it is mine; it will not leave it ontologically unscathed inasmuch as it is for-consciousness. In accord with the arcana of election, the end result will be happy or unhappy, but the conflict remains of an empirical order. Accordingly, Luther sees it *concluding successfully;* the ego must be "emptied," "annihilated" (*sch.* 3,7). Given the ego, I am lost; given the self, I am saved. "The inner sense {*sens propre*} . . . should be destroyed, the one which, overly indulging us, judges us poorly" (*sch.* 3,4, cor.). The ego can only take pleasure in itself; in the absence of extrinsic intervention, it will never know that it is naturally it own prisoner, knowing, loving, seeking nothing but itself. It doesn't have a good appreciation of itself. Only liberating justification judges rightly. It reveals the ego, and it reveals the ego enclosed in itself. The ego liberated from its confusions would be the self—thus the destroyed ego. The affirmation of the self, and even my life, demands the negation of the ego, even unto its death. The being of one requires the non-being of the other. "This ancient being must be extinguished in its root." This is a radical liberation because it unfolds the folding back upon the self that defines radical evil. Luther does not hesitate to say that the granting of the self "frees us from the tendency for evil" (*sch.* 3,21). In this way the self will triumph over its adversary after all. Moreover, the self "suppresses man himself" (*sch.* 7,1), that is to say, his identity. It substitutes itself for the ego as an emigrant substitutes one civic identity for another. "Someone who emigrates from one town to another dies to the law of the one he leaves" (*gl.* 7,2). We can thus leave the city of the ego! The ancient command to "die to oneself and to all things" (*sch.* 10,10) indeed signifies here a death in being. "God imparts life only to the dead—not to those who consider themselves such, but to those that are dead" (*sch.* 10,19). Such was the crisis that caused Luther to be reborn. He had been freed *from* the ego, *for* the self. The subject is reborn, and the self born, once the ego is annihilated. Given the self, the ego is no longer. By considering the facts in accordance with imputation, the gift of the one rules the fate of the other. One of these facts alone will be attributed to us. What is being? The reality that is destined for me. Being is equivalent to being given.

The conflict still remains of an empirical order—and the attempt at a solution remains too elegant—by not considering the *a priori* traits in consciousness. The deduction of categories from the quasi-spontaneity in the originary act of the "I obey" has shown that, no matter what fact is imputed, I already have something singling out its modality: *both* "I posit," namely, the present ego that is imputable by the word that condemns, *and* "I let-be," namely, the self to come that is imputable by the word that saves. This categorial duality no more fractures being-for-consciousness than does the empirical duality parallel to it. Kant will provide a complex table of *a priori* acts, which certainly does not mean that being emerges from it tripled into possibility, existence, and necessity. In the analysis of these traits, being will be seated on the side of the imperative subject. What is being in Luther? An *a priori* act in a dual modality—positing and letting-be, acts that conjunctively determine all phenomenal givenness. Being is equivalent to determining the given.

The "either-or" is *a posteriori* because it is imputative, and the "both-and" is *a priori* because it is imperative—what does this solution by imputation and the categories for pointing it out clear up? No doubt it clarifies my eventual destiny and its subjective conditions. But this is not the question, not the entire question. The question is to know the hegemonic strategies that the turn toward consciousness engenders. Luther articulates being in a dualist manner, and this with vehemence, but he does not articulate its symmetry between the ontic given and its ontological givenness. This givenness itself proves to be fractured dissymmetrically. From where, then, does the *dis* of the disjunction and the disparate, which breaks hegemony, enter into being-for-consciousness?

The Lutheran pathos wants being to signify autonomy, and only autonomy—and that it also signify heteronomy, and only heteronomy. But in this dualism of obedience, *autonomy and heteronomy are not opposed as the categorial act and the empirical given* (it remains to be seen if even in emancipatory dualism, in Kant, they are opposed in such a manner). The pathos affecting transcendentalism from its inception appears when we examine the respective places of autonomous and heteronomous enunciation. From where speaks he who says "me" and whose discourse becomes entirely autological? And from where speaks he who says "you" and whose discourse also becomes entirely heterological?

In the type of discord that results from two laws in conflict and for which all laws of superior authority are lacking—a discord that we call a differend—the simultaneous applicability of the two laws exists only for the chronicler, seen from the outside (or for the owl of Minerva that flies over the field of battle once the operations have ended). The parties to the conflict do not say *"simul."* They say "either-or." To recognize the claims of the adversarial party as valid would already be to sort out the differend and prepare an amicable settlement. When Luther says "justified and sinners, simultaneously," in whose place does he speak? From the side of the party ready for some sort of compromise, because it already sees itself entering through the great open doors of paradise? How could this be so when the torments of the "both-and" have only started with the discovery of passive justification? He speaks instead of the outside, as a "good philosopher."[86] The *simul* marks the autological-heterological conflict only indirectly.

In the place of who, in a differend, do we then say "either-or"? In the place of the litigant, of course. To be in a differend with someone is to challenge him with "either you, or me." This is how the ego opposes itself to the self. Taking the side of passive justification, Luther can roundly conclude on the necessity of annihilating the ego. But his statements on the reality of the self and the unreality of the ego that he offers dogmatically carry us far from the *simul*. "Sinners and justified, simultaneously"—"the justified thus putting the sinner to death." The contradiction is flagrant in this author whose talent one suspects would carry him less to rigor than polemics. What spirit! etc. When commentators feel the untenable, they endeavor to trace a middle road between the simultaneity of traits (nevertheless dogmatic), and the annihilation (equally dogmatic) of one of the facts for the sake of the other. Luther "wanted to say" "the total subsumption of our knowledge under the word of God"[87]—so, we have neither the simultaneity of positing–letting-be, nor the negation of the ego, but the subsumption of it under the self. We would like to understand, not only what it means to subsume knowledge completely under the word of God (we fear we have understood—biblical integrism[88]), but above all how this program, thinking of itself as the reconciler, will finally come to prove both the *simul* and the "either-or" right. But we will never be able to, since it is the program of reconciliation that is absurd.

We will have grasped Luther, and with him, the functioning of the differend in every critical, dualistic ontology when we grasp by what logic one can and must continue on to the "either-or" after already having said "both-and." This logic constitutes the regime in which the strategy of spontaneous givenness (Luther's "me" alone, thus the ego; Kant's categorial *Position*) does not cease to counter that of a givenness received from the outside (Luther's "you" alone, thus the self; in Kant it is the sensible *Setzung*). Still speaking only of the regime of passive consciousness, the transcendental differend in it opposes not what is posited categorially to the empirical given, but *the logic of self-positing to that of allo-donation*. It divides the system of consciousness into two equally totalizing, *a priori* functions. Such a linkage puts into play an imperative logic of being, a logic fractured in its very authority.

The heterogeneity of positing and givenness emphasized by Luther makes it such that neither of these can be unlearned through self-discipline, nor contained, limited, or be deprived of the allegiance that the subject pledges it in its entirety—in other words, it makes it such that both remain rebels to subsumption. Under the hegemony of consciousness, two incommensurable legalities hold us simultaneously. Consciousness proclaims what is, and it also receives what is.

As the good philosopher, Luther can describe this autological-heterological transcendentalism. But also as the party to the differend, on the other hand, Luther can but plead for the self and "letting-be–givenness" over against the ego and "positing." Out of what mouth comes the discourse that cries out "extermination," "suppression," "put to death"? From the mouth of the prosecutor, the representative of the efficient, extrinsic word. What "either-or" will be sharper than that concerning the very being of the parties? Their conflict subsists on the death that they mutually seek out. "When God gives life, he does it by killing" (*SA* 633). In the conflict of disparate givennesses, Luther remains the preacher that can take part and take sides. (In the proceedings that Kant initiates against speculative reason, in which reason officiates both as the accused and as judge, the role of the prosecutor will be curiously lacking. Hence there is a less acute sense of the differend than in Luther, even if the statement of the transcendental disparity *in terms of being* is the masterpiece of the Kantian critical dualism that is maintained, while being refined, from the precritical writings to the last moment of the critical system).

It is only in appearance that transcendental logic stretches like a membrane between the outside and the inside, here—in the subject—the categories of positing and allowing, and there—in the given—the phenomena of the ego and the self. In truth, according to the broken imperative ontology, everything is played out in the subject. *Here,* in consciousness, the ego posits and imposes itself; its essence is ontological and consists in saying "me" in the mortal hubris that swells apperceptive quasi-spontaneity to the point of exclusivity. *Here,* again in consciousness, the self lets-be and lets itself be given; its heterological essence amounts to saying "you."

Life *and* death—life *or* death: It is impossible to get a grip on an issue in the light of such a dilemma. All the poignancy of the Lutheran reform resides in this possibility of reconciling the *normative* statements, of which one reiterates the "me" even in death and the other the "you" until life. These statements—"me," "you"—would allow themselves to be embellished with some meta-truth only by having recourse to a speculative absolute. Hegel, who would engineer this path, at least knew the violence he inflicted upon Luther; what this latter had begun, he wrote, "spirit, more advanced in its maturation," carried to a good end as concept.[89] But in Luther, he who says "me" is not the determinate other, posited in the face of the same that is the "you." Luther never ceases denouncing dyadic alterity, the face-to-face, as the egotistical, metaphysical fiction *par excellence.* Hegel turns the disparate into a contradiction marking a provisional moment in the formation of the concept. He resolves the insoluble.

But does not the differend between being as normative self-positing and as allodonation that is equally normative get resolved naturally through the recourse to apperception? If Luther enthrones the apperceptive I as the ultimate referent for the modern age, what is more consistent, it seems, than to submit to this authority the conflict plunging modern consciousness in its characteristic torments? What is the use of an ultimate referent if not to serve as arbiter? But this is the wrong way to understand how the hegemonic regime functions in general, and that of consciousness in particular. These regimes remain fantasmic in their role of engineering life by holding death in check. It imparts to the differend a misleading respite. They have been delegated to promote a jurisdiction that states "here and there": here life, and there—as remote as a single thing can be—death. These regimes do not negate death, they make a specialty of relegating it to those things that are absent. Their public function is *containment.* More expressively than the tragic one in Parmenides or erratic nature in the Romans, the pathetic consciousness in Luther, because it is heteronomous, affirms life and death as disparate strategies. Fantasms legislate by marking strategic relations in being, not by sanctioning some one particular strategy against some other particular strategy. The recourse to the norming norm, namely, the apperceptive where apperception is a hybrid synthesis, provides everything, save a resolution to the differend.

There is no transcendentalism unless the other of consciousness is given to it, not produced by it. After Luther, this other—the spatio-temporal manifold—is given to sensibility. In the emancipatory critique, the originary apperceptive simplicity, though synthetic as well, apparently suffers no damage; it is only the unifying form of the acts issuing from the subject itself. Such at least is the confidence that Kant has in his enterprise. In the face of the sensibly given, subjective autonomy guarantees the integrity of the "I think." Such a guarantee of simplicity is lacking in the pre-emancipatory critique. The other is certainly given to me from outside, but it is so at the very hub of the system of consciousness, not in its sensible periphery where my free choice brings itself to bear on my body and on my possessions in time and space. The other appears in consciousness as one of the terms synthesized by the "I obey," whereby it breaks the hub. Here is where Luther teaches moderns to think the other otherwise.

The great philosophical lesson to be learned from Luther resides in this differend between heterogeneous and nevertheless simultaneous strategies of consciousness. His transcendental dualism does not oppose the subject to some "thing" confronting it as its other; rather, it divides it against itself. It splits being, not into spirit and nature, not into things thought and extended things, not into subject and object, but into an irreducible double bind. This is what straight-off breaks self-consciousness, the foundation of an age. Here also is what will end up bringing down its reign. To mark the immanence of this break, thus its necessity, Luther can only assimilate the natural given to one of the two strategies resulting from the "I obey," the one in which the ego posits itself. The differend resulting from the transcendental logic that once was constituted to take account of the experience of the salvation here *remains* without appeal. It will be necessary to wait for the emancipatory work of Kant to formalize it in terms of the autonomy of reason. In the interior of the field of spontaneous consciousness, the passage from one transcendentalism to the other will upset its elements, beginning with the mode and the content of the experience. But the influence of consciousness on phenomenon, as the separation that renders it an enemy to itself, remains—and this in spite of the relapse to the logic of things in Descartes. Consciousness becomes normative for being when experience is understood as receiving givens—be they spiritual or sensible—for an originarily synthetic, apperceptive act. Its normativity is fractured as soon as the phenomenality of phenomena has to be constituted in reference to two subjective poles deploying this originary synthesis in order for experience to retain its primacy. In Luther, these two poles are the *a priori* acts determining the ego and the self as the two facts of consciousness; in Kant, these two poles are the two "roots" with the two concepts of being (also irreducible) that follow from them.

It is not difficult to say in what respect the broken reference is more than a Lutheran curiosity—why it necessarily extends throughout the transcendental project.

The critical turn sees phenomena as being what I posit, and in this it constitutes me as the "possessor of the world." But it also sees the subject as remaining liable {*passible*}, whereby the pathetic enters into the hegemony.

If normative consciousness is broken in its heteronomic development, what then is left of its autonomous regime? Will the modern fantasm reign as a simple, univocal hegemony under the emancipatory nomism?

B

The Regime of Spontaneous Consciousness:

"I, the Possessor of the World"

Introduction

> "If I say 'I think', 'I act', etc., then either the word 'I' is used falsely, or I am free. . . . If I say: 'I do this,' that signifies spontaneity in the transcendental sense."[90]
>
> —Kant

Did not the Enlightenment finally discover the infrangible referent? The ancients let themselves be mystified by the gods or God. From Parmenides to Proclus, Greek polytheism is caught up in the search for a foundation within the limits of simple reason, just as Christian monotheism is from Augustine to Luther. Modernity comes to enfranchise reason, to give autonomy to man, to emancipate people. . . . The rational subject, spontaneously prescribing its laws to nature just as it does to itself—now here we have the legislating agent who succeeds where beliefs have only failed, namely in centering the ensemble of phenomena upon a simple focal point such as an intuition. My act, the "I-think," is originary because it does not refer me to any referent other than myself; it is foundational without being a being; and how could a pure act be breakable, erratic, tragic? How could it impose any sort of double bind? Do we not, with this act, have in hand the ultimate source of phenomenality, namely, a formal process which is nothing if not a presence to me, if not a consciousness of my own thought?

The gaze which I cast upon myself not only accompanies (*con-*) all that can be given to my knowledge (*-scientia*), but above all it constitutes it. The modern age is endowed with a freedom that remained until then outside the world. There are no experiences unless, within my originary consciousness, I prescribe to them the forms according to which they must be given to me. It is a gaze that is solely mine and universally efficacious because originarily free. Is not the simple normative bind which philosophers were charged to secure thereby brought to bear? Even more, through the regime of universal representation am I not made, as Kant said, "possessor of the world"?[91]

Perhaps. Nevertheless it is a terrifying normativity and possession. The terror of the ancients had to do with the lot the Fates could dispatch to us; that of the medievals had to do with the judgment which could befall us at the end of time. The terror of freedom has its source only in itself. It concerns nothing other than the experience of emancipation, namely, our legislative autonomy.

As is well-known, to make the law is gratifying to the one who makes it. On the other hand, legislation can be severe when it is brought to bear *upon* you, at your expense. That autonomy does not represent the culmination of all normative research can be seen already in the more or less subtle ways of being exposed to the caprices of others. Nothing is more frightening (*erschrecklich*), Kant observes, than the power held by one rational agent to impose his will upon another rational agent. "Much harsher than the yoke of [natural] necessity is the subjection of one man to the will of another . . . to the point of depriving him of his own will." But why more frightening? Because in legislative freedom there is nothing like an endpoint. "The evils of nature follow certain laws . . . , but man's willfulness [*Eigensinn*] is deprived of rules. . . . [In subjection] the cause of my unhappiness is endowed with reason." In natural disasters, reason preserves the comfort of eventually being able to understand the chain of causes and effects. To grasp why—is that not the properly human way of arriving at a conclusion about what happens to us? On the other hand, no such terminus faces that other cause, namely, the freedom of the other (*autrui*)—the intersubjective freedom which, in the imaginary museum of modernity, nevertheless simultaneously occupies the place of the Mona Lisa and that of an illuminating apparatus, a place of choice where all that acts and all that is at stake is concentrated (experience being a *Handeln*), and the illuminating apparatus which allows everything to be seen (the truth proceeding from the system of *a priori* acts). And yet, I remain exposed to the freedom of the other, without appeal, to the point of being able to be reduced to "nothing more than a simple pawn." Under elective freedom, whose terror paralyzed Luther, the Enlightenment thinkers exhibited lordly freedom in its crude violence, a violence capable of transforming me into a tool. "Supposing that he [the master] were good, who would guarantee me that he would not venture to do otherwise?"[92]

Even worse—and even clearer still—I remain exposed to the freedom *in me,* "the willfulness of man is deprived of rules." Here is the man of the Enlightenment become, for himself, a source of torments. This, above all, signifies the pattern of the subjectivist differend, whose conditions it will be necessary to seek in the critical turn.

The grand project of emancipation sees our legislative spontaneity as independent of nature. Freedom and nature: the same and its other? If this binomial, on which the modern philosopher lives, should turn out to be more complicated, if freedom should instead incorporate nature and, pathetically, expel it in the same movement—if Kant *must, and must not* cram nature into freedom, and this for reasons following from the critical project itself—then in that case emancipation would aggravate the torments of consciousness above and beyond every heteronomous terror. Autonomy would be binomial, a double law. Its commandment and its commission, its claims and its mandates, all that by which e-man-cipation evokes the hands of the legislative subject would refer to an ambidextrous agent whose one hand knows not what the other does. Self-consciousness, the condition of *universal* legislation, does not know how this very consciousness—the "consciousness that I have of existing"—*singularizes* us as well.

No modern philosopher has caused more ink to be spilled than Kant. Where, then, could his transcendentalism still conceal some secret if not in trivialities? The two centuries which have lived with the autonomous I, have they not transcribed and retranscribed without end, in theory and in practice, the lines of force which this I inscribes both within itself and outside of it?

To speak only of "theory," it happens that the transcriptions and descriptions strangely leave much to be desired. Whereas "practice" has extended its lines of force around the globe, the very import of the new foundation assured to experience by Kant remains surprisingly uncertain. Kant never doubted that he perfected the institution of the truly ultimate condition of all phenomena. "Self-consciousness in general therefore is the representation of that which is the condition of all unity, and is itself unconditioned" (A 401). However, as Copernicus invites him to do and as every reader, be this only of the three *Critiques,* can affirm with amazement, Kant never ceases to experiment. The emancipatory reversal in the way of thinking consists in *attempting* legislations. "We must therefore test whether we may not have more success in the tasks of metaphysics if we suppose that objects must conform to our knowledge" (BXVI). Kant justifies the experimental method; moreover, he also uses it by engaging unceasingly in experiments, some of which would appear to have been solved by him, and others having to remain outside of his field of inquiry; finally, he commissions the subject to test its freedom. Henceforth, autonomy is inscribed upon flags and heteronomy upon black-bordered announcements of death. What is other to my spontaneity (the salutary agent in Luther) turns into the product constituted by my spontaneity. No longer does any sign signal to me from an elsewhere other than within me. Hence the new torment—at least if the thetic freedom in me addresses to itself black-bordered notes announcing the death of heteronomous powers; it is a new torment if its constitutive activity is itself exhausted, in more than one sense, in bordering and rebordering them in black, pathetically; it is a new torment if, in regard to its own singular being, it is bereft of all rules.

Kant justifies experimentation through a transmutation of truth. Kant does not abandon the criteria for the adequation of truth any more than does Luther. Also as in Luther, however, truth as agreement or conformity no longer links the words which I say and the things which are; it links representations. Transcendental logic is a "logic of the truth" (B 87) in that my conceptual representations unify my sensorial representations. The interpretive syntheses which result there do indeed aim at things in themselves, but they do not reach them. Where Luther would say, "just as I hear the word—according to the ego or the self—so do I have the truth," Kant would say, "just as I synthesize experience, so do I possesses the true." Truth by coherence thus precedes truth by conformity. In the system of conditions for linking my representations, necessity and universality no doubt protect me in advance against the arbitrary. But these conditions themselves follow no rules other than those of their internal coherence: "Transcendental reason consequently admits of no other test than the endeavor to harmonize its assertions." (B 452) The centering of experiences upon the subject is authorized, then, to attempt a system of conditions. The attempt will fail, however, if, while the system is being put to the test, inconsistencies appear. Kant admits and presupposes the "nominal" definition (which is to say the received, or by convention—even provisional definition) of truth by conformity, but he puts into practice a completely different conception of it. Where, indeed, will critical reason turn to gauge its non-empirical assertions concerning the empirical and to see whether or not they hold? All that it can do is turn toward itself and ask whether the rules it follows in unifying its own representations pass the test of the sensed connection. Kant uses a "real" conception of truth, such as can be experimented with. Truth means, first of all, coherence.

Kantian experimentation also brings itself to bear on the *supreme* referents, the ideas of the soul, of the world, of God—to which it is a question of allotting their respective places under the *ultimate* referent, self-consciousness. In terms of their precritical status, which is still evident in the *Critique of Pure Reason,* these ideas lose their referential function in the subsequent works. If one is to believe a solemn declaration in the preface to the second edition, this *Critique* was supposed to abolish the knowledge that one had taken great pains to extricate from those ideas, and it was supposed to carve out a place for belief. Outside of such belief, reason remains caught in a systematic struggle against itself, namely, a dialectical struggle whose critique, which is also dialectical (like the leeward drift of a ship which hinders it from going with . . . the drift [93]), can at the very most isolate the antinomial forces and point to the impossibility of their resolution. Now, only two years later, the opuscule *Answer to the Question: What is Enlightenment*? opens with the definition: "*Aufklärung* signifies man's liberation from his self-incurred tutelage." (One thinks to read here an echo of Voltaire: "It is difficult to free fools from the chains which they venerate.") The Transcendental Dialectic has amply demonstrated that reason incurs its own tutelage, that this tutelage is *historical* and that it can be raised up through "the courage of making use of its own understanding"[94]—this is precisely what the Dialectic has also amply demonstrated to be impossible! It is permissible to draw from here at least this moral concerning terminological usage: The opposition of "systematic and historical" is to be ranked among the numerous distinctions of limited suitability. And it is necessary to draw from there another consequence concerning methodological usage: transcendental experimentation is of unlimited suitability.

Finally, the ultimate referent finds itself called upon to test its freedom. To say that the I acts spontaneously is to say that it begins absolutely.[95] Like every other hegemonic law, that of the transcendental I is posited, archic. Just like the theticism of the Greek one or Latin nature, the gesture through which we posit ourselves as an instance of commencement-commandment always runs the risk of turning into a false movement. Accordingly, that which after Kant is called finitude—the mark of my death—comes from subjective, legislative spontaneity turning into a false movement, not only on this or that occasion, but essentially and always. The I tests its autonomy in everything: in knowledge as pure apperception; in instrumental activity, by the technical expertise for according means to ends; in moral action, as the "no one"; and finally, in the community of those who judge together, through its "intelligible substrate".[96] It is the *pollachôs legati* of originary autonomy that remains the most difficult to sort out in the critical enterprise. So, it would be a pitiful dogmatic turn to trace the plurivalent I back to the univocal by decreeing, as the interpreters do, the equation of the apperceptive I = the practical actor = the moral person = the intelligible substrate. One would thus really fall from formal, ultimate conditions back under supreme, entitative conditions (where Kant takes refuge in morality; but as we will see, freedom is not first of all a moral function). Kant nowhere pretends to have established autonomy as one and the same in understanding, praxis, morality and judgment. Such a reduction to the univocal would be pitiful because it would obliterate the loftiness of self-consciousness. Like the highest science in Aristotle, the unity of the autonomous I remains *sought after,* and it must remain so. Apperception, instrumental reason, the moral self, *Grund:* one set out in search of the unity of the subject and meets up with something like a committee. . . . By invoking experimentation, Kant explicitly recognized—as did Aristotle for the one—the fantasmic status of the new hegemony. We see that the I is always testing its autonomy in the non-superimposable, dualistic constellations which ensue in these diverse domains. The other of pure apperception is the sensorial given whose "intuitive manifold" I master; the other of technical reason, the end for which I always employ the means and which always refers to new ends; the other of the person, the phenomenal I whose desires I must humble; the other of the noumenal substrate, the factual community where judgments are negotiated through the force of persuasion. There is a fourfold danger for autonomy in this manifold of intuition, this heteronomy of an advantageous end, this tendency to give myself over to inclination, and, finally, this discursive back and forth in which common sense is at work. Those, then, are so many figures under which the other is buried in the legislative subject. There is also a fourfold temptation to let that other rule in it. Temptations and tests are already coupled in the Lutheran terror; now, under the regime of spontaneous consciousness, the wide, open doors of paradise, where extrinsic efficacy imputes election to me alone, are once again closed. The more intervention there is from the outside, the more absolution. Incurred through ourselves, our torments remain to be suffered until . . . we learn the human condition.

To grasp the pathos in emancipation, we must first see in what respect spontaneity is equivalent to freedom (chapter 3). Originary freedom is terrifying to itself. How are we to understand this terror? Does Kant transmute the forces that fracture the I? Nothing forbids us from once again calling these forces the self and the ego.

Then we must see in what respect spontaneity is equivalent to being (chapter 4). The conflict of the self and ego plunges us into torments. Do these very torments direct us toward what "being" means for Kant and perhaps for modernity? In that case, the self and the ego would reflect the strategies of being which are natality and mortality. Spontaneity is shattered upon these ultimates.

The self remains a matter of causality (freedom giving itself universal laws) and the ego, one of willfulness (freedom seized by the radical tendency to singularize itself, "deprived of rules"). Under the emancipatory transcendental regime, the self and the ego lose all exteriority with respect to the I. They now name the I itself, insofar as it maintains relations with itself. From one transcendentalism to another—from the soteriological to the critical—there is a displacement, a reorientation and a difference in stress, but not an abandoning of these facts of consciousness. On the contrary, severed from the alien efficacy that saves or condemns, the self and the ego are now revealed to be really our own, to be really *facta,* that which free consciousness always makes of itself. They are literally pronouns, "in the place of the name" of consciousness. The self no longer arrives to us as alien, it is the I *testing* its autonomy. No longer is the ego a simple inclination, it is the I *being tested,* tempted by its autonomy.

CHAPTER 3

The Torments of Autonomy

In the twentieth century, we imagine that we have achieved a science of mind through demonstrating that the mind functions like a computer; the nineteenth century invested its hope for an impeccable science of mind in the analogy with the steam engine (as one dreams of a thermodynamic, hydraulic model of the unconscious); the eighteenth century invested such hope in the analogy with a building. Science instructs, because it shelters; it does so according to an order. But which? The only edifying order will be that which reason constructs for itself. Such is the diagram of a programmer or, in a more traditionally modern vein, the plan of an architect (the ideal architectonic in Kant allies itself not with Aristotelian *techné,* but with ideas such as the "mathematizable society" in Condorcet, his contemporary). The experimental method requires that reason resemble something fabricated rather than a natural organism, such as a tree with its trunk and root. . . .

Beginning with the first pages drafted in accordance with the new method (the "Transcendental Theory of Method" in the first *Critique*) Kant quite clearly announced the goal concerning truth, such as he set it out for himself by reversing the way of thinking. He proposed to establish a system of conditions that are true because coherent, namely, the "architectonic of pure reason" (B 860ff.). In delineating the foundations of self-consciousness,[97] then the respective divisions of sensibility and understanding, and finally, the stage of ideas, this critical metaphysician proceeds as Vico had urged him to do. He states that in every experience, it is we who constitute the true—*verum factum,* that which we make is true. The true and the fabricated are convertible. Here again, it is necessary to bear in mind the multivalences. The self and the ego are *facts* {*faits*} of consciousness; the moral law, that is *made* {*fait*} by reason; the true that is known because *made* {*fait*} by us ourselves. . . . It is a plural 'making' {*faire*} in which a freedom that is itself plural manifests itself. The scientific philosopher will try out different models. He will put to the test some particular complex representation of multiple processes in which each *a priori* act is lodged in an ensemble by internal necessity, and he will see whether this subjective domiciling permits him to explain our experiences sensibly.

The transcendental subject, such as Kant puts to the test, is indeed composed of mutually supportive acts, each of which depends upon the others and forms a system with them. But as soon as it passes beyond declarations of method, the Kantian science of reason can no longer satisfy itself with simple systematic criteria. It will be a science of the subject only if all of the acts also emanate from a unique origin. If they do not, then it will be impossible to examine them by asking "Who?" The transcendental architectonic must envision a conjunction of topical acts for every act of knowledge and for every possible action. Whether these acts determine givens (nature) or the giver (freedom), their conjunction will render them *mine*. When it comes to the demand for originary unicity, it will be a matter of the new centering of phenomena upon subjective legislation. It will also be a matter of my autonomy. Accordingly, in the crucial passage from the analysis of knowledge to that of action, Kant insists that in both, "in the final analysis, it can be only a question of one and the same reason, differentiated only in its application."[98] To be more precise, it can be a question only of one and the same trans-regional, autonomous freedom.

Experimental reason demands a *systemic* subject which spontaneous reason (which must answer for its acts) can only annul on account of its need for an originary *rootedness*. A house puts down roots. The question of "Who?" brings to an end the work of plans and diagrams. It leads back to the metaphors of branches, trunk, stems, and roots.

On pre-regional unification: the self reconsidered

The self answers to the Kantian question of "Who?" and it does so in the middle voice. We know the sensible object by effectuating the synthetic unity of intuitions, and we restrain our inclinations by effectuating an imperative synthesis of instincts. *Who* is thus efficacious? It is not the "I" known through internal experience which announces itself in the direct voice. This "I" remains an object, categorized as substance and empirically determined according to its passing states. The culture of the "I," which makes of it an individual self, begins with John Locke. Obviously, Kant had to deal with this.

Is then the self, which is the spontaneous subject and which determines all objects, that which is unknown, the intelligible thing in itself? The two stems of our spatio-temporal knowledge are rooted far from space and time in the noumenal self (B 29). It is there, moreover, that the moral syntheses, the imperatives, are formed. We act upon an object of the will by effectively submitting our inclinations to the idea of a law. Here again, who is it that is efficacious? A cursory look at the *Groundwork of the Metaphysics of Morals,* one might say, suffices to convince us that the same self is the noumenal source of morality. Is not the foundation of knowledge just as much as that of morals to be sought, then, in the belief for which, at the very beginning of his critical system, Kant proposed to open up a place? He acknowledged that the self was the ineffable origin of both our cognitive and moral freedom. To grasp that origin, Kant had to abolish knowledge {*savoir*}. In the case of the beautiful, the sublime, and natural teleology, it is true that that origin—our "intelligible substrate"—is *symbolized*. It remains that for want of sensible verification, we can never *know* {*connaître*} it. Nevertheless, beginning from the fact of moral experience, we can demonstrate that it is necessary to believe such a self is ineffable, that is, to believe ourselves a person, acting through imperative syntheses.

Why then do the pages concerning the self appear to be so embarrassed? At the end of the *Groundwork,* Kant asks: "How is the categorical imperative possible?" The answer: "The sole presupposition that one can give for it is . . . the idea of freedom." It is impossible to go back beyond that presupposition so as to bring it, in its turn, to some still more originary condition. "How is that presupposition itself possible? This is what no human reason can ever grasp." If there is embarrassment, one will say, this can be only because freedom cannot be deduced. Such is the embarrassment of finite reason which blushes when faced with the enclosure within which the project of the Enlightenment keeps it confined. Critical reflection observes moral liberty at work, watching it legislate—"you should." That suffices to reassure us that the causality coming from ourselves is real (and not only possible, as the critique of theoretical reason shows it to be). It is a wasted effort to attempt to ascertain, moreover, "how freedom itself, as causality of a will, is possible," a wasted effort, because such a knowledge could be obtained only by plunging the gaze into "the world of intelligibles." Kant leaves the responsibility for such exaltations (*herumschwärmen*) to others. It remains for us to consider the *effect* of that cause which is our intellect in its freedom, namely, the moral law. This "proceeds from our will inasmuch as it is intelligent, which is to say from our authentic self."[99] Thus, the self has departed, once again, from the one and only scene of consciousness, our world.

If such was Kant's last word about the self, the transcendental and hence ultimate origin of our acts would be haloed afresh with the old Platonic solar brilliance, and this halo would be magnified into a supreme authority, that is, into a transcendent origin surrounded only, as Nietzsche will say, by the fogs of Königsberg. The emancipatory project consists in anchoring nature and freedom "in one and the same reason," in the faculty of syntheses; but emancipation will have failed miserably if the acts of reason must diverge and diversify themselves as do the strings in the hand of a marionette puppeteer; it would be a monstrative subject that itself was not revealed to the observing subject because it does not fall under the laws constitutive of phenomenality.

In the face of his greatest wager—perhaps his only genuine one—which is freedom, Kant surprisingly enclosed himself in the either-or of the phenomenal and noumenal. "The freedom of the will is suprasensible . . . it is the spiritual nature of the soul,"[100] he will write the year of his death. But how can we hope to understand our free legislation toward ourselves by departing in this way from that arena where all is played out, namely, from consciousness as the origin of representations? Again, the issue is the experimental method. Kantian belief might well hang itself on the transcendental freedom of the soul; does not the entire critical enterprise point at least toward an original freedom which is, nevertheless, transcendental? But how are we to grasp this freedom?

Kant never doubted that it was necessary, given the threat of heteronomy, to root freedom in the self. But on the other hand, what remained a problem about which he was very hesitant was how to implant freedom. To begin with, it is necessary to clarify the motive for his hesitations. By doing so, we will gain a notion of the self as an *originally free transcendental function*. Indeed, according to the critical turn, the self will no longer be some "thing," neither in time nor outside of time, but will itself be constitutive of all that is produced in time. Now, the mutual references between self-consciousness, freedom, and the self make it difficult to grasp the nomothetic function in which the I-think is summarized. Kant describes this function according to a very ancient figure of thought, that of the one and the many. The one which is the I-think must be "able to accompany" the multiple. How are we to understand such a passage from the one and ultimate law to its incidences? Finally, it will be necessary to ask whether the self does not exercise a *causality sui generis* which, to contrast it with heteronomous efficacy in Luther, we will be able to qualify as autonomous efficacy.

a. Between the Grotto and the Whirlwind. Trying successive models, Kant works on the self more than on any other subjective constituent. Let us take another look at this. Is it necessary to understand the self modestly through *analogy* with some intelligible cause? "The concept of an intelligible world is only one *point of view*" for grasping, in us, the legislative relation as such.[101] The self would amount, then, to a simple way of seeing what critical reflection would adopt to take hold of the production of rules. This is a perspectivist solution and as such too feeble, seeing that it would reduce the self to an "as if." Now, Kant never speaks, nor may he speak of the properly transcendental domain in the mode of "as if."

Is it necessary, then, to insert the self into the architectonic as a "fact of reason,"[102] a precious piece of furniture found in a room on the highest floor? The sentiment of respect would mark it out there on high as *a given*. There it would ally itself with the moral law through its immediately known presence, in honor of which, in this single, unique case, critical reason would have to suspend the search for conditions governing representation. This time, the solution is too strong. The self would appear in consciousness as a megalith from an unknown hand. Even according to Kant, this would also be a deliberately paradoxical solution (*widersinnig*). In a system of conditions where understanding represents and interprets the givens, but where no given is ever co-present to the understanding, a brute fact—and an intelligible fact to boot—quite simply has no place at all. If Kant were to retain it definitively, this attempt would confirm the fragmentation of consciousness. This would be to turn truth as coherence into a network of conditions. Through what affinity could the apperceptive freedom accompanying my representations still be recognized in the freedom dictating the moral law, a freedom unknown to reflection in being a donor beyond donation, beyond the world? This is literally an unwieldy solution. It dismisses the noble goal of arriving at a "unitary vision of all the rational faculties (both theoretical and practical) and of deducing all starting from a single principle."[103] That single principle can consist only in autonomy taken in a meta-regional, but not at all a meta-transcendental, sense. Only a source of autonomous actions which is neither phenomenal nor noumenal will determine, directly from itself, the formal "I" and will constitute it as a free self, the agent of all emancipations. On the contrary, to locate freedom in a fact of reason amounts to limiting not only subjective autonomy to pragmatic spontaneity, but also that spontaneity only to morality—and consequently, because it is formal it would limit the ultimate authority to a supreme authority since it is the one most dense in thinkable contents.

In whatever sense one takes the word *Faktum,* one ends by binding transcendental freedom and therefore the self. Having taxed one's ingenuity to unknot this difficulty, one will always finish by tightening the knot.

Indeed, on the one hand Kant reattaches this "fact" to the question, quite usual in jurisprudence, of *quid facti.* Hence, for him, a fact is that which is the case—a being. And with that, we have already tightened up the reist knot. Luther said *Tatsache* (from the verb *tun,* 'to do') and underlined the process rather than the case, namely, the phylogenetic process in the ego (a *factum* because fabricated) and the ontogenetic process in the self (*effectum* because bestowed). Just as, in respect to Luther, the phrase "facts of consciousness" accords, consequently, with the dismissal of the logic of things, so too in Kant the "fact of reason," understood as a given, reintroduces reist connotations into the very heart of the new logic.

On the other hand, if the moral law—unknowable, but intelligible—is *facta,* 'made,' as Kant has also said, then this can be only through an agent that is itself intelligible. Thus, the noumenal knot is tightened up. Is it fitting to identify the self purely and simply with "the person as a reasonable and responsible being (*Wesen*)?"[104] Indeed, such is the path upon which Kant ends up setting out. But we have just seen the price that must be paid. Is it not the most certain path by which to leave the terrain of *a priori* acts and once again to stand firmly on that of things or of beings, all the ideas of which overwhelm our finite reason by passing forever beyond its grasp? In one manner or another, the self is confined, suppressed, strangled.

So in the end, neither of the two solutions thematizes *transcendental* freedom.[105]

Kant describes the transcendental question as a problem of judgment, which is to say, of language. If for Luther consciousness lives on the extrinsic word passing close to the ear, in Kant it lives on the secret syntheses, acquired through and in reason (in the broad sense of the term "pure reason," hence of *Gemüt*). In its *a priori* determinations, the autonomous subject is a subject that judges, which is to say, that speaks. It forms cognitive, imperative (hypothetical-instrumental or categorical-moral), and aesthetic statements. It is true that by such judgments Kant understands mental acts, rather than words and syllables, carriers of sense which are put end to end with an eye toward communication. Now, this mentalist figure of language points precisely toward his conception of the self. Critique must succeed in grasping this self without making concessions either to the transports of exalted spirits ravaging Sweden at the time, or to the psychological platitudes on the other side of the English Channel—without, then, reducing it to a content of experience which the critique would desire to be either privileged or ordinarily associative. Between the grotto of Scylla, where Swedenborg crouches, and the vortex of Charybdis, where the empiricists spin in circles, critique will recover the identity of a speaker who advances by joining, modestly, predicates to subjects. The transcendental speaker answers to the questions: Who judges? Who enunciates? Who speaks?

Thus, one will understand the self only by listening to it make itself a transcendental, logical subject that gives itself predicates. The Kantian approach therefore is concerned with how to insert the self into the fabric of *a priori* conditions without installing it either in the spiritual high waters or the psychological downstream of those conditions. The coherence of this fabric forms "transcendental truth"(B 185). Kant endeavors to give to the self a web of pure propositions in which it would appear as a subject of statements: I think, I bind, I should, I can, I judge. . . . The self in Kant no more coincides with the formal "I" than it does in Luther. Instead it is the consciousness of a process. In saying *Ich verbinde,* "I am conscious of the identical self . . . which amounts to saying that I have consciousness of the originary, synthetic unity of apperception" (B 134). The origin is a process of enunciation in the middle voice: "it thinks." In contradistinction to what occurs in Luther, I am authentically myself not in receiving myself, free from the effects of the law, but in freely giving myself laws (of which morals are only a limited case). In legislation, the self alone speaks and the speaker is neither perspectivist, nor factual, nor entitative, but concretely occurring in the sense of an originary function. It announces itself in consciousness. With the act of originarily legislative enunciation, we have the *transcendental self.*

If, as Kant never ceases saying, the issue of the entire critique resides in *judgments;* and if, as both current usage and "metaphysical deduction" attest, judgments are linguistic performances; then all the *a priori* forms of the cognitive subject (still to speak only of it) are born in the middle voice of originary enunciation: space and time, the categories and the ideas. On the strength of the linguistic character of our *a priori* syntheses, Kant can dismiss, back to back, the two traditional claimants—rationalist and empiricist—to the rank of origin. The forms, notably the categories, are neither innate nor learned. No longer are they the truths of reason clearly and distinctly perceived, but rather the products derived from our sensorial impressions through association. Along the Cartesian pathway, the subject loses the contingent novelty of experience; along the pathway of Hume, it loses its necessity and universality. Between these two impracticable pathways, Kant seeks the source of forms in an act. At times he calls this act, dismissing both innatism and occasionalism, *acquisito originaria.*[106]

Kant describes three phases of this act—as so many moments of *enunciation in the middle voice in which the self declares itself.* Now, here is the program he takes on at the beginning of the Analytic of Concepts: "We shall therefore follow up the pure concepts to their first seeds and predispositions in the human understanding, in which they lie prepared, till at last, on the occasion of experience, they are developed, and by the same understanding are exhibited in their purity" (B 91). Thus the categories are born. Beginning from simple arrangements in the understanding, they are developed with experience so as to be exposed, finally, in all purity, independently of experience. What type of process is composed of these phases? What is excluded is that it is a question of genesis. The Analytic would turn on psychologism if it compiled a simple genetic account. In contrast, disposition, development, and exposition record very precisely the mental moments of enunciation.

Now, to enunciate is to act. Transcendental logic aims to describe a system of acts through which I inform beforehand all concretely occurring givens. Through this system of acts, I make a phenomenon from the sensuous manifold. Accordingly, we have seen that to be mine, the forms of immanent action can proceed only from a single origin—an origin meant not in the sense of some transcendent spiritual nature, but in the sense of occurrence, *oriri*. The origin is the transcendental event. The logic that singles it out must give an account of an occurring act, unifying the forms into a focal point.

Kant called the unity of an act that gathers together diverse forms into a judgment, a function. And, indeed, there are as many judgments as there are exercises of that logical focalization: "By giving a thorough exposition of the functions of unity in judgments we will have found all the functions of the understanding" (B 94). Judgments are statements; it is necessary, then, to describe the transcendental self as the *enunciating function of enunciated functions.*

b. "To be able to accompany." With that subordination of multiple (categorial) functions to an ultimate (apperceptive) function, one has the problem to which Kant consecrated the decisive and, alas, in its two versions, the most obscure section of the *Critique,* namely, the transcendental deduction of the categories[107] This compact text presupposes, so to speak, that our heads are not empty, and this not only in fact, but in principle. They are filled with representations (in the broad sense, which is to say, with thoughts). Are there not, among these abundant contents, some that on their own we would count as knowledge? If so, which, and which sorts of knowledge?

In accordance with the transcendental idealism as well as the empirical realism to which Kant refers (but about which it will be necessary to ask—and this will be the whole question—whether in his works each of them does not invoke two disparate notions of being), the deduction is supposed to establish that the use of our *a priori* concepts is limited, and can only but be limited, to statements about the conditions rendering experience possible. What must be proven about these synthetic statements, or—seeing as they are thoughts to begin with—about these propositions is that they are not futile, cognitively speaking. Formal logic already enriches our knowledge beyond sensible experience and prior to it; however, transcendental logic expands upon it *in the service* of experience. Our heads are full, not only of experiences and their traces, but, to begin with, the rules for tracing experience. The proof is given by showing that the *a priori* syntheses have sense only insofar as they work on intuitions. That excludes allegedly analytic modes of knowledge as deprived of sense because not empirically verifiable. Accordingly, one readily describes the deduction as being prior to the demonstration of the possibility of *applying* the pure concepts to the manifold of intuition. It is at this high point that the deduction comes to an end.[108] However, applicability was already decided with the first step in the downward-moving procedure beginning from the I-think, namely, from that which leads from simple self-consciousness—from the simple consciousness of the self, as well—to the multiple forms of the understanding.[109] It has been decided in that procedure (perhaps in a circular fashion, but the circle is inevitable when one runs through a closed ensemble of functions) by the status that transcendental idealism assigns to the categories, which is to say, precisely by their objective status. Applicability is thus only coincident to *nomothetic justification,* which is, namely, that henceforth self-consciousness makes the law of all laws. Wherever it is a question of such an ultimate reference, the figure of henological thought remains pertinent. Likewise, that *a priori* judgments are applied to intuitions and that they exhaust their legitimacy therein proceeds from the way in which Kant makes the most ancient problem in philosophy his own, namely, that of the one legislating over the many. Such is the first issue of the deduction. Kant indeed submits this old ontological problem to critique. He inscribes it within the system of *a priori* acts and sorts through its elements. He does not, however, undermine the figure "the one and the many." On the contrary, he works on it expressly in order to achieve the ennoblement of the modern hegemonic fantasm. Degrees of being are transmuted henceforth into functions, essences into judgments and thus into statements, universals into operations of the understanding, the magnified hypostasis into a maximized subjective event, and subordinated particulars into subsumed intuitions.

If the deduction treats of application only secondarily, that means it is no longer a text about representation in the narrow sense. It does not speak of mental entities which render present upon the mental landscape that which is first present outside the mind. It is a legislative text. It shows what the consequences and implications are of subjective theticism, not for representation in the sense that was just mentioned, but for that which makes, in the last instance, the law. It is offered—as are others, notably Cartesian ones—as an instituting document for referential consciousness. That institution, which thus will have taken two and a half centuries to be accomplished (the fantasm which it exalts will reign, intact, for a much shorter time than that)—that epochal institution of self-consciousness, is perfected by the deduction.

One hardly ever reads it this way. Nevertheless, if the deduction itself is often obscure, the criteria which it must satisfy are not. It must show not only that our heads are not empty, but also that self-consciousness contains a knowledge of the conditions of experience such that it (1) lets reducible, objective principles filter into knowledge (in the plural, these principles are the categories for which all that matters here is that there is more than one; in nomothetic justification, their number is of little importance); and (2) that it lets a principle for these principles filter into knowledge (one, simple, identical; the I-think, for which all that counts in this justification is that it is irreducible and thus ultimate). Through the expectations that Kant himself invests in it, the deduction is decreed a doctrine of principles. The *relation* of the one to the many is the place where the principial position has the power to be this principle, and since the beginning of philosophy has been the most unyielding problem in henology. Faithful to his habit of saying the essential in the first paragraphs, Kant summarizes this relation in these perplexing words, which open the deduction: "The 'I think' must *be capable* of accompanying all my representations" (B 131, my emphasis).

"To be capable of accompanying"—how are we to understand this? It is Kant who emphasizes it. A curious beginning to a document of enthronement. Could not the I-think also be capable of not accompanying my representations? Kant seems to expose it to what is transitory. Is it necessary to envisage a focal point connected in some way to an on/off switch? Would there then be anything in it that was still formal? The nomothesis seems stillborn. A fair number of commentators understand the phrase in the sense that it would be *possible* for self-consciousness to become actual, but that it would not have to remain so. The words of the opening—"*to be capable* of accompanying"—do they not show the empiricist to be right and do they not inevitably turn attention to psychology? The problem which arises here is decisive for grasping self-consciousness as an act which the self exercises so that this self is confounded, as we shall see, with transcendental freedom.

Among the elementary questions which give rise to the turn toward the legislative I, there is, to begin with, that of the "who"—who says "I" in the I-think? Kant responds that it is the self, to which the two other questions of the "what" and the "how" are linked: *What* is the self? If it centers upon itself all phenomenal laws, it will be that for which there are phenomena; it will be self-consciousness. And finally, *how* does it legislate? Response: freely. In its positings, the self is originally legislative freedom.

Before continuing, a brief remark. Kant achieves the institution of the modern hegemony by showing in what way it was illegitimate to draw from the cogito conclusions concerning the real identity of the speaker who therein asserted himself, an identity through which, in Descartes, the first person singular still refers to a being, a thing.[110] Through his project for a science of *a priori* acts, Kant discards the logic of things (although in his project there are occasional relapses into that very logic). The new logic permits him to call by name the attempt to arrive at the sort of certitude of self that one has of a thinking thing. The name he uses is "transcendental illusion." In reflecting upon conditions that the act of thought presupposes, one will arrive, always and only, at acts and at a self which is expressed in the middle voice. The deduction will be limited to developing only the formal and functional implications of the I-think.

Now, as it should be with an instituting discourse, practical readings of Kant abound. Nevertheless, two tendencies were brought to bear there early on. They persist today, at times intersecting. On the one hand, one reads in it a "logic." The forms of sensibility—space and time—are displaced, in this case, into the understanding. The thing-in-itself goes into the refuse heap of outdated medieval ideas; against metaphysics, one retains only the forms, functions, concepts, and methods as well as the criteria of validation in argumentation; and one denies that self-consciousness, the condition of all reasoning, could ever itself become actual. For transcendental apperception, that signifies that self-consciousness is the act in which we think together what the understanding conceives. Thus self-consciousness is not differentiated into anything according to the conceived contents; therefore, it is a formally and materially neutral thought. Thus, it would be the simple logical place for multiple, objective productions, the place where I make mine all that is conceived. Such is the critical tendency, first cultivated by the Neo-Kantians of the last century. On the other hand, one reads Kant as a David Hume who would have succeeded. Self-consciousness is temporalized by memory; subjective spontaneity assigns—against formalism—practical ends; the ideas are prefaced with an "as if"; all discussions of criteria {*critériologie*} cover only the entities which are the case in the world; and having self-consciousness means that, through the I-think, I can pay attention to each of my thoughts in their singularity. . . . This is the Kant that would speak the truth about empiricism insofar as it gets along without an ultimate authority. The rules of the understanding suffice to assure science, with their provenance being of little importance (accordingly, one will replace the categories with the unity, the identity, the diversity, the resemblance, the totality, etc., of that which is found to be the case). One can certainly turn the sciences, advancing with the confirmation or invalidation of each hypothesis into the economy of a single, sovereign position. Moreover, it is a tempered empiricism that the Anglo-Saxon Kantians of today, having descended from logical positivism, are inclined to mix into curious intersectings.

So, the "logical" Kant is purged of his great discovery—the finitude of the subject—due to that incontrovertible condition of all experience, namely, time. Besides, if it is of the order of formal or general logic—not transcendental logic—the new ultimate referent here will be as ancient as the Organon of Aristotle. As for the Kant who spoke the truth about empiricism, it fell to him, wonderfully it seems, to do the work of deconstruction. He would only have to show the discontinuities which render consciousness irregular *in principle,* and the ultimate authority would be conquered by impurity. The polar solidity of the principle would find itself invaded by contingency and thus would vanish. To have self-consciousness is to appropriate one's thoughts and experiences, to recognize them as one's own; however, nobody practices such recognition twenty-four hours a day. Therefore, just as I can, and can not, pay attention to that which unfolds upon the screen of my mental cinema, so I can, and can not, advise myself that these episodes are my own. And that is the ultimate referent traced back to *a* possible experience, and thereby immediately transgressed. The appropriation would be dispersed, frustrated by a strategy of expropriation. The grand procedure of "making-mine" would auto-deconstruct through the compromises, often noted, of transcendentalism with psychologism.

Below, we will encounter once again a legislative-transgressive differend under the regime of self-consciousness, but it will prove to be somewhat more complicated. If Kant teaches that apperception can, and can not, be produced, then apperception would effectively lose its legislative status. In that case, there would be *nothing to violate.* There would be no law other than the network of forms. Now, without an ultimate law, from whence will these forms draw their power of determination? Lawlessness was Kant's *bête noire,* the source of horrors and labors that are equally interminable. It was also the source of a conception of the strongest sort of law. With an intermittent apperception there is no more law and therefore no more noun to transgress, to contaminate, to render fragile—nothing to combine, pathetically, as Kant will do in respect to being, with its disparate contrary. By reading Kant as an empiricist, the law is not deconstructed; it falls into a pit of thoughtlessness where brute facts alone make the law.

Nevertheless, a self-consciousness which *is capable* of accompanying thoughts does not reduce Kantian formalism to nothing. The deduction begins by posing self-consciousness as a process that always relates itself—this is what "to be capable" signifies—effectively to the contents of the understanding. If I say that to heat the earth, the sun must be able to emit a heat of at least five thousand degrees, I say that if it heats our planet, it must be done in a certain way. I describe its way of being. In the same way, Kant describes the way of being of consciousness. To serve as the ultimate authority, it must be capable of accompanying—*it must be such that it accompanies*—my thoughts. The cited words suggest neither that the I-think accompanies my cogitations as a latent, abstract, logical moment, determining their compatibility, nor even that it introduces time into apperception. We remain far, and should so remain, from the "person" according to John Locke, who knows his identity by linking together through memory the phases of his life. Whether or not I actually notice the concomitance which is consciousness, it arises from originary, not empirical apperception.

Nor do Kant's words suggest this emergency exit: to postulate the stable "I" around which thoughts would be grouped under the form of this or that judgment—under twelve forms centered upon an inert axis. There is nothing there to posit such an axis, for Kant never speaks of the "I" as such in the deduction! He speaks of acts, of *Handlungen*. What is invariable is the "being able to accompany" itself, which is precisely an active relation of the one to the many. From the very beginning the *können* establishes the occurrent referent. Accordingly, the self, self-consciousness, and freedom intersect in the I-think understood as capability. The categories are the forms through which the I-think acts, that through which it "forms" syntheses. The referential one is instituted here as the action to which whosoever links the terms in a proposition commits himself.

To be able to accompany is to translate, without mediation, originary acting into derived actions. Unity means to make a unity: to unify. And without freedom, there is no such making-one. There would be nothing to deduce if self-consciousness were not, in this way, essentially unifying, and that is the point of departure for Kantian legislation. Even further, legislation *is* the immediate action of the I-think upon the categories.

Philosophy always begins when one takes note of the conditions under which one is living. To be able not to accompany my thought then also means being able not to philosophize (which implies—and no matter what Hegel does with it—a reflexivity in Kantian self-consciousness). But to notice this is the work of empirical apperception, in which, consequently, the genesis of philosophy begins. Genetic commencement does not mean, however, systematic initiant.

c. Initial activity. "To be able to accompany" describes a spontaneous doing that is absolutely first. Primacy—here, in a word, is modernity—such that one can never say *I have* experience, but rather must say *I constitute* experience.*[111] Who makes it initially? Neither the empirical I who signs "Immanuel Kant," as we have seen, nor the noumenal I who must believe itself destined to immortality. The subject who constitutes experience can be only the transcendental self.

Experience is either unitary or impossible (A 110). Now, I become aware of its unity by conferring unity upon it. Action falls within the province of the self. There is, then, something pleonastic about the phrase "self-consciousness." In Kantian ap-

*The French expression used here, *faire l'expérience*, is usually translated simply as 'to experience.' However, I make use of the more awkward 'constitute experience' to emphasize the activity that Schürmann means to bring out. Similarly, Schürmann plays on the ambiguity of the word *faire* to mean either 'to make' or 'to do'; the former meaning has a certain priority in his reading of modern consciousness. I will occasional use 'activity' to preserve some of this ambiguity.

perception the redundancy indicates reflexivity. There are those that contest this. However, without it, how are we to understand *begleiten*? How are we to understand the *ad* in *ac*companiment and in *ap*perception?* Also, reflexivity emphasizes inseparably—or separately only through critique—the elements of the *a priori* effectuation, which are the effectuated cognitive synthesis, the act which it effects, as well as the effectuating agent. The agent that constitutes experience is reflected *in* what it makes (unity), *through* its doing (unifying). Hence the complexity of the self in contradistinction to the I as a simple referential pole.

The agent defined by reflective doing is not, then, to be confounded with that spiritual being which, in every experience, I must *believe* myself to be. This is, moreover, why reflexivity does not mean that the spirit represents itself to itself as an object. I would fall again into the Cartesian transcendental illusion of affirming that the conceptual activity through which I represent objects of experience to myself can itself be given as an object. Even further, that would be to destroy in thought the very character—or event—of thinking. So to grasp the self it is of no use to analyze either objectivity or the identity of conditions between experience and its object. It is necessary to grasp the origin of experience, namely, the originary activity. The transcendental agent is this unifier of the forms of unity that I *think* necessarily is.

The I-think is objective. It signifies that I think something (whereby it is distinguished from the Cartesian cogito). Every experience must be reconnected with its transitivity to be true. The I-think differs from the transcendental subject which is defined by its formal identity with the object (the supreme principle of all synthetic judgments). But both—the I-think and the subject—remain irreducible to me so that I have consciousness of myself in enunciating synthetic judgments, that is, to the *transcendental self.* How, in apperceptive activity, is the self linked to the I-think and the subject?

If, through reflexivity, we represent to ourselves the originary synthetic enunciation as the very gesture of our determining spontaneity, then the self is equivalent to spontaneity. It is, as we have seen, what constitutes experience, "the determining self" (*das bestimmende Selbst,* A 402). Representation and reflection here mean that the self determines through enunciating and it also hears the determinations that it enunciates. Which is to say that it is transcendentally responsible since it cannot not respond to (and for) the interlocutor which it is for itself. The ancient dialogue of the soul with itself[112] traverses critical desubstantiation. The consequence: In place of a dialogue reflecting the subsistent norm, autonomous reflection legislates by positing the subjective norm.

The reorientation of the speaker back to the interlocutor is the initial activity through which the self is distinguished from the I, which, as the simple pole of transitive consciousness, does nothing. We are sovereign in enunciating synthetic judgments, whereby the self differs from the transcendental subject, which is the form of every objective perception. Essentially spontaneous and autonomous, the self designates that formal primitiveness in which I am actively myself. So, for Kant, what is primi-

*The "ac" and "ap" both stem from the Latin prefix "ad," with the "d" yielding a doubled consonant in the modern word.

tive in us—which is to say "the first born"—is the legislator which we are. In enunciating itself, representing itself, and reflecting on itself, the self is the bestower of law.

On that account, it bears a more precise name which, it is true, multiplies the difficulties. The spiritual nature of this being behind legislative spontaneity—this spontaneity itself is called *freedom*—has really escaped us. In its name, the moderns submit themselves to the world, but they do not do so in the name of a noumenal agent. To speak of the transcendental self is to speak of freedom effectuating judgments. Self-consciousness thus becomes consciousness *of* the self in subsumptions, subordinations, and submissions as free acts.

The notorious difficulties concerning freedom in Kant concern its unicity. Under penalty of fragmenting me, there cannot be *plural* freedoms in me—a cognitive one for subsuming intuitions, an instrumental one for subordinating ends, a moral one for submitting and "humiliating" desires. Now, the awkwardness with which Kant engages this debate is just as notorious. The classic place for this is his critique of the antinomy in which naturally metaphysical reason goes astray. Does every change in us and around us proceed only according to the laws of nature, or is it necessary to reserve as well some place for a "free causality"? These alternatives are irresolvable, at least in the cosmological context where Kant raises them. However, if one notes the identification card of this freedom whose being antithetical to reason does not prove its impossibility, one will be seized by a certain conceptual vertigo. "Suppose that there were a freedom in the *transcendental* sense. . . . [emphasis added]" Such freedom would be a dynamic source of actions, following from the succession of being and non-being which characterizes the changes in the world. One would have an origin which would not be preceded by any law, spontaneously producing a series of effects: "Nature and transcendental freedom differ as do conformity to laws and lawlessness" (B 475). That which gives the laws must itself remain beyond the law, *arché anarcheos*. From all evidence, in this gap Kant prepares for the freedom of the moral person, a freedom which he will then call, more precisely, *transcendent*.[113]

This term "transcendental" is a clumsy turn of phrase in the discussion of the third antinomy, and it distorts the great problem of originary freedom.[114] In the texts, one would search in vain for "transcendental" freedom without metonomy. But what does spontaneity signify? Does it mean to begin a series of effects observable in the world *ex nihilo—ap'anarchian, ap'anomian,* as an uncaused cause? This is not the way Kant himself taught us to distinguish clearly between idealism and realism. Freedom that conforms to critical idealism will be a pure function. Its doing will be confined to giving forth the rules for rendering beings observable, but obviously it will not effectuate observable beings. But how, then, are we to grasp it as one and the same, diversifying itself regionally into pure theoretical, pragmatic, and practical legislations? This is a question of the effect in this or that particular acting—cognitive, instrumental, and moral—which, it is crucial to see, does not in the least bear upon the split between the noumenal and phenomenal. Rather, it involves the predicative figures in which the function of all functions is expressed as being initial, initiative, synthetic, originary, spontaneous, autonomous, and, in that sense, free. Since the middle voice renders it initially reflexive, this event occurs in consciousness, neither upstream from it in the intelligible sphere nor downstream in the world. Thus the legislating event alone is to be called the transcendental self.

The embarrassed gesture of Kant that excludes as being out of reach every *deduction of practical freedom from an originary freedom* is, consequently, hardly plausible. "Man in himself" (*an sich selbst*), he writes, is "conscious of his freedom."[115] It is hard to see how the first function of consciousness could thus merge with a being *an sich,* in itself, in which one can only believe. This spiritual being alone is founder. The self is opposed to a foundation (*Grund*) as the finite is to the infinite. It is free not through the absence of foundation, but through reflexivity. In contradistinction to spirit, consciousness never goes beyond the limits, traced by it, of legality. Therefore, it is necessary to wrest the self away from the in-itself in order to understand the self.

In regard to the self, even more than to God and the world, Kant struggles against the least concession which might seem to enlist him in the dishonorable league of exalted spiritualists (this suggests, and the remark about "lawlessness" proves, how much he feared his theory of the noumenon, under the ideal of the soul, coming close to them). The very coherence of the *a priori* system—the truth, then—demands that we separate the self from the in-itself. The systematic truth demands that a condition of free auto-legislation govern the diverse regional laws in consciousness. In our cognitive judgments, that first condition of autonomy is the responsibility of pure apperception. Accordingly, Kant does not fail to underline its doing so *{le faire}*. Cognitive autonomy is only possible as work. The originary self acts. It links, binds. The same first condition of autonomy is also at work in moral action. There, however, unexpected currents disturb the demarcation traced between the free *being,* which is the spiritual person, and free *acting* enunciating the imperative. Nevertheless it is necessary to delineate clearly this *chorismos* in autonomy. It is a question of systematically primary freedom. It can scarcely be both a simple "point of view" and a "fact of reason"—made by reason—and "the person" besides. Kant must have had profound reasons for these uncertainties at the very crux of the system.

One will have expected something like a topology of freedom. Indeed, such a topology is at work wherever I judge. By pure judgments, Kant understands operations, namely, those for reuniting, by means of the copula, certain represented contents even prior to all experience. Contrary to Kantian usage, would it not be necessary, then, to reserve the expression "transcendental freedom" for the initial spontaneity realizing such syntheses? It would then be diversified according to types of acting: theoretical (knowledge), pragmatic (technical know-how), and practical (moral acting). In other words, is it not fitting to inscribe the specifically cognitive, instrumental, and moral laws in a generic freedom as so many of its occurrences? By initial freedom we should understand that spontaneity effectuating the syntheses, whatever the region of phenomena to subsume might be. It is a primitive event about which one can say, in all tranquillity and without risk of exaltation, that it does not prohibit us from *believing* a soul transcendent, but that it makes us *think* transcendental autonomy: the self. Through the consciousness of the "I," we know that the syntheses belong to us; but through the consciousness of the "self," we know that we effectuate them.

Self-consciousness can have no other content than transcendental, originarily initial freedom. Through its reflexivity, it is that freedom.

What is missing in Kant, however, is the clear linking of freedom to the *verum factum*. By fleeing into morality, the thought of the originary event finds a refuge that protects it from an overt, critical nomothesis. If not, how could Kant's obstinate resolve to thematize freedom only through moral autonomy be explained? Why set up freedom stringently in the face of natural determinism if, even though we know this determinism, we indeed *make* the true by composing judgments for saying what is? Ever since the Copernican revolution in thinking, to posit aboriginally moral freedom almost amounts to a subterfuge for not enduring, however so solemnly declared, the new hegemony: self-consciousness, which is to say, consciousness of the self. Kant asserts it like a censure. It is forbidden to recognize a freedom which remains neutral with regard to the great debate between nature and morality, a freedom which precedes these as an event (in the middle voice) precedes both making (cognitive) and acting (moral). The censure intervenes at the precise turn where freedom, which generally initiates, comes to produce its specifically practical syntheses—those where we no longer say that which is, but that which ought to be. Kant presents this turn as the shift toward freedom plain and simple, whereas doing, always initial, turns only toward a more specific initiative: toward acting, which is a species of doing. Not that Kant silently passes over subjective initiative itself. On the contrary, he thematizes it each time he responds to the question of how the *a priori* syntheses are possible. However, whereas he calls it by its name, "freedom," in respect to the instrumental and moral syntheses, he silences its name in developing its first occurrence in the cognitive syntheses. As a result, one no longer sees what is essential, namely, whether cognitive, instrumental or moral, doing originarily falls within the province of one and the same freedom.

Kant's question "What can I know?" inquires into doing just as much as does the explicit question "What ought I to do?" The latter concerns the objective efficacy I exercise in regard to things (*Sachen*) not endowed with reason as well as to beings (*Wesen*) endowed with reason. The efficacy toward myself operating upon representations also is double. It is cognitive when I submit a schema to a principle, and it is moral when I submit a maxim to a norm. Likewise, in admitting that objective efficacy demands that the appeal to the in-itself intervene (which is another question entirely), how can we not recognize in the two intra-subjective operations, which precede the objective ones, the work of one and the same transcendental freedom? And since, as modern, freedom remains an attribute but no longer modifies any being, how is one not to recognize in all *a priori* judgments, prior to their diversity, the agent which is the self?

Reconsidered from the point of view of autonomy, the self is endowed with what, to the contrary, the Lutheran critique banished from it with vehemence, namely, the efficacy of a subjective doing in the final instance.

One sees the topical permutation that transformation inflicts upon the elements of transcendentalism. From being unconditionally bad in the pre-emancipatory project, autonomy becomes unconditionally good with the emancipatory turn. By forming synthetic judgments *a priori*, I cannot be mistaken. This is why the spontaneity of the self is absolutely good. It is so as a function preceding moral goodness (in relation to which the self therefore is neither good nor evil). Thus initiatory autonomy, the principle of the Enlightenment, is established—the new *radical good*. The rational will which Kant declares expressly—and apodictically—"good without qualification" is, then, always only the specific occurrence of the self in the moral domain. It serves there as the criterion for morals. On that account, certainly, it will be first in the order of their foundations. But it will not be first in the order of conditions. If in Kant there is no reasoning that leads from transcendental autonomy, which is unconditionally good, to the moral will, which is good without qualification, it is because he intends to preserve the immediate obviousness of the foundation of morals. In his critique of knowledge, he had not been as peremptory. There, he did not fear seeking a spontaneous condition (pure apperception) for the principles of intuition, however evident they may have been (B 200).

Just as evident is the continuity with the classical kinetic approach. To put it in the strongest terms, which is to say the most massively metaphysical terms, autonomy transcendentalizes the efficient cause. The causative self remains irreducible, certainly, both to the *causa phaenomenon* (the empirical character) as well as to the *causa noumenon* (the intelligible character). Nevertheless, that these two causes, the natural and the moral, receive their being from consciousness is the very sense of the Copernican turn. Kant says as much elsewhere. For example, he described his deduction of categories as "the attempt (*Versuch*) . . . to keep open to reason the whole field of activity by which it pursues ends (*zweckmässige Tätigkeit*)" (B 128). Whoever speaks of telic activity speaks of a cause—self-consciousness *moves* itself to effect syntheses. This practice at the very heart of the theory remains a blind spot in Kant.[116] One would say that he recoils in the face of the originarily free function, instituted, nevertheless, by the very call to subjective legislation. Would that be because he detects there what one would have to call a transcendental cause? Then it would be necessary to distinguish between two uncaused causes, a noumenal and a transcendental cause—between the personality and the self. One cannot help asking if causal freedom is as exclusively technical-instrumental and practical-moral as Kant would wish it. If there is an impasse concerning the self, for which despite renewed attempts he cannot find a way out, would this then constitute an aporia traversing his concept of freedom? Might it be possible that trans-regional freedom *must and must not* be a cause?

It must be, otherwise no synthesis—no "S is P"—could ever be effectuated. No experience could be constituted. And it must not be, under penalty of opening wide the doors, not at all of paradise, but of the hell that is anomie.

Kant took great pains to bar the pathways to that hell. He recognized, as we have seen, a salutary absence of laws in transcendent freedom (which he called "transcendental") through which I give myself the moral law: "Nature and transcendental freedom differ between themselves as do conformity to laws and transgression of law." Transgression naturalizes us as inhabitants of the intelligible world where anomie no longer menaces souls. Anomie also no longer menaces transcendental freedom properly speaking, namely, the self as the initiating function of the categories. The self is the event of a relation which consciousness establishes with itself and from whence are born the *a priori* forms. It differs from these forms only as enunciating differs from what is enunciated. The self remains not only inscribed in the nomic fabric of these forms, it is the very texture of that fabric considered in terms of *texere:* being made {*se faisant*}. Anomie still menaces, diabolically,[117] the will as free from submission to desires. "The willfulness of man is deprived of rules." Like Luther before him, Kant detects "radical evil" in this tendency.

Before examining the torments and the pathos with which this evil affects originary freedom, let us raise, in Kant, a parallel to the polysemic concept of cause which we have just seen. The categorical act through which I measure *a priori* every maxim indicates a *noumenal cause;* actions are the effects of that act, and it lodges us in an "incomprehensible" world. On the other hand, the categorial act through which I measure *a priori* all experiences leads me to know *phenomenal causes;* the schema are its effects, and it renders our world comprehensible to us. But the self acts in these two acts. It is the *transcendental cause,* the effects of which are all the subjective functions, and which makes us comprehensible to ourselves as "determining." Kant causes a rigorously parallel polysemy to be subject to the other categories. Take, for instance, the very first one in the table of categories—unity. A person is one, in the noumenal sense; in gathering together the sense manifold, experience is one in the categorial sense; consciousness is one, finally, in the transcendental sense.

I have said ultimate referents are distinguished from supreme referents through their relational nature. Perhaps God, man, and the world reign supreme in Kant. However, self-consciousness, insofar as it is reflected and is determined through that relation as a transcendental cause—as self—reigns here as the fantasm of last resort.

Only, here again, the legislative strategy is inscribed in a differend with a transgressive strategy which is also a cause, with the ego.

On a pre-individual singularization: the ego reconsidered

"The willfulness of man is deprived of rules." *Eigensinn* certainly has something to do with freedom. But the sense through which I seek what is mine, and in which one may see again a manifestation of the ego, is certainly of a nature entirely other than the transcendental self. The ego is no more posited as the determinate negation of the self here than it is in Luther. How, then, is it posited? How is it opposed to the self?

The emancipatory audacity of the project of autonomy can best be seen in the axiom "You should, therefore you can." On the strength of that conviction, two centuries ago the West entered into the Age of Reason, an advance perhaps no less decisive than the Bronze Age following that of the age of the reindeer, inasmuch as henceforth we make the materials for mastering nature ourselves. . . . The moderns have ceased to endure the strange cavalcades consuming the subject unto death. The self and the ego are both born from our own freedom. There certainly was boldness in the Lutheran hero of faith who upheld, without natural assistance, the double bind—"You should, but you cannot." The law has never cut short all attenuating circumstances, thereby defying the old judicial wisdom which requires that *ultra posse nemo obligatur.*

But the Kantian axiom, and with it the modern pathos, goes even further. Having to . . . and being able to . . . come from me. Emancipated autonomy signifies not only a *determining* freedom through which I state the law for myself, it also signifies that I have what is necessary for understanding the law, namely, a liberty that is also *determinable.* The project would collapse if the self and the ego surrendered themselves to some mutually negating struggle. Then is not a nostalgia for ancient heteronomies necessary if one is once again to practice the bad faith of diagnosing the perfectly liberated subjects as having some pathology—a subject spontaneous both in its function of commanding and of obedience?

And yet, as enlightened and emancipated as I may be, I never stop seeking elsewhere than in myself for the reference points for acting. The eye puts itself on the lookout for well-formed lines; the ear for words that please—I never stop desiring. Well, for Kant, to desire is to submit. The figure that attracts me and the word that flatters are so many intruders demanding the self to work upon them (the medium of maxims). We don't need the Enlightenment in order to ascertain the innumerable episodes in which the *singularizing spontaneity* of willfulness gets the better of the *universalizing spontaneity* of reason. Yet critical Enlightenment thinkers clarify the transcendental architectonic. In doing so they serve to situate the placement of that door opening on to the other, which is desire. This is the receptivity from whence reason actively opens itself to the singular, whereby it is singularized. The ego will oppose, in a differend, the legislation of the self to an equally transcendental counter-strategy.

Kant is able to *describe* willfulness as the inextirpable tendency to relapse into heteronomy. And so, as early as his first notes that are already attuned to the inverted way of thinking (six years before the publication of the *Critique of Pure Reason*[118]), he affirms the systematic necessity of what he will later call radical evil, the tendency not only to pride ourselves on the given (sensible) rather than on what we give ourselves (the moral law), but also to exalt into a maxim such a preference for the singular and the heteronomous. With this decisive step, evil no longer resides in sensibility, but in legislation as well, that of maxims contrary to the law. Under the regime of transcendental autonomy, how are we to understand this other of the self that persists in freedom and is signaled by desire?

The affective-affectable aperture through which attractions take hold of us is not simple. Desire, though exiled into the sphere of being possessed, is not for all that placed squarely in some zone of pure passivity. Kant sees in desire the same structure—the conjunction of receptivity and spontaneity—that is in every process that implies sensibility, be it cognitive or pragmatic. Now, how must spontaneity function so that I can be subject to affects coming to me essentially from elsewhere? If the willfulness of man is deprived of rules, it is because desire, which spontaneously puts us at the mercy of exogenous determinations, is deprived of them. For there to be affects, there must be in me a faculty of impulses that are as arbitrary as the attracting-determining objects I stay close to are contingent.

In other words, it is necessary that in addition to the rational will (*Wille*) there be in us an arbitrary will (*Willkür,* A 802) always ready to follow the latest stimulus. There must be a free will in the sense of indifference that permits us to conform or not to conform to the moral law. If we were constituted differently, without desire and consequently sheltered from excessive assaults, the moral law would not take the form of duty in us, which is to say, the form of a constraint. At issue in this neutral will is the dictate with which will I will go along—with the one that I state and in which, as voluntarily autonomous, I realize my advantage, or with the one through which I hear impulses and through which, just as voluntarily heteronomous, I go beyond the law and lose myself. It is as if the terms of the *simul* are themselves inverted from the moment that the murmur of alien, singular, solicitations can no longer be reduced in us to the silence that, since it is a unifying voice, the universal expresses through the sovereign and imperative voice.

So we have the return of a singularizing heteronomy—therefore, of the ego—the explication of which remains, in Kant, as much an embarrassment as is universalizing autonomy—hence, as is the self. It is permissible to suspect in both cases that the motives of embarrassment are the same, namely, to keep the moral law pure.

Kant attempts an explanation of this shattered spontaneity through an inverted Christology, namely, by way of two natures in the same subject (inverted, because the subject is ourselves, the saint having no more than one nature). The tendency to heteronomy does not affect all beings, which are themselves finite and living under the moral law. A "saintly will" would be exempt from it. The only ones delivered unto extreme alterity are those subjects in whom "the moral principles must be engendered, spread and reinforced."[119] If we suffer those torments where the rational will enters into conflict with the will serving desire, it is because we are born with dispositions placing us at the mercy of stimulants. Appeals to heteronomy strike at the perfectibility of the human species, the perfectibility of which the grand project of the Enlightenment took upon itself. Accordingly, the arbitrary will is defined through the contiguity of that *specific,* actually inherited nature (of which anthropology treats) to the *transcendent* nature allying us to rational beings (of which the metaphysics of morals treats). Following the example of the self, is there a place for the *transcendental* ego between anthropology and metaphysics?

The doctrine of two natures belongs to moral anthropology. It furnishes Kant with an *explanans* sufficiently malleable for giving an account of several, traditionally formidable, problems—starting from that *explanandum* which is the most formidable of all: evil. There again, however, Kant quietly skirts around the terrain tidied up by him, where the pure functions precede both specific heredity and the practical personality. At times, as we shall see, he falls into a hereditary etiology of evil and thus aims short of transcendental freedom; at other times, he falls into a metaphysical explanation, and thus aims beyond it.

a. Reason infected by willfulness. For Kant, as for Luther (and Augustine) before him, evil is born in the love of the self. However, in contradistinction to the Christian tradition, Kant recognizes a self-love {*amour propre*} that is rational and is good without qualification, namely, the love of the self {*amour de soi*} as the moral person. The will that is good because it is rational takes for its end the single person. The good thus restricts itself to the subjectivist and intersubjectivist sphere—a restriction that results from the emancipatory turn in transcendentalism, along with the anti-Lutheran chasm which ensues (autonomy is now esteemed good and heteronomy bad). So the arbitrary will can be set up in regard to the legislating will in three manners that are equally originary.[120]

All three produce "dispositions relating themselves immediately to desire," and all three give birth to a specific form of evil. Their study is incumbent upon moral anthropology, which exposes in us traits that are both favorable and unfavorable to the application of the law.

We can, quite simply, renounce submitting desire to the law. In that case, the love of the self remains "mechanical." The consequences of this are "bestial vices," notably "savage anomie (in relations with the other)." The rational will can also change itself into an implement for forcing the respect of our fellow creatures. Thus it serves "the comparative love of the self (for which reason is required)." The consequence of this is the *de facto* perversion in which reason works in the service of mundane interests. The analogy with the tradition is obvious: Augustine showed in love the possibility of a culpable inversion between the goods of usage and the goods of pleasure; Luther, between the flesh and the spirit. Kant follows this heritage in seeing the source of all evil in the instrumentalization of the supreme good. However, from the moment that, in the name of the Enlightenment, heteronomy must remain subordinated to autonomy, the *de facto* perversion no longer suffices to explain evil. Accordingly, Kant departs from the tradition in anchoring radical evil in a certain function—general-anthropological, not universal-metaphysical—of the supreme good which is the rational will. The necessity of this additional step[121] results from the chasm in question. Since evil can no longer be traced back, uniformly, to love of the self, it is necessary to seek its root in a relation which the rational will maintains with the arbitrary will. The third type introduces heteronomy right into the general function of reason, the anthropological function which Kant calls "the heart of man." Radical evil consists in the tendency to give oneself, in full consciousness, maxims subordinating legislative reason to the motives of desire. The question will be: Lodged thus in reason, can evil exert its ravages without contaminating the transcendental space?

In terms of the two natures, evil consists in subordinating the transcendent or intelligible nature in us to our specific, empirical nature. Both "push" (*treiben*) the arbitrary will; they act upon it through impulses (*Triebfedern*). This is the enlightened version of divine and satanic cavalcades, which makes it possible for the individual, in reality, to let himself be pushed from one side to the other. Following my intelligible nature, I can obey the law; but following the nature of the species, I can also obey my predilections. If there were in me only the impetus of the rational will, my autonomy would remain infallible and my acting good without a struggle. If there were only the impetus of desired objects, heteronomy would remain infrangible and acting would remain mechanical. It is crucial to see that their simultaneous efficacy alone affects the two driving forces of one moral coefficient. The transcendentalization of the *simul* is recognized in this, that deprived of the other, each would operate through simple necessity: automatic conformity of the saintly will to the moral law, or the equally automatic satisfaction of desire through sensible objects. Good and evil do not reside, then, in these impulses themselves, but in the manner of submitting them one to the other. The will that seeks pleasure is good only on the condition of its conformity to the law. The will that conforms to the law in principle is evil, only on the sole condition that it seeks to find there its pleasure. "On principle," radical evil is a secret premise of reason—a tendency (*Hang*)—from which no descendant of Adam escapes. Can it henceforth be described in the simple terms of moral anthropology?

In any case we see how deeply into us willfulness, that through which we seek only what is ours, reaches: as far as into reason itself. Rational self-love, having the person for its end, thus finds itself radically obstructed by a love of the self, likewise rational, but which subordinates, on principle, the person to the satisfaction of desirable ends. Kant calls that tendency moral egoism. In this sense, he attributes it to the ego. "The moral egoist limits all ends to himself. He sees profit only in that which is useful to him. Pursuing his sole advantage and his own happiness, he is a eudaimonist who does not place the supreme motive determining his will in the representation of duty."[122] Useful ends determine us from outside. The Kantian egoist is then, curiously, he who gives his heart to heteronomy. This is a question of inner disposition, however, or of first intention (*Gesinnung*), but not of the object. As in Augustine and Luther, radical evil has, in Kant, no object if it is not my empirical I. Intention radically bent back upon myself— such is, as it is in Luther, willfulness (*Eigensinn*). Only, for Kant, the egoistic perversion of ends taints with instrumental heteronomy a love of self that is good because rational, whereas Luther would have seen only perdition. "Enlightened" willfulness is only the moral occurrence of the perversion between autonomy and heteronomy. Further on, it will be necessary to examine its ontological strategies. From this moment on, we can describe the ego as the inextirpable tendency to introduce the other, as a motive and a means, right into the heart of reason. Now, if that perforation of reason always individualizes it, we must then ask whether such an anthropological destiny does not suppose, as its condition, a *properly transcendental,* thus pre-individual, *singularization* at work within reason itself.

b. The time of the ego. For Kant, with such a perforation and such a singularization, what can be made of the grand project of finally taking possession of the sovereign good promised, in vain, by philosophers since antiquity is precisely the government of the self, autarchy.[123] One sees how the distinction between two natures, intelligible and specific, is crucial for him. They do not fall under the same genus. One marks our eternal destiny, the other our temporal destiny. They are opposed to each other, then, as the world of intelligibles is opposed to the world of sense. We must *believe* ourselves to be of an intelligible nature, but we have *experience* of our specific nature. The first is accessible to a metaphysical apprehension only under the sign of the "as if"; the other is accessible to anthropological knowledge. That distinction permits Kant to maintain, in the same subjective reason, both a will that is good because it is spontaneously legislative and a will that is inclined to evil because radically receptive—without, for all that, moral reason getting corrupted. The polysemy of the concept of nature has repercussions for that of the subject, since the subjective conditions of autonomous reason are of the noumenal order and those of heteronomous reason of an empirical one. It also has repercussions for the concept of character. In a sense strictly parallel to the two natures, Kant opposes the intelligible character in us to the specific character—calling the intelligible, here again, "transcendental" (A 538f.) instead of "transcendent." This is a new elision of the transcendental sphere, properly speaking, that the theory of the two natures conceals precisely in making use of it. Accordingly, that will be the place to ask whether such an elision is not completely interested. Did Kant not pay the price for keeping intact the freedom posited as the "spontaneity of the subject as thing in itself"?[124] His dualism discovers a shattered spontaneity in the will, a discovery which, in assigning freedom to the thing in itself, Kant is eager to cover over. The torments of freedom turned against itself are masked under the more premodern, indeed, Augustinian, conflict between our intelligible existence which allies us to pure, rational beings and our specific history, incurred since Adam.

But first, with the time of the ego, let us raise a second *explanandum* which that theory helps to illuminate.

Through the ego, I appropriate to myself the maxim of always seeking my advantage, a maxim marking the human species ever since the Fall. Now, understood in this way, the ego not only has a history, as in Luther, but it is the very motor of our history. The age of Kant trusts in progress as in the resultant pacification of rapacious forces in conflict. On account of the discords born from that radical tendency, each enunciates in the very depths of his being this rule of conduct for private usage: In every circumstance, I should seek that which is agreeable to me. Such a maxim is able to confer advantages, on the condition, however, of remaining unsaid. Stated in public, it loses its profitability. It is suppressed. "Moral evil has this property, inseparable from its essence, that in its intentions (notably towards others similarly disposed) it is contrary to itself and destroys itself; from whence it gives way to the [moral] principle of the good, even if this occurs only through slow progress."[125] This is a ruse in the proper sense, for if it is out in the open, it produces only ravages. But with a minimum of understanding, the wolves of Hobbes grasp that it is necessary to turn the motto of profit into a secret maxim; they enter, then, into an "unsociable sociability."[126] The ego goes *underground*. To protect himself from the fangs of his fellow creatures, the egoist submits himself to agreements. With them, he fashions a world whose policed order guarantees the alchemical transformation of evil into good. Even a nation of devils, provided they are endowed with understanding, will comprehend the benefits of the law. Disguising their motives, they succeed in founding a state.[127] The enlightened version of the great work is "Vices of particular advantage to the public."[128]

The ego sets into motion the progress in which evil, however inextirpable, will bring public life into agreement asymptotically with the good, however undemonstrably. Driven back in me, into the sphere of secret intentions, the ego advances the history outside of me toward the noumenal republic. In spite of our motives, intelligible destiny enlists specific, unavowable nature and makes use of it. Autonomous consciousness thus breaks with the temporality of passive consciousness. As in Luther, the ego institutes duration. But Kant constructs that duration beginning from an ideal future and not from the fall of the species with Adam. If the Enlightenment exalts spontaneity, it is so that the people will govern themselves; hence, in Kant, the inversion in the order of temporal dimensions concerns the ideal status of republicanism. In the terms of the first, Latin historicization of a hegemonic fantasm: the time of the ego, because it serves the grand, emancipatory cause in spite of our motives, is the time of the possible which will be, and not that of the memories of what was. Just as the events of 47 B.C.E. (the dictatorship of Caesar, the end of the Roman republic) had constrained Cicero to a retrospective view of history, so those of 1789 confirmed the audacity of a view toward the not-yet. For Kant, history is as exclusively of the political order as it was for Cicero. But from classic republican theory to modern theory, the originary sites of time are inverted. In the Kantian doctrine, only the future opens and founds historic duration: "The expectation of that which will come . . . is the most decisive mark of human advantage."[129] In the Augustinian terms expounded in the Enlightenment, this means that corrupt nature advances toward the recovery of intact nature through the conflicts the former instigates. The crises in the terrestrial city moves it toward the heavenly city. The ego stretches itself and endures, here again; but that which allies me with the devil belabors time to the greater advantage of the suprasensible ideal. Its mechanics—such as the "invisible hand" of the market according to Adam Smith—will make the city progress toward the noumenal republic.

The ego carries that out by way of an emancipatory crisis. The conflict of interests, brought to a certain maturity, opens an unprecedented possibility, namely, that of a conversion from legality to morality. Humanity up until now, says Kant, has lived for the sole end of a happiness faithfully reflecting the customs of the environment. For that, it has engaged us in incessant struggles that show that nature has regard only for the survival of the species, not for the good life. Now, this very conflict of instincts leads to a threshold. "Man advances in his labor to the point where his comportment renders him worthy of life and of his well-being." "Worthy of well-being" is the formula signifying "that all of our maxims correspond to the moral law"—a happy monotony of generations having had to struggle for their sole immediate advantage. "A social accord, pathologically forced, is transformed into a moral whole." Therefore, it is as if there were a stage in the progress beginning from which enlightened man no longer trusts in his instincts alone. He will have discovered his equality with all rational, and hence reasonable, beings. Modern man has passed over this threshold, "nature has made him come forth from her womb."[130] Accordingly, Kant does not hesitate to give a date to this crisis where the ideal of the noumenal republic can finally begin its work of regulation—or, in the terms fitting an enlightened Augustine, the date where "the ethical city of God" has the chance to be substituted for the market administered by devils. "If one asks which age is the best in the entire history of the Church up until now, I respond without hesitation: it is ours."[131]

The conversion of egoism into morality doubly realizes the Copernican turn, both in politics and in ethics. If Kant accorded a limitless admiration to the French Revolution (but not without moral reprobation), it is because it translated the critical, transcendental revolution into the public domain.[132] He saw in the enthusiasm of the spectating European public a "historic sign" (*signum prognosticon*), a sign which would permit him to believe that the people had acquired a new inner moral disposition. The same conversion, submitting the ego to the supreme principle of morality as such—to the principle of autonomy—can and must be produced again in the private domain. Kant describes it with clearly autobiographical accents. An "unstable condition of the instincts" precedes such a conversion, and it requires a "solemn vow." It happens unexpectedly like a "new birth, . . . through, so to speak, an explosion." "Perhaps they are few in number those who, before their thirtieth year, have exerted themselves in view of that revolution and fewer still are those who have solidly consolidated it before their fortieth."[133]

The ego is temporalized, then, beginning from the future. Inscribed within the limits of simple reason, it surpasses itself not toward some parousia, but only toward an ideal, namely, autonomy both in the individual character and in collective government. Accordingly, its duration binds it around the revolution in the manner of the thinking—concretized in the public and individual emancipation wherein the age for which paradise is reason feels itself "entirely reborn."

So here we now have Kant aiming above, properly speaking, transcendental freedom to give evil, no longer a hereditary etiology, but a metaphysical explication. The time of the ego is born from an act (*Tat*), itself modeled, it is true, upon the biblical story in which radical evil would be an "intelligible act, preceding all experience," "knowable only by reason."[134] This last trait of the ego is again reputed to attach it—as in Luther, but with a different reasoning—to the nature of the species, in such a way that I singularize that nature in willing the perversion of the moral good through pragmatic advantage; which is to say, by submitting the rational will to instinct. Indeed, by invoking the act knowable only through reason, Kant has already moved elsewhere.

So, according to the major distinctions of Kant himself, how would an "intelligible act" "preceding all experience" figure amongst the simple anthropological givens? It is evident that here Kant has departed from the movement of the doctrine of hereditary sin. He has left the anthropological terrain. He speaks now of evil in the very vocabulary of the *a priori* science. As a result, one can no longer refrain from asking if radical evil does not penetrate reason more profoundly than is admitted by the distinction between a science of empirical deeds and an other of the noumenal act. We must ask ourselves if its radicality is not the fact of—if it is not made by—freedom as a pure initiatory function. In that case, the ego would no longer be coupled with the self so as to haunt it from the extra-rational, anthropological margin, but from within. The incommensurability of the self and the ego would have obliged Kant to oscillate between the language of the anthropologist and that of the metaphysician. He would have instituted the *fundamentum concussum* of shattered transcendental spontaneity, but in turn he would have denied it by distorting it, from above (through the intelligible) to preserve freedom intact, and from below (through anthropology) to save dualism. He would have withdrawn to the noumenal terrain where souls are at stake to give an account of the good, and to the terrain where the history of the human species unfolds to give an account of evil.[135]

Yet, he himself has more to say about this.

How is the ego posited? How does it oppose itself to the self? To respond, it will be necessary to avoid not only casting an eye to souls, but also to avoid narrating the

Fall. If the act which enroots evil in us is "knowable only by reason," then the ego will be opposed not only to the legislative self through instinctual impulses, and it will be posited not only as the incitement to transgress the law for the sake of happiness; rather, the ego as a whole will be a transgressive strategy obedient to the other of consciousness and introducing it *into consciousness* through a singularization preceding all experience, and therefore a pre-individual singularization. It will wound the self in turning transcendental freedom against itself.

c. Freedom turned against itself. Thus Kant here comes to distinguish between two natures as if between two thinkable, and hence rational, durations. Furthermore, the functions of the self and of the ego remain mutually exclusive and without genus. They will be opposed in thought without a principle of subsumption. No longer will they be allowed to be divide up between the moral will (*Wille*) and the free will (*Willkür*). The latter undetermines us, whereas the ego, as we have just seen, determines us singularly. This, then, is our reason, pathetically an enemy of itself.

To read the lines which open the *Transcendental Aesthetic* (A 19), one could easily harbor the impression that the other of the subject touches our spontaneity only on its exterior margin, sensibility. Does Kant not say there that intuition is related immediately to givens and that consciousness, which depends upon time and space, finds itself therein relegated to a subaltern rank, serving intuition as a means? If such were the last word on heteronomy, then heteronomy would oppose to autonomy a symmetrical negation of the type inside-outside. Morality would fall from there into impossibility. We would be angels, wearied only by a skin and five senses. If morality is necessary, it is because the other of the autonomous subject possesses that subject itself even in its "heart." According to the principle of autonomy, heteronomy will mark our anthropological-practical nature only if we ourselves have incurred it and do not cease incurring it. To establish that evil is lodged in our freedom itself, it suffices to have demonstrated its radical tendency. Indeed, the root of the transcendental subject is its spontaneous freedom.[136] Every construction of a nature depraved as a result of some ancient fault not only would reinstate fatality, but would send us back again to the side short of the emancipatory threshold, to lose evil in the mechanics of history rather than to recognize us as responsible for *our heteronomy, freely willed in our autonomy.*

The rootedness of the ego in my autonomy blocks forever the attempts to exile evil outside of my acts where I am most myself. It is impossible, after the critical turn, to ascribe it to entitative givens—to innate insufficiencies; to some substantial being; to the absence of substantial being; to a cosmic flaw heightening, through contrast, the harmony of all; to a simple human illusion; to the pitiless march of history; to an intra-divine abyss. . . . These are so many attempts to objectify evil, as if it could be tracked down in some arrangement of beings. Where is evil? The metaphysical genius in us looks everywhere, except in our rational will. Though thus enrooted, evil does not figure amongst our representations. It cannot be contemplated either from within or from without. When Kant speaks of an intelligible act from whence it is born, one therefore must not expect a theory concerning some noumenal being that is, on that account, *universal*. Nothing would be more absurd than to posit a sort of corruption contaminating the intelligible substrate. The intelligibility here is that of my nature as a *singular* agent.[137]

The person is "intelligible" because noumenal, and the act too is "intelligible," but it generates egoism—these two perspectives are in a differend over the same free reason. The universal and the singular do not form a pair. The first of these intelligibles shows what we are in principle as finite, rational beings; the other, that at which we in fact make reason work. Oddly, Kant seeks to situate the protagonists of this conflict concerning the disparate intelligible within a metaphysics of morals and a moral anthropology. Is that not, however, an evasion? Reason of the noumena—reason of the species: This territorialization encroaches upon the transcendental terrain. This distribution of good and evil within reason indeed shows in what sense it would be false to oppose the two natures as reason and sensibility are opposed. It shows also in what sense it would be false to anchor evil (à la Schelling) in the "intelligible ground," the noumenal *Wesen*. According to the Kantian institution, however, upon what sole territory are there, legitimately, conditions preceding all experience? Under penalty of falling again into full-blown speculation, it cannot be upon the terrain of the person. It is the person that unites the intelligible and sensible strategies through subsumption—by being constituted as the end of the self. The originally egoistic agent—the ego—unites them through perversion, by constituting itself in its subjective ground as the preferential end. Now, just like the person, the ego also "precedes every act falling under the senses." Henceforth, the two types of ends articulate in reason the negation through which the same is opposed to an incommensurable other. Only *transcendental spontaneity* wills the universal law which it gives to itself and, contrary to itself, it also wills the singularization of this very law in view of our advantages. The self and the ego shatter spontaneity.

That we subordinate the law to the ego is not, then, only a fact of observation. What is remarkable here is that one cannot avoid seeing both moral legislation and its egoistic employment as emanating from the same spontaneous reason. Both, indeed, are "made" by it. Through the rational origin (*Vernunftursprung*) of evil, free spontaneity enters into an unequal conflict with itself. It loses its measure. The two natures in a single reason reveal their asymmetry, following from their respective activities. The one legislates "objectively" through universalization; the other acts upon the law "subjectively" through singularization. Metaphysics thematizes only the prescriptive nature in us, without having to describe what we concretely make of the law. The nature of man to which it is necessary to impute the ego is, in contrast, "the subjective ground (*Grund*) of the employment of his own freedom as such (under moral, objective laws), which precedes every act falling under the senses."[138] This is the hybrid construction that is the ground of the species and that each would copy according to the model supposed of Adam. Is the ego a matter of a simple employment of freedom? The incongruity with the *Grund*, which gives to the explication more than a metaphysical air, is only too flagrant.

So we have a properly transcendental hybrid that temporalizes freedom doubly. If they are the deeds of the same spontaneity, the self and the ego introduce discordant times into freedom. Kant, who seeks to unfold two durations in the same reason, said so. But he said so in opposing the permanence of the moral order, where we are at home with ourselves as rational beings, to the human history engaged through the ego. The time of the moral law is eternity, rationalized in conformity with critical subjectivism. "Like the reason which is itself formed from the concept of the moral point of view," "the moral order of ends" is eternal.[139] To that is opposed the more complex time in which radical evil rages. The ego commences to endure, always already. "Ever since" the free will conformed to desire, we have a history. However, following the critical project further, that act *in illo tempore* inscribes Adam's fall within the limits of simple reason. Kant must grasp, then, the *arché* of duration as an ineffable decision taken, made, willed by each individual. This is the ineffable traversed by the fissure of universal versus singular. If there were communication, it would put an end to autonomy, responsibility, imputability. We have, each for himself, decided initially, *ab initio,* in our free initiative and then in our initial freedom, that it would be better to occupy ourselves with our affairs than with the moral law. Singular, and yet archic, this decision commences and commands the time of the ego. Through the conflicts which ensue, the ego makes us advance toward a time of history—which is itself ineffable, as is the noumenal republic. To the self that wills universal-ideal ineffability is adjoined the ego that wills singular-fundamental ineffability. If it is true that in Kant time originarily infects reason, perhaps it does not then suffice to stop at the imagination as it enacts the three ecstases. Is that not to trace once more the subjective functions back to a single, spontaneous source? Is that not to deny again that reason suffers? In contrast, the conflictual temporalizations in freedom raise up this tragic denial. A pathetic fault shatters the modern *arché* which is spontaneity.

Kant transcendentalizes the Pauline pathos of the will divided against itself. "The good which I desire [hear here, "to follow the universalizable law"], I do not do, but that which I do not desire [hear here, "to singularize the law for myself"], I do" (Romans 7:19). I do not desire to singularize the law, but that is what I do, and thus I desire it as well. Kant *could not* give an account of the will—nor, consequently, of freedom—thus turned against itself if he were to content himself with proceeding on the one hand as a metaphysician of the intelligible ground and on the other as an anthropologist of consequences after Adam. To situate the two wills in that way is to send the antagonists back into their two respective camps. It is also, here again, quietly to skirt the agonal terrain which he himself cleared out, namely, that of the critical transcendentalism in which reflection has to do not with natures, but with functions.

The pathos of spontaneity can again be shown regarding what we have seen in regard to enunciation. Kant recognized the pathos there, and then he denied it, and so sorts these out by ordering the adverse enunciative functions. Take the axiom that crushes every attenuating circumstance: "You should, therefore you can." Duty commands us from the moment that transcend*ent* freedom incorporates us into the "*corpus mysticum* of rational beings. . . ." (A 808). As for capability {*le pouvoir*}, it speaks through the mouth of the human species. Transcendent nature says "you should." Anthropological nature responds "I am capable"—and I am not capable—of that which I should to do, namely, to subsume the impulses of the ectypal body under the sovereignty of that archetypal, mystical body. Thus Kant reduces to silence the first, enunciative function in which we recognized transcendental freedom.

Having eluded the question of initial autonomy, Kant can only give sporadic indications about the task that systematically is nevertheless first, namely, inscribing the *moral* conflict, where the rational will must impose itself upon sensible solicitations, in the *transcendental* conflict opposing autonomy and heteronomy within the same reason. Radical evil always designates only the moral incidence of heteronomy. And yet, in the explication that he gives of it—through recourse to two natures in a single subject, to enlightened theandrism—Kant oddly avoids embarking upon the grand road of scientific philosophy that is outlined through his turn toward self-consciousness. Thus we must say there that freedom divided against itself *expresses* anew the universal law and it *expresses* the singularization that contravenes it. It places itself in the double bind. A self-contradicting event that permits doubt as to whether the hyperbolic-specific allocation of two enunciative durations resolves the critical problem, namely, that in all of our actions, it is always the same reason that acts. Self-contradicting freedom permits us to doubt that consciousness, even as emancipated, dictates the law uniformly.

"You ought, therefore you can"—this axiom joins moral autonomy and moral heteronomy without, however, rendering transcendental freedom problematic. How are we to grasp the originarily practical condition of the tendency in us to dispose of autonomy, a tendency in which Kant recognizes radical evil? If this evil is only the moral figure of heteronomy working on spontaneous consciousness in all of its functions, then the regime of that consciousness will suffer systematic torments. When all is said and done, emancipatory audacity will have afforded the pathetic differend only symptomatic remissions, like a tranquilizer.

The self is the strategy of originally imperative statements, those in which I command myself to carry out the syntheses, whether they are cognitive, pragmatic, or moral. Kant recognized in the moral domain an equally imperative strategy—the ego—which contaminates reason with an incommensurable alterity. Now, if transcendental freedom can be originarily only one, then a heteronomous determination affects all the subjective functions—and not only the moral, and not only through their being put to use. "The willfulness of man is deprived of rules"—an observation that is not, at first, at all anthropological. It falls within the province of the new logic, doubly imperative, but not symmetrically. It is both autological and heterological.

Far from the Lutheran ego becoming the Kantian *Sinnlichkeit,* and far from the new hegemonic law banishing its contamination to its outside, to the contingency of our hereditary history, the self and the ego are opposed as two incommensurable strategies within the same originarily transcendental freedom. That is where the affinity between Kant and Luther is to be found. With the disparate thus introduced into the archic authority, and to better understand the modern pathos, it will be necessary to try to see whether shattered spontaneity does not give certain indices for taking up the question of being. Luther remained allergic to that question. Nevertheless, no one since the Greek tragics has been as explicit as he was about intolerable originary differing, borne, endured, in torments; nor about death as an ultimate counter-strategy, opposing natality as an equally ultimate strategy that posits the law; nor finally, about the singular temporalizing us. In Kant, the torments, the incommensurability of ultimate strategies, the work of singularization as well as the conflict without resolution which ensues—all this attains in being the hegemony of emancipated consciousness.

How are we then to understand the Kantian thesis that being is . . . a thesis?

CHAPTER 4

The Differend in Being-for-Consciousness

"Finite spirit is that which is not active otherwise than in suffering."[140]
—Kant

Kant, it is said, supposedly recoiled before an abyss into which he glimpsed, and then denied. It is as if he shied away from his own discovery of the temporality of being. His retreat may be seen particularly in the revisions to which he submitted the deduction of the categories in the second edition of the *Critique of Pure Reason*.[141]

However, by examining what he says in all of his statements regarding the question of being itself—and not only regarding the role of the imagination—we find that from the first to the second edition, he takes, quite to the contrary, a step forward, and a giant step at that, toward an abyss traversing being itself.

At many decisive points in this second edition, Kant inserts remarks about being—about "existence"—which do not square with the doctrine of modalities. Those remarks occur in a note to the new Preface, in the Refutation of Idealism, in the new Deduction, and finally, apropos of the Paralogisms. In those revisions, he conjoins with existence as the second category of modality a notion of being that points elsewhere than toward the understanding. Kant forthrightly affirms the character of this other being, irreducible to the predicative functions: "the existence here is not a category" (B 423n). In this context, it is a question of consciousness, the ultimate condition of all spontaneous acting. There, Kant considers self-consciousness as a *given*—not, however, as an empirical-psychic given, because then it would fall directly under the categories, nor, any longer, as a noumenal-intelligible given, for then it would be pure spirit. Consciousness is given in every use that we make of our faculties.

Kant is exceedingly clear in making the distinction that the existence of the given is not a category. Quite to the contrary, where the text presents numerous circumlocutions—much *ambo agere,* the pursuit of two paths—it is in regard to other distinctions, namely that an existence that is given is neither noumenon nor phenomenon. Those two paths are the very ones by which, in regard to freedom, we have seen Kant skirt around the transcendental terrain. We see the same thing here. Kant formulates the theorem about existence that "[t]he mere, but empirically determined, consciousness of my own existence proves the existence of objects in space outside of me" (B 275). Here we have the existence of consciousness (and thus of precategorial being) being determined like that of an object of experience.

Henceforth, the reflex of evasion is common in Kant. With full clarity, he sees a certain originary break through which the critical turn puts us, in the final instance, in a double bind. He then evades the pathetic condition he perceived and escapes to the terrains adjacent to the transcendental, at times the terrain of the thing-in-itself, at others the terrain of appearance. It will be necessary to ask oneself if, here again, Kant has not recognized, and then denied, an originary *pathein,* a suffering which affects transcendental being.

There is no lack of suggestive readings which recuperate, set aside, glean from, and blow out of proportion, or even seek to integrate and smooth over, the passages on precategorial being. The most suggestive of these sees the "discovery of a concrete subject which does not have a tenable place within the system."[142]

Before thus banishing precategorial being from the system, let us give the "system" a chance. Let us see if the other being—other than categorial—does not rather belong here, and essentially so at that. The point of departure in Kant allows us to maintain that being thus understood occupies the central place in the system, the place toward which the first lines of the Aesthetic point (the intuited given is "that to which all thought as a means is directed . . ." (A 19). In precategorial being it is a matter, right from the beginning, of givenness as such.

It is said that the systematic point of departure for the critique, which is never questioned, is experience. In a word, for Kant, it goes without saying that we have sensory experiences. Now, if precategorial being signifies givenness, then it responds directly to the attempt to render problematic that in view of which thought is made into a means, which is to say, it responds to the attempt to render problematic the fact that there is experience. The critical project would then begin with the recognition that being escapes our spontaneity, which nevertheless posits it. Being escapes spontaneity because the given can only occur {*survenir*}; but spontaneity still posits being, for in accordance with the grand plan of seeking, henceforth, the unconditioned in ourselves, the subject must "make" all that happens to it.

Hence in Kant we have a double comprehension of being. In the last *Critique,* posited being will be called *Position* (*CJ,* A 336),[143] a word I translate as 'thesis.' Thetic, categorial being is a thesis. On the other hand, Kant calls precategorial being that is given *Setzung.* I translate this as 'position.' The hegemony of subjective spontaneity means that I also posit given being. That is, in letting myself give something—in letting myself effect something—I do not remain passive. In allowing I actively receive that which occurs. Subjective spontaneity *turns received being against thetic being.* This is how the Kantian gesture that succeeds in instituting the modern referent remains, despite everything, faithful to the tragic truth, the truth of the conflict between the ultimates that have hold of us without recourse. Kant thematizes these as the impulse (of natality) toward autonomy, and then again as the impulse (of mortality) toward heteronomy. The first leads us to legislate universally. The second always returns us to the singular that occurs and is given outside of the universal, categorical law that the understanding declares. The differend between the conflictual strategies of being will turn transcendental logic into a broken imperative ontology.

Once the reflexive source of the laws of being—the self—is recognized as corrupted by a counter-law—the ego—what becomes, then, of its normative simplicity? What becomes of the thesis of the self as nomothesis? Consequently, it is necessary to ask if the differend that turns freedom against itself and ruins its simplicity will affect being? To see whether it does, we will begin at the end, namely, at the single goal that Kant never ceased to pursue throughout his critical works. That goal is rational legislation.

To legislate is to impose an order prescribing what ought to be. A juridical law decrees what must not be done, and therefore what must be done. It drafts the models to which action ought to conform and which, recognized or not, binds the actions of everyone. A law constrains even a dissident; it turns one into a dissident. But juridical laws have the power to obligate only by virtue of a law validating them in the final instance. Such a validation is transcendental if the subject, prior to all theoretical or practical experience, imposes the marks of objectivity on nature and those of personality upon itself. In Kant, pure reason legislates in the strongest sense. It spontaneously makes itself the order according to which all that can show itself will show itself. Outside of the objectivity that it constitutes, there is no natural object; outside of the personality which it confers, no moral person. Reason is not only realized in theoretical experiences and in practical injunctions but even nature and the person owe their being to it.

Now, the spontaneity that constitutes and confers would neither constitute nor confer anything at all if it did not receive a given. Hence the two parts of the critical project are transcendental idealism and critical realism. Accordingly, each time he skirts around the terrain which he himself cleared out, Kant breaks his silence only to speak of reception, which amounts to speaking of an *unsubsumable other* against which spontaneity collides. In reception, the received given brings along another being. Hence the torments in autonomous consciousness.

It is also said that critique has substituted a formal act for the ancient, substantial referents, ordering the world through their full presence to it: apperception for theory, and hence for the order of nature; and the "making" of the "fact of reason" for practice, and hence for that of the person. Kant never abandoned the search for an ultimate measure for being. Rather, he deflected it from the demiurge or creator measuring his works, toward reason measuring its acts. And consequently one says, in the end, that he replaced dogmatic metaphysics with critical metaphysics, which is to say, with the metaphysics of experience. This metaphysics encompasses theory and practice, a distinction henceforth irrelevant to the investigation of the new sovereignty. Something is only to the extent that it conforms to the self-consciousness dictating its rules to experience.

Given this understanding of being-for-consciousness, the simplicity in the normative referent is preserved and with it the determination of being as presence. The I-think remains near to my representations. The validating law is in the last instance fully present to the laws that it validates (the categories) and, in that way, to the syntheses that it carries out. Presence is all the more efficacious in being non-reist, for I am much nearer to the work that I make than I ever will be to a thing. Transcendental activity alone can guarantee the immediacy of presence. In this sense, Kantian subjective spontaneity would have succeeded magnificently, metaphysically, where speculation about substances inevitably collides with their irremediable diversity, and presence with the fragility of being that characterizes the last of the Aristotelian categories: relation.

In Kant, things are no different when it comes to the question of being than they are with that of originary freedom, for he evades it just as obstinately as he responds to it. He evades it by repeating, from the works of youth through those of old age, that being is thesis, that it gives itself neither to intellectual intuition nor to conceptual analysis, that in contradistinction to the other categories, those of modality are not real predicates, and that appearances as objects of possible experience is *all there is.*

However, in distinguishing between being as thesis and as position, Kant also *answers* the question of being. Thesis results from subjective spontaneity. It is the modal act of the self positing some thing in relation to thought, some possible, existing, or necessary thing. Kant says the other designates the actuality "of the thing in itself." In the second edition of this text, he adds "(outside of this concept)." We will have to come back to these words. Let us note here only that the *an sich selbst* scarcely corresponds with the parallel text in the *Critique of Pure Reason,* ". . . something real that is given, given indeed to thought in general, and so not as appearance, nor as thing in itself (noumenon), but as something which actually exists" (B 423n). Whatever may be the status one will have to accord to that which gives, or is given, *Setzung* refers the subject to what is other than itself, to heterogeneity; it is a reference in which we recognized the work of the ego. That this text is not, in the work of Kant, a *hapax legomenon,* but that it expresses the agony (the *agôn,* the struggle, just as much as the decline presaging the end) in his theticism, is what must be shown in order to establish, under the hegemony of self-consciousness, the pathetic condition of being. If to the question "what is being?" Kant actually gives two answers, that will then be one too many for the new referent to reign in utter simplicity.

Categorial being, *Dasein,* is one of the fundamental modes of the synthesizing of the given in the unity of an objective experience. This dynamic category is not only a law of all possible experience, but also, inseparably, a law of every possible object of experience. Such laws are synthetic because they are thetic; the pro-position is a position that one advances. *Satz* is a *Setzung.* So, like the other categories, that of *Dasein* has objective validity only if linked to the pure forms of intuition—to time and to space—thus constituting what can become a phenomenon for us. This is Kant's doctrinal answer[144] to the question of being.

Parallel to this doctrinal response, however, Kant gives another, one that precedes his critical revolution and remains operative in every step of the transcendental project. It is related to what one commentator has been able to describe as the "subversive" strategy in the critique, a strategy that "installs in the very upsurge of reason a radical non-presence to the self."[145]

On givenness as position

In the opuscule *Of the Sole Possible Foundation for a Proof Demonstrating the Existence of God,*[146] Kant develops an initial notion of givenness. The presuppositions of this text, seven years prior to the "Copernican turn," are in line neither with Kant's subsequent critique of the argument, called ontological, nor with the transcendental method as such. Nevertheless, there is continuity with the critical system with regard to one issue, namely, that it is impossible to conceive of being as a real predicate and that consequently it adds no thought contents to what we conceive.

His demonstration there for establishing that being does not figure amongst the real predicates begins with a given that is reminiscent of the idealities in Leibniz. It begins with the propositions of logic, mathematics, and axiomatic geometry, linked through universal and necessary connections. Kant reasons, then, neither starting from actual things, as does the Aristotelian tradition, nor from being as the necessary content of thought, as does Descartes. He takes his point of departure from the universal possibilities, which is to say, from the formal presuppositions of every actual thing. The argument proceeds *a priori,* founded neither in observation nor in a postulated correspondence between concepts and things,[147] but in the pure relations between concepts. Absolute existence can be attained through a rationalist procedure that depends upon the system of rules for thought inasmuch as *this system is given.*

If some given rule of connections between concepts existed, even if it were only that of the true opposed to the false, material existence would itself be given as well. "If all existence is denied, it follows from this that nothing at all is posited, nothing is given: with no matter there to be thought upon, all possibility vanishes entirely" (A 18f.). In other words, one can very well deny, in one fell swoop, both the actual and the possible without on that account falling into contradiction. It is only contradictory to maintain that the actual exists without the possible or the possible without the actual. Apodicticity results not from *what* is thought (as in Descartes), but from *the fact that* there are contents of thought arranged through necessary links. In the absence of this genus of givens, there quite simply would be no thought. "For something to be possible, but for nothing to be actual, this is a contradiction, seeing that if nothing were to exist, nothing thinkable would be given" (A 19). It should be noted that in the first citation "posited" is equivalent to "given," and that the second extends this equation to "to exist."

Kant speaks here, then, of positing (*Setzen*) as one speaks of it in Aristotelian logic, where ways of saying reflect, without thereby creating a problem, ways of being. "This thing posited" signifies, then, "this thing being the case." If I posit—if it is the case—that all human beings must die, and if moreover I suppose—if it is the case—that I am human, then something specific follows from this for me. In other words, and it is the corollary of being as simple givenness, for the precritical Kant to posit does not at all denote a subjective, thetic act; it is not at all a making, a legislating, a thesis; and it certainly is not some spontaneity in the spirit that posits. Critical *Position,* in the sense of a rule that the understanding dictates, still remains out of reach. Precritical being is simple and it is described by the equation *Setzung*

= *Gegebensein* = *Dasein*. To be "posited" is equivalent to being "given," which is equivalent to "existing."

It goes without saying that this equation of three terms changes *contents*, changes the "matter for thinking," as soon as Kant passes over the critical threshold. Prior to this crossing over, the contents are ideal entities actually conceived. Afterwards, they are sensible entities actually perceived. Before, *Dasein* as position means "being there in reason." Afterwards, it means "being there in time." Nevertheless, both before and after the crisis, being signifies *that which there is to be received*.

In order for the argument, which in this treatise establishes the existence of God, to be complete, the apodictic principle—being as position-givenness-existence, as that which there is to be received—needs to be developed in two directions. From what any given thing might be, Kant must pass on to absolute givenness; and from existence, he must pass to essence. These two moments of the proof, which distance Kant as much from Anselm as from Descartes, are not going to occupy us here. What is important in this treatise for his comprehension of being persists at the core of the transcendental method, namely, that without a givenness from which to begin, consciousness will fall into the impossible. Indeed, after the critical turn, givenness will no longer furnish us with a system of idealities. Being will be understood in the sense of a position no longer absolute, but merely relative, namely, relative to our experience. As the first trace of the other (other than categorial) meaning of being in the critical Kant, we can at least recall that being signifies givenness as such. This is also called position, owing to the influence which logic has not ceased to exercise upon ontology. The concept of "to give–to posit–to exist"—let us state it briefly, of givenness— cannot be analyzed any further. It can only be endowed with negative determinations. Each part of the *Critique of Pure Reason* contributes to such a negative determination such that givenness there proves to be precognitive, precategorial, and prepredicative. The most revealing question (and which motivated the revisions of the second edition) will concern the existing I. However, in seeking to understand how the I is given, what is to be grasped above all is how that which is, is given.

The singular, limit of doing

The critical turn now adjoins another being to being as givenness-position, namely, the category, the thesis. To understand this adjoining wherein modern pathos is excavated, it is necessary to recall, at first, the two paradoxical suppositions acknowledged at the beginning of the entire critical enterprise, suppositions Kant never justifies. Rather, in his experimentation[148] he puts these two premises directly to work. They are: (1) The object of experience is accessible to us only according to the thetic forms, originarily prescribed first by the understanding, and then by sensibility; (2) Our spontaneity is not, for all that, the origin of things which, to the contrary, must be given to us. Objective being has a double origin, not exactly within consciousness and outside of it, but rather within it to the extent that it acts in utter purity—to the extent that it legislates spontaneously—and within it, again, to the extent that it receives, that it accommodates, what is given. Indeed, sense reception mixes together a certain acting and a certain passivity. It mixes formal intuitions with the forms of intuition. Hence there is, under the label of empirical realism, an impurity, a material contamination, a limit to doing. As early as his methodological about-face toward self-consciousness, Kant both installs himself within the new arena and, with a step to the side, evades it. Installation and evasion, where being undergoes the pathetic divide between the universal that is a thesis and the singular that is given.

The critique is supposed to show that knowledge {*savoir*} and verification—the *a priori* syntheses and experience—cease to be opposed as mutually exclusive from the moment that one admits the two suppositions in question. One will note that their dualism opposes neither the subject to the object, nor even the faculty of rules to sensibility, but subjective spontaneity to a certain *passivity in receptivity* that is equally subjective. Due to this passivity, hegemony trembles. The object, which is not produced by us in its entirety, becomes knowable through the traits that we spontaneously impose upon it. It must obey the universal rules that issue from us. Nevertheless, in order for us to know it, it must be given to us in its singularity. Now, the singular as singular always resists subsumption. Thus, something eludes the rules guaranteeing true, certain, universal, necessary knowledge. Kant describes this surplus of being as the "material" of all givenness. Yet, distinctions such as form-matter are such commonplaces that once one inhabits them, one forgets to ask exactly which terrain is being occupied. If one looks more closely, this terrain turns out to be fractured. The conditions of the thought object are the conditions of the received object, but they are not those of the being singularized in givenness. It is there that the other of consciousness arises, the heterogeneous given, of which one can say, as did Luther, *"wen es trifft, den trifft's"* ("it strikes who it strikes").

To give an account of *spontaneity,* Kant elaborates a subtle system. Apperception, the source of all doing, is diversified into categories, then into the receptive activity formalized by time and space—these categories and forms are mediated in their turn by the schemata. By his own admission, however, he spent less time on *givenness:* "But in the above proof [the transcendental deduction] there is one feature from which I could not abstract, the feature, namely, that the manifold to be intuited must be *given* prior to the synthesis of the understanding and independently of it; how this takes place remains here undetermined" (B 145). Givenness remains problematic. With it, the simple footing of the subjectivist regime remains indeterminate. These problems are knotted together in affection. It is in affection that position now turns aside from givenness and that makes the regime tremble.

How is the manifold given? "That remains here indeterminate." This is again one of those cases, it seems, wherein finite reason collides with the wall that separates us from purely rational hypothetical beings endowed with intellectual intuition. Were we equipped like them, we would see directly the essence of that which is given. Accordingly, just as with the root of the two branches of consciousness that is unknown to us because it is noumenal, one is eager to conclude that, equally, givenness means noumenal givenness. Kant explicitly encourages such a reading (for example, B 306f.). Such a conclusion, nonetheless, is entirely premature. Kant's urgings in this direction have the same status as his propaedeutic to belief in opposition to doctrine. We can legitimately consider appearance as "appearance of," in which case we give in to belief and substitute ideation for finite reason. To begin with, however, we should consider appearance as "appearance to." In that case, we reflect upon what happens to us and thought allies transcendental idealism with empirical realism. To suspend belief and to reflect in this way is to turn it into cognitive propositions about *that which* appears. We can say that there are syntheses, but not what is maintained at their root (at least given the hypothesis of common rootedness, it is only a matter of belief; given our hypothesis of a radical differend, nothing can be, strictly speaking, maintained). Similarly, we can say that "it gives" {*ça donne*} but not *what* is given {*ce qui (se) donne*}. Givenness "remains here indeterminate" because the given occurs as something about which one speaks in the middle voice.

Two proofs by absurdity show this impossibility of making an entitative statement about that which gives (gives itself). If one wishes to argue that what we receive in affection is the knowable object—the phenomenon—then one pretends to know, prior to all syntheses, the manner of being of an object of which one says, in other respects, that this same manner of being is determined only by the thetic and synthetic conditions of knowledge {*connaître*}. This is a beautiful circle in which the empiricists are hellishly tormented and that renders critique useless. If, in contrast, one were to argue that in affection it is the thing, from out of its insurmountable epistemic distance, that we receive—the noumena, the supernatural essence—then one will become a speculative metaphysician before even taking a stab at the work of critique. Once again a beautiful circle that the intuitionists of every age draw around the ideation that they postulate. Critique should refrain from such metaphysics. It should pave the way to a non-intuitionist metaphysics. In both cases, one is responding to the question about what affects us by putting the cart before the horse. As a result, the transcendental ground is left in disarray under the trampling hooves that chase away common sense forever.

The natural metaphysician in us gains an advantage, however doubtful, from saying that what affects the senses is the thing such as it is. The advantage is of *resolving*, now, the paradox between position and givenness—both of which are operative in sense reception. Critique rests upon this paradox. For critique this profit is doubtful, even fatal, because in this case the origin in us abdicates its sovereignty and hands it over to an origin outside of us. This is what happens in the explication, already cited, according to which the *Ding an sich selbst*—therefore, the intelligible in principle, the noumenon—would be given. We would be affected in our sense intuition by "the-thing-in-itself (outside of the concept)."[149] Such is this triumph of the intelligible outside of us, which is as dubious as Alexander's gesture at Gordon makes it, namely, the gesture of solving by severing, which is the prerogative of authority and which constitutes it as such. Whosoever is assigned the office of consolidating the public order through recourse to some ultimate authority must postulate it as simple. He must deny multiple constraints that are knotted together. On the other hand, to endure paradox and eventually the tragic, and thus to retain the agonic condition of being—this is the task incumbent upon the philosopher (and as a consequence if he is critical, he is pathetically inept at exercising royalty).

However, the options for giving an account of affection do not stop only at noumenon and phenomenon. They bind spontaneity to receptivity, and in the latter, they bind formal positing to material subjection. Kant certainly names what affects us. As early as the first version of the Transcendental Deduction he explains that we cannot place ourselves, so to speak, outside of our representations and compare them to that from which they issue. Thus, it is left to us to describe, with a certain ignorance, what affects us as "something in general = X" (A 104). Now, the phrase casts us upon the high seas. Kant means to speak of the transcendental object. However, it is far from clear what one may understand by that.

On the one hand, it occurs to him to identify, without ceremony, the transcendental object with the thing-in-itself (A 366). Even more, there would be *some number* of transcendental objects, which is to say, objects other than those that affect us—the intelligible totalities that are God, the world, the soul. On the other hand, however, he describes the transcendental object as "a correlate of the unity of apperception" (A 250). Modeled on that unity, it results purely from our spontaneity. We adjoin it *a priori* to apperception in order to exit from self-consciousness and its thetic arena. Thus, he designates the opening through which the other of the subject can appear in the subject.

That last notion alone is evidently critical. By noumena, it is always necessary to understand the correlate of non-finite reason and by the thing-in-itself, that of non-finite understanding. The transcendental object, for its part, is correlated to such powers as those with which rational, finite beings are endowed, namely, to an understanding that, in order to know, must be allied with sensibility. The thetic gesture that posits the transcendent object opens consciousness to givenness, and it does so before those powers perform their work of synthesis. And it is here that everything gets complicated. Posited and given in reception, but how? Is it posited by us, given to us? Is the transcendental object native to consciousness or rather is it of a foreign, external source and influence? If it is native, then it seems that we will never step out of the arena of consciousness. How, then, is one to avoid solipsism? If it is foreign, how is one to avoid substantialism—it is of little importance whether that old penchant of the natural metaphysician in us persists out in the open or in concealment?

"Affection," "to be affected," implies "suffering," hence, passivity. To say that what affects us must be material is to thematize givenness only in view to the sensory apparatus. To understand the transcendental object and with it given being, it is necessary to try to delimit the acting and what is undergone in reception. Then we will be able to grasp in experience the limit where *spontaneous doing remains in discord with the singularization that is suffered.* It is an incongruous disparity that renders affection pathetic.

There is here something which affects me. In the Aesthetic, such is the point of departure for all critical reflection (*krisis,* through which we assign to each function its place in the *a priori* system). In thinking this, we are more modest than when believing; in perceiving, more modest than when forming the experience upon which to reflect; and finally, in letting ourselves be affected by the "something = X," more modest still than in perceiving. In affection, our doing is exhausted, and the regime of spontaneous consciousness is subverted. Transcendental doing consists in linking perceived appearances in accordance with rules so that "experience is possible only through the representation of a necessary connection of perceptions" (B 218). As for affection, where doing collides against the singular, it—affection—occurs on this side of such connections. Yet it is accompanied by the indistinct sensation of a modification in external sense as well as in internal sense. The diffuse consciousness of these modifications obviously does not suffice to know appearances; this simple consciousness nevertheless delivers to us its own certitude of actual reality (without the schema of actuality), namely, that something is there that has not yet fallen under our doing, nor, therefore, under spatial-temporal organization. This is an indistinct consciousness that does not yet allow us to distinguish between *pure materiality* and *singular materials*. In the "sensory manifold," the universal—the transcendental matter (B 322) for all finite consciousness—is mixed with the singular without the subject opening the space between understanding and sensibility, the space where the particular is born. In the entangling of the universal with the singular, the interstice between faculties required for subsumption does not yet appear. In this respect the transcendental object differs from phenomena. It gives them a framework wherein the incongruity that characterizes their reception is preserved. Indeed, the paradox between autogenetic spontaneity and allogenetic givenness is summed up in the materiality of the transcendental object. The two work to constitute this object—spontaneity—because we fashion for ourselves the material framework for all quantification, and givenness because what is perceived brings along its singular materials, the origin of which is not in us.[150] It is necessary to see that to speak here of "object" and of "perceived" is to speak through analogies—outside of the laws of objectification and particularization. By (actively) positing materiality as the sensible zone of our heteronomy, we let ourselves be touched (passively) by an intuited, singular material. This is an incontrovertible suffering that inserts finite reason into the world. Hence the pre-eminence that intuition has over thought. The immediacy of the singular is due to *pathein* and passivity. I know—I *constitute* experience—always through a mediated action, mediated by the transcendental object whose material conjoins active auto-affection and passive allo-affection.

Now, this suffering remains the great denial of modernity. The subject that is posited as the "possessor of the world" is pathetic, but not at all through an excess of rational enlightenment. At times, the complaint is made that modern reason overexposes phenomena to the point that they lose all their own density, as well as all mystery. According to the Kantian pathology of the modern condition,[151] such an overexposure can, to the contrary, only fail. It is only from an empirical anthropology and an empirical cosmology, thus only from a theology transmuted into morality, that Kant expects explications—enlightenment, in that sense—concerning the self, the world, and God. The Kant of *a priori* criticism recognized the suffering that renders the Enlightenment tragic, even though he denied with great vehemence that our spontaneity shatters itself upon the irrecuperable singular.

How does the denial work here? It works through the retreat into belief. To be affected, but not yet under spatial-temporal conditions—is that not to establish immediately "the objective reality of noumena"? It is thus that Kant is read, that he was and is read, and so it is thus that the torments of spontaneity are denied. If the given is noumenal, referential simplicity will be saved anew. But will the transcendental project leave it at that as well? Ever since the very first one there have been readers who have complained about Kant's point of departure for the entire critique: "*Without* this presupposition (of the noumenon), I could not enter into the *Critique,* and *with* this presupposition, I cannot remain there."[152] Kant acquiesces in advance to the first half of the objection. He denies that there has been a denial. Without the noumenon, he writes, "we should be landed in the absurd conclusion that there can be appearance without anything that appears" (B XXVI f). The force of the denial is obvious in the sleight of hand played upon appearance. From the pure event of appearing (in the infinitive sense), it is reified into that which appears (in the nominative sense). A dodge that is not, however, indispensable.

A Kant who would have held himself firmly to his critical project without this after-thought that turns the negative sense of noumenon into the positive is a Kant who would have responded to the objection by saying that without the presupposition of the *transcendental object* you cannot enter into the *Critique,* but with it you can very well remain there. . . . It goes without saying that even for the Kant who gets to eat his transcendental cake and yet have it noumenally too, sensory affection does not produce consciousness of the noumenon as such. Like simple sensation, it remains blind. It lacks the concept, which is to say, the act of grasping-together[153] the sensory manifold. No longer does the consciousness of being, implicated in affection, already achieve the formal constitution of the object. Here, *awareness of being* is shown to be irreducible precisely to the *concept of being.* Being given singularly is out of sync with being universally conceived. All that will be permitted to remain in the *Critique* without malaise or denial will be the event of givenness in its immediate occurrence, namely, the event descending from "possible givens," in the treatise of 1763, that now passes through the ordeal of turning toward legislative spontaneity. The ordeal remains incomplete in Kant. Complete, it would have had to dismiss the realism of universals in favor of their idealism, and it would have had to confine philosophy, without compromises, solely to the realism of experience. Hence the new status of matter each time Kant stops compromising about the critical project—with status here being in the *plural,* for we posit transcendental matter as the condition for undergoing singular materials.

It is necessary, then, to understand the transcendental object not as a being, but as the material clearing in which experience can be produced. It is neither noumenon, nor the thing-in-itself, nor phenomena, nor cause. Such are the negative terms through which he mires in darkness the clear light of pure apperception. And here it is stated in positive terms. The correlate of apperception is likewise one; it also must be able to accompany all experience; it also remains unknowable through want of the categorial-sensible space wherein it might appear and perform the work of subsumption; and finally, every concept is also missing from it, and not on account of some supernatural essence, but because it precedes categorization, and hence particularization. We may note this motif of uncognizability, namely, that the transcendental object lacks strict objectivity resulting from a synthesis. This motif is much stronger than the enlightened belief on behalf of which Kant performs his dance of seven veils around the noumenon. It is also the motif on account of which Kant can describe the process of *givenness* as *position;* the singular sensory material does not reach us (could not be given) were it not for an anticipation (from a position) of universal materiality. Givenness and position do not concern two matters, but two ways of considering the material constitution of the world. The two ways are distinguished as spontaneity and passivity—suffering—in receiving the world. Posited spontaneously, materiality is common to all sensations. It is transcendental matter. As for the singular material, it is suffered passively, able to be dated and located in its occurrence. One may see therein the distinction, however transcendentalized, between prime matter and secondary matter. *Materia prima* becomes, then, the one object, but without objectivity—pure, non-extended material—such that we posit it in advance of every synthesis, when we are gripped by a singular material intuitively given.

If this is so, then we see that it is denial that is speaking in the either-or between empirical affection and noumenal affection. Skirting around the terrain that one is supposed to harrow—that of transcendental conditions as legislative functions—is the Kantian version of tragic denial.

There is an ambiguity in the status of what affects us that accompanies the critique from its earliest steps. The Transcendental Aesthetic, states Kant, "already of itself establishes the objective reality of noumena" (A 249). Now, what sort of gaze would be necessary to be able to penetrate the immediacy of sensations so that this immediacy would furnish the noumenal reality? It would require an abundantly perspicacious gaze, the very sort that Kant calls belief. To the extent that all experience is necessarily experience *of* something, we are in principle to believe that the noumenon appears in appearance; we are to believe that that from which we form *a posteriori* syntheses for our knowledge possesses in itself, even though beyond our grasp, a core of intelligibility. In analyzing the simple material encounter, however, nothing authorizes a parallel piercing through of appearances. On the contrary, one discovers here the liminal occurrence of the pathos that characterizes receptivity. To receive the given, as we have seen, the subject must make itself active in positing the transcendental matter and passive in suffering, through it, such singular material. Taking the side for the whole, Kant gathers the asymmetrical duality under the label *Setzung* and distinguishes it as a whole from the *Position* "in relation to our concept" (*CJ* 336), hence from the categorial.[154]

We see Kant dodge the transcendental terrain when, in the second edition of the text, he adds in regard to position the parenthesis "(outside of the concept)." Objects are supposed to emerge *desubstantialized* from the liminality between posited matter and given matter. Well, this is the entire problem. To say that there is givenness is something quite different (less so from the substantialist point of view; more so from the transcendental) from saying that sensation establishes the objective reality of noumena outside of the concept. There is givenness, "so" the noumenal causes sensation—such a "so" always plunges us anew into transcendental illusion.

Elsewhere, in regard to internal givenness, Kant is equally peremptory, but this time in the opposite direction. It is regarding internal givenness that the second edition accomplishes the decisive step toward incongruous being. In pure apperception (overdetermined still more so than its corollary, the transcendental object), "I am conscious of myself, not as I appear to myself, *nor as I am in myself,* but only that I am" (B 157 emphasis added). Here there is more than a reference to the core of intelligibility in the given. The either-or between appearance and the in-itself is revoked. There is a *tertium dator* between phenomenal and noumenal being. An indistinct consciousness of being no longer points us to the exterior sensory given, but to the subject and its own materials, "my representation."

The "thought of something in general = X" is systematically operative, if not put into words, as early as the Aesthetic. The materiality to which it makes an appeal permits ontological givenness to be described negatively as precognitive. The doctrinal concept of being thereby is enfeebled under the heteronomy and passivity that the singular inflicts upon us. The singular reaches us not only from outside of consciousness. "I, the possessor of the world"—that is what expropriates me first of all from within. Thus tragic denial takes its specifically modern form: pathos.

The singular in consciousness

In the Analytic of Concepts, this same non-doctrinal comprehension of being is sharpened—or rendered still more enigmatic—with regard to the source of all spontaneity, namely, the I-think. "The 'I think' expresses the act of determining my existence" (B 158n).

Kant moves from the "I think" to the "I am." This is one of the most difficult problems of the system. Hesitations, which are not fortuitous and that hinder Kant from placing himself squarely on critical terrain, are mixed with the refutation of dogmatic idealism. The explication of consciousness that I have of myself must be reconstructed, so obscure are the connections. Thus in the cited phrase, if it is not the categorial, then which act? If it is neither noumenal nor phenomenal, then which I-am? And if it does not denote the modality, then which existence?

To anticipate the reconstruction, the I-am turns out to be the content of a consciousness that synthesizes pure apperception with the material given in internal sense. Now, here is where everything goes awry. Such a consciousness will remain necessarily indeterminate, since—and this is the core of the problem—it passes over the determining functions which are the categories; the I-am will then escape the concept, and the syntheses, judgments; the I-think will do more than accompany, it will determine the mental material as mine, without, for all that, producing knowledge; and finally, this material of internal sense will never accede to experience, properly speaking. Why such tiptoeing around? The answer is not far off. Perhaps here it is a matter, more than ever, of avoiding torments.

Let us begin with the fluctuations in Kant when it comes to situating these elements in the subjective apparatus. The singular given within is our thoughts that come and go, a coming-and-going that marks out in us the limit of acting and suffering. Kant situates the consciousness of the mental manifold sometimes in the understanding (B 419), and at other times in internal sense (B 68). This may be the height of confusion, but it is a *hapax legomenon* in the *Critique*. Even though it is pure, apperception is supposed to furnish consciousness with "acts and inner determinations" (B 574). The indistinctness about the place where the singular is given makes it almost impossible to demarcate pure apperception in relation to empirical apperception, and then in relation to internal sense. Even worse, elsewhere he counts both apperception and internal sense amongst the "sources of knowledge" and declares that both are employed both transcendentally and empirically (A 115). There is a pernicious ubiquity of the mental manifold, and hence of the singular suffered, within the subjective apparatus. It is practically everywhere. Might this be because, in the I-am, doing essentially collides against a suffering, namely, against a sensibility with regard to the given?

As for the internal material, the line between doing and suffering is, in every case, more unstable and shifting than for the external. In contrast, Kant clearly describes activity and passivity; whatever the faculty may be in which it occurs, we have "consciousness of what we *suffer* to the extent that we are affected by the play of our thoughts." No one escapes the assault of his own cognitions. They arise, a perpetual cinema. Like the external senses, internal sense suffers whatever happens to it. Hence—such, at least, as the systems allows it—it is distinguished from pure apperception, "the consciousness of what we *constitute*."[155] The topography is clear, then, in that it opposes the passive part in empirical consciousness to transcendental consciousness, which is entirely active. As pure spontaneity, this consciousness remains sheltered from assault. Only this is not how it goes for the elementary consciousness telling me *that I am* (hence the necessity of an analysis according to the understanding of being, rather than according to the constitution of experience). Which act, then, determines my act prior to all categorial intervention? It is, as we have seen, the source of all acts: pure apperception. To act always means to limit a material. Furthermore, the work of this entirely spontaneous act consists in limiting the thoughts which come and go. Now, by analogy with the extrinsic manifold, one could say even prior to all temporalization and categorization that this work modifies an undifferentiated "matter." This is the work of pure singularization exercising itself upon the transcendental subject, comparable to what is exercised upon the materiality of the transcendental object. *A priori* self-consciousness prepares a noematic milieu for thoughts to occur, a milieu which is again analogous to prime matter. A passivity is thereby introduced into the hegemonic referent, which accords poorly with the modern prestige of making and of doing—an originary passivity which, if its necessity is confirmed, would be inflicted upon modernity like an ontological evil. It would corrupt the ultimate fantasm that is instituted as pure spontaneity. Ontological suffering must therefore be denied.

Instituting itself so as to take possession of the world, self-consciousness can only suffer anguish since it must submit to, suffer, an external and internal plethora. Hence the strategies of evasion in Kant, to declare the noumenon the other which touches me, or to squelch it under the thetic regime.

Here is the denial at work. In philosophy, the needs of an ultimate authority always require it to establish that being is one. Well, in Kant, more interested than any other in securing the source of laws, this unity must be made by us; henceforth, being will be thesis. We "posit [*setzen*] those representations in time" (B 67); this compact formula unites positing with its other: givenness. There is denial here because through his *thesis that being is thesis* Kant censures givenness, assault, afflux, suffering, sensibility, and passivity.[156] And there is the disavowal of denial, because Kant calls all heteronomous traces in us pathological. In its less compressed form, the formula would say that we posit the universal duration in which the mental singular, not yet temporalized, is given. Whatever the topographical shift might be, the frontier between activity and passivity therefore traverses the reception of the mental manifold. In this, it is strictly parallel to the fault line in extrinsic reception. To receive, as one recalls, is to posit (actively) the transcendental condition for letting oneself be touched (passively) by an intuited singular. Auto-affection conjoins these disparates: universal, noematic matter and a fleeting, singular material. It places the I-am under the double bind of legislation and givenness. Legislation means, then, that in order to receive the manifold, the I-think makes itself the "transcendental subject of thoughts = X" (A 346). And givenness means that representations happen to me.

These—singulars and the heteronomous—representations occur less through their genesis in external sensation—less through *repraesentare* in the strict sense—than through an assault. The place of cleavage at the heart of that spontaneity where doing collides with the other of all spontaneity is *the awareness that I am*. Something is there in the occurrence that assails me, my being. In suffering the precategorial assault of being, it is impossible to distinguish between me and what happens to me. Hence the indistinct consciousness of my existence. Hence also the shattering of spontaneity.

As is customary, when it is a question of the transcendental status proper to the heteronomous singular, the clarity of Kantian distinctions instead becomes the exception. Moreover, in the domain of the mental singular, Kant tends more than ever to blur the empirical and the transcendent, thereby once again evading the transcendental. Might this incoherence be attributed to a drafting process notorious for its rapidity?[157] The evasion, from which all the difficulties follow, is too systematic for that. One can witness here a gesture of censure—*the* stroke of censure that Kant draws across the architectonic canvas that, nevertheless, he himself puts in place. Indeed, more visibly than ever, he recoils in the face of the evidence of a conflictual, transcendental condition of being.

Thus, in regard to "my existence," does he not describe the I of metaphysical psychology—the transcendent I—as the substrate of all empirical judgment?[158] This is in complete disagreement with his theory of judgment. Critical discourse does not equip us, nor can it, with predicates that single out some property of an intelligible substrate existing on its own. Thoughts would be of such properties and within internal experience, they would modify this transcendent I. One sees the absurdity that follows from this, namely, that I delimit my noumenal identity through empirical predicates. This is a delimitation that would deliver the unknowable essence over to internal observation. That alliance of the transcendent and empirical concerning "my existence" is, consequently, a dead end.

Within being it is a question here of what is proper to an appropriation. As we have seen, we posit the representational materials of internal sense in the mind. This is a position parallel (if one leaves the provenance of representations to the side) to that of external sense. Yet in mental givenness, doing is associated with a sensibility and—as strange as it may seem in speaking of "my" thoughts—with a heteronomy, which is to say that sensibility and heteronomy are both the transcendentals. This is because, following the example of the external manifold, these thoughts that occur are anonymous and disarm me. Within the formal framework of the transcendental subject, these thoughts are brought about in an event, as in the middle voice, distancing the voice and its effects from the imperative I-think, from the transitive I-speak, in short, from the spontaneity legislating the world. A singularizing sensibility inflicts expropriation and havoc upon the strategy of appropriation and of the proper. Hence the torments in spontaneous consciousness.

The only pure consciousness would be the I-am, if it weren't for such heteronomous, impure, fleeting mental material: "The sensation which appertains to sensibility serves as the base for that existential proposition." What sensation? "An *indeterminate empirical* intuition" (B 422n; emphasis added). Pure apperception stabilizes the shifting scene of mental representations, but not through a category. The possessor of the world encounters the intra-mental limit of doing, the limit of its sovereignty. With *pathein* thus introduced into hegemonic consciousness, Kant *must* avoid the transcendental terrain. If not, then that would be the end of the referent making the law into an ultimate authority. Kant must treat being, which is not simple, as a simple thesis. Being is disparate, not as sensible multiplicity is, but as the hybrid universal-singular is, namely, as a cross between posited transcendental matter and given sense materials. Their originary admixture, which is not a composition, confounds the nomothetic maximization of emancipated doing.

The entire Kantian gnoseology, it is true, rests upon the hybrid since experience is defined through the synthesis of the intuited with the *a priori* functions. Here, however, something else is at issue. In the indeterminate intuition of being, the understanding lacks its rules of operation. One must bear in mind this hybrid of auto-affection, namely, the I-think, expressing the act which determines the mental assault undergone and, thereby, my indeterminate existence. Auto-affection is hybrid because the I-think is diversified into categories; "my existence," however, cannot mean the phenomenal object that is constituted and that singles out the category of existence—any more than in regard to the external sense manifold, the consciousness of being has as its content completed experience. "My existence" can be given neither in an intellectual intuition, nor—since the I-think determines it—to formal consciousness. The existing I will be neither noumenal nor logical. No longer will it be the synthesized empirical I, the observation of which—the experience of the self—would require that intuition, effectuated through internal sense, be conjoined to a pure concept of the understanding. Those elements which constitute phenomenality remain excluded from auto-affection. Auto-affection gives me only a confused consciousness that I am. Obviously we are far—as far as transcendental idealism is from material idealism (B 274)—from the clear intuition of "I think–I am." Rather, the thinking subject is included in what is given. Accordingly, Kant adds these words, entirely fitting, however cryptic, which indicate the other being, the being suffered: "existence here is still not a category" (B 467f). An enigmatic remark because it murmurs the suggestion that Kant opposes a sensible intuition of existence to the Cartesian intuition, *cogitans sum*. Is this not to go against the axiom according to which being is not a real predicate and that, consequently, it gives nothing to be grasped in intuition? Not at all. The being which is the object of an indeterminate, empirical intuition does not contravene that axiom. Kant says that, as pure sensation, existence precedes all experience and therefore all synthesis. Besides idealism, that suffices to exclude, if need be, substantialism and hence any sensible intuition of being. This denial itself also is excluded. Indeed, the neo-Aristotelian murmur about being (which "would fall" afresh into the senses) would in effect silence the conflict.

At the end of these eliminations, there remains a single candidate for the title of "what exists": the "it moves" which I experience (but which I do not observe) as *my own* within my mental life. It is something in general; not a universal, but an occurrence of singular givens retained in their occurrence, not as singulars. There is something there of the tragic and of the enigmatic, too. Of the tragic because the law of what is proper to me finds itself here subverted by the "it" that happens to me and therefore by an alienating counter-law of which I am not master. Of the enigmatic because the critical vulgate requires that the categorial doctrine exhaust the transcendental problem of being. Consequently, in internal intuition one is no longer dealing with that doctrinal concept which would have self-consciousness rule, simply. Rather, one is dealing with a gnoseological arrangement of the differend between appropriation and expropriation. The indistinct presence of my mental life to my consciousness opposes a counterpoint of ignorance to the highest level of knowledge. In the face of the subject making the law—in the face of the law—the occurring plurality appears outside of the laws of appearance, contravening them.

In an effort to neutralize the differend which he recognizes and which he denies, Kant does not permit himself to fall again into the Cartesian illusion and to move from function to beings. Yet he maintains a givenness of being in apperceptive unity, which seems more than a simple "focal point." The I-think functions as a proposition about existence independently of every recourse to modalities; independently of the category of existence. Kant justifies that strange synthesis while describing the existing I as given in an indeterminate way and, nevertheless, impossible to reify into a thing thought (B 423n). More than a focal point, less than a thing—how are we to understand this? To see this clearly, let us finally ask, about the singular in consciousness: What determination? What indetermination?

Is the determination (*Bestimmtheit,* the being-determined) of the I-think, through simple auto-position, able to prescribe what ought to be? If primary spontaneity is determined, it obviously will not be so, through the rules of the understanding. The source of all determinations, in its turn, will not be able to be determined categorially. It is pure determination and, on that account, pure sovereignty—it is the origin of every law and of every order. Nevertheless, if its nature is that it "determines my existence," then the I-think will have to be adjoined to an indeterminate givenness as equi-originary. The I-am *singularizes* the I-think, the universal legislator. Such is the disparity that Kant seeks to grasp, in the second edition, through the revisions concerning being. The existing I designates the as-yet indistinct presence of an indeterminate sensation to thought. Being only their proto-synthesis, this presence remains deprived of conceptual articulation. This is only the case because the I of apperception, the non-empirical subject of every empirical judgment, is not, so to speak, alone. There is already an other at the origin. By virtue of the I-am and consequently by virtue of singularization, the I-think is lacking in normative simplicity which, in Kant, is expressed by the mute surfeit of representations.

Kant notes that the new logic calls for a new ontology where "existence is not yet a category," but he scarcely thematizes the precategorial sensation of existence upon which, nevertheless (and according to his own words), the consciousness that I have of being rests. Accordingly, this ontology would require an indirect conceptual apparatus for keeping hold of the singular, an apparatus that remains beyond the reach of the theticism of the autonomous subject. Be that as it may, if in givenness existence is not yet a category, and if givenness signifies singularization, then categorial ontology is only half of the critical discourse about being. Kant sketches out the other half when he attempts to treat what is the singular in that event that is the representational upsurge. Two incongruous halves—categorial being and other being—a pathetic double bind.

With a sensation of existence being produced on this side of the understanding, we see how far we are from Descartes. Kant conjoins consciousness, the place of the pure I-think, to the I-am, which is not pure since its material is offered to internal sense. The givenness of the indeterminate "real thing," "designated as such in the proposition 'I think'," happens prior to every act of experience and every synthesis (B 423n). We are far from Descartes, for the I-think differs conflictually from the I-am, just as apperception differs from the *a priori* sensibility where I belong to the sense manifold, and just as the universal law differs from the law of the singular. The event of givenness that thought serves fractures the unity of the *cogitans sum* into a transcendental differend.

Time turned against itself

The categories, which are the tools of subsumption, have no grip on this differend. It follows that auto-presence is *scarcely*[159]—with sensibility and sufferance—in a position to guarantee the ultimate normative referent. In order for the I-think to succeed in linking[160] nature and, eventually, praxis in conformity with an imperative ontology, it must be able to assure the subject full possession first of itself and then of the world. But the differential other, which it necessarily must suffer, is precisely what intervenes in possession. Since this other brings with it its own law—givenness—it can inscribe itself only as the differend with the spontaneity that posits the subject and opposes the object.

We see how the question of being, addressed to the spontaneity of the I-think which is the grand conquest of the Enlightenment, reveals the same pathetic condition the question of freedom revealed. At what point are we touched by that suffering? If, at the highest point of our mind, the self and the ego corrupt the simplicity of originary freedom, and if, in its subsumptive work, the positing of being collides with the givenness suffered, then what is the consequence for the "unknown root" of this mind (B 29)? The twisted trunk of a tree can only indicate a root equally twisted.

Let us look again briefly at official, transcendental ontology. For the highest point of our mind to be able, singly, to put us in possession of the world, the tree, at the apperceptive summit and at the unknown root, must *put into place* all that is in us and around us. The root in regard to which one has interrogated so much must symbolize existence as pure presence of the self to itself. If such an auto-possession could be established, then the proximity of the representing subject to its representations would have to be understood in the strongest sense, namely, as the possession of the world, which is to say, as the joy of phenomena being constituted through our own normative activity. Thus we saw above that only functions and their transcendental logic, and not beings and their logic of things, can assure presence and proximity and therefore the perfect pleasure of possession.

Now, in regard to the root that ought to guarantee all this, Kant once again undoes the regime of appropriative activity.

If he wanted—and since he needed—to argue for full and permanent presence, then to whom or what would the title rights belong? In Kant, the unknown is in principle not mysterious. It is always the noumenon. Kant speaks clearly when he declares that the root of our powers is unknown. He means that the two transcendental branches of the mind emerge from a common transcendent root.[161] To read this root as symbolizing being as presence would be in accord with the voyager between two worlds that Kant often is; he would like this a great deal. We have seen him too often surveying the border of the metaphysical thicket that abuts the plains where everything functions to make the parturition of metaphysical-empirical monsters still astounding.[162] But, in the very name of the new hegemony, the reader must, for his part, know what he is doing when he warrants these excursions outside of the transcendental ground that Kant nevertheless conquered. If one intends to follow the Kantian impulse toward the *Grund* without, however, betraying diacritical sobriety, then the demythologized rootedness would be the poetic presence—not noumenal, but functional—of the I-think to itself and, consequently, to the empirical given that is linked to it. The two branch activities of the mind would emerge from a making, *poiein,* which would render me present to myself as well as to the manifold given. They would authorize me to possess the world.

Now, can thetic being guarantee possession by means of the functions of a making that is centered in this way? The positing and givenness which work on it certainly are functions; however, worked on diversely in this way, the initial making *is not simple*. Hence, the difference between the I-think and I-am is not resolved into a normativity, but is dramatized in a differend. The reasons for this are the disparate tractions that turn the I-am against itself, namely, the ultimate pulls of universalization and singularization. Their divergence, which a phenomenology of ultimates would describe by natality-mortality, can only repudiate particularization, the sole constituent of phenomenality. As a result, the root found at the edge of the thicket proves fragile and poetic presence "scarcely" a presence. Rootedness takes place only painfully. It almost does not succeed. And it renders us liable to that pain one has in making excursions onto the metaphysical ground, which consist in losing phenomenality. It suffices to consider how presence to the self becomes determined presence in order to see the subject broken in its auto-possession. And he who does not possess himself will never possess the other of himself. And so we have here the one who will oblige us to rethink rootedness.

In order for the existent subject to take full possession of himself, in order for it to be close to itself without any gap, and hence nomothetic—for this to be the case, it would be necessary that it be determined completely (*durchgängig*). But such will never be the case. The indeterminate presence of the I-am precedes not only knowledge, but even thought and apperception. If it were otherwise, the I-think would no longer determine existence, which however it is said to do. The nomothetic act from which both theoretical and practical rules derive is the auto-institution of the I-think as a differential function acting upon the I-am. We ought to "regard ourselves as *legislating* completely *a priori* in regard to our *existence,* and as even determining that existence . . ." (B 430). It is a determination which, in consequence of the categorial eclipse, can only fail at its task, which is subsumption. This is exactly why presence to the self remains indeterminate. Thus my sensed and as yet unarticulated existence precedes awareness (apperception) even more so than introspection (experience). *Being as indeterminate givenness precedes being as thesis.* It precedes the category provided with a schema. On one side, there is the determining I-think positing and deploying itself in twelve rules of appropriation, and on the other, "my existence" receiving a determination not its own {*impropre*}, in short, that is expropriative. The second concept of being in Kant opens a zone of singularization in the universally legislative subject. Indeterminate existence, given transcendentally to internal sensation, opposes to apperception a counterpoint of ignorance as the highest point of consciousness. This givenness tears apart critical ontology. It opposes a counter-law of indistinction to the originary law, which for the self consists in saying distinctly "I bind" and therefore "I think."

So it is that the subject posits "entirely *a priori*" the I-think as the origin of all possible laws, and thus that the I-am opposes to it, from within, a sensibility that destroys auto-presence, *the subject subjugating itself* to itself. This is the pathos of autonomy, which precedes the imperatives for subordinating and humiliating the ego under the moral law. Without this double strategy—the I-think emerging from indeterminate presence and, due to sensibility-passivity, scarcely determining it—there would be neither legislation nor law. But with it, the law loses its simplicity, its respectability.

Respect sinks away in an enforced silence. To obtain a semblance of complete determination, it is necessary to suppress the *pathein* that rebels against subsumption, and to enunciate only the *setzen*. This is a rebellion and an act of denial that will succeed only on the condition of maximizing theticism into pure, subjective spontaneity. Thus heteronomy is obliterated and the nomothesis is won. But (what follows from this question will not be pursued for heuristic morality) how is one to respect laws derived from the arch-violent gesture that is always tragic denial?

What follows is sufficiently troubling, even without being regarded morally. To elevate denial and to avow that we suffer the singular *a priori* is to go against the law from within. This counter-law, the indeterminateness of being that is suffered singularly, is the condition of impossibility in epochal sovereignty. It co-constitutes—and hence destitutes beforehand—every law, rule, and norm. Indeed, from whence does the transcendental legislator draw its power of legislating? From the me that I am, the subject subjugated to the self that legislates.

Yet one can say still more about the transcendental difference as differend. And we should, at least, if the foundations demand to be retraced back to the point of their phenomenological emergence. The analysis of the existing me has shown that indeterminate givenness and auto-determination constitute two equally incontrovertible moments of being, and that therefore the emancipated subject suffers a rupture, and the Kantian doctrine of being as category suffers a subversion.

The phenomenological reasons for the originary breach and displacement are not difficult to inventory. Once again, they concern the moment of passivity toward our singularization. We have recognized therein the counter-strategy of dispossession that unsettles from within the subjectivist strategies for possessing the world. Passivity, systematically necessary in the hegemonic institution, exposes the autonomous subject to heteronomy, not empirically or anthropologically, but in its transcendental constitution. The expropriation in appropriation shatters immediately, and from inside, the regime that self-consciousness exercises. It contaminates the ultimate referent with an irremediable pathology. What is this suffering? There is only one originary phenomenon, but it is not a phenomenon properly speaking, which always and in everything works on us through expropriation and singularization; which inflicts upon us a passivity without issue and renders us sensitive at the very heart of aprioric "making"; and which places us at the mercy of that upon which no "making" or "doing" ever will take hold: death.

Whence the ravages—the outbursts of which we will see later on in Heidegger—that plunge hegemonic consciousness into its torments.

Since Vico (but already in latency since the *Physics* and *Politics* of Aristotle), the prestige of making and of acting has not ceased to increase. It is because *poiein* and *prattein* can be conceived, whereas the radical *pathein/paschein*—the origin of suffering—denies the concept. This is another reason, phenomenologically stronger than noumenal belief, for speaking of the "unknown" root of our faculties. These faculties delve deep into something unconceivable, not crypto-essentialist, but terribly close to us in having to do with our singularity. They delve deep into the everydayness that Heidegger described as weakened by *Entzug,* the "withdrawal," the "undertow." This pull, drawing too close for it to be conceived, is mortality. Philosophers are not exactly eager to examine, analyze, discuss, interpret, prove, or refute it, as they are wont to do with the effects of natality, effects among which doing and acting occupy, precisely, the first rank.

With the sole exception of Luther. However, for him, expropriation is what saves. In the *simul iustus et peccator,* in the differend between the self and the ego, passivity is attached to a strategy of restitution. It draws us toward the fully present justification. Following the Pauline he-who-loses-wins, singularization and mortality signify salvation. All subjective doing, on the other hand, originates from our tendency to set ourselves up as the dispensers of justice to ourselves. What draws us toward destruction is the initiative in us, on the strength of which we always begin. The ego that condemns us is *posited* by us; extrinsically, but nonetheless at the heart of consciousness, the self which saves was *given* to us. In Kant, these relations are inverted. The self—the principle of initiative, of integrity, and of possession which acts and conveys that which is (being, which is subsumptive because categorial)—is posited by us; what is given to us is the ego, which also reaches into the heart of consciousness, but as a principle of disintegration and dispossession that exposes us to what is other than us (being, which is suffering because singular). In Luther, the complex of heteronomy, passivity, givenness, the non-native, the inconceivable allogene, and the singular, lead to the triumph *over* death. In Kant, this complex gives the victory to death. Or rather, it ramifies and circulates death throughout the two stems as well as their branches. It constitutes us as mortals without appeal; at least without transcendental appeal.

This is because the primitive presence to self knots the universal to the singular in such a way that it disrupts the quest for a full, subjective auto-possession. The foundation, or the essence[163] of the subject is fissured. Shot through with indetermination, the thesis of the self will come up against a nomothesis just as fissured by the transgressive strategy.

This is why the rootedness of the stems can no longer be imagined as simple. In place of a taproot holding the faculties together with a view to possessing the world, we have instead a fascicled root, dividing itself into more than one strand. Twisted, split, it follows the ultimates of experience, which are natality and mortality.

Whereby it turns time against itself.

Indeed, if the non-subsumable other touches us through singularization and hence through being-for-death, then the complex of subsumptions—judgments, syntheses, imperatives, all that in Kant works to unify—proceeds from that ultimate which is natality. By leaving noumenal belief to its articles of censure and of violence and therefore confining ourselves only to a transcendental critique, the root of our *Gemüt* runs aground upon the philosophical labor of reducing to one the conflictual dyad between being posited and being given. It miscarries there because the duality is a disparity that does not allow a generic noun ("being" is neither a noun nor a genus) to be hung over it, and because the time that pulls toward death is other than what carries us along from birth. The time of death exposes me to the singularizing assault; through the time of natality, I posit subsumptive universals. How could such an agony, which exposes me even while I am positing, install me as the possessor of the world? How could a freedom thus turned agonally, temporally against itself emanate from a regime of simply normative being?

More profoundly than the ancients, perhaps, the moderns seem to have always known that under the law something is hidden that isn't pretty. Machiavelli and Hobbes trusted the echo of what happens to the law when it is anchored in the solitary subject: it becomes savage, not respectable. The transcendental critique took it upon itself to rehabilitate the law. But it must pay the price of rendering wild the very ground—being as spontaneity—into which emancipated self-consciousness puts down its roots.[164] The undersides of the law are not unknown to us. Knowledge of them comes to us with the phenomenological ultimates, with being-for-death in a struggle against being-for-birth. It is a knowledge that confirms modern autonomy as essentially tragic because pathetically divided in its freedom and in its being.

In each of us there is the natural metaphysician whose purpose is to bring such an originary wildness to order. Philosophy hearkens to this hope. Since our means of dominating otherness {*l'autre*} and the other {*l'autrui*} have increased beyond the bounds of any dream in the Enlightenment, philosophy devotes itself with increasing ardor to theories of action and of pragmatism wherein the practical I no longer feels itself exposed to anything at all. What impresses us, as moderns, and that from whence proceed both the natural metaphysician and the philosophers, its delegates, is our efficiency. We perceive in it no limits. "The tragic" crosses our lips at the very most as a literary theme, or it accompanies a shrug of the shoulders in the face of a misfortune. The man who legislates for nature ought to possess himself fully. He has a hand in the world, but he does not feel himself to be in the hands of anything. When one posits spontaneity in the ultimate authority, the authority which remains empty is the one that causes suffering. "The tragic" serves as a formula, then, for covering this emptiness. The transcendental critique recognizes the other that places us at its mercy, but it denies it as soon as it recognizes it. Now, have all of the conditions of possibility been stated once the traits of action have been inventoried, namely, the traits that are communicable, functional, interactive, reifying, instrumental. . . ? These are so many phenomena for which philosophy never ceases to raise, in a thousand ways, the normative question. Just as numerous, however, are the phenomena upon which we have no grasp at all: the finite world in which we are placed, all that about which we say "it happens" and which reduces us to passivity. In German, an event that suddenly occurs and puts us at its mercy is called a *Widerfahrnis*.[165] That is rarely encountered in a pure state. A war has its causes in those who unleash it; the climatic change, amongst others, in the leaders who clamor for yet "more studies!" even though the planet already advances, tranquilly, toward asphyxia. Acting and suffering are intertwined in what happens to us. But what is the ultimate condition of sensibility? How is it adjoined to the conditions of possibility through which, since Kant, one understands the condition of activity? It is in a differend that sensibility and possibility respond to the ancient question: What is being?

Hence, Kant seems to have seen. And then he seems to have denied what he saw. Witness the agonies that result from transcendental idealism, whose system opens us to the other of our spontaneity as it submits thought to singular givenness, and then to sensibility. In this way spontaneity enters into a pathetic discord with itself. The time of being turns singularization against universalization and it does so radically, at the root.

Recanting the denial

Kant could not help but deny the tragic because it is a matter of a suffering at the root of the legislative subject. And yet, he himself did the spadework on the ground in the transcendental geography into which this root plunges, the terrain where singulars can show themselves without being transformed into particular cases of a common posit. This occurs in the Transcendental Dialectic and then in the third *Critique*. Does Kant then recant the denial of the radical, normative double bind?

Pathetic theticism can be seen quite clearly in the Transcendental Dialectic. There

Kant repeats the formula of the non-doctrinal concept of being, a formula taken up from the precritical writings: "'*Being*' is obviously not a real predicate" (B 626). "Real" no more designates here the first category of quality than "being" designates the second category of modality. Empirically, we know what a thing is when we join, to the logical subject that singles out substance, the predicates that single out its properties. To formulate such judgments about the supreme being and to establish some "ontological proof," we must know *a priori* the realities (in the plural) of that being, which is to say, its thinkable properties. If that were possible, these properties—which the Scholastics called perfections—would permit a complete determination of that being. Its concept would be realized, then, as an "entire concept of all reality," even better, of all realities. Now, from the moment that the categories (of the understanding) do not, by definition, have a place in the dialectic (of reason), and the criterion of actuality remains sense givenness, "being" can no longer be counted amongst the *a priori* predicates. *Sein* differs from categorial *Dasein* (or from *Existenz*) in that it does not at all allow itself to be attached *a priori* to any concept,[166] neither formally, like all of the categories, nor materially, as perfection. To refute the ontological proof of the existence of God, it suffices, then, for Kant to take up again his precritical equation between being and position. In the critical context, being-posited (*Gesetztsein*) signifies that sensibility is affected by some given. We have seen that "position" emphasizes the act of making in the receiving, which is to say in "givenness." Affection accedes to language through the copula. Under its critical form, the equation then amounts to expressing the equivocal, the inadequate, the non-equivalent—literally, the inequity between being as category and being as precognitive, precategorial, prepredicative singular givenness.

Apart from the sporadic assertions of the second edition of the *Critique of Pure Reason,* the givenness of the singular is only implied within the doctrinal meaning of being, for it is recognized only through the intensity of the denial, of the suppression, of the censure, of the endlessly striving theticism of triumphant, spontaneous autonomy. On the other hand, and in keeping with the presentiment that Hannah Arendt had[167] in the *Critique of the Faculty of Judgment,* Kant prepared himself to retain explicitly the singular. Contrary to being that is knowable because it is categorial and predicative, and contrary, therefore, to phenomenal being, the being of the singular becomes the very issue of that faculty (for example, *CJ,* A 346). Does Kant henceforth recant the denial through which he strikes at transcendental sensibility and hence singularization? His itinerary in that regard begins with the precritical declaration that being is not a predicate at all. Then he specifies that it is not a "real" predicate, but only the being-given that marks out the copula. Finally (prior to the posthumous work where being will be an *idea* made by us), he clearly lays out, though only in passing, the disparate strategies of universalization and singularization. This is why the distinction between categorial thesis and extra-categorial givenness was able to serve as a guy wire for us in reading the first *Critique* in terms of the third.

Thesis indicates here the capacity that the mind has for representing to itself some phenomenon, for gaining access to it. It is not necessary, then, to mix the sense of *Position* here, as I have said, with the sense that the word has in the *Critique of*

Pure Reason, where it refers only to givenness. The *Position* of one hundred thalers is to have them in the pocket (B 627). In contrast, in the third *Critique* such an extra-mental actuality is called *Setzung.* "The actual . . . signifies the *Setzung* of a thing in itself (outside of the concept)" (*CJ* B 340). *Position* emphasizes, then, the relation of a conceived representation to the understanding, and hence, the possible; *Setzung* emphasizes the relation to sensibility of the material one suffers, and hence the actual. Thus the singular is recognized in its contingency and randomness (in this case, the random chance of "falling upon" a being organized in a teleological way, which is to say, upon a living organism). The fault line, as we have also seen, traverses receptivity. It splits it into making and suffering. The reflective judgments, as well as the distinction between activity and passivity in reception, offer the framework for rehabilitating the singular in its being-given. Even more than making, suffering invests givenness with a properly transcendental status.

As always when it is a matter of differences and oppositions, it is necessary to guard against the pitfalls to which our languages, slackened by the grand plays and the great antithetic battles, are disposed. Indeed, the double bind of *Position* and *Setzung* gives the point of departure to the great Kantian bifurcations—understanding-sensibility, inside-outside, subject-object, being-duty, thinking-knowing, spontaneity-receptivity, activity-passivity. . . . The double bind forces these disjunctions, but opposes non-disjunctive terms to itself. It does not disjoin a genus. No commonness, no *koinon,* between being posited and being given. The architectonic imagery, with its adjacencies and partitions, serves here no better than does the botanical imagery with its forkings and branchings. This is because the double bind does not establish any correspondence, which is why it foils the ontology of the adequate response, of responsibility through adequation, and of the reciprocity between stems. What is witnessed therein is that *Position,* the immediate act of the self, is simple. It is the thesis of a possible. However, simplicity is lacking in *Setzung,* which is the mediate act of the self to which the extrinsic suffered is intermixed. Simplicity remains irrecuperable for theticism. Sovereign, spontaneous consciousness is imposed through particularizing subsumptions in which it posits and opposes. However, if "being" means "being-given," then this sovereignty proves to be a delusion. It has to suffer the other. Spontaneity shatters upon the extra-thetic. In order to recant the pathogenic denial, it would be necessary for Kant to pursue most resolutely the *alterity which he sees* when he declares that the transcendental subject is assembled from "two entirely heterogeneous pieces" (*CJ* A 336). The assemblage is made through collocations and dislocations, according to whether I retain the given as a particular or as a singular. The given "is" both of these, though precisely as a heterogeneous being. The disparate normativity that it would be necessary to recognize and to love in order to recant the tragic denial, boils down to this ontological heterogeneity.

In contrast, to maximize the I-think into a dispenser from whence the world proceeds and is possessed, a network of laws decreed and enacted by me—that only succeeds at the cost of denying heterogeneity, sensibility, suffering, givenness, the singular. In spite of the semantic polarities, the universalizing-singularizing double bind in its twisting of receptivity is not, therefore, dualist. The only tolerable herbalistic metaphor would rather lead from the sporadic to the scattered.

One can say that at each turn of his itinerary Kant always returns to being as givenness. In the first as in the third *Critique* (in the second, "being-given" signifies the "fact" of reason), the decisive turn is taken with the dialectic where the categories are, at any rate, put to the side. It is only once the non-subsumptive judgments are discovered, however, that he can describe givenness as what it has been all along, namely the *there* of singulars. Being means neither to subsist as noumenon (Kant, the last Scholastic), nor to be perceived (Kant, the material idealist), nor to be singled out by an act of the understanding (Kant, the epistemologist), nor to collide with sensibility (Kant, the dogmatic empiricist). When he recognizes singular givenness, being means being-given to reflective judgment. The discovery of these judgments, even if it does not lead to an explicit theory of the singular,[168] marks out the margin of categorial ontology and hence the border of the regime of spontaneity which makes of the world a subjective possession. In reflective judgments, the universal is not held in advance as it is in determinate judgments; it always has to be sought amongst the occurrences having no precedent or common measure. Reflecting in this way, I seek some one singular to which to compare some other singular. To tell you how much your nape delighted me, I say, "as in Piero della Francesca."

To say "as" in that way is to weaken the subsumptive mechanism in which the singular is lost beforehand. Lost to what? Lost, absorbed, denied in the monomaniacal, particularizing strategy in which, however, we possess life, language, and conceivable being. As for standard singulars—"rich like Cressus," "built like Hercules"—and as for their multifocal strategies, reflective judgment does not maximize these. Here I treat such an angel of Piero, Cressus and Hercules *as if* in them I had hold of universals.

What remains to feign no longer is the *simple* bind, to deny no longer that there has been denial by affirming life as if death were not, but to bear in mind the undertow of mortality in the thetic impulse even of natality. Tragic knowing consists in this.

Kant with Aeschylus henceforth—and by way of Luther? In a rough way, yes. Suffering, once rehabilitated to its rank equal to that of making and doing, opens up the transcendental differend. It offers nothing to console, nor to consolidate. Allegiance to the conflictual strategies of being places us under an autonomous spontaneity that is not therapeutic by having recourse to an intelligible substrate, but that is shattered and on that account, more gravely pathogenic than any anterior hegemony. Its pathos proceeds from us.

By way of conclusion, let us return to the Kantian paradox stated at the beginning. The only way we have access to the object of experience is in accordance with thetic forms, and yet our spontaneity is not the origin of things which must, to the contrary, be given to us. This paradox is knotted together in the relation of the transcendental object to affection. To eliminate neither spontaneity nor subjective sensibility, the transcendental object which affects us must be understood as the anticipation of some sort of sense material. Anticipation signifies activity and material signifies passivity. In their collocation, difference is transmuted into differend.

To recant the denial would mean to know the particular and the singular as consigned to unconnected places. To particularize a universal we have in hand in advance, our judgments restate the ancient difference between *einai* and *on*, or between *esse* and *ens*. Consequently, one can speak of a transcendental difference in Kant. All the figures of the ontological difference—henologic, naturalistic, and transcendental figures—only work to unfold an ambiguity grammatically rolled up into the present participle. In most Indo-European languages, the participle "being" can function either as a noun (a being) or as a verb ("being old, he believed himself wise"). Now, as a result of the Kantian revolution in our way of thinking, this transcendental difference inflicts an introversion upon the traditional terms of difference. It is no longer the verb—*Dasein* as categorial *act,* as the act of conceiving—that singles out the indeterminate, but the noun, namely, the being that is given. This unknown something encountered in sensation is indeterminate. In the transcendental difference, to determine is to make. We make the true by applying a category to a sense manifold, by subsuming it under a predicate. Contrary to that, in the Aristotelian tradition as well as in Heidegger, the verb *(einai, esse, sein)* designates the indeterminate and the noun *(to on, ens, das Seiende)* designates the determinate. In both the metaphysical and the phenomenological difference, a being determines—"forms" (Aristotle), "orders" *(epechein,* Heidegger)—the process of being, which remains neutral.

The Kantian reversal of the poles of the determinate and indeterminate openly testifies to the subjectivist turn. Determining is what *I do:* categorizing. The "something = X" which *I suffer* remains indeterminate. Hence the suffering, recognized less overtly, in consequence of which the reversal barely functions. The subject which aspires to universal determination remains, in the nomothesis itself on account of which it succeeds, shot through with indetermination. Hence again the fragile ontology in Kant, fractured by sensibility into a determinate, verbal "singling out" and a nominal, indeterminate "given," to which a category cannot be applied. Hence, above all and finally, the failed interment. The root does not hold *simply.* It remains, not a difference legislating uniformly between normative making and a normed given, but the differend between this making which determines and the suffering which undetermines. The singular which one can only suffer transgresses thetic legislation in advance.

To annul the denial would amount to retaining that legislative-transgressive mingling at the core of the Kantian nomothesis. But that does not amount to suggesting that the law precedes an empirically occurring infraction,[169] nor that some Dionysian chaos undermines our Apollonian investments in order. If Kant were satisfied with the first transgression, flat because hypo-transcendental, he would fall into positivist truism; if he anticipated the second, precipitous because hyper-transcendental, he would submit to some principial dualism. In retaining an *a priori* sensibility with regard to the suffered singular, we obviously are no longer trying to describe a genesis of consciousness, not a "chaotic and anarchic" given over which the light of understanding would triumph. Rather, it is a matter of understanding legislation and transgression as two simultaneous moments of the nomothetic I-think that nevertheless are irreducible. In Kant, the ontological obscurity in which the I-am founders conceals from the Enlightenment the double bind which he nevertheless recognized. In the order of being, the I-am is a *condition* of the I-think and is, in the order of the law, also the *object.* As a presence to the indeterminate self, the I-am gives rise, literally, to thought; but as the target and the issue of determination, it is bound by thought. The Kantian I-think would have no being if not *by virtue of* the singular I-am which, in this sense, precedes it; but it would have nothing upon which to legislate if it were not *for* this very I-am, which in a sense succeeds it. Insofar as it emerges from the I-am, the cogito does not legislate. It owes the spontaneity, to which its prestige is attached in the order of the law, to a preceding passivity in the order of being. It is in this respect that the I-think is subjugated to the I-am, which works on it from out of an originary transgression. A plural labor, singularizing, dispersing. A labor equi-aprioric as well, without which the legislating I-think would not be.

What follows for the question of normativity? Kant inscribes, polemically, the question of being in the either-or between metaphysics and critique.[170] But in metaphysics as in critique, that which possesses being by prior right is normative. Indeed, if his revolution in the way of thinking were limited to the attempt to give a better account of experience, if the revolution did not immediately reverse the directing of that more ancient question, if it did not commence by bringing what one understands by "being" to bear on the subject, then the rules of experience would never have the force of law. We lack the hegemony to distinguish, as one does in moral theory, between norm and condition, between a deliberative measure ("treat each as an end, and not only as a means") and a coercive measure. According to its Kantian institution, autonomous spontaneity can guide our decisions only because, as our condition, it constrains us in advance.[171] Condition *is* norm. Legislative spontaneity *is* transcendental freedom. The Kantian revolution alters the terms of ontology and hence adds a chapter to it. It places whatever is and can be under imperative self-consciousness. Its emprise is such that it "makes" all things be. This is the normativity which follows from the reversal of direction in the raising of the question of being.

Now, consciousness makes these neither as things, nor as phenomena constituted by our syntheses. The judicative authority is not *simply* ultimate. How, then, does consciousness make all things? It weaves them into the faille of the "I-think–I-am," where the I-think is posited while the I-am is given in an indistinct sensation. There is indeed a distribution of epistemic and ontologic conditions. However, it is not between metaphysical and critical philosophy, but between the I conscious of its spontaneity and the I suffering itself as given. Such is the irony (but such is the essence of tragedy) in my possession of the world. Full thetic presence, determined without remainder, would be underscored by the equation "I think = I am."[172] In contradistinction to this, Kant did not just recognize opaque suffering, mutely other, impenetrable in its provenance; he also distanced it from the I-think, underscoring the inadequation of subjectivist normativity. Material occurrence is joined to the nomothesis as its remainder, impossible to cast aside as ousiological refuse. There is a poverty of the thesis of being to which must be added, though in another register, givenness; there is a poverty, inversely, of the I-am to which auto-determination is added. And precisely in such an addition—with autonomy as a principle and sensibility toward heteronomy as a co-constitutive transcendental surplus—we see the Kantian pathetic ontology. The hegemonic referent is broken here upon a double referential function. Being occurs both "samely" and "otherly." Without anti-predicative paranormativity, thetic and "systematic" normativity could not be.[173] But the *para* destabilizes the securing of the *tithémi*. The possessor of the world trembles from a dispossession, and hence from powerlessness.

It is said that Kant knew how to play the part of the rational and irrational, that he was more lucid than a Descartes about the irrational that bores holes all over self-consciousness and perforates it. Well-seen, well-said—except that here the polarity of rational and irrational goes over to the side of the differend where being as verb (the copula, B 100) signifies autonomy and being as noun (the being that I am) signifies the zone of heteronomy that is added to it as equi-originary. "To redress" that allocation of being and beings would amount to restoring spontaneity to sense givenness and thus to nature. This would be an anti-subjectivist counter-revolution. But centered thus upon subjective activity, the thesis that being is would necessarily shut its eyes to the suffered other, upon which it feeds. Thetic normativity has no access to this other normativity, which is sheltered in advance from the reign of spontaneity.

In the Platonic ascent I *raise myself up* toward the light to really belong to it, to become its own. The subjectivist turn reverses the photonic emanation. I *project* Enlightenment upon the world and thereby make it my own (finally, in Nietzsche, according to the prayer of Zarathustra, the sun *will mount* toward me, in that I appropriate it to myself). To possess the world would be to shine upon it, to constitute the *phainesthai* of phenomena, to be posited as the source of their brightness. I would possess it thus only on the condition of shining upon it through the manifestation of my intact autonomy. Consequently, theoretical values and practical norms would be in possession of what is called their validity. Now, my precategorial existence touches upon intact existence, tainting it. The I-think shines—determines and rules—but it lacks the immediacy of being. The I-am is given—for determining and ruling—as a neighboring being so as to secure ontological anchoring, but it lacks the spontaneity for making the law. Henceforth, it is not self-presence that is sovereign, but the differend in self-consciousness, a shattered measure, broken between thetic normativity and proximity to pain.

This is the pathetic legislation where archic spontaneity, singularly harassed, tormented from within, is estranged in anarchy.

II

The Diremption

On Double Binds without a Common Noun (Heidegger)

Introduction: Proteus Alone Can Save Us Now

"Only a God can save us now"[1]
—Heidegger

For a century and a half—since the deaths of Hegel and Goethe—hegemonic fantasms have suffered a polymorphous suspension. Hölderlin declared that he had received from the gods a knowledge heavier than he could digest, a knowledge which had to do with a certain condition of being becoming obvious in this late modernity; then Russians appeared, calling themselves nihilists and anarchists; lastly, Nietzsche announced that the true world had become a fable. . . . The half-century which elapsed between Hegel's death in 1831 and August 5, 1881, when the thought came to Nietzsche that the world is made up of incessant constellations of forces—these five decades are doubtless the most difficult ones to understand in our entire history. One might say that gazes then dared to wrest themselves away from authorities that were posited as consoling and consolidating, and that once again they allowed themselves to bear witness to the truly primary condition, the tragic condition that, since Euripides, the functionaries of humanity had busied themselves with banalizing by subsuming it under a genus (*"mors et alia huiusmodi,"* 'death and other things of that kind {*genre*},' Thomas Aquinas will say in a sovereign manner[2]). The fracture that death inflicts on any ultimate thesis or position is declared in discourses unheard of until the middle of the nineteenth century. Hölderlin and Nietzsche felt as if they were stricken by the oldest of obvious facts—that of the mortal labor that exerts the disparate on life. The tragic is defined, as was seen, by that labor.

How could the truth of this suspension, which has become our manifest destiny, be gathered up? Here, even more than was the case with the destitution of the *hen* and *natura,* it is important to read carefully. That the Greek "one" and the Latin "nature" lost their power to impose a regime troubles hardly anyone but those persons nostalgic for an immutable order (a nostalgia which illustrates how slow fantasms are in dying off). But whoever takes the hegemony of self-consciousness to task should beware. The utopianists of an ideal discursive community are watching, avatars of the philosophical bureaucracy assigned to transcendental and reflexive service.

One must take note immediately of a certain *pars pro toto* in contemporary discussions concerning ultimate normative groundings. The new functionaries of humanity issuing from Kantian criticism speak of intersubjectivity, transcendental reflection, and communicative rationality—always of a self-consciousness, if a socialized one—but that is evidently not the only referent stemming from the Reformation and the

Enlightenment which is at stake when they add: "If that is no longer, all is lost." Normative regimes in general would sink away with the primacy of the reflective subject. For want of social integration through consensus, everything is sinking away, they cry out in Frankfurt. Everything, that is to say, every form of a *koinon* which would generate obligations. Indeed, everything has sunk away, answered the genealogist of conscience in Paris not long ago: "The search for a form of morals which would be acceptable to everyone, in the sense that everyone should submit to it, appears catastrophic to me."[3] On both sides of the line of demarcation that appeared in the nineteenth century—a line which was to separate for some time a constructive and a deconstructive thinking—they are in agreement. The fate of hegemonies *tout court* is what is at stake in the hegemony of self-consciousness.

An attentive reading becomes necessary, for a thinking of the tragic differend might prove to be more faithful to the critical and emancipatory turn which established modernity than the theses of dialectical reconciliation and pragmatic consensus.

If indeed it did turn out that with the eclipse of referential self-consciousness, we experience the *kenosis,* the emptying out of any ultimate authority—if, *pars pro toto,* the "end of the subject" means the "end of hegemonies"—then it is not, properly speaking, a *destitution* that has been going on for a century and a half. To destitute an authority is always to oppose a No to a prior Yes, it is always a counter-thesis, an anti-authoritarian reaction. The *counter* and *anti* gestures necessarily operate right in the middle of that which they commit themselves to denying. No one is more solidly fixated on the figure of the father, the male, or of principles, than he who claims to have freed himself from it. Thus one need only remember how the regimes of the one and nature gave way to the disparate which dislocated them, beginning with their respective establishments, to understand that their destitutions were always a phoenix's tale. From the ashes of the Greek hegemony, the Latin hegemony emerges, and from the ashes of the latter, modern self-consciousness emerges. There is a thetic relapse without which no new regime could be put into place (yet which does not *take up* the destituted positions in any synthesis).

On the other hand, if the contemporary age genuinely shows the exhaustion of normative positions, there can no longer be such a relapse in the thinking that gives in to it. No more can the investment be withdrawn from some ultimate authority and transferred to some safer place. What comes to pass for us is not the destitution of one fantasm after another, but a *diremption* that deprives us henceforth of any fantasmic recourse. By "diremption," I only mean secondarily the will not to want to posit, which is only another posture of the will. "Diremption" means first of all an expiration has happened, the annihilation of normative acts that cleanses the tragic condition. If there is a task and a possibility of thinking today, it can only be that of letting normative consciousness collapse—not by putting a stop to philosophy so as to pass on, either to the science (the Anglo-Saxon temptation), or to literature (the French temptation), but by learning not to have wholehearted faith in semantic maximization itself (which is the temptation in any Western language).

How is one to live, under the sign of Proteus? How does one let the positions, which for our peace of mind focus on some particular focal sense of being, collapse?

These are daunting questions, but they are nevertheless secondary in relation to this question, which is graver still: *How is one to think*? Not "What is one to think?" Not "Which datum is to be borne in mind and followed?" But rather: How is one to bear in mind that which gives itself without submitting it straight away to subsumptions? Only the lover of the disparate has stopped denying the diremption—which has already been legislating, in any case, for a century and a half.

Philosophy (or whatever takes its place) can contribute to this apprenticeship. Once thetic candor has been lost, the conversation with texts remains. Then what is to be read to better understand how the normative hold is coming undone around us? We have just seen a first criterion for reading. To proceed first upon the great awakenings of Hölderlin, then of Nietzsche, without for all that losing from one's view the transcendental problematic in view of which these awakenings were possible, one would need a text that would inscribe referential consciousness into the lineage of the fantasms which have guided our history—a topological text. It should also have to allow the diremption which has become our epochal lot to be linked to normative topology. Lastly, it would have to be a text which helps the tragic truth emerging from under the diremption to be born in mind, the tug of death ceaselessly stealing life away from fantasmic attraction.

Riveted to a monstrous site

> . . . the as yet unnameable which is proclaiming itself and which can do so, as is necessary whenever a birth is in progress—only under the species of the non-species, in the formless, mute, nascent and terrifying form of monstrosity.[4]

I find these expectations, as well as some others, to be satisfied by a text of Heidegger, the *Beiträge zur Philosophie* (*Contributions to Philosophy*), written between 1936 and 1938.[5]

Why Heidegger rather than any other? Because Nietzsche spoke, from a site which is already no longer ours, of there being new nights, then of their falling upon the natural metaphysician that lies dormant in us, nights having to do precisely with that "nature" and the maximizing thrusts by which it awakens; because the Husserl of the *Crisis* did not put the primacy of subjectivity and consciousness into question; because Wittgenstein made it a point of honor to neglect history; and, finally, because all three only got rid of the very question of metaphysics—the question of being—by speaking an Indo-European language and therefore using the copula "is" without interpreting it.

Why this text of Heidegger rather than any other? It certainly is not because, following certain commentators, I consider it his masterwork.[6]

Far from it. But, in a sense, because of this "far from it." Here is the sense of this. First, these *Contributions* date from the years when Heidegger has behind him what he would later call his greatest blunder; when, circumspectly, he dared in his courses to imply criticisms of the regime; and when he was writing under the most intense, combined influence of Hölderlin and Nietzsche. Next, this text deserves one's attention for the overdetermined legacy it bequeaths to us. Indeed there is something disconcerting about it. Its elevated tone easily veers to exaltation ("No one understands what 'I' am thinking here." *BzP* 8) The idiolect is more ponderous than in any of his other writings. At times one might think one were reading a piece of Heideggerian plagiarism, so encumbered is it with ellipses and overwrought phrases. The uneven treatment of trivialities—in the sense of the *trivium:* grammar, logic, and rhetoric—makes for difficult reading. An atrophy of grammar (the undernourishment of the sentence, often stripped of predicates) and a cacotrophy of logic (malnourishment of the rules of discourse so as to make them perish) are indeed accompanied by a hypertrophy (overnourishment) of rhetoric. Litotes, hyperbole, questions left open, periods parceled out, nouns reduced to their verbal origins, these oratorical techniques are meant to undo the work of construction in philosophical discourse.

The masterwork of the thinking of being? *Far* from it—but doubtless Heidegger's most significant. Far, as is the periphery from the center in the metaphysical arena. The text begins by tracing this periphery: We are living in "the age of the transition from metaphysics to the historical thinking of being" (*BzP* 3). Thus traced by the closure, which is epochally impossible to leap over in order to place oneself abruptly outside it and so to assert an absolute break. . . . Centripetal forces, however, which there is reason to believe are not foreign to those that drew Heidegger to the administrative center of a model university, never cease to pull his thinking back from the periphery, such that the railing that encloses our site accounts for all the embarrassments of this text. They, just as much as the attempts to think otherwise, are what make it significant.

Why this text rather than another? Because it states with the greatest urgency—I do not say the greatest clarity[7]—the differend within being itself encountered in the establishment of the modern hegemony in Luther and Kant. It never ceases to vary the double bind, the effect of the everyday ultimates that are natality and mortality—thus it never ceases varying the originary dissension of being.

One hears it said that phenomenology remains incapable of any critical discourse, particularly as far as political regimes are concerned. Its very method condemns it from the outset to mere descriptions, whatever might be the realm to which one "applies" it. It can only remain mute in debates concerning the forms of public life.

In Heidegger's case, this objection is just not pertinent. His phenomenology speaks of "worlds"—of regions of manifestation, of economies, of plays, of gathering, of contextualizations. We always find ourselves inscribed in various worlds, each of which phenomenalizes according to its own laws. Now, to free these irreducibly multiple worlds, Heidegger has to argue against all ultimate fantasms posited as trans-regional. The epochal serialization of these fantasms provides him with a powerful tool against totalitarianism. Indeed, *totalitarianism exalts the regional political referent to the point of identifying it with the modern epochal referent.* National Socialism raises the collective subject to the rank of the standard sense of being, conferring upon it the function that subjectivity has for modernity.

What makes the *Contributions* symptomatic is that Heidegger, while denouncing it, also gives in to exaltation. I will come back at length to the advances he makes in thinking otherwise than in reference to an exalted fantasm. Here, on the other hand, are some of the gravitational forces that carry this text toward the very center of the arena that they delimit and that they measure at the limit, forces spelled out quite bluntly in the form of a four-point inventory. After each such sketch of a focalizing strategy, I shall indicate in a few words—before returning to it below—the dispersive counter-strategy monstrously allied with it.

Who? The center where, as Heidegger never stops repeating, metaphysical strategies have always been hatched has been and remains "man"—the concept of representable beings endowed with attributes and capable of perfecting themselves (be it by ascending toward the universal, by entering into themselves or, yet again, by progress). Now, in these pages Heidegger just as tirelessly repeats: Who? Who are we? A question not to be confused, to be sure, with this other one: What? What are we? The What will end up pointing in the direction of the ego, and the Who in the direction of the self understood as a possible *gift of time*. But this other response—other than humanist—will appear only at the end of a series of detours, of complex decelerations and accelerations in an itinerary of utterances that still issue, one must say, from the most solid center of entitative doctrines of man, precisely where representation and attributive logic sustain the thesis of perfectibility. "No one understands what 'I' am thinking here." In this utterance, the I who is thinking and who signs with his initials *M. H.* places himself within a pair of quotation marks, holding the hegemony of the subject at bay, precisely at the distance that is supposed to separate historial-concretely occurring thinking from all historicist-entitative representation. In other statements, the quotation marks disappear. To lay out just one sample of that more ancient cloth, forming a text with the logic of things and the thesis of perfectibility that this logic helps to weave: decision.

In historial phenomenology this word is to be taken literally. It designates the epochal breaks "cleaving" eras of truth. The question "Who?" does not arise there, as this phenomenology is concerned with arrangements of concealing-unconcealing and not with agents.

But it happens that alongside this aletheiological semantics of caesurae-decisions one reads, for instance: "Who decides? Each and every one." Suddenly the sum total of beings capable of making a decision is the answer to the question "Who?" Is not the persistence of the subject in its most entitative form blatant indeed? And what is at stake in that decision, posited as one posits an act? "The rescue of beings"—that is, here again, of a collective subject, for these beings are "the West." It is difficult not to construe a decision such as this on the model of self-consciousness, for it appeals most strongly to the agent and to effects emanating from it, formulated as an alternative: either "found truth and recreate beings in their totality," or else succumb to "anesthesia," the lack of creative and founding efficacy, carrying the gravest consequences (*BzP* 100f.). Whence the call, also reiterated, to creators (*die Schaffenden*) and founders (*die Gründer*).[8]

The select few are to create and found the site from which the many will then decide where to go. The model is generally "political" and no doubt specifically "populist" (political populism being defined by a leader and a pack of unconditionals, with which the people identify themselves instinctively). What does it presuppose here?

One might well believe oneself in the thick of an anthropology of capacities, where the possible denotes acts that are within our power: "Who is capable (*wer vermag*), and when, and how . . . ?" (*BzP* 353). Yet *Being and Time* had taught us to inquire in another way about ourselves and about the possible than in accordance with our powers (*Vermögen*). Again, what is brought into focus is acting on a goal, an end, on an instituting. "Why? (an appeal to grounding)" (*BzP* 258). Yet *Kant and the Problem of Metaphysics* had taught us to understand groundings, too, in another way. Then, in order to "overthrow today's man as he has been until today," man "must depart from his current fundamental constitution." Is this not pushing the effort of freedom, as the seat of acts *in potestate nostra,* to the extreme? Lastly, the anthropologism is obvious when Heidegger suspects his contemporaries of not measuring up. Departing from his mode of being "is perhaps already something impossible for the man of today" (*BzP* 248). Yet *On the Essence of Truth* had taught us to understand freedom in another way.

But there is a counter-strategy, a rather centrifugal one that will inscribe the self in discordant times and will thereby wrest it from the modern hegemony of self-consciousness. The double bind of appropriation and expropriation will constitute it as tragic.

The last god. (1) The final section of the *Contributions*[9] is entitled "The Last God." The phrase recalls first of all the theology of salvation as Rudolf Bultmann had practiced it along with Heidegger in their weekly sessions in Marburg a decade earlier, a theology of *eschata* (last things), not in the sense of an denouement at the end of time but in the sense of the plenitude of salvation offered in the instant. (2) The phrase is, however, overdetermined by an intimation of essence. Moreover, it connotes the possibility that widely differing experiences of the divine conveyed by both the Greek and the biblical traditions can be gathered together in a single nucleus (*das Gottwesen, BzP* 406) and extracted from their speculative and religious strait-jacket. This resurgence of Husserlian idealist essentialism in the notion of *Wesen* is as provisional as it is unexpected. (3) Lastly, there occurs a return of the theory of *kairos* (the opportune moment) which Heidegger, in the early 1920s, had hoped to make the core of a never-written study on Aristotle. The word "last" is indeed to be understood in a temporal sense, not as the end point of some time span, but an instant marking an epoch. Everything which, for the past two and a half millennia, has been held to provide salvation would then be reduced to its quintessence, as it were, and gathered together in a now. This critical moment, when the phenomenological truth of the divine in its numerous past forms could become what is proper (*eigen*) to a historial-type man, would be the event (*Ereignis*) to come. It was thought to be a possible event, for which Heidegger during the mid-1930s was attempting to prepare. Concerning the last god, he takes up an expression of the prophet Elijah (I Kings 19: 12), and speaks of this god's "passage" (*Vorbeigang*).

There again we find a counter-strategy. It will sketch (but without providing any definite outline) a more pagan god, one that Heidegger does not name, a god venerated since remote antiquity for its resistance (through flexibility) to any representation and cooptation—Proteus. Toward the end of his life, might Heidegger have meant to say that only Proteus can save us now? . . .

The people. This becomes an issue for Heidegger as a direct consequence of the question of being.

In the first beginning—with the Greeks—where they figured out problems, the phenomena of the city and of being overlapped in many ways. They shared the same "poietic" and linguistic characters (by being uttered, being is set to work, and the city is above all the space instituted by speech); the same "technical" manifestation of *phusis* (*techné* inscribing within limits whatever shows itself); the same agonistic character due to the undertow affecting both the city (its archaic past in the sense of the pre-Doric, i.e., of the heroic) as well as being (its "expropriation"); lastly, they shared the same nomic essence, as both are sites of a gathering (*legein,* whence a certain redundancy in defining man as a living being, either "endowed with *logos*" or "political"). These are but so many intersecting meanings reflected by the proximity of words (*polis—pelein*[10]). They are but so many features, too, connecting "the founding act of a State" with the act that makes language a work.[11] At the Greek beginning, there is being as both extra-discursive and discursive gathering: the kinship of Solon and Homer.

The same features would also mark the new beginning, the repetition, the retrieval, the refounding, after a long history of forgetfulness. Now, one must clearly see the motivation of the role assigned to Germany in this other beginning. As the young Hegel as well as Marx had first observed, followed unanimously by the subsequent tradition, nineteenth-century Germany had no being of its own. Heidegger shares this view. For him, Germany still has no being in accordance with any of the features just mentioned.[12] In Hegelian terms (turned, however, against the system of objective Spirit), the state remains for Heidegger an abstract *notion* of everydayness. But only a concrete gathering, in the sense of the everyday, can become phenomenal. The properly political phenomenon will therefore be, not the state, but the people. Put the other way around, the type of gathering capable of becoming a phenomenon in accordance with the features mentioned will be termed "people." The philosophical impetus behind Heidegger's administrative commitments is to be sought in the kinship these features suggest between the question of being and the question of politics, a kinship rooted in *legein.*

The founding in the realm of language, responding to the Greek epic, thus bears the name of Hölderlin. For a few months, Heidegger also thought he could name the new Solon. The *Volk,*[13] at any rate, is to be understood as a gathering brought about by a founding utterance (*techné* assigning its limits to "natural" language), in incessant struggle with the dispersive concealment traversing from within every poetic as well as every political configuration.

The return of representational thinking is obvious here, as it already was in the case of the Who and of god. One cannot help feeling disturbed as one recalls that the step beyond *Being and Time* was meant precisely to disencumber thinking from the remnants of subjectivism that still burdened the Existential Analytic. This text re-establishes the prestige of the particular for the Who, god, and the people, and even if in the *Contributions* Heidegger seeks to retain the singular more firmly than ever—more pathetically, as will be seen. "Particular" implies a "particularized universal." There is the universal "people," particularized in the Greek, the Roman, the German. . . . Contrary to what one might believe at first sight, it is not due to his attention to the entitative that Heidegger here undermines the very phenomenological project he unrelentingly claims for himself (singular beings alone—the temple of Paestum, this pitcher, that bridge, to cite some well-known examples—allow one to *diasozein ta phainomena*); it is due to the representation of ideal entities. Germany must particularize the idea. How can we fail to be puzzled by this return of the common dished up to our apprehensions? With the logic of representable things reinstated, how can one fail to fear that one has stepped back into the midst of "special metaphysics"?

Now, yet again there is a counter-strategy. Heidegger will never undo the tie linking *pelein* to *polis*. The question of politics and that of being will always raise for him one and the same problem of "gathering." A thinking of being, however, which has been disengaged from subjectivism—if such a thinking is at all to come within our reach—forces one to think the political in another way. The strategies of decentering in the *Contributions* grapple with this transition. The gathering can no longer take place around, or by, or on, a self-conscious subject such as the people.

*The contingency of Da-sein.** The task of particularizing the idea remains, for "the 'people' is not yet the essence of the people" (*das noch nicht volkhafte 'Volk', BzP* 398). The quotation marks signal Heidegger's disenchantment with the movement of the day. In 1936, the essence of the people—without quotation marks this time, as one commonly speaks of things common—remains as yet to be established; and the *via remotionis,* which consists in removing the particularizing conditions so as, as one says, to concoct an idea, remains the royal path. The mutation in human being is a long time in coming, since it can be conjectured that the uprising (*Aufbruch*) of 1933 had not fulfilled its promises. It will indeed be "a principle of the people" (*ein 'völkische Prinzip', BzP* 42) that will provide the standard for the wholly other human being, but one has henceforth to await the domination by the founders to come. What would they have to found? With the people, Heidegger places the *there,* with which the Existential Analytic formerly had broken up subjectivist solipsism, under the sign of the "not yet." The postponement of the *there* holds the Who in suspension just as it delays the passage of the last god and puts off until some remote tomorrow the popular uprising. "*Man* is transformed by the founding of Da-sein" (*BzP* 230). It is only when the "people" have become a people (no more quotation marks, for we "dare to use immediate speech," *BzP* 239) that Da-sein shall be. "Da-sein is nothing but *instant* and history" (*BzP* 323), instant as an eruption of a human essence that never existed before, history as it thereby founds the other beginning, other than the Greek beginning. The *there* thus remains still "to be prepared" (*BzP 231*) and Da-sein—in an explicit critique of *Being and Time*—"the ground of a determinate human-being: of the one that is yet to come" (*BzP* 300). Such is now the surprising contingency of Da-sein. It may, and it may not, come to be.

*"Être-là" is the French translation of Heidegger's German "Dasein." Normally left untranslated in English, "Dasein" refers to human existence. Etymologically viewed, it means "Being-there," as does the French "Être-là." Heidegger gives special emphasis to the etymological sense by writing, with some consistency in the *Contributions*, "Da-sein." It is impossible to distinguish in the French translation between the emphasized and unemphasized occurrences. I have consulted the German to establish this distinction in Heidegger's text, and in most instances have rendered the French "Être-là" as "Da-sein."

Is so stripping Da-sein of its transcendental structure and singularizing it as ontic tantamount to taking a step back so as to leap further?

Leaping onto some post-subjectivist terrain? It seems doubtful. No longer transcendental, phenomenology risks becoming merely descriptive. One can see this in the collapse of the historial into the historiological only to be raised up from it. The historial is always measured by the scale of truth giving and withholding itself from thinking. The modes of these givings and these refusals spell out epochs, thereby determining what, at any given time, it is possible and impossible for humans to do, to will, to experience. As to the historiological, it is measured along a different scale, one that is just the converse of the epochal play of concealing-unconcealing. Here facts such as inventions, revolutions, and other seizures of power, as the will of leaders or the consensus of rational agents, etc., determine the historiological periods. Thus each time Heidegger ventures in his last writings to *date* the beginning (for instance, with Parmenides[14]) and the end (for instance, "in three hundred years"[15]) of the history of being's withdrawal, there lurks a risk of succumbing to a second-order historical positivism, where facts of thinking mark turning points in history.

Now, if January 30, 1933, did not mark the anticipated beginning, the breakthrough to a new type of human still remains possible at a later date. Accordingly, Heidegger does not hesitate to describe the forms of power, both exoteric and esoteric, capable of leading us there. In order to stand up to the cultural isomorphism that has come to envelop the planet, "the domination of the 'freed' (that is to say, uprooted and egotistic) masses is to be established and maintained through the shackles of 'organization'." So much for government {*pouvoir public*}. Simultaneously another, more hidden, domination is needed for the sake of the renewal ahead. "Here, it is a matter of preparing the [founders] to come, who will create new sites on which to stand within being itself." And he adds that both forms of domination "have to be willed by those who know" (*BzP* 61f.). Willed to what end? To found *Da-sein* {German in original} henceforth understood as an ontic possibility.[16]

Reading *Being and Time,* who would have ever thought that a few years later Heidegger would go on to submit Da-sein to the will of a few? This establishment of a contingent will ruling over the *there* determines the anthropologism, the theologism, and the populism we have just seen.

A counter-strategy remains. It extracts the *there* from the hegemony of self-consciousness. The *there* arises as a possibility, Heidegger will say, from the fractured instant. The temporality (*Temporalität*) of being that remained out of reach for an analytic starting from ecstatic temporality (*Zeitlichkeit*) will then become thinkable by means of the double bind that points out that fracturing, which is to say, it will become thinkable as tragic temporality.

Concerning an analogous shift in another text written during the same years, a similar contamination of Heideggerian deconstruction by subjectivity has been judged fatal.[17] Fatal, yes, if *fatum* is meant to render *Geschick,* destiny (an awkward Latinization, though). But fatal in the sense that the persistence of the human, divine, national, historical subject would lead to the ruin, even the death, of the deconstructive project, that it would thereby suffer a fatal blow—this seems to me much more difficult to argue. One might as well assert that attributive grammar is itself harmful or deadly for thinking (and indeed it is for thinking that claims to implant itself firmly outside the metaphysical closure). What could be more "metaphysical," indeed, than to determine a grammatical subject by means of a predicate? It is therefore indispensable to grasp the "destinal" necessity which, after 1934, continues in Heidegger to encumber the *other* thinking with the system of the *same.*

The double level of writing (for the public and for the initiate), the tactics for mastery on both of these levels, the calculation of dates, the conjunction of preparatory knowing and willing, the creation (not the reception) of sites in being, and finally the kerygma announcing a type of humanity to come—all of these obviously form a system, and a "system" in just the sense Heidegger has tirelessly sought to dismantle. With the eidetics of the Who, of god, of the people and of factual history, do we not hold the branches of a tree-diagram modeled on Porphyry or Descartes, simply revised on the drawing board of historical consciousness?

Perhaps so—at least if the trunk of this new *arbor Porphyreana* were to promise, in its turn, an eidetics of being. On this point, however, there is no compromise, no contamination, no hesitation at all. Being, in the *Contributions,* is understood as "event." It can be said in many ways, of course, but never as the starting point of a dieresis. The event-like tree trunk grafted with eidetic branches thus shows itself to be monstrous. It possesses that monstrousness that Jacques Derrida himself, in the lines quoted in the above epigraph, has so pertinently shown to be an epochal necessity, and that never ceases to turn these Heideggerian contributions to politics into limpings.

A "terrible warning"

"There is *nothing* to be expected from antiquity or from what follows it, if not the terrible warning. . . ." (*BzP* 73)

Let us now turn to *pathein* and its rehabilitation. No textual ensemble of Heidegger is more painful than the *Contributions.* A twofold pain rings through it, one measurable in millennia, the other in a few years.

The pain of a confinement. If the tradition that has come down to us from antiquity offers no more than a terrible warning, it is because the words in our dictionaries, the rules of their concatenation in sentences, the meaningful linking together of these sentences in discourse, and lastly, the "public function" of discourse—all of this very ancient legacy always and only consolidates the regimes of the same. It perpetuates tragic denial. Whoever seeks to think otherwise than in the service of a hegemony has nothing more to expect from the Greek vulgate that girds our epochal possibilities. The girdle is too tight; the encircling wall is impossible to jump. Whether overtly or covertly, the enclosure assigned to us continues to arrange everydayness in accordance with the morphology of the same and its inexhaustible ruses of subsumption. All that remains is to traverse that enclosure up to its very boundaries and to trace the internal disturbances of its arrangements.

One of our myths may be the belief that the morphogenesis of the same has occurred along a trajectory running from Homer to Socrates. But to break its confining power, it will not suffice to demythologize that genesis. Quite the opposite. What is terrifying is the logic of the same as it has been adapting itself to every new hegemony since the Greeks, including the most finely honed demystifications. No less terrifying is the blindness in the face of the dysfunctions of the same (which is as old as its logic)—in the face of the morphogenesis of the other. Just as, in an earlier phenomenological project of Heidegger, a tool revealed its essence when broken, so too the warning speaks in these *dysfunctions*. One will respond to that warning coming from the tradition only by laboring in pain. Only "the courage for the ancient" will eventually make possible "the freedom for the new" (*BzP* 434). In terms of the agonal demonstration of the *Contributions*, only a system of the subject altered from its common trunk up by a thinking of the non-common event will be in a position to prepare another site. Only the monstrosity of such a graft, denaturing the law of the same, will enable us to grasp the monstrous stakes to which he felt emboldened in the years when, striking the pose of the one who had leapt outside their closure, he proclaimed the confinement within the Who, god, the people, and history to be broken, as all were declared outmoded in their received configurations.

The pain of the failed uprising. In 1936, the lesson of tradition had just shown itself to be terrible indeed. The expected leap toward the other had proved to be but a weighty fall back into the same. With the *Contributions*, Heidegger has left us his most vehement debate, albeit highly ambiguous, with National Socialism as the system of the same and its violent subsumptions. The pain is that of a dreadful awakening, of having been duped. The impulse (*Stoß*) toward the extra-territorial shows itself to have been only a gradual sinking into the extreme fixation of—and upon—hegemonic subjectivism. "The total vision of the world" simply established "the giganticism of operational machination" (*das Riesenhafte der Machenschaft, BzP* 40). Later on he will explain that he had hoped Hitler would lead Germany upon "the terrain of a renovation and a gathering for the sake of the West's responsibility";[18] for the sake of a new *response*, that is, to the most ancient of legacies. With the uprising thus unmasked as a deception and his commitment as an error, Heidegger finds himself back on the old isomorphic ground, only more hardened than ever. Just as in other texts from the mid-1930s, he describes the hemisphere in terms of thetic foundationalism from which, through a profusion of quotation marks, he now takes his distance in the most polemical fashion: "The 'populist' 'organization' of science 'itself' moves along the same path as the 'Americanist' 'organization'" (*BzP* 149); along the same path also described as leading from Judaism to Christianity, then to Bolshevism (which, through this line of descent, shows itself to be "originarily Western"), and finally to the "reign of reason as equalization of everything" (*BzP* 54).[19] Both positive uniformity and disenchantment echo in the already cited declaration of the recluse ("No one understands what 'I' am thinking here") seeking to set himself off as sharply as possible from what the world around him has become.

A sharp pain seizes his thinking when he tries to set himself apart. This is what we have just seen in terms of that place where the logic of the same leads. It has proved terrifying in its all-assimilating cunning, as was brought to bear too close to home, namely, precisely on the Heideggerian wager. The pain speaks through the biting, unwitting irony of the title, *Contributions to Philosophy*. Having wagered on a discontinuity in the manner of thinking, Heidegger ends up *contributing* to the institutionalized zenith of referential self-consciousness. He comes to make his contribution to the public function of the philosopher. The zenith, invested with the expectation of a reversal, exacerbates a thinking which, riveted to the monstrous site, seeks to tear itself away from it. Whence the strategies of philosophical reriveting which, like uncontrollable discharges, keep intersecting in this text with the counter-strategies of "the other thinking."

A phenomenology of normative regimes, moving to the limits of the confinement that is over two thousand years old, would by itself be monstrous. It would seek to advance toward another terrain along the paths laid out by the principles of identity and non-contradiction, namely, by the principles of the same. The wager Heidegger had placed on diffraction had turned into an investment in the most effectively focalizing focal sense, which is what was most senseless about it; from then on, the pain is doubled. The play of functions and dysfunctions, no longer in ancient or modern texts, but at the level of Heidegger's utterance itself, makes this utterance the most pathetic document of broken hegemony. Perhaps one should say it is the crack where hegemony bursts through, because, unlike the Greek, Latin, and modern regimes, a nomothesis never ceases to come to light in a thinking which proceeds non-thetically. It is an inversion which does not prevent this awkwardly contributing text from bearing witness to theticism as well as to the disruptions which have always ruined its integrative power.

It is plausible, as has been conjectured (it is however no more than conjecture), that the professed break with National Socialism and what Heidegger will later call the "turn" in the question of being amounted to one and the same shift in his thinking.[20] To raise the basic question (What is being?), the guiding question (What is the being of beings?) is only concerned indirectly with the beings that we are. It is concerned with the historial. The second beginning, which was supposed to respond to the Greek beginning, had failed; as a consequence, the guiding question indeed becomes: Having come to this monstrous site, how are we to understand being? The starting point remains everydayness, only now insofar as it has a history with a definite contemporary effect. This leads to the vast detour through the epochs of truth and their normative dispositions, so as to arrive at the basic question. This also accounts for the projecting of Da-sein into a future now construed as merely possible. Regardless of whether this reorientation was motivated by disenchantment, it is radical.

More important than motives, however, are conditions. These concern self-consciousness and the monstrosity of a passage to its limits, disfiguring it. The Existential Analytic turns out to have been but Heidegger's penultimate concession to subjectivist transcendentalism, and thus to the metaphysics of consciousness. The final concession came in 1933 with the urgency of a *carpe diem*. Both concessions concern the very question from which any problematic of self-consciousness emerges: Who am I? It is a question to which *Being and Time* replied: Most of the time I am "they," doing as "they" do and living as "they" live. The question clearly veers to the ontic, with the presumed *kairos* of 1933. A great divide then opens up between the "until now" and the "henceforth." Thus, concerning the self, until now "self-assurance" has been such that no experience could transplant man "to a region never yet trodden." Henceforth, however, "no opposition [. . .] to the certainty concerning man is *more dangerous* than the question: Who are we?" (*BzP* 53f.). It seems the question is dangerous, first of all, to anyone who raises it, for it exposes him to the lure of such treacherous answers as the one to which Heidegger had succumbed. Furthermore, it is dangerous in that it perpetuates the modern hegemony. It is also dangerous because, according to the assumption itself of a closure, by trying to transplant oneself, one is implanted in a history condemned elsewhere as offering no more than a terrible lesson. Lastly, the question is dangerous (but it would be futile to attempt to enumerate all the dangers of metaphysics pushed to its limits) for the question of being itself, which risks being confined within the Greco-German bifrontality.

Now, the Heidegger of the *Contributions* falls unhesitatingly—yet as we shall see, not without also *monstrously repeating them*—into all these traps at once: "The danger of the question of who we are is at the same time—if it be true that in distress, danger can summon the supreme effort—the sole path to come to ourselves and thereby to pave the way for the originary rescue of the West, that is to say, for its justification from out of its history" (ibid.). To justify the West from out of its history, such is precisely the ambiguity of the liminal operation. History is at once a terrible warning and a legitimizing canon. Moreover, this is the new guiding question, now labeled pathetically in the terms of the last of the hegemonies. Who are we? Who am I? How are we to understand ourselves? How are we to become conscious of ourselves, to "come to ourselves"? These are but so many concessions to the modern hegemony which necessarily undermine the new guiding question. That question is raised, no longer in accordance with metaphysics (What is the being of beings?) nor in accordance with fundamental ontology (What is the being of Da-sein?), but in accordance with the chronological and geographical coordinates of a people. What is our being in these days when the great uprising is proclaimed? The question of subjective beings—to whose obstructive effect on the question of being, however, Heidegger will never cease drawing attention—is retained here over and against and, especially, parallel to the question of being as event. He addresses it to the *subject,* to the focal meaning of being for the moderns, and to this subject at a precise date and place, to a subject determined as ontic.

It must be said that this way of breaking with the fad of the day is ineffectual. It would be hard to conclude that treacherous responses have vanished. On the contrary, the wager remains.

There persists, first of all, the conviction that the uprising of 1933 was headed in the right direction. "For us"—that is, for Heidegger—the question, "Who are we?" remains so essential that "it loses the dissident appearance toward the new German will" (ibid.). It is known that Heidegger never shared the biological and racist consequences of this new will. His polemic follows from this: In his rectoral address, he had placed his hopes on a renewal of science, but pseudo-biology had disabused him of that; then self-criticism led him to see the essential continuity, grounded in the interest of mastery, between modern science and eugenics. But it is also known that he believed himself, in some sense, to understand the Nazis better than they understood themselves. Heidegger never contested "the truth" and "the inner greatness" of the movement, on which he had wagered.[21] The wager appears here in its "supreme" form, paradoxically justifying Western history through the beginning that would dismiss it.

What persists here is the hegemony of the self-conscious agent with the subjectivist centering it imprints on thinking. Coming to ourselves and "originarily" saving the West, which is to say, through repeating its origins—doesn't this assertion consolidate the "we" of the *"subiectum"* which elsewhere in the same text Heidegger attempts precisely to "shake" (*BzP* 444)? It is hard to see how such a questioning would lead to the undoing of the referent that has made for modernity.

Moreover, where does one who worries about his own "being" stand so as to come to himself, and from where does he speak? Is not his platform all too familiar? It is the bastion of the *same*. It looms over the whole landscape of questions of identity. Yet from there, how could one expect to break the enclosure encircling the entire problematic of beings? Doesn't this third danger present itself pre-emptorily before the search for *another* "foothold" (*Fußpunkt, BzP* 265)?

Lastly, how is one to think the other that is the event, if the "supreme" resides in the German "Who" that responds to the Greek "Who"? (In 1945, when he acknowledged his earlier extravagant hope in National Socialist "responsibility," Heidegger reiterated that it had indeed been for him a matter of "responding" in that sense.) Do not these comparisons first of all erect a barrier of calculative answers against the question of being? The essence of calculative reason is to measure the small by the big, the particular by the universal, the superficial by the deep, the low by the high, all beings by one model being. Now, no metaphysical standard (the one, nature, consciousness, or any others) ever has been marked as ontic so clearly as is the posited rise of one people, in the sixth century B.C.E., and the rise of another, posited again, in the twentieth century.

These are but a few of what one would be tempted to call contradictions in the *Contributions to Philosophy*. In what follows, I shall keep hold of them and sharpen them, for I know of no other text that offers so painfully to our thinking the great repression of the tradition of tragic being. Heidegger lends his voice both to the forces of repression as well as to those of the repressed. The pain remains unabated, for the same adversity traverses, from within, both the site of the text and the thought that echoes there. The distress of the site and the pathos of thinking indicate one and the same epochal monstrosity. The agonistic dissension in terms of which Heidegger from then on understood being, in turn, becomes manifest in this monstrosity.

An addendum to the extravagant expectations: Heidegger was only partly mistaken when, for a few months in the 1930s, he expected a new beginning of the West responding to Homer and Solon. He was by no means mistaken about what was *terminal* in the movement. To speak only of philosophy, where is one to turn, since the 1930s, to find a thought that raises even so much as the question of the conditions of what has befallen us? Neither the accountants of pragmatic *problem-solving* {English in original}, nor the sociologists of critical theory, nor the deconstructors flirting more and more with literary criticism, nor the doxographers of philosophy, nor those nostalgic for natural law, even catch a glimpse of the tragic condition of being in view of which Heidegger had to "err greatly."[22] However embarrassed—because of being embarrassed—his attempts at recanting the tragic denial from which all fantasms stem may have been, the Heidegger who emerged from the break and the turning had at least learned to think otherwise the one question *originarily* bound to remain open (If other questions resist closing—those of death and of evil—it is because they follow from this one.): the question of being.[23] Of what other figure of our century can it be said that 1933 and its aftermath opened his eyes to what there is of being—like the blinded Oedipus, to quote him again, who had "one eye too many, perhaps"?

Before these months of blindness, I find no trace of an originary agonistic dissension (*Streit, Zwist, Riß, Zwietracht*), either in *Being and Time,* or in the texts immediately following it. Later, however, the lesson is never forgotten. In the repetition of thetic epochs, it fractures {*fissure*} so-called uniformly normative principles; under the legislation of diremption, this dissension fractures being as event. One indication among others for this is the historializing of feelings, moods, and tones. In *Being and Time, Stimmungen* were (mediately) revelatory of being. Now after 1934, Heidegger recognizes that they have a history. What are the feelings that henceforth determine us? They are, for good reason, fright, restraint, and reverential awe (*das Erschrecken,*[24] *die Verhaltenheit, die Scheu*). Together these constitute the foreboding (*die Ahnung, BzP* 14), that anticipates being as the event of an *agôn* or a *polemos* turned against itself, the event of an internal return-turnabout-turning.[25] He did not have to wait for the exterminations of 1942 to ask whether philosophy was still possible. What is still possible is a thinking that seeks to grasp the truth of being from out of the monstrous site to which we find ourselves riveted.

The beings-beingness-being *difference* would not have been thinkable without Greek philosophy. The *differend*—which itself is gaping, between appropriating and expropriating strategies in being itself—would have remained unthought without the theticism which became excessive in the twentieth century. The memorial, the deconstruction, the "working through," every repetition of the gesture of being, were thus inadequate to this differend. It was in the face of the task of "*letting*" the differend "become our distress" that there was "nothing more to hope for from antiquity" (*BzP* 73). In the half-century since the *Contributions,* the excessiveness of position taking has taken on other forms of giganticism and of operative machination, extending institutionalized violence beyond Europe. Riveted as we are to the site of a planetary self-destruction which has become an imminent possibility, the old tragic knowledge has come back within our reach, the knowledge that within every constellation laying down the law, the transgressive pull backwards toward the No pulls us more powerfully toward death than the universalizing and normative Yes binds us to life.

Better than any of the past fantasmic destitutions, the diremption of any and all ultimately authoritative referents foreseen in the nineteenth century and darkening the twentieth is the realization of the differend for which Heinrich Hertz provided the model.[26]

This model, we may recall, sets disparate strategies into opposition within subsumptive references, strategies as disparate as were the irreconcilable laws that took hold of the Greek tragic hero, leading him toward a place of impossible knowledge (toward the *Wesen,* Hertz said) whose blankness made and makes up all his knowledge.

Perhaps as a result of the rude awakening of 1934, this differend is clearly traced out in the *Contributions*. It is traced twice, first along the regime which today is undergoing the loss of its normative power—the regime of consciousness, and second according to the other thinking, that of being as event.

Thus what is pathetic about consciousness will have to be reconsidered first of all, to understand in what way, according to Heidegger, this pathos ruins the hegemony that still surrounds us. To discern the *historial differend* in it, I shall ask: How do the contraries that have no genus—again, the self and the ego, even if disparate in a different way than at the moment of their modern institution—aggravate the pathos of consciousness beyond what is normatively viable? What retrospective gaze does diremption allow one to cast on the totality of normative fantasms? Which life ended up making us the last of these fantasms? And, at the moment when referential regimes turn out to be an epoch-making illusion, how does diremption henceforth lay down the law?

Then I will briefly touch upon what could be called questions of method, covering topology and the conditions of non-referential thinking.[27]

Lastly, it will be necessary to ask Heidegger to where the thinking of the possible freed up by diremption leads. It will then be a matter of raising some questions about the potential that the *discordance of times* harbors in the event. These questions will have to do with the event, the singular, the incongruous other, and expropriation, as well as with the "law" of being as event, the law of the double bind—without any consoling and consolidating fantasm—where natality bears us toward the figures of the common, but where mortality always pulls us back from those figures and singularizes us.

CHAPTER 5

On the Historial Differend

On the late modern pathology: the self as other

"By the event alone do we become ourselves." (*BzP* 230)

In this remark, Heidegger pushes modern hegemony to its extreme limit. We must try to grasp this "our selves" (*wir selbst*) as pointing toward the self (*das Selbst*), and we must try to grasp the event—strangely instrumentalized here by the self—as the strife between appropriation (*Ereignung*) and expropriation (*enteignet,* ibid.). Instrumentalization pulls the event under the modern hegemony, where everything becomes a tool for self-assertion. At the same time, if the strife in question is in one way or another the condition of the self, then "to become oneself" must have been an agonistic pursuit ever since the institution of modernity.

The text moves to the limits of the subjectivist dynasty, where its "principle" (*BzP* 336) becomes monstrous. This movement to the limits can easily be traced. It follows a chain of excesses that leads toward a *possible* Da-sein. The regime that constituted modernity obviously gets disfigured by the giganticism of technocratic rationality. But it gets disfigured more essentially by a movement that is excessive in a different way, in a way that is still guided by the principial economy even while rendering it unrecognizable from within: monstrous. The giganticism where the uniformity imposed by *archai* triumphs thus is not to be confused with the monstrous, where the archic is altered by the anarchic. This alteration alone prefigures another economy, with a broken *arché*. The denial of that break has moved and still moves totalizing phenomenalization as the condition for its apogee—the condition, if there truly is an apogee, for its perigee as well. What remains to be understood is the self, without denying the originary double bind. The focal meaning having served since the Enlightenment in order to take stock of phenomena found itself pushed aside from its very emergence, as was seen, by counter-strategies to which the focal meaning itself gave rise. Their linkage reveals, at the heart of the grip {*saisie*} making up the epoch, a diremption {*dessaisie*} Heidegger later will say marks the end of all epochal history.[28] This end can best be understood by following the modern pathos to its limit.

A last warning before attempting to link together the steps by which Heidegger proceeds to disfigure self-consciousness as well as the self. Here it is a matter of a topical sequence in his very own text, not a thematic concatenation of statements "about" the self and the *topoi* it occupies as the ego's non-generic other. At that level of themes and places {*lieux dits*}, to the contrary, Heidegger hardly misses an opportunity to refute whoever would dwell on modern self-consciousness as a springboard toward another thinking (*BzP* 67ff.). No matter that this "whoever" is Heidegger himself. . . . Indeed, the text speaks at times from a topos which can only be called subjectivist and at times from another, event-like, topos. Hence the difficulty in reading these *Contributions*. Hence, too, their incomparable symptomatic status.

Here, then, are some of the displacements by which Heidegger works on the self-conscious subject, and pushes its regime to the limit where it becomes unrecognizable.

At first he speaks from the place where a certain collective subject becomes problematic to itself—a subject of the imaginary institution circumscribed by the Meuse, Memel, the Adige, and the Baelt; a place involving Berlin and a time measured by a span of three or four years; a problem, lastly, that concerns the identity of that subject. It is a "proper" place in the strict sense of that word, a universal "idiot" as is all identification with that subjectivist *idion* that is most difficult to shake, most unreflective and most murderous: "my" people.

This proper place exceeds itself as soon as it is inscribed within the history of principial representations. The reign of the conscious, reflexive, rational subject, whether intimate or collective, amounts to an "illusory reign" (*Scheinherrschaft*). This *Schein* will have to be examined more closely, for here is the referent that has caused our age to be included among the fantasms. Just as one had to dispel the transcendental illusion of certain earlier totalizing fantasms in order to establish the modern focal sense of being, so "this illusory reign must some day be broken" so as to destitute it (*BzP* 336). The break in the topical sequence is striking. From the question "Who are we?" a question in which the "we" *functions,* Heidegger moves on to a *dysfunction,* to the breakable subjective regime. The self-conscious subject problematizing its identity has transmuted itself into "ourselves," no longer as we have become (a question following a certain seizure of power), but as one position among others (modern reason "willing to posit itself on itself," ibid.) in a long thetic history. This position is as fragile as the ancient hegemonic theses were. This second place exceeds the first, just as epochal diachrony exceeds its synchronic figures. The possible break which is prior to the immediate "we" provides the central feature to the gesture of being and to every deconstruction.

The epochal place is exceeded in turn. Something hides and at the same time shows itself under the whole "*psyché-noûs-animus-spiritus-cogitatio*-consciousness-subject-ego-spirit-person" semantic genesis. If these are but so many epochal illusions, they still have their own truth. For "what we call Da-sein" (*BzP* 314) is in accord with them while at the same time holding itself back from explicit thematization. Again, we have a new textual site, which is literally decisive. It separates *Da-sein's* age-old latency from its coming to light. But—and this is how the closure is articulated here—even if the "consciousness-subject-ego" complex exercises only an illusory reign, *Da-sein* is not yet, which is to say, is not yet taken to disengage normative regimes. Kant, awaking from his dogmatic slumber, demonstrated the mechanisms that generate illusions, mechanisms that nevertheless remained indefeasible to the most sober reason. Heidegger, at least in his transgressive strategy, invests more heavily in criticism. He intends to disengage the very mechanism of "philosophy" by "contributing" to it a supplement gathered from its own grindings. Whence the title of the book, *as he understands it*. Heidegger speaks with the voice of a chronicler as he describes the preparatory excess that may one day allow Da-sein to found itself: "we see these centuries complete this breaking" of referential subjectivity (*BzP* 336). The breaking of the referential subject and the tragic double bind announcing itself in normative dysfunction are not yet, but are possible for us—a breaking and a double bind which are summed up in Da-sein.

A question, before letting this last link loose: What is the understanding of being to which this sequence of topical excesses leads? To answer, it suffices to return to the title page of the *Contributions to Philosophy*. The text, we may recall, is addressed to two distinct audiences, the many and the few. I said that with this classification of reading subjects Heidegger, while trying to dismiss its subsumptive logic, *classifies* a good number of his own strategies as being of subjectivist ancestry. Now, this segregation {of audiences} is crucial to the fact that the book bears two titles, one exoteric, the other esoteric. Only the first is "public." Here is the second title: *Vom Ereignis* (*Of the Event*). But "the event," we also know, points precisely beyond the lineage of representations stretching from *psyché* to "person" via the "consciousness-subject-ego" complex. The title Heidegger calls "essential" thus does not prolong that lineage. It breaks with it. This break is highly overdetermined since it is meant to render obsolete not only the lineage issuing from *psyché*, but also fundamental ontology and the ahistorical Da-sein of the Existential Analytic, as well as the role of a university rector as place-holder and guide of the people, the German collective subject, and a good many other rhapsodic offspring of subjectivism (rhapsodic, both in the ancient sense of a discourse patched together, and in the modern sense of a composition celebrating popular identity). By so juxtaposing, beginning with the titles, the words "philosophy" and "event," Heidegger's text singles out the grafting that sums up the task of his thinking.

The chain of excesses pulled along by event-like being does not end with historicized Da-sein. One link remains, which can only exacerbate the monstrousness of the site. The advance that the people, the epoch, and Da-sein merely serve to prepare is to eventually alter humans. Indeed, *Da-sein* is still only the fractured "ground" of the "Human being yet to come" (*BzP* 300, again an explicit critique of *Being and Time*[29]). The final link adds to the chain of displacements a possibility that remains beyond reach in two ways: Da-sein exceeds the epoch, as a result of which essential being-human remains as yet groundless.

Toward what, then, may man transmute himself? How is one to describe his possible shape, exceeding as it does the epoch of technicity? Its description will have to deal with the event, but how? Or rather: Where? Indeed, the *there* obviously designates a place. Once the subject has been transformed into Da-sein, the latter will prepare the place where man can let himself be appropriated by the event. Heidegger calls this possible being-human, still out of reach but appropriated by the *Ereignis*, the *self*.

A warning against a utopian reading should be added here. Phrases such as "up until now" and "not yet" abound in the text. To the extent that they concern the popular uprising on which, for a few months, Heidegger had counted, these expressions imply an assessment or a historicist protocol. History would have had to be told upstream and downstream from a certain electoral victory in the early 1930s. With the shifts, first toward the historial-epochal, then toward Da-sein and the event, these very phrases, on the other hand, have nothing at all to do with that sort of accounting that since the end of the nineteenth century one calls historical positivism. On the contrary, "Any recollection of being and language is but an advance (*ein Vorstoß*) so as to reach our 'station' in being itself" (*BzP* 501). The series of topical excesses is then by no means to be read as tracing a line toward some epiphanic morrow, be it *ou*-topic or *eu*-topic. For Heidegger it is always and solely a matter of showing possibilities inscribed in our own place, possibilities that have become obvious as a result of that electoral victory, since, once the scales have fallen from the eyes, all hegemonies prove to be fantasmic.

A further warning is called for, which seems less obvious at first sight, but is indispensable, namely, against an autonomistic reading. The shifts in question lead to the self. Now, ever since the moderns first began to speak of it, the self has fallen under the either/or of a patient (in Luther) and an agent (in Kant). The emancipated self, as we saw, would be the proper name of my freedom. There, the subject would come to itself, reside in itself, would act for itself. The self born from the Enlightenment would be the source of identity for both cognitive and moral activities. As a practical principle of identity it would provide the ultimate condition for acts which, because they were autonomous, would be fully responsible.

Heidegger, at least in his transgressive strategies, thinks the self in another way. "The 'by oneself' is but a deceptive display." A display: Something else is going on behind the autonomy flaunted by the moderns. The other, *heteron,* exceeding the *auton* of the autonomous subject, in reality precedes it and works upon it from within. To speak in the transcendental idiom, but turned against subjectivist transcendentalism, in order for its acts to be representable in reflection and imputable to it, the self must already have been constituted in advance. "Constituted": The passive form of the past participle says something more essential than autonomy. It bespeaks a heteronomy that persists at the very heart of, prior to, and underneath, all spontaneity, a heteronomy that renders the autonomy-reflexivity-responsibility-emancipation complex deceptive. "The *reflexive relation* stated in the 'self'—to 'oneself', with 'oneself', for 'oneself'—has its essence in *appropriation*" (*BzP* 320). The self appears only in a historial constellation of being, which appropriates it and makes it its own, only following which can the self reflect and thus turn back upon itself, persist close to itself, and assert itself for itself. This is not to say that the self amounts once again to an act of grace giving us an identity from outside. Nevertheless, heteronomy (as will be seen concerning the law) and receptivity (as will be seen concerning the "other beginning") say something truer than modern self-possession. Autonomy and heteronomy, then, must not be construed as the two cases of one genus, but as two traits—a discordant play of attraction and retraction—marking our pathetic site as well as the tragic condition of being that this site reveals.

The modern pathology places phenomena, and the self first of all, on disparate terrains, under the archic-anarchic double bind. Within the subjectivist arena, the ego remains the other of the archic self. Thus at the limit of this arena, the self still experiences the pull of the consciousness from which it was born, but which henceforth it is pulled back toward a privation (*ex-*, *an-*). A topic without a general topography places the self within the event of appropriation-expropriation and leads to *the other as anarchic self.*

In what way the self exceeds our site can be glimpsed by attending to some semantic associations Heidegger connects to "appropriation." "By the event of appropriation alone do we become ourselves." What does this mean? First of all, and in a certain agreement with tradition, this is to say that the self *is* not, but comes to be. It comes about not, to be sure, through a new *paideia* given to the ephebe as his own against the barbarians, nor by a new education given to Emile against culture. The self as Heidegger understands it comes about suddenly. Appropriation (*Ereignung*) happens as an event (*Ereignis*). As for ownness (*das Eigene*), this denotes nothing attributive. It is topological. It concerns one's "own place," the *there*. These associations, too, lead outside of the metaphysics of property (for instance, of a substance), of propriety (the purity or clarity of a simple idea) and of power (for example, of ancient pretor, a word translated from the Greek *archontate*). Belonging to being freed from these, as it were, improper connotations, Da-sein properly (*eigentlich*) becomes a self. Disenframed from the system of consciousness and the ego, the self becomes other. It responds to being *qua* event.

Whatever the "positive" descriptions that will be given of the event, the statements that have been noted already give it a "negative" significance (to be found, moreover, in Heidegger until his very last writings). The event is the aggregate of phenomena as it comes about, shorn of every subsumptive authority.

In response to this stripping, what may emerge is the anarchic self as what is at stake in the other responsibility (other than that of the autonomous subject). Its incompatibility with the hegemony of the cogito is obvious. The self finds itself disconnected from any focal meaning, placed outside of referential consciousness, and "defined" by this severance and this outside-consciousness. It is made finite, rendered just as singular as being is *qua* event. The self, Heidegger writes, "belongs" to the event, which in turn "makes use of" it (*BzP* 251). Each remains unthinkable without the other. The series of excesses starting with the anxiousness of a collective subject asking itself "Who are we? " leads to the mutual constitution of singulars.

With the self so violently demarcated from any philosophy of the subject, the pathos of the contemporary question of "Who?" is already at hand. Who are we when the referents, traversed just as violently by the divide that accounts for the monstrousness of our site, collapse? In one form or another these referents answered the question "What is man?" The modern answer to that "What?" has been that man is the ego capable of representing itself as the focal meaning in the constitution of phenomena. Now, Heidegger observes, "it is by no means a foregone conclusion that the 'self' can be determined through the representation of the 'ego'." By no means a foregone conclusion—an astonishing *understatement* when it is a question of the sharpest pain alienating the self from the ego. It is a question of our epochal figure of the tragic. Indeed the common genus is lacking that would encompass the questions What? (answer: ego) and Who? (answer: self). Both of these questions, to be sure, concern us. But only the first leads "to determinations setting the standard," to normative determinations. The other question, to the contrary, plunges us "into the distress of the abandonment by being" (*BzP* 68). Who are we? "Not yet" the self; thus, always deprived of this possible gift—but this gift is nothing but the diremption itself—whereby Da-sein will be deterritorialized. In other words, to mark the pathos that makes us unsteady in these times of weakened hegemonies, no continuous fabric envelops the ego and the self. No continuous discourse links philosophy, which establishes the old "'self'-certainty (*Selbstgewißheit*) proper to the 'ego'" to the other thinking "recollecting the self" (*Selbstbesinnung, BzP* 48); hence, it may be added, a certain historial necessity of textual discontinuities in the *Contributions*. As for self-assertion (*Selbstbehauptung*[30]), it then falls entirely within the operative machination that constitutes the current events not only in Germany, but in the entire hemisphere. As for the possible (which in 1936 Heidegger has reasons, unimaginable in 1927, to call "higher than the actual"[31]), the other that clashes with the ego is the self. To trace the gap between them is thinking's hitherto unheard-of responsibility, its unconsoling, unconsolidating, and unedifying service.

A public service it is, for if the "other beginning" remains out of reach to reform the people of the 1930s, this is not to say that the possible does not *manifest itself.* Only the most thoughtless positivism will deny that the possible manifests itself. The anarchic self manifests itself, on the contrary, by the retraction it exerts upon normative consciousness. It declares itself in that the world of the moderns has never been able to confront the standard of the autonomous ego. That on the fringes of the territory laid out by the cogito, a mere possibility—the self, another modern achievement[32]—possesses such subtractive powers implies of course that the possible is understood, not in the historicist manner, as a future, but in the historial manner, as a "to-come." The self is, and has been, to-come ever since the very establishment of normative consciousness. In the counter-strategies that have passed through the transcendental strategy toward order, since its establishment, the anarchic self has revealed itself as something concretely possible. The possible is never nothing, it is a *posse* (just as *Möglichkeit* is a *Macht,* a power). In Heidegger it therefore holds a status strictly paralleling that of "concealment" in truth understood as unconcealment, operating in the manner of a singularization concealed in all unconcealed phenomenalization, always and already powerful, even if unthought; and subverting from within the true which the ego founds as the opposite of the false. Concealment supplements the symmetrical contraries of true and false as a dissymmetrical contrary. Similarly, the self supplements the symmetrical opposites of consciousness (ego) and object (representation) as an opposite impossible to measure by the standard of consciousness, and having no common measure. To ask for a "leap" in thinking, so that it may reach what has been forgotten by oppositional logic, amounts in any case to receiving *the other, thought otherwise than as a determinate negation*. How could one fail to recognize in this foreign other—impossible to reconcile, to pair, to amalgamate, or to sublate—the very logic of the tragic?

And how could one fail to recognize in it the pathos which, over the four centuries of modernity, has turned consciousness against itself? The ego and the self have shown themselves to be contradictory since Luther and not complying with the principle of non-contradiction. The pertinence of propositions about one in no way entails the non-pertinence of propositions about the other. Is it betting too much on this other logic of disparates to see its full deployment in the pathologies of the twentieth century? The normative fracture that announced itself in the "facts of consciousness" in Luther would then reveal, after the hypertrophy of spiritualizations in German Idealism, its full pathogenic potential. Today the discourses abound that exude the aspiration toward the groundless that, in our historial site, take the place of Spirit, of its inspirations and its reconciliations. But none have expressed the tragic in its modern form as has Heidegger. None, indeed, has expressed the pathos that separates being fantasized as universal ego from being singularized as the event of a becoming-self.

Fantasms of the same: the integrative violence of the law

> "As regards the founding of the essence of the truth of being,
> 'logic' itself is an illusion, even though the most necessary illusion
> that the history of being has known up to now." (*BzP* 461)

In these lines, Heidegger states one feature common to all ultimate representations. The Greek one, Latin nature, and modern self-consciousness are linked to this "most necessary illusion" that logic, itself understood as the corpus of norms for truth, has been. Indeed, according to the opinion common in philosophy, henology puts the principle of non-contradiction to work (even in Heidegger, Parmenides is held to be the beginning of "the destitution of *phusis*"[33]); *natura* is organized according to the principle of continuity, a logical principle in the sense of a teleological order; lastly, autonomous consciousness would be summed up in its *a priori* forms, in transcendental logic. If Heidegger sees the above as being so many epochal figures of the same illusion, it is because he considers them in terms of the other "logic" of being *qua* event. His critique supposes that with regard to the principial—in particular, transcendental—*logos,* he take a step back toward the tragic *logos*. This distance alone allows him to describe logic as "an illusion of an essence *even deeper* than the 'dialectical illusion' made visible by Kant" (ibid.). One could not state better the radicalization he brings to bear on the modern critique of totalizing speculations.

For Kant, the illusion of totalizing speculations unceasingly mocked and tormented (*zwackt und äfft,* B 397) reason, and their megalomania kept the natural metaphysician in us alive, as every search for conditions necessarily postulated the unconditioned. In Heidegger, postulates *per thesin* trick us out of a "more necessary" historial necessity because they bear upon being independently of its fixation around the normative ego and its antecedents. More necessary does not mean being anchored yet more deeply in the architectonic of consciousness than the ideas of soul, world, and God. If necessity were still to be gauged by some *arch-techné,* that would be the end of the Heideggerian project of a radical *Aufklärung,* a project that assigns to thinking the task of preparing an anarchic economy of being. Here necessity, as will be seen concerning the categories of modality, results not from a system of *a priori* acts, but from the double bind of life and death.

How, then, does the logical illusion arise from this double bind?

Concerning each hegemony, I have described the fantasm of the universal which commands it. For Heidegger, commanding here means that logic proves to be illusory in its *work of subsumption.* To show how, one would only need to point out in the logic of the same (a) the interest that speaks through it, (b) the understanding of being reflected in it, as well as (c) the linguistic shifts in the course of history that displace it. These incursions into "metaphysical" territory—which constitute this terrain as such, but that is another problem—aim at anything but arriving at some verdict on the past. What is at stake each time is rather our own historial possibility carved out indirectly by these incursions.

a. In logical subsumptions (a pleonasm, anyway) an interest declares itself. Heidegger suggests this, first, when speaking as a symptomatologist of modern times. "The dread before being has never been as great as today. The proof: The gigantic arrangement by which we attempt to surmount this dread" (*BzP* 139). He then describes the gigantic therapeutic contrivance in terms of fabrication, as an "operative machination" (*Machenschaft:* a word that expresses at once making—*poiesis* and *techné,* sinister maneuvering,[34] as well as the collapse of *phusis* into "that which produces itself," *BzP* 126f). Later he describes the same thetic contrivance as "positive enframing" (*Gestell*). One still has to be able to recognize one and the same phenomenon behind both descriptions. It becomes apparent in the dread that has become unbearable, it pushes on the most rigid institutionalized fixity, it is called "need for security." "The unwavering assurance against all insecurity" (*BzP* 203) is sought in the logical fixation of being, conceived to make fixed phenomena true. In what attracts us as logically true, the interest in safety grips us not only from within (by the need for consolation) and from without (by the need for consolidation). It also drives the entire history of truth from the time *phusis* came to denote self-production up to the time of the global reach of contemporary technology. The referents propped up by the historical illusions therefore are not at all disinterested. If they have been able to maintain themselves over quasi-pharaonic millennia, it is because they have served as points of reference for damming up anguish in the face of instability. Whence a first indirect feature of "the essence of the truth of being" as event. It has to be thought of otherwise than as guaranteeing stability (otherwise too, of course, than as some determinate negation of the stable, as is flux, becoming, or movement). As is known, Heidegger reads contemporary technology as providing the extreme form of truth by adequation. As mathematizable, nature is adequate to the subject. "The technicity of modern technology follows from a new mutation in the essence of truth." Again, what has to be understood here is which truth, and with which necessary consequence, is thereby denied: "*alétheia* alone, by virtue of its agonistic way of being, makes 'tragedy' possible and necessary."[35]

b. The understanding of being reflected in the logic of subsumption can only have been fashioned to satisfy, without remainder, the need for assurance-security-safety;

without remainder, hence the attraction (and the word) of the universal. The illusion, one and unique in this, arises when one "posits something before oneself, in its *koinon* and its *katholou*" (*BzP* 477); it arises when one turns an aggregate of "this" and "that" toward what is common to them from a general point of view. Whether such positing of the common and general operates by way of defining, predicating, or naming, it always results from the maximizing thrust of languages. This prompts a most troubling question: On what basis have the common and general "assumed (*angemaßt*) an eminent rank" (ibid.)? What has been the basis for this hubris (*Anmaßung*) of the universal posited as the common measure (*Maß*) of the true?[36] At stake are the conditions of manifestation, not some explanatory etiology.

As the illusion stemming from natality, which is an ultimate of everydayness, the *regional* games of the particular and the universal open the space for all speech. Without common regional representations, there is no language, and consequently no worlds. But to characterize these representations as a labor of subsumption and as an opposition of universal and particular is to do a disservice to regional plays, for thereby their irreducible diversity is lost. In order to single out a regional nomic strategy, it is better to speak not of a universal and its particular cases, but of an economy and the phenomena which make it up. Worlds are constituted by assemblages which are made and unmade—which come undone under the tugging {*retrait*} of mortality.

The critique that starts off from the ultimates of everydayness, however, dismantles *ultimate* subsumptions. One must ask of these: From where did their hubris come to us? To respond in historical terms, it came from the ancient construction of causes and the modern construction of conditions. To respond in terms of being, it came from the representation of a true beingness that is both cause and condition of beings. To respond in terms of the ultimates of everydayness, it comes from the denial of the tugging of mortality that always singularizes the phenomena that arrange themselves to make a world. Thus the sway of the illusion is only secondarily due to the concatenation of epochs. It is due first of all to the fact that the truth of being has been cleansed of its intrinsic discord (which cleansing is nothing other than *epechein*, the very suspension of truth), that is, cleansed by the concealment-unconcealment that the step back toward the event is to restore to it. Being could appear as a reliable ground only once rid of tragic antagonisms. Once it is reduced to the same and integrates all alterity under the dominion of a *logos* such that one can conceive of nothing more common, it renders services of assurance.

c. Regarding the shifts that have displaced the illusion of the same in accordance with the predominant languages, Heidegger enumerates rather than justifies them: "Beings: in their *arising* into their own (Greekness); *caused* by some sort of supreme being from out of its essence (Middle Ages); the factual as *object* (modernity)—the truth of being concealing itself more and more" (*BzP* 171). First of all we should note here that the eclipse of being in its conflictual truth begins with the *phuein* of beings. From the preclassical Greeks onwards, the unconcealed that is self-identical provided the standard to which phenomena must conform in order to be true. More noteworthy still is the historicist-historial amphibology in which these words on the linguistic shifts put *die Sprache*. When read as historicist, the epochalization is linked to easily datable of translations. A *logos* of the same that binds and obligates us for the period of its eminence then is pressed into the service of a retrospective and descriptive phenomenology. This positivist stratum (but, as in Michel Foucault, it is a second-order positivism) remains part and parcel of any inquiry into hegemonic fantasms. When read historially, on the other hand, the epochalization is instead linked to "the word as what founds history," to speech, that is, as it wrests from concealment an economy of unconcealment. Here, the same has a power of obligation only insofar *{dans la mesure}*[37] as conflictual truth binds us in advance, "in silence," forgotten, denied, and prior to any spoken language. According to the first reading, *Sprache* has to be translated as 'tongue' *{langue}*, according to the second, as 'language' *{langage}*. Neither of these two epochal concatenations is construed somehow above history (which is why the very status of the "history of being" is missed by those who see it as posited "in an idealist heaven . . . *above* or *behind* real history"[38]). Rather the past, which has modulated beingness, is first read from the viewpoint of fantasized beings and a second time from that of being that is sundered. According to the first reading, speaking amounts to "humanizing beings"; according to the second, speech has already and always wrought "the most originary dehumanization of man as a 'factual living entity'" (*BzP* 510). What is dehumanized is the phenomenological gaze. The phenomenological gaze shifts from the focal {meaning of being} that is always a posture of "man," toward what is originary, toward the event *giving rise* to all such postures that standardize the conflictual essence of the truth so as to norm the true.

Hence the advantage, as will be seen below, of beginning the investigation of the agonistic event by an examination of "topology." Hence, above all, the relentless *historial differend* that twists one's words as soon as one asks: What sets the standard? Because of the diversity of answers—"it is the one," "it is nature," "it is self-consciousness"—the differend is not superelevated into the event. If the latter remains nameless and unnameable, it is because it synthesizes nothing. It sets its standard, but one that is singular and originary without being simple. There is then nothing more equivocal, and by the very equivocalness that accounts for differing, than Heidegger's formula: "*so ist die Sprache Massetzung*" (ibid.). It twists one's words because, following the first strategy that construes the history of beingness from beings, it must be translated as "thus a tongue posits the standard." Law-making *logos* is illusory because of its factual and entitative multiplicity. Following the second strategy, which receives from the event the double bind that debilitates all fantasms, the phrase must be translated instead as "thus language sets the standard." Understood this way, what sets the standard is the unique dissension emphasized by the word *alétheia*. Any *logos* laying down the law uniformly remains illusory because it camouflages and deceives the rent between unconcealing and concealing. The *singulare tantum,* which is the logical illusion, has its condition in that other *singularlum tantum*—that entirely other singular—that is fractured being.

The double bind of natality and mortality manifests for us the event in its dissension of appropriation-expropriation; truth is also manifested there in its conflict of unconcealment-concealment. How, then, does the logical illusion arise from the double bind? By the thoughtlessness (*Gedankenlosigkeit*) of life positing itself as if the expropriating and concealing undertow were not. Thus by tragic denial.

The task of thinking, then, amounts to the repetition of this polymorphic undertow.

The task is complicated by its polymorphism. Thus Heidegger speaks of the event at times in the plural (designating the foundations of epochs where being suspends [*epéchein*] its conflictual truth, all the while granting an economy), and at times in the singular (designating that which "keeps the standard" [ibid.] in this refusing and this granting). If the shifts in our past have displaced the logical illusion in accordance with hegemonic bearings, in retrospect their sequence gestures in the direction of a forgotten, entirely other bearing. Fantasms have been able to make the law only inasmuch as they hold to being itself as event ("*das steht beim Seyn selbst*," *BzP* 492).

One happily labels epochal phenomenology as being contextualist, relativist, and thus as nihilist. Does not historial differing oppose attractions-retractions lacking any common name? Now, from where does this differend come? Again, it is manic denial of *tragic truth* that leads one to cry nihilism in reading Heidegger. There is a historial differend, first of all because the "there is" is undermined in event-like differing. Is it so extravagant to see, in the normative dispersion that befalls us, the sign of a graver, more irreparable discordance? Obviously one can remain indifferent to the conditions under which one is living and go on with *business as usual*. The normative dispersion of which one complains today on the political right as well as on the left nonetheless contains a lesson. Whether one looks at it diachronically or synchronically, it manifests a tearing in the condition of being that undermines any rootedness in advance. Following the scheme of hiding and showing, which truth is, the strife between unconcealment and concealment in originary truth is a strife for which "being itself" remains nameless. From the epochal to the aletheiological, the differend steps back as if from the conditioned to the condition.

Acquiescence to the originary discordance is Heidegger's whole concern. Thus one should not rush to state, in some facile formula, that of which it consists (see chapter 6). Beforehand, it will prove useful to look closely at the *concordance* forced by fantasms, which results from the integrative violence of the law that spreads isomorphism.

In jumping from strategy to strategy, the *Contributions* not only thematize the monstrous passage to the normative limits, but they carry it to completion. Thus Heidegger first speaks *under* the regime of self-consciousness, revealing the double bind of the self and the ego in their disparity. Then all of a sudden he speaks from somewhere else. The disparate then no longer opposes adversarial thrusts fracturing one referent or another from within, but it opposes the normative referents to themselves. From where is he speaking then? Where is he who says that ultimate norms are illusions whose institution and destitution is due to being itself? By all evidence, such a discourse no longer issues from the epochal influence of consciousness. If it still did, how could it render that influence problematic? The procedure may instead be comparable to the question "What is metaphysics?" Later he will say that to raise it is "in a sense, to have left metaphysics."[39] In a sense. . . . The same is true here. In order to ask "What are these fantasmic illusions that are more necessary than the transcendental illusions?" the question can no longer be raised in the broad daylight of transcendental subjectivism. From what place, then? Not, to be sure, from some extra-metaphysical satellite or some new wave washing beyond the anti-subjectivist tidal wave. These are but so many reactive effects to that "old sun" (unless it is the moon of the night of the world), the ego. Heidegger does not leave the terrain where the substitutes for the Platonic sun continue to rule—and how could one? Instead he speaks from that blank place (*"offene Stelle," BzP* 510) that has been gaping in consciousness from the time of its referential institution. He speaks from the place of the innermost rent (*"der innigste Riss,"*[40] ibid.) in the modern theticism of the same, a rent first apparent in Kant with the disparate modes of positing (*Setzung* and *Position*), where night erupts into the obviousness of the blazing midday sun. This is something quite different from declaring cheerfully that metaphysics has ended and that one has only to decide to change terrain by abruptly placing oneself outside.

Principial theticism becomes problematic beginning with the site—our own, which is anything but stable—where the fragility of modern normative "achievements" has become the most widely shared bit of knowledge about the world. Just as in the experience of Oedipus, something about this new state of affairs opens one's eyes. Beginning with the blank place in pathetic consciousness, Heidegger will end up being able to describe the discordance within the event, which translates into cracks passing through all epochal referents. But, and this alone is important here, speaking from that blank rent he can still describe the referents themselves, both in their attempted subsumptive effectiveness and in their hubris. With a strong dose of polemics, he traces them back to key Greek concepts such as *harmonia, eudaimonia,* and *entelecheia:* "[T]he fissuring of being *must not be patched up by the fantasized illusion of reconciliation, of 'happiness' and of false accomplishment*" (*BzP* 406). So much for the equalizing beginning. The allusions to the Stoics, to Plato, and to Aristotle are barely concealed. Beingness has been fantasized as reconciling what occurrent being fissures. Then, here is what he has to say about the normative force of these illusory reconciliations: The subject runs "the danger of revolving around itself and of idolizing what are only conditions for its permanence, to the point of turning them into its *unconditioned*" (*BzP* 398). This time, Heidegger reads the genealogical history from its end where the subject revolves around itself, making the world its own representations. Whether it designates the individual or the people, the ego raises its own identity to the level of an idol, postulating it as an ultimate condition for the sake of consoling and consolidating itself. But the description is obviously valid for any equalization posited as normative. Heidegger does not hesitate to name a few of these illusions—so many versions of logolatry—that have served to turn the occurrent tragic into some guarantee of the same.[41] How is being understood in a way that it can lend itself in this way to the fantasms of the same? "Strictly speaking, only what endures in being present is" (*BzP* 115). Fantasms invade thinking only after all topological irregularities have been smoothed over, only after the event bitter with discordance has been leveled off into the similar and the same.

The event only gives rise to historial illusions once stabilized into beingness. Heidegger links these places of the same, these commonplaces, to languages or even names of philosophers.[42] Reading him, one can therefore speak unhesitatingly of hegemonies in the plural. Nevertheless, all that interests him in all historial differing is the violence due to which occurrent being has collapsed into stable beingness. In this sense, for two and a half thousand years we have lived but a single fantasmic hegemony: the one that has forced all phenomena into the isomorphic.

Fantasms are born of a comparison (*Vergleichen*) that always amounts to an equalization (*Gleichmachen*), and this by means of a calculative relation to some referent posited as remaining the same (*ein Gleiches, BzP* 151).

What indeed is a representation to be called whose job is to force into an isomorphism all other representations measured by its yardstick? What is there that is, by essence, *the same* for an entire class of cases and before which all are *equal*? Such a representation is called a law. To speak of equality before the law amounts, then, to yet another pleonasm. The law is defined by the equality it imposes on subjects and cases, just as its subjects and cases are defined by the law that equalizes them. "All men are mortal," "The square of the hypotenuse is equal to the sum of the squares of the other two sides of a right-angled triangle," "Oviparous animals reproduce by means of eggs that hatch outside the female's body; viviparous animals reproduce by bringing forth living young," "Thou shalt not kill." . . . In every case, a law gives shape to the same, and it always makes the cases, facts, particulars, subjects, human practices, and natural processes for which it "obtains" the same. Without integrative violence there is no law and without the law there is no isomorphism. To obtain, to be valid and fit—this all means to be strong, to exercise integrative violence. What then is more violent than a "value" posited in order to impose on disparates some shape of the same?

Such is at least the work of the law as it appears through the strict reciprocity between a normative referent and the isomorphic. Seen from the perspective of the event that clears an opening, it will appear in an entirely different light (chapter 7), not for the universal concordance among particular cases, but for the discordance among phenomena set into an economy and singularized at the same time (the "same" time, which will bring the to-come into the present and thereby will turn time against itself).

On the isomorphic: archic and anarchic

"What is, when the struggle for standards dies out?" (*BzP* 28)

The explicit project of making the world uniform institutes the modern age. Thus, why qualify the understanding of substances facing the subject if not to make them equal (*iso*) in their forms (*morphé*), that is, uniform, isomorphic? In Kant, the uniformization of phenomena is obtained through the inner sense. Only what is temporalized is a datum and only what can be ordered in calculable succession or simultaneity is temporalized. As for the acts of the understanding, there are powerful reasons why the first of these acts must concern what can be measured and calculated. Since the subject knows only perceptions that are measurable in their spatial and temporal extension, the first Kantian category has to be that of quantity. Thus, the uniform and the quantifiable must not be treated as mere consequences of the "Copernican turn" toward the legislating subject. Quite the reverse. Only because every phenomenon has to be accessible to calculation—because its phenomenality is summed up in its calculability—does the subject have to occupy the place of legislator. Establishing itself as the spontaneous source of the laws of being, the subject will be certain that these laws will be the same everywhere.

The modern regularity of phenomena results, then, from an act of anticipation, from an *a priori* positing. For Heidegger, the spontaneous subject is defined by this theticism alone. "*Positing* a rule in advance" (*BzP* 161) is the one gesture that constitutes both the autonomous agent and the datum it renders uniform. Now, a rule prescribing what ought to be is called a "norm." The isomorphic is the *normal*. To see how the uniform is related to norms, one must pick up the thread of the historial. Step by step, it leads from modern universal *mathesis* to a certain abyss.

The Cartesian and Kantian institution of the project of mathematization—thus the thesis of a science that is universal because it quantifies—matches its utter success in the twentieth century. Heidegger describes today's planetary deployment of this project in terms of "giganticism" and "operative machination." Understood in this way, the isomorphic appears as the terminus of the modern trajectory. It is the mode of being in which triumphs the focusing of phenomena upon self-consciousness.[43] The question cited in the epigraph above, "What is, when the struggle for standards dies out?" emphasizes the extinguishing of the struggle. There is no longer a struggling for norms, since everything amounts to the same. This emphasis can support itself with reference to many of Heidegger's polemics. Doesn't he argue quite simply that National Socialism, Americanism, Bolshevism, Judaism, and Christianity all are moving along the same path, and that thus they have ceased to fight among themselves to set the standard for life? What prevails in their gray-on-gray is the normalization of nature construed transcendentally by intuitive temporalization and categorial quantification. Isomorphism characterizes an epoch, the one in which self-consciousness—the "I think"—sets the standard.

However, the historial thread leads, to be sure, much further back. Normalization is ancient. Prior to forcing conformity to the subject, it forced conformity to the type. If Heidegger traces a genealogy that leads from the type (from the *idea*) to the subject (to transcendental idealism) and, finally, to "operative machinations" (to the ideal of performance and output), it is because the interests that have worked on it from within since the beginning reveal themselves at the end of history. Here these interests have to do with theses and the isomorphic, that is to say, with norms and the normal. The violence of the thetic ideal as the master of meaning resides in its formalism. A para-*digm* shows (*deik-*) how to define something, it formalizes that to which it is applied, informs it by imposing a name on it, makes it conform to what it ought to be—in short, makes it uniform and standardizes it. Such is *archic isomorphism,* the uniformity imposed by a type, an idea, a model, a cause, or some other variety of *arché*—by a hegemonic fantasm.

The historial critique espies an illusion at the heart of this very uniformity imprinted by the ideal on what passes for the real. To believe that a normative difference separates the ideal and the real is, properly speaking, the illusion "of an essence still deeper than the 'dialectical illusion'." This is because, in retrospect, the lineage issuing from the Platonic *idea* was not driven by the focal meaning of an age posited as great, hegemonic, normative, ideal—it was not driven by the ultimate referents. There could be neither norms nor the normalized unless being had from the outset been made isomorphic according to possible operations of measurement. It must lend itself to such operations. But it can only be prepared for this by a prior constraint and a prior reduction. The isomorphic does not follow from a referent posited as archic, but includes this referent. Being must be understood beforehand in an algebraic manner (*algebra* coming from an Arabic word signifying precisely constraint and reduction). When he states that algebra contains the key to all knowledge, Descartes is merely axiomatizing the most ancient pre-understanding of being. What could be more calculating than to say, for example, here is the one, it sums things up? Here is nature, it is what is greatest, it sets the standard? The prestige of the normative reveals, from its rise in ancient Greece, the prestige of the calculable. The simple screening of ideals will never reveal this. "Ideals," Heidegger writes, "are of an essence that is not properly historial (*geschichtlich*), but historiological (*historisch*)" (*BzP* 443). Their respective promotion and sphere of influence can be inventoried just like that of all leaders—leaders of states, of armies, or of other ranks, all of whom are subject to factual history. The historial, on the other hand, does not lend itself to calculative reason as something to inventory. It concerns "'only' what pertains to being: to the decisive, the un-decided, the uncertain" (ibid.), words strictly signifying the caesurae setting epochs apart. What is not to be missed in contemporary "giganticism" is the epiphany of its norms and the normal—that their difference is the very content of the illusion in which a leading referent governs the defining, predicating, and naming of the logical illusion accompanying the common, the *koinon,* in all its variations.

There occurs indeed, Heidegger writes, a veritable "'wizardry' of what is universally valid" (*BzP* 343) as the common designates at once the form unifying particular cases into a class—making them uniform—and the standard serving as their yardstick. The isomorphic endlessly extends the universal in the first sense; in the second sense, fantasms maximize it unendingly. Thus the historial thread, unraveled back as far as the Greeks, reveals a duplicity under the long career of the common. Perhaps this double game of the same becomes obvious only once the normalized extensiveness and the normative intensiveness of the *koinon* have obviously collapsed into the one-dimensional. Then, "being as what is the most common" (its boundless extensiveness) makes it that "all beings are being being most intensely" (its supreme intensiveness) (*BzP* 444 and 136). When each being counts as *ontôs on,* then all are equivalent, equally valid, and indifferent (*gleichgültig*). This is the moment of the decisive crisis when, once and for all, "the struggle for standards dies out."

With the detour via the genealogy of being as idea, the emphasis lies rather on the first part of the question cited, namely, "What is?" Answer: Under the theticism of the idea and of all that has been endowed with value ever since, only the isomorphic is. The history of being, however, gives this answer a fuller resonance than the modern mathematization of phenomena around the ego. In the twentieth century—and for Heidegger, in the mid-1930s—it becomes unmistakable that by tracing the normalized back to its norm, one goes literally from the similar to the same. Hence the truth of archic isomorphism becomes clear. It has never served anything but an illusion covering up thetic, integrative violence.

The collapse of the normative difference into isomorphism is thus ancient. Only today it is deepening into an abyss. Heidegger responds to isomorphism with a No and a Yes that are equally vehement. No, for the world rendered uniform makes being-there (*Da-sein*) difficult and rare, it perverts it into being-gone (*Weg-sein, BzP* 323). Yes, since for the phenomenologist of being, *there is* nothing other than singulars. This *there is,* to be sure, is not nothing. It "is" being itself as an event that phenomenalizes and rephenomenalizes singulars according one constellation, then another constellation. But a universal and most intense being, which would measure everything according to the top and the bottom of a scale—such a normative being lacks all phenomenality. Or, rather, it possesses only fantasmic phenomenality, like a historial illusion.

The motive of the vehemence that prompted Heidegger to wager on a certain political movement becomes clearer. If beingness in the shape of one fantasm or another has kept us spellbound for over two thousand years, the work of disenchanting the world was already completed in the first half of the twentieth century. Giganticism and operational machinations had taken care of it quite effectively. They had already displayed, in the full light of day, the evidence for all beings henceforth being worth the being that is most of all. Did the movement in question not promise a break with that tedium by resituating the "we"?

The isomorphism of the most monotonous indistinctness at least conveys this truth about being: There is no use probing for its depth in the direction of *archai* and ultimate authorities. The whole problematic of the profound and the superficial proves to be essentially calculative, as it amounts to measuring one being against another. If one is to think otherwise, then nothing must be sought behind phenomena; they themselves are to be preserved in the caesura in which the event of contextualization-decontextualization arranges them. Thinking emancipates itself from the normative "difference" (*Unterscheidung*) between beings and their beingness by stepping back from occurrent being toward the "decision" (*Entscheidung, BzP* 455)—a decision that one would never have needed to open a text of Heidegger in order to conceive of as a human initiative. Rather, it shows quite clearly the heterogeneity in the twofold step back by which Heidegger transmutes the ancient theme of the *a priori*. Difference allows one to move from beings to the depth that is *illusory—which is archic because thetic*—of beingness; the decision, on the other hand, moves from these illusions to their *phenomenal condition,* to the "time" deeper than history (*unterzeitlich, BzP* 108)*—that is anarchic because occurrent.*

The Yes to the isomorphic understood this way—that is, to the collapse of normative beingness into normalized beings—sustains the narrative that is the history of being. "There was once a time when beingness became what was most of all (*ontôs on*)." From that point on, "being has had the character of beingness." And how has the latter been understood? "Always and solely as *koinon,* as that which is common and thus ordinary for all beings" (*BzP* 243, 425, 75). Now if being has been posited as beingness (as one posits a foundation) and beingness in turn is represented as a being, then the ancient question "What is the being of beings?" is only the title of a management program applied to beings that have been tacitly understood[44] to be all worth the same, but among which this or that one had to be promoted for the sake of consoling the soul and consolidating the city. The question "What is the being of beings?" is thus embarrassing for its redundancy. The way it has been reiterated by the civil servants of mankind has made them go round in circles among beings that are strictly equivalent.

The ambiguity with regard to isomorphism could not be stated more pathetically. On the one hand, it tells the truth about beings. No system of qualities except an illusory one ranks them, and the theticism that promotes one or the other among them has never been anything but an act of arch-violence that selects one representation and confers upon it an immutable value. It is an act whose essential hubris has not failed to burst forth with the epochal breaks undergone by such haltings. Yes to the anarchic isomorphism in which beings remain unclassifiable—*alike in this*—and resist subsumption under some signifying cluster.

On the other hand, however, with an entire lexicon placed in quotation marks, Heidegger denounces isomorphism. Thus, in the mid-1930s, "a renewal of 'culture' is being 'called for' and its rooting in the 'people' is being busily pursued with the aim of communicating it to everyone" (*BzP* 496). Tirades like this abound. Their target is, of course, what Heidegger felt to be the betrayal committed by the National Socialists. Instead of singularizing the German people so that they might respond to the Greek people, the party had subjected them to a "popularization" (ibid.) as flat as in America or the Soviet Union. The uprising did indeed take place, but it ended up perverting everything. Rather than letting the singular be the first *(das Erste)*, the leaders posited a stupefying focal meaning: the essence of the masses (*das Massenhafte, BzP* 122). It inflated collective subjectivism to the extreme, placing itself thereby in the direct genealogical descent of the normative idea and of the normalized common, hence, of archic isomorphism.

There is nothing "post-modern" about the archic-anarchic split. Rather, it pushes the modern contradictory figures of the self and the ego to the limit, where they oppose each other as the baseless and the illusory base. Since the inception of nascent modernity, the self has been and remains a pure possibility. It is a singular that resists subsumption. It is only as an event. The ego, rather, raises itself up into a universal, and is the actual agent of all subsumption. It is only duration, "the eternal—the simple prolongation of the same, the empty *et cetera*" (*BzP* 121), empty as all beings are that are epochally promoted to the rank of beingness.

Now Heidegger proceeds otherwise than by rallying to the chorus of those who call for new norms. Faced with the collapse of hegemonies, he raises the oldest question in philosophy and asks "Which *condition of being* announces itself in the modern pathos?" Our monstrous site makes this an unavoidable question. It will find its answer in a discordance of times that acknowledges being *qua* event.

Anarchic isomorphism, in which the singular yields only to incommensurable moments of time, announces itself as a possibility in archic isomorphism, the mere aftereffect of a universal ruling as the one great, profound, efficient standard—a standard indicating in its turn the algebraic presupposition that is as old as is the illusion of logic.

In other words, the occurrent announces itself in the indifferent and the indistinct. This is why the tragic condition of being cannot even become a problem so long as some hegemony goes without saying, impervious to questioning. But anarchic isomorphism does not fit with the indifferent produced by the archic reference. They clash monstrously, which describes our site. The baseless and the illusory base hold us in their double bind, which describes our pathos.

What *is,* then, when the struggle for the standards that *archai* were—ultimate referents, normative foci, hegemonic fantasms—dies away? What comes to be *is* the possibility that the struggle of discordant contrariness can openly flare up, the event whose essence is the tragic.

Under the isomorphic that we are living, knowledge {*savoir*} has collapsed into knowledges {*connaissances*}, and these, in turn, into information. Thinking will find knowledge again—and everdayness, a self—by placing itself underneath the double bind of the ultimates conjoined in the event.

On the other that is being: what the diremption reveals

"Being and beings by no means allow themselves to be distinguished immediately because in no way do they relate immediately to one another. (*BzP* 477)

Once the normative difference in which beings would "relate" immediately to "being" has been recognized as the theticism of beingness, varied over the centuries *cum ira et studio,* then differing itself becomes thinkable. We have already seen some of its elements: the contrariness, without common genus, of self and ego; the gap between the singular and the particular; the denial that promoted all illusorily subsuming fantasms; the technological isomorphism in which the normative difference between a posited law and the disparate sup-posed by it collapses. What remains is briefly to spell out that *historial* differend, and see how it points toward a more originary *discordance.* We do this in order to answer the question: What does the diremption reveal?

One must remember first of all that in Heidegger, the vast suspicion toward anything that has passed as an ultimate authority harbors a significance for manifestation. The destructive exercise serves to reveal us as bearers of a potential that lies ahead of us; it does not show ourselves to be the victims of a mystification behind us. To recognize the broken hegemonies under which the West has grown up means to us that it is possible to retain the differend as such, to sustain it. Thus to catch a glimpse of what the diremption reveals, it suffices to listen to the one—the historial "they"—who speaks in the name of what the French so aptly call *une idée arrêtée,* the halt decreed to institute the rule of one or another ideality. What does this metaphysician, that is in each one of us, say? The genealogy of fantasms shows what—this metaphysician speaks of everything and nothing, with the name of the idea wanting to mean everything, but the halt, *l'arrêt,* saying nothing (except a libidinal investment in order[45]). What is then glimpsed is a condition freed of halts and decrees, of all *epéchein* closing off questioning, a condition in which being, as it does not subsume them under a name, does not relate in any immediate way to phenomena. It is this non-relationship that diremption reveals. What does this mean?

To a retrospective reading, the isomorphic in technological giganticism brings to light an inner discord that works on historial time as if from underneath (*unterzeitlich*). An epochal step back leads from the historial differend to the originary temporal discordance, to being as time, the one and only issue in Heidegger. Understanding this step back will mean understanding that in all coming to presence, the singularization to come undoes givens in advance. Solely to serve the needs of the exposition, this discordance can be put, term by term, into parallel with Heinrich Hertz's complaint about electromagnetism: the force received by an antenna can be used quite efficiently by treating it as wavelike, but it can be used just as efficiently by treating it as particles. The either/or of the two models does not lead to any practical problem. It is painful, on the other hand, for whoever inquires into the essence (*Wesen*) of that force. There isn't a more general representation than waves and particles that allows these disparate contraries to be subsumed under it. Thus the question of their common noun must remain just that—a question.

Such is also the case for Heidegger. Due to the originary phenomenalizing-singularizing strife, being "is not immediately related" to beings. The lesson of technological giganticism is there to show beings detached from any simple ordering. Thus in the absence of normative immediacy, the "question of being" can only remain an open one. Only those to whom this or that representation is everything, and therefore binds everything, also have an answer to everything. Now, what would a hypothetically immediate relation be—a *simple bond*? The entire lineage of historial illusions is there to supply examples. Consider nature again. Understood as a normative principle of continuity between regions of experience, nature would relate immediately to each of the beings that it homologizes: the soul, the city, humankind, the cosmos. Nature is held to subsume their diversity under its teleological regime. To the genealogist, however, the order of ends it imposes has in turn been *posited* for the sake of an end, that is, for the sake of immediately relating this ultimate referent to each being. But—and Heidegger places all the weight on this "decision"—the event with no common standard is in stark contrast with beingness; or—following a play of graphemes—being that remains a question (*Seyn*) without common measure is in stark contrast with referential being (*Sein*), the common noun of beings.

One readily believes that the ontological difference is Heidegger's last word on being. But to understand thereby the being "of beings" is to miss right away *the other that is being*. It has been construed according to the very old schema of an immediate, subsumptive, normative, nominative, and entitative relation—in a word, according to the *single bond*. But does this key really open the doors to the oldest question in philosophy, or does it rather force the lock? Greek, Latin, and modern texts have provided no lack of solutions to the problem of being—according to Heidegger, one and all forcing and distorting it beyond any possible *diasozein*. It is always beingness whose numerous modulations have provided the answers, not without having first turned the question of a verb and its temporalizing strategies into that of a noun and its immobilizing strategy. Thus the "ontological" difference between nature and an act thought to be natural answers first of all to the question "In the name of what?" and then (that is to say only on the strength of an authoritative name) it also responds to the question "What is being?" Being is not nature, nor does it integrate ends, and therefore it does not *differ* from beings to which it immediately relates, except once it has been obliterated for the sake of beingness which has itself been fantasized in accordance with the interests of order and stability.[46]

In the lines quoted above, being remains an open question, as the question of *Wesen* remained open for Hertz. Just as for Hertz, the impossibility of getting his bearings on this one problem worthy of investigation is due to disparate contraries. The ego can be put to good use. The revolutions of the eighteenth century and their institutional effects are there to prove it. The self can also be put to good use. Luther and his anti-institutional effects are there to prove it. But one can make only pathetic use of the self paired with the ego. Their common referent, consciousness, only succeeds in integrating them at the cost of a violence that warps the self, that reduces the disparate to archic isomorphism, that turns being into some fantasm of beingness, and buries its otherness in irrevocable forgetfulness.

"What then?" one may ask. "Then" there is an institutionalized violence that is irrevocable.

Under the epochal figure of the differend, there lies hidden an old anguish: Where are we going? In terms of discordant forces: Where is the pathos that defines us—that is itself a symptom of the monstrous epoch—taking us? Or again, aiming more directly at the forgetfulness concealed by this pathos and this monstrousness: If the question of being remains a question, in differend with the non-subsumable disparate, then to which terrain is it leading us? By way of a response, Heidegger designates an abyss. But the *abyssus* is a theme as old as *angustia*. Put side by side, the two words "abyss" and "anguish" may even produce some handsome literary effects, though perhaps a bit old-fashioned. The exact terrain traversed by this abyss needs therefore to be mapped out and its trail traced with some precision.

Its terrain is the terrain of all terrains: "The abyss is the *originary unity* of space and time." As to its trail, it follows a lack, a flight: "The abyss is the ground staying away" (*BzP* 379). The abyssal engraves a line of flight in every name of beingness.

An operation of diachronic geography consists in inscribing some terrain in *space and time*. In this sense these constitute the terrain of all possible terrains. The inscription of a spatio-temporal figure requires that space and time precede it as essentially isomorphic. Such has been, at least, the modern way of construing them. Space and time must be forms (not contents) of magnitude (pure extensions), infinite (not structured from within) and given (neither acquired, nor abstracted). To speak of space and time is to speak of empty dimensions preceding every experience and making it available to possible measurement. Inscribing a phenomenon in it amounts to calculating the place it occupies in these dimensions. Our epochal arrangement joins space and time together to obtain the empty frame within which every object figures in advance as one piece in a combinatory of extensions. For the subject, nothing has being unless it fills the *a priori* void in accordance with the dimensions of "in front of," "next to," "above," or "below," as well as "before," "after," or "simultaneously." For the moderns, the originary unity of space and time resides in the subject who prescribes them to every object of possible experience in view of its universal *mathesis*, that is, in view of the phenomenalization constituted by measurement, and thus by the category of quantity.

Heidegger, we saw, translates the transcendental illusion into a historial one, whereby it shows itself as the motive of a certain epoch and a certain destiny. He does not proceed otherwise with spatial and temporal apriorism. By virtue of its mathematizing goal, it offers the perfect tool for containing, repressing, and mastering the tragic. The interest presiding over this "containment" becomes blatant when one observes the representations of space and time at work. No great suspicion is needed here to notice that the questions of Where and When have never been as neutral as they were posited to be. They have, on the contrary, always and essentially worked to the advantage of one or another historial fantasm and its regime. Where and When are referential questions. Do the questions of Where and When refer to a focalizing center? The empty magnitude they open has indeed been structured according to the Aristotelian *pros hen* or to Kantian reflection. How then can the paradox of such a structured void even be thought of if not on the basis of some structuring authority—the one as substance, the subject as consciousness—that orders phenomena? Spatio-temporal mathematization has never been innocently "theoretical," nor disinterested. It is comprehensible only as a labor, the labor of strengthening hegemonies.

Ever since philosophers have spoken of them, space and time have served to submit being to number and calculation. The Aristotelian *pou* and *pote* are categories; in beingness, they emphasize what is countable and measurable, either according to front, back, etc. . . . or to before and after. Conceived with a view to ontometry, space and time cannot be anything in themselves, but yet must be structured. Thus ousiology structures them on the basis of relations observed in natural motions; the Transcendental Aesthetic does so on the basis of relations dictated by the acts of the spontaneous subject. Yet in both, space and time are constructed as *that in which* something becomes a phenomenon, determining in advance the possible proportions of its phenomenality. Whether it is ousiological or transcendental, beingness differs from beings in that it arranges them into referential juxtapositions and successions.

Now the step back from beingness reinscribes the spatio-temporal problematic within the question of being. At the monstrous limit of universal mathematization, space-time turns into the singular "place of an instant" (*Augenblicksstätte, BzP* 375), where the event occurs. That turning moves from time (isomorphic because measurable) to the abyss of incommensurable times. This abyss is what is revealed by diremption and the dwelling it assigns to us.

"The abyss is *the originary unity* of space and time." "Originary" in what sense? The origin, it seems, will have to be thought otherwise than as substance and as founding subject, for "the abyss is the ground staying away." Therefore, *Abgrund* has, first of all, a negative connotation. It designates the collapse of bedrock that could serve as a bottom on which to posit the normative difference.

In this difference, as it has propped up all hegemonies, the normative-nominative other is significant. In them our bases {*assises*} tell us what we are and what to do. The originary *Grund* makes those who find stability therein autochthonous. To the sedentary, it guarantees a common name. Among aboriginals there can be no diversity, nothing disparate. The earth (the origin and basis of their spatio-temporal body) endows them with more than a name; it normalizes those it names, it lays down their law. The common name puts proper nouns in the vocative mode. In the *Abgrund,* on the other hand, the foundation upon which autochthony goes without saying, owing to an obviously common name, slips away. In describing the origin of time and space as abyssal, Heidegger cuts short the idyll of the {native} soil, because he cuts out the significant, vocative effects of common names. How, then, is one to think of an origin that signifies literally nothing?

In order to deactivate signification understood as normative, and hence to disengage the clutch connecting being and ought-to-be, Heidegger preferred for a few years to strike out the word *Seyn*—a striking out that set the style for much of French writing for over a decade. Just about anything was then put "under erasure," the name of the father obviously, that of capital, of spirit, and in their sweep any sign naïvely charged with meaning. The wave of erasures was followed by that of palimpsests. The word crossed out rhymed only too well with the repressed, whose fragmented return one had to prove capable of deciphering. Such is the way of fashion. However, literary effects are one thing; the question of diremption and of the condition of being it makes for us, is quite another. At least in reading Heidegger, only the other that is being remains nameless. In dissension with itself, it no longer lends itself to normative positings.

Such a negation of the name of the *arché* no longer amounts (contrary to what I have been reproached for[47]) to spilling over into some mysticism of the origin. How could this be so when anarchy designates the inner break—which has already happened from the very beginning—within bases and underpinnings? The other that being is does not counter *archai* with a determinate negation. Such negations only come into play with archic beings, "father" and "capital" included. So, the anarchic and the archic "by no means allow themselves to be distinguished immediately because in no way do they relate immediately to one another."

To say that "being" does not name a being, that it is not a name, is to strip it of the very power that has instituted all hegemonies: the subsumptive power. The holding together, *synecheia,* of presents and absents toward which Parmenides' chariot advanced; the vast continuity of ends that Cicero sought to gather from the Rome that was, and Augustine from the Jerusalem to be; the non-imputation of the ego faced with the self, in Luther, and its absorption into the freedom of the self in Kant—all these outlinings of an ultimate power synthesizing disparate forces are broken up by being discordant in themselves and thus nameless. It is their conflictual origin itself, abyssal, empty of content, impossible to invoke as an appellate authority. With the name, power also fades away. Beneath the other that is being, the forces laying down their laws remain disparate. Heidegger's retrospective reading shows that we have always lived under the *historial differing* where conflictuality remains tragic because it is deprived of any adjudicating fantasm.

"The abyss" designates this inner conflictuality of being in several ways, all of which pertain to the event.

Where the ground slips away, something unfathomable opens up. To speak of the abyss is then to recognize a retraction toward a measureless No that wins out over the attraction of the Yes and of measure, "the originary No that belongs to being itself and hence to the event" is deployed in the abyss (*BzP* 388).

The event, which is abyssal because it is non-foundational (*abgründig*), also is structured from within by the "momentary places." The event does serve as the origin of space and time, but not as an axis reducing them to some focal point. A transmutation throws spatio-temporal representations off their received axes. Heidegger turns the pure dimensions of universal mathematization into singular traits so as to singularize the event. The monstrosity of our historial site appears nowhere more clearly than when the Aristotelian categories of Where and When, together with their Kantian offspring, get converted—perverted perhaps, certainly subverted—into *singular traits ajoining the event.* It will be necessary to recognize in the singularization to come the deadly effect that turns time against itself and thereby transmutes presence into event. Now, unlike what some read into Heidegger, there is nothing harmonious in this jointure. The "emptiness of the abyss" indeed points to the event as "joined together" (*gefügt, BzP* 381); yet, since its jointure occurs through strife, this still means that any aeonic[48] terrain sinks away from under the here and the now.

The abyss thus leads toward the caesura-decision where being absents itself from hegemonies. Heidegger redirects the appanage of the German mystics: "The 'void' is just as much, and properly speaking, the fullness of what remains still undecided and to be decided: the abyssal" (ibid.). The abyss exerts no power at all, but it harbors the fullness of the possible.[49]

Heidegger calls the locus of that decision *Da-sein*—which diremption reveals. Da-sein continues to "be away" as long as man seeks to posit himself on some univocally normative foundation. Da-sein's own place is the abyss of the ground lost and of singularization regained. At the risk of losing itself unto death (not out of a willing, like Leonidas, but out of a knowing, like Oedipus), Da-sein must keep the groundless. "Holding firmly onto the abyss belongs to the essence of Da-sein" (*BzP* 460). Here we see our abode, assigned to us by diremption.

What is abyssal, finally, is the tragic contrariety itself that through all these strategies Heidegger seeks to rehabilitate in being, beyond theticism. On this point, there is no "influence" to deconstruct. The renunciation of all names that lay down the law and the subsequent affirmation of tragic being remains without precedent in the doctrines of first conditions. The event, then, equals originary dissension. "Being: the event." "Abyss: as the time-space of dissension" (*BzP* 346).

Those are so many manners in which the incongruity of death is adjoined to life. Strictly speaking, the undertow it exerts no longer gives rise to a differend, but to a discordance—if at least by differend one understand the conflict of disparate laws calling for an impossible common authority. I speak of a differend only to describe this call and the referents that are posited to fulfill it in an illusory manner. "What will I do?" Antigone asks, caught between the laws of the family religion and those of the city. The generic law is lacking. "What then is electromagnetic force?" asks Heinrich Hertz, caught between two incongruous yet equally useful models. The answer to the question of *Wesen* is lacking.

Is it reading too much into Heidegger's sudden awakening in the mid-1930s to view it as the attempt to think a discordant originary condition without any affinity with some ultimate nominative-normative authority? He would then be echoing the Sophocles of *Oedipus at Colonus*. In this tragedy, the most difficult for us moderns to understand, all questioning has ceased. Discordance has been accepted, even affirmed, and it breaks the hero. Something analogous happens to Heidegger after his failing. Concerning the entry into the singular "momentary place," he asks: "In what way [does this occur] in Greek tragedy?" (*BzP* 374). He seeks to accept and to assert in being the discordance of appropriation-expropriation. But to learn to retain the labor of subtraction that breaks them, "'rational animals' must first *become* mortals."[50]

Before tracing the discord that the nocturnal, so retained, introduces into the diurnal, some remarks may be useful to clarify the status of a thinking that is content not only with retrospection nor even historiality, but that understands itself as "transitional" (*übergänglich, BzP* 463) thinking. To avoid the simplifications of a "resolute leap" outside the "metaphysical closure" dear to the advocates of post-modernity, one needs to ask in what sense the condition of being that diremption reveals places us in transit as well as, perhaps, makes us transitional beings. Hence: In transit, wherefrom and whereto? And which transition?

CHAPTER 6

What, the Deferred *There*?

On topology

> "Every beginning is in itself complete, unsurpassable. Beginnings escape historicist recording not because they are trans-temporal and eternal, but because they are greater than eternity. As *thrusts of time* they grant to being, by spatializing it, the openness in which it conceals itself. The proper founding of this time-space is called Da-sein." (*BzP* 17)

Da-sein is not yet. Such is the surprising reinterpretation of the *there* in the *Contributions*. The reader remembering *Being and Time* can only be jolted: How is the *there* deferred? The *Da* designates a possible place (*topos*). Topology is the phenomenology of this possible place.

It matters little whether the reinterpretation would have occurred that way without the expectations Heidegger had invested in the political movement of the day and without the harsh awakening that ensued. What does matter, however, is the "terrible warning," the thetic hubris culminating in planetary technicity. Would Creon have *seen* the conflicting laws of city and family without first having been *blinded* in his nomothesis against Antigone? Would Agamemnon have seen them thus without too having been blinded in his nomothesis against Iphigenia? The Greeks did not speak of *hubris eutuches* (*felix culpa*). Yet this would have been an apt description of the tragic crisis. Not that it leads to a happy ending. But what does the hero see who, late in the day, confesses his excesses? He stops denying that there is, that there has always been, a legal double bind. If the word *pathei mathos,* 'suffering to understand,'[51] does not speak of denial, nevertheless it states its consequences: suffering and knowledge. In the crisis marked by guilt and sorrow, hubristic blindness turns—or may turn—into the visionary blindness embodied in Tiresias and Oedipus. Being as dissension is seen by bloodied eye sockets alone and is affirmed by silence.

Heidegger had hoped for a German response to the Greek beginning. Little did he suspect how right he would prove to be. . . . Far from repeating in late modernity the old gesture going from Homer to Solon, "the history of being" ended up by making us retrace the tragic crisis: hubristic blindness and guilt, followed by the clear—or at least possible and urgent—vision of originary unconcealment-concealment. Suddenly it is no longer *Rede* that is first and silence a mere modification;[52] like the heroes of

Aeschylus and Sophocles, our age has had to learn the ineluctability of legislation-transgression. Hence, "language is grounded in silence" (*BzP* 510). Like Oedipus at Colonus, the other thinking vows "not to break silence concerning things forbidden."[53] The undertow that ruins normative referents from within remains unspeakable. The legislator on whom certain texts of Heidegger had counted had not "properly founded" a new site. As a result, *topos* needed to be understood otherwise. Thus there was an awakening to the topical fissuring that legislators—and in their service, philosophical functionaries—have always made it their job to cover up. The hubristic blindness that had led to the statement, "The Führer himself alone *is* the German reality of today and of tomorrow as well as its law,"[54] turns into the tragic blindness that sees the retraction of death in the attraction for life; that sees concealment in unconcealment and expropriation in appropriation; or again (but these are no longer Heidegger's words) the singularization to come in every phenomenal constellation, hence the transgressive thrust in every aggregate making up a world.

The topological inquiry asks: How is the *there* deferred? In order to answer, the inquiry follows the itinerary formed by the tragic crisis. It looks back toward beginnings that have initiated epochs and discovers in them an ambivalence breeding hubris. Then it seeks to grasp the critical "thrust of time" where tragic denial bursts forth. Lastly, it finds its own task in keeping alive the question of the possible *there* and of its discordant spacings.

Recapitulative topology. This asks: What was the fracture in being that in its Greek, Latin, and modern ministry, the philosophical civil service repressed? In this its retrodictive task, topology spells out the double bind marking epochal beginnings. Although these are "in themselves what is complete, unsurpassable," they are indeed never simple, as we have seen. The era of the Greek *hen* opens with the discordance between the laws in force and their contraries subverting them; the era of *natura* opens with a teleological continuity posited as stable and a no-longer or not-yet *nasci* that renders it precarious; lastly, the era of modern self-consciousness opens with the autonomous ego, dispossessed straight off by the heteronomous self. In epochal beginnings, the *instituting* discourse remains faithful to incongruous phenomenalizations and singularizations. It stakes out "an opening where being is concealed." It emphasizes the legislative-transgressive double bind and in this is analogous to the opening of the dramas of Creon, Agamemnon, Eteocles . . .

Instituted discourse, on the other hand, represses the legislative tragedy. In this repression, Heidegger detects the fantasmic work of "logic." Henology, then the cosmic *logos,* and lastly transcendental logic, disguise originary dissension. The one, turned into a master-idea or a first substance, subsumes multiple data to itself; nature incorporates erratic distensions into itself, assigning to each in turn its end; and consciousness submits the sensing self to itself like a simple modification of the ego. Such positions repeat the hubristic moment in tragedy when the heroic edict brings the conflict between city and family back to order. This is a precarious order, though, which prompts the return of the repressed. In the same way, even as it sustains an epoch, every hegemonic referent unfailingly also calls for singulars to assert themselves against subsumption, whereby it calls for its own self-destitution.

In its recapitulative work, topology inquires into the places and regions of experience where philosophers have settled with the aim of absolutizing one given phenomenon and denying incongruous laws. Among these *topoi* one finds axiomatic geometry, substantial motion, the history of republican Rome and the spiritual Jerusalem, the observation of the self by itself, and many more. From the topography of these strongholds—like Creon, settled in his royalty—the normative *chargés d'affaires* have been able to exalt one representation beyond measure, to declare it the standard of all measurement, and to subject the singular to it. The totalizing illusion is the result of a cacography.[55]

Critical topology. Here the *topoi* to be situated and described are reduced to only one—to that caesura-place from which the topologist of the present speaks, who asks: How can the double bind formerly glimpsed (the repressed "having-been") today become imminent (the "to-come" that is to be safeguarded)? This is a decisive place where phenomenology does not, to be sure, turn into yet another instituting discourse, but a transitive one. In this *krisis,* some problems disappear, while others, and formidable ones, emerge. All have to do with the oneness without genus of a discourse trying to remain faithful to the singular that is happening to us.

What disappears is the very possibility of obliterating dissension. The hypothesis of an epochal closure gives to the tragic double bind that singular feature, never before seen, of archic-anarchic monstrosity. This bifrontal character of our site results from a "thrust of time." The phrase answers to the perplexity in which historial thinking begins. Things are one way, then suddenly they are an entirely different way. . . .[56] In topological terms, we find ourselves inscribed within one horizon—one "space-time"—and then suddenly reinscribed within another horizon. There is nothing there but the singular, a *terra deserta* that is no longer ours, a *terra incognita* that is not yet ours, and a transition in which an entire collectivity lives as if holding its breath. No one *nomos* governs this nomadism where allocations and assignments to discontinuous planes follow one another without warning or mediation. Reinscription, however, institutes a possibility that remains to be seized. To *whom* can and ought the "proper founding" be entrusted? No longer to any particular hero. The possible concerns the way of being of an entire age. In Heidegger, what answers to the question "Who?" is a site (not a subject, which would answer instead to the question "What?")—it is a conflictual site to which one can only let oneself be assigned. When such allocation occurs, *Da-sein* is.

Now, this allocation happens right before our eyes: "In technological reasoning {*im Ge-stell*}, we perceive a first and oppressing flash of the event {of appropriation}."[57] We perceive there the *event,* namely, of appropriation-expropriation; we perceive it in a *flash,* for technicity pushes both totalizing subsumption and singularizing dispersion to their extremes; the flash is *oppressive* because such a double bind extends violence; and it is *first* because "there where the danger grows so also is what saves," namely, the knowledge of the legislative diremption.

However, critical topology, combining the discourses of peril and of salvation in this way, encounters formidable difficulties. To trace the break between the archic terrain and the conflictual anarchic condition, two languages are needed—an epochal bilingualism. Heidegger says we have yet to become "dwellers in the time-space from which the gods have flown" (*BzP* 52). This means first of all that we have to learn to speak in both ways of the flaw that ruins hegemonies. Our century is readily described as one of great destructions, and one's reflection would have to suffer from a hopeless case of anorexia to characterize it otherwise. But if to think is to concentrate on the conditions under which one is living, then it is worthwhile to ask: How did we arrive at this? To this question, topology answers by pointing to the *krisis* around which the history of being turns, and which makes of us its in-dwellers. Critical topology implies that in the twentieth century, the double bind beneath every monofocal position becomes more obvious than ever, which in turn implies that the tragic denial at the foundation of order imposes itself all the more. Institutionalized brutality, guilt, an isomorphism that stifles reflection; then, the turning that moves outside of the same and its laws; lastly, the lesson learned from collapses, the vision of empty sockets and the silent affirmation of the legislation-transgression that diremption bequeathed to us. All this is afforded only to a bifocal phenomenological thinking. It is a thinking, for Heidegger does no more than linger upon the site and its conditions; it is phenomenological, since it gathers what shows itself there; and it is bifocal, since what shows itself is the emptying-out of normative epochs (another pleonasm: an epoch—a suspension of conflictual truth—always results from an idea that puts a stop to questioning, a halt posited, a decree, a thesis and, in that sense, a norm) and the possible *there,* deferred.

The difficulties have less to do with the circular character of this topology (which surmises a transition to be at work and then discovers symptoms verifying the surmise). Not every hermeneutical circle is vicious. The difficulties arise rather from the fact that topology can be retrospective and critical only because it is essentially anticipatory. In the vocabulary of representation, which is the promoting agency behind any maximized meaning, the meta-narrative instructing us about the stage whence we come, just as the semi-narrative about the possible *exit* that we are living (semi-, since narrative speech remains suspended at the exit of representation), both have their condition on a discontinuous plane upon which we are already summoned, brought to court. Both the analytic of the hegemonies that once were and that of the diremption that is suppose the pre-eminence of the possible over the actual.

By virtue of the temporal discontinuity that it singles out, this pre-eminence requires there be an "approach in order to reach our 'station' in being itself and thereby our history" (*BzP* 501). Only the contingent future, which is the eventual, occurrent *topos,* can teach us about our past and about our present. So long as the *there* has not been seized upon as our own possibility, one will never "measure what has happened in the history of metaphysics: the prelude to the event itself" (*BzP* 174), a prelude that has always deferred the *there* and anarchy.

Heidegger is not saying that soon, perhaps in the year 2000,* we shall reach our station in being. He is saying that the tragic *there* is possible, that it always has been so, that it is even more clearly so in the age of the diremption that is our own, and that there is no bearer of salvation (*salvus,* as 'whole,' which is what the tragic gaze

*Schürmann is writing this in the early 1990s.

becomes after the crisis) other than that possibility. To speak of the deferred *there* does not mean to postpone anything until later, any more than being-towards-death or the singularization to come indicate episodes to occur later on.

Deferred in what way then? The question is one of anticipation.

Anticipatory topology. This deals with a possible historial locus, one already given, yet still to be occupied; thus it is a locus spaced out from within. Its description is first of all negative, since *topos* here no longer signifies any region of beings whose relations can be maximized to produce some archic referent. "In the other beginning, some being or some region or district can no longer set the standard, any more than can beings as such" (*BzP* 248). The difficulty consists in understanding anticipation without any utopian or millennial postponements. This requires a clear understanding of the negations in the lines just quoted.

What is denied under their obvious apophatism? The hyperbolic use of one being—proper (such as the Platonic Good), regional (such as the movable in Aristotle), or general (such as beings in general whose Why left Leibniz at a loss)—posited as normative. They are aimed against maximization by representation. The transition doesn't make us go from one common {*noun*} to another as Hegel described it—the "great men," he wrote, "see the very truth of their age and their world, the next genus, so to speak, which is already formed in the womb of time." Here, there is no *genus* to come.

But what is thereby being denied, above all, is a certain phenomenology of simple manifestation one may be tempted to read into Heideggerian "giving." Such a phenomenology, answering the ancient question of being *qua* being, would run like this: Heidegger relates *geben* to *phain-* and *phu*—the Greek 'showing' and 'rising'—that indicate manifestation; then he inverts the relations of grounding (as attested to, moreover, by the lines quoted), anchoring not manifestation in one being that shows itself most noteworthy, but rather this being, as well as all others, in manifestation. Being *qua* being would consist in simple giving (*es gibt,* 'there is') as underscored by these verbs in the middle voice: "to show oneself," "to rise." To answer to the question of being, presencing by itself would have to be born in mind, apart from any consideration for present beings.[58]

This is all well and good. Still, reconstructions such as this say nothing about the *intrinsic contrariety* of being for the sake of which Heidegger never ceased to renew his idiom. Being is indeed showing, arising, manifesting, presencing, self-giving; but it is all that in a "fissured" mode, in "dissension," as "unconcealment-concealment," "appropriation-expropriation," in the "strife," the *pòlemos* and the *agôn* by which the No asserts itself and death declares itself. Heidegger's apophatism does not harbor some negative haplology (*haploon,* 'simple')[59]; it puts simplicity out of operation. With their negations, the lines quoted do suggest that being alone is *maßgebend,* setting the standard. But "Yes and No are an essential property of being itself, and the No even more originarily than the Yes" (*BzP* 178). How could apophatic utterances, then, ever exalt a simple standard, retrieve a simple condition beneath epochal regimes, prepare a simple place? The *thought* of the double bind that is being may indeed be simple (*einfach, schlicht,* etc.), just as the sight of Oedipus blinded could be simple and safe. But if, in the other beginning, it is no longer a being that "gives" as an ultimate authority—gives the standard, gives food for thought, gives rise to . . . —nor any thesis about being that binds uniformly, then the great awakening after the compromises of 1933–34 leads outside of all simply normative regimes. It leads toward a conflictual normativity, the knowledge of which is more ancient in the West than any theticism of the same.

To speak of the deferred *there* is to entertain the possibility that the denial of the transgressive other may exhaust itself, a denial that has provided the impetus to every hegemony of the same, while its exhaustion has always secretly shattered normative power. To attempt the possible means here to destabilize affirmation, the firm, firmness, and to rehabilitate under the Yes the undertow of the No. The possible undercuts the effects of positive discourse. Hence the silence of the tragic hero fleeing into that *non-place* for the ancients, the desert, a non-place, not moving (like the island of some messianic society) into an ever-greater distance as a result of a poorly calculated arrival, but deferred under the mode of the possible and therefore in a differend with itself. This is something completely different than a utopia and a completely different apophasis. Negating and questioning are all that remains to anyone seeking to retain the disparate, for Heidegger, a negating that posits no dialectical nescience and a questioning that presupposes no maieutic prescience. The topology of the possible does not work with a theodolite. Like the desert where Oedipus wanders, the anticipated conflictual *topos* is closed to prospection. In the *Contributions,* it is described through 'fissuring' (*Zerklüftung*), a word that stresses time more than space. To be deferred is the very temporality of the tragic *there,* the discord of times (see below). Within it is the originary strife whose vision blinds one and whose knowledge strikes one silent.

Now if such is the originary condition, then why state it in the future tense? Witness the proliferation of topical postponements. At present, we can at most prepare the "place of questioning" (*BzP* 85), where "those to come" will prepare themselves, those who in turn will prepare "new standpoints in being," wherein alone can "the strife of earth and world be sustained" (*BzP* 62), a strife out of which may issue the tragic *there.* This series of sites—*Frageort, Standort, Da*—has nothing to do with a speculation on the morrows. In anticipatory topology, the emphasis remains on the possible site and its discontinuity, rather than on actual terrains and their contiguity. Statements in the future tense concern a potential that is given now. They are not meant to put the other beginning off indefinitely, but to aggravate here and now the discontinuity between regimes of the same whose institutionalized hypertrophy Heidegger had just helped to promote and the occurrent discordance by which he henceforth understands being.

If topology is concerned with the place where the conflictual event can be sustained, at least one misunderstanding regarding Heidegger is excluded. What guarantee is there, one may object, that the anarchic possible will not prove more violent still than the archic actual? Many things are possible, not all equally desirable. Does Heidegger justify them in advance, whatever they may be?

The question is meaningless. It reduces the guiding category of modality, the possible, to what derives from it, the actual. One worries about what will happen to public order *if* the legitimizing referents were to turn out fractured. This amounts to misconstruing the status of the possible, since conflictual being *already* grips and breaks us, just as it has always gripped and broken us: "We are already moving, although still only transitionally, within another truth" (*BzP* 18). In instituting planetary totalitarianism, we would merely be once again answering the possible with denial. Global archi-cracy would only extend and deepen the actual. Creon forces and enforces the public order by denying its transgressive other; but what would there even be to deny if the tragic double bind did not hold him always and already? The conflictually possible is to come only because it is our most ancient condition. It breaks with the actual as the event breaks with constant presence; as the singular breaks with subsumption; as originary discordance does with any focal meaning; and as the acknowledgment of what is (its letting-be) breaks with thetic repression (positing being).

The question of factual legitimizations proves meaningless, for it asks, "Such a fact, such a deed—in the name of what?" Common names always maximize relations between actual beings. Topology, for its part, "maximizes" the possible.[60] The maximal possibility, which will never be translated into an actual economy, would be to comply equally with the claims of singulars as with the fantasms of the common. Topology does not legitimize facts by referring them to a name. It legitimizes the feasible in anticipating that nameless possibility. What common name, indeed, could one give to ultimates in differend? The whole problem of legitimization gets transmuted. The site of the event is substituted for the site of norms, the former site always already having arisen and spread itself out under the evidence of principles collapsing into the isomorphic: "Being comes to be in the event. This implies that a site has arisen: unexpected, singular, alienating us with regard to the instant and only thus spreading itself out" (*BzP* 260). It is true that the site so anticipated can no longer guarantee any tranquillity of order. But this is not to say that its topology justifies anything and everything. Its criteria of responsibility were set forth by Aeschylus, Sophocles, Heraclitus, and Parmenides. It heeds other imperatives: "The things absent, behold them nevertheless as firmly present" (Parmenides 4,1). In the thetic impulse, which is the effect of natality, behold the undertow of mortality. In the site mapped out by the law behold the other, "unmapping" all laws, namely, the singularization to come that alienates us from the lures of normative presence.

"Therefore must we not turn our thinking around to completely different zones and standards and manners of being so as to belong to the necessities that are dawning here?" (*BzP* 204). Such is the onus of anticipatory topology. It is a matter of belonging to the possible, more powerful than any actual denial.[61] But in this possible, a "not yet" stands out from the "already." The instrumental nature of normative single bonds has long since become obvious, but yet we are not ready to acknowledge its tragic double binds. Hence, "The locus of decision still remains to be founded" (*BzP* 187). But also, "To think this way already requires, to be sure, a standpoint where it will no longer be possible to be lured by all the 'good' and the 'progressive' and the 'gigantic' that are being achieved" (*BzP* 140). In what passes for good, progressive, gigantic—no doubt this must mean in the technological giganticism that passes for progressive and hence for good— necessities arise that compel one to think otherwise. The everydayness that breaks with the cluster of "good" (Plato), "progress" (early modernity), and "giganticism" (late modernity) is already ours, already a necessity in the sense that everyone is living it; but it still remains for us to grasp it. Isn't the possible defined by such a graft of the *not yet* onto an *already*? And doesn't it thereby shatter the concordance of times? To say a cataclysm is possible is to say that at present things are holding up, but that the conditions of their collapse are already there. In Heidegger, the conditions—the zones and the standards and the modes of being—are brought together so that the illusion that normativity can be found in values, progress, and technology collapses. Insofar as they remain still to be grasped, these conditions are situated ahead of us (*ante*); hence anticipation. They fissure the subjectivist *topos* that continues to pass for bedrock; hence topology.

To establish oneself expressly on the fissured ground is what Heidegger now understands by "Da-sein." This establishing marks the other beginning. It is a matter of a disjunction—a twofold disjunction—that Heidegger was to attempt ever anew over the forty years to follow.

On the one hand, the *fundamentum concussum* remains to be disjoined from any foundation luring us as *inconcussum*. This is an archeological labor of disjunction that frees plateaus in collision from under the numerous foundations posited since the Greeks, that frees, that is, the strife between world and earth. On the *world*-map of fantasmic arenas, Heidegger traces out especially the bases of the modern enclosure, thereby freeing under the discourse established since the sixteenth and seventeenth centuries the *earthly* restraint that has inhibited each of the great founding discourses, as if rendering it mute. Historial critique is responsible for the archeological disjunction. It has its site and its hour, namely, the "thrust of time" making us late moderns feel the collision of plateaus that are presupposed beneath every posited foundation.

On the other hand, the forces in collision themselves remain to be disjoined. Heideggerian responsibility consists in a response to that destabilizing thrust in which normative positings suffer their deposal, making the disparate underneath referential subjectivity obvious. To respond to what is happening to us then means to free up the originary double bind in its various figures: appropriation-expropriation in the event; the world-earth strife and the gods-humans conflict in history; unconcealment-concealment in truth; the discordance of phenomenalization-singularization in manifestation. . . . This polemological disjunction is the responsibility of anticipatory critique. It separates dislocating strategies so that Da-sein can belong to the originary (Heraclitean) *polemos*.

Our stupefaction with the isomorphic that we ourselves bring about shows just how far away such a responsible belonging remains. Hence the appeal to "found the historial place for the history to come" (*BzP* 60), to "create that time-space, the site for the essential instants" (*BzP* 98). Later, Heidegger will describe the founding instance of history, in an abbreviated form, as the "entry into the event"[62] (abbreviated, since the event conjoins mutually hostile tractions). This entry would be as compact as all beginnings have been. What is to be retained in that compactness is the conflictuality glimpsed, then infallibly repressed, in the Greek, Latin, and modern beginnings.

Stupefaction grows exponentially in the consumer of ideas who has seen everything and read everything. There may be something charming about a blasé high school student; later, it is better to have learned how to read. For example, on truth and its site: "the truth of being [has still] to find a site that is coming to be in Da-sein" (*BzP* 90). One may vaguely recall that Heidegger, at least when read in translation, liked to speak of authenticity, that this has doubtless something to do with truth, and that there were decades when fashion required that one "be true." Hence one may think that thoroughfare to have closed down, "coming to be" in nothing. Speed reading may however make one miss the essential—here, the conflictuality without agreement that is truth. Unconcealment-concealment has yet to find its site, the condition of being for which both Hölderlin and Nietzsche "had to leave, before their time, the clarity of their days" (*BzP* 204). Such being-true would describe proven-to-be and truthful beings—genuine existence—only with difficulty. The site of truth is rather "the *there* in its abyssal character" (*BzP* 240). The conflictual *gives rise to* or *allows for* what is bottomless.

Such places are imparted rarely. It is one thing to describe the conflict that broke tragic heroes first, Hölderlin and Nietzsche later. It is another thing entirely for an age to find itself allotted the double bind. Topology carries out the description; the event carries out the allocation.

What then is one to understand by "allows for"? Here again, very popular misconceptions lie in wait for the reader of Heidegger. One of these has to do with the desire for grace. To 'allow for' (*verstatten*) means, to be sure, to impart, assign, permit, grant. Now, for what does the event allow? If it is for unconcealment-concealment—and if the event is itself appropriation-expropriation—then our site (*Stätte*) is never granted to us in a mode other than that of disaccord and discordance. To allow oneself to be charmed by the Heideggerian "there is" and "favor" amounts again to reading poorly. Each place is allotted with grace, but never without disgrace either.

Another misconception has to do with the desire for a solid ground. Heideggerian nostalgia would want to attach the people to its soil, as the Athenians were attached to Attica. And indeed, does he not celebrate rural rootedness? Yet the history of broken hegemonies and their diremption knows no privilege, no *lex priva,* no law deprived of its transgressive other. The "there is" always occurs, and the gift that assigns is always taken back as well. The *es gibt* always sunders one's abode. Only diremption brings this condition to light. How, then, is it so easy for theticism to overlook allocation-dislocation? It is that denial intervenes normally, equipped with the apparatus of norms and the normal. In Aeschylus and Sophocles, it took an act of parricide or fratricide to do away with the denial. To us, it seems, even a world on the way to self-destruction does not suffice.

These two misconceptions suffice to suggest the whole difficulty of topology. This is again a matter of desire, as one wishes Heidegger's "other thinking" to succeed where theticism could only fail. Having heard talk of metaphysical closure, one expects an investigation of contiguous historical arenas; and, having read his exhortations to keep oneself ready for a "gift," one expects the demonstration of an entry into the good graces of fate. But Heidegger describes laws that always fracture the unconditioned. Grace thus has to be thought of otherwise than as healing. The "thrusts of time" bring no therapy to the truth of being that is dissension. Remaining riveted to a monstrous site (according to the hypothesis itself of closure), one expects moreover a "philosophy of the one" capable of edifying. However, Heidegger shows how edification has proved hubristic and the platform it presupposed anything but solid. This is, as it were, the advantage of our monstrosity. Coming from afar, already won over by the polemical truth of being, how can we persist in the tragic denial from which were born the edicts of a Creon as well as all normative positings, including that of *Blut und Boden*? The cunning of theticism means that, beneath their illusory edification, these positings bring about destructions and that they bar access to the dislocated site. How can earth be thought of otherwise than as solid ground?

"Why does the earth remain silent in this destruction? Because it is not permitted the strife with a world and because the truth of being does not find there a site" (*BzP* 277ff.).

"Now, in the transition toward the other beginning . . ."[63]

"The greatest event is always the beginning . . . The unused power [of the latter] harbors the richest possibilities: the only salvation." (*BzP* 57ff.)

The transition toward the other beginning means the possible assent to conflictual being. The only salvation is that diremption is recognized as legislating. This thought raises some formidable difficulties, of course. I am no longer speaking, at least directly, of Heidegger's political wagers. The difficulties are philosophical, and they are intertwined like so many threads lying on the border of the text—of the transcendental text—that tightens itself around referential consciousness. With the *there* recontextualized out of subjectivism, shouldn't this cloth unravel and be relegated to the archive of fantastic yarns {*étoffes fantaisie*}? Now, sometimes surreptitiously, sometimes with no further ado, Heidegger sews the seams back together even as he strives to tear its fiber.

With the transitional Now, the rallying point {*feu et lieu*} of moderns, their home and focal point—the *I think*—undergoes displacements somewhat in the manner of an ethnic group which, after a shift in borders, is still there but already elsewhere; or again, like a childhood memory wandering off in a conversation, continuing, in the new site, but no longer going without saying.

These are difficulties of the path (*hodos*) along (*meta*) which one eventually comes to the *there;* difficulties of "method," then. That "eventually" is what will cause all the concern, as will be seen. I take them up here, in a chapter devoted to what one might call with some hesitation problems of method (one hesitates, for the beginning of a history is not really a "problem," and the thinking that seeks to collect it does not choose a "method"). To dispel any misunderstandings on our course, let us bear in mind from the outset that the difficulties in question arise from the event of expropriation-appropriation. These differences have to do with the strategy of birth that the *ad-* and *Er-* acknowledge (*ap-propriation, Er-eignis*). They will thus be just as grave in the following chapter, which will treat the temporal conjunction of birth-death, namely, conjunctions of the *ad-* with the *ex-*, or of the *Er-* with the *Ent-* (*ex-propriation, Ent-eignis*).

There is the difficulty, precisely. Heidegger draws an eventual path whose graph transcribes occurrent conflictuality. The eventual {*l'éventuel*}—the other beginning—is the contingent; the occurrent {*l'événementiel*} is the originary. It asks: How is the other beginning linked to the event of appropriation? It thus traces a step back from the conditioned to its condition. Now isn't that the very scheme of the most traditional *a priori* doctrine? Doesn't the passage out of the modern hegemony fail as soon as it has been sketched?

There is no doubt that the *a priori* remains the scheme by which one grasps the other beginning. Heidegger says it in many ways. For example: "'The events' ('*Ereignisse*') of history are nothing but the thrusts coming from the event of appropriation (*Er-eignung*) itself" (*BzP* 463). Thus the whole effort to free originary conflictuality—the unthought of the tradition—is summed up in the possibility of making the conditioning thrust that has remained in operation our own, if forgotten, underneath all the conditioned thrusts that have made our history. Heidegger does not hesitate to evoke something like an unswaying march toward the *there,* the place where the unthought will emerge from forgottenness: "Being as event of appropriation is the victory of the unavoidable" (*BzP* 228).

The difficulties are summed up in this victory. How might one understand a victory of the condition over the conditioned? Kant declared: Wherever there is experience, its condition is transcendental apperception; it has always been so, only covered up with the dogmatism of entitative doctrines. Now, the discovery of this first and universal condition defines the Enlightenment, and today, at the end of the eighteenth century, the possibility thus comes to light of an entire people freeing themselves from the chains they forged, attached, and adored. When each person will have learned to think for himself, a cosmopolitanism will ensue through which all peoples will begin a common history anew, otherwise. They will *enter into transcendental apperception,* will let themselves be appropriated by it, will make of it the sole content of their experience. What meaning could it have for Kant to make this declaration? One sees immediately how absurd an "entry into the event of appropriation" would be, so long as it is linked to "events," just as transcendentalism links experiences to the I-think. It would be a witticism lacking any wit to proclaim "the entry into the I-think." Or rather, it would be the worst kind of wit, that which would turn the *Aufklärung* into *Schwärmerei;* that is, the Enlightenment into exalted inspiration.

Let us admit that the filiation with the *a priori,* notably of the transcendental sort, is only a loose thread in the unraveling cloth of modernity. Let us admit also that the analogy, even if more elastic, according to which events would receive their structure from the *Ereignis,* just as experiences do from the cogito—that even this elasticity is too tightly bound around a thinking that from the beginning declares itself to be an attempt, an experimentation, a trial, a *Versuch* (there again, like transcendental critique): "In the age of the transition from metaphysics toward the thinking of the history of being, one can only make an *attempt*" (*BzP* 3, first page of the text). Nonetheless, a duality remains between the *initial power* concealing the richest possibilities and some *initium* establishing an epoch or closing off epochs. The unthought does indeed split up into (a) the originary unused which, through transition, becomes (b) our possible site.

What is excluded, moreover, is constructing this duality according to the model of the so-called ontological difference. *The* event would bring event*s* together, just as being brings beings together. This is a solution that in fact is not one because the (possible) other beginning is not at all a being, because the event is not the event "of" anything, and because the whole talk of appropriation-expropriation, with its incidences of unconcealment-concealment, world-earth, etc. . . , consists in retaining conflictuality—the possible *there*—as our only standard. "[I]n Da-sein measurement resides: that is, as the ground of the strife between world and earth" (*BzP* 510). The ontological difference, in turn, does not allow for some "entry into being." What could such an entry mean? It would connote some sort of ontophany—an absurdity. To describe the other beginning as an entry into the event, on the other hand, is not absurd. This signifies the emplacement of thinking, that is, of everyday life emancipated from obsessive denials under the tragic double bind.

Still another path offers itself, which goes back as far as the *a priori*. It has to do more directly with "living beings capable of dying," consoling themselves maniacally (for that is cheating death) as "living beings endowed with reason."

There is no death where life cannot already be found; there is no new birth, no palingenesis, where the initiative power that natality is could not be found. The latter is the condition of everything new in life, of everything that begins, of every beginning. It is above all in the biblical tradition that the duality of natality-birth was recognized as a linguistic phenomenon. To go straight to the *locus classicus:* "The son of God was never anything but Yes" (II Corinthians 1:19). An originary Yes, because "in the beginning was the word" (John 1:1). All plural words are just responses to the singular word, God's Word. In John's statement, the most speculative of all the Scriptures, the imperfect of the verb "to be" singles out that duality of word and words. *The* word would conceal something like an affirmative power from which all other words would derive their capacity for affirming or negating. One sees that, in the word that is–was–will be *in arché,* there can be no negation. The archic word will be a pure "Yes." Every negation presupposes a prior affirmation; if the originary utterance were "No," our propositions would lose their very space, and there would be no language. It is only to a "Yes" that one can answer Yes or No.

Doesn't one have, with this first *logos,* the Yes, the matrix that Heidegger follows each time he speaks of an originary gift? A unique and silent Yes would precede every proposition. Yes—let us translate it as. There is manifestation, showing, arising, coming forth, opening. There is natality. The No's that forgetting, occlusion, and mortality are can only come afterwards. Every phenomenon presupposes a *phainesthai.* Stamped by the occurrent "there is," we are capable of noticing what there is, the givens, the eventual. The occurrent would work on the eventual in the manner of a univocal norm. Heidegger indeed says, "Silence is the most hidden keeper of standards (*Maß-halten*)—it keeps the sole measure (*das Maß*) by virtue of which it alone can then posit scales (*Maßstäbe*). And it is thus that language is measure-positing (*Maßsetzung*)" (*BzP* 510). It is a positing language, because every statement is held by the silent gift. No need of transcendentalism or ontology. With language, we are always practicing an absolute performative whose only content—unless it is its form—is acquiescence. We are beings who begin, say Yes, acquiesce, are born essentially, and that is why we are capable of continually beginning anew (and ending), reacquiescing (and denying), being born again (and dying).

A dead end remains, nevertheless. We have read it. In occurrent being, the No is "more originary" than the Yes (*BzP* 247). A new paganism, perhaps (if it is pagan to say that death triumphs over life); an end of consolations, certainly.

The difference between appropriation and the other beginning will neither be an *a priori* nor an ontological or performative one. One would have to be able to give a description of it that would underscore the strategy in being that gets things going, and thus also underscores these departures without, however, evoking any of the three archic constructions I have just mentioned; this description, moreover, would have to be plain enough to swear by the latest colors of intellectual ready-to-wear fashion. It will have to state the duality of natality-birth, a difference that thus takes account of an *initium* or an *incipit*—an initiating or inceptive difference.

In relation to the *a priori,* ontological, and performative figures, the initiating or inceptive difference essentially implies history.

The accumulation of difficulties as they have thus presented themselves might be lightened by separating two steps. First of all (1) I will follow the initiating anteriority of *the* event of appropriation over event*s* in history. I shall ask: How does occurrent natality (appropriation) precede the eventual birth (the other beginning)? This is a question of precedence, since Heidegger is never at a loss for declarations and allusions indicating that the entry into the *there* should be written in the future tense. Then (2) I will recall that the eventual does not mean an imminent historiological beginning, but an always immanent historial possibility. I will then ask: How does the possibility of the other beginning overdetermine the originary that determined the first beginning? It is an overdetermination that can still be read in the double play of possibility, likewise written sometimes in the singular, sometimes in the plural. "Being is possibility," which is why one must take on the "decision of one of the concealed possibilities" (*BzP* 475ff.). Overdetermination means something that is both more supple and more violent than a condition. It means the monstrous unraveling of the text that established modernity.

The determination of givens by their conditions as well as their overdetermination by the gift vary the very ancient scheme of transcendence. The latter always opens a gap. A duality that, Heidegger says, is to be taken *and* left. "In transitional thinking, however, we must endure this duality: *at first,* attack the first clarification with the help of this distinction, and *then* precisely jump over it . . . by a leap that makes one enter into the event of Da-sein" (*BzP* 251).

A note for the benefit of the heralds of the "post-modern": That transcendence is to be taken *and* to be left does not add it to the menu of free samples. The other beginning is hardly a mishmash of borrowings in which an empty eclecticism seeks to pass off conceptual laziness as playful boldness. It is true that there are features of wit, playfulness, if one wishes, in the readings of texts offered by Heidegger, notably in his etymologizing associations.[64] But for all that they do not bespeak an "anything goes" attitude. By overdetermining received ideas, all one is doing is wandering among the dilapidated monuments of metaphysics, like the cats in the Colosseum of Rome. Heidegger gives a strong reading of the historiological {*historiques*} answers to the "guiding question"—What is the being of beings?—with a view toward "the transition towards the basic question": What is the time of being? (*BzP* 169). A time that is nevertheless just as irrecoverable for archic needs, since it is discordant in itself.

Before taking up the transition to the deferred *there,* and then the initiating or inceptive difference, here is a brief terminological reminder. It has to do with the "beginning" and how it is distinct from the "origin" and the "start." These relations are essential to the project of the *Contributions,* in which the Heideggerian discourse understands itself as instituting, opening up the era of the diremption recognized as legislating. Heidegger would wish it to be followed by an instituted discourse, which would sustain a new history.

The words *Anfang,* 'beginning,' and *anfänglich,* 'initial,' are literal translations—and, in Heidegger, deconstructions—of *principium.* The Latin word indicates what reason 'grasps first,' its *primum captum.* To begin with the beginning would then mean to apprehend principles. The German words, on the other hand, do not immediately emphasize any direct or indirect object. *Anfangen* and "to begin" are verbs in the middle voice: "it" begins (first moment). In Heidegger, such turns of phrases in the middle voice always signal the turning in his itinerary. A grasping with a direct object, a *Fangen,* does follow, to be sure (second moment); only the Heideggerian usage inverts its direction. The issue then is no longer grasping, but letting oneself be grasped. Hence the task for thinking (third moment) is to grasp what holds it in its grip, to take hold of it anew.

Now, what does thinking thus know initially? Not this or that matter that may show itself as present, but the coming-to-presence of every this and of all that. This coming-to-presence is the phenomenological origin, *Ursprung,* of phenomena, their always eclipsed manifestation. It occurs, it is an event, *the* event. To begin otherwise will be to begin with the origin understood in this way. "The thought of being *qua* event is the initial thought" (*BzP* 31). The first beginning is in no way to be described in the imperfect tense. It designates the procedure that considers principles—notably hegemonic ones—and that, beginning with their being intuitively grasped, passes on to discursive demonstrations. Thus the other beginning would consist in "the more originary repetition of the first beginning" (*BzP* 57).[65] Why more originary? Because it takes its point of departure from what is *manifestly* first, namely, intrinsically conflictual manifestation (and not some simple positing). It thus repeats in the phenomenological mode the "second sailing" of the *Phaedo.* Thinking sets off anew, this time not, to be sure, from principles and causes, but from the event of showing and hiding that always grasps it wherever something shows itself.

Lastly, the many event*s* spell out segments of history. The latter is emphasized when one start (*Beginn*) follows another. Grasping is now to be written in the plural, and the new departure in the past, present, or future tenses. For instance "today, in the beginning of the decisive segment of modern times. . . ." (*BzP* 493). In such a beginning, a new economy grasps us and holds us. According to the most summary statements of the history of being, there was only one beginning, which was the one that instituted "metaphysics" in the fifth and fourth centuries B.C.E. in Greece. But each institution that establishes an epoch is also a start.

The beginning, the origin, and the start converge in the transition that is possible today. The question from then on is knowing if "the beginning becomes a start and a linking-up" (*BzP* 179)—a linking up to the originary grasp by means of grasping anew.

1. Now, conjugated in this way, don't the three manners of coming first lead toward the *there*? The other beginning seems indeed to link up without any snags to the "metaphysical closure." An enclosure would be closed up, and something new would begin. Is it not with the transition toward more open breathing spaces that one can most easily sum up the themes that made Heidegger the mentor of some followers of 1968--the themes of the border of epochal confinement, the leap and the break, the essence of technology being equated with that of metaphysics, the possible higher than the actual, the other thinking and the other acting, natality, and the determination in the last instance by the to-come; in short, doesn't that transition sum up the theme of the place that Heideggerian topology describes as the *there*? Doesn't closure evoke a previous stage, and the beginning, a stage ahead of us? Heidegger did not always steer clear of such broadly sketched contractions, and his judicious readers have not held themselves back from noting the shortcuts and the compressions to which one must subject a complex history in order to constitute a solid and consistent two-thousand-year era, a metaphysical block.[66] And yet. . . . To speak of myself first, the readings that I have attempted above on Greek, Latin, and German texts should have demonstrated that if there are breaks, they fracture the very terrains of *the* metaphysics. A break inside of it, not from it. Then comes Heidegger's graph—he never praised some *trans lineam* passage. The topology of the conflictual *there* should suffice to dispel simplicities about the contiguity of arenas and the resolute leap over their confines.

All this does not prevent, but rather demonstrates, the fact that the other beginning does not designate a simple departure. How, then, is it related to the deferred *there*?

It would seem as if Heidegger proceeds by means of a sort of self-deconstruction within the *Contributions* itself.

There is a constructing moment. The reign of referents posited as universally normative—metaphysics—has only produced violence and isomorphism. Now, for a century, another destiny has been prepared, responding to the one instituted in Greece, and the response has become actual since the new Solon has occupied the chancellery in Berlin. Thus the German people found a new destiny for the healing of the West. The other beginning—isn't this the way we should understand "the only salvation" that is quoted above in the epigraph? According to this mad hope, postulated as all therapeutic agents have been, the nomic function would henceforth have passed from the universal that normalizes, to *a singular being*, whether it be the individual whose name is on everybody's lips ("the Führer alone is the law") or the collectivity to which everyone must be able to show that they have belonged for three uncontaminated generations. It seems that the diremption of hegemonic referents would be marked by the institution of a singular referent.

There is a deconstructive moment that is the immediate result of his disenchantment with the most abruptly normalizing events of the day. *Singular being* has never ceased to lay down the law; since before the Greek start where the first beginning was grasped, this other destiny has held us in the way that a possibility does; no hegemonic fantasm ever reigned simply, for all were broken from within; and no subsumption ever was able to obliterate the precarious—because it is discordant in itself—event of contextualization-decontextualization. Thus deconstructed, the nomic function instead passes over to that conflictual event that gives the measure, gives the time, gives rise to a site, and gives food for thought, the event of appropriation in presence and of expropriation out of it. By "other beginning" one must understand a manner of being that always complies with this other, agonal singular. It is a manner of being that is always necessarily postponed because it is essentially possible. The other beginning thus means, it seems, the deferred *there*.

The phenomenological truth of the constructing moment consists in what I have called anarchic isomorphism: There are only singular beings. Life nourishes itself on finite increments, not on infinite maximizations. Among the multitude of phenomena, it bears in mind a few points of reference and constitutes regions around them. Outside of these there is no life. To understand the nourishment by means of singular referents, one has only to call to mind ethical and aesthetic judgments. In them, one compares some given being to another one that is also given, chosen as a sample, and made into a canon. Such is the case with *paideia*. It aims at making the ephebe "as virtuous as" one of the prudent ancients, Pericles for instance. Such is also the case with Kantian reflective judgments. That French-style garden is "as beautiful as" Versailles.[67] Increasing *this* to measure *that,* and *that* other one too, without for all that leveling the one and the other in their singularity—therein lies the violence that nourishes not only language, but life. By means of such a model (*Exemplum*) one divines, Kant says, an idea of the imagination, a necessarily vague representation. An idea of reason, on the other hand, is illustrated by an example (*Beispiel*). The imaginary increment is thus not to be confused with the conceptual maximization by which theticism holds up some beings as a supreme, trans-regional referent, or some particular relation of beings as an ultimate referent.[68] In Heidegger, this constructing moment obviously loses its phenomenological truth each time that the other beginning finds itself directly or indirectly identified with the *start* that occurred in 1933. Then it, too, maximizes subjectivity and puts the thetic idea to work.

The phenomenological truth of the deconstructing moment can be read in the admittedly ambiguous lines quoted above as an epigraph. The greatest event is "always" the beginning. What does that mean? Always: Each time that a new economy is instituted in our history? So that means, with the Greeks, first of all, and with the slow gestation in process since Hölderlin, next? *Or rather* "always" in the way that a condition is "always"? The ambiguity bears on the way in which the beginning is tied to the event. According to the first reading, the beginning would be inscribed in the plural and as episodic; according to the second, in the singular and as *a priori*.

Now, in seeking to link being and history together, Heidegger can only undo the link between the episodic and the *a priori*. It would be idealist theticism, indeed, to treat history as an absolute condition. Thus the other beginning cannot be inscribed factually like *data* and dates, nor trans-factually like *posita* and the *a priori*. It indicates the effort of not searching for being behind anything at all, of thinking the condition otherwise than as ground or background, and therefore otherwise than as an autonomous and autarchic instance that is authoritative thanks to its being an ultimate authority. In order to cease positing, as if being could be reached by some operation on beings (whether incrementally or through maximization), the pairing of "empirical given" and "*a priori* condition" has to be unlearned. But that is precisely where the difficulties lie. How might one think a singularity that is not akin to that of a *this,* a condition weaned from the lineage of *a priori* positings?

There is nothing ambiguous about the abrupt response given, in the lines quoted as an epigraph, to the either-or between given event*s* that are datable as starts are, and *the* event that gives as only the origin gives. Both starts and the origin are a matter of the "unused power" of the beginning.

What is happening? Heidegger is seeking to erase the distinction between the empirical and transcendental one finds in modernity. There is only the freshness of phenomena occurring, a never used, unusable power that always conceals "the richest possibilities." What occurs is an overdetermination of the *institution*—a start, a new historical departure—by *appropriation,* by the strategy of natality in the originary event.[69] Such an overdetermination no longer varies the *a priori*. Hence the necessity of speaking of an initiating or inceptive difference.

The difference is obvious when the *other* in "the other beginning" (a) indicates a decision in the sense of a historical passage, that is, "the transition from modernity to its other"; then when this other (b) is incorporated into being that is itself decisional {*décisoire*}. "Should another beginning occur, because the essence of being itself is de-cision?" (*BzP* 92). A "decision" between historial eras, a "de-cision" between the *ad-* and the *ex-* in the event of appropriation-expropriation, the graphic play indicates the difference by which the conflictual tractions in being make up the very possibility of being born and dying in their innumerable forms.

More briefly, "The other beginning of thinking always remains only that which can be divined by anticipating it (*das Geahnte*) and nevertheless that which has already been decided" (*BzP* 4). It is (a) imminent as the *birth* of a possible economy, and it has (b) always and already occurred as a trait of *natality* in a splitting off and seceding from the trait of mortality in agonal being. Because it points to these two ways of beginning, the "other beginning" is itself differential, but because it isn't based on any archic thesis, this difference no longer has anything *a priori* about it.

2. Henceforth, how does the eventual that is always possible (a birth) differ therein from the occurrent that conceals every possibility (natality)? Following three paths that open up will make this clearer.

The first path picks up the so-called ontological difference and traces the course of its fading away. One could not have a more massive formula: "In the other beginning, all beings are sacrificed to being" (*BzP* 230). It may leave us at a loss. All beings are condemned to be sacrificed to being?

The formula reorients the manner of questioning. The first beginning is marked by the guiding question (*Leitfrage*): What is the being of beings? The answers are: It is the idea, it is substance . . . always a figure of beingness. The West was born from wonderment at being. Only a manner of questioning is to be sacrificed in the dread one has in the face of being,[70] a dread from which astonishment eventually will be reborn. The other beginning appears with the basic question (*Grundfrage, BzP* 75ff.): What is the essencing (*Wesung*) of being? What appears there is natality (the "principle" of birth, if one may use that word here), in strife with mortality. Why "basic"? It is a matter of another grounding. In the first beginning, being (*Sein*) was grounded on beings. In the other beginning, being (*Seyn*) "grounds" itself on its own dissension. Its agonal self-grounding requires a change in orthography, the use of quotation marks, fragmented sentences, and all kinds of expedients, in order to denature the representations of beingness, that is, in order to sacrifice the foundational recourse to beings.

Now, what is more *instituting* than a way of questioning? All epochal scansions have resulted from the attention given to some newly irresistible representation. Thus the transitional question (*Übergangsfrage*), "Why are there beings rather than nothing?" (*BzP* 509), makes the gaze that is fixed upon representable things veer off. It no longer asks what the being of beings is. To follow this veering off beyond the ontological difference is precisely the way of questioning that ends up cutting off ultimate references. What would happen if, instead of discrediting some single referent of beings so as to accredit another—instead of becoming tired of what is "out" and getting excited over what is "in" for the usual return to school this fall—our attention were to dwell on the tragic conflictuality that is being? One is told that thoughtlessness, which denies the tragic, stems from human frailty, and so on, that only "limit-situations" sometimes awaken thinking and lead it to inquire into "what is tragic." But is there any place on the monstrous site that has been allotted to us where one does not find those limit-situations? By questioning oneself about the strife that goes on in those situations, the other beginning is instituted.

However, the beginning does get more complicated with the present demise of archic economies and the birth of a possible anarchic economy. It differentiates itself, not into beings and being, but into institution and appropriation. The sort of public destitution that the West has always counterattacked by instituting thesis after thesis would be *born* ("other beginning" in the sense of a start) from a thinking which would be more attentive to conditions than to promotions. And the event would cease to be intractable, manifesting itself as a trait of *natality* ("other beginning" in the sense of origin).

The withering away of the ontological difference directs one's phenomenological gaze toward what begins every phenomenal manifestation: the strategy of appropriation in occurrent being. Of what other way of looking at life may it be said that it left the thetic obsession behind? Of what other way of looking may it be said that it makes another economy of life possible?

The second path uncovered follows the guiding thread of truth. Under the heading of "*From the first to the other beginning,*" Heidegger writes the following: "In the *first beginning,* truth (as unconcealment) is a characteristic of beings. . . . In the *other beginning,* truth is recognized and grounded as the truth of being, just as being itself is recognized and grounded there as the being of truth—that is, as *the event turned against itself.* To that belongs the intrinsic transgression of the fissuring, and thus the *abyss*" (*BzP* 185).

Let us bear in mind the words "recognized" and "grounded" from these programmatic lines. They bespeak the overdetermination of the eventual by the occurrent, and thus the difference between birth and natality.

In the other beginning—as was seen concerning what diremption reveals—the contrariety, the intrinsic transgressivity of the event, its fissuring, and its abyssal character were recognized. What does that mean, if not that the double bind has always occurred, but that it goes unnoticed, *incognito,* so long as one understands truth as a quality that affects unconcealed beings? Retreating behind hegemonies, the long-lasting power of the double bind nevertheless never ceased to signal their departure. Conflictual truth, remaining in its suspended retreat, has not been exhausted in the epochal economies. One thinks to grasp—intuitively, principially—the one, nature, consciousness, or another of these supremely unconcealed beings, first; but it is the appropriation in the event that *always begins.* Hence the injunction to recognize its unconcealing labor. Such is the role of the instituting discourse which, while only prefacing it, Heidegger nevertheless claims as his own.

Again we have an injunction to "ground" this labor. That would be the role of an instituted discourse, taking over from Heidegger's preparatory gesture. The other beginning indicates the awakening to the tragic condition; but with an awakening, everything is only beginning. Once you are seized by conflictual truth, how will you follow it up? Such is the question that will decide if the other beginning can be translated into another history, not, "What will you say next?" Rather, the linkage is made by "grounding the *there*", by enduring an economy without consolation. By which standards or norms are you going to orient yourself now? Heidegger answers: "The endurance of being itself bears its standard in itself, insofar as being still needs a standard" (*BzP* 12)—insofar as the event turned back against itself can still be called a standard. The conflictual economy is born from itself; once it has been recognized, it remains to be loved in the patience of sensitive mortals, and, in this sense, to be grounded.

The third path uncovered carves up the sediments of the origin-beginning-start according to an expressly topological incision, an incision going from the *not-there* to the *there.*

In the Greek start, "the name 'Da-sein' receives its content in the first beginning—*essencing itself (there) by arising, unconcealed*," in a word, *phusis* (*BzP* 296). What arises of itself and endures in front of the gaze is what is there, in sight. In the manner that the Greeks thought of action, this arising is the origin of phenomena. Their instituting thinking was astonished only by this arising; and instituted thinking then wondered at duration. In the discourses stemming from the Greek institution, "Da-sein" means a modality of present beings, the fact that they last and are effectively available. To guarantee this duration, one maximized the trait of appropriation in being, and in doing so denied the withdrawal of death.

With the diremption of the tutelage over presence, Da-sein becomes what is at stake in an eventual start: in an entry, a new departure, a birth. An entry into what? Into an origin no longer reduced to arising alone, but suffered as the dissension between arising and withdrawal. No meditation leads from *phusis* to *Da-sein* so understood, neither the passage through metaphysical *actualitas,* nor some return to the premetaphysical act. How to live, how to think? By beginning with dissension. That is what Da-sein in the other beginning signifies.

Da-sein signifies, moreover, the very gap between the two beginnings. It is "the *krisis* between the first and the other beginning" (ibid.), due to which its notion itself becomes differential. As crisis, it overdetermines the eventual with the occurrent. It overdetermines the eventual, for where could one find the patience today to endure the double bind? And through the occurrent, for "being itself essentially comes to be as *the event of grounding the there*" (*BzP* 183). The initiating or inceptive difference can be expressed in terms of grounding. The occurrent grounding calls for eventual founders, just as the originary appropriation calls for a start.

If the *there* thus marks the gap between the first and the other beginning, it announces the break that the possible always introduces into the actual. Like the question of being ("formerly" a guiding question, "now" a basic question) and truth ("formerly" the unconcealed in its arising, "now" unconcealment-concealment), the *there* also undergoes the historical sundering ("formerly" the given granted to us, "now" the gift in discord with itself). The two beginnings make Da-sein equivocal. One only speaks of it in a shattered voice that demands a break in hearing, a break that exacerbates the tearing and equivocity rather than mediating or remedying them.

Being, truth, and the *there* appeared equivocal formerly and now, not because a univocal origin would appear unclear in the first beginning and lucid in the second, but because that origin itself harbors what is equivocal, unclear, and sundered. If one speaks of different things at each end—formerly and now—while compelling languages to make them mutually translatable, then the foreshortenings that collect "metaphysics" into one chunk go awry. Now, the possible: Heidegger strove for forty years to free the conflictual *there* that breaks us and broke each hegemony. An otherness without genus divides up the guardians of beingness (formerly, always actual, not-there) and the agonal freedom of being (now, always possible, there). Powerful territorial interests {*intérêts de fiefs*} therefore are needed in order to be able to detect in the origin turned against itself the obsession, always and again, of a presence rescued from dislocations. How could an origin that would be "its own worst enemy" guarantee a simple and full presence?

What lesson can be learned from these three paths that have been uncovered that will help one understand the initiating or inceptive difference?

The lesson has to do with time—with the temporal essencing (*Wesung*) of being. The origin is indeed its own worst enemy, thanks to time. It is not difficult to see that, if being means the *polemos* of appropriation and expropriation, and if it is to be understood as time, then time itself will be polemical. The difference between birth and natality announces this discordance of times, that is, the originary differend by which time is something that one can never enjoy. Its undertow means that it is always lacking. The *difference* is of a temporal kind inasmuch as it deploys itself in history, since occurrent appropriation, as was seen, there gives rise to an eventual future, to the grounding of an anarchic economy. The *differend* is what introduces strife into the originary event itself. It is a temporal strife that is "prior" to history (by an initiating or inceptive anteriority) and toward which all of Heidegger's argument is directed.

As concerns the possible economy, this strife is expressed by an analogy, namely, that the time of being is just as polemical as is the truth of being. In the other beginning, "the 'truth' of being is named 'time'" (*BzP* 183). What does that mean? One would have to be illiterate not to understand: just as truth is conflictual in itself, the same holds for time. The terms of the analogy coincide, which means that it isn't an analogy. The aletheiological *truth* of being is that it comes about, turned against itself. In the turning-against, the discordance of *times* manifests itself, becomes thinkable with the turning in the economy.

It is an other, discordant time; an other, concealing-revealing truth; an other Dasein, deferred by the possible; an other being, turned against itself; an other originary speaking, where the No holds itself up against the Yes—these are so many figures of the double bind becoming the sole phenomenological issue with the other beginning (this other beginning is "other" than historical alterity, and thus an other otherness). The driving figure in this series remains that of time. Thus, if one remembers that the pride of thinking lay precisely in ending all polemics by providing intuition with an unshakable and constraining referent, one will understand the substitution that results from the other beginning: "No longer 'thinking'—but 'time'" (ibid.). From one beginning to the other, the focal meaning that sums up "thinking" (in quotes and therefore intuitive and discursive) gives way to the discordance that is "time" (in quotes, this time, to cross out the associations of instant and intuition, as well as duration and discourse).

What do the three paths uncover, then? They first suggest an eventual birth, that is, "that the *truth* of being is grounded and that this grounding is accomplished as Dasein" (*BzP* 176). Epochal history, where the ravages of appropriation-expropriation were covered up, would be lifted just as one lifts a curfew. A start, then, of another "'age of the world,' which means another history of being" (*BzP* 158). The three paths uncover the difference as Heidegger's vocabulary presents it, a difference in the beginning between the start (the birth when time comes) and the origin (the natality by which time happens). But they especially indicate that in truth, all begins with dissension. From the outset of manifestation, occurrent natality turns against itself. A conflictual origin makes it such that nothing begins simply. Once it has been rethought as *Anfang,* the *principium* that was summoned and mandated loses its power to command and its mandate. The three paths move toward an origin that makes one "leave peace behind," an origin that is literally "frightening."

Only principial investments make one believe that dread has been cast off. The discourse instituted in Athens has buried beneath its constitutive positings every figure of a deconstituting origin. But the deciphering that is resolutely faithful to phenomena reveals that one can find no instance of an autonomous, simple origin that is uniformly a source and a condition of beings. *Diasôzein* did not find it in the first beginning: "Unity is not an originary determination of the being of beings." It does not find it in the other beginning either: "Since the other beginning, this un-shaken and un-questioned determination (unity) can and must be submitted to questioning" (*BzP* 459f.). Simple unity does not manifest itself, it is posited. The art of positing it is the "trick of the trade." Now, the tragic conflict that set all the epochs on their way shows itself in the new departure beyond epochs. With the diremption that befalls us, originary, dreadful strategies appear.

CHAPTER 7

On the Discordance of Times

On the singularizing "momentary sites"

"Being—the remarkable error to believe that being must always 'be'. . . . Being is what is most rare because most singular. Thus no one appreciates the few moments in which a site founds itself and comes to be." (*BzP* 255)

The discordance of times sums up for Heidegger the origin that is dreadful because it is turned against itself, the tragic origin that diremption frees.

Now the issue is to understand how the ultimate that mortality is effects such a turning and undermines time. As everyone knows, time is what we always lack. Now Heidegger looks to what everyone knows for a hint of the condition of being. One must carefully follow his criticism of the "always 'being'." Discordance and diremption are indeed at play in the "what is most rare" and "the most singular."

The *there* of the tragic double bind is deferred, we can recall, by the modal category under which Heidegger places it in the *Contributions:* that of the possible, higher than the actual. Accordingly, its temporality is structured by the priority—a simple consequence of the possible as Heidegger understood it—of the future over the present. Still, this priority is only the penultimate word on time. The last word belongs to the discordance that defines the event and hence the *there*.

On the one hand, it is essential for the *there* to be deferred. On the other, however, we have seen that its contingency makes it depend on "thrusts of time" that occur or do not occur. To "enter into the *there*" will therefore amount to making one's own a singular condition that is not simple.

In the lines quoted, Heidegger is translating the originary *agôn* into a reading tactic. He is pathetically turning against the tradition commonplaces received from it, thereby hoping to prepare a place out of the common, the *koinon,* the universal, the general, and the generic. The remarkable error announced in these lines with regard to being—remarkable because it is the most traditional—is expressed by two philosophemes that are just as remarkably traditional. One has to do with time, the other with space.

The issue of time is deceptively introduced by one of the most classical antitheses, that of being-always and of the instant. Heidegger is obviously not proposing an nth permutation of the disjunction of the genus "time" into fixed everlastingness and the fleeting now. Since these lines neither invert nor even preserve the framework of the pairings of *aiôn-nûn* or the *sempiternitas-nunc,* it is equally obvious that such a framework no longer fits the temporality of the anticipated place. They do not invert the coefficients of those opposites, transforming what would endure into the negative and the fleeting into the positive—to turn against does not mean to invert. Nor do they preserve the framework, for being "is" not, "it unfolds" (*west*) or does not unfold. Rather, Heidegger twists the framework of the genus time so as to prepare to overcome it (double meaning of the verb *verwinden:* 'to twist,' 'to overcome'). To apply to the tradition the terms inherited from it thus does not serve to refute it. They serve another strategy, since in the rare instants in question, dissension founds a site for itself, wherein "being unfolds." Such founding can only be received, and the "founders" can do no more than respond to it. It is pointless to look for any doxographic antecedent serving as a handrail for this sort of transitional strategy.

As to the issue of space, it too emerges from a classical binary schema since the "site" follows the "moment." Does this not amount to having the representation of space derive once again from that of time? If so, Heidegger would be transmuting rather than permuting an old pair, but still a pair. Do these lines not reduce space and time to the atomic, space to a given site and time to a given moment? If so, Heidegger then would be passing—yet another classical disjunction—from the demonstrable to the merely ostensible. He would be abandoning the dieresis starting from a genus and leading to its components in order to confine himself to the components alone: to deictic objects. His polemic against the prestige of continuous duration is well-known. But even if, rather than totalizing time and space, one were to retain what is most minuscule about them and transmute them into "momentary sites" {*lieux d'instants*}, wouldn't one still be wandering amongst the very representations that have sustained the career of *mathesis*?

A whole set of problems arises here that go to the core of ultimate fantasms, and thus the law. They thematize the withdrawal that *singularization* exerts, that condition in the event that we know by virtue of our mortality. One will remember that it was the work of the singular that thwarted the subsumption beneath the references to the one, nature, and consciousness. Now the "momentary sites" thematize singularization for itself and thus the diremption of the universal as well as of its subsumptive and particularizing mechanisms.

One will also remember that underneath these hegemonies, the singular caused the failure of normative constructions that in each case were worked on precisely by time. It is an epochally variable labor, for in Parmenides it called for the narration of an intrigue with its reversals of fortune and outcome; in Cicero and Augustine, the chronicle of the *res gestae* and the *res gerendae;* in Luther and Kant, lastly, the reception of a singular presented to the subject—in the former a reception in the spirit opposed to reason, and in the latter in the internal sense opposed to the understanding. According to each of these arrangements, the singular was *given,* and in its givenness, was to be *left alone.* That marked its recalcitrance to co-optation, as subsuming referents are never given but posited. Under a normative regime, it would be a mistake {*contresens*} to "let be" the law-making authority. Letting-be would subvert it like that laughter (*gelôs*) to which—the tragic breaking through where one would least expect it—the legislator Lycurgus had a statue erected right in the middle of austere Sparta.[71]

In an age when it becomes possible to let ultimate positings be, the singular is again allied with time. Thus, under hegemonies just as under diremption, their alliance is given, not constructed. However, time and the singular combine their strategies differently when they are pushed to the monstrous limit of hegemonies. Concerning this givenness again, Heidegger uses quotation marks to set off the other, foreign to the tradition: "'time' in an originary sense . . . gives truth" (*BzP* 200). If by truth here Heidegger means *alétheia* and its history, then one sees how the profound and profundity should henceforth be understood: "Time," in the originary sense of the moment, works as if from below (*unterzeitlich, BzP* 108) on the aletheological time fragmented into epochs. This "time" below time will be profound. It will be originary because it structures unconcealment-concealment in its epoch-making configurations. In this "time" that gives we see the singular that is not simple. But what does this mean?

It is a different arrangement in which every accent of the singular becomes unrecognizable. First, the moment. We will see its being fissured by an intrinsic function of refusal. Obviously, time works the singular otherwise and elsewhere than according to the plot, the chronicle, or *a priori* intuition. The work of the moment is originary in comparison to times such as these as well as some others. Truth originates in it. The moment fashions not the true in its successive or simultaneous positings, but aletheiological truth in its constellations wrested from concealment. Hence the quotation marks. The event of the gift and the refusal is singular without being simple. And then there is givenness. It remains opposed, to be sure, to any thesis,[72] and it is indeed of the singular that Heidegger says that it gives itself. But which singular? "Being gives itself" (*BzP* 220), whereas in the plot, the chronicle, and intuition, it was always and only beings that were given. In other words, what is given is the agonal function in its unobstructed purity—diremption. Lastly, letting. Parmenides' chariot lets singular absents (*apeonta*) be firmly present; the citizen of Cicero's and Augustine's *res publica* lets a singular city be memorialized; the Lutheran believer lets God act alone; the Kantian subject lets itself be affected by sensible singulars. . . . In these counter-strategies that undermine normative systems, it is "he who knows," then "he who remembers," then "he who believes," then "he who thinks for himself"—each and every time, it is the human being—who, under one figure or another, lets the singular be what it is. The letting-be that has weakened hegemonies has nevertheless borrowed from them their "humanist" character, even and especially in its ascetic forms. Nothing of the sort remains in transitional thinking. It is the "other" of beings, Heidegger says, that "lets beings be beings" (*BzP* 264). *Who* does this? No longer humans, but the appropriative strategy in the event—the contextualization in which alone phenomena appear. As for *Gelassenheit,* it is of course an attitude as well, and thus something that is "ours." Yet it modifies no subject. It is a trait of thinking, not an attribute of that being that is a person nor an activity done to those beings facing that person. It "lets being be as event" (*BzP* 391, 118). Just as time and givenness, "letting" stresses what is singularly discordant. This singularity is the most difficult to think yet is what for the forty years following the *Contributions* will distinguish the exorbitance of Heidegger's project. He never ceased leaving the civil service of humanity; he will turn the closed orbit of particulars focused on a principle into the open trajectory of singularization.

In this turn and this turning lies the transitional character of the project. The universal that had provided principles turns into the uniqueness of a singular, into "the out-of-the-ordinary of what happens only once and just this once" (*das Einmalige und Diesmalige, BzP* 463). How should this be understood if its uniqueness lies in an agonal origin? Heidegger's laconic assessment of poverty—we "still" lack everything: the capacity to listen, language, speech, names (ibid.)—hardly helps to further the question, even when advanced as a simple question. Europe in the late twentieth century likes to think of itself as involved in attempts to "think otherwise." Thus whoever has leafed through the philosophers finds no reason to doubt their partisanship when one reads that the other is being, and that it is this for a singularity fractured from within. So much of the most abstract sort has been said about being that one might as well add that it "is" once and just this once, and that in this uniqueness and rarity it shatters itself, shatters us, and that it has always shattered every hegemony. This otherness is apparently so ethereal that it no longer rouses anybody. And partisanship may become all the more halting as one grasps, even if not altogether and at once what is meant by the otherness of a singular that is neither a being nor simple, at least one of its implications. For example, that we lack words (whence Heidegger's "sigetics"). Is this what we are to say about our language? Or even that the ground on which we might stand to raise its question is shaky (therefore the "abyss"). Should that be said of our intellectuals? And this despite its being quite a blow to principles (hence "anarchism"). Is this what we are to say about our values? . . . Despite the fact that in the midst of the verbal hodgepodge, some striking words still please us, as long as the year was a good one and that they are surrounded with attractively arranged clarifications? These are but so many ways of avoiding the blows that the twentieth century has inflicted on its languages, its intellectuals, and its values—ways of avoidance for which one may beg neither for patience nor for sympathy because time is precisely what is lacking.

Now, how could time come to be lacking if it were not essentially traversed by an undertow that steals it away from us? To raise just this one question is to have grasped the originary tragedy. In temporal terms, it is to have grasped the *fissured* instant. One might get a clearer view by having spatialization follow singularization, that is, by returning to the site where history has lodged us today.

How is one then to understand being as singular, as happening only once and just this once? By returning precisely to what happens once and just this once. And Heidegger has amply described this. What is happening to us is the monstrosity of the historial site and the pathos of being-human to which it gives rise. Generalized standardization has led to our expulsion from any standard meaning of being. We experience a dispersion that marks the end of epochs. This is his starting point, never put into question after the erring of the 1930s, and into whose conditions he keeps inquiring obstinately. As was seen, the point of departure presents for us a possibility: that of Dasein. It is the possibility that the self might belong to the conflictual event and to the double bind. Now, whoever speaks of the event speaks of precariousness. And what is Heidegger's way of speaking of the precarious site? He speaks of it by disengaging the individuation in which the condition remains a universally conceivable principle, shrunken by some co-principle (matter, time, haecceity . . .) into some object that is no longer displayable. In the event, on the other hand, the condition itself is singular. It is expropriation. As undeniable to the site we inhabit, it turns being against itself, and in*ters* in advance every phenomenon of the *world*. Recognizing ourselves as assigned to that site without denying it—that will be the way to become a self.

By approaching the question of time from that of space, the site and the self have to be thought of together. The site grants the self, but the event also "needs" the self (*BzP* 245), uses it, makes use of it, and wears it away. Hence the self is neither actual nor simple. We know singular being, happening only once and just this once, through the bifrontality of the site that diremption lays out for us. It is a historical site that makes polyphemes of us, those who speak in multiple voices because we have incorporated disparate contraries. Being incorporates nothingness, it "casts around itself only and solely nothingness" (*BzP* 471). Similarly, appropriation incorporates expropriation and, again, the *there* (*das Da*) incorporates the not-there (*das Weg*). The knowledge we incorporate from this strife is, according to Heidegger, too close to be directly thinkable—perhaps also too painful (unless, like the tragic heroes, we need an even sharper pain)—yet it nonetheless instructs us as to our possibility. It is the knowledge of an agonal self and of its agony.

Just as the suspension that is the *epoché* has its condition in the concealment that is *léthé*, so indeed the monstrousness of the site has its condition in the agonal contrariety of being. Now Heidegger attempts to understand the originary *agôn* in spatial and temporal terms, namely, as an abyssal site and as a discordance of times. The reflections on space and time serve, therefore, as much more than surgical strikes against what is isomorphically mathematizable. The singular that is being neither occurs nor is it to be understood outside of the momentary sites thus fractured, outside the momentary sites of the self, that is, of the tragic *there*.

Thus the distinctions between place and time become blurred. In any economy of what is possible to do and to be, the site carves out a narrowly limited space for us. The place is the share of the possible that is assigned to us, whether this "us" designates the rare founders (notably poets and statesmen), the few who hear and understand them, the many to whom they address themselves or, yet again, all those situated by an epoch. The *there* determines the "we" (thereby erasing all entitative and subjectivist connotations from the "we"). At the point of insertion into a given economy, very few of the phenomena making up a world are within our reach. The *there* is severely restricted by the infinite number of possibles remaining out of reach, that is, by what is impossible in the economy. To say that "the *there* is assigned" (*das Da wird zugewiesen*) is to speak of an "assigned clearing" (*zugewiesene Lichtung, BzP* 240). Allocation, then, no longer owes anything to the natural *topos* occupied by a substance (Aristotle), nor to transcendental ideality spatializing a phenomenon given to the subject (Kant). Allocating and assigning are verbs that, after the crisis, Heidegger conjugates in the passive voice just as the assigning "of" being gets declined in the subjective genitive case. A place gives a configuration to finitude as it is destined to us.

This is how the site reveals its affinity with the moment. An insertion into a given economy always occurs, and can only occur, punctually, at one given point (topical insertion) as well as at the right moment (historial insertion). This double reduction to the spatial and temporal point is tantamount to saying that the tragic *there* is neither spatial nor temporal in the sense of the four dimensions. Rather, it occurs each time anew and each time as singular—singularized by the to-come, as we will see below. An allocation to the site is effected by an economic rearrangement of the beings making up a world. It happens unexpectedly as a thrust (*Ruck, Stoß*—the Platonic *exaiphnês* historicized). These thrusts make up the truth of "natality,"[73] the occurrent truth of this maximizing impulse that, in its Greek, Latin, and modern figures signaled the point of inception of all fantasms.

This also suggests how Heidegger can speak of the event both in the plural and in the singular. In the plural, since the sudden reversals in history are innumerable; in the singular, since we hold being—being holds us and has us in its double bind—only through these displacements at the heart of its economy. What Heidegger calls being must be understood as a phenomenal arrangement that takes shape in sudden advents, so that always "its unfolding must be awaited as a thrust" (*BzP* 242). Retrospectively, the momentary sites articulate the history of being, marking ever new departures, small and great. Prospectively they charge it with another new beginning, one in which no denial would normalize the fissured site and discordant times.

The entry into the double bind can be missed, as it has been missed ever since we have needed univocal referents. In this—brutally univocal—sense, for close to twenty-five centuries the tragic *there* has had neither place nor time. Momentary sites can be made ours or not. Thus there is a recurrence of the subjectivist-occurrent monstrosity when Heidegger designates by a proper name the subject (Hölderlin more than anyone else) who has been able to grasp those momentary sites. But all the while relapsing into it, Heidegger still delimits the monstrous by means of the transition toward a possible economy in which the agonic event would be sustained in its singularity. "Already the place (Da-sein) is being created into whose builder and guardian the human subject must transform itself" (*BzP* 242). This "already" and this "place" come together in the "momentary site," in what is possible for us.

This is why the tragic *there* is well described in locutions stressing delay, such as "preparing," "awaiting," "entering into," "not yet." . . . They emphasize the transitional character. A historial constellation centered on the subject and its subsumptions is decentered so as to free the singular from all subsumptive mechanics and hence to free disparity. What remains is to comply pathetically with the hegemonic subjectivism that is collapsing upon itself and thus is pulling back. By appealing to the founders, Heidegger is evoking the flexibility of such compliance. "Founding the *there*" thus does not mean anchoring a site on some unshakable foundation. Founding means making one's own, even to the monstrous limits of the possible, the narrow strip of terrain upon which it is given to us to advance. In terms of the law, founding is not a nomic but a nomadic act—a breakthrough of squatters knowing themselves to be removable and singularizable since they are {settled} outside any univocal law.

Nothing suggests the diremption undergone by the representations of the universal and the general better than this transmutation of place and moment into features of a possible *there*. As an ontological trait of being-in-the-world (*Being and Time*) the *there* denoted precisely the most common character of a certain being. It denoted the existential—that is, universal and necessary—condition of finite transcendence. As the possible momentary site, however, it comes to denote the non-generalizable other of all that has passed for universal and necessary. It names the event occurring only once and just this once. Heidegger thus seeks to turn the *there* from a common noun into a proper name. This violence done to the deictic adverb only reflects the violence of the boundary on which we live. Thus the monstrousness of our site translates easily into a series of alternatives, each pointing to either side of the epochal caesura. The limit where theticism reveals its fictitious impulses provides a place and a moment for an either-or (which obviously has nothing to do with any choice put before a free will). The alternatives thematize the other of any subsumptive universal that is without genus. May it suffice, as a mere indication, to mention the two that have to do with the questions, "Who are we?" and "What is being?" Heidegger writes that it is a matter of knowing "whether man wants to remain a 'subject' *or* if he is to found Da-sein; . . . if beings accept being as what is 'most general,' thereby handing it over to 'ontology' and submerging it, *or* if being is to come to word in its singularity, and, like that which happens only once, determine beings" (*BzP* 90f.).

What is more traditional in philosophy than theories on the dimensions of the phenomena of the here and now? Heidegger removes these dimensions from the dominion of theories. It is a lesson in deconstruction to see him work through the legacy of "place and moment" and to conjoin them in the "momentary site." This conjunction destroys them as forms, whether apophantic, transcendental, or other. Not being the site and time *of* anything, they no longer lend themselves to subsumptions. The singular event, thought from out of the singular *there*—that is the other of the ontological tradition. Space and time thus come to lie beyond the reach of normative co-optation. Concerning the expropriating trait riddling the event of appropriation, a trait that sunders all normativity from within, it will be necessary to try to retrace the temporal conditions of this other right down to its fissured place of emergence. It suffices, however, to have understood this singular that is not simple—the event of the tragic *there*—to see that being will no longer be thinkable as the other *of beings*. Instead of their ontological and normative difference, what will have to be thought is a temporal and dispersive discordance. Reading the opening paragraphs of the lecture "Time and Being" (1961), one may be left with the impression that it was only with his last word on the question of being that Heidegger found an access to the site from which he could raise it "without regard for a grounding of being in beings."[74] With the *Contributions,* such a reading of the texts no longer holds. I continue to believe that Heidegger is to be read backward, from the last to the first writings. By reading him in this way, one glimpses precisely the motives and paths that led him to raise the question of being for its own sake and out of itself, motives arising from the singular, and paths prompted by the many ways of accentuating the internal conflict arising from singularization.

With the momentary sites of this *singularum tantum*—with being as event turned against itself—one also sees how Heidegger substitutes ultimates for the *a priori*. A description that sets out from beings in order to inscribe them within an *a priori* construct only transcribes the latter into a mere postscript (*Nachtrag, BzP* 174) to the "givens" that, for the needs of normativity, are then declared "*a posteriori.*" This is not to say that, from the perspective of the other beginning, being no longer precedes beings in any way at all. It precedes them—whereby it announces the conflictual origin—as the strife of nothingness and being precedes any access to phenomenal beings struggling against their singularization. This is another kind of anteriority, by which being finds itself "alienated from beings" (*BzP* 258), foreign to them, no longer crowning them with a referent and no longer backing them up with some authoritative common noun. "For its other, being has non-being" (*BzP* 267). This is what the analytic of ultimates teaches us: Non-being singularizes being like death singularizes these living beings that, for good reasons, Parmenides (*brotoi*), Augustine ("we are dead, in the soul and in the body"[75]), Luther (by confessing to God, believing him to be dead to himself) and Heidegger call mortals.

As long as one does not see that non-being—in terms of ultimates, mortality—singularizes the event because it *fissures* it, one will not understand how "something of this sort is possible: to think being itself in its way of unfolding, without taking its point of departure to be in beings" (*BzP* 429). Until Heidegger's last writings, these ties between the singular event, the expropriating undertow that traverses it like a backdraft of death, and its foreignness from beings were to be strengthened. These bonds substitute the tragic double bind for fantasmic norms.

The "fissured" moment

"He is lucky who can belong to the fateful fissuring of being." (*BzP* 416)

There may be a subtle way, even if it was as old as Homer, of co-opting the singular for normative needs. Heidegger lapses into this, as I have said, when he exalts the singularity of a collective subject. This co-optation became a doctrine with Kant. While the subsumptive judgments operated on cases of a universal and constituted them as particulars, reflective judgments, in turn, do not do such violence to phenomena. They measure one given singular by the yardstick of some other one. It is so when we admire a woman "as beautiful as Helen," a man "as courageous as Achilles," "as strong as Ajax." . . . By means of such comparisons, a paradigmatic singular authorizes aesthetic assessments as well as political allegiances—at least if one is to believe an interpreter who is seductive in her boldness.[76] Doesn't Heidegger follow an analogous strategy not only when, in his subjectivist intrications, he has the Germans answer to the Greeks (and *for* the Greeks), but again when, in his anti-subjectivist and deconstructive strategy, he singularizes being, gathers it up from the momentary sites and awaits a decisive *there* that is as singular as the Greek decisive *there* was?

Greek Da-sein, he indeed says, did not last. It was only "a great and unique moment" (*BzP* 196). Doesn't the height of the beginning serve as a model for the beginning anew that is possible and imminent today? Germany was not able to rise "as high as Greece." But doesn't the rule of that singular that the sixth century was, remain? Isn't it in relation to a *that* that one may denounce *this* which we have become and prepare an eventually possible *there*? Isn't technology judged to be monotonous, offering only giganticism and machinery, because it is measured more or less tacitly against that Greek moment when being first made itself into event? Thus, because Heidegger fragments duration just as he singularizes being, history is only made up of "moments that are rare and quite far from one another." The question, then, is: Do we stand "before the door of a new moment?" (*BzP* 342). Aren't the mournful No that answers this question during the Thirties, as well as the Yes to the optative, both to be measured by the rule of the singular Greek *there*? Such a standard no longer results, to be sure, from reflection. But nonetheless it seems to entitle one to judge one singular in relation to another, a normative relation, where the authoritative noun would henceforth be that proper name, "Greece."

However widespread this view of Heidegger haughtily saying "the Greeks and I"—or nostalgically, which is more banal—is, it is highly problematic. Heidegger defends himself against this charge many times. His denial bears precisely on surreptitiously re-established normativity. "Even in that highest [Greek] time, only moments—uniqueness—, not a state and a rule" (*BzP* 507). This uniqueness is what is problematic. Does it serve to exalt a rare measure-moment or to fracture every measure?

It suffices indeed to remember the tragic choice in order to understand what is unclear about the denial of a rule. Hubristic blindness is never far. Cannot the singular moments to which a "thrust of time" gives rise serve as a model to follow? What makes them essentially ill-suited to have a normative function?

What makes them so are the fissures.

"He is lucky who can belong to the fateful fissuring of being." I read these words from the last section of the *Contributions*[77] as summing up the tragic condition for which Heidegger paid so dearly to discover. Don't they present the very morality of "Oedipus at Colonus"? The entire story of Oedipus, decipherer of the riddle asked by the Sphinx, revolves around that other riddle: Who am I? One remembers the last warning given by Jocasta: "Unhappy man, may you never know who you are."[78] Now, having reached Colonus, Oedipus has accepted who he is: not the dispenser of justice who saved Thebes, but the defiler who brought it to the verge of ruin. He made its fateful destiny his own. Unhappy for having denied the ancestral allegiance, he then becomes happy because of his belonging to the fateful fissuring of the ancestral and the civil laws, gratified with apotheosis, and enthroned as the patron hero of Athens. Would it be demanding too much of Heidegger's text to read the *unselig* ('fateful') as a reminder of the description that Oedipus gives of himself, *ego tlamôn* ("I, unhappy"[79])? Is Heidegger perhaps putting himself on stage here? It is not asking too much of the text, in any case, to understand that he answers the question of

Who?—therefore, the question of the self—in terms of the belonging to a fateful, dire conflict in being itself, a conflict that, once hubristic denial has been exposed, defines the tragic double bind.

In the "fracturings," everything is at stake. For Heidegger, what is at stake therein is a certain continuity in his research, the lesson learned from erring, the second departure in his thinking that ensues from erring, and lastly, his place in the history of philosophy. What is also at stake there is the human condition as it results from being dissociated from any figure of the common.

From his dissertation on Duns Scotus to his last lectures, Heidegger sought the categories with which to raise the question of being in its relation to time. Of his two best-known answers, the first (*Being and Time*) bases itself on the "existentialia" of temporality, namely, the ecstases; the second (*Time and Being*), on the "traits" of the event that are appropriation and expropriation. Now, under the heading of "fissurings" (*Zerklüftungen*), the Heidegger of the *Contributions* ventures an answer to the categorial problem, without which the conflictuality of appropriation-expropriation remains incomprehensible in its quite precisely tragic bearing—as it has remained, in fact, uncomprehended, at least in the commentators of which I am aware. It would seem as if, in those fateful years, Heidegger had an ear out for a German Homer, then to he whom Heidegger seems to have taken to be a German Solon, and that he himself ends up speaking in the voice of Sophocles.

The fissurings emphasize the discordances of time. They emphasize being by temporal appropriation and expropriation. In order to see what this determinative labor is, one must ask by what *katêgorein* these fissurings emphasize the discordances. Heidegger connects them to categories, yet also separates them from the categories, since fissurings have to structure the singular and the moment. One would be mistaken to see this as a problem of application and to construe them according to the model of form and content.

One must be able to think the temporal characteristics of being while jettisoning the formalism and representations of the universal that being conveys. The same jettisoning already opposed the "momentary sites" to the empty forms of space and time. Thus: "[T]he fissuring of being . . . does not project a table of empty categories" (*BzP* 237).

The thinking that is other than formalizing and subsumptive thinking remains difficult in that it reassigns the entire old problem of the categories to the transitional site. It has to single out the singular without turning it into anything particular. Thus the lists that Heidegger substitutes for the tables of forms are in this respect less instructive—indeed, quite eclectic (as when he speaks of the "fissuring of being into uniqueness, freedom, contingency, necessity, possibility and actuality," ibid.[80])—than the status he grants to them. They receive their justification from the transitional thrust that befalls us, a thrust toward an economy of the self (of the tragic *there*) which, more than ever, remains deadened in that of the ego. Hence the embarrassed borrowings, in quotation marks, from Kantian transcendentalism: "To attempt the impossible and to grasp the essence of being with the help of 'metaphysical' 'modalities'. . . ." An impossible attempt, which in truth the bifrontality of the site nevertheless renders unavoidable. In attempting, then, to grasp the event with the categories of modality, its fissuring will mean "the supreme actuality of the highest possible, as possible, and thereby the first necessity" (*BzP* 244). This is less obscure than it appears, if one at least does remember *toward what* the new categorization is to lead: toward the event without common noun because it is fissured from within, toward the singularization without genus, toward the moment without the frame of a "before" and an "after."

What *katêgorein,* then? The transitional archic-anarchic *historizes* the categories of modality. According to their *a priori* use, the possible is more than the actual, and the actual is more than the necessary. Now, this received use measures the possible as well as the necessary by the actual. It is here that the fissuring makes a dent in the *a priori,* that kingmaker behind the scenes of all normative hegemonies. Once the *a priori*—that is, thetic—gesture is recognized as the historial illusion *par excellence,* what remains of the modalities? The actual then signifies the now of the caesura-decision, and the possible signifies the double bind of the conflictual moment; and with the *a priori* theses being revealed as illusory, the turning that is outside of distress (*Not*) will be necessary (*not-wendig*). In an initial approximation, the fissurings thus emphasize the event as the advent of a post-epochal site, as the figure of being destined to us.

This transitional historialization displaces "priorities," as one says. In conformity with the prestige of the actual and presence, beingness was determined by *energeia, actualitas,* and *Wirklichkeit.* Impervious to phenomena, this prestige is all too redolent of theticism. So the guiding category becomes that of the necessary, signifying, as we will see, the turning (priority will come back to the possible, finally, with the function of singularization to come).

In the face-to-face encounter with the Greek beginning, the fissurings respond to traits that are already agonistic, such as *phusis* and *logos* (*BzP* 236). Temporalized by history, they allow one to cast a retrospective and transitional glance over the gesture of being. They occur twice. In the Greek institution, they retain the transgressive strategies that hegemonic univocity represses, and in the contemporary diremption, they anticipate the anarchy whose rediscovered conflictuality today ruins every "archy."

Now, in Heidegger, historial temporalization always and only serves as the access to occurrent temporality. To respond to the normative ruination that befalls us, one must decide either to feign the old subsumptive theticism or let agonic truth be. Either categorization of beingness, or fissuring of being. There is no passageway leading from one term of this alternative to the other. If there were one, it would link the nascent economy of disparates to hegemonies. But, as we have seen, to begin with the monstrous double bind of technicity is an entirely different departure than beginning with the simple bind emanating from some subsumptive principle. The either-or allows one to glimpse the vehemence of the other thinking, a vehemence that asserts the loss of all consoling and consolidating moments. "The fissuring of being must not be submerged underneath the invented illusion of adjustments" (*BzP* 406). The adjustments, compromises, balancings (*Ausgleiches*) would also be—and were—amicable settlements. Against this amicability of uniformly legislating referents (one loves consoling agents—the one, term of anagogical *erôs;* nature, the goal of right *dilectio;* the realm of consciousnesses, loved as an end in itself)—Heidegger turns "the fateful fissuring."

To do more than glimpse the tear whose fissurings lacerate the fantasized tissue of beingness, it is enough to ask: Which is the differend that above all it is no longer something to be settled in an amicable manner?

Like every differend, the one that the fissurings emphasize opposes law to law, and it splits what passes as being self-identical. In translating Heidegger, 'differend' (which is the gerund of *dis-ferre,* bearing from here/there, dispersing) does a good job of rendering *Ausfälligkeit* (falling outside, but also and especially projection, invective, a scattered exit from here to/from there). Whoever posits the identical will make a show of positive thinking, and whoever exalts values will show signs of rallying. The differend, however, appears when, beneath the excess of thetic violence, exaltation falls back and rallyings are dispersed. Having been a party to such excess, Heidegger knows whereof he speaks: "Well, now what is needed is the *great turning-back,* which is beyond any 'transvaluation of all values'." What is needed is a turn (*Kehre*) in the manner of thinking. The turning-back (*Umkehrung*) shows being turned (*kehrig*) against itself. It shows it in a differend. Hence the attempt to think the "*event turned against itself,* to which the intrinsic differend of fracturing belongs" (*BzP* 185). Differing thus cleaves being with regard to itself, just as the tragic hero was his law and his counter-law all at once (Oedipus passing for being self-identical, but divided against himself as the investigator of regicide according to the law of the city, and the object of the investigation according to the ancestral law of his lineage).

The following questions are to be kept alive while the philosophical charge of categorization mutates into the responsibility of fissuring: What need of mastery dispatched philosophers in the search of categories of being, and what distress has stripped {*déssaisie*} us of it, reopening the tragic fissuring? What has happened to us so that in the twentieth century the reference to some ultimate meaning appears as a catch-all that has been able to frame every sort of "given"? More directly, the first of these questions is addressed to the most penetrating thinker of this century: How is one to understand that he had to be implicated in naked thetic violence to have his eyes opened to the other need, to tragic distress, more ancient than the wish for a univocal norm? And the second question is addressed to us: Which blindings will we have to pass through to learn how to see? How far will *hubris* and errancy (*Irre, BzP* 430; *Wirrnis, BzP* 98) have to go, as they verge on becoming planetary, so that we might learn to think time and its condition, singularization by mortality, differently?

One of the numerous ways Heidegger has of keeping such questions alive is lodging them within the reach or the distance of a leap. Such is the case with the new departure that another, no longer subsumptive, thinking might take. Since the passageways still only serve one figure of the universal that goes hand in hand with another such figure, the leap is necessary (*notwendig*) because it alone is capable of turning (*wenden*) the distress (*Not*). "*In the other beginning,* what matters is the leap into the fissuring in-between of the turning of the event" (*BzP* 231). We should understand this as meaning that an other thinking matters, a thinking that never sidesteps or repairs the double bind, that answers for being fissured by time, that submits to the law of expropriation that unmakes our world, a law turned against the law of appropriation that makes the world, a turning that is the event. All that is asked of us is to be-there in the site of the diremption that is already ours. The leap thus does not lead to anywhere else. It is summed up in the detachment toward normative positings: "fracturing opens itself . . . that *totally detaches* itself from being as the most 'general' determination" (*BzP* 278). "All" that is asked of us is to forget varying the normative difference and to learn the differend as the originary temporal condition.

If there is in Heidegger an antecedent to the fissuring of being, it is to be found in ecstatic temporality. To be sure, this antecedence only appears from a retrospective reading of the Existential Analytic. It nevertheless points toward the discordance of times.

In the *Contributions,* the conflictuality of appropriation-expropriation not only pertains to time, but is explicitly tied to the "ecstases." As we saw, once they have been dissociated from the mathematical project, space and time appear in their common origin: the tragic *there*—a possible place that thereby cannot be dissociated from time. In order to become phenomenal, it requires "momentary sites." In the plural, these designate the events that mark epochal caesurae. Their temporality is, then, of a historial order. But for Heidegger, the historial is always derived. It stems from the occurrent. That means that (as in Kant, but for reasons pertaining to singular being, not to the subsuming subject) time is more originary than space. The event is granted as a moment "before" taking place. Phenomena are fissured because they are temporal, they announce themselves, tarry, and leave. That they can come (let themselves be appropriated) and go (let themselves be expropriated) has to do with the event in the singular, which no longer connotes epochs. The event distinguishes itself from any fixed presence by internal strife, just as *alétheia*-truth distinguishes itself from *adequatio*-truth by the internal strife between concealment and unconcealment. Fissuring works on the moment so that time is always lacking.

Their work always takes over that of the ecstases by a complexity other than the one they confer upon the moment. Fissured time suffers more from negations than ecstatic time does, the fissuring reveals "the *most hidden* essence of the *No*—as 'not yet' and 'no more'" (*BzP* 410). In *Being and Time,* through the implication of the world ecstatic temporality was demarcated from the retentions and protentions of consciousness. Consequently, what one calls past and future were interwoven in such a manner that the world *that had been* unfolded the possible *in front* of us. The to-come presented to projects a world that has already happened. These interweavings resulted from the trait that Heidegger then called being-unto-death. Now, this trait will end up retracing "the most intimate finitude of being" (ibid.) and thus by literally derailing its representations of infinitude. In order to single out the negative power by which the No of the not-yet and the no-more wins over the Yes of a phenomenally given world, Heidegger no longer speaks of "ecstases," but of "displacements" *(Entrückungen). "The moment:* in it displacements are placed" (*BzP* 384). Time is essentially lacking because it essentially expropriates itself in the direction of the not-yet and the no-more. The ecstases gave being-there a ground (*Grund*); fissuring, for its part, is abyssal (*abgründig*).

Fissuring strips the old problematic of the moment not only of every construction of duration based on its parts (as well as of the speculations on the *nunc stans* that only modify the old opposition between that and duration into a hyperbolic paradox), but also of every centering of time on the *there*. One must see clearly that the fissurings take over the categories of modality due to the new contingency of the *there*. As no longer given, the *there* no longer anchors phenomena. Being possible, it exposes them to time. The problematic inherited from the moment, that proved itself by supporting all regimes of the common noun with one prop or another, is thus placed by Heidegger under the law of the No. It is a transgressive law, since it opens the abyss of the "displacement toward what refuses itself (which the essence of temporalization precisely consists in)" (*BzP* 384). Read carefully: The essence of temporalization consists in the undertow toward "that which refuses itself." It can obviously no longer be a matter of *some* moments, of epochal turnings, that articulate history. The moment fissured by "what refuses itself" has no date. It cannot be placed anywhere on a diachronic line. Discordant with itself, it is the condition and the origin of all negative experience. One might also translate *entrücken* as *ravir* (ravish), to forcibly carry away. The fissured moment, then, is the condition and the origin of the *ravages* wrought by death.

Ontologies varied being according to its regimes. By naming what is most universal—and thereby what was the ultimate normative authority—they served to support order. They varied the name of the beingness that makes the law. Now, what happens to the regimes of life when being is to be understood as the singular event, without a name, mortally turned against itself (*kehrig;* turned back against itself, *widerwendig;* adverse, *gegenwendig*)? In short, how does appropriating-expropriating time lay down the law?

Beingness as a name or a noun always led to one and the same correlate: a world stabilized by constant presence. Heidegger transmutes this law of univocity into a law of contrariety. Hence its stakes, which are unthinkable without this law, are the anarchism ruining the principle of the Führer, the monstrousness of the epochal site, the pathos of the latecomer moderns that we are, the diremption of hegemonies, the fissured temporality of being, a certain priority of the No and of death over the affirmative and maximizing impulse of life. These are so many reasons for being twice as careful. If, with the event, the contrariety of appropriation and expropriation lays down the law, one must heed three questions more than others: The event of what? Whither expropriation? Which law and which counter-law?

The event of what?

"Now, being—up until now in the form of beingness, that which is most general and most familiar—becomes, as event, the most singular and the most alienating." (*BzP* 177)

Caution is required, if only because Heidegger exudes a certain overcautiousness with regard to the "proper" and "appropriation," too akin to property, possession, and full presence. However, doesn't the word *Ereignis,* 'event,' come from *eigen,* 'proper' or 'ownness'? And doesn't Heidegger go so far as to understand it as *Eigentum,* 'property'—and the latter, in the manner of *Fürstentum,* 'principality,' which is to say, despite everything, as "sovereign center" (*BzP* 311)? Monstrosity has a strong back if these vertebrae are grafted onto "the most alienating" being (*das Befremdlichste*).

However, it is not the proper that, under the diremption, proves to be an illusion. To wager on the attraction of the proper, while at the same time denying the withdrawal that alienates and expropriates—now that is the illusion.

Caution is required not only with regard to the connotations of a word. One must also remain attentive to its use. Where I distinguished between the terms "event" and "appropriation," Heidegger's vocabulary fluctuates considerably. One encounters *Ereignis, Er-eignis, Ereignung, Eignung, eineignen,* and still more variants. The first of these uses is the most heavily overdetermined. *Ereignis* is written, as we saw, sometimes in the singular (originary condition of phenomena) and sometimes in the plural (epochal beginnings, "thrusts" in history). But Heidegger also lapses into synecdoche, since phrasings in the singular sometimes designate the event of the originary strife of appropriation and expropriation, sometimes appropriation alone. In the latter case (analyzed above with regard to the "other beginning"), *Ereignis* and its cognates emphasize the part for the structural whole. Here what will be at issue is this structural whole, the originary conflict of which I will note some incidences. Finally, in the next section, I will return to alienation taken by itself, and thus to expropriation (*Ent-eignung, enteignen,* etc. . . .)

The illusion of pure property, of possession, and of simple presence can arise only by disregarding the synecdoche. One starts to talk about the metaphysics of the proper only if one takes the part for the whole, that is, if one sets up as a noun-referent the strategy of being by which natality gathers particular phenomena, makes them come to pass and belong to some others, and in that sense appropriates them to one another. But that strategy of the proper would be null and void—and being would not have to come to pass—if it weren't for the counter-strategy of mortality in the event, and thus of disavowal, exclusion, expulsion, and singularization, namely, what Heidegger here calls alienation. Thus one would be mistaken about the event—the issue guiding his thinking up until the last writings—so long as one proceeds as if it were obvious that the originary condition of phenomena must be simple.

The non-simple, conflictual *Ereignis* is best deciphered by observing it at work. In what way is it both appropriating and what is most alienating? To see more clearly, one should ask *of what* is being the event. One will then discover a structure of avowal inevitably calling for disavowal—just as Oedipus could only disavow the queen, his bride, and with her his entitlements to the city, when he ends up by acknowledging his mother and his hereditary rights. His belonging to the Labdacides expropriated him from Thebes, made him a foreigner there, and thus alienated him, just as, inversely, belonging to the *polis* expropriates him from his *oikos,* alienates him from his household. Such is the tragic double bind rendering the hero unrecognizable to himself, and unknown. Such is also the work of the event, giving life only by inflicting death, and—which the civil service of theticism forgets to add—inflicting death even while natality, by means of the fantasms "of what is most general and most familiar," gives life.

The appropriating-expropriating event is Heidegger's answer to the question already cited: "To what extent does this come about in Greek tragedy" (*BzP* 374)? Ever since Nietzsche there has been agreement that in its primitive state tragedy always and only offered a vision of the sufferings of Dionysus, even if in human guise. Once the dythrambic heritage was lost, Euripides no longer hesitated to put the god directly on stage and have him direct his own epiphany. Regarding *The Bacchantes* (perhaps not a very fortunate example) one has even described the conflict that makes up the essence of tragedy in the following way: "If the universe of the Same is not willing to integrate into itself this element of alterity that every group, every human being carries within itself. . . , then the stable, the regular, the identical tip over and collapse, which is the Other in its hideous form, absolute alterity, the return of the chaos that appears as the sinister truth, the authentic and terrifying side of the Same."[81] To what extent does the appropriating-alienating event come to pass in Greek tragedy? Through the collisions of the same and its disparate other, collisions that came to call for its integration and reconciliation only when the conflictual urgency abated with the Athenian rationalism of the last years of the fifth century.

The originary condition is always the event of discordant laws. This is how Heidegger responds to the sinister truth of regimes of the same, experienced too close up for the lesson to be able to be forgotten.

Here, now, are some of the phenomenal regions where the alienating work of the event is observed (just in the *Contributions* there are indeed others that could be mentioned): the alterity in the self, the chiasm of the strife and contrariety in what one can only call the proto-four-fold, and finally the disjunction between the event and such unexpected epochs. An originary agony reveals itself running from the self to the constellation of world-earth-humans-gods and to the thrusts that make history. It indeed deals with time, but not as the one in agony would say: from here to my death. . . . Rather, the momentary sites and its fissurations refer to their condition, the discordance of times. The agony is what those who inhabit the monstrous site have to keep alive (last section) by resolutely placing themselves under the legislative-transgressive diremption.

The self. "The recursive relation that the 'self' names (to 'oneself,' near 'oneself,' for 'oneself') has its essence in *appropriation* (*Eignung*)" (*BzP* 320). With these words, Heidegger first of all offers us a doxographic summary, then he designates a functional feature that persists throughout the doctrines of the self, and finally he states its condition which has not been thematized by received conceptions. This condition fractures the subjectivist self encountered above along with the last god, the people, and the contingent *there.*

Given the summary, it is difficult not to suspect an allusion to the heteronomous, autonomous, and then dialectical self of modern subjectivism. *Das Selbst* is not received from another and comes "to" itself (Luther); it constitutes itself in its legislative freedom, remaining "near" itself (Kant); and it is reflected "for" itself through art, religion, and philosophy (Hegel). In these recursive relations, however, one and the same function characterizes it, the relation to *that to which* it returns—that Heidegger himself also calls the ego. The self marks an alterity in the subject. Through orthographic displacements, he refers to consciousness cleaving itself so it can be found more easily. This functional feature, the recursive relation, has not changed since the institution of modernity. Now, Heidegger emphasizes this relation only to discover its condition, namely, the agonistic event that the self makes its own and that constitutes it.

One sees him go right up to the limit of the field where the contest is waged between heteronomy and autonomy, including the empty result that is their speculative reconciliation. It is a going-to-the-limit that, all together, implies a rejection and a projection, a rejection of these received positions, for in them "the decisional character" is missing in the self, and a projection of a drilling down to the phenomenal origin, for "self-being is more originary than every I, you and we." But here we see that the rejection and projection oddly converge on an immediate belonging-together, since the I, the you, and the we indicate "the powerlessness to sustain *property* (*Eigentum*)" (*BzP* 321). This convergence on the proper seems not to go along well with the alienation occurring in the event.

What more does self-being as originary property need in order to demonstrate the metaphysics of the same? The one origin, the multiple of the I-you-we that emerges there, the bond of property attaching this derived multiplicity to its source—not to forget the allusion to the old schema of *a priori* levels when self-being is qualified by "more originary"—don't these pieces make up a system? And don't they thereby invoke others that have made their demonstrations by assuring hegemonic regimes? Wouldn't the identity of self-being, prior to "recursive relations," as well as the full presence, prior to the relations "to," "near" and "for," naturally complete the system? The "more" that it needs is the patience for the gestation of an other thinking being worked out under the common nouns of the same.

Subjectivist constructions of the self lack "the decisional character." One needs patience, "for the pre-eminence of the consciousness of the 'ego' is only too tenacious" (ibid.). In other words, the search for a common noun—self-consciousness—a search from which the self and ego are born, assiduously works against the question of an origin that would be other than subsumptive. The diremption of the same, the *decision,* indicates this. This word, which here is used neither in the sense of epochal caesurae nor in the sense of a voluntaristic decisionism, points toward the event as it cleaves the self. We have seen this with regard to the differed *there,* what is decisional is the manner of being itself. It therefore seems that the origin, the constituting condition, essencing—all the deconstructions of the *a priori*—have to be understood as modes of *caedere,* of splitting and the scission.

It is one thing to observe that the self gushes its syntax, as if naturally, into a throng of preposition such as *to, near, for,* or even to observe that it is naturally linked to the ego, thus to ascertain its relational structure. It is another thing, however, to find the condition that accounts for this relationality (of which reflexivity is always but one figure). I do not think one can get a hold of things here without bearing in mind the readings of Luther and Kant ventured above. Consciousness has never reigned over the phenomena that it constitutes in any but a fractured way, and these reading have as their goal the weakening of this tenacity. As the ultimate condition (post-transcendental "condition," post-hegemonic "ultimate") of the transcendental differend that these readings have intended to bring to light, Heidegger offers the discordance that turns the event against itself. He says that by bringing together the descriptions of this discordance, self-being emerges from the "*contrariety of the struggle in fissuring*" (ibid.). The self sustains the originary discordance, finds itself appropriated by it, and thus alienated from itself. Herein we can see Heidegger's idiom of the proper and appropriation has cast off the cords attaching it to the logic of the same and full presence. This idiom is no more than a borrowing serving to place every phenomenon within conflictuality. To speak of the decisional self is to divide its allegiance, to make of it a henchman of the differend. It is also to dissociate the "proper" from every positing of the identical. The proper reveals its gaps when one asks: *What* does the event alienate all the while making it its own? The answer: The self, the deputy {*lieu-tenant*} of the ultimate discordance between the proper and the foreign.

In this first response we will bear in mind that the recursive relations—to oneself, near oneself, for oneself—would remain unthinkable if they did not issue from being turned against itself and which is their condition. Hence the alienation. It makes us the uneasy bearers of an essence that is its own worst enemy. The self is related to "the event and its turning" (*BzP* 31), answers to it, makes of it the very issue of its responsibility. It survives only by suffering the decision and the agonistic fissuring.

The proto-four-fold. "Being unfolds as the appropriation (*Er-eignung*) of gods and humans to their encounter. The strife of world and earth emerges in the lighting of the concealment of the in-between that springs from and along with the mutually opposing appropriation. And it is only in the time-play-space of this strife that the appropriation is preserved or lost" (*BzP* 477).

We will begin with the end which, without mentioning it, once more thematizes the self. The agonistic appropriation (note the synecdoche) can be preserved and it can be lost. By preserving it, being-there is won, the self becomes our property, the differend is sustained. Lost means not being there. The last cited phrase thus places in the *agôn* the issue that, in the earlier writings, have been translated as 'authenticity' (*Eigentlichkeit*)—an association to a focalizing *autos* that here would be more out of place than ever since the event displaces the self outside of existence and its modifications. It places it at the intersection of a strife and a contrariety.

Because of *The Origin of the Work of Art,* we know that strife he is talking about. It opposes the world and the earth. How are we to understand this strife here? In terms, to be sure, of projects of which the "world" emphasizes the totalizing opening and the "earth" emphasizes foreclosure (*BzP* 482). But their strife is complex. "On each side of this strife one finds what we know from metaphysics as the sensible and non-sensible" (ibid.). It is, in short, a deconstruction of the intelligible and sensible *chorismos,* transforming it into the contrariety of gods and humans (later, in the commentaries on Hölderlin and under the heading of the *Geviert,* in the contrariety of "divinities and mortals"). Heidegger engages in an operation of double slackening that will be easily missed by those who imagine he is laying out some geographic bearings in four cardinal points. The landscape of the "four-fold" as well as its antecedents in the *Contributions* is more furrowed than that. It is a nomadic landscape that has made use of but one compass. Thus the emphasis is not placed on the number "four," nor on the Platonic ancestry of "gods" and "men," nor on the Kantian anchor of the "world" and "earth" (in brief, it is a matter of freedom and nature, thus of the opposition of history and nature, which are themselves deconstructed[82]). The emphasis is placed on the disparate nouns—the *onomata* and the *nomoi.* Gods, humans, world, earth—these are so many nouns imposing their laws but whose crisscrossing differends fracture the legislating univocity. From the self to the four-fold, one thus passes from a double allegiance to a multiple allegiance. We must not miss this dispersion at the origin that binds us or else we will understand nothing of discordant times: "the originary truth of being" in which "'man until now' collapses" (*BzP* 294). The dispersive agony results from a complex *agôn,* since contrariety overdetermines the strife. Their quadruple conflict can either play itself out in the openness of the *there* or be closed off in the not-there.

The event of what, and since when? It suffices to see that the law of the gods *is not* that of humans—if not, then why speak of contrariety—and that the law of the world *is not* that of the earth—if not, why speak about strife? "Here, there is no more 'encounter'" (*BzP* 311), but something less accommodating —the event of the chiasm between this strife and this contrariety.

There is suffering on all sides in the event that hands each to the others, gods and men, world and earth. The axis of the contrariety that opposes the first of these crosses the axis of the strife where the second of these confront each other. Whatever direction one follows on these crossed axes, one always meets a noun common to the subsumptive power that is fractured. It may suffice to point out some key phrases.

Thus, for the gods. They suffer the "distress" (*Notschaft, BzP* 460) of needing the event opening to them the in-between that separates them from men. And so it is with men as well. They suffer the "alienation" (*Befremdung, BzP* 465) making them strangers to themselves. Understood in terms of the decisional event—in terms of the self—they no longer recognize themselves as what they have believed themselves to be for millennia—masters of creation, living beings endowed with reason, legislators of nature. . . . The nouns "gods" and "man" no longer designate classes of beings. Their in-between, Heidegger says, is "the simple bursting" of the common in the event whose dislocations singularize phenomena (*BzP* 485). It is also the pain of the world, for in the event every projection of openness suffers a "belonging that refuses" (*verweigernde Zugehörighkeit,* ibid.) in the enclosed area that makes it finite. Projections here are weakened in a completely different way than by "being-thrown" (*Being and Time*). They lose their totalizing essence. So finally we have the pain of the earth, which still has to be "taken over in its suffering" (*Übernahme als Erleiden, BzP* 260). It marks the withdrawal that closes up every phenomenon in itself.

One may say that in these phrases Heidegger is seeking to "square" the tragic. The Greek double bind opposed family law to public law, the heroic *daimon* to the civil *ethos,* or simply the clan to the nascent city. Now, Heidegger here multiplies the bonds and conflictual allegiances. Hence his polymorphic tactics meant to circumvent this figure of thinking that is most effective for reinforcing identity, namely, determinate negation. Due to the alterity in the four-fold, it would be a mistake to construe "contrariety" as an opposition between some figure of the same and its apparent other. Even if they have need of them, the gods do not go together with men. The contrariety between these two does not indicate their mutual phenomenal constitution. Such would be to represent them as classes of beings, as genera, or as species, and that would truly be to quash the singularity of their occurrent fulgurations. The same goes for the strife. The world and earth are no more opposed, determined over against each other. If they were terms in this sense, they would inevitably lead to subsumptions. But the event does not allow for the superimposition of any grand authority, not the principle of non-contradiction any more than the principle of identity. In contrariety and the strife of the four nouns, Heidegger ventures to think what is never identical to itself. This is, moreover, why the singular is his penultimate word and singularization—thus time—his last word.

But what are we to make of the plural, "gods" and "men." Isn't there here a stubbornness of the *koinon* by way of a classificatory relapse? Perhaps—if these plurals had anything to do with numbers, even if innumerable numbers.[83] Now, the chiastic event gives the lie to these commonplaces, bursting them. Every allegiance to the four nouns is to be sustained as *defied* by the disparity that faces it: the allegiance to the gods by that to men, the allegiance to the world by that to the earth. It certainly has to do with phenomenal constitution, but with a constitution through quadruple discord. *Who or what* sustains the contrariety and the strife? This is precisely the question that places a focalizing despotism out of play.

There may be a perverse way of recovering from the tragic by nevertheless raising its gaps up into some unity. This would consist in retaining nothing of the four-fold except for the 'gathering,' *legein*. This is perverse because Heidegger really does say that the event gathers together gods and men, world and earth. The Greek word itself, moreover, shifts things without a hitch from "gathering" to "speaking," and for Heidegger isn't it poetic speaking that unifies the four-fold? He even situates the origin of language in their four-fold exchange (*BzP* 510). However, it is a curious origin that is then immediately described as "the most intimate *rift*" (ibid.). Indeed the axes of contrariety and the strife cross on *logos*. But they may be traced back to a new figure of the one only at the cost of a most interesting *non sequitur*. In the four-fold, *legein* does not mean "gathering into the one." Contrariety and the strife indicate there how one must think *legein* (but this would require other arguments and other readings), not the reverse. The gathering has to be extricated from *pros hen* relations. And what is the interest that leads to the leveling out of the *agôn* in the name of *legein*? Such an operation would reduce the four-fold to a bad isomorph, to the uni-dimensionality of the one favored by generalized "logic." But the event makes the common *logos* bloom into the good isomorphism for which there are only disparate singulars. The interest would be to plaster over one more time, even if in a different way than under the hegemonies, the crevices of the phenomenal condition.[84] Contrariety and the strife, on the other hand, cleave *legein* with agonistic dissensions that have no remedy. By singling them out, Heidegger removes the plasterwork.

Is this the regime of the same, or an agonizing struggle and gaps due to contrariety and strife? Beginning in the mid-1930s this was and would remain for Heidegger the decisive question. And even in the end he will see the great danger on the side of the same and its univocal law, not on the side of the disparate where multiple names lay down the laws in differend. The event of what, since when? It is the event of and since the agonizing struggle that is onomastic *inasmuch as* it is nomic.

Of times out of joint. ". . . an essential temporal discordance at the interior of the 'time' of the history of being" (*BzP* 128), such is the event. In other words, Heidegger *disjoins* historical and epochal "time" in relation to occurrent, originary time turned against itself.

Discordance works on history through new departures and ruptures. Here again it is difficult to do without the schema of condition and conditioned. We have just seen two instances of this conditioning at work. It drives modern subjectivism right down to the double bind of the self, and it also drives the intersection of ancient and modern dualisms right down to the quadruple bond of the proto-four-fold. Is originary time disjoined from the "time" of epochal history in the same way that a condition for possibility is disjoined from what it makes possible? Or rather, is one once again plying the apriorist's trade by thus appealing to time's discordance as if to a condition?

Apriorism isn't at all a threat, for the historial is nowhere to be found in the "*a posteriori*." It has nothing to do with empirical history. Heidegger steps back from the facts that historically are the case toward the historial which, for its part, is disjoined from the event. It is a temporal figure of the double step back: beings-beingness-being.

Moreover, apriorism is irrelevant with regard to what the event alienates in relation to the familiar conceptions of being, thus in relation to beingness. The *leap* between these conceptions and occurrent being sets out, as if on a second heading, beyond the normative *difference* between beings and their beingness. And so also with time. There is no common standard that belongs to both the time of the event—the appropriating-expropriating discordance—and the "time" of the regimes of beingness, regimes that are in every instance posited as arranging what happens to be the case in a historical era in a lasting order.

Finally, the step back from epochs demolishes apriorism since it tears apart, as we have seen, the originary condition. If one must understand being (*Seyn,* ibid.) as contrarieties and strifes, then it will no longer be able to install it in the archive of *a priori* theses. Its inscription is out of sync with the titles that, to serve the needs of ultimate concordance, philosophers have customarily used to name being (*Sein*)—thereby aiming solely at beingness (*Seiendheit*). This is because its inscription is out of sync with what one has customarily called "time." Hence, above all, the quotation marks around this word in a segment of the phrase cited.

As for the history of being, if it is articulated into epochs rather than being a duration, then no genus, no focalizing condition, and no analogy will extend *Sein* toward *Seyn*. Similarly, no genus, no focalizing condition, and no analogy will extend "time" posited as lasting and isomorphic toward occurrent, polymorphic time. Hence the disjointure rather than apriorism.

The disjointure of "time" and time hollows out a gap in which theses—which is to say, normative decrees {*arrêtés*}—are swallowed up. Whoever speaks of epochs speaks of thetic decrees. Quotation marks thus do not dethematize duration in history because they thematize its *destitutions*. They mark a departure leading beyond or on this side of epochal articulations—or rather outside of them if, however, it is possible to think the outside other than as the twin of the inside. Only a wrenching of thinking allows one to pass from the "time" that is concerned with epochal history to originary time, which is *Ereignis*—to agonistic, polemical freeings. So, it is not as an *a priori* that temporal discordance fissures the referential positings around which epochs have built their hegemonic concordances.

How then is one to take the temporal withdrawal outside of the historial—the step back toward the event? With regard to this disjointure of time, it is still rather difficult to loosen the shackles of certain received idioms. But it is also here that everyone knows, with an originary knowledge, what we are speaking about. Time, its own worst enemy. It being a question of such a condition, one no longer ventures apriorism. The idiom of "conditions" will be misleading only if one speaks according to the *a priori* schema of difference, instead of the leap inserting us into the differend, and therefore in the strife, contrariety, antagonism, the fission of focal meanings and the fissuring of the moment. How is it that discordance is the event? It is by virtue of the normative attractions and suspensive withdrawals that dislocate history. In a vocabulary that is no longer Heidegger's, it is the event that makes hegemonic institutions and destitutions possible.

Originary time—once again, Heidegger's singular preoccupation—can be understood only by grasping the manner in which it works on historial "time." In other words, the event can be understood only by following the disjointure of time. The text we have cited speaks about operative machination. This, Heidegger says in that text, is the last among the "determinate figures" of beingness (*BzP* 128). Such figures have had the function of settling the event as one settles a lawsuit. They have served to make it permanent, as if discordance could be subjected to some all-encompassing law. In the constructions of "time," it therefore ever again is a matter of subsumption. Under every fantasmic positing there is a name of beingness that imposes on the event a common denominator that reduces time to continuity. Before indicating what we should do and be, these thetic figures have served to order the spaces of time. It is a kinetic order unifying time spans according to a before and after; it is a perpetual order unifying through the infinite repetition of the same moment; it is an eternal order immobilizing the moment; it is an ideal order unifying time spans by linking together intuitions. . . . These are so many *technical* figures by which one has been able to make a temporal arrangement win out over the non-positive event outside every arrangement. It is impossible not to so dispose of time as one disposes of an asset; it is impossible not to mete it out in portions that follow one after the other. But what is the price we pay for this asset? The price paid is the repression of what everyone knows, namely, that one never disposes of time which, rather, breaks us, just as it has all along broken ultimate authorities. It is only the thetic philosophers who, as it were, flout that most intimate knowledge we have as mortals (and that makes us such). One can also say about theticism that it is disjoined—in the form of a denial—with regard to appropriation and expropriation. To recall the lesson of the transcendental illusion, a temporal illusion presiding over all normative theses and thus over the most recent one, namely, operative machination, it is the illusion that time lends itself to *techné.*

To prove theses innocent, Heidegger seeks to "*de-pose*" (*ent-setzen,* a wordplay on the German translation of the Greek *deinon,* 'terrifying') the forces of concordance built up into referents. How does this deposition proceed without which, he says, there will be neither event, nor decision, nor antagonism (*BzP* 470)?

The diremption that is happening to us indicates the answer. How would the figures of permanence be destituted if time did not essentially suffer from a suction outside presence—therefore, if temporal discordance did not "condition" history? Epochal theses can weaken and fail because time comes to be lacking, essentially. Precisely in this it is their condition, and it is precisely here that we see the ordinary knowledge that deposes the fantasms of permanence. What is conditioned, then, is the undertows that undermine from within every historial order; these are the double and quadruple binds, as well as all the experiences in which the ravages of mortality sap the impulses of natality.

In the condition so altered, Heidegger certainly has in mind the tragedians before the philosophers. But what is being sought out there is the memorial of the unthought within the spaces of time allotting to each portion its moment in a sequence. Thus Aristotle allots it the space and time necessary for perceptible movement, and Kant the space of the time of perception. What is still forgotten here, there, and elsewhere is the condition of these spaces of time, namely that something like portions and bits of time can take shape and can be disfigured. This taking shape—not the shape—temporalizes appropriation just as the effacement of shape temporalizes expropriation. From the normative point of view, the originary double bind appears as the destiny of institutions and destitutions.

A phenomenology that starts out from the diremption that is happening to us can only alter the idiom of condition and conditioned. If institutions and destitutions are what are conditioned, this will hardly be lost by setting out in search of a simple condition. Hence the discordance is still described as the *condition of difference.* As we have seen, it is a condition in three stages, and, from beings to beingness, is nomic; every maximal representation lays down the law. From figures of beingness to the event, the condition is dysnomic.

Whatever the variant may be (henological, natural, transcendental), difference separates a normative region from the givens that it serves to norm and normalize.

In Aristotle, this region is that of physical movement in which the *pros hen* reigns. In Kant, it is that of mathematical judgments in which the spontaneous syntheses carried out by self-consciousness reign. The leap into discordance is what disjoins the configuring-disfiguring event—a disjointure that signals the farewell to normative genera, the welcome of a condition outside normative generics and normalizing generality. In difference, an *a priori* figure determines beforehand every empirical moment and thereby particularizes it; in discordance, the moment remains refractory to determination because it is fissured and thereby singularized. If Heidegger considers old ontological materials by carving them up in two ways—one slice constitutive of the same (beings and beingness) and one slice cutting away the other (beingness and event)—one sees therein the temporal expectations, namely, that the indivisible moment (a being) is counted, its configurations (beingness) are represented, whereas the fissured moment (the event) is suffered. Or, by worsening the *phusis* (bursting open) into a "splitting up": Spatio-temporal givens are numbered, their space-time is given a figure, whereas the "fissuring, splitting open, of being itself" suddenly happens, disfigured, destitute, and killed (see *BzP* 103). Just as is the case with all the consoling and consolidating illusions that are its offspring, one must persevere in wrenching time from representation, for it is in this that it has *figured* as the gold for every investment, every technology, every calculation —for every operative machination.

To speak of an essential temporal discordance within the "time" of the history of being is therefore to allude to its condition that is non-aprioric because fractured. Heidegger makes more than an allusion when he states without beating around the bush: "There would be no history if being, as event of appropriation (*Er-eignis*), didn't bear it along" (*BzP* 242). The event bears along history. . . . One will still be tempted to include such formulation in the cubbyhole of "transcendentalism without a subject," just as one will include in that of irrationalism everything that deals with discordance, with the leap of thought that it demands, with the fissuring from which it is born, with the double and quadruple bind by which it devastates us, with the institutions and destitutions that ravage continuous history—in a word, with all that has dealt with the tragic. But the readings conducted above on Parmenides, Cicero, and Augustine, as well as on Luther and Kant, should have shown that there is more to the originary dissension than a fad.

On the basis of evidence these same readings will have demonstrated the traditional fierce determination to "sort out" the differend on whose temporal essence we have touched here. These are all-inclusive sortings-out by which life has countered (with the excess that always defines desire) one arrangement to all others, an arrangement in whose grip we are, and are gripped doubly. Discordance arranges the stopping points {*arrêts*} in the history of being; but because it is death—we will see this more precisely without delay—that works on its points of fixation {*arrêtés*}, discordance is still taking care of our life referents just as one says of a killer that he is going to take care of you . . . including the farewell.

To conclude with the event, it may suffice to place a few markers that extend its *agon* both above and below our monstrous site. Up above, for "it is only within the in-between of the contrariety of gods and men as the basis of the strife between world and earth that history is at play" (*BzP* 479). And below, for being will be, "one day, the event itself" (*BzP* 269), namely, when the diremption has really deprived us—a future pointing toward an age already more than a century old—of normative hegemonies. Welcome to the exclusives, to the irreconcilables that make up the condition of hegemonic institutions and destitutions.

The present brought back down to earth is already ours, even if we are still imperturbably late in relation to the phenomenal economy that is without *archê* and of which the evidence is mounting. Perhaps history has never learned anything about large communities. Nevertheless, their lessons are there, lessons about the fantasmic regimes whose slow retreat constitutes the monstrosity of our site—with a millstone they covered over "history properly speaking—the struggle for the appropriation of man by being." But by intractably suffering destitution, they will also serve as a "prelude to the event itself as the unfolding of being" (*BzP* 309, 174). There is a lesson about the anarchic economy whose possibility constitutes our liberty. When we abandon ourselves to discordant times, "then the event of appropriation (*Er-eignis*) is, for a moment, the event (*Ereignis*). This moment is *the time of being*" (*BzP* 508).

Yet one more time—how is time such that mortals never stop lacking it? What marker can one glean from the *tempus fugit* so as to think "the time of being"?

Whither expropriation?

> "Being itself must unfold by turning against itself, and the basis for this is appropriation as the denial which is an injunction. If so, then the Not and the No would even be what is most originary in being." (*BzP* 247)

We will never rise above the tragic condition; this means we will never *raise it* up to some encompassing thesis. The lines above suggest why. Again it is necessary not to be mistaken about the "more original" No.

Isn't Heidegger here making even more deadening the weight of an ultimate authority, only occurring in the negative, instead of dispersing it in strifes and contrarieties? Doesn't he say that a simple impulse works on the event of appropriation—not the attraction of a Yes given from on high (thus the affirmative, and therefore what we call positive and that we like), but rather a pull that is negative because it draws us toward the Not and the No? Could a "refusal that is an injunction" be originary—an injunction that enjoins us to do as "being itself," to say no? What more would be needed here to prove metaphysical nihilism? It is a dark vision, one may add, that has too great a sense for rude awakenings.

When one word—the No, more originarily—suffices to set loose a series of associations, these are inevitably the clichés that one has at hand (and like a pick-axe). The "No" is not a continuation of doctrines of the negative just as the "originary" is not a continuation of the doctrine of principles. Every doctrine presupposes a "eureka!" that cuts questioning short. But there is no bedrock, be it as a fundamental *nihil* (moreover, an impossible concept, as I have shown), that can stop Heidegger's exploratory drilling. It would be a better idea to suspend the associations that are all too spontaneously grafted onto the negative, the Not, and the No. If there is anything dazzling about the No for thought, it will be in the manner of Oedipus—by a question remaining a question.

This question is the only one that Heidegger ever sought to raise—that of the time of being.

A good many years after the *Contributions,* he will ask with regard to the event of appropriation-expropriation: "Whither expropriation?"[85] The "ex-" alone points to the question of a directionality given to phenomena. The event, we have just seen, expresses the conflictual constitution of phenomena—wherein the modern problematic persists (for example, the self), conflictual in that it twists and splits its vanishing point (for example, the proto-four-fold). In appropriation we would like to think we find the condition that makes it possible for a focal meaning to institute itself, in expropriation the condition for its destitution. If this is so, then the No alienates first of all the hegemonic titles and, through these, the integrative violence of the law. Just as is the law that it undermines from within, the No is an injunction, and also a law. It turns the law against itself, originarily.

Does this mean that expropriation enjoys a certain priority? Let's let apriorism be, even though it raises its "civil servant's" head everywhere. Heidegger instead seeks to think the pull in the *agôn* that makes a phenomenon's self-identity illusory. Phenomena bear within themselves the mark of the other, which does not mesh with their *phainesthai.* The "ex-" and the directionality that it emphasizes point to a removal outside their simple being-given. In a word—but this word, too, has to be understood in discontinuity with its precursors—they point to the work of *heteronomy* in the event.

Now, to expropriate a phenomenon toward what is other than it—is this not in a sense the very definition of every hegemonic focalization? Take once more the example of referential *natura.* Doesn't it rule precisely by expropriating the phenomenal given *toward* this fantasmic position? What pull of "ex-," what traction outside what is clearly and widely known, would be more brutal than the integration of givens that are within sight into the telic snares literally neither seen nor known? One recalls how the Latins, following the Stoics in this, went on to derive the law of a phenomenon outside of it. An organ doesn't belong just to itself, but to this other, which is the body assigning it to its end; similarly, the body does not belong just to itself, but to this other, which is the soul or mind assigning it to its end, and so forth until the other is the city, the end of minds, humanity the end of cities. . . . The thetic law is always imposed as the other of what shows itself. Therefore, isn't heteronomy the very spinal cord of theticism, and perhaps the whipcord for every subsumption?

Now, suffering diremption, the *heteron* brings the thetic gesture to a sudden end. Heteronomy changes directions. For example, 'refusal' (*Verweigerung*) is a word that is reminiscent of *epechein,* 'suspension,' not to be confused with tragic denial (*Verleugnung*); for in being that is turned against itself, the archic function can only be repudiated. Appropriation would have to be retained *as* refusal. What does this mean if not that a discord more originary than any focalizing heteronomy renders the law powerless? A unified, trans-agonal rule gets its normativity from bad makeovers, from an illusory heteronomy like that of an origin in which affirmation would win out over refusal. We deny refusal through thetic affirmations—a tactic that literally has made the epoch. It has also made silence. It has brought an evil silence down upon denial. In order to do so, the functionary of theticism takes to the heights—ultimate referents are posited as the other of phenomena on which one can count and which, therefore, are placed above them. What is to be struck dumb from this height? The expropriation at work *in* phenomenality. On the other hand, with refusal winning out over affirmation and denial (but it remains to be seen what this means), it is impossible to exalt some universal *heteron* and to confer its powers of making-over, subsumption, obligation, and obliteration. Hence the injunction not to forget what each person knows, even if dimly, namely, that in the final reckoning when there is nothing left to count nor to count on, the Not and the No always prevail.

So, whither expropriation? Toward what other, by what heteronomy? Here again epochal history can render its heuristic services. Heidegger always unfolds the historial in terms of and with a view to the moment that is ours, in terms of and with a view to diremption. This unites diverse destinies of heteronomy.

First of all, diremption is happening to us in that the destructions of the twentieth century reveal the consequences of the theticism that the West has lived. In this sense, it represents an end of something. The fabric of the world no longer joins us in correlations to this *heteron* that has an enveloping orientation. Through a shift in the everyday, perceptible since Hölderlin,[86] thetic heteronomy has ceased to play and to display the world. In this kenosis of the sovereign other, quarrels about heteronomy—whether it is good because salutary (Luther) or bad because contingent (Kant)—shape up as the penultimate episode. Whether it builds as sovereign an identity outside the subject or in the subject, or whether it repudiates these, in each instance theticism abandons phenomena. It imposes on them a law foreign to them, which thereby is nothing but *hubris,* a maximized representation (*aufspreizen, BzP* 120). With fantasmic heteronomies the diremption also undermines their correlate—the autonomy that lays down the law.

Moreover, diremption reveals a heteronomy that no is no longer correlated to anything. "In this age, 'beings'—called the 'real' and 'life' and 'values'—are expropriated of being" (ibid.). In letting all landmarks fall by the wayside, diremption is now what inflicts an expropriation on phenomena. Hence the destitution of our historial site. Again—whither expropriation? Toward this *heteron* where phenomena lose their place and are generalized, as are the real, life, values . . . a *heteron* that Heidegger calls "operational machination." It is a transitional epoch in which hegemonic attachments are undone but in which tragic binds are born in "the calculation, the rapidity and the claim-staking of the masses" (ibid.). It is an era of lawlessness (*Ungebundenheit,* ibid.) that is not to be confused with the era of anarchy, which is what is historially possible for us. The latter is defined by the multiple nomic bonds that can no longer be relieved by any fiction of the same—neither that of the thetically fictive nor that of an anomic isomorph.

Finally, diremption prepares the other that singularizes every phenomena by drawing it outside its own identity—the other that is the conflictual event. Through this function it frees the originary Not and the No. There is a turning at work under the ancient weakening of principles and under their contemporary collapse—being that is "turning against itself." To live this "against" is precisely that for which transitional thinking prepares. Diremption enjoins us to let ourselves by taken hold of by "the originary Not belonging to being itself and thus to the event" (*BzP* 388). Whoever says Not or No denies, of course. Thus it remains difficult not to think the turning-against as some sort of negation. What we must finally see is that the "against" opposes not determinate, but disparate functions.

How come all this is not just pure speculation? In other words, how is it that we know the disparity that gives rise to the Not and the No? It's not so hard to say.

Humans know full well what turns being against itself, fissures the moment, introduces dissension into the self as well as contrariety and strife into the four-fold, what conceals all truth and destabilizes all identity, which makes the old autarchy and modern autonomy crumble. It is called "death." It's not hard to *say*. But death also is just as difficult to think as is being which, in death, breaks us. Yet for Heidegger, death is what it is necessary to try to understand if one wants to understand the time of being: "Death—the highest and most extreme testimonial of being" (*BzP* 284).

Two paths to a better understanding of this testimonial suggest themselves.

Heidegger first of all gives another sketch of being-for-death, the condition and "thorn" of historiality (*BzP* 282). This path leads far back into the Christian tradition. The debt is obvious despite the metaphysical detour by which it has come to us—according to the tradition, the resurrection has, on the contrary, extracted this thorn. The metaphor has been salvaged for what I have called the analytic of ultimates, thus in order to express that the historial has its condition in being-for-death.

The other path also diverts a procedure that is quite old. Heidegger there pursues and alters categorial inquiry so that diremption is this "current" epoch charged with a transitional "possibility" that prepares what is agonally "necessary." Diverted from critical transcendentalism, where its categories of modality sanction the understanding to say what is, actuality, possibility, and necessity come to mark out its horizon with the question: whither expropriation?

The historial and categorial paths for tracing expropriation converge on the *there*, the site dislocated by the agonistic origin. As a repetition of what is most violent, the modalities point toward the condition that fractures history. Ontologies see in this only a heaping up into a "pallid and empty pell-mell" the traits that nevertheless indicate being-for-death. In their phenomenological truth, these categories single out "fundamental determinations of the fissuring and their reflections in the *there* that for the most part go unnoticed" (*BzP* 282f). Thus, it is a question of taking note of the actual, the possible, and the necessary as traces of death.

With regard to *actuality*, this means that the wearing away of fantasms leaves us destitute as only mortals are destitute. Currently there is an *agôn* in which fantasmic maximization militates against the singularization that confuses in advance every thrust toward hegemony. In the era of operational machination, disparate impulses bring themselves to bear on isomorphism. This current situation—this current frenzy—takes away any chance for normative success from the theses stemming from natality, with the result that their wearing away makes the condition of mortality appear in our laws and norms. *Possibility* is what situates our condition ahead of us. The possible is what can come to be, namely, being itself in its fissured momentariness (*BzP* 475). Thus what is to come for us would be what appropriation expresses by our death. In terms of the ultimates, mortality is what always and again still has to be grasped. And *necessity,* finally, characterizes the ineluctable. What is necessary is the conformity of phenomena to the conditions of being—to the turning of the distress (*Not-wendig-keit*). So understood, the necessary is possible, immanent in the actuality of our site. Categorial discourse indeed continues to single out being, but by linking it entirely to the contingency of the *there.* So we see where the historial path, retraced by the categorial procedure, leads. It takes us back to the ultimates of ordinary experience—to *Dasein* understood as the site (Colonus) where the double injunction of an origin turned against itself is made our own.

One sees the breakthrough in relation to *Being and Time.* The Existential Analytic traced the quasi-transcendental functions back to their simple source—the *there* as the site of finite transcendence. In the *Contributions,* on the other hand, the traits of Da-sein do no more than "testify" to the fundamental determinations of being. The latter can also be characterized by phenomenal accord and delusion, in differend. They alone are necessary. According to the *originary* analysis of modal categories, necessity is indeed the guiding one; actuality and possibility derive from ultimates in differend. According to the *historial* analysis, as we may recall, it was, to the contrary, the category of possibility that was the guiding one; actuality and necessity derived from conflicts that have burst open our century. Hence, to speak of being-for-death amounts to our way of conveying disillusionment, expropriation, alienation, the No and the Not that first of all name a trait of being itself—the tugging away {re-*trait*} operative in every contexture making up a world.

The *there,* the place of the differend of natality and mortality, is founded (neither in the active nor the passive voices, but in the middle voice) or it is not founded. Its precariousness indicates well enough that being is originarily riddled by a tugging that weakens it. "Being unfolds as *the event where the there is founded*—in short—as event" (*BzP* 247). The *there* remains contingent because it is fissured by a heteronomic strategy. To retrace the historial path with the aid of the modalities thus amounts to pulling the existential organization out by the root (*ursprüngliche Verwurzelung*). Being itself no longer lends itself as a ground for operations of extirpation.

This is, now, the work of the No. It even deprives us of this last offshoot of the modern focalization, the literally radical *Dasein.*

Memento mori: One could hardly find a better expression for what has been and what remains the phenomenological labor under philosophical theticism. From whence does the heteronomic strategy touch us? We know and yet we don't know. "Man knows it in the diverse forms of death" (*BzP* 324). As mortals we "know" the strange and alienating other, yet with a knowledge that is doubly indirect. I have never seen my death, and as for the *heteron,* the other from which it comes, death only makes it take on diverse forms. Is this other, the originarily alienating withdrawal, thinkable without forms? Can one put one's finger (since it is a matter of monstration) on the unconditioned condition of heteronomy, on the origin for which Da-sein "is broken upon being" (*BzP* 486)? Everyone knows that death is a question of time. But which time and how? We must redouble our attention, for here it has to do with the time of being independently of any subjectivist or crypto-subjectivist reference. It has to do with the temporal condition that turns being against itself.

The appeal is blatant, from the temporal ecstases (*Being and Time* § 65) to being "turning against itself." Having-been occurs in ecstatic temporality. Dasein always overtakes itself so as to come back to what it has been. In this sense, existential temporality (*Zeitlichkeit*) is already turned against itself.

In occurrent temporality (*Temporalität*), this structure is displaced outside existence. The lines cited above in the epigraph say so: "Being itself must unfold by turning against itself." Then follows the words according to which the No is "more originary." Indeed, it is a blatant appeal in the form of a displacement—in the existential analytic, the future was more originary due to its arising from this origin of all temporality, which is death. How can one not then see that to speak of a No more originary than being is to desubjectify the passing ahead toward death? Could this be to speak of a No-more, of a temporalizing Not?

Through this passing-ahead, the future was the most originary of the ecstases; in an analogous manner, the Not will be the most originary in the time of being, in the event. In both instances, the same question is at issue—how is time constituted? Both give the same answer—it is constituted through the passing-ahead toward the No-more and the Not. Only, between these two, the passing-ahead changes contexts. Finite transcendence, or being-in-the-world, is temporalized by death; as for the event, it is temporalized by an expropriation without a subject. Yet in both instances time arises from the imminent negation of being. Thus, it is only with regard for the *constitution of time* that the Not is "what in being is most originary." There is no more nihilism in this phrase than there is in temporalization through anticipatory resoluteness.

Can we catalogue understandings of time in terms of time being constituted by slipping off toward the Not? In the catalogue of time, Plato's (*Timaeus*) is cosmological, that of Augustine (*Confessions*) is psychic and mentalist, that of Descartes and Kant is isomorphic inasmuch as it is subjectivist, that of *Being and Time* is existential. . . . The most complex notion of time is no doubt found in Aristotle.[87]

If the time of being is constituted by the originary Not—by the future thematized outside of existence—then its occurrent understanding is aptly described as tragic. It is an apt description not only because it preserves the phenomenological point of departure in time, but above all apt in that it singles out time's double work in allotting us our proper site and alienating us toward, in sum, the improper.

Thus one need not be stymied by the apparent contradiction between an expropriating Not that would be *more originary* than the appropriative Yes and the double bind in which, as the differend always requires, a No and a Yes are mutually antagonistic and *co-originary*. In keeping with ecstatic temporality, the future is the most originary of the three manners of being outside the self because it constitutes time;

but the three ecstases are co-originally intertwined in co-determining existence. Thus, the event. Expropriation toward the No-more fissures the moment whereby it constitutes occurrent temporality. But co-originary appropriation and expropriation bring about the *agôn* toward which diremption alienates ultimate authorities.

What is it with time that mortals never stop lacking it? By way of a response, one would need a noun that expressed in some way the ultimate condition by virtue of which we are mortals. But *nouns* make up the very archive of norms in which notions of time are, in any case, classed only in some appendix that could be labeled "Here all is stable." The instructions for use might have as its first line the denial of an originary Not.

To seek a common noun of the Not may only hatch a monstrosity. But a deictic noun, a noun that shows?

We should note the difficulties Heidegger brings upon himself when, to singularize being, he seeks to break the *koinon* by introducing heteronomy into it. Because of these difficulties, the question of the drift and direction in which expropriation pulls (which is to say, its drift understood in the sense of orientation) must remain a question.[88] Expropriation whither? Here still are some markers.

Expropriation toward death? Certainly toward singular death—which is mine even though non-subjective. But we have seen that it can't help but "testify" to occurrent expropriation. It indicates this expropriation: Death as my extreme possibility "harbors the most profound indication of the essence of nothingness" (*BzP* 325).

Expropriation, then, toward nothingness? This seems to be Heidegger's strategy here. If the event turned against itself repeats the network of the existential outside-the-self—the imminence of what has been, the return from what is to come—then it is a negative labor that turns the event against itself. Death harbors the indication of this labor. Wanting to *pair up* nothingness and being would still be pure speculation. A deictic nothing, a *singularum tantum* will always be incommensurable *{dispars}*. Nothingness must be able to be pointed out. Only then will its labor be originary in the tragic sense, fracturing the conditioned since the condition is fractured first of all. The post-transcendental idiom here ties your tongue all the while letting it loose. Such a negative and monstrative condition has always remained unthought, but it is not unthinkable. One must recall that the deictic status of nothingness followed from the double bind of the ultimates, known to all, and was conveyed by the dissension of being, by the dislocation of the *there,* by the strife of chiastic contraries, by fissuration and temporal discordance, by the nomic differend. Nothing can become a phenomenon without these traits of denegation working on it from within. It is an intimate labor, all the better known for my death. But it can also be pointed out in what one calls 'evil' *{le mal}* (curious common noun, of which the generic illusion no doubt says to philosophers that this is the problem for which they have not yet found a solution . . .). So there's no need for a vigorous imagination to describe the function that, beneath the diverse figures of the expropriative undertow, always takes the present away from us and shields us from the present. This is a singularizing function. The "drift" of this—isn't it nothingness? One says that it is to there that those who die slip away. How is one to think the expropriation drawing all phenomena in the direction of nothingness? Above all, how is one to understand singularization in such a pulling along?

A few years after the *Contributions* Heidegger will make one knit one's brows by declaring that the essence of being is nothing. One takes this to mean that being is not a being, that it can't be counted among beings. Isn't this the better-known Heideggerian lesson that being differs from beings, that these alone are something and that being is consequently nothing? The words says it quite well—nothing, no thing—being is not a being. Now, Heidegger observes, this "negative" determination of nothingness follows precisely the same sort of reisms according to which a given thing possesses or does not possess some given quality. Attributive logic really has no hope of teaching us anything about the origin of phenomena, about their manifestation—*phainesthai*—or their upsurgence—*oriri*—where the condition is burst apart. This logic presupposes that one describes phenomena as givens, that the phenomenal means the actual, and that being is understood as the actuality of givens. Hence the task, he says, of "determining in a more originary manner the mutual belonging together of being and nothingness. The polemic against attributive logic thus serves to make nothingness problematic independently of the relation between being and beings, independently of the ontological difference. It is a new problematization that is announced in a cascade of rhetorical questions[89] pointing in the direction of the event turned against itself: "What if being itself were what withdrew itself, and essentially came to be as denegation? . . . And would 'nothingness' be, by virtue of *this no-thing-ness* of being itself, full of that allotting 'power' from which emerges . . . all 'creation' (the becoming-beings of beings)" (*BzP* 246)? Here nihilation (*Nichtung*) has nothing to do with the so-called ontological difference. The cascade falls from the other side of a barricade sheltering the question of being from "vulgar," describable, creatable, expandable phenomena so that beings become even more so beings—maximizable—and in any case pouring over us as what alone is of interest. How is it that the Not is greater than the Yes? What is ruled out is every differential determination.

Actual phenomena are thus held in check, or placed between parentheses. To grasp the originarily transgressive No in being, it is useful to linger briefly over the traditional privilege of the actual over the possible and to linger over the interest that is professed in it, for the normative fantasms become for Heidegger just as problematic through transcendentalism (and thus through Kant) as the Not, the No-more, and nothingness become through kineticism, and thus through Aristotle. It is there, in the analysis of physical change, that the possible and non-being show themselves temporalized by the future. Dissociated from kineticism, this temporalization will allow us to thematize singularization.

Non-being, the Not, and nothingness have gained widespread acceptance for more than two millennia, so that they appear in the analysis of possible change, inscribed in actual givens. No doubt the presupposition of Aristotelian kineticism is that of reducing beforehand the possible to what can be *rendered* actual, and thus reducing actual-being to what has been made so—to fabricated being. A lintel, a column, and a pile of sand are possible in a block of marble on the condition that an order, an architect, a workshop, hammers and chisels, etc., intervene. Kineticism reduces the possible to the makable. In other words, it reduces the logic of attribution and approval to technology. In Heidegger's words, the Yes to the actual signifies the "Yes of 'making'" (*BzP* 246) in which one holds together the interest that pushes to normative maximization and the bases for its critique.

To maximize such a Yes is not without interest. What is most interesting about beings is always what one can do with them. Hence the great archic gesture is essentially an archi-technic gesture—it posits a primordial Yes that is completely ordered, complete with an order to be realized, replete with an organization that is to be actualized. Here is the technological core of all classical paradigms. As for the bases of its critiques, when some Yes exalted in this manner uniformly lays down the law, it is things (by way of their representation) that set the standard; it is approval that universalizes the actual; it is the producible (by way of a metabasis) that passes for all beings—the better made, according to the order of possibles, the better the being; and finally it is nothingness (by way of attributive logic) that signifies the negation of beings, the no-thing, the non-product, the non-actual. Aristotelian *dunamis* has governed the proper usage of nothingness in philosophy and has precluded the knowledge of a No greater than the Yes.

Thus the secular variations on the actual and the possible have this in common, namely, that they treat the possible in the manner of the actual and according to it—equal to it, less good than it, or better than it. These variations treat the possible either as the actual itself that then figures among the possibles (for example, the best of worlds), or as an actuality that is defective because it is not (a unicorn), or again as a better actuality that will be (messianic society).

If the actual enjoys an advantage over the possible, it is that both are measured by our interest in fabrication. Thus the possible is that of which I can make something. It indeed bespeaks the orientation toward the future, but it does not bespeak a fidelity to phenomena. Therefore to think the possible temporalized by the future without immediately subjecting it to technical interests, it is necessary to suspend the exclusivity of the actualizable and the actual. This is the price one must pay so that nothing, which is the possible, can show itself to be singularizing.

Hence the efforts by Heidegger to wrench nothingness both from difference and from kineticism. "Nihilation belongs to being itself" (*BzP* 118). Nothingness does not characterize being as other than beings any more than it denotes the other of actual-being. It is, rather, the essence of the other that being is. And it is this as a function—nihil*ation*—that breaks the prestige of the common, of the general and generic, of all universalizing fantasms. It is this by singularizing being.

Singularizing it how? To dissolve thetic specters and remain faithful to the possible "higher than the actual," the deictically legislating function—co-legislating tragically—will have to bear on time. On *a* time, rather, at least if the discord of appropriation and expropriation is originarily described as a discordance of time*s*.

Consequently, expropriation toward the future? The pre-eminence of the future was the part that kineticism expresses correctly. Yet it is necessary not to distort this pre-eminence by maximizing it. At least since Plato the consummate moment has offered itself to humans fleeing their mortality. Finally, no more future, full presence at the end of the journey—such would be happiness. Joy spoiled in advance by the knowledge that is revealed by the analytic of ultimates. The moment is fissured and humbles this hubris that, in the form of the *nun* or the *aion,* seeks to "build the present up into an eternity" (*BzP* 493). To declare a consummate moment, to enrich it to the point that there is nothing to come that it lacks—this is the way that denial strikes a blow at temporal dissension. Hence, as Heidegger seeks to understand being as time—and time as the fissured moment—the conclusion seems obvious: The negative strategies in being are due to futurizing. The possible to come (the singular phenomenon upon which theories of contingent futures supposedly touch) expresses the primary and ultimate condition for which we are always lacking time. If the possible to come names that *toward which* expropriation pulls us, then the discordance of times signifies that the prestige of the present is broken on the future—the time of the singular in strife with the fantasms of stability.

Yet difficulties remain. "Nothingness" and "future" are not deictic nouns. They don't point out anything. To represent these traits in objects of ostentation would be to treat them once more as we do beings. But the pullings that turn the origin against itself remain intractable, even if they overdo the theories of proper noun. Proper nouns are used in making statements and they presuppose a given object. Now, nothingness and the future structure givenness, but they are not givens. The tradition says "you, o death," and thereby it recognizes my singularization. But it would still be necessary to say "o nothingness, o future"—"o" each time followed by a singular. The difficulties in thinking expropriation are due to the unyielding schemas of subsumption.

In differend with itself, the ultimate moment remains shot through by a refusal that resists analysis. At most we experience it by giving in to the ineluctable capitulation—"The *refusal,* as the proximity of the ineluctable, makes being-there into the vanquished" (*BzP* 412). If the condition of being—the condition that being is—necessarily places us under the double bind, it is because it is itself simultaneously gift and refusal, and because it therefore eludes philosophy, tragically ("our father Parmenides" expropriated, so to speak, by Aeschylus and Sophocles).

Expropriation toward death, toward nothingness, toward the future—these attempts at a response do not really get at the freeing impulse that turns time against itself. On the other hand, there no longer is any need to turn the alienating injunction stemming from the No-more and the Not into a problem. It draws phenomena toward the possible to come and in doing so temporalizes them. But this is not to say that it wins out over the appropriative injunction of the Yes any more than in the existential analytic the future as the "primary meaning" of time annuls having-been, being-present and the "to-come," which are co-originary (*Being and Time* § 65).

The double bind remains: "But has there been a man capable of sustaining both of these"—both the strategy of the gift that "grounds its freedom" (*BzP* 412) and the counter-strategy of refusal that has conquered it in advance? Both the impulse to let ourselves be matriculated in the world and the expulsion from its matrix? Both the legislation by an instituting thrust that appropriates us and the transgression toward the non-common to come that has expropriated us in advance?

To respond to these questions, or at least to keep them alive, we must try to see more clearly into singularization. The impulse of hegemonic destitutions like that of diremption is to be found there. There is where the originary impulse of the tragic condition is.

The singularization to come

"The singularity of the Not follows from the singularity of being
to which it belongs, and therefore the singularity of the other.
The one *and* the other impose their constraints." (*BzP* 267)

What breaks hegemonies and places us under the legislation of diremption? In other words, what binds us with bonds that are impossible to loosen and at the same time impossible to maximize into a universal, simple focal meaning. These lines express it three times over—it is singularity—an amassing of singularities that impose their constraints.

By way of conclusion and to understand this "and" of the double bind, we will retrace the path—as one traces steps—that lead back from the modern pathology toward the originary dissension, a path this time informed by the temporalization through the future where nothingness works on the possible. How is one to understand diremption that legislates? This can only be as legislation-transgression.

By departing from the monstrous site that is ours—such has been, at least, the reading that I have proposed—the *Contributions* succeed where *Being and Time* had failed. A heuristic temporality which is no longer either subjectivist nor existential permits him to carry out a step back toward the temporality of being. What heuristic temporality it this? It is that of our monstrous age in which a non-thetic possibility is announced in an ultra-thetic present. For Heidegger, as for Nietzsche before him, a declining normative consciousness plainly marks the kenosis of hegemonic fanstasms. It marks their diremption. But it also points toward a hiatus that spaces and temporalizes from within what perennial philosophers have pursued as an ultimate *a priori* moment. Our historical site is characterized by the spacing out of the "not-there" and the "there." It is this gap that gives a spatial shape to this temporal monster that ultra-theticism, disfigured by the collapse into itself of a maximum meaning, is. The heuristic function of the technical age that is used to sketch out the step back from phenomena toward their conditions is embodied in the economy thus spaced out and differed {*différée*} from within.

Now, incongruous spaces and times (which is the argument in the *Contributions* that seems to me to be really worth consideration) can be brought into sync only by a *condition that is in itself incongruous.* As we have seen, Heidegger folds space over onto time and describes this condition, as we have also seen, as the event of appropriation and expropriation.

It is a condition about which the lines cited above tell us that it binds us. It binds us in the way that a law does. The same lines also say that this law is not simple. It binds us through an amassing—"and"—of constraints. Take, for example, the conditioned.

Waning modernity knows itself *tied up* by paralyzing planetary forces {*emprises*}, apparently without end, and at the same time *unbound* by idealities in the name of which we nevertheless continue to kill each other. What is the condition of this bind-unbinding arrangement? It can only be a function in discord with itself that, under diremption, lays down the law *and* carries on regardless of it. After his failing, Heidegger responds to the old question of being as being with this nomic monster: the originary, and in this sense ultimate, disparity of a legislation-transgression.

I have suggested how the law was born from tragic denial. A certain elation in Agamemnon sacrificing his daughter remains the eloquent index of this denial. In the exhilaration of the slaughter, the law of the city is affirmed against that of the household—a legislative hubris for which Agamemnon will pay dearly at the return of the expedition. Moreover, we should keep in mind the lesson of the ultimates in differend, for life always sustains itself by repressing the death that transgresses, just as the deputies of the common are always instituted by denying those allegiances that singularize them outside the common, and as a focal meaning always effaces the dispersive other. It is a question, now, of conditions—in the originary conflictuality by which Heidegger understands being, what legislation is this and what transgression?

The double bind arises from singularities thought not as a dispersion of givens, but as dispersive functions. Being as well as the other in it, which is the Not—and this is what has to be understood—bind us through singulariz*ations*.

We have encountered some figures of the singularizing function. There was an epochal figure: the destitution that a hegemonic fantasm undergoes. A historial figure: the diremption of every fantasm and of every hegemony. A figure in ordinary experience: my death. Now, is there a figure of singularization that makes all these possible? It would be an unfigurable figure whose function would nevertheless inform us about the legislative and the transgressive that "impose their constraints." The originary function of singularization is best retraced in language. Therefore, we will try to follow the indications that Heidegger gives with regard to the Yes and the No—indications of a certain manner of saying Yes and a certain manner of saying No. Here the No shows itself to be larger than the Yes, just as the anarchic possible is higher than the archic actual. It is a "No" also with no speakers, just as the anarchic possible dispenses with maximizers.

In my singularization, my world says No to me; in the destituting singularization, an epochal world says No to its fantasm; in the singularization that dirempts us, the phenomenal world says No to the natural metaphysician; and in originary singularization? Let's return to the legislative function and then to the transgressive.

Legislation. To the genealogist of normative representations, philosophical hubris declares itself in legislative, not transgressive, acts. The decrees that have served successively to legitimize order in the West were imposed by the same terror as those with which Iphigenia cast glances at her sacrificers. These decrees have been elevated to ultimate referents for their epoch, excessively. The *Urstiftung* as Heidegger understands it became the responsibility of philosophers, the institution of a subsumptive meaning. By retracing these institutions it has become apparent that the law of laws in each instance comes from a maximal affirmation, namely, from a Yes inflating some one or other finite phenomenon to normative dimensions. In terms of these operations of maximization and centering, Heidegger can qualify the whole corps of philosophies of order as humanistic (an expression, moreover, that is pleonastic in this genealogy, philosophy having had for its mission the placing of things at the disposition of man).

Legislative hubris thus appears, one could say, in the comparative and superlative. In the comparative because, if man has brought all things around him to a halt according to one or another particular order—if he has asserted himself as being the measure—then it is because he has and continues to posit himself as being worth more—a comparison of worth and value by which he validates his hegemony in the constitution of phenomenality. But "humanist" excess reaches the superlative when man gives airs of leaping beyond his own shadow and claiming to plant himself by himself on a post-hegemonic terrain, when he makes the post-subjectivist, post-thetic economy again into a matter of assertion. Then, Heidegger asks, would "the hubris of the giving of the measure (*Anmaßung der Maßgabe*) not be *even* greater there where man is simply posited as the measure?" (*BzP* 25). The denial of the transgressive No and the Not thus curiously reaches its peak when the loss of norms becomes a common conviction, when one has agreed to shake off ancient and modern fixations and when it is okay—or even already a bit old-fashioned—to speak of transgression. There is something even more exhilarating than Agamemnon's elation. This is when, with no more ado than the commander at Aulis, one proclaims complete the withering away of metaphysics along with its thetic and normative games, and when we are invited to takes measures to assert henceforth our individuality. An assertion and a denial that add to its theses. They really tie themselves up in knots in poses and positions struck, and measures taken which nevertheless are declared old hat.

The lesson to be drawn from this legislative excess is that there is a violence of self-assertion that is impossible to unlearn and another violence that, in its convulsions, the West perhaps already has been in the process of unlearning for more than a century.

It is impossible to elude regional violences—the micro-violence whereby a bodily organ asserts itself, or the macro-violence whereby a collectivity asserts itself. Micro and macro are that from which language lives. One must not forget that Thebes once again became livable through the laws that Oedipus, the *tyrant,* gave to it. Life is nourished and the concepts of our languages are serialized by extensions of meaning moving gradually forward. These polymorphically integrative violences result from the ultimate phenomenological trait of natality. Regional affirmations, with no trace of megalomania, make us say Yes to what offers one sense here, another one there. Yes to the sense in some particular domain, then in some other one. In other words, it is impossible to leave the *polis* or the concept without suffering a *factual singularization*.

Quite different is the violence of a trans-regional law maximized in terms of a regional meaning—as normative subjectivity asserts itself, megalomaniacally, starting with the modest experience of the "I think." Late modernity is working at recovering from this univocal Yes. It is hard work, punctuated with relapses of every magnitude. The Führer differed from the Greek *tyrannos* precisely by the nomothetic affirmation of a collective subject elevated to an ultimate instance. Between Aulis and Berlin, the political, regional code is exalted into a trans-regional, encompassing self-assertion. Hence the Heidegger of the *Contributions,* having just recovered from this properly modern hyperbolic self-assertion and from normative subjectivity, devoted himself to recalling the counter-law by which the singular always subverts such subsumptive instances. Under thetic self-assertion he recalled a certain singularizing, no longer factual, but *functional* No.

"Other thinking" tries to bear in mind the lesson learned from legislating through hegemonic fantasms. It is *impossible to deny* denial in ultimate referents since the necrology of their destitutions can be documented just as much as can the genealogy of their institutions. Hence the step back from theses and decrees leads from a simply subsumptive Yes to a conflict in which the No is adjoined to the Yes so as to fracture its power of subsumption. Thus it is a functional "No."

Here is what we have for legislative assertions instituting an epoch: "The ordinary Yes is immediately and thoughtlessly maximized into *this* pure and simple Yes that lends to every No its measure" (*BzP* 246). Heidegger thus distinguishes between two Yeses. One is usually tacitly or explicitly pronounced in the face of what is the case. Yes, she is beautiful; yes, right now I think so; yes, my country. It is a constative yes by which we give our assent to what is. The correlative No, we can add, is the strict counterpart to it: No, she is not as ugly as her mother; no, I am not singing right now; no, I am not French. The other Yes results from an operation that is more complex than constatation. First of all, there is only one—it is the *schlechthin* {pure and simple}Yes, he says. Afterwards its correlation to the No changes into a determination because this Yes makes something "out of every No." For its part, the No remains multiple, but the Yes takes on the position of an ultimate instance for all the constative Yeses and No's. Finally, what the single Yes does to the multiple No's is to impose its measure on them. This is a complex operation, for unicity, determination in the final instance and measurement are nothing phenomenal. They are no longer gleaned from what shows itself as being the case. The Yes-measure—the assertion of an ultimate referent—results (and this now is the key word) from a maximization beginning with an assent in the face of some thing that shows itself. The Yes-measure is *aufgesteigert.* It becomes thetic, assertoric. For Heidegger, the fidelity to phenomena ends with this operation and speculation begins. To say that one can repudiate—namely, particulars—only after having affirmed—namely, a universal—is precisely the subsumptive operation, an operation in which one posits as law an assertoric Yes *in relation* solely to which every No is a No. The "oblivion of being" is summed up in the No thus made secondary.

It is worth noting that, for Heidegger, such legislative maximizations are never formal in the sense of taking the form of a neutral structure. They always elevate a content. In this operation one passes from the "yes, she is beautiful" to the fullness of the *kalokagathia;* one passes from the "yes, I think so" to the thickness of the *cogito;* and from the "yes, my country" to the *über alles*. . . .

It is just as worthwhile to note that, in this critique of assertoric maximization, the possibility of a Yes phenomenologically anterior to every negation never arises anywhere. For Heidegger, it is simply a matter of being true to phenomena, not only to these or those among them, nor to this or that region of experience, but to this inescapable phenomenon that is "the bond of the one *and* the other"—the double bind. A Yes that would be an originary word (*Urwort*[90]) remains literally out of the question from the moment the question of being takes its point of departure from the ultimates of everydayness (being-for-birth or natality, and being-for-death or mortality), which alone are originary and alone are neutral, for they alone are truly familiar to all. Hence the phenomenological project is older than assertoric theticism. It is a project that is neither speculative nor elective—to rehabilitate the No as the other of being at the heart of being, to rehabilitate the disparate Yes-No whose differend turns every law against itself.

Then which No? The origin of the law in the event of appropriation-expropriation unsettles principles of order such as unicity, final determination and standardization. It makes them function against—by a non-dialectical "against"—the most efficient ordering mechanisms: against oppositional negation. Heidegger restores to the Yes its belonging to the No, denied by the legislative fiat that relates these to the law of which Agamemnon made himself the champion at Aulis. Only, this restoration undermines forevermore all *tranquilitas ordinis*. In the face of the theses of a subsumptive and prescriptive order, the No can be described only as singularizing and transgressive.

Transgression. Two senses have to be excluded when speaking of "transgression," and a third will have to be preserved.

a. Heidegger's sarcasm concerning any extra-territoriality posited by mere fiat, the target of which was clear in the 1930s, has by no means lost its relevance. It could easily be redirected today. There are those who have made of transgression *the* law. . . . Yet this does not guarantee faithfulness to expropriation in the event. If in our day and age such faithfulness is best learned by inquiring into the distant origins of technicity and into the possibility it harbors, then transgression is not to be taken here in the sense where, for instance, Michel Foucault "preludes" to it (and excellently).[91] Transgression does not denote here the passage beyond some closure, not the *trans lineam*.

b. Another strategy of the *trans*- is more complex. In the part of the *Contributions* entitled "The Leap," one of the sections is headed "Excess in the Essence of Being" (*BzP* 249). Heidegger says that we must understand excess (*Übermaß*) not as a quantitative surplus, but as a measure that "refuses to be evaluated and to be measured." The paradox—a standard of measure beyond all measurement—is ancient. It recalls the step beyond being (*epekeina tes ousias*) as construed by the Alexandrians and their epigones. This paradox, however, pertains to the core of every doctrine of principles. A standard is a principle only if it is not in turn measured by some other standard. Whence the warning: "The excess is not the beyond [which would define] some supra-sensible realm." In other words, as Heidegger understands it, the excess places the sequence of intelligible "befores and afters" out of play. It does so as it places representations of universals and their hierarchy out of play. And nevertheless the excess is entirely prescriptive, "binding" (*Erzwingung*). Therefore it cannot be a question of a prescription or an *a priori* bond like that exerted, for example, by the

Greek *agathon* and the *hen*. Every principle, every norm and law, is a prescriptive, binding instance—on the condition, however, that it reign *simply*. Now, simplicity is just what Heidegger challenges in the excess. The blow dealt to the prestige of simplicity undoes the *a priori* in Heidegger even more than does anti-subjectivism. One may well fail to see this, for his phrasings have here a familiar ring. Only nothingness, "because it belongs to being, has a rank equal to it." Is this not reminiscent of the Dionysian *huper-on*, treated as a *huper-metron*? One would say so, and not simply because of the appeal to "rank." Indeed, nothingness is to be understood, he continues, "*as the excess of pure refusal*" (*BzP* 245). In Dionysus the Areopagite, the prefix *huper-* compounds the distance marked by the more ancient *epekeina*. The prefix moves the term to which it is attached out of reach. It designates an ultimate focusing that refuses to yield to our thought[92]—a refusal that, to the Neoplatonic mainstream, exalts simplicity.

Now, this precise and venerable lexicon here gets diverted from simplicity. Heidegger writes that the excess "opens the *strife* and keeps open the space for every strife" (*BzP* 249). That, then, is how it binds beings. It commits them to discord. Not, to be sure, to the war of wolves where each singular confronts all the others, but to the *polemos* of life and death permeating every singular and singularizing them. The excess bespeaks the polemical essence of the event. Here we are far from the doctrine of principles and from its most rigorous argument, where the ascent through negations produces an instance reachable in the excess (*huperochê*). A simple bond? How could it be since the event itself is not simple? It is rather a double constraint or double bind, phrased here as that of being and nothingness.

c. By transgression one therefore must understand the co-normativity of the law's disparate other under the very reign of the law. But what does this mean? If being is characterized by the discordant temporal attraction and withdrawal within manifestation, then whether one is speaking of theoretical or practical laws, of natural or positive laws, they are all and always deferred and spaced from within by their singularizing negation, just as an epochal hegemony is, from its establishment onward, deferred and spaced from within by its decline to come. Such a decline occurs when the fantasm promoted to the normative rank for an epoch suddenly appears as one commonplace representation among others (just as a psychoanalysis is said to be finished when the analyst is no longer the referent of maximized knowledge that he was and becomes a professional occupying some particular apartment, pursuing, banally, his living just like others). Take as another example the *natura* of "natural law"—it is singularized when the Scotists detected an essential contingency in it. Its referential prestige was done in by this. In every normative positing, the possible singularization at the heart of an actually legislating phenomenal economy exercises a transgressive withdrawal.

Who says No? To answer according to the historial heuristic, when the Greek, Latin, or modern integration collapsed, a world said No to the fantasm that had instituted it. The representation that appeared to be most common was singularized. To answer according to the existential heuristic, through being-towards-death I anticipate my expulsion from every sense-giving context. My world says No to me. It is a destitution without a rebel, transgression without an offender, negation without speakers, expropriation without expropriators.

For this disparity of strategies sundering *Ereignis,* I find it difficult to endorse readings according to which the Heideggerian double bind would be an engagement of symmetrical contraries. The event temporalizes phenomena through the loss of the world; it is a *possible,* singularizing loss inscribed beforehand in being-in-the-world. The strategies of contextualization and decontextualization are not opposed at the heart of one and the same genus only if one brings one's reading to a halt at the point where words are symmetrical. But this would be to leap squarely over the decontextualizing, singularizing, temporalizing—and therefore transgressive—factor of the possible. One will no longer say that in the singularization to come the possible reflects the actual as its antithesis; such would then be to leap over the possibilizing factor in the everyday: *my* death. Things are different here. In Heidegger, death as mine temporalizes phenomena because it is absolutely *singular.* Consequently it is impossible to treat the singular as a determinate negation of the universal. The opposite of the universal is the particular. It takes a neglect of the persistent tie between temporalization and singularization to append these conflictual strategies neatly to the list, long since antiquity, of terms that are mutually exclusive within a genus and conjointly exhaustive of a genus.

For Heidegger, ancient tragic conflicts remain the model (in the sense of a module) for originary disparity. The law of the household and the law of the city can be construed as opposing one another so as to better be sublated only if they are revised by the dialectic of objective spirit under the authority of the modern state. Aeschylus's heroes, for their part, perish from that conflict without there being any higher instance. Antigone's law remains in a differend, without genus, with that of Creon. The same is true of the phenomenalizing attraction and dephenomenalizing withdrawal in *Ereignis*—it is an irreducible differend that is being itself.

Knowing that we possess everything—our world will end up by saying to us and thus already says to us: No. Understood in this way, transgression by the singularization to come de-poses or de-posits (*ent-setzen*) hegemonic referents as it again arouses the dread (*das Entsetzen*) in those in whom Da-sein becomes, then, the event. "This de-posing occurs only from out of being itself—even more, this itself is nothing other than what de-poses and what dis-mays" (*BzP* 482), nothing other than legislation-transgression.

It remains to be seen in what respect this double bind is originary. It will be so only if the Yes, just as much as the No, "speaks to us" well before every instituting discourse and thus every speaker.

Legislation-transgression. Faced with the apparatus put in place by the univocal law, tragic knowledge never had a chance. Is it not, perhaps, legitimate in the city?[93] At the very most, it will act through sporadic discursive interventions, through what Heidegger calls "other thinking." Thus the semblance of univocity disperses. The law takes back the nocturnal withdrawal that denies it the attraction for the diurnal order. It loses its ordering power. Appropriation makes the law by integrating some particular phenomena and then some others into a provisional economy, namely, by saying Yes to them. But the expropriation to come already breathes its No into them.

This Yes-No signals the double normative bind, and in many ways.

First, in tearing apart referential fantasms, the disparity of Yes-No puts an end to the *contents* that have been promoted to the ultimate rank. Rehabilitating the No as co-originary with the Yes does not amount to declaring the ugly equal to the beautiful, or thoughtlessness equal to the "I think." In this sense, originary differing remains formal and neutral. It works upon everydayness the way a category works upon the empirical—except for the fact that everydayness can no more be treated as an empirical given than the late modern pathology can make the differend burst out into the open. Therefore one must force the received lexicon and recognize in the differend of Yes-No not only the condition of possibility of phenomena, but also their condition of impossibility. The "phenomenological" phenomena, which are the ultimates that everyone knows, are not described as some beautiful woman, some act of thinking, or some country. If the differend works on phenomena without their condition being formally one, then it will neither determine them nor measure them materially (as would the *eidos* that makes beautiful things beautiful, or nature which makes acts natural, etc). It works on them by destroying from within the apriorism that posits some focal meaning. By the same stroke, it destroys what we understand as contents. The conflict of natality and mortality in everydayness, along with the conflict of positing and letting-be in the epoch of extreme theticism, *reveal* the event turned back against itself—turned against a formal Yes as only an equally formal No can be.

But it is not an equal No. Apparently in a blatant inconsistency, Heidegger indeed declares the No greater than the Yes. I have already indicated these sensational phrases. They do indicate that singularization always wins out over the phenomenalization making a world. But how does it win? Received wisdom, which holds that death always ends by winning out over life, is one thing. Quite another is the question of conditions: How is one to think an expropriating withdrawal in the event that is "greater" than the appropriating attraction?

One feature at least about the co-originary, yet unequal, No and Yes is *not* hard to see, namely, that their unequalness prevents them from recycling oppositional figures in which the principle of non-contradiction combines with the principle of the excluded middle to produce a binary division within some genus posited as ultimate. But does Heidegger then undertake an inverse secondarization of normative theses, devising a primary No followed by a Yes that would feed upon it and, in turn, confirm it—Yes to No, hence twice No? Such a Mephistophelization of being as originary catastrophe[94] would not only be absurd, but it would, moreover, once again disjoin the tragically co-originary laws and counter-laws.

How then is one to think nothingness or the No as "the other" of equivalences and oppositions put into place by Aristotle's physics? The other manner will place it neither vis-à-vis actual things as their technological negation, nor anterior to the Yes as its catastrophic annihilation.

How is one to place it? What must the place of the No be? Phenomenologically, it is always *to come*. Nothingness and the No are immanent to the world as is a possibility, thus they are imminent. The distortion Heidegger inflicts on the correct usage of the actual and the possible responds to the dephenomenalizing trait that always twists in advance a phenomenal edifice, a given habitat. To respond to the uneven phenomena whose coupling our lexicon forces—in order to demonstrate responsibility—it is necessary to begin where they begin to blur: with the possible as what is under revision.

To say that the possible is "higher than the actual" (*Being and Time* § 7) is already to break apart this old pair. The possible is displaced. It no longer abuts the actual, nor follows from it. Rather, it designates the simple opening where, as one says, all is possible—not that entitative "all" that is still representable, but the gap between my habitable world and this same world undoing itself. Severed from the entitative, the possible no longer signifies this particular column or lintel latent in the block of marble, awaiting the passage, the choice, and the hand of the architect Ictinus—it no longer signifies *any* possibilities capable of being made actual. Therefore, there is the new link from the possible to the future—"higher" than the actual because indifferent to present and absent moments as well as to the actual and to the eventually actual.

Now (and this is the key moment of the argument), as severed from the actualizable-makable, the possible is not simple. It is *the formal discordance of times,* the present opening, but opening to the future. Not bipolar presence-absence, but the to-come itself. Temporally discordant in this way, it (literally) derails the everyday through the traits of natality and morality, just as it derails the truth through unconcealment and concealment. The possible always "pulls" doubly. There is the attraction (*Bezug*) of the Yes, and the withdrawal (*Entzug*) of the No (*BzP* 183, 293). Is this a new symmetrical duality? Only the most rigidly stratified retina could read the double pulls prompted by the possible yet again according to the geometry of determinate negation. Rather, they undo, once and for all, bipolar mechanics. It should suffice to recall the dissymmetrical turns of phrase: birth is "for death"; "The clearing, for concealment" (*BzP* 351); "the without-ground, the way of originarily being the ground" (*BzP* 379); the Not "more originary than being" (*BzP* 247); the No "of an essence still deeper than the Yes" (*BzP* 178). . . . "For," "more originary," "deeper"—one will not be able to suggest that these propositions and comparatives are coupled with contraries. None of the bipolar models received from the tradition would survive were it to be arranged in the form of "Yes *for* No" or "No, *deeper* than Yes." What sense would it make to say that the microbiological fullness of honey is "for" the biological No of ashes? Or that ashes are "deeper," "more originary" than honey? That would do away with their symmetry (with their being structured, according to Lévi-Strauss)—as, indeed, with the discordance of time, it does away with the symmetry of Yes and No.

The speculative baggage of comparatives still remains. One might quite naturally say that if the No is the contrary equal of the Yes, and if it does not follow the Yes as if dependent on it, then it can only precede it as does a condition. Thus the No would end up rendering the Yes secondary. But what is it that can be described according to locations such as "above," "equal to," and "below"? We have just seen such gradations always serve to represent beings. It being a question of traits permeating the "to-come," the propositions and comparatives in question, on the other hand, no longer posit any sort of scale. More originary cannot mean, then, primordial—on the first order—as a first cause is toward proximate causes. As the paradigm of binary oppositions withers away, so does that of progressively deficient similitudes trailing off from some maximal position. As we have already seen, it is unthinkable that death, concealment, the ground-less, nothingness, and the No might occupy a "primordial" place.

The phenomenologically originary can only pertain to manifestation. Only there will we speak of a No more originary than the Yes. At first glace, there has been nothing more familiar since Heraclitus. The No wins in that manifestation as such never becomes manifest. Coming to presence loves to hold itself back.

There also has been nothing more evident—and with an evidence "aimed at" in every phenomenology of intentionality, since visibility has always been espied before every visible content. The attraction of the Yes signifies appearance. *Yes, there is manifestation* states what is, moreover, a double tautology, for "yes," "there is," and "manifestation" all bespeak the same phenomenalization. The contrary statement would assert: No, there is no manifestation; appearance does not happen. No one yet has, as far as I know, thus drawn a veil over the world. Phenomenologists are those that observe that *No, there is no manifestation of manifestation*. Heidegger would agree. Only, if manifestation is constituted not from out of a stabilizing self-consciousness, but by precarious contextualizations and recontextualizations, then one should add: *There is a No that weakens all manifestation*. This statement, without denying manifestation nor tautologizing non-manifestation, proceeds to another place. To see where, we must, following the same project of phenomenology, not only look at how we speak, but about what we speak.

Now, here, the withdrawal of the No is more familiar and still more obvious, but with a familiarity and an obviousness that are situated in everydayness, not in the history of philosophy or the method of phenomenology. This is why this withdrawal is most decisive for the understanding of being. In what respect does the No pull *otherwise* than the Yes? Inquiring into manifestation and the No in the everyday, there is revealed an alterity (which accounts as much for the *kruptesthai philei* of Heraclitus as for Husserlian intentionality) in which the entire tragic condition of being is at play.

What is Heidegger speaking *about* when he speaks of *phuein* or of manifestation? Always of singulars forming constellations, which is to say, singulars phenomenalizing themselves by entering into an economy—this entry into presence was to remain his sole and persistent issue. This entry works on singulars by regionalizing them; it inscribes them in a context—in a world—and thereby makes phenomena of them. This is what Marcel Duchamp understood so well when he mounted a bicycle wheel on a stool and exhibited it in a museum. A bicycle wheel is made for turning around a greased axis, held in a metal fork and serving the purpose of locomotion. "Yes" to that object of spokes and a rim when it composes a world, contextualized between the asphalt on which it advances and the cars between which it allows you to thread your way. It is there that it appears, phenomenalized in accordance with what it is. But a No traverses its phenomenalization as the possibility of a being dislodged, a dislodging that here exiles it to a stool in an exposition and that singularizes it there. The singularization always to come in phenomena signifies the No to their world;

better—it is the *No that signifies to them their world* (their "own" world, but without any appropriating subject or full presence).

To call a being "singular in its world," or beings "singulars in their world," would be nonsensical—it would amount to a sense overdetermined by a non-sense. That overdetermination is the tragic (that Rimbaud emphasized when he said "We are not in the world."). There solitude takes root, more originary than love. Only a phenomenon in its world has meaning. Singularization ruins {*abîme*} meaning, but it is a *mise en abîme* at the point of emergence, thus already emergent.

Here then is how Heidegger remains faithful to the philosophers' ancient quest for conditions while at the same time dispatching the *a priori,* universality, the ultimate instance, simplicity, univocity, as well as all other corollaries of normative theticism. Factual decontextualization—such as occurs in Duchamp's "ready-made" or in my own terminal entropy—can happen only because the decontextualizing No is first of all a trait of being. Singularization, as possible, always disrupts from within any actual phenomenality bestowed by a world. Nothingness has to be more originary than being because *it singularizes being into an event.* Such singularization is the pathetic stakes of the *Contributions to Philosophy.* Each time Heidegger speaks of the supreme danger, it is this of which he is speaking.

Singularization is indeed the other belonging to no genus, essentially alienating being in its *Wesen.* What parity, symmetry, determinate negation, contrariety, contradiction—or what hierarchy of particulars under a universal principle—could couple the singular with the phenomenon? Thus one must not let oneself be duped by the *lexical* pairing when the double bind is described as appropriation-expropriation, unconcealment-concealment, being-nothingness, Yes-No, legislation-transgression. In each of these pairs that are not pairs at all, the first word designates the phenomenality that a being owes to its world and the second designates its singularization to come.

This singularization spells out a liability in phenomena, namely, that they can suffer expulsion from their world. As an originary trait, it expresses the fact that dispossession is always imminent, that full possession never happens. From the viewpoint of the everyday, such an expulsion is called death; from the point of view of the event of being, such eviction is called "expropriation"; from the viewpoint of epochal hegemonies, it is called "destitution"; and for the modern epoch, finally, it signifies the diremption that deprives us of fantasm-referents.

These are but so many retractions brought about by the possible, hence the future. Whether Heidegger is speaking of the singular or whether he speaks of time, the same *differend* is at issue, namely, of the disparate laws in which nomic being always opens up a world, but in which the Not—more originarily nomic in that it singularizes phenomena toward their *exit*—strips this world, forever and always, of its reconciling, consoling, and consolidating foci.

The tragic world is not an anomic world. It is doubly nomic. What is received and harbored binds and obligates us just as much as the open; "What closes up on itself opens up as that which holds and binds" (*BzP* 260).

As for the world of the twentieth century, Heidegger doubtless lets himself get carried away a bit when he suggests that today singularization becomes pathological to the point that ours is hardly a world anymore, that things can no longer become phenomena in accordance with what they are. "Operational machinations are unbounded" (*Ungebundenheit der Machenshaften, BzP* 120), he says. The phrase makes sense if it is meant to suggest a vanishing of the deictic character of contemporary language, as words get detached from everyday experience. Concocted by technicity, life becomes impenetrable to experience to the point that a thick mutism covers over its originary condition. The phrase makes less sense if it suggests that technicity today leaves things under the *simple* bind of their *singularization*. If these words mean to say that "operative machinations" exhaust all phenomenalization, that they nullify worldhood anew—even if differently than in subjectivistic solipsism—then the phrase cannot but prompt headaches. At least it enables one to understand why, according to the *Contributions,* Da-sein is not yet. It will be, when an age recognizes itself in all clarity as placed in a phenomenal economy without denying in it the singularization to come. This is the knowledge that alone would vouchsafe phenomena.

"The one *and* the other impose their constraint," says the epigraph above. We have seen whence every univocal law is born—from the hubris that denies mortifying singularization as if it were not. Idealists of all times have been the model functionaries of order, declaring flatly that the singular has no being. Now, the unlearning of this hubris (an unlearning that Heidegger calls *Gelassenheit*) restores to the law its disparate other and hence the double bind. From beneath tragic denial, it restores the tragic truth that always ends by singularizing the hero to the point of killing him.

Such occurs with Agamemnon. At Aulis, the blood ties singularize him in the phenomenal economy constituted by the armies under his command. Conversely, the constraints of arms singularize him in that other phenomenal economy, constituted by Clytemnestra and the house of Atreus, at Mycenae. At Aulis, his nomic allegiance to what was militarily univocal effaces the singular No pleading with him through the eyes of Iphigenia, bound and gagged. A few years later, he will find himself singularized in quite the same manner, in the net set by Aegisthus. In each case, the denial that promotes the law singularizes the man of law.

This is also what Michel Foucault said: "Only a fiction can make us believe that laws are made to be respected. . . . Illegalism constitutes an absolutely positive element in social functioning, whose role the general strategy of society includes in advance."[95] It is an illegalism upon which the singular lives—under the law and outside the law simultaneously.

When Heidegger says that "the event alone is binding" (*BzP* 416), one must take this to mean that only the disparate event in its appropriation and expropriation is binding; in terms of the law—only the originary, legislative-transgressive double bind is binding.

Conclusion

On the conditions of evil: denying dispossession

By way of conclusion, it will be useful to return to an ambition stated in the General Introduction, namely, to learn more deeply about the conditions of sufferings that humans have inflicted upon themselves on a small and grand scale. The natural metaphysician in us might scoop up those conditions—the plural must not be effaced—with one stroke of the shovel and summarily call them evil. By remembering tragic denial one can, it seems to me, sort out that shovelful and in the process gain some precision.

Indeed, one can go at it differently, I think, than by inquiring into the facts or invoking their ideas. One can go at it through a phenomenology of ultimates. At the risk of taking a turn either into some neo-positivism or into a paleo-idealism, here is how we work in philosophy. We seek to grasp the irreducible traits in the everyday and put them to the test of a historical and systematic investigation. The analytic of ultimates, in other words, provides the tools to the topology of double normative binds. As for the incantations of the right and the left, according to which "we need norms" in order to understand, judge, and act, the response of the phenomenologist has always been and should be that to learn how to think and do, *Einsicht* (perspicacity, inspection, circumspection; much less {a matter of} intuition or awareness), suffices.

Ethics and morals, then, no longer belong to philosophy.

The ambition to learn about the conditions of evil—conditions that are neither ethical nor moral, but phenomenological—has guided all the preceding analyses and reflections. To mimic the gnostics' question (mimes being experts in demythologizing): How did evil enter the world? The topology of double normative binds begins not with the narrative of some primitive fall, but with a certain primitive scene with which, and through which, to work; namely, the conflict of the heroic and democratic laws of the Athens of the fifth century, such as they are represented in the theater of Aeschylus and Sophocles. For example, Agamemnon slitting his daughter's throat, *in the name of*... precisely what? In the name of what is called "values," no doubt the nation (more than the *polis,* less than the state), certainly the army, inevitably honor, plus perhaps Greek expansionism and the Ionian colonization.... One makes the decisive cut to promote a common noun capable of laying down the law. Now, it is by the same bloody cut that Agamemnon also cuts himself off from the law of the Atrides. He "de-cides" {*trache*} between the two following laws: *for* that of the phenomenality constituted at Aulis, and *against* the one at Mycene, where other obligations would have compelled him to act differently. We should also reiterate that at Aulis his function as leader determines and universalizes him, that it inserts him into a world that makes sense, but that at Aulis, the undeniable allegiance—nevertheless denied—to family lineage also singularized him. The other bond expels him beforehand from the world of weapons and battleships, the world that in sacrificing his daughter he extols as unequivocally normative. To think this double bind for itself is really to get at the heart of tragic knowledge.

Here, then, we see wherein those ultimates of ordinary experience are revealed that we know, however poorly. They are revealed in the *maximization* of some name that sets our bearings and that contextualizes a world, but also in the *singularization* outside any context, outside the world.

How did evil enter the world? Not in a narratable coming, not by that erstwhile king too cowardly to sustain the double bind. Evil comes in an incredible move, when one cuts off singularization; when one blinds oneself against it; when, in the name of a jealous fantasm that subsumes everything that can become a phenomenon, one strikes a decisive blow—a fantasm that henceforth will command exclusive allegiance, that will integrate making, doing, and knowing in a masterable arrangement, and in this sense appropriates the world; when we deny the expropriation that wrests us from this world.

Was sacrificing Iphigenia right or wrong? It is more instructive to see that it is the *barrage of values that makes one do these sorts of things*. The primal scene does not allow "the problem of evil" to be placed, from the outset and without question, within the confines of "morality"—as if evil were a matter of *mores*, of moral standards, habits, and practices, or even of disposition and intentions, as though such practices and intentions would be clarified by a theory, juxtaposable, for example, to a political theory, as if they would be accessible to investigation or speculation. A theoretical pigeonholing that makes orderings pass for explanations. "Morally speaking, he was wrong," but "politically speaking. . . ." Having reached this lofty post from which one can skim over discourses one calls secondary, unfounded in themselves, how is one to discern what is good and what is evil? Obviously by recourse to some primary discourse that deals with a grounding principle. Now, topology has shown these principles, in the name of which the various cases are put in order, to be fragile. They owe their sovereignty to tragic denial.

A metaphysics of supreme referents differs from a phenomenology of ultimates as negation (*Verneinung*[1]) differs from denial (*Verleugnung*). Negating norms is a metaphysical operation that depends on a prior thetic act. On the other hand, denying a knowledge involves no such precursory normative thesis. It is not an operation of determinate negation. Hence the analysis of denials—and with them, of evil—is the responsibility of a phenomenology that studies how, under the aegis of a simple normativity, hegemonic fantasms have never ceased to modulate an originary differend into double binds.

I have spoken of *destitution* to describe what happens to such a fantasm when it loses its force of law. *Diremption* signifies the loss of every hegemony—the possibility that we have been living for more than a century. In the destitutions and in diremption, the ultimate trait of mortality is manifested, along with the singularizing condition that manifests itself in everydayness as *dispossession.*

The great detour through hegemonies will not have been in vain if it has been able to recover a precursory knowledge without which there would be nothing to deny. When the integrative fantasms are destituted, a dispossession is revealed that always pulls on phenomena like a groundswell, depriving them of their world. It is a dispossession of habitable phenomenalities that remains systematically operative in every positing of an integrative law. The law thereby finds itself already placed in abeyance, already forbidden. Such is the uneasy charm of theticism—to argue positions *by force of necessity* and all at once to recognize and to silence the everyday knowledge that we have of the originary differend.

In order to think evil one is left with, on the surface, a host of questions to which everyone keeps returning: What is the good life? What are proper conduct and right intention. . . as well as, in the depths, a dispossession that keeps returning? Is what is called evil to be attributed to this dispossession? At first sight, nothing would seem more plausible. Evil strips us of the good life, a just world, of love just as if it anticipated death. Accordingly, by paying attention to ordinary experience, we know better than to exalt now this, now that, colossal referent and, like dwarfs, to put our trust in it. We know better than to rank evil among the special issues dealt with in a special branch of philosophy, itself understood as a branch of the human sciences in the shadow of a hegemony posited so as to integrate (at least by right) knowledges, just as the human sciences are posited so as to integrate lifeworlds.

Now, the depths don't instruct us much better than does the surface. Something in us, to be sure, applauds when, with resignation, we are told that evil is a special problem indeed. Were it not, it would be everywhere—a thought more difficult still to resign oneself to, unbearable. But something in us agrees as well that the "problem" in question does not belong in any discipline of knowledge, as the problem of motion belongs in physics and as the study of insects does in entomology. This is because we have a knowledge of evil, but no scientific knowledge. It certainly stands in league with the complex of destitution-diremption-expropriation-dephenomenalization, a complex of which dispossession stresses the origin in everyday experience. But in league how exactly? Deep etiologies have a superficiality about them, namely, that they promise they will consummate a prior knowing in a scientific knowledge—a promise impossible to keep. Instead of consummately intelligible transparence, they serve up, through successive pronouncements, a breathtaking parade of ultimate instances.

What we need is neither superficial surveys nor deep burrowings, but the work of *Einsicht*—insight, which is the work of inspection, circumspection. For this, as I have said, one must try to grasp irreducible traits in the everyday, and then put them to the test of a historical and systematic investigation. Borrowing from Hannah Arendt (who on this point corrected, not without irony, Heidegger), I have called these traits "natality" and "mortality." The first, the archic trait, prompts us toward new commencements and sovereign commandments. It makes us magnify norms and principles. The second always wrests us from the world of such archic referents. It is the singularizing, dispersing, desolating, evicting, dephenomenalizing, exclusory trait. The two do not pair off. One does not oppose the other as a determinate negation. They are originary, yet not binary, traits. They do not split a genus in half. They do not pull in opposite directions, falling within the domain of one and the same initial positing and thus under one and the same science (*oppositorum eadem est scientia*[2]). Thus there is no better heuristic than one that wonders: How is it possible that I have begun to be? How it is possible that I will finish being? Now, the larger is the figure of these traits that make-possible, the more easily will they be read. This is why I have gone to those pages where the natal impulse has made itself really colossal—on those pages where the ramparts have been erected against temporality and next to which one could hope for nothing grander.

In those documents of maximization, the trait of mortality can be read as well, although written less large. It is indeed inscribed there, even if reduced, poorly erased, denied. Having nevertheless seen it at work in the Greek, Latin, and modern institutions, it was useful to go to the pages that document the collapse of these hegemonies under the *return of the denied*.

As to good and evil, they cannot be parceled out according to phenomenologically originary traits gleaned from everydayness. How could natality be the pure and simple good? The maximizations to which it sweeps us away, kill. Nor can mortality, which leads us back to singulars,[3] be equated with evil in its naked state. The primitive scene suggests it, the destiny of hegemonies confirms it, the exhaustion of certain illustrious ideologies illustrates it, and our ordinary ambivalences toward death proves it—that these equations are false. Hence the last decade of the twentieth century has its own peculiar way of calling us back to the senselessness that we know, namely, that a meaning is not something one posits or composes, but something that comes about as a world phenomenalizes itself, and that we always receive it only to find ourselves, in advance, expelled from it.

As if the lesson of those institutions of which nothing more magnificent can be conceived and which for a while went without saying before collapsing under the return of the denied—thus, as if that lesson from history were not ponderous enough, the twentieth century has added to it. It has incurred a diremption of referential authorities of which one can ask if it will not be enough, in the end, to make us recover from the denial and to learn to say "yes" to dispossession. Who, "us"? There has been no lack of moments in history in which a "yes" to the universalizing-singularizing double bind was lived by all.[4] Who then still needs to learn what they already know? The thetic metaphysician in us will have to learn tragic thinking.

To the thetic impulse of natality we owe our normative referents. It is the link that sets us free. Is it not a bit hasty, then, to assert that this impulse does not amount to the good as such? It is the impulse that unifies life. Correlatively, can one dare assert that singularization, which for all that amounts to the loss of love, home, and country, of health and of life—that this withdrawal, this subtraction, is not evil pure and simple? These correlations fed the gigantomachia concerning the focal meaning of being in the nineteenth century, when the normative apparatus began to realize the profits of desire. The young Nietzsche still held keenly that out of unification comes the good and out of individuation comes the evil.[5]

Evil is be to be dispossessed. The equation frames things all too well, and also is in sync with the common opinion in each of the linguistic eras that philosophy has gone through. For the Greeks, evil meant to be dispossessed of the good, to be at the very bottom of the ladder crowned by the one; for the Latins, dispossession of the grand telic continuity was what drew whomever to work contrary to nature; for the moderns, finally, dispossession in the Enlightenment is what turns one radically away from self-consciousness. Each time the good posits itself, which is why it lays down the law. Common opinion in philosophy also knows that evil opposes itself to this self-positing—at least so long as alterity means negation and so long as one denies the very denial that has promoted the ultimate referents. Evil arises when the one, nature, and self-consciousness are damaged in their full canonical presence. It is nothing but a misuse of these normative instances, about which our life is supposed to have taught us that one gains by letting them radiate in their simple obviousness. "Evil is the evil use of the good."[6]

Now, the investigations above have taught us something quite different. Philosophers cannot think for us. They can show us ways of thinking that we wouldn't have imagined. Is it not precisely thetic desire—the impulse that has posited simply binding referents—that speaks in the wish that self-positing and therefore the normatively obvious should shine? But their simplicity turns out to have been produced, and is rough-hewn. Consequently, with regard to the non-simplicity of the good there is a truth that we know but that we do not understand. It teaches us—and philosophers, reread in the light of this knowledge of ultimates, teach us—that the law extends its subsumptive power by virtue of its very positedness. Whoever says law (*das Gesetz*) says positing (*das Gesetzte*), and whoever says positing says "stop" and "decree," a thetic blow and a tragic denial. Knowledge should prevent us from being startled when (the lesson of the tragics) the good reveals itself amidst double binds. Thus, let's put the polarity of good and evil in abeyance. It is about evil that the analytic of ultimates can instruct us.

Perhaps the first who, in the nineteenth century, thought in a different way than by paying homage to some form of "unitary ground" (although to render homage to ethics), and who practiced an alterity other than determinate negation, was Kierkegaard. "Any discourse about a superior unity that would reconcile absolute contradictions is a metaphysical assault on ethics."[7] Instead of metaphysical grounding, there is to be ethical seriousness. Now, "seriousness is: the singular."[8] The good is no longer met anywhere on the subsumptive scale—neither at the top where the universal was good because obvious—nor below where it was particularized. Instead of the clarity of the good there was "the dread of the good."[9] Dread, since the serious good demands of me that I singularize myself, just as Abraham singularized himself by agreeing to sacrifice Isaac. Who, then, is speaking when individuation is treated as evil? The natural metaphysician is speaking again, full of dread this time but promptly hushing dread under the therapeutic megalomania of the desire that no longer tolerates the serious. Desire wants a maximum of sense. It can't help but deny the inversion of the primal scene where the good comes to be equivalent to the singular. Still, from one sacrifice to the other, from Agamemnon's to Abraham's, the *simply* normative function passes from the common to the singular.

We see how hard it becomes to arbitrate. Evil—the obscuring of principles in their simple obviousness, or the singularizing dread that is gagged, like Iphigenia, by tragic denial? A narrator of hegemonies, it is true, might arbitrate without any great metaphysical hardship. He might say that until normative self-consciousness began to wane (roughly until the deaths of Hegel and Goethe), singularization and individuation smacked of evil. Then, with the destitution of the modern referent, masters of suspicion appeared who inverted everything. Not unlike Kierkegaard, they placed the singular at the top of the ladder of values and the universal, the one, the unifier of every fantasm, at the bottom. Yet the hegemonies cannot be recounted as one recounts periods in factual history. They do not stretch time into duration. Their history is not the historian's. What intelligibility that clarifies the ultimate conditions of evil would be gained with this sort of information about the normative inversion that occurred in the nineteenth century? None.

In truth, if natality and mortality are phenomenologically originary, we do know what to make of the inversion thesis (a thesis it is). To report that sometime after 1830 values got inverted, the bottom of the ladder now counting for the top and the top for the bottom—such storytelling is not exactly free of any interest. It allows one to classify one's neighbor, if he locates his referents up high, as "still a metaphysician," for two centuries now, a professional insult. But, the interest in the simplicity of the ultimate passes its verdict, "still an X," which in its turn is a thoroughly metaphysical insult. Let us rather say that, in Kierkegaard's words, one should dare to hear the voices of dread beneath that of desire. They are discordant voices from which one profits by letting oneself be instructed. They testify to the *orietur* that always attracts us toward some focal meaning, as well as to the *morietur* that then withdraws us from it.

The two incongruent clusters of attraction-natality-maximization-appropriation and withdrawal-mortality-singularization-expropriation, then the denial of this whole second cluster as well as the exaltation of attractive, maximally normative theses. These then are conditions of evil other than ethical or moral.

There are, to be sure, others and those that we do not understand are the more numerous. In any case, *the* condition of evil does not exist for an analytic of ultimates. No more, one may add, than exists *the* demonstration or *the* phenomenology. It would therefore be beside the point to object by saying, "You set out from the premises of natality-mortality, only to step from the descriptive to the prescriptive and so end up with normative double binds taken over from simple ultimate instances." The objection is beside the point, first of all, because philosophy consists in submitting what you already know to a rigorous thinking of the elements of experience; an argumentative circle is thus not vicious if it allows one to understand conditions better. Furthermore, it is one thing to state primary propositions that are held to be true, but it is quite another to begin from originary traits with which everyone is familiar;

natality and mortality are thus not premises for deductive reasoning. Lastly, these traits cannot be described like givens; the conditions of evil just mentioned therefore do not result from a metabasis beginning with what can be described.

Kierkegaard can help one undo entanglements, knitted by a long tradition, that tie evil to the singular, namely, to individuation, and thus to one single condition of evil. But in order to descry the originary dissension that destroys from within any simply normative positing, an analytic is needed that informs everyday knowledge with a historical topology.

On impossible normative simplicity

I will conclude with a few brief reminders so as to schematize this analytic such as we have cast it in accordance with different languages. First, singulars and singularities follow phenomenologically from singulariz*ation* (from the pull of mortality); then as originary, singularization works on theticism in its very dynamic and deprives us once and for all of a simple appellate authority; and then, recognizing the singular as irreducible to the particular and hence to subsumption—a recognition that was oblique under the hegemonies depending on how they arrived at their limits where they are dirempted today and that was anguished or jubilant—in no way means that one can somehow escape from under norms that are posited as sovereign and deposed beforehand by their singular extraction. And lastly, there is *no evil* for which one has to posit some simple and encompassing meaning (this is the very attraction of natality), but the formula "the ultimate is simple" kills; it poses as if singularization were not. With these reminders, the first underscores the future, the next a certain anarchy, the third the tragic double bind persisting in every historical arrangement, and the last the tragic hubris of normative theses.

"Develop your singularities," one was told not long ago in Paris as well as in California. What followed and what follows, analytically, is "respect singularities." What was not said and what nevertheless requires philosophy if its task is to render explicit the knowledge of conditions: From where does such an imperative come? What makes it possible, convincing? Therefore, no time was lost in Frankfurt to retort: "In the name of what? Spell out your valid arguments." But in the name, in the values, and in the subjective (or intersubjective) authority upon which critical theoreticians end up falling back, topology recognizes so many *productions* with which theticism gratifies us.[10] Just as any other thetic referent, the one invoked in the name of consensus through discursive rationality, or through communicative action, can be posited only at the cost of denying the foreignness of the singular reference. This reference enters into constitutive strategies that are entirely different from subjectivist ones. They can be detected, provided one ceases maximizing self-consciousness, including one in the form of a universal pragmatics. Now, to reach an origin other than a posited and positive one, there is not a great many choices of method. One needs to try to go back to what one has always known, even if poorly: my singularization *to come*.

Polymorphous singularities are constituted,[11] and monomorphous theses get destituted, not, to be sure, by time "as such." That would amount to declaring yet again a magnitude rather than to gleaning a trait. Only the expropriating withdrawal toward my death, hence time as contretemps, confers my singularity. The singular "I" thus implies neither fullness nor property. It is not some sort of freedom, nor the self. Rather it comes about with the dephenomenalizing strategy in ordinary experience, with the expropriation outside my own world. Social theorists have always recognized this, albeit indirectly, when they say that the world—community or collectivity, family, civil society, state—does not come about through accretion and that, in all idealist rigor, the individual has no being. Singularities are always only dispossessed singularities for a thinking that recognizes originary time in the expropriation to come. Therefore, what singularizes me is not some particular asset of which I can make a show. My world always being on the verge of expelling me, the singular instead has its being through the temporality of imminence. I am "I," singularly dispossessed.

Natality and mortality, which are the ultimates in differend, thus have different concerns regarding the future. Putting to death—this is not a popular thought, since norms and values are proclaimed from all sides—falls within the domain of the first; this is at least the case when one kills "in the name of . . ." Thus, one has been able to speak of the banality with regard to exterminations. We have to understand this—evil becomes banal once a common focalization is exalted and singularization denied. Putting the other to death is easily accepted when a fantasm has won the day and when it obsesses the collective field of vision. On the other hand, the single death suffered, mine, coming now, falls under the domain of mortality.[12] We will never stop investing more and more in maximizations unless we have enough confidence in philosophy to expect it to be able to dissolve the hubris behind any simple normative meaning—that it can analyze it, trace it back to its elements, disclose its denial, and thus from under the prestige of common nouns rehabilitate singularization.

In philosophy we may just as well put our pens away if we give up inquiring into the ultimate conditions of experience. But we cease to so inquire when we maximize this or that representation that happens to be thought of highly. Such theticism is gratifying, and essentially so, for it crowns with an ultimate guarantee our fantasmic investments a little like the FDIC guarantees bank accounts. There exists today a whole philosophical industry, administered by the "functionaries of humanity" (Husserl) whose purpose is to sanction institutions and usages. But something unsteady remains about gratifications, since during the interval they last they require that one blind oneself to negative experience. Such is the secret that accounts for the lineage of archic positings: They condense the true, the beautiful, and the good at the extreme. And how could one not enjoy this—a literally marvelous exaltation like the ascent to the ideas—which includes, of course, the ascent toward the ideal of perfect intersubjective communication.

Yet it is concerning just such marvels that in everydayness we do *know better*. If pleasure demands that I deny negative experience, then this kind of experience has already been recognized. Otherwise there could be no denying it. In addition, everyone knows that it will have, and therefore already has, the last word. As a result, the platform from which fantasmic maximizations are hoisted up, and from which normative arguments therefore depart, has always been carved out in advance to serve more or less magnificent—because more or less magnifiable—interests.

The nineteenth century's objective idealism recognized the systematic need to trace the conditions of negative experience back to the "ground" (for Schelling, freedom). However, it is not difficult to see that by splitting the sovereign principle into originary ground and non-ground (*Urgrund* and *Ungrund*), one only applies to evil the same subsumptive exaltation to which we owe all hegemonic fantasms. Evil in turn gets maximized and introduced into the ultimate referent. Thus, in Schelling, the absolute will universalizes ends and reasons, just as it then singularizes itself through original sin. Obviously one hardly escapes theticism by coupling absolute evil with the good. To make that escape it is necessary to remain faithful to the irreducible phenomena, the traits of natality and mortality. But then the ultimate condition will no longer be absolutely archic.

Whether explicitly or tacitly and whatever its variant, a doctrine of principles cannot do without a concept of anarchy. In such a doctrine, this concept only sums up the axiom that forbids indefinite regression toward more and more primitive conditions. In theticism, the first *arché* is anarchic, since if, in its turn, it had an *arché,* it would no longer be first.

The anarchy that appears not to have to truncate the phenomenologically originary conditions is something quite different, for singularization works on every normative position from within. The call to remain faithful to singularization clashes with the call for principles legislating simply; the dissonance is ultimate that deprives us and has always deprived us of a simple appellate authority. The origin thus proves to be *anarchic because in dissension with itself.*

The eras of philosophy, shaped by the languages in which it has been spoken, can best be described through fantasmic theticism. A posited fantasm, as has been shown, always regulates a given epochal arrangement. As has also been shown, the way a given arrangement is linked to the regulative positing mutates ceaselessly.[13] Under the hegemony of the Greek *hen,* unification through narratable stages that a voyager traverses (Parmenides) differs from unification by conformation (Plotinus). Under the hegemony of Latin *natura,* the telic continuum of soul-body-city-humanity-cosmos (Cicero as spokesman for the Roman Stoics) differs from integration by graduated universalization (Meister Eckhart). Under the hegemony of modern self-consciousness, lastly, the subsumption exercised by the received self (Luther) or spontaneous self (Kant) differs from the economy of the self as singularized (Heidegger).

Just as varying in each case is the destabilizing undertow by which singularization undermines these normative referents. In a topological inquiry, it pulls these maxims back to their respective places of extraction, the fantasm of *hen* to the remembrance of things absent (perhaps the ostracized), that of *natura* to a particular city that was or another that will be, that of self-consciousness, lastly, toward the self actually either bestowed or fashioned. A maximization thus cannot but remain faithful to its singular provenance, although it does so with an oblique fidelity, one covered up with a pomp and circumstance that passes for obvious so as to make one forget the humble condition from which a hegemony has been elevated.

Therefore, the topologist does more than describe shifting territories and the breaks between them. Were he to rest content with descriptions, he would be precluded from investigating conditions. Now, if these conditions are not simple, how are they to be understood and expressed? It has seemed to me that they are most easily read in the elementary functions of maximization and singularization such as they traverse the history of referential theses. I have suggested that these functions reproduce, in broad strokes, the traits of everyday experience—the first (maximization) phenomenalizing experience and thus giving to life a world; the other (singularization) mortifying. Hence, whether one recognizes or denies the counter-strategies stemming from mortality, we remain faithful to the *polemos* of ultimates in all that we do and can do. Whatever may be the epochal order it conditions, the originary condition thus shows itself to be polemically turned against itself. It is not just that "beneath the rule: abuse" (Bertolt Brecht), but in both its essence and incidences, transgression occurs outside legislation. It is not a matter of abuse by some agent, but rather that the rule abuses itself in its ruling. To rule is to speak in the name of the common. It is to simplify the manifold, produce evidence, and thereby make oneself understood. The tragic authors saw an unruliness at the heart of the rule, a "dark light" (Hölderlin) at the core of the evident. They tell us: *You cannot understand. You must understand.* What? That any name laying down the law contains in it its own forces of abandonment. That we always inhabit a fugal world, one slipping away even while it shelters us, a fleeting world. The ultimates that are at the beginning of thought—maximizing natality, singularizing mortality—remain incomprehensibles; they apprehend *it*. But that about which one cannot speak is what the tragic authors have expressed, and it has to be expressed.

The ceaseless rearrangements within any given language epoch show themselves only to a preunderstanding of ultimates. The same is true of the breaks when, instead of Greek, one started speaking Latin in philosophy; then, much later, a modern vernacular language. The originary double bind can be verified, put to the test of these historical sites. Having a preunderstanding of it does not provide a fixed grid, but the dynamics of allocations and dislocations that in each case make an epoch. Outside the epochal articulations, these traits remain indeed untreatable. To solidify them into theoretical objects would require rubbing out the linguistic ruptures and ordaining some philosophical Volapük. How could one even take stock of the refigurations and breaks as such, unless one has an antecedent knowledge that allows one to read both the trait that weaves a world and the one that tears it?

Now if we know ourselves to be so incongruously bound, there is something comical about those beautiful urges to force a solution wherein one resorts to an ultimate authority so as to escape from the double bind. Comical, inasmuch as they look so much alike. The one seeks to raise itself up to some speculatively panoramic viewpoint that looks out over particular normed terrains, terrains upon which to speculate so as to realize a profit in private consolation and public consolidation. The other seeks to elude all these sorts of terrains. Both of them have only turned the tragic condition, in which being-for-birth and being-for-death hold us in their grip, into a differend. This is, moreover, why "anarchy" does not mean and cannot be taken to mean the consigning of the *archai* to the philosophical tools henceforth obsolete and then going off to settle happily in a place deprived of principles.[14] The analytic of ultimates holds forth {*épiloge*} upon hegemonic fantasms, but an epilogue to fantasms as such is literally unthinkable, just as it is unthinkable not to enlist universals into the service of some consoling and consolidating noun. All common nouns are capable of this, for we think and speak under the fantasmogenic impetus of natality. It is, however, possible to enlarge one's way of thinking[15] beyond the fantasied common. In our languages, verbs in the middle voice always lead their speaker out of simple nominative lawmaking. It is, then, possible to think for itself the double bind that we know. With eyes opened by the hubristic sufferings that our age has inflicted on itself—as Oedipus at Colonus wants his eyes open and who thought of his eyes as open—is it possible to love the ultimates in differend?

Natality never ceases to give and give us again a world in which to dwell. It does this by extolling nouns around which to rally—they are called "general ideas." Of these, the best would be the most general, hence also the simplest. It would give us the best of all worlds. But one immediately sees—and Europe has seen all its consequences—that this "best world" kills. The thetic drive mutilates thinking. Just as desire, of which it is the public agent, theticism has no use for remaining faithful to phenomena, a faithfulness that is called thinking. It singles out some pithy meaning, augments it, institutes it as an authority, bestows hegemony on it. Such compounding of thought produces *mortal* fantasms—mortal not only in that they perish, but also in that they put to death.

The knowledge that the ultimate is not simple, that it cannot be being, that it is so fashioned only by an act of thetic denial—the metaphysician in us resists this knowledge. The tragic authors had no fear of what they knew. Beneath the profusion of plots they show one and the same nomic differend, first *de-cided* for the sake of institutions, then suffered, recognized, accepted, embraced, *loved*. For them, the institution of a blinding meaning itself resulted from a blindness: hubris.

Thinking becomes urgent, one would like to say easy, once hubris has been committed. Then Antigone all of a sudden speaks in the voice of Creon and Creon in the voice of Antigone.[16] The Furies, avengeresses according to the terrible heroic code, suddenly plead for the democratic order, and Athena, the city's namesake, turns into the advocate of the *deinon* in institutions.[17] Is this discursive permutation a reconciliation of opposites? Hardly, for these oppositions do not amount to determinate negations, but to thought being faithful to disparate ultimates. In the aftermath of hubris committed (totalitarianisms, it seems, being behind us in Europe), a new questions can be raised: How could thoughtlessness ever go so far? Concerning these aftermaths, we enjoy today an indisputable prerogative. At the beginning of the twenty-first century in the West, we are rather well-stationed to recover—if that were possible—from denial and thoughtlessness. Looking back from hubris toward tragic knowing, the *singular* can suddenly show itself incongruously *in differend with the world.*

> No one was able to remember when and how long ago Akaky Akakievich had entered the ministry, nor who had recommended him. The directors, department heads, division managers and other administrators came and went; he was always seen in the same place, in the same position, at the very same duty of a copying clerk. No respect was shown him in the office. The porters, far from getting up from their seats when he came in, took no more notice of him than if a fly had flown across the room. The

head clerk's assistant would throw papers under his nose without even bothering to say "Copy this." The younger clerks jeered and made jokes at him to the best of their clerkly wit. They would scatter bits of paper on his head and exclaim "Snow falling!" Akaky Akakievich, however, remained impassive. Only when one of them jolted his arm and hindered him from doing his work, he simply said:

"What have I done to you?"

There was something strange in these words. He uttered them in such a poignant tone that one young man, new to the office and who, following the example of the rest, had allowed himself to tease him, suddenly stopped as though cut to the heart. From that moment on, the world appeared to him in a different light.[18]

Notes

Volume One

General Introduction

1. As far as I know, the expression "double bind" was coined in 1956 by Gregory Bateson. I retain the three formal traits he gives to this concept in *Steps to an Ecology of Mind,* London, 1972, pp. 206. First there is a primary injunction that decrees the law; then there is a secondary injunction decreeing a law in conflict with the first; and finally, there is a third injunction "prohibiting the victim from escaping from the field" constituted by the first two injunctions. Obviously I do not make use of these traits as they are applied in social psychology.

2. Friedrich Hölderlin, "In leiblicher Bläue," *Sämtliche Werke,* ed. F. Beissner, v. 2, Stuttgart, 1951, p. 373. The translations of foreign language texts in these notes are mine (with some exceptions) even when I refer to a published French version. I will not indicate the particular modifications I've made to existing translations.

3. Aeschylus, *Agamemnon,* v. 177 (cf. v. 250f).

4. Friedrich Nietzsche, *The Gay Science,* II, section 57.

5. G. W. F. Hegel, *Grundlinien der Philosophie des Rechts,* Preface; *Werke,* ed. Glockner, 3rd ed., Stuttgart, 1952, vol. VII, p. 35.

6. There can be no tragic sense without a sharp sense of our temporality, and therefore of our historicity. This was as true in the Attic age as it is for our age. Here is one indication among many. There are debates in the "philosophy of mind" concerning obligations toward the collective that are in conflict with those toward the individual self. They raise the question inspired by Descartes: How is it possible to render our beliefs objective? To reformulate the question in terms of perspectives (subjective and objective) on ourselves: How is one to make the perspective of the particular person ensconced in the world agree with objective vision of the same world, such that this vision encompasses both the person and his perspective? The current state of the sciences requires a "fresh" analysis of the tensions between these two perspectives, an analysis that one conducts at great expense through "thought experiments" (thought experiments of this sort: What would remain of me if a part of someone else's brain were implanted in me?). One discovers that it would be a good idea to temper both the subjective and objective; that a "convergence" of the personal and impersonal points of view is necessary (cf. Thomas Nagel, *The View from Nowhere,* Oxford, 1986, as well as *Equality and Partiality,* Oxford, 1991). This is argumentative freshness that has no sense of how stale it is. First of all, the smallest historical airing would show that the dilemma between the subjective and objective has its own date of birth and its own presuppositions, that this dualism is hardly the alpha and omega of philosophy pure and simple, and that the blackboard on which philosophy is inscribed is never erased (in these authors it would be easy to show this blackboard hugely engraved by a scientistic ideology)—in short, that the history of philosophy still remains the best guardrail against prejudices passing for common sense. Then and above all, one can only be disappointed to read with perfect clarity statements using the very same terms that constitute the tragic conflict when one then sees these authors unimaginatively conclude that we need a *mixed point of view* (Nagel, *Equality and Partiality,* p. 75), a little bit of loyalty to the universal, a little bit to the singular. More imaginative, because it does not obliterate the "obstinate relation to death" (with the temporalization and historialization that follows from it), is the linking of the singular to the universal such as it is expressed in the views of Michel Foucault, with whom I will conclude below.

7. Aristotle, *Nichomachean Ethics,* X, 7; 1177 b 33 (one could call this a critical resumption of Plato, *Theaetetus,* 176 b; *Republic* VI, 500 c.). The metaphysician in us has nothing to fear from his critics. Allying themselves with desire, he promises *apantkein,* to render "mortality" null and void.

8. Samuel Beckett, *Worstward Ho,* New York, 1983, p. 8.

9. "To be a principle is to be the cause of multiple effects without itself having any antecedents," Aristotle, *Metaphysics* V, 26; 1024 a 1–3.

10. See the example of an infinite regression taken from Indian cosmology to which John Locke opposes philosophy: The Earth rests upon an elephant, which hangs on a tortoise. . . . (*An Essay Concerning Human Understanding,* II, 13, 19 and II, 23, 2). Fichte and Hegel take up this example.

11. This entry into the public lists occurred with Pythagoras. As for the distinction between the supreme referent and an ultimate referent, here is an example. On the 4th of October, 1582, there occurred an event the likes of which hadn't happened since Julius Caesar: at midnight, the calendar passed to the 15th of October. Thus ten days were banished from our history. Pope Gregory XIII used this measure to eliminate

an error in the Julian calendar that was based on an incorrect calculation of planetary movement. According to theories at that time, the supreme function can be reduced to the demiurge (Plato), to the cosmic cycle (Aristotle), to hypothesized *nous* (Plotinus), or to the creator (Augustine). But the ultimate function, which constitutes the phenomenality of time strictly speaking, fell to the great cosmic cycle (Plato), to the before and after of sensible substance in movement (Aristotle), to the life of the soul (Plotinus), or the distensions of *memoria-contuitus-expectatio* of the soul (Augustine). From this last point of view, the notion of time in the Gregorian calendar—which is our calendar—remains Platonic (which does not exclude a great diversity of those notions in other domains). The supreme reference names the cause of time—in each case it is a being. The ultimate reference expresses its condition—it is always a relation among processes.

12. In Edmund Husserl, *Die Krisis der europaeischen Wissenschaften und die transzendentale Phaenomenologie,* The Hague, 1954, p. 15.

13. ". . . today *the truth* can only be had through certain ancient books," Leo Strauss, *Persecution and the Art of Writing,* New York, 1952, p. 154.

14. One no longer writes treatises like *De Consolatione philosophiae*. But perhaps the interests of consolation remain more widespread among philosophers than it appears. Take the example of Wittgenstein. Bertrand Russell recounts that Wittgenstein "used to come to my rooms at midnight, and for hours he would walk backwards and forwards like a tiger . . . on one such evening after an hour or so of dead silence, I said to him: 'Wittgenstein, are you thinking about logic or about your sins?' 'Both,' he said, and then reverted to silence" (*Portraits from Memory and Other Essays,* London and New York, 1956, p. 23). It's necessary to listen—I think about logic *because* I think about my sins? This seems to be the lesson even of the *Tractatus,* in which education makes up an integral part of the logical argument. In Wittgenstein, logic once again finds one of its most traditional features—the power to console. As for the consolidation of public life, it would be difficult to find fault with William Butler Yeats, who said "civilization is hooped together by manifold illusion," in "Meru" (*The Poems,* edited by R. J. Finneran, New York, 1983, p. 289).

15. Aristotle, *On Generation and Corruption,* I, 2; 316 a 6f.

16. Nietzsche says the normative illusion is born from a double gesture. An image is *exalted* into a handy metaphor like a coin, and then the individual thereby is repudiated (*Über Wahrheit und Lüge im aussermoralischen Sinn,* KGW, vol. III, 2, pp. 373ff.). He adds that every people posits such an illusion above itself, *in its language* (ibid.).

17. The *pros hen* has been judiciously rendered as *focal meaning* by G. E. L. Owen in his article that is still outstanding, "Logic and Metaphysics in Some Early Works of Aristotle," in *Aristotle and Plato in the Mid-Fourth Century,* edited by I. Düring and G. E. L. Owen, Göteborg, 1960, p. 169. In speaking of a "focal meaning of being," I nevertheless mean to preserve not only the ultimate relationality Aristotle established, but also the fantasmic character Kant detected therein (*focus imaginarius, Critique of Pure Reason,* B 672). The citation of Cicero is taken from *The Laws,* II, 1.

18. Michel Foucault, *The Archaeology of Knowledge,* trans. A. M. Sheridan, New York, 1972, p. 14.

19. Hannah Arendt, "On Hannah Arendt" (transcription of a debate held in Toronto in 1972), in *Hannah Arendt: The Recovery of Public Realm,* edited by M. A. Hill, New York, 1979, p. 306.

20. Kant, *Reflexionen* (*Anthropologie*), no. 1034.

21. Aristotle, reader of the "philosophers of nature," declared that it was the observation of becoming that furnished, notably Anaxagoras, with the schemas with which to think the mixture (*Physics,* I, 4; 187 a 26–35). Thus Aristotle slips his own initial question under that of Anaxagoras. But this sleight of hand trick played on his forerunner does not, for all that, invalidate the statement *of method* according to which a doxographer must always ask: "Given a particular conceptual edifice, to what phenomenal region does it remain faithful?"

22. Martin Heidegger, "Vom Wesen und Begriff der Φύσις Aristotles, Physik B, 1" in *Holzwege,* Frankfurt, Klostermann, 1967, p. 312; *The Principle of Reason,* trans. R. Lilly, Indiana University Press, Bloomington, 1991, p. 63.

23. Cf. Aristotle, *On Interpretation* II, 16 a 20, and III, 16 b 6.

24. Jacques Derrida, *Margins of Philosophy,* trans. Alan Bass, Chicago, The University of Chicago Press, 1987, p. 135. Derrida seems to speak here as a chronicler of what was going on in France at the time he signed this text—"May 12, 1968."

25. Such was Bertrand Russell's verdict about Wittgenstein after reading the *Tractatus*. Disconcerted by the hybrid genre of the book, Russell suspected that Wittgenstein had gone over to mysticism so as not to have to ponder it any more. "I think (although he wouldn't agree) that what he likes best in mysticism is its power to make him stop thinking," Bertrand Russell, in a letter cited by Ray Monk, *Ludwig Wittgenstein: The Duty of Genius,* Oxford, 1990, p. 183.

26. Contrary to an opinion widely held since antiquity, the word "philosophy" does not mean what

Augustine and many others have read into it: "For the Greeks, the love of wisdom bore the name of 'philosophy'" (*Confessions*, III, 4, 8). *Philein* signifies here not "to love," but "to appropriate," (*suos*, in Latin, *suus*, in French *sien*). The *philosophos* is the one who pursues a knowledge in order to make it his own. Cf. the passages of Herodotus I, 30 and Thucydides II, 40 cited by Wolfgang Schadewaldt, *Die Anfänge der Philosophie bei den Griechen*, Frankfurt, 1978, p. 13. The French translator of Thucydides renders passage II, 40 as, "We cultivate the beautiful in its simplicity, and things of the spirit without lacking firmness" (*La Guerre de Péloponèse*, trans. J. de Romilly, vol. II, 1, Paris, 1962, p. 29). According to Schadewaldt, it is necessary instead to read it as, "We make the beautiful ours (*philoxlomen*) in all simplicity; and we make knowledge (*philosophomen*) ours without softness." Schadewaldt adds, "One often understands [the verb *philosophein*] as signifying 'to love wisdom.' Today we know that this is wrong. . . . The *philosophos* has a view to appropriating a knowledge in the sense that he pursues it" (ibid.).

27. Samuel Beckett, *Ill Seen Ill Said*, New York, 1981, p. 40.

28. It is necessary to keep the redundancy in the expression "normative tradition." Indeed, the tradition will have to be understood not as a pedigree of proper names but as the infrastructure of the measure-taking in virtue of which this pedigree has been able to maintain itself across the ages. *Maßnahme* first of all signifies the institution of a measure through a fundamental theticism; then there is the adequation to the measure thus posited through moral conformity; finally the thesis is put into force through legal measures.

29. Eudoxus of Knidos, Fragments 121 and 124, in *Die Fragmente des Eudoxus von Knidos*, ed. F. Lasserre, Berlin, 1956, pp. 67ff. Simplicius relates that the expression summed up a charge Plato addresses to the astronomers. "He posed this problem to the mathematicians: What are the circular, uniform and perfectly regular movements that one does well to take as hypotheses, so that one can preserve the appearances presented by the planets?" (Cf. Pierre Duhem, *Sozein ta phainomena. Essai sur la notion de théorie physique de Platon à Galilée*, Paris, 1982, pp.) 1ff. I have had recourse to this phrase in the sense that Aristotle gives to it ("follow the phenomena," *Metaphysics*, I, 5; 986 b 31), in order to characterize not only the role of hypotheses, but the entire labor of phenomenology in the sense of *ta phainomenon legein*—'to gather together and say that which shows itself from itself.'

30. Wurzel alles Übels
   Einig zu sein ist göttlich und gut; woher ist die Sucht denn
   Unter den Menschen, dass nur Einer und Eines nur sei?

F. Hölderlin, *Sämtliche Werke*, vol. 1, 1946, p. 305. See also the Conclusion below.

31. Anton Chekhov, "Une banale histoire," in *Le Duel et autre nouvelles*, trans. E. Parayre, Paris, 1971, p. 314.

32. Sophocles, *Oedipus at Colonus*, lines 624, 1526, 74.

33. By natality, Hannah Arendt means the impulse of the active life: labor, work, action. Natality—"the principle of beginning"—is the condition "of institutions and of laws and generally of all that deals with the community of men"; it is the "miracle that saves the world," for "the faculty of action is ontologically rooted in it." Mortality makes our finitude and lays out the singular life in a narratable history (*Condition de l'homme moderne*, trans. G. Fradier, Paris, 2nd. ed., 1983, pp. 17, 200, 215, 277f). In *On Violence* (New York, 1970), she identifies *homo natalis* as the man which, for her, essentially commences: *homo politicus*. Arendt doesn't say so, but the evidence is that this distinction was inspired by Heidegger. "Dasein factically exists natively (*geburtig*), and it is natively even if it has already died in the sense of being-towards-death." Natality and mortality are opposed as are being-towards-birth—Heidegger says "being for the beginning" (*Sein zum Anfang*)—and being-towards-death (*Sein zum Tode*) (*Being and Time*, *§ 72*). It is true that Heidegger does not give the same breadth of analysis to being-towards-birth as he does to being-towards-death.

34. *initium [. . .] ut esset, creatus fuit homo*, Augustine, *The City of God*, ed. R. W. Dyson (Cambridge, Cambridge University Press, 1998), XII, 21, 4. Pendant to this is the definition of man that situates him midway between the angels, with whom he shares rationality, and beasts, with whom he shares mortality: *animale rationale mortale* (*City of God*, IX, 13, 3).

35. Epicurus, Letter to Menoice (124b–127a); Diogenes Laertius, *Lives and Opinions of Philosophers*, X, 124f.

36. Augustine, *Confessions*, XI, 14,17.

37. Aristotle, *Metaphysics*, XI, 3; 1061 a 10f. In distinguishing between first philosophy, which is theology, and the—impossible—science of being *qua* being, I follow Pierre Aubenque. With regard to Aristotle, he writes that "the search for unity takes the place of the unity itself," *Le Problem de l'etre chez Aristote*, 2nd ed. Paris, 1966, p. 504.

38. Ibid., X, 2; 1053 b 20f.

39. Ibid., VI, 2; 1026 a 33—b 2.

40. Ibid., XI, 3; 1061 a 18.

41. "Rational living beings must still become mortals," M. Heidegger, "The Thing" in *Poetry, Language, Thought,* trans. Albert Hofstadter, 179. The point seems to be directed at Kant rather than Aristotle; Heidegger lays the blame on reason as the agent of progress. Man perfects himself, said Kant, "in making himself, who is an animal capable of rationality (*animal rationabile*), into the reasonable animal (*animal rationale*)" (*Anthropologie in pragmatischer Hinsicht,* A 315; AA v. VII, p. 321). Not without sarcasm, Heidegger replies that to progress is to go toward death . . .

42. Nietzsche, *The Birth of Tragedy,* section 10.

43. Heidegger, *On Time and Being,* trans. J. Stambaugh, New York, pp. 43.

44. The difference that is said to be ontological, such as Heidegger expresses it in reference to the normative or traditional metaphysical difference between "beings" and their "beingness" (*onta-ousia-entia-entitas, die Seienden-die Seiendheit*), consists in taking a step back toward "being" (*parousia, esse, das Sein*). The first step backwards in relation to phenomena lays bare their founding condition; the second, which is heteromorphic to the first, lays bare their temporal condition.

45. Sophocles, *Antigone,* lines 243, 332f., 1046; *Oedipus Rex,* line 545; *Philoctetes,* line 440; *Oedipus at Colonus,* line 806. Many French translations foolishly speak of "marvelous things." More appropriate is its translation as "formidable," which I have borrowed from Jacques Lacan (*Le Seminaire, Livre VII,* Paris, 1986, p. 320), on the condition that we take this word *both* literally (*deinon* comes from *deos,* 'fear,' in Latin *formido*), *and* in the sense of French high school students' jargon of "formidable." Hölderlin first translated it as *gewaltig,* and then as *ungeheuer.* Karl Reinhardt prefers *unheimlich.* What is important is to retain the double sense. In *Antigone,* the mutual bloodbath between Polynices and Etéocles, the edicts of Creon, and Antigone's transgression are indeed frightful *deina* . . . ; the invention of ships to traverse the seas, of the plow to work the earth, of the city to perfect nature . . . are admirable *deina* (lines 334ff.).

46. Heidegger, *On Time and Being,* p. 6.

47. Jean-Pierre Vernant and Pierre Vidal-Naquet, *Mythe et tragédie en Grèce ancienne,* vol. II, Paris, 1986, p. 105.

48. Aeschylus, *Agamemnon,* vv. 205–211, in the translation of Paul Mazon, *Eschyle,* Paris, 1925, vol. II, p. 17.

49. Heinrich Hertz, *Die Prinzipien der Mechanik,* Leipzig, 1894, p. 9. On the use Wittgenstein makes of these lines, see G. P. Baker and P. M. S. Hacker, *Wittgenstein: Understanding and Meaning,* Oxford, 1980, pp. 16f. and 492f.

50. The translator emphasizes the sudden change in Agamemnon's attitude by the liberal rendering of *themis* as 'without crime.' On the other hand, he attenuates the phrase *orgen periorgos epithumein,* which means 'to desire most passionately in passion.' See the parallel constructions and the commentary in Eduard Fraenkel, *Aeschylus: Agamemnon,* Oxford, 1950, v. I, p. 103, and v. II, pp. 123f.

51. For the ancients, the desert where Oedipus wandered is the non-place *par excellence.* It is not adjoined like a third place to the *polis* and to the *oikos;* the double bind, as we have seen, indeed excludes not only every encompassing law but also every law by which to escape (see above, note 1). For Aristotle, the tragic journey finally comes down to a matter of misfortune (*dustuchia Poetics,* XIII, 1453 a 25). He is writing at the moment when the conflict between the heroic past of Athens and its democratic present has been resolved; this is why he can consider Euripides, who no longer has any sense of this conflict, as "the most tragic of poets." There is a certain platitude in Aristotle's theory of tragedy that can be explained by the influence, here again, of the *Physics.* Victor Goldschmidt has shown that "tragedy is treated as a natural substance," whose changes Aristotle tried to explain in terms of causes (*Temps physique et temps tragique chez Aristote,* Paris, 1982, pp. 218 and to 29).

52. Ludwig Wittgenstein, *Philosophical Investigations,* § 94. I do not always follow Pierre Klossowski's French translation (*Tractatus logico-philosophicus* and *Investigations philosophiques,* Paris, 1961). The numbers in parentheses refer to sections.

53. "The more precisely we consider the language of facts, the stronger becomes the differend (*Widerstreit*) between this language and our demands. The differend becomes unbearable. . . . Philosophy is a struggle against the bewitchment of our understanding by our language" (§§ 107 and 109). The superior law, seeming to control the terms in conflict, can only be a chimera. This is what I call a fantasm. In Heidegger the differend emphasizes the incongruity between, on the one hand, the particular subsumable under the universal and, on the other hand, the singular (in the present instance, freedom): "The particular, of course, is always other than the universal, but this being an other does not signify a differend (*Widerstreit*)," *Vom Wesen des menschlichen Freiheit* (course from the summer of 1930), *Gesamtausgabe,* vol. 31, Frankfurt, 1982, p. 30. So as to return to it frequently, I retain both the fantasmic status of the term posited as encompassing as well as the first instance of the differend, the incongruity of the particular and the singular.

54. Not only *nomos,* the law, and *onoma,* the name or noun, but also the word "nomad" are derived from the Indo-European root **nem*. Cf. Emmanuel Laroche, *Histoire de la racine *NEM en grec ancien,* Paris, 1949, pp. 115–129.
55. Bertolt Brecht, *The Life of Galileo,* first scene.
56. The structure of this differend must not be confused with that of tragic conflict. Universals are opposed to each other in ideologies. But in tragic conflicts, the bonds of the *oikos* singularizes man from civic law, and inversely the bonds of the *polis* singularizes man from familial law. Tragic conflict is paradigmatic not for this particular chiasm, but for the *singularization* that it effects.
57. Remark in the posthumous work, cited by Baker and Hacker, *Wittgenstein: Understanding and Meaning,* pp. 552f.
58. Wittgenstein, "Bermerkungen über Frazers 'The Golden Bough'," *Synthese* XVII (1967), p. 242.
59. On this "presupposition," see the Conclusion below.
60. Fantasized as a durable and universal foundation, being always comes down to some type of beingness. As for being *qua* event, it is necessary to understand this as singularizing time.
61. That Oedipus *unwittingly* transgresses the familial law during his reign in no way changes the hubristic status of the law that re-established peace in Thebes—the law of the city is born from tragic denial.
62. "Song of Death," in *Japanese Poetry,* trans. C. H. Page, Cambridge, 1923, p. 130.
63. Friedrich Nietzsche, *Werke in drei Bänden,* ed. K. Schlechta, Munich, 1956, vol. III, p. 338.
64. Martin Heidegger, *Parmenides, Gestamtausgabe* vol. 54, Frankfurt, 1982, p. 134.
65. J. Derrida, *Parages,* Paris, 1986, p. 254.
66. Through the differential *polos,* a philosophical thought takes up a position that it does not question but from which it draws all its questions. We have seen that for Aristotle this is physical movement in its thetic difference from the one that is being (cf. above, note 29); for Kant it is sensible experience in its difference from the "I think." The fact from which the medievals set out is that of created being and its difference, again a thetic one, from pure being: "The *esse* is not explained, it is what explains everything else," wrote Etienne Gilson (*Philosophie de la chrétienté,* Paris, 1949, pp. 291f). For the Heidegger after *Being and Time,* upon whom the readings below will converge, the difference is no longer thetic. The difference is between, on the one hand, the historial site of waning modernity and, on the other hand, the originary phenomenological traits of natality and mortality. Once theticism has been sent packing, what remains to be understood is this difference and its conditions. Hence the question that takes the step back from this difference is: What makes the contemporary exhaustion of normative referents possible, an exhaustion that translates the traits of natality and mortality into an epoch? Answer: Perhaps a certain sobriety that knows itself to be bound only by the ultimates in differend.
67. This also is the case with Heraclitus, though less severely. But Heraclitus emphasizes, appropriately, the *polemos* that is the one—its polemic essence. To see how philosophers have remained faithful to originary singulars even while giving themselves over to theticism—to see how they have broken their mandate to secure principles even as they satisfy the same—it is necessary to examine the nomotheses.
68. Meister Eckhart, *Die deutschen und lateinischen Werke,* ed. Deutsche Forschungsgemeinschaft. LW = Lateinische Werke. LW I, p. 612.
69. Meister Eckhart, LW III, p. 16.
70. There are those who would like to push the transcendental turn in German philosophy back to Meister Eckhart. The author who most clearly puts forth this reading is Joachim Kopper (*Die Metaphysik Meister Eckharts,* Saarbrüken, 1955, and elsewhere). But if Eckhart does desubstantialize the contents of metaphysics, he does not for all that transcendentalize them. It is, surely, with him that the destitution of referential *natura* comes to pass, but he is not that point of transition to the new referent, which will be self-consciousness.
71. Without the slightest hesitation, Sartre resubscribes to the modern hegemony. "The 'I think, therefore I am' became methodological for me. . . . The first truth, which is an unconditional truth, is established by the contact of consciousness with itself" (*Sartre, un film realise par A. Astruc et M. Contat,* Gallimard, Paris, 1977, p. 85).
72. "Smith vs. Board of School Commissioners of Mobile County, Alabama" and "Smith vs. George Wallace, Governor of Alabama," *Federal Supplement,* vol. 655, 1986 (S.D. Alabama, 1987), pp. 942, 945f., 974 and 987–990. The concept of secular humanism goes back to the pioneer of American pedagogical pragmatism, John Dewey, whose article "Religion in Our Schools" had been presented to the court (pp. 956–958). Dewey himself describes his secularism as religious. He wrote that "we become militant for our new religion" whose essence comes down to "value processing." There is an instrumentalization in this secular religion whose goal was to eliminate sources of friction from public life. To liberate the egalitarian society from enslavement to the past, it was also necessary to prohibit the reading of all books written before 1900 (ibid.). As for the concept of religion, American tribunals prefer to rely

on Paul Tillich for his definition as "ultimate concern" (cf. ibid. pages 941, 966f, 979), a definition that is so general that indeed one can hardly imagine which doctrines would not be able to be subsumed under this concept. The judgment in question was overturned by the United States Court of Appeals for the 11th Circuit on Aug. 26, 1987.

There is no doubt that I would not have undertaken to write this book if I had not lived, as a stranger, in the midst of the most ideologically brutal of Western people at the century's end—of a people who equally brutally deny not only singularities, but even their own ideological fantasms and maximizations.

73. G. W. F. Hegel, *Grundlinien der Philosophie des Rechts,* I, 3, §§ 95–103; *Werke,* vol. VII, pp. 149–161. It's true that Hegel became persuaded by some legal scholars and modified his position in the *Encyclopedia.*

Part One. In the Name of the One: The Greek Hegemonic Fantasm

I. Its Institution

1. Plato, *Sophist* 241 d. In this same dialogue, the Stranger from Elea claims that singular beings are and are not. By so introducing an "other of being" that does not fall under the disjunction of being and nothingness, he commits "parricide" toward Parmenides (ibid.).

2. In the references within parentheses, the first number refers to Parmenides' Fragment, and the second number to the line as found in Hermann Diels and Walter Kranz, *Die Fragmente der Vorsokratiker,* 6th ed., Berlin, 1951 (designated below by the letters *'VS'*).

3. Plato, *Sophist,* 246 a.

4. Even the henologue would have to be content with pronouncing the single aspirated consonant "hhhhhhh." This is what was said by Proclus (according to Theodore d'Asine), who saw the three letters of the word "HEN" corresponding to the hypostatic triad. The first hypostasis, which is unpronounceable, would then be formed by the inarticulable aspiration "H"; the second hypostasis by the pronounceable vowel "E"; the third hypostasis by the consonant "N" that can be pronounced only with—"consonant" with—the vowel that precedes it (Proclus, *Commentary on the 'Parmenides',* 52,9; see his *Commentary on the 'Timaeus',* II, 274.

5. Homer, *Iliad,* III 30ff and 396ff.

6. For example, see ibid., I, 76 and 103.

7. Karl Reinhardt, *Parmenides und die Geschichte der griechischen Philosophie* (1916), 4th ed., Frankfurt, 1985, above all, pp. 208–210.

8. Kurt Riezler, *Parmenides* (1933), 2nd ed., augmented by Hans-Georg Gadamer, Frankfurt, 1970, p. 54.

9. Pierre Aubenque has forcefully indicated the priority of being, which is the issue in Parmenides, over the other issue, namely the one: "Therefore being, and not at first unity." ("Syntaxe et sémantique de l'être dans le poème de Parménide," in Pierre Aubenque, ed., *Etudes sur Parménide,* Paris, 1987, vol. 2, p. 108). Now, such an "either-or" supposes that one understands the present participle as a substantive verb—which, moreover, is what Aubenque does ("Parmenides speaks of being or, more precisely, of beings," ibid., p. 106). Below, I shall propose a more *differential* reading of the present participle. If *eon* simply designates beings, then, yes, the one will be an attribute, then a predicate, of beings (cf. ibid., p. 129). By taking such an ousiologic stance, however, one locks oneself from the beginning within a narrow circle of possible significations of being; in the case at issue, it is between the alternative of a verificative use and the copula. As a result, though, one deprives oneself of the very possibility of asking if there is not in Parmenides another understanding of being that is foreign to Aristotle. If, on the other hand, the present participle includes a difference, then *being* will be what makes the *one,* which "holds together" contraries (8, 6). The "either-or" will dissipate under the structural affinity—which is not an identity—between being and the one. This is why I shall speak of being "as one." We might also say, "being, namely, the one."

10. K. Reinhardt, *Parmenides und die Geschichte,* p. 35. The three paths would consist "in two contradictories and their mixture: *estin, ouk estin, esti te kai ouk estin,*" ibid., p. 71.

11. Such is, at least, the view of Kathleen Freeman, *The Pre-socratic Philosophers,* Oxford, 1946, p. 46, p. 144.

12. Jean Beaufret, *Dialogue avec Heidegger* vol. I, *Philosophie grecque,* Paris, 1973, p. 70.

13. Martin Heidegger, *Parmenides* (course of 1942–43), *Gesamtausgabe,* vol 54, Frankfurt, 1982, pp. 69–71; English, trans. André Schuwer and Richard Rojcewicz (Bloomington, Indiana University Press, 1992) pp. 47–49. This edition includes the original pagination.

14. K. Reinhardt, *Parmenides und die Geschichte*, pp. 30f.
15. *VS*, A 14.
16. "The root *phu*-implies only existence," G. S. Kirk, *Heraclitus: The Cosmic Fragments*, Cambridge, 1954, p. 228. Again one must add that this is existence not in the sense of the fact of being, but in the sense of a *coming to being* as is borne out by the three occurrences of this root in Parmenides (10,1; 16,3; 19,1).
17. K. Riezler doesn't hesitate to translate *doxa* (8,51) as *Setzungen, Parmenides*, p. 34.
18. "Of all things the measure is man, of things that are that they are, and of things that are not that they are not" (*Protagoras*, VS B 1; trans. Rosamond Kent Sprague, Columbia, University of South Carolina Press, 1972, p. 18.). Plato presents these words as if they were a doctrine of perception (*Theaetetus* 152 a), but obviously it is a matter of a theticism dealing with being.
19. Lambros Couloubaritis has distinguished in the text four, then six, then eight paths of Parmenides ("Les multiples chemins de Parménide," in Aubenque, ed., *Etudes sur Parménide*, vol. II, pp. 31, 41). The integration of the doxic path into the aletheological path that I am suggesting renders superfluous at least the distinction between the *doxa* of mortals and *doxa* as a discourse on appearance (ibid., p. 35). Mortals trust in the "famous doxic burst," thus in the appearance of the present. Now, the aletheological perspective does not at all confuse this appearing with the false. It only joins to it the absent that does not appear. "Glory, aspect offered by a thing, the fact of being considered, the view that one forms." All these senses of *doxa* (ibid., p. 34) describe the *pareonta* in view of which the man who knows adds the vision of the *apeonta* (4, 1).
20. Hans Schwabl, a commentator praised by H.-G. Gadamer, writes "There, where it is a question of being [therefore, on the second segment of the journey] it can no longer be a question of light and night." ("Sein und Doxa bei Parmenides," in *Um die Begriffswelt der Vorsokratiker*, ed. Hans-Georg Gadamer, Darmstadt, 1968, p. 396.) The day and night would be only "decrees" (*Setzungen*) of mortals (ibid., p. 418). This is in keeping with Fragment 9 but directly contradicts the expression "gateway of night and of day" (1, 11), which is to say, the gateway where the night ends and the day begins. For the same reason we cannot follow Heribert Boeder (*Topologie der Metaphysik*, Freiburg, 1980), for whom Parmenides describes a descent into Hades (pp. 99, 107). What do these authors make of the verse: "Leaving the house of night for the light" (1, 9)?
21. Nestor-Luis Cordero, *Les Deux Chemins de Parménide*, Paris, 1984, thinks that *pylai* designates two gateways: "[I]t is a question of a gateway that allows one to leave the path of the night and the gateway that opens toward the path of the day" (p. 179). Besides the misinterpretation of the Greek (the plural *oikoi*, for example, often means 'the house'), the reading contradicts the very thesis of this author who, like others (and contrary to K. Reinhardt), claims that Parmenides teaches two and not three paths. If there are two gateways to cross, by what path does one traverse the "no-man's land" separating them if not by some version of a third segment?
22. Jean Beaufret (*Parmenides: Le Poème*, Paris, 1955, p. 38) seems to contest that the path of the day is the same as that of being and consequently he also speaks of four paths in Parmenides. Unfortunately, no argument is given to show this construction.
23. The editors of *VS* (vol. I, p. 229) cite Homer, *Odyssey*, X, 86ff.
24. Cf. Hjalmar Frisk, *Griechisches etymologisches Wörterbuch*, Heidelberg, 1956, pp. 340f.
25. Cf. Alexander Mourelatos, *The Route of Parmenides*, New Haven, 1970, p. 22.
26. With similar details, Homer describes the gateway that Penelope crosses in order to begin looking for Ulysses' ship before beginning the shooting match that will decide her fate (*Odyssey*, 21, 42–50). Such descriptions mark a decisive turn in the epic narrative (cf. Otfrid Becker, *Das Bild des Weges und verwandte Vorstellungen im frühgriechischen Denken, Hermes Einzelschriften*, IV [1937], p. 139.
27. K. Reinhardt's view is that this path has nothing to do with those described in Fragments 2 and 6 (*Parmenides und die Geschichte*, p. 46n).
28. We might say that the doxic and aletheological segments are described respectively by the verse from King Lear:

> ". . . we'll talk with them too,
> Who loses and who wins; who's in, who's out:
> And take upon us the mystery of things" (Act V Scene 3, lines 14–16)

29. M. Heidegger, *Being and Time*, § 21, trans. Macquerrie and Robinson, New York, Harper, 1962, p. 128.
30. One thinks of the words of Virginia Woolf: "It is fatal for anyone to be a man or a woman pure and simple. One must be woman-manly, or man-womanly" (*A Room of One's Own*, New York, 1957, p. 108).
31. I infer the definite article (*ta*) before *apeonta* and render it as 'the things.' For reasons that I have just established, I thereby avoid both the monism of being and the Platonic dualism between opinion and

knowledge. The Platonizing violence that the vast majority of commentators inflict upon Parmenides reaches its peak when one claims that one must understand *pareonta* as intelligibles.

32. Immanuel Kant, *Critique of Pure Reason,* B XXXIII.

33. Aristotle, *Metaphysics,* IV, 5; 1009 b 21ff, where he relates Fragment 16 according to which men "think" what the mixture of their members—of their senses, of the day and the night in them (cf. Schwabl, "Sein und Doxa bei Parmenides," pp. 416f)—offers them. We are always aware of "a relation between mixtures of contraries" (K. Reinhardt, pp. 76f).

34. Cf. M. Heidegger, *Parmenides,* pp. 132f. Pursuing a topology of being, Heidegger does not link politics to *doxa.* "The *polis* itself is only the pole of the *pelein,* the manner in which the being of beings is combined, through its unconcealment and concealment, in a place where the history of a community is gathered" (p. 142). In the same sense, see M. Heidegger, *Hölderlins Hymne 'Der Isther,' Gesamtausgabe,* vol. 53, Frankfurt, 1984, pp. 88 and 100.

35. The text of 6, 3 is defective. The editors of *VS* give us *eirgo* and Cordero (*Les Deux Chemins,* pp. 170f.) gives us *archei.* Both versions are equally conjectural. That of Cordero is used by the author to show what he calls his "position" on Parmenides, stated in his title, namely, that the poem teaches only two paths. This is more of a dogmatic than a philological maneuver.

36. In this translation of VIII, 54, I follow H.-G. Gadamer and H. Schwabl; cf. K. Riezler, *Parmenides,* p. 35n.

37. On "the in-between" of Platonic *doxa,* see *Republic,* 478 d–479 d.

38. "In Parmenides we find that this one is determined as thinking, or that what thinks is what is . . . although the unity of being and thinking is still conceived there as the one, the immobile, the rigid," G. W. F. Hegel, *Vorlesungen über die Philosophie der Religion, Sämtliche Werke,* ed. Hermann Glockner, Stuttgart, 1927–29, vol. 16, p. 515. See below, note 78.

39. For Aristotle, Parmenidean being is "sensible" (*On the Heavens* III, 1, 298 b 1). This reading is followed today, notably by John Burnet (*Early Greek Philosophy,* 1892, 4th ed., London, 1930 and 1957, p. 178) and Pierre Aubenque ("Syntaxe et sémantique. . . ," *Etudes sur Parménide,* p. 117). It is true that one can translate this second statement (8,34) as a double reference to thinking. "[T]hinking, and thinking that that [the object of thought] is, is all one," H. Fränkel, "Parmenidesstudien," *Nachtrag von der Gesellschaft der Wissenschaften zu Göttingen* (1930), pp. 186f. On the difficulties raised by the interpretation of Parmenidean being as given in experience, see Kurt von Fritz, "Noûs, Noeîn and their Derivatives in Presocratic Philosophy," *Classical Philology* XL (1945), pp. 237f.

40. This term is used in anatomy where it designates the fibro-cartilaginous articulations of the vertebral column. They are not very moveable because the body (*phusis*) of one bone runs up against that of another.

41. Kurt von Fritz, whose work on the ancient conceptions of *noûs* is authoritative, does not hesitate to speak of the "'intuitive' nature of *noûs*" in Parmenides, notably in Fragment 2. This is a usage that reflects the even older, Homeric meaning of the verb *noeîn,* 'to realize a situation,' (*saisir une situation, gewahrwerden*). Along with this received conception, Parmenides is the first to *practice* "discursive thinking, which is a part of the function of *noûs*." By such conjunctions as "*gar, epei, oûn, toûd'heineka, houneke* in almost every sentence," he has placed argumentation in the service of intuition."He was the first to consciously include reasoning within the activity of *noûs*" (p. 241f.). Subsequent philosophers will undertake to add their respective contributions to intuitive thinking and discursive reasoning. In Aristotle, once again, it seems preferable to translate *noeîn* with words derived from the Latin *intuere,* and to render *noûs* as 'intuition.' Cf. P. Aubenque, *Le Problème de l'être chez Aristote,* pp. 56–59.

42. "Parmenides . . . says that a corpse does not perceive the light, heat, or sounds, but that it perceives their contraries: the cold, silence, and so forth" (*VS,* A 46).

43. *VS,* A 46. This Fragment of Theophrastes attributes to Parmenides the equation between *aisthanesthai* and *phroneîn.* But since Parmenides nowhere else distinguishes between *phroneîn* and *noeîn,* he can no longer, if we follow Theophrastes, distinguish between *aisthanesthai* and *noeîn.* Cf. von Fritz, "Noûs, Noeîn and their Derivatives," p. 240.

44. Kant will repeat that receptivity does not mean pure passivity, nor does spontaneity mean pure activity.

45. Martin Heidegger, *Qu'appelle-t-on penser?* (trans. A. Becker and G. Granel, Paris, 1959), p. 221.

46. Jean Beufret, *Dialogue,* vol. I, p. 71.

47. See the texts of Herodotus, Thucydides, and Xenophanes cited by K. Riezler, *Parmenides,* p. 55.

48. A. Mourelatos, *The Route of Parmenides,* p. 26.

49. See above, General Introduction, note 54.

50. Translations of Plato into English stemming from the school of Leo Strauss (for in the United States it is one) interpret *mûthos* as 'likely account,' an interpretation linked to the conviction of these commentators that there is an esoteric doctrine concealed beneath Plato's exoteric doctrine: "Plato hides his

opinion," Leo Strauss, *City and Man*, Chicago, 1964, p. 59. But does the goddess in Parmenides so hide her intentions? Listening to her describe her teaching about *doxa*, one might think so: "From here on, learn the denominative representations of mortals, by hearing the misleading series (*kosmon apatelon*) of my words" (8, 51f.). Does she not admit thereby that she is getting ready to speak of unreliable *doxai* in a discourse that itself is unreliable? We have only to read on. She anticipates the reaction of the disconcerted listener: "as if the unity [of contraries] could not be" (8, 54). Her discourse is "filled with cunning" for a mortal who conceals from himself what every division into contraries presupposes, namely, their prior unity. The goddess's *mûthos* is not esoteric but cunning in the sense of a detour. She can speak to us about the unity, of which we are tacitly aware, only by using the expedient of the oppositions that make up our actual condition.

51. Cf. Denis O'Brien, "Introduction à la lecture de Parménide: Les deux voies de l'être et du non-être," in *Etudes sur Parménide*, vol. 1, pp. 262ff.

52. Emile Benveniste, *Le vocabulaire des institutions indo-européennes*, vol. II, Paris, 1969, p. 102.

53. Ibid., p. 109.

54. *Iliad*, XVI, 386.

55. Solon, Fragment 11 (Ernst Diehl, *Anthologia Lyrica Graeca* [Leipzig, 1954], p. 35).

56. Which absents? I have already said that the heroic laws are excluded and in this sense absent at the moment that democracy gets going. Nevertheless, one can make this reading more specific with a hypothesis. Parmenides died around 470. Now, far away in Athens, Cleisthenes managed to get a punitive measure of ostracism adopted in 508 that was applied for the first time twenty years later (cf. Aristotle, *On the Republic of Athens*, 22, 1–4). If the neuter *apeonta* resonates in the masculine "the ostracized," then the observation in terms of which Parmenides will have maximized the *hen suneches* will have generally been that of the tragic conflict, and more specifically, that of the practice of ostracism.

57. Aristotle criticizes Parmenides for having recognized only two explanatory principles of phenomena, hot and cold (*Metaphysics*, I, 5; 986 b 34f.). By substituting these material *archai* for the declarative contraries that, for Parmenides, are night and day, Aristotle turns him into a natural philosopher. Thus, since our source for the hypothetical title *Peri Phuseôs* is Simplicius, the leading classifier of the "Presocratics" as "Prearistotelians," we can be certain that for Simplicius, *phusis* designated the totality of things moved by themselves. This may be one reason to doubt that this title is genuine.

58. See the texts (notably Herodotus, 2, 52) cited by Walter Pötscher, "Das Person-Bereichdenken in der frügriechischen Periode," *Weiner Studien, Zeitschrift für klassische Philologie* 72 (1959), p. 7.

59. In Homer, *moîra* can indicate a portion of time or even of meat. *Iliad*, X, 253; XIX, 418; XX, 260. Cf. E. R. Dodds, *The Greeks and the Irrational*, Berkeley, 1951, pp. 7f.

60. Cf. Walter Pötscher, "Moira, Thémis und *timé* im homerischen Denken," *Wiener Studien, Zeitschrift für klassische Philologie* 73 (1960), pp. 14–30.

61. This was the interpretation of Eduard Zeller, *Die Philosophie der Griechen* (1844–52), 4th ed., Leipzig, 1876, p. 517. I follow Leonardo Taràn in saying that *péras*, in Parmenides, has nothing to do with spatial or temporal extension. *Parmenides: A Text with Translation, Commentary, and Critical Essays*, Princeton, 1965, pp. 151–54. I cannot agree with Taràn, however, when he states that these limits are those of the "law of identity," imposed by "logical necessity" (ibid., pp. 151, 159).

62. A. J. Festugière, *Contemplation et vie contemplative selon Platon*, Paris, 1967, p. 29.

63. The root from which the noun *péras* is derived also yields verbs such as *perao*, 'to pass across,' *peior*, 'to pierce,' ' to walk along a path from one end to the other,' *peraino*, 'to bring to term,' *peraioo*, 'to translate,' ' to traverse.' It also yields the adverb *péra*, 'beyond,' and, in Latin, the prefix *per-*, 'across,' as in 'to perforate,' as well as the French preposition *par* and the German *fahren*, 'to travel,' *führen*, 'to drive,' *Furt*, 'ford.' For this sense of *péras* as opening, cf. Marcel Détienne and Jean-Pierre Vernant, *Les ruses de l'intelligence: le métis des Grecs*, Paris, 1974, pp. 271–80.

64. Plato, *Timeaus* 47 e–f.

65. Aeschylus, *Prometheus* 514 (2) 27f. and Plato, *Laws*, 818 e.

66. "This great saying of Heraclitus, the *hen diapheron eautô* [the One differing in itself], only a Greek could discover it." Friedrich Hölderlin, "Hyperion," in *Sämtliche Werke*, vol. 3, ed. F. Beissner, Stuttgart, 1958, p. 85.

67. These lines (6, 8f.) are not easy to understand. K. Reinhardt reads them in the way I read the circle described in Fragment 2. "The analysis forms a circle: it starts from beings and returns to beings, and each of the three ways, upon which one can set out, leads back to the starting point: *to on éstin*" (K. Reinhardt, *Parmenides und die Geschichte*, p. 60). H. Schwabl sees that the end of Fragment 6 (but not Fragment 5) is aimed at the contradiction that consists in joining nonbeing to being, but he limits its scope to the "Ionian tradition," therefore to their speculative juxtaposition. But what is at stake in Fragment 6 is two-headedness, hence the doxic confusion between being and nonbeing ("Sein und Doxa bei Parmenides,"p. 413). N.-L. Cordero, the author who takes up Reinhardt's most criticized assumption and pushes it to the

limit, that is, reading the Fragments as rudimentary logic, sees in 6, 9 a denunciation of vicious circles in reasoning (*Les Deux Chemins,* p. 182). Whatever questions we may pose to Parmenides, we need to distinguish clearly between two circles, the inevitable return of all thinking, always, to the question of being (Fragment 5), and the doxic gyrations where one follows this or that preponderating force, taken as being itself, only to brush aside the path as soon as some other force comes to flush it out.

68. K. Reinhardt, *Parmenides und die Geschichte,* p. 26.

69. "Daß ich erkenne, was die Welt
Im innersten zusammenhält."

Faust, I, lines 382–83.

70. *Iliad* I, 443. Cf. Felix Heinimann, *Nomos und Physis: Herkunft und Bedeutung einer Antithese im griechischen Denken des fünften Jahrhunderts,* 4th ed., Basel, 1945; reprint Darmstadt, 1980, p. 43.

71. In Plato, the young Socrates sums up Parmenides' thesis as follows: "You say that the whole is one" (*hen phès einai to pân, Parmenides* 128a). The Parmenides who appears in the dialogue replies by stating his own hypothesis and asking, "If I begin from the one and admit either that it is one or that it is not one (*eite hen éstin eite mè hen*), what follows from that?" (ibid., 137 b). Neither the thesis that posits the unity of beings in their totality nor the hypotheses that posit the unity of each being in its singularity is sanctioned by Parmenides's poem.

72. Melissus, who called himself a disciple of Parmenides, understood the one as signifying the spatial-temporal expanse. Our lack of sources prevents us from knowing whether he posed questions analogous to those of the Kantian antinomies, but his conception of the expanse of the world entails turning the 'limit' (*péras*) into its contrary, the 'unlimited' (*apeiron*). *VS,* B 2, 3. Cf. Julius Stenzel, *Metaphysik des Altertums,* Munich, 1931, pp. 65ff.

73. M. Heidegger, *Chemins qui ne mènent nulle part,* trans. W. Brockmeier, Paris, 1962, p. 182.

74. Numa-Denis Fustel de Coulanges, *La Cité antique,* 2nd. ed., Paris, 1927, p. 396.

75. From this is derived *nomisma,* the money that circulates because it is worth something, a derivation analogous to the German one in which *Geld,* 'money,' stems from *gelten,* 'to counts as,' 'be worth.' This broad sense does not exclude narrower ones. In Pindar, a contemporary of Parmenides, *nomos* can signify precisely the "constitution" of a city. Cf. the texts cited by F. Heinimann, *Nomos und Physis,* p. 71.

76. This saying of Xenophanes illustrates the agonistic nature of Greek dialectic in general: "He who carries off such compensation, if only for driving horses, does not merit them compared to me. Indeed, our wisdom is more noble than the vigor of a man or a horse. No, there is no sense in such a custom [*nomos*]. It is a mistake to place bodily strength above noble wisdom" (*VS,* B 2, 10–14). To establish oneself as the unbeatable champion of dialectic, one must refute not so much an argument as someone. The dialectician reveals the internal contradictions of the opponent's argument, yet the *nomos* allying disputations of the race course and the struggle—a custom to which Socrates will owe a good part of his reputation—would require, moreover, that one never retreat in the face of *ad hominem* arguments.

77. Aristophanes, *The Clouds,* lines 1075–1078.

78. *VS,* B 44.3.

79. In Plato, Hippias says, "the law tyrannizes men and often violates nature" (*Protagoras* 337 c). Callicles refers to animals to illustrate true justice—which consists in the strongest having the advantage—and to demonstrate that laws are contrary to nature (*Gorgias,* 483d).

80. See below, Part Two, Introduction, note 1.

81. During the lifetime of Parmenides, Cleisthenes, who is called the founder of Athenian democracy, instituted the isonomy, the principle of the equality of all before the law. To put it into force, he sought to shift the legislative power from the families and phratries to a new administrative unit, the deme. The phylarchs, the leaders of the Attic tribes, opposed him. Hence, the following century would see attempts to restore phyletic power through oligarchic *coups d'Etat.* The ancient nobility would finally carry the day thanks to a defeat—the conquest of Athens that ended the Peloponnesian War and led to the tyranny of the Thirty. (Plato, the anti-democrat, will see in this history of the last two centuries a reason for legitimizing a mixed oligarchic/monarchic constitution. This is why, as Cornelius Castoriadis puts it, to see Plato as the founder of Greek political thought is like declaring Charles Maurras the father of the French Revolution—or the Daughters of the American Revolution as the mothers of the American Revolution.) How could Parmenides, as the thinker of the first normative system, not seek to establish which is the legitimate regime, the democratic or the oligarchic one? One good reason it seems to me is that, with regard to the norm that is the one, these contraries are held together. Similarly, it is for good reason that Hamlet, the hero *par excellence* whose tragic knowledge paralyzes action, hesitates to become the dispenser of justice toward the illegitimate king. Measured by "the eternal essence of things"—"horrible truth"—to punish the guilty is a ridiculous task: "Dionysian man resembles Hamlet. Both have once truly cast an eye into the essence of things, and they have known. Henceforth they are revolted by action for

their action cannot change the eternal essence of things. . . . To have known is what kills action; action supposes that one is veiled by an illusion—such is the doctrine of Hamlet—the true knowledge, the gaze cast upon the true horror, gets the upper hand on every driving motive to act, in Hamlet just as in Dionysian man." (Nietzsche, *The Birth of Tragedy,* sec. 7).

82. *VS,* B 129. The editors question the validity of this Fragment.

83. F. Hölderlin, *Andenken* ("Des dunkeln Lichtes voll," *Sämtliche Werke*, vol. II, [1953], p. 197); letter of December 4, 1801, to Casimir Böhlendorf (ibid., vol. 6 [1969], p. 457)

84. Heidegger, *Parmenides,* p. 125.

85. Michel Foucault, "Des supplices aux cellules," *Le Monde,* February 21, 1975, p. 16; reprinted in *Dits et Ecrits* vol II, Paris, 1994, pp. 718–19

86. For the details, see, for example, J. Wiesner, "Die Negation der Entstehung des Seienden. Studien zu Parmenides B 8, 5–21," *Archiv für Geschichte der Philosophie* 52 (1970), pp. 1–34. It is less easy to specify where the list of signs stops, in the text, than to say where it begins. The best thing may be to reduce it to three lines (8, 3–5). We then have to deal with just four affirmative predicates, "now," "all of the same measure," "one," and "holding together." But so as not to avoid the difficulties, I will follow Kurt Riezler (*Parmenides* pp. 50–55) and will take verses 3–5, 22–27, 29f., 32f., 37f. and 42–49 of Fragment 8 as enumerating the signs.

87. Cf. Plato, *Meno* 80 a–86 c, *Theatetus* 149 a; Aristotle, *Topics* VI 6; 145 b16–20; *Metaphysics* III 1; 995 a 23–b3.

88. See above, note 72.

89. G. E. L. Owen, "Eleatic Questions," *Classical Quarterly* 10 (1960), p. 100. Owen repeats this image of a ladder that is to be tossed aside and equates it with that of "signposts" in "Plato and Parmenides on the Timeless Present," *The Monist* 50 (1966), p. 322. This solution has been called "the easy way out hypothesis" by Denis O'Brien, in "L'être et l'éternité," Aubenque (ed.), *Etudes sur Parménide,* vol. II, p. 137. It is such, inasmuch as the signs are supposed to point toward the one that the goddess will reveal. Their provisory character, on the other hand, is firmly established by the linking together of the itinerary and by the segment of this itinerary where the traveler encounters them.

90. K. Riezler, *Parmenides,* p. 51. The Platonizing tendency of Riezler's interpretation has been demonstrated by Hans-Georg Gadamer, "Riezler: Parmenides," *Gnomon* 2 (1936), pp. 77–86. This demonstration applies equally to D. O'Brien, *Etudes sur Parménides,* vol. II, pp. 149 and 161.

91. See the variations in N.-L. Cordero, *Les Deux Chemins,* p. 26 n.

92. "One" was not a number for the Greeks. It was either the unit segment that one applied a certain number of times to obtain a number, or the number thereby obtained as an encompassing unity. Aristotle will take up the ambiguity of the word "one" in arithmetic. There the word will serve as a measure for each number for which it constitutes the smallest part, but it can also serve to designate any divisible whole whatsoever because it contains some plurality. "Both the unity of measure and the one are principles." *Metaphysics* XIV 1, 1088 a 7f. The same equivocation strikes its non-arithmetical uses. "One" can designate some particular phenomenon—for example, an Athenian independently of his city or even in opposition to it—but it can also designate the whole—Athens—as constituted of parts and even in opposition to them.

93. Hans-Georg Gadamer, *Um die Begrifftswelt,* p. 370.

94. *Archein,* that Hölderlin's words describe best: "As you begin, so you shall remain" ("Wie du anfiengst, wirst du bleiben," "Der Rhein," line 48; *Sämtliche Werke,* vol II [1951], p. 143.

95. "The interlocking rings . . . must have represented a kind of archetype indefinitely repeating itself, as well as the totality of the cosmos in each individual thing." K. Reinhardt, *Parmenides und die Geschichte,* p. 19. *VS* gives references to Aetius and Cicero.

96. Meister Eckhart, *Sermons,* trans. J. Ancelet-Hustache, vol. 1, Paris, 1974, p. 123 (modified).

97. A panoramic view over all the parts of time: "The now in which God made the first man, and the now in which the last man must perish, and the now in which I speak, they are all equal in God [as well as for] the man who dwells in one and the same light with God," ibid., p. 54 (trans. modified). A panoramic view over all the parts of space: "What is beyond the seas is no further from this power than what is present [here]," ibid., p. 221 (trans. modified).

98. Parmenides precedes the debut of metaphysics (for example, Heidegger, *Parmenides,* p. 113). "Heraclitus and Parmenides were not yet 'philosophers.' Why? Because they were the greatest of thinkers." *Was is das—die Philosophie?,* Pfullingen, 1956, p. 15. Metaphysics begins with Parmenides (for example, *Sein und Zeit,* Tübingen, 1957, 8th ed., p. 171), so that a post-metaphysical thinking must "detach itself from every 'it is'" (*Acheminenement vers la Parole,* trans. J. Beaufret, W. Brockmeier, F. Fédier, Paris, 1976, p. 139). Regarding the ambiguity of the place of Parmenides in relation to metaphysics, see, for example, "La Thèse de Kant sur l'être," trans. L. Braun and M. Haar, *Questions II,* Paris, 1968, pp. 112–16.

99. N.-L. Cordero, *Les Deux Chemins* p. 38.

100. Victor Goldschmidt, "Sur le problème du 'système de Platon,'" *Rivista critica di Storia della Filosofia* 5 (1950), p. 178; "Temps historique et temps logique dans l'interprétation des systèmes philosophiques," *Actes du Congrès International de Philosophie de Bruxelles* (1953), vol. XII, pp. 7–13; *Le système stoïcien et l'idée de temps,* Paris, 1979, 4th ed., pp. 64–67, 118.

101. "[The identity of thought and being] is the profound thought [in Parmenides]. Thinking produces itself, and what is produced is a thought. Thinking is therefore identical with its being, for nothing is outside being, that great affirmation." G. W. F. Hegel, *Vorlesungen über die Geschichte der Philosophie,* vol. 17, pp. 309, 312. Gerold Prauss shrewdly observes that in so making being a position, Hegel places Parmenides on the terrain of *doxa* and makes him one of the "two-headed" ones. "Hegels Parmenides-Deutung," *Kant-Studien* 57 (1966), pp. 282–84.

102. For example, Eric Havelock, "Parmenides and Odysseus," *Harvard Studies in Classical Philology* XLII (1958), pp. 133–43.

103. Hegel, *Vorlesungen über die Geschichte der Philosophie,* vol. 17, pp. 312f.

104. Paul Ricoeur, *Time and Narrative,* vol. 1, trans. Kathleen McLaughlin and David Pellauer, Chicago, University of Chicago Press, 1985, pp. 43f.

105. Parmenides "sees the two kingdoms, that of truth and that of sensory enticements, spread out at his feet" (K. Reinhardt, *Parmenides und die Geschichte,* p. 152). Reinhardt goes too far in his Platonizing when he describes these two kingdoms as "two worlds" (ibid., p. 213).

106. Carl Schmidt, *Verfassungsrechtliche Aufsätze,* Berlin, 1958, distinguishes three basic senses of this root, 'to take,' 'to distribute,' and 'to pasture.' As such, they designate steps in the constitution of any juridical system—the laws of distribution (*suum cuique*), then the law of exploitation (*usus*) (ibid., pp. 491, 502) follow the initial taking possession of some good (*appropriatio primeava*). As for the modern word "nomad," it is derived from *nomados,* a genitive form of the adjective *nomas*—in the last of our three senses: 'grazing'—but also traveling in search of grazing land.' See also above, General Introduction, note 54.

107. Cf. Emile Benveniste, "Expression indo-duropéenne de l"éternité,'" *Bulletin de la Société de Linguistique de Paris* XXXVIII (1937), pp. 103–12.

108. Zeno conceived his aporias "against the detractors who mocked Parmenides for the incoherent implications resulting from his thesis (that only the one is), in order to prove to them that their contrary thesis (that only the many is) traps them into even more ridiculous contradictions" (K. Riezler, *Parmenides,* p. 79).

109. "To follow a story is to move forward in the midst of contingencies and peripeteia guided by an expectation that finds its fulfillment in the 'conclusion' of the story" (Ricoeur, *Time and Narrative,* p. 66).

110. Oskar Becker, "Gefüge," in *Dasein und Dawesen,* Pfüllingen, 1963, p. 136.

111. This is what Paul Ricoeur calls *mimesis*[1]. *Time and Narrative,* pp. 54–64.

112. Antonio Capizzi not only raises these questions, he answers them in great detail in his *Introduzione a Parmenide,* Bari, 1975, and *La Porta di Parmenide,* Rome, 1975.

113. Cf. above note 71.

114. Friedrich Nietzsche, *Thus Spoke Zarathustra,* Part III, "On the Spirit of Gravity."

115. See General Introduction, note 7.

116. Martin Heidegger, "Protocole d'un séminaire," trans. Jean Lauxerois and Claude Roël, in *Questions IV,* Paris, 1976, p. 78.

117. Jean-François Lyotard, *Le Différend,* Paris, p. 127.

118. K. Riezler, *Parmenides,* p. 59.

119. M. Heidegger, "Protocole," p. 77.

120. Democritus, *VS,* Fragment 118.

121. The sense of tragic necessity is already lost in Euripides: "Happy are those who, through research (*istorias*), have attained knowledge (*mathèsis*)" (*VS* Fragment 910). Democritus, with admirable precision, describes this *mathèsis* as "knowing and speaking in terms of causes" (*VS,* Fragment 118). The word sums up, one could say, the Western ideal itself. In the words of Virgil, "Happy is he who can know the causes of things (*fellix qui potuit rerum cognoscere causas, Georgics,* 2, 490). The philosophies of order (an expression that is, moreover, pleonastic) owe their long career to the intuitively obvious fact that no system can be comprehended by itself. A pile of stones does not explain a house, nor do the vocal cords explain grammar. To know a cause is precisely what defeats mortality in us (cf. *anthanzein* above, General Introduction, note 7).

II. Its Destitution

1. Two centuries after Plotinus, Proculus will devote himself to summing up the Greek heritage in honor of which he is called the first of the Scholastics. Nevertheless, this is a poor reason to argue for an end—epochal institutions and destitutions are not computed in terms of centuries; and for the thought of Proclus itself, its formalist obsession, especially with the reduction to triads, renders its Neoplatonism sterile.

2. Marinus, *Vie de proclus,* chap. X, ed. V. Cousin, *Procli philosophi platonici opera inedita,* Paris, 1864, col. 20, 15.

3. In these references to the works of Plotinus, the Roman numerals after the abbreviation *En* refer to the *Enneads,* and numerals that follow to the tractates; the numerals within brackets refer to the chronological arrangement of the tractates; then come the references to sections and lines. I do not always follow the translation by Emile Bréhier, *Enneades,* vol. I–VI, Paris, 1924–38.

4. Plotinus's questionis irreducible to the one asked by Leibniz: "[W]hy are there beings rather than nothing?" (*Principes de la nature et de la grâce,* § 7). Leibniz inquired into the principle beyond the multiple that takes account of the multiple. Plotinus's question does not thematize the multiple. It stops short of the inexplicable *in the principle itself.* Despite "mysticism," this question is also irreducible to the astonishment of Wittgenstein. "'[H]ow extraordinary that anything should exist' or 'how extraordinary that the world should exist'" (cited by R. Monk, *Ludwig Wittgenstein: The Duty of Genius,* London, 1990, p. 277).

5. Cf. Plato, *Republic* 358 a; 571 a; 580 b.

6. Cf. Plato, *Philebus* 64 e.

7. Cf. Augustine, *Confessions,* Book VII, chapter 10, 16.

8. Here is evidence that Porphyry was repulsed by the idea of incarnation: "How can one allow that the divine would become an embryo, then after his birth, that it would be enveloped in swaddling clothes, all soiled by blood, by bile—and still worse?" *Against the Christians,* Fragment 77; cf. Pierre Hadot, *Plotin ou la simplicité du regard,* Paris, 1963, p. 24.

9. Cf. the words of Goethe, who we know was a good reader of Plotinus: "[W]e have life in the colored reflection" ("Am farbingen Abglanz haben wir das Leben," *Faust* II, line. 4727)—colors spreading out before us light, which in itself is too compact.

10. Marsilio Ficino conceived of a progressive scale, with no gaps, of luminous values. On it the pure "splendor" shades off into "brilliance," then into "brightness," into "white," "yellow," and thus following throughout the whole spectrum to the point where light exhausts itself in "black" (*Opera,* vol. I, Basel, 1591, pp. 825f; Cf. André Chastel, *Marsile Ficin et l'art,* Geneva-Lille, 1954, p. 103). Moreover, between the degrees it seems necessary to insert at every turn an infinity of nuances. This is, *grosso modo,* a Neoplatonistic construction but not a Plotinian one.

11. M. Heidegger, *Chemins qui ne mènent nulle part,* trans. W. Brockmeier, Paris, 1962, p. 281. In stressing certain points, this chapter fleshes out an article that was itself something of an embryo of the present book ("L'henologie comme dépassement de la métaphysique," *Les Etudes philosophiques* XXXVII (1982), pp. 331–350.

12. M. Heidegger, *Chemins,* pp. 380f. With regard to the duality contained in the participle, cf. M. Heidegger, *Qu'appelle-t-on penser?,* pp. 202–204. The present participle is the site of the difference, at least in Greek, Latin, English, German. . . . In French, the ambiguity effects the infinitive: "il faut *être* sage," "c'est *un être* sage."

13. Substance (*ousia*) is that which "is" most intensely and authentically (*ontôs on*). *En*. VI, 3 [44], 6, 1 and 30.

14. I borrow this expression from Pierre Aubenque, "Plotin et le dépassement de l'ontologie grecque classique," in *Le Néoplatonism,* Paris, 1971, p. 102.

15. Pierre Hadot, *Porphyre et Victorinus,* Paris, 1968, vol. II, p. 104 (translation slightly modified). For the change in attribution, see Pierre Hadot, "Lêtre et l'étant dans le néoplatonism," in *Etudes néoplatoniciennes,* Neufchâtel, 1971, p. 30.

16. Cf. above, General Introduction, note 22.

17. ". . . the closure of metaphysics, that, in transgressing it, such boldness of the *Enneads* seems to indicate," Jacques Derrida, *Marges—de philosophie,* Paris, 1972, p. 206.

18. Plato, *Parmenides,* 142 b.

19. It is the accession to a nominative—here as in all epochal hegemonies—that makes for equivocal normativity. The prestige of the one among philosophers has to do with its representation being indispensable for conceiving an order. So if the one is not a noun or a name, it cannot be represented; to act "in the name of the one" thus will no longer be able to mean "to act in accordance with the order."

20. *En*. VI, 6 [34], 3, 1–7. For a commentary, see Pierre Hadot, *Plotin,* pp. 29 and 32ff.

21. Heidegger describes the three terms in several manners: "beings, beingness, being"; or "that which is present, the mode of presence, the coming to presence" (*das Anwesende, die Anwesenheit, das Anwesen*); or again "that which is manifest, the character of being manifest, the manifesting" (*das Offengare, die Offenbarkeit, das Offenbaren*), cf. "Protocol d'un séminaire sur la conférence 'Temps et Etre'" (trans. J. Lauxerois and C. Roëls, *Questions IV*, p. 59, here is unintelligible). Heidegger makes an allusion to the *hen* as singular event, for example, in the lines cited above as an epigraph to this chapter.

22. "In a battle, in the midst of a route, a soldier stops himself, another stops, and yet another, until the army is returned to its initial order" (Aristotle, *Second Analytic,* II, 19; 100 a 11–13). In Aristotle the image serves to illustrate how an *arché* essentially works. On the other hand, in the examples of it that inspired Plotinus—and even if he often speaks of the *arché,* calling the one the "principle of being" (*arché ontos, En.* VI, 9 [9], 9,1)—the *arché* is a matter of contextualization, of phenomenalization.

23. Even "when you think [the one] as Intelligence or as God, it is still something more" (*En.* VI, 9 [9], 6, 12).

24. See above, chapter 5, note 107.

25. Plotinus does not hesitate to attribute efficient, formal, or final causality to the one. As for matter, paradoxically it is said to resemble the one. It is also devoid of form (*En.* I, 8 [51], 8, 21 and II, 5 [25], 4, 12), non-being (*En.* II, 5 [25], 4, 11), without limit (*En.* I, 8 (51), 3, 13) and simple potency (*En.* II, 5 [25], 5 5). But "when we designated it a cause, we are saying something not about it, but to us, namely, that something of it reaches us" (*En.* VI, 9 [9], 3, 49).

26. "Time is the number of a movement according to a before and after," Aristotle, *Physics* IV, 11; 220 a 24. This definition is foundational, at least if "in the history of Western metaphysics there has never been an interpretation of movement more difficult to think than Aristotle's," M. Heidegger "Ce qu'est et comment se détermine la *phusis*" (trans. F. Fédier, *Questions II*), p. 245.

27. Augustine, *Confessions,* XII, 8, 8.

28. Cf. *The City of God,* XI, 6 and *The Trinity,* IV, 18, 24. In his treatise on time, Plotinus calls eternity *adiastatos,* 'non-extended' (*En.* III, 7 [45], 3, 15).

29. *Confessions,* XI, 26, 33 and 20, 26.

30. Heidegger cites the *Physics* ("if there were no soul, time would be impossible," IV, 14) as well as the *Confessions* (XI 26, 33) as examples of the "ordinary" concept of time (curiously, elsewhere he does not hesitate to amalgamate these two conceptions, cf. *Die Grundprobleme der Phänomenologie, Gesamtausgabe,* vol. 24, Frankfurt, 1975, p. 327). He adds that "in principle, the interpretation of Dasein as temporality is not situated outside the horizon of the ordinary concept of time," *Being and Time,* § 82 (*Sein und Zeit,* Halle, 1941, p. 427).

31. Heidegger, *Chemins,* p. 59; *Nietzsche,* trans. P. Klossowski, Paris, 1971, vol. II, p. 337.

32. Heidegger, "Séminare du Thor, 1969" (trans. J. Beaufret, *Questions IV*), pp. 268f.

33. "Each time, the event brings together the temporal limit in which history grasps the guarantee of an epoch" (*Nietzsche,* vol. II, p. 398).

34. *En.* III, 7 [45], 11, 42–46. By translating *bios* as 'state of life,' I follow Hans Jonas, "Plotin über Ewigkeit und Zeit," in *Politische Ordnung und menschliche Existenz, Festgabe für Erik Vögelin,* ed. A. Dempf, et al, Munich, 1962, pp. 310f.

35. *Chronoun, En.* III 7 [45], 11, 30. According to H. R. Schwyzer ("Plotinos," *Realenzyclopädie der klassichen Altertumswissenschaft* XXI/1 col. 525, 14), this verb is probably a neologism coined by Plotinus himself.

36. One may object that Plato already conceived of time as "the moving image of eternity" (*Timaeus* 37 d) and that, if the manner of thinking new with Plotinus consists in reattaching time to eternity as a copy to its model, it amounts to the most traditional Platonism. The objection has been struck down through the forceful philosophical arguments of Rémi Brague. The so-called definition of time in the *Timaeus* was "constituted" by Plotinus, and is "based on an error in the assignation of the grammatical subject" (*Du temps chez Platon et Aristote,* Paris, 1982, pp. 24 and 69).

37. In the youthful works one nevertheless finds many paraphrases of ascending movement such as Plato describes in the *Symposium. Cf. En.* I, 6 [1], 7–8 and elsewhere.

38. *En.* III, 7 [45], 5, 16–22. The reading proposed here of the distinction between perpetuity (*aidiotès*) and eternity (*aion*) as two *logoi* stemming from the mediating hypostasis differs from those which do not admit of any difference of meaning between the two terms (see, for example, H. Jonas, "Plotin über Ewigkeit und Zeit," p. 297, note 3). The double character of eternity as a middle term, which is what I intend to establish, would give an architectonic foundation to the remark by Werner Beierwaltes, *Plotin: Über Ewigkeit und Zeit,* Frankfurt, 1967, pp. 156–158, according to which these terms are two nouns for the same *Sache,* only viewed from two different perspectives. The Latin authors will have recourse to the opposition between perpetuity and eternity to distinguish, for example, between *sempiternitas mundi* and *aeternitas dei.* So far as the substantive form of the verb *to einai* in this citation is concerned, it confirms

the distinction I made above between negative henology and negative theology. Plotinus equates "being" to eternity, to God, to constant life, which is to say, to hypostatic Intelligence. The same equation leads him again to speak of *to d'estin* (ibid. 6, 18) and of the *esti monon* (ibid. 3, 34), both of which refer to eternity.

39. "It is first of all necessary to find out what eternity is, for once the immobile model is known, its image—which we understand is time—will be more clearly apprehended. But if we imagine what time is before having contemplated what eternity is, one can, through recollection, pass from the sensible back to the intelligible so as to represent the being that time resembles, if it is true that time is a copy of eternity," ibid. 1, 16–24. Plotinus does not engage in this ascending, inductive reasoning.

40. *Peri to hen* (*En.* III, 7 [45], 6, 2f). Eternity is *kentro-eidès,* it is turned toward the center around which it traces the periphery.

41. Whatever is in time being "lacks" (*elleipein,* ibid. 4, 15), "attracts" being (*helkon to einai* 4, 31), must constantly "acquire" being (*epiktasthai,* 4, 20), and "aspires" to being (*ephesei tini ousias,* 4, 31) as that which is to come (*ephesis tou mellontos,* 4, 34). These expressions have allowed Hans Jonas to write that "for Plotinus, the future is what is properly temporal in time, the future is the mode in which time temporalizes itself" ("Plotin über Ewigkeit und Zeit," p. 298). To possess their end is therefore not the fate of sensible things; here the Aristotelian concept of *entelecheia* does not apply to the sublunary world.

42. Eternity differs from time in that thinking is not subject to the future, to the not-yet—the noetic act is identical to its object, the *noeton.* On the other hand, eternity also differs from the one since noetic identity unites two terms. "Intelligence is number, but essential multiplicity has the essential one as its principle. This essential multiplicity is the intelligence and the intelligible taken together, if indeed there is a duality" (*En* III, 8 [30], 9, 4f).

43. The "nature" of the Latins and the "self-consciousness" of the moderns, as we will see, are such ultimate referents with content.

44. The affinity with Heidegger as well as the distance in relation to him are equally obvious. *Gelassenheit*—'serenity,' 'releasement,' 'letting-be'—constitutes for Heidegger, beginning in the middle of the 1930s, not only the essential trait of thought (which is to say, of *Dasein* such as he understands that term then), but also, and even more decisively, the trait of being as event. Heidegger seems to want to link *lassen* to the verb *parechein,* which means 'to offer,' 'make possible,' 'to expose' (cf. "La Doctrine de Platon sur la verité," in trans. A. Préau, *Questions II,* p. 152), rather than to *eaein.* Nevertheless, this affinity in the manner in which man fulfills his life as well as his act of being seems to me to bring Heidegger close to Plotinus on one crucial point. One cannot distinguish between the one and unification as one does between substance and its act; similarly, Heideggerian *Sein* is not some thing ("the wholly other of all beings is nothingness; but this nothingness is unfolded as being," trans. R. Munier, *Questions I,* Paris, 1968, p. 304), but a process: *letting*-be present, *Anwesen*lassen (with the emphasis placed on the 'letting,' cf. "Séminare du Thor, 1969," in trans. J. Beaufret, *Questions IV,* p. 300). Of course, "to unite" (Plotinus) and "being" (Heidegger) belong to two universes of thought between which there are at the most resemblances of configurations. But without dwelling too long here on the obvious distance, we can say that the figure of "thinking" is identical to that of being, whether one describes their formal identity as union (Plotinus) or as letting-be (Heidegger). We may add that Meister Eckhart, the "missing link" between Plotinus and Heidegger in this matter, who states most clearly the occurrent character of the identity between the essence of being and the essence of "something in man"; cf. below, "The Double Bind of Principle and Origin."

45. *En.* III, 8 [30], 10,1. The way the word *dunamis* is used here is irreducible to what Aristotle makes of it. By describing the one in terms of its "potency," Plotinus means to speak neither of hyletic potentiality waiting to be actualized (cf. Aristotle, *Metaphysics* VIII, 2; 1042 b 9), nor of the kinetics to which the conceptual pair belongs that is translated as "actuality and potentially" (cf. ibid. IV, 12; 1019 a 15). In German, the Plotinian *dunamis* is better translated as *Ermöglichung.* In the present context, the way Plotinus uses this word amounts to an excessive appropriation of Plato, who wrote: "As for potency, I only consider that to which it refers and what its effects are." The use by Plotinus is excessive because for Plato there are numerous *dunameis,* "the strongest being knowledge" (*Republic* V, 477 c–d). When all is said and done, in Plotinus there can be but one single *dunamis,* the one.

46. See above, General Introduction, note 29.

47. Porphyry, *The Life of Plotinus,* § 23, 16f. The entire treatise, *En.* VI, 9 [9], describes, in the developments actually indicating experience, the union of the individual soul with the one.

48. Giorgio Agamben, *La Communauté qui vient,* Paris, 1990, pp. 68f. I bear this description in mind, but not all the connotations of the "whomever" that Agamben gives it—especially the relationship to the idea.

49. There certainly is *no* reference to "the origin of the Principle" (as George Leroux would have it, *Plotin: Traité sur la liberte et la volonté de l'Un* (*Ennéade* VI, 8 [39]), Paris, 1990, p. 25). Whatever

could this *arché* be that is more originary than originary—an *arché* beyond the anarchic *arché* that is the one (but that Leroux calls "the Principle"), itself beyond the metaphysical *arché* that is the Intellect? Neither does it have anything to do with a conjunction of "history and ontology" (p. 63), nor the search for a genetic beginning.

50. Philip Merlan, "Plotinus" in the *Encyclopedia of Philosophy*, New York and London, 1967, vol. VI, pp. 352 and 259.

51. Porphyry, *The Life of Plotinus*, § 2, 26.

52. This does not mean that with his doctrine of free will Plotinus has "placed something in the one that *is not the one itself*" (Th. Gollwitzer, *Plotins Lehre von der Willensfreiheit*, 2 volumes [vol. I, Kempten, 1900; vol. II Kaiserslautern, 1902], vol. II, p. 48). Rather than positing the other *of* the one, we have to try to think the other *in* the one. If we do not, we will come to the conclusion, quite as regrettable as that of Gollwitzer, namely, that there is a "dualism of principles" in the one (ibid. p. 51).

53. In the very first monotheistic speculations the term *anarchos* denoted first of all the perpetuity of the world, of time, or of destiny. But in doing so it also connoted the essence of God as absolute *arché* (cf. Philo of Alexandria, *On the Eternity of the World*, X, 53 and XV, 75).

54. The tractate *En*. VI, 8 begins with a warning: We must not confuse these two terms with those of the Aristotelian idiom (1, 13). In the one, *dunamis* results from willing (9, 44) which, for it, is always an act and therefore *energeia*. The two terms are not opposed—they converge on the free will.

55. See *Lexicon Plotinianum*, ed. J. H. Sleeman and G. Pollet, Louvain, 1980 col. 850f.

56. Plotinus does not speak of the one as being simple "in itself," namely, essentially simple (cf. the *Lexicon Plotinianum.*, under *haplous*).

57. To say "the one *and* its act . . ." (for example, *En* VI, 8 [39], 16, 30) may make one think (it is here that some objections are directed at Plotinus) that there is a duality in the one (ibid. 13, 3); or even that it is subject to chance and accident (7, 32); that it could be other than it is (21, 1ff.) or, on the contrary, that its acting necessarily follows from its being (7, 37); or that it is invested with accidents (16, 18). . . . Such misinterpretations are inevitable as soon as one neglects the *epikeina*, Plotinus says, and *treats the one as a being* (11, 7).

58. The Intellect is beings, and in this sense 'the whole' (*to pan*). It is also, properly speaking, the hypostatic level dialecticized: "[I]n becoming someone, you are no longer the whole. You add a negation to it. You become the whole only by rejecting this negation" (*En*. VI, 5 [23], 12, 22). "The dialectic bears upon the good and its contrary. . . . It is fixed in the intelligible, and it is there that it limits its activity. . . . But when it gathers itself into the one, it considers from on high the logic that treats of propositions and syllogisms, and it abandons them as one leaves to others the art of teaching to write" (*En*. I, 3 [20], 4, 6f).

59. On the complex constellations between freedom and necessity in Plotinus as well as between the will and automatism, see H. F. Müller, "Plotinus über Notwendigkeit und Freiheit," *Neue Jahrbücher für das klassiche Altertum XXXIII* (1914), pp. 462–488. Elsewhere, the author is not unaware of the conflict between the universal and the singular ("not only the soul of the world, but also the individual soul is supreme principle," p. 465), but he ends up by *reconciling* its double bind in "a personal God" (p. 488).

60. Etiological discourse confined itself to the Intellect. The causes are ideas. Even liberty, thought in terms of the one, undermines the prestige of Aristotle's *Physics* which till then was uncontested. As G. Leroux has done well to remark, Plotinus was the first to stop incorporating freedom "into physics" (*Plotin: Traité sur la liberte*, p. 49).

61. Similarly, we will soon see the reverse program—namely, the return of imitative being (the sensible) to the being imitated (the intelligible)—exhausts ethics.

62. On the teleological notion of "the whole" in the middle and late Stoics, see below, chapter 8.

63. "He who complains about the nature of the world therefore does not know what he is doing nor the extent of his audacity. He is unaware of the continuous order of things, from the first to the second, then to the third, and so on up till the last ones. Therefore, one must not insult beings because they are inferior to the first ones. One has to accept with gentleness the nature of all beings" (*En*. II, 9 [33] 13, 1f). The "continuous order of things" obviously signifies here the hypostatic architecture and not, as in the Stoics, the great chain of individual-family-city-nation-humanity-nature-world-God formed by the principle of a continuous telocracy. As for being "gentle" (*paros*), in the hypostatic architecture, this quality determines the relation of the superior to the inferior. It is, notably, the technical term with which to describe our relations to the body and to society. See P. Hadot, *Plotin ou la simplicité du regard*, pp. 132–135.

64. It has in fact been possible to sustain a continuity in the sense of freedom running throughout the three hypostases. Although in other respects excellent in its philological as well as exegetical precision, it is here that we see the philosophical weakness of G. Leroux's book. "The structure of the treatise consists in transferring to the One . . . the predicates of human freedom taken up by ethics" (*Plotin: Traité sur la liberte* p. 13). This thesis eliminates *inessential* freedom from the one for the sake of an "act eternally

identical to its essence" (p. 94, contrary to other remarks by this author, what he says here is true). Plotinus dedicated three tractates to moral or ethical freedom: "On Destiny" (*En.* III, 1 [3]), "On Providence" (*En.* III, 2–3 [47f]), and "Difficulties Relative to the Soul" (*En.* IV, 3–4 [27f]).

65. Plotinus borrows these expressions from Plato and Aristotle so as to speak of freedom. They are difficult to translate—to *eph'hèmin*—or *ep'autois*—as well as *to autoexousion* to signify 'what is within our power.' Plato also attaches it both to *boulèsis,* 'intention,' and through it, to *logos.* By *ekousion* he means what we deliberately do, with conviction and without constraint; by *thelesis* he means the mobility of action that is 'as it should be' (see the references to Plato, *En.* IV, [39], 18, 42); and finally, *eleutheron* describes all acts that are opposed to the condition of the slave.

66. *En.* IV, 3 [27], 12,1. The mirror of Dionysus is an Orphic symbol of dismemberment.

67. *En.* III, 6 [26], 5, 1 and I, 1 [53] 3, 16. Paul Oskar Kristeller, author of one of the best studies on freedom in Plotinus (*Der Begriffe der Seele in der Ethik Plotins,* Tübingen, 1929), so reduces henology to ethics as to give a reconstruction of its that is as partial as it is biased, partial because the freedom *of the one* thereby suffers an eclipse; biased because the doctrine of the Soul gets transformed into a philosophy of consciousness.

68. Ever since Plato, philosophers have exhorted one to "care for death" (*melete thanatou, Phaedo,* 81). Montaigne declares "that to philosophize, is to learn to die" (*Essais,* I, 20). In the face of this, they have also taught us that to philosophize is "to mature in view of another birth" (*in alium maturescimus partum*) (Seneca, *epist.* 102, 23). To die in the singular and by its gripping assault—to be reborn to a non-captive life freed from these assaults thanks to the knowledge of the universal. But in Plotinus these exhortations are relevant only to the gap between the Soul and Intellect, the gap where the dispersive separation is transformed into solitude. At least in reading the tractates on freedom and will of the one they lose all relevance for the passage beyond the Intellect and thus beyond beings. Advancing—or retreating, or climbing up, in brief, changing place—*epekeina tês ousias,* we "see" in the one, not the shining universal in all simplicity and all purity, but the origin of this freedom which *detaches* the Soul, which *isolates* the Intellect, and introduces the *whomever* into the one.

69. The intoxication of love, says Plotinus, dulls the Intellect, making it forgetful of distinctions. The *thinking Intellect* knows and recognizes otherness (between knowing and known), whereas the *loving Intellect* is "confused" about otherness (*En.* VI, 7 [38], 35, 24 and 33).

70. In the way Plotinus reads Plato's *Symposium, ekplettesthai* increases to the extent that the soul raises itself up, "wanting to unite with the one, what terror in joy" (*En.* I, 6 [1], 7, 14). "That we might seize it itself [. . .], we will be terrified of it" (*En.* VI, 8 [39], 19, 2–8). John Rist has done a good job of showing, first of all, that it is indeed a matter of terror and not of astonishment, as Bréhier translates it, and that secondly this terror results from desire willing possession (*Eros and Psyché,* Toronto, 1964, p. 98).

71. This is the interpretation of John Rist (*Human Value,* Leiden, 1982, p. 109). To preserve an ultimate foundation in henology, despite the freedom and will of the one, we have few options. One must reduce the one either to the predicates of willing or to a describable being. This second reduction was effected by Hilary Armstrong, according to whom love—and thus the will—by itself makes the subject more closely present to itself than can knowledge (*The Architecture of the Intelligible Universe in the Philosophy of Plotinus,* Cambridge, 1940, p. 13). In these two cases one ends up necessarily negating *epekeina,* thus by pulling the one down to the Intellect.

72. Individual souls are "sisters"—not parts, as the Stoics taught—of the soul of the world (*En.* IV, 3 [27], 6, 13). The whole treatise V, 7 [18] is dedicated to demonstrating that the Intellect contains ideas, even of singular things.

73. Angelius Silesius repeats a general Neoplatonic exhortation when he writes:

> Daß du nicht Menschen liebst, das tust du recht und wohl.
> Die Menschenheit ists, die man im Menschen lieben soll.

"That you do not love men, in this you do well / it is humanity that you must love in man" (*Pèlerin cherubinique. Cherubinischer Wandersmann,* Paris, 1946, p. 86), a general Neoplatonic exhortation, but no longer a Plotinian one.

74. Werner Beierwaltes, *Denken des Einen,* Frankfurt, 1985, p. 145.

75. On two occasions in the tractates on freedom and will Plotinus affirms that the one is *monachon* (VI, 8 [39], 7, 38 and 9,10), the word the French translators render as *seul,* 'alone.' This translation does not capture its semantic precision. Plotinus preserves the Aristotelian use where the word signifies 'only' or 'in a single way,' in an 'in definable' sense (see, for example, *Metaphysics,* Z, 15; 1040 a 29, as well as the commentary by L. Robin, *Aristote,* Paris, 1944, pp. 144f). The one is in its own way, in that it does not fall under the elements of the definition—is outside genera. R. Harder translates *monarchon* still more correctly as *einzigartig,* 'of the singular species.'

76. Willy Theiler attributes the argument to Plotinus himself, who supposedly is engaged in a *Gedan-*

kenexperiment. Plotinus would then be considering the hypothesis of a "sub-freedom," restricted to the Intellect and thus submitted to polymorphic thought, rather than a "hyper-freedom" (notes to Richard Harder, *Plotins Schriften,* Hamburg, 1956–71, vol. IVB, p. 372). Emile Bréhier, for his part, attributed the opposing argument to the gnostics (*Plotin, Ennéades,* Paris, 1923–38, vol. VI, 2, p. 120). The two attributions raise more problems than they solve.

77. See J. Rist, *Human Value,* p. 107.

78. According to the German editor, Plotinus had in mind here "the Epicureans" to whom—with the same gesture of exclusion as in the tractate VI, 8, more than half of which nevertheless seems to be dedicated to them—he would not even have had to "pay serious attention." (R. Harder, *Plotins Schriften,* vol. I, b, p. 473).

79. H. Jonas, "Plotin über Ewigkeit und Zeit," p. 314. The remark by Derrida cited above (note 17), ". . . the closure of metaphysics, that, in transgressing it, such boldness of the *Enneads* seems to indicate" may be able to emphasize this very originary gap. It would therefore be necessary to read, in the citation, quotation marks around the word "audacity." Indeed, it is the *tolma* in the one that no metaphysical discourse can capture.

80. Translation by Bréhier. The word "principle" is not in the text (which only says *to skoteinon*), but here it is useful, and lacking anything better, I will have recourse to it.

81. In this refutation of atomism, one should translate *dunamis* as 'force' rather than as 'power.'

82. Naguib Baladi describes audacity as "the force of the One" and consequently speaks of the "audacious force" ("Origine et signification de l'audace chez Plotin," in *Le Néoplatonisme,* Paris, 1971, pp. 92 and 97). It is not quite clear what status the author means to give to this supplementary *dunamis.* So, when he claims that the audacious is "not only of thought, but also of being" (p. 90), it is no doubt necessary to understand it is as ". . . but also *of the one.*"

83. In Plotinus's architectonic of the world, *logos* signifies first of all "pivots" between hypostases (cf.. Hans Früchtel, *Weltenwurf und Logos,* Frankfurt, 1970, pp. 25, 41f, and elsewhere).

84. G. Agamben, *La Communauté qui vient,* p. 9.

85. W. Beierwaltes, *Denken des Einen,* p. 142.

86. In the whole of the *Enneads,* the use of this word is so rare that the translator of VI, 8 simply lets it pass. Cf. G. Leroux, *Plotin: Traité sur la liberte,* pp. 173 and 337f.

Part Two. In the Name of Nature: The Latin Hegemonic Fantasm

1. In general, the Sophists subordinated conventions to natural necessity (even if, among the different Sophists, this necessity does not designate the same thing). In this sense with them one can surely speak of the normativity of nature (see Antiphon, *VS* II, 87, B 44, as well as the discourse by Hippias in Plato's *Protagorus* 337 c 7f and by Callicles in the *Gorgias* 483 b–484 c). But above all the Sophists present themselves as experts in ethical and pedagogical matters. Their instructions on how to acquire virtue were especially directed at political excellence. According to them, the acquisition of this depended on three factors: natural disposition (*phusis*), instruction (*didaché*), and exercise (*askêsis*). In accordance with the expertise on which they prided themselves, they ranked the last two of these above the first (cf. for example, *Critias, VS* II, 88, B 9). Consequently it would be a mistake to attribute to the Sophists a normativity substantively irreducible to nature.

We could even say that in a general manner with the Greeks, the linking together of *phusis-metron-diké* takes the place of what later will be called the law of nature. Through this linking together, the experience of positive law doubtlessly tends to be extrapolated toward the cosmos—a maximization that we will see very much at work in the Romans. The chief witness of this sort of extension of measurement would be Solon (see Fragment 11 cited above, chapter 2, note 55, as well as Fragment 16 cited above, note 3; Fragments 54 and 94 of Heraclitus may have been inspired by these Fragments). Whatever obeys the same *metron,* the same principle of order, is *symmetrical*—a notion that is equally mathematical, juridical, and cosmic. So, even when enlisting "nature" to translate *phusis,* the linking together in question does not permit us simply to treat nature as an ultimate referent.

It is with Plato that the expressions "according to nature" and "against nature" signify a norm, above all in the sexual legislation of *The Laws* (for example, 636 a–b). But even there *phusis* functions differently than as a referent establishing the continuity of ends. It is conceived systematically in terms of animals (cf. K. J. Dover, *Greek Homosexuality,* Harvard University Press, Cambridge, 1989, pp. 165–167 and 185f). Thus, in the words of the pseudo-Aristotelian *Problemata* (IV, 6), "those who are effeminate by nature . . . are constituted contrary to nature." The cause here is on the order of anatomy. According to them, sperm is secreted in the rectum. "They feel desire in a different place from seminal secretion. Being similar to women in this respect, this is why they are insatiable. Because the liquid is basically less abundant, it is not poured outside and cools off quickly" (cited and commented on by Dover, ibid. pages 170ff.). Nature attains hegemony not through zoological extrapolation, but through teleological universalization beginning with Roman Republican experience.

2. The first of these two notions, perhaps the creation of Aristotle (*Physics,* II, 1), refers to the sum of extra-human givens, or even just to the world of bodies in movement (for example, *On the Heavens* I, 1; 268 a 1ff. and III, 1; 298 a 27ff.). In following the second, Aristotle for example says that "*phusis* has made all things with a view to man" (*Politics,* I, 8; 1256 b 22; cf. *Physics,* II, 2; 194 a 35; and more generally, *Metaphysics,* V, 4).

In Aristotle there is a primacy of *phusis* in this sense that physical movement remains the guiding phenomenon for his entire philosophy. The study of kinetics provided him with his schemes for thinking and his vocabulary. Hence, we can understand the term "metaphysics" differently (there being no evidence of this term before the first century of our era)—neither as an exterior, classificatory designation of books arranged in a library *above* those dealing with physics, nor as a systematic and Platonizing program for going *beyond* physical phenomena. The group of texts entitled *Metaphysics* develop, in scattered treatises, certain principles discovered with regard to movement. Perhaps the "meta" is then not to be understood as an "above," or as a "beyond," but as an "after" in the sense of a corollary to the study that is to guide all knowledge, a corollary to the analysis of *kinésis.* Understood in this way, the *Metaphysics* would signify some "Supplements to the Physics." A primacy of *phusis,* yes, but in the organization of knowledge, not in some normativity for acting.

3. It is true, in a certain manner, that this principle of continuity is at the very origin of Greek democracy. Solon, the paradigmatic figure of the enlightened legislator, will not only give Athenians their laws, but also explain what the public work of a legitimizing authority is—it is an identical "measure" that administers both human and extra-human processes. "What is most difficult to catch sight of is the invisible measure of knowledge, the sole guardian in all things of the limit" (Fragment 16). Now, this measure that is difficult to see imposes a necessity on the acts of man that is as ineluctable as what links antecedents and consequences in nature: "[F]rom the clouds falls the power of snow or hail, and the thunder from the bright lightning. Men who grow too big bring ruin to the city, and by their own ignorance a people falls into the servitude of a single person" (Fragment 10). Here the affairs of the city obey the same order as do atmospheric phenomena. In this, Solon indeed incorporates into one and the same point of view natural and political events, measuring the legitimacy of the latter in terms of the regularity of the former. But obviously this does not mean that nature here works upon action as does a maximal norm. Rather, this norm is the "measure." It recalls the *logos* of Heraclitus which, exactly, likes to hide itself (*VS,* B 123). So, if this *logos* is also *nomos, diké* and *phusis* (*VS* B 30, 31, 33, 94, 114, 123), it is because its essence consists in "homologating," and in this respect it remains a figure of the one (B 50). The Stoics, who will be examined below, were inspired by its Heraclitean origins. The good life is the one homologated by nature (Zeno: *to homologoumenos* or *akolouthôs to phusei zên, SVF* I, 45, 21). But the expression *nomos phuseôs* does not occur in the ancient Stoics (it is attributed to Zeno by Cicero, *On the Nature of the Gods,* I, 14, 36). Also, as Otto Rieth has shown very well (*Grundbegriffe der stoischen Ethik,* Berlin, 1933, pp. 70ff.), the meaning of the principle of Stoic continuity is still henological. With the passage from the ancient Stoics to the middle Stoics, normative nature will substitute for the normative one—for us, given the fortuitous selection of extant documents *such as exposited by Cicero.* Just as we lack supporting documents to judge the justice of this exposition, we have been able to say that Cicero himself is "the legitimate father of the theory of natural law," Ernest Fortin, "Augustine, Thomas Aquinas, and the Problem of Natural Law," *Mediaevalia,* IV (1978), p. 183.

4. See above, chapter 1, note 16.

5. In this respect, the Platonic innovation consists in identifying *phusis* with the ideas. Thus Plato speaks of the *phusis* of a number or of duty (*Republic* VII, 525 c and V, 476 b), understanding by that their truthful being, their essence. The loss of the city indicates what is "just by nature" (*phusei dikaion, Republic* VI, 501 b 2). But one cannot deduce from this an ultimate normativity of "nature." On the contrary, nature remains subordinated to the *techné* of the demiurge, and this not only in the *Timaeus* (cf. *Sophist* 265 c–e and *Phaedo* 99 d–e). The expression "natural law" is found twice in Plato, but opposed to that of "moral law." In the *Timaeus* (83 e), it is applied to the purifying virtues of excreting bodily liquids; in the *Gorgias* (483 e), it designates the strongest law.

6. For the works of Cicero, the abbreviation *Law* refers to *De legibus,* the abbreviation *Rep.* to *De republica,* and the abbreviation *Off.* to *De Officiis.* The bilingual edition *De la republique, Des lois* (trans. Charles Appuhn, Paris, 1954) is of unequaled quality. Books within these texts are indicated by Roman numerals, and sections are indicated by Arabic numerals. A similar convention will be used to refer to the works of Augustine: *The City of God* (*City*) and *Confessions* (*Conf.*)

7. Cf. Vitruve, *De l'architecture,* Book I, chapter 1, 7.

8. "From the concept of the true will be born a great and immutable joy," Seneca, *On the Happy*

Life 4, 5. There is no source of happiness that will compete with nature, for which the truth is the principle of continuity. Conversely, "we cannot call a man happy who is thrown outside the truth" (5, 2).

9. Because philosophers know the immutable telic continuity, their life is but a note accompanying death—*tota phiosophorum vita commentatio mortis est* (Cicero, *Tusculanes*, I, 74). See also the *Letters* of Seneca (74, 17; 36, 10; 102, 24–26; 114, 26; etc.), as well as the resonances in Montaigne, a come-lately Stoic: "[T]o philosophize is to learn to die" (*Essays*, I, 20).

10. Francis Bacon, *De dignitate et augmentis scientiarium*, III, 5; *The Works of Lord Bacon*, vol. 2,1,1841, p. 340.

11. The given order, too, is *thesis*, it is true, but this inasmuch as it depends on an anterior principle "according to nature"; the posited order depends on an anterior principle "according to free choice" (*pros ton tuchon*, Aristotle, *Metaphysics*, V, 11; 1018 b 9f). Needless to say, for Aristotle only the first thesis is in conformity with being.

12. Aeschylus, *The Persians*, lines 744–751.

13. *"tagrapta kasphala theôn nomima,"* Sophocles, *Antigone*, lines 441f.

14. Even for King Lear, carrying the dead Cordelia, his daughter, in his arms, there is nothing left to do but "howl, howl, howl, howl" (Act V, Scene 3, line 257). It was as if Lear were dead ("You do me wrong to take me out of the grave," Act IV, Scene 7, line 45); seeing Cordelia, he comes back to life ("Fair daylight. . . ," Act IV, Scene 7, line 53). Does this resurrection serve as some sort of *Aufhebung* reconciling life and death? It would be a strange reconciliation that linked the "howl, howl, . . ." and revealed the irreparable, "never, never, never, never, never" (Act V, Scene 3, line 309). Lear himself says what he has seen—"that heaven's vault should crack" (Act V, Scene 3, line 259). Like Creon, and just as belatedly, he saw the vault, or the foundation, broken.

15. Cf. above, Wittgenstein's meta-regional usage of the contradiction between thermodynamic and mechanical principles, General Introduction, notes 52–53.

16. Apulée, *Platon et sa doctrine*, II, 22.

17. "I call fiction (*plasma*) the violence done to truth with a view to satisfying a hypothesis," Aristotle, *On the Heavens*, III, 7; 306 a 12.

18. Such is the view of Pierre Aubenque: "[I]t is no exaggeration to say that the contemplation of 'visible gods' played, for Aristotle, the role of the *cogito* in Descartes: that of a 'certain and unshakable foundation' . . . ," *Le Problème de l'être chez Aristote*, Paris, 1966, p. 339.

19. *"transilire mortalitatem suam",* Seneca, Letter 6, 1; cf. *Natural Questions* I, Preface, 17.

I. Its Institution

20. *The Laws*, I, 22, 58; Cf *Tusculanes* and 1, 5–7, and *De officiis*, and 1,153. To correctly translate the latter title remains an undertaking destined to failure (cf. below, note 28). Therefore, I will cite it in the Latin.

21. Cicero, *De finibus bonorum et malorum*, III, 19.

22. The work follows very closely the *Peri Kathekiontos* (lost) of Panaetius of Rhodes.

23. The solution to Kant is found in Max Pohlenz, *Antikes Führertum*, Leipzig, 1934, p. 129. We leave open whether, as Pohlenz thinks (ibid.), the imperative is valid only for the great number of weak people incapable of transmuting impulses arising from the body into pure rational judgments. Cicero comments on the distinction between *kathékon* and *kathortoma*, in *De finibus bonorum et malorum*, III, 24 c and 32 b.

24. For a Greek, it is true that "ethics of the site" would be a pleonasm, *êthos* designating the place that one occupies in the city; but the shift that I seek to retrace has to do with *our nature* as it assigns us our place. The Greeks knew nothing of such an assigning agent.

25. Panaetius of Rhodes, cited by Seneca, *Letter* 116, 5. For the general sense of *kathékon* in the Stoics, see the description of Diogenes Laertius. "[T]hey call fitting that which, once accomplished, can be rationally defended: for example, that which is consistent with the processes of physical life (*zoé*) such as one finds also in plants and animals. Also in these, indeed, one observes acts that are fitting. Moreover, we say that the first to have employed this term "fitting" was Zeno. He used it in its etymological sense: 'to happen to someone' (*kata tinas hékein*). There would be therein, finally, an activity arising from dispositions which were in accord with nature (*kata phusin*)," *Lives and Opinions of Philosophers*, VII, 107f.

26. Cicero, *De finibus bonorum et malorum*, III, 16.

27. Ernst Bernert, *De vi atque usu vocabuli officii*, Breslau, 1930, pp. 4–9 and 25–42.

28. "Quod cur factum sit, ratio probabilis reddi possit," *De Officiis*, I, 8. The phrase goes back to Panaetius. The word that Cicero translates *eulogon* as is *probabilis* (which I have translated as 'well-founded'). This is one of the lax points in his translations, for which it was standard fare in the nineteenth

century to call Cicero "superficial, moreover boasting about his inconsistency," "messy," etc. (cf. *Das neue Cicerobild*, ed. Karl Büchner, Darmstadt, 1971, pp. 22f. and 60). All that interests us here is the new constellation of Latin terminology.

29. *De Officiis*, I, 107. In the following, the numbers in parentheses refer to sections of this First Book.

30. "The ones are prized for their quickness on the course, the others for their vigor in battle. In their aspect, the ones have dignity, the others charm. . . . Socrates was likable and cheerful, witty in conversation: this is what the Greeks call *eirôn*—always skillful at pretending. Pythagoras and Pericles acquired great authority without ever letting themselves be given to gaiety. As for Hannibal . . ." (107f).

31. Cicero, *De natura deorum*, II, 12, 33.

32. Letter to Atticus 16, 14, 3.

33. One can see this in Augustine himself where we will nevertheless soon see the fidelity to singulars. The things in time "are far below [eternal things], and even they are not" (*nec sunt, Confessions*, XI, 6, 8).

34. Augustine, *De vera religione*, 39, 72.

35. This nascent Latin interiority obviously is not to be confused with post-Cartesian interiority. The first is instituted under the postulate of a *freedom in me that I am not*, that nevertheless is more intimately present to me than I am not it. On the other hand, modern interiority situates the freedom that I am over against *mechanisms in me that I am not*, or at least not truly. In the nineteenth century, the *Bildung* of this interiority produces the idealist fervor in Germany and that of the private journal in France. The drama, or the comedy, of the mind assailed by the infernal sexual machine has been staged by Descartes, not by Paul or Augustine. Cognitive freedom and mechanic necessity are opposed in an *other alterity* that is not that of a strange freedom in me and of my exterior corrupted by my own faults. If today interiority makes us tremble less, it is not because we will have learned to count beyond the two in this domain, but rather because both—mind-computer and body-producer (an excellent example, Daniel Dennet, *Consciousness Explained*, Boston, 1981)—have been automated. In the twentieth century, and in a still different alterity, interiority in its turn is mechanized.

36. Augustine, *De diversis quaestionibus*, LXXXIII, 35, 1.

37. Augustine, *Confessions*, VI, 10, 16. The references in parentheses in the following refer to the *Confessions*.

38. Augustine, *De libre arbitre*. The references in parentheses in the following refer to the First Book. In distinguishing between a conversion to philosophy (summer 386) and another conversion to Christianity (spring 391), I follow Henri-Irénée Marrou, who does not hesitate to say that during this half-decade Augustine "was but a philosopher" (*Saint Augustine et la fin de la culture antique*, Paris, 1938, p. 168). No doubt the Christian was gradually born in him. The major part of Book Two and Book Three, written four crucial years after Book One, retrace Book One, which was then judged to be insufficiently Christian.

39. In section 9, 19 alone, Augustine employs the following expressions to designate the ideal influence over the self: *summum potestam habere, exserere principatum, regnum mentis, subiugatio libidinum, subiici indomitum, dominatus cupiditatum*.

40. Normative nature is "divine reason or the will of God prescribing that the natural order be conserved and proscribing departing from it" (*Contra Faustum Manichaeum*, 22, 27). It is no accident that the most developed reflections on normative nature are found in the treatises against the Manicheans. In opposition to Mani, Augustine seeks to show that a bad nature would be a contradiction in terms: "[I]t is obvious that it is necessary to blame not the thing that one uses badly, but the one who uses badly" (*De libre arbitre*, I, 16, 34).

41. *La Genese au sens litteral*, IV, 3, 7.

42. See, for example, *De libre arbitre*, II, 19, 53.

43. Cicero, *Rep.*, V, 1, 2. Already in Plato, the perfect city would have to be only in discourse. But this was because the *politeîa* could not exist historically. Whereas in Cicero, if all the being it has is in discourse, this is because, having really existed just a short time before, it is no longer.

44. Cicero, *De legibus*, III, 1, 2f.; I, 10, 30.

45. Cicero, *Rep.*, II, 1, 1–37, 63, and practically all of Book Two. The Roman Constitution fused three forms traditionally considered good: the royalty (*regnum*), the aristocracy (*dominatus optimatium*), and the popular state (*civitas popularis*), cf. *Rep.*, I, 26, 42–27, 43. The happy fusion of these forms in Rome is a theme that Cicero takes up at Polybus (ibid., I, 21, 34); see the excellent study of Kurt von Fritz, *The Theory of the Mixed Constitution in Antiquity*, New York, 1954.

46. Ibid., III, 3,5. Scipio begins his narrative with another point against Plato: "I'm going to go back to the origins of the Roman people. Indeed I will more easily attain the goal that I have in view in showing you our Republic at its birth, in its growth, in its adulthood, and finally in its full vigor, then if, like Socrates in Plato, I were to concoct the ideal State." (II, 1, 3) For the *somnium Scipionis*, see ibid. VI, 9, 9–26, 29.

47. Leo Strauss, *Naturrecht und Geschichte*, Frankfurt, 1977, p. 142n. In the United States there has arisen from Strauss a veritable movement whose goal is the formation of a fundamentalist elite. The movement is not confined to university circles (cf. below, note 67). Being a sacralized text is a function that falls to a group of "great books" from Plato to Thomas Aquinas (cf. above, General Introduction, note 13), but also to the American Constitution. As their fundamentalism requires, *the Straussians* read these texts extremely defensively and polemically against every historical method.

48. See Strauss, *Naturrecht*, p. 248 (*Laws*, III, 1, 3).

49. Cicero's philosophical sympathies extended to the skepticism of the new academy. This is not to say that his theticism turned nature into a positive law as Carneades promotes it during his "philosophical mission" in Rome (*Rep.*, III, 5,8–18,28). The false movement no longer amounts to a strategy of hiding his true intentions, a strategy that Cicero elsewhere confesses to practice (*Tusculanes*, 5, 10f). Rather, it is a matter of one's not being able to posit the ecumenical destiny of Roman constitutional underpinnings without declaring the singular to be universal. An artistic trick, Augustine will say with sarcasm (see the lines of the *City of God* II, 21,82, cited below).

50. *The City of God*, XIV, 28, 56. The references in parentheses that follow refer to this work.

51. For example, in the first works, "all nature as nature is good" (*De libre arbitre*, III, 13, 36); and, for example, in the last works, "the will of the great creator is the nature of each created thing" (*City of God*, XXI, 8, 2).

52. The constitution of time through the anticipation of the city is difficult to reconcile with his constitution in the *mens* or the *anima* and by *memoria* (*Confessions*, XI, 20, 26). The gap can be seen when Augustine twists Cicero's own words in his mouth. *De finibus bonorum et malorum*—a Ciceronian title—what are these? Augustine answers, we must listen to "what response the City of God gives . . . : we do *not yet* see our good" (XIX, 4, 1). The word that he turns around is "end." He turns its from goal or target into outcome or consummation. That there is a gap here can only be because, in *The City of God*, even more explicitly than in the *Confessions*, time is constituted in terms of the future.

53. In Books XI to XXII of *The City of God*, Augustine recounts the history of two cities, the heavenly and worldly, their birth (*de exortu*, XI–XIV), their historical trajectory (*de excursu*, XV–XVIII), and their respective ends (*de debitis finibus*, XIX–XXII).

54. In the organization of life justice has changed: "[W]e must regulate our life well, which is why it is written: 'The just live by faith'" (XIX, 4, 1).

55. Significant in this regard are the corrections Augustine makes to a list of definitions of peace, borrowed from Varron. This compiler had defined peace through a far-reaching homologization. Peace "naturally" extends from the harmony in the body to the vegetative and sensitive soul (*anima*), to the rational soul (*animus*), to the cohabitation of the soul with the body, to the household, then to the city, and finally to the cosmos (*mundus*) whose order results, according to him, from the harmony between men and gods. Now, Augustine corrects two points in this list. Between the peace in the household and the city he the inserts the definition of peace between men and God: the eruption of the singular; and for the last point on the list he substitutes the peace promised in the heavenly city: the eruption of *time* (XIX, 13,1). This last eruption is new in the development of Augustine himself who, about thirty years earlier had even described the peace between man and God as the trait "difficult to understand," characteristic of the wise man even in present life (*De libre arbitre*, I, 10, 21). During his conversions (at first to philosophy, then to Christianity), Augustine gradually acquired as an attitude a cautious approach, and with it the marks of mortality that are singularization and time. These marks are expelled anew from the normative fantasm where nature is equated with the principle of continuity, which is equated with the order guaranteeing the peace: "The peace of all things is the tranquility of order; order is the arrangement of equal and unequal beings, assigning to each the place that suits them" (XIX, 13, 1).

56. H.-X. Arquillière defines political Augustinianism as the "tendency to absorb natural right into supranatural justice, the law of the State into that of the Church" (*L'Augustinisme politique*, Paris, 1972, p. 54). The terms of this definition are not the happiest, the distinction between the natural and the supranatural being contrary to the unitary conception of nature in Augustine.

57. "Thus Cain was the first born of two parents of the human race. He took the side of the city of man; Abel, who followed, belonged to the City of God" (XV, 1, 2). With this Augustine concludes on a diachrony that is both ontogenic and phylogenic. "[E]very man is born *first* to the world, not to God" (*Contra Iulianum* VI, 4).

58. The pre-Alexandrian Greek does not have a word to express this. Certainly desire (*erôs*), deliberation (*boulê*), vow (*ethelô*), as well as some traits of the parts of the soul in Plato prefigure it, the *logistikon*, as domination; the *thumoeides*, as spontaneity; and the *epithumêtikon*, as the choice of an object (see *Pheadrus*, 246ff.). But it would be excessive if one sees it at work under these words, so to speak, as under so many pseudonyms. As for the "free will of the one" in Alexandrian henology, see above, chapter 7.

59. When, in the fourteenth century, hegemonic *natura* is destituted, teleology amounts to a simple

projection of the human will onto psychic processes. Once finality is coupled to the will as to its correlate, to speak of an *intentio,* of an *inclinatio,* of an *appetere* that are natural will necessarily amount to pure metaphors (see in Anneliese Maier, *Metaphysiche Hintergründe der spätscholastischen Naturphilosophie,* Rome, 1955, the excellent study "Finalkausalität und Naturgesetz," above all pages 310–335).

60. *Second Analytics,* I, 10; 76 a 31.

61. *Metaphysics,* A 2; 982 a 21f.

62. *Second Analytics,* I, 9; 76 a 16.

63. P. Aubenque, *Le Problème de l'être,* p. 250.

64. *Topics* I, 2; 101 b 1f.

65. "The human discourse on being signifies being only in a multiple manner and in the mode of dispersion," for "the genera are irreducible and incommunicable to each other," (P. Aubenque, *Le Problème de l'être,* pp. 198 and 223).

66. "The discovery of nature is as old as philosophy, [. . .] man could not live without reflecting on first things"; however, "in modern times, we have abandoned the idea that nature is the measure (Leo Strauss, *Naturrecht und Geschichte,* pp. 93 and 123). Strauss declares the unity of "classical philosophy" so as to demarcate roughly the ancients and the moderns (for the crude interests that are behind this operation, see the following note).

67. On the influence that the followers of Leo Strauss exerted on the American government under the presidency of Ronald Reagan, see *Newsweek* magazine, August 3, 1987. The author describes the network of followers in the chief governmental agencies and he provides examples of political options they were successful in getting adopted during this period. He asks: "Why are there so many Straussians in the Reagan Administration?" Answer: "The members of this club sometimes speak as if they preferred an aristocratic government" (p. 61). On the role of Straussians in the administration of {the first} President Bush, see *The New York Times,* September 9, 1992, p. A15. Leo Strauss himself never made a secret of his plans: "The goal of liberal education should be to found an aristocracy in the society of the democratic masses" (*Liberalism Ancient and Modern,* New York, 1968, p. 4). When it is a question of rehabilitating the old philosophical order, "natural law" obviously offers itself as the masterpiece.

68. Regarding this context, see Basile N. Tatakis, *Panétius de Rhodes, le fondeur du moyen stoïcisme: sa vie et son œuvre,* Paris, 1931.

69. Cicero, *De Officiis,* III, 13.

70. Diogenes Laertius, *Lives of the Philosophers,* VII, 110.

71. On the classical Stoic vocabulary thus redirected for usage by the larger public, see M. Pohlenz, *Antikes Führertum,* p. 129.

72. Cf. *Confessions* VII, 8,20–9,21. The "weakness" in the will capable, by right if not by fact, of totalizing itself has been suggested by X. Léon-Dufour, "Grâce et libre arbitre chez Saint Augustin," *Recherches de Sciences Religieuses* XXXIII (1946), pp. 129–163. However, the author does not draw from this the conclusion that we find important here, namely, that with autonomous totalization failing, the will thereby finds itself placed back among *heteronomous singulars* in relation to its power. The nonfulfillment of the will and the alien singular that comes to compensate for it will furnish, as we will see below, Luther with his point of departure.

73. This is Hannah Arendt's argument in *Der Liebesbegriff bei Augustinus,* Berlin, 1929, *passim* (cf. for example, p. 79). The argument would have been stronger if, in this dissertation as in her later writings, first, Arendt had not confused the "world" constituted by labor, work, and action—therefore the public sphere—with the "world" in the sense of John (a dual sense stated by Augustine: *omnes dilectores mundi mundus vocantur, Commentaire sur la Première Epître de S. Jean,* II 12) and second, if she had not silently passed over precisely that liberating effect that has been, since Augustine, the doctrine of two kingdoms. In the theocratically inclined monotheisms, the political and scientific spheres have not been able, even up till the present day, to detach themselves from the book that alone legitimizes their knowledge as well as their labor, work, and action; on the other hand, the doctrine of two kingdoms, the parallelism between the city of God and the earthly city, has, as it were, provided the road map for liberating, after more than a millennium of struggle, this secular state (as well as the autonomous sciences) whose downgrading Arendt deplores in Augustine.

74. *Confessions* VIII, 5, 12; *De musica* VI, 19 (*secunda, et quasi affabricata natura).*

75. "*inconcussa naturae lex*" (*De doctrina christiana* I, 27, and elsewhere).

76. *Soliloquiorum* I, 2, 7.

77. *De diversis quaestionibus* 83, 35, 1.

78. *Ennarrations in Psalmos* CXLI, 15.

79. H. Arendt, *Der Liebesbegriff,* p. 27f. The communion of believers, she again writes, "lays claim to *every* man—in contradistinction to every secular community," ibid., p. 76; cf. Augustine, *Sermon,* 34, 7.

80. Ibid, p. 28. She cites this phrase from the *Confessions:* "If souls please you, then they are loved

in God, because they also are subjected to change and that, fixed only in themselves, they must become stable: otherwise, they will slip away and perish" (*Confessions* IV, 12, 18). The expression *in illo fixae stabiliuntur* shows what the nomothesis is all about: positing an unshakable point of reference. Arendt comments, in terms of meaning and significance, "The beloved receives an originary meaning only once it is made fixed and stable in this way. . . . Every adventitious question arising concerning others will inquire only after their being before God, not after their intra-worldly significance" (H. Arendt, *Der Liebesbegriff*, pp. 71, 79).

81. See above, note 73, as well as H. Arendt, *La Vie de l'esprit*, vol. II: *Le Vouloir*, Paris, 1983, chapter 10.

82. *City of God*, XIX, 4, 4. One must not miss the movement of interiorization. Except for the substitution of *caro* for *hormé*, this definition is certainly inspired by the Greeks. In the *Nichomachean Ethics* (Book V), Aristotle defines justice as the virtue that, in the forms later called distributive and communicative, rules our relations to others (*pros heteron*). Distribution—Augustine repeated this as far back as the dialogues of his youth (*De libre arbitre* V, XIII, 27: *sua cuique tribuere*)—is when an authority gives to each in the city what they are due. In the *City of God*, following in this respect the adjustments made by the Stoics, the field that the definition covers is displaced. Justice must rule the interaction between forces of the soul. Thus there is a displacement toward interiority. The *iustus ordo naturae* designates the system of telic subordinations in which the flesh finds its end in the spirit, and in which both find their common end in God. This is an interiorization that best marks the parallax.

83. Augustine, *Contra Faustum Manicheaum*, 22, 27.

84. "The city of the godless . . . has no true justice" (*City*, XIX, 24). In the collective history of salvation, just as in the individual *anagôgè*, intelligence is universalized on the basis of contingent givens. "Proper refinement [of the human race] comes about through certain temporal stages (*per quosdam articulos temporum*); the character of these is that one raises oneself up from temporal things to the intelligence of eternal things, and from the visible to the invisible" (*City*, X, 14). One raises oneself up from the particular to the common by progressing (*proferre*) through contingent singulars. This is the version of the double bind that will torment Kant when he will ask, "Does the human race progress continually toward the better?" The goal will be noumenal, but the progress toward it will no less be "inferred" from contingencies such as the revolution of 1789 (*Le conflit des facultés*, Paris, pp. 141f. and 145).

85. This is the definition of joy in which desire, pleasure, and charity are blended together: "To enjoy is to be attached to some being by love, for this very being," *De doctrina christiana*, I, 4. Curiously, charity is called on to be blurred: "Charity makes us desire to see its object and to take the highest pleasure in it" *Soliloquiorum* I, 6, 13. Charity thus is effaced in the face of the joy that it alone makes us desire. Augustine was aware of and reformulated in a good many sentences the teaching of Diotima in the *Symposium*—love annuls itself in the enjoyment of the object. But this says nothing about the end of the gap hollowed out by the Augustinian ascent, nor about the agent that endows this end with prerogatives of *lex inconcussa*, nor, above all, about its accessibility.

86. A. Nygren (*Eros und Agape*, 2 vols., Gütersloh, 1930) has been rightly criticized for a narrowly "egoist" conception of Platonic eros. Yet it is necessary to add that *agapê*, at least in its Latin equivalents, really is "egoist," and this too—it is my will, loving my own good—restored *natura*—that becomes accessible only in others (with a capital letter or not, depending on the case).

87. In contrast with interiority, Jean-Pierre Vernant gives a good example of the public singularization to come. In Sparta, the warriors wore long hair to appear "larger, more noble and more terrible" (Xenophon). Now, Vernant adds, they must have appeared thus once dead on the battlefield. It was a matter of preparing oneself for a "beautiful death" to come. Vernant cites the report of a spy sent to Sparta by Xerxes on the eve of the battle. The spy saw the men peacefully combing their hair. To the amazement of the Persian king in the face of this account, he answered, "Such is the custom at Sparta; when they are on the verge of risking their lives, these men take care of their hairdo" (Herodotus). Living, the Hoplite fought in rows strictly equal to each other; he became an individual through heroic death (*L'Individu, la mort, l'amour*, Paris, 1989, p. 67). It is with the Christian Latins, and with the interweavingss of the will and time that we have just seen, that the singularization to come passes into an interior register.

II. Its Destitution

1. My citations follow the critical edition, *Meister Eckhart, Die deutschen und lateinischen Werke* (ed. the Deutsche Forschungsgemeinschaft, Stuttgart, 1936ff.). I refer to German texts in this edition with the cipher *DW* (*Die deutschen Werke*), and to the Latin texts with the cipher *LW* (*Die lateinischen Werke*), following one or the other with the number of the volume and then the page number. For the German sermons I have used the translation by Jeanne Ancelet-Hustache, *Maître Eckhart: Sermons* (3 volumes, Paris, 1974, 1978, 1979) using the cipher *S;* for the German treatises, I refer to Jeanne Ancelet-

Hustache, *Maître Eckhart: Les Traités* (Paris, 1971) with the cipher *T.* However, I do not always follow these translations.

2. As regards ultimate referents, which is a good way of distinguishing them from supreme referents, it is not the intention that counts. . . . The papal bull that appeared after the death of Eckhart and condemned twenty-eight propositions attributed to him, mentioned a retraction that he was supposed to have made at the end of his life; he was supposed to have proclaimed, in other words, his intention of orthodoxy (cf. the text of the bull *In Agro Dominico* of March 29, 1329, ed. H. Denifle and F. Ehrle in *Archiv für Literatur-und Kirchengeschichte des Mittelsalters,* vol. II, Berlin, 1886, p. 640). Eckhart never wanted to challenge the supreme referents. Quite another question is whether Eckhart's discourse is still articulated under the influence of *natura,* the ultimate referent. Now, this is where we need not fear the rejoinder that he delivered to the judges of the Inquisition. He accused them of "a certain malice or gross ignorance," of a "stunted and stupid intelligence" . . . (G. Théry, "Edition critiques des pièces relatives au procès d'Eckhart contenues dans le manuscrit 33b de la bibliotèque de Soest," *Archives d'Histoires doctrinale et littéraire du Moyen Age,* I [1926–1927], pp. 196–248). They understood quite well that he attacked sovereign nature. If his discourse is read as if it still unquestioningly found its place under this influence, Eckhart becomes quite simply unintelligible—which is not something that can be said of any of the Scholastics before him.

3. By including Eckhart among the Christian Neoplatonists, one gains hardly anything more than a vague concept of vertical integration. Of course, he places himself in the lineage of Plotinus when he affirms that "what is prior and superior receives nothing at all of what is posterior"; the superior "descends with its properties into what is inferior and posterior. It assimilates cause and agent as what is effective and as patient" (*LW* I,155). Vertical integration therefore means that each thing is assimilated by the level above, which serves as its end. But by stopping with what is exclusive about formal and final causality, one no less misses what is essential about it. First of all, and speaking only of nature, Eckhart does indeed recognize the ascendant causality: "Nature does not make leaps; it always begins by effecting what is lowest and thus effecting up to what is highest" (*DW* I,298f; *S* I,161). We will see how to understand this effective nature (the beginning of chapter 12). Next, it is far from being a hypostasis, but is a continuous gradation according to "nobility" (for example, *DW* II,174; *S* II,29). Finally and above all, as a refrain Eckhart repeats "being and pure nature." There, he speaks neither of the universe integrated by finality, nor of the active principle, but of something completely different: of the neo-Aristotelian act of being that is reconsidered and rearticulated (see chapter 13). This act removes the normativity from the principle of hierarchization whereby nature is denatured.

4. The cipher *Pf* refers to Franz Pfeiffer, *Deutsche Mystiker des vierzehnten Jahrhunderts,* 2 volumes, vol. II: *Meister Eckhart, Predigten und Traktate,* Leipzig, 1857, and Aalen, 1962. This edition, of which some of the texts are not unanimously considered to be authentic, is usable inasmuch as the critical edition has not been produced.

5. The distinction between God and the godhead—or divinity—is quite classic. Paul assimilated the *theiotès* to the *aorata* and to the *dunamis,* "the invisible essence [of God], which is to say his eternal power in his divinity. . . ." (Romans 1:20; cf. Col. 2:9). The Latin translations sometimes write *deitas* and sometimes *divinitas.* In Thomas Aquinas, *deitas* signifies the *essentia dei* opposed to the action of God (*Commentary on the Epistles to the Romans,* I, 6). Eckhart aims at this distinction between *actus* and *agere* ("God acts, the godhead does not act," *Pf* 181,10). He says *wesen,* a word that denotes being as divine essence.

6. Regarding Meister Eckhart as a neo-Aristotelian, see Bernhard Welte, "Meister Eckhart als Aristoteliker," in *Auf der Spur des Ewigens,* Frieburg, 1965, pp. 197ff.

7. Aristotle mentions the difference between infinitive (*einai*) and nominative (*to on*) forms of the verb "to be," even if he does not take it up or develop it as such (cf. P. Aubenque, *Le Problème de l'être chez Aristote,* pp. 170, note 3; 184, note 4; and elsewhere).

8. The obligation *is incumbent upon* God prior to its emanating from him. *Got muoz,* 'God must,' is in Eckhart one of the phrases that point toward being as divine essence, thus toward the godhead beyond God (see the analysis by Shizuteru Ueda, "Über den Sprachgebrauch Meister Eckharts," *Glaube, Geist, Geschichte. Festschrift für Ernst Benz,* Leiden, 1967, pp. 266f.).

9. We have been able to see in Eckhart the development of self-consciousness inasmuch as it prescribes its forms to knowledge (Joachim Kopper, *Die Metaphysik Meister Eckharts,* Saarbrücken, 1955; and "Die Analysis der Sohnesgeburt bei Meister Eckhart," *Kant Studien* 57 [1966], pp. 100–112).

10. "The poet, great Initiator," René Char, *Fureur et Mystère,* Paris, 1962, p. 83.

11. See above, General Introduction, p. 9. In France, there had been something like a flurry of confessions when Roland Barthes, Jacques Derrida, and Michel Foucault ("each time I have tried to carry out a theoretical work, it has been in terms of elements of my own experience," 1981) published that they would not have sought to "think otherwise" if they had not belonged to a "minority," if they had not found

themselves on the margins, cf. *Roland Barthes par Roland Barthes*, Paris, 1975, p. 134; J. Derrida and G. Bennington, *Jacques Derrida*, Paris, 1991, for example, pp. 57, 278f, 300f; Didier Eribon, *Michel Foucault*, Paris, 1989, p. 46.

12. The keyword of the alchemist is "transmutation." This can be characterized by four principal objectives: to convert the base metals into noble metals, to do better than nature, to heal the human body, and to spiritually perfect the alchemist himself (see the texts cited by Robert Halleux, *Typologie des sources du moyen-âge occidental, Les Textes alchimiques* fasc. 32, Turnhout, 1979, pp. 43f.). In what follows I will confine myself to the first and last of these objectives.

13. At the beginning of the fourteenth century, writes A. Maier (see above, chapter 10, note 59), the axiom *omnes agens agit propter finem* loses its relevance (*Metaphysische Hintergründe*, pp. 277ff.). If there are no ends except for the will, then only those agents endowed with a will will act with a view to an end. Hence the natural processes will be explained only by the chain of efficient causes. The great telic continuity is undone by the impact of the will "discovered" by the Romans.

14. We have frequently remarked that Aristotle and alchemy are in concert in Western medieval culture. The great issue during the twelfth century upon which these two legacies converge (both were transmitted by the Arabs) is the intelligibility of the formless—of what in both traditions is called prime matter. In contradistinction to Aristotelian *prote hule*, alchemical *prima materia* is characterized not by the absence of all form, but—at least according to certain texts—by the form that is the quintessence (cf. Wilhelm Ganzenmüller, *Die Alchemie im Mittelalter*, Paderborn, 1938, pp. 179f.). It is a different prime matter, spiritualized. The Aristotelian quintessence becomes immanent to the body (cf. F. S. Taylor, *The Idea of the Quintessence*, London, 1953, pp. 246ff.). Accordingly, Albertus Magnus sought to complete Aristotle's *Physics* with his *Book of Minerals* (see the annotated translation of this work by D. Wyckoff, *Albertus Magnus. Book of Minerals*, Oxford, 1967). He defines alchemy as the science of "reducing those metals, which in minerals are corrupted and imperfect, to their perfection" (*Libellus de alchimia* II; ed. Borgnet, Paris, 1890–99, vol. 37, p. 547). Aquinas counts alchemy not among the sciences, but among the arts that apply physical science (*Commentary on 'De Trinitate' de Boethius*, q. 5, art. 1, third and fifth answers, and art. 3, fifth objection). In this he follows the usage of the alchemists themselves who call it *ars regia*.

15. Alchemy prepares modern chemistry for the experimental method—at least a certain experimental method—but not for the conception of nature. Thus, the "Transmission of ancient science" (this is its subtitle), in the sense that M. Berthelot understands it (*La Chimie au Moyen Age*, 3 vols., Paris, 1893), is here untimely. To read alchemical texts as the first stammerings of modern chemistry is to confuse the contrary movement in history.

16. Take for example the summary in the *Encyclopedia Universalis* that we see here: "[T]he reading of these treatises were meant to sketch out an initiatory work. The masters wanted their disciples to mobilize all their intellectual and spiritual forces. . . . They were supposed to tear themselves away from their time and even more from themselves" (*s.v.* "Alchemy").

17. Beginning with the twelfth century, "alchemical ideology belongs to the whole of culture—just as much to the popular culture as to the learned culture of the Middle Ages." It reaches its peak—before being condemned by the letter of decree by John XXII *Spondent quas non exhibent*—precisely during the time of Meister Eckhart (R. Halleux, *Les Textes alchimiques* pp. 133 and 124f). In other words, it reaches its peak at the very moment where, in the explanation of becoming, "one henceforth does without hypothetical causes and final tendencies" (A. Maier, *Metaphysiche Hintergründe*, pp. 334f).

18. *Biblitèque des philosophes chimiques* (Paris, 1741), cited by Titius Burckhardt, *Alchemy*, trans. W. Stoddaert, London, 1967, p. 96.

19. "This stone is not stone, and although it may be precious, it is sold for nothing," *Turba philosophorum* (cited by W. Ganzenmüller, *Die Alchemie im Mittelalter*, p. 176).

20. This is the first principle in the *Table Emeraude*, an authoritative document for medieval alchemists and which is presented as having been revealed to Hermes Trisgegistus (cf. J. F. Ruska, *Tabula Smaragdina*, Heidelberg, 1926).

21. According to Plutarch, the old name of Egypt was *Chèmia* (*De Iside et Osiride*, 33, 364 c; cf. A. J. Hopkins, *Alchemy, Child of Greek Philosophy*, New York, 1934, p. 94). According to another possible derivation, the word would stem from the Greek verb *chéô*, 'to flow,' 'to melt.'

22. The singular could only be determined by another singular (Love). Thus in Angelius Silesius, who elsewhere puts certain themes of Eckhart in verse:

> Ich weiß, daß ohne mich Gott nicht ein Nu kann leben:
> werd' ich zunicht,—er muß vor Not den Geist aufgeben.
>
> (" I know that, without me, God could not live for an instant: / if I were to become nothing, he would necessarily have to give up the ghost").

> Nichts ist als ich und Du—und wenn wir zwei nicht sein,
> so ist Gott nicht mehr Gott und fällt der Himmel ein.
>
> ("Nothing exists other than me and you—and if we two were not, / Then God would cease to be God and the Heavens would collapse.").

Such a reciprocal determination of singulars is absent in texts of Eckhart.

23. *"Vivere militare est,"* Seneca, Letter 96, 5.

24. When he had to defend himself against the accusations concerning certain points of his teaching, he says "that there is in the soul something such that, if it were completely so, it would be uncreated, I have understood and I understand is in accordance with the truth, and even in a way that conforms to that of the doctors, my colleagues; namely, if it was an intelligence through essence. But I have never said that there was in the soul something of the soul which is not created and not creatable. . . ," cited by M.-H. Laurent, "Autour du procès de Maître Eckhart," *Divus Thomas* XXXIX, Piacenza, 1936, p. 345.

25. Eckhart, *Commentaries on Genesis,* II, n. 139.

26. Thomas Aquinas, *Disputed Questions of the Truth,* q. 23, art. 6. In these remarks on the deduction of the law I am drawing on Part II, I of the *Summa Theologica,* questions 90 to 105. The cipher "I" refers to the Part One and the cipher "II-I" refers to Part Two, first division; the ciphers are followed by the number of the Question (q.) and the Article (art.). For the details, see the apparatus and excellent commentary of the bilingual Latin-German edition, *Die deutsche Thomas-Ausgabe,* vol. 13: *Das Gesetz,* Heidelberg and Köln, 1977.

27. See, for example, Bonaventure: "God gives laws, not through the will, but through the highest reason (*maxima ratione*)," *Collections in Hexaemeron* 21, 10.

28. "The essence of God is his being," *Summa contra Gentiles,* I, 22, § "Hanc autem."

29. It is true that we have been able to retrace this bit of evidence to Porphyry, who would have passed it on to Aquinas by way of Boethius. Cf. Pierre Hadot, "La distinction de l'être et de l'étant dans le *De Hebdomadibus* de Boèce," *Die Metaphsik im Mittelalter,* ed. P. Wilpert, Berlin, 1963, p. 147ff.

30. Cf. T. Burckhardt, *Alchemy,* pp. 68f.

31. *Eigenschaft* in Middle-High German, just as *propriété* in French, signifies both the attribute and the possession.

32. "Natural right," in distinction to "natural law," follows from the "insitting-seating"—a right that each being has to the site circumscribed by its position.

33. Cf. Vladimir Lossky, *Théologie négative et connaissance de Dieu chez Maître Eckhart,* Paris, 1960, pp. 339f.

34. For an ancient Greek, to be master of oneself is to go to the *bouleuthérion,* to the *agora,* and to the Pnyx; it is not to go into the fields, to fight in the phalanx, or to slap the cook.

35. In all this we see again the doctrine of the complete return to oneself, according to Aquinas, whom Eckhart, moreover, calls his "excellent professor," "venerable brother" (*LW* I,151) and "colleague" (above, chapter 11, note 24).

36. A precious stone "that possesses a great force through its bearing, its insitting in itself" is distinguished from simple tuff by a rough outline of reflexivity. Every formally hierarchical metaphysics supposes that one level receives its being by contemplating the level that precedes it. A precious stone "turns its head and looks above itself." For a modern, it is a strange mineral reflexivity that places a jewel by itself to contemplate . . . what? The algae, no doubt, the lower fringe of the class of living beings that is above all that is inorganic. In Neoplatonic tradition, it is not exactly unheard of to say that a thing is constituted in continuous stages by reflection; it is here that it has its share of perfection, that it takes part, participation.

37. For an analysis of these phrases as well as the references, I allow myself to refer to my *Maître Eckhart ou la joie errante,* Paris, 1972, pp. 207–227.

38. In Eckhart formal causality communicates the sole order that is nature. This causality does not communicate being. Thus it contracts the four natures according to Scotus Erigenus, which is generally presupposed by the Scholastics even if they vary it. Nature which creates but is not created therefore is, for Eckhart, the only creator; on the other hand, intermediate nature is—both created and creators—reduced to filling up the holes in the formal landscape of nature.

39. The triangular identification between God, pure space, and light is found in certain Neoplatonics. Simplicius cites the phrase of Proclus: "The purest light in the body is place" (*Commentary on the* Physics, 621, 32), and Sextus Empiricus attributes to Aristotle the doctrine—hardly Aristotelian—according to which "the first God is the place of all things" (*Contra les mathématiciens,* 10,33); Cf. Pierre Duhem, *Le système du monde,* vol. V, Paris, 1917, p. 231.

40. In all this, Eckhart makes the Aristotelian heavens indeterminate. For Aristotle, the heavens and the earth naturally pull on substances—the heavens toward the above, the earth toward the below (*Physics,*

211f.). The substance has reached its natural place when it ceases to be so moved. Eckhart also maintains that the heavens, not being contained by anything, have no place. But as he abandons kineticism, the ascendant orientation of natural movement does not interest him. The heavens lose their role of absolute limit and thus of telic determination.

41. A French translation of this text does not hesitate to render *naturaliter* meekly as "here it is a question of the law of nature," even if this means omitting the second *naturaliter* two lines later (*L'œuvre latine de Maître Eckhart,* vol. I, Paris, 1984, before, p. 395).

42. If "you seek something by [means of] God, it is as if you were to make of God a candle in order to seek something with it, and when one has found that which one seeks, one throws the candle away" (*DW* I,69; *S* I,65).

43. With the candor of an entirely Roman pragmatism, Seneca instrumentalizes telic nature: "[S]erve the order and order will serve you" (*serva ordinem et ordo te servabit*), cited by H. Deku, *Wahrheit und Unwahrheit der Tradition,* Ottilien, 1986, p. 380.

44. In Cicero, exteriority in relation to the thetic city is assured by factual memory; in Augustine it is assured by anticipatory memory.

45. Which is to say, when one stops advancing what Anglo-Saxon philosophers call *claims.*

46. In God, "the highest angels and the gnat and the soul are equal" (*DW* II,493; *S* II,146).

47. Binary opposites fall under one and the same science: *"oppositorum eadem est scientia"* (*LW* I, 149). As for the opposition of antecedents and consequence, of *buillition-ébuillition* {heating-boiling}, one may again read into this a resonance with alchemy. In the alambic, the *buillition* produces liquefaction and indistinction; then the distillate is drained into distinct *ébullitions.*

48. In writing his self-defense, he repeats that it is necessary to be detached from property: "[I]n the nudity of his essence which is above every noun {*nom*}, God penetrates and falls into the naked essence of the soul, which also is without a proper name {*nom*}." Responding to the summonses, he adds that "there is something moral in this." This is a response that could hardly have been satisfactory to those who had summoned him, for he again explains himself through the removal of what is proper. It is necessary "to love God without means and without any property entailing a means" (G. Théry "Edition critique des pièces relatives au procès d'Eckhart," p. 258).

49. For example, DW I,109; and 165; 193; 194; 199; 200, etc. . . .; *S* I,85; 109; 121; 123, etc. . . .

50. DW V, 411; T 163. In place of "being" (*wesen*) that one expects and that I have placed in brackets, Eckhart says "property" (*Eigenschaft*). Accordingly, the French translator who usually renders *Eigenschaft* with formulations such is 'attachment to what is my own' seems in the present text to want to have her cake and eat it to—both indeterminate being and property—by translating the word here as "the being proper to God." This is not the only uncertainty in the treatise *On Non-Attachment.* A little later on Eckhart describes non-attachment in terms that seem to arise directly from the Stoic tradition (DW V, 411f.: T 163f.).

51. Just as above (note 23), the "if . . ." announces the change from a principial strategy to an originary strategy.

52. The words that I have replaced with an ellipsis, because they divert our attention from context, are "of the whole godhead." This is because the concept of the godhead is greatly overdetermined in Eckhart (see the excellent analysis of the distinction 'God and godhead' in Bernard Welte, *Meister Eckhart, Gedanken zu seinen Gedanken,* Freiburg, 1979, pp. 175–248).

53. This is an Aristotelian schema, of course, passed on by the School. "[T]he known and its actuality of being known, and the knowing and its actuality of being a knowing are one and the same," Thomas Aquinas, *Commentary on Aristotle's* De Anima, no. 724.

54. See the passages of his various documents of justification edited by O. Karrer and H. Piesch, *Meister Eckharts Rechtfertigungssdchrift vom Jahre 1326,* Erfurt, 1927, pp. 65f. and 99f., as well as by G. Théry, "Edition critiques," p. 185.

55. See the text cited above, chapter 12, note 41.

56. The inconsistency in the image is due to the use of paradigms. We also see it in Plotinus: "[A]n image (*eikôn*) loses its consistency (*oudè ménei*) when it neither belongs to another nor is found in the other" (*En.* V, 3 [49], 8, 12f.). It is the paradigmatic other to which it refers.

57. The collapse here will happen later (see below, vol. II, chapter 5, the section on the isomorph).

58. Eckhart does not share Thomas Aquinas's nervousness concerning the priority of the intellect or the will in God. Sometimes he affirms one and sometimes the other.

59. An anthropomorphism modeled on that of the Scotists could be conceived in Eckhart something like this: Through the caress of pure nature freedom finds its "rest" in the ground of God. It finds there its own ground which, because of the indeterminacy, cannot be counted among the attributes of the foundational God. Consequently, the freedom of the ground of God is one thing else, and the freedom of the foundational God is something else again. But for all this, we are not hailing Duns Scotus here

and bifurcating theology into a theology of powers (*potestas absoluta* receiving the possibles—*potestas ordinata* leading toward the nature that is in fact); this could not be the case because the entire semantic field of "purity" in Eckhart is precisely what effaces anthropomorphisms.

60. See above, note 24.

61. "Piercing through" is not something that we do at certain times, or that certain people do. One muddles everything by rendering *durchbrechen* (as does one French translator) as *'faire sa percée'* [make a breakthrough].

62. This meaning of the word has been documented at least as far back as late Middle-High German.

63. See above, Introduction to Part Two, note 9; also, in Maurice Blondel, this turning away of non-attachment for the sake of a "pure, cosmic objectivism.": "[T]he purity of inner non-attachment is the organ of perfect vision—mortification thus is the genuine metaphysical experiment" (*L'Action,* Paris, 1893, pp. 442, 383).

64. See above, chapter 12, note 38.

65. This is one of the reasons why I'm not convinced that "when Meister Eckhart wants to go beyond determinations, the movement that he suggests remains enclosed, it seems, in ontic transcendence" (Jacques Derrida, *L'Écriture et la différence,* Paris, 1967, p. 217).

66. Michel Foucault, *Naissance de la clinique,* Paris, 1963, p. 202. Reinscribed in the analytic of ultimates which is the concern of the topology of normative double binds, Foucault's words obviously gain a significance beyond only that of modernity.

Volume Two

1. "Wir fassen ein Gesetz begierig an, Das unsrer Leidenschaft zur Waffe dient."

Goethe, *Iphigenia in Tauris,* V,3, line 1832f.

2. Among ultimate referents, *natura* is probably the one that has most evidently been maximized from a proper noun—at least if, as I indicated in the first volume, Latin nature-as-law has been extrapolated from the *nasci* ('birth,' 'genesis,' 'ancestral history') of republican Rome. Below I will speak of self-consciousness, a familiar phenomenon, and in that sense it has been a common noun in use ever since the Deutero-Homer; but it has been the name of an ultimate referent only since the sixteenth century.

3. See above, Volume One, General Introduction, note 33.

4. See below, for example, the analysis of the imperative "Extend your hand" in Luther.

5. For instance, the Greek "one." In the first volume, I suggested that in Parmenides the *hen* is instituted beginning with an experience of inclusion and exclusion reminiscent of ostracism. The goddess would say: Those whom you exclude from your world, keep them present to thought as much as those you include.

Part Three. In the Name of Consciousness: The Modern Hegemonic Fantasm

1. *Dictata super Psalterium* (ps. 77); *WAS,* vol. 3, p. 593. The edition I use is Martin Luther, *Werke. Kritische Gesamtausgabe,* Weimar, 1883ff. The cipher *WAS (Weimarer Ausgabe,* First Section, *Schriften*) refers to the writings, and *WAB* (*Weimarer Ausgabe,* Fourth Section, *Briefwechsel*) refers to the correspondence.

2. Erasmus Alberus, cited by Heinz Otto Burger, "Luther as an Event in Literary History," *Martin Luther: 450th Anniversary of the Reformation,* Bad Godesberg 1967, p. 124.

3. Friedrich Nietzsche, *Beyond Good and Evil,* sect. 247. Hegel already called Luther's translation of the Bible the German "popular book," *Volksbuch, allemand* (*Lectures on the Philosophy of Religion*), Part Three, "The Absolute Religion," *Samtliche Werke* (*Jubilaumsausgabe*), new edition by H. Glockner, vol. 16, Stuttgart, 1928, p. 290). Again with regard to the translation of the Bible, Hegel also states, "Only that is mine which is stated in my mother tongue" (*Lectures on the Philosophy of History*; ibid., vol. 19, Stuttgart, 1928, p. 218). The same elegy from Goethe's mouth: "What God states in the Koran is true: 'No people has been sent a prophet if not in its own language.' Accordingly, the Germans become a people thanks only to Luther" (letter to Blumenthal dated May 28th, 1819). The eighteenth century did not judge otherwise. "It is he (Luther) that awakened and unbound the sleeping giant that was the German language," J. G. Herder, "Fragment" of 1767 (*Sämtliche Werke,* ed. B. Suphan, Berlin, 1877ff., vol. 1, p. 372).

4. Heinrich Heine, "Of Germany" (*Historisch-kritische Gesamtausgabe,* Hamburg, 1979, vol. VIII/1, p. 284). Writing for the German public, Heine called the freedom of mind that had produced the French Revolution "the elder daughter" of the German Reformation ("Die romantische Schule," ibid., p. 143).

The Lutheran hymn *Our God Is a Fortress* was "the Marseillaise of the Reformation," and if there should never be a German revolution, freedom will have found its language thanks to the translation of the Bible: "As this book is in the hands of the poorest classes, they have no need of scholarly lessons to be able to express themselves. This state of affairs will have remarkable consequences when the political revolution erupts here. Everywhere, freedom will be able to speak, and its language will be Biblical" ("Zur Geschichte der Religion und Philosophie in Deutschland," ibid., pp. 40).

5. Heinrich Bornkamm, *Luther als Schriftsteller,* Heidelberg, 1965, p. 17 (one will find some bibliographic indications concerning Luther's German in relation to the history of the language, ibid., p. 14, note 26).

6. The expression was in use at the beginning of the century. Robert Winkler understands it thus: "Kant is the philosopher of Protestantism," for, "what Kant states in a general way about knowledge and the object, Luther states in relation to God and the actuality of God" ("Der Transzendentalismus bei Luther," in Festschrift G. Wobbermin, *Luther, Kant, Schleiermacher in ihrer Bedeutung für den Protestantismus,* Berlin, 1939, p. 34; cf. Julius Kaftan, *Kant, der Philosoph des Protestantismus,* Berlin, 1904). Paradoxically, the expression does not aptly characterize Kant's writings on religion. In them, he instead follows Erasmus, a veritable "Nathan the Sage" of the sixteenth century, against Luther's intransigent dogmatism. Also, Lessing, author of *Nathan the Sage,* calls for a post-Lutheran liberation: "You, Luther, . . . you freed us from the yoke of tradition; who will now come to liberate us from the unbearable yoke of the letter?" (G. E. Lessing, "The Parabole. Appendix against Goeze" (*Werke,* ed. J. Petersen and W. V. Olshausen, Berlin, 1925, vol. 23, p. 160). Lessing himself, as well as Kant, will be able to don the mantel of the second liberator; but Erasmus already had the rights to it. Only Erasmus, as W. Dilthey will observe, "was able only to point out the path to a distant future; he could not satisfy the present" ("The Natural System of the Sciences of the Mind in the Seventeenth Century," *Gesammelte Schriften,* vol. II, ed. G. Misch, Berlin, 1914, p. 218). As for the considerable literature around the "transcendentalist" interpretation of Luther, in general it props itself, directly or indirectly, on the work of Reinhold Seeberg, *Lehrbuch der Dogmengeschichte. T. IV, sect. 1: Die Entstehung des protestantischen Lehrbegriffs,* second edition, corrected, Leipzig, 1917. By "transcendentalism" Seeberg understood the Protestant principle in accordance with which the subject of all biblical and theological enunciations is always "me"—me as created, justified, pardoned, saved, etc. This *pro me* is repeated with insistence in Luther's *Small Catechism,* from 1529 onward the most widely propagated book among Protestants. Its adversaries decried the cult of me (for example., Paul Hacker, *Das Ich im Glauben bei Martin Luther,* Vienna, 1966, pp. 23f.). This will be one of the reasons below to distinguish between "I," "ego," and "self."

7. I could not resign myself to follow without modification any of the existing French translations.

8. The word may have the same root as *mnémè,* memory. See the play on words in the *Iliad.* "Tell, muses, . . . who were the chiefs of the Daneans. . . . Their crowd, I would not be able to point out . . . unless the Olympian muses (*moûsai*) . . . remind me (*mnèsaiath*) how many were there that came to Illios," *Iliad* 2, 484–492. *Moûsa* would thus come from the same root as the Latin words *monere* and *mens* (cf. *Der kleine Pauly,* ed. K. Ziegler, W. Sontheimer, and H. Gärtner, Munich, 1975, vol. III, col. 1476).

9. In what concerns both the intervention of a second hand and the interest this lends to themes such as responsibility and law, there is—apart from one notable exception—agreement among the major commentators on Homer in our century: Werner Jaeger, *Scripta minora,* Rome, 1960, vol. I, pp. 321–324, reprint of a text from 1926; Rudolf Pfeiffer, *Ausgewahlte Schriften,* Munich, 1955, pp. 15f., reprint of a text from 1928; and Wolfgang Schadewaldt (postface to his German translation of the *Odyssey, Die Odyssee,* Hamburg, 1958, pp. 327ff., idem, *Hellas und Hesperien,* Stuttgart, 1970, vol. I, pp. 42–105, reprint of texts published between 1958 and 1960; idem, "Dialog Schule-Wissenschaft: Klassische Sprachen und Literaturen," *Fortwirkende Antike* vol. VI, 1972, pp. 33–59. The notable exception is Karl Reinhardt, *Tradition und Geist,* Göttingen, 1960, p. 88, reprint of a text from 1948, who, nevertheless, also observes that the passages such as the narrative of the infractions on the Island of Thrinacie are a matter "of another [literary] nature."

10. Theodor Adorno and Max Horkheimer read into the *Odyssey* the act of the birth of the self. "The constitution of the self" is supposedly accomplished there by "the mastery of nature within man," *Dialektik der Auflärung,* new edition, Frankfurt, 1981, pp. 66, 69. They cite the verses: "He spoke, reprimanding the heart in his breast, / And soon, his heart, remained assured like an anchor / In patience. But it returned to him (*autos*) with all its sense" (20, 22–24). They detect here the prefiguration of a self seeking to impose itself upon affects. This is not only to substantialize the *autos* in spite of the language, it is above all to read Homer through an entirely modern concept of nature. Self-consciousness does not mean consciousness *of the* self, and even less does it mean consciousness of a self-dominating impulses. To be convinced of how absurd it is to superimpose on Greek texts a modern concept of the self, it should suffice to read the opening lines, this time, of the *Iliad:* "Sing, goddess, the anger of Pelus's son Achilles

/ and its devastations, which brought countless woes upon the Achaeans, / hurled in their multitudes to the house of Hades strong souls / of heroes, and made themselves spoil / for dogs and every bird, and the will of Zeus was accomplished / since that time when first there stood in division of conflict / Atreus' son the lord of men and brilliant Achillus. If this *autoi* conceals an allusion to the self, then the self is rotting in the sun and is devoured by dogs, while the spirit sinks away to Hades!

11. See Fragment 11 of Solon, cited above, chapter 1, note 46.

12. A whole school of commentators judged the Deutero-Homer to be a rather clumsy poet; see the references in Schadewaldt —who does not share this opinion—*Hellas und Hesperien*, vol. I, p. 63, note. 6.

13. Friedrich Hölderlin, "Der Rhein," *Sämtliche Werke*, vol. II (1953), p. 152.

14. Vittorio Hösle, *Die Vollendung der Tragödie im Spatwerk des Sophokles*, Stuttgart, 1984, pp. 30–36.

15. Hannah Arendt, *La Vie de l'esprit*, vol. I: *La Pensée*, trans. L. Lotringer, Paris, 1981, p. 149.

16. Cf. Kurt von Fritz, "*Noos* and *Noein* in the Homeric poems," *Classical Philology*, XXXVIII (1943), pp. 85 and 91.

I. Its Institution

17. These two texts of Luther, although written in Latin, are "entirely permeated with his German," cf. above, note 2. In *WAS*, the *Commentary to the Letter to the Romans* comprises vol. 56 (1938). In the text, I cite this in parentheses according to the scholium (*sch.*) and, should the case arrive, the corollary (*cor.*), or by the gloss (*gl.*). *On the Free Serf* is found in *WAS*, vol. 18 (1908), pp. 551–787. I cite it, also within parentheses in the text, by the cipher *SA*, followed by the page in *WAS*.

18. Hans Blumenberg cites these lines as an example of the "Copernican paradigm," *Lebenszeit und Weltzeit*, Frankfurt, 1986, p. 188.

19. René Descartes, *Discourse on Method*, IV, 1.

20. M. Luther, letter no. 3451 to Melanchthon (March 5, 1540); *WAB*, vol. 9, p. 70. Here, *conscientia* designates the moral consciousness.

21. Philippe Ariès recounts the turn in regard to the representation of the Last Judgment in Christianity. "[T]he idea of judgment swept over" the Middle Ages; then, in the fifteenth century, "man became his own judge," *L'Homme devant la mort*, Paris, 1977, pp. 104 and 112. The intellectual ontogenesis of Martin Luther recapitulates wondrously this cultural phylogenesis.

22. The psychoanalyst Erik Erikson believes that Luther's anxieties led him to an "extreme totalism: the enshrinement of God in the dreaded role of the father and who you can never trust. With this, the buckle is buckled, repression returns in full force," *Young Man Luther*, New York, 1958, p. 164. On the Oedipus complex in Luther, see ibid., pp. 73, 77, 123.

23. "Preface"; *WAS* vol. 54, p. 186. It consists of a commentary from the elderly Luther, for the edition of his Latin works (1545), on the new intelligence of the *justitia Dei* as it had come to him in reading Romans 1:17. On the dating of this new intelligence out of which, strictly speaking, the Reformation was born, see Gerhard Ebeling's article "Luther" in *Die Religion in Geschichte und Gegenwart*, vol. IV, 1960, pp. 495–520. The texts of the *Commentary on Romans* that I cite are alone sufficient to exclude any date later than 1515. As Gerhard Müller observed, the definition of justice in the Preface of 1545 corresponds in all rigor to that of the commentary of 1515 on Romans 1:17 ("Neuere Literatur zur Theologie des jungen Luther," *Kerygma und Dogma*, XI [1965], pp. 334ss.). Man in the face of the law is to be counted among ". . . these travellers, for which lies open / The familiar empire of dark futures," Charles Beaudelaire, *Les Fleurs du mal*, "Bohemiens en voyage."

24. The distinction between *sub lege* and *in lege* situations comes from Augustine (*Commentary on the Psalms* 1, 2 and elsewhere). The configurations of the law in Luther could form a true dilemma only because the decalogue and the law "inscribed in the heart" not only have the same ends, but are also both extrinsic to the I. On teleology as the unifying factor of the forms of the law, see Gerhard Ebeling, *Luther*, Tübingen, 1964, pp. 153f.

25. "I call *transcendental* all knowledge that, in general, is concerned less with objects than in our manner of knowing them to the extent that this manner should be possible *a priori*," Immanuel Kant, *Critique of Pure Reason*, "Introduction" (A 11); *AA*, vol. III, p. 43. I follow the convention used in all the literature on Kant—except, unfortunately, in the French translation of the *Critique* by A. Tremesaygues and B. Pacaud, Paris, 1971—in citing the first edition (Riga, 1781) with the cipher A and the second (Riga, 1787) with the cipher B. For Kant's other works I also indicate beforehand the reference to the first edition of the work (cipher: A), and then that of the *Akademie-Ausgabe* (cipher: *AA*): *Kants Gesammelte Schriften*, ed. Preußische Akademie der Wissenschaften, Leipzig, 1902ff.

26. M. Luther, *The Great Catechism*, "The First Commandment," *WAS*, vol. 30/I, pp. 132f. These lines have not gone without provoking controversy. See the attempt at clarification in Gerhard Ebeling, "Was

heißt einen Gott haben oder was ist Gott?," in G. Ebeling, *Wort und Glaube,* Tübingen, 1969, vol. II, pp. 287–304.

27. The "hidden" God is no longer that of the *via negativa* or Neoplatonic apophasis. One sees this in the unconcealment that Luther opposes to concealment. What God is not hidden? "He is nothing other than [my act of] believing in him." This is a phenomenal God who, contrary to that of the *via affirmativa* or of the cataphasis, cannot be endowed with attributes. The opposition of "hidden" and "unhidden" disengages being and essence, the *an sit* and the *quid sit,* etc., because it disengages predicative logic. Proceeding in the same direction, Philip Melanchthon will state that it is pointless to inquire into questions such as the unicity of God, the Trinity, Creation, the Incarnation. Such problems are beyond our ken and are ones from which scholastics have derived nothing but their vanity (*Loci communes,* ed. D. Th. Kolbe, Leipzig, 1900, p. 63). Faith has but one object: "You do not believe in the proper manner if you do not believe that salvation has been given to you" (ibid., p. 175).

28. Immanuel Kant, *Critique of Pure Reason* (A 158); *AA,* vol. III, p. 146.

29. Luther, *Commentary on the Letter to the Galatians* (3, 6); *WAS,* vol. 40/1, p. 360.

30. Aristotle, *Metaphysics,* XII, 9; 1075a 4, and *De anima,* III, 4; 430 a 33f.

31. The polemic that Luther engages in against the Jews indicates once again consciousness as the source of being. The Scripture is *present* to them since they read it, but it remains closed to them. Seeking to render themselves entitatively just in satisfying the law, they do not *represent* it in a self-consciousness knowing itself as reputed to be just. Consequently, to the extent that the subject does not admit the divine promises are truthful (in the prophets), they are nothing, they do not show themselves, they do not become phenomena, they are not. They come to be when we confess them fulfilled.

32. Luther continues: "It would be in vain for Christ to have been given and crucified for us a thousand times if the word of God did not come to distribute it and offer it to me in saying: 'All this belongs to you'," *The Great Catechism,* "Of the Sacrament of the Altar," *WAS,* vol. 30/I, p. 226. The key role of extrinsic speech demarcates definitively this theory of subjective appropriation from the mystical Rhenish tradition that will inspire Angelus Silesius to the contrary one century after Luther: "Christ could be born a thousand times in Bethlehem, / If he is not born in you, it is your loss forever." *L'errant chérubinique,* trans. Roger Munier, Paris, 1970, p. 50. Here one sees some of the themes, only in the *Commentary on the Epistle to the Romans,* where the two principal concepts of this Rhenish heritage come up, those of detachment (*Abgeschiedenheit*) and of letting-be (*Gelassenheit*). You ought "not to desire what would be yours" (*sch.* 9,3), but "to become nothing, stripped and virgin to all things," "emptied of all forms" (*sch.* 3,7), and "dying to all things" (*sch.* 15,4); you ought "to deny all that is not God" and "to turn yourself away from all things" (*sch.* 8,7); "when our projects are finally rendered silent and our works lie at rest, then we become pure receptacles in the eyes of God" (*sch.* 8,26); "one should at all times allow oneself to be, remaining without knowing, without sensation, without understanding" (*sch.* 10,2). For all that, including the *raptus* (*sch.* 5,5), it would be simple to indicate the parallel texts in Meister Eckhart. But Luther alters this heritage in integrating it into the thought of a positive word and of hearing.

33. Luther, *Commentary on the First Book of Moses; WAS,* vol. 44, p. 246.

34. "Letters are dead words, oral discourse renders words alive" (*The Last Speeches of David; WAS,* vol. 54, p. 74), since "the voice is the soul of the word" (*Operationes in psalmos, ps.* 11,7; *WAS,* vol. 5, p. 379).

35. "I am Lutheran and, by philosophy, entirely anchored in Lutheranism," G. W. F. Hegel, letter to Tholuck of July 3, 1826 (in Wilhelm Lutgert, *Die Religion des deutschen Idealismus,* vol. III, Gütersloh, 1925, p. 464). The Lutheran anchoring of German Idealism is twofold, by the principle of subjectivity and by that of objectivation. For idealism, this last principle is concerned with speech to the extent that the mind reaches its actuality only in being concretized in the sensible. But in Luther the entire conception of speech would collapse if he conceived the mind as capable of objectivating itself from within. On the contrary, it is necessary that the concrete—which is nothing other than speech—be revealed to him from outside. The idealists believed it possible to find, in reformed thought, the concrete only by way of the detour through a speculative interiorization of the non-interiorizable.

36. Arguments about the knowledge of God in terms of nature—veiled knowledge—in no way constitute a foreign, medieval, and as yet unreformed element in Luther's thought. This knowledge fulfills a systematic function, although completely different than in the Scholastics (it authorizes no "proof of the existence of God"). It comes to view with the discovery of the law. Veiled by the condemnatory imperative, it remains not only uncertain, but its logic—as we will see regarding the ego—leads to idolatry. One can discern three places of this indirect knowledge: in exterior nature, in history, and in moral consciousness (Rudolf Malter *Das reformatorische Denken und die Philosophie,* Bonn, 1980, pp. 277f).

37. He violently rejected all complicity with philosophy, which is only "a study of vanity and perdition" (*sch.* 8,19). This can be said only from the point of view of faith, not of the law. The law, at least in its form "inscribed in the heart," manifests itself as the opposite of reason and invites philosophical explication.

But the philosopher will never know that the law leads to death. That is the reason that his profession binds him to the "wisdom of the flesh, that is the revolt against God" (Romans 8:7).

38. Augustine, *Soliloquies,* II, 7.

39. The Word of God is present in all talk of faith, and even in all talk pertaining to law (on the diverse modes of this presence, see Gerhard Ebeling, *Evangelische Evangelienauslegung: Eine Untersuchung zu Luthers Hermeneutik,* Munich, 1942, and Darmstadt, 1962, pp. 362ff.). However, the *logos* is no longer ours in any way. Above all, it is no longer our "first domestic good," *prôton oikeîon,* as the Stoics said.

40. There is a "lapsus" only if we absurdly turn into a "work" the *potentia obœdientialis* toward which the cited expressions point and which cause difficulty. The act of this faculty, the "I obey," will, to the contrary, appear as the originary and *a priori* synthesis in consciousness from which the modifications regarding speech are deployed. It makes consciousness be one, wherein it will prove itself to be the keystone of pre-emancipatory transcendentalism—mirroring the ultimate, emancipatory "I think."

41. Such was the thesis of Ernst Troeltsch, for example, *Gesammelte Schriften,* Tübingen, 1922, p. 248.

42. It is true that Luther, despite being imbued with Dionysian Neoplatonism, dedicates himself to the detailed construction of a universe in which eight degrees of the good are erected . . . in order to hasten immediately to raze the edifice in declaring these goods to be so many traps for faith. "[M]an—and it is horrible—fabricates idols for himself" (*sch.* 8,7).

43. Aristotle, *Metaphysics,* I, 2; 982 a 5.

44. In the opposite direction, that is to say, no longer that "all our understanding should be regulated by objects" but, to the contrary, "the object should be regulated by the manner of our power of intuition," *Critique of Pure Reason,* B XVIf. In just these two pages, the words 'try,' 'attempt,' 'attempting' (*Versuch, versuchen*) recur five times.

45. "There exists in God neither cause nor foundation serving as the rule nor standard for his will. . . . Rather, His will is the rule for all things. . . . Everything that occurs, because he desires it as such, will be just" (*SA* 712). Events occur through what Scotus called the *necessitas consequentis* (*absoluta, simplex*), not through *necessitas consequentiae* (*relativa, conditionis*), cf. Duns Scotus, *Commentary on the Sentences,* 1. I, dist. 39, qu. 5. Luther draws from it the "strong" conclusion of a voluntary predestination, against the "weak" version of a simple prescience that would accord to man some practical autonomy.

46. Augustine, *Confessions,* VII, 9,13.

47. Man is a beast of burden: "When he is mounted by God, he desires and goes where God wants. . . . When Satan is in the saddle, he desires and goes where Satan wants. . . . The riders themselves fight to keep him and possess him" (*SA* 635). One should read into this no more than the affirmation of God as "supremely mobile" (cf. Alfred Adam, "Die Herkunft des Lutherwortes vom menschlichen Willen," *Lutherjahrbuch,* XXIX [1962], pp. 25–34).

48. Ludwig Feuerbach cites Luther: "If you believe it, you possess it; if you do not believe it, you do not have it; if you believe it, it is; if you do not believe it, it is not." He continues: "It follows that faith in beatitude or, what comes to the same, in divinity, is only the certitude of my own beatitude and my divinity. . . . Believing signifies nothing more than transforming [the statement]: 'There exists one God, a Christ' into [the statement] 'I am a God, I am a Christ'," *Sämtliche Werke,* ed. W. Bolin and Fr. Jodl, vol. VII, Stuttgart, 19XX, pp. 353–369. This transformation will reduce the initial religious production of the divine to the human. Feuerbach saw well the transcendental turn—"Luther places all the stress on the 'for us'" (ibid., p. 318–326)—as well as the parallel with the Cartesian *cogito,* "my believing is my being" (ibid., vol. III, 14). But in Luther, no more than in Descartes or Kant, we cannot infer a subjective production from simple conditions.

49. In Meister Eckhart, detachment is receptive and poietic at the same time, as is its model, the Aristotelian *noûs* (cf. Schürmann, *Maître Eckhart ou la joie errante,* Paris, 1972, pp. 29–36 and 45–54).

50. *Praelectio in Psalmos* (*ps.* 45); *WAS* vol. 40/II, p. 527.

51. Werner Elert, *Morphologie des Luthertums,* Munich 1931, vol. I, p. 75.

52. Sermon for Saint Martin 1516; *WAS,* 1, p. 100.

53. *Dictata super Psalterium* (*ps.* 50); *WAS* vol. 3, p. 290.

54. Ibid.

55. French has an expression, *les Lumières* {the Enlightenment}, only for speaking of the *Aufklarung* in the sense of a period in the history of ideas. It does not have a word to render its programmatical sense, independent of the confidence in progress as it marked the eighteenth century. It happens that in Luther's context, we can make up for this lack, not unhappily, by borrowing from Roman law the term *emancipation* (a *mancipatio* was a legal transaction by which one freed a thing—a good or a person—from under the seizure of someone so that it could be taken in hand, *manu capere,* by another; *emancipatio* designated the freeing, especially by a son, from under all seizure, especially of the paterfamilias). Luther's transcendentalism is critical, but it remains pre-emancipatory; consciousness is still placed under the

hand of God. To observe its effects, one needs only read the condemnations he heaps upon the revolting peasantry (*Against the Murderous and Brigand Peasant Hordes; WAS,* vol. 18, pp. 357–361). His rejection of all practical emancipation is founded on the theory of the two regimes, itself the consequence of theonomy in self-consciousness.

56. *Commentary on the Letter to the Galatians* (3,19); *WAS,* vol. 40/1, p. 481.

57. *Operationes in Psalmos* (*ps.* 5, 9); *WAS,* vol. 5, p. 144.

58. In speaking of the self and the ego, of the principles of life and death, I only hear Luther speaking. One would do well not to seek here some allusion to terminologies that only subsequently saw the light of day.

59. It goes without saying that facts of consciousness have nothing to do with the "facts of salvation"—facts and gestures registered in the Scriptures and whose supposed efficiency Luther counts among the reist illusions.

60. In the transcendental sense, writes one commentator, the mind "is entirely disintellectualized, emptied of every representation of an active power. It is really nothing more than a 'place'," Wilfried Joest, *Ontologie der Person bei Luther,* Göttingen 1967, p. 185.

61. Certain commentators wanted to establish in Luther a natural knowledge of God through the universal fact of moral consciousness (see, for example, Ernst Wolf, *Peregrinatio. Studien zur reformatorischen Theologie und zum Kirchenproblem,* vol. 1, Munich 1954, p. 17.). Such a demonstration would have little to offer. For the premoderns, it goes without saying that a cognitive certainty is attached to desire; we experience a "natural desire to see God"—thus we see God. In Luther, desire and knowledge are determined otherwise. What in us desires to see? Obviously, the ego. As for the self, it instead desires to understand. It knows *a priori* that *submission* to a word can take one to the peak. It is an other desire, because heteronomous; a different peak also, because humiliating (but it is not the desire to be humiliated, which is a contortion of the ego). To seek to demonstrate a natural knowledge of God on the basis of moral consciousness thus would be to pass beyond the originary phenomenon in Luther—beyond the "I obey" that orients self-consciousness toward the word.

62. Shakespeare, *Hamlet,* Act 1, Scene 5.

63. It is thus difficult to follow Heidegger when he suggests that Luther inaugurates the modern search for *certitude,* a search in which Descartes would take part, so to speak, only by broaching secularization: "The truth of beings, in the sense of the certitude of the self of subjectivity, is at root, as certainty (*certitudo*), the justification of representation and of what it represents before its own clarity. Justification (*iustificatio*) is the fulfillment of *iustitia* and, in this manner, justice itself. . . . At the beginning of modern times there awakens with new vigor the question: How, in the whole of beings—which means, before the foundation that is, of all beings, most (God)—can man become and be certain of his solidity, that is to say of his salvation? This question of the certitude of salvation is precisely that of justification" (*Chemins qui ne mènent nulle part,* trans. W. Brockmeier lightly modified, Paris, 1962, p. 201). Elsewhere Heidegger traces out something like a genealogy of subjective certitude posited over against objective nature, a genealogy prepared by Occam and proceeding from Luther to Galileo, then to Descartes (*Seminar at Thor,* 1968, trans. J. Beaufret, *Questions IV,* Paris, 1976, p. 220f.). The search for solidity, thus for permanence, defines the ego. Far from making it his key question, Luther *denounces* such a search as the very essence of the "flesh." On the event of the word that "strikes," see the lines cited below, note 65.

64. Following Rudolph Malter, all categorial discourse amounts only to "subsuming, through theory, the totality of what falls under our own egotistical comprehension, *Das reformatorische Denken. . . ,* p. 83.

65. "You ask: When and how God sends his word? I say: Question your experience. If the word cleaves and strikes and wakens the heart, then it has been sent by God. But it neither strikes nor wounds everyone. It strikes whom it strikes (*wen es trifft, den triffts*)" (*Interpretation of Psalm 109; WAS* vol. 1, 695).

66. *Sermon for the Second Day of Easter 1523; WAS* vol. 12, p. 497.

67. In accordance with the opinion common among his readers, Luther displaces the vocabulary of "speculative" mysticism toward a theology of biblical speech. The quest of a Tauler, especially, would aim at the *fruitio Dei*—in short, what I call the ego. See, for example, Horst Quiring, "Luther und die Mystik," *Zeitschrift für systematische Theologie* XIII [1936], pp. 150–240. Things are nevertheless more complicated. In one of its two guiding themes, the Rhenish tradition (and already the Greek patristic tradition) teaches the birth of the Word in the soul. In this sense, this mysticism really does constitute a theology of speech—overdetermined, certainly, by ancient, Neoplatonic, metaphysical tropes of the *logos*. But it is a misinterpretation to amalgamate, in one and the same critique of "spiritual pleasure," Dionysian and Rhenish heritages.

68. When he deals with the problem of the categories (in the *Regulae*), he does so by "transcribing" Aristotle (see Jean-Luc Marion, *Sur l'ontologie grise de Descartes,* Paris, 1981, §13, pp. 78ff.).

69. René Descartes, Third *Meditation; AT,* vol. 7, p. 40. Many times over, Descartes suggests that he understands his doctrine of innate ideas as the transposition into human consciousness of the exemplar-

ism of the essences pre-existing in the divine intellect (cf. *AT*, vol. 4, p. 350; vol. 5, p. 152; vol. 7, pp. 166, 181). This metaphysics of ideal existants, in Descartes, is but the pendant to his material idealism of time and space from which Kant will part: "The formal idealism (that I also call transcendental) effectively puts an end to the Cartesian material idealism." (*Prolegomena*, § 49 [*A* 141]; *AA*, vol. IV, p. 337. On the only figure of innatism accepted in Kant, cf. below, note 117.

70. Immanuel Kant, *What does it mean to orient oneself in thought?* endnote (*A* 330); *AA*, vol. VIII, pp. 146f.

71. It is the subtitle of the work by Robert Spaemann and Reinhard Loew, *Die Frage Wozu? Geschichte und Wiederentdeckung des teleologischen Denkens*, Munich, 1981.

72. The champion of "classical" philosophy so understood is indeed Leo Strauss. He seeks to resuscitate the conception of natural law as based upon a "teleological vision" (*Natural Right and History*, Chicago, 1950, pp. 7f., 143–147). According to Strauss, it is important to resuscitate it in order to hold mass society in check: "Liberal education is the necessary effort to establish an aristocracy at the heart of mass democratic society" (*Liberalism Ancient and Modern*, New York, 1968, p. 4). How so? By a doctrine that is as easy to *convey as evident* as is that of teleology. Accordingly, his own works rank among "this particular type of literature in which the truth concerning all crucial things is presented exclusively between the lines" (*Persecution and the Art of Writing*, New York, 1952, p. 25). And what is the crucial truth that Leo Strauss himself presents exclusively between the lines? This "truth" is that the historic division between the classical and modern epochs, and thus that the "teleologial vision" itself of which the divsion marks a loss and a mourning, are but *tools of public intervention* to constitute the new aristocracy and to confer on it full powers (with this corollary that does not lack piquancy: the arch-modern, Nietzsche, is struck down precisely for having turned truth into a tool of power).

73. Nostalgia going to "the absolute authority of the sages," Leo Strauss, *Natural Right*, p. 185. The call to absolute power had been discreetly watered down by the German translators of the work.

74. *Probatio* to the first conclusion of the *Disputation of Heidelberg*, published by Erich Vogelsang, *Luther, Werke in Auswahl*, vol. 5, 3rd ed., Berlin, 1963, pp. 403f.; see the *Conclusion prima* in *WAS*, vol. 1, pp. 355f.

75. Under the influence of the ego, consciousness remains unhappy. It seeks to satisfy itself absolutely by means of the absolute—as it is missing it.

76. See the lines cited above, note 47. From the transcendentalist perspective, which alone interests us here, the parable lends itself to misunderstanding because of the decisionism that it suggests.

77. Francesco Petrarca, *Prose*, ed. G. Martellotti, Milan, 1955, pp. 28f., 66.

78. See above, note 63. Luther renders problematic, not certitude by faith, but certitude by election; cf. W. Elert, *Morphologie des Luthertums*, vol. I, pp. 76–78, with the discussion of the *Commentary on the Letter to the Romans* and of the *Interpretation of Psalm 109* (*WAS*, vol. 9, p. 191).

79. In the *Disputatio contra scholasticam theologiam*, Luther describes men as naturally enslaved by their actions; *WAS* vol. 1, p. 226, thesis 39.

80. From this point of view, the affinity with Kant would be greater in Erasmus, against whom Luther directs *SA*. The author of the *Diatribe Concerning the Free Will*, writes Luther, "does not see, either in the Old or in the New Testament, anything but laws and good commandments for the formation of men in view of good morals. But of what pertains to the new birth, to the restoration, to the regeneration, of all the work of the Spirit, he sees nothing" (*SA* 693). Erasmus attracts Luther's thunder because he maintains that Scripture "should be understood through a sensible interpretation, not purely and simply accepted" (*SA* 731). See also above, note 6.

81. "That the free will is nothing . . . an empty concept" (*SA* 756).

82. Luther "himself realized in the social order of the Church that which, in the civil order, he so fervently fought: a 'peasant uprising' . . . [is responsible] for all nonsense in matters of knowledge, in brief, of the plebianism of the spirit . . ." (*The Gay Science*, no. 358).

83. "The mind is held captive by the truth," *De Captivitate Babylonica*, *WAB*, vol. 6, p. 561. We have in mind the distinction between truth and sense in Hannah Arendt. The truth constrains the understanding to adherence, while sense liberates thought (*La Vie de l'esprit*, vol. 1: *La Pensée*, trans. by L. Lotringer, Paris, 1981, pp. 30 and 70–83).

84. See above, Volume One, General Introduction, note 4.

85. One falsely restrains Luther's project by seeing in it only a soteriology. The exclusive efficiency of God is at work, both in the creation and in the justification (*SA* 753). As a result, he must set out upon the contemptible terrain of being. Hence the question: How are the commonplaces concerning being in movement, repeated by Luther without a warning, to be harmonized with the turn, taken with vehemence, toward being-for-consciousness? Answer: nature is transcendentalized in accordance with the future through its "sighs," just as the self is through the "promise."

86. "Bene philosophari" (*Disputation de Heidelberg*, thesis 30; *WAS* vol. 1, p. 355); "optimi philosophi"

(*sch.* 8,19); "philosophizing outside Christ is like fornicating outside marriage. The creature in man rejoices (*frui*) but it serves (*uti*) nothing," (*Probatio* to the first conclusion of the *Disputation de Heidelberg; Werke in Auswahl,* vol. 5, p. 404).

87. Malter, *Das reformatorische Denken,* p. 143.

88. Faith is at the end of a gun. "If they (the peasants) are demented to the point of not wanting to hear the Word, they will hear the whip and the gun, and that will be good for them" (letter to Joannes Rühel of May 30, 1525; *WAB* vol. 3, p. 515). See also his program for university reform, namely, "to banish entirely" all the works dealing with "natural things," notably the *Physics, Metaphysics,* the *De Anima,* and the *Ethics* of Aristotle. This last book above all, "worse than any other, it goes straight to the encounter of God's grace and Christian virtue." "In the schools and the tribunals" also, the evangelists should have the last word (*An den christlichen Adel deutscher Nation,* no. 25; *WAS,* vol. 6, pp. 457f. and 460).

89. "What Luther had begun with as faith, in the sentiment and according to the witness of the Spirit, is the same thing as the mind, advanced further in its maturation, that seeks to grasp in the concept so as to liberate itself thereby in the present and find himself," "Preface" to Hegel, *Grundlinien der Philosophie des Rechts: Sämtliche Werke,* vol. 7, Stuttgart 1928, p. 36.

90. Immanuel Kant, *Metaphysik,* course notes, *AA* vol. XXVIII, p. 269 (for the abbreviations used in the references to Kant, see note 25 above). This course dates from the beginning of the 1770s. Just as in his inaugural dissertation, Kant here proposed a speculative proof of human freedom, only "subjectively unknowable." Even if a such a proof does not pass the critical threshold, the cited lines clearly state the epistemological and moral unity of freedom and hence the unicity of spontaneity. My purpose will be to show that the *one* freedom remains presupposed beyond the threshold, but that this freedom, transcendental in the critical sense, is shattered in its spontaneity through its dependence on given, heteronomous being.

91. "Ich, der Inhaber der Welt," *Opus postumum, AA* vol. XXI, p. 45, l. 25. The Cartesian project of a *dominion* (through the sciences, we are able to make ourselves "as the masters and possessors of nature") is enlarged into the *constitution* of the world.

92. Immanuel Kant "On Freedom" (*AA* vol. XX, pp. 91f.).

93. More formidable still is the multivalence of "reason" in the process that the Enlightenment had intended for it. It thereby combines incompatible charges. Reason, as critical, is seated as judge and jury; as speculative, it is the accused as well as its lawyer; as reflexive, it is plaintiff and prosecutor; as transcendental, it is acquitted; but finally, insofar as it remains naturally, irremediably metaphysical, it is condemned as something outside of the law. Kant acquits it as *Verstand* in the transcendental deduction; he condemns it as *Vernunft* in the dialectic.

94. *Response to the Question: What Is Enlightenment*? (*A* 481); *AA* vol. VIII, p.33.

95. In all the branches of critical philosophy, the unconditioned function is the responsibility of subjective spontaneity. If in knowledge self-consciousness is "the condition of all unity, itself unconditioned" (*A* 401), then it is because self-consciousness is pure spontaneity. Likewise in morality. Now, Kant was satisfied to juxtapose theoretical and practical spontaneity without once raising the question of its unicity. Commentators follow him in that with a few rare exceptions. Two notable exceptions: Gerold Prauss, *Kant über Freiheit als Autonomie,* Frankfurt/M., 1983, and Henry Allison, *Kant's Theory of Freedom,* Cambridge, 1990.

96. Autonomy is contained analytically in spontaneity, not the inverse. In all of the branches of critical transcendentalism, Kant seeks to show that only the law that *we impose* is efficacious (toward nature) and obligatory (toward ourselves). So, without autonomy, there is no spontaneous legislation.

97. Gérard Granel (*L'Équivoque de la pensée kantienne,* Paris, 1970) devoted himself to a "deconstruction of [Kantian] pure reason." In the process he discovered (1) an absence of foundation (pp. 115f.) as well as (2) an equivocation between the language of representation and the language of phenomenality (pp.110f. and elsewhere). A blundering book, not only because it seeks to illuminate the *Critique* by way of the *Dissertation* of 1770, but also because (1) it states and then denies what the real foundation of Kantian critical thought is—that which no reader can ignore, namely, *that there is experience.* There is a foundation in the world (whatever Granel says of it) which, it is true (with Granel this time), (2) indeed divides univocal being. Through this "laying out straight" of the univocal, Granel's project touches my own purpose, though evidently at a distance, which is to lay open the conflictual foundation of the transcendental critique. Now, there again, the route taken by Granel is not at all viable since he reads into Kant what he wants to find there: "We do not say—once again—that these affirmations were *in* Kant *in the explicit form* in which we give them. Rather, we say that Kant is in them (p.109)." Whosoever wishes to give demonstrations by means of argumentative strategies must advance upon an unassailable textual base; and who, advancing thus, becomes disquieted by the absence of a *simple* foundation in Kant, must interrogate the sense of being that the influence of representation imposes and that, indeed, Kant prepares himself to shatter for the sake of phenomenality.

98. *Groundwork of the Metaphysics of Morals,* "Preface" (A XIV); *AA,* vol. IV, p.391f.
99. Ibid., "Of the Extreme Limit of all Practical Philosophy" (A 120–125); *AA,* vol. IV, pp. 458–461.
100. *What Are the Real Advancements . . .* (A 97–99); *AA,* vol. xx, p.292.
101. *Groundwork,* (A 119f.); *AA,* vol. IV, pp. 458–461.
102. *Critique of Pure Practical Reason,* "7. Principle of Pure Practical Reason. Note" (A 56); *AA,* vol. V, p. 31.
103. Ibid., "Critical Elucidation of the Analytic of Pure Practical Reason" (A 162); *AA,* vol. V, p. 91.
104. *Religion within the Limits of Simple Reason,* I, 1 (A 14); *AA,* vol. VI, p. 26. According to the context, I translate *vernünftig* sometimes as 'rational,' sometimes as 'reasonable.'
105. Kant, for whom there are plenty of convergences between theoretical and practical freedom, does not hesitate to suggest that here and there, it is one. Thus it occurs to him to suggest that freedom can be established simply by reflecting upon our rationality. Transcendental freedom "is the hypothesis required for all rules, and, consequently for every employment of the understanding," even if it "belongs to beings in which the foundation for acting consists in their being conscious of a rule" (*Reflexionen* No. 4904, *AA,* vol. XVIII, p. 24). One would have expected nothing less, and he affirms that transcendental freedom overhangs moral freedom: "To suppress transcendental freedom is to abolish all practical freedom" (B 562). But how is one to understand transcendental freedom? It is "the ability to begin a state of affairs *from oneself*" (B 561); according to the context, it is a causal capability. Also, spontaneity, the very essence of apperception, does not at all allow itself to be reduced to cosmological efficacy. Spontaneity is rather its principle—and at times, Kant seems to want to characterize even the I-think with efficacy (for example, in saying that theoretical laws cover "that which becomes, through us, actual," (*Critiques of Judgement* A 339). One would have, then, a transcendental freedom diversified into epistemic (*Handeln*) and moral (*Tun*) spontaneity. However, one can only remain perplexed in seeing (1) that Kant never problematizes the unicity of theoretical and practical spontaneity; (2) that in treating of causality, he reduces the transcendental to the cosmological; (3) that, correlatively, in apperception, he systematically passes over causality without comment; and finally (4) that, consequently, a homonymy traverses the concept of freedom.
106. *Über eine Entdeckung . . .* (A 71); *AA,* vol. VIII, p. 223. Cf. *Opus Postumum, AA,* vol. XXII, p. 76.
107. For the attempts to reconstruct Kant's argumentative course in the deduction, a topic that is not mine, one should refer to the works of Dieter Henrich, notably, *Identität und Objektivität. Eine Untersuchung zu Kants transzendentaler Deduktion,* Heidelberg, 1976.
108. His goal is to demonstrate that the object comes to being, as an object of experience, according to the laws of the understanding, and that these laws are objectively real, §§ 26–27.
109. To look at the last phrase of § 15, which immediately precedes the deduction properly speaking: "We must seek that still higher unity, namely, in that which itself contains the foundation for the unity of different concepts in judgments, and therefore contains the foundation for possibility of the understanding, including in its logical usage" (B 131). *Sogar in seinem logischen Gebrauche.* Consequently, the foundation which is pure apperception renders possible, more evidently still, the unity of judgments in transcendental logic, the unity in categorical usage.
110. This shift—the metabasis from the middle voice to the noun—was seen clearly by Thomas Hobbes, who drew this conclusion from the Cartesian cogito: "I go for a walk [middle voice], therefore I am the walk [noun]" (*Third Objections,* objection 2; *AT* vol. VII, p. 172). It is true that Kant himself thought to declare, straightaway, pure apperception identical to the noumenon. "In transcendental apperception, the soul is *substantia noumenon;* therefore, it does not have permanence in time, which appertains only to objects in space." (*Reflexionen* no. 6001, *AA,* vol. XVIII, pp. 420ff.). As often in the French tradition, here spiritualism has given proof of an even greater faithfulness *sui generis* to the tragic condition. "We burn with the desire to find a solid foundation and a lasting, ultimate base so as to build there a tower, high enough so that it will rise up into the infinite; but all of our foundations fall apart, and the earth opens up to their destruction." (Pascal, *Pensées,* II, 72)
111. "*Mann kann nicht sagen eine Erfahrung haben, sondern sie machen*" (*Opus Postumum, AA,* vol. XXII, p. 107). The posthumous work which is dominated by the project of an *a priori* construction of an "indirect matter" has formulas in it that could suggest an absolute self-positing: "That outside of me there is still something; it is a product made by me. I make myself, myself. [. . .] We all make ourselves" (ibid. p. 82). We remain, nonetheless, far from Fichte. I *posit* myself in such a way that I can be *given* in sensible intuition. In the context, Kant seeks to construct an *a priori* proof of the existence of aether, an indirect matter for experience. In that case, 'to make' signifies *poîein.* But the axiom also is suitable to *Handeln, prattein,* and hence to all of the phases of the Kantian critique. It illustrates how Kant appropriates the sentence in which Vico summarized the method of Galileo: "*verum ipsum factum*" (*De antiquissima Italorum sapientia,* 1709). Let us add that when Kant defines the human—following Rousseau and against

Aristotle—as *animal liberum,* he opposes himself doubly to Luther, against the *animal obœdiens,* and for (rational) salvation through works.

112. Cf. Plato, *Gorgias* 482; *Sophist* 263f.; *Theaetetus* 189f.; as well as in Kant himself, but according to a purely empirical analysis. "[T]o think is to speak with oneself." (*Anthropology in a Pragmatic Perspective,* A 109).

113. *Critique of Practical Reason,* I, 3 (A 189f.); *AA,* vol. V, pp. 105f.

114. The proportion "nature : transcendent freedom :: conformity to laws : originary anomie" will warp, again in the nineteenth century, a large part of the debate about freedom as the determinate other of nature.

115. *Anthropology,* I, 1 "On Being Conscious of One's Self," (A 3); *AA,* vol. VII, p. 127.

116. Hence, for example, the hiatus between the two definitions, *ad extra* and *ad intra,* of freedom, as the capacity to produce effects in the world and as the self-legislation of the volitional will.

117. One knows the word according to which "even a race of devils (if only they are endowed with understanding)" would be capable of organizing themselves into a nation, *Of Perpetual Peace* (A 60); *AA,* vol. VIII, p. 366. The submission of the will to willfulness (to *Eigensinn*) through the calculations of the understanding is, for Kant, diabolical.

118. See the texts of 1775 cited by Eric Weil, *Problèmes kantiens,* Paris, 1970, pp. 144f.

119. *Metaphysics of Morals,* Introduction (A 11); *AA,* vol. VI, p.127.

120. The following citations are taken from *Religion within the Limits of Reason Alone* I, 1 (A 13–18); *AA,* vol. VI, pp. 25–28.

121. A good number of his contemporaries, and even the most admiring, were disturbed by Kant's effort to anchor evil in the very heart of the autonomous subject. Thus Goethe: "With that spot of radical evil, Kant has insultingly besmirched his philosophical great coat" (Letter to Herder, 1793).

122. *Anthropology,* I, 2 (A 8); *AA,* vol. VII, pp. 129f. The editors cite a manuscript that carries this addendum: "a eudaimonist, *very poorly advised in his principle, . . .*"

123. In Descartes, the menace that, in the form of the evil genius, haunts rational subjectivism might well be madness, whether this would be from the inside of reason or like its Great Exclusion (strictly speaking, in Descartes, there can be a "maddening" counter-strategy only in the context of the *Meditations*). In Kant, where subjectivism demands ordering forms not only in the understanding, but also in sensibility, the menace signifies that sensibility could carry reason into "chaos and shadows" (A X). No longer is the menace one of private madness, but of public disorder, due to the lack of power for putting laws into force, of anarchy in the commom sense of the word. What we find there is a leitmotif which, like a phobia, interferes with the Kantian procedure at each important turn; cf. B XXXVII, A 100f., 111F., 121; *Perpetual Peace,* A 12, 19 (note), 62, 72 (note); *The Conflict of Faculties,* A 18 and 41 (note). This last text above all illustrates that, for Kant, "anarchy" results from the faculty of judgment abandoning itself to inclinations. But when I speak of the ego in Kant, it is not a question of such abandon, but rather of the conditions of heteronomy in transcendental freedom.

124. *Critique of Practical Reason,* A 178.

125. *Of Perpetual Peace,* Appendix, I (A 88); *AA,* vol. VIII, p. 379. Goethe's Mephistopheles is presented as "the spirit who always negates," but who, being a part of that force that desires evil, always accomplishes the good:

> "Ich bin der Geist, der stets verneint."
> ". . . Ein Teil von jener Kraft,
> Die stets das Böse will und stets das Gute schafft."

Faust, Part I, lines 1338 and 1336f.

126. *Idea of A Universal History. . . ,* Fourth Thesis (A 392); *AA,* vol. VIII, pp. 20f.

127. See above, note 117.

128. This is the subtitle of Bernard de Mandeville, *Fable des abeilles* (1714).

129. *The Probable Beginning of Human History* (A 9); *AA,* vol. VIII, p, 113.

130. See the following texts: *Account Rendered by Herder: 'Ideas Concerning the Philosophy of Human History'* (A 155); *AA,* vol. VIII, p.64; *Idea of A Universal History. . . ,* Third Thesis (A 391 and 393), *AA,* vol. VIII, pp. 20f; *Religion. . . ,* Note to the First Section (B 52); *AA,* vol. VI, p. 46. *The Probable Beginning . . .* (A 11) *AA,* vol. VIII, p.114. See also the description by Nietzsche of a possible inversion of political "maxims": *The Wanderer and His Shadow,* no. 284.

131. *Religion. . . ,* III, 2 (A 174 and 188); *AA,* vol. VI, pp. 124 and 131.

132. We know the fortunes that this distribution of revolutionary work on either side of the Rhine—political work in France, philosophical work in Germany—experienced in the nineteenth century. The French worked to refine the people by allying politics with that most bloody commodity of exportation, religion; the English did so by allying their parliamentarianism with mercantilism. The Germans, upon

a base of nationalized weakness and under the cover of moral reprobation, are always ready to desire to change the world through their simple essence (*Und es mag am deutschen Wesen / Einmal noch die Welt genesen,* E. Geibel), the essence of poets and of thinkers (*das Volk der Dichter und Denker*).

133. *Anthropology,* II, A, 3 (A 270f.); *AA,* vol. VII, p.294.

134. *Religion,* I, 3, note (A 36) and I, 2 (A 23); *AA,* vol. VI, pp. 39 and 31.

135. In coming to a close, the nineteenth century will lament with interminable sighs the broken foundation of the self and the heteronomy that touches it. Thus Ralph Waldo Emerson: "Everything intercepts us from ourselves."

136. In regard to the "root" again, Kant evades the transcendental terrain. The two branches of the spirit plunge into one "common root, unknown, however, by us" (B 29); now, according to the critical project, all that that treats of things in themselves is unknown; the two branches are enrooted, then, "perhaps" in our intelligible substrate. Evil is "radically" other, namely through a tendency affecting the species. In both—in regard to the noumenon and in regard to the species—radicality, putting out creeping roots rather than sending down a taproot, leads, strangely, outside of the ground that is, properly speaking, transcendental.

137. On singularization as a strategy of radical evil, see the passage of Hölderlin cited in Volume One, General Introduction, note 30.

138. Kant continues: "If then we say that by nature man is good, or that by nature, he is evil, that only signifies that he encloses in himself a first ground (unexplorable by us) for the acceptation of maxims, whether good or evil (contrary to the law); and he does so in a general manner, inasmuch as man, by such a sign that through that nature he expresses at the same time the character of his species" *Religion. . . ,* I (A 6f.); *AA,* vol. VI, p. 21. In regard to that single nature of the species, Kant speaks of "innate" dispositions, ibid. I, 2, and 3 (A 23 and 25); *AA,* vol. VI, pp. 31–33.

139. *The End of All Things* (A 496f.); *AA,* vol. VIII, p. 327.

140. *Opus Postumum, AA,* vol. XXI, p.76.

141. M. Heidegger, *Kant and the Problem of Metaphysics,* trans. Richard Taft, Bloomington, 1997, § 31.

142. Paul Ricoeur, "Kant et Husserl,", *Kantstudien,* XLVI (September 1954), p. 53.

143. The abbreviation *CJ,* following the page numbers in the first edition, refers to the *Critique of Judgment.*

144. In Kant, that which can be proven without recourse to appearances—that which is demonstrated or deduced *a priori*—constitutes an element of doctrine.

145. John Sallis, *The Gathering of Reason,* Athens, Ohio University Press, 1980, p. 166f.

146. Kant, *Der einzig mögliche Beweisgrund zu einer Demonstration des Daseins Gottes* (1763), *AA,* vol. II, pp. 63–163. For what follows, see above all A 1–16.

147. Descartes himself postulated this correspondence in an explicit reference to his ontological proof. At the beginning of the Second Responses, under the title "Reasons that prove the existence of God and the distinction between spirit and the human body, disposed in a geometric way," he writes: "IX. When we say that some attribute is contained in the nature or the concept of a thing, it is the same to say that that attribute is true of that thing and that one can be assured that it is in it" (*œvres de Descartes, publiées per Charles Adam & Paul Tannery,* Paris, Cerf, 1897–1910, vol. IX, p. 125). The Kant of 1763 speaks in a voice more rationalist than that of Descartes.

148. See the lines of the second Preface (B XVI), capital for the hypothetic method in philosophy, cited above.

149. It is true that when he denies that being is a real predicate, Kant speaks, oddly, of the thing "in itself" (*an sich selbst*) so as to designate the phenomenal givenness susceptible of being determined according to possibility, existence, and necessity (*Critique of Pure Reason* B 626). However, as the parenthesis indicates "(outside of the concept)," in the text of the *Critique of Judgment* the phrase really serves him as a way to escape to the noumenal terrain.

150. The Kant of the *Opus Postumum* draws back a notch (but, under the threat of solipsism, he obviously cannot remove) the discord and displacement between spontaneity and givenness by hypostasizing an *a priori* matter: aether.

151. In this chapter, I will call pathologic not the acting affected "by the movements of sensibility" (B 562), but the cleavage between spontaneity and passivity, the transcendental figure of the tragic.

152. Friedrich Jacobi, *David Hume über den Glauben oder: Idealismus und Realismus* (Breslau, 1787), pp. 222f. The internal contradictions in Kant—as long as we understand appearance and the thing in itself as being *two types of beings*—have been presented most clearly by H. Vaihinger, *Commentar zu Kants Kritik der reinen Vernunft,* Stuttgart, 1881–92, vol. 2, notably p. 53. They have been traced back, judiciously, to ways of *considering* experience by Henry Allison, *Kant's Transcendental Idealism,* New Haven and London, 1983, pp. 247ff.

153. 'Concept' comes from *con-capere*, just as *Begriff* comes from *greifen*, 'to seize.'

154. A new terminological difficulty: In the *Critique of Pure Reason*, the receptive spontaneity in sensorial affection is called *Position*, to which categorial thesis is opposed. In contrast, in the *Critique of Judgment* it is this thesis that Kant calls *Position*, and in that same work, he calls *Setzung* the position in sensorial affection. A terminological chiasm thus is produced between the first and the last *Critique*. In 1787, Kant had used *Setzung* to speak of a work of investment that reason effectuated upon itself; and he used *Position* to speak of the existence of the given outside of consciousness. Consider the text on position as self-affection (B 67f). In the space of ten lines, the verb *setzen* occurs there five times. It designates (1) the intuition in internal sense as the investment (*besetzen*, ibid.) of that sense with relations; (2) an act concerning, not the thing in itself, but representation in its temporality ("die Zeit, in die [*sic*] wir diese Vorstellungen setzen"); (3) affection not through extrinsic givenness, but intrinsic givenness; time is that through which the mind affects itself ("die Art, wie das Gemüt durch eigene Tätigkeit, nämlich dieses Setzen seiner Vorstellung, mithin durch sich selbst affiziert wird"). It is always a question of a 'positing in the mind' (*Setzen im Gemüte*). For extra-mental *Position*, we recall the phrase in regard to the ontological proof: "*Being* is evidently not a real predicate. . . , it is simply the position [*Position*] of a thing" (B 626). In 1790, *Setzen* denotes extra-mental being and *Position*, categorial—and in that sense, mental—being.

155. *Anthropologie*, § 24; AA, vol. VII, p. 1161 [my emphasis both times]. The question of knowing if internal sense has a "sensible manifold" in it, or whether it receives it from outside, appears to me to be poorly posed. Thoughts certainly have their *genesis* in external givenness; this does not prevent *noesis* from being produced in internal sense.

156. In Kant there consequently is no need to go looking for "the other of reason" in the body, as do the brothers Hartmut and Gernot Böhme, *Das Andere der Vernunft*, Frankfurt, 1983.

157. Composed "in three or four months, so to speak, on the fly," cited in Ernst Cassirer, *Kants Leben und Lehre*, Berlin, 1918, and Darmstadt, 1975, p. 145.

158. "All internal experience is (or has) a judgment in which the predicate is empirical and of which the subject is the I. Independently of experience, there remains, then, only the I of rational psychology; the I being the substrate of all empirical judgments." (*Reflexionen* no. 5453; *AA*, vol. XVIII, p. 186).

159. The penal code (in modern German, *Strafgesetz*) comes from the Latinism, *peinliche Gerichtsordnung: poena*, punishment, pain.

160. On the opposition between "constraint"—or "bond"—and "free," see the excellent pages in Friedrich Kaulbach, *Der philosophische Begriff der Bewegung*, Cologne, 1965, pp. 23ff.

161. B 430. It is only in the very late works that Kant ceased to conceive of the noumenon as transcendent. The noumenon "is not a particular object existing outside of my representations, but only the idea of the abstraction of the sensorial, to the extent that [that abstraction] is recognized as necessary" (*Opus Postumum*, *AA*, vol. XXII, p. 23). Furthermore, he calls it only a subjective and only a logical residue left by the work of phenomenal constitution. This is what accords poorly with "the distinction separating all objects in general into phenomena and noumena." (B 294).

162. Kant dies at the moment when he turns his back for good on that border. The theory in the *Opus Postumum* that most of all led to a shrugging of the shoulders—the *a priori* proof of the existence of aether—no longer owes anything to metaphysical nostalgia. As one commentator has said, Kant's responses to the problems of physical objects in the posthumous work "accord better with the situation in physics *today* than with the physical conception of the world in his time," Vittorio Mathieu, *Kant's Opus Postumum*, Frankfurt, 1989, p. 137.

163. In the section, "General Remarks Concerning the Passage from Rational Psychology to Cosmology," Kant designates the originary moment of indeterminate self-presence, not without a certain vagueness, as "the basis of thought" (*der Grund des Denkens*) and as "essence itself" (*das Wesen selbst*). Through such turns of phrase he seems to seek to preserve the existing, singular I—the indistinct I-think-I-am—not only from its hypostatization into noumenon, but moreover from its reduction to simple phenomena.

164. Following an indication of Heidegger, one can excavate even deeper and analyze, following the root, the soil into which it plunges. The remark, it is true, concerns Descartes (M. Heidegger, "Introduction to 'Qu'est-ce que la métaphysique?': Le retour au fondement de la métaphysique," trans. R. Munier, *Questions I*, Paris, 1968, p. 23.). If, applied to Kant, the soil represents being, for him it is no longer uniform; it does not have a single form and function.

165. Cf. Wilhelm Kamlah, *Philosophische Anthropologie: Sprachkritische Grundlegung und Ethik* (Zurich, 1972).

166. Heinz Heimsoeth, "Christian Wolffs Ontologie und die Prinzipienforschung I. Kants" in *Kant-studien, Ergänzungsheft* 71 (1956), cites Kant's course on metaphysics, published under the direction of Pölitz, to maintain that the categories of modality "are not predicates" (p. 27). According to the *Critique*, however, "the categories of modality have this peculiarity, that they do not in the least augment, as a

determination of the object, the concept to which they are joined *as predicates*. . . ." (B 266; my emphasis). The problem bears on the Kantian distinction between reality and actuality. A real predicate adds to the subject of a proposition a thinkable content; a modal predicate affirms its possibility, existence, or actual necessity. The category of *Dasein*, which can be thought *a priori* and which is a predicate, does not augment any concept. It gives us nothing to know.

167. 'Intuited' {*pressenti*}, because she is concerned with the status of the singular only in political discourse.

168. Kant knew himself to be too much of "a functionary of humanity" for that.

169. Evidently, Kant is able to conceive of the interplay of legislation-transgression only by joining it to universal morality and individual maxims or actions (cf. *Groundwork of the Metaphysics of Morals*, *B* 57–59, 113). "Material" transgression, to which he again makes an appeal in reconstructing evolution: "Before reason was awakened, . . . there was no transgression at all" (*Of the Conjectural Beginning of Human History*, *A* 13). The closest that he comes to a "formal" transgression is through the distinction between two sites of the will, both above and on this side of the law that it gives to itself (*Groundwork*, *B* 72).

170. The constitution of our *Wesen*, says Kant with irony, is a problem that is "something of an embarrassment to metaphysicians, but not to the transcendental philosopher; the latter makes no claims to explain the possibility of things, but he satisfies himself with establishing the modes of knowledge through which the possibility of experience is conceived of as possible (*die Möglichkeit der Möglichkeit der Erfahrung begreifen*)," *Opus Postumum*, *AA*, vol. XXI, p. 76. For two centuries, the word "metaphysics" has been used halfheartedly to make it perfectly clear that we are concerned only with "being." Well, Kant himself, asking how possibility is possible, has to speak as a philosopher of being.

171. That does not mean to say that obligation collapses into "necessitation," but really that moral theory is not ontologically independent, cf. *Groundwork*, *A* 123.

172. *Opus Postumum*, *AA*, vol. XXII, p. 115. In the posthumous work, Kant describes that equation both as "intuition" and "in opposition to all intuition" (ibid.). The givenness of the other submits here to a topographical rearrangement, but it is not in the least absorbed into some positing of the pure self. About self-affection and self-positing in the last works, see V. Mathieu, *Kants Opus Postumum*, pp. 162–188.

173. That which indicates—against Paul Ricoeur—the "systematic" necessity of the heterogeneous concepts of being. Cf. above, note 142.

II. The Diremption

1. Martin Heidegger, "Only a God Can Save Us Now" (interview with *Der Spiegel*), trans. D. Schendler, *The Graduate Faculty Philosophy Journal* VI (1977).

2. Thomas Aquinas, *Summa Theologica*, II, 1, q, 42, art. 2.

3. Michel Foucault, "Le retour de la morale" (interview), in *Les Nouvelles*, June 28, 1984, p. 41.

4. Jacques Derrida, *Writing and Difference*, trans. A. Bass, Chicago, University of Chicago Press, 1978, p. 293 (translation modified).

5. Martin Heidegger, *Beiträge zur Philosophie*, "Gesamtausgabe," vol. 65, Frankfurt, 1989; referred to as *Contributions*, cited hereafter as *BzP*.

6. For a quarter of a century, Otto Pöggeler has kept his readers in suspense. The *Beiträge* alone, he claimed, contained Heidegger's genuine thinking, which the lectures and public courses merely made accessible to a more general audience (*Der Denkweg Martin Heideggers*, Pfullingen, 1963, p. 145). The *Contributions* were said to constitute his "major work proper" (*das eigentliche Hauptwerk*)," "Heidegger und die hermeneutische Theologie," in *Verifikationen: Festschrift für Gerhard Ebeling*, Tübingen, 1982, p. 481.

7. In *Identity and Difference*, he will say that the difference between being and beings "essentially stems" from a gift which sets aside everything in its approach (*auseinander-zueinander*). Thus the differend is more originary than the difference.

8. "What we found and create . . . alone will be true, open" (*BzP* 315).

9. The final part of Heidegger's manuscript, at least. The editor of the volume has, indeed, rearranged the order of the chapters (cf. the postscript, *BzP* 514).

10. See above, Volume One, chapter 1, note 34.

11. M. Heidegger, *Poetry, Language, Thought*, trans. A. Hofstadter, New York, Harper & Row, 1971, p. 62.

12. The modern nation-states seem to be taken by Heidegger as avatars of Roman republicanism, if not of Roman Caesarism: "[T]he Roman relation to beings is managed by the *imperium*," he wrote in 1942–43; from this imperial conception of being stems Roman law (*ius* deriving from *iubeo*, 'I command'). Now this "Roman essence of truth finds its completion . . . in the 19th century," *Parmenides*

(lecture course of 1942–43, *"Gesamtausgabe,"* vol. 54), V. Klostermann, Frankfurt, 1982, pp. 65, 86. On Heidegger's deliberate obliteration of the concept of state, see the following note.

13. There's no need to get one's hackles up over this word. Its theoretical usefulness goes back a long way. It has to do with German quarrels over matters of state. From at least the time of Friedrich List, 'political economy' has been rendered in German as *Volkswirtschaft;* the 'League of Nations' was the *Völkerbund;* since Kant, 'international law' has been *Völkerrecht;* and so on. In German theorists of the eighteenth and nineteenth centuries, the word "people" has no ethnic connotations. It was a terminological choice due primarily to negative motives. One has only to open Adam Smith to see how fluid the concept of nation was at the time (in France, these lexical difficulties were solved in 1789, with those who longed for the Ancien Régime speaking of "kingdom," the bourgeois speaking of "nation," the proletariat speaking of "fatherland," and anyone demanding political rights speaking of "people"). As for the concept of state, it was no better suited to the Germans because of their *Kleinstaaterei* and their *Vielstaaterei*—the proliferation of their mini-states. In the social sciences as in philosophy, *Volk* was used to avoid these semantic difficulties. In opposition to the word's univocal use under National Socialism, Heidegger appeals to its polysemy. The "abandonment by being," he writes, shows up in particular in the "total insensitivity to *polysemy* (*Vieldeutigkeit*)." Thus the word "people" evokes at once that which characterizes "the community, the race, that which is low and inferior, the nation, that which endures" (*BzP* 117). This *pollachôs legetai* is instructive since the last of these ways in which "the people" is said barely conceals a polemic against what does not endure: the state—from which Heidegger had just withdrawn his services. Neither in *Being and Time* (§ 74) nor in *BzP* can the word *Volk* be taken without other considerations to support the thesis of a persistent ultra-nationalism on Heidegger's part.

14. Cf. above, Volume I, chapter 4, note 98, as well as the lines from *BzP* 473 quoted below, note 33.

15. "Only a God Can Save Us Now," p. 21.

16. The *there* (*da*) thus takes the place of what in *Being and Time* Heidegger had called *eigentlich,* usually translated as the 'authentic'; the *not-there* (*weg*) takes the place of the 'inauthentic' (*BzP* 323).

17. Jacques Derrida deems "fatal" the removal of quotation marks from the word *spirit* in Heidegger after *Being and Time* (*De l'esprit,* Paris, Galilée, 1987). There he insists heavily on this (cf. pp. 24, 65, 66, 87, 90, 100). There may be something of a rhetorical tactic in both the charge and his insistence; they serve to distance himself from Heidegger, to "leave metaphysics." This is a French rather than German tactic—but who inhabits this "French landscape" that Derrida circumscribes by a kind of Maginot operation?—for which, Derrida declares, one only needs to "decide [*sic*] to change terrain, in a discontinuous and eruptive manner, abruptly installing oneself outside and asserting the absolute rupture and difference" (*Marges—de la philosophie,* Paris, 1972, pp. 162ff.). What could possibly sanction such a decision? What would be its conditions and its means? And if the questions of authorization and condition belong to the very metaphysics one is to break with, what could be said of the opposition of inside and outside? Has not Derrida himself reiterated the extent to which *logos* ties every statement back to the "old ground"? One might just as well argue that the logic of our languages remains "fatal" to us. And this may well be so, but more radically fatal than a misplacing of quotation marks or, especially, of decision. Doubtless a more local quarrel is also being carried out behind the scenes. Derrida is obviously demarcating himself from French philosophy which, as one knows, had been spiritualist until the arrival in France of Marx, Freud, and Nietzsche. So be it. This doesn't prevent the Derrida seeking to inscribe National Socialism within the spiritualist tradition—in order to leave this tradition by "entwining" the style that changes terrain with the style that deconstructs without changing terrain—*from responding poorly.* I find the responsibility regarding the monstrous site that is ours better kept by the Derrida who observes that the "the simple practice of language ceaselessly reinstates the 'new' terrain on the oldest ground" (ibid.).

I have said that the text quoted from *Marges* can be read as a chronicle of the French scene at the date when it is signed "May 12, 1968." This doesn't prevent the announcement of a place or a time that "absolutely breaks" with the present from remaining a troubling leitmotif in Derrida (cf. the "Exergue" to *De la Grammatologie,* Paris, 1967, p. 14). In the subjectivist allegiance commanded by Heideggerian *spirit* just as by Derridean *decision* and *choice,* etc. (*Margins,* loc. cit.—without quotation marks) must be seen an object lesson demonstrating that our monstrous epochal arrangement holds us ruthlessly. No text, however, administers this lesson more harshly than the *Contributions.*

18. M. Heidegger, "Lettre au rectorat académique de l'Université Albert-Ludwig," trans. J. M. Vaysse, *L'Herne,* Paris, 1983, p. 105.

19. Note in these bold equations the ambiguity regarding Judaism. Heidegger likens it to *Russentum*—which contains a still latent spiritualism—as "non-Western"; but he also sees in it a common source of everything Western: "Bolshevism is actually Jewish; but then Christianity too is at bottom Bolshevik!" (ibid.).

20. Cf. Philippe Lacoue-Labarthe, *La Fiction du politique,* Paris, 1987, p. 160. More subtle, at first sight, in his chronology, even if his typology is overly simplifying, is the scale of Heidegger's reorienta-

tions after *Being and Time,* as retraced by Jürgen Habermas ("Heidegger—Werk und Weltanschauung," preface to Victor Farias, *Heidegger und der Nationalsozialismus,* Frankfurt, 1989, pp. 18–29): new paganism, rupture with academic philosophy, and neo-conservative diagnosis of the present time since 1929; application of certain existentials to the collective destiny since the beginning of the thirties; narrowing of *Dasein* to the German destiny and call to guides since 1933; critique of reason under the influence of Nietzsche, Greco-German bifrontality under that of Hölderlin, and a disappointed turning back to the "spirit" of National Socialism since 1935; apocalyptic expectation of salvation since approximately 1940; fatalism in the face of history since 1943; and, finally, a quietist obedience to the sendings of being since 1945. It so happens that the *Contributions* perturb this chronology on the topic of the two themes that precisely were incompatible, according to the ideological critique, with what, according to the latter, the Heideggerian "*Weltanschauung*" of the thirties would have been, the "history of being"—"a concept with which Heidegger presents himself after the war"—and the "waiting" (Habermas, pp. 20, and 27). On the contrary, these are two guiding themes in the *Contributions* (see, e.g., *BzP* 231, 69). The lesson to be drawn from this: Beware of ultimately authoritative explanations by ideological forces; it comes very close to ideology.

The *Contributions* confirm, even while adding to it an important specification, the two shifts in Heidegger's itinerary as he described them himself (from the "meaning" of being, to its "truth," then to its "topology"; "Séminaire du Thor," 1969, trans. J. Beaufret, *Questions IV,* pp. 268ff. The specification bears on the role of Nietzsche in these reorientations. Starting in 1929, and for a decade, Nietzsche allows Heidegger to pathetically free himself from subjectivist transcendentalism. Hence the historial critique, the understanding of epochs as constellations of forces (around ultimate referents), the genealogy of the suspension of meaning, and even the style. In 1939, on the other hand, that is, right in the middle of the lectures on Nietzsche, the relation changes completely. Then Nietzsche will be the spokesman of metaphysics hardened into planetary technology, into voluntarism, into the theticism of values, etc.

21. M. Heidegger, *An Introduction to Metaphysics,* trans. R. Manheim, New Haven, Yale University Press, 1959, p. 199.

22. M. Heidegger, *Poetry, Language, Thought,* p. 9.

23. The tragic condition of being could become problematic for Sartre only as the pathos of freedom blinded—as is the case for the whole tradition stemming from Descartes—by blind forces; nor could it for Habermas, who amalgamates into a mono-phenomenon the non-rational, irrational, the critique of the Enlightenment, and crypto-fascism; nor could it for the analytic philosophers who greet the very question of the human condition—and *a fortiori* that of being that determines it—with a shrug of the shoulders.

24. One may suspect this to be a translation of Sophocles' *deinon* (*Antigone,* l. 332f.).

25. Here are some key formulations of that (literally) crucial thought: "the event turned back into itself" (*das in sich kehrige Ereignis, BzP* 185); "the event beating against itself" (*das in sich gegenschwingende Ereignis, BzP* 261); "the turning-against" (*die Wider-kehre, BzP* 407); "the 'en-counter'" (*die Entgegnung, BzP* 470); "the counter-turning" (*das Gegenwendige, BzP* 247). Each time the "counter" and "against" are non-dialectical.

26. See above, Volume One, General Introduction, note 49.

27. The method and the thinking remain those of the phenomenologist who "sees and grasps only that which *is*" (*BzP* 242). That requires, Heidegger says, that he "no longer stop at good and evil, at the decadence and the rescue of the tradition, at benevolence and violence" (ibid.)—not out of immorality, but because the moral attitude "shrinks" evil and thereby even ends up "magnifying" it (*BzP* 117ff.), thus depriving itself of any space in which to respond to it. Heidegger's method and thinking remain "non moral" (*BzP* 284), for "moral" responsibility is a paltry *response* to the destiny of being that is coming upon us. Phenomenological "seriousness" could not be better stated. Seeing and grasping that which is, is responding—by thinking otherwise—to the condition that is made for us. Such is the other responsibility, in which the "other thinking" is summed up. On what one calls "the question of evil," see the Conclusion below.

28. M. Heidegger, *On Time and Being,* trans. J. Stambaugh, New York, Harper and Row, 1972, p. 41.

29. The self-criticism is twofold. On the one hand, those who would dwell in the *there* "are yet to be prepared. What is Da-sein, if not the *grounding* of the being of *these* beings?" (*BzP* 903). The *Da* is announced in the future. On the other hand, the grounding designated by the *there* is no longer radical in the sense of an axial root. We will see this in regard to the "fissuring"; it no longer furnishes phenomena "originary rootedness" (*ursprüngliche Verwurzelung, Being and Time* § 72).

30. Cf. the title of the inaugural address as academic rector: M. Heidegger, "The Self-Assertion of the German University," trans. K. Harries, *Review of Metaphysics* 38 (1985), p. 467. In the *Contributions,* Heidegger refers to it twice as if to a text having the same status as his publications and his courses (*BzP* 55, 144). The continuity concerns the founding role that falls to philosophy in relation to the sciences (cf. *Being and Time,* § 69). The "Address" is cited to condemn every science deprived of this foundation,

therefore, in order to condemn racist biology. A science that sees itself as "populist" cannot help but worsen the forgetfulness of being and the destruction of the truth. The *Contributions* distance themselves from the "Address" in that it appeared impossible to ground the modern sciences in that way. They also distance themselves from it above all in that the "Address" is without doubt the only Heideggerian text in which every figure of death—being-for-death, concealment, evil, expropriation—is absent. In Heidegger, accepting the rectorate marked the moment of tragic denial. The tragic double bind found no place in self-affirmation, understood as the identification of the guided with the guide. This affirmation was supposed to bring the lieutenant of the Führer into solidarity with his university, just as at Aulis the denial of the family brought Agamemnon into solidarity with his armies. In 1933 Heidegger did the work of consolidation, betting on natality in the popular uprising as if mortality were not.

31. *Being and Time,* § 7.

32. The modern self is only illusory ("*vermeintlich*," *BzP* 118).

33. *"Entmachung der phusis"* (*BzP* 115). In Parmenides, "being is already the being that is most of all" (*BzP* 473).

34. The word obviously alludes to *mechanê* in the sense both of machines and of maneuvers, like those to which Agamemnon fell victim (*mechanêma,* Aeschylus, *The Libation Bearers,* line 981). The tragic machinery-machinations bind the victim with "chains no bronzesmith made" (ibid. line 492). The victim is caught in a net that is also a trap. In the German vocabulary of hunting, one would say he is *gestellt.* The two words Heidegger uses to describe contemporary technology, *Machenschaft* and *Gestell,* connote tracking down prey and the hunting trap.

35. M. Heidegger, *Parmenides,* pp. 74, 134.

36. There is a beautiful irony here, hubris traditionally signifying not the setting up of a standard or ultimate authority, but its transgression.

37. The standard that the event gives, as we will see further, is the double bind in which expropriation by mortality weakens appropriation by natality.

38. Jürgen Habermas, "Heidegger—Werk und Weltanschauung," p. 20.

39. M. Heidegger, "Introduction" to "What Is Metaphysics?" According to the *Contributions,* "the questioning conversation" with the Greeks "already requires the leap" into the other beginning (*BzP* 169).

40. The word comes from Hölderlin.

41. For example, "the suprasensory world, the Ideas, God, the moral law, the authority of reason, progress, the happiness of the greatest number, culture, civilization," M. Heidegger, *The Question Concerning Technology and Other Essays,* trans. W. Lovitt, New York, Harper and Row, 1977, p. 65.

42. In the list cited (preceding note), it would be easy to put names to each of the enumerated representations.

43. "In giganticism is displayed the grandeur of the *subiectum* sure of itself and building everything upon its own representation and production" (*BzP* 441). *Machenschaft* should be understood as "the schema of thoroughgoing calculative explainability through which, in each being, everything blends together uniformly" (*BzP* 132).

44. "All have agreed no longer to raise any questions" (*BzP* 491), a statement not suggesting, to be sure, some consensus among subjects.

45. In this regard, nothing is more instructive than to frequent the colloquia of analytic philosophy in the United States. In order to reassure that their presentations will be "professional," they are obliged to begin with the words "I am going to argue. . . ." Then, in the course of their demonstration, they indicate the possible bifurcations in the discourse: "If I had continued on with X, I would have come to undesirable conclusions; *therefore,* I continue with Y." The confession is touching in its candor. The point of departure (always decisive in philosophy) is a desire, and argumentation serves to reinforce it. How then, is one to render the word *argument* {English in original}? As *raisonnement,* as one often reads it? Nothing is more naive. *To argue a case* {English original} is to plead a cause. Professional discourse is a pleading. One chooses a subject (usually linked, more or less, to what Americans consider their "values" as well as to their institutions, but that is another matter) and an opponent has to be proven wrong. As at the bar in court, one must persuade by the force of one's *claims* {English original} (of positions claimed). In contradistinction to Greek sophistry, rhetoric serves to institute a proceeding in which it is a matter not of convincing, but of confusing. The good *argument* {English original}—a tight one, and giving the appearance of an irresistible deduction—is the one that leaves the opponent without any recourse. It is not a matter of winning the adversary over to your side, but of your side winning. The investment of desire in discourse can scarcely be more obvious than in this *adversary method* {English original}. One will find pleaders—in the second degree—for philosophy so placed in the service of "desirable conclusions" in Richard Rorty (*Consequences of Pragmatism,* Minneapolis, 1982, pp. 219f) and Robert Nozik (*Philosophical Explanations,* Cambridge, 1981, p. 4). With Husserl, the philosopher-king turned himself into a functionary; in America, he becomes a lawyer.

46. This is an example of the telescoping of being-beingness-beings in a single referent: the Scholastic *esse* defined as "pure act," then represented as *entitas,* and finally bearing the name—God—of *summum ens.*

47. G. Vatimo, "Nietzsche interprèt de Heidegger," in *Heidegger: Questions ouvertes,* Paris, 1988, pp. 94f.

48. The Greek *aiôn* designates a figure of time made up of natural phases: phases of a pregnancy, of a life, etc. According to Emile Benveniste, the word denotes in Homer the vital force that determines a period that is counted in months or years—not the opposite. "It is the persistence of the *aïôn* that will measure the duration of a life," cf. the article cited above (Volume One, chapter 5, note 107), p. 109. On the other hand, the Heideggerian moment enters into no *Gestell,* be it natural or transcendental.

49. Meister Eckhart described the sum of ideas in God as "the abyss of his godhead and the fullness of his being (*wesen*) and his nature," sermon *Qui audit me* DW I, p. 194 (*Meister Eckhart: Sermons and Treatises,* trans. M. O'C. Walshe, vol. 2, London, Watkins, 1981, p. 84; translation slightly modified). In Heidegger as well, *Abgrund* always designates a fullness of possibilities, but in the mode of an arrival and a future, not in the paradigmatic mode, as that from which everything comes about.

50. M. Heidegger, "The Thing," *Essais et conférences,* trans. A. Préau, Paris, Gallimard, 1958, p. 213.

51. Aeschylus, *Agamemnon,* line 177 (cf. lines 250f.). See above, Volume One, General Introduction, note 3.

52. M. Heidegger, *Being and Time,* § 34.

53. Sophocles, *Oedipus at Colonus,* line 624.

54. Quoted in G. Schneeberger, *Nachlese zu Heidegger,* Bern, 1962, p. 136.

55. According to Kant, the transcendental illusion is always the result of a cacography. The natural metaphysician in us goes off to search for a major premise in the realm of logic, and a minor premise in the realm of phenomenal experience; these heteronomous sites are then joined into a third, and one concludes that there is a noumenal being (the soul, the world, and God).

56. Faced with the "thrusts of time," how could one continue to believe, according to the old saying, that scientific knowledge is obtained by causes? Imponderable causes such as those that the thrusts obey. Consider the following etiology, which is obviously not one: "Communism was not vanquished by military force, but by the life, by the spirit of human beings, by conscience, by the resistance that being as well as human beings offers to manipulation. It was vanquished by a revolt of color, authenticity, history in all of its variety, of human individuality against imprisonment within a uniform ideology" (Vaclav Havel, speech at the World Economic Forum, Davos, February 4 1992.). Faced with such an etiology, Democritus's laughter would doubtless fall silent (cf. above, Volume One, chapter 5, notes 120, 121).

57. M. Heidegger, "The Principle of Identity" in *Identity and Difference,* trans. Joan Stambaugh, New York, Harper and Row, 1969, p. 38 {translation modified}.

58. That Heidegger goes rather far in this disregard for beings will be shown by a "knowing seriousness" that will no longer "collide with the good and bad, with the decline and salvation of the tradition, with benevolence and brutality . . ." (*BzP* 242).

59. For recent attempts to read into Heidegger just such a negative haplology, see Jacques Derrida, *Of Spirit: Heidegger and The Question* (trans. G. Bennington and R. Bowlby, Chicago, University of Chicago Press, 1989), pp. 108–113, and *Psyché,* Paris, Galilée, 1987, p. 592 (the latter page having left me most perplexed, coming from an author whose subtleness in reading is often praised). In trying to demarcate himself from Heidegger, Derrida ends up subscribing to the oldest prejudices about *Dasein* and *Seyn,* the first supposedly serving an anthropology, and the second serving a theology.

60. Michel Foucault called upon his readers "to imagine and to construct what we could be" ("Why Study Power: The Question of the Subject," in H. Dreyfus and P. Rabinow, *Michel Foucault: Beyond Structuralism and Hermeneutics,* Chicago, University of Chicago Press, 1982, p. 216). He had in view the "power to be" as laid out by the system of knowledge and practices within which we find ourselves inscribed. Such "power to be" is finite: "There is not a single culture in the world in which everything is permitted" (*Histoire de la folie à l'âge classique,* 2nd ed., Paris, 1972, p. 578). Even so, the latitudes offered within such a system ask to be exhausted. Fully grasping what is possible presupposes "freeing thinking from what it thinks silently" (*L'usage des plaisirs,* Paris, 1984, p. 15), that is to say, from the actual conjunctions between knowledge and power. How could one fail to see in this topological notion of the possible an echo of Heidegger, who, Foucault stated elsewhere, "has always been for me the essential philosopher" (interview, *Le Nouvel Observateur,* June 28, 1984, p. 40)?

61. Note the amphibology of "power." In "anti-cipation," the object of *capere* is the same as that of the verbs "to ground," "to create," etc. . . . The topographical *power of the possible* that one must grasp in order to contest an epochal regime. Under the sovereignty of a "prin-ciple," on the other hand, the object of the *capere* is an ultimate referent, the hegemonic *power of the actual* that one must grasp to submit oneself to that regime.

62. M. Heidegger, *On Time and Being*, p. 41.
63. *BzP* 458.
64. A better example, but not the only one, is the shift—one does not dare to speak of translation—from *sophon* to "destinal" [Heidegger, *Essais et conférences*, pp. 262f.]. The middle term of this association is the German word *geschickt*, 'able,' but also 'sent.' The primitive meaning of *sophia* would be knowledge which makes one able. Now, such knowledge by which one is well-versed in the art of the doable varies from one era to another; it is thus *geschickt* to us, epochally destined. It is true that in ancient times, *sophon* designated a know-how. But the shift from this practical meaning to "destiny" only makes sense on the basis of the polysemy of the German word.
65. "The originary appropriation of the first beginning means the implantation into the other beginning" (*BzP* 171).
66. On the Heideggerian constitution of "metaphysics" as the object (and therefore the result, of an arch-metaphysical operation), see for example Karl-Otto Apel, *Transformation der Philosophie*, Frankfurt, 1976, vol. I, p. 259; and Paul Ricoeur, *La métaphore vive*, Paris, 1975, p. 395.
67. According to Kant, English-style gardens border on the grotesque due to an excess of freedom in imagination (*Critique of Judgment*, A 70), whereas in French-style gardens, one can see perfectly how imagination imposes its idea on nature, which is the meaning of genial "purposiveness without purpose."
68. Hannah Arendt could give a political reading of the *Critique of Judgment* only at the cost of transforming the status of freedom. From an idea of reason in Kant, it is turned by Arendt into an idea of the imagination. It is only by means of such a displacement that one can speak of the "rare moments of freedom" such as the "citizen's unions" in America around 1776, the popular societies in Paris between 1789 and 1793, the begardes and beguines communes beginning in the twelfth century and the Commune of 1871, the Soviets of 1905 and 1917, and the German Councils of 1918 (H. Arendt, *Über die Revolution*, Munich, 1963, pp. 335–338), to which she later added May 1968, so many models displaying freedom as a *reflective* idea of the imagination. But these rare moments do not provide examples of *regulative* freedom, the idea of reason. A regulating principle totalizes, and in that sense subsumes experience. Now, such as it was lived in the attempts and communes, for instance, freedom does not allow itself to be extended thus to every possible experience.
69. Even if this overdetermination may end up instructing us on the *ad-* in *ap*propriation, it is appropriate to discuss the other beginning in the wake of topology, and therefore in a chapter devoted to what one would call problems of method.
70. "The fundamental tonality of the first beginning is *wonderment:* that beings are. . . . The fundamental tonality of the other beginning is *dread:* dread at the abandonment by being" (*BzP* 46).
71. Plutarch, *Lycurgus*, XXIV, 4.
72. Thus, reading retrospectively, every normative standard was never anything but a thesis; since before Plato, being was only *thesei on* (*BzP* 184); in Plato, both the *epekeina* and the *chorismos* only result from the prior *positing* of the idea as universal (*BzP* 216); the teleological system, in turn, amounts to "an anthropological system of ends" (*BzP* 142); what passes for "possible" has always been *posited* in advance by the will (*BzP* 108); "nature" itself is only an *Ansetzung*, a positing (*BzP* 163); as to the sciences, all of them always turn beings into a *positum* and in this respect they are essentially positive, mathematics included (*BzP* 145); the laws which they claim to "read" are ex-pounded by them (*heraus-stellen, BzP* 161). Transitional thinking, lastly, will first have to de-pose (*ab-setzen, BzP* 483) beings; and of being itself, it can only expect dread (*ent-setzen, BzP* 267), which is one of the connotations of what I call the singularization to come.
73. I have said that "natality" in Hannah Arendt translates *Gebürtigkeit* in *Being and Time*, § 72 (cf. above, volume One, General Introduction, note 33). The figure of "self-affirmation" (*Selbstbehauptung*) is tied to it. It is, however, only with the "thrusts of time" in the *Contributions* that Heidegger explicitly singles out the condition of the impulse toward the new. This condition is distinct, to be sure, from "natality," a subjectivist notion in Arendt. But rather than a "counter-echo" to Heidegger (Jacques Taminiaux, "Arendt, disciple de Heidegger?," in *Etudes phénoménologiques* no. 2 [1985], p. 121), it is a matter of the most decisive displacement outside of the problematic of the I and the We. The "thrusts of time" desubjectivize and historicalize *kairos* which, as I also said, Heidegger had intended in 1921 to retain as a key notion for a study on Aristotle. They also answer the question of the political. As the received regimes henceforth end up being the same, only an economic arrangement that is impossible to conceive and to want will bring us out of the isomorphic . . .
74. M. Heidegger, *On Time and Being*, p. 13; cf. ibid., p. 48.
75. Augustine, *De Trinitate*, Bk. IV, ch. III, 5.
76. Hannah Arendt, *Lectures on Kant's Political Philosophy*, Chicago, 1982, pp. 76f., 84f.
77. The last section, at least in Heidegger's manuscript, as the editor rearranged the text (cf. above, note 9).

78. Sophocles, *Oedipus Rex*, line 1068.

79. ibid., l. 1333.

80. According to another enumeration, being is fissured into "uniqueness, rarity, instantaneousness, coming-about [*survenue*] and advent, restraint and freedom, expiration and necessity" (*BzP* 118).

81. Jean-Pierre Vernant and Pierre Vidal-Naquet, *Mythe et tragédie en Grèce ancienne,* vol. II, Paris, 1986, p. 259.

82. On the opposition between history and nature, see *BzP* 277, 349, 399. The metaphysical scheme from which the four-fold derives can be described in Kantian vocabulary. If the ancient *chorismos* between "intelligible" and "sensible" can be found on each side of the modern opposition of "freedom" and "nature," then the four terms are intelligible freedom (*libertas noumenon*), deconstructed into "gods" or "divinities"; sensible freedom (*libertas indifferentiae*), deconstructed into "humans" or "mortals"; intelligible nature (posited essences), deconstructed into the "world"; sensible nature (given perceptions), deconstructed into "earth." Beneath the appearance of a systematic chiasm, this filiation nonetheless runs the risk of camouflaging the essential: the gaps without common genus.

83. The proto-four-fold of the *Contributions* also features "the god", instead of the plural; and Heidegger himself oscillates there between "humans," "man," and "Da-sein"—to which one might have to add "confusion" (*Wirrnis*), since Heidegger opposes the world to the earth just as he opposes love to death, as well as the god to confusion and, lastly, history to exploitable nature (*BzP* 399). When he happens to designate one of the four terms as "the god", it seems that one should not think of the "last god." The latter is never part of the four names.

84. Heidegger calls that a "feeble (*schwächlich*) operation of mediation and rescue" (*BzP* 241).

85. "Protocol," (Heidegger, *Questions IV*), p. 77.

86. Hölderlin's name serves to legitimize the diremption: "Amidst all that is unsupported, where is the questioning of the truth of being to find support for the claim that the thrust of being has already been able to induce a first shuddering into our history? Again we come to something unique, that Hölderlin has to become the sayer that he is" (*BzP* 485). Hölderlin finds himself installed in a strange, trans-temporal present. He "is," not he "was"—the other beginning. He even signifies the event: "[U]nder the name of Hölderlin, the unique putting-up-for-decision happens—'happens,' not 'happened'" (*ereignet, nicht etwa ereigenete, BzP* 464).

87. Victor Goldschmidt, *Temps physique et temps tragique chez Aristote,* Paris, 1982; "Temps historique et temps logique dans l'interpétation des systèmes philosophiques," *Actes du Congrès international de philosophie de Bruxelles,* 1953, vol. XII, pp. 7–13. The author develops no less than seven notions of time in Aristotle: physical, doxic, categorial, cosmological, ethical, logical, and finally tragic notions.

88. "Expropriation to where?" The narrator (cautioned by Heidegger) continues: "Nothing more can be said of the direction and the sense of this question" ("Protocol," loc. cit.).

89. When reading an author, one must know how to spot the tropes where he sums up his thinking. In Kant, it usually occurs in the opening paragraph of a section, a chapter, or even a work; in Heidegger, in rhetorical questions.

90. According to Franz Rosenszweig, the Yes, in the sense of *sic,* of *amen,* of "it is good," is the "originary word" (*das Urwort;* [*Der Stern der Erlösung,* Heidelberg, 1921, First Part, p. 37 and Second Part, p. 51] cf. his *The Star of Redemption,* trans. W. Hallo, New York, 1970, pp. 27, 127). The translator renders *Urwort* indiscriminately as "archetypal word" and as "arch-word." Both renderings carry connotations that are too Greek for the context.

91. Cf. Michel Foucault, "Preface to Transgression," in *Language, Counter-Memory, Practice,* ed. D. F. Bouchard, Ithaca, Cornell University Press, 1977, pp. 29ff.

92. The two main works by Pseudo-Dionysius Areopagite both open with hymns in which the prefix 'above' (*huper-*) and the adverb 'beyond' (*epekeina*) abound. God is "He who is beyond every being" (*ho pantôn epékeina*), he is "above the unknowable" (*huperagnoston*), "above the most evident" (*huperphanestaton*), etc. (*On Mystical Theology,* I, 1); He is "the non-being cause of every being, beyond beings" and "beyond thought" (*The Divine Names,* I, 1), from Pseudo-Dionysius Areopagite, *The Divine Names and Mystical Theology,* trans. John D. Jones, Milwaukee, Marquette University Press, 1980, pp. 109, 211, translations slightly modified.

93. See Yeats's line quoted above, Volume One, General Introduction, note 14.

94. A catastrophe is, literally, an overturning. Now, for something to be overturned it must first be. Logically, therefore, a negation cannot assert itself as originary; operations of negation as well as affirmation require a Yes as their transitive object. In phenomenological terms, an originary No, making the Yes secondary, would annul the *phainesthai* itself and hence the world. As for Mephistopheles, Goethe shows himself to be a good theologian when he has this spirit, who always negates ("*ich bin der Geist, der stets verneint*"), state that from time to time he does like to see that old gentleman, God ("*Von Zeit zu Zeit seh' ich den Alten gern,*" *Faust,* Part One, lines 1338 and 350). This is because the No feeds off the Yes. The reverse would be senseless.

95. Michel Foucault, "Des supplices aux cellules," *Le Monde,* February 21, 1975, p. 16; reprinted in *Dits et Ecrits,* vol II, Paris, 1994, pp. 718–19 (cf. above, Volume I, chapter 3, note 85).

Conclusion

1. Goethe, spokesman in this for the natural metaphysician in us, has Mephistopheles describe himself as "that spirit which always negates" (*ich bin der Geist, der stets verneint, Faust,* First Part, l. 1338). That spirit negates the good, whereby evil not only becomes knowable but, as professional metaphysicians say, also relates itself to the good: "As the opposite of the good, evil pertains to the order of the knowable as well as of the good" (*malum ex hoc ipso quod bono opponitur habet rationem cognoscibilis et boni,* Thomas Aquinas, *On Truth,* q. 2, art. 15, 2nd reply). In metaphysical theticism (a pleonastic phrase in any case), the other is always the other *of* some primary positing.

2. See above. The generic unicity of opposites is necessary for scientific knowledge {*connaissance*}. As for knowing {*savoir*}, it grasps disparate opposites without a genus. Only polymorphic discourses accede to such knowledge. Inversely, *Wissen* becomes *Wissenschaft* by subjecting the ultimates of tragic knowing to the principles of non-contradiction, of identity, and of the excluded middle.

3. An argument that would relate evil to good as mortality is related to natality would do no more than disguise phenomenologically a metaphysics of identity. If evil amounts to a singularization that is equi-originary with the good, then how is one to avoid relapsing into some gnostic dialectic? That would be a red herring, for, to say it again, the singular is inscribed in a differend with the particular. Therefore it remains insusceptible to the dialectic. The singular is opposed to universal not as is the contradictory nor as is the contrary, but as is the incongruous.

4. See above the enumeration of "the rare moments of freedom" according to Hannah Arendt, ch. 6, note 68.

5. See the text cited above.

6. "*Malum est male uti bono*," Augustine, *On the Nature of the Good,* Bk. I, ch. 36 (PL vol. 42, col. 562).

7. Søren Kierkegaard, *Diary,* entry dated August 1, 1835.

8. *Gesammelte Werke,* ed. E. Hirsch, vol. 30, Düsseldorf, 1950ff., p. 9.

9. *Der Begriff Angst,* Jena 1923, pp. 117ff. and 135ff.

10. The words 'value,' *Wert, valeur* pass from the vocabulary of political economy into that of philosophy during the time of Hume and Kant. This idiom is not only contemporaneous with the institution of the modern hegemony, it is one of that institution's immediate effects. Hence, in wanting to develop "arguments of validity" in terms of communication, one never ceases turning in circles within the arena of hegemonic self-consciousness. With such arguments, it is still subjectivity that sniffs its own traces—the values it has posited with the transcendental turn.

11. It would be no less a thetic operation to speculate on *the* sexual difference, as if singularities were safe as long as one proves capable of counting up to two and posits no longer the (male) one, but the (female) other. Such an operation constitutes the very recipe of theticism. In speaking of sexualities, common nouns such as "feminism" can only perpetuate binary models and hence the most crudely metaphysical antitheses.

12. On the discrepancy between death that is about to be dealt on a large scale, banal as a consequence of a common belief, and death as imminently suffered, see the novel by Christa Wolf, *Cassandra,* trans. Jan van Heurck (New York, Farrar, Straus, Giroux, 1984). I know of no better illustration of the two incongruous kinds of futurity.

13. Tracing the complexities of those internal mutations would devolve not on a topology, but on a more empirical archaeology.

14. For an example of anarchy understood as an "outside" where on is implanted by a resolute "decision," see above.

15. In Kant, the 'expanded way of thinking' (*die erweiterte Denkungsart*) consists in a judgment that takes singulars into account, cf. *Critique of Judgment,* sections 40 and 77.

16. Sophocles, *Antigone,* lines 504–509, 734–741 and 937.

17. Aeschylus, *The Eumenides,* lines 517, 696ff.

18. Nikolai Gogol, "The Overcoat," *The Collected Tales and Plays,* trans. C. Garnett, rev. L. J. Kent, New York, 1964, pp. 564 f. (translation slightly modified and abbreviated).

Index of Names

Index of Terms

REINER SCHÜRMANN (1941–1993) was Professor of Philosophy at the Graduate Faculty of the New School for Social Research and author of *Heidegger on Being and Acting: From Principles to Anarchy*, *Meister Eckhart: Mystic and Philosopher*, and *Les Origines*.

REGINALD LILLY is Associate Professor of Philosophy at Skidmore College. He is editor of *The Ancients and the Moderns* and translator of *The Principle of Reason* by Martin Heidegger and *The Song of the Earth* by Michel Haar.

www.ingramcontent.com/pod-product-compliance
Lightning Source LLC
LaVergne TN
LVHW042156080826
844660LV00042B/1140

9780253215475